Education State Rankings
2011–2012

Other titles in the State Fact Finder series

City Crime Rankings

Crime State Rankings

Health Care State Rankings

State Rankings

Education State Rankings
2011–2012

PreK–12 Education in the 50 United States

Kathleen O'Leary Morgan

and

Scott Morgan

Editors

Los Angeles | London | New Delhi
Singapore | Washington DC

Los Angeles | London | New Delhi
Singapore | Washington DC

FOR INFORMATION:

CQ Press

An Imprint of SAGE Publications, Inc.

2455 Teller Road

Thousand Oaks, California 91320

E-mail: order@sagepub.com

SAGE Publications Ltd.

1 Oliver's Yard

55 City Road

London, EC1Y 1SP

United Kingdom

SAGE Publications India Pvt. Ltd.

B 1/I 1 Mohan Cooperative Industrial Area

Mathura Road, New Delhi 110 044

India

SAGE Publications Asia-Pacific Pte. Ltd.

33 Pekin Street #02-01

Far East Square

Singapore 048763

Acquisitions Editor: Sarah J. Walker

Production Editor: Belinda Josey

Copy Editor: Tracy Villano

Indexer: Scott Morgan

Cover Designer: Silverander Communications

Marketing Manager: Christopher O'Brien

Tables on pages 42–47, 180–181, 377, 390, 392–393, 414, and 427–429 reprinted with permission of the National Education Association © 2011. All rights reserved.

Printed in the United States of America

ISBN 978-1-60871-728-6

This book is printed on acid-free paper.

11 12 13 14 15 10 9 8 7 6 5 4 3 2 1

Contents

Detailed Table of Contents

IV. SAFETY AND DISCIPLINE

Introduction and Methodology

Education State Rankings 2011–2012 analyzes the latest education data for each of the fifty states. The book provides state-by-state rankings of roughly 440 education factors in the following seven categories: districts and facilities, finance, graduates and achievement, safety and discipline, special education, staff, and students.

Purpose of This Book

Education State Rankings 2011–2012 translates complicated and often convoluted statistics into meaningful information that is easy to understand. Too often reference books offer data without providing enough information to put the data into context. The purpose of this book is to serve as a resource for researchers, legislators, policy analysts, journalists, and community members that allows individuals to access basic facts and compare the status of their state's educational system to that of other states and the nation as a whole. There are two principal approaches to using these rankings: The first is to examine how a state is doing relative to all other states; the second is to compare a state to itself over a period of time. Both approaches are important for achieving a good understanding of how and whether a state is making progress in each category.

These data and rankings can be used in a variety of ways, by a variety of audiences, including the following:

- Education policymakers can use them to help identify education problems for further study.
- State governments can determine whether their students' educational progress is on par with the rest of the nation.
- The federal government can use the data to allocate grant funding.
- The media can rely upon these results to report and compare education rankings across states and years.

The Data and Their Limitations

The data featured in *Education State Rankings 2011–2012* were chosen specifically by the editors from a variety of government and private-sector sources. Although the data provide more than a snapshot of the status of education across the nation, they are not inclusive of all the possible education data that might be available.

Previous editions of *Education State Rankings* have used the term "smartest" when describing some states' place within the overall rankings. We no longer use this term because it is purely descriptive. At no point do we attempt to explain *why* a particular state is doing better or less well in education than other states or against the national average. Such an explanation—currently sought by education policy experts and other social science researchers—is beyond the scope of this book. While our selection of factors clearly affects the rankings, we believe the rankings provide a solid measurement of how the fifty states are faring with regard to education. Researchers, practitioners, and others can confidently use the data to understand education issues and guide policy decisions.

Methodology

As noted previously, the rankings in *Education State Rankings 2011–2012* are based on seven overall categories, which are broken down into nineteen factors that reflect general public school system expenditures and revenue, ratio of students to teachers, rate of student attendance and graduation, and the general academic proficiency of the student population. We reduced the number of factors from twenty to nineteen as the data available for fourth-grade writing scores were from 2002. The scores for eighth-grade writing have been updated, so while we continue to use those scores, we have decided to drop the fourth-grade figures as the data are outdated. These factors are divided into two groups: those that are "negative," for which a high ranking would be considered troublesome for a state, and those that are "positive," for which a high ranking would be considered a good sign for a state:

Negative Factors
- Public High School Dropout Rate
- Special Education Pupil-Teacher Ratio
- Percent of Public Elementary and Secondary School Staff Who Are School District Administrators
- Public Elementary School Pupil-Teacher Ratio
- Public Secondary School Pupil-Teacher Ratio

Positive Factors
- Public Elementary and Secondary School Revenue per $1,000 Personal Income

- Percent of Public Elementary and Secondary School Current Expenditures Used for Instruction
- Percent of Population Graduated from High School
- Average Freshman Graduation Rate for Public High Schools
- Percent of Public School Fourth Graders Proficient or Better in Reading
- Percent of Public School Eighth Graders Proficient or Better in Reading
- Percent of Public School Fourth Graders Proficient or Better in Mathematics
- Percent of Public School Eighth Graders Proficient or Better in Mathematics
- Percent of Public School Fourth Graders Proficient or Better in Science
- Percent of Public School Eighth Graders Proficient or Better in Science
- Percent of Public School Eighth Graders Proficient or Better in Writing
- Average Teacher Salary as a Percent of Average Annual Pay of All Workers
- Percent of School-Age Population in Public Schools
- Average Daily Attendance as a Percent of Fall Enrollment in Public Elementary and Secondary Schools

The nineteen factors involve a rate or percentage of frequency so the numbers are not biased toward population size, and the positive and negative nature of each factor is taken into account as part of the formula. Once we calculate the score for each individual factor, we add the scores to determine the state's overall ranking, with a positive score indicating a positive outlook for a state and demonstrating that the state is above the national average.

"Comparison Score" Methodology

The methodology for determining the state education rankings involves a multi-step process in which rates for each of the nineteen factors listed above are processed through a formula that measures how a state compares to the national average for a given category. The end result is that the farther below the national average a state's education ranking is, the lower it ranks overall. The farther above the national average a state's education ranking is, the higher it ranks overall. The methodology used for the most recent edition of the book has been used for the previous editions of *Education State Rankings*. The editors subjectively determine which factors are "negative" and which are "positive," as negative and positive factors are treated differently in the formula.

The methodology for *Education State Rankings* is described here in detail. The formula below is used for these calculations:

$$\frac{\text{State Rate} - \text{National Rate}}{\text{National Rate}} * 100$$

The following are steps for the "comparison score" calculation and examples that illustrate the calculations. Negative values are given in parentheses.

1. Using the state of New Jersey as an example, consider the following two factors, one positive and one negative: *Positive Factor:* Percent of Public School Fourth Graders Proficient or Better in Mathematics in 2009 is 49.0; *Negative Factor:* Public Secondary School Pupil-Teacher Ratio in 2009 is 10.2.

2. The percent difference between the state rate and the national rate for all nineteen factors is then computed. For the positive factor of Percent of Public School Fourth Graders Proficient or Better in Mathematics, New Jersey's rate of 49.0 is divided by the national rate of 38.0 for a percent difference of 1.2895. For the negative factor of Public Secondary School Pupil-Teacher Ratio, New Jersey's rate of 10.2 is divided by the national rate of 12.1 for a percent difference of 0.843.

3. The number "1" is then subtracted from the percent difference for each factor so that states whose results match the national average will equal 0 instead of 1. The results are then multiplied by 100 for a more manageable number. For the positive factor in our example, 1 is subtracted from 1.2895 to equal 0.2895, which is then multiplied by 100 to equal 28.947. For the negative factor, 1 is subtracted from 0.843 to equal (.157), which is then multiplied by 100 to equal (15.702).

4. These numbers are then scaled to 1/19 of the index by multiplying each score by 5.26% (because there are nineteen equally weighted factors, each factor is multiplied by 5.26 or 1/19). For the positive factor, 28.947 times 0.0526 equals 1.5235. For the negative factor, (15.702) times 0.0526 equals (.8264) or (0.83).

5. The negative factors are then multiplied by negative one (–1). Positive factors are not multiplied by anything. Therefore, New Jersey's score for the positive factor of Percent of Public School Fourth Graders Proficient or Better in Mathematics in 2009 remains 1.52. New Jersey's score for the negative factor of Public Secondary School Pupil-Teacher Ratio in 2009 is 0.83, or (0.83) multiplied by –1. (Both of these scores have been rounded to the second decimal place.) Remember that a positive score illustrates that the state scored higher than the national average on a positive factor and lower than the national average on a negative factor. Therefore, New Jersey's score of 1.52 for the positive factor of Percent of Public School Fourth Graders Proficient or Better in Mathematics (a positive score on a positive factor) illustrates that New Jersey has a higher than the national average score. New Jersey's score of 0.83 for the negative factor of Public Secondary School Pupil-Teacher Ratio (a positive score on a negative factor) illustrates that New Jersey has a lower than the national average score for the number of pupil to teachers in public secondary schools.

6. The final comparison score for each state is the sum of the individual scores for the nineteen equally weighted factors ("Score" on the Education Rankings tables on the following pages). This way, the states are assessed on how they stack up against the national average. In the case of New Jersey, the score is 21.81 (note that we only illustrated the calculations of two of the nineteen factors here). The interpretation of these scores is that the higher the state score, the further

above the national score; the lower the score, the further below the national score. A score of zero is equal to the national score. With a score of 21.81, New Jersey is significantly above the national average.

The scores are then sorted to produce the rankings. Note that the rankings do not indicate the actual difference between the scores, only their order, providing a means by which education trends can be gauged in differing communities. Since New Jersey's score of 21.81 is the highest of all fifty states, New Jersey is the highest ranked state in these education rankings.

The *2011–2012 Education State Rankings* table on page xviii provides the results of all the state scores as well as the scores from the previous year. All states are ranked from highest to lowest, with any ties among the states listed alphabetically for a given ranking. Negative numbers are reported in parentheses. Data reported as "NA" are not available or could not be calculated. In tables with national totals (as opposed to rates, per capita data, or the like), a separate column shows the percentage of the national total represented by each state. This "% of USA" column is particularly interesting when compared with a state's share of the nation's population for a particular year.

To further assist readers, source information and footnotes are provided at the bottom of each page. National totals, rates, and percentages are prominently displayed at the top of each table. Every other line in each table is shaded in gray for easier reading. In addition to the data and rankings, the volume offers numerous information-finding tools, including a thorough table of contents, table listings at the beginning of each chapter, a glossary of education terms, and a detailed index.

Following the *Education State Rankings* are 441 tables comparing the states in numerous categories. A directory of the data sources used by the editors is included, providing addresses, telephone numbers, and websites.

2011–2012 Education State Rankings

2011–12	State	2010–11	Score	2011–12	State	2010–11	Score
40	Alabama	38	(7.06)	11	Montana	8	8.95
46	Alaska	45	(16.98)	17	Nebraska	19	5.16
47	Arizona	47	(17.45)	43	Nevada	44	(11.23)
35	Arkansas	34	(2.71)	4	New Hampshire	6	13.47
48	California	49	(18.44)	1	New Jersey	1	21.81
23	Colorado	22	2.26	49	New Mexico	48	(20.13)
7	Connecticut	2	12.13	12	New York	13	8.36
37	Delaware	39	(5.03)	26	North Carolina	26	0.05
29	Florida	28	(1.56)	22	North Dakota	21	3.59
27	Georgia	25	(0.55)	14	Ohio	10	7.99
38	Hawaii	42	(6.04)	34	Oklahoma	32	(2.49)
16	Idaho	14	6.02	31	Oregon	31	(1.88)
42	Illinois	24	(8.00)	6	Pennsylvania	7	12.28
18	Indiana	20	4.91	20	Rhode Island	17	4.39
10	Iowa	15	9.13	36	South Carolina	35	(4.13)
8	Kansas	9	10.93	41	South Dakota	40	(7.93)
24	Kentucky	23	0.78	25	Tennessee	27	0.24
45	Louisiana	46	(12.67)	33	Texas	33	(2.19)
15	Maine	16	7.96	30	Utah	36	(1.72)
28	Maryland	30	(1.30)	2	Vermont	3	18.05
3	Massachusetts	4	16.04	13	Virginia	11	8.15
39	Michigan	41	(6.28)	32	Washington	37	(2.00)
9	Minnesota	12	9.70	44	West Virginia	43	(11.40)
50	Mississippi	50	(33.09)	5	Wisconsin	5	12.41
21	Missouri	18	4.23	19	Wyoming	29	4.72

POSITIVE (+) AND NEGATIVE (–) FACTORS CONSIDERED:
Public Elementary and Secondary School Revenue per $1,000 Personal Income (Table 53) +
Percent of Public Elementary and Secondary School Current Expenditures Used for Instruction (Table 135) +
Percent of Population Graduated from High School (Table 182) +
Averaged Freshman Graduation Rate for Public High Schools (Table 187) +
Percent of Public School Fourth Graders Proficient or Better in Reading (Table 214) +
Percent of Public School Eighth Graders Proficient or Better in Reading (Table 228) +
Percent of Public School Fourth Graders Proficient or Better in Mathematics (Table 242) +
Percent of Public School Eighth Graders Proficient or Better in Mathematics (Table 256) +
Percent of Public School Fourth Graders Proficient or Better in Science (Table 270) +
Percent of Public School Eighth Graders Proficient or Better in Science (Table 278) +
Percent of Public School Eighth Graders Proficient or Better in Writing (Table 286) +
Average Teacher Salary as a Percent of Average Annual Pay of All Workers (Table 393) +
Percent of School-Age Population in Public Schools (Table 413) +
Average Daily Attendance as a Percent of Fall Enrollment in Public Elementary and Secondary Schools (Table 428) +
Public High School Dropout Rate (Table 196) –
Special Education Pupil-Teacher Ratio (Table 366) –
Percent of Public Elementary and Secondary School Staff Who Are School District Administrators (Table 401) –
Public Elementary School Pupil-Teacher Ratio (Table 423) –
Public Secondary School Pupil-Teacher Ratio (Table 424) –

Previous Education State Rankings

STATE	'11–'12	'10–'11	'09–'10	'08–'09	'07–'08	'06–'07	'05–'06	'04–'05	'03–'04	'02–'03
Alabama	40	38	37	39	42	45	43	44	46	41
Alaska	46	45	44	44	44	46	44	45	23	25
Arizona	47	47	47	48	48	50	50	48	45	44
Arkansas	35	34	32	36	37	32	37	36	38	38
California	48	49	45	45	45	47	46	43	44	29
Colorado	23	22	25	30	23	27	23	21	35	27
Connecticut	7	2	4	4	3	3	2	2	3	1
Delaware	37	39	27	29	30	28	25	27	19	43
Florida	29	28	30	26	31	29	36	39	40	47
Georgia	27	25	34	37	40	41	40	38	36	40
Hawaii	38	42	42	43	43	42	42	42	43	45
Idaho	16	14	19	17	14	20	28	29	30	22
Illinois	42	24	17	28	35	35	32	24	27	33
Indiana	18	20	22	19	22	24	26	17	13	9
Iowa	10	15	11	11	11	9	14	8	8	11
Kansas	8	9	9	18	21	15	13	15	15	14
Kentucky	24	23	26	27	32	31	35	37	37	28
Louisiana	45	46	46	46	46	44	45	46	47	49
Maine	15	16	15	8	7	5	5	11	6	5
Maryland	28	30	31	16	17	18	19	18	18	30
Massachusetts	3	4	2	1	2	2	3	1	1	7
Michigan	39	41	40	40	26	39	27	31	20	20
Minnesota	9	12	14	12	10	13	6	7	12	12
Mississippi	50	50	50	50	50	48	49	47	48	48
Missouri	21	18	21	20	18	22	21	26	28	31
Montana	11	8	8	7	8	7	9	10	4	3
Nebraska	17	19	20	15	15	11	12	13	11	13
Nevada	43	44	48	49	49	49	47	49	49	46
New Hampshire	4	6	7	9	12	12	15	14	26	19
New Jersey	1	1	1	3	4	4	4	4	5	4
New Mexico	49	48	49	47	47	43	48	50	50	50
New York	12	13	16	13	16	16	10	6	10	26
North Carolina	26	26	43	31	28	23	22	25	21	24
North Dakota	22	21	23	22	19	21	20	19	24	21
Ohio	14	10	12	25	25	34	31	20	22	41
Oklahoma	34	32	39	38	39	36	39	40	39	32
Oregon	31	31	38	41	38	40	38	35	32	23
Pennsylvania	6	7	10	10	9	10	11	9	7	15
Rhode Island	20	17	18	14	13	14	16	23	16	10
South Carolina	36	35	41	32	33	26	29	32	41	36
South Dakota	41	40	13	24	24	17	18	22	31	34
Tennessee	25	27	29	34	36	30	41	41	42	39
Texas	33	33	28	35	29	25	24	33	34	16
Utah	30	36	35	33	34	38	33	28	25	17
Vermont	2	3	3	2	1	1	1	3	2	2
Virginia	13	11	5	6	5	6	7	12	17	37
Washington	32	37	33	23	27	33	30	30	33	35
West Virginia	44	43	36	42	41	37	34	33	29	18
Wisconsin	5	5	6	5	6	8	8	5	8	6
Wyoming	19	29	24	21	20	19	17	16	14	8

I. Districts and Facilities

Public Elementary and Secondary Education Agencies in 2010

National Total = 17,807 Agencies*

ALPHA ORDER

RANK	STATE	AGENCIES	% of USA
33	Alabama	171	1.0%
45	Alaska	54	0.3%
9	Arizona	642	3.6%
21	Arkansas	295	1.7%
2	California	1,190	6.7%
24	Colorado	262	1.5%
31	Connecticut	200	1.1%
47	Delaware	40	0.2%
42	Florida	75	0.4%
30	Georgia	206	1.2%
50	Hawaii	1	0.0%
36	Idaho	142	0.8%
3	Illinois	1,076	6.0%
16	Indiana	387	2.2%
17	Iowa	371	2.1%
19	Kansas	327	1.8%
32	Kentucky	194	1.1%
38	Louisiana	123	0.7%
25	Maine	255	1.4%
48	Maryland	25	0.1%
15	Massachusetts	393	2.2%
6	Michigan	855	4.8%
12	Minnesota	558	3.1%
35	Mississippi	165	0.9%
11	Missouri	565	3.2%
13	Montana	502	2.8%
22	Nebraska	294	1.7%
49	Nevada	18	0.1%
23	New Hampshire	280	1.6%
8	New Jersey	675	3.8%
40	New Mexico	108	0.6%
5	New York	879	4.9%
26	North Carolina	231	1.3%
27	North Dakota	228	1.3%
4	Ohio	1,047	5.9%
10	Oklahoma	584	3.3%
28	Oregon	221	1.2%
7	Pennsylvania	798	4.5%
46	Rhode Island	52	0.3%
41	South Carolina	103	0.6%
34	South Dakota	166	0.9%
37	Tennessee	140	0.8%
1	Texas	1,280	7.2%
39	Utah	117	0.7%
18	Vermont	357	2.0%
29	Virginia	207	1.2%
20	Washington	310	1.7%
44	West Virginia	57	0.3%
14	Wisconsin	461	2.6%
43	Wyoming	61	0.3%

RANK ORDER

RANK	STATE	AGENCIES	% of USA
1	Texas	1,280	7.2%
2	California	1,190	6.7%
3	Illinois	1,076	6.0%
4	Ohio	1,047	5.9%
5	New York	879	4.9%
6	Michigan	855	4.8%
7	Pennsylvania	798	4.5%
8	New Jersey	675	3.8%
9	Arizona	642	3.6%
10	Oklahoma	584	3.3%
11	Missouri	565	3.2%
12	Minnesota	558	3.1%
13	Montana	502	2.8%
14	Wisconsin	461	2.6%
15	Massachusetts	393	2.2%
16	Indiana	387	2.2%
17	Iowa	371	2.1%
18	Vermont	357	2.0%
19	Kansas	327	1.8%
20	Washington	310	1.7%
21	Arkansas	295	1.7%
22	Nebraska	294	1.7%
23	New Hampshire	280	1.6%
24	Colorado	262	1.5%
25	Maine	255	1.4%
26	North Carolina	231	1.3%
27	North Dakota	228	1.3%
28	Oregon	221	1.2%
29	Virginia	207	1.2%
30	Georgia	206	1.2%
31	Connecticut	200	1.1%
32	Kentucky	194	1.1%
33	Alabama	171	1.0%
34	South Dakota	166	0.9%
35	Mississippi	165	0.9%
36	Idaho	142	0.8%
37	Tennessee	140	0.8%
38	Louisiana	123	0.7%
39	Utah	117	0.7%
40	New Mexico	108	0.6%
41	South Carolina	103	0.6%
42	Florida	75	0.4%
43	Wyoming	61	0.3%
44	West Virginia	57	0.3%
45	Alaska	54	0.3%
46	Rhode Island	52	0.3%
47	Delaware	40	0.2%
48	Maryland	25	0.1%
49	Nevada	18	0.1%
50	Hawaii	1	0.0%
	District of Columbia	59	0.3%

Source: U.S. Department of Education, National Center for Education Statistics
"Numbers and Types of Public Elementary and Secondary Education Agencies" (http://nces.ed.gov/pubs2011/2011346.pdf)
*For school year 2009-2010. Agencies include regular school districts, regional education service agencies, state operated agencies, federally operated agencies, and "other" agencies. Some states include each charter school as a separate agency.

Regular Public Elementary and Secondary School Districts in 2010

National Total = 13,629 Districts*

ALPHA ORDER

RANK	STATE	DISTRICTS	% of USA
35	Alabama	133	1.0%
43	Alaska	53	0.4%
23	Arizona	224	1.6%
21	Arkansas	244	1.8%
2	California	958	7.0%
28	Colorado	178	1.3%
30	Connecticut	169	1.2%
48	Delaware	19	0.1%
41	Florida	67	0.5%
26	Georgia	180	1.3%
50	Hawaii	1	0.0%
36	Idaho	116	0.9%
3	Illinois	869	6.4%
17	Indiana	294	2.2%
13	Iowa	361	2.6%
15	Kansas	316	2.3%
29	Kentucky	174	1.3%
40	Louisiana	69	0.5%
20	Maine	246	1.8%
47	Maryland	24	0.2%
21	Massachusetts	244	1.8%
7	Michigan	551	4.0%
14	Minnesota	337	2.5%
32	Mississippi	152	1.1%
9	Missouri	523	3.8%
12	Montana	417	3.1%
19	Nebraska	253	1.9%
49	Nevada	17	0.1%
26	New Hampshire	180	1.3%
6	New Jersey	603	4.4%
38	New Mexico	89	0.7%
4	New York	696	5.1%
37	North Carolina	115	0.8%
25	North Dakota	185	1.4%
5	Ohio	615	4.5%
8	Oklahoma	532	3.9%
24	Oregon	190	1.4%
10	Pennsylvania	500	3.7%
46	Rhode Island	32	0.2%
39	South Carolina	85	0.6%
31	South Dakota	156	1.1%
33	Tennessee	140	1.0%
1	Texas	1,032	7.6%
45	Utah	41	0.3%
18	Vermont	291	2.1%
34	Virginia	134	1.0%
16	Washington	295	2.2%
42	West Virginia	55	0.4%
11	Wisconsin	425	3.1%
44	Wyoming	48	0.4%

RANK ORDER

RANK	STATE	DISTRICTS	% of USA
1	Texas	1,032	7.6%
2	California	958	7.0%
3	Illinois	869	6.4%
4	New York	696	5.1%
5	Ohio	615	4.5%
6	New Jersey	603	4.4%
7	Michigan	551	4.0%
8	Oklahoma	532	3.9%
9	Missouri	523	3.8%
10	Pennsylvania	500	3.7%
11	Wisconsin	425	3.1%
12	Montana	417	3.1%
13	Iowa	361	2.6%
14	Minnesota	337	2.5%
15	Kansas	316	2.3%
16	Washington	295	2.2%
17	Indiana	294	2.2%
18	Vermont	291	2.1%
19	Nebraska	253	1.9%
20	Maine	246	1.8%
21	Arkansas	244	1.8%
21	Massachusetts	244	1.8%
23	Arizona	224	1.6%
24	Oregon	190	1.4%
25	North Dakota	185	1.4%
26	Georgia	180	1.3%
26	New Hampshire	180	1.3%
28	Colorado	178	1.3%
29	Kentucky	174	1.3%
30	Connecticut	169	1.2%
31	South Dakota	156	1.1%
32	Mississippi	152	1.1%
33	Tennessee	140	1.0%
34	Virginia	134	1.0%
35	Alabama	133	1.0%
36	Idaho	116	0.9%
37	North Carolina	115	0.8%
38	New Mexico	89	0.7%
39	South Carolina	85	0.6%
40	Louisiana	69	0.5%
41	Florida	67	0.5%
42	West Virginia	55	0.4%
43	Alaska	53	0.4%
44	Wyoming	48	0.4%
45	Utah	41	0.3%
46	Rhode Island	32	0.2%
47	Maryland	24	0.2%
48	Delaware	19	0.1%
49	Nevada	17	0.1%
50	Hawaii	1	0.0%
	District of Columbia	1	0.0%

Source: U.S. Department of Education, National Center for Education Statistics
"Numbers and Types of Public Elementary and Secondary Education Agencies" (http://nces.ed.gov/pubs2011/2011346.pdf)
*For school year 2009-2010. Regular school districts are agencies responsible for providing free public education for school-age children residing within their jurisdiction. Included in these figures are districts that reported having no students. This can occur when a small district has no pupils or contracts with another district to educate the students under its jurisdiction.

Regular Public School Districts Providing Pre-Kindergarten to 12th Grade Education in 2010
National Total = 10,629 Districts*

ALPHA ORDER

RANK	STATE	DISTRICTS	% of USA
28	Alabama	132	1.2%
41	Alaska	53	0.5%
34	Arizona	102	1.0%
17	Arkansas	244	2.3%
8	California	401	3.8%
21	Colorado	178	1.7%
31	Connecticut	116	1.1%
48	Delaware	17	0.2%
38	Florida	67	0.6%
20	Georgia	179	1.7%
50	Hawaii	1	0.0%
33	Idaho	109	1.0%
9	Illinois	382	3.6%
13	Indiana	291	2.7%
11	Iowa	361	3.4%
14	Kansas	289	2.7%
24	Kentucky	169	1.6%
37	Louisiana	69	0.6%
19	Maine	206	1.9%
47	Maryland	24	0.2%
22	Massachusetts	177	1.7%
4	Michigan	522	4.9%
12	Minnesota	333	3.1%
26	Mississippi	148	1.4%
6	Missouri	450	4.2%
42	Montana	52	0.5%
15	Nebraska	253	2.4%
49	Nevada	16	0.2%
38	New Hampshire	67	0.6%
18	New Jersey	227	2.1%
35	New Mexico	89	0.8%
2	New York	644	6.1%
32	North Carolina	115	1.1%
27	North Dakota	146	1.4%
3	Ohio	612	5.8%
7	Oklahoma	425	4.0%
23	Oregon	172	1.6%
5	Pennsylvania	498	4.7%
46	Rhode Island	28	0.3%
36	South Carolina	85	0.8%
25	South Dakota	155	1.5%
30	Tennessee	124	1.2%
1	Texas	974	9.2%
44	Utah	41	0.4%
45	Vermont	36	0.3%
29	Virginia	129	1.2%
16	Washington	248	2.3%
40	West Virginia	55	0.5%
10	Wisconsin	369	3.5%
43	Wyoming	48	0.5%

RANK ORDER

RANK	STATE	DISTRICTS	% of USA
1	Texas	974	9.2%
2	New York	644	6.1%
3	Ohio	612	5.8%
4	Michigan	522	4.9%
5	Pennsylvania	498	4.7%
6	Missouri	450	4.2%
7	Oklahoma	425	4.0%
8	California	401	3.8%
9	Illinois	382	3.6%
10	Wisconsin	369	3.5%
11	Iowa	361	3.4%
12	Minnesota	333	3.1%
13	Indiana	291	2.7%
14	Kansas	289	2.7%
15	Nebraska	253	2.4%
16	Washington	248	2.3%
17	Arkansas	244	2.3%
18	New Jersey	227	2.1%
19	Maine	206	1.9%
20	Georgia	179	1.7%
21	Colorado	178	1.7%
22	Massachusetts	177	1.7%
23	Oregon	172	1.6%
24	Kentucky	169	1.6%
25	South Dakota	155	1.5%
26	Mississippi	148	1.4%
27	North Dakota	146	1.4%
28	Alabama	132	1.2%
29	Virginia	129	1.2%
30	Tennessee	124	1.2%
31	Connecticut	116	1.1%
32	North Carolina	115	1.1%
33	Idaho	109	1.0%
34	Arizona	102	1.0%
35	New Mexico	89	0.8%
36	South Carolina	85	0.8%
37	Louisiana	69	0.6%
38	Florida	67	0.6%
38	New Hampshire	67	0.6%
40	West Virginia	55	0.5%
41	Alaska	53	0.5%
42	Montana	52	0.5%
43	Wyoming	48	0.5%
44	Utah	41	0.4%
45	Vermont	36	0.3%
46	Rhode Island	28	0.3%
47	Maryland	24	0.2%
48	Delaware	17	0.2%
49	Nevada	16	0.2%
50	Hawaii	1	0.0%
	District of Columbia	1	0.0%

Source: U.S. Department of Education, National Center for Education Statistics
    "Numbers and Types of Public Elementary and Secondary Education Agencies" (http://nces.ed.gov/pubs2011/2011346.pdf)
*For school year 2009-2010. Includes districts with beginning ranges of pre-kindergarten, kindergarten, or first grade and completion of 12th grade.

Percent of Regular Public Elementary and Secondary School Districts Providing Pre-Kindergarten to 12th Grade Education in 2010
National Percent = 78.0%*

RANK	STATE	PERCENT
20	Alabama	99.2
1	Alaska	100.0
44	Arizona	45.5
1	Arkansas	100.0
46	California	41.9
1	Colorado	100.0
43	Connecticut	68.6
33	Delaware	89.5
1	Florida	100.0
18	Georgia	99.4
1	Hawaii	100.0
29	Idaho	94.0
45	Illinois	44.0
21	Indiana	99.0
1	Iowa	100.0
31	Kansas	91.5
24	Kentucky	97.1
1	Louisiana	100.0
39	Maine	83.7
1	Maryland	100.0
42	Massachusetts	72.5
26	Michigan	94.7
22	Minnesota	98.8
23	Mississippi	97.4
37	Missouri	86.0
49	Montana	12.5
1	Nebraska	100.0
28	Nevada	94.1
48	New Hampshire	37.2
47	New Jersey	37.6
1	New Mexico	100.0
30	New York	92.5
1	North Carolina	100.0
41	North Dakota	78.9
17	Ohio	99.5
40	Oklahoma	79.9
32	Oregon	90.5
16	Pennsylvania	99.6
35	Rhode Island	87.5
1	South Carolina	100.0
18	South Dakota	99.4
34	Tennessee	88.6
27	Texas	94.4
1	Utah	100.0
50	Vermont	12.4
25	Virginia	96.3
38	Washington	84.1
1	West Virginia	100.0
36	Wisconsin	86.8
1	Wyoming	100.0

RANK	STATE	PERCENT
1	Alaska	100.0
1	Arkansas	100.0
1	Colorado	100.0
1	Florida	100.0
1	Hawaii	100.0
1	Iowa	100.0
1	Louisiana	100.0
1	Maryland	100.0
1	Nebraska	100.0
1	New Mexico	100.0
1	North Carolina	100.0
1	South Carolina	100.0
1	Utah	100.0
1	West Virginia	100.0
1	Wyoming	100.0
16	Pennsylvania	99.6
17	Ohio	99.5
18	Georgia	99.4
18	South Dakota	99.4
20	Alabama	99.2
21	Indiana	99.0
22	Minnesota	98.8
23	Mississippi	97.4
24	Kentucky	97.1
25	Virginia	96.3
26	Michigan	94.7
27	Texas	94.4
28	Nevada	94.1
29	Idaho	94.0
30	New York	92.5
31	Kansas	91.5
32	Oregon	90.5
33	Delaware	89.5
34	Tennessee	88.6
35	Rhode Island	87.5
36	Wisconsin	86.8
37	Missouri	86.0
38	Washington	84.1
39	Maine	83.7
40	Oklahoma	79.9
41	North Dakota	78.9
42	Massachusetts	72.5
43	Connecticut	68.6
44	Arizona	45.5
45	Illinois	44.0
46	California	41.9
47	New Jersey	37.6
48	New Hampshire	37.2
49	Montana	12.5
50	Vermont	12.4
	District of Columbia	100.0

Source: CQ Press using data from U.S. Department of Education, National Center for Education Statistics
"Numbers and Types of Public Elementary and Secondary Education Agencies" (http://nces.ed.gov/pubs2011/2011346.pdf)
*For school year 2009-2010. Regular school districts are agencies responsible for providing free public education for school-age children residing within their jurisdiction.

Public Elementary and Secondary Schools in 2010

National Total = 98,817 Schools*

<table>
<tr><td colspan="4">ALPHA ORDER</td><td colspan="4">RANK ORDER</td></tr>
<tr><th>RANK</th><th>STATE</th><th>SCHOOLS</th><th>% of USA</th><th>RANK</th><th>STATE</th><th>SCHOOLS</th><th>% of USA</th></tr>
<tr><td>23</td><td>Alabama</td><td>1,600</td><td>1.6%</td><td>1</td><td>California</td><td>10,068</td><td>10.2%</td></tr>
<tr><td>44</td><td>Alaska</td><td>506</td><td>0.5%</td><td>2</td><td>Texas</td><td>8,619</td><td>8.7%</td></tr>
<tr><td>15</td><td>Arizona</td><td>2,248</td><td>2.3%</td><td>3</td><td>New York</td><td>4,730</td><td>4.8%</td></tr>
<tr><td>32</td><td>Arkansas</td><td>1,120</td><td>1.1%</td><td>4</td><td>Illinois</td><td>4,405</td><td>4.5%</td></tr>
<tr><td>1</td><td>California</td><td>10,068</td><td>10.2%</td><td>5</td><td>Florida</td><td>4,043</td><td>4.1%</td></tr>
<tr><td>21</td><td>Colorado</td><td>1,793</td><td>1.8%</td><td>6</td><td>Michigan</td><td>3,879</td><td>3.9%</td></tr>
<tr><td>31</td><td>Connecticut</td><td>1,165</td><td>1.2%</td><td>7</td><td>Ohio</td><td>3,796</td><td>3.8%</td></tr>
<tr><td>50</td><td>Delaware</td><td>217</td><td>0.2%</td><td>8</td><td>Pennsylvania</td><td>3,244</td><td>3.3%</td></tr>
<tr><td>5</td><td>Florida</td><td>4,043</td><td>4.1%</td><td>9</td><td>New Jersey</td><td>2,590</td><td>2.6%</td></tr>
<tr><td>11</td><td>Georgia</td><td>2,461</td><td>2.5%</td><td>10</td><td>North Carolina</td><td>2,550</td><td>2.6%</td></tr>
<tr><td>49</td><td>Hawaii</td><td>289</td><td>0.3%</td><td>11</td><td>Georgia</td><td>2,461</td><td>2.5%</td></tr>
<tr><td>39</td><td>Idaho</td><td>742</td><td>0.8%</td><td>12</td><td>Minnesota</td><td>2,433</td><td>2.5%</td></tr>
<tr><td>4</td><td>Illinois</td><td>4,405</td><td>4.5%</td><td>13</td><td>Missouri</td><td>2,427</td><td>2.5%</td></tr>
<tr><td>18</td><td>Indiana</td><td>1,961</td><td>2.0%</td><td>14</td><td>Washington</td><td>2,318</td><td>2.3%</td></tr>
<tr><td>26</td><td>Iowa</td><td>1,468</td><td>1.5%</td><td>15</td><td>Arizona</td><td>2,248</td><td>2.3%</td></tr>
<tr><td>28</td><td>Kansas</td><td>1,419</td><td>1.4%</td><td>16</td><td>Wisconsin</td><td>2,242</td><td>2.3%</td></tr>
<tr><td>24</td><td>Kentucky</td><td>1,542</td><td>1.6%</td><td>17</td><td>Virginia</td><td>2,164</td><td>2.2%</td></tr>
<tr><td>25</td><td>Louisiana</td><td>1,488</td><td>1.5%</td><td>18</td><td>Indiana</td><td>1,961</td><td>2.0%</td></tr>
<tr><td>41</td><td>Maine</td><td>649</td><td>0.7%</td><td>19</td><td>Massachusetts</td><td>1,836</td><td>1.9%</td></tr>
<tr><td>27</td><td>Maryland</td><td>1,447</td><td>1.5%</td><td>20</td><td>Oklahoma</td><td>1,795</td><td>1.8%</td></tr>
<tr><td>19</td><td>Massachusetts</td><td>1,836</td><td>1.9%</td><td>21</td><td>Colorado</td><td>1,793</td><td>1.8%</td></tr>
<tr><td>6</td><td>Michigan</td><td>3,879</td><td>3.9%</td><td>22</td><td>Tennessee</td><td>1,772</td><td>1.8%</td></tr>
<tr><td>12</td><td>Minnesota</td><td>2,433</td><td>2.5%</td><td>23</td><td>Alabama</td><td>1,600</td><td>1.6%</td></tr>
<tr><td>34</td><td>Mississippi</td><td>1,085</td><td>1.1%</td><td>24</td><td>Kentucky</td><td>1,542</td><td>1.6%</td></tr>
<tr><td>13</td><td>Missouri</td><td>2,427</td><td>2.5%</td><td>25</td><td>Louisiana</td><td>1,488</td><td>1.5%</td></tr>
<tr><td>37</td><td>Montana</td><td>828</td><td>0.8%</td><td>26</td><td>Iowa</td><td>1,468</td><td>1.5%</td></tr>
<tr><td>32</td><td>Nebraska</td><td>1,120</td><td>1.1%</td><td>27</td><td>Maryland</td><td>1,447</td><td>1.5%</td></tr>
<tr><td>42</td><td>Nevada</td><td>636</td><td>0.6%</td><td>28</td><td>Kansas</td><td>1,419</td><td>1.4%</td></tr>
<tr><td>45</td><td>New Hampshire</td><td>484</td><td>0.5%</td><td>29</td><td>Oregon</td><td>1,301</td><td>1.3%</td></tr>
<tr><td>9</td><td>New Jersey</td><td>2,590</td><td>2.6%</td><td>30</td><td>South Carolina</td><td>1,206</td><td>1.2%</td></tr>
<tr><td>36</td><td>New Mexico</td><td>855</td><td>0.9%</td><td>31</td><td>Connecticut</td><td>1,165</td><td>1.2%</td></tr>
<tr><td>3</td><td>New York</td><td>4,730</td><td>4.8%</td><td>32</td><td>Arkansas</td><td>1,120</td><td>1.1%</td></tr>
<tr><td>10</td><td>North Carolina</td><td>2,550</td><td>2.6%</td><td>32</td><td>Nebraska</td><td>1,120</td><td>1.1%</td></tr>
<tr><td>43</td><td>North Dakota</td><td>517</td><td>0.5%</td><td>34</td><td>Mississippi</td><td>1,085</td><td>1.1%</td></tr>
<tr><td>7</td><td>Ohio</td><td>3,796</td><td>3.8%</td><td>35</td><td>Utah</td><td>1,046</td><td>1.1%</td></tr>
<tr><td>20</td><td>Oklahoma</td><td>1,795</td><td>1.8%</td><td>36</td><td>New Mexico</td><td>855</td><td>0.9%</td></tr>
<tr><td>29</td><td>Oregon</td><td>1,301</td><td>1.3%</td><td>37</td><td>Montana</td><td>828</td><td>0.8%</td></tr>
<tr><td>8</td><td>Pennsylvania</td><td>3,244</td><td>3.3%</td><td>38</td><td>West Virginia</td><td>759</td><td>0.8%</td></tr>
<tr><td>48</td><td>Rhode Island</td><td>321</td><td>0.3%</td><td>39</td><td>Idaho</td><td>742</td><td>0.8%</td></tr>
<tr><td>30</td><td>South Carolina</td><td>1,206</td><td>1.2%</td><td>40</td><td>South Dakota</td><td>714</td><td>0.7%</td></tr>
<tr><td>40</td><td>South Dakota</td><td>714</td><td>0.7%</td><td>41</td><td>Maine</td><td>649</td><td>0.7%</td></tr>
<tr><td>22</td><td>Tennessee</td><td>1,772</td><td>1.8%</td><td>42</td><td>Nevada</td><td>636</td><td>0.6%</td></tr>
<tr><td>2</td><td>Texas</td><td>8,619</td><td>8.7%</td><td>43</td><td>North Dakota</td><td>517</td><td>0.5%</td></tr>
<tr><td>35</td><td>Utah</td><td>1,046</td><td>1.1%</td><td>44</td><td>Alaska</td><td>506</td><td>0.5%</td></tr>
<tr><td>47</td><td>Vermont</td><td>323</td><td>0.3%</td><td>45</td><td>New Hampshire</td><td>484</td><td>0.5%</td></tr>
<tr><td>17</td><td>Virginia</td><td>2,164</td><td>2.2%</td><td>46</td><td>Wyoming</td><td>363</td><td>0.4%</td></tr>
<tr><td>14</td><td>Washington</td><td>2,318</td><td>2.3%</td><td>47</td><td>Vermont</td><td>323</td><td>0.3%</td></tr>
<tr><td>38</td><td>West Virginia</td><td>759</td><td>0.8%</td><td>48</td><td>Rhode Island</td><td>321</td><td>0.3%</td></tr>
<tr><td>16</td><td>Wisconsin</td><td>2,242</td><td>2.3%</td><td>49</td><td>Hawaii</td><td>289</td><td>0.3%</td></tr>
<tr><td>46</td><td>Wyoming</td><td>363</td><td>0.4%</td><td>50</td><td>Delaware</td><td>217</td><td>0.2%</td></tr>
<tr><td></td><td></td><td></td><td></td><td></td><td>District of Columbia</td><td>233</td><td>0.2%</td></tr>
</table>

Source: U.S. Department of Education, National Center for Education Statistics
   "Numbers and Types of Public Elementary and Secondary Schools" (http://nces.ed.gov/pubs2011/2011345.pdf)
*For school year 2009-2010.

Regular Public Elementary and Secondary Schools in 2010

National Total = 89,018 Schools*

ALPHA ORDER

RANK	STATE	SCHOOLS	% of USA
25	Alabama	1,370	1.5%
45	Alaska	450	0.5%
14	Arizona	1,939	2.2%
32	Arkansas	1,082	1.2%
1	California	8,472	9.5%
21	Colorado	1,683	1.9%
33	Connecticut	1,049	1.2%
50	Delaware	182	0.2%
6	Florida	3,398	3.8%
11	Georgia	2,248	2.5%
49	Hawaii	285	0.3%
40	Idaho	633	0.7%
4	Illinois	4,017	4.5%
17	Indiana	1,875	2.1%
23	Iowa	1,410	1.6%
24	Kansas	1,407	1.6%
29	Kentucky	1,238	1.4%
27	Louisiana	1,260	1.4%
41	Maine	619	0.7%
26	Maryland	1,321	1.5%
19	Massachusetts	1,755	2.0%
7	Michigan	3,332	3.7%
22	Minnesota	1,666	1.9%
34	Mississippi	928	1.0%
12	Missouri	2,181	2.5%
36	Montana	822	0.9%
31	Nebraska	1,087	1.2%
42	Nevada	593	0.7%
43	New Hampshire	484	0.5%
10	New Jersey	2,359	2.7%
37	New Mexico	808	0.9%
3	New York	4,591	5.2%
9	North Carolina	2,531	2.8%
44	North Dakota	474	0.5%
5	Ohio	3,653	4.1%
18	Oklahoma	1,786	2.0%
28	Oregon	1,256	1.4%
8	Pennsylvania	3,132	3.5%
48	Rhode Island	298	0.3%
30	South Carolina	1,136	1.3%
39	South Dakota	676	0.8%
20	Tennessee	1,704	1.9%
2	Texas	7,518	8.4%
35	Utah	862	1.0%
47	Vermont	307	0.3%
16	Virginia	1,883	2.1%
15	Washington	1,885	2.1%
38	West Virginia	693	0.8%
13	Wisconsin	2,136	2.4%
46	Wyoming	336	0.4%

RANK ORDER

RANK	STATE	SCHOOLS	% of USA
1	California	8,472	9.5%
2	Texas	7,518	8.4%
3	New York	4,591	5.2%
4	Illinois	4,017	4.5%
5	Ohio	3,653	4.1%
6	Florida	3,398	3.8%
7	Michigan	3,332	3.7%
8	Pennsylvania	3,132	3.5%
9	North Carolina	2,531	2.8%
10	New Jersey	2,359	2.7%
11	Georgia	2,248	2.5%
12	Missouri	2,181	2.5%
13	Wisconsin	2,136	2.4%
14	Arizona	1,939	2.2%
15	Washington	1,885	2.1%
16	Virginia	1,883	2.1%
17	Indiana	1,875	2.1%
18	Oklahoma	1,786	2.0%
19	Massachusetts	1,755	2.0%
20	Tennessee	1,704	1.9%
21	Colorado	1,683	1.9%
22	Minnesota	1,666	1.9%
23	Iowa	1,410	1.6%
24	Kansas	1,407	1.6%
25	Alabama	1,370	1.5%
26	Maryland	1,321	1.5%
27	Louisiana	1,260	1.4%
28	Oregon	1,256	1.4%
29	Kentucky	1,238	1.4%
30	South Carolina	1,136	1.3%
31	Nebraska	1,087	1.2%
32	Arkansas	1,082	1.2%
33	Connecticut	1,049	1.2%
34	Mississippi	928	1.0%
35	Utah	862	1.0%
36	Montana	822	0.9%
37	New Mexico	808	0.9%
38	West Virginia	693	0.8%
39	South Dakota	676	0.8%
40	Idaho	633	0.7%
41	Maine	619	0.7%
42	Nevada	593	0.7%
43	New Hampshire	484	0.5%
44	North Dakota	474	0.5%
45	Alaska	450	0.5%
46	Wyoming	336	0.4%
47	Vermont	307	0.3%
48	Rhode Island	298	0.3%
49	Hawaii	285	0.3%
50	Delaware	182	0.2%
	District of Columbia	208	0.2%

Source: U.S. Department of Education, National Center for Education Statistics
    "Numbers and Types of Public Elementary and Secondary Schools" (http://nces.ed.gov/pubs2011/2011345.pdf)
*For school year 2009-2010.

Title I Eligible Public Elementary and Secondary Schools in 2010

National Total = 64,811 Schools*

ALPHA ORDER

RANK	STATE	SCHOOLS	% of USA
25	Alabama	925	1.4%
42	Alaska	359	0.6%
16	Arizona	1,251	1.9%
27	Arkansas	829	1.3%
2	California	6,044	9.3%
31	Colorado	674	1.0%
35	Connecticut	547	0.8%
49	Delaware	175	0.3%
7	Florida	2,606	4.0%
11	Georgia	1,531	2.4%
48	Hawaii	196	0.3%
38	Idaho	524	0.8%
4	Illinois	3,194	4.9%
15	Indiana	1,384	2.1%
24	Iowa	958	1.5%
18	Kansas	1,178	1.8%
21	Kentucky	1,079	1.7%
17	Louisiana	1,191	1.8%
36	Maine	544	0.8%
39	Maryland	409	0.6%
22	Massachusetts	1,038	1.6%
5	Michigan	2,899	4.5%
26	Minnesota	873	1.3%
30	Mississippi	706	1.1%
20	Missouri	1,111	1.7%
32	Montana	634	1.0%
37	Nebraska	528	0.8%
43	Nevada	333	0.5%
40	New Hampshire	404	0.6%
13	New Jersey	1,430	2.2%
28	New Mexico	751	1.2%
3	New York	4,259	6.6%
9	North Carolina	1,971	3.0%
44	North Dakota	303	0.5%
6	Ohio	2,863	4.4%
19	Oklahoma	1,157	1.8%
33	Oregon	612	0.9%
8	Pennsylvania	2,453	3.8%
47	Rhode Island	232	0.4%
23	South Carolina	992	1.5%
34	South Dakota	607	0.9%
14	Tennessee	1,429	2.2%
1	Texas	6,594	10.2%
45	Utah	276	0.4%
46	Vermont	250	0.4%
29	Virginia	735	1.1%
12	Washington	1,486	2.3%
41	West Virginia	370	0.6%
10	Wisconsin	1,558	2.4%
50	Wyoming	173	0.3%

RANK ORDER

RANK	STATE	SCHOOLS	% of USA
1	Texas	6,594	10.2%
2	California	6,044	9.3%
3	New York	4,259	6.6%
4	Illinois	3,194	4.9%
5	Michigan	2,899	4.5%
6	Ohio	2,863	4.4%
7	Florida	2,606	4.0%
8	Pennsylvania	2,453	3.8%
9	North Carolina	1,971	3.0%
10	Wisconsin	1,558	2.4%
11	Georgia	1,531	2.4%
12	Washington	1,486	2.3%
13	New Jersey	1,430	2.2%
14	Tennessee	1,429	2.2%
15	Indiana	1,384	2.1%
16	Arizona	1,251	1.9%
17	Louisiana	1,191	1.8%
18	Kansas	1,178	1.8%
19	Oklahoma	1,157	1.8%
20	Missouri	1,111	1.7%
21	Kentucky	1,079	1.7%
22	Massachusetts	1,038	1.6%
23	South Carolina	992	1.5%
24	Iowa	958	1.5%
25	Alabama	925	1.4%
26	Minnesota	873	1.3%
27	Arkansas	829	1.3%
28	New Mexico	751	1.2%
29	Virginia	735	1.1%
30	Mississippi	706	1.1%
31	Colorado	674	1.0%
32	Montana	634	1.0%
33	Oregon	612	0.9%
34	South Dakota	607	0.9%
35	Connecticut	547	0.8%
36	Maine	544	0.8%
37	Nebraska	528	0.8%
38	Idaho	524	0.8%
39	Maryland	409	0.6%
40	New Hampshire	404	0.6%
41	West Virginia	370	0.6%
42	Alaska	359	0.6%
43	Nevada	333	0.5%
44	North Dakota	303	0.5%
45	Utah	276	0.4%
46	Vermont	250	0.4%
47	Rhode Island	232	0.4%
48	Hawaii	196	0.3%
49	Delaware	175	0.3%
50	Wyoming	173	0.3%
	District of Columbia	186	0.3%

Source: U.S. Department of Education, National Center for Education Statistics
"Numbers and Types of Public Elementary and Secondary Schools" (http://nces.ed.gov/pubs2011/2011345.pdf)
*For school year 2009-2010. Title I schools are eligible for Title I federal funding to assist disadvantaged students. Includes schools with and without school-wide Title I programs.

Percent of Public Elementary and Secondary Schools
That Are Title I Eligible in 2010
National Percent = 65.6%*

ALPHA ORDER

RANK	STATE	PERCENT
35	Alabama	57.8
21	Alaska	70.9
37	Arizona	55.6
18	Arkansas	74.0
33	California	60.0
46	Colorado	37.6
43	Connecticut	47.0
8	Delaware	80.6
29	Florida	64.5
32	Georgia	62.2
26	Hawaii	67.8
22	Idaho	70.6
19	Illinois	72.5
22	Indiana	70.6
27	Iowa	65.3
6	Kansas	83.0
24	Kentucky	70.0
10	Louisiana	80.0
4	Maine	83.8
49	Maryland	28.3
36	Massachusetts	56.5
17	Michigan	74.7
47	Minnesota	35.9
28	Mississippi	65.1
45	Missouri	45.8
13	Montana	76.6
42	Nebraska	47.1
39	Nevada	52.4
5	New Hampshire	83.5
38	New Jersey	55.2
2	New Mexico	87.8
1	New York	90.0
12	North Carolina	77.3
34	North Dakota	58.6
16	Ohio	75.4
29	Oklahoma	64.5
43	Oregon	47.0
15	Pennsylvania	75.6
20	Rhode Island	72.3
7	South Carolina	82.3
3	South Dakota	85.0
8	Tennessee	80.6
14	Texas	76.5
50	Utah	26.4
11	Vermont	77.4
48	Virginia	34.0
31	Washington	64.1
40	West Virginia	48.7
25	Wisconsin	69.5
41	Wyoming	47.7

RANK ORDER

RANK	STATE	PERCENT
1	New York	90.0
2	New Mexico	87.8
3	South Dakota	85.0
4	Maine	83.8
5	New Hampshire	83.5
6	Kansas	83.0
7	South Carolina	82.3
8	Delaware	80.6
8	Tennessee	80.6
10	Louisiana	80.0
11	Vermont	77.4
12	North Carolina	77.3
13	Montana	76.6
14	Texas	76.5
15	Pennsylvania	75.6
16	Ohio	75.4
17	Michigan	74.7
18	Arkansas	74.0
19	Illinois	72.5
20	Rhode Island	72.3
21	Alaska	70.9
22	Idaho	70.6
22	Indiana	70.6
24	Kentucky	70.0
25	Wisconsin	69.5
26	Hawaii	67.8
27	Iowa	65.3
28	Mississippi	65.1
29	Florida	64.5
29	Oklahoma	64.5
31	Washington	64.1
32	Georgia	62.2
33	California	60.0
34	North Dakota	58.6
35	Alabama	57.8
36	Massachusetts	56.5
37	Arizona	55.6
38	New Jersey	55.2
39	Nevada	52.4
40	West Virginia	48.7
41	Wyoming	47.7
42	Nebraska	47.1
43	Connecticut	47.0
43	Oregon	47.0
45	Missouri	45.8
46	Colorado	37.6
47	Minnesota	35.9
48	Virginia	34.0
49	Maryland	28.3
50	Utah	26.4
	District of Columbia	79.8

Source: CQ Press using data from U.S. Department of Education, National Center for Education Statistics
    "Numbers and Types of Public Elementary and Secondary Schools" (http://nces.ed.gov/pubs2011/2011345.pdf)
*For school year 2009-2010. Title I schools are eligible for Title I federal funding to assist disadvantaged students. Includes schools with and without school-wide Title I programs.

Title I School-Wide Public Elementary and Secondary Schools in 2010

National Total = 44,512 Schools*

ALPHA ORDER

RANK	STATE	SCHOOLS	% of USA
18	Alabama	879	2.0%
37	Alaska	310	0.7%
19	Arizona	873	2.0%
22	Arkansas	715	1.6%
2	California	4,245	9.5%
29	Colorado	438	1.0%
43	Connecticut	192	0.4%
46	Delaware	155	0.3%
3	Florida	2,399	5.4%
11	Georgia	1,254	2.8%
45	Hawaii	180	0.4%
28	Idaho	468	1.1%
8	Illinois	1,371	3.1%
16	Indiana	954	2.1%
24	Iowa	538	1.2%
20	Kansas	754	1.7%
14	Kentucky	1,008	2.3%
12	Louisiana	1,116	2.5%
34	Maine	389	0.9%
38	Maryland	304	0.7%
26	Massachusetts	507	1.1%
7	Michigan	1,589	3.6%
41	Minnesota	277	0.6%
23	Mississippi	686	1.5%
27	Missouri	501	1.1%
33	Montana	395	0.9%
39	Nebraska	299	0.7%
40	Nevada	288	0.6%
48	New Hampshire	115	0.3%
32	New Jersey	396	0.9%
21	New Mexico	716	1.6%
6	New York	1,595	3.6%
5	North Carolina	1,790	4.0%
50	North Dakota	78	0.2%
4	Ohio	1,975	4.4%
15	Oklahoma	987	2.2%
30	Oregon	420	0.9%
10	Pennsylvania	1,335	3.0%
47	Rhode Island	122	0.3%
17	South Carolina	927	2.1%
36	South Dakota	339	0.8%
9	Tennessee	1,344	3.0%
1	Texas	6,282	14.1%
42	Utah	201	0.5%
44	Vermont	183	0.4%
31	Virginia	407	0.9%
13	Washington	1,069	2.4%
35	West Virginia	369	0.8%
25	Wisconsin	518	1.2%
49	Wyoming	79	0.2%

RANK ORDER

RANK	STATE	SCHOOLS	% of USA
1	Texas	6,282	14.1%
2	California	4,245	9.5%
3	Florida	2,399	5.4%
4	Ohio	1,975	4.4%
5	North Carolina	1,790	4.0%
6	New York	1,595	3.6%
7	Michigan	1,589	3.6%
8	Illinois	1,371	3.1%
9	Tennessee	1,344	3.0%
10	Pennsylvania	1,335	3.0%
11	Georgia	1,254	2.8%
12	Louisiana	1,116	2.5%
13	Washington	1,069	2.4%
14	Kentucky	1,008	2.3%
15	Oklahoma	987	2.2%
16	Indiana	954	2.1%
17	South Carolina	927	2.1%
18	Alabama	879	2.0%
19	Arizona	873	2.0%
20	Kansas	754	1.7%
21	New Mexico	716	1.6%
22	Arkansas	715	1.6%
23	Mississippi	686	1.5%
24	Iowa	538	1.2%
25	Wisconsin	518	1.2%
26	Massachusetts	507	1.1%
27	Missouri	501	1.1%
28	Idaho	468	1.1%
29	Colorado	438	1.0%
30	Oregon	420	0.9%
31	Virginia	407	0.9%
32	New Jersey	396	0.9%
33	Montana	395	0.9%
34	Maine	389	0.9%
35	West Virginia	369	0.8%
36	South Dakota	339	0.8%
37	Alaska	310	0.7%
38	Maryland	304	0.7%
39	Nebraska	299	0.7%
40	Nevada	288	0.6%
41	Minnesota	277	0.6%
42	Utah	201	0.5%
43	Connecticut	192	0.4%
44	Vermont	183	0.4%
45	Hawaii	180	0.4%
46	Delaware	155	0.3%
47	Rhode Island	122	0.3%
48	New Hampshire	115	0.3%
49	Wyoming	79	0.2%
50	North Dakota	78	0.2%
	District of Columbia	181	0.4%

Source: U.S. Department of Education, National Center for Education Statistics
"Numbers and Types of Public Elementary and Secondary Schools" (http://nces.ed.gov/pubs2011/2011345.pdf)
*For school year 2009-2010. Title I school-wide schools are those in which all of the pupils enrolled are eligible for Title I federal funding, which assists disadvantaged students.

Percent of Public Elementary and Secondary Schools
That Are Title I School-Wide Schools in 2010
National Percent = 45.0%*

RANK	STATE	PERCENT
18	Alabama	54.9
13	Alaska	61.3
31	Arizona	38.8
9	Arkansas	63.8
28	California	42.2
39	Colorado	24.4
47	Connecticut	16.5
6	Delaware	71.4
15	Florida	59.3
21	Georgia	51.0
12	Hawaii	62.3
11	Idaho	63.1
36	Illinois	31.1
22	Indiana	48.6
33	Iowa	36.6
19	Kansas	53.1
8	Kentucky	65.4
4	Louisiana	75.0
14	Maine	59.9
43	Maryland	21.0
37	Massachusetts	27.6
30	Michigan	41.0
50	Minnesota	11.4
10	Mississippi	63.2
44	Missouri	20.6
24	Montana	47.7
38	Nebraska	26.7
27	Nevada	45.3
40	New Hampshire	23.8
48	New Jersey	15.3
1	New Mexico	83.7
34	New York	33.7
7	North Carolina	70.2
49	North Dakota	15.1
20	Ohio	52.0
17	Oklahoma	55.0
35	Oregon	32.3
29	Pennsylvania	41.2
32	Rhode Island	38.0
2	South Carolina	76.9
25	South Dakota	47.5
3	Tennessee	75.8
5	Texas	72.9
45	Utah	19.2
16	Vermont	56.7
46	Virginia	18.8
26	Washington	46.1
22	West Virginia	48.6
41	Wisconsin	23.1
42	Wyoming	21.8

RANK	STATE	PERCENT
1	New Mexico	83.7
2	South Carolina	76.9
3	Tennessee	75.8
4	Louisiana	75.0
5	Texas	72.9
6	Delaware	71.4
7	North Carolina	70.2
8	Kentucky	65.4
9	Arkansas	63.8
10	Mississippi	63.2
11	Idaho	63.1
12	Hawaii	62.3
13	Alaska	61.3
14	Maine	59.9
15	Florida	59.3
16	Vermont	56.7
17	Oklahoma	55.0
18	Alabama	54.9
19	Kansas	53.1
20	Ohio	52.0
21	Georgia	51.0
22	Indiana	48.6
22	West Virginia	48.6
24	Montana	47.7
25	South Dakota	47.5
26	Washington	46.1
27	Nevada	45.3
28	California	42.2
29	Pennsylvania	41.2
30	Michigan	41.0
31	Arizona	38.8
32	Rhode Island	38.0
33	Iowa	36.6
34	New York	33.7
35	Oregon	32.3
36	Illinois	31.1
37	Massachusetts	27.6
38	Nebraska	26.7
39	Colorado	24.4
40	New Hampshire	23.8
41	Wisconsin	23.1
42	Wyoming	21.8
43	Maryland	21.0
44	Missouri	20.6
45	Utah	19.2
46	Virginia	18.8
47	Connecticut	16.5
48	New Jersey	15.3
49	North Dakota	15.1
50	Minnesota	11.4

District of Columbia	77.7

Source: CQ Press using data from U.S. Department of Education, National Center for Education Statistics
    "Numbers and Types of Public Elementary and Secondary Schools" (http://nces.ed.gov/pubs2011/2011345.pdf)
*For school year 2009-2010. Title I school-wide schools are those in which all of the pupils enrolled are eligible for Title I federal
funding, which assists disadvantaged students.

Special Education Public Elementary and Secondary Schools in 2010

National Total = 2,089 Schools*

ALPHA ORDER

RANK	STATE	SCHOOLS	% of USA
15	Alabama	41	2.0%
45	Alaska	2	0.1%
23	Arizona	20	1.0%
38	Arkansas	4	0.2%
5	California	146	7.0%
33	Colorado	9	0.4%
13	Connecticut	56	2.7%
24	Delaware	19	0.9%
3	Florida	170	8.1%
10	Georgia	72	3.4%
40	Hawaii	3	0.1%
26	Idaho	15	0.7%
4	Illinois	147	7.0%
17	Indiana	38	1.8%
35	Iowa	7	0.3%
29	Kansas	10	0.5%
29	Kentucky	10	0.5%
17	Louisiana	38	1.8%
48	Maine	1	0.0%
16	Maryland	40	1.9%
22	Massachusetts	23	1.1%
2	Michigan	197	9.4%
1	Minnesota	276	13.2%
40	Mississippi	3	0.1%
11	Missouri	68	3.3%
45	Montana	2	0.1%
20	Nebraska	28	1.3%
29	Nevada	10	0.5%
49	New Hampshire	0	0.0%
9	New Jersey	73	3.5%
37	New Mexico	6	0.3%
6	New York	105	5.0%
27	North Carolina	14	0.7%
19	North Dakota	34	1.6%
12	Ohio	64	3.1%
38	Oklahoma	4	0.2%
45	Oregon	2	0.1%
28	Pennsylvania	12	0.6%
40	Rhode Island	3	0.1%
29	South Carolina	10	0.5%
35	South Dakota	7	0.3%
24	Tennessee	19	0.9%
21	Texas	25	1.2%
8	Utah	86	4.1%
49	Vermont	0	0.0%
14	Virginia	42	2.0%
7	Washington	103	4.9%
40	West Virginia	3	0.1%
33	Wisconsin	9	0.4%
40	Wyoming	3	0.1%

RANK ORDER

RANK	STATE	SCHOOLS	% of USA
1	Minnesota	276	13.2%
2	Michigan	197	9.4%
3	Florida	170	8.1%
4	Illinois	147	7.0%
5	California	146	7.0%
6	New York	105	5.0%
7	Washington	103	4.9%
8	Utah	86	4.1%
9	New Jersey	73	3.5%
10	Georgia	72	3.4%
11	Missouri	68	3.3%
12	Ohio	64	3.1%
13	Connecticut	56	2.7%
14	Virginia	42	2.0%
15	Alabama	41	2.0%
16	Maryland	40	1.9%
17	Indiana	38	1.8%
17	Louisiana	38	1.8%
19	North Dakota	34	1.6%
20	Nebraska	28	1.3%
21	Texas	25	1.2%
22	Massachusetts	23	1.1%
23	Arizona	20	1.0%
24	Delaware	19	0.9%
24	Tennessee	19	0.9%
26	Idaho	15	0.7%
27	North Carolina	14	0.7%
28	Pennsylvania	12	0.6%
29	Kansas	10	0.5%
29	Kentucky	10	0.5%
29	Nevada	10	0.5%
29	South Carolina	10	0.5%
33	Colorado	9	0.4%
33	Wisconsin	9	0.4%
35	Iowa	7	0.3%
35	South Dakota	7	0.3%
37	New Mexico	6	0.3%
38	Arkansas	4	0.2%
38	Oklahoma	4	0.2%
40	Hawaii	3	0.1%
40	Mississippi	3	0.1%
40	Rhode Island	3	0.1%
40	West Virginia	3	0.1%
40	Wyoming	3	0.1%
45	Alaska	2	0.1%
45	Montana	2	0.1%
45	Oregon	2	0.1%
48	Maine	1	0.0%
49	New Hampshire	0	0.0%
49	Vermont	0	0.0%
	District of Columbia	10	0.5%

Source: U.S. Department of Education, National Center for Education Statistics
"Numbers and Types of Public Elementary and Secondary Schools" (http://nces.ed.gov/pubs2011/2011345.pdf)
*For school year 2009-2010.

Percent of Public Elementary and Secondary Schools
That Are Special Education Schools in 2010
National Percent = 2.1%*

ALPHA ORDER

RANK ORDER

RANK	STATE	PERCENT		RANK	STATE	PERCENT
14	Alabama	2.6		1	Minnesota	11.3
38	Alaska	0.4		2	Delaware	8.8
28	Arizona	0.9		3	Utah	8.2
38	Arkansas	0.4		4	North Dakota	6.6
23	California	1.5		5	Michigan	5.1
35	Colorado	0.5		6	Connecticut	4.8
6	Connecticut	4.8		7	Washington	4.4
2	Delaware	8.8		8	Florida	4.2
8	Florida	4.2		9	Illinois	3.3
10	Georgia	2.9		10	Georgia	2.9
26	Hawaii	1.0		11	Maryland	2.8
18	Idaho	2.0		11	Missouri	2.8
9	Illinois	3.3		11	New Jersey	2.8
19	Indiana	1.9		14	Alabama	2.6
35	Iowa	0.5		14	Louisiana	2.6
32	Kansas	0.7		16	Nebraska	2.5
34	Kentucky	0.6		17	New York	2.2
14	Louisiana	2.6		18	Idaho	2.0
45	Maine	0.2		19	Indiana	1.9
11	Maryland	2.8		19	Virginia	1.9
24	Massachusetts	1.3		21	Ohio	1.7
5	Michigan	5.1		22	Nevada	1.6
1	Minnesota	11.3		23	California	1.5
43	Mississippi	0.3		24	Massachusetts	1.3
11	Missouri	2.8		25	Tennessee	1.1
45	Montana	0.2		26	Hawaii	1.0
16	Nebraska	2.5		26	South Dakota	1.0
22	Nevada	1.6		28	Arizona	0.9
49	New Hampshire	0.0		28	Rhode Island	0.9
11	New Jersey	2.8		30	South Carolina	0.8
32	New Mexico	0.7		30	Wyoming	0.8
17	New York	2.2		32	Kansas	0.7
35	North Carolina	0.5		32	New Mexico	0.7
4	North Dakota	6.6		34	Kentucky	0.6
21	Ohio	1.7		35	Colorado	0.5
45	Oklahoma	0.2		35	Iowa	0.5
45	Oregon	0.2		35	North Carolina	0.5
38	Pennsylvania	0.4		38	Alaska	0.4
28	Rhode Island	0.9		38	Arkansas	0.4
30	South Carolina	0.8		38	Pennsylvania	0.4
26	South Dakota	1.0		38	West Virginia	0.4
25	Tennessee	1.1		38	Wisconsin	0.4
43	Texas	0.3		43	Mississippi	0.3
3	Utah	8.2		43	Texas	0.3
49	Vermont	0.0		45	Maine	0.2
19	Virginia	1.9		45	Montana	0.2
7	Washington	4.4		45	Oklahoma	0.2
38	West Virginia	0.4		45	Oregon	0.2
38	Wisconsin	0.4		49	New Hampshire	0.0
30	Wyoming	0.8		49	Vermont	0.0

District of Columbia 4.3

Source: CQ Press using data from U.S. Department of Education, National Center for Education Statistics
"Numbers and Types of Public Elementary and Secondary Schools" (http://nces.ed.gov/pubs2011/2011345.pdf)
*For school year 2009-2010.

Vocational Public Elementary and Secondary Schools in 2010

National Total = 1,417 Schools*

ALPHA ORDER

RANK	STATE	SCHOOLS	% of USA
7	Alabama	72	5.1%
36	Alaska	3	0.2%
1	Arizona	207	14.6%
20	Arkansas	23	1.6%
5	California	75	5.3%
30	Colorado	6	0.4%
22	Connecticut	16	1.1%
30	Delaware	6	0.4%
10	Florida	53	3.7%
37	Georgia	1	0.1%
42	Hawaii	0	0.0%
25	Idaho	11	0.8%
10	Illinois	53	3.7%
17	Indiana	29	2.0%
42	Iowa	0	0.0%
37	Kansas	1	0.1%
2	Kentucky	124	8.8%
30	Louisiana	6	0.4%
18	Maine	27	1.9%
19	Maryland	24	1.7%
13	Massachusetts	39	2.8%
15	Michigan	38	2.7%
25	Minnesota	11	0.8%
3	Mississippi	90	6.4%
8	Missouri	66	4.7%
42	Montana	0	0.0%
42	Nebraska	0	0.0%
37	Nevada	1	0.1%
42	New Hampshire	0	0.0%
9	New Jersey	55	3.9%
37	New Mexico	1	0.1%
30	New York	6	0.4%
37	North Carolina	1	0.1%
28	North Dakota	9	0.6%
6	Ohio	73	5.2%
42	Oklahoma	0	0.0%
42	Oregon	0	0.0%
4	Pennsylvania	87	6.1%
25	Rhode Island	11	0.8%
13	South Carolina	39	2.8%
35	South Dakota	4	0.3%
21	Tennessee	21	1.5%
42	Texas	0	0.0%
30	Utah	6	0.4%
23	Vermont	15	1.1%
12	Virginia	49	3.5%
23	Washington	15	1.1%
16	West Virginia	31	2.2%
29	Wisconsin	8	0.6%
42	Wyoming	0	0.0%

RANK ORDER

RANK	STATE	SCHOOLS	% of USA
1	Arizona	207	14.6%
2	Kentucky	124	8.8%
3	Mississippi	90	6.4%
4	Pennsylvania	87	6.1%
5	California	75	5.3%
6	Ohio	73	5.2%
7	Alabama	72	5.1%
8	Missouri	66	4.7%
9	New Jersey	55	3.9%
10	Florida	53	3.7%
10	Illinois	53	3.7%
12	Virginia	49	3.5%
13	Massachusetts	39	2.8%
13	South Carolina	39	2.8%
15	Michigan	38	2.7%
16	West Virginia	31	2.2%
17	Indiana	29	2.0%
18	Maine	27	1.9%
19	Maryland	24	1.7%
20	Arkansas	23	1.6%
21	Tennessee	21	1.5%
22	Connecticut	16	1.1%
23	Vermont	15	1.1%
23	Washington	15	1.1%
25	Idaho	11	0.8%
25	Minnesota	11	0.8%
25	Rhode Island	11	0.8%
28	North Dakota	9	0.6%
29	Wisconsin	8	0.6%
30	Colorado	6	0.4%
30	Delaware	6	0.4%
30	Louisiana	6	0.4%
30	New York	6	0.4%
30	Utah	6	0.4%
35	South Dakota	4	0.3%
36	Alaska	3	0.2%
37	Georgia	1	0.1%
37	Kansas	1	0.1%
37	Nevada	1	0.1%
37	New Mexico	1	0.1%
37	North Carolina	1	0.1%
42	Hawaii	0	0.0%
42	Iowa	0	0.0%
42	Montana	0	0.0%
42	Nebraska	0	0.0%
42	New Hampshire	0	0.0%
42	Oklahoma	0	0.0%
42	Oregon	0	0.0%
42	Texas	0	0.0%
42	Wyoming	0	0.0%
	District of Columbia	4	0.3%

Source: U.S. Department of Education, National Center for Education Statistics
    "Numbers and Types of Public Elementary and Secondary Schools" (http://nces.ed.gov/pubs2011/2011345.pdf)
*For school year 2009-2010.

Percent of Public Elementary and Secondary Schools
That Are Vocational Schools in 2010
National Percent = 1.4%*

RANK	STATE	PERCENT
5	Alabama	4.5
28	Alaska	0.6
1	Arizona	9.2
14	Arkansas	2.1
27	California	0.7
35	Colorado	0.3
22	Connecticut	1.4
10	Delaware	2.8
23	Florida	1.3
40	Georgia	0.0
40	Hawaii	0.0
20	Idaho	1.5
24	Illinois	1.2
20	Indiana	1.5
40	Iowa	0.0
37	Kansas	0.1
3	Kentucky	8.0
33	Louisiana	0.4
6	Maine	4.2
18	Maryland	1.7
14	Massachusetts	2.1
26	Michigan	1.0
32	Minnesota	0.5
2	Mississippi	8.3
11	Missouri	2.7
40	Montana	0.0
40	Nebraska	0.0
36	Nevada	0.2
40	New Hampshire	0.0
14	New Jersey	2.1
37	New Mexico	0.1
37	New York	0.1
40	North Carolina	0.0
18	North Dakota	1.7
17	Ohio	1.9
40	Oklahoma	0.0
40	Oregon	0.0
11	Pennsylvania	2.7
8	Rhode Island	3.4
9	South Carolina	3.2
28	South Dakota	0.6
24	Tennessee	1.2
40	Texas	0.0
28	Utah	0.6
4	Vermont	4.6
13	Virginia	2.3
28	Washington	0.6
7	West Virginia	4.1
33	Wisconsin	0.4
40	Wyoming	0.0

RANK	STATE	PERCENT
1	Arizona	9.2
2	Mississippi	8.3
3	Kentucky	8.0
4	Vermont	4.6
5	Alabama	4.5
6	Maine	4.2
7	West Virginia	4.1
8	Rhode Island	3.4
9	South Carolina	3.2
10	Delaware	2.8
11	Missouri	2.7
11	Pennsylvania	2.7
13	Virginia	2.3
14	Arkansas	2.1
14	Massachusetts	2.1
14	New Jersey	2.1
17	Ohio	1.9
18	Maryland	1.7
18	North Dakota	1.7
20	Idaho	1.5
20	Indiana	1.5
22	Connecticut	1.4
23	Florida	1.3
24	Illinois	1.2
24	Tennessee	1.2
26	Michigan	1.0
27	California	0.7
28	Alaska	0.6
28	South Dakota	0.6
28	Utah	0.6
28	Washington	0.6
32	Minnesota	0.5
33	Louisiana	0.4
33	Wisconsin	0.4
35	Colorado	0.3
36	Nevada	0.2
37	Kansas	0.1
37	New Mexico	0.1
37	New York	0.1
40	Georgia	0.0
40	Hawaii	0.0
40	Iowa	0.0
40	Montana	0.0
40	Nebraska	0.0
40	New Hampshire	0.0
40	North Carolina	0.0
40	Oklahoma	0.0
40	Oregon	0.0
40	Texas	0.0
40	Wyoming	0.0
	District of Columbia	1.7

Source: CQ Press using data from U.S. Department of Education, National Center for Education Statistics
    "Numbers and Types of Public Elementary and Secondary Schools" (http://nces.ed.gov/pubs2011/2011345.pdf)
*For school year 2009-2010.

Alternative Education Public Elementary and Secondary Schools in 2010

National Total = 6,293 Schools*

ALPHA ORDER

RANK	STATE	SCHOOLS	% of USA
12	Alabama	117	1.9%
22	Alaska	51	0.8%
19	Arizona	82	1.3%
37	Arkansas	11	0.2%
1	California	1,375	21.8%
15	Colorado	95	1.5%
24	Connecticut	44	0.7%
38	Delaware	10	0.2%
4	Florida	422	6.7%
11	Georgia	140	2.2%
46	Hawaii	1	0.0%
18	Idaho	83	1.3%
8	Illinois	188	3.0%
34	Indiana	19	0.3%
22	Iowa	51	0.8%
46	Kansas	1	0.0%
10	Kentucky	170	2.7%
9	Louisiana	184	2.9%
45	Maine	2	0.0%
21	Maryland	62	1.0%
34	Massachusetts	19	0.3%
6	Michigan	312	5.0%
3	Minnesota	480	7.6%
20	Mississippi	64	1.0%
13	Missouri	112	1.8%
43	Montana	4	0.1%
41	Nebraska	5	0.1%
27	Nevada	32	0.5%
49	New Hampshire	0	0.0%
14	New Jersey	103	1.6%
26	New Mexico	40	0.6%
29	New York	28	0.4%
43	North Carolina	4	0.1%
49	North Dakota	0	0.0%
40	Ohio	6	0.1%
41	Oklahoma	5	0.1%
25	Oregon	43	0.7%
36	Pennsylvania	13	0.2%
39	Rhode Island	9	0.1%
33	South Carolina	21	0.3%
31	South Dakota	27	0.4%
29	Tennessee	28	0.4%
2	Texas	1,076	17.1%
16	Utah	92	1.5%
46	Vermont	1	0.0%
7	Virginia	190	3.0%
5	Washington	315	5.0%
27	West Virginia	32	0.5%
17	Wisconsin	89	1.4%
32	Wyoming	24	0.4%

RANK ORDER

RANK	STATE	SCHOOLS	% of USA
1	California	1,375	21.8%
2	Texas	1,076	17.1%
3	Minnesota	480	7.6%
4	Florida	422	6.7%
5	Washington	315	5.0%
6	Michigan	312	5.0%
7	Virginia	190	3.0%
8	Illinois	188	3.0%
9	Louisiana	184	2.9%
10	Kentucky	170	2.7%
11	Georgia	140	2.2%
12	Alabama	117	1.9%
13	Missouri	112	1.8%
14	New Jersey	103	1.6%
15	Colorado	95	1.5%
16	Utah	92	1.5%
17	Wisconsin	89	1.4%
18	Idaho	83	1.3%
19	Arizona	82	1.3%
20	Mississippi	64	1.0%
21	Maryland	62	1.0%
22	Alaska	51	0.8%
22	Iowa	51	0.8%
24	Connecticut	44	0.7%
25	Oregon	43	0.7%
26	New Mexico	40	0.6%
27	Nevada	32	0.5%
27	West Virginia	32	0.5%
29	New York	28	0.4%
29	Tennessee	28	0.4%
31	South Dakota	27	0.4%
32	Wyoming	24	0.4%
33	South Carolina	21	0.3%
34	Indiana	19	0.3%
34	Massachusetts	19	0.3%
36	Pennsylvania	13	0.2%
37	Arkansas	11	0.2%
38	Delaware	10	0.2%
39	Rhode Island	9	0.1%
40	Ohio	6	0.1%
41	Nebraska	5	0.1%
41	Oklahoma	5	0.1%
43	Montana	4	0.1%
43	North Carolina	4	0.1%
45	Maine	2	0.0%
46	Hawaii	1	0.0%
46	Kansas	1	0.0%
46	Vermont	1	0.0%
49	New Hampshire	0	0.0%
49	North Dakota	0	0.0%
	District of Columbia	11	0.2%

Source: U.S. Department of Education, National Center for Education Statistics
   "Numbers and Types of Public Elementary and Secondary Schools" (http://nces.ed.gov/pubs2011/2011345.pdf)
*For school year 2009-2010.

Percent of Public Elementary and Secondary Schools
That Are Alternative Education Schools in 2010
National Percent = 6.4%*

ALPHA ORDER

RANK	STATE	PERCENT
13	Alabama	7.3
9	Alaska	10.1
29	Arizona	3.6
35	Arkansas	1.0
2	California	13.7
17	Colorado	5.3
27	Connecticut	3.8
20	Delaware	4.6
8	Florida	10.4
16	Georgia	5.7
42	Hawaii	0.3
6	Idaho	11.2
22	Illinois	4.3
35	Indiana	1.0
30	Iowa	3.5
48	Kansas	0.1
7	Kentucky	11.0
5	Louisiana	12.4
42	Maine	0.3
22	Maryland	4.3
35	Massachusetts	1.0
12	Michigan	8.0
1	Minnesota	19.7
15	Mississippi	5.9
20	Missouri	4.6
39	Montana	0.5
40	Nebraska	0.4
18	Nevada	5.0
49	New Hampshire	0.0
25	New Jersey	4.0
19	New Mexico	4.7
38	New York	0.6
46	North Carolina	0.2
49	North Dakota	0.0
46	Ohio	0.2
42	Oklahoma	0.3
31	Oregon	3.3
40	Pennsylvania	0.4
32	Rhode Island	2.8
33	South Carolina	1.7
27	South Dakota	3.8
34	Tennessee	1.6
4	Texas	12.5
10	Utah	8.8
42	Vermont	0.3
10	Virginia	8.8
3	Washington	13.6
24	West Virginia	4.2
25	Wisconsin	4.0
14	Wyoming	6.6

RANK ORDER

RANK	STATE	PERCENT
1	Minnesota	19.7
2	California	13.7
3	Washington	13.6
4	Texas	12.5
5	Louisiana	12.4
6	Idaho	11.2
7	Kentucky	11.0
8	Florida	10.4
9	Alaska	10.1
10	Utah	8.8
10	Virginia	8.8
12	Michigan	8.0
13	Alabama	7.3
14	Wyoming	6.6
15	Mississippi	5.9
16	Georgia	5.7
17	Colorado	5.3
18	Nevada	5.0
19	New Mexico	4.7
20	Delaware	4.6
20	Missouri	4.6
22	Illinois	4.3
22	Maryland	4.3
24	West Virginia	4.2
25	New Jersey	4.0
25	Wisconsin	4.0
27	Connecticut	3.8
27	South Dakota	3.8
29	Arizona	3.6
30	Iowa	3.5
31	Oregon	3.3
32	Rhode Island	2.8
33	South Carolina	1.7
34	Tennessee	1.6
35	Arkansas	1.0
35	Indiana	1.0
35	Massachusetts	1.0
38	New York	0.6
39	Montana	0.5
40	Nebraska	0.4
40	Pennsylvania	0.4
42	Hawaii	0.3
42	Maine	0.3
42	Oklahoma	0.3
42	Vermont	0.3
46	North Carolina	0.2
46	Ohio	0.2
48	Kansas	0.1
49	New Hampshire	0.0
49	North Dakota	0.0

District of Columbia   4.7

Source: CQ Press using data from U.S. Department of Education, National Center for Education Statistics
"Numbers and Types of Public Elementary and Secondary Schools" (http://nces.ed.gov/pubs2011/2011345.pdf)
*For school year 2009-2010.

Public Elementary and Secondary Magnet Schools in 2010

Reporting States Total = 2,213 Schools*

ALPHA ORDER

RANK	STATE	SCHOOLS	% of USA
17	Alabama	31	1.4%
23	Alaska	13	0.6%
NA	Arizona**	NA	NA
13	Arkansas	40	1.8%
NA	California**	NA	NA
18	Colorado	25	1.1%
10	Connecticut	54	2.4%
25	Delaware	3	0.1%
2	Florida	363	16.4%
8	Georgia	78	3.5%
NA	Hawaii**	NA	NA
25	Idaho	3	0.1%
5	Illinois	104	4.7%
19	Indiana	24	1.1%
NA	Iowa**	NA	NA
14	Kansas	35	1.6%
12	Kentucky	41	1.9%
7	Louisiana	83	3.8%
29	Maine	1	0.0%
6	Maryland	87	3.9%
NA	Massachusetts**	NA	NA
1	Michigan	477	21.6%
9	Minnesota	76	3.4%
22	Mississippi	19	0.9%
14	Missouri	35	1.6%
NA	Montana**	NA	NA
NA	Nebraska**	NA	NA
19	Nevada	24	1.1%
NA	New Hampshire**	NA	NA
NA	New Jersey**	NA	NA
27	New Mexico	2	0.1%
NA	New York**	NA	NA
4	North Carolina	125	5.6%
NA	North Dakota**	NA	NA
NA	Ohio**	NA	NA
NA	Oklahoma**	NA	NA
NA	Oregon**	NA	NA
11	Pennsylvania	53	2.4%
NA	Rhode Island**	NA	NA
NA	South Carolina**	NA	NA
NA	South Dakota**	NA	NA
16	Tennessee	32	1.4%
NA	Texas**	NA	NA
19	Utah	24	1.1%
27	Vermont	2	0.1%
3	Virginia	166	7.5%
NA	Washington**	NA	NA
NA	West Virginia**	NA	NA
24	Wisconsin	4	0.2%
NA	Wyoming**	NA	NA

RANK ORDER

RANK	STATE	SCHOOLS	% of USA
1	Michigan	477	21.6%
2	Florida	363	16.4%
3	Virginia	166	7.5%
4	North Carolina	125	5.6%
5	Illinois	104	4.7%
6	Maryland	87	3.9%
7	Louisiana	83	3.8%
8	Georgia	78	3.5%
9	Minnesota	76	3.4%
10	Connecticut	54	2.4%
11	Pennsylvania	53	2.4%
12	Kentucky	41	1.9%
13	Arkansas	40	1.8%
14	Kansas	35	1.6%
14	Missouri	35	1.6%
16	Tennessee	32	1.4%
17	Alabama	31	1.4%
18	Colorado	25	1.1%
19	Indiana	24	1.1%
19	Nevada	24	1.1%
19	Utah	24	1.1%
22	Mississippi	19	0.9%
23	Alaska	13	0.6%
24	Wisconsin	4	0.2%
25	Delaware	3	0.1%
25	Idaho	3	0.1%
27	New Mexico	2	0.1%
27	Vermont	2	0.1%
29	Maine	1	0.0%
NA	Arizona**	NA	NA
NA	California**	NA	NA
NA	Hawaii**	NA	NA
NA	Iowa**	NA	NA
NA	Massachusetts**	NA	NA
NA	Montana**	NA	NA
NA	Nebraska**	NA	NA
NA	New Hampshire**	NA	NA
NA	New Jersey**	NA	NA
NA	New York**	NA	NA
NA	North Dakota**	NA	NA
NA	Ohio**	NA	NA
NA	Oklahoma**	NA	NA
NA	Oregon**	NA	NA
NA	Rhode Island**	NA	NA
NA	South Carolina**	NA	NA
NA	South Dakota**	NA	NA
NA	Texas**	NA	NA
NA	Washington**	NA	NA
NA	West Virginia**	NA	NA
NA	Wyoming**	NA	NA
	District of Columbia	5	0.2%

Source: U.S. Department of Education, National Center for Education Statistics
   "Numbers and Types of Public Elementary and Secondary Schools" (http://nces.ed.gov/pubs2011/2011345.pdf)
*For school year 2009-2010. Magnet schools are those designed to attract students of different racial/ethnic backgrounds for the purpose of reducing racial isolation, or to provide an academic or social focus on a specific theme (e.g., performing arts).
**Not available or not applicable.

Percent of Public Elementary and Secondary
That Are Magnet Schools in 2010
Reporting States Percent = 2.2%*

ALPHA ORDER

RANK	STATE	PERCENT
17	Alabama	1.9
13	Alaska	2.6
NA	Arizona**	NA
9	Arkansas	3.6
NA	California**	NA
21	Colorado	1.4
7	Connecticut	4.6
21	Delaware	1.4
2	Florida	9.0
10	Georgia	3.2
NA	Hawaii**	NA
26	Idaho	0.4
15	Illinois	2.4
24	Indiana	1.2
NA	Iowa**	NA
14	Kansas	2.5
12	Kentucky	2.7
5	Louisiana	5.6
27	Maine	0.2
4	Maryland	6.0
NA	Massachusetts**	NA
1	Michigan	12.3
11	Minnesota	3.1
18	Mississippi	1.8
21	Missouri	1.4
NA	Montana**	NA
NA	Nebraska**	NA
8	Nevada	3.8
NA	New Hampshire**	NA
NA	New Jersey**	NA
27	New Mexico	0.2
NA	New York**	NA
6	North Carolina	4.9
NA	North Dakota**	NA
NA	Ohio**	NA
NA	Oklahoma**	NA
NA	Oregon**	NA
20	Pennsylvania	1.6
NA	Rhode Island**	NA
NA	South Carolina**	NA
NA	South Dakota**	NA
18	Tennessee	1.8
NA	Texas**	NA
16	Utah	2.3
25	Vermont	0.6
3	Virginia	7.7
NA	Washington**	NA
NA	West Virginia**	NA
27	Wisconsin	0.2
NA	Wyoming**	NA

RANK ORDER

RANK	STATE	PERCENT
1	Michigan	12.3
2	Florida	9.0
3	Virginia	7.7
4	Maryland	6.0
5	Louisiana	5.6
6	North Carolina	4.9
7	Connecticut	4.6
8	Nevada	3.8
9	Arkansas	3.6
10	Georgia	3.2
11	Minnesota	3.1
12	Kentucky	2.7
13	Alaska	2.6
14	Kansas	2.5
15	Illinois	2.4
16	Utah	2.3
17	Alabama	1.9
18	Mississippi	1.8
18	Tennessee	1.8
20	Pennsylvania	1.6
21	Colorado	1.4
21	Delaware	1.4
21	Missouri	1.4
24	Indiana	1.2
25	Vermont	0.6
26	Idaho	0.4
27	Maine	0.2
27	New Mexico	0.2
27	Wisconsin	0.2
NA	Arizona**	NA
NA	California**	NA
NA	Hawaii**	NA
NA	Iowa**	NA
NA	Massachusetts**	NA
NA	Montana**	NA
NA	Nebraska**	NA
NA	New Hampshire**	NA
NA	New Jersey**	NA
NA	New York**	NA
NA	North Dakota**	NA
NA	Ohio**	NA
NA	Oklahoma**	NA
NA	Oregon**	NA
NA	Rhode Island**	NA
NA	South Carolina**	NA
NA	South Dakota**	NA
NA	Texas**	NA
NA	Washington**	NA
NA	West Virginia**	NA
NA	Wyoming**	NA

District of Columbia	2.1

Source: CQ Press using data from U.S. Department of Education, National Center for Education Statistics
"Numbers and Types of Public Elementary and Secondary Schools" (http://nces.ed.gov/pubs2011/2011345.pdf)
*For school year 2009-2010. Magnet schools are those designed to attract students of different racial/ethnic backgrounds for the purpose of reducing racial isolation, or to provide an academic or social focus on a specific theme (e.g., performing arts).
**Not available or not applicable.

Public Elementary and Secondary Charter Schools in 2010

National Total = 4,952 Schools*

ALPHA ORDER

RANK	STATE	SCHOOLS	% of USA
NA	Alabama**	NA	NA
30	Alaska	25	0.5%
3	Arizona	504	10.2%
25	Arkansas	38	0.8%
1	California	813	16.4%
9	Colorado	158	3.2%
32	Connecticut	18	0.4%
32	Delaware	18	0.4%
4	Florida	412	8.3%
18	Georgia	63	1.3%
29	Hawaii	31	0.6%
26	Idaho	36	0.7%
23	Illinois	39	0.8%
20	Indiana	53	1.1%
37	Iowa	9	0.2%
27	Kansas	35	0.7%
NA	Kentucky**	NA	NA
14	Louisiana	77	1.6%
NA	Maine**	NA	NA
22	Maryland	42	0.8%
19	Massachusetts	62	1.3%
6	Michigan	294	5.9%
8	Minnesota	181	3.7%
40	Mississippi	1	0.0%
21	Missouri	48	1.0%
NA	Montana**	NA	NA
NA	Nebraska**	NA	NA
27	Nevada	35	0.7%
35	New Hampshire	15	0.3%
17	New Jersey	70	1.4%
15	New Mexico	72	1.5%
10	New York	140	2.8%
13	North Carolina	96	1.9%
NA	North Dakota**	NA	NA
5	Ohio	323	6.5%
32	Oklahoma	18	0.4%
12	Oregon	102	2.1%
11	Pennsylvania	134	2.7%
36	Rhode Island	12	0.2%
23	South Carolina	39	0.8%
NA	South Dakota**	NA	NA
31	Tennessee	20	0.4%
2	Texas	536	10.8%
15	Utah	72	1.5%
NA	Vermont**	NA	NA
38	Virginia	3	0.1%
NA	Washington**	NA	NA
NA	West Virginia**	NA	NA
7	Wisconsin	206	4.2%
38	Wyoming	3	0.1%

RANK ORDER

RANK	STATE	SCHOOLS	% of USA
1	California	813	16.4%
2	Texas	536	10.8%
3	Arizona	504	10.2%
4	Florida	412	8.3%
5	Ohio	323	6.5%
6	Michigan	294	5.9%
7	Wisconsin	206	4.2%
8	Minnesota	181	3.7%
9	Colorado	158	3.2%
10	New York	140	2.8%
11	Pennsylvania	134	2.7%
12	Oregon	102	2.1%
13	North Carolina	96	1.9%
14	Louisiana	77	1.6%
15	New Mexico	72	1.5%
15	Utah	72	1.5%
17	New Jersey	70	1.4%
18	Georgia	63	1.3%
19	Massachusetts	62	1.3%
20	Indiana	53	1.1%
21	Missouri	48	1.0%
22	Maryland	42	0.8%
23	Illinois	39	0.8%
23	South Carolina	39	0.8%
25	Arkansas	38	0.8%
26	Idaho	36	0.7%
27	Kansas	35	0.7%
27	Nevada	35	0.7%
29	Hawaii	31	0.6%
30	Alaska	25	0.5%
31	Tennessee	20	0.4%
32	Connecticut	18	0.4%
32	Delaware	18	0.4%
32	Oklahoma	18	0.4%
35	New Hampshire	15	0.3%
36	Rhode Island	12	0.2%
37	Iowa	9	0.2%
38	Virginia	3	0.1%
38	Wyoming	3	0.1%
40	Mississippi	1	0.0%
NA	Alabama**	NA	NA
NA	Kentucky**	NA	NA
NA	Maine**	NA	NA
NA	Montana**	NA	NA
NA	Nebraska**	NA	NA
NA	North Dakota**	NA	NA
NA	South Dakota**	NA	NA
NA	Vermont**	NA	NA
NA	Washington**	NA	NA
NA	West Virginia**	NA	NA
	District of Columbia	99	2.0%

Source: U.S. Department of Education, National Center for Education Statistics
    "Numbers and Types of Public Elementary and Secondary Schools" (http://nces.ed.gov/pubs2011/2011345.pdf)
*For school year 2009-2010. Charter schools provide free public elementary/secondary education under a charter granted by the state legislature or other appropriate authority.
**Not available or not applicable.

Percent of Public Elementary and Secondary
That Are Charter Schools in 2010
National Percent = 5.0%*

<table>
<tr><td colspan="4">ALPHA ORDER</td><td colspan="4">RANK ORDER</td></tr>
<tr><td>RANK</td><td>STATE</td><td></td><td>PERCENT</td><td>RANK</td><td>STATE</td><td></td><td>PERCENT</td></tr>
<tr><td>NA</td><td>Alabama**</td><td></td><td>NA</td><td>1</td><td>Arizona</td><td></td><td>22.4</td></tr>
<tr><td>17</td><td>Alaska</td><td></td><td>4.9</td><td>2</td><td>Hawaii</td><td></td><td>10.7</td></tr>
<tr><td>1</td><td>Arizona</td><td></td><td>22.4</td><td>3</td><td>Florida</td><td></td><td>10.2</td></tr>
<tr><td>22</td><td>Arkansas</td><td></td><td>3.4</td><td>4</td><td>Wisconsin</td><td></td><td>9.2</td></tr>
<tr><td>9</td><td>California</td><td></td><td>8.1</td><td>5</td><td>Colorado</td><td></td><td>8.8</td></tr>
<tr><td>5</td><td>Colorado</td><td></td><td>8.8</td><td>6</td><td>Ohio</td><td></td><td>8.5</td></tr>
<tr><td>33</td><td>Connecticut</td><td></td><td>1.5</td><td>7</td><td>New Mexico</td><td></td><td>8.4</td></tr>
<tr><td>8</td><td>Delaware</td><td></td><td>8.3</td><td>8</td><td>Delaware</td><td></td><td>8.3</td></tr>
<tr><td>3</td><td>Florida</td><td></td><td>10.2</td><td>9</td><td>California</td><td></td><td>8.1</td></tr>
<tr><td>30</td><td>Georgia</td><td></td><td>2.6</td><td>10</td><td>Oregon</td><td></td><td>7.8</td></tr>
<tr><td>2</td><td>Hawaii</td><td></td><td>10.7</td><td>11</td><td>Michigan</td><td></td><td>7.6</td></tr>
<tr><td>17</td><td>Idaho</td><td></td><td>4.9</td><td>12</td><td>Minnesota</td><td></td><td>7.4</td></tr>
<tr><td>36</td><td>Illinois</td><td></td><td>0.9</td><td>13</td><td>Utah</td><td></td><td>6.9</td></tr>
<tr><td>28</td><td>Indiana</td><td></td><td>2.7</td><td>14</td><td>Texas</td><td></td><td>6.2</td></tr>
<tr><td>38</td><td>Iowa</td><td></td><td>0.6</td><td>15</td><td>Nevada</td><td></td><td>5.5</td></tr>
<tr><td>31</td><td>Kansas</td><td></td><td>2.5</td><td>16</td><td>Louisiana</td><td></td><td>5.2</td></tr>
<tr><td>NA</td><td>Kentucky**</td><td></td><td>NA</td><td>17</td><td>Alaska</td><td></td><td>4.9</td></tr>
<tr><td>16</td><td>Louisiana</td><td></td><td>5.2</td><td>17</td><td>Idaho</td><td></td><td>4.9</td></tr>
<tr><td>NA</td><td>Maine**</td><td></td><td>NA</td><td>19</td><td>Pennsylvania</td><td></td><td>4.1</td></tr>
<tr><td>27</td><td>Maryland</td><td></td><td>2.9</td><td>20</td><td>North Carolina</td><td></td><td>3.8</td></tr>
<tr><td>22</td><td>Massachusetts</td><td></td><td>3.4</td><td>21</td><td>Rhode Island</td><td></td><td>3.7</td></tr>
<tr><td>11</td><td>Michigan</td><td></td><td>7.6</td><td>22</td><td>Arkansas</td><td></td><td>3.4</td></tr>
<tr><td>12</td><td>Minnesota</td><td></td><td>7.4</td><td>22</td><td>Massachusetts</td><td></td><td>3.4</td></tr>
<tr><td>39</td><td>Mississippi</td><td></td><td>0.1</td><td>24</td><td>South Carolina</td><td></td><td>3.2</td></tr>
<tr><td>32</td><td>Missouri</td><td></td><td>2.0</td><td>25</td><td>New Hampshire</td><td></td><td>3.1</td></tr>
<tr><td>NA</td><td>Montana**</td><td></td><td>NA</td><td>26</td><td>New York</td><td></td><td>3.0</td></tr>
<tr><td>NA</td><td>Nebraska**</td><td></td><td>NA</td><td>27</td><td>Maryland</td><td></td><td>2.9</td></tr>
<tr><td>15</td><td>Nevada</td><td></td><td>5.5</td><td>28</td><td>Indiana</td><td></td><td>2.7</td></tr>
<tr><td>25</td><td>New Hampshire</td><td></td><td>3.1</td><td>28</td><td>New Jersey</td><td></td><td>2.7</td></tr>
<tr><td>28</td><td>New Jersey</td><td></td><td>2.7</td><td>30</td><td>Georgia</td><td></td><td>2.6</td></tr>
<tr><td>7</td><td>New Mexico</td><td></td><td>8.4</td><td>31</td><td>Kansas</td><td></td><td>2.5</td></tr>
<tr><td>26</td><td>New York</td><td></td><td>3.0</td><td>32</td><td>Missouri</td><td></td><td>2.0</td></tr>
<tr><td>20</td><td>North Carolina</td><td></td><td>3.8</td><td>33</td><td>Connecticut</td><td></td><td>1.5</td></tr>
<tr><td>NA</td><td>North Dakota**</td><td></td><td>NA</td><td>34</td><td>Tennessee</td><td></td><td>1.1</td></tr>
<tr><td>6</td><td>Ohio</td><td></td><td>8.5</td><td>35</td><td>Oklahoma</td><td></td><td>1.0</td></tr>
<tr><td>35</td><td>Oklahoma</td><td></td><td>1.0</td><td>36</td><td>Illinois</td><td></td><td>0.9</td></tr>
<tr><td>10</td><td>Oregon</td><td></td><td>7.8</td><td>37</td><td>Wyoming</td><td></td><td>0.8</td></tr>
<tr><td>19</td><td>Pennsylvania</td><td></td><td>4.1</td><td>38</td><td>Iowa</td><td></td><td>0.6</td></tr>
<tr><td>21</td><td>Rhode Island</td><td></td><td>3.7</td><td>39</td><td>Mississippi</td><td></td><td>0.1</td></tr>
<tr><td>24</td><td>South Carolina</td><td></td><td>3.2</td><td>39</td><td>Virginia</td><td></td><td>0.1</td></tr>
<tr><td>NA</td><td>South Dakota**</td><td></td><td>NA</td><td>NA</td><td>Alabama**</td><td></td><td>NA</td></tr>
<tr><td>34</td><td>Tennessee</td><td></td><td>1.1</td><td>NA</td><td>Kentucky**</td><td></td><td>NA</td></tr>
<tr><td>14</td><td>Texas</td><td></td><td>6.2</td><td>NA</td><td>Maine**</td><td></td><td>NA</td></tr>
<tr><td>13</td><td>Utah</td><td></td><td>6.9</td><td>NA</td><td>Montana**</td><td></td><td>NA</td></tr>
<tr><td>NA</td><td>Vermont**</td><td></td><td>NA</td><td>NA</td><td>Nebraska**</td><td></td><td>NA</td></tr>
<tr><td>39</td><td>Virginia</td><td></td><td>0.1</td><td>NA</td><td>North Dakota**</td><td></td><td>NA</td></tr>
<tr><td>NA</td><td>Washington**</td><td></td><td>NA</td><td>NA</td><td>South Dakota**</td><td></td><td>NA</td></tr>
<tr><td>NA</td><td>West Virginia**</td><td></td><td>NA</td><td>NA</td><td>Vermont**</td><td></td><td>NA</td></tr>
<tr><td>4</td><td>Wisconsin</td><td></td><td>9.2</td><td>NA</td><td>Washington**</td><td></td><td>NA</td></tr>
<tr><td>37</td><td>Wyoming</td><td></td><td>0.8</td><td>NA</td><td>West Virginia**</td><td></td><td>NA</td></tr>
</table>

District of Columbia   42.5

Source: CQ Press using data from U.S. Department of Education, National Center for Education Statistics
"Numbers and Types of Public Elementary and Secondary Schools" (http://nces.ed.gov/pubs2011/2011345.pdf)
*For school year 2009-2010. Charter schools provide free public elementary/secondary education under a charter granted by the state legislature or other appropriate authority.
**Not available or not applicable.

Average Size of Public Elementary and Secondary Schools in 2010

National Average = 546.8 Students*

ALPHA ORDER				RANK ORDER		
RANK	STATE	STUDENTS		RANK	STATE	STUDENTS
19	Alabama	553.0		1	Florida	797.7
46	Alaska	261.3		2	Georgia	740.7
18	Arizona	554.5		3	Nevada	715.5
32	Arkansas	444.2		4	California	712.0
4	California	712.0		5	Utah	668.7
28	Colorado	484.2		6	Virginia	665.6
23	Connecticut	525.3		7	South Carolina	637.3
9	Delaware	633.9		8	Texas	637.0
1	Florida	797.7		9	Delaware	633.9
2	Georgia	740.7		10	Hawaii	633.7
10	Hawaii	633.7		11	Maryland	626.8
34	Idaho	428.9		12	New York	595.4
25	Illinois	519.4		13	North Carolina	589.0
16	Indiana	558.7		14	Tennessee	578.4
41	Iowa	341.2		15	New Jersey	574.1
42	Kansas	339.8		16	Indiana	558.7
20	Kentucky	550.1		17	Pennsylvania	558.1
26	Louisiana	518.3		18	Arizona	554.5
43	Maine	297.5		19	Alabama	553.0
11	Maryland	626.8		20	Kentucky	550.1
24	Massachusetts	520.4		21	Mississippi	532.8
30	Michigan	477.0		22	Washington	527.6
27	Minnesota	489.5		23	Connecticut	525.3
21	Mississippi	532.8		24	Massachusetts	520.4
35	Missouri	418.1		25	Illinois	519.4
50	Montana	172.4		26	Louisiana	518.3
44	Nebraska	288.7		27	Minnesota	489.5
3	Nevada	715.5		28	Colorado	484.2
36	New Hampshire	408.2		29	Ohio	481.4
15	New Jersey	574.1		30	Michigan	477.0
37	New Mexico	407.2		31	Rhode Island	473.8
12	New York	595.4		32	Arkansas	444.2
13	North Carolina	589.0		33	Oregon	437.7
48	North Dakota	197.5		34	Idaho	428.9
29	Ohio	481.4		35	Missouri	418.1
40	Oklahoma	366.0		36	New Hampshire	408.2
33	Oregon	437.7		37	New Mexico	407.2
17	Pennsylvania	558.1		38	West Virginia	406.8
31	Rhode Island	473.8		39	Wisconsin	406.3
7	South Carolina	637.3		40	Oklahoma	366.0
49	South Dakota	182.7		41	Iowa	341.2
14	Tennessee	578.4		42	Kansas	339.8
8	Texas	637.0		43	Maine	297.5
5	Utah	668.7		44	Nebraska	288.7
45	Vermont	280.5		45	Vermont	280.5
6	Virginia	665.6		46	Alaska	261.3
22	Washington	527.6		47	Wyoming	260.3
38	West Virginia	406.8		48	North Dakota	197.5
39	Wisconsin	406.3		49	South Dakota	182.7
47	Wyoming	260.3		50	Montana	172.4
					District of Columbia	333.9

Source: U.S. Department of Education, National Center for Education Statistics
   "Numbers and Types of Public Elementary and Secondary Schools" (http://nces.ed.gov/pubs2011/2011345.pdf)
*For school year 2009-2010. Includes primary, middle, high, and other schools.

Membership Size of Largest Public Elementary and Secondary Schools in 2010

National Average Largest School = 3,260 Students*

ALPHA ORDER			RANK ORDER		
RANK	STATE	STUDENTS	RANK	STATE	STUDENTS
32	Alabama	2,510	1	Pennsylvania	8,539
38	Alaska	2,276	2	Ohio	8,115
9	Arizona	4,276	3	Illinois	8,077
15	Arkansas	3,333	4	New York	8,076
6	California	4,899	5	Colorado	5,006
5	Colorado	5,006	6	California	4,899
24	Connecticut	2,854	7	Texas	4,697
43	Delaware	2,044	8	Indiana	4,389
10	Florida	4,186	9	Arizona	4,276
13	Georgia	3,482	10	Florida	4,186
30	Hawaii	2,639	11	Virginia	4,067
25	Idaho	2,789	12	Massachusetts	4,029
3	Illinois	8,077	13	Georgia	3,482
8	Indiana	4,389	14	New Jersey	3,336
40	Iowa	2,266	15	Arkansas	3,333
39	Kansas	2,267	16	New Hampshire	3,315
41	Kentucky	2,169	17	South Carolina	3,265
35	Louisiana	2,355	18	Minnesota	3,262
49	Maine	1,426	19	Nevada	3,243
21	Maryland	3,007	20	Oregon	3,193
12	Massachusetts	4,029	21	Maryland	3,007
27	Michigan	2,669	22	Utah	2,982
18	Minnesota	3,262	23	North Carolina	2,948
44	Mississippi	1,975	24	Connecticut	2,854
34	Missouri	2,378	25	Idaho	2,789
45	Montana	1,956	25	New Mexico	2,789
31	Nebraska	2,513	27	Michigan	2,669
19	Nevada	3,243	28	Washington	2,655
16	New Hampshire	3,315	29	Tennessee	2,643
14	New Jersey	3,336	30	Hawaii	2,639
25	New Mexico	2,789	31	Nebraska	2,513
4	New York	8,076	32	Alabama	2,510
23	North Carolina	2,948	33	Wisconsin	2,408
42	North Dakota	2,113	34	Missouri	2,378
2	Ohio	8,115	35	Louisiana	2,355
36	Oklahoma	2,343	36	Oklahoma	2,343
20	Oregon	3,193	37	South Dakota	2,338
1	Pennsylvania	8,539	38	Alaska	2,276
47	Rhode Island	1,853	39	Kansas	2,267
17	South Carolina	3,265	40	Iowa	2,266
37	South Dakota	2,338	41	Kentucky	2,169
29	Tennessee	2,643	42	North Dakota	2,113
7	Texas	4,697	43	Delaware	2,044
22	Utah	2,982	44	Mississippi	1,975
50	Vermont	1,394	45	Montana	1,956
11	Virginia	4,067	46	West Virginia	1,883
28	Washington	2,655	47	Rhode Island	1,853
46	West Virginia	1,883	48	Wyoming	1,550
33	Wisconsin	2,408	49	Maine	1,426
48	Wyoming	1,550	50	Vermont	1,394
				District of Columbia	1,483

Source: U.S. Department of Education, National Center for Education Statistics
"Numbers and Types of Public Elementary and Secondary Schools" (http://nces.ed.gov/pubs2011/2011345.pdf)
*For school year 2009-2010. Includes primary, middle, high, and other schools.

Membership Size of Smallest Public Elementary and Secondary Schools in 2010

National Average Smallest School = 10 Students*

ALPHA ORDER

RANK	STATE	STUDENTS
3	Alabama	55
26	Alaska	3
21	Arizona	4
5	Arkansas	21
35	California	1
18	Colorado	6
35	Connecticut	1
1	Delaware	109
35	Florida	1
35	Georgia	1
15	Hawaii	8
31	Idaho	2
35	Illinois	1
6	Indiana	19
35	Iowa	1
35	Kansas	1
13	Kentucky	11
21	Louisiana	4
21	Maine	4
11	Maryland	12
21	Massachusetts	4
26	Michigan	3
35	Minnesota	1
11	Mississippi	12
8	Missouri	16
35	Montana	1
31	Nebraska	2
20	Nevada	5
35	New Hampshire	1
16	New Jersey	7
35	New Mexico	1
7	New York	18
26	North Carolina	3
31	North Dakota	2
21	Ohio	4
14	Oklahoma	9
35	Oregon	1
18	Pennsylvania	6
2	Rhode Island	60
9	South Carolina	14
26	South Dakota	3
35	Tennessee	1
35	Texas	1
26	Utah	3
10	Vermont	13
16	Virginia	7
35	Washington	1
4	West Virginia	30
31	Wisconsin	2
35	Wyoming	1

RANK ORDER

RANK	STATE	STUDENTS
1	Delaware	109
2	Rhode Island	60
3	Alabama	55
4	West Virginia	30
5	Arkansas	21
6	Indiana	19
7	New York	18
8	Missouri	16
9	South Carolina	14
10	Vermont	13
11	Maryland	12
11	Mississippi	12
13	Kentucky	11
14	Oklahoma	9
15	Hawaii	8
16	New Jersey	7
16	Virginia	7
18	Colorado	6
18	Pennsylvania	6
20	Nevada	5
21	Arizona	4
21	Louisiana	4
21	Maine	4
21	Massachusetts	4
21	Ohio	4
26	Alaska	3
26	Michigan	3
26	North Carolina	3
26	South Dakota	3
26	Utah	3
31	Idaho	2
31	Nebraska	2
31	North Dakota	2
31	Wisconsin	2
35	California	1
35	Connecticut	1
35	Florida	1
35	Georgia	1
35	Illinois	1
35	Iowa	1
35	Kansas	1
35	Minnesota	1
35	Montana	1
35	New Hampshire	1
35	New Mexico	1
35	Oregon	1
35	Tennessee	1
35	Texas	1
35	Washington	1
35	Wyoming	1
	District of Columbia	27

Source: U.S. Department of Education, National Center for Education Statistics
"Numbers and Types of Public Elementary and Secondary Schools" (http://nces.ed.gov/pubs2011/2011345.pdf)
*For school year 2009-2010. Includes primary, middle, high, and other schools.

Public Primary Schools in 2010

National Total = 52,306 Schools*

ALPHA ORDER

ALPHA ORDER

RANK	STATE	SCHOOLS	% of USA
29	Alabama	707	1.4%
49	Alaska	171	0.3%
16	Arizona	1,131	2.2%
33	Arkansas	547	1.0%
1	California	5,619	10.7%
19	Colorado	1,027	2.0%
30	Connecticut	661	1.3%
50	Delaware	111	0.2%
5	Florida	2,026	3.9%
11	Georgia	1,305	2.5%
48	Hawaii	181	0.3%
41	Idaho	354	0.7%
4	Illinois	2,527	4.8%
15	Indiana	1,137	2.2%
25	Iowa	759	1.5%
24	Kansas	764	1.5%
26	Kentucky	754	1.4%
28	Louisiana	712	1.4%
39	Maine	383	0.7%
23	Maryland	886	1.7%
18	Massachusetts	1,039	2.0%
7	Michigan	1,846	3.5%
22	Minnesota	912	1.7%
35	Mississippi	456	0.9%
12	Missouri	1,243	2.4%
38	Montana	423	0.8%
32	Nebraska	619	1.2%
40	Nevada	371	0.7%
43	New Hampshire	294	0.6%
9	New Jersey	1,506	2.9%
35	New Mexico	456	0.9%
3	New York	2,540	4.9%
10	North Carolina	1,411	2.7%
44	North Dakota	271	0.5%
6	Ohio	1,999	3.8%
21	Oklahoma	971	1.9%
27	Oregon	733	1.4%
7	Pennsylvania	1,846	3.5%
47	Rhode Island	190	0.4%
31	South Carolina	657	1.3%
42	South Dakota	336	0.6%
20	Tennessee	1,007	1.9%
2	Texas	4,326	8.3%
33	Utah	547	1.0%
45	Vermont	220	0.4%
14	Virginia	1,194	2.3%
17	Washington	1,125	2.2%
37	West Virginia	447	0.9%
13	Wisconsin	1,236	2.4%
46	Wyoming	194	0.4%

RANK ORDER

RANK	STATE	SCHOOLS	% of USA
1	California	5,619	10.7%
2	Texas	4,326	8.3%
3	New York	2,540	4.9%
4	Illinois	2,527	4.8%
5	Florida	2,026	3.9%
6	Ohio	1,999	3.8%
7	Michigan	1,846	3.5%
7	Pennsylvania	1,846	3.5%
9	New Jersey	1,506	2.9%
10	North Carolina	1,411	2.7%
11	Georgia	1,305	2.5%
12	Missouri	1,243	2.4%
13	Wisconsin	1,236	2.4%
14	Virginia	1,194	2.3%
15	Indiana	1,137	2.2%
16	Arizona	1,131	2.2%
17	Washington	1,125	2.2%
18	Massachusetts	1,039	2.0%
19	Colorado	1,027	2.0%
20	Tennessee	1,007	1.9%
21	Oklahoma	971	1.9%
22	Minnesota	912	1.7%
23	Maryland	886	1.7%
24	Kansas	764	1.5%
25	Iowa	759	1.5%
26	Kentucky	754	1.4%
27	Oregon	733	1.4%
28	Louisiana	712	1.4%
29	Alabama	707	1.4%
30	Connecticut	661	1.3%
31	South Carolina	657	1.3%
32	Nebraska	619	1.2%
33	Arkansas	547	1.0%
33	Utah	547	1.0%
35	Mississippi	456	0.9%
35	New Mexico	456	0.9%
37	West Virginia	447	0.9%
38	Montana	423	0.8%
39	Maine	383	0.7%
40	Nevada	371	0.7%
41	Idaho	354	0.7%
42	South Dakota	336	0.6%
43	New Hampshire	294	0.6%
44	North Dakota	271	0.5%
45	Vermont	220	0.4%
46	Wyoming	194	0.4%
47	Rhode Island	190	0.4%
48	Hawaii	181	0.3%
49	Alaska	171	0.3%
50	Delaware	111	0.2%
	District of Columbia	133	0.3%

Source: U.S. Department of Education, National Center for Education Statistics
   "Numbers and Types of Public Elementary and Secondary Schools" (http://nces.ed.gov/pubs2011/2011345.pdf)
*Estimate for school year 2009-2010. Primary grades are determined by states and range from a low of pre-kindergarten to a high of 8th grade.

Average Size of Public Primary Schools in 2010

National Average = 450.8 Students*

ALPHA ORDER		RANK ORDER	

RANK	STATE	STUDENTS	RANK	STATE	STUDENTS
16	Alabama	473.0	1	Florida	627.5
39	Alaska	317.5	2	Georgia	621.2
10	Arizona	509.1	3	Utah	574.4
25	Arkansas	416.3	4	Nevada	558.5
7	California	530.6	5	Texas	549.0
28	Colorado	409.0	6	South Carolina	532.3
29	Connecticut	404.8	7	California	530.6
8	Delaware	511.4	8	Delaware	511.4
1	Florida	627.5	9	Hawaii	510.4
2	Georgia	621.2	10	Arizona	509.1
9	Hawaii	510.4	11	North Carolina	505.8
32	Idaho	363.3	12	Virginia	502.9
23	Illinois	424.2	13	New York	499.4
21	Indiana	435.3	14	Mississippi	489.0
43	Iowa	298.7	15	Tennessee	477.6
41	Kansas	303.3	16	Alabama	473.0
19	Kentucky	454.7	17	Louisiana	465.3
17	Louisiana	465.3	18	Maryland	463.5
45	Maine	223.5	19	Kentucky	454.7
18	Maryland	463.5	20	New Jersey	440.2
27	Massachusetts	412.4	21	Indiana	435.3
31	Michigan	386.5	22	Pennsylvania	430.0
26	Minnesota	415.6	23	Illinois	424.2
14	Mississippi	489.0	24	Washington	419.7
36	Missouri	349.7	25	Arkansas	416.3
50	Montana	162.4	26	Minnesota	415.6
44	Nebraska	243.0	27	Massachusetts	412.4
4	Nevada	558.5	28	Colorado	409.0
42	New Hampshire	299.4	29	Connecticut	404.8
20	New Jersey	440.2	30	Ohio	402.4
34	New Mexico	358.0	31	Michigan	386.5
13	New York	499.4	32	Idaho	363.3
11	North Carolina	505.8	33	Oklahoma	359.7
49	North Dakota	172.9	34	New Mexico	358.0
30	Ohio	402.4	35	Oregon	354.7
33	Oklahoma	359.7	36	Missouri	349.7
35	Oregon	354.7	37	Wisconsin	344.2
22	Pennsylvania	430.0	38	Rhode Island	337.3
38	Rhode Island	337.3	39	Alaska	317.5
6	South Carolina	532.3	40	West Virginia	311.7
48	South Dakota	176.0	41	Kansas	303.3
15	Tennessee	477.6	42	New Hampshire	299.4
5	Texas	549.0	43	Iowa	298.7
3	Utah	574.4	44	Nebraska	243.0
47	Vermont	209.4	45	Maine	223.5
12	Virginia	502.9	46	Wyoming	217.0
24	Washington	419.7	47	Vermont	209.4
40	West Virginia	311.7	48	South Dakota	176.0
37	Wisconsin	344.2	49	North Dakota	172.9
46	Wyoming	217.0	50	Montana	162.4
				District of Columbia	294.3

Source: U.S. Department of Education, National Center for Education Statistics
   "Numbers and Types of Public Elementary and Secondary Schools" (http://nces.ed.gov/pubs2011/2011345.pdf)
*Estimate for school year 2009-2010. Primary grades are determined by states and range from a low of pre-kindergarten to a high of 8th grade.

Percent of Public Schools That Are Primary Schools in 2010

National Percent = 59.3%*

ALPHA ORDER

ALPHA ORDER

RANK	STATE	PERCENT
45	Alabama	52.5
50	Alaska	38.0
23	Arizona	59.2
47	Arkansas	50.7
3	California	67.0
17	Colorado	61.0
10	Connecticut	63.6
16	Delaware	61.3
12	Florida	62.9
27	Georgia	58.4
9	Hawaii	63.7
38	Idaho	56.0
11	Illinois	63.1
18	Indiana	60.9
44	Iowa	54.1
39	Kansas	55.4
14	Kentucky	62.0
36	Louisiana	56.6
15	Maine	61.9
2	Maryland	67.1
23	Massachusetts	59.2
34	Michigan	56.8
39	Minnesota	55.4
49	Mississippi	49.4
33	Missouri	57.4
46	Montana	51.5
20	Nebraska	60.6
12	Nevada	62.9
18	New Hampshire	60.9
8	New Jersey	63.9
35	New Mexico	56.7
39	New York	55.4
37	North Carolina	56.3
32	North Dakota	57.5
42	Ohio	54.9
43	Oklahoma	54.4
26	Oregon	58.5
23	Pennsylvania	59.2
5	Rhode Island	64.4
29	South Carolina	58.0
48	South Dakota	50.1
22	Tennessee	60.2
31	Texas	57.8
6	Utah	64.3
1	Vermont	71.7
7	Virginia	64.0
21	Washington	60.3
4	West Virginia	64.6
29	Wisconsin	58.0
28	Wyoming	58.1

RANK ORDER

RANK	STATE	PERCENT
1	Vermont	71.7
2	Maryland	67.1
3	California	67.0
4	West Virginia	64.6
5	Rhode Island	64.4
6	Utah	64.3
7	Virginia	64.0
8	New Jersey	63.9
9	Hawaii	63.7
10	Connecticut	63.6
11	Illinois	63.1
12	Florida	62.9
12	Nevada	62.9
14	Kentucky	62.0
15	Maine	61.9
16	Delaware	61.3
17	Colorado	61.0
18	Indiana	60.9
18	New Hampshire	60.9
20	Nebraska	60.6
21	Washington	60.3
22	Tennessee	60.2
23	Arizona	59.2
23	Massachusetts	59.2
23	Pennsylvania	59.2
26	Oregon	58.5
27	Georgia	58.4
28	Wyoming	58.1
29	South Carolina	58.0
29	Wisconsin	58.0
31	Texas	57.8
32	North Dakota	57.5
33	Missouri	57.4
34	Michigan	56.8
35	New Mexico	56.7
36	Louisiana	56.6
37	North Carolina	56.3
38	Idaho	56.0
39	Kansas	55.4
39	Minnesota	55.4
39	New York	55.4
42	Ohio	54.9
43	Oklahoma	54.4
44	Iowa	54.1
45	Alabama	52.5
46	Montana	51.5
47	Arkansas	50.7
48	South Dakota	50.1
49	Mississippi	49.4
50	Alaska	38.0

District of Columbia	67.2

Source: CQ Press using data from U.S. Department of Education, National Center for Education Statistics
   "Numbers and Types of Public Elementary and Secondary Schools" (http://nces.ed.gov/pubs2011/2011345.pdf)
*Estimated percent of regular public schools for school year 2009-2010. Primary grades are determined by states and range
from a low of pre-kindergarten to a high of 8th grade.

Public Middle Schools in 2010

National Total = 16,451 Schools*

ALPHA ORDER

RANK	STATE	SCHOOLS	% of USA
22	Alabama	269	1.6%
49	Alaska	36	0.2%
23	Arizona	268	1.6%
31	Arkansas	224	1.4%
2	California	1,358	8.3%
20	Colorado	296	1.8%
33	Connecticut	194	1.2%
47	Delaware	39	0.2%
7	Florida	580	3.5%
9	Georgia	493	3.0%
48	Hawaii	38	0.2%
41	Idaho	113	0.7%
4	Illinois	775	4.7%
15	Indiana	347	2.1%
21	Iowa	289	1.8%
25	Kansas	253	1.5%
30	Kentucky	229	1.4%
27	Louisiana	243	1.5%
40	Maine	114	0.7%
28	Maryland	234	1.4%
17	Massachusetts	333	2.0%
6	Michigan	607	3.7%
25	Minnesota	253	1.5%
34	Mississippi	192	1.2%
12	Missouri	383	2.3%
29	Montana	231	1.4%
38	Nebraska	126	0.8%
42	Nevada	108	0.7%
43	New Hampshire	97	0.6%
11	New Jersey	445	2.7%
35	New Mexico	173	1.1%
3	New York	856	5.2%
10	North Carolina	484	2.9%
46	North Dakota	41	0.2%
5	Ohio	729	4.4%
16	Oklahoma	334	2.0%
32	Oregon	211	1.3%
8	Pennsylvania	554	3.4%
45	Rhode Island	58	0.4%
24	South Carolina	258	1.6%
36	South Dakota	167	1.0%
19	Tennessee	303	1.8%
1	Texas	1,690	10.3%
37	Utah	131	0.8%
50	Vermont	26	0.2%
14	Virginia	349	2.1%
18	Washington	329	2.0%
39	West Virginia	121	0.7%
13	Wisconsin	375	2.3%
44	Wyoming	69	0.4%

RANK ORDER

RANK	STATE	SCHOOLS	% of USA
1	Texas	1,690	10.3%
2	California	1,358	8.3%
3	New York	856	5.2%
4	Illinois	775	4.7%
5	Ohio	729	4.4%
6	Michigan	607	3.7%
7	Florida	580	3.5%
8	Pennsylvania	554	3.4%
9	Georgia	493	3.0%
10	North Carolina	484	2.9%
11	New Jersey	445	2.7%
12	Missouri	383	2.3%
13	Wisconsin	375	2.3%
14	Virginia	349	2.1%
15	Indiana	347	2.1%
16	Oklahoma	334	2.0%
17	Massachusetts	333	2.0%
18	Washington	329	2.0%
19	Tennessee	303	1.8%
20	Colorado	296	1.8%
21	Iowa	289	1.8%
22	Alabama	269	1.6%
23	Arizona	268	1.6%
24	South Carolina	258	1.6%
25	Kansas	253	1.5%
25	Minnesota	253	1.5%
27	Louisiana	243	1.5%
28	Maryland	234	1.4%
29	Montana	231	1.4%
30	Kentucky	229	1.4%
31	Arkansas	224	1.4%
32	Oregon	211	1.3%
33	Connecticut	194	1.2%
34	Mississippi	192	1.2%
35	New Mexico	173	1.1%
36	South Dakota	167	1.0%
37	Utah	131	0.8%
38	Nebraska	126	0.8%
39	West Virginia	121	0.7%
40	Maine	114	0.7%
41	Idaho	113	0.7%
42	Nevada	108	0.7%
43	New Hampshire	97	0.6%
44	Wyoming	69	0.4%
45	Rhode Island	58	0.4%
46	North Dakota	41	0.2%
47	Delaware	39	0.2%
48	Hawaii	38	0.2%
49	Alaska	36	0.2%
50	Vermont	26	0.2%
	District of Columbia	27	0.2%

Source: U.S. Department of Education, National Center for Education Statistics
"Numbers and Types of Public Elementary and Secondary Schools" (http://nces.ed.gov/pubs2011/2011345.pdf)
*Estimate for school year 2009-2010. Middle school grades are determined by states and range from a low of 4th grade to a high of 9th grade.

Average Size of Public Middle Schools in 2010

National Average = 574.8 Students*

ALPHA ORDER				RANK ORDER		
RANK	STATE	STUDENTS		RANK	STATE	STUDENTS
25	Alabama	533.5		1	Florida	883.4
38	Alaska	460.1		2	Nevada	858.8
23	Arizona	559.0		3	California	802.5
35	Arkansas	465.4		4	Utah	795.0
3	California	802.5		5	Hawaii	767.1
32	Colorado	481.8		6	Georgia	749.7
20	Connecticut	584.4		7	Virginia	722.6
9	Delaware	682.3		8	Maryland	698.1
1	Florida	883.4		9	Delaware	682.3
6	Georgia	749.7		10	North Carolina	648.4
5	Hawaii	767.1		11	Texas	620.5
31	Idaho	489.7		12	New Jersey	609.5
34	Illinois	470.4		13	South Carolina	601.6
18	Indiana	591.3		14	Pennsylvania	598.9
46	Iowa	337.0		15	New York	597.9
44	Kansas	361.1		16	Massachusetts	595.6
21	Kentucky	568.8		17	Tennessee	591.9
29	Louisiana	496.4		18	Indiana	591.3
45	Maine	355.4		19	Minnesota	589.3
8	Maryland	698.1		20	Connecticut	584.4
16	Massachusetts	595.6		21	Kentucky	568.8
28	Michigan	513.3		22	Washington	567.0
19	Minnesota	589.3		23	Arizona	559.0
27	Mississippi	515.7		24	Rhode Island	556.9
33	Missouri	474.5		25	Alabama	533.5
50	Montana	126.2		26	Oregon	516.3
41	Nebraska	380.6		27	Mississippi	515.7
2	Nevada	858.8		28	Michigan	513.3
36	New Hampshire	460.9		29	Louisiana	496.4
12	New Jersey	609.5		30	Ohio	490.8
40	New Mexico	388.9		31	Idaho	489.7
15	New York	597.9		32	Colorado	481.8
10	North Carolina	648.4		33	Missouri	474.5
43	North Dakota	363.6		34	Illinois	470.4
30	Ohio	490.8		35	Arkansas	465.4
42	Oklahoma	375.5		36	New Hampshire	460.9
26	Oregon	516.3		37	West Virginia	460.2
14	Pennsylvania	598.9		38	Alaska	460.1
24	Rhode Island	556.9		39	Wisconsin	416.9
13	South Carolina	601.6		40	New Mexico	388.9
49	South Dakota	158.2		41	Nebraska	380.6
17	Tennessee	591.9		42	Oklahoma	375.5
11	Texas	620.5		43	North Dakota	363.6
4	Utah	795.0		44	Kansas	361.1
47	Vermont	315.0		45	Maine	355.4
7	Virginia	722.6		46	Iowa	337.0
22	Washington	567.0		47	Vermont	315.0
37	West Virginia	460.2		48	Wyoming	292.0
39	Wisconsin	416.9		49	South Dakota	158.2
48	Wyoming	292.0		50	Montana	126.2
					District of Columbia	310.1

Source: U.S. Department of Education, National Center for Education Statistics
"Numbers and Types of Public Elementary and Secondary Schools" (http://nces.ed.gov/pubs2011/2011345.pdf)
*Estimate for school year 2009-2010. Middle school grades are determined by states and range from a low of 4th grade to a high of 9th grade.

Percent of Public Schools That Are Middle Schools in 2010

National Percent = 18.6%*

ALPHA ORDER

RANK	STATE	PERCENT
13	Alabama	20.0
50	Alaska	8.0
45	Arizona	14.0
8	Arkansas	20.8
42	California	16.2
37	Colorado	17.6
22	Connecticut	18.7
6	Delaware	21.5
32	Florida	18.0
5	Georgia	22.0
46	Hawaii	13.4
33	Idaho	17.9
16	Illinois	19.4
27	Indiana	18.6
11	Iowa	20.6
29	Kansas	18.3
21	Kentucky	18.8
17	Louisiana	19.3
28	Maine	18.4
35	Maryland	17.7
19	Massachusetts	19.0
22	Michigan	18.7
43	Minnesota	15.4
8	Mississippi	20.8
35	Missouri	17.7
1	Montana	28.1
47	Nebraska	12.3
29	Nevada	18.3
12	New Hampshire	20.1
20	New Jersey	18.9
6	New Mexico	21.5
22	New York	18.7
17	North Carolina	19.3
48	North Dakota	8.7
13	Ohio	20.0
22	Oklahoma	18.7
41	Oregon	16.9
34	Pennsylvania	17.8
15	Rhode Island	19.7
3	South Carolina	22.8
2	South Dakota	24.9
31	Tennessee	18.1
4	Texas	22.6
43	Utah	15.4
49	Vermont	8.5
22	Virginia	18.7
37	Washington	17.6
40	West Virginia	17.5
37	Wisconsin	17.6
10	Wyoming	20.7

RANK ORDER

RANK	STATE	PERCENT
1	Montana	28.1
2	South Dakota	24.9
3	South Carolina	22.8
4	Texas	22.6
5	Georgia	22.0
6	Delaware	21.5
6	New Mexico	21.5
8	Arkansas	20.8
8	Mississippi	20.8
10	Wyoming	20.7
11	Iowa	20.6
12	New Hampshire	20.1
13	Alabama	20.0
13	Ohio	20.0
15	Rhode Island	19.7
16	Illinois	19.4
17	Louisiana	19.3
17	North Carolina	19.3
19	Massachusetts	19.0
20	New Jersey	18.9
21	Kentucky	18.8
22	Connecticut	18.7
22	Michigan	18.7
22	New York	18.7
22	Oklahoma	18.7
22	Virginia	18.7
27	Indiana	18.6
28	Maine	18.4
29	Kansas	18.3
29	Nevada	18.3
31	Tennessee	18.1
32	Florida	18.0
33	Idaho	17.9
34	Pennsylvania	17.8
35	Maryland	17.7
35	Missouri	17.7
37	Colorado	17.6
37	Washington	17.6
37	Wisconsin	17.6
40	West Virginia	17.5
41	Oregon	16.9
42	California	16.2
43	Minnesota	15.4
43	Utah	15.4
45	Arizona	14.0
46	Hawaii	13.4
47	Nebraska	12.3
48	North Dakota	8.7
49	Vermont	8.5
50	Alaska	8.0

District of Columbia	13.6

Source: CQ Press using data from U.S. Department of Education, National Center for Education Statistics
"Numbers and Types of Public Elementary and Secondary Schools" (http://nces.ed.gov/pubs2011/2011345.pdf)
*Estimated percent of regular public schools for school year 2009-2010. Middle school grades are determined by states and range from a low of 4th grade to a high of 9th grade.

Public High Schools in 2010

National Total = 16,077 Schools*

<table>
<tr><td colspan="4">ALPHA ORDER</td><td colspan="4">RANK ORDER</td></tr>
<tr><td>RANK</td><td>STATE</td><td>SCHOOLS</td><td>% of USA</td><td>RANK</td><td>STATE</td><td>SCHOOLS</td><td>% of USA</td></tr>
<tr><td>27</td><td>Alabama</td><td>270</td><td>1.7%</td><td>1</td><td>California</td><td>1,209</td><td>7.5%</td></tr>
<tr><td>46</td><td>Alaska</td><td>51</td><td>0.3%</td><td>2</td><td>Texas</td><td>1,128</td><td>7.0%</td></tr>
<tr><td>14</td><td>Arizona</td><td>401</td><td>2.5%</td><td>3</td><td>New York</td><td>916</td><td>5.7%</td></tr>
<tr><td>25</td><td>Arkansas</td><td>279</td><td>1.7%</td><td>4</td><td>Ohio</td><td>776</td><td>4.8%</td></tr>
<tr><td>1</td><td>California</td><td>1,209</td><td>7.5%</td><td>5</td><td>Illinois</td><td>645</td><td>4.0%</td></tr>
<tr><td>22</td><td>Colorado</td><td>290</td><td>1.8%</td><td>6</td><td>Michigan</td><td>633</td><td>3.9%</td></tr>
<tr><td>36</td><td>Connecticut</td><td>164</td><td>1.0%</td><td>7</td><td>Pennsylvania</td><td>602</td><td>3.7%</td></tr>
<tr><td>50</td><td>Delaware</td><td>27</td><td>0.2%</td><td>8</td><td>Missouri</td><td>485</td><td>3.0%</td></tr>
<tr><td>12</td><td>Florida</td><td>450</td><td>2.8%</td><td>9</td><td>North Carolina</td><td>469</td><td>2.9%</td></tr>
<tr><td>15</td><td>Georgia</td><td>383</td><td>2.4%</td><td>10</td><td>Oklahoma</td><td>461</td><td>2.9%</td></tr>
<tr><td>49</td><td>Hawaii</td><td>39</td><td>0.2%</td><td>10</td><td>Wisconsin</td><td>461</td><td>2.9%</td></tr>
<tr><td>40</td><td>Idaho</td><td>120</td><td>0.7%</td><td>12</td><td>Florida</td><td>450</td><td>2.8%</td></tr>
<tr><td>5</td><td>Illinois</td><td>645</td><td>4.0%</td><td>13</td><td>Minnesota</td><td>431</td><td>2.7%</td></tr>
<tr><td>17</td><td>Indiana</td><td>337</td><td>2.1%</td><td>14</td><td>Arizona</td><td>401</td><td>2.5%</td></tr>
<tr><td>19</td><td>Iowa</td><td>316</td><td>2.0%</td><td>15</td><td>Georgia</td><td>383</td><td>2.4%</td></tr>
<tr><td>18</td><td>Kansas</td><td>333</td><td>2.1%</td><td>16</td><td>New Jersey</td><td>340</td><td>2.1%</td></tr>
<tr><td>29</td><td>Kentucky</td><td>213</td><td>1.3%</td><td>17</td><td>Indiana</td><td>337</td><td>2.1%</td></tr>
<tr><td>30</td><td>Louisiana</td><td>212</td><td>1.3%</td><td>18</td><td>Kansas</td><td>333</td><td>2.1%</td></tr>
<tr><td>41</td><td>Maine</td><td>109</td><td>0.7%</td><td>19</td><td>Iowa</td><td>316</td><td>2.0%</td></tr>
<tr><td>33</td><td>Maryland</td><td>186</td><td>1.2%</td><td>20</td><td>Virginia</td><td>306</td><td>1.9%</td></tr>
<tr><td>24</td><td>Massachusetts</td><td>282</td><td>1.8%</td><td>21</td><td>Washington</td><td>302</td><td>1.9%</td></tr>
<tr><td>6</td><td>Michigan</td><td>633</td><td>3.9%</td><td>22</td><td>Colorado</td><td>290</td><td>1.8%</td></tr>
<tr><td>13</td><td>Minnesota</td><td>431</td><td>2.7%</td><td>23</td><td>Tennessee</td><td>284</td><td>1.8%</td></tr>
<tr><td>31</td><td>Mississippi</td><td>200</td><td>1.2%</td><td>24</td><td>Massachusetts</td><td>282</td><td>1.8%</td></tr>
<tr><td>8</td><td>Missouri</td><td>485</td><td>3.0%</td><td>25</td><td>Arkansas</td><td>279</td><td>1.7%</td></tr>
<tr><td>34</td><td>Montana</td><td>168</td><td>1.0%</td><td>26</td><td>Nebraska</td><td>276</td><td>1.7%</td></tr>
<tr><td>26</td><td>Nebraska</td><td>276</td><td>1.7%</td><td>27</td><td>Alabama</td><td>270</td><td>1.7%</td></tr>
<tr><td>43</td><td>Nevada</td><td>98</td><td>0.6%</td><td>28</td><td>Oregon</td><td>249</td><td>1.5%</td></tr>
<tr><td>44</td><td>New Hampshire</td><td>88</td><td>0.5%</td><td>29</td><td>Kentucky</td><td>213</td><td>1.3%</td></tr>
<tr><td>16</td><td>New Jersey</td><td>340</td><td>2.1%</td><td>30</td><td>Louisiana</td><td>212</td><td>1.3%</td></tr>
<tr><td>38</td><td>New Mexico</td><td>152</td><td>0.9%</td><td>31</td><td>Mississippi</td><td>200</td><td>1.2%</td></tr>
<tr><td>3</td><td>New York</td><td>916</td><td>5.7%</td><td>32</td><td>South Carolina</td><td>195</td><td>1.2%</td></tr>
<tr><td>9</td><td>North Carolina</td><td>469</td><td>2.9%</td><td>33</td><td>Maryland</td><td>186</td><td>1.2%</td></tr>
<tr><td>36</td><td>North Dakota</td><td>164</td><td>1.0%</td><td>34</td><td>Montana</td><td>168</td><td>1.0%</td></tr>
<tr><td>4</td><td>Ohio</td><td>776</td><td>4.8%</td><td>35</td><td>South Dakota</td><td>166</td><td>1.0%</td></tr>
<tr><td>10</td><td>Oklahoma</td><td>461</td><td>2.9%</td><td>36</td><td>Connecticut</td><td>164</td><td>1.0%</td></tr>
<tr><td>28</td><td>Oregon</td><td>249</td><td>1.5%</td><td>36</td><td>North Dakota</td><td>164</td><td>1.0%</td></tr>
<tr><td>7</td><td>Pennsylvania</td><td>602</td><td>3.7%</td><td>38</td><td>New Mexico</td><td>152</td><td>0.9%</td></tr>
<tr><td>47</td><td>Rhode Island</td><td>46</td><td>0.3%</td><td>39</td><td>Utah</td><td>132</td><td>0.8%</td></tr>
<tr><td>32</td><td>South Carolina</td><td>195</td><td>1.2%</td><td>40</td><td>Idaho</td><td>120</td><td>0.7%</td></tr>
<tr><td>35</td><td>South Dakota</td><td>166</td><td>1.0%</td><td>41</td><td>Maine</td><td>109</td><td>0.7%</td></tr>
<tr><td>23</td><td>Tennessee</td><td>284</td><td>1.8%</td><td>42</td><td>West Virginia</td><td>105</td><td>0.7%</td></tr>
<tr><td>2</td><td>Texas</td><td>1,128</td><td>7.0%</td><td>43</td><td>Nevada</td><td>98</td><td>0.6%</td></tr>
<tr><td>39</td><td>Utah</td><td>132</td><td>0.8%</td><td>44</td><td>New Hampshire</td><td>88</td><td>0.5%</td></tr>
<tr><td>48</td><td>Vermont</td><td>44</td><td>0.3%</td><td>45</td><td>Wyoming</td><td>61</td><td>0.4%</td></tr>
<tr><td>20</td><td>Virginia</td><td>306</td><td>1.9%</td><td>46</td><td>Alaska</td><td>51</td><td>0.3%</td></tr>
<tr><td>21</td><td>Washington</td><td>302</td><td>1.9%</td><td>47</td><td>Rhode Island</td><td>46</td><td>0.3%</td></tr>
<tr><td>42</td><td>West Virginia</td><td>105</td><td>0.7%</td><td>48</td><td>Vermont</td><td>44</td><td>0.3%</td></tr>
<tr><td>10</td><td>Wisconsin</td><td>461</td><td>2.9%</td><td>49</td><td>Hawaii</td><td>39</td><td>0.2%</td></tr>
<tr><td>45</td><td>Wyoming</td><td>61</td><td>0.4%</td><td>50</td><td>Delaware</td><td>27</td><td>0.2%</td></tr>
<tr><td></td><td></td><td></td><td></td><td></td><td>District of Columbia</td><td>26</td><td>0.2%</td></tr>
</table>

Source: U.S. Department of Education, National Center for Education Statistics
   "Numbers and Types of Public Elementary and Secondary Schools" (http://nces.ed.gov/pubs2011/2011345.pdf)
*Estimate for school year 2009-2010. High school grades are determined by states and range from a low of 7th grade to a high of 12th grade.

Average Size of Public High Schools in 2010

National Average = 856.3 Students*

ALPHA ORDER				RANK ORDER		
RANK	STATE	STUDENTS		RANK	STATE	STUDENTS
25	Alabama	740.5		1	Florida	1,589.7
36	Alaska	595.8		2	California	1,474.3
28	Arizona	734.5		3	Maryland	1,336.1
42	Arkansas	473.7		4	Hawaii	1,330.7
2	California	1,474.3		5	Virginia	1,236.7
24	Colorado	741.7		6	Georgia	1,183.8
12	Connecticut	959.1		7	Nevada	1,176.3
9	Delaware	1,091.8		8	New Jersey	1,152.8
1	Florida	1,589.7		9	Delaware	1,091.8
6	Georgia	1,183.8		10	Texas	1,059.9
4	Hawaii	1,330.7		11	South Carolina	1,042.7
37	Idaho	585.2		12	Connecticut	959.1
14	Illinois	942.0		13	Tennessee	946.1
17	Indiana	940.1		14	Illinois	942.0
43	Iowa	452.0		15	Utah	941.1
44	Kansas	415.0		16	Rhode Island	940.8
23	Kentucky	878.3		17	Indiana	940.1
27	Louisiana	737.0		18	Washington	936.8
41	Maine	508.6		19	New York	909.3
3	Maryland	1,336.1		20	Massachusetts	904.8
20	Massachusetts	904.8		21	Pennsylvania	887.5
26	Michigan	739.9		22	North Carolina	879.1
35	Minnesota	603.4		23	Kentucky	878.3
31	Mississippi	672.1		24	Colorado	741.7
40	Missouri	546.0		25	Alabama	740.5
48	Montana	261.0		26	Michigan	739.9
47	Nebraska	349.4		27	Louisiana	737.0
7	Nevada	1,176.3		28	Arizona	734.5
30	New Hampshire	727.5		29	West Virginia	730.8
8	New Jersey	1,152.8		30	New Hampshire	727.5
38	New Mexico	581.3		31	Mississippi	672.1
19	New York	909.3		32	Oregon	668.7
22	North Carolina	879.1		33	Ohio	667.2
50	North Dakota	191.4		34	Vermont	608.8
33	Ohio	667.2		35	Minnesota	603.4
46	Oklahoma	356.5		36	Alaska	595.8
32	Oregon	668.7		37	Idaho	585.2
21	Pennsylvania	887.5		38	New Mexico	581.3
16	Rhode Island	940.8		39	Wisconsin	577.2
11	South Carolina	1,042.7		40	Missouri	546.0
49	South Dakota	221.7		41	Maine	508.6
13	Tennessee	946.1		42	Arkansas	473.7
10	Texas	1,059.9		43	Iowa	452.0
15	Utah	941.1		44	Kansas	415.0
34	Vermont	608.8		45	Wyoming	379.5
5	Virginia	1,236.7		46	Oklahoma	356.5
18	Washington	936.8		47	Nebraska	349.4
29	West Virginia	730.8		48	Montana	261.0
39	Wisconsin	577.2		49	South Dakota	221.7
45	Wyoming	379.5		50	North Dakota	191.4
					District of Columbia	523.6

Source: U.S. Department of Education, National Center for Education Statistics
   "Numbers and Types of Public Elementary and Secondary Schools" (http://nces.ed.gov/pubs2011/2011345.pdf)
*Estimate for school year 2009-2010. High school grades are determined by states and range from a low of 7th grade to a high of 12th grade.

Percent of Public Schools That Are High Schools in 2010

National Percent = 18.2%*

ALPHA ORDER

ALPHA ORDER / RANK ORDER

RANK	STATE	PERCENT	RANK	STATE	PERCENT
15	Alabama	20.0	1	North Dakota	34.8
50	Alaska	11.3	2	Nebraska	27.0
13	Arizona	21.0	3	Minnesota	26.2
4	Arkansas	25.9	4	Arkansas	25.9
44	California	14.4	5	Oklahoma	25.8
28	Colorado	17.2	6	South Dakota	24.8
38	Connecticut	15.8	7	Kansas	24.1
43	Delaware	14.9	8	Iowa	22.5
48	Florida	14.0	9	Missouri	22.4
30	Georgia	17.1	10	Mississippi	21.6
49	Hawaii	13.7	10	Wisconsin	21.6
20	Idaho	19.0	12	Ohio	21.3
36	Illinois	16.1	13	Arizona	21.0
25	Indiana	18.1	14	Montana	20.4
8	Iowa	22.5	15	Alabama	20.0
7	Kansas	24.1	15	New York	20.0
27	Kentucky	17.5	17	Oregon	19.9
32	Louisiana	16.8	18	Michigan	19.5
26	Maine	17.6	19	Pennsylvania	19.3
47	Maryland	14.1	20	Idaho	19.0
36	Massachusetts	16.1	21	New Mexico	18.9
18	Michigan	19.5	22	North Carolina	18.7
3	Minnesota	26.2	23	Wyoming	18.3
10	Mississippi	21.6	24	New Hampshire	18.2
9	Missouri	22.4	25	Indiana	18.1
14	Montana	20.4	26	Maine	17.6
2	Nebraska	27.0	27	Kentucky	17.5
33	Nevada	16.6	28	Colorado	17.2
24	New Hampshire	18.2	28	South Carolina	17.2
44	New Jersey	14.4	30	Georgia	17.1
21	New Mexico	18.9	31	Tennessee	17.0
15	New York	20.0	32	Louisiana	16.8
22	North Carolina	18.7	33	Nevada	16.6
1	North Dakota	34.8	34	Virginia	16.4
12	Ohio	21.3	35	Washington	16.2
5	Oklahoma	25.8	36	Illinois	16.1
17	Oregon	19.9	36	Massachusetts	16.1
19	Pennsylvania	19.3	38	Connecticut	15.8
39	Rhode Island	15.6	39	Rhode Island	15.6
28	South Carolina	17.2	40	Utah	15.5
6	South Dakota	24.8	41	West Virginia	15.2
31	Tennessee	17.0	42	Texas	15.1
42	Texas	15.1	43	Delaware	14.9
40	Utah	15.5	44	California	14.4
46	Vermont	14.3	44	New Jersey	14.4
34	Virginia	16.4	46	Vermont	14.3
35	Washington	16.2	47	Maryland	14.1
41	West Virginia	15.2	48	Florida	14.0
10	Wisconsin	21.6	49	Hawaii	13.7
23	Wyoming	18.3	50	Alaska	11.3

District of Columbia   13.1

Source: CQ Press using data from U.S. Department of Education, National Center for Education Statistics
"Numbers and Types of Public Elementary and Secondary Schools" (http://nces.ed.gov/pubs2011/2011345.pdf)
*Estimated percent of regular public schools for school year 2009-2010. High school grades are determined by states and range from a low of 7th grade to a high of 12th grade.

"Other" Public Schools in 2010

National Total = 3,380 Schools*

ALPHA ORDER

RANK	STATE	SCHOOLS	% of USA
12	Alabama	101	3.0%
4	Alaska	192	5.7%
10	Arizona	112	3.3%
30	Arkansas	28	0.8%
3	California	206	6.1%
17	Colorado	70	2.1%
34	Connecticut	21	0.6%
44	Delaware	4	0.1%
5	Florida	166	4.9%
22	Georgia	55	1.6%
31	Hawaii	26	0.8%
26	Idaho	45	1.3%
21	Illinois	58	1.7%
25	Indiana	46	1.4%
28	Iowa	38	1.1%
29	Kansas	30	0.9%
34	Kentucky	21	0.6%
14	Louisiana	92	2.7%
41	Maine	13	0.4%
40	Maryland	15	0.4%
12	Massachusetts	101	3.0%
6	Michigan	163	4.8%
24	Minnesota	51	1.5%
16	Mississippi	76	2.2%
22	Missouri	55	1.6%
49	Montana	0	0.0%
49	Nebraska	0	0.0%
41	Nevada	13	0.4%
44	New Hampshire	4	0.1%
18	New Jersey	67	2.0%
32	New Mexico	23	0.7%
2	New York	272	8.0%
7	North Carolina	143	4.2%
46	North Dakota	3	0.1%
8	Ohio	140	4.1%
36	Oklahoma	20	0.6%
20	Oregon	59	1.7%
9	Pennsylvania	118	3.5%
47	Rhode Island	1	0.0%
33	South Carolina	22	0.7%
47	South Dakota	1	0.0%
15	Tennessee	78	2.3%
1	Texas	346	10.2%
27	Utah	41	1.2%
38	Vermont	17	0.5%
38	Virginia	17	0.5%
11	Washington	109	3.2%
37	West Virginia	19	0.6%
19	Wisconsin	60	1.8%
43	Wyoming	10	0.3%

RANK ORDER

RANK	STATE	SCHOOLS	% of USA
1	Texas	346	10.2%
2	New York	272	8.0%
3	California	206	6.1%
4	Alaska	192	5.7%
5	Florida	166	4.9%
6	Michigan	163	4.8%
7	North Carolina	143	4.2%
8	Ohio	140	4.1%
9	Pennsylvania	118	3.5%
10	Arizona	112	3.3%
11	Washington	109	3.2%
12	Alabama	101	3.0%
12	Massachusetts	101	3.0%
14	Louisiana	92	2.7%
15	Tennessee	78	2.3%
16	Mississippi	76	2.2%
17	Colorado	70	2.1%
18	New Jersey	67	2.0%
19	Wisconsin	60	1.8%
20	Oregon	59	1.7%
21	Illinois	58	1.7%
22	Georgia	55	1.6%
22	Missouri	55	1.6%
24	Minnesota	51	1.5%
25	Indiana	46	1.4%
26	Idaho	45	1.3%
27	Utah	41	1.2%
28	Iowa	38	1.1%
29	Kansas	30	0.9%
30	Arkansas	28	0.8%
31	Hawaii	26	0.8%
32	New Mexico	23	0.7%
33	South Carolina	22	0.7%
34	Connecticut	21	0.6%
34	Kentucky	21	0.6%
36	Oklahoma	20	0.6%
37	West Virginia	19	0.6%
38	Vermont	17	0.5%
38	Virginia	17	0.5%
40	Maryland	15	0.4%
41	Maine	13	0.4%
41	Nevada	13	0.4%
43	Wyoming	10	0.3%
44	Delaware	4	0.1%
44	New Hampshire	4	0.1%
46	North Dakota	3	0.1%
47	Rhode Island	1	0.0%
47	South Dakota	1	0.0%
49	Montana	0	0.0%
49	Nebraska	0	0.0%
	District of Columbia	12	0.4%

Source: U.S. Department of Education, National Center for Education Statistics
"Numbers and Types of Public Elementary and Secondary Schools" (http://nces.ed.gov/pubs2011/2011345.pdf)
*Estimate for school year 2009-2010. "Other" schools are all schools not falling within primary, middle, or high school categories. This includes ungraded schools.

Percent of Public Schools That Are "Other" Schools in 2010

National Percent = 3.8%*

ALPHA ORDER

RANK	STATE	PERCENT
4	Alabama	7.5
1	Alaska	42.7
7	Arizona	5.9
29	Arkansas	2.6
30	California	2.5
19	Colorado	4.2
38	Connecticut	2.0
34	Delaware	2.2
13	Florida	5.2
30	Georgia	2.5
2	Hawaii	9.2
6	Idaho	7.1
41	Illinois	1.4
30	Indiana	2.5
27	Iowa	2.7
34	Kansas	2.2
40	Kentucky	1.7
5	Louisiana	7.3
37	Maine	2.1
42	Maryland	1.1
9	Massachusetts	5.8
14	Michigan	5.0
22	Minnesota	3.1
3	Mississippi	8.2
30	Missouri	2.5
49	Montana	0.0
49	Nebraska	0.0
34	Nevada	2.2
45	New Hampshire	0.8
25	New Jersey	2.8
24	New Mexico	2.9
7	New York	5.9
11	North Carolina	5.7
46	North Dakota	0.6
20	Ohio	3.8
42	Oklahoma	1.1
16	Oregon	4.7
20	Pennsylvania	3.8
47	Rhode Island	0.3
39	South Carolina	1.9
48	South Dakota	0.1
16	Tennessee	4.7
18	Texas	4.6
15	Utah	4.8
12	Vermont	5.5
44	Virginia	0.9
9	Washington	5.8
27	West Virginia	2.7
25	Wisconsin	2.8
23	Wyoming	3.0

RANK ORDER

RANK	STATE	PERCENT
1	Alaska	42.7
2	Hawaii	9.2
3	Mississippi	8.2
4	Alabama	7.5
5	Louisiana	7.3
6	Idaho	7.1
7	Arizona	5.9
7	New York	5.9
9	Massachusetts	5.8
9	Washington	5.8
11	North Carolina	5.7
12	Vermont	5.5
13	Florida	5.2
14	Michigan	5.0
15	Utah	4.8
16	Oregon	4.7
16	Tennessee	4.7
18	Texas	4.6
19	Colorado	4.2
20	Ohio	3.8
20	Pennsylvania	3.8
22	Minnesota	3.1
23	Wyoming	3.0
24	New Mexico	2.9
25	New Jersey	2.8
25	Wisconsin	2.8
27	Iowa	2.7
27	West Virginia	2.7
29	Arkansas	2.6
30	California	2.5
30	Georgia	2.5
30	Indiana	2.5
30	Missouri	2.5
34	Delaware	2.2
34	Kansas	2.2
34	Nevada	2.2
37	Maine	2.1
38	Connecticut	2.0
39	South Carolina	1.9
40	Kentucky	1.7
41	Illinois	1.4
42	Maryland	1.1
42	Oklahoma	1.1
44	Virginia	0.9
45	New Hampshire	0.8
46	North Dakota	0.6
47	Rhode Island	0.3
48	South Dakota	0.1
49	Montana	0.0
49	Nebraska	0.0

District of Columbia 6.1

Source: CQ Press using data from U.S. Department of Education, National Center for Education Statistics
   "Numbers and Types of Public Elementary and Secondary Schools" (http://nces.ed.gov/pubs2011/2011345.pdf)
*Estimated percent of regular public schools for school year 2009-2010. "Other" schools are all schools not falling within primary, middle, or high school categories. This includes ungraded schools.

Private Elementary and Secondary Schools in 2010

National Total = 33,366 Schools*

ALPHA ORDER

RANK	STATE	SCHOOLS	% of USA
19	Alabama	578	1.7%
46	Alaska	123	0.4%
27	Arizona**	360	1.1%
34	Arkansas	224	0.7%
1	California	3,644	10.9%
23	Colorado	488	1.5%
25	Connecticut	405	1.2%
44	Delaware	135	0.4%
4	Florida	1,962	5.9%
14	Georgia	823	2.5%
44	Hawaii	135	0.4%
36	Idaho**	197	0.6%
7	Illinois	1,733	5.2%
11	Indiana	910	2.7%
33	Iowa	230	0.7%
31	Kansas	263	0.8%
28	Kentucky	358	1.1%
24	Louisiana	458	1.4%
39	Maine	163	0.5%
15	Maryland	795	2.4%
13	Massachusetts	830	2.5%
9	Michigan	1,069	3.2%
21	Minnesota	524	1.6%
29	Mississippi	316	0.9%
16	Missouri	693	2.1%
42	Montana	153	0.5%
35	Nebraska**	221	0.7%
41	Nevada	157	0.5%
30	New Hampshire	285	0.9%
8	New Jersey	1,385	4.2%
37	New Mexico	187	0.6%
3	New York	2,016	6.0%
17	North Carolina	667	2.0%
49	North Dakota	47	0.1%
6	Ohio**	1,759	5.3%
32	Oklahoma	252	0.8%
22	Oregon	497	1.5%
2	Pennsylvania	2,276	6.8%
39	Rhode Island	163	0.5%
26	South Carolina	398	1.2%
48	South Dakota	75	0.2%
20	Tennessee	525	1.6%
5	Texas	1,852	5.6%
38	Utah	184	0.6%
47	Vermont	119	0.4%
10	Virginia	915	2.7%
18	Washington	656	2.0%
43	West Virginia	137	0.4%
12	Wisconsin	894	2.7%
50	Wyoming	39	0.1%

RANK ORDER

RANK	STATE	SCHOOLS	% of USA
1	California	3,644	10.9%
2	Pennsylvania	2,276	6.8%
3	New York	2,016	6.0%
4	Florida	1,962	5.9%
5	Texas	1,852	5.6%
6	Ohio**	1,759	5.3%
7	Illinois	1,733	5.2%
8	New Jersey	1,385	4.2%
9	Michigan	1,069	3.2%
10	Virginia	915	2.7%
11	Indiana	910	2.7%
12	Wisconsin	894	2.7%
13	Massachusetts	830	2.5%
14	Georgia	823	2.5%
15	Maryland	795	2.4%
16	Missouri	693	2.1%
17	North Carolina	667	2.0%
18	Washington	656	2.0%
19	Alabama	578	1.7%
20	Tennessee	525	1.6%
21	Minnesota	524	1.6%
22	Oregon	497	1.5%
23	Colorado	488	1.5%
24	Louisiana	458	1.4%
25	Connecticut	405	1.2%
26	South Carolina	398	1.2%
27	Arizona**	360	1.1%
28	Kentucky	358	1.1%
29	Mississippi	316	0.9%
30	New Hampshire	285	0.9%
31	Kansas	263	0.8%
32	Oklahoma	252	0.8%
33	Iowa	230	0.7%
34	Arkansas	224	0.7%
35	Nebraska**	221	0.7%
36	Idaho**	197	0.6%
37	New Mexico	187	0.6%
38	Utah	184	0.6%
39	Maine	163	0.5%
39	Rhode Island	163	0.5%
41	Nevada	157	0.5%
42	Montana	153	0.5%
43	West Virginia	137	0.4%
44	Delaware	135	0.4%
44	Hawaii	135	0.4%
46	Alaska	123	0.4%
47	Vermont	119	0.4%
48	South Dakota	75	0.2%
49	North Dakota	47	0.1%
50	Wyoming	39	0.1%
	District of Columbia	86	0.3%

Source: U.S. Department of Education, National Center for Education Statistics
    "Characteristics of Private Schools in the United States" (http://nces.ed.gov/pubs2011/2011339.pdf)
*For school year 2009-2010.
**Interpret data for these states with caution.

II. Finance

Estimated Public Elementary and Secondary School Revenue in 2011

National Total = $596,271,055,000*

ALPHA ORDER					RANK ORDER			
RANK	STATE	REVENUE	% of USA		RANK	STATE	REVENUE	% of USA
26	Alabama	$7,708,230,000	1.3%		1	California	$65,025,080,000	10.9%
48	Alaska	1,428,694,000	0.2%		2	Texas	50,739,496,000	8.5%
20	Arizona	10,282,861,000	1.7%		3	New York	49,390,908,000	8.3%
32	Arkansas	5,443,570,000	0.9%		4	Pennsylvania	29,142,038,000	4.9%
1	California	65,025,080,000	10.9%		5	Florida	27,072,769,000	4.5%
22	Colorado	8,850,607,000	1.5%		6	Illinois	25,323,620,000	4.2%
21	Connecticut	9,549,219,000	1.6%		7	New Jersey	24,737,623,000	4.1%
43	Delaware	2,059,526,000	0.3%		8	Georgia	22,328,160,000	3.7%
5	Florida	27,072,769,000	4.5%		9	Michigan	19,992,857,000	3.4%
8	Georgia	22,328,160,000	3.7%		10	Ohio	18,678,687,000	3.1%
42	Hawaii	2,325,252,000	0.4%		11	Virginia	17,089,869,000	2.9%
41	Idaho	2,497,169,000	0.4%		12	Massachusetts	15,455,655,000	2.6%
6	Illinois	25,323,620,000	4.2%		13	Maryland	15,089,122,000	2.5%
17	Indiana	11,261,263,000	1.9%		14	North Carolina	12,926,407,000	2.2%
30	Iowa	5,658,991,000	0.9%		15	Washington	12,358,213,000	2.1%
31	Kansas	5,518,663,000	0.9%		16	Wisconsin	11,501,060,000	1.9%
27	Kentucky	7,044,472,000	1.2%		17	Indiana	11,261,263,000	1.9%
24	Louisiana	8,213,937,000	1.4%		18	Missouri	10,878,776,000	1.8%
40	Maine	2,865,602,000	0.5%		19	Minnesota	10,800,973,000	1.8%
13	Maryland	15,089,122,000	2.5%		20	Arizona	10,282,861,000	1.7%
12	Massachusetts	15,455,655,000	2.6%		21	Connecticut	9,549,219,000	1.6%
9	Michigan	19,992,857,000	3.4%		22	Colorado	8,850,607,000	1.5%
19	Minnesota	10,800,973,000	1.8%		23	Tennessee	8,632,049,000	1.4%
34	Mississippi	4,673,684,000	0.8%		24	Louisiana	8,213,937,000	1.4%
18	Missouri	10,878,776,000	1.8%		25	South Carolina	7,855,646,000	1.3%
47	Montana	1,532,470,000	0.3%		26	Alabama	7,708,230,000	1.3%
38	Nebraska	3,390,496,000	0.6%		27	Kentucky	7,044,472,000	1.2%
37	Nevada	3,463,673,000	0.6%		28	Oregon	6,673,541,000	1.1%
39	New Hampshire	2,899,938,000	0.5%		29	Oklahoma	6,360,106,000	1.1%
7	New Jersey	24,737,623,000	4.1%		30	Iowa	5,658,991,000	0.9%
35	New Mexico	4,160,913,000	0.7%		31	Kansas	5,518,663,000	0.9%
3	New York	49,390,908,000	8.3%		32	Arkansas	5,443,570,000	0.9%
14	North Carolina	12,926,407,000	2.2%		33	Utah	5,179,715,000	0.9%
50	North Dakota	1,144,747,000	0.2%		34	Mississippi	4,673,684,000	0.8%
10	Ohio	18,678,687,000	3.1%		35	New Mexico	4,160,913,000	0.7%
29	Oklahoma	6,360,106,000	1.1%		36	West Virginia	3,474,982,000	0.6%
28	Oregon	6,673,541,000	1.1%		37	Nevada	3,463,673,000	0.6%
4	Pennsylvania	29,142,038,000	4.9%		38	Nebraska	3,390,496,000	0.6%
44	Rhode Island	1,844,393,000	0.3%		39	New Hampshire	2,899,938,000	0.5%
25	South Carolina	7,855,646,000	1.3%		40	Maine	2,865,602,000	0.5%
49	South Dakota	1,335,949,000	0.2%		41	Idaho	2,497,169,000	0.4%
23	Tennessee	8,632,049,000	1.4%		42	Hawaii	2,325,252,000	0.4%
2	Texas	50,739,496,000	8.5%		43	Delaware	2,059,526,000	0.3%
33	Utah	5,179,715,000	0.9%		44	Rhode Island	1,844,393,000	0.3%
46	Vermont	1,698,057,000	0.3%		45	Wyoming	1,775,607,000	0.3%
11	Virginia	17,089,869,000	2.9%		46	Vermont	1,698,057,000	0.3%
15	Washington	12,358,213,000	2.1%		47	Montana	1,532,470,000	0.3%
36	West Virginia	3,474,982,000	0.6%		48	Alaska	1,428,694,000	0.2%
16	Wisconsin	11,501,060,000	1.9%		49	South Dakota	1,335,949,000	0.2%
45	Wyoming	1,775,607,000	0.3%		50	North Dakota	1,144,747,000	0.2%
						District of Columbia	935,721,000	0.2%

Source: National Education Association, Washington, D.C.
    "Rankings and Estimates" (Copyright © 2011, NEA, used with permission, http://www.nea.org/home/44479.htm)
*Estimates for school year 2010-2011.

Estimated Per Capita Public Elementary and Secondary School Revenue in 2011
National Per Capita = $1,929*

ALPHA ORDER

RANK	STATE	PER CAPITA
39	Alabama	$1,630
17	Alaska	2,015
46	Arizona	1,540
25	Arkansas	1,870
33	California	1,745
35	Colorado	1,737
4	Connecticut	2,708
8	Delaware	2,310
47	Florida	1,449
10	Georgia	2,253
30	Hawaii	1,789
43	Idaho	1,601
20	Illinois	1,956
32	Indiana	1,747
23	Iowa	1,872
21	Kansas	1,942
41	Kentucky	1,623
28	Louisiana	1,813
12	Maine	2,183
5	Maryland	2,630
7	Massachusetts	2,331
18	Michigan	2,013
15	Minnesota	2,042
44	Mississippi	1,579
29	Missouri	1,810
45	Montana	1,564
23	Nebraska	1,872
50	Nevada	1,305
11	New Hampshire	2,191
2	New Jersey	2,833
14	New Mexico	2,046
6	New York	2,523
48	North Carolina	1,367
31	North Dakota	1,751
42	Ohio	1,620
38	Oklahoma	1,708
36	Oregon	1,731
9	Pennsylvania	2,307
33	Rhode Island	1,745
37	South Carolina	1,709
40	South Dakota	1,629
49	Tennessee	1,362
19	Texas	2,012
27	Utah	1,830
3	Vermont	2,728
13	Virginia	2,149
26	Washington	1,832
22	West Virginia	1,904
16	Wisconsin	2,029
1	Wyoming	3,242

RANK ORDER

RANK	STATE	PER CAPITA
1	Wyoming	$3,242
2	New Jersey	2,833
3	Vermont	2,728
4	Connecticut	2,708
5	Maryland	2,630
6	New York	2,523
7	Massachusetts	2,331
8	Delaware	2,310
9	Pennsylvania	2,307
10	Georgia	2,253
11	New Hampshire	2,191
12	Maine	2,183
13	Virginia	2,149
14	New Mexico	2,046
15	Minnesota	2,042
16	Wisconsin	2,029
17	Alaska	2,015
18	Michigan	2,013
19	Texas	2,012
20	Illinois	1,956
21	Kansas	1,942
22	West Virginia	1,904
23	Iowa	1,872
23	Nebraska	1,872
25	Arkansas	1,870
26	Washington	1,832
27	Utah	1,830
28	Louisiana	1,813
29	Missouri	1,810
30	Hawaii	1,789
31	North Dakota	1,751
32	Indiana	1,747
33	California	1,745
33	Rhode Island	1,745
35	Colorado	1,737
36	Oregon	1,731
37	South Carolina	1,709
38	Oklahoma	1,708
39	Alabama	1,630
40	South Dakota	1,629
41	Kentucky	1,623
42	Ohio	1,620
43	Idaho	1,601
44	Mississippi	1,579
45	Montana	1,564
46	Arizona	1,540
47	Florida	1,449
48	North Carolina	1,367
49	Tennessee	1,362
50	Nevada	1,305

| | District of Columbia | 1,532 |

Source: CQ Press using data from National Education Association, Washington, D.C.
"Rankings and Estimates" (Copyright © 2011, NEA, used with permission, http://www.nea.org/home/44479.htm)
*Estimates for school year 2010-2011. Per capita calculated with 2010 population.

Estimated Per Pupil Public Elementary and Secondary School Revenue in 2011

National Per Pupil = $12,129*

ALPHA ORDER

RANK	STATE	PER PUPIL		RANK	STATE	PER PUPIL
40	Alabama	$10,403		1	Wyoming	$20,096
33	Alaska	10,823		2	Vermont	19,829
44	Arizona	9,597		3	New York	18,691
25	Arkansas	11,849		4	New Jersey	18,109
39	California	10,455		5	Maryland	17,950
38	Colorado	10,487		6	Connecticut	16,871
6	Connecticut	16,871		7	Pennsylvania	16,521
9	Delaware	16,024		8	Massachusetts	16,214
41	Florida	10,329		9	Delaware	16,024
15	Georgia	13,215		10	Maine	15,291
17	Hawaii	12,981		11	New Hampshire	15,005
49	Idaho	8,755		12	Virginia	13,644
23	Illinois	12,019		13	Minnesota	13,333
35	Indiana	10,708		14	Rhode Island	13,288
28	Iowa	11,515		15	Georgia	13,215
29	Kansas	11,473		16	Wisconsin	13,190
36	Kentucky	10,701		17	Hawaii	12,981
27	Louisiana	11,699		18	New Mexico	12,727
10	Maine	15,291		19	North Dakota	12,433
5	Maryland	17,950		20	West Virginia	12,259
8	Massachusetts	16,214		21	Missouri	12,036
22	Michigan	12,029		22	Michigan	12,029
13	Minnesota	13,333		23	Illinois	12,019
45	Mississippi	9,413		24	Washington	11,904
21	Missouri	12,036		25	Arkansas	11,849
32	Montana	10,905		26	Oregon	11,820
30	Nebraska	11,394		27	Louisiana	11,699
50	Nevada	7,582		28	Iowa	11,515
11	New Hampshire	15,005		29	Kansas	11,473
4	New Jersey	18,109		30	Nebraska	11,394
18	New Mexico	12,727		31	South Carolina	10,964
3	New York	18,691		32	Montana	10,905
46	North Carolina	9,196		33	Alaska	10,823
19	North Dakota	12,433		34	South Dakota	10,782
42	Ohio	9,758		35	Indiana	10,708
43	Oklahoma	9,686		36	Kentucky	10,701
26	Oregon	11,820		37	Texas	10,516
7	Pennsylvania	16,521		38	Colorado	10,487
14	Rhode Island	13,288		39	California	10,455
31	South Carolina	10,964		40	Alabama	10,403
34	South Dakota	10,782		41	Florida	10,329
47	Tennessee	8,885		42	Ohio	9,758
37	Texas	10,516		43	Oklahoma	9,686
48	Utah	8,821		44	Arizona	9,597
2	Vermont	19,829		45	Mississippi	9,413
12	Virginia	13,644		46	North Carolina	9,196
24	Washington	11,904		47	Tennessee	8,885
20	West Virginia	12,259		48	Utah	8,821
16	Wisconsin	13,190		49	Idaho	8,755
1	Wyoming	20,096		50	Nevada	7,582

District of Columbia   12,278

Source: CQ Press using data from National Education Association, Washington, D.C.
   "Rankings and Estimates" (Copyright © 2011, NEA, used with permission, http://www.nea.org/home/44479.htm)
*Estimates for school year 2010-2011. Based on student membership.

Estimated Public Elementary and Secondary School
Current Expenditures in 2011
National Total = $532,223,619,000*

ALPHA ORDER

RANK	STATE	EXPENDITURES	% of USA
24	Alabama	$7,026,567,000	1.3%
46	Alaska	1,471,406,000	0.3%
25	Arizona	6,908,908,000	1.3%
29	Arkansas	5,512,621,000	1.0%
1	California	54,040,359,000	10.2%
22	Colorado	8,092,091,000	1.5%
20	Connecticut	8,484,231,000	1.6%
44	Delaware	1,794,300,000	0.3%
6	Florida	23,914,328,000	4.5%
9	Georgia	18,536,859,000	3.5%
43	Hawaii	2,116,966,000	0.4%
41	Idaho	2,310,612,000	0.4%
4	Illinois	25,064,787,000	4.7%
15	Indiana	10,926,879,000	2.1%
31	Iowa	4,843,755,000	0.9%
32	Kansas	4,451,177,000	0.8%
27	Kentucky	6,327,541,000	1.2%
23	Louisiana	7,427,166,000	1.4%
39	Maine	2,816,994,000	0.5%
13	Maryland	12,834,707,000	2.4%
12	Massachusetts	14,133,979,000	2.7%
8	Michigan	19,969,147,000	3.8%
18	Minnesota	9,644,663,000	1.8%
34	Mississippi	3,973,714,000	0.7%
19	Missouri	8,516,020,000	1.6%
48	Montana	1,401,496,000	0.3%
38	Nebraska	3,110,016,000	0.6%
36	Nevada	3,695,616,000	0.7%
40	New Hampshire	2,666,511,000	0.5%
5	New Jersey	24,203,175,000	4.5%
35	New Mexico	3,709,570,000	0.7%
2	New York	46,905,790,000	8.8%
14	North Carolina	11,671,670,000	2.2%
50	North Dakota	817,604,000	0.2%
10	Ohio	18,207,449,000	3.4%
30	Oklahoma	5,457,661,000	1.0%
28	Oregon	6,187,494,000	1.2%
7	Pennsylvania	23,519,622,000	4.4%
42	Rhode Island	2,193,529,000	0.4%
26	South Carolina	6,890,102,000	1.3%
49	South Dakota	1,153,542,000	0.2%
21	Tennessee	8,154,262,000	1.5%
3	Texas	44,042,836,000	8.3%
33	Utah	4,143,321,000	0.8%
45	Vermont	1,494,070,000	0.3%
11	Virginia	14,720,696,000	2.8%
16	Washington	10,762,364,000	2.0%
37	West Virginia	3,222,734,000	0.6%
17	Wisconsin	10,281,284,000	1.9%
47	Wyoming	1,419,502,000	0.3%

RANK ORDER

RANK	STATE	EXPENDITURES	% of USA
1	California	$54,040,359,000	10.2%
2	New York	46,905,790,000	8.8%
3	Texas	44,042,836,000	8.3%
4	Illinois	25,064,787,000	4.7%
5	New Jersey	24,203,175,000	4.5%
6	Florida	23,914,328,000	4.5%
7	Pennsylvania	23,519,622,000	4.4%
8	Michigan	19,969,147,000	3.8%
9	Georgia	18,536,859,000	3.5%
10	Ohio	18,207,449,000	3.4%
11	Virginia	14,720,696,000	2.8%
12	Massachusetts	14,133,979,000	2.7%
13	Maryland	12,834,707,000	2.4%
14	North Carolina	11,671,670,000	2.2%
15	Indiana	10,926,879,000	2.1%
16	Washington	10,762,364,000	2.0%
17	Wisconsin	10,281,284,000	1.9%
18	Minnesota	9,644,663,000	1.8%
19	Missouri	8,516,020,000	1.6%
20	Connecticut	8,484,231,000	1.6%
21	Tennessee	8,154,262,000	1.5%
22	Colorado	8,092,091,000	1.5%
23	Louisiana	7,427,166,000	1.4%
24	Alabama	7,026,567,000	1.3%
25	Arizona	6,908,908,000	1.3%
26	South Carolina	6,890,102,000	1.3%
27	Kentucky	6,327,541,000	1.2%
28	Oregon	6,187,494,000	1.2%
29	Arkansas	5,512,621,000	1.0%
30	Oklahoma	5,457,661,000	1.0%
31	Iowa	4,843,755,000	0.9%
32	Kansas	4,451,177,000	0.8%
33	Utah	4,143,321,000	0.8%
34	Mississippi	3,973,714,000	0.7%
35	New Mexico	3,709,570,000	0.7%
36	Nevada	3,695,616,000	0.7%
37	West Virginia	3,222,734,000	0.6%
38	Nebraska	3,110,016,000	0.6%
39	Maine	2,816,994,000	0.5%
40	New Hampshire	2,666,511,000	0.5%
41	Idaho	2,310,612,000	0.4%
42	Rhode Island	2,193,529,000	0.4%
43	Hawaii	2,116,966,000	0.4%
44	Delaware	1,794,300,000	0.3%
45	Vermont	1,494,070,000	0.3%
46	Alaska	1,471,406,000	0.3%
47	Wyoming	1,419,502,000	0.3%
48	Montana	1,401,496,000	0.3%
49	South Dakota	1,153,542,000	0.2%
50	North Dakota	817,604,000	0.2%
	District of Columbia	1,051,924,000	0.2%

Source: National Education Association, Washington, D.C.
   "Rankings and Estimates" (Copyright © 2011, NEA, used with permission, http://www.nea.org/home/44479.htm)
*Estimates for school year 2010-2011.

Estimated Per Capita Public Elementary and Secondary School Current Expenditures in 2011
National Per Capita = $1,722*

ALPHA ORDER

RANK	STATE	PER CAPITA
35	Alabama	$1,486
9	Alaska	2,076
50	Arizona	1,035
15	Arkansas	1,894
40	California	1,450
31	Colorado	1,588
3	Connecticut	2,406
12	Delaware	2,013
47	Florida	1,280
16	Georgia	1,871
27	Hawaii	1,628
36	Idaho	1,481
14	Illinois	1,936
25	Indiana	1,695
29	Iowa	1,602
33	Kansas	1,567
39	Kentucky	1,458
26	Louisiana	1,640
7	Maine	2,146
6	Maryland	2,237
8	Massachusetts	2,131
13	Michigan	2,011
20	Minnesota	1,823
45	Mississippi	1,342
42	Missouri	1,417
41	Montana	1,430
24	Nebraska	1,717
44	Nevada	1,392
11	New Hampshire	2,015
1	New Jersey	2,772
19	New Mexico	1,824
5	New York	2,396
49	North Carolina	1,234
48	North Dakota	1,251
32	Ohio	1,579
37	Oklahoma	1,465
28	Oregon	1,605
17	Pennsylvania	1,862
10	Rhode Island	2,075
34	South Carolina	1,499
43	South Dakota	1,407
46	Tennessee	1,287
23	Texas	1,747
38	Utah	1,464
4	Vermont	2,400
18	Virginia	1,851
30	Washington	1,595
22	West Virginia	1,765
21	Wisconsin	1,814
2	Wyoming	2,592

RANK ORDER

RANK	STATE	PER CAPITA
1	New Jersey	$2,772
2	Wyoming	2,592
3	Connecticut	2,406
4	Vermont	2,400
5	New York	2,396
6	Maryland	2,237
7	Maine	2,146
8	Massachusetts	2,131
9	Alaska	2,076
10	Rhode Island	2,075
11	New Hampshire	2,015
12	Delaware	2,013
13	Michigan	2,011
14	Illinois	1,936
15	Arkansas	1,894
16	Georgia	1,871
17	Pennsylvania	1,862
18	Virginia	1,851
19	New Mexico	1,824
20	Minnesota	1,823
21	Wisconsin	1,814
22	West Virginia	1,765
23	Texas	1,747
24	Nebraska	1,717
25	Indiana	1,695
26	Louisiana	1,640
27	Hawaii	1,628
28	Oregon	1,605
29	Iowa	1,602
30	Washington	1,595
31	Colorado	1,588
32	Ohio	1,579
33	Kansas	1,567
34	South Carolina	1,499
35	Alabama	1,486
36	Idaho	1,481
37	Oklahoma	1,465
38	Utah	1,464
39	Kentucky	1,458
40	California	1,450
41	Montana	1,430
42	Missouri	1,417
43	South Dakota	1,407
44	Nevada	1,392
45	Mississippi	1,342
46	Tennessee	1,287
47	Florida	1,280
48	North Dakota	1,251
49	North Carolina	1,234
50	Arizona	1,035
	District of Columbia	1,723

Source: CQ Press using data from National Education Association, Washington, D.C.
"Rankings and Estimates" (Copyright © 2011, NEA, used with permission, http://www.nea.org/home/44479.htm)
*Estimates for school year 2010-2011. Per capita calculated with 2010 population.

Estimated Per Pupil Public Elementary and Secondary School Current Expenditures in 2011
National Per Pupil = $10,826*

ALPHA ORDER

RANK	STATE	PER PUPIL
35	Alabama	$9,483
22	Alaska	11,147
50	Arizona	6,448
14	Arkansas	11,999
42	California	8,689
33	Colorado	9,588
8	Connecticut	14,989
10	Delaware	13,960
40	Florida	9,124
23	Georgia	10,971
17	Hawaii	11,819
46	Idaho	8,101
16	Illinois	11,896
27	Indiana	10,390
30	Iowa	9,856
38	Kansas	9,254
32	Kentucky	9,612
25	Louisiana	10,578
7	Maine	15,032
6	Maryland	15,268
9	Massachusetts	14,828
13	Michigan	12,015
15	Minnesota	11,905
48	Mississippi	8,003
36	Missouri	9,422
29	Montana	9,973
26	Nebraska	10,452
47	Nevada	8,089
11	New Hampshire	13,797
2	New Jersey	17,717
21	New Mexico	11,346
1	New York	17,750
45	North Carolina	8,303
41	North Dakota	8,880
34	Ohio	9,512
44	Oklahoma	8,311
24	Oregon	10,959
12	Pennsylvania	13,334
5	Rhode Island	15,803
31	South Carolina	9,616
37	South Dakota	9,310
43	Tennessee	8,393
39	Texas	9,128
49	Utah	7,056
3	Vermont	17,447
19	Virginia	11,753
28	Washington	10,367
20	West Virginia	11,369
18	Wisconsin	11,791
4	Wyoming	16,066

RANK ORDER

RANK	STATE	PER PUPIL
1	New York	$17,750
2	New Jersey	17,717
3	Vermont	17,447
4	Wyoming	16,066
5	Rhode Island	15,803
6	Maryland	15,268
7	Maine	15,032
8	Connecticut	14,989
9	Massachusetts	14,828
10	Delaware	13,960
11	New Hampshire	13,797
12	Pennsylvania	13,334
13	Michigan	12,015
14	Arkansas	11,999
15	Minnesota	11,905
16	Illinois	11,896
17	Hawaii	11,819
18	Wisconsin	11,791
19	Virginia	11,753
20	West Virginia	11,369
21	New Mexico	11,346
22	Alaska	11,147
23	Georgia	10,971
24	Oregon	10,959
25	Louisiana	10,578
26	Nebraska	10,452
27	Indiana	10,390
28	Washington	10,367
29	Montana	9,973
30	Iowa	9,856
31	South Carolina	9,616
32	Kentucky	9,612
33	Colorado	9,588
34	Ohio	9,512
35	Alabama	9,483
36	Missouri	9,422
37	South Dakota	9,310
38	Kansas	9,254
39	Texas	9,128
40	Florida	9,124
41	North Dakota	8,880
42	California	8,689
43	Tennessee	8,393
44	Oklahoma	8,311
45	North Carolina	8,303
46	Idaho	8,101
47	Nevada	8,089
48	Mississippi	8,003
49	Utah	7,056
50	Arizona	6,448
	District of Columbia	13,803

Source: National Education Association, Washington, D.C.

"Rankings and Estimates" (Copyright © 2011, NEA, used with permission, http://www.nea.org/home/44479.htm)

*Estimates for school year 2010-2011. Based on student membership.

U.S. Department of Education Grants for State Assessments in 2011

National Total = $385,950,536*

ALPHA ORDER

RANK	STATE	GRANTS	% of USA
23	Alabama	$6,333,266	1.6%
47	Alaska	3,537,277	0.9%
14	Arizona	7,726,173	2.0%
34	Arkansas	5,069,585	1.3%
1	California	30,244,931	7.8%
22	Colorado	6,551,376	1.7%
29	Connecticut	5,476,919	1.4%
45	Delaware	3,603,729	0.9%
4	Florida	14,796,652	3.8%
8	Georgia	10,269,793	2.6%
41	Hawaii	3,871,726	1.0%
38	Idaho	4,237,837	1.1%
5	Illinois	12,238,873	3.1%
13	Indiana	7,729,895	2.0%
32	Iowa	5,118,260	1.3%
33	Kansas	5,100,444	1.3%
26	Kentucky	5,984,843	1.5%
24	Louisiana	6,237,611	1.6%
42	Maine	3,825,814	1.0%
19	Maryland	6,981,686	1.8%
17	Massachusetts	7,236,907	1.9%
9	Michigan	10,040,252	2.6%
21	Minnesota	6,740,334	1.7%
31	Mississippi	5,193,703	1.3%
18	Missouri	7,169,892	1.8%
44	Montana	3,649,089	0.9%
37	Nebraska	4,318,452	1.1%
35	Nevada	4,923,542	1.3%
40	New Hampshire	3,875,823	1.0%
11	New Jersey	9,139,615	2.3%
36	New Mexico	4,505,267	1.2%
3	New York	15,765,500	4.0%
10	North Carolina	9,644,744	2.5%
48	North Dakota	3,424,063	0.9%
7	Ohio	11,096,071	2.8%
27	Oklahoma	5,680,866	1.5%
28	Oregon	5,533,264	1.4%
6	Pennsylvania	11,308,440	2.9%
43	Rhode Island	3,670,712	0.9%
25	South Carolina	6,134,580	1.6%
46	South Dakota	3,576,728	0.9%
16	Tennessee	7,383,337	1.9%
2	Texas	22,888,175	5.9%
30	Utah	5,445,475	1.4%
49	Vermont	3,391,858	0.9%
12	Virginia	8,413,984	2.2%
15	Washington	7,598,877	1.9%
39	West Virginia	4,141,396	1.1%
20	Wisconsin	6,951,770	1.8%
50	Wyoming	3,383,472	0.9%

RANK ORDER

RANK	STATE	GRANTS	% of USA
1	California	$30,244,931	7.8%
2	Texas	22,888,175	5.9%
3	New York	15,765,500	4.0%
4	Florida	14,796,652	3.8%
5	Illinois	12,238,873	3.1%
6	Pennsylvania	11,308,440	2.9%
7	Ohio	11,096,071	2.8%
8	Georgia	10,269,793	2.6%
9	Michigan	10,040,252	2.6%
10	North Carolina	9,644,744	2.5%
11	New Jersey	9,139,615	2.3%
12	Virginia	8,413,984	2.2%
13	Indiana	7,729,895	2.0%
14	Arizona	7,726,173	2.0%
15	Washington	7,598,877	1.9%
16	Tennessee	7,383,337	1.9%
17	Massachusetts	7,236,907	1.9%
18	Missouri	7,169,892	1.8%
19	Maryland	6,981,686	1.8%
20	Wisconsin	6,951,770	1.8%
21	Minnesota	6,740,334	1.7%
22	Colorado	6,551,376	1.7%
23	Alabama	6,333,266	1.6%
24	Louisiana	6,237,611	1.6%
25	South Carolina	6,134,580	1.6%
26	Kentucky	5,984,843	1.5%
27	Oklahoma	5,680,866	1.5%
28	Oregon	5,533,264	1.4%
29	Connecticut	5,476,919	1.4%
30	Utah	5,445,475	1.4%
31	Mississippi	5,193,703	1.3%
32	Iowa	5,118,260	1.3%
33	Kansas	5,100,444	1.3%
34	Arkansas	5,069,585	1.3%
35	Nevada	4,923,542	1.3%
36	New Mexico	4,505,267	1.2%
37	Nebraska	4,318,452	1.1%
38	Idaho	4,237,837	1.1%
39	West Virginia	4,141,396	1.1%
40	New Hampshire	3,875,823	1.0%
41	Hawaii	3,871,726	1.0%
42	Maine	3,825,814	1.0%
43	Rhode Island	3,670,712	0.9%
44	Montana	3,649,089	0.9%
45	Delaware	3,603,729	0.9%
46	South Dakota	3,576,728	0.9%
47	Alaska	3,537,277	0.9%
48	North Dakota	3,424,063	0.9%
49	Vermont	3,391,858	0.9%
50	Wyoming	3,383,472	0.9%
	District of Columbia	3,274,725	0.8%

Source: U.S. Department of Education, Budget Office
"Fiscal Year 2010-2012 State Tables" (http://www2.ed.gov/about/overview/budget/statetables/index.html)
*Estimates for fiscal year 2011 appropriation. Includes $19,512,933 in grants to U.S. territories and Indian tribe set-aside.

U.S. Department of Education College and Career Ready Students (Title I)
Grants to Local Educational Agencies in 2011
National Total = $14,463,416,198*

ALPHA ORDER

RANK	STATE	GRANTS	% of USA
19	Alabama	$225,736,068	1.6%
47	Alaska	35,863,502	0.2%
11	Arizona	314,893,989	2.2%
27	Arkansas	156,581,557	1.1%
1	California	1,626,853,420	11.2%
29	Colorado	153,342,588	1.1%
33	Connecticut	107,015,653	0.7%
45	Delaware	42,389,903	0.3%
4	Florida	740,529,196	5.1%
9	Georgia	526,093,785	3.6%
42	Hawaii	47,568,135	0.3%
39	Idaho	54,119,573	0.4%
5	Illinois	642,998,237	4.4%
15	Indiana	256,458,543	1.8%
37	Iowa	76,708,378	0.5%
32	Kansas	110,730,631	0.8%
18	Kentucky	226,124,814	1.6%
13	Louisiana	298,919,404	2.1%
40	Maine	52,443,462	0.4%
25	Maryland	182,670,903	1.3%
21	Massachusetts	219,019,366	1.5%
8	Michigan	535,793,852	3.7%
26	Minnesota	158,755,544	1.1%
24	Mississippi	193,877,333	1.3%
17	Missouri	244,238,099	1.7%
43	Montana	44,589,031	0.3%
38	Nebraska	61,731,920	0.4%
34	Nevada	97,380,933	0.7%
46	New Hampshire	40,527,335	0.3%
12	New Jersey	299,988,553	2.1%
31	New Mexico	113,837,748	0.8%
3	New York	1,168,409,107	8.1%
10	North Carolina	390,839,738	2.7%
48	North Dakota	34,097,283	0.2%
6	Ohio	570,011,835	3.9%
28	Oklahoma	154,672,779	1.1%
30	Oregon	146,453,623	1.0%
7	Pennsylvania	546,045,342	3.8%
41	Rhode Island	49,541,517	0.3%
20	South Carolina	220,623,764	1.5%
44	South Dakota	43,701,783	0.3%
14	Tennessee	274,585,354	1.9%
2	Texas	1,348,969,431	9.3%
36	Utah	80,211,532	0.6%
49	Vermont	33,280,977	0.2%
16	Virginia	245,997,415	1.7%
23	Washington	211,174,588	1.5%
35	West Virginia	93,226,662	0.6%
22	Wisconsin	213,279,005	1.5%
50	Wyoming	32,551,783	0.2%

RANK ORDER

RANK	STATE	GRANTS	% of USA
1	California	$1,626,853,420	11.2%
2	Texas	1,348,969,431	9.3%
3	New York	1,168,409,107	8.1%
4	Florida	740,529,196	5.1%
5	Illinois	642,998,237	4.4%
6	Ohio	570,011,835	3.9%
7	Pennsylvania	546,045,342	3.8%
8	Michigan	535,793,852	3.7%
9	Georgia	526,093,785	3.6%
10	North Carolina	390,839,738	2.7%
11	Arizona	314,893,989	2.2%
12	New Jersey	299,988,553	2.1%
13	Louisiana	298,919,404	2.1%
14	Tennessee	274,585,354	1.9%
15	Indiana	256,458,543	1.8%
16	Virginia	245,997,415	1.7%
17	Missouri	244,238,099	1.7%
18	Kentucky	226,124,814	1.6%
19	Alabama	225,736,068	1.6%
20	South Carolina	220,623,764	1.5%
21	Massachusetts	219,019,366	1.5%
22	Wisconsin	213,279,005	1.5%
23	Washington	211,174,588	1.5%
24	Mississippi	193,877,333	1.3%
25	Maryland	182,670,903	1.3%
26	Minnesota	158,755,544	1.1%
27	Arkansas	156,581,557	1.1%
28	Oklahoma	154,672,779	1.1%
29	Colorado	153,342,588	1.1%
30	Oregon	146,453,623	1.0%
31	New Mexico	113,837,748	0.8%
32	Kansas	110,730,631	0.8%
33	Connecticut	107,015,653	0.7%
34	Nevada	97,380,933	0.7%
35	West Virginia	93,226,662	0.6%
36	Utah	80,211,532	0.6%
37	Iowa	76,708,378	0.5%
38	Nebraska	61,731,920	0.4%
39	Idaho	54,119,573	0.4%
40	Maine	52,443,462	0.4%
41	Rhode Island	49,541,517	0.3%
42	Hawaii	47,568,135	0.3%
43	Montana	44,589,031	0.3%
44	South Dakota	43,701,783	0.3%
45	Delaware	42,389,903	0.3%
46	New Hampshire	40,527,335	0.3%
47	Alaska	35,863,502	0.2%
48	North Dakota	34,097,283	0.2%
49	Vermont	33,280,977	0.2%
50	Wyoming	32,551,783	0.2%
	District of Columbia	48,999,648	0.3%

Source: U.S. Department of Education, Budget Office
   "Fiscal Year 2010-2012 State Tables" (http://www2.ed.gov/about/overview/budget/statetables/index.html)
*Estimates for fiscal year 2011 appropriation. Includes $668,961,577 in grants to U.S. territories and Indian tribe set-aside. Title I schools are eligible for Title I federal funding to assist disadvantaged students.

U.S. Department of Education Grants for Improving Teacher Quality in 2011

National Total = $2,468,054,000*

ALPHA ORDER

RANK	STATE	GRANTS	% of USA
21	Alabama	$38,743,831	1.6%
39	Alaska	11,562,580	0.5%
20	Arizona	38,878,497	1.6%
29	Arkansas	23,659,435	1.0%
1	California	270,981,109	11.0%
28	Colorado	27,353,126	1.1%
31	Connecticut	22,673,316	0.9%
39	Delaware	11,562,580	0.5%
4	Florida	110,257,126	4.5%
9	Georgia	64,698,714	2.6%
39	Hawaii	11,562,580	0.5%
39	Idaho	11,562,580	0.5%
5	Illinois	99,684,668	4.0%
17	Indiana	41,706,110	1.7%
35	Iowa	18,898,938	0.8%
33	Kansas	19,348,902	0.8%
22	Kentucky	38,136,939	1.5%
11	Louisiana	54,419,039	2.2%
39	Maine	11,562,580	0.5%
24	Maryland	34,923,613	1.4%
13	Massachusetts	43,963,725	1.8%
7	Michigan	96,339,187	3.9%
25	Minnesota	33,144,043	1.3%
23	Mississippi	36,009,086	1.5%
15	Missouri	42,199,520	1.7%
39	Montana	11,562,580	0.5%
38	Nebraska	11,839,523	0.5%
37	Nevada	12,360,167	0.5%
39	New Hampshire	11,562,580	0.5%
10	New Jersey	55,220,523	2.2%
34	New Mexico	19,135,206	0.8%
3	New York	196,797,290	8.0%
12	North Carolina	54,029,160	2.2%
39	North Dakota	11,562,580	0.5%
8	Ohio	91,322,787	3.7%
27	Oklahoma	28,018,537	1.1%
30	Oregon	23,655,193	1.0%
6	Pennsylvania	98,302,355	4.0%
39	Rhode Island	11,562,580	0.5%
26	South Carolina	30,729,833	1.2%
39	South Dakota	11,562,580	0.5%
16	Tennessee	41,832,263	1.7%
2	Texas	201,174,961	8.2%
36	Utah	16,017,963	0.6%
39	Vermont	11,562,580	0.5%
14	Virginia	43,456,153	1.8%
19	Washington	39,890,148	1.6%
32	West Virginia	20,545,828	0.8%
18	Wisconsin	39,917,347	1.6%
39	Wyoming	11,562,580	0.5%

RANK ORDER

RANK	STATE	GRANTS	% of USA
1	California	$270,981,109	11.0%
2	Texas	201,174,961	8.2%
3	New York	196,797,290	8.0%
4	Florida	110,257,126	4.5%
5	Illinois	99,684,668	4.0%
6	Pennsylvania	98,302,355	4.0%
7	Michigan	96,339,187	3.9%
8	Ohio	91,322,787	3.7%
9	Georgia	64,698,714	2.6%
10	New Jersey	55,220,523	2.2%
11	Louisiana	54,419,039	2.2%
12	North Carolina	54,029,160	2.2%
13	Massachusetts	43,963,725	1.8%
14	Virginia	43,456,153	1.8%
15	Missouri	42,199,520	1.7%
16	Tennessee	41,832,263	1.7%
17	Indiana	41,706,110	1.7%
18	Wisconsin	39,917,347	1.6%
19	Washington	39,890,148	1.6%
20	Arizona	38,878,497	1.6%
21	Alabama	38,743,831	1.6%
22	Kentucky	38,136,939	1.5%
23	Mississippi	36,009,086	1.5%
24	Maryland	34,923,613	1.4%
25	Minnesota	33,144,043	1.3%
26	South Carolina	30,729,833	1.2%
27	Oklahoma	28,018,537	1.1%
28	Colorado	27,353,126	1.1%
29	Arkansas	23,659,435	1.0%
30	Oregon	23,655,193	1.0%
31	Connecticut	22,673,316	0.9%
32	West Virginia	20,545,828	0.8%
33	Kansas	19,348,902	0.8%
34	New Mexico	19,135,206	0.8%
35	Iowa	18,898,938	0.8%
36	Utah	16,017,963	0.6%
37	Nevada	12,360,167	0.5%
38	Nebraska	11,839,523	0.5%
39	Alaska	11,562,580	0.5%
39	Delaware	11,562,580	0.5%
39	Hawaii	11,562,580	0.5%
39	Idaho	11,562,580	0.5%
39	Maine	11,562,580	0.5%
39	Montana	11,562,580	0.5%
39	New Hampshire	11,562,580	0.5%
39	North Dakota	11,562,580	0.5%
39	Rhode Island	11,562,580	0.5%
39	South Dakota	11,562,580	0.5%
39	Vermont	11,562,580	0.5%
39	Wyoming	11,562,580	0.5%
	District of Columbia	11,562,580	0.5%

Source: U.S. Department of Education, Budget Office
   "Fiscal Year 2010-2012 State Tables" (http://www2.ed.gov/about/overview/budget/statetables/index.html)
*Estimates for fiscal year 2011 appropriation. Includes $137,476,299 in grants to U.S. territories and Indian tribe set-aside. The purpose of these grants is to help increase the academic achievement of all students by helping schools and school districts ensure that all teachers are highly qualified to teach. State and local educational agencies receive funds on a formula basis, as does the state agency for higher education.

Public Elementary and Secondary School Revenue in 2009

National Total = $590,947,579,000*

ALPHA ORDER

RANK ORDER

RANK	STATE	REVENUE	% of USA
26	Alabama	$7,184,885,000	1.2%
44	Alaska	2,158,835,000	0.4%
21	Arizona	8,719,722,000	1.5%
32	Arkansas	4,732,685,000	0.8%
1	California	71,453,144,000	12.1%
22	Colorado	8,262,667,000	1.4%
19	Connecticut	9,501,924,000	1.6%
45	Delaware	1,674,367,000	0.3%
4	Florida	26,487,591,000	4.5%
10	Georgia	17,968,445,000	3.0%
40	Hawaii	2,689,758,000	0.5%
42	Idaho	2,181,398,000	0.4%
5	Illinois	26,371,090,000	4.5%
15	Indiana	12,710,067,000	2.2%
31	Iowa	5,527,244,000	0.9%
30	Kansas	5,613,161,000	0.9%
27	Kentucky	6,705,234,000	1.1%
24	Louisiana	7,931,699,000	1.3%
41	Maine	2,551,991,000	0.4%
14	Maryland	13,141,453,000	2.2%
12	Massachusetts	15,170,426,000	2.6%
9	Michigan	18,647,707,000	3.2%
18	Minnesota	10,170,640,000	1.7%
34	Mississippi	4,380,745,000	0.7%
20	Missouri	9,396,217,000	1.6%
47	Montana	1,595,318,000	0.3%
37	Nebraska	3,446,377,000	0.6%
33	Nevada	4,441,108,000	0.8%
39	New Hampshire	2,716,562,000	0.5%
6	New Jersey	25,651,702,000	4.3%
36	New Mexico	3,703,462,000	0.6%
2	New York	55,677,184,000	9.4%
11	North Carolina	15,410,562,000	2.6%
50	North Dakota	1,104,033,000	0.2%
8	Ohio	22,150,278,000	3.7%
29	Oklahoma	6,028,778,000	1.0%
28	Oregon	6,104,185,000	1.0%
7	Pennsylvania	25,473,158,000	4.3%
43	Rhode Island	2,166,937,000	0.4%
25	South Carolina	7,656,698,000	1.3%
49	South Dakota	1,255,234,000	0.2%
23	Tennessee	8,081,576,000	1.4%
3	Texas	47,930,801,000	8.1%
35	Utah	4,234,810,000	0.7%
48	Vermont	1,507,266,000	0.3%
13	Virginia	15,000,778,000	2.5%
16	Washington	11,925,646,000	2.0%
38	West Virginia	3,096,506,000	0.5%
17	Wisconsin	10,781,347,000	1.8%
46	Wyoming	1,673,170,000	0.3%

RANK	STATE	REVENUE	% of USA
1	California	$71,453,144,000	12.1%
2	New York	55,677,184,000	9.4%
3	Texas	47,930,801,000	8.1%
4	Florida	26,487,591,000	4.5%
5	Illinois	26,371,090,000	4.5%
6	New Jersey	25,651,702,000	4.3%
7	Pennsylvania	25,473,158,000	4.3%
8	Ohio	22,150,278,000	3.7%
9	Michigan	18,647,707,000	3.2%
10	Georgia	17,968,445,000	3.0%
11	North Carolina	15,410,562,000	2.6%
12	Massachusetts	15,170,426,000	2.6%
13	Virginia	15,000,778,000	2.5%
14	Maryland	13,141,453,000	2.2%
15	Indiana	12,710,067,000	2.2%
16	Washington	11,925,646,000	2.0%
17	Wisconsin	10,781,347,000	1.8%
18	Minnesota	10,170,640,000	1.7%
19	Connecticut	9,501,924,000	1.6%
20	Missouri	9,396,217,000	1.6%
21	Arizona	8,719,722,000	1.5%
22	Colorado	8,262,667,000	1.4%
23	Tennessee	8,081,576,000	1.4%
24	Louisiana	7,931,699,000	1.3%
25	South Carolina	7,656,698,000	1.3%
26	Alabama	7,184,885,000	1.2%
27	Kentucky	6,705,234,000	1.1%
28	Oregon	6,104,185,000	1.0%
29	Oklahoma	6,028,778,000	1.0%
30	Kansas	5,613,161,000	0.9%
31	Iowa	5,527,244,000	0.9%
32	Arkansas	4,732,685,000	0.8%
33	Nevada	4,441,108,000	0.8%
34	Mississippi	4,380,745,000	0.7%
35	Utah	4,234,810,000	0.7%
36	New Mexico	3,703,462,000	0.6%
37	Nebraska	3,446,377,000	0.6%
38	West Virginia	3,096,506,000	0.5%
39	New Hampshire	2,716,562,000	0.5%
40	Hawaii	2,689,758,000	0.5%
41	Maine	2,551,991,000	0.4%
42	Idaho	2,181,398,000	0.4%
43	Rhode Island	2,166,937,000	0.4%
44	Alaska	2,158,835,000	0.4%
45	Delaware	1,674,367,000	0.3%
46	Wyoming	1,673,170,000	0.3%
47	Montana	1,595,318,000	0.3%
48	Vermont	1,507,266,000	0.3%
49	South Dakota	1,255,234,000	0.2%
50	North Dakota	1,104,033,000	0.2%
	District of Columbia	801,008,000	0.1%

Source: U.S. Bureau of the Census, Governments Division
   "Public Education Finances: 2009" (http://www.census.gov/govs/school/)

*Revenue includes all money received by a school system from external sources (net of refunds) other than from issuance of debt or liquidation of investments. Does not include noncash transactions such as receipt of services, commodities, or other "receipts in-kind." Excludes duplicative interschool system transactions.

Per Capita Public Elementary and Secondary School Revenue in 2009

National Per Capita = $1,925*

ALPHA ORDER

RANK	STATE	PER CAPITA		RANK	STATE	PER CAPITA
44	Alabama	$1,526		1	Alaska	$3,091
1	Alaska	3,091		2	Wyoming	3,074
49	Arizona	1,322		3	New Jersey	2,946
37	Arkansas	1,638		4	New York	2,849
18	California	1,933		5	Connecticut	2,701
35	Colorado	1,644		6	Vermont	2,424
5	Connecticut	2,701		7	Maryland	2,306
24	Delaware	1,892		8	Massachusetts	2,301
47	Florida	1,429		9	Hawaii	2,077
28	Georgia	1,828		10	Rhode Island	2,057
9	Hawaii	2,077		11	New Hampshire	2,051
48	Idaho	1,411		12	Illinois	2,043
12	Illinois	2,043		13	Pennsylvania	2,021
15	Indiana	1,979		14	Kansas	1,991
27	Iowa	1,838		15	Indiana	1,979
14	Kansas	1,991		16	Maine	1,936
42	Kentucky	1,554		17	Texas	1,934
30	Louisiana	1,766		18	California	1,933
16	Maine	1,936		19	Minnesota	1,931
7	Maryland	2,306		20	Ohio	1,919
8	Massachusetts	2,301		21	Nebraska	1,918
25	Michigan	1,870		22	Wisconsin	1,907
19	Minnesota	1,931		23	Virginia	1,903
46	Mississippi	1,484		24	Delaware	1,892
41	Missouri	1,569		25	Michigan	1,870
38	Montana	1,636		26	New Mexico	1,843
21	Nebraska	1,918		27	Iowa	1,838
33	Nevada	1,680		28	Georgia	1,828
11	New Hampshire	2,051		29	Washington	1,790
3	New Jersey	2,946		30	Louisiana	1,766
26	New Mexico	1,843		31	North Dakota	1,707
4	New York	2,849		32	West Virginia	1,702
36	North Carolina	1,643		33	Nevada	1,680
31	North Dakota	1,707		34	South Carolina	1,679
20	Ohio	1,919		35	Colorado	1,644
39	Oklahoma	1,635		36	North Carolina	1,643
40	Oregon	1,596		37	Arkansas	1,638
13	Pennsylvania	2,021		38	Montana	1,636
10	Rhode Island	2,057		39	Oklahoma	1,635
34	South Carolina	1,679		40	Oregon	1,596
43	South Dakota	1,545		41	Missouri	1,569
50	Tennessee	1,284		42	Kentucky	1,554
17	Texas	1,934		43	South Dakota	1,545
45	Utah	1,521		44	Alabama	1,526
6	Vermont	2,424		45	Utah	1,521
23	Virginia	1,903		46	Mississippi	1,484
29	Washington	1,790		47	Florida	1,429
32	West Virginia	1,702		48	Idaho	1,411
22	Wisconsin	1,907		49	Arizona	1,322
2	Wyoming	3,074		50	Tennessee	1,284
					District of Columbia	1,336

Source: CQ Press using data from U.S. Bureau of the Census, Governments Division
"Public Education Finances: 2009" (http://www.census.gov/govs/school/)
*Revenue includes all money received by a school system from external sources (net of refunds) other than from issuance of debt or liquidation of investments. Does not include noncash transactions such as receipt of services, commodities, or other "receipts in-kind." Excludes duplicative interschool system transactions.

Public Elementary and Secondary School Revenue per $1,000 Personal Income in 2009
National Ratio = $47.74*

ALPHA ORDER

RANK	STATE	RATIO
35	Alabama	$45.31
1	Alaska	70.67
47	Arizona	38.89
15	Arkansas	50.48
38	California	44.36
48	Colorado	38.48
28	Connecticut	47.38
31	Delaware	46.83
50	Florida	35.89
12	Georgia	52.61
20	Hawaii	49.25
40	Idaho	43.30
27	Illinois	47.58
6	Indiana	56.94
23	Iowa	48.30
17	Kansas	50.00
22	Kentucky	48.31
32	Louisiana	46.78
10	Maine	52.95
25	Maryland	47.97
34	Massachusetts	45.43
11	Michigan	52.78
36	Minnesota	44.97
21	Mississippi	48.48
42	Missouri	42.91
33	Montana	46.77
24	Nebraska	48.21
43	Nevada	42.37
29	New Hampshire	47.15
5	New Jersey	57.40
7	New Mexico	55.50
4	New York	59.45
30	North Carolina	46.90
45	North Dakota	41.48
9	Ohio	53.21
37	Oklahoma	44.81
39	Oregon	43.85
16	Pennsylvania	50.15
19	Rhode Island	49.28
13	South Carolina	51.61
46	South Dakota	39.75
49	Tennessee	36.90
18	Texas	49.54
26	Utah	47.64
3	Vermont	61.85
41	Virginia	43.00
44	Washington	41.53
8	West Virginia	54.14
14	Wisconsin	50.53
2	Wyoming	62.05

RANK ORDER

RANK	STATE	RATIO
1	Alaska	$70.67
2	Wyoming	62.05
3	Vermont	61.85
4	New York	59.45
5	New Jersey	57.40
6	Indiana	56.94
7	New Mexico	55.50
8	West Virginia	54.14
9	Ohio	53.21
10	Maine	52.95
11	Michigan	52.78
12	Georgia	52.61
13	South Carolina	51.61
14	Wisconsin	50.53
15	Arkansas	50.48
16	Pennsylvania	50.15
17	Kansas	50.00
18	Texas	49.54
19	Rhode Island	49.28
20	Hawaii	49.25
21	Mississippi	48.48
22	Kentucky	48.31
23	Iowa	48.30
24	Nebraska	48.21
25	Maryland	47.97
26	Utah	47.64
27	Illinois	47.58
28	Connecticut	47.38
29	New Hampshire	47.15
30	North Carolina	46.90
31	Delaware	46.83
32	Louisiana	46.78
33	Montana	46.77
34	Massachusetts	45.43
35	Alabama	45.31
36	Minnesota	44.97
37	Oklahoma	44.81
38	California	44.36
39	Oregon	43.85
40	Idaho	43.30
41	Virginia	43.00
42	Missouri	42.91
43	Nevada	42.37
44	Washington	41.53
45	North Dakota	41.48
46	South Dakota	39.75
47	Arizona	38.89
48	Colorado	38.48
49	Tennessee	36.90
50	Florida	35.89

District of Columbia   19.85

Source: U.S. Bureau of the Census, Governments Division
"Public Education Finances: 2009" (http://www.census.gov/govs/school/)
*Revenue includes all money received by a school system from external sources (net of refunds) other than from issuance of debt or liquidation of investments. Does not include noncash transactions such as receipt of services, commodities, or other "receipts in-kind."

Per Pupil Public Elementary and Secondary School Revenue in 2009

National Per Pupil = $12,250*

ALPHA ORDER

RANK	STATE	PER PUPIL	RANK	STATE	PER PUPIL
44	Alabama	$9,636	1	New York	$20,645
6	Alaska	16,576	2	Wyoming	19,238
47	Arizona	8,882	3	New Jersey	18,874
42	Arkansas	9,976	4	Connecticut	17,373
26	California	11,588	5	Vermont	17,108
39	Colorado	10,171	6	Alaska	16,576
4	Connecticut	17,373	7	Massachusetts	16,270
12	Delaware	14,335	8	Maryland	15,574
40	Florida	10,098	9	Rhode Island	15,312
32	Georgia	10,893	10	Pennsylvania	15,023
11	Hawaii	14,987	11	Hawaii	14,987
49	Idaho	8,141	12	Delaware	14,335
17	Illinois	12,457	13	New Hampshire	13,725
19	Indiana	12,360	14	Maine	13,666
28	Iowa	11,337	15	Ohio	12,811
23	Kansas	11,939	16	Minnesota	12,664
41	Kentucky	10,010	17	Illinois	12,457
22	Louisiana	11,967	18	Wisconsin	12,435
14	Maine	13,666	19	Indiana	12,360
8	Maryland	15,574	20	Virginia	12,146
7	Massachusetts	16,270	21	Michigan	11,987
21	Michigan	11,987	22	Louisiana	11,967
16	Minnesota	12,664	23	Kansas	11,939
46	Mississippi	8,919	24	Nebraska	11,796
36	Missouri	10,457	25	North Dakota	11,664
29	Montana	11,266	26	California	11,588
24	Nebraska	11,796	27	Washington	11,510
38	Nevada	10,305	28	Iowa	11,337
13	New Hampshire	13,725	29	Montana	11,266
3	New Jersey	18,874	29	New Mexico	11,266
29	New Mexico	11,266	31	West Virginia	10,984
1	New York	20,645	32	Georgia	10,893
35	North Carolina	10,613	33	Oregon	10,862
25	North Dakota	11,664	34	South Carolina	10,719
15	Ohio	12,811	35	North Carolina	10,613
45	Oklahoma	9,353	36	Missouri	10,457
33	Oregon	10,862	37	Texas	10,314
10	Pennsylvania	15,023	38	Nevada	10,305
9	Rhode Island	15,312	39	Colorado	10,171
34	South Carolina	10,719	40	Florida	10,098
43	South Dakota	9,913	41	Kentucky	10,010
48	Tennessee	8,324	42	Arkansas	9,976
37	Texas	10,314	43	South Dakota	9,913
50	Utah	7,954	44	Alabama	9,636
5	Vermont	17,108	45	Oklahoma	9,353
20	Virginia	12,146	46	Mississippi	8,919
27	Washington	11,510	47	Arizona	8,882
31	West Virginia	10,984	48	Tennessee	8,324
18	Wisconsin	12,435	49	Idaho	8,141
2	Wyoming	19,238	50	Utah	7,954
				District of Columbia	18,069

Source: U.S. Bureau of the Census, Governments Division
   "Public Education Finances: 2009" (http://www.census.gov/govs/school/)
*Based on student membership. Revenue includes all money received by a school system from external sources (net of refunds) other than from issuance of debt or liquidation of investments. Does not include noncash transactions such as receipt of services, commodities, or other "receipts in-kind."

Public Elementary and Secondary School
Revenue from Federal Sources in 2009
National Total = $55,900,112,000*

ALPHA ORDER

RANK	STATE	REVENUE	% of USA
23	Alabama	$728,795,000	1.3%
39	Alaska	312,667,000	0.6%
16	Arizona	1,044,140,000	1.9%
31	Arkansas	534,510,000	1.0%
1	California	9,745,250,000	17.4%
29	Colorado	560,538,000	1.0%
35	Connecticut	403,017,000	0.7%
48	Delaware	109,682,000	0.2%
5	Florida	2,694,566,000	4.8%
8	Georgia	1,644,548,000	2.9%
36	Hawaii	392,837,000	0.7%
42	Idaho	218,777,000	0.4%
3	Illinois	3,346,509,000	6.0%
10	Indiana	1,403,839,000	2.5%
33	Iowa	431,142,000	0.8%
37	Kansas	378,810,000	0.7%
24	Kentucky	719,997,000	1.3%
14	Louisiana	1,238,259,000	2.2%
41	Maine	245,063,000	0.4%
25	Maryland	694,846,000	1.2%
15	Massachusetts	1,181,681,000	2.1%
6	Michigan	2,094,714,000	3.7%
28	Minnesota	575,703,000	1.0%
26	Mississippi	675,576,000	1.2%
21	Missouri	758,650,000	1.4%
45	Montana	195,705,000	0.4%
40	Nebraska	297,732,000	0.5%
34	Nevada	425,133,000	0.8%
47	New Hampshire	146,867,000	0.3%
17	New Jersey	1,014,556,000	1.8%
32	New Mexico	519,973,000	0.9%
4	New York	3,197,833,000	5.7%
12	North Carolina	1,377,661,000	2.5%
46	North Dakota	160,294,000	0.3%
9	Ohio	1,531,263,000	2.7%
20	Oklahoma	768,972,000	1.4%
27	Oregon	656,298,000	1.2%
7	Pennsylvania	1,811,141,000	3.2%
43	Rhode Island	206,225,000	0.4%
22	South Carolina	734,602,000	1.3%
44	South Dakota	201,889,000	0.4%
19	Tennessee	870,374,000	1.6%
2	Texas	4,913,841,000	8.8%
30	Utah	535,223,000	1.0%
50	Vermont	102,453,000	0.2%
18	Virginia	914,507,000	1.6%
11	Washington	1,385,421,000	2.5%
38	West Virginia	355,325,000	0.6%
13	Wisconsin	1,258,519,000	2.3%
49	Wyoming	108,333,000	0.2%

RANK ORDER

RANK	STATE	REVENUE	% of USA
1	California	$9,745,250,000	17.4%
2	Texas	4,913,841,000	8.8%
3	Illinois	3,346,509,000	6.0%
4	New York	3,197,833,000	5.7%
5	Florida	2,694,566,000	4.8%
6	Michigan	2,094,714,000	3.7%
7	Pennsylvania	1,811,141,000	3.2%
8	Georgia	1,644,548,000	2.9%
9	Ohio	1,531,263,000	2.7%
10	Indiana	1,403,839,000	2.5%
11	Washington	1,385,421,000	2.5%
12	North Carolina	1,377,661,000	2.5%
13	Wisconsin	1,258,519,000	2.3%
14	Louisiana	1,238,259,000	2.2%
15	Massachusetts	1,181,681,000	2.1%
16	Arizona	1,044,140,000	1.9%
17	New Jersey	1,014,556,000	1.8%
18	Virginia	914,507,000	1.6%
19	Tennessee	870,374,000	1.6%
20	Oklahoma	768,972,000	1.4%
21	Missouri	758,650,000	1.4%
22	South Carolina	734,602,000	1.3%
23	Alabama	728,795,000	1.3%
24	Kentucky	719,997,000	1.3%
25	Maryland	694,846,000	1.2%
26	Mississippi	675,576,000	1.2%
27	Oregon	656,298,000	1.2%
28	Minnesota	575,703,000	1.0%
29	Colorado	560,538,000	1.0%
30	Utah	535,223,000	1.0%
31	Arkansas	534,510,000	1.0%
32	New Mexico	519,973,000	0.9%
33	Iowa	431,142,000	0.8%
34	Nevada	425,133,000	0.8%
35	Connecticut	403,017,000	0.7%
36	Hawaii	392,837,000	0.7%
37	Kansas	378,810,000	0.7%
38	West Virginia	355,325,000	0.6%
39	Alaska	312,667,000	0.6%
40	Nebraska	297,732,000	0.5%
41	Maine	245,063,000	0.4%
42	Idaho	218,777,000	0.4%
43	Rhode Island	206,225,000	0.4%
44	South Dakota	201,889,000	0.4%
45	Montana	195,705,000	0.4%
46	North Dakota	160,294,000	0.3%
47	New Hampshire	146,867,000	0.3%
48	Delaware	109,682,000	0.2%
49	Wyoming	108,333,000	0.2%
50	Vermont	102,453,000	0.2%
	District of Columbia	75,856,000	0.1%

Source: U.S. Bureau of the Census, Governments Division
   "Public Education Finances: 2009" (http://www.census.gov/govs/school/)
*Includes federal revenue passed through state governments as well as federal outlays directly received. Includes all such revenue received by a school system from federal sources (net of refunds) other than from issuance of debt or liquidation of investments. Does not include noncash transactions such as receipt of services, commodities, or other "receipts in-kind."

Per Capita Public Elementary and Secondary School Revenue from Federal Sources in 2009
National Per Capita = $182*

ALPHA ORDER

RANK ORDER

RANK	STATE	PER CAPITA	RANK	STATE	PER CAPITA
33	Alabama	$155	1	Alaska	$448
1	Alaska	448	2	Hawaii	303
32	Arizona	158	3	Louisiana	276
22	Arkansas	185	4	California	264
4	California	264	5	Illinois	259
48	Colorado	112	5	New Mexico	259
47	Connecticut	115	7	South Dakota	249
43	Delaware	124	8	North Dakota	248
35	Florida	145	9	Mississippi	229
25	Georgia	167	10	Wisconsin	223
2	Hawaii	303	11	Indiana	219
38	Idaho	142	12	Michigan	210
5	Illinois	259	13	Oklahoma	209
11	Indiana	219	14	Washington	208
37	Iowa	143	15	Montana	201
40	Kansas	134	16	Wyoming	199
25	Kentucky	167	17	Texas	198
3	Louisiana	276	18	Rhode Island	196
21	Maine	186	19	West Virginia	195
44	Maryland	122	20	Utah	192
23	Massachusetts	179	21	Maine	186
12	Michigan	210	22	Arkansas	185
50	Minnesota	109	23	Massachusetts	179
9	Mississippi	229	24	Oregon	172
42	Missouri	127	25	Georgia	167
15	Montana	201	25	Kentucky	167
27	Nebraska	166	27	Nebraska	166
30	Nevada	161	28	Vermont	165
49	New Hampshire	111	29	New York	164
45	New Jersey	117	30	Nevada	161
5	New Mexico	259	30	South Carolina	161
29	New York	164	32	Arizona	158
34	North Carolina	147	33	Alabama	155
8	North Dakota	248	34	North Carolina	147
41	Ohio	133	35	Florida	145
13	Oklahoma	209	36	Pennsylvania	144
24	Oregon	172	37	Iowa	143
36	Pennsylvania	144	38	Idaho	142
18	Rhode Island	196	39	Tennessee	138
30	South Carolina	161	40	Kansas	134
7	South Dakota	249	41	Ohio	133
39	Tennessee	138	42	Missouri	127
17	Texas	198	43	Delaware	124
20	Utah	192	44	Maryland	122
28	Vermont	165	45	New Jersey	117
46	Virginia	116	46	Virginia	116
14	Washington	208	47	Connecticut	115
19	West Virginia	195	48	Colorado	112
10	Wisconsin	223	49	New Hampshire	111
16	Wyoming	199	50	Minnesota	109

District of Columbia   126

Source: CQ Press using data from U.S. Bureau of the Census, Governments Division
"Public Education Finances: 2009" (http://www.census.gov/govs/school/)
*Includes federal revenue passed through state governments as well as federal outlays directly received. Includes all such revenue received by a school system from federal sources (net of refunds) other than from issuance of debt or liquidation of investments. Does not include noncash transactions such as receipt of services, commodities, or other "receipts in-kind."

Public Elementary and Secondary School Revenue from Federal Sources per $1,000 Personal Income in 2009
National Ratio = $4.52*

RANK	STATE	RATIO
27	Alabama	$4.60
1	Alaska	10.23
26	Arizona	4.66
17	Arkansas	5.70
9	California	6.05
45	Colorado	2.61
50	Connecticut	2.01
43	Delaware	3.07
37	Florida	3.65
22	Georgia	4.82
5	Hawaii	7.19
28	Idaho	4.34
10	Illinois	6.04
7	Indiana	6.29
35	Iowa	3.77
42	Kansas	3.37
18	Kentucky	5.19
4	Louisiana	7.30
19	Maine	5.08
48	Maryland	2.54
39	Massachusetts	3.54
13	Michigan	5.93
46	Minnesota	2.55
3	Mississippi	7.48
40	Missouri	3.46
15	Montana	5.74
31	Nebraska	4.16
32	Nevada	4.06
46	New Hampshire	2.55
49	New Jersey	2.27
2	New Mexico	7.79
41	New York	3.41
30	North Carolina	4.19
11	North Dakota	6.02
36	Ohio	3.68
16	Oklahoma	5.72
24	Oregon	4.71
38	Pennsylvania	3.57
25	Rhode Island	4.69
21	South Carolina	4.95
6	South Dakota	6.39
34	Tennessee	3.97
19	Texas	5.08
11	Utah	6.02
29	Vermont	4.20
44	Virginia	2.62
22	Washington	4.82
8	West Virginia	6.21
14	Wisconsin	5.90
33	Wyoming	4.02

RANK	STATE	RATIO
1	Alaska	$10.23
2	New Mexico	7.79
3	Mississippi	7.48
4	Louisiana	7.30
5	Hawaii	7.19
6	South Dakota	6.39
7	Indiana	6.29
8	West Virginia	6.21
9	California	6.05
10	Illinois	6.04
11	North Dakota	6.02
11	Utah	6.02
13	Michigan	5.93
14	Wisconsin	5.90
15	Montana	5.74
16	Oklahoma	5.72
17	Arkansas	5.70
18	Kentucky	5.19
19	Maine	5.08
19	Texas	5.08
21	South Carolina	4.95
22	Georgia	4.82
22	Washington	4.82
24	Oregon	4.71
25	Rhode Island	4.69
26	Arizona	4.66
27	Alabama	4.60
28	Idaho	4.34
29	Vermont	4.20
30	North Carolina	4.19
31	Nebraska	4.16
32	Nevada	4.06
33	Wyoming	4.02
34	Tennessee	3.97
35	Iowa	3.77
36	Ohio	3.68
37	Florida	3.65
38	Pennsylvania	3.57
39	Massachusetts	3.54
40	Missouri	3.46
41	New York	3.41
42	Kansas	3.37
43	Delaware	3.07
44	Virginia	2.62
45	Colorado	2.61
46	Minnesota	2.55
46	New Hampshire	2.55
48	Maryland	2.54
49	New Jersey	2.27
50	Connecticut	2.01

| | District of Columbia | 1.88 |

Source: U.S. Bureau of the Census, Governments Division
   "Public Education Finances: 2009" (http://www.census.gov/govs/school/)
*Includes federal revenue passed through state governments as well as federal outlays directly received. Includes all such revenue received by a school system from federal sources (net of refunds) other than from issuance of debt or liquidation of investments. Does not include noncash transactions.

Per Pupil Public Elementary and Secondary School Revenue from Federal Sources in 2009
National Per Pupil = $1,159*

RANK	STATE	PER PUPIL
35	Alabama	$977
1	Alaska	2,401
27	Arizona	1,064
24	Arkansas	1,127
7	California	1,581
50	Colorado	690
48	Connecticut	737
37	Delaware	939
30	Florida	1,027
33	Georgia	997
2	Hawaii	2,189
43	Idaho	816
7	Illinois	1,581
13	Indiana	1,365
40	Iowa	884
44	Kansas	806
25	Kentucky	1,075
3	Louisiana	1,868
16	Maine	1,312
42	Maryland	823
17	Massachusetts	1,267
14	Michigan	1,347
49	Minnesota	717
12	Mississippi	1,375
41	Missouri	844
11	Montana	1,382
31	Nebraska	1,019
34	Nevada	986
46	New Hampshire	742
45	New Jersey	747
6	New Mexico	1,582
21	New York	1,186
36	North Carolina	949
4	North Dakota	1,693
39	Ohio	886
20	Oklahoma	1,193
22	Oregon	1,168
26	Pennsylvania	1,068
9	Rhode Island	1,457
29	South Carolina	1,028
5	South Dakota	1,594
38	Tennessee	896
28	Texas	1,057
32	Utah	1,005
23	Vermont	1,163
47	Virginia	740
15	Washington	1,337
18	West Virginia	1,260
10	Wisconsin	1,452
19	Wyoming	1,246

RANK	STATE	PER PUPIL
1	Alaska	$2,401
2	Hawaii	2,189
3	Louisiana	1,868
4	North Dakota	1,693
5	South Dakota	1,594
6	New Mexico	1,582
7	California	1,581
7	Illinois	1,581
9	Rhode Island	1,457
10	Wisconsin	1,452
11	Montana	1,382
12	Mississippi	1,375
13	Indiana	1,365
14	Michigan	1,347
15	Washington	1,337
16	Maine	1,312
17	Massachusetts	1,267
18	West Virginia	1,260
19	Wyoming	1,246
20	Oklahoma	1,193
21	New York	1,186
22	Oregon	1,168
23	Vermont	1,163
24	Arkansas	1,127
25	Kentucky	1,075
26	Pennsylvania	1,068
27	Arizona	1,064
28	Texas	1,057
29	South Carolina	1,028
30	Florida	1,027
31	Nebraska	1,019
32	Utah	1,005
33	Georgia	997
34	Nevada	986
35	Alabama	977
36	North Carolina	949
37	Delaware	939
38	Tennessee	896
39	Ohio	886
40	Iowa	884
41	Missouri	844
42	Maryland	823
43	Idaho	816
44	Kansas	806
45	New Jersey	747
46	New Hampshire	742
47	Virginia	740
48	Connecticut	737
49	Minnesota	717
50	Colorado	690
	District of Columbia	1,711

Source: U.S. Bureau of the Census, Governments Division
   "Public Education Finances: 2009" (http://www.census.gov/govs/school/)
*Based on student membership. Includes federal revenue passed through state governments as well as federal outlays directly received. Includes all such revenue received by a school system from federal sources (net of refunds) other than from issuance of debt or liquidation of investments. Does not include noncash transactions such as receipt of services, commodities, or other "receipts in-kind."

Percent of Public Elementary and Secondary School Revenue from Federal Sources in 2009
National Percent = 9.5%*

RANK	STATE	PERCENT
25	Alabama	10.1
5	Alaska	14.5
13	Arizona	12.0
17	Arkansas	11.3
8	California	13.6
39	Colorado	6.8
49	Connecticut	4.2
42	Delaware	6.6
24	Florida	10.2
31	Georgia	9.2
4	Hawaii	14.6
26	Idaho	10.0
10	Illinois	12.7
19	Indiana	11.0
35	Iowa	7.8
41	Kansas	6.7
22	Kentucky	10.7
2	Louisiana	15.6
27	Maine	9.6
48	Maryland	5.3
35	Massachusetts	7.8
18	Michigan	11.2
45	Minnesota	5.7
3	Mississippi	15.4
34	Missouri	8.1
12	Montana	12.3
33	Nebraska	8.6
27	Nevada	9.6
47	New Hampshire	5.4
50	New Jersey	4.0
7	New Mexico	14.0
45	New York	5.7
32	North Carolina	8.9
5	North Dakota	14.5
38	Ohio	6.9
9	Oklahoma	12.8
20	Oregon	10.8
37	Pennsylvania	7.1
30	Rhode Island	9.5
27	South Carolina	9.6
1	South Dakota	16.1
20	Tennessee	10.8
23	Texas	10.3
11	Utah	12.6
39	Vermont	6.8
44	Virginia	6.1
15	Washington	11.6
16	West Virginia	11.5
14	Wisconsin	11.7
43	Wyoming	6.5

RANK	STATE	PERCENT
1	South Dakota	16.1
2	Louisiana	15.6
3	Mississippi	15.4
4	Hawaii	14.6
5	Alaska	14.5
5	North Dakota	14.5
7	New Mexico	14.0
8	California	13.6
9	Oklahoma	12.8
10	Illinois	12.7
11	Utah	12.6
12	Montana	12.3
13	Arizona	12.0
14	Wisconsin	11.7
15	Washington	11.6
16	West Virginia	11.5
17	Arkansas	11.3
18	Michigan	11.2
19	Indiana	11.0
20	Oregon	10.8
20	Tennessee	10.8
22	Kentucky	10.7
23	Texas	10.3
24	Florida	10.2
25	Alabama	10.1
26	Idaho	10.0
27	Maine	9.6
27	Nevada	9.6
27	South Carolina	9.6
30	Rhode Island	9.5
31	Georgia	9.2
32	North Carolina	8.9
33	Nebraska	8.6
34	Missouri	8.1
35	Iowa	7.8
35	Massachusetts	7.8
37	Pennsylvania	7.1
38	Ohio	6.9
39	Colorado	6.8
39	Vermont	6.8
41	Kansas	6.7
42	Delaware	6.6
43	Wyoming	6.5
44	Virginia	6.1
45	Minnesota	5.7
45	New York	5.7
47	New Hampshire	5.4
48	Maryland	5.3
49	Connecticut	4.2
50	New Jersey	4.0
	District of Columbia	9.5

Source: U.S. Bureau of the Census, Governments Division
"Public Education Finances: 2009" (http://www.census.gov/govs/school/)
*Includes federal revenue passed through state governments as well as federal outlays directly received. Includes all such revenue received by a school system from federal sources (net of refunds) other than from issuance of debt or liquidation of investments. Does not include noncash transactions such as receipt of services, commodities, or other "receipts in-kind."

Public Elementary and Secondary School
Federal Government Revenue for Child Nutrition Programs in 2009
National Total = $10,687,460,000*

ALPHA ORDER

RANK	STATE	REVENUE	% of USA
13	Alabama	$215,581,000	2.0%
41	Alaska	30,813,000	0.3%
11	Arizona	234,527,000	2.2%
24	Arkansas	154,456,000	1.4%
1	California	1,525,463,000	14.3%
29	Colorado	120,748,000	1.1%
34	Connecticut	81,857,000	0.8%
43	Delaware	24,587,000	0.2%
3	Florida	626,434,000	5.9%
5	Georgia	490,526,000	4.6%
40	Hawaii	34,123,000	0.3%
37	Idaho	59,392,000	0.6%
6	Illinois	382,803,000	3.6%
14	Indiana	214,585,000	2.0%
33	Iowa	88,407,000	0.8%
31	Kansas	106,801,000	1.0%
19	Kentucky	194,242,000	1.8%
17	Louisiana	210,070,000	2.0%
39	Maine	40,231,000	0.4%
26	Maryland	139,848,000	1.3%
25	Massachusetts	151,942,000	1.4%
12	Michigan	230,303,000	2.2%
28	Minnesota	128,484,000	1.2%
21	Mississippi	185,579,000	1.7%
20	Missouri	192,166,000	1.8%
44	Montana	24,434,000	0.2%
38	Nebraska	57,027,000	0.5%
35	Nevada	71,803,000	0.7%
46	New Hampshire	21,245,000	0.2%
15	New Jersey	214,063,000	2.0%
50	New Mexico	775,000	0.0%
4	New York	547,631,000	5.1%
7	North Carolina	375,162,000	3.5%
47	North Dakota	15,078,000	0.1%
9	Ohio	296,344,000	2.8%
23	Oklahoma	169,334,000	1.6%
30	Oregon	111,397,000	1.0%
8	Pennsylvania	338,883,000	3.2%
42	Rhode Island	27,277,000	0.3%
18	South Carolina	205,480,000	1.9%
45	South Dakota	21,617,000	0.2%
10	Tennessee	251,895,000	2.4%
2	Texas	1,335,402,000	12.5%
32	Utah	95,097,000	0.9%
48	Vermont	13,751,000	0.1%
16	Virginia	211,757,000	2.0%
22	Washington	179,980,000	1.7%
36	West Virginia	71,088,000	0.7%
27	Wisconsin	139,227,000	1.3%
49	Wyoming	13,112,000	0.1%

RANK ORDER

RANK	STATE	REVENUE	% of USA
1	California	$1,525,463,000	14.3%
2	Texas	1,335,402,000	12.5%
3	Florida	626,434,000	5.9%
4	New York	547,631,000	5.1%
5	Georgia	490,526,000	4.6%
6	Illinois	382,803,000	3.6%
7	North Carolina	375,162,000	3.5%
8	Pennsylvania	338,883,000	3.2%
9	Ohio	296,344,000	2.8%
10	Tennessee	251,895,000	2.4%
11	Arizona	234,527,000	2.2%
12	Michigan	230,303,000	2.2%
13	Alabama	215,581,000	2.0%
14	Indiana	214,585,000	2.0%
15	New Jersey	214,063,000	2.0%
16	Virginia	211,757,000	2.0%
17	Louisiana	210,070,000	2.0%
18	South Carolina	205,480,000	1.9%
19	Kentucky	194,242,000	1.8%
20	Missouri	192,166,000	1.8%
21	Mississippi	185,579,000	1.7%
22	Washington	179,980,000	1.7%
23	Oklahoma	169,334,000	1.6%
24	Arkansas	154,456,000	1.4%
25	Massachusetts	151,942,000	1.4%
26	Maryland	139,848,000	1.3%
27	Wisconsin	139,227,000	1.3%
28	Minnesota	128,484,000	1.2%
29	Colorado	120,748,000	1.1%
30	Oregon	111,397,000	1.0%
31	Kansas	106,801,000	1.0%
32	Utah	95,097,000	0.9%
33	Iowa	88,407,000	0.8%
34	Connecticut	81,857,000	0.8%
35	Nevada	71,803,000	0.7%
36	West Virginia	71,088,000	0.7%
37	Idaho	59,392,000	0.6%
38	Nebraska	57,027,000	0.5%
39	Maine	40,231,000	0.4%
40	Hawaii	34,123,000	0.3%
41	Alaska	30,813,000	0.3%
42	Rhode Island	27,277,000	0.3%
43	Delaware	24,587,000	0.2%
44	Montana	24,434,000	0.2%
45	South Dakota	21,617,000	0.2%
46	New Hampshire	21,245,000	0.2%
47	North Dakota	15,078,000	0.1%
48	Vermont	13,751,000	0.1%
49	Wyoming	13,112,000	0.1%
50	New Mexico	775,000	0.0%
	District of Columbia	14,633,000	0.1%

Source: U.S. Bureau of the Census, Governments Division
   "Public Education Finances: 2009" (http://www.census.gov/govs/school/)
*Federal revenue passed through state governments. Includes payments by the Department of Agriculture for the National School Lunch, Special Milk, School Breakfast, and Ala Carte Programs. Excludes the value of donated commodities.

Percent of Public Elementary and Secondary School Federal Revenue Used for Child Nutrition Programs in 2009
National Percent = 19.1%*

ALPHA ORDER

RANK	STATE	PERCENT
2	Alabama	29.6
47	Alaska	9.9
15	Arizona	22.5
3	Arkansas	28.9
34	California	15.7
19	Colorado	21.5
22	Connecticut	20.3
16	Delaware	22.4
13	Florida	23.2
1	Georgia	29.8
49	Hawaii	8.7
10	Idaho	27.1
43	Illinois	11.4
35	Indiana	15.3
21	Iowa	20.5
5	Kansas	28.2
11	Kentucky	27.0
30	Louisiana	17.0
33	Maine	16.4
23	Maryland	20.1
40	Massachusetts	12.9
45	Michigan	11.0
17	Minnesota	22.3
7	Mississippi	27.5
12	Missouri	25.3
41	Montana	12.5
26	Nebraska	19.2
32	Nevada	16.9
36	New Hampshire	14.5
20	New Jersey	21.1
50	New Mexico	0.1
29	New York	17.1
8	North Carolina	27.2
48	North Dakota	9.4
25	Ohio	19.4
18	Oklahoma	22.0
30	Oregon	17.0
27	Pennsylvania	18.7
38	Rhode Island	13.2
6	South Carolina	28.0
46	South Dakota	10.7
3	Tennessee	28.9
8	Texas	27.2
28	Utah	17.8
37	Vermont	13.4
13	Virginia	23.2
39	Washington	13.0
24	West Virginia	20.0
44	Wisconsin	11.1
42	Wyoming	12.1

RANK ORDER

RANK	STATE	PERCENT
1	Georgia	29.8
2	Alabama	29.6
3	Arkansas	28.9
3	Tennessee	28.9
5	Kansas	28.2
6	South Carolina	28.0
7	Mississippi	27.5
8	North Carolina	27.2
8	Texas	27.2
10	Idaho	27.1
11	Kentucky	27.0
12	Missouri	25.3
13	Florida	23.2
13	Virginia	23.2
15	Arizona	22.5
16	Delaware	22.4
17	Minnesota	22.3
18	Oklahoma	22.0
19	Colorado	21.5
20	New Jersey	21.1
21	Iowa	20.5
22	Connecticut	20.3
23	Maryland	20.1
24	West Virginia	20.0
25	Ohio	19.4
26	Nebraska	19.2
27	Pennsylvania	18.7
28	Utah	17.8
29	New York	17.1
30	Louisiana	17.0
30	Oregon	17.0
32	Nevada	16.9
33	Maine	16.4
34	California	15.7
35	Indiana	15.3
36	New Hampshire	14.5
37	Vermont	13.4
38	Rhode Island	13.2
39	Washington	13.0
40	Massachusetts	12.9
41	Montana	12.5
42	Wyoming	12.1
43	Illinois	11.4
44	Wisconsin	11.1
45	Michigan	11.0
46	South Dakota	10.7
47	Alaska	9.9
48	North Dakota	9.4
49	Hawaii	8.7
50	New Mexico	0.1

| | District of Columbia | 19.3 |

Source: CQ Press using data from U.S. Bureau of the Census, Governments Division
   "Public Education Finances: 2009" (http://www.census.gov/govs/school/)
*Federal revenue passed through state governments. Includes payments by the Department of Agriculture for the National School Lunch, Special Milk, School Breakfast, and Ala Carte Programs. Excludes the value of donated commodities. Figured as a percent of all federal revenue whether passed through state governments or received directly.

Federal Government Revenue for Public Elementary and Secondary School Compensatory (Title I) Programs in 2009
National Total = $12,369,968,000*

RANK	STATE	REVENUE	% of USA
15	Alabama	$225,992,000	1.8%
41	Alaska	46,541,000	0.4%
10	Arizona	284,306,000	2.3%
26	Arkansas	140,696,000	1.1%
1	California	1,897,719,000	15.3%
25	Colorado	145,457,000	1.2%
28	Connecticut	118,348,000	1.0%
46	Delaware	32,575,000	0.3%
4	Florida	693,962,000	5.6%
49	Georgia	580,000	0.0%
36	Hawaii	54,851,000	0.4%
39	Idaho	49,977,000	0.4%
5	Illinois	685,974,000	5.5%
12	Indiana	231,772,000	1.9%
33	Iowa	72,986,000	0.6%
31	Kansas	100,193,000	0.8%
48	Kentucky	1,829,000	0.0%
9	Louisiana	310,526,000	2.5%
38	Maine	51,326,000	0.4%
22	Maryland	186,107,000	1.5%
13	Massachusetts	230,607,000	1.9%
7	Michigan	417,159,000	3.4%
29	Minnesota	112,236,000	0.9%
23	Mississippi	185,973,000	1.5%
20	Missouri	202,797,000	1.6%
40	Montana	46,795,000	0.4%
35	Nebraska	58,135,000	0.5%
32	Nevada	86,217,000	0.7%
44	New Hampshire	35,035,000	0.3%
11	New Jersey	263,197,000	2.1%
27	New Mexico	125,348,000	1.0%
3	New York	1,194,992,000	9.7%
8	North Carolina	369,743,000	3.0%
43	North Dakota	37,707,000	0.3%
NA	Ohio**	NA	NA
21	Oklahoma	196,953,000	1.6%
24	Oregon	147,450,000	1.2%
6	Pennsylvania	524,765,000	4.2%
37	Rhode Island	54,307,000	0.4%
19	South Carolina	205,034,000	1.7%
42	South Dakota	44,597,000	0.4%
14	Tennessee	227,557,000	1.8%
2	Texas	1,356,940,000	11.0%
34	Utah	58,998,000	0.5%
45	Vermont	32,600,000	0.3%
16	Virginia	225,772,000	1.8%
18	Washington	216,535,000	1.8%
30	West Virginia	103,263,000	0.8%
17	Wisconsin	217,610,000	1.8%
47	Wyoming	30,411,000	0.2%

RANK	STATE	REVENUE	% of USA
1	California	$1,897,719,000	15.3%
2	Texas	1,356,940,000	11.0%
3	New York	1,194,992,000	9.7%
4	Florida	693,962,000	5.6%
5	Illinois	685,974,000	5.5%
6	Pennsylvania	524,765,000	4.2%
7	Michigan	417,159,000	3.4%
8	North Carolina	369,743,000	3.0%
9	Louisiana	310,526,000	2.5%
10	Arizona	284,306,000	2.3%
11	New Jersey	263,197,000	2.1%
12	Indiana	231,772,000	1.9%
13	Massachusetts	230,607,000	1.9%
14	Tennessee	227,557,000	1.8%
15	Alabama	225,992,000	1.8%
16	Virginia	225,772,000	1.8%
17	Wisconsin	217,610,000	1.8%
18	Washington	216,535,000	1.8%
19	South Carolina	205,034,000	1.7%
20	Missouri	202,797,000	1.6%
21	Oklahoma	196,953,000	1.6%
22	Maryland	186,107,000	1.5%
23	Mississippi	185,973,000	1.5%
24	Oregon	147,450,000	1.2%
25	Colorado	145,457,000	1.2%
26	Arkansas	140,696,000	1.1%
27	New Mexico	125,348,000	1.0%
28	Connecticut	118,348,000	1.0%
29	Minnesota	112,236,000	0.9%
30	West Virginia	103,263,000	0.8%
31	Kansas	100,193,000	0.8%
32	Nevada	86,217,000	0.7%
33	Iowa	72,986,000	0.6%
34	Utah	58,998,000	0.5%
35	Nebraska	58,135,000	0.5%
36	Hawaii	54,851,000	0.4%
37	Rhode Island	54,307,000	0.4%
38	Maine	51,326,000	0.4%
39	Idaho	49,977,000	0.4%
40	Montana	46,795,000	0.4%
41	Alaska	46,541,000	0.4%
42	South Dakota	44,597,000	0.4%
43	North Dakota	37,707,000	0.3%
44	New Hampshire	35,035,000	0.3%
45	Vermont	32,600,000	0.3%
46	Delaware	32,575,000	0.3%
47	Wyoming	30,411,000	0.2%
48	Kentucky	1,829,000	0.0%
49	Georgia	580,000	0.0%
NA	Ohio**	NA	NA
	District of Columbia	29,518,000	0.2%

Source: U.S. Bureau of the Census, Governments Division
"Public Education Finances: 2009" (http://www.census.gov/govs/school/)
*National total is only for states shown separately. This is federal revenue passed through state governments. Revenue authorized by Title I of the Elementary-Secondary Education Act. Includes basic, concentration, and migratory education grants.
**Not available.

Percent of Public Elementary and Secondary School Federal Revenue Used for Compensatory (Title I) Programs in 2009
National Percent = 22.1%*

ALPHA ORDER

RANK	STATE	PERCENT
3	Alabama	31.0
45	Alaska	14.9
12	Arizona	27.2
17	Arkansas	26.3
37	California	19.5
20	Colorado	25.9
5	Connecticut	29.4
4	Delaware	29.7
22	Florida	25.8
49	Georgia	0.0
46	Hawaii	14.0
30	Idaho	22.8
34	Illinois	20.5
43	Indiana	16.5
42	Iowa	16.9
16	Kansas	26.4
48	Kentucky	0.3
24	Louisiana	25.1
33	Maine	20.9
13	Maryland	26.8
37	Massachusetts	19.5
36	Michigan	19.9
37	Minnesota	19.5
11	Mississippi	27.5
15	Missouri	26.7
27	Montana	23.9
37	Nebraska	19.5
35	Nevada	20.3
27	New Hampshire	23.9
20	New Jersey	25.9
26	New Mexico	24.1
1	New York	37.4
13	North Carolina	26.8
29	North Dakota	23.5
NA	Ohio**	NA
23	Oklahoma	25.6
31	Oregon	22.5
7	Pennsylvania	29.0
17	Rhode Island	26.3
9	South Carolina	27.9
32	South Dakota	22.1
19	Tennessee	26.1
10	Texas	27.6
47	Utah	11.0
2	Vermont	31.8
25	Virginia	24.7
44	Washington	15.6
6	West Virginia	29.1
41	Wisconsin	17.3
8	Wyoming	28.1

RANK ORDER

RANK	STATE	PERCENT
1	New York	37.4
2	Vermont	31.8
3	Alabama	31.0
4	Delaware	29.7
5	Connecticut	29.4
6	West Virginia	29.1
7	Pennsylvania	29.0
8	Wyoming	28.1
9	South Carolina	27.9
10	Texas	27.6
11	Mississippi	27.5
12	Arizona	27.2
13	Maryland	26.8
13	North Carolina	26.8
15	Missouri	26.7
16	Kansas	26.4
17	Arkansas	26.3
17	Rhode Island	26.3
19	Tennessee	26.1
20	Colorado	25.9
20	New Jersey	25.9
22	Florida	25.8
23	Oklahoma	25.6
24	Louisiana	25.1
25	Virginia	24.7
26	New Mexico	24.1
27	Montana	23.9
27	New Hampshire	23.9
29	North Dakota	23.5
30	Idaho	22.8
31	Oregon	22.5
32	South Dakota	22.1
33	Maine	20.9
34	Illinois	20.5
35	Nevada	20.3
36	Michigan	19.9
37	California	19.5
37	Massachusetts	19.5
37	Minnesota	19.5
37	Nebraska	19.5
41	Wisconsin	17.3
42	Iowa	16.9
43	Indiana	16.5
44	Washington	15.6
45	Alaska	14.9
46	Hawaii	14.0
47	Utah	11.0
48	Kentucky	0.3
49	Georgia	0.0
NA	Ohio**	NA

District of Columbia 38.9

Source: CQ Press using data from U.S. Bureau of the Census, Governments Division
"Public Education Finances: 2009" (http://www.census.gov/govs/school/)

*National percent is only for states shown separately. This is federal revenue passed through state governments. Revenue authorized by Title I of the Elementary-Secondary Education Act. Includes basic, concentration, and migratory education grants.
**Not available.

Federal Government Revenue for Public Elementary and Secondary School Vocational Programs in 2009
National Total = $641,094,000*

ALPHA ORDER

ALPHA ORDER

RANK	STATE	REVENUE	% of USA
14	Alabama	$16,040,000	2.5%
40	Alaska	2,785,000	0.4%
11	Arizona	20,812,000	3.2%
21	Arkansas	9,557,000	1.5%
1	California	64,202,000	10.0%
28	Colorado	6,789,000	1.1%
27	Connecticut	6,969,000	1.1%
33	Delaware	4,028,000	0.6%
3	Florida	42,286,000	6.6%
NA	Georgia**	NA	NA
35	Hawaii	3,660,000	0.6%
37	Idaho	3,571,000	0.6%
8	Illinois	28,924,000	4.5%
18	Indiana	12,048,000	1.9%
30	Iowa	5,594,000	0.9%
45	Kansas	1,684,000	0.3%
NA	Kentucky**	NA	NA
20	Louisiana	9,730,000	1.5%
44	Maine	2,219,000	0.3%
15	Maryland	13,215,000	2.1%
19	Massachusetts	10,806,000	1.7%
9	Michigan	21,606,000	3.4%
47	Minnesota	314,000	0.0%
29	Mississippi	6,681,000	1.0%
16	Missouri	13,136,000	2.0%
39	Montana	2,925,000	0.5%
38	Nebraska	3,042,000	0.5%
32	Nevada	4,704,000	0.7%
34	New Hampshire	3,831,000	0.6%
22	New Jersey	9,146,000	1.4%
25	New Mexico	7,667,000	1.2%
5	New York	33,866,000	5.3%
10	North Carolina	21,605,000	3.4%
42	North Dakota	2,395,000	0.4%
4	Ohio	36,369,000	5.7%
7	Oklahoma	30,072,000	4.7%
23	Oregon	8,044,000	1.3%
6	Pennsylvania	30,545,000	4.8%
36	Rhode Island	3,596,000	0.6%
17	South Carolina	13,038,000	2.0%
46	South Dakota	962,000	0.2%
12	Tennessee	19,178,000	3.0%
2	Texas	56,696,000	8.8%
26	Utah	7,641,000	1.2%
41	Vermont	2,757,000	0.4%
13	Virginia	18,669,000	2.9%
24	Washington	7,682,000	1.2%
NA	West Virginia**	NA	NA
31	Wisconsin	5,483,000	0.9%
43	Wyoming	2,229,000	0.3%

RANK ORDER

RANK	STATE	REVENUE	% of USA
1	California	$64,202,000	10.0%
2	Texas	56,696,000	8.8%
3	Florida	42,286,000	6.6%
4	Ohio	36,369,000	5.7%
5	New York	33,866,000	5.3%
6	Pennsylvania	30,545,000	4.8%
7	Oklahoma	30,072,000	4.7%
8	Illinois	28,924,000	4.5%
9	Michigan	21,606,000	3.4%
10	North Carolina	21,605,000	3.4%
11	Arizona	20,812,000	3.2%
12	Tennessee	19,178,000	3.0%
13	Virginia	18,669,000	2.9%
14	Alabama	16,040,000	2.5%
15	Maryland	13,215,000	2.1%
16	Missouri	13,136,000	2.0%
17	South Carolina	13,038,000	2.0%
18	Indiana	12,048,000	1.9%
19	Massachusetts	10,806,000	1.7%
20	Louisiana	9,730,000	1.5%
21	Arkansas	9,557,000	1.5%
22	New Jersey	9,146,000	1.4%
23	Oregon	8,044,000	1.3%
24	Washington	7,682,000	1.2%
25	New Mexico	7,667,000	1.2%
26	Utah	7,641,000	1.2%
27	Connecticut	6,969,000	1.1%
28	Colorado	6,789,000	1.1%
29	Mississippi	6,681,000	1.0%
30	Iowa	5,594,000	0.9%
31	Wisconsin	5,483,000	0.9%
32	Nevada	4,704,000	0.7%
33	Delaware	4,028,000	0.6%
34	New Hampshire	3,831,000	0.6%
35	Hawaii	3,660,000	0.6%
36	Rhode Island	3,596,000	0.6%
37	Idaho	3,571,000	0.6%
38	Nebraska	3,042,000	0.5%
39	Montana	2,925,000	0.5%
40	Alaska	2,785,000	0.4%
41	Vermont	2,757,000	0.4%
42	North Dakota	2,395,000	0.4%
43	Wyoming	2,229,000	0.3%
44	Maine	2,219,000	0.3%
45	Kansas	1,684,000	0.3%
46	South Dakota	962,000	0.2%
47	Minnesota	314,000	0.0%
NA	Georgia**	NA	NA
NA	Kentucky**	NA	NA
NA	West Virginia**	NA	NA
	District of Columbia	2,296,000	0.4%

Source: U.S. Bureau of the Census, Governments Division
   "Public Education Finances: 2009" (http://www.census.gov/govs/school/)
*National total is only for states shown separately. This is federal revenue passed through state governments. Revenue from the Carl Perkins Vocational Education Act. Includes revenue from Title II (Basic Grants) and Title III-E (Tech-Prep Education).
**Not available.

Percent of Public Elementary and Secondary School Federal Revenue Used for Vocational Programs in 2009
National Percent = 1.1%*

ALPHA ORDER

ALPHA ORDER

RANK ORDER

RANK	STATE	PERCENT		RANK	STATE	PERCENT
6	Alabama	2.2		1	Oklahoma	3.9
34	Alaska	0.9		2	Delaware	3.7
9	Arizona	2.0		3	Vermont	2.7
12	Arkansas	1.8		4	New Hampshire	2.6
42	California	0.7		5	Ohio	2.4
26	Colorado	1.2		6	Alabama	2.2
14	Connecticut	1.7		6	Tennessee	2.2
2	Delaware	3.7		8	Wyoming	2.1
18	Florida	1.6		9	Arizona	2.0
NA	Georgia**	NA		9	Virginia	2.0
34	Hawaii	0.9		11	Maryland	1.9
18	Idaho	1.6		12	Arkansas	1.8
34	Illinois	0.9		12	South Carolina	1.8
34	Indiana	0.9		14	Connecticut	1.7
25	Iowa	1.3		14	Missouri	1.7
45	Kansas	0.4		14	Pennsylvania	1.7
NA	Kentucky**	NA		14	Rhode Island	1.7
41	Louisiana	0.8		18	Florida	1.6
34	Maine	0.9		18	Idaho	1.6
11	Maryland	1.9		18	North Carolina	1.6
34	Massachusetts	0.9		21	Montana	1.5
31	Michigan	1.0		21	New Mexico	1.5
47	Minnesota	0.1		21	North Dakota	1.5
31	Mississippi	1.0		24	Utah	1.4
14	Missouri	1.7		25	Iowa	1.3
21	Montana	1.5		26	Colorado	1.2
31	Nebraska	1.0		26	Oregon	1.2
29	Nevada	1.1		26	Texas	1.2
4	New Hampshire	2.6		29	Nevada	1.1
34	New Jersey	0.9		29	New York	1.1
21	New Mexico	1.5		31	Michigan	1.0
29	New York	1.1		31	Mississippi	1.0
18	North Carolina	1.6		31	Nebraska	1.0
21	North Dakota	1.5		34	Alaska	0.9
5	Ohio	2.4		34	Hawaii	0.9
1	Oklahoma	3.9		34	Illinois	0.9
26	Oregon	1.2		34	Indiana	0.9
14	Pennsylvania	1.7		34	Maine	0.9
14	Rhode Island	1.7		34	Massachusetts	0.9
12	South Carolina	1.8		34	New Jersey	0.9
44	South Dakota	0.5		41	Louisiana	0.8
6	Tennessee	2.2		42	California	0.7
26	Texas	1.2		43	Washington	0.6
24	Utah	1.4		44	South Dakota	0.5
3	Vermont	2.7		45	Kansas	0.4
9	Virginia	2.0		45	Wisconsin	0.4
43	Washington	0.6		47	Minnesota	0.1
NA	West Virginia**	NA		NA	Georgia**	NA
45	Wisconsin	0.4		NA	Kentucky**	NA
8	Wyoming	2.1		NA	West Virginia**	NA

District of Columbia   3.0

Source: CQ Press using data from U.S. Bureau of the Census, Governments Division
    "Public Education Finances: 2009" (http://www.census.gov/govs/school/)

*National percent is only for states shown separately. This is federal revenue passed through state governments. Revenue from the Carl Perkins Vocational Education Act. Includes revenue from Title II (Basic Grants) and Title III-E (Tech-Prep Education).
**Not available.

Percent of Public Elementary and Secondary School Federal Revenue Distributed through States in 2009
National Percent = 93.0%*

ALPHA ORDER

RANK	STATE	PERCENT
9	Alabama	97.0
50	Alaska	45.6
44	Arizona	84.1
16	Arkansas	95.5
18	California	94.9
40	Colorado	89.2
33	Connecticut	91.2
1	Delaware	100.0
29	Florida	92.4
14	Georgia	95.9
45	Hawaii	72.2
25	Idaho	93.5
11	Illinois	96.3
3	Indiana	98.9
20	Iowa	94.4
21	Kansas	94.2
22	Kentucky	94.0
38	Louisiana	89.3
32	Maine	91.6
17	Maryland	95.3
11	Massachusetts	96.3
34	Michigan	90.9
34	Minnesota	90.9
27	Mississippi	92.7
28	Missouri	92.5
49	Montana	68.9
43	Nebraska	85.3
10	Nevada	96.8
8	New Hampshire	97.1
5	New Jersey	98.2
48	New Mexico	70.5
4	New York	98.5
36	North Carolina	89.6
46	North Dakota	71.8
23	Ohio	93.7
36	Oklahoma	89.6
19	Oregon	94.5
23	Pennsylvania	93.7
6	Rhode Island	97.8
2	South Carolina	99.5
47	South Dakota	70.8
14	Tennessee	95.9
30	Texas	92.2
30	Utah	92.2
26	Vermont	92.9
42	Virginia	87.6
38	Washington	89.3
7	West Virginia	97.3
13	Wisconsin	96.2
41	Wyoming	87.8

RANK ORDER

RANK	STATE	PERCENT
1	Delaware	100.0
2	South Carolina	99.5
3	Indiana	98.9
4	New York	98.5
5	New Jersey	98.2
6	Rhode Island	97.8
7	West Virginia	97.3
8	New Hampshire	97.1
9	Alabama	97.0
10	Nevada	96.8
11	Illinois	96.3
11	Massachusetts	96.3
13	Wisconsin	96.2
14	Georgia	95.9
14	Tennessee	95.9
16	Arkansas	95.5
17	Maryland	95.3
18	California	94.9
19	Oregon	94.5
20	Iowa	94.4
21	Kansas	94.2
22	Kentucky	94.0
23	Ohio	93.7
23	Pennsylvania	93.7
25	Idaho	93.5
26	Vermont	92.9
27	Mississippi	92.7
28	Missouri	92.5
29	Florida	92.4
30	Texas	92.2
30	Utah	92.2
32	Maine	91.6
33	Connecticut	91.2
34	Michigan	90.9
34	Minnesota	90.9
36	North Carolina	89.6
36	Oklahoma	89.6
38	Louisiana	89.3
38	Washington	89.3
40	Colorado	89.2
41	Wyoming	87.8
42	Virginia	87.6
43	Nebraska	85.3
44	Arizona	84.1
45	Hawaii	72.2
46	North Dakota	71.8
47	South Dakota	70.8
48	New Mexico	70.5
49	Montana	68.9
50	Alaska	45.6

| | District of Columbia | 98.0 |

Source: CQ Press using data from U.S. Bureau of the Census, Governments Division
"Public Education Finances: 2009" (http://www.census.gov/govs/school/)
*Includes all such revenue received by a school system from federal sources (net of refunds) other than from issuance of debt or liquidation of investments. Does not include noncash transactions such as receipt of services, commodities, or other "receipts in-kind."

Public Elementary and Secondary School Revenue from State Sources in 2009
National Total = $276,153,850,000*

ALPHA ORDER

RANK	STATE	REVENUE	% of USA
19	Alabama	$4,161,103,000	1.5%
40	Alaska	1,357,747,000	0.5%
22	Arizona	3,806,064,000	1.4%
28	Arkansas	3,530,487,000	1.3%
1	California	40,084,244,000	14.5%
25	Colorado	3,634,018,000	1.3%
26	Connecticut	3,606,594,000	1.3%
44	Delaware	1,047,418,000	0.4%
8	Florida	9,047,586,000	3.3%
11	Georgia	7,739,086,000	2.8%
37	Hawaii	2,205,032,000	0.8%
39	Idaho	1,459,554,000	0.5%
10	Illinois	7,879,160,000	2.9%
16	Indiana	5,804,809,000	2.1%
33	Iowa	2,545,353,000	0.9%
29	Kansas	3,291,485,000	1.2%
21	Kentucky	3,870,440,000	1.4%
27	Louisiana	3,568,903,000	1.3%
43	Maine	1,107,152,000	0.4%
17	Maryland	5,697,257,000	2.1%
15	Massachusetts	5,974,489,000	2.2%
6	Michigan	10,130,740,000	3.7%
13	Minnesota	6,590,788,000	2.4%
34	Mississippi	2,334,363,000	0.8%
20	Missouri	3,927,189,000	1.4%
47	Montana	765,177,000	0.3%
42	Nebraska	1,182,776,000	0.4%
35	Nevada	2,272,415,000	0.8%
45	New Hampshire	1,002,239,000	0.4%
4	New Jersey	10,401,527,000	3.8%
32	New Mexico	2,615,320,000	0.9%
2	New York	25,768,345,000	9.3%
9	North Carolina	8,229,140,000	3.0%
50	North Dakota	407,374,000	0.1%
5	Ohio	10,226,228,000	3.7%
31	Oklahoma	3,014,993,000	1.1%
30	Oregon	3,117,315,000	1.1%
7	Pennsylvania	9,858,461,000	3.6%
48	Rhode Island	765,069,000	0.3%
24	South Carolina	3,654,658,000	1.3%
49	South Dakota	412,798,000	0.1%
23	Tennessee	3,800,870,000	1.4%
3	Texas	19,708,771,000	7.1%
36	Utah	2,224,007,000	0.8%
41	Vermont	1,336,424,000	0.5%
14	Virginia	6,317,714,000	2.3%
12	Washington	7,146,416,000	2.6%
38	West Virginia	1,793,917,000	0.6%
18	Wisconsin	4,785,070,000	1.7%
46	Wyoming	945,765,000	0.3%

RANK ORDER

RANK	STATE	REVENUE	% of USA
1	California	$40,084,244,000	14.5%
2	New York	25,768,345,000	9.3%
3	Texas	19,708,771,000	7.1%
4	New Jersey	10,401,527,000	3.8%
5	Ohio	10,226,228,000	3.7%
6	Michigan	10,130,740,000	3.7%
7	Pennsylvania	9,858,461,000	3.6%
8	Florida	9,047,586,000	3.3%
9	North Carolina	8,229,140,000	3.0%
10	Illinois	7,879,160,000	2.9%
11	Georgia	7,739,086,000	2.8%
12	Washington	7,146,416,000	2.6%
13	Minnesota	6,590,788,000	2.4%
14	Virginia	6,317,714,000	2.3%
15	Massachusetts	5,974,489,000	2.2%
16	Indiana	5,804,809,000	2.1%
17	Maryland	5,697,257,000	2.1%
18	Wisconsin	4,785,070,000	1.7%
19	Alabama	4,161,103,000	1.5%
20	Missouri	3,927,189,000	1.4%
21	Kentucky	3,870,440,000	1.4%
22	Arizona	3,806,064,000	1.4%
23	Tennessee	3,800,870,000	1.4%
24	South Carolina	3,654,658,000	1.3%
25	Colorado	3,634,018,000	1.3%
26	Connecticut	3,606,594,000	1.3%
27	Louisiana	3,568,903,000	1.3%
28	Arkansas	3,530,487,000	1.3%
29	Kansas	3,291,485,000	1.2%
30	Oregon	3,117,315,000	1.1%
31	Oklahoma	3,014,993,000	1.1%
32	New Mexico	2,615,320,000	0.9%
33	Iowa	2,545,353,000	0.9%
34	Mississippi	2,334,363,000	0.8%
35	Nevada	2,272,415,000	0.8%
36	Utah	2,224,007,000	0.8%
37	Hawaii	2,205,032,000	0.8%
38	West Virginia	1,793,917,000	0.6%
39	Idaho	1,459,554,000	0.5%
40	Alaska	1,357,747,000	0.5%
41	Vermont	1,336,424,000	0.5%
42	Nebraska	1,182,776,000	0.4%
43	Maine	1,107,152,000	0.4%
44	Delaware	1,047,418,000	0.4%
45	New Hampshire	1,002,239,000	0.4%
46	Wyoming	945,765,000	0.3%
47	Montana	765,177,000	0.3%
48	Rhode Island	765,069,000	0.3%
49	South Dakota	412,798,000	0.1%
50	North Dakota	407,374,000	0.1%
	District of Columbia**	NA	NA

Source: U.S. Bureau of the Census, Governments Division
    "Public Education Finances: 2009" (http://www.census.gov/govs/school/)
*Consists only of revenue originating from state governments. Includes all such revenue received by a school system (net of refunds) other than from issuance of debt or liquidation of investments. Does not include noncash transactions such as receipt of services, commodities, or other "receipts in-kind."
**Not applicable.

Per Capita Public Elementary and Secondary School Revenue from State Sources in 2009
National Per Capita = $900*

ALPHA ORDER

RANK	STATE	PER CAPITA
23	Alabama	$884
2	Alaska	1,944
48	Arizona	577
8	Arkansas	1,222
12	California	1,084
42	Colorado	723
14	Connecticut	1,025
10	Delaware	1,183
50	Florida	488
37	Georgia	787
4	Hawaii	1,702
18	Idaho	944
46	Illinois	610
20	Indiana	904
26	Iowa	846
11	Kansas	1,168
21	Kentucky	897
35	Louisiana	794
28	Maine	840
16	Maryland	1,000
19	Massachusetts	906
15	Michigan	1,016
7	Minnesota	1,252
36	Mississippi	791
44	Missouri	656
38	Montana	785
43	Nebraska	658
25	Nevada	860
40	New Hampshire	757
9	New Jersey	1,195
6	New Mexico	1,301
5	New York	1,319
24	North Carolina	877
45	North Dakota	630
22	Ohio	886
29	Oklahoma	818
30	Oregon	815
39	Pennsylvania	782
41	Rhode Island	726
31	South Carolina	801
49	South Dakota	508
47	Tennessee	604
34	Texas	795
33	Utah	799
1	Vermont	2,149
31	Virginia	801
13	Washington	1,072
17	West Virginia	986
26	Wisconsin	846
3	Wyoming	1,738

RANK ORDER

RANK	STATE	PER CAPITA
1	Vermont	$2,149
2	Alaska	1,944
3	Wyoming	1,738
4	Hawaii	1,702
5	New York	1,319
6	New Mexico	1,301
7	Minnesota	1,252
8	Arkansas	1,222
9	New Jersey	1,195
10	Delaware	1,183
11	Kansas	1,168
12	California	1,084
13	Washington	1,072
14	Connecticut	1,025
15	Michigan	1,016
16	Maryland	1,000
17	West Virginia	986
18	Idaho	944
19	Massachusetts	906
20	Indiana	904
21	Kentucky	897
22	Ohio	886
23	Alabama	884
24	North Carolina	877
25	Nevada	860
26	Iowa	846
26	Wisconsin	846
28	Maine	840
29	Oklahoma	818
30	Oregon	815
31	South Carolina	801
31	Virginia	801
33	Utah	799
34	Texas	795
35	Louisiana	794
36	Mississippi	791
37	Georgia	787
38	Montana	785
39	Pennsylvania	782
40	New Hampshire	757
41	Rhode Island	726
42	Colorado	723
43	Nebraska	658
44	Missouri	656
45	North Dakota	630
46	Illinois	610
47	Tennessee	604
48	Arizona	577
49	South Dakota	508
50	Florida	488

District of Columbia**   NA

Source: CQ Press using data from U.S. Bureau of the Census, Governments Division
   "Public Education Finances: 2009" (http://www.census.gov/govs/school/)
*Consists only of revenue originating from state governments. Includes all such revenue received by a school system (net of refunds) other than from issuance of debt or liquidation of investments. Does not include noncash transactions such as receipt of services, commodities, or other "receipts in-kind."
**Not applicable.

Public Elementary and Secondary School Revenue from State Sources per $1,000 Personal Income in 2009
National Ratio = $22.31*

ALPHA ORDER

RANK	STATE	RATIO
15	Alabama	$26.24
2	Alaska	44.44
44	Arizona	16.97
5	Arkansas	37.65
21	California	24.88
45	Colorado	16.92
38	Connecticut	17.98
9	Delaware	29.29
50	Florida	12.26
26	Georgia	22.66
3	Hawaii	40.38
11	Idaho	28.97
48	Illinois	14.22
16	Indiana	26.01
31	Iowa	22.24
8	Kansas	29.32
13	Kentucky	27.89
33	Louisiana	21.05
25	Maine	22.97
34	Maryland	20.80
40	Massachusetts	17.89
12	Michigan	28.67
10	Minnesota	29.14
17	Mississippi	25.84
39	Missouri	17.93
27	Montana	22.43
46	Nebraska	16.55
32	Nevada	21.68
42	New Hampshire	17.39
24	New Jersey	23.28
4	New Mexico	39.20
14	New York	27.51
18	North Carolina	25.04
47	North Dakota	15.31
23	Ohio	24.56
29	Oklahoma	22.41
30	Oregon	22.39
36	Pennsylvania	19.41
41	Rhode Island	17.40
22	South Carolina	24.63
49	South Dakota	13.07
43	Tennessee	17.35
35	Texas	20.37
19	Utah	25.02
1	Vermont	54.84
37	Virginia	18.11
20	Washington	24.89
7	West Virginia	31.37
27	Wisconsin	22.43
6	Wyoming	35.08

RANK ORDER

RANK	STATE	RATIO
1	Vermont	$54.84
2	Alaska	44.44
3	Hawaii	40.38
4	New Mexico	39.20
5	Arkansas	37.65
6	Wyoming	35.08
7	West Virginia	31.37
8	Kansas	29.32
9	Delaware	29.29
10	Minnesota	29.14
11	Idaho	28.97
12	Michigan	28.67
13	Kentucky	27.89
14	New York	27.51
15	Alabama	26.24
16	Indiana	26.01
17	Mississippi	25.84
18	North Carolina	25.04
19	Utah	25.02
20	Washington	24.89
21	California	24.88
22	South Carolina	24.63
23	Ohio	24.56
24	New Jersey	23.28
25	Maine	22.97
26	Georgia	22.66
27	Montana	22.43
27	Wisconsin	22.43
29	Oklahoma	22.41
30	Oregon	22.39
31	Iowa	22.24
32	Nevada	21.68
33	Louisiana	21.05
34	Maryland	20.80
35	Texas	20.37
36	Pennsylvania	19.41
37	Virginia	18.11
38	Connecticut	17.98
39	Missouri	17.93
40	Massachusetts	17.89
41	Rhode Island	17.40
42	New Hampshire	17.39
43	Tennessee	17.35
44	Arizona	16.97
45	Colorado	16.92
46	Nebraska	16.55
47	North Dakota	15.31
48	Illinois	14.22
49	South Dakota	13.07
50	Florida	12.26
	District of Columbia**	NA

Source: U.S. Bureau of the Census, Governments Division
"Public Education Finances: 2009" (http://www.census.gov/govs/school/)
*Consists only of revenue originating from state governments. Includes all such revenue received by a school system (net of refunds) other than from issuance of debt or liquidation of investments. Does not include noncash transactions such as receipt of services, commodities, or other "receipts in-kind."
**Not applicable.

Per Pupil Public Elementary and Secondary School Revenue from State Sources in 2009
National Per Pupil = $5,725*

ALPHA ORDER

RANK	STATE	PER PUPIL
25	Alabama	$5,580
4	Alaska	10,425
47	Arizona	3,877
10	Arkansas	7,442
16	California	6,501
40	Colorado	4,473
14	Connecticut	6,594
6	Delaware	8,967
49	Florida	3,449
38	Georgia	4,691
2	Hawaii	12,286
28	Idaho	5,447
48	Illinois	3,722
24	Indiana	5,645
33	Iowa	5,221
11	Kansas	7,001
22	Kentucky	5,778
31	Louisiana	5,385
19	Maine	5,929
13	Maryland	6,752
17	Massachusetts	6,407
15	Michigan	6,512
7	Minnesota	8,207
37	Mississippi	4,752
41	Missouri	4,370
30	Montana	5,403
45	Nebraska	4,048
32	Nevada	5,273
36	New Hampshire	5,064
9	New Jersey	7,653
8	New Mexico	7,956
5	New York	9,555
23	North Carolina	5,667
42	North Dakota	4,304
20	Ohio	5,914
39	Oklahoma	4,678
26	Oregon	5,547
21	Pennsylvania	5,814
29	Rhode Island	5,406
34	South Carolina	5,116
50	South Dakota	3,260
46	Tennessee	3,915
43	Texas	4,241
44	Utah	4,177
1	Vermont	15,169
35	Virginia	5,115
12	Washington	6,897
18	West Virginia	6,363
27	Wisconsin	5,519
3	Wyoming	10,874

RANK ORDER

RANK	STATE	PER PUPIL
1	Vermont	$15,169
2	Hawaii	12,286
3	Wyoming	10,874
4	Alaska	10,425
5	New York	9,555
6	Delaware	8,967
7	Minnesota	8,207
8	New Mexico	7,956
9	New Jersey	7,653
10	Arkansas	7,442
11	Kansas	7,001
12	Washington	6,897
13	Maryland	6,752
14	Connecticut	6,594
15	Michigan	6,512
16	California	6,501
17	Massachusetts	6,407
18	West Virginia	6,363
19	Maine	5,929
20	Ohio	5,914
21	Pennsylvania	5,814
22	Kentucky	5,778
23	North Carolina	5,667
24	Indiana	5,645
25	Alabama	5,580
26	Oregon	5,547
27	Wisconsin	5,519
28	Idaho	5,447
29	Rhode Island	5,406
30	Montana	5,403
31	Louisiana	5,385
32	Nevada	5,273
33	Iowa	5,221
34	South Carolina	5,116
35	Virginia	5,115
36	New Hampshire	5,064
37	Mississippi	4,752
38	Georgia	4,691
39	Oklahoma	4,678
40	Colorado	4,473
41	Missouri	4,370
42	North Dakota	4,304
43	Texas	4,241
44	Utah	4,177
45	Nebraska	4,048
46	Tennessee	3,915
47	Arizona	3,877
48	Illinois	3,722
49	Florida	3,449
50	South Dakota	3,260

District of Columbia**   NA

Source: U.S. Bureau of the Census, Governments Division
    "Public Education Finances: 2009" (http://www.census.gov/govs/school/)
*Based on student membership. Consists only of revenue originating from state governments. Includes all such revenue received by a school system (net of refunds) other than from issuance of debt or liquidation of investments. Does not include noncash transactions such as receipt of services, commodities, or other "receipts in-kind."
**Not applicable.

Percent of Public Elementary and Secondary School Revenue from State Sources in 2009
National Percent = 46.7%*

RANK	STATE	PERCENT
11	Alabama	57.9
7	Alaska	62.9
33	Arizona	43.6
3	Arkansas	74.6
15	California	56.1
32	Colorado	44.0
43	Connecticut	38.0
8	Delaware	62.6
48	Florida	34.2
36	Georgia	43.1
2	Hawaii	82.0
5	Idaho	66.9
50	Illinois	29.9
29	Indiana	45.7
28	Iowa	46.1
10	Kansas	58.6
13	Kentucky	57.7
30	Louisiana	45.0
34	Maine	43.4
34	Maryland	43.4
41	Massachusetts	39.4
16	Michigan	54.3
6	Minnesota	64.8
18	Mississippi	53.3
38	Missouri	41.8
23	Montana	48.0
47	Nebraska	34.3
20	Nevada	51.2
44	New Hampshire	36.9
40	New Jersey	40.5
4	New Mexico	70.6
26	New York	46.3
17	North Carolina	53.4
44	North Dakota	36.9
27	Ohio	46.2
22	Oklahoma	50.0
21	Oregon	51.1
42	Pennsylvania	38.7
46	Rhode Island	35.3
24	South Carolina	47.7
49	South Dakota	32.9
25	Tennessee	47.0
39	Texas	41.1
19	Utah	52.5
1	Vermont	88.7
37	Virginia	42.1
9	Washington	59.9
11	West Virginia	57.9
31	Wisconsin	44.4
14	Wyoming	56.5

RANK	STATE	PERCENT
1	Vermont	88.7
2	Hawaii	82.0
3	Arkansas	74.6
4	New Mexico	70.6
5	Idaho	66.9
6	Minnesota	64.8
7	Alaska	62.9
8	Delaware	62.6
9	Washington	59.9
10	Kansas	58.6
11	Alabama	57.9
11	West Virginia	57.9
13	Kentucky	57.7
14	Wyoming	56.5
15	California	56.1
16	Michigan	54.3
17	North Carolina	53.4
18	Mississippi	53.3
19	Utah	52.5
20	Nevada	51.2
21	Oregon	51.1
22	Oklahoma	50.0
23	Montana	48.0
24	South Carolina	47.7
25	Tennessee	47.0
26	New York	46.3
27	Ohio	46.2
28	Iowa	46.1
29	Indiana	45.7
30	Louisiana	45.0
31	Wisconsin	44.4
32	Colorado	44.0
33	Arizona	43.6
34	Maine	43.4
34	Maryland	43.4
36	Georgia	43.1
37	Virginia	42.1
38	Missouri	41.8
39	Texas	41.1
40	New Jersey	40.5
41	Massachusetts	39.4
42	Pennsylvania	38.7
43	Connecticut	38.0
44	New Hampshire	36.9
44	North Dakota	36.9
46	Rhode Island	35.3
47	Nebraska	34.3
48	Florida	34.2
49	South Dakota	32.9
50	Illinois	29.9
	District of Columbia**	NA

Source: U.S. Bureau of the Census, Governments Division
   "Public Education Finances: 2009" (http://www.census.gov/govs/school/)
*Consists only of revenue originating from state governments. Includes all such revenue received by a school system (net of refunds) other than from issuance of debt or liquidation of investments. Does not include noncash transactions such as receipt of services, commodities, or other "receipts in-kind."
**Not applicable.

State Government Revenue for Public Elementary and Secondary School Formula Assistance Programs in 2009
National Total = $187,040,174,000*

ALPHA ORDER

RANK	STATE	REVENUE	% of USA
21	Alabama	$3,212,334,000	1.7%
39	Alaska	950,712,000	0.5%
18	Arizona	3,480,659,000	1.9%
32	Arkansas	1,889,039,000	1.0%
1	California	22,210,994,000	11.9%
19	Colorado	3,361,980,000	1.8%
33	Connecticut	1,499,346,000	0.8%
45	Delaware	781,384,000	0.4%
22	Florida	2,972,138,000	1.6%
7	Georgia	6,581,518,000	3.5%
38	Hawaii	952,649,000	0.5%
34	Idaho	1,140,822,000	0.6%
14	Illinois	4,202,459,000	2.2%
12	Indiana	4,785,468,000	2.6%
30	Iowa	2,154,623,000	1.2%
25	Kansas	2,532,973,000	1.4%
27	Kentucky	2,404,689,000	1.3%
20	Louisiana	3,240,916,000	1.7%
43	Maine	881,295,000	0.5%
23	Maryland	2,846,746,000	1.5%
17	Massachusetts	3,533,120,000	1.9%
4	Michigan	8,558,665,000	4.6%
10	Minnesota	4,955,773,000	2.6%
29	Mississippi	2,208,243,000	1.2%
26	Missouri	2,427,088,000	1.3%
48	Montana	555,236,000	0.3%
44	Nebraska	878,495,000	0.5%
37	Nevada	1,019,521,000	0.5%
41	New Hampshire	890,363,000	0.5%
8	New Jersey	5,605,986,000	3.0%
28	New Mexico	2,323,256,000	1.2%
3	New York	16,093,222,000	8.6%
6	North Carolina	7,894,666,000	4.2%
49	North Dakota	366,444,000	0.2%
5	Ohio	8,237,453,000	4.4%
31	Oklahoma	2,140,900,000	1.1%
24	Oregon	2,803,884,000	1.5%
9	Pennsylvania	5,236,733,000	2.8%
46	Rhode Island	633,763,000	0.3%
40	South Carolina	942,152,000	0.5%
50	South Dakota	347,697,000	0.2%
16	Tennessee	3,540,885,000	1.9%
2	Texas	16,449,267,000	8.8%
42	Utah	886,235,000	0.5%
35	Vermont	1,123,669,000	0.6%
11	Virginia	4,870,242,000	2.6%
13	Washington	4,648,474,000	2.5%
36	West Virginia	1,088,996,000	0.6%
15	Wisconsin	4,087,830,000	2.2%
47	Wyoming	609,172,000	0.3%

RANK ORDER

RANK	STATE	REVENUE	% of USA
1	California	$22,210,994,000	11.9%
2	Texas	16,449,267,000	8.8%
3	New York	16,093,222,000	8.6%
4	Michigan	8,558,665,000	4.6%
5	Ohio	8,237,453,000	4.4%
6	North Carolina	7,894,666,000	4.2%
7	Georgia	6,581,518,000	3.5%
8	New Jersey	5,605,986,000	3.0%
9	Pennsylvania	5,236,733,000	2.8%
10	Minnesota	4,955,773,000	2.6%
11	Virginia	4,870,242,000	2.6%
12	Indiana	4,785,468,000	2.6%
13	Washington	4,648,474,000	2.5%
14	Illinois	4,202,459,000	2.2%
15	Wisconsin	4,087,830,000	2.2%
16	Tennessee	3,540,885,000	1.9%
17	Massachusetts	3,533,120,000	1.9%
18	Arizona	3,480,659,000	1.9%
19	Colorado	3,361,980,000	1.8%
20	Louisiana	3,240,916,000	1.7%
21	Alabama	3,212,334,000	1.7%
22	Florida	2,972,138,000	1.6%
23	Maryland	2,846,746,000	1.5%
24	Oregon	2,803,884,000	1.5%
25	Kansas	2,532,973,000	1.4%
26	Missouri	2,427,088,000	1.3%
27	Kentucky	2,404,689,000	1.3%
28	New Mexico	2,323,256,000	1.2%
29	Mississippi	2,208,243,000	1.2%
30	Iowa	2,154,623,000	1.2%
31	Oklahoma	2,140,900,000	1.1%
32	Arkansas	1,889,039,000	1.0%
33	Connecticut	1,499,346,000	0.8%
34	Idaho	1,140,822,000	0.6%
35	Vermont	1,123,669,000	0.6%
36	West Virginia	1,088,996,000	0.6%
37	Nevada	1,019,521,000	0.5%
38	Hawaii	952,649,000	0.5%
39	Alaska	950,712,000	0.5%
40	South Carolina	942,152,000	0.5%
41	New Hampshire	890,363,000	0.5%
42	Utah	886,235,000	0.5%
43	Maine	881,295,000	0.5%
44	Nebraska	878,495,000	0.5%
45	Delaware	781,384,000	0.4%
46	Rhode Island	633,763,000	0.3%
47	Wyoming	609,172,000	0.3%
48	Montana	555,236,000	0.3%
49	North Dakota	366,444,000	0.2%
50	South Dakota	347,697,000	0.2%
	District of Columbia**	NA	NA

Source: U.S. Bureau of the Census, Governments Division
"Public Education Finances: 2009" (http://www.census.gov/govs/school/)
*Revenue from general noncategorical state assistance programs such as foundation, minimum or basic formula support, apportionment, equalization, flat or block grants, and state public school fund distributions. This category also includes revenue dedicated from major state taxes, such as income and sales taxes.
**Not applicable.

Percent of Public Elementary and Secondary School
State Government Revenue Used for Formula Assistance Programs in 2009
National Percent = 67.7%*

ALPHA ORDER

RANK	STATE	PERCENT
23	Alabama	77.2
31	Alaska	70.0
5	Arizona	91.5
41	Arkansas	53.5
39	California	55.4
4	Colorado	92.5
47	Connecticut	41.6
27	Delaware	74.6
49	Florida	32.9
12	Georgia	85.0
46	Hawaii	43.2
22	Idaho	78.2
42	Illinois	53.3
19	Indiana	82.4
13	Iowa	84.6
25	Kansas	77.0
35	Kentucky	62.1
6	Louisiana	90.8
21	Maine	79.6
44	Maryland	50.0
38	Massachusetts	59.1
14	Michigan	84.5
26	Minnesota	75.2
2	Mississippi	94.6
36	Missouri	61.8
29	Montana	72.6
28	Nebraska	74.3
45	Nevada	44.9
9	New Hampshire	88.8
40	New Jersey	53.9
9	New Mexico	88.8
34	New York	62.5
1	North Carolina	95.9
7	North Dakota	90.0
20	Ohio	80.6
30	Oklahoma	71.0
8	Oregon	89.9
43	Pennsylvania	53.1
18	Rhode Island	82.8
50	South Carolina	25.8
15	South Dakota	84.2
3	Tennessee	93.2
17	Texas	83.5
48	Utah	39.8
16	Vermont	84.1
24	Virginia	77.1
32	Washington	65.0
37	West Virginia	60.7
11	Wisconsin	85.4
33	Wyoming	64.4

RANK ORDER

RANK	STATE	PERCENT
1	North Carolina	95.9
2	Mississippi	94.6
3	Tennessee	93.2
4	Colorado	92.5
5	Arizona	91.5
6	Louisiana	90.8
7	North Dakota	90.0
8	Oregon	89.9
9	New Hampshire	88.8
9	New Mexico	88.8
11	Wisconsin	85.4
12	Georgia	85.0
13	Iowa	84.6
14	Michigan	84.5
15	South Dakota	84.2
16	Vermont	84.1
17	Texas	83.5
18	Rhode Island	82.8
19	Indiana	82.4
20	Ohio	80.6
21	Maine	79.6
22	Idaho	78.2
23	Alabama	77.2
24	Virginia	77.1
25	Kansas	77.0
26	Minnesota	75.2
27	Delaware	74.6
28	Nebraska	74.3
29	Montana	72.6
30	Oklahoma	71.0
31	Alaska	70.0
32	Washington	65.0
33	Wyoming	64.4
34	New York	62.5
35	Kentucky	62.1
36	Missouri	61.8
37	West Virginia	60.7
38	Massachusetts	59.1
39	California	55.4
40	New Jersey	53.9
41	Arkansas	53.5
42	Illinois	53.3
43	Pennsylvania	53.1
44	Maryland	50.0
45	Nevada	44.9
46	Hawaii	43.2
47	Connecticut	41.6
48	Utah	39.8
49	Florida	32.9
50	South Carolina	25.8

District of Columbia**   NA

Source: CQ Press using data from U.S. Bureau of the Census, Governments Division
    "Public Education Finances: 2009" (http://www.census.gov/govs/school/)
*Revenue from general noncategorical state assistance programs such as foundation, minimum or basic formula support, apportionment, equalization, flat or block grants, and state public school fund distributions. This category also includes revenue dedicated from major state taxes, such as income and sales taxes.
**Not applicable.

State Government Revenue for Public Elementary and Secondary School Compensatory Programs in 2009
National Total = $6,223,719,000*

ALPHA ORDER

RANK	STATE	REVENUE	% of USA
13	Alabama	$85,866,000	1.4%
29	Alaska	0	0.0%
18	Arizona	22,239,000	0.4%
9	Arkansas	196,498,000	3.2%
2	California	1,317,966,000	21.2%
29	Colorado	0	0.0%
21	Connecticut	12,602,000	0.2%
29	Delaware	0	0.0%
29	Florida	0	0.0%
29	Georgia	0	0.0%
24	Hawaii	4,278,000	0.1%
29	Idaho	0	0.0%
6	Illinois	271,921,000	4.4%
17	Indiana	26,514,000	0.4%
22	Iowa	10,311,000	0.2%
29	Kansas	0	0.0%
29	Kentucky	0	0.0%
29	Louisiana	0	0.0%
29	Maine	0	0.0%
3	Maryland	938,937,000	15.1%
29	Massachusetts	0	0.0%
5	Michigan	277,966,000	4.5%
8	Minnesota	215,330,000	3.5%
16	Mississippi	27,202,000	0.4%
29	Missouri	0	0.0%
23	Montana	8,241,000	0.1%
27	Nebraska	374,000	0.0%
20	Nevada	13,635,000	0.2%
29	New Hampshire	0	0.0%
1	New Jersey	1,535,587,000	24.7%
28	New Mexico	93,000	0.0%
29	New York	0	0.0%
12	North Carolina	86,639,000	1.4%
29	North Dakota	0	0.0%
4	Ohio	437,611,000	7.0%
19	Oklahoma	21,003,000	0.3%
29	Oregon	0	0.0%
14	Pennsylvania	59,932,000	1.0%
29	Rhode Island	0	0.0%
11	South Carolina	158,211,000	2.5%
25	South Dakota	1,576,000	0.0%
29	Tennessee	0	0.0%
29	Texas	0	0.0%
15	Utah	31,550,000	0.5%
29	Vermont	0	0.0%
7	Virginia	269,766,000	4.3%
10	Washington	190,432,000	3.1%
26	West Virginia	1,439,000	0.0%
29	Wisconsin	0	0.0%
29	Wyoming	0	0.0%

RANK ORDER

RANK	STATE	REVENUE	% of USA
1	New Jersey	$1,535,587,000	24.7%
2	California	1,317,966,000	21.2%
3	Maryland	938,937,000	15.1%
4	Ohio	437,611,000	7.0%
5	Michigan	277,966,000	4.5%
6	Illinois	271,921,000	4.4%
7	Virginia	269,766,000	4.3%
8	Minnesota	215,330,000	3.5%
9	Arkansas	196,498,000	3.2%
10	Washington	190,432,000	3.1%
11	South Carolina	158,211,000	2.5%
12	North Carolina	86,639,000	1.4%
13	Alabama	85,866,000	1.4%
14	Pennsylvania	59,932,000	1.0%
15	Utah	31,550,000	0.5%
16	Mississippi	27,202,000	0.4%
17	Indiana	26,514,000	0.4%
18	Arizona	22,239,000	0.4%
19	Oklahoma	21,003,000	0.3%
20	Nevada	13,635,000	0.2%
21	Connecticut	12,602,000	0.2%
22	Iowa	10,311,000	0.2%
23	Montana	8,241,000	0.1%
24	Hawaii	4,278,000	0.1%
25	South Dakota	1,576,000	0.0%
26	West Virginia	1,439,000	0.0%
27	Nebraska	374,000	0.0%
28	New Mexico	93,000	0.0%
29	Alaska	0	0.0%
29	Colorado	0	0.0%
29	Delaware	0	0.0%
29	Florida	0	0.0%
29	Georgia	0	0.0%
29	Idaho	0	0.0%
29	Kansas	0	0.0%
29	Kentucky	0	0.0%
29	Louisiana	0	0.0%
29	Maine	0	0.0%
29	Massachusetts	0	0.0%
29	Missouri	0	0.0%
29	New Hampshire	0	0.0%
29	New York	0	0.0%
29	North Dakota	0	0.0%
29	Oregon	0	0.0%
29	Rhode Island	0	0.0%
29	Tennessee	0	0.0%
29	Texas	0	0.0%
29	Vermont	0	0.0%
29	Wisconsin	0	0.0%
29	Wyoming	0	0.0%
	District of Columbia**	NA	NA

Source: U.S. Bureau of the Census, Governments Division
"Public Education Finances: 2009" (http://www.census.gov/govs/school/)
*Revenue for "at risk" or other economically disadvantaged students including migratory children. Also includes monies from state programs directed toward the attainment of basic skills and categorical education excellence and quality education programs that provide more than staff enhancements--such as materials and resource centers.
**Not applicable.

Percent of Public Elementary and Secondary School
State Government Revenue Used for Compensatory Programs in 2009
National Percent = 2.3%*

ALPHA ORDER

RANK	STATE	PERCENT
12	Alabama	2.1
27	Alaska	0.0
18	Arizona	0.6
3	Arkansas	5.6
8	California	3.3
27	Colorado	0.0
24	Connecticut	0.3
27	Delaware	0.0
27	Florida	0.0
27	Georgia	0.0
25	Hawaii	0.2
27	Idaho	0.0
7	Illinois	3.5
21	Indiana	0.5
22	Iowa	0.4
27	Kansas	0.0
27	Kentucky	0.0
27	Louisiana	0.0
27	Maine	0.0
1	Maryland	16.5
27	Massachusetts	0.0
10	Michigan	2.7
8	Minnesota	3.3
14	Mississippi	1.2
27	Missouri	0.0
15	Montana	1.1
27	Nebraska	0.0
18	Nevada	0.6
27	New Hampshire	0.0
2	New Jersey	14.8
27	New Mexico	0.0
27	New York	0.0
15	North Carolina	1.1
27	North Dakota	0.0
4	Ohio	4.3
17	Oklahoma	0.7
27	Oregon	0.0
18	Pennsylvania	0.6
27	Rhode Island	0.0
4	South Carolina	4.3
22	South Dakota	0.4
27	Tennessee	0.0
27	Texas	0.0
13	Utah	1.4
27	Vermont	0.0
4	Virginia	4.3
10	Washington	2.7
26	West Virginia	0.1
27	Wisconsin	0.0
27	Wyoming	0.0

RANK ORDER

RANK	STATE	PERCENT
1	Maryland	16.5
2	New Jersey	14.8
3	Arkansas	5.6
4	Ohio	4.3
4	South Carolina	4.3
4	Virginia	4.3
7	Illinois	3.5
8	California	3.3
8	Minnesota	3.3
10	Michigan	2.7
10	Washington	2.7
12	Alabama	2.1
13	Utah	1.4
14	Mississippi	1.2
15	Montana	1.1
15	North Carolina	1.1
17	Oklahoma	0.7
18	Arizona	0.6
18	Nevada	0.6
18	Pennsylvania	0.6
21	Indiana	0.5
22	Iowa	0.4
22	South Dakota	0.4
24	Connecticut	0.3
25	Hawaii	0.2
26	West Virginia	0.1
27	Alaska	0.0
27	Colorado	0.0
27	Delaware	0.0
27	Florida	0.0
27	Georgia	0.0
27	Idaho	0.0
27	Kansas	0.0
27	Kentucky	0.0
27	Louisiana	0.0
27	Maine	0.0
27	Massachusetts	0.0
27	Missouri	0.0
27	Nebraska	0.0
27	New Hampshire	0.0
27	New Mexico	0.0
27	New York	0.0
27	North Dakota	0.0
27	Oregon	0.0
27	Rhode Island	0.0
27	Tennessee	0.0
27	Texas	0.0
27	Vermont	0.0
27	Wisconsin	0.0
27	Wyoming	0.0
	District of Columbia**	NA

Source: CQ Press using data from U.S. Bureau of the Census, Governments Division
"Public Education Finances: 2008" (http://www.census.gov/govs/school/index.html)
*Revenue for "at risk" or other economically disadvantaged students including migratory children. Also includes monies from state programs directed toward the attainment of basic skills and categorical education excellence and quality education programs that provide more than staff enhancements--such as materials and resource centers.
**Not applicable.

State Government Revenue for Public Elementary and Secondary School Special Education Programs in 2009
National Total = $16,470,528,000*

RANK	STATE	REVENUE	% of USA
34	Alabama	$1,925,000	0.0%
38	Alaska	0	0.0%
36	Arizona	470,000	0.0%
16	Arkansas	219,709,000	1.3%
2	California	3,005,934,000	18.3%
21	Colorado	126,818,000	0.8%
10	Connecticut	516,669,000	3.1%
35	Delaware	512,000	0.0%
5	Florida	934,889,000	5.7%
38	Georgia	0	0.0%
15	Hawaii	274,246,000	1.7%
31	Idaho	3,846,000	0.0%
9	Illinois	645,667,000	3.9%
25	Indiana	34,957,000	0.2%
32	Iowa	3,383,000	0.0%
12	Kansas	419,679,000	2.5%
38	Kentucky	0	0.0%
26	Louisiana	26,176,000	0.2%
27	Maine	11,322,000	0.1%
13	Maryland	391,583,000	2.4%
38	Massachusetts	0	0.0%
4	Michigan	979,114,000	5.9%
8	Minnesota	784,204,000	4.8%
33	Mississippi	3,251,000	0.0%
23	Missouri	114,456,000	0.7%
30	Montana	4,698,000	0.0%
19	Nebraska	183,542,000	1.1%
22	Nevada	116,805,000	0.7%
38	New Hampshire	0	0.0%
6	New Jersey	875,486,000	5.3%
38	New Mexico	0	0.0%
1	New York	3,511,335,000	21.3%
37	North Carolina	57,000	0.0%
28	North Dakota	9,378,000	0.1%
38	Ohio	0	0.0%
38	Oklahoma	0	0.0%
38	Oregon	0	0.0%
3	Pennsylvania	1,031,782,000	6.3%
38	Rhode Island	0	0.0%
17	South Carolina	210,526,000	1.3%
24	South Dakota	47,796,000	0.3%
38	Tennessee	0	0.0%
38	Texas	0	0.0%
18	Utah	199,645,000	1.2%
20	Vermont	141,996,000	0.9%
11	Virginia	473,709,000	2.9%
7	Washington	791,649,000	4.8%
29	West Virginia	6,418,000	0.0%
14	Wisconsin	366,896,000	2.2%
38	Wyoming	0	0.0%

RANK	STATE	REVENUE	% of USA
1	New York	$3,511,335,000	21.3%
2	California	3,005,934,000	18.3%
3	Pennsylvania	1,031,782,000	6.3%
4	Michigan	979,114,000	5.9%
5	Florida	934,889,000	5.7%
6	New Jersey	875,486,000	5.3%
7	Washington	791,649,000	4.8%
8	Minnesota	784,204,000	4.8%
9	Illinois	645,667,000	3.9%
10	Connecticut	516,669,000	3.1%
11	Virginia	473,709,000	2.9%
12	Kansas	419,679,000	2.5%
13	Maryland	391,583,000	2.4%
14	Wisconsin	366,896,000	2.2%
15	Hawaii	274,246,000	1.7%
16	Arkansas	219,709,000	1.3%
17	South Carolina	210,526,000	1.3%
18	Utah	199,645,000	1.2%
19	Nebraska	183,542,000	1.1%
20	Vermont	141,996,000	0.9%
21	Colorado	126,818,000	0.8%
22	Nevada	116,805,000	0.7%
23	Missouri	114,456,000	0.7%
24	South Dakota	47,796,000	0.3%
25	Indiana	34,957,000	0.2%
26	Louisiana	26,176,000	0.2%
27	Maine	11,322,000	0.1%
28	North Dakota	9,378,000	0.1%
29	West Virginia	6,418,000	0.0%
30	Montana	4,698,000	0.0%
31	Idaho	3,846,000	0.0%
32	Iowa	3,383,000	0.0%
33	Mississippi	3,251,000	0.0%
34	Alabama	1,925,000	0.0%
35	Delaware	512,000	0.0%
36	Arizona	470,000	0.0%
37	North Carolina	57,000	0.0%
38	Alaska	0	0.0%
38	Georgia	0	0.0%
38	Kentucky	0	0.0%
38	Massachusetts	0	0.0%
38	New Hampshire	0	0.0%
38	New Mexico	0	0.0%
38	Ohio	0	0.0%
38	Oklahoma	0	0.0%
38	Oregon	0	0.0%
38	Rhode Island	0	0.0%
38	Tennessee	0	0.0%
38	Texas	0	0.0%
38	Wyoming	0	0.0%
	District of Columbia**	NA	NA

Source: U.S. Bureau of the Census, Governments Division
  "Public Education Finances: 2009" (http://www.census.gov/govs/school/)
*Revenue for the education of students with special needs, such as those with physical and mental disabilities.
**Not applicable.

Percent of Public Elementary and Secondary School
State Government Revenue Used for Special Education Programs in 2009
National Percent = 6.0%*

ALPHA ORDER

RANK	STATE	PERCENT
34	Alabama	0.0
34	Alaska	0.0
34	Arizona	0.0
20	Arkansas	6.2
17	California	7.5
23	Colorado	3.5
2	Connecticut	14.3
34	Delaware	0.0
11	Florida	10.3
34	Georgia	0.0
5	Hawaii	12.4
31	Idaho	0.3
15	Illinois	8.2
28	Indiana	0.6
32	Iowa	0.1
4	Kansas	12.8
34	Kentucky	0.0
27	Louisiana	0.7
26	Maine	1.0
19	Maryland	6.9
34	Massachusetts	0.0
12	Michigan	9.7
6	Minnesota	11.9
32	Mississippi	0.1
24	Missouri	2.9
28	Montana	0.6
1	Nebraska	15.5
22	Nevada	5.1
34	New Hampshire	0.0
14	New Jersey	8.4
34	New Mexico	0.0
3	New York	13.6
34	North Carolina	0.0
25	North Dakota	2.3
34	Ohio	0.0
34	Oklahoma	0.0
34	Oregon	0.0
10	Pennsylvania	10.5
34	Rhode Island	0.0
21	South Carolina	5.8
7	South Dakota	11.6
34	Tennessee	0.0
34	Texas	0.0
13	Utah	9.0
9	Vermont	10.6
17	Virginia	7.5
8	Washington	11.1
30	West Virginia	0.4
16	Wisconsin	7.7
34	Wyoming	0.0

RANK ORDER

RANK	STATE	PERCENT
1	Nebraska	15.5
2	Connecticut	14.3
3	New York	13.6
4	Kansas	12.8
5	Hawaii	12.4
6	Minnesota	11.9
7	South Dakota	11.6
8	Washington	11.1
9	Vermont	10.6
10	Pennsylvania	10.5
11	Florida	10.3
12	Michigan	9.7
13	Utah	9.0
14	New Jersey	8.4
15	Illinois	8.2
16	Wisconsin	7.7
17	California	7.5
17	Virginia	7.5
19	Maryland	6.9
20	Arkansas	6.2
21	South Carolina	5.8
22	Nevada	5.1
23	Colorado	3.5
24	Missouri	2.9
25	North Dakota	2.3
26	Maine	1.0
27	Louisiana	0.7
28	Indiana	0.6
28	Montana	0.6
30	West Virginia	0.4
31	Idaho	0.3
32	Iowa	0.1
32	Mississippi	0.1
34	Alabama	0.0
34	Alaska	0.0
34	Arizona	0.0
34	Delaware	0.0
34	Georgia	0.0
34	Kentucky	0.0
34	Massachusetts	0.0
34	New Hampshire	0.0
34	New Mexico	0.0
34	North Carolina	0.0
34	Ohio	0.0
34	Oklahoma	0.0
34	Oregon	0.0
34	Rhode Island	0.0
34	Tennessee	0.0
34	Texas	0.0
34	Wyoming	0.0

District of Columbia**   NA

Source: CQ Press using data from U.S. Bureau of the Census, Governments Division
"Public Education Finances: 2009" (http://www.census.gov/govs/school/)
*Revenue for the education of students with special needs, such as those with physical and mental disabilities.
**Not applicable.

State Government Revenue for Public Elementary and Secondary School Vocational Programs in 2009
National Total = $875,618,000*

ALPHA ORDER

RANK	STATE	REVENUE	% of USA
33	Alabama	$0	0.0%
33	Alaska	0	0.0%
14	Arizona	10,383,000	1.2%
12	Arkansas	19,641,000	2.2%
20	California	4,512,000	0.5%
11	Colorado	20,401,000	2.3%
19	Connecticut	4,776,000	0.5%
33	Delaware	0	0.0%
2	Florida	121,886,000	13.9%
33	Georgia	0	0.0%
16	Hawaii	7,390,000	0.8%
15	Idaho	8,552,000	1.0%
7	Illinois	44,232,000	5.1%
25	Indiana	2,814,000	0.3%
24	Iowa	2,962,000	0.3%
33	Kansas	0	0.0%
22	Kentucky	3,375,000	0.4%
33	Louisiana	0	0.0%
33	Maine	0	0.0%
33	Maryland	0	0.0%
31	Massachusetts	287,000	0.0%
8	Michigan	35,488,000	4.1%
26	Minnesota	1,105,000	0.1%
6	Mississippi	49,763,000	5.7%
9	Missouri	27,424,000	3.1%
29	Montana	895,000	0.1%
33	Nebraska	0	0.0%
32	Nevada	139,000	0.0%
17	New Hampshire	6,772,000	0.8%
33	New Jersey	0	0.0%
33	New Mexico	0	0.0%
33	New York	0	0.0%
33	North Carolina	0	0.0%
18	North Dakota	5,995,000	0.7%
23	Ohio	3,213,000	0.4%
9	Oklahoma	27,424,000	3.1%
33	Oregon	0	0.0%
5	Pennsylvania	61,922,000	7.1%
33	Rhode Island	0	0.0%
1	South Carolina	240,373,000	27.5%
30	South Dakota	822,000	0.1%
27	Tennessee	982,000	0.1%
33	Texas	0	0.0%
4	Utah	69,467,000	7.9%
13	Vermont	10,907,000	1.2%
3	Virginia	76,729,000	8.8%
28	Washington	979,000	0.1%
21	West Virginia	4,008,000	0.5%
33	Wisconsin	0	0.0%
33	Wyoming	0	0.0%

RANK ORDER

RANK	STATE	REVENUE	% of USA
1	South Carolina	$240,373,000	27.5%
2	Florida	121,886,000	13.9%
3	Virginia	76,729,000	8.8%
4	Utah	69,467,000	7.9%
5	Pennsylvania	61,922,000	7.1%
6	Mississippi	49,763,000	5.7%
7	Illinois	44,232,000	5.1%
8	Michigan	35,488,000	4.1%
9	Missouri	27,424,000	3.1%
9	Oklahoma	27,424,000	3.1%
11	Colorado	20,401,000	2.3%
12	Arkansas	19,641,000	2.2%
13	Vermont	10,907,000	1.2%
14	Arizona	10,383,000	1.2%
15	Idaho	8,552,000	1.0%
16	Hawaii	7,390,000	0.8%
17	New Hampshire	6,772,000	0.8%
18	North Dakota	5,995,000	0.7%
19	Connecticut	4,776,000	0.5%
20	California	4,512,000	0.5%
21	West Virginia	4,008,000	0.5%
22	Kentucky	3,375,000	0.4%
23	Ohio	3,213,000	0.4%
24	Iowa	2,962,000	0.3%
25	Indiana	2,814,000	0.3%
26	Minnesota	1,105,000	0.1%
27	Tennessee	982,000	0.1%
28	Washington	979,000	0.1%
29	Montana	895,000	0.1%
30	South Dakota	822,000	0.1%
31	Massachusetts	287,000	0.0%
32	Nevada	139,000	0.0%
33	Alabama	0	0.0%
33	Alaska	0	0.0%
33	Delaware	0	0.0%
33	Georgia	0	0.0%
33	Kansas	0	0.0%
33	Louisiana	0	0.0%
33	Maine	0	0.0%
33	Maryland	0	0.0%
33	Nebraska	0	0.0%
33	New Jersey	0	0.0%
33	New Mexico	0	0.0%
33	New York	0	0.0%
33	North Carolina	0	0.0%
33	Oregon	0	0.0%
33	Rhode Island	0	0.0%
33	Texas	0	0.0%
33	Wisconsin	0	0.0%
33	Wyoming	0	0.0%
	District of Columbia**	NA	NA

Source: U.S. Bureau of the Census, Governments Division
"Public Education Finances: 2009" (http://www.census.gov/govs/school/)
*Revenue for state vocational education assistance programs including career education programs.
**Not applicable.

Percent of Public Elementary and Secondary School
State Government Revenue Used for Vocational Programs in 2009
National Percent = 0.3%*

ALPHA ORDER

RANK	STATE	PERCENT
25	Alabama	0.0
25	Alaska	0.0
17	Arizona	0.3
11	Arkansas	0.6
25	California	0.0
11	Colorado	0.6
21	Connecticut	0.1
25	Delaware	0.0
5	Florida	1.3
25	Georgia	0.0
17	Hawaii	0.3
11	Idaho	0.6
11	Illinois	0.6
25	Indiana	0.0
21	Iowa	0.1
25	Kansas	0.0
21	Kentucky	0.1
25	Louisiana	0.0
25	Maine	0.0
25	Maryland	0.0
25	Massachusetts	0.0
16	Michigan	0.4
25	Minnesota	0.0
3	Mississippi	2.1
9	Missouri	0.7
21	Montana	0.1
25	Nebraska	0.0
25	Nevada	0.0
9	New Hampshire	0.7
25	New Jersey	0.0
25	New Mexico	0.0
25	New York	0.0
25	North Carolina	0.0
4	North Dakota	1.5
25	Ohio	0.0
7	Oklahoma	0.9
25	Oregon	0.0
11	Pennsylvania	0.6
25	Rhode Island	0.0
1	South Carolina	6.6
19	South Dakota	0.2
25	Tennessee	0.0
25	Texas	0.0
2	Utah	3.1
8	Vermont	0.8
6	Virginia	1.2
25	Washington	0.0
19	West Virginia	0.2
25	Wisconsin	0.0
25	Wyoming	0.0

RANK ORDER

RANK	STATE	PERCENT
1	South Carolina	6.6
2	Utah	3.1
3	Mississippi	2.1
4	North Dakota	1.5
5	Florida	1.3
6	Virginia	1.2
7	Oklahoma	0.9
8	Vermont	0.8
9	Missouri	0.7
9	New Hampshire	0.7
11	Arkansas	0.6
11	Colorado	0.6
11	Idaho	0.6
11	Illinois	0.6
11	Pennsylvania	0.6
16	Michigan	0.4
17	Arizona	0.3
17	Hawaii	0.3
19	South Dakota	0.2
19	West Virginia	0.2
21	Connecticut	0.1
21	Iowa	0.1
21	Kentucky	0.1
21	Montana	0.1
25	Alabama	0.0
25	Alaska	0.0
25	California	0.0
25	Delaware	0.0
25	Georgia	0.0
25	Indiana	0.0
25	Kansas	0.0
25	Louisiana	0.0
25	Maine	0.0
25	Maryland	0.0
25	Massachusetts	0.0
25	Minnesota	0.0
25	Nebraska	0.0
25	Nevada	0.0
25	New Jersey	0.0
25	New Mexico	0.0
25	New York	0.0
25	North Carolina	0.0
25	Ohio	0.0
25	Oregon	0.0
25	Rhode Island	0.0
25	Tennessee	0.0
25	Texas	0.0
25	Washington	0.0
25	Wisconsin	0.0
25	Wyoming	0.0

District of Columbia** NA

Source: CQ Press using data from U.S. Bureau of the Census, Governments Division
   "Public Education Finances: 2009" (http://www.census.gov/govs/school/)
*Revenue for state vocational education assistance programs including career education programs.
**Not applicable.

State Government Revenue for Public Elementary and Secondary School Transportation Programs in 2009
National Total = $4,587,770,000*

ALPHA ORDER

RANK	STATE	REVENUE	% of USA
6	Alabama	$299,660,000	6.5%
17	Alaska	58,442,000	1.3%
33	Arizona	0	0.0%
33	Arkansas	0	0.0%
2	California	620,119,000	13.5%
19	Colorado	44,836,000	1.0%
16	Connecticut	59,639,000	1.3%
14	Delaware	71,486,000	1.6%
4	Florida	460,902,000	10.0%
33	Georgia	0	0.0%
18	Hawaii	47,205,000	1.0%
13	Idaho	73,225,000	1.6%
3	Illinois	493,629,000	10.8%
31	Indiana	14,000	0.0%
27	Iowa	8,120,000	0.2%
33	Kansas	0	0.0%
29	Kentucky	690,000	0.0%
33	Louisiana	0	0.0%
33	Maine	0	0.0%
9	Maryland	224,828,000	4.9%
8	Massachusetts	264,706,000	5.8%
33	Michigan	0	0.0%
15	Minnesota	64,164,000	1.4%
33	Mississippi	0	0.0%
10	Missouri	157,755,000	3.4%
24	Montana	12,475,000	0.3%
32	Nebraska	1,000	0.0%
30	Nevada	121,000	0.0%
33	New Hampshire	0	0.0%
7	New Jersey	283,924,000	6.2%
11	New Mexico	106,021,000	2.3%
33	New York	0	0.0%
26	North Carolina	11,856,000	0.3%
23	North Dakota	17,763,000	0.4%
33	Ohio	0	0.0%
33	Oklahoma	0	0.0%
25	Oregon	11,908,000	0.3%
1	Pennsylvania	710,688,000	15.5%
33	Rhode Island	0	0.0%
20	South Carolina	39,149,000	0.9%
33	South Dakota	0	0.0%
33	Tennessee	0	0.0%
33	Texas	0	0.0%
12	Utah	75,306,000	1.6%
28	Vermont	1,211,000	0.0%
33	Virginia	0	0.0%
5	Washington	321,482,000	7.0%
22	West Virginia	21,710,000	0.5%
21	Wisconsin	24,735,000	0.5%
33	Wyoming	0	0.0%

RANK ORDER

RANK	STATE	REVENUE	% of USA
1	Pennsylvania	$710,688,000	15.5%
2	California	620,119,000	13.5%
3	Illinois	493,629,000	10.8%
4	Florida	460,902,000	10.0%
5	Washington	321,482,000	7.0%
6	Alabama	299,660,000	6.5%
7	New Jersey	283,924,000	6.2%
8	Massachusetts	264,706,000	5.8%
9	Maryland	224,828,000	4.9%
10	Missouri	157,755,000	3.4%
11	New Mexico	106,021,000	2.3%
12	Utah	75,306,000	1.6%
13	Idaho	73,225,000	1.6%
14	Delaware	71,486,000	1.6%
15	Minnesota	64,164,000	1.4%
16	Connecticut	59,639,000	1.3%
17	Alaska	58,442,000	1.3%
18	Hawaii	47,205,000	1.0%
19	Colorado	44,836,000	1.0%
20	South Carolina	39,149,000	0.9%
21	Wisconsin	24,735,000	0.5%
22	West Virginia	21,710,000	0.5%
23	North Dakota	17,763,000	0.4%
24	Montana	12,475,000	0.3%
25	Oregon	11,908,000	0.3%
26	North Carolina	11,856,000	0.3%
27	Iowa	8,120,000	0.2%
28	Vermont	1,211,000	0.0%
29	Kentucky	690,000	0.0%
30	Nevada	121,000	0.0%
31	Indiana	14,000	0.0%
32	Nebraska	1,000	0.0%
33	Arizona	0	0.0%
33	Arkansas	0	0.0%
33	Georgia	0	0.0%
33	Kansas	0	0.0%
33	Louisiana	0	0.0%
33	Maine	0	0.0%
33	Michigan	0	0.0%
33	Mississippi	0	0.0%
33	New Hampshire	0	0.0%
33	New York	0	0.0%
33	Ohio	0	0.0%
33	Oklahoma	0	0.0%
33	Rhode Island	0	0.0%
33	South Dakota	0	0.0%
33	Tennessee	0	0.0%
33	Texas	0	0.0%
33	Virginia	0	0.0%
33	Wyoming	0	0.0%
	District of Columbia**	NA	NA

Source: U.S. Bureau of the Census, Governments Division
"Public Education Finances: 2009" (http://www.census.gov/govs/school/)
*Payments for various state transportation aid programs such as those that compensate the school system for part of its transportation expense and those that provide reimbursement for transportation salaries or school bus purchase.
**Not applicable.

Percent of Public Elementary and Secondary School State Government Revenue Used for Transportation Programs in 2009
National Percent = 1.7%*

ALPHA ORDER

RANK	STATE	PERCENT
1	Alabama	7.2
10	Alaska	4.3
29	Arizona	0.0
29	Arkansas	0.0
19	California	1.5
20	Colorado	1.2
17	Connecticut	1.7
3	Delaware	6.8
5	Florida	5.1
29	Georgia	0.0
16	Hawaii	2.1
6	Idaho	5.0
4	Illinois	6.3
29	Indiana	0.0
26	Iowa	0.3
29	Kansas	0.0
29	Kentucky	0.0
29	Louisiana	0.0
29	Maine	0.0
13	Maryland	3.9
8	Massachusetts	4.4
29	Michigan	0.0
23	Minnesota	1.0
29	Mississippi	0.0
12	Missouri	4.0
18	Montana	1.6
29	Nebraska	0.0
29	Nevada	0.0
29	New Hampshire	0.0
15	New Jersey	2.7
11	New Mexico	4.1
29	New York	0.0
27	North Carolina	0.1
8	North Dakota	4.4
29	Ohio	0.0
29	Oklahoma	0.0
25	Oregon	0.4
1	Pennsylvania	7.2
29	Rhode Island	0.0
22	South Carolina	1.1
29	South Dakota	0.0
29	Tennessee	0.0
29	Texas	0.0
14	Utah	3.4
27	Vermont	0.1
29	Virginia	0.0
7	Washington	4.5
20	West Virginia	1.2
24	Wisconsin	0.5
29	Wyoming	0.0

RANK ORDER

RANK	STATE	PERCENT
1	Alabama	7.2
1	Pennsylvania	7.2
3	Delaware	6.8
4	Illinois	6.3
5	Florida	5.1
6	Idaho	5.0
7	Washington	4.5
8	Massachusetts	4.4
8	North Dakota	4.4
10	Alaska	4.3
11	New Mexico	4.1
12	Missouri	4.0
13	Maryland	3.9
14	Utah	3.4
15	New Jersey	2.7
16	Hawaii	2.1
17	Connecticut	1.7
18	Montana	1.6
19	California	1.5
20	Colorado	1.2
20	West Virginia	1.2
22	South Carolina	1.1
23	Minnesota	1.0
24	Wisconsin	0.5
25	Oregon	0.4
26	Iowa	0.3
27	North Carolina	0.1
27	Vermont	0.1
29	Arizona	0.0
29	Arkansas	0.0
29	Georgia	0.0
29	Indiana	0.0
29	Kansas	0.0
29	Kentucky	0.0
29	Louisiana	0.0
29	Maine	0.0
29	Michigan	0.0
29	Mississippi	0.0
29	Nebraska	0.0
29	Nevada	0.0
29	New Hampshire	0.0
29	New York	0.0
29	Ohio	0.0
29	Oklahoma	0.0
29	Rhode Island	0.0
29	South Dakota	0.0
29	Tennessee	0.0
29	Texas	0.0
29	Virginia	0.0
29	Wyoming	0.0

District of Columbia**   NA

Source: CQ Press using data from U.S. Bureau of the Census, Governments Division
    "Public Education Finances: 2009" (http://www.census.gov/govs/school/)
*Payments for various state transportation aid programs such as those that compensate the school system for part of its transportation expense and those that provide reimbursement for transportation salaries or school bus purchase.
**Not applicable.

Public Elementary and Secondary School
Revenue from Local Sources in 2009
National Total = $258,893,617,000*

RANK	STATE	REVENUE	% of USA
28	Alabama	$2,294,987,000	0.9%
48	Alaska	488,421,000	0.2%
20	Arizona	3,869,518,000	1.5%
40	Arkansas	667,688,000	0.3%
3	California	21,623,650,000	8.4%
19	Colorado	4,068,111,000	1.6%
16	Connecticut	5,492,313,000	2.1%
46	Delaware	517,267,000	0.2%
5	Florida	14,745,439,000	5.7%
9	Georgia	8,584,811,000	3.3%
49	Hawaii	91,889,000	0.0%
47	Idaho	503,067,000	0.2%
4	Illinois	15,145,421,000	5.9%
15	Indiana	5,501,419,000	2.1%
26	Iowa	2,550,749,000	1.0%
32	Kansas	1,942,866,000	0.8%
30	Kentucky	2,114,797,000	0.8%
24	Louisiana	3,124,537,000	1.2%
37	Maine	1,199,776,000	0.5%
12	Maryland	6,749,350,000	2.6%
10	Massachusetts	8,014,256,000	3.1%
13	Michigan	6,422,253,000	2.5%
25	Minnesota	3,004,149,000	1.2%
36	Mississippi	1,370,806,000	0.5%
18	Missouri	4,710,378,000	1.8%
42	Montana	634,436,000	0.2%
31	Nebraska	1,965,869,000	0.8%
33	Nevada	1,743,560,000	0.7%
34	New Hampshire	1,567,456,000	0.6%
6	New Jersey	14,235,619,000	5.5%
44	New Mexico	568,169,000	0.2%
1	New York	26,711,006,000	10.3%
14	North Carolina	5,803,761,000	2.2%
45	North Dakota	536,365,000	0.2%
8	Ohio	10,392,787,000	4.0%
29	Oklahoma	2,244,813,000	0.9%
27	Oregon	2,330,572,000	0.9%
7	Pennsylvania	13,803,556,000	5.3%
38	Rhode Island	1,195,643,000	0.5%
23	South Carolina	3,267,438,000	1.3%
41	South Dakota	640,547,000	0.2%
21	Tennessee	3,410,332,000	1.3%
2	Texas	23,308,189,000	9.0%
35	Utah	1,475,580,000	0.6%
50	Vermont	68,389,000	0.0%
11	Virginia	7,768,557,000	3.0%
22	Washington	3,393,809,000	1.3%
39	West Virginia	947,264,000	0.4%
17	Wisconsin	4,737,758,000	1.8%
43	Wyoming	619,072,000	0.2%

RANK	STATE	REVENUE	% of USA
1	New York	$26,711,006,000	10.3%
2	Texas	23,308,189,000	9.0%
3	California	21,623,650,000	8.4%
4	Illinois	15,145,421,000	5.9%
5	Florida	14,745,439,000	5.7%
6	New Jersey	14,235,619,000	5.5%
7	Pennsylvania	13,803,556,000	5.3%
8	Ohio	10,392,787,000	4.0%
9	Georgia	8,584,811,000	3.3%
10	Massachusetts	8,014,256,000	3.1%
11	Virginia	7,768,557,000	3.0%
12	Maryland	6,749,350,000	2.6%
13	Michigan	6,422,253,000	2.5%
14	North Carolina	5,803,761,000	2.2%
15	Indiana	5,501,419,000	2.1%
16	Connecticut	5,492,313,000	2.1%
17	Wisconsin	4,737,758,000	1.8%
18	Missouri	4,710,378,000	1.8%
19	Colorado	4,068,111,000	1.6%
20	Arizona	3,869,518,000	1.5%
21	Tennessee	3,410,332,000	1.3%
22	Washington	3,393,809,000	1.3%
23	South Carolina	3,267,438,000	1.3%
24	Louisiana	3,124,537,000	1.2%
25	Minnesota	3,004,149,000	1.2%
26	Iowa	2,550,749,000	1.0%
27	Oregon	2,330,572,000	0.9%
28	Alabama	2,294,987,000	0.9%
29	Oklahoma	2,244,813,000	0.9%
30	Kentucky	2,114,797,000	0.8%
31	Nebraska	1,965,869,000	0.8%
32	Kansas	1,942,866,000	0.8%
33	Nevada	1,743,560,000	0.7%
34	New Hampshire	1,567,456,000	0.6%
35	Utah	1,475,580,000	0.6%
36	Mississippi	1,370,806,000	0.5%
37	Maine	1,199,776,000	0.5%
38	Rhode Island	1,195,643,000	0.5%
39	West Virginia	947,264,000	0.4%
40	Arkansas	667,688,000	0.3%
41	South Dakota	640,547,000	0.2%
42	Montana	634,436,000	0.2%
43	Wyoming	619,072,000	0.2%
44	New Mexico	568,169,000	0.2%
45	North Dakota	536,365,000	0.2%
46	Delaware	517,267,000	0.2%
47	Idaho	503,067,000	0.2%
48	Alaska	488,421,000	0.2%
49	Hawaii	91,889,000	0.0%
50	Vermont	68,389,000	0.0%
	District of Columbia	725,152,000	0.3%

Source: U.S. Bureau of the Census, Governments Division
"Public Education Finances: 2009" (http://www.census.gov/govs/school/)
*Revenue raised locally including taxes and charges. Includes all such revenue received by a school system from local sources (net of refunds) other than from issuance of debt or liquidation of investments. Does not include noncash transactions such as receipt of services, commodities, or other "receipts in-kind."

Per Capita Elementary and Secondary School Revenue from Local Sources in 2009
National Per Capita = $843*

ALPHA ORDER

RANK	STATE	PER CAPITA
44	Alabama	$487
26	Alaska	699
35	Arizona	587
48	Arkansas	231
36	California	585
21	Colorado	810
2	Connecticut	1,561
37	Delaware	584
22	Florida	795
16	Georgia	873
50	Hawaii	71
46	Idaho	325
7	Illinois	1,173
17	Indiana	857
18	Iowa	848
28	Kansas	689
43	Kentucky	490
27	Louisiana	696
14	Maine	910
5	Maryland	1,184
4	Massachusetts	1,215
31	Michigan	644
38	Minnesota	570
45	Mississippi	464
24	Missouri	787
30	Montana	651
11	Nebraska	1,094
29	Nevada	660
6	New Hampshire	1,183
1	New Jersey	1,635
47	New Mexico	283
3	New York	1,367
32	North Carolina	619
20	North Dakota	829
15	Ohio	900
33	Oklahoma	609
33	Oregon	609
10	Pennsylvania	1,095
9	Rhode Island	1,135
25	South Carolina	716
23	South Dakota	788
39	Tennessee	542
13	Texas	941
40	Utah	530
49	Vermont	110
12	Virginia	986
42	Washington	509
41	West Virginia	521
19	Wisconsin	838
8	Wyoming	1,137

RANK ORDER

RANK	STATE	PER CAPITA
1	New Jersey	$1,635
2	Connecticut	1,561
3	New York	1,367
4	Massachusetts	1,215
5	Maryland	1,184
6	New Hampshire	1,183
7	Illinois	1,173
8	Wyoming	1,137
9	Rhode Island	1,135
10	Pennsylvania	1,095
11	Nebraska	1,094
12	Virginia	986
13	Texas	941
14	Maine	910
15	Ohio	900
16	Georgia	873
17	Indiana	857
18	Iowa	848
19	Wisconsin	838
20	North Dakota	829
21	Colorado	810
22	Florida	795
23	South Dakota	788
24	Missouri	787
25	South Carolina	716
26	Alaska	699
27	Louisiana	696
28	Kansas	689
29	Nevada	660
30	Montana	651
31	Michigan	644
32	North Carolina	619
33	Oklahoma	609
33	Oregon	609
35	Arizona	587
36	California	585
37	Delaware	584
38	Minnesota	570
39	Tennessee	542
40	Utah	530
41	West Virginia	521
42	Washington	509
43	Kentucky	490
44	Alabama	487
45	Mississippi	464
46	Idaho	325
47	New Mexico	283
48	Arkansas	231
49	Vermont	110
50	Hawaii	71

District of Columbia   1,209

Source: CQ Press using data from U.S. Bureau of the Census, Governments Division
"Public Education Finances: 2009" (http://www.census.gov/govs/school/)
*Revenue raised locally including taxes and charges. Includes all such revenue received by a school system from local sources (net of refunds) other than from issuance of debt or liquidation of investments. Does not include noncash transactions such as receipt of services, commodities, or other "receipts in-kind."

Public Elementary and Secondary School Revenue from Local Sources per $1,000 Personal Income in 2009
National Ratio = $20.91*

<table>
<tr><td colspan="3">ALPHA ORDER</td><td colspan="3">RANK ORDER</td></tr>
<tr><td>RANK</td><td>STATE</td><td>RATIO</td><td>RANK</td><td>STATE</td><td>RATIO</td></tr>
<tr><td>41</td><td>Alabama</td><td>$14.47</td><td>1</td><td>New Jersey</td><td>$31.86</td></tr>
<tr><td>37</td><td>Alaska</td><td>15.99</td><td>2</td><td>New York</td><td>28.52</td></tr>
<tr><td>31</td><td>Arizona</td><td>17.26</td><td>3</td><td>Nebraska</td><td>27.50</td></tr>
<tr><td>48</td><td>Arkansas</td><td>7.12</td><td>4</td><td>Connecticut</td><td>27.39</td></tr>
<tr><td>43</td><td>California</td><td>13.42</td><td>5</td><td>Illinois</td><td>27.33</td></tr>
<tr><td>25</td><td>Colorado</td><td>18.95</td><td>6</td><td>New Hampshire</td><td>27.20</td></tr>
<tr><td>4</td><td>Connecticut</td><td>27.39</td><td>7</td><td>Rhode Island</td><td>27.19</td></tr>
<tr><td>41</td><td>Delaware</td><td>14.47</td><td>8</td><td>Pennsylvania</td><td>27.18</td></tr>
<tr><td>24</td><td>Florida</td><td>19.98</td><td>9</td><td>Georgia</td><td>25.14</td></tr>
<tr><td>9</td><td>Georgia</td><td>25.14</td><td>10</td><td>Ohio</td><td>24.96</td></tr>
<tr><td>50</td><td>Hawaii</td><td>1.68</td><td>11</td><td>Maine</td><td>24.89</td></tr>
<tr><td>46</td><td>Idaho</td><td>9.99</td><td>12</td><td>Indiana</td><td>24.65</td></tr>
<tr><td>5</td><td>Illinois</td><td>27.33</td><td>13</td><td>Maryland</td><td>24.64</td></tr>
<tr><td>12</td><td>Indiana</td><td>24.65</td><td>14</td><td>Texas</td><td>24.09</td></tr>
<tr><td>17</td><td>Iowa</td><td>22.29</td><td>15</td><td>Massachusetts</td><td>24.00</td></tr>
<tr><td>30</td><td>Kansas</td><td>17.31</td><td>16</td><td>Wyoming</td><td>22.96</td></tr>
<tr><td>39</td><td>Kentucky</td><td>15.24</td><td>17</td><td>Iowa</td><td>22.29</td></tr>
<tr><td>27</td><td>Louisiana</td><td>18.43</td><td>18</td><td>Virginia</td><td>22.27</td></tr>
<tr><td>11</td><td>Maine</td><td>24.89</td><td>19</td><td>Wisconsin</td><td>22.20</td></tr>
<tr><td>13</td><td>Maryland</td><td>24.64</td><td>20</td><td>South Carolina</td><td>22.02</td></tr>
<tr><td>15</td><td>Massachusetts</td><td>24.00</td><td>21</td><td>Missouri</td><td>21.51</td></tr>
<tr><td>28</td><td>Michigan</td><td>18.18</td><td>22</td><td>South Dakota</td><td>20.29</td></tr>
<tr><td>44</td><td>Minnesota</td><td>13.28</td><td>23</td><td>North Dakota</td><td>20.15</td></tr>
<tr><td>40</td><td>Mississippi</td><td>15.17</td><td>24</td><td>Florida</td><td>19.98</td></tr>
<tr><td>21</td><td>Missouri</td><td>21.51</td><td>25</td><td>Colorado</td><td>18.95</td></tr>
<tr><td>26</td><td>Montana</td><td>18.60</td><td>26</td><td>Montana</td><td>18.60</td></tr>
<tr><td>3</td><td>Nebraska</td><td>27.50</td><td>27</td><td>Louisiana</td><td>18.43</td></tr>
<tr><td>34</td><td>Nevada</td><td>16.63</td><td>28</td><td>Michigan</td><td>18.18</td></tr>
<tr><td>6</td><td>New Hampshire</td><td>27.20</td><td>29</td><td>North Carolina</td><td>17.66</td></tr>
<tr><td>1</td><td>New Jersey</td><td>31.86</td><td>30</td><td>Kansas</td><td>17.31</td></tr>
<tr><td>47</td><td>New Mexico</td><td>8.52</td><td>31</td><td>Arizona</td><td>17.26</td></tr>
<tr><td>2</td><td>New York</td><td>28.52</td><td>32</td><td>Oregon</td><td>16.74</td></tr>
<tr><td>29</td><td>North Carolina</td><td>17.66</td><td>33</td><td>Oklahoma</td><td>16.69</td></tr>
<tr><td>23</td><td>North Dakota</td><td>20.15</td><td>34</td><td>Nevada</td><td>16.63</td></tr>
<tr><td>10</td><td>Ohio</td><td>24.96</td><td>35</td><td>Utah</td><td>16.60</td></tr>
<tr><td>33</td><td>Oklahoma</td><td>16.69</td><td>36</td><td>West Virginia</td><td>16.56</td></tr>
<tr><td>32</td><td>Oregon</td><td>16.74</td><td>37</td><td>Alaska</td><td>15.99</td></tr>
<tr><td>8</td><td>Pennsylvania</td><td>27.18</td><td>38</td><td>Tennessee</td><td>15.57</td></tr>
<tr><td>7</td><td>Rhode Island</td><td>27.19</td><td>39</td><td>Kentucky</td><td>15.24</td></tr>
<tr><td>20</td><td>South Carolina</td><td>22.02</td><td>40</td><td>Mississippi</td><td>15.17</td></tr>
<tr><td>22</td><td>South Dakota</td><td>20.29</td><td>41</td><td>Alabama</td><td>14.47</td></tr>
<tr><td>38</td><td>Tennessee</td><td>15.57</td><td>41</td><td>Delaware</td><td>14.47</td></tr>
<tr><td>14</td><td>Texas</td><td>24.09</td><td>43</td><td>California</td><td>13.42</td></tr>
<tr><td>35</td><td>Utah</td><td>16.60</td><td>44</td><td>Minnesota</td><td>13.28</td></tr>
<tr><td>49</td><td>Vermont</td><td>2.81</td><td>45</td><td>Washington</td><td>11.82</td></tr>
<tr><td>18</td><td>Virginia</td><td>22.27</td><td>46</td><td>Idaho</td><td>9.99</td></tr>
<tr><td>45</td><td>Washington</td><td>11.82</td><td>47</td><td>New Mexico</td><td>8.52</td></tr>
<tr><td>36</td><td>West Virginia</td><td>16.56</td><td>48</td><td>Arkansas</td><td>7.12</td></tr>
<tr><td>19</td><td>Wisconsin</td><td>22.20</td><td>49</td><td>Vermont</td><td>2.81</td></tr>
<tr><td>16</td><td>Wyoming</td><td>22.96</td><td>50</td><td>Hawaii</td><td>1.68</td></tr>
<tr><td></td><td></td><td></td><td></td><td>District of Columbia</td><td>17.97</td></tr>
</table>

Source: U.S. Bureau of the Census, Governments Division
"Public Education Finances: 2009" (http://www.census.gov/govs/school/)
*Revenue raised locally including taxes and charges. Includes all such revenue received by a school system from local sources (net of refunds) other than from issuance of debt or liquidation of investments. Does not include noncash transactions such as receipt of services, commodities, or other "receipts in-kind."

Per Pupil Elementary and Secondary School Revenue from Local Sources in 2009
National Per Pupil = $5,367*

ALPHA ORDER

RANK	STATE	PER PUPIL
43	Alabama	$3,078
35	Alaska	3,750
34	Arizona	3,942
48	Arkansas	1,407
38	California	3,507
24	Colorado	5,007
2	Connecticut	10,042
28	Delaware	4,429
16	Florida	5,621
21	Georgia	5,204
50	Hawaii	512
46	Idaho	1,877
9	Illinois	7,154
18	Indiana	5,350
20	Iowa	5,232
30	Kansas	4,132
42	Kentucky	3,157
25	Louisiana	4,714
12	Maine	6,425
7	Maryland	7,999
4	Massachusetts	8,595
31	Michigan	4,128
36	Minnesota	3,741
44	Mississippi	2,791
19	Missouri	5,242
27	Montana	4,480
11	Nebraska	6,729
32	Nevada	4,046
8	New Hampshire	7,919
1	New Jersey	10,474
47	New Mexico	1,728
3	New York	9,904
33	North Carolina	3,997
15	North Dakota	5,667
14	Ohio	6,011
39	Oklahoma	3,483
29	Oregon	4,147
6	Pennsylvania	8,141
5	Rhode Island	8,449
26	South Carolina	4,574
22	South Dakota	5,059
37	Tennessee	3,513
23	Texas	5,016
45	Utah	2,771
49	Vermont	776
13	Virginia	6,290
41	Washington	3,275
40	West Virginia	3,360
17	Wisconsin	5,464
10	Wyoming	7,118

RANK ORDER

RANK	STATE	PER PUPIL
1	New Jersey	$10,474
2	Connecticut	10,042
3	New York	9,904
4	Massachusetts	8,595
5	Rhode Island	8,449
6	Pennsylvania	8,141
7	Maryland	7,999
8	New Hampshire	7,919
9	Illinois	7,154
10	Wyoming	7,118
11	Nebraska	6,729
12	Maine	6,425
13	Virginia	6,290
14	Ohio	6,011
15	North Dakota	5,667
16	Florida	5,621
17	Wisconsin	5,464
18	Indiana	5,350
19	Missouri	5,242
20	Iowa	5,232
21	Georgia	5,204
22	South Dakota	5,059
23	Texas	5,016
24	Colorado	5,007
25	Louisiana	4,714
26	South Carolina	4,574
27	Montana	4,480
28	Delaware	4,429
29	Oregon	4,147
30	Kansas	4,132
31	Michigan	4,128
32	Nevada	4,046
33	North Carolina	3,997
34	Arizona	3,942
35	Alaska	3,750
36	Minnesota	3,741
37	Tennessee	3,513
38	California	3,507
39	Oklahoma	3,483
40	West Virginia	3,360
41	Washington	3,275
42	Kentucky	3,157
43	Alabama	3,078
44	Mississippi	2,791
45	Utah	2,771
46	Idaho	1,877
47	New Mexico	1,728
48	Arkansas	1,407
49	Vermont	776
50	Hawaii	512

District of Columbia   16,358

Source: U.S. Bureau of the Census, Governments Division
"Public Education Finances: 2009" (http://www.census.gov/govs/school/)
*Based on student membership. Revenue raised locally including taxes and charges. Includes all such revenue received by a school system from local sources (net of refunds) other than from issuance of debt or liquidation of investments. Does not include noncash transactions such as receipt of services, commodities, or other "receipts in-kind."

Percent of Public Elementary and Secondary School Revenue from Local Sources in 2009
National Percent = 43.8%*

ALPHA ORDER

RANK	STATE	PERCENT
37	Alabama	31.9
46	Alaska	22.6
22	Arizona	44.4
48	Arkansas	14.1
42	California	30.3
14	Colorado	49.2
1	Connecticut	57.8
40	Delaware	30.9
5	Florida	55.7
18	Georgia	47.8
50	Hawaii	3.4
45	Idaho	23.1
3	Illinois	57.4
24	Indiana	43.3
21	Iowa	46.1
35	Kansas	34.6
38	Kentucky	31.5
28	Louisiana	39.4
19	Maine	47.0
11	Maryland	51.4
9	Massachusetts	52.8
36	Michigan	34.4
43	Minnesota	29.5
39	Mississippi	31.3
13	Missouri	50.1
27	Montana	39.8
4	Nebraska	57.0
29	Nevada	39.3
2	New Hampshire	57.7
6	New Jersey	55.5
47	New Mexico	15.3
17	New York	48.0
31	North Carolina	37.7
15	North Dakota	48.6
20	Ohio	46.9
32	Oklahoma	37.2
30	Oregon	38.2
8	Pennsylvania	54.2
7	Rhode Island	55.2
25	South Carolina	42.7
12	South Dakota	51.0
26	Tennessee	42.2
15	Texas	48.6
34	Utah	34.8
49	Vermont	4.5
10	Virginia	51.8
44	Washington	28.5
41	West Virginia	30.6
23	Wisconsin	43.9
33	Wyoming	37.0

RANK ORDER

RANK	STATE	PERCENT
1	Connecticut	57.8
2	New Hampshire	57.7
3	Illinois	57.4
4	Nebraska	57.0
5	Florida	55.7
6	New Jersey	55.5
7	Rhode Island	55.2
8	Pennsylvania	54.2
9	Massachusetts	52.8
10	Virginia	51.8
11	Maryland	51.4
12	South Dakota	51.0
13	Missouri	50.1
14	Colorado	49.2
15	North Dakota	48.6
15	Texas	48.6
17	New York	48.0
18	Georgia	47.8
19	Maine	47.0
20	Ohio	46.9
21	Iowa	46.1
22	Arizona	44.4
23	Wisconsin	43.9
24	Indiana	43.3
25	South Carolina	42.7
26	Tennessee	42.2
27	Montana	39.8
28	Louisiana	39.4
29	Nevada	39.3
30	Oregon	38.2
31	North Carolina	37.7
32	Oklahoma	37.2
33	Wyoming	37.0
34	Utah	34.8
35	Kansas	34.6
36	Michigan	34.4
37	Alabama	31.9
38	Kentucky	31.5
39	Mississippi	31.3
40	Delaware	30.9
41	West Virginia	30.6
42	California	30.3
43	Minnesota	29.5
44	Washington	28.5
45	Idaho	23.1
46	Alaska	22.6
47	New Mexico	15.3
48	Arkansas	14.1
49	Vermont	4.5
50	Hawaii	3.4

District of Columbia   90.5

Source: U.S. Bureau of the Census, Governments Division
    "Public Education Finances: 2009" (http://www.census.gov/govs/school/)
*Revenue raised locally including taxes and charges. Includes all such revenue received by a school system from local sources (net of refunds) other than from issuance of debt or liquidation of investments. Does not include noncash transactions such as receipt of services, commodities, or other "receipts in-kind."

Public Elementary and Secondary School Local Source Revenue from Property Taxes in 2009
National Total = $168,767,677,000*

ALPHA ORDER

RANK	STATE	REVENUE	% of USA
30	Alabama	$1,043,592,000	0.6%
43	Alaska	0	0.0%
15	Arizona	3,169,024,000	1.9%
39	Arkansas	405,905,000	0.2%
2	California	16,038,031,000	9.5%
14	Colorado	3,323,314,000	2.0%
43	Connecticut	0	0.0%
35	Delaware	435,191,000	0.3%
5	Florida	12,452,512,000	7.4%
9	Georgia	5,941,223,000	3.5%
43	Hawaii	0	0.0%
37	Idaho	414,072,000	0.2%
4	Illinois	13,799,888,000	8.2%
12	Indiana	4,186,392,000	2.5%
20	Iowa	1,686,808,000	1.0%
23	Kansas	1,506,567,000	0.9%
24	Kentucky	1,473,780,000	0.9%
28	Louisiana	1,173,329,000	0.7%
33	Maine	504,809,000	0.3%
43	Maryland	0	0.0%
43	Massachusetts	0	0.0%
10	Michigan	5,492,955,000	3.3%
19	Minnesota	1,801,162,000	1.1%
29	Mississippi	1,050,314,000	0.6%
13	Missouri	3,645,315,000	2.2%
40	Montana	390,430,000	0.2%
22	Nebraska	1,580,047,000	0.9%
25	Nevada	1,469,207,000	0.9%
27	New Hampshire	1,256,778,000	0.7%
6	New Jersey	11,678,659,000	6.9%
34	New Mexico	442,388,000	0.3%
3	New York	15,434,453,000	9.1%
43	North Carolina	0	0.0%
36	North Dakota	432,925,000	0.3%
8	Ohio	8,411,117,000	5.0%
21	Oklahoma	1,642,175,000	1.0%
18	Oregon	1,833,322,000	1.1%
7	Pennsylvania	11,014,689,000	6.5%
41	Rhode Island	101,069,000	0.1%
17	South Carolina	2,506,295,000	1.5%
32	South Dakota	525,199,000	0.3%
43	Tennessee	0	0.0%
1	Texas	20,950,962,000	12.4%
26	Utah	1,264,881,000	0.7%
42	Vermont	1,853,000	0.0%
43	Virginia	0	0.0%
16	Washington	2,723,516,000	1.6%
31	West Virginia	867,339,000	0.5%
11	Wisconsin	4,284,208,000	2.5%
38	Wyoming	411,982,000	0.2%

RANK ORDER

RANK	STATE	REVENUE	% of USA
1	Texas	$20,950,962,000	12.4%
2	California	16,038,031,000	9.5%
3	New York	15,434,453,000	9.1%
4	Illinois	13,799,888,000	8.2%
5	Florida	12,452,512,000	7.4%
6	New Jersey	11,678,659,000	6.9%
7	Pennsylvania	11,014,689,000	6.5%
8	Ohio	8,411,117,000	5.0%
9	Georgia	5,941,223,000	3.5%
10	Michigan	5,492,955,000	3.3%
11	Wisconsin	4,284,208,000	2.5%
12	Indiana	4,186,392,000	2.5%
13	Missouri	3,645,315,000	2.2%
14	Colorado	3,323,314,000	2.0%
15	Arizona	3,169,024,000	1.9%
16	Washington	2,723,516,000	1.6%
17	South Carolina	2,506,295,000	1.5%
18	Oregon	1,833,322,000	1.1%
19	Minnesota	1,801,162,000	1.1%
20	Iowa	1,686,808,000	1.0%
21	Oklahoma	1,642,175,000	1.0%
22	Nebraska	1,580,047,000	0.9%
23	Kansas	1,506,567,000	0.9%
24	Kentucky	1,473,780,000	0.9%
25	Nevada	1,469,207,000	0.9%
26	Utah	1,264,881,000	0.7%
27	New Hampshire	1,256,778,000	0.7%
28	Louisiana	1,173,329,000	0.7%
29	Mississippi	1,050,314,000	0.6%
30	Alabama	1,043,592,000	0.6%
31	West Virginia	867,339,000	0.5%
32	South Dakota	525,199,000	0.3%
33	Maine	504,809,000	0.3%
34	New Mexico	442,388,000	0.3%
35	Delaware	435,191,000	0.3%
36	North Dakota	432,925,000	0.3%
37	Idaho	414,072,000	0.2%
38	Wyoming	411,982,000	0.2%
39	Arkansas	405,905,000	0.2%
40	Montana	390,430,000	0.2%
41	Rhode Island	101,069,000	0.1%
42	Vermont	1,853,000	0.0%
43	Alaska	0	0.0%
43	Connecticut	0	0.0%
43	Hawaii	0	0.0%
43	Maryland	0	0.0%
43	Massachusetts	0	0.0%
43	North Carolina	0	0.0%
43	Tennessee	0	0.0%
43	Virginia	0	0.0%
	District of Columbia	0	0.0%

Source: U.S. Bureau of the Census, Governments Division
   "Public Education Finances: 2009" (http://www.census.gov/govs/school/)
*Revenue from taxes based on ownership of property and measured by its value. Includes general property taxes relating to property as a whole, real and personal, tangible or intangible, whether taxed at a single rate or at classified rates, and taxes on selected types of property, such as motor vehicles or certain or all intangibles.

Percent of Public Elementary and Secondary School Local Source Revenue from Property Taxes in 2009
National Percent = 65.2%*

ALPHA ORDER

RANK	STATE	PERCENT
38	Alabama	45.5
43	Alaska	0.0
13	Arizona	81.9
35	Arkansas	60.8
28	California	74.2
14	Colorado	81.7
43	Connecticut	0.0
9	Delaware	84.1
7	Florida	84.4
31	Georgia	69.2
43	Hawaii	0.0
10	Idaho	82.3
2	Illinois	91.1
27	Indiana	76.1
33	Iowa	66.1
23	Kansas	77.5
30	Kentucky	69.7
40	Louisiana	37.6
39	Maine	42.1
43	Maryland	0.0
43	Massachusetts	0.0
6	Michigan	85.5
36	Minnesota	60.0
26	Mississippi	76.6
24	Missouri	77.4
34	Montana	61.5
17	Nebraska	80.4
8	Nevada	84.3
18	New Hampshire	80.2
11	New Jersey	82.0
22	New Mexico	77.9
37	New York	57.8
43	North Carolina	0.0
16	North Dakota	80.7
15	Ohio	80.9
29	Oklahoma	73.2
21	Oregon	78.7
20	Pennsylvania	79.8
41	Rhode Island	8.5
25	South Carolina	76.7
11	South Dakota	82.0
43	Tennessee	0.0
4	Texas	89.9
5	Utah	85.7
42	Vermont	2.7
43	Virginia	0.0
18	Washington	80.2
1	West Virginia	91.6
3	Wisconsin	90.4
32	Wyoming	66.5

RANK ORDER

RANK	STATE	PERCENT
1	West Virginia	91.6
2	Illinois	91.1
3	Wisconsin	90.4
4	Texas	89.9
5	Utah	85.7
6	Michigan	85.5
7	Florida	84.4
8	Nevada	84.3
9	Delaware	84.1
10	Idaho	82.3
11	New Jersey	82.0
11	South Dakota	82.0
13	Arizona	81.9
14	Colorado	81.7
15	Ohio	80.9
16	North Dakota	80.7
17	Nebraska	80.4
18	New Hampshire	80.2
18	Washington	80.2
20	Pennsylvania	79.8
21	Oregon	78.7
22	New Mexico	77.9
23	Kansas	77.5
24	Missouri	77.4
25	South Carolina	76.7
26	Mississippi	76.6
27	Indiana	76.1
28	California	74.2
29	Oklahoma	73.2
30	Kentucky	69.7
31	Georgia	69.2
32	Wyoming	66.5
33	Iowa	66.1
34	Montana	61.5
35	Arkansas	60.8
36	Minnesota	60.0
37	New York	57.8
38	Alabama	45.5
39	Maine	42.1
40	Louisiana	37.6
41	Rhode Island	8.5
42	Vermont	2.7
43	Alaska	0.0
43	Connecticut	0.0
43	Hawaii	0.0
43	Maryland	0.0
43	Massachusetts	0.0
43	North Carolina	0.0
43	Tennessee	0.0
43	Virginia	0.0

District of Columbia   0.0

Source: CQ Press using data from U.S. Bureau of the Census, Governments Division
        "Public Education Finances: 2009" (http://www.census.gov/govs/school/)
*Revenue from taxes based on ownership of property and measured by its value. Includes general property taxes relating to property as a whole, real and personal, tangible or intangible, whether taxed at a single rate or at classified rates, and taxes on selected types of property, such as motor vehicles or certain or all intangibles.

Public Elementary and Secondary School Local Source Revenue
from Other Local Taxes in 2009
National Total = $7,134,268,000*

ALPHA ORDER				RANK ORDER			
RANK	STATE	REVENUE	% of USA	RANK	STATE	REVENUE	% of USA
12	Alabama	$36,747,000	0.5%	1	Pennsylvania	$1,676,021,000	23.5%
25	Alaska	0	0.0%	2	Louisiana	1,604,626,000	22.5%
25	Arizona	0	0.0%	3	Georgia	1,578,031,000	22.1%
20	Arkansas	1,251,000	0.0%	4	Iowa	545,855,000	7.7%
5	California	401,423,000	5.6%	5	California	401,423,000	5.6%
14	Colorado	22,775,000	0.3%	6	Kentucky	381,100,000	5.3%
25	Connecticut	0	0.0%	7	Ohio	364,401,000	5.1%
25	Delaware	0	0.0%	8	Missouri	202,120,000	2.8%
25	Florida	0	0.0%	9	Nebraska	144,658,000	2.0%
3	Georgia	1,578,031,000	22.1%	10	New York	50,430,000	0.7%
25	Hawaii	0	0.0%	11	South Carolina	48,816,000	0.7%
25	Idaho	0	0.0%	12	Alabama	36,747,000	0.5%
13	Illinois	27,046,000	0.4%	13	Illinois	27,046,000	0.4%
21	Indiana	910,000	0.0%	14	Colorado	22,775,000	0.3%
4	Iowa	545,855,000	7.7%	15	South Dakota	19,549,000	0.3%
25	Kansas	0	0.0%	16	Mississippi	17,793,000	0.2%
6	Kentucky	381,100,000	5.3%	17	Wyoming	4,212,000	0.1%
2	Louisiana	1,604,626,000	22.5%	18	Nevada	3,395,000	0.0%
24	Maine	11,000	0.0%	19	Vermont	2,329,000	0.0%
25	Maryland	0	0.0%	20	Arkansas	1,251,000	0.0%
25	Massachusetts	0	0.0%	21	Indiana	910,000	0.0%
25	Michigan	0	0.0%	22	Washington	654,000	0.0%
25	Minnesota	0	0.0%	23	West Virginia	115,000	0.0%
16	Mississippi	17,793,000	0.2%	24	Maine	11,000	0.0%
8	Missouri	202,120,000	2.8%	25	Alaska	0	0.0%
25	Montana	0	0.0%	25	Arizona	0	0.0%
9	Nebraska	144,658,000	2.0%	25	Connecticut	0	0.0%
18	Nevada	3,395,000	0.0%	25	Delaware	0	0.0%
25	New Hampshire	0	0.0%	25	Florida	0	0.0%
25	New Jersey	0	0.0%	25	Hawaii	0	0.0%
25	New Mexico	0	0.0%	25	Idaho	0	0.0%
10	New York	50,430,000	0.7%	25	Kansas	0	0.0%
25	North Carolina	0	0.0%	25	Maryland	0	0.0%
25	North Dakota	0	0.0%	25	Massachusetts	0	0.0%
7	Ohio	364,401,000	5.1%	25	Michigan	0	0.0%
25	Oklahoma	0	0.0%	25	Minnesota	0	0.0%
25	Oregon	0	0.0%	25	Montana	0	0.0%
1	Pennsylvania	1,676,021,000	23.5%	25	New Hampshire	0	0.0%
25	Rhode Island	0	0.0%	25	New Jersey	0	0.0%
11	South Carolina	48,816,000	0.7%	25	New Mexico	0	0.0%
15	South Dakota	19,549,000	0.3%	25	North Carolina	0	0.0%
25	Tennessee	0	0.0%	25	North Dakota	0	0.0%
25	Texas	0	0.0%	25	Oklahoma	0	0.0%
25	Utah	0	0.0%	25	Oregon	0	0.0%
19	Vermont	2,329,000	0.0%	25	Rhode Island	0	0.0%
25	Virginia	0	0.0%	25	Tennessee	0	0.0%
22	Washington	654,000	0.0%	25	Texas	0	0.0%
23	West Virginia	115,000	0.0%	25	Utah	0	0.0%
25	Wisconsin	0	0.0%	25	Virginia	0	0.0%
17	Wyoming	4,212,000	0.1%	25	Wisconsin	0	0.0%
					District of Columbia	0	0.0%

Source: U.S. Bureau of the Census, Governments Division
    "Public Education Finances: 2009" (http://www.census.gov/govs/school/)
*Revenue from taxes other than property taxes.

Percent of Public Elementary and Secondary School Local Source Revenue from Other Local Taxes in 2009
National Percent = 2.8%*

ALPHA ORDER

RANK	STATE	PERCENT
12	Alabama	1.6
21	Alaska	0.0
21	Arizona	0.0
17	Arkansas	0.2
11	California	1.9
16	Colorado	0.6
21	Connecticut	0.0
21	Delaware	0.0
21	Florida	0.0
3	Georgia	18.4
21	Hawaii	0.0
21	Idaho	0.0
17	Illinois	0.2
21	Indiana	0.0
2	Iowa	21.4
21	Kansas	0.0
4	Kentucky	18.0
1	Louisiana	51.4
21	Maine	0.0
21	Maryland	0.0
21	Massachusetts	0.0
21	Michigan	0.0
21	Minnesota	0.0
14	Mississippi	1.3
7	Missouri	4.3
21	Montana	0.0
6	Nebraska	7.4
17	Nevada	0.2
21	New Hampshire	0.0
21	New Jersey	0.0
21	New Mexico	0.0
17	New York	0.2
21	North Carolina	0.0
21	North Dakota	0.0
8	Ohio	3.5
21	Oklahoma	0.0
21	Oregon	0.0
5	Pennsylvania	12.1
21	Rhode Island	0.0
13	South Carolina	1.5
10	South Dakota	3.1
21	Tennessee	0.0
21	Texas	0.0
21	Utah	0.0
9	Vermont	3.4
21	Virginia	0.0
21	Washington	0.0
21	West Virginia	0.0
21	Wisconsin	0.0
15	Wyoming	0.7

RANK ORDER

RANK	STATE	PERCENT
1	Louisiana	51.4
2	Iowa	21.4
3	Georgia	18.4
4	Kentucky	18.0
5	Pennsylvania	12.1
6	Nebraska	7.4
7	Missouri	4.3
8	Ohio	3.5
9	Vermont	3.4
10	South Dakota	3.1
11	California	1.9
12	Alabama	1.6
13	South Carolina	1.5
14	Mississippi	1.3
15	Wyoming	0.7
16	Colorado	0.6
17	Arkansas	0.2
17	Illinois	0.2
17	Nevada	0.2
17	New York	0.2
21	Alaska	0.0
21	Arizona	0.0
21	Connecticut	0.0
21	Delaware	0.0
21	Florida	0.0
21	Hawaii	0.0
21	Idaho	0.0
21	Indiana	0.0
21	Kansas	0.0
21	Maine	0.0
21	Maryland	0.0
21	Massachusetts	0.0
21	Michigan	0.0
21	Minnesota	0.0
21	Montana	0.0
21	New Hampshire	0.0
21	New Jersey	0.0
21	New Mexico	0.0
21	North Carolina	0.0
21	North Dakota	0.0
21	Oklahoma	0.0
21	Oregon	0.0
21	Rhode Island	0.0
21	Tennessee	0.0
21	Texas	0.0
21	Utah	0.0
21	Virginia	0.0
21	Washington	0.0
21	West Virginia	0.0
21	Wisconsin	0.0
	District of Columbia	0.0

Source: CQ Press using data from U.S. Bureau of the Census, Governments Division
"Public Education Finances: 2009" (http://www.census.gov/govs/school/)
*Revenue from taxes other than property taxes.

Public Elementary and Secondary School Local Source Revenue
from Parent Government Contributions in 2009
National Total = $45,826,172,000*

ALPHA ORDER

RANK	STATE	REVENUE	% of USA
18	Alabama	$0	0.0%
12	Alaska	420,634,000	0.9%
15	Arizona	3,354,000	0.0%
18	Arkansas	0	0.0%
10	California	854,000,000	1.9%
18	Colorado	0	0.0%
6	Connecticut	4,950,734,000	10.8%
18	Delaware	0	0.0%
18	Florida	0	0.0%
18	Georgia	0	0.0%
18	Hawaii	0	0.0%
18	Idaho	0	0.0%
18	Illinois	0	0.0%
17	Indiana	636,000	0.0%
18	Iowa	0	0.0%
18	Kansas	0	0.0%
18	Kentucky	0	0.0%
18	Louisiana	0	0.0%
11	Maine	628,339,000	1.4%
4	Maryland	6,293,112,000	13.7%
3	Massachusetts	6,356,428,000	13.9%
18	Michigan	0	0.0%
18	Minnesota	0	0.0%
16	Mississippi	2,905,000	0.0%
18	Missouri	0	0.0%
18	Montana	0	0.0%
18	Nebraska	0	0.0%
18	Nevada	0	0.0%
13	New Hampshire	226,517,000	0.5%
9	New Jersey	880,389,000	1.9%
18	New Mexico	0	0.0%
1	New York	8,815,469,000	19.2%
5	North Carolina	5,125,672,000	11.2%
18	North Dakota	0	0.0%
18	Ohio	0	0.0%
18	Oklahoma	0	0.0%
18	Oregon	0	0.0%
18	Pennsylvania	0	0.0%
8	Rhode Island	1,062,505,000	2.3%
18	South Carolina	0	0.0%
18	South Dakota	0	0.0%
7	Tennessee	2,195,077,000	4.8%
18	Texas	0	0.0%
18	Utah	0	0.0%
18	Vermont	0	0.0%
2	Virginia	7,287,119,000	15.9%
18	Washington	0	0.0%
18	West Virginia	0	0.0%
14	Wisconsin	11,426,000	0.0%
18	Wyoming	0	0.0%

RANK ORDER

RANK	STATE	REVENUE	% of USA
1	New York	$8,815,469,000	19.2%
2	Virginia	7,287,119,000	15.9%
3	Massachusetts	6,356,428,000	13.9%
4	Maryland	6,293,112,000	13.7%
5	North Carolina	5,125,672,000	11.2%
6	Connecticut	4,950,734,000	10.8%
7	Tennessee	2,195,077,000	4.8%
8	Rhode Island	1,062,505,000	2.3%
9	New Jersey	880,389,000	1.9%
10	California	854,000,000	1.9%
11	Maine	628,339,000	1.4%
12	Alaska	420,634,000	0.9%
13	New Hampshire	226,517,000	0.5%
14	Wisconsin	11,426,000	0.0%
15	Arizona	3,354,000	0.0%
16	Mississippi	2,905,000	0.0%
17	Indiana	636,000	0.0%
18	Alabama	0	0.0%
18	Arkansas	0	0.0%
18	Colorado	0	0.0%
18	Delaware	0	0.0%
18	Florida	0	0.0%
18	Georgia	0	0.0%
18	Hawaii	0	0.0%
18	Idaho	0	0.0%
18	Illinois	0	0.0%
18	Iowa	0	0.0%
18	Kansas	0	0.0%
18	Kentucky	0	0.0%
18	Louisiana	0	0.0%
18	Michigan	0	0.0%
18	Minnesota	0	0.0%
18	Missouri	0	0.0%
18	Montana	0	0.0%
18	Nebraska	0	0.0%
18	Nevada	0	0.0%
18	New Mexico	0	0.0%
18	North Dakota	0	0.0%
18	Ohio	0	0.0%
18	Oklahoma	0	0.0%
18	Oregon	0	0.0%
18	Pennsylvania	0	0.0%
18	South Carolina	0	0.0%
18	South Dakota	0	0.0%
18	Texas	0	0.0%
18	Utah	0	0.0%
18	Vermont	0	0.0%
18	Washington	0	0.0%
18	West Virginia	0	0.0%
18	Wyoming	0	0.0%
	District of Columbia	711,856,000	1.6%

Source: U.S. Bureau of the Census, Governments Division
   "Public Education Finances: 2009" (http://www.census.gov/govs/school/)
*Tax receipts and other amounts appropriated by a parent government and transferred to its dependent school system. Although most of this revenue comes from property tax collections, the exact amounts derived from taxes or other revenue sources available to parent governments for their school systems frequently cannot be determined from state education agency accounting records and are therefore shown as parent government contributions.

Percent of Public Elementary and Secondary School Local Source Revenue from Parent Government Contributions in 2009
National Percent = 17.7%*

ALPHA ORDER

RANK	STATE	PERCENT
17	Alabama	0.0
6	Alaska	86.1
16	Arizona	0.1
17	Arkansas	0.0
13	California	3.9
17	Colorado	0.0
3	Connecticut	90.1
17	Delaware	0.0
17	Florida	0.0
17	Georgia	0.0
17	Hawaii	0.0
17	Idaho	0.0
17	Illinois	0.0
17	Indiana	0.0
17	Iowa	0.0
17	Kansas	0.0
17	Kentucky	0.0
17	Louisiana	0.0
9	Maine	52.4
2	Maryland	93.2
7	Massachusetts	79.3
17	Michigan	0.0
17	Minnesota	0.0
14	Mississippi	0.2
17	Missouri	0.0
17	Montana	0.0
17	Nebraska	0.0
17	Nevada	0.0
11	New Hampshire	14.5
12	New Jersey	6.2
17	New Mexico	0.0
10	New York	33.0
5	North Carolina	88.3
17	North Dakota	0.0
17	Ohio	0.0
17	Oklahoma	0.0
17	Oregon	0.0
17	Pennsylvania	0.0
4	Rhode Island	88.9
17	South Carolina	0.0
17	South Dakota	0.0
8	Tennessee	64.4
17	Texas	0.0
17	Utah	0.0
17	Vermont	0.0
1	Virginia	93.8
17	Washington	0.0
17	West Virginia	0.0
14	Wisconsin	0.2
17	Wyoming	0.0

RANK ORDER

RANK	STATE	PERCENT
1	Virginia	93.8
2	Maryland	93.2
3	Connecticut	90.1
4	Rhode Island	88.9
5	North Carolina	88.3
6	Alaska	86.1
7	Massachusetts	79.3
8	Tennessee	64.4
9	Maine	52.4
10	New York	33.0
11	New Hampshire	14.5
12	New Jersey	6.2
13	California	3.9
14	Mississippi	0.2
14	Wisconsin	0.2
16	Arizona	0.1
17	Alabama	0.0
17	Arkansas	0.0
17	Colorado	0.0
17	Delaware	0.0
17	Florida	0.0
17	Georgia	0.0
17	Hawaii	0.0
17	Idaho	0.0
17	Illinois	0.0
17	Indiana	0.0
17	Iowa	0.0
17	Kansas	0.0
17	Kentucky	0.0
17	Louisiana	0.0
17	Michigan	0.0
17	Minnesota	0.0
17	Missouri	0.0
17	Montana	0.0
17	Nebraska	0.0
17	Nevada	0.0
17	New Mexico	0.0
17	North Dakota	0.0
17	Ohio	0.0
17	Oklahoma	0.0
17	Oregon	0.0
17	Pennsylvania	0.0
17	South Carolina	0.0
17	South Dakota	0.0
17	Texas	0.0
17	Utah	0.0
17	Vermont	0.0
17	Washington	0.0
17	West Virginia	0.0
17	Wyoming	0.0

District of Columbia 98.2

Source: CQ Press using data from U.S. Bureau of the Census, Governments Division
"Public Education Finances: 2009" (http://www.census.gov/govs/school/)
*Tax receipts and other amounts appropriated by a parent government and transferred to its dependent school system. Although most of this revenue comes from property tax collections, the exact amounts derived from taxes or other revenue sources available to parent governments for their school systems frequently cannot be determined from state education agency accounting records and are therefore shown as parent government contributions.

Public Elementary and Secondary School Local Source Revenue
from Nonschool Local Government in 2009
National Total = $5,923,935,000*

ALPHA ORDER

RANK	STATE	REVENUE	% of USA
3	Alabama	$634,846,000	10.7%
41	Alaska	0	0.0%
24	Arizona	27,262,000	0.5%
32	Arkansas	8,067,000	0.1%
6	California	341,736,000	5.8%
29	Colorado	13,697,000	0.2%
5	Connecticut	389,053,000	6.6%
41	Delaware	0	0.0%
41	Florida	0	0.0%
9	Georgia	186,276,000	3.1%
41	Hawaii	0	0.0%
40	Idaho	140,000	0.0%
41	Illinois	0	0.0%
4	Indiana	502,089,000	8.5%
33	Iowa	5,977,000	0.1%
18	Kansas	105,022,000	1.8%
23	Kentucky	32,551,000	0.5%
22	Louisiana	35,130,000	0.6%
30	Maine	9,916,000	0.2%
41	Maryland	0	0.0%
1	Massachusetts	993,333,000	16.8%
25	Michigan	22,995,000	0.4%
14	Minnesota	153,617,000	2.6%
27	Mississippi	20,887,000	0.4%
13	Missouri	156,331,000	2.6%
16	Montana	132,311,000	2.2%
26	Nebraska	22,330,000	0.4%
35	Nevada	2,616,000	0.0%
39	New Hampshire	296,000	0.0%
8	New Jersey	234,151,000	4.0%
41	New Mexico	0	0.0%
7	New York	234,869,000	4.0%
41	North Carolina	0	0.0%
28	North Dakota	20,868,000	0.4%
17	Ohio	112,538,000	1.9%
11	Oklahoma	173,499,000	2.9%
19	Oregon	75,360,000	1.3%
15	Pennsylvania	144,333,000	2.4%
41	Rhode Island	0	0.0%
10	South Carolina	177,708,000	3.0%
36	South Dakota	2,299,000	0.0%
2	Tennessee	648,779,000	11.0%
20	Texas	64,811,000	1.1%
38	Utah	299,000	0.0%
37	Vermont	1,043,000	0.0%
41	Virginia	0	0.0%
30	Washington	9,916,000	0.2%
34	West Virginia	5,337,000	0.1%
21	Wisconsin	60,905,000	1.0%
12	Wyoming	160,742,000	2.7%

RANK ORDER

RANK	STATE	REVENUE	% of USA
1	Massachusetts	$993,333,000	16.8%
2	Tennessee	648,779,000	11.0%
3	Alabama	634,846,000	10.7%
4	Indiana	502,089,000	8.5%
5	Connecticut	389,053,000	6.6%
6	California	341,736,000	5.8%
7	New York	234,869,000	4.0%
8	New Jersey	234,151,000	4.0%
9	Georgia	186,276,000	3.1%
10	South Carolina	177,708,000	3.0%
11	Oklahoma	173,499,000	2.9%
12	Wyoming	160,742,000	2.7%
13	Missouri	156,331,000	2.6%
14	Minnesota	153,617,000	2.6%
15	Pennsylvania	144,333,000	2.4%
16	Montana	132,311,000	2.2%
17	Ohio	112,538,000	1.9%
18	Kansas	105,022,000	1.8%
19	Oregon	75,360,000	1.3%
20	Texas	64,811,000	1.1%
21	Wisconsin	60,905,000	1.0%
22	Louisiana	35,130,000	0.6%
23	Kentucky	32,551,000	0.5%
24	Arizona	27,262,000	0.5%
25	Michigan	22,995,000	0.4%
26	Nebraska	22,330,000	0.4%
27	Mississippi	20,887,000	0.4%
28	North Dakota	20,868,000	0.4%
29	Colorado	13,697,000	0.2%
30	Maine	9,916,000	0.2%
30	Washington	9,916,000	0.2%
32	Arkansas	8,067,000	0.1%
33	Iowa	5,977,000	0.1%
34	West Virginia	5,337,000	0.1%
35	Nevada	2,616,000	0.0%
36	South Dakota	2,299,000	0.0%
37	Vermont	1,043,000	0.0%
38	Utah	299,000	0.0%
39	New Hampshire	296,000	0.0%
40	Idaho	140,000	0.0%
41	Alaska	0	0.0%
41	Delaware	0	0.0%
41	Florida	0	0.0%
41	Hawaii	0	0.0%
41	Illinois	0	0.0%
41	Maryland	0	0.0%
41	New Mexico	0	0.0%
41	North Carolina	0	0.0%
41	Rhode Island	0	0.0%
41	Virginia	0	0.0%
	District of Columbia	0	0.0%

Source: U.S. Bureau of the Census, Governments Division
  "Public Education Finances: 2009" (http://www.census.gov/govs/school/)
*Revenue from local governments other than a parent government.

Percent of Public Elementary and Secondary School Local Source Revenue from Nonschool Local Government in 2009
National Percent = 2.3%*

RANK	STATE	PERCENT
1	Alabama	27.7
38	Alaska	0.0
29	Arizona	0.7
22	Arkansas	1.2
16	California	1.6
33	Colorado	0.3
8	Connecticut	7.1
38	Delaware	0.0
38	Florida	0.0
15	Georgia	2.2
38	Hawaii	0.0
38	Idaho	0.0
38	Illinois	0.0
6	Indiana	9.1
36	Iowa	0.2
9	Kansas	5.4
18	Kentucky	1.5
23	Louisiana	1.1
28	Maine	0.8
38	Maryland	0.0
5	Massachusetts	12.4
31	Michigan	0.4
11	Minnesota	5.1
18	Mississippi	1.5
13	Missouri	3.3
3	Montana	20.9
23	Nebraska	1.1
36	Nevada	0.2
38	New Hampshire	0.0
16	New Jersey	1.6
38	New Mexico	0.0
27	New York	0.9
38	North Carolina	0.0
12	North Dakota	3.9
23	Ohio	1.1
7	Oklahoma	7.7
14	Oregon	3.2
26	Pennsylvania	1.0
38	Rhode Island	0.0
9	South Carolina	5.4
31	South Dakota	0.4
4	Tennessee	19.0
33	Texas	0.3
38	Utah	0.0
18	Vermont	1.5
38	Virginia	0.0
33	Washington	0.3
30	West Virginia	0.6
21	Wisconsin	1.3
2	Wyoming	26.0

RANK	STATE	PERCENT
1	Alabama	27.7
2	Wyoming	26.0
3	Montana	20.9
4	Tennessee	19.0
5	Massachusetts	12.4
6	Indiana	9.1
7	Oklahoma	7.7
8	Connecticut	7.1
9	Kansas	5.4
9	South Carolina	5.4
11	Minnesota	5.1
12	North Dakota	3.9
13	Missouri	3.3
14	Oregon	3.2
15	Georgia	2.2
16	California	1.6
16	New Jersey	1.6
18	Kentucky	1.5
18	Mississippi	1.5
18	Vermont	1.5
21	Wisconsin	1.3
22	Arkansas	1.2
23	Louisiana	1.1
23	Nebraska	1.1
23	Ohio	1.1
26	Pennsylvania	1.0
27	New York	0.9
28	Maine	0.8
29	Arizona	0.7
30	West Virginia	0.6
31	Michigan	0.4
31	South Dakota	0.4
33	Colorado	0.3
33	Texas	0.3
33	Washington	0.3
36	Iowa	0.2
36	Nevada	0.2
38	Alaska	0.0
38	Delaware	0.0
38	Florida	0.0
38	Hawaii	0.0
38	Idaho	0.0
38	Illinois	0.0
38	Maryland	0.0
38	New Hampshire	0.0
38	New Mexico	0.0
38	North Carolina	0.0
38	Rhode Island	0.0
38	Utah	0.0
38	Virginia	0.0
	District of Columbia	0.0

Source: CQ Press using data from U.S. Bureau of the Census, Governments Division
"Public Education Finances: 2009" (http://www.census.gov/govs/school/)
*Revenue from local governments other than a parent government.

Public Elementary and Secondary School Local Source Revenue from School Lunch Charges in 2009
National Total = $6,968,057,000*

ALPHA ORDER

RANK	STATE	REVENUE	% of USA
19	Alabama	$128,944,000	1.9%
50	Alaska	12,869,000	0.2%
24	Arizona	115,724,000	1.7%
33	Arkansas	57,171,000	0.8%
2	California	505,643,000	7.3%
26	Colorado	98,646,000	1.4%
21	Connecticut	123,728,000	1.8%
49	Delaware	17,413,000	0.2%
3	Florida	355,543,000	5.1%
11	Georgia	224,068,000	3.2%
44	Hawaii	22,094,000	0.3%
38	Idaho	30,751,000	0.4%
8	Illinois	276,516,000	4.0%
13	Indiana	206,310,000	3.0%
23	Iowa	115,869,000	1.7%
28	Kansas	92,386,000	1.3%
25	Kentucky	111,211,000	1.6%
35	Louisiana	50,622,000	0.7%
40	Maine	27,431,000	0.4%
20	Maryland	126,939,000	1.8%
17	Massachusetts	151,201,000	2.2%
12	Michigan	215,114,000	3.1%
14	Minnesota	198,029,000	2.8%
32	Mississippi	58,407,000	0.8%
16	Missouri	158,238,000	2.3%
45	Montana	20,657,000	0.3%
30	Nebraska	64,255,000	0.9%
37	Nevada	36,465,000	0.5%
36	New Hampshire	43,231,000	0.6%
6	New Jersey	307,668,000	4.4%
41	New Mexico	26,486,000	0.4%
5	New York	308,718,000	4.4%
9	North Carolina	276,445,000	4.0%
43	North Dakota	23,620,000	0.3%
7	Ohio	304,632,000	4.4%
29	Oklahoma	82,496,000	1.2%
34	Oregon	55,536,000	0.8%
4	Pennsylvania	326,878,000	4.7%
47	Rhode Island	18,680,000	0.3%
27	South Carolina	95,259,000	1.4%
39	South Dakota	27,637,000	0.4%
18	Tennessee	136,265,000	2.0%
1	Texas	655,676,000	9.4%
31	Utah	63,559,000	0.9%
46	Vermont	19,167,000	0.3%
10	Virginia	253,145,000	3.6%
22	Washington	119,875,000	1.7%
42	West Virginia	26,160,000	0.4%
15	Wisconsin	175,898,000	2.5%
48	Wyoming	17,917,000	0.3%

RANK ORDER

RANK	STATE	REVENUE	% of USA
1	Texas	$655,676,000	9.4%
2	California	505,643,000	7.3%
3	Florida	355,543,000	5.1%
4	Pennsylvania	326,878,000	4.7%
5	New York	308,718,000	4.4%
6	New Jersey	307,668,000	4.4%
7	Ohio	304,632,000	4.4%
8	Illinois	276,516,000	4.0%
9	North Carolina	276,445,000	4.0%
10	Virginia	253,145,000	3.6%
11	Georgia	224,068,000	3.2%
12	Michigan	215,114,000	3.1%
13	Indiana	206,310,000	3.0%
14	Minnesota	198,029,000	2.8%
15	Wisconsin	175,898,000	2.5%
16	Missouri	158,238,000	2.3%
17	Massachusetts	151,201,000	2.2%
18	Tennessee	136,265,000	2.0%
19	Alabama	128,944,000	1.9%
20	Maryland	126,939,000	1.8%
21	Connecticut	123,728,000	1.8%
22	Washington	119,875,000	1.7%
23	Iowa	115,869,000	1.7%
24	Arizona	115,724,000	1.7%
25	Kentucky	111,211,000	1.6%
26	Colorado	98,646,000	1.4%
27	South Carolina	95,259,000	1.4%
28	Kansas	92,386,000	1.3%
29	Oklahoma	82,496,000	1.2%
30	Nebraska	64,255,000	0.9%
31	Utah	63,559,000	0.9%
32	Mississippi	58,407,000	0.8%
33	Arkansas	57,171,000	0.8%
34	Oregon	55,536,000	0.8%
35	Louisiana	50,622,000	0.7%
36	New Hampshire	43,231,000	0.6%
37	Nevada	36,465,000	0.5%
38	Idaho	30,751,000	0.4%
39	South Dakota	27,637,000	0.4%
40	Maine	27,431,000	0.4%
41	New Mexico	26,486,000	0.4%
42	West Virginia	26,160,000	0.4%
43	North Dakota	23,620,000	0.3%
44	Hawaii	22,094,000	0.3%
45	Montana	20,657,000	0.3%
46	Vermont	19,167,000	0.3%
47	Rhode Island	18,680,000	0.3%
48	Wyoming	17,917,000	0.3%
49	Delaware	17,413,000	0.2%
50	Alaska	12,869,000	0.2%
	District of Columbia	865,000	0.0%

Source: U.S. Bureau of the Census, Governments Division
"Public Education Finances: 2009" (http://www.census.gov/govs/school/)
*Gross collections from cafeteria sales to children and adults.

Percent of Public Elementary and Secondary School Local Source Revenue from School Lunch Charges in 2009
National Percent = 2.7%*

ALPHA ORDER

RANK	STATE	PERCENT
6	Alabama	5.6
34	Alaska	2.6
27	Arizona	3.0
3	Arkansas	8.6
40	California	2.3
36	Colorado	2.4
40	Connecticut	2.3
21	Delaware	3.4
36	Florida	2.4
34	Georgia	2.6
2	Hawaii	24.0
5	Idaho	6.1
47	Illinois	1.8
17	Indiana	3.8
11	Iowa	4.5
8	Kansas	4.8
7	Kentucky	5.3
48	Louisiana	1.6
40	Maine	2.3
45	Maryland	1.9
45	Massachusetts	1.9
23	Michigan	3.3
4	Minnesota	6.6
13	Mississippi	4.3
21	Missouri	3.4
23	Montana	3.3
23	Nebraska	3.3
44	Nevada	2.1
31	New Hampshire	2.8
43	New Jersey	2.2
10	New Mexico	4.7
50	New York	1.2
8	North Carolina	4.8
12	North Dakota	4.4
28	Ohio	2.9
18	Oklahoma	3.7
36	Oregon	2.4
36	Pennsylvania	2.4
48	Rhode Island	1.6
28	South Carolina	2.9
13	South Dakota	4.3
16	Tennessee	4.0
31	Texas	2.8
13	Utah	4.3
1	Vermont	28.0
23	Virginia	3.3
20	Washington	3.5
31	West Virginia	2.8
18	Wisconsin	3.7
28	Wyoming	2.9

RANK ORDER

RANK	STATE	PERCENT
1	Vermont	28.0
2	Hawaii	24.0
3	Arkansas	8.6
4	Minnesota	6.6
5	Idaho	6.1
6	Alabama	5.6
7	Kentucky	5.3
8	Kansas	4.8
8	North Carolina	4.8
10	New Mexico	4.7
11	Iowa	4.5
12	North Dakota	4.4
13	Mississippi	4.3
13	South Dakota	4.3
13	Utah	4.3
16	Tennessee	4.0
17	Indiana	3.8
18	Oklahoma	3.7
18	Wisconsin	3.7
20	Washington	3.5
21	Delaware	3.4
21	Missouri	3.4
23	Michigan	3.3
23	Montana	3.3
23	Nebraska	3.3
23	Virginia	3.3
27	Arizona	3.0
28	Ohio	2.9
28	South Carolina	2.9
28	Wyoming	2.9
31	New Hampshire	2.8
31	Texas	2.8
31	West Virginia	2.8
34	Alaska	2.6
34	Georgia	2.6
36	Colorado	2.4
36	Florida	2.4
36	Oregon	2.4
36	Pennsylvania	2.4
40	California	2.3
40	Connecticut	2.3
40	Maine	2.3
43	New Jersey	2.2
44	Nevada	2.1
45	Maryland	1.9
45	Massachusetts	1.9
47	Illinois	1.8
48	Louisiana	1.6
48	Rhode Island	1.6
50	New York	1.2

District of Columbia   0.1

Source: CQ Press using data from U.S. Bureau of the Census, Governments Division
   "Public Education Finances: 2009" (http://www.census.gov/govs/school/)
*Gross collections from cafeteria sales to children and adults.

Public Elementary and Secondary School Local Source Revenue from Tuition and Transportation Fees in 2009
National Total = $1,224,456,000*

ALPHA ORDER

RANK	STATE	REVENUE	% of USA
35	Alabama	$4,023,000	0.3%
46	Alaska	299,000	0.0%
43	Arizona	1,177,000	0.1%
28	Arkansas	8,833,000	0.7%
8	California	58,773,000	4.8%
5	Colorado	81,326,000	6.6%
34	Connecticut	4,398,000	0.4%
48	Delaware	0	0.0%
21	Florida	12,553,000	1.0%
15	Georgia	30,137,000	2.5%
48	Hawaii	0	0.0%
33	Idaho	4,662,000	0.4%
11	Illinois	48,029,000	3.9%
23	Indiana	10,738,000	0.9%
19	Iowa	15,651,000	1.3%
26	Kansas	9,703,000	0.8%
27	Kentucky	9,168,000	0.7%
24	Louisiana	10,362,000	0.8%
31	Maine	6,426,000	0.5%
18	Maryland	20,486,000	1.7%
2	Massachusetts	104,960,000	8.6%
13	Michigan	43,290,000	3.5%
3	Minnesota	94,401,000	7.7%
32	Mississippi	5,782,000	0.5%
16	Missouri	24,185,000	2.0%
36	Montana	3,350,000	0.3%
42	Nebraska	1,547,000	0.1%
25	Nevada	9,769,000	0.8%
29	New Hampshire	8,488,000	0.7%
1	New Jersey	106,919,000	8.7%
38	New Mexico	2,959,000	0.2%
14	New York	41,538,000	3.4%
48	North Carolina	0	0.0%
44	North Dakota	1,076,000	0.1%
4	Ohio	84,042,000	6.9%
12	Oklahoma	47,448,000	3.9%
17	Oregon	21,615,000	1.8%
9	Pennsylvania	52,354,000	4.3%
45	Rhode Island	1,047,000	0.1%
22	South Carolina	10,926,000	0.9%
40	South Dakota	2,362,000	0.2%
30	Tennessee	7,081,000	0.6%
7	Texas	68,227,000	5.6%
20	Utah	14,090,000	1.2%
41	Vermont	2,206,000	0.2%
10	Virginia	49,520,000	4.0%
6	Washington	72,050,000	5.9%
39	West Virginia	2,579,000	0.2%
37	Wisconsin	3,079,000	0.3%
47	Wyoming	224,000	0.0%

RANK ORDER

RANK	STATE	REVENUE	% of USA
1	New Jersey	$106,919,000	8.7%
2	Massachusetts	104,960,000	8.6%
3	Minnesota	94,401,000	7.7%
4	Ohio	84,042,000	6.9%
5	Colorado	81,326,000	6.6%
6	Washington	72,050,000	5.9%
7	Texas	68,227,000	5.6%
8	California	58,773,000	4.8%
9	Pennsylvania	52,354,000	4.3%
10	Virginia	49,520,000	4.0%
11	Illinois	48,029,000	3.9%
12	Oklahoma	47,448,000	3.9%
13	Michigan	43,290,000	3.5%
14	New York	41,538,000	3.4%
15	Georgia	30,137,000	2.5%
16	Missouri	24,185,000	2.0%
17	Oregon	21,615,000	1.8%
18	Maryland	20,486,000	1.7%
19	Iowa	15,651,000	1.3%
20	Utah	14,090,000	1.2%
21	Florida	12,553,000	1.0%
22	South Carolina	10,926,000	0.9%
23	Indiana	10,738,000	0.9%
24	Louisiana	10,362,000	0.8%
25	Nevada	9,769,000	0.8%
26	Kansas	9,703,000	0.8%
27	Kentucky	9,168,000	0.7%
28	Arkansas	8,833,000	0.7%
29	New Hampshire	8,488,000	0.7%
30	Tennessee	7,081,000	0.6%
31	Maine	6,426,000	0.5%
32	Mississippi	5,782,000	0.5%
33	Idaho	4,662,000	0.4%
34	Connecticut	4,398,000	0.4%
35	Alabama	4,023,000	0.3%
36	Montana	3,350,000	0.3%
37	Wisconsin	3,079,000	0.3%
38	New Mexico	2,959,000	0.2%
39	West Virginia	2,579,000	0.2%
40	South Dakota	2,362,000	0.2%
41	Vermont	2,206,000	0.2%
42	Nebraska	1,547,000	0.1%
43	Arizona	1,177,000	0.1%
44	North Dakota	1,076,000	0.1%
45	Rhode Island	1,047,000	0.1%
46	Alaska	299,000	0.0%
47	Wyoming	224,000	0.0%
48	Delaware	0	0.0%
48	Hawaii	0	0.0%
48	North Carolina	0	0.0%
	District of Columbia	598,000	0.0%

Source: U.S. Bureau of the Census, Governments Division
"Public Education Finances: 2009" (http://www.census.gov/govs/school/)
*Current charges for tuition and transportation fees paid by individuals.

Percent of Public Elementary and Secondary School Local Source Revenue from Tuition and Transportation Fees in 2009
National Percent = 0.5%*

RANK	STATE	PERCENT
35	Alabama	0.2
40	Alaska	0.1
46	Arizona	0.0
6	Arkansas	1.3
28	California	0.3
5	Colorado	2.0
40	Connecticut	0.1
46	Delaware	0.0
40	Florida	0.1
23	Georgia	0.4
46	Hawaii	0.0
9	Idaho	0.9
28	Illinois	0.3
35	Indiana	0.2
14	Iowa	0.6
17	Kansas	0.5
23	Kentucky	0.4
28	Louisiana	0.3
17	Maine	0.5
28	Maryland	0.3
6	Massachusetts	1.3
13	Michigan	0.7
2	Minnesota	3.1
23	Mississippi	0.4
17	Missouri	0.5
17	Montana	0.5
40	Nebraska	0.1
14	Nevada	0.6
17	New Hampshire	0.5
11	New Jersey	0.8
17	New Mexico	0.5
35	New York	0.2
46	North Carolina	0.0
35	North Dakota	0.2
11	Ohio	0.8
3	Oklahoma	2.1
9	Oregon	0.9
23	Pennsylvania	0.4
40	Rhode Island	0.1
28	South Carolina	0.3
23	South Dakota	0.4
35	Tennessee	0.2
28	Texas	0.3
8	Utah	1.0
1	Vermont	3.2
14	Virginia	0.6
3	Washington	2.1
28	West Virginia	0.3
40	Wisconsin	0.1
46	Wyoming	0.0

RANK	STATE	PERCENT
1	Vermont	3.2
2	Minnesota	3.1
3	Oklahoma	2.1
3	Washington	2.1
5	Colorado	2.0
6	Arkansas	1.3
6	Massachusetts	1.3
8	Utah	1.0
9	Idaho	0.9
9	Oregon	0.9
11	New Jersey	0.8
11	Ohio	0.8
13	Michigan	0.7
14	Iowa	0.6
14	Nevada	0.6
14	Virginia	0.6
17	Kansas	0.5
17	Maine	0.5
17	Missouri	0.5
17	Montana	0.5
17	New Hampshire	0.5
17	New Mexico	0.5
23	Georgia	0.4
23	Kentucky	0.4
23	Mississippi	0.4
23	Pennsylvania	0.4
23	South Dakota	0.4
28	California	0.3
28	Illinois	0.3
28	Louisiana	0.3
28	Maryland	0.3
28	South Carolina	0.3
28	Texas	0.3
28	West Virginia	0.3
35	Alabama	0.2
35	Indiana	0.2
35	New York	0.2
35	North Dakota	0.2
35	Tennessee	0.2
40	Alaska	0.1
40	Connecticut	0.1
40	Florida	0.1
40	Nebraska	0.1
40	Rhode Island	0.1
40	Wisconsin	0.1
46	Arizona	0.0
46	Delaware	0.0
46	Hawaii	0.0
46	North Carolina	0.0
46	Wyoming	0.0
	District of Columbia	0.1

Source: CQ Press using data from U.S. Bureau of the Census, Governments Division
"Public Education Finances: 2009" (http://www.census.gov/govs/school/)
*Current charges for tuition and transportation fees paid by individuals.

Public Elementary and Secondary School
Local Source Revenue from Other Charges in 2009
National Total = $6,473,678,000*

ALPHA ORDER

RANK	STATE	REVENUE	% of USA
13	Alabama	$185,625,000	2.9%
35	Alaska	19,437,000	0.3%
19	Arizona	123,986,000	1.9%
26	Arkansas	82,427,000	1.3%
3	California	535,874,000	8.3%
10	Colorado	233,476,000	3.6%
43	Connecticut	4,552,000	0.1%
50	Delaware	816,000	0.0%
1	Florida	807,429,000	12.5%
7	Georgia	265,204,000	4.1%
49	Hawaii	1,324,000	0.0%
44	Idaho	4,220,000	0.1%
8	Illinois	251,656,000	3.9%
18	Indiana	135,353,000	2.1%
29	Iowa	42,570,000	0.7%
34	Kansas	22,681,000	0.4%
38	Kentucky	11,032,000	0.2%
40	Louisiana	8,043,000	0.1%
47	Maine	3,325,000	0.1%
15	Maryland	177,406,000	2.7%
31	Massachusetts	37,076,000	0.6%
5	Michigan	304,867,000	4.7%
12	Minnesota	190,983,000	3.0%
20	Mississippi	119,294,000	1.8%
11	Missouri	230,796,000	3.6%
30	Montana	37,561,000	0.6%
27	Nebraska	73,939,000	1.1%
24	Nevada	86,698,000	1.3%
46	New Hampshire	3,678,000	0.1%
9	New Jersey	237,202,000	3.7%
32	New Mexico	23,441,000	0.4%
21	New York	110,274,000	1.7%
25	North Carolina	86,133,000	1.3%
33	North Dakota	22,879,000	0.4%
2	Ohio	575,134,000	8.9%
14	Oklahoma	185,437,000	2.9%
22	Oregon	100,272,000	1.5%
28	Pennsylvania	62,129,000	1.0%
45	Rhode Island	3,993,000	0.1%
17	South Carolina	143,471,000	2.2%
37	South Dakota	18,101,000	0.3%
6	Tennessee	288,562,000	4.5%
4	Texas	320,351,000	4.9%
39	Utah	8,108,000	0.1%
42	Vermont	5,219,000	0.1%
36	Virginia	18,284,000	0.3%
16	Washington	152,514,000	2.4%
41	West Virginia	6,846,000	0.1%
23	Wisconsin	96,147,000	1.5%
48	Wyoming	2,799,000	0.0%

RANK ORDER

RANK	STATE	REVENUE	% of USA
1	Florida	$807,429,000	12.5%
2	Ohio	575,134,000	8.9%
3	California	535,874,000	8.3%
4	Texas	320,351,000	4.9%
5	Michigan	304,867,000	4.7%
6	Tennessee	288,562,000	4.5%
7	Georgia	265,204,000	4.1%
8	Illinois	251,656,000	3.9%
9	New Jersey	237,202,000	3.7%
10	Colorado	233,476,000	3.6%
11	Missouri	230,796,000	3.6%
12	Minnesota	190,983,000	3.0%
13	Alabama	185,625,000	2.9%
14	Oklahoma	185,437,000	2.9%
15	Maryland	177,406,000	2.7%
16	Washington	152,514,000	2.4%
17	South Carolina	143,471,000	2.2%
18	Indiana	135,353,000	2.1%
19	Arizona	123,986,000	1.9%
20	Mississippi	119,294,000	1.8%
21	New York	110,274,000	1.7%
22	Oregon	100,272,000	1.5%
23	Wisconsin	96,147,000	1.5%
24	Nevada	86,698,000	1.3%
25	North Carolina	86,133,000	1.3%
26	Arkansas	82,427,000	1.3%
27	Nebraska	73,939,000	1.1%
28	Pennsylvania	62,129,000	1.0%
29	Iowa	42,570,000	0.7%
30	Montana	37,561,000	0.6%
31	Massachusetts	37,076,000	0.6%
32	New Mexico	23,441,000	0.4%
33	North Dakota	22,879,000	0.4%
34	Kansas	22,681,000	0.4%
35	Alaska	19,437,000	0.3%
36	Virginia	18,284,000	0.3%
37	South Dakota	18,101,000	0.3%
38	Kentucky	11,032,000	0.2%
39	Utah	8,108,000	0.1%
40	Louisiana	8,043,000	0.1%
41	West Virginia	6,846,000	0.1%
42	Vermont	5,219,000	0.1%
43	Connecticut	4,552,000	0.1%
44	Idaho	4,220,000	0.1%
45	Rhode Island	3,993,000	0.1%
46	New Hampshire	3,678,000	0.1%
47	Maine	3,325,000	0.1%
48	Wyoming	2,799,000	0.0%
49	Hawaii	1,324,000	0.0%
50	Delaware	816,000	0.0%
	District of Columbia	5,054,000	0.1%

Source: U.S. Bureau of the Census, Governments Division
  "Public Education Finances: 2009" (http://www.census.gov/govs/school/)
*Amounts received from the public for performance of specific services benefiting the person charged and sales of commodities and services. Excludes school lunch sales, tuition, and transportation fees (shown separately). Includes revenue from the sale and rental of textbooks and receipts from centrally administered student activity funds.

Percent of Public Elementary and Secondary School Local Source Revenue from Other Charges in 2009
National Percent = 2.5%*

ALPHA ORDER

RANK	STATE	PERCENT
5	Alabama	8.1
20	Alaska	4.0
22	Arizona	3.2
1	Arkansas	12.3
26	California	2.5
9	Colorado	5.7
50	Connecticut	0.1
47	Delaware	0.2
10	Florida	5.5
23	Georgia	3.1
33	Hawaii	1.4
36	Idaho	0.8
29	Illinois	1.7
26	Indiana	2.5
29	Iowa	1.7
35	Kansas	1.2
38	Kentucky	0.5
44	Louisiana	0.3
44	Maine	0.3
25	Maryland	2.6
38	Massachusetts	0.5
14	Michigan	4.7
7	Minnesota	6.4
2	Mississippi	8.7
13	Missouri	4.9
8	Montana	5.9
21	Nebraska	3.8
12	Nevada	5.0
47	New Hampshire	0.2
29	New Jersey	1.7
19	New Mexico	4.1
43	New York	0.4
32	North Carolina	1.5
17	North Dakota	4.3
10	Ohio	5.5
4	Oklahoma	8.3
17	Oregon	4.3
38	Pennsylvania	0.5
44	Rhode Island	0.3
16	South Carolina	4.4
24	South Dakota	2.8
3	Tennessee	8.5
33	Texas	1.4
38	Utah	0.5
6	Vermont	7.6
47	Virginia	0.2
15	Washington	4.5
37	West Virginia	0.7
28	Wisconsin	2.0
38	Wyoming	0.5

RANK ORDER

RANK	STATE	PERCENT
1	Arkansas	12.3
2	Mississippi	8.7
3	Tennessee	8.5
4	Oklahoma	8.3
5	Alabama	8.1
6	Vermont	7.6
7	Minnesota	6.4
8	Montana	5.9
9	Colorado	5.7
10	Florida	5.5
10	Ohio	5.5
12	Nevada	5.0
13	Missouri	4.9
14	Michigan	4.7
15	Washington	4.5
16	South Carolina	4.4
17	North Dakota	4.3
17	Oregon	4.3
19	New Mexico	4.1
20	Alaska	4.0
21	Nebraska	3.8
22	Arizona	3.2
23	Georgia	3.1
24	South Dakota	2.8
25	Maryland	2.6
26	California	2.5
26	Indiana	2.5
28	Wisconsin	2.0
29	Illinois	1.7
29	Iowa	1.7
29	New Jersey	1.7
32	North Carolina	1.5
33	Hawaii	1.4
33	Texas	1.4
35	Kansas	1.2
36	Idaho	0.8
37	West Virginia	0.7
38	Kentucky	0.5
38	Massachusetts	0.5
38	Pennsylvania	0.5
38	Utah	0.5
38	Wyoming	0.5
43	New York	0.4
44	Louisiana	0.3
44	Maine	0.3
44	Rhode Island	0.3
47	Delaware	0.2
47	New Hampshire	0.2
47	Virginia	0.2
50	Connecticut	0.1

District of Columbia — 0.7

Source: CQ Press using data from U.S. Bureau of the Census, Governments Division
"Public Education Finances: 2009" (http://www.census.gov/govs/school/)

*Amounts received from the public for performance of specific services benefiting the person charged and sales of commodities and services. Excludes school lunch sales, tuition, and transportation fees (shown separately). Includes revenue from the sale and rental of textbooks and receipts from centrally administered student activity funds.

Public Elementary and Secondary School Total Expenditures in 2009

National Total = $604,856,342,000*

ALPHA ORDER

RANK	STATE	EXPENDITURES	% of USA
26	Alabama	$7,806,113,000	1.3%
41	Alaska	2,396,412,000	0.4%
20	Arizona	9,580,393,000	1.6%
32	Arkansas	4,980,644,000	0.8%
1	California	71,850,888,000	11.9%
22	Colorado	8,633,794,000	1.4%
21	Connecticut	9,107,330,000	1.5%
45	Delaware	1,732,081,000	0.3%
4	Florida	28,867,429,000	4.8%
9	Georgia	19,011,396,000	3.1%
42	Hawaii	2,318,671,000	0.4%
44	Idaho	2,078,446,000	0.3%
5	Illinois	26,867,583,000	4.4%
17	Indiana	10,948,807,000	1.8%
31	Iowa	5,513,550,000	0.9%
30	Kansas	5,816,078,000	1.0%
27	Kentucky	6,829,740,000	1.1%
25	Louisiana	7,935,780,000	1.3%
40	Maine	2,545,450,000	0.4%
14	Maryland	12,482,460,000	2.1%
12	Massachusetts	14,837,791,000	2.5%
10	Michigan	18,788,035,000	3.1%
16	Minnesota	11,005,880,000	1.8%
34	Mississippi	4,552,756,000	0.8%
19	Missouri	10,134,666,000	1.7%
47	Montana	1,607,907,000	0.3%
37	Nebraska	3,500,576,000	0.6%
33	Nevada	4,574,369,000	0.8%
39	New Hampshire	2,595,350,000	0.4%
6	New Jersey	25,391,366,000	4.2%
36	New Mexico	3,940,618,000	0.7%
2	New York	57,346,173,000	9.5%
13	North Carolina	14,836,575,000	2.5%
50	North Dakota	1,079,302,000	0.2%
8	Ohio	22,255,659,000	3.7%
29	Oklahoma	5,934,574,000	1.0%
28	Oregon	6,699,599,000	1.1%
7	Pennsylvania	25,004,158,000	4.1%
43	Rhode Island	2,148,881,000	0.4%
24	South Carolina	8,413,203,000	1.4%
49	South Dakota	1,261,764,000	0.2%
23	Tennessee	8,581,791,000	1.4%
3	Texas	53,423,805,000	8.8%
35	Utah	4,417,005,000	0.7%
48	Vermont	1,475,296,000	0.2%
11	Virginia	15,291,282,000	2.5%
15	Washington	12,201,225,000	2.0%
38	West Virginia	3,119,908,000	0.5%
18	Wisconsin	10,678,772,000	1.8%
46	Wyoming	1,649,649,000	0.3%

RANK ORDER

RANK	STATE	EXPENDITURES	% of USA
1	California	$71,850,888,000	11.9%
2	New York	57,346,173,000	9.5%
3	Texas	53,423,805,000	8.8%
4	Florida	28,867,429,000	4.8%
5	Illinois	26,867,583,000	4.4%
6	New Jersey	25,391,366,000	4.2%
7	Pennsylvania	25,004,158,000	4.1%
8	Ohio	22,255,659,000	3.7%
9	Georgia	19,011,396,000	3.1%
10	Michigan	18,788,035,000	3.1%
11	Virginia	15,291,282,000	2.5%
12	Massachusetts	14,837,791,000	2.5%
13	North Carolina	14,836,575,000	2.5%
14	Maryland	12,482,460,000	2.1%
15	Washington	12,201,225,000	2.0%
16	Minnesota	11,005,880,000	1.8%
17	Indiana	10,948,807,000	1.8%
18	Wisconsin	10,678,772,000	1.8%
19	Missouri	10,134,666,000	1.7%
20	Arizona	9,580,393,000	1.6%
21	Connecticut	9,107,330,000	1.5%
22	Colorado	8,633,794,000	1.4%
23	Tennessee	8,581,791,000	1.4%
24	South Carolina	8,413,203,000	1.4%
25	Louisiana	7,935,780,000	1.3%
26	Alabama	7,806,113,000	1.3%
27	Kentucky	6,829,740,000	1.1%
28	Oregon	6,699,599,000	1.1%
29	Oklahoma	5,934,574,000	1.0%
30	Kansas	5,816,078,000	1.0%
31	Iowa	5,513,550,000	0.9%
32	Arkansas	4,980,644,000	0.8%
33	Nevada	4,574,369,000	0.8%
34	Mississippi	4,552,756,000	0.8%
35	Utah	4,417,005,000	0.7%
36	New Mexico	3,940,618,000	0.7%
37	Nebraska	3,500,576,000	0.6%
38	West Virginia	3,119,908,000	0.5%
39	New Hampshire	2,595,350,000	0.4%
40	Maine	2,545,450,000	0.4%
41	Alaska	2,396,412,000	0.4%
42	Hawaii	2,318,671,000	0.4%
43	Rhode Island	2,148,881,000	0.4%
44	Idaho	2,078,446,000	0.3%
45	Delaware	1,732,081,000	0.3%
46	Wyoming	1,649,649,000	0.3%
47	Montana	1,607,907,000	0.3%
48	Vermont	1,475,296,000	0.2%
49	South Dakota	1,261,764,000	0.2%
50	North Dakota	1,079,302,000	0.2%
	District of Columbia	805,362,000	0.1%

Source: U.S. Bureau of the Census, Governments Division
"Public Education Finances: 2009" (http://www.census.gov/govs/school/)
*Includes current spending (including salaries, benefits, services, and supplies), capital outlay, and "other." "Other" includes payments to state and local governments and interest on school system indebtedness.

Per Capita Public Elementary and Secondary School
Total Expenditures in 2009
National Per Capita = $1,970*

ALPHA ORDER

RANK	STATE	PER CAPITA
39	Alabama	$1,658
1	Alaska	3,431
48	Arizona	1,453
33	Arkansas	1,724
19	California	1,944
34	Colorado	1,718
5	Connecticut	2,589
17	Delaware	1,957
45	Florida	1,557
21	Georgia	1,934
29	Hawaii	1,790
50	Idaho	1,345
11	Illinois	2,081
36	Indiana	1,705
27	Iowa	1,833
12	Kansas	2,063
43	Kentucky	1,583
30	Louisiana	1,767
22	Maine	1,931
8	Maryland	2,190
7	Massachusetts	2,250
25	Michigan	1,885
10	Minnesota	2,090
47	Mississippi	1,542
37	Missouri	1,693
40	Montana	1,649
18	Nebraska	1,948
32	Nevada	1,731
16	New Hampshire	1,959
4	New Jersey	2,916
15	New Mexico	1,961
3	New York	2,935
44	North Carolina	1,582
38	North Dakota	1,669
23	Ohio	1,928
41	Oklahoma	1,610
31	Oregon	1,751
14	Pennsylvania	1,984
13	Rhode Island	2,040
26	South Carolina	1,844
46	South Dakota	1,553
49	Tennessee	1,363
9	Texas	2,156
42	Utah	1,586
6	Vermont	2,373
20	Virginia	1,940
28	Washington	1,831
35	West Virginia	1,714
24	Wisconsin	1,888
2	Wyoming	3,031

RANK ORDER

RANK	STATE	PER CAPITA
1	Alaska	$3,431
2	Wyoming	3,031
3	New York	2,935
4	New Jersey	2,916
5	Connecticut	2,589
6	Vermont	2,373
7	Massachusetts	2,250
8	Maryland	2,190
9	Texas	2,156
10	Minnesota	2,090
11	Illinois	2,081
12	Kansas	2,063
13	Rhode Island	2,040
14	Pennsylvania	1,984
15	New Mexico	1,961
16	New Hampshire	1,959
17	Delaware	1,957
18	Nebraska	1,948
19	California	1,944
20	Virginia	1,940
21	Georgia	1,934
22	Maine	1,931
23	Ohio	1,928
24	Wisconsin	1,888
25	Michigan	1,885
26	South Carolina	1,844
27	Iowa	1,833
28	Washington	1,831
29	Hawaii	1,790
30	Louisiana	1,767
31	Oregon	1,751
32	Nevada	1,731
33	Arkansas	1,724
34	Colorado	1,718
35	West Virginia	1,714
36	Indiana	1,705
37	Missouri	1,693
38	North Dakota	1,669
39	Alabama	1,658
40	Montana	1,649
41	Oklahoma	1,610
42	Utah	1,586
43	Kentucky	1,583
44	North Carolina	1,582
45	Florida	1,557
46	South Dakota	1,553
47	Mississippi	1,542
48	Arizona	1,453
49	Tennessee	1,363
50	Idaho	1,345

| | District of Columbia | 1,343 |

Source: CQ Press using data from U.S. Bureau of the Census, Governments Division
   "Public Education Finances: 2009" (http://www.census.gov/govs/school/)
*Includes current spending (including salaries, benefits, services, and supplies), capital outlay, and "other." "Other" includes
payments to state and local governments and interest on school system indebtedness.

Per Pupil Elementary and Secondary School
Total Expenditures in 2009
National Per Pupil = $12,539*

ALPHA ORDER

RANK	STATE	PER PUPIL
41	Alabama	$10,469
4	Alaska	18,401
45	Arizona	9,759
40	Arkansas	10,498
28	California	11,653
38	Colorado	10,627
6	Connecticut	16,652
9	Delaware	14,829
36	Florida	11,005
29	Georgia	11,525
15	Hawaii	12,919
50	Idaho	7,757
17	Illinois	12,692
37	Indiana	10,647
33	Iowa	11,308
19	Kansas	12,370
43	Kentucky	10,196
24	Louisiana	11,974
13	Maine	13,631
10	Maryland	14,793
7	Massachusetts	15,913
21	Michigan	12,078
12	Minnesota	13,704
46	Mississippi	9,269
34	Missouri	11,279
32	Montana	11,355
23	Nebraska	11,982
39	Nevada	10,614
14	New Hampshire	13,112
3	New Jersey	18,683
22	New Mexico	11,987
1	New York	21,264
42	North Carolina	10,218
31	North Dakota	11,403
16	Ohio	12,871
47	Oklahoma	9,207
25	Oregon	11,922
11	Pennsylvania	14,747
8	Rhode Island	15,184
26	South Carolina	11,778
44	South Dakota	9,965
48	Tennessee	8,839
30	Texas	11,496
49	Utah	8,296
5	Vermont	16,746
18	Virginia	12,381
27	Washington	11,776
35	West Virginia	11,067
20	Wisconsin	12,316
2	Wyoming	18,968

RANK ORDER

RANK	STATE	PER PUPIL
1	New York	$21,264
2	Wyoming	18,968
3	New Jersey	18,683
4	Alaska	18,401
5	Vermont	16,746
6	Connecticut	16,652
7	Massachusetts	15,913
8	Rhode Island	15,184
9	Delaware	14,829
10	Maryland	14,793
11	Pennsylvania	14,747
12	Minnesota	13,704
13	Maine	13,631
14	New Hampshire	13,112
15	Hawaii	12,919
16	Ohio	12,871
17	Illinois	12,692
18	Virginia	12,381
19	Kansas	12,370
20	Wisconsin	12,316
21	Michigan	12,078
22	New Mexico	11,987
23	Nebraska	11,982
24	Louisiana	11,974
25	Oregon	11,922
26	South Carolina	11,778
27	Washington	11,776
28	California	11,653
29	Georgia	11,525
30	Texas	11,496
31	North Dakota	11,403
32	Montana	11,355
33	Iowa	11,308
34	Missouri	11,279
35	West Virginia	11,067
36	Florida	11,005
37	Indiana	10,647
38	Colorado	10,627
39	Nevada	10,614
40	Arkansas	10,498
41	Alabama	10,469
42	North Carolina	10,218
43	Kentucky	10,196
44	South Dakota	9,965
45	Arizona	9,759
46	Mississippi	9,269
47	Oklahoma	9,207
48	Tennessee	8,839
49	Utah	8,296
50	Idaho	7,757
	District of Columbia	18,167

Source: CQ Press using data from U.S. Bureau of the Census, Governments Division
"Public Education Finances: 2009" (http://www.census.gov/govs/school/)
*Based on student membership. Includes current spending (including salaries, benefits, services, and supplies), capital outlay, and "other." "Other" includes payments to state and local governments and interest on school system indebtedness.

Public Elementary and Secondary School Current Expenditures in 2009

National Total = $517,708,299,000*

ALPHA ORDER

RANK	STATE	EXPENDITURES	% of USA
25	Alabama	$6,728,969,000	1.3%
43	Alaska	2,033,374,000	0.4%
22	Arizona	7,735,635,000	1.5%
32	Arkansas	4,443,722,000	0.9%
1	California	61,071,012,000	11.8%
23	Colorado	7,146,967,000	1.4%
20	Connecticut	8,190,255,000	1.6%
45	Delaware	1,454,873,000	0.3%
4	Florida	23,498,048,000	4.5%
10	Georgia	16,036,166,000	3.1%
41	Hawaii	2,250,087,000	0.4%
44	Idaho	1,904,422,000	0.4%
6	Illinois	23,218,026,000	4.5%
17	Indiana	9,706,715,000	1.9%
30	Iowa	4,755,348,000	0.9%
31	Kansas	4,685,472,000	0.9%
27	Kentucky	5,930,403,000	1.1%
24	Louisiana	7,003,000,000	1.4%
40	Maine	2,389,734,000	0.5%
14	Maryland	11,373,754,000	2.2%
11	Massachusetts	13,968,798,000	2.7%
9	Michigan	16,642,564,000	3.2%
18	Minnesota	9,331,434,000	1.8%
33	Mississippi	3,985,744,000	0.8%
19	Missouri	8,734,145,000	1.7%
46	Montana	1,432,675,000	0.3%
38	Nebraska	2,938,103,000	0.6%
34	Nevada	3,652,056,000	0.7%
39	New Hampshire	2,443,217,000	0.5%
5	New Jersey	23,440,277,000	4.5%
36	New Mexico	3,107,149,000	0.6%
2	New York	50,690,599,000	9.8%
13	North Carolina	12,543,171,000	2.4%
50	North Dakota	968,881,000	0.2%
8	Ohio	19,011,682,000	3.7%
29	Oklahoma	5,310,369,000	1.0%
28	Oregon	5,627,387,000	1.1%
7	Pennsylvania	21,596,546,000	4.2%
42	Rhode Island	2,087,690,000	0.4%
26	South Carolina	6,716,042,000	1.3%
49	South Dakota	1,082,630,000	0.2%
21	Tennessee	7,751,563,000	1.5%
3	Texas	39,984,644,000	7.7%
35	Utah	3,488,395,000	0.7%
47	Vermont	1,397,548,000	0.3%
12	Virginia	13,582,801,000	2.6%
15	Washington	9,958,400,000	1.9%
37	West Virginia	2,950,686,000	0.6%
16	Wisconsin	9,713,099,000	1.9%
48	Wyoming	1,274,683,000	0.2%

RANK ORDER

RANK	STATE	EXPENDITURES	% of USA
1	California	$61,071,012,000	11.8%
2	New York	50,690,599,000	9.8%
3	Texas	39,984,644,000	7.7%
4	Florida	23,498,048,000	4.5%
5	New Jersey	23,440,277,000	4.5%
6	Illinois	23,218,026,000	4.5%
7	Pennsylvania	21,596,546,000	4.2%
8	Ohio	19,011,682,000	3.7%
9	Michigan	16,642,564,000	3.2%
10	Georgia	16,036,166,000	3.1%
11	Massachusetts	13,968,798,000	2.7%
12	Virginia	13,582,801,000	2.6%
13	North Carolina	12,543,171,000	2.4%
14	Maryland	11,373,754,000	2.2%
15	Washington	9,958,400,000	1.9%
16	Wisconsin	9,713,099,000	1.9%
17	Indiana	9,706,715,000	1.9%
18	Minnesota	9,331,434,000	1.8%
19	Missouri	8,734,145,000	1.7%
20	Connecticut	8,190,255,000	1.6%
21	Tennessee	7,751,563,000	1.5%
22	Arizona	7,735,635,000	1.5%
23	Colorado	7,146,967,000	1.4%
24	Louisiana	7,003,000,000	1.4%
25	Alabama	6,728,969,000	1.3%
26	South Carolina	6,716,042,000	1.3%
27	Kentucky	5,930,403,000	1.1%
28	Oregon	5,627,387,000	1.1%
29	Oklahoma	5,310,369,000	1.0%
30	Iowa	4,755,348,000	0.9%
31	Kansas	4,685,472,000	0.9%
32	Arkansas	4,443,722,000	0.9%
33	Mississippi	3,985,744,000	0.8%
34	Nevada	3,652,056,000	0.7%
35	Utah	3,488,395,000	0.7%
36	New Mexico	3,107,149,000	0.6%
37	West Virginia	2,950,686,000	0.6%
38	Nebraska	2,938,103,000	0.6%
39	New Hampshire	2,443,217,000	0.5%
40	Maine	2,389,734,000	0.5%
41	Hawaii	2,250,087,000	0.4%
42	Rhode Island	2,087,690,000	0.4%
43	Alaska	2,033,374,000	0.4%
44	Idaho	1,904,422,000	0.4%
45	Delaware	1,454,873,000	0.3%
46	Montana	1,432,675,000	0.3%
47	Vermont	1,397,548,000	0.3%
48	Wyoming	1,274,683,000	0.2%
49	South Dakota	1,082,630,000	0.2%
50	North Dakota	968,881,000	0.2%
	District of Columbia	739,339,000	0.1%

Source: U.S. Bureau of the Census, Governments Division
    "Public Education Finances: 2009" (http://www.census.gov/govs/school/)
*Includes salaries, benefits, services, and supplies. Census expanded its usual "current expenditures" concept for education finance reports to include all current public elementary and secondary education outlays regardless of the specific unit of government that actually makes the expenditure.

Per Capita Public Elementary and Secondary School Current Expenditures in 2009
National Per Capita = $1,686*

ALPHA ORDER

RANK	STATE	PER CAPITA
39	Alabama	$1,429
1	Alaska	2,911
50	Arizona	1,173
30	Arkansas	1,538
20	California	1,652
40	Colorado	1,422
5	Connecticut	2,328
22	Delaware	1,644
46	Florida	1,268
24	Georgia	1,631
14	Hawaii	1,737
48	Idaho	1,232
12	Illinois	1,798
31	Indiana	1,511
27	Iowa	1,581
19	Kansas	1,662
42	Kentucky	1,375
28	Louisiana	1,559
11	Maine	1,813
8	Maryland	1,996
7	Massachusetts	2,119
18	Michigan	1,669
13	Minnesota	1,772
43	Mississippi	1,350
37	Missouri	1,459
36	Montana	1,469
23	Nebraska	1,635
41	Nevada	1,382
10	New Hampshire	1,845
2	New Jersey	2,692
29	New Mexico	1,546
3	New York	2,594
44	North Carolina	1,337
32	North Dakota	1,498
21	Ohio	1,647
38	Oklahoma	1,440
35	Oregon	1,471
17	Pennsylvania	1,713
9	Rhode Island	1,982
34	South Carolina	1,472
45	South Dakota	1,333
49	Tennessee	1,231
26	Texas	1,613
47	Utah	1,253
6	Vermont	2,248
15	Virginia	1,723
33	Washington	1,494
25	West Virginia	1,621
16	Wisconsin	1,718
4	Wyoming	2,342

RANK ORDER

RANK	STATE	PER CAPITA
1	Alaska	$2,911
2	New Jersey	2,692
3	New York	2,594
4	Wyoming	2,342
5	Connecticut	2,328
6	Vermont	2,248
7	Massachusetts	2,119
8	Maryland	1,996
9	Rhode Island	1,982
10	New Hampshire	1,845
11	Maine	1,813
12	Illinois	1,798
13	Minnesota	1,772
14	Hawaii	1,737
15	Virginia	1,723
16	Wisconsin	1,718
17	Pennsylvania	1,713
18	Michigan	1,669
19	Kansas	1,662
20	California	1,652
21	Ohio	1,647
22	Delaware	1,644
23	Nebraska	1,635
24	Georgia	1,631
25	West Virginia	1,621
26	Texas	1,613
27	Iowa	1,581
28	Louisiana	1,559
29	New Mexico	1,546
30	Arkansas	1,538
31	Indiana	1,511
32	North Dakota	1,498
33	Washington	1,494
34	South Carolina	1,472
35	Oregon	1,471
36	Montana	1,469
37	Missouri	1,459
38	Oklahoma	1,440
39	Alabama	1,429
40	Colorado	1,422
41	Nevada	1,382
42	Kentucky	1,375
43	Mississippi	1,350
44	North Carolina	1,337
45	South Dakota	1,333
46	Florida	1,268
47	Utah	1,253
48	Idaho	1,232
49	Tennessee	1,231
50	Arizona	1,173
	District of Columbia	1,233

Source: CQ Press using data from U.S. Bureau of the Census, Governments Division
"Public Education Finances: 2009" (http://www.census.gov/govs/school/)

*Includes salaries, benefits, services, and supplies. Census expanded its usual "current expenditures" concept for education finance reports to include all current public elementary and secondary education outlays regardless of the specific unit of government that actually makes the expenditure.

Public Elementary and Secondary School Current Expenditures per $1,000 Personal Income in 2009
National Ratio = $41.29*

ALPHA ORDER

RANK	STATE	RATIO
22	Alabama	$41.73
1	Alaska	66.30
47	Arizona	34.21
15	Arkansas	44.12
42	California	36.97
49	Colorado	33.02
32	Connecticut	40.64
34	Delaware	40.17
50	Florida	31.14
8	Georgia	46.85
31	Hawaii	40.75
41	Idaho	37.72
25	Illinois	41.60
17	Indiana	43.20
27	Iowa	41.36
23	Kansas	41.69
19	Kentucky	42.26
28	Louisiana	41.17
6	Maine	49.03
26	Maryland	41.43
24	Massachusetts	41.64
11	Michigan	46.16
35	Minnesota	39.41
16	Mississippi	43.90
36	Missouri	39.10
21	Montana	41.76
29	Nebraska	41.05
45	Nevada	34.63
18	New Hampshire	42.29
4	New Jersey	51.97
9	New Mexico	46.51
3	New York	53.71
39	North Carolina	37.95
43	North Dakota	36.10
14	Ohio	44.97
40	Oklahoma	37.78
33	Oregon	40.26
20	Pennsylvania	41.88
9	Rhode Island	46.51
13	South Carolina	44.98
48	South Dakota	34.13
44	Tennessee	35.01
30	Texas	41.02
38	Utah	38.07
2	Vermont	56.93
37	Virginia	38.71
46	Washington	34.46
5	West Virginia	51.10
12	Wisconsin	45.02
7	Wyoming	47.01

RANK ORDER

RANK	STATE	RATIO
1	Alaska	$66.30
2	Vermont	56.93
3	New York	53.71
4	New Jersey	51.97
5	West Virginia	51.10
6	Maine	49.03
7	Wyoming	47.01
8	Georgia	46.85
9	New Mexico	46.51
9	Rhode Island	46.51
11	Michigan	46.16
12	Wisconsin	45.02
13	South Carolina	44.98
14	Ohio	44.97
15	Arkansas	44.12
16	Mississippi	43.90
17	Indiana	43.20
18	New Hampshire	42.29
19	Kentucky	42.26
20	Pennsylvania	41.88
21	Montana	41.76
22	Alabama	41.73
23	Kansas	41.69
24	Massachusetts	41.64
25	Illinois	41.60
26	Maryland	41.43
27	Iowa	41.36
28	Louisiana	41.17
29	Nebraska	41.05
30	Texas	41.02
31	Hawaii	40.75
32	Connecticut	40.64
33	Oregon	40.26
34	Delaware	40.17
35	Minnesota	39.41
36	Missouri	39.10
37	Virginia	38.71
38	Utah	38.07
39	North Carolina	37.95
40	Oklahoma	37.78
41	Idaho	37.72
42	California	36.97
43	North Dakota	36.10
44	Tennessee	35.01
45	Nevada	34.63
46	Washington	34.46
47	Arizona	34.21
48	South Dakota	34.13
49	Colorado	33.02
50	Florida	31.14
	District of Columbia	18.03

Source: U.S. Bureau of the Census, Governments Division
    "Public Education Finances: 2009" (http://www.census.gov/govs/school/)
*Includes salaries, benefits, services, and supplies. Census expanded its usual "current expenditures" concept for education finance reports to include all current public elementary and secondary education outlays regardless of the specific unit of government that actually makes the expenditure.

Per Pupil Public Elementary and Secondary School Current Expenditures in 2009
National Per Pupil = $10,499*

ALPHA ORDER

RANK	STATE	PER PUPIL
36	Alabama	$8,870
3	Alaska	15,552
48	Arizona	7,813
40	Arkansas	8,712
29	California	9,657
39	Colorado	8,718
6	Connecticut	14,531
13	Delaware	12,257
37	Florida	8,760
30	Georgia	9,650
11	Hawaii	12,399
49	Idaho	7,092
18	Illinois	10,835
34	Indiana	9,369
28	Iowa	9,707
26	Kansas	9,951
38	Kentucky	8,756
20	Louisiana	10,533
12	Maine	12,304
9	Maryland	13,449
7	Massachusetts	14,118
21	Michigan	10,483
15	Minnesota	11,098
45	Mississippi	8,075
32	Missouri	9,529
24	Montana	10,059
25	Nebraska	10,045
44	Nevada	8,422
14	New Hampshire	11,932
2	New Jersey	16,271
33	New Mexico	9,439
1	New York	18,126
41	North Carolina	8,587
23	North Dakota	10,151
19	Ohio	10,560
47	Oklahoma	7,885
27	Oregon	9,805
10	Pennsylvania	12,512
8	Rhode Island	13,707
35	South Carolina	9,277
43	South Dakota	8,507
46	Tennessee	7,897
42	Texas	8,540
50	Utah	6,356
4	Vermont	15,175
17	Virginia	10,930
31	Washington	9,550
22	West Virginia	10,367
16	Wisconsin	11,078
5	Wyoming	14,573

RANK ORDER

RANK	STATE	PER PUPIL
1	New York	$18,126
2	New Jersey	16,271
3	Alaska	15,552
4	Vermont	15,175
5	Wyoming	14,573
6	Connecticut	14,531
7	Massachusetts	14,118
8	Rhode Island	13,707
9	Maryland	13,449
10	Pennsylvania	12,512
11	Hawaii	12,399
12	Maine	12,304
13	Delaware	12,257
14	New Hampshire	11,932
15	Minnesota	11,098
16	Wisconsin	11,078
17	Virginia	10,930
18	Illinois	10,835
19	Ohio	10,560
20	Louisiana	10,533
21	Michigan	10,483
22	West Virginia	10,367
23	North Dakota	10,151
24	Montana	10,059
25	Nebraska	10,045
26	Kansas	9,951
27	Oregon	9,805
28	Iowa	9,707
29	California	9,657
30	Georgia	9,650
31	Washington	9,550
32	Missouri	9,529
33	New Mexico	9,439
34	Indiana	9,369
35	South Carolina	9,277
36	Alabama	8,870
37	Florida	8,760
38	Kentucky	8,756
39	Colorado	8,718
40	Arkansas	8,712
41	North Carolina	8,587
42	Texas	8,540
43	South Dakota	8,507
44	Nevada	8,422
45	Mississippi	8,075
46	Tennessee	7,897
47	Oklahoma	7,885
48	Arizona	7,813
49	Idaho	7,092
50	Utah	6,356
	District of Columbia	16,408

Source: U.S. Bureau of the Census, Governments Division
  "Public Education Finances: 2009" (http://www.census.gov/govs/school/)
*Based on student membership. Includes salaries, benefits, services, and supplies. For this per pupil calculation, Census has excluded expenditures for adult education, community services, and other nonelementary-secondary programs.

Percent Change in Per Pupil Public Elementary and Secondary School Current Expenditures: 2005 to 2009 (Adjusted for Inflation)
National Percent Change = 9.8% Increase*

RANK	STATE	PERCENT CHANGE
13	Alabama	14.3
1	Alaska	30.7
17	Arizona	13.6
42	Arkansas	5.7
35	California	9.0
47	Colorado	2.7
13	Connecticut	14.3
48	Delaware	2.3
28	Florida	10.6
33	Georgia	9.4
4	Hawaii	25.5
46	Idaho	2.8
30	Illinois	10.3
50	Indiana	(3.1)
26	Iowa	10.8
7	Kansas	17.6
22	Kentucky	12.0
3	Louisiana	26.1
26	Maine	10.8
5	Maryland	24.7
15	Massachusetts	14.1
48	Michigan	2.3
10	Minnesota	16.6
24	Mississippi	11.8
21	Missouri	12.4
17	Montana	13.6
29	Nebraska	10.4
15	Nevada	14.1
11	New Hampshire	15.0
39	New Jersey	7.3
19	New Mexico	13.4
8	New York	16.9
34	North Carolina	9.2
20	North Dakota	13.3
44	Ohio	3.8
36	Oklahoma	8.5
32	Oregon	10.0
37	Pennsylvania	7.9
6	Rhode Island	20.3
24	South Carolina	11.8
38	South Dakota	7.6
41	Tennessee	6.8
40	Texas	7.0
31	Utah	10.1
9	Vermont	16.7
23	Virginia	11.9
11	Washington	15.0
43	West Virginia	4.8
45	Wisconsin	3.5
2	Wyoming	29.4

RANK	STATE	PERCENT CHANGE
1	Alaska	30.7
2	Wyoming	29.4
3	Louisiana	26.1
4	Hawaii	25.5
5	Maryland	24.7
6	Rhode Island	20.3
7	Kansas	17.6
8	New York	16.9
9	Vermont	16.7
10	Minnesota	16.6
11	New Hampshire	15.0
11	Washington	15.0
13	Alabama	14.3
13	Connecticut	14.3
15	Massachusetts	14.1
15	Nevada	14.1
17	Arizona	13.6
17	Montana	13.6
19	New Mexico	13.4
20	North Dakota	13.3
21	Missouri	12.4
22	Kentucky	12.0
23	Virginia	11.9
24	Mississippi	11.8
24	South Carolina	11.8
26	Iowa	10.8
26	Maine	10.8
28	Florida	10.6
29	Nebraska	10.4
30	Illinois	10.3
31	Utah	10.1
32	Oregon	10.0
33	Georgia	9.4
34	North Carolina	9.2
35	California	9.0
36	Oklahoma	8.5
37	Pennsylvania	7.9
38	South Dakota	7.6
39	New Jersey	7.3
40	Texas	7.0
41	Tennessee	6.8
42	Arkansas	5.7
43	West Virginia	4.8
44	Ohio	3.8
45	Wisconsin	3.5
46	Idaho	2.8
47	Colorado	2.7
48	Delaware	2.3
48	Michigan	2.3
50	Indiana	(3.1)

| | District of Columbia | 15.1 |

Source: CQ Press using data from U.S. Bureau of the Census, Governments Division
"Public Education Finances: 2009 and 2005" (http://www.census.gov/govs/school/)
*School years 2008-2009 and 2004-2005. Adjusted for inflation to 2009 dollars using 1982-1984 as the index base period.

Percent Change in Per Pupil Public Elementary and Secondary School Current Expenditures: 2000 to 2009 (Adjusted for Inflation)
National Percent Change = 23.3% Increase*

ALPHA ORDER

RANK ORDER

RANK	STATE	PERCENT CHANGE
21	Alabama	27.1
7	Alaska	42.8
25	Arizona	24.6
20	Arkansas	27.8
29	California	23.1
45	Colorado	13.5
12	Connecticut	32.5
30	Delaware	22.5
28	Florida	23.6
34	Georgia	20.7
2	Hawaii	53.4
50	Idaho	9.1
33	Illinois	21.0
49	Indiana	9.5
36	Iowa	19.0
17	Kansas	28.6
37	Kentucky	18.7
4	Louisiana	49.6
14	Maine	30.0
6	Maryland	44.0
10	Massachusetts	34.2
48	Michigan	9.8
23	Minnesota	26.3
16	Mississippi	29.3
26	Missouri	24.5
15	Montana	29.9
24	Nebraska	25.5
39	Nevada	17.9
8	New Hampshire	42.0
22	New Jersey	27.0
13	New Mexico	31.8
5	New York	44.9
44	North Carolina	15.1
9	North Dakota	39.8
32	Ohio	21.1
41	Oklahoma	17.3
46	Oregon	12.0
18	Pennsylvania	28.4
11	Rhode Island	33.5
31	South Carolina	21.8
27	South Dakota	23.7
38	Tennessee	18.6
47	Texas	11.5
40	Utah	17.8
2	Vermont	53.4
19	Virginia	28.3
35	Washington	19.9
41	West Virginia	17.3
43	Wisconsin	15.2
1	Wyoming	57.6

RANK	STATE	PERCENT CHANGE
1	Wyoming	57.6
2	Hawaii	53.4
2	Vermont	53.4
4	Louisiana	49.6
5	New York	44.9
6	Maryland	44.0
7	Alaska	42.8
8	New Hampshire	42.0
9	North Dakota	39.8
10	Massachusetts	34.2
11	Rhode Island	33.5
12	Connecticut	32.5
13	New Mexico	31.8
14	Maine	30.0
15	Montana	29.9
16	Mississippi	29.3
17	Kansas	28.6
18	Pennsylvania	28.4
19	Virginia	28.3
20	Arkansas	27.8
21	Alabama	27.1
22	New Jersey	27.0
23	Minnesota	26.3
24	Nebraska	25.5
25	Arizona	24.6
26	Missouri	24.5
27	South Dakota	23.7
28	Florida	23.6
29	California	23.1
30	Delaware	22.5
31	South Carolina	21.8
32	Ohio	21.1
33	Illinois	21.0
34	Georgia	20.7
35	Washington	19.9
36	Iowa	19.0
37	Kentucky	18.7
38	Tennessee	18.6
39	Nevada	17.9
40	Utah	17.8
41	Oklahoma	17.3
41	West Virginia	17.3
43	Wisconsin	15.2
44	North Carolina	15.1
45	Colorado	13.5
46	Oregon	12.0
47	Texas	11.5
48	Michigan	9.8
49	Indiana	9.5
50	Idaho	9.1

District of Columbia   21.5

Source: CQ Press using data from U.S. Bureau of the Census, Governments Division
"Public Education Finances: 2009 and 2000" (http://www.census.gov/govs/school/)
*School years 2008-2009 and 1999-2000. Adjusted for inflation to 2009 dollars using 1982-1984 as the index base period.

Public Elementary and Secondary School
Current Expenditures as a Percent of Total Expenditures in 2009
National Percent = 85.6%*

ALPHA ORDER

RANK	STATE	PERCENT
27	Alabama	86.2
33	Alaska	84.9
43	Arizona	80.7
16	Arkansas	89.2
32	California	85.0
40	Colorado	82.8
13	Connecticut	89.9
37	Delaware	84.0
42	Florida	81.4
36	Georgia	84.4
2	Hawaii	97.0
9	Idaho	91.6
25	Illinois	86.4
19	Indiana	88.7
27	Iowa	86.2
44	Kansas	80.6
24	Kentucky	86.8
22	Louisiana	88.2
7	Maine	93.9
10	Maryland	91.1
5	Massachusetts	94.1
20	Michigan	88.6
34	Minnesota	84.8
23	Mississippi	87.5
27	Missouri	86.2
17	Montana	89.1
39	Nebraska	83.9
45	Nevada	79.8
5	New Hampshire	94.1
8	New Jersey	92.3
48	New Mexico	78.8
21	New York	88.4
35	North Carolina	84.5
14	North Dakota	89.8
31	Ohio	85.4
15	Oklahoma	89.5
37	Oregon	84.0
25	Pennsylvania	86.4
1	Rhode Island	97.2
45	South Carolina	79.8
30	South Dakota	85.8
12	Tennessee	90.3
50	Texas	74.8
47	Utah	79.0
3	Vermont	94.7
18	Virginia	88.8
41	Washington	81.6
4	West Virginia	94.6
11	Wisconsin	91.0
49	Wyoming	77.3

RANK ORDER

RANK	STATE	PERCENT
1	Rhode Island	97.2
2	Hawaii	97.0
3	Vermont	94.7
4	West Virginia	94.6
5	Massachusetts	94.1
5	New Hampshire	94.1
7	Maine	93.9
8	New Jersey	92.3
9	Idaho	91.6
10	Maryland	91.1
11	Wisconsin	91.0
12	Tennessee	90.3
13	Connecticut	89.9
14	North Dakota	89.8
15	Oklahoma	89.5
16	Arkansas	89.2
17	Montana	89.1
18	Virginia	88.8
19	Indiana	88.7
20	Michigan	88.6
21	New York	88.4
22	Louisiana	88.2
23	Mississippi	87.5
24	Kentucky	86.8
25	Illinois	86.4
25	Pennsylvania	86.4
27	Alabama	86.2
27	Iowa	86.2
27	Missouri	86.2
30	South Dakota	85.8
31	Ohio	85.4
32	California	85.0
33	Alaska	84.9
34	Minnesota	84.8
35	North Carolina	84.5
36	Georgia	84.4
37	Delaware	84.0
37	Oregon	84.0
39	Nebraska	83.9
40	Colorado	82.8
41	Washington	81.6
42	Florida	81.4
43	Arizona	80.7
44	Kansas	80.6
45	Nevada	79.8
45	South Carolina	79.8
47	Utah	79.0
48	New Mexico	78.8
49	Wyoming	77.3
50	Texas	74.8
	District of Columbia	91.8

Source: CQ Press using data from U.S. Bureau of the Census, Governments Division
   "Public Education Finances: 2009" (http://www.census.gov/govs/school/)
*Includes salaries, benefits, services, and supplies. Census expanded its usual "current expenditures" concept for education finance reports to include all current public elementary and secondary education outlays regardless of the specific unit of government that actually makes the expenditure.

Public Elementary and Secondary School Capital Expenditures in 2009

National Total = $68,044,563,000*

ALPHA ORDER

RANK	STATE	EXPENDITURES	% of USA
21	Alabama	$924,956,000	1.4%
39	Alaska	303,165,000	0.4%
14	Arizona	1,312,659,000	1.9%
37	Arkansas	409,763,000	0.6%
2	California	8,881,265,000	13.1%
18	Colorado	1,035,058,000	1.5%
27	Connecticut	763,075,000	1.1%
40	Delaware	254,460,000	0.4%
4	Florida	4,533,913,000	6.7%
6	Georgia	2,712,073,000	4.0%
48	Hawaii	68,584,000	0.1%
45	Idaho	111,190,000	0.2%
5	Illinois	2,884,993,000	4.2%
22	Indiana	899,628,000	1.3%
29	Iowa	672,339,000	1.0%
20	Kansas	958,961,000	1.4%
28	Kentucky	720,114,000	1.1%
23	Louisiana	824,390,000	1.2%
46	Maine	108,016,000	0.2%
19	Maryland	961,161,000	1.4%
33	Massachusetts	589,413,000	0.9%
15	Michigan	1,280,455,000	1.9%
16	Minnesota	1,187,008,000	1.7%
35	Mississippi	493,773,000	0.7%
17	Missouri	1,120,105,000	1.6%
41	Montana	158,151,000	0.2%
36	Nebraska	488,293,000	0.7%
32	Nevada	633,545,000	0.9%
44	New Hampshire	112,359,000	0.2%
11	New Jersey	1,499,241,000	2.2%
26	New Mexico	784,529,000	1.2%
3	New York	5,463,718,000	8.0%
10	North Carolina	1,647,148,000	2.4%
47	North Dakota	95,977,000	0.1%
7	Ohio	2,552,105,000	3.8%
34	Oklahoma	568,720,000	0.8%
25	Oregon	803,096,000	1.2%
8	Pennsylvania	2,411,908,000	3.5%
50	Rhode Island	24,161,000	0.0%
13	South Carolina	1,318,784,000	1.9%
43	South Dakota	154,459,000	0.2%
30	Tennessee	652,210,000	1.0%
1	Texas	9,297,597,000	13.7%
24	Utah	821,593,000	1.2%
49	Vermont	64,170,000	0.1%
12	Virginia	1,418,914,000	2.1%
9	Washington	1,818,982,000	2.7%
42	West Virginia	157,049,000	0.2%
31	Wisconsin	648,807,000	1.0%
38	Wyoming	372,507,000	0.5%

RANK ORDER

RANK	STATE	EXPENDITURES	% of USA
1	Texas	$9,297,597,000	13.7%
2	California	8,881,265,000	13.1%
3	New York	5,463,718,000	8.0%
4	Florida	4,533,913,000	6.7%
5	Illinois	2,884,993,000	4.2%
6	Georgia	2,712,073,000	4.0%
7	Ohio	2,552,105,000	3.8%
8	Pennsylvania	2,411,908,000	3.5%
9	Washington	1,818,982,000	2.7%
10	North Carolina	1,647,148,000	2.4%
11	New Jersey	1,499,241,000	2.2%
12	Virginia	1,418,914,000	2.1%
13	South Carolina	1,318,784,000	1.9%
14	Arizona	1,312,659,000	1.9%
15	Michigan	1,280,455,000	1.9%
16	Minnesota	1,187,008,000	1.7%
17	Missouri	1,120,105,000	1.6%
18	Colorado	1,035,058,000	1.5%
19	Maryland	961,161,000	1.4%
20	Kansas	958,961,000	1.4%
21	Alabama	924,956,000	1.4%
22	Indiana	899,628,000	1.3%
23	Louisiana	824,390,000	1.2%
24	Utah	821,593,000	1.2%
25	Oregon	803,096,000	1.2%
26	New Mexico	784,529,000	1.2%
27	Connecticut	763,075,000	1.1%
28	Kentucky	720,114,000	1.1%
29	Iowa	672,339,000	1.0%
30	Tennessee	652,210,000	1.0%
31	Wisconsin	648,807,000	1.0%
32	Nevada	633,545,000	0.9%
33	Massachusetts	589,413,000	0.9%
34	Oklahoma	568,720,000	0.8%
35	Mississippi	493,773,000	0.7%
36	Nebraska	488,293,000	0.7%
37	Arkansas	409,763,000	0.6%
38	Wyoming	372,507,000	0.5%
39	Alaska	303,165,000	0.4%
40	Delaware	254,460,000	0.4%
41	Montana	158,151,000	0.2%
42	West Virginia	157,049,000	0.2%
43	South Dakota	154,459,000	0.2%
44	New Hampshire	112,359,000	0.2%
45	Idaho	111,190,000	0.2%
46	Maine	108,016,000	0.2%
47	North Dakota	95,977,000	0.1%
48	Hawaii	68,584,000	0.1%
49	Vermont	64,170,000	0.1%
50	Rhode Island	24,161,000	0.0%
	District of Columbia	66,023,000	0.1%

Source: U.S. Bureau of the Census, Governments Division
    "Public Education Finances: 2009" (http://www.census.gov/govs/school/)

*Includes expenditures for construction of buildings, roads, and other improvements; purchases of equipment, land, and structures; and payments for capital leases. Includes amounts for additions, replacements, and major alterations to structures; however, maintenance and repairs to such structures are considered current operation expenditures.

Per Capita Public Elementary and Secondary School Capital Expenditures in 2009
National Per Capita = $222*

ALPHA ORDER

ALPHA ORDER

RANK	STATE	PER CAPITA
24	Alabama	$196
2	Alaska	434
23	Arizona	199
38	Arkansas	142
14	California	240
22	Colorado	206
20	Connecticut	217
8	Delaware	287
13	Florida	245
10	Georgia	276
49	Hawaii	53
48	Idaho	72
18	Illinois	223
39	Indiana	140
17	Iowa	224
5	Kansas	340
33	Kentucky	167
28	Louisiana	184
47	Maine	82
32	Maryland	169
44	Massachusetts	89
40	Michigan	128
16	Minnesota	225
33	Mississippi	167
27	Missouri	187
35	Montana	162
12	Nebraska	272
14	Nevada	240
46	New Hampshire	85
31	New Jersey	172
3	New Mexico	390
9	New York	280
30	North Carolina	176
37	North Dakota	148
19	Ohio	221
36	Oklahoma	154
21	Oregon	210
25	Pennsylvania	191
50	Rhode Island	23
7	South Carolina	289
26	South Dakota	190
42	Tennessee	104
4	Texas	375
6	Utah	295
43	Vermont	103
29	Virginia	180
11	Washington	273
45	West Virginia	86
41	Wisconsin	115
1	Wyoming	684

RANK ORDER

RANK	STATE	PER CAPITA
1	Wyoming	$684
2	Alaska	434
3	New Mexico	390
4	Texas	375
5	Kansas	340
6	Utah	295
7	South Carolina	289
8	Delaware	287
9	New York	280
10	Georgia	276
11	Washington	273
12	Nebraska	272
13	Florida	245
14	California	240
14	Nevada	240
16	Minnesota	225
17	Iowa	224
18	Illinois	223
19	Ohio	221
20	Connecticut	217
21	Oregon	210
22	Colorado	206
23	Arizona	199
24	Alabama	196
25	Pennsylvania	191
26	South Dakota	190
27	Missouri	187
28	Louisiana	184
29	Virginia	180
30	North Carolina	176
31	New Jersey	172
32	Maryland	169
33	Kentucky	167
33	Mississippi	167
35	Montana	162
36	Oklahoma	154
37	North Dakota	148
38	Arkansas	142
39	Indiana	140
40	Michigan	128
41	Wisconsin	115
42	Tennessee	104
43	Vermont	103
44	Massachusetts	89
45	West Virginia	86
46	New Hampshire	85
47	Maine	82
48	Idaho	72
49	Hawaii	53
50	Rhode Island	23
	District of Columbia	110

Source: CQ Press using data from U.S. Bureau of the Census, Governments Division
"Public Education Finances: 2009" (http://www.census.gov/govs/school/)

*Includes expenditures for construction of buildings, roads, and other improvements; purchases of equipment, land, and structures; and payments for capital leases. Includes amounts for additions, replacements, and major alterations to structures; however, maintenance and repairs to such structures are considered current operation expenditures.

Per Pupil Elementary and Secondary School
Capital Expenditures in 2009
National Per Pupil = 1,411*

ALPHA ORDER

ALPHA ORDER | | | RANK ORDER | | |
RANK	STATE	PER PUPIL	RANK	STATE	PER PUPIL
27	Alabama	$1,240	1	Wyoming	$4,283
3	Alaska	2,328	2	New Mexico	2,386
23	Arizona	1,337	3	Alaska	2,328
39	Arkansas	864	4	Delaware	2,179
17	California	1,440	5	Kansas	2,040
24	Colorado	1,274	6	New York	2,026
20	Connecticut	1,395	7	Texas	2,001
4	Delaware	2,179	8	South Carolina	1,846
10	Florida	1,728	9	Washington	1,756
12	Georgia	1,644	10	Florida	1,728
49	Hawaii	382	11	Nebraska	1,671
48	Idaho	415	12	Georgia	1,644
22	Illinois	1,363	13	Utah	1,543
38	Indiana	875	14	Minnesota	1,478
21	Iowa	1,379	15	Ohio	1,476
5	Kansas	2,040	16	Nevada	1,470
34	Kentucky	1,075	17	California	1,440
26	Louisiana	1,244	18	Oregon	1,429
45	Maine	578	19	Pennsylvania	1,422
30	Maryland	1,139	20	Connecticut	1,395
44	Massachusetts	632	21	Iowa	1,379
40	Michigan	823	22	Illinois	1,363
14	Minnesota	1,478	23	Arizona	1,337
36	Mississippi	1,005	24	Colorado	1,274
25	Missouri	1,247	25	Missouri	1,247
32	Montana	1,117	26	Louisiana	1,244
11	Nebraska	1,671	27	Alabama	1,240
16	Nevada	1,470	28	South Dakota	1,220
46	New Hampshire	568	29	Virginia	1,149
33	New Jersey	1,103	30	Maryland	1,139
2	New Mexico	2,386	31	North Carolina	1,134
6	New York	2,026	32	Montana	1,117
31	North Carolina	1,134	33	New Jersey	1,103
35	North Dakota	1,014	34	Kentucky	1,075
15	Ohio	1,476	35	North Dakota	1,014
37	Oklahoma	882	36	Mississippi	1,005
18	Oregon	1,429	37	Oklahoma	882
19	Pennsylvania	1,422	38	Indiana	875
50	Rhode Island	171	39	Arkansas	864
8	South Carolina	1,846	40	Michigan	823
28	South Dakota	1,220	41	Wisconsin	748
43	Tennessee	672	42	Vermont	728
7	Texas	2,001	43	Tennessee	672
13	Utah	1,543	44	Massachusetts	632
42	Vermont	728	45	Maine	578
29	Virginia	1,149	46	New Hampshire	568
9	Washington	1,756	47	West Virginia	557
47	West Virginia	557	48	Idaho	415
41	Wisconsin	748	49	Hawaii	382
1	Wyoming	4,283	50	Rhode Island	171
				District of Columbia	1,489

Source: CQ Press using data from U.S. Bureau of the Census, Governments Division
"Public Education Finances: 2009" (http://www.census.gov/govs/school/)

*Based on student membership. Includes expenditures for construction of buildings, roads, and other improvements; purchases of equipment, land, and structures; and payments for capital leases. Includes amounts for additions, replacements, and major alterations to structures; however, maintenance and repairs to such structures are considered current operation expenditures.

Public Elementary and Secondary School
Capital Expenditures as a Percent of Total Expenditures in 2009
National Percent = 11.2%*

ALPHA ORDER

RANK	STATE	PERCENT
20	Alabama	11.8
14	Alaska	12.7
13	Arizona	13.7
36	Arkansas	8.2
15	California	12.4
18	Colorado	12.0
35	Connecticut	8.4
9	Delaware	14.7
6	Florida	15.7
10	Georgia	14.3
49	Hawaii	3.0
43	Idaho	5.3
26	Illinois	10.7
36	Indiana	8.2
16	Iowa	12.2
5	Kansas	16.5
27	Kentucky	10.5
28	Louisiana	10.4
47	Maine	4.2
38	Maryland	7.7
48	Massachusetts	4.0
40	Michigan	6.8
24	Minnesota	10.8
24	Mississippi	10.8
22	Missouri	11.1
29	Montana	9.8
11	Nebraska	13.9
12	Nevada	13.8
45	New Hampshire	4.3
42	New Jersey	5.9
2	New Mexico	19.9
32	New York	9.5
22	North Carolina	11.1
34	North Dakota	8.9
21	Ohio	11.5
30	Oklahoma	9.6
18	Oregon	12.0
30	Pennsylvania	9.6
50	Rhode Island	1.1
6	South Carolina	15.7
16	South Dakota	12.2
39	Tennessee	7.6
4	Texas	17.4
3	Utah	18.6
45	Vermont	4.3
33	Virginia	9.3
8	Washington	14.9
44	West Virginia	5.0
41	Wisconsin	6.1
1	Wyoming	22.6

RANK ORDER

RANK	STATE	PERCENT
1	Wyoming	22.6
2	New Mexico	19.9
3	Utah	18.6
4	Texas	17.4
5	Kansas	16.5
6	Florida	15.7
6	South Carolina	15.7
8	Washington	14.9
9	Delaware	14.7
10	Georgia	14.3
11	Nebraska	13.9
12	Nevada	13.8
13	Arizona	13.7
14	Alaska	12.7
15	California	12.4
16	Iowa	12.2
16	South Dakota	12.2
18	Colorado	12.0
18	Oregon	12.0
20	Alabama	11.8
21	Ohio	11.5
22	Missouri	11.1
22	North Carolina	11.1
24	Minnesota	10.8
24	Mississippi	10.8
26	Illinois	10.7
27	Kentucky	10.5
28	Louisiana	10.4
29	Montana	9.8
30	Oklahoma	9.6
30	Pennsylvania	9.6
32	New York	9.5
33	Virginia	9.3
34	North Dakota	8.9
35	Connecticut	8.4
36	Arkansas	8.2
36	Indiana	8.2
38	Maryland	7.7
39	Tennessee	7.6
40	Michigan	6.8
41	Wisconsin	6.1
42	New Jersey	5.9
43	Idaho	5.3
44	West Virginia	5.0
45	New Hampshire	4.3
45	Vermont	4.3
47	Maine	4.2
48	Massachusetts	4.0
49	Hawaii	3.0
50	Rhode Island	1.1

District of Columbia 8.2

Source: CQ Press using data from U.S. Bureau of the Census, Governments Division
"Public Education Finances: 2009" (http://www.census.gov/govs/school/)

*Includes expenditures for construction of buildings, roads, and other improvements; purchases of equipment, land, and structures; and payments for capital leases. Includes amounts for additions, replacements, and major alterations to structures; however, maintenance and repairs to such structures are considered current operation expenditures.

Public Elementary and Secondary School "Other" Expenditures in 2009

National Total = $19,103,480,000*

RANK	STATE	EXPENDITURES	% of USA
28	Alabama	$152,188,000	0.8%
37	Alaska	59,873,000	0.3%
10	Arizona	532,099,000	2.8%
30	Arkansas	127,159,000	0.7%
2	California	1,898,611,000	9.9%
13	Colorado	451,769,000	2.4%
27	Connecticut	154,000,000	0.8%
44	Delaware	22,748,000	0.1%
6	Florida	835,468,000	4.4%
23	Georgia	263,157,000	1.4%
50	Hawaii	0	0.0%
36	Idaho	62,834,000	0.3%
7	Illinois	764,564,000	4.0%
16	Indiana	342,464,000	1.8%
33	Iowa	85,863,000	0.4%
26	Kansas	171,645,000	0.9%
24	Kentucky	179,223,000	0.9%
31	Louisiana	108,390,000	0.6%
40	Maine	47,700,000	0.2%
29	Maryland	147,545,000	0.8%
21	Massachusetts	279,580,000	1.5%
5	Michigan	865,016,000	4.5%
11	Minnesota	487,438,000	2.6%
35	Mississippi	73,239,000	0.4%
20	Missouri	280,416,000	1.5%
45	Montana	17,081,000	0.1%
34	Nebraska	74,180,000	0.4%
19	Nevada	288,768,000	1.5%
41	New Hampshire	39,774,000	0.2%
12	New Jersey	451,848,000	2.4%
39	New Mexico	48,940,000	0.3%
3	New York	1,191,856,000	6.2%
9	North Carolina	646,256,000	3.4%
46	North Dakota	14,444,000	0.1%
8	Ohio	691,872,000	3.6%
38	Oklahoma	55,485,000	0.3%
22	Oregon	269,116,000	1.4%
4	Pennsylvania	995,704,000	5.2%
42	Rhode Island	37,030,000	0.2%
15	South Carolina	378,377,000	2.0%
43	South Dakota	24,675,000	0.1%
25	Tennessee	178,018,000	0.9%
1	Texas	4,141,564,000	21.7%
32	Utah	107,017,000	0.6%
47	Vermont	13,578,000	0.1%
18	Virginia	289,567,000	1.5%
14	Washington	423,843,000	2.2%
48	West Virginia	12,173,000	0.1%
17	Wisconsin	316,866,000	1.7%
49	Wyoming	2,459,000	0.0%

RANK	STATE	EXPENDITURES	% of USA
1	Texas	$4,141,564,000	21.7%
2	California	1,898,611,000	9.9%
3	New York	1,191,856,000	6.2%
4	Pennsylvania	995,704,000	5.2%
5	Michigan	865,016,000	4.5%
6	Florida	835,468,000	4.4%
7	Illinois	764,564,000	4.0%
8	Ohio	691,872,000	3.6%
9	North Carolina	646,256,000	3.4%
10	Arizona	532,099,000	2.8%
11	Minnesota	487,438,000	2.6%
12	New Jersey	451,848,000	2.4%
13	Colorado	451,769,000	2.4%
14	Washington	423,843,000	2.2%
15	South Carolina	378,377,000	2.0%
16	Indiana	342,464,000	1.8%
17	Wisconsin	316,866,000	1.7%
18	Virginia	289,567,000	1.5%
19	Nevada	288,768,000	1.5%
20	Missouri	280,416,000	1.5%
21	Massachusetts	279,580,000	1.5%
22	Oregon	269,116,000	1.4%
23	Georgia	263,157,000	1.4%
24	Kentucky	179,223,000	0.9%
25	Tennessee	178,018,000	0.9%
26	Kansas	171,645,000	0.9%
27	Connecticut	154,000,000	0.8%
28	Alabama	152,188,000	0.8%
29	Maryland	147,545,000	0.8%
30	Arkansas	127,159,000	0.7%
31	Louisiana	108,390,000	0.6%
32	Utah	107,017,000	0.6%
33	Iowa	85,863,000	0.4%
34	Nebraska	74,180,000	0.4%
35	Mississippi	73,239,000	0.4%
36	Idaho	62,834,000	0.3%
37	Alaska	59,873,000	0.3%
38	Oklahoma	55,485,000	0.3%
39	New Mexico	48,940,000	0.3%
40	Maine	47,700,000	0.2%
41	New Hampshire	39,774,000	0.2%
42	Rhode Island	37,030,000	0.2%
43	South Dakota	24,675,000	0.1%
44	Delaware	22,748,000	0.1%
45	Montana	17,081,000	0.1%
46	North Dakota	14,444,000	0.1%
47	Vermont	13,578,000	0.1%
48	West Virginia	12,173,000	0.1%
49	Wyoming	2,459,000	0.0%
50	Hawaii	0	0.0%
	District of Columbia	0	0.0%

Source: U.S. Bureau of the Census, Governments Division
   "Public Education Finances: 2009" (http://www.census.gov/govs/school/)
*Current spending for other than elementary-secondary education instruction and support services activities. This includes food services, enterprise operations, community services (e.g., swimming pools and libraries), and adult education.

Per Capita Public Elementary and Secondary School "Other" Expenditures in 2009
National Per Capita = $62.22*

RANK	STATE	PER CAPITA
33	Alabama	$32.32
6	Alaska	85.72
8	Arizona	80.67
23	Arkansas	44.01
20	California	51.37
4	Colorado	89.91
24	Connecticut	43.77
40	Delaware	25.70
22	Florida	45.07
38	Georgia	26.77
50	Hawaii	0.00
28	Idaho	40.65
16	Illinois	59.22
18	Indiana	53.32
36	Iowa	28.55
14	Kansas	60.89
26	Kentucky	41.54
43	Louisiana	24.13
31	Maine	36.18
39	Maryland	25.89
25	Massachusetts	42.40
5	Michigan	86.76
3	Minnesota	92.56
41	Mississippi	24.81
21	Missouri	46.83
46	Montana	17.52
27	Nebraska	41.29
2	Nevada	109.25
35	New Hampshire	30.03
19	New Jersey	51.89
42	New Mexico	24.35
13	New York	60.99
11	North Carolina	68.89
44	North Dakota	22.33
15	Ohio	59.94
47	Oklahoma	15.05
10	Oregon	70.35
9	Pennsylvania	78.99
32	Rhode Island	35.16
7	South Carolina	82.95
34	South Dakota	30.37
37	Tennessee	28.27
1	Texas	167.12
29	Utah	38.43
45	Vermont	21.84
30	Virginia	36.74
12	Washington	63.60
48	West Virginia	6.69
17	Wisconsin	56.04
49	Wyoming	4.52

RANK	STATE	PER CAPITA
1	Texas	$167.12
2	Nevada	109.25
3	Minnesota	92.56
4	Colorado	89.91
5	Michigan	86.76
6	Alaska	85.72
7	South Carolina	82.95
8	Arizona	80.67
9	Pennsylvania	78.99
10	Oregon	70.35
11	North Carolina	68.89
12	Washington	63.60
13	New York	60.99
14	Kansas	60.89
15	Ohio	59.94
16	Illinois	59.22
17	Wisconsin	56.04
18	Indiana	53.32
19	New Jersey	51.89
20	California	51.37
21	Missouri	46.83
22	Florida	45.07
23	Arkansas	44.01
24	Connecticut	43.77
25	Massachusetts	42.40
26	Kentucky	41.54
27	Nebraska	41.29
28	Idaho	40.65
29	Utah	38.43
30	Virginia	36.74
31	Maine	36.18
32	Rhode Island	35.16
33	Alabama	32.32
34	South Dakota	30.37
35	New Hampshire	30.03
36	Iowa	28.55
37	Tennessee	28.27
38	Georgia	26.77
39	Maryland	25.89
40	Delaware	25.70
41	Mississippi	24.81
42	New Mexico	24.35
43	Louisiana	24.13
44	North Dakota	22.33
45	Vermont	21.84
46	Montana	17.52
47	Oklahoma	15.05
48	West Virginia	6.69
49	Wyoming	4.52
50	Hawaii	0.00

District of Columbia	0.00

Source: CQ Press using data from U.S. Bureau of the Census, Governments Division
"Public Education Finances: 2009" (http://www.census.gov/govs/school/)
*Current spending for other than elementary-secondary education instruction and support services activities. This includes food services, enterprise operations, community services (e.g., swimming pools and libraries), and adult education.

Per Pupil Elementary and Secondary School "Other" Expenditures in 2009
National Per Pupil = $396*

ALPHA ORDER

RANK	STATE	PER PUPIL
32	Alabama	$204
10	Alaska	460
7	Arizona	542
25	Arkansas	268
22	California	308
5	Colorado	556
24	Connecticut	282
35	Delaware	195
20	Florida	319
41	Georgia	160
50	Hawaii	0
30	Idaho	234
17	Illinois	361
18	Indiana	333
38	Iowa	176
15	Kansas	365
25	Kentucky	268
40	Louisiana	164
28	Maine	255
39	Maryland	175
23	Massachusetts	300
5	Michigan	556
3	Minnesota	607
44	Mississippi	149
21	Missouri	312
46	Montana	121
29	Nebraska	254
2	Nevada	670
33	New Hampshire	201
19	New Jersey	332
44	New Mexico	149
12	New York	442
11	North Carolina	445
43	North Dakota	153
14	Ohio	400
47	Oklahoma	86
9	Oregon	479
4	Pennsylvania	587
27	Rhode Island	262
8	South Carolina	530
35	South Dakota	195
37	Tennessee	183
1	Texas	891
33	Utah	201
42	Vermont	154
30	Virginia	234
13	Washington	409
48	West Virginia	43
15	Wisconsin	365
49	Wyoming	28

RANK ORDER

RANK	STATE	PER PUPIL
1	Texas	$891
2	Nevada	670
3	Minnesota	607
4	Pennsylvania	587
5	Colorado	556
5	Michigan	556
7	Arizona	542
8	South Carolina	530
9	Oregon	479
10	Alaska	460
11	North Carolina	445
12	New York	442
13	Washington	409
14	Ohio	400
15	Kansas	365
15	Wisconsin	365
17	Illinois	361
18	Indiana	333
19	New Jersey	332
20	Florida	319
21	Missouri	312
22	California	308
23	Massachusetts	300
24	Connecticut	282
25	Arkansas	268
25	Kentucky	268
27	Rhode Island	262
28	Maine	255
29	Nebraska	254
30	Idaho	234
30	Virginia	234
32	Alabama	204
33	New Hampshire	201
33	Utah	201
35	Delaware	195
35	South Dakota	195
37	Tennessee	183
38	Iowa	176
39	Maryland	175
40	Louisiana	164
41	Georgia	160
42	Vermont	154
43	North Dakota	153
44	Mississippi	149
44	New Mexico	149
46	Montana	121
47	Oklahoma	86
48	West Virginia	43
49	Wyoming	28
50	Hawaii	0
	District of Columbia	0

Source: CQ Press using data from U.S. Bureau of the Census, Governments Division
    "Public Education Finances: 2009" (http://www.census.gov/govs/school/)
*Based on student membership. Current spending for other than elementary-secondary education instruction and support services activities. This includes food services, enterprise operations, community services (e.g., swimming pools and libraries), and adult education.

Public Elementary and Secondary School
"Other" Expenditures as a Percent of Total Expenditures in 2009
National Percent = 3.2%*

ALPHA ORDER

RANK	STATE	PERCENT
29	Alabama	1.9
23	Alaska	2.5
3	Arizona	5.6
20	Arkansas	2.6
20	California	2.6
4	Colorado	5.2
34	Connecticut	1.7
41	Delaware	1.3
17	Florida	2.9
39	Georgia	1.4
50	Hawaii	0.0
14	Idaho	3.0
18	Illinois	2.8
12	Indiana	3.1
36	Iowa	1.6
14	Kansas	3.0
20	Kentucky	2.6
39	Louisiana	1.4
29	Maine	1.9
43	Maryland	1.2
29	Massachusetts	1.9
5	Michigan	4.6
7	Minnesota	4.4
36	Mississippi	1.6
18	Missouri	2.8
45	Montana	1.1
25	Nebraska	2.1
2	Nevada	6.3
38	New Hampshire	1.5
33	New Jersey	1.8
43	New Mexico	1.2
25	New York	2.1
7	North Carolina	4.4
41	North Dakota	1.3
12	Ohio	3.1
46	Oklahoma	0.9
9	Oregon	4.0
9	Pennsylvania	4.0
34	Rhode Island	1.7
6	South Carolina	4.5
28	South Dakota	2.0
25	Tennessee	2.1
1	Texas	7.8
24	Utah	2.4
46	Vermont	0.9
29	Virginia	1.9
11	Washington	3.5
48	West Virginia	0.4
14	Wisconsin	3.0
49	Wyoming	0.1

RANK ORDER

RANK	STATE	PERCENT
1	Texas	7.8
2	Nevada	6.3
3	Arizona	5.6
4	Colorado	5.2
5	Michigan	4.6
6	South Carolina	4.5
7	Minnesota	4.4
7	North Carolina	4.4
9	Oregon	4.0
9	Pennsylvania	4.0
11	Washington	3.5
12	Indiana	3.1
12	Ohio	3.1
14	Idaho	3.0
14	Kansas	3.0
14	Wisconsin	3.0
17	Florida	2.9
18	Illinois	2.8
18	Missouri	2.8
20	Arkansas	2.6
20	California	2.6
20	Kentucky	2.6
23	Alaska	2.5
24	Utah	2.4
25	Nebraska	2.1
25	New York	2.1
25	Tennessee	2.1
28	South Dakota	2.0
29	Alabama	1.9
29	Maine	1.9
29	Massachusetts	1.9
29	Virginia	1.9
33	New Jersey	1.8
34	Connecticut	1.7
34	Rhode Island	1.7
36	Iowa	1.6
36	Mississippi	1.6
38	New Hampshire	1.5
39	Georgia	1.4
39	Louisiana	1.4
41	Delaware	1.3
41	North Dakota	1.3
43	Maryland	1.2
43	New Mexico	1.2
45	Montana	1.1
46	Oklahoma	0.9
46	Vermont	0.9
48	West Virginia	0.4
49	Wyoming	0.1
50	Hawaii	0.0
	District of Columbia	0.0

Source: CQ Press using data from U.S. Bureau of the Census, Governments Division
"Public Education Finances: 2009" (http://www.census.gov/govs/school/)

*Current spending for other than elementary-secondary education instruction and support services activities. This includes food services, enterprise operations, community services (e.g., swimming pools and libraries), and adult education.

Public Elementary and Secondary School Current Expenditures for Salaries, Wages, and Benefits in 2009
National Total = $419,521,844,000*

ALPHA ORDER

RANK	STATE	EXPENDITURES	% of USA
25	Alabama	$5,406,569,000	1.3%
43	Alaska	1,590,951,000	0.4%
22	Arizona	6,026,752,000	1.4%
32	Arkansas	3,227,001,000	0.8%
1	California	49,747,108,000	11.9%
23	Colorado	5,669,994,000	1.4%
20	Connecticut	6,550,055,000	1.6%
45	Delaware	1,160,901,000	0.3%
6	Florida	18,131,246,000	4.3%
10	Georgia	13,191,839,000	3.1%
41	Hawaii	1,767,188,000	0.4%
44	Idaho	1,568,599,000	0.4%
4	Illinois	22,012,312,000	5.2%
16	Indiana	8,219,413,000	2.0%
29	Iowa	4,005,183,000	1.0%
31	Kansas	3,621,540,000	0.9%
27	Kentucky	5,059,592,000	1.2%
24	Louisiana	5,600,754,000	1.3%
40	Maine	1,888,031,000	0.5%
14	Maryland	9,643,759,000	2.3%
12	Massachusetts	11,023,549,000	2.6%
9	Michigan	13,633,593,000	3.2%
18	Minnesota	7,504,813,000	1.8%
33	Mississippi	3,155,097,000	0.8%
19	Missouri	6,974,880,000	1.7%
47	Montana	1,072,607,000	0.3%
38	Nebraska	2,300,890,000	0.5%
34	Nevada	3,038,324,000	0.7%
39	New Hampshire	1,898,749,000	0.5%
5	New Jersey	18,307,921,000	4.4%
37	New Mexico	2,473,481,000	0.6%
2	New York	40,853,507,000	9.7%
13	North Carolina	10,424,845,000	2.5%
50	North Dakota	763,549,000	0.2%
8	Ohio	15,179,298,000	3.6%
30	Oklahoma	3,797,169,000	0.9%
28	Oregon	4,494,292,000	1.1%
7	Pennsylvania	16,553,097,000	3.9%
42	Rhode Island	1,669,115,000	0.4%
26	South Carolina	5,403,623,000	1.3%
49	South Dakota	822,444,000	0.2%
21	Tennessee	6,201,819,000	1.5%
3	Texas	31,935,693,000	7.6%
35	Utah	2,900,557,000	0.7%
46	Vermont	1,073,676,000	0.3%
11	Virginia	11,714,482,000	2.8%
15	Washington	8,300,794,000	2.0%
36	West Virginia	2,477,614,000	0.6%
17	Wisconsin	7,887,517,000	1.9%
48	Wyoming	1,064,196,000	0.3%

RANK ORDER

RANK	STATE	EXPENDITURES	% of USA
1	California	$49,747,108,000	11.9%
2	New York	40,853,507,000	9.7%
3	Texas	31,935,693,000	7.6%
4	Illinois	22,012,312,000	5.2%
5	New Jersey	18,307,921,000	4.4%
6	Florida	18,131,246,000	4.3%
7	Pennsylvania	16,553,097,000	3.9%
8	Ohio	15,179,298,000	3.6%
9	Michigan	13,633,593,000	3.2%
10	Georgia	13,191,839,000	3.1%
11	Virginia	11,714,482,000	2.8%
12	Massachusetts	11,023,549,000	2.6%
13	North Carolina	10,424,845,000	2.5%
14	Maryland	9,643,759,000	2.3%
15	Washington	8,300,794,000	2.0%
16	Indiana	8,219,413,000	2.0%
17	Wisconsin	7,887,517,000	1.9%
18	Minnesota	7,504,813,000	1.8%
19	Missouri	6,974,880,000	1.7%
20	Connecticut	6,550,055,000	1.6%
21	Tennessee	6,201,819,000	1.5%
22	Arizona	6,026,752,000	1.4%
23	Colorado	5,669,994,000	1.4%
24	Louisiana	5,600,754,000	1.3%
25	Alabama	5,406,569,000	1.3%
26	South Carolina	5,403,623,000	1.3%
27	Kentucky	5,059,592,000	1.2%
28	Oregon	4,494,292,000	1.1%
29	Iowa	4,005,183,000	1.0%
30	Oklahoma	3,797,169,000	0.9%
31	Kansas	3,621,540,000	0.9%
32	Arkansas	3,227,001,000	0.8%
33	Mississippi	3,155,097,000	0.8%
34	Nevada	3,038,324,000	0.7%
35	Utah	2,900,557,000	0.7%
36	West Virginia	2,477,614,000	0.6%
37	New Mexico	2,473,481,000	0.6%
38	Nebraska	2,300,890,000	0.5%
39	New Hampshire	1,898,749,000	0.5%
40	Maine	1,888,031,000	0.5%
41	Hawaii	1,767,188,000	0.4%
42	Rhode Island	1,669,115,000	0.4%
43	Alaska	1,590,951,000	0.4%
44	Idaho	1,568,599,000	0.4%
45	Delaware	1,160,901,000	0.3%
46	Vermont	1,073,676,000	0.3%
47	Montana	1,072,607,000	0.3%
48	Wyoming	1,064,196,000	0.3%
49	South Dakota	822,444,000	0.2%
50	North Dakota	763,549,000	0.2%
	District of Columbia	531,866,000	0.1%

Source: CQ Press using data from U.S. Bureau of the Census, Governments Division
"Public Education Finances: 2009" (http://www.census.gov/govs/school/)
*Current spending for compensation of school system officers and employees. Consists of gross compensation before deductions for withheld taxes, retirement contributions, or other purposes. Also includes benefits such as contributions on behalf of employees for retirement coverage, Social Security, group health and life insurance, tuition reimbursement, workers' compensation, and unemployment compensation.

Per Capita Public Elementary and Secondary School Current Expenditures for Salaries, Wages, and Benefits in 2009
National Per Capita = $1,366*

ALPHA ORDER

RANK ORDER

RANK	STATE	PER CAPITA	RANK	STATE	PER CAPITA
38	Alabama	$1,148	1	Alaska	$2,278
1	Alaska	2,278	2	New Jersey	2,102
50	Arizona	914	3	New York	2,091
40	Arkansas	1,117	4	Wyoming	1,955
19	California	1,346	5	Connecticut	1,862
39	Colorado	1,128	6	Vermont	1,727
5	Connecticut	1,862	7	Illinois	1,705
24	Delaware	1,312	8	Maryland	1,692
49	Florida	978	9	Massachusetts	1,672
20	Georgia	1,342	10	Rhode Island	1,585
17	Hawaii	1,364	11	Virginia	1,486
46	Idaho	1,015	12	New Hampshire	1,433
7	Illinois	1,705	13	Maine	1,432
28	Indiana	1,280	14	Minnesota	1,425
21	Iowa	1,332	15	Wisconsin	1,395
26	Kansas	1,285	16	Michigan	1,367
35	Kentucky	1,173	17	Hawaii	1,364
29	Louisiana	1,247	18	West Virginia	1,361
13	Maine	1,432	19	California	1,346
8	Maryland	1,692	20	Georgia	1,342
9	Massachusetts	1,672	21	Iowa	1,332
16	Michigan	1,367	22	Ohio	1,315
14	Minnesota	1,425	23	Pennsylvania	1,313
43	Mississippi	1,069	24	Delaware	1,312
36	Missouri	1,165	25	Texas	1,289
42	Montana	1,100	26	Kansas	1,285
27	Nebraska	1,281	27	Nebraska	1,281
37	Nevada	1,150	28	Indiana	1,280
12	New Hampshire	1,433	29	Louisiana	1,247
2	New Jersey	2,102	30	Washington	1,246
31	New Mexico	1,231	31	New Mexico	1,231
3	New York	2,091	32	South Carolina	1,185
41	North Carolina	1,111	33	North Dakota	1,180
33	North Dakota	1,180	34	Oregon	1,175
22	Ohio	1,315	35	Kentucky	1,173
45	Oklahoma	1,030	36	Missouri	1,165
34	Oregon	1,175	37	Nevada	1,150
23	Pennsylvania	1,313	38	Alabama	1,148
10	Rhode Island	1,585	39	Colorado	1,128
32	South Carolina	1,185	40	Arkansas	1,117
47	South Dakota	1,012	41	North Carolina	1,111
48	Tennessee	985	42	Montana	1,100
25	Texas	1,289	43	Mississippi	1,069
44	Utah	1,042	44	Utah	1,042
6	Vermont	1,727	45	Oklahoma	1,030
11	Virginia	1,486	46	Idaho	1,015
30	Washington	1,246	47	South Dakota	1,012
18	West Virginia	1,361	48	Tennessee	985
15	Wisconsin	1,395	49	Florida	978
4	Wyoming	1,955	50	Arizona	914

District of Columbia   887

Source: CQ Press using data from U.S. Bureau of the Census, Governments Division
   "Public Education Finances: 2009" (http://www.census.gov/govs/school/)
*Current spending for compensation of school system officers and employees. Consists of gross compensation before deductions for withheld taxes, retirement contributions, or other purposes. Also includes benefits such as contributions on behalf of employees for retirement coverage, Social Security, group health and life insurance, tuition reimbursement, workers' compensation, and unemployment compensation.

Per Pupil Public Elementary and Secondary School Current Expenditures for Salaries, Wages, and Benefits in 2009
National Per Pupil = $8,697*

ALPHA ORDER

RANK	STATE	PER PUPIL		RANK	STATE	PER PUPIL
37	Alabama	$7,251		1	New York	$15,149
4	Alaska	12,216		2	New Jersey	13,471
47	Arizona	6,139		3	Wyoming	12,236
43	Arkansas	6,802		4	Alaska	12,216
24	California	8,068		5	Vermont	12,187
40	Colorado	6,979		6	Connecticut	11,976
6	Connecticut	11,976		7	Massachusetts	11,822
12	Delaware	9,939		8	Rhode Island	11,794
41	Florida	6,912		9	Maryland	11,429
27	Georgia	7,997		10	Illinois	10,398
13	Hawaii	9,846		11	Maine	10,110
49	Idaho	5,854		12	Delaware	9,939
10	Illinois	10,398		13	Hawaii	9,846
29	Indiana	7,993		14	Pennsylvania	9,762
23	Iowa	8,215		15	New Hampshire	9,593
32	Kansas	7,703		16	Virginia	9,485
35	Kentucky	7,553		17	Minnesota	9,345
22	Louisiana	8,450		18	Wisconsin	9,097
11	Maine	10,110		19	West Virginia	8,789
9	Maryland	11,429		20	Ohio	8,779
7	Massachusetts	11,822		21	Michigan	8,764
21	Michigan	8,764		22	Louisiana	8,450
17	Minnesota	9,345		23	Iowa	8,215
45	Mississippi	6,423		24	California	8,068
31	Missouri	7,762		25	North Dakota	8,067
33	Montana	7,574		26	Washington	8,011
30	Nebraska	7,875		27	Georgia	7,997
39	Nevada	7,050		27	Oregon	7,997
15	New Hampshire	9,593		29	Indiana	7,993
2	New Jersey	13,471		30	Nebraska	7,875
36	New Mexico	7,524		31	Missouri	7,762
1	New York	15,149		32	Kansas	7,703
38	North Carolina	7,179		33	Montana	7,574
25	North Dakota	8,067		34	South Carolina	7,565
20	Ohio	8,779		35	Kentucky	7,553
48	Oklahoma	5,891		36	New Mexico	7,524
27	Oregon	7,997		37	Alabama	7,251
14	Pennsylvania	9,762		38	North Carolina	7,179
8	Rhode Island	11,794		39	Nevada	7,050
34	South Carolina	7,565		40	Colorado	6,979
44	South Dakota	6,495		41	Florida	6,912
46	Tennessee	6,388		42	Texas	6,872
42	Texas	6,872		43	Arkansas	6,802
50	Utah	5,448		44	South Dakota	6,495
5	Vermont	12,187		45	Mississippi	6,423
16	Virginia	9,485		46	Tennessee	6,388
26	Washington	8,011		47	Arizona	6,139
19	West Virginia	8,789		48	Oklahoma	5,891
18	Wisconsin	9,097		49	Idaho	5,854
3	Wyoming	12,236		50	Utah	5,448
					District of Columbia	11,998

Source: CQ Press using data from U.S. Bureau of the Census, Governments Division
   "Public Education Finances: 2009" (http://www.census.gov/govs/school/)
*Based on student membership. Current spending for compensation of school system officers and employees. Consists of gross compensation before deductions for withheld taxes, retirement contributions, or other purposes. Also includes benefits such as contributions on behalf of employees for retirement coverage, Social Security, group health and life insurance, tuition reimbursement, workers' compensation, and unemployment compensation.

Percent of Public Elementary and Secondary School Current Expenditures Used for Salaries, Wages, and Benefits in 2009
National Percent = 81.0%*

ALPHA ORDER

RANK	STATE	PERCENT
21	Alabama	80.3
39	Alaska	78.2
41	Arizona	77.9
49	Arkansas	72.6
16	California	81.5
32	Colorado	79.3
22	Connecticut	80.0
29	Delaware	79.8
44	Florida	77.2
14	Georgia	82.3
37	Hawaii	78.5
13	Idaho	82.4
1	Illinois	94.8
5	Indiana	84.7
6	Iowa	84.2
43	Kansas	77.3
3	Kentucky	85.3
22	Louisiana	80.0
34	Maine	79.0
4	Maryland	84.8
35	Massachusetts	78.9
15	Michigan	81.9
20	Minnesota	80.4
33	Mississippi	79.2
26	Missouri	79.9
48	Montana	74.9
38	Nebraska	78.3
10	Nevada	83.2
42	New Hampshire	77.7
40	New Jersey	78.1
31	New Mexico	79.6
18	New York	80.6
11	North Carolina	83.1
36	North Dakota	78.8
29	Ohio	79.8
50	Oklahoma	71.5
26	Oregon	79.9
46	Pennsylvania	76.6
22	Rhode Island	80.0
19	South Carolina	80.5
47	South Dakota	76.0
22	Tennessee	80.0
26	Texas	79.9
11	Utah	83.1
45	Vermont	76.8
2	Virginia	86.2
9	Washington	83.4
7	West Virginia	84.0
17	Wisconsin	81.2
8	Wyoming	83.5

RANK ORDER

RANK	STATE	PERCENT
1	Illinois	94.8
2	Virginia	86.2
3	Kentucky	85.3
4	Maryland	84.8
5	Indiana	84.7
6	Iowa	84.2
7	West Virginia	84.0
8	Wyoming	83.5
9	Washington	83.4
10	Nevada	83.2
11	North Carolina	83.1
11	Utah	83.1
13	Idaho	82.4
14	Georgia	82.3
15	Michigan	81.9
16	California	81.5
17	Wisconsin	81.2
18	New York	80.6
19	South Carolina	80.5
20	Minnesota	80.4
21	Alabama	80.3
22	Connecticut	80.0
22	Louisiana	80.0
22	Rhode Island	80.0
22	Tennessee	80.0
26	Missouri	79.9
26	Oregon	79.9
26	Texas	79.9
29	Delaware	79.8
29	Ohio	79.8
31	New Mexico	79.6
32	Colorado	79.3
33	Mississippi	79.2
34	Maine	79.0
35	Massachusetts	78.9
36	North Dakota	78.8
37	Hawaii	78.5
38	Nebraska	78.3
39	Alaska	78.2
40	New Jersey	78.1
41	Arizona	77.9
42	New Hampshire	77.7
43	Kansas	77.3
44	Florida	77.2
45	Vermont	76.8
46	Pennsylvania	76.6
47	South Dakota	76.0
48	Montana	74.9
49	Arkansas	72.6
50	Oklahoma	71.5

District of Columbia 71.9

Source: CQ Press using data from U.S. Bureau of the Census, Governments Division
   "Public Education Finances: 2009" (http://www.census.gov/govs/school/)
*Current spending for compensation of school system officers and employees. Consists of gross compensation before deductions for withheld taxes, retirement contributions, or other purposes. Also includes benefits such as contributions on behalf of employees for retirement coverage, Social Security, group health and life insurance, tuition reimbursement, workers' compensation, and unemployment compensation.

Public Elementary and Secondary School Current Expenditures for Salaries and Wages in 2009
National Total = $310,334,051,000*

ALPHA ORDER

RANK	STATE	EXPENDITURES	% of USA
26	Alabama	$3,809,370,000	1.2%
44	Alaska	945,159,000	0.3%
22	Arizona	4,678,519,000	1.5%
32	Arkansas	2,557,025,000	0.8%
1	California	37,561,531,000	12.1%
23	Colorado	4,592,653,000	1.5%
21	Connecticut	4,700,781,000	1.5%
46	Delaware	808,034,000	0.3%
4	Florida	13,804,733,000	4.4%
9	Georgia	10,422,791,000	3.4%
41	Hawaii	1,268,293,000	0.4%
42	Idaho	1,175,778,000	0.4%
5	Illinois	13,580,369,000	4.4%
16	Indiana	5,581,282,000	1.8%
28	Iowa	3,074,306,000	1.0%
31	Kansas	2,867,777,000	0.9%
27	Kentucky	3,806,572,000	1.2%
24	Louisiana	4,167,267,000	1.3%
40	Maine	1,342,120,000	0.4%
14	Maryland	7,013,377,000	2.3%
13	Massachusetts	7,571,711,000	2.4%
10	Michigan	9,267,692,000	3.0%
18	Minnesota	5,326,075,000	1.7%
33	Mississippi	2,397,815,000	0.8%
17	Missouri	5,467,499,000	1.8%
45	Montana	829,685,000	0.3%
37	Nebraska	1,747,173,000	0.6%
34	Nevada	2,212,218,000	0.7%
39	New Hampshire	1,374,939,000	0.4%
6	New Jersey	13,455,477,000	4.3%
36	New Mexico	1,880,079,000	0.6%
2	New York	28,868,481,000	9.3%
12	North Carolina	8,350,984,000	2.7%
50	North Dakota	592,357,000	0.2%
8	Ohio	11,202,314,000	3.6%
30	Oklahoma	2,924,128,000	0.9%
29	Oregon	3,008,542,000	1.0%
7	Pennsylvania	12,261,616,000	4.0%
43	Rhode Island	1,161,789,000	0.4%
25	South Carolina	4,166,600,000	1.3%
49	South Dakota	645,345,000	0.2%
20	Tennessee	4,803,518,000	1.5%
3	Texas	27,264,612,000	8.8%
35	Utah	2,051,962,000	0.7%
47	Vermont	793,675,000	0.3%
11	Virginia	8,686,523,000	2.8%
15	Washington	6,191,751,000	2.0%
38	West Virginia	1,649,211,000	0.5%
19	Wisconsin	5,164,944,000	1.7%
48	Wyoming	782,886,000	0.3%

RANK ORDER

RANK	STATE	EXPENDITURES	% of USA
1	California	$37,561,531,000	12.1%
2	New York	28,868,481,000	9.3%
3	Texas	27,264,612,000	8.8%
4	Florida	13,804,733,000	4.4%
5	Illinois	13,580,369,000	4.4%
6	New Jersey	13,455,477,000	4.3%
7	Pennsylvania	12,261,616,000	4.0%
8	Ohio	11,202,314,000	3.6%
9	Georgia	10,422,791,000	3.4%
10	Michigan	9,267,692,000	3.0%
11	Virginia	8,686,523,000	2.8%
12	North Carolina	8,350,984,000	2.7%
13	Massachusetts	7,571,711,000	2.4%
14	Maryland	7,013,377,000	2.3%
15	Washington	6,191,751,000	2.0%
16	Indiana	5,581,282,000	1.8%
17	Missouri	5,467,499,000	1.8%
18	Minnesota	5,326,075,000	1.7%
19	Wisconsin	5,164,944,000	1.7%
20	Tennessee	4,803,518,000	1.5%
21	Connecticut	4,700,781,000	1.5%
22	Arizona	4,678,519,000	1.5%
23	Colorado	4,592,653,000	1.5%
24	Louisiana	4,167,267,000	1.3%
25	South Carolina	4,166,600,000	1.3%
26	Alabama	3,809,370,000	1.2%
27	Kentucky	3,806,572,000	1.2%
28	Iowa	3,074,306,000	1.0%
29	Oregon	3,008,542,000	1.0%
30	Oklahoma	2,924,128,000	0.9%
31	Kansas	2,867,777,000	0.9%
32	Arkansas	2,557,025,000	0.8%
33	Mississippi	2,397,815,000	0.8%
34	Nevada	2,212,218,000	0.7%
35	Utah	2,051,962,000	0.7%
36	New Mexico	1,880,079,000	0.6%
37	Nebraska	1,747,173,000	0.6%
38	West Virginia	1,649,211,000	0.5%
39	New Hampshire	1,374,939,000	0.4%
40	Maine	1,342,120,000	0.4%
41	Hawaii	1,268,293,000	0.4%
42	Idaho	1,175,778,000	0.4%
43	Rhode Island	1,161,789,000	0.4%
44	Alaska	945,159,000	0.3%
45	Montana	829,685,000	0.3%
46	Delaware	808,034,000	0.3%
47	Vermont	793,675,000	0.3%
48	Wyoming	782,886,000	0.3%
49	South Dakota	645,345,000	0.2%
50	North Dakota	592,357,000	0.2%
	District of Columbia	474,713,000	0.2%

Source: U.S. Bureau of the Census, Governments Division
"Public Education Finances: 2009" (http://www.census.gov/govs/school/)
*Current spending for compensation of school system officers and employees. Consists of gross compensation before deductions for withheld taxes, retirement contributions, or other purposes.

Per Capita Public Elementary and Secondary School Current Expenditures for Salaries and Wages in 2009
National Per Capita = $1,011*

ALPHA ORDER

RANK	STATE	PER CAPITA
42	Alabama	$809
4	Alaska	1,353
50	Arizona	709
36	Arkansas	885
18	California	1,016
29	Colorado	914
5	Connecticut	1,336
30	Delaware	913
48	Florida	745
12	Georgia	1,060
20	Hawaii	979
47	Idaho	761
13	Illinois	1,052
38	Indiana	869
15	Iowa	1,022
17	Kansas	1,017
37	Kentucky	882
27	Louisiana	928
16	Maine	1,018
7	Maryland	1,231
8	Massachusetts	1,148
25	Michigan	930
19	Minnesota	1,011
41	Mississippi	812
30	Missouri	913
39	Montana	851
22	Nebraska	972
40	Nevada	837
14	New Hampshire	1,038
1	New Jersey	1,545
24	New Mexico	936
2	New York	1,477
35	North Carolina	890
28	North Dakota	916
23	Ohio	971
44	Oklahoma	793
45	Oregon	786
21	Pennsylvania	973
9	Rhode Island	1,103
30	South Carolina	913
43	South Dakota	794
46	Tennessee	763
11	Texas	1,100
49	Utah	737
6	Vermont	1,276
10	Virginia	1,102
26	Washington	929
34	West Virginia	906
30	Wisconsin	913
3	Wyoming	1,438

RANK ORDER

RANK	STATE	PER CAPITA
1	New Jersey	$1,545
2	New York	1,477
3	Wyoming	1,438
4	Alaska	1,353
5	Connecticut	1,336
6	Vermont	1,276
7	Maryland	1,231
8	Massachusetts	1,148
9	Rhode Island	1,103
10	Virginia	1,102
11	Texas	1,100
12	Georgia	1,060
13	Illinois	1,052
14	New Hampshire	1,038
15	Iowa	1,022
16	Maine	1,018
17	Kansas	1,017
18	California	1,016
19	Minnesota	1,011
20	Hawaii	979
21	Pennsylvania	973
22	Nebraska	972
23	Ohio	971
24	New Mexico	936
25	Michigan	930
26	Washington	929
27	Louisiana	928
28	North Dakota	916
29	Colorado	914
30	Delaware	913
30	Missouri	913
30	South Carolina	913
30	Wisconsin	913
34	West Virginia	906
35	North Carolina	890
36	Arkansas	885
37	Kentucky	882
38	Indiana	869
39	Montana	851
40	Nevada	837
41	Mississippi	812
42	Alabama	809
43	South Dakota	794
44	Oklahoma	793
45	Oregon	786
46	Tennessee	763
47	Idaho	761
48	Florida	745
49	Utah	737
50	Arizona	709

District of Columbia 792

Source: CQ Press using data from U.S. Bureau of the Census, Governments Division
"Public Education Finances: 2009" (http://www.census.gov/govs/school/)
*Current spending for compensation of school system officers and employees. Consists of gross compensation before deductions for withheld taxes, retirement contributions, or other purposes.

Per Pupil Elementary and Secondary School Current Expenditures for Salaries and Wages in 2009
National Per Pupil = $6,433*

ALPHA ORDER				RANK ORDER		
RANK	STATE	PER PUPIL		RANK	STATE	PER PUPIL
43	Alabama	$5,109		1	New York	$10,704
9	Alaska	7,257		2	New Jersey	9,900
47	Arizona	4,766		3	Vermont	9,009
39	Arkansas	5,390		4	Wyoming	9,002
24	California	6,092		5	Connecticut	8,595
37	Colorado	5,653		6	Maryland	8,312
5	Connecticut	8,595		7	Rhode Island	8,209
15	Delaware	6,918		8	Massachusetts	8,120
41	Florida	5,263		9	Alaska	7,257
19	Georgia	6,318		10	Pennsylvania	7,232
12	Hawaii	7,067		11	Maine	7,187
49	Idaho	4,388		12	Hawaii	7,067
18	Illinois	6,415		13	Virginia	7,033
38	Indiana	5,428		14	New Hampshire	6,946
20	Iowa	6,306		15	Delaware	6,918
23	Kansas	6,100		16	Minnesota	6,632
36	Kentucky	5,683		17	Ohio	6,479
21	Louisiana	6,288		18	Illinois	6,415
11	Maine	7,187		19	Georgia	6,318
6	Maryland	8,312		20	Iowa	6,306
8	Massachusetts	8,120		21	Louisiana	6,288
28	Michigan	5,958		22	North Dakota	6,258
16	Minnesota	6,632		23	Kansas	6,100
46	Mississippi	4,882		24	California	6,092
25	Missouri	6,085		25	Missouri	6,085
31	Montana	5,859		26	Nebraska	5,980
26	Nebraska	5,980		27	Washington	5,976
42	Nevada	5,133		28	Michigan	5,958
14	New Hampshire	6,946		29	Wisconsin	5,957
2	New Jersey	9,900		30	Texas	5,867
35	New Mexico	5,719		31	Montana	5,859
1	New York	10,704		32	West Virginia	5,850
34	North Carolina	5,751		33	South Carolina	5,833
22	North Dakota	6,258		34	North Carolina	5,751
17	Ohio	6,479		35	New Mexico	5,719
48	Oklahoma	4,537		36	Kentucky	5,683
40	Oregon	5,354		37	Colorado	5,653
10	Pennsylvania	7,232		38	Indiana	5,428
7	Rhode Island	8,209		39	Arkansas	5,390
33	South Carolina	5,833		40	Oregon	5,354
44	South Dakota	5,097		41	Florida	5,263
45	Tennessee	4,947		42	Nevada	5,133
30	Texas	5,867		43	Alabama	5,109
50	Utah	3,854		44	South Dakota	5,097
3	Vermont	9,009		45	Tennessee	4,947
13	Virginia	7,033		46	Mississippi	4,882
27	Washington	5,976		47	Arizona	4,766
32	West Virginia	5,850		48	Oklahoma	4,537
29	Wisconsin	5,957		49	Idaho	4,388
4	Wyoming	9,002		50	Utah	3,854
					District of Columbia	10,708

Source: U.S. Bureau of the Census, Governments Division
"Public Education Finances: 2009" (http://www.census.gov/govs/school/)
*Based on student membership. For this per pupil calculation, Census has excluded expenditures for salaries and wages for adult education, community services, and other nonelementary-secondary programs.

Percent of Public Elementary and Secondary School Current Expenditures Used for Salaries and Wages in 2009
National Percent = 59.9%*

ALPHA ORDER

RANK	STATE	PERCENT
38	Alabama	56.6
50	Alaska	46.5
19	Arizona	60.5
30	Arkansas	57.5
14	California	61.5
5	Colorado	64.3
32	Connecticut	57.4
45	Delaware	55.5
27	Florida	58.7
3	Georgia	65.0
39	Hawaii	56.4
12	Idaho	61.7
28	Illinois	58.5
30	Indiana	57.5
4	Iowa	64.6
16	Kansas	61.2
6	Kentucky	64.2
23	Louisiana	59.5
41	Maine	56.2
12	Maryland	61.7
47	Massachusetts	54.2
43	Michigan	55.7
34	Minnesota	57.1
21	Mississippi	60.2
8	Missouri	62.6
29	Montana	57.9
23	Nebraska	59.5
18	Nevada	60.6
40	New Hampshire	56.3
32	New Jersey	57.4
19	New Mexico	60.5
35	New York	57.0
2	North Carolina	66.6
17	North Dakota	61.1
25	Ohio	58.9
46	Oklahoma	55.1
48	Oregon	53.5
36	Pennsylvania	56.8
44	Rhode Island	55.6
10	South Carolina	62.0
22	South Dakota	59.6
10	Tennessee	62.0
1	Texas	68.2
26	Utah	58.8
36	Vermont	56.8
7	Virginia	64.0
9	Washington	62.2
42	West Virginia	55.9
49	Wisconsin	53.2
15	Wyoming	61.4

RANK ORDER

RANK	STATE	PERCENT
1	Texas	68.2
2	North Carolina	66.6
3	Georgia	65.0
4	Iowa	64.6
5	Colorado	64.3
6	Kentucky	64.2
7	Virginia	64.0
8	Missouri	62.6
9	Washington	62.2
10	South Carolina	62.0
10	Tennessee	62.0
12	Idaho	61.7
12	Maryland	61.7
14	California	61.5
15	Wyoming	61.4
16	Kansas	61.2
17	North Dakota	61.1
18	Nevada	60.6
19	Arizona	60.5
19	New Mexico	60.5
21	Mississippi	60.2
22	South Dakota	59.6
23	Louisiana	59.5
23	Nebraska	59.5
25	Ohio	58.9
26	Utah	58.8
27	Florida	58.7
28	Illinois	58.5
29	Montana	57.9
30	Arkansas	57.5
30	Indiana	57.5
32	Connecticut	57.4
32	New Jersey	57.4
34	Minnesota	57.1
35	New York	57.0
36	Pennsylvania	56.8
36	Vermont	56.8
38	Alabama	56.6
39	Hawaii	56.4
40	New Hampshire	56.3
41	Maine	56.2
42	West Virginia	55.9
43	Michigan	55.7
44	Rhode Island	55.6
45	Delaware	55.5
46	Oklahoma	55.1
47	Massachusetts	54.2
48	Oregon	53.5
49	Wisconsin	53.2
50	Alaska	46.5
	District of Columbia	64.2

Source: CQ Press using data from U.S. Bureau of the Census, Governments Division
"Public Education Finances: 2009" (http://www.census.gov/govs/school/)
*Current spending for compensation of school system officers and employees. Consists of gross compensation before deductions for withheld taxes, retirement contributions, or other purposes.

Public Elementary and Secondary School Current Expenditures for Employee Benefits in 2009
National Total = $109,187,793,000*

ALPHA ORDER

RANK	STATE	EXPENDITURES	% of USA
20	Alabama	$1,597,199,000	1.5%
37	Alaska	645,792,000	0.6%
25	Arizona	1,348,233,000	1.2%
36	Arkansas	669,976,000	0.6%
1	California	12,185,577,000	11.2%
28	Colorado	1,077,341,000	1.0%
19	Connecticut	1,849,274,000	1.7%
45	Delaware	352,867,000	0.3%
7	Florida	4,326,513,000	4.0%
12	Georgia	2,769,048,000	2.5%
43	Hawaii	498,895,000	0.5%
44	Idaho	392,821,000	0.4%
3	Illinois	8,431,943,000	7.7%
14	Indiana	2,638,131,000	2.4%
29	Iowa	930,877,000	0.9%
35	Kansas	753,763,000	0.7%
26	Kentucky	1,253,020,000	1.1%
23	Louisiana	1,433,487,000	1.3%
40	Maine	545,911,000	0.5%
15	Maryland	2,630,382,000	2.4%
10	Massachusetts	3,451,838,000	3.2%
6	Michigan	4,365,901,000	4.0%
16	Minnesota	2,178,738,000	2.0%
34	Mississippi	757,282,000	0.7%
21	Missouri	1,507,381,000	1.4%
48	Montana	242,922,000	0.2%
39	Nebraska	553,717,000	0.5%
33	Nevada	826,106,000	0.8%
41	New Hampshire	523,810,000	0.5%
4	New Jersey	4,852,444,000	4.4%
38	New Mexico	593,402,000	0.5%
2	New York	11,985,026,000	11.0%
18	North Carolina	2,073,861,000	1.9%
50	North Dakota	171,192,000	0.2%
9	Ohio	3,976,984,000	3.6%
30	Oklahoma	873,041,000	0.8%
22	Oregon	1,485,750,000	1.4%
8	Pennsylvania	4,291,481,000	3.9%
42	Rhode Island	507,326,000	0.5%
27	South Carolina	1,237,023,000	1.1%
49	South Dakota	177,099,000	0.2%
24	Tennessee	1,398,301,000	1.3%
5	Texas	4,671,081,000	4.3%
31	Utah	848,595,000	0.8%
47	Vermont	280,001,000	0.3%
11	Virginia	3,027,959,000	2.8%
17	Washington	2,109,043,000	1.9%
32	West Virginia	828,403,000	0.8%
13	Wisconsin	2,722,573,000	2.5%
46	Wyoming	281,310,000	0.3%

RANK ORDER

RANK	STATE	EXPENDITURES	% of USA
1	California	$12,185,577,000	11.2%
2	New York	11,985,026,000	11.0%
3	Illinois	8,431,943,000	7.7%
4	New Jersey	4,852,444,000	4.4%
5	Texas	4,671,081,000	4.3%
6	Michigan	4,365,901,000	4.0%
7	Florida	4,326,513,000	4.0%
8	Pennsylvania	4,291,481,000	3.9%
9	Ohio	3,976,984,000	3.6%
10	Massachusetts	3,451,838,000	3.2%
11	Virginia	3,027,959,000	2.8%
12	Georgia	2,769,048,000	2.5%
13	Wisconsin	2,722,573,000	2.5%
14	Indiana	2,638,131,000	2.4%
15	Maryland	2,630,382,000	2.4%
16	Minnesota	2,178,738,000	2.0%
17	Washington	2,109,043,000	1.9%
18	North Carolina	2,073,861,000	1.9%
19	Connecticut	1,849,274,000	1.7%
20	Alabama	1,597,199,000	1.5%
21	Missouri	1,507,381,000	1.4%
22	Oregon	1,485,750,000	1.4%
23	Louisiana	1,433,487,000	1.3%
24	Tennessee	1,398,301,000	1.3%
25	Arizona	1,348,233,000	1.2%
26	Kentucky	1,253,020,000	1.1%
27	South Carolina	1,237,023,000	1.1%
28	Colorado	1,077,341,000	1.0%
29	Iowa	930,877,000	0.9%
30	Oklahoma	873,041,000	0.8%
31	Utah	848,595,000	0.8%
32	West Virginia	828,403,000	0.8%
33	Nevada	826,106,000	0.8%
34	Mississippi	757,282,000	0.7%
35	Kansas	753,763,000	0.7%
36	Arkansas	669,976,000	0.6%
37	Alaska	645,792,000	0.6%
38	New Mexico	593,402,000	0.5%
39	Nebraska	553,717,000	0.5%
40	Maine	545,911,000	0.5%
41	New Hampshire	523,810,000	0.5%
42	Rhode Island	507,326,000	0.5%
43	Hawaii	498,895,000	0.5%
44	Idaho	392,821,000	0.4%
45	Delaware	352,867,000	0.3%
46	Wyoming	281,310,000	0.3%
47	Vermont	280,001,000	0.3%
48	Montana	242,922,000	0.2%
49	South Dakota	177,099,000	0.2%
50	North Dakota	171,192,000	0.2%
	District of Columbia	57,153,000	0.1%

Source: U.S. Bureau of the Census, Governments Division
"Public Education Finances: 2009" (http://www.census.gov/govs/school/)
*Amounts paid by the school system for fringe benefits. These amounts are not included in salaries and wages paid directly to employees. Includes contributions on behalf of employees for retirement coverage, Social Security, group health and life insurance, tuition reimbursement, workers' compensation, and unemployment compensation.

Per Capita Public Elementary and Secondary School Current Expenditures for Employee Benefits in 2009
National Per Capita = $356*

ALPHA ORDER

RANK	STATE	PER CAPITA
24	Alabama	$339
1	Alaska	925
49	Arizona	204
44	Arkansas	232
25	California	330
48	Colorado	214
5	Connecticut	526
17	Delaware	399
43	Florida	233
34	Georgia	282
20	Hawaii	385
39	Idaho	254
2	Illinois	653
16	Indiana	411
29	Iowa	309
36	Kansas	267
33	Kentucky	290
26	Louisiana	319
14	Maine	414
10	Maryland	462
6	Massachusetts	524
13	Michigan	438
14	Minnesota	414
38	Mississippi	257
40	Missouri	252
41	Montana	249
30	Nebraska	308
28	Nevada	313
18	New Hampshire	395
4	New Jersey	557
32	New Mexico	295
3	New York	613
46	North Carolina	221
37	North Dakota	265
22	Ohio	345
42	Oklahoma	237
19	Oregon	388
23	Pennsylvania	340
8	Rhode Island	482
35	South Carolina	271
47	South Dakota	218
45	Tennessee	222
50	Texas	188
31	Utah	305
12	Vermont	450
21	Virginia	384
27	Washington	316
11	West Virginia	455
9	Wisconsin	481
7	Wyoming	517

RANK ORDER

RANK	STATE	PER CAPITA
1	Alaska	$925
2	Illinois	653
3	New York	613
4	New Jersey	557
5	Connecticut	526
6	Massachusetts	524
7	Wyoming	517
8	Rhode Island	482
9	Wisconsin	481
10	Maryland	462
11	West Virginia	455
12	Vermont	450
13	Michigan	438
14	Maine	414
14	Minnesota	414
16	Indiana	411
17	Delaware	399
18	New Hampshire	395
19	Oregon	388
20	Hawaii	385
21	Virginia	384
22	Ohio	345
23	Pennsylvania	340
24	Alabama	339
25	California	330
26	Louisiana	319
27	Washington	316
28	Nevada	313
29	Iowa	309
30	Nebraska	308
31	Utah	305
32	New Mexico	295
33	Kentucky	290
34	Georgia	282
35	South Carolina	271
36	Kansas	267
37	North Dakota	265
38	Mississippi	257
39	Idaho	254
40	Missouri	252
41	Montana	249
42	Oklahoma	237
43	Florida	233
44	Arkansas	232
45	Tennessee	222
46	North Carolina	221
47	South Dakota	218
48	Colorado	214
49	Arizona	204
50	Texas	188

District of Columbia   95

Source: CQ Press using data from U.S. Bureau of the Census, Governments Division
    "Public Education Finances: 2009" (http://www.census.gov/govs/school/)
*Amounts paid by the school system for fringe benefits. These amounts are not included in salaries and wages paid directly to employees. Includes contributions on behalf of employees for retirement coverage, Social Security, group health and life insurance, tuition reimbursement, workers' compensation, and unemployment compensation.

Per Pupil Public Elementary and Secondary School Current Expenditures for Employee Benefits in 2009
National Per Pupil = $2,263*

ALPHA ORDER

RANK	STATE	PER PUPIL
25	Alabama	$2,142
1	Alaska	4,959
47	Arizona	1,373
45	Arkansas	1,412
27	California	1,976
49	Colorado	1,326
7	Connecticut	3,381
12	Delaware	3,021
38	Florida	1,649
36	Georgia	1,679
16	Hawaii	2,780
42	Idaho	1,466
3	Illinois	3,983
20	Indiana	2,565
29	Iowa	1,909
39	Kansas	1,603
31	Kentucky	1,871
24	Louisiana	2,163
14	Maine	2,923
11	Maryland	3,117
4	Massachusetts	3,702
15	Michigan	2,807
17	Minnesota	2,713
41	Mississippi	1,542
37	Missouri	1,678
35	Montana	1,715
30	Nebraska	1,895
28	Nevada	1,917
18	New Hampshire	2,646
6	New Jersey	3,570
33	New Mexico	1,805
2	New York	4,444
44	North Carolina	1,428
32	North Dakota	1,809
23	Ohio	2,300
48	Oklahoma	1,354
19	Oregon	2,644
21	Pennsylvania	2,531
5	Rhode Island	3,585
34	South Carolina	1,732
46	South Dakota	1,399
43	Tennessee	1,440
50	Texas	1,005
40	Utah	1,594
9	Vermont	3,178
22	Virginia	2,452
26	Washington	2,036
13	West Virginia	2,939
10	Wisconsin	3,140
8	Wyoming	3,235

RANK ORDER

RANK	STATE	PER PUPIL
1	Alaska	$4,959
2	New York	4,444
3	Illinois	3,983
4	Massachusetts	3,702
5	Rhode Island	3,585
6	New Jersey	3,570
7	Connecticut	3,381
8	Wyoming	3,235
9	Vermont	3,178
10	Wisconsin	3,140
11	Maryland	3,117
12	Delaware	3,021
13	West Virginia	2,939
14	Maine	2,923
15	Michigan	2,807
16	Hawaii	2,780
17	Minnesota	2,713
18	New Hampshire	2,646
19	Oregon	2,644
20	Indiana	2,565
21	Pennsylvania	2,531
22	Virginia	2,452
23	Ohio	2,300
24	Louisiana	2,163
25	Alabama	2,142
26	Washington	2,036
27	California	1,976
28	Nevada	1,917
29	Iowa	1,909
30	Nebraska	1,895
31	Kentucky	1,871
32	North Dakota	1,809
33	New Mexico	1,805
34	South Carolina	1,732
35	Montana	1,715
36	Georgia	1,679
37	Missouri	1,678
38	Florida	1,649
39	Kansas	1,603
40	Utah	1,594
41	Mississippi	1,542
42	Idaho	1,466
43	Tennessee	1,440
44	North Carolina	1,428
45	Arkansas	1,412
46	South Dakota	1,399
47	Arizona	1,373
48	Oklahoma	1,354
49	Colorado	1,326
50	Texas	1,005

District of Columbia — 1,289

Source: U.S. Bureau of the Census, Governments Division
"Public Education Finances: 2009" (http://www.census.gov/govs/school/)

*Amounts paid by the school system for fringe benefits. These amounts are not included in salaries and wages paid directly to employees. Includes contributions on behalf of employees for retirement coverage, Social Security, group health and life insurance, tuition reimbursement, workers' compensation, and unemployment compensation.

Percent of Public Elementary and Secondary School Current Expenditures Used for Employee Benefits in 2009
National Percent = 21.1%*

ALPHA ORDER

ALPHA ORDER

RANK	STATE	PERCENT
12	Alabama	23.7
2	Alaska	31.8
40	Arizona	17.4
48	Arkansas	15.1
29	California	20.0
48	Colorado	15.1
17	Connecticut	22.6
9	Delaware	24.3
36	Florida	18.4
41	Georgia	17.3
20	Hawaii	22.2
27	Idaho	20.6
1	Illinois	36.3
5	Indiana	27.2
32	Iowa	19.6
47	Kansas	16.1
24	Kentucky	21.1
28	Louisiana	20.5
16	Maine	22.8
15	Maryland	23.1
8	Massachusetts	24.7
7	Michigan	26.2
14	Minnesota	23.3
34	Mississippi	19.0
41	Missouri	17.3
43	Montana	17.0
35	Nebraska	18.8
17	Nevada	22.6
22	New Hampshire	21.4
26	New Jersey	20.7
33	New Mexico	19.1
13	New York	23.6
44	North Carolina	16.5
39	North Dakota	17.7
25	Ohio	20.9
45	Oklahoma	16.4
6	Oregon	26.4
31	Pennsylvania	19.9
9	Rhode Island	24.3
36	South Carolina	18.4
45	South Dakota	16.4
38	Tennessee	18.0
50	Texas	11.7
9	Utah	24.3
29	Vermont	20.0
19	Virginia	22.3
23	Washington	21.2
3	West Virginia	28.1
4	Wisconsin	28.0
21	Wyoming	22.1

RANK ORDER

RANK	STATE	PERCENT
1	Illinois	36.3
2	Alaska	31.8
3	West Virginia	28.1
4	Wisconsin	28.0
5	Indiana	27.2
6	Oregon	26.4
7	Michigan	26.2
8	Massachusetts	24.7
9	Delaware	24.3
9	Rhode Island	24.3
9	Utah	24.3
12	Alabama	23.7
13	New York	23.6
14	Minnesota	23.3
15	Maryland	23.1
16	Maine	22.8
17	Connecticut	22.6
17	Nevada	22.6
19	Virginia	22.3
20	Hawaii	22.2
21	Wyoming	22.1
22	New Hampshire	21.4
23	Washington	21.2
24	Kentucky	21.1
25	Ohio	20.9
26	New Jersey	20.7
27	Idaho	20.6
28	Louisiana	20.5
29	California	20.0
29	Vermont	20.0
31	Pennsylvania	19.9
32	Iowa	19.6
33	New Mexico	19.1
34	Mississippi	19.0
35	Nebraska	18.8
36	Florida	18.4
36	South Carolina	18.4
38	Tennessee	18.0
39	North Dakota	17.7
40	Arizona	17.4
41	Georgia	17.3
41	Missouri	17.3
43	Montana	17.0
44	North Carolina	16.5
45	Oklahoma	16.4
45	South Dakota	16.4
47	Kansas	16.1
48	Arkansas	15.1
48	Colorado	15.1
50	Texas	11.7

District of Columbia — 7.7

Source: CQ Press using data from U.S. Bureau of the Census, Governments Division
"Public Education Finances: 2009" (http://www.census.gov/govs/school/)
*Amounts paid by the school system for fringe benefits. These amounts are not included in salaries and wages paid directly to employees. Includes contributions on behalf of employees for retirement coverage, Social Security, group health and life insurance, tuition reimbursement, workers' compensation, and unemployment compensation.

Public Elementary and Secondary School Current Expenditures for Instruction in 2009
National Total = $311,891,097,000*

ALPHA ORDER

RANK	STATE	EXPENDITURES	% of USA
26	Alabama	$3,836,398,000	1.2%
44	Alaska	1,129,756,000	0.4%
22	Arizona	4,296,503,000	1.4%
32	Arkansas	2,417,974,000	0.8%
1	California	35,617,964,000	11.4%
23	Colorado	4,108,304,000	1.3%
20	Connecticut	5,054,397,000	1.6%
45	Delaware	877,678,000	0.3%
4	Florida	13,884,278,000	4.5%
9	Georgia	10,063,924,000	3.2%
40	Hawaii	1,402,305,000	0.4%
43	Idaho	1,157,633,000	0.4%
6	Illinois	13,520,105,000	4.3%
18	Indiana	5,548,292,000	1.8%
29	Iowa	2,914,176,000	0.9%
30	Kansas	2,883,104,000	0.9%
27	Kentucky	3,468,191,000	1.1%
24	Louisiana	4,051,985,000	1.3%
41	Maine	1,383,650,000	0.4%
14	Maryland	6,899,346,000	2.2%
11	Massachusetts	8,885,949,000	2.8%
10	Michigan	9,422,685,000	3.0%
17	Minnesota	5,815,987,000	1.9%
33	Mississippi	2,317,710,000	0.7%
19	Missouri	5,175,127,000	1.7%
47	Montana	855,803,000	0.3%
36	Nebraska	1,887,427,000	0.6%
35	Nevada	2,145,779,000	0.7%
39	New Hampshire	1,546,316,000	0.5%
5	New Jersey	13,800,343,000	4.4%
37	New Mexico	1,807,514,000	0.6%
2	New York	35,195,372,000	11.3%
13	North Carolina	7,943,541,000	2.5%
50	North Dakota	579,830,000	0.2%
8	Ohio	10,734,314,000	3.4%
31	Oklahoma	2,836,912,000	0.9%
28	Oregon	3,291,310,000	1.1%
7	Pennsylvania	12,803,821,000	4.1%
42	Rhode Island	1,224,158,000	0.4%
25	South Carolina	3,854,229,000	1.2%
49	South Dakota	645,912,000	0.2%
21	Tennessee	4,809,809,000	1.5%
3	Texas	23,895,853,000	7.7%
34	Utah	2,169,434,000	0.7%
46	Vermont	859,433,000	0.3%
12	Virginia	8,194,237,000	2.6%
15	Washington	5,984,072,000	1.9%
38	West Virginia	1,759,397,000	0.6%
16	Wisconsin	5,857,285,000	1.9%
48	Wyoming	744,877,000	0.2%

RANK ORDER

RANK	STATE	EXPENDITURES	% of USA
1	California	$35,617,964,000	11.4%
2	New York	35,195,372,000	11.3%
3	Texas	23,895,853,000	7.7%
4	Florida	13,884,278,000	4.5%
5	New Jersey	13,800,343,000	4.4%
6	Illinois	13,520,105,000	4.3%
7	Pennsylvania	12,803,821,000	4.1%
8	Ohio	10,734,314,000	3.4%
9	Georgia	10,063,924,000	3.2%
10	Michigan	9,422,685,000	3.0%
11	Massachusetts	8,885,949,000	2.8%
12	Virginia	8,194,237,000	2.6%
13	North Carolina	7,943,541,000	2.5%
14	Maryland	6,899,346,000	2.2%
15	Washington	5,984,072,000	1.9%
16	Wisconsin	5,857,285,000	1.9%
17	Minnesota	5,815,987,000	1.9%
18	Indiana	5,548,292,000	1.8%
19	Missouri	5,175,127,000	1.7%
20	Connecticut	5,054,397,000	1.6%
21	Tennessee	4,809,809,000	1.5%
22	Arizona	4,296,503,000	1.4%
23	Colorado	4,108,304,000	1.3%
24	Louisiana	4,051,985,000	1.3%
25	South Carolina	3,854,229,000	1.2%
26	Alabama	3,836,398,000	1.2%
27	Kentucky	3,468,191,000	1.1%
28	Oregon	3,291,310,000	1.1%
29	Iowa	2,914,176,000	0.9%
30	Kansas	2,883,104,000	0.9%
31	Oklahoma	2,836,912,000	0.9%
32	Arkansas	2,417,974,000	0.8%
33	Mississippi	2,317,710,000	0.7%
34	Utah	2,169,434,000	0.7%
35	Nevada	2,145,779,000	0.7%
36	Nebraska	1,887,427,000	0.6%
37	New Mexico	1,807,514,000	0.6%
38	West Virginia	1,759,397,000	0.6%
39	New Hampshire	1,546,316,000	0.5%
40	Hawaii	1,402,305,000	0.4%
41	Maine	1,383,650,000	0.4%
42	Rhode Island	1,224,158,000	0.4%
43	Idaho	1,157,633,000	0.4%
44	Alaska	1,129,756,000	0.4%
45	Delaware	877,678,000	0.3%
46	Vermont	859,433,000	0.3%
47	Montana	855,803,000	0.3%
48	Wyoming	744,877,000	0.2%
49	South Dakota	645,912,000	0.2%
50	North Dakota	579,830,000	0.2%
	District of Columbia	330,698,000	0.1%

Source: U.S. Bureau of the Census, Governments Division
"Public Education Finances: 2009" (http://www.census.gov/govs/school/)
*Includes payments from all funds for instruction. This includes salaries, employee benefits, supplies, materials, and contractual services. Excludes capital outlay, debt service, and interfund transfers. Instruction covers regular, special, and vocational programs offered in both the academic year and summer school. Excluded are support services (e.g., instructional staff support and administration) and other support activities as well as adult education and community services.

Per Capita Public Elementary and Secondary School Current Expenditures for Instruction in 2009
National Per Capita = $1,016*

ALPHA ORDER

RANK	STATE	PER CAPITA
40	Alabama	$815
2	Alaska	1,617
50	Arizona	651
38	Arkansas	837
24	California	964
39	Colorado	818
4	Connecticut	1,437
21	Delaware	992
48	Florida	749
18	Georgia	1,024
12	Hawaii	1,083
48	Idaho	749
15	Illinois	1,047
33	Indiana	864
22	Iowa	969
19	Kansas	1,023
42	Kentucky	804
28	Louisiana	902
14	Maine	1,050
8	Maryland	1,211
7	Massachusetts	1,348
26	Michigan	945
11	Minnesota	1,104
44	Mississippi	785
33	Missouri	864
32	Montana	878
13	Nebraska	1,051
41	Nevada	812
9	New Hampshire	1,167
3	New Jersey	1,585
29	New Mexico	899
1	New York	1,801
36	North Carolina	847
31	North Dakota	896
27	Ohio	930
46	Oklahoma	769
35	Oregon	860
20	Pennsylvania	1,016
10	Rhode Island	1,162
37	South Carolina	845
43	South Dakota	795
47	Tennessee	764
24	Texas	964
45	Utah	779
5	Vermont	1,382
16	Virginia	1,040
30	Washington	898
23	West Virginia	967
17	Wisconsin	1,036
6	Wyoming	1,369

RANK ORDER

RANK	STATE	PER CAPITA
1	New York	$1,801
2	Alaska	1,617
3	New Jersey	1,585
4	Connecticut	1,437
5	Vermont	1,382
6	Wyoming	1,369
7	Massachusetts	1,348
8	Maryland	1,211
9	New Hampshire	1,167
10	Rhode Island	1,162
11	Minnesota	1,104
12	Hawaii	1,083
13	Nebraska	1,051
14	Maine	1,050
15	Illinois	1,047
16	Virginia	1,040
17	Wisconsin	1,036
18	Georgia	1,024
19	Kansas	1,023
20	Pennsylvania	1,016
21	Delaware	992
22	Iowa	969
23	West Virginia	967
24	California	964
24	Texas	964
26	Michigan	945
27	Ohio	930
28	Louisiana	902
29	New Mexico	899
30	Washington	898
31	North Dakota	896
32	Montana	878
33	Indiana	864
33	Missouri	864
35	Oregon	860
36	North Carolina	847
37	South Carolina	845
38	Arkansas	837
39	Colorado	818
40	Alabama	815
41	Nevada	812
42	Kentucky	804
43	South Dakota	795
44	Mississippi	785
45	Utah	779
46	Oklahoma	769
47	Tennessee	764
48	Florida	749
48	Idaho	749
50	Arizona	651

District of Columbia	551

Source: CQ Press using data from U.S. Bureau of the Census, Governments Division
   "Public Education Finances: 2009" (http://www.census.gov/govs/school/)
*Includes payments from all funds for instruction. This includes salaries, employee benefits, supplies, materials, and contractual services. Excludes capital outlay, debt service, and interfund transfers. Instruction covers regular, special, and vocational programs offered in both the academic year and summer school. Excluded are support services (e.g., instructional staff support and administration) and other support activities as well as adult education and community services.

Per Pupil Public Elementary and Secondary School Current Expenditures for Instruction in 2009
National Per Pupil = $6,369*

ALPHA ORDER

RANK	STATE	PER PUPIL
39	Alabama	$5,142
6	Alaska	8,675
48	Arizona	4,376
42	Arkansas	5,089
29	California	5,776
43	Colorado	5,047
4	Connecticut	8,872
12	Delaware	7,475
37	Florida	5,293
25	Georgia	6,052
10	Hawaii	7,813
49	Idaho	4,320
19	Illinois	6,330
35	Indiana	5,389
27	Iowa	5,977
21	Kansas	6,128
38	Kentucky	5,178
23	Louisiana	6,114
15	Maine	7,059
8	Maryland	8,177
5	Massachusetts	8,737
24	Michigan	6,057
14	Minnesota	7,242
46	Mississippi	4,719
31	Missouri	5,759
26	Montana	6,043
18	Nebraska	6,460
44	Nevada	4,979
13	New Hampshire	7,434
2	New Jersey	9,337
33	New Mexico	5,498
1	New York	12,524
34	North Carolina	5,470
22	North Dakota	6,126
28	Ohio	5,940
47	Oklahoma	4,401
32	Oregon	5,690
11	Pennsylvania	7,516
9	Rhode Island	7,906
36	South Carolina	5,330
41	South Dakota	5,097
45	Tennessee	4,954
39	Texas	5,142
50	Utah	4,075
3	Vermont	9,184
17	Virginia	6,630
30	Washington	5,775
20	West Virginia	6,241
16	Wisconsin	6,756
7	Wyoming	8,565

RANK ORDER

RANK	STATE	PER PUPIL
1	New York	$12,524
2	New Jersey	9,337
3	Vermont	9,184
4	Connecticut	8,872
5	Massachusetts	8,737
6	Alaska	8,675
7	Wyoming	8,565
8	Maryland	8,177
9	Rhode Island	7,906
10	Hawaii	7,813
11	Pennsylvania	7,516
12	Delaware	7,475
13	New Hampshire	7,434
14	Minnesota	7,242
15	Maine	7,059
16	Wisconsin	6,756
17	Virginia	6,630
18	Nebraska	6,460
19	Illinois	6,330
20	West Virginia	6,241
21	Kansas	6,128
22	North Dakota	6,126
23	Louisiana	6,114
24	Michigan	6,057
25	Georgia	6,052
26	Montana	6,043
27	Iowa	5,977
28	Ohio	5,940
29	California	5,776
30	Washington	5,775
31	Missouri	5,759
32	Oregon	5,690
33	New Mexico	5,498
34	North Carolina	5,470
35	Indiana	5,389
36	South Carolina	5,330
37	Florida	5,293
38	Kentucky	5,178
39	Alabama	5,142
39	Texas	5,142
41	South Dakota	5,097
42	Arkansas	5,089
43	Colorado	5,047
44	Nevada	4,979
45	Tennessee	4,954
46	Mississippi	4,719
47	Oklahoma	4,401
48	Arizona	4,376
49	Idaho	4,320
50	Utah	4,075
	District of Columbia	7,460

Source: U.S. Bureau of the Census, Governments Division
    "Public Education Finances: 2009" (http://www.census.gov/govs/school/)

*Based on student membership. Includes payments from all funds for instruction. This includes salaries, employee benefits, supplies, materials, and contractual services. Excludes capital outlay, debt service, and interfund transfers. Instruction covers regular, special, and vocational programs offered in both the academic year and summer school. Excluded are support services (e.g., instructional staff support and administration) and other support activities as well as adult education and community services.

Public Elementary and Secondary School Current Expenditures for Instruction per $1,000 Personal Income in 2009
National Ratio = $25.19*

ALPHA ORDER

RANK	STATE	RATIO
34	Alabama	$24.19
2	Alaska	36.98
48	Arizona	19.16
17	Arkansas	25.79
41	California	22.11
49	Colorado	19.13
25	Connecticut	25.20
31	Delaware	24.55
50	Florida	18.81
6	Georgia	29.47
20	Hawaii	25.68
40	Idaho	22.98
33	Illinois	24.39
29	Indiana	24.86
23	Iowa	25.47
20	Kansas	25.68
28	Kentucky	24.99
36	Louisiana	23.90
7	Maine	28.71
26	Maryland	25.19
14	Massachusetts	26.61
13	Michigan	26.67
19	Minnesota	25.72
22	Mississippi	25.65
38	Missouri	23.63
27	Montana	25.09
15	Nebraska	26.40
46	Nevada	20.47
12	New Hampshire	26.84
4	New Jersey	30.88
11	New Mexico	27.09
1	New York	37.58
35	North Carolina	24.18
43	North Dakota	21.79
18	Ohio	25.78
44	Oklahoma	21.09
37	Oregon	23.64
24	Pennsylvania	25.21
8	Rhode Island	27.84
16	South Carolina	25.98
47	South Dakota	20.46
42	Tennessee	21.96
30	Texas	24.70
32	Utah	24.40
3	Vermont	35.27
39	Virginia	23.49
45	Washington	20.84
5	West Virginia	30.76
10	Wisconsin	27.45
9	Wyoming	27.63

RANK ORDER

RANK	STATE	RATIO
1	New York	$37.58
2	Alaska	36.98
3	Vermont	35.27
4	New Jersey	30.88
5	West Virginia	30.76
6	Georgia	29.47
7	Maine	28.71
8	Rhode Island	27.84
9	Wyoming	27.63
10	Wisconsin	27.45
11	New Mexico	27.09
12	New Hampshire	26.84
13	Michigan	26.67
14	Massachusetts	26.61
15	Nebraska	26.40
16	South Carolina	25.98
17	Arkansas	25.79
18	Ohio	25.78
19	Minnesota	25.72
20	Hawaii	25.68
20	Kansas	25.68
22	Mississippi	25.65
23	Iowa	25.47
24	Pennsylvania	25.21
25	Connecticut	25.20
26	Maryland	25.19
27	Montana	25.09
28	Kentucky	24.99
29	Indiana	24.86
30	Texas	24.70
31	Delaware	24.55
32	Utah	24.40
33	Illinois	24.39
34	Alabama	24.19
35	North Carolina	24.18
36	Louisiana	23.90
37	Oregon	23.64
38	Missouri	23.63
39	Virginia	23.49
40	Idaho	22.98
41	California	22.11
42	Tennessee	21.96
43	North Dakota	21.79
44	Oklahoma	21.09
45	Washington	20.84
46	Nevada	20.47
47	South Dakota	20.46
48	Arizona	19.16
49	Colorado	19.13
50	Florida	18.81
	District of Columbia	8.20

Source: U.S. Bureau of the Census, Governments Division
"Public Education Finances: 2009" (http://www.census.gov/govs/school/)
*Includes payments from all funds for instruction. This includes salaries, employee benefits, supplies, materials, and contractual services. Excludes capital outlay, debt service, and interfund transfers. Instruction covers regular, special, and vocational programs offered in both the academic year and summer school. Excluded are support services (e.g., instructional staff support and administration) and other support activities as well as adult education and community services.

Percent of Public Elementary and Secondary School Current Expenditures Used for Instruction in 2009
National Percent = 60.2%*

ALPHA ORDER

RANK	STATE	PERCENT
44	Alabama	57.0
47	Alaska	55.6
48	Arizona	55.5
49	Arkansas	54.4
35	California	58.3
41	Colorado	57.5
11	Connecticut	61.7
17	Delaware	60.3
28	Florida	59.1
6	Georgia	62.8
7	Hawaii	62.3
15	Idaho	60.8
36	Illinois	58.2
43	Indiana	57.2
14	Iowa	61.3
12	Kansas	61.5
32	Kentucky	58.5
39	Louisiana	57.9
39	Maine	57.9
16	Maryland	60.7
3	Massachusetts	63.6
45	Michigan	56.6
7	Minnesota	62.3
38	Mississippi	58.1
26	Missouri	59.3
23	Montana	59.7
2	Nebraska	64.2
30	Nevada	58.8
4	New Hampshire	63.3
29	New Jersey	58.9
36	New Mexico	58.2
1	New York	69.4
4	North Carolina	63.3
21	North Dakota	59.8
46	Ohio	56.5
50	Oklahoma	53.4
32	Oregon	58.5
26	Pennsylvania	59.3
31	Rhode Island	58.6
42	South Carolina	57.4
23	South Dakota	59.7
10	Tennessee	62.0
21	Texas	59.8
9	Utah	62.2
12	Vermont	61.5
17	Virginia	60.3
20	Washington	60.1
25	West Virginia	59.6
17	Wisconsin	60.3
34	Wyoming	58.4

RANK ORDER

RANK	STATE	PERCENT
1	New York	69.4
2	Nebraska	64.2
3	Massachusetts	63.6
4	New Hampshire	63.3
4	North Carolina	63.3
6	Georgia	62.8
7	Hawaii	62.3
7	Minnesota	62.3
9	Utah	62.2
10	Tennessee	62.0
11	Connecticut	61.7
12	Kansas	61.5
12	Vermont	61.5
14	Iowa	61.3
15	Idaho	60.8
16	Maryland	60.7
17	Delaware	60.3
17	Virginia	60.3
17	Wisconsin	60.3
20	Washington	60.1
21	North Dakota	59.8
21	Texas	59.8
23	Montana	59.7
23	South Dakota	59.7
25	West Virginia	59.6
26	Missouri	59.3
26	Pennsylvania	59.3
28	Florida	59.1
29	New Jersey	58.9
30	Nevada	58.8
31	Rhode Island	58.6
32	Kentucky	58.5
32	Oregon	58.5
34	Wyoming	58.4
35	California	58.3
36	Illinois	58.2
36	New Mexico	58.2
38	Mississippi	58.1
39	Louisiana	57.9
39	Maine	57.9
41	Colorado	57.5
42	South Carolina	57.4
43	Indiana	57.2
44	Alabama	57.0
45	Michigan	56.6
46	Ohio	56.5
47	Alaska	55.6
48	Arizona	55.5
49	Arkansas	54.4
50	Oklahoma	53.4

District of Columbia 44.7

Source: CQ Press using data from U.S. Bureau of the Census, Governments Division
    "Public Education Finances: 2009" (http://www.census.gov/govs/school/)
*Includes payments from all funds for instruction. This includes salaries, employee benefits, supplies, materials, and contractual services. Excludes capital outlay, debt service, and interfund transfers. Instruction covers regular, special, and vocational programs offered in both the academic year and summer school. Excluded are support services (e.g., instructional staff support and administration) and other support activities as well as adult education and community services.

Public Elementary and Secondary School Current Expenditures for Salaries, Wages, and Benefits for Instruction in 2009
National Total = $279,065,950,000*

ALPHA ORDER

RANK	STATE	EXPENDITURES	% of USA
26	Alabama	$3,475,572,000	1.2%
44	Alaska	997,996,000	0.4%
22	Arizona	3,911,631,000	1.4%
32	Arkansas	2,105,291,000	0.8%
1	California	31,712,415,000	11.4%
24	Colorado	3,641,182,000	1.3%
20	Connecticut	4,564,037,000	1.6%
45	Delaware	816,172,000	0.3%
7	Florida	11,456,224,000	4.1%
9	Georgia	9,170,995,000	3.3%
41	Hawaii	1,211,363,000	0.4%
43	Idaho	1,071,714,000	0.4%
4	Illinois	12,192,382,000	4.4%
17	Indiana	5,370,069,000	1.9%
29	Iowa	2,710,187,000	1.0%
31	Kansas	2,397,039,000	0.9%
27	Kentucky	3,287,988,000	1.2%
23	Louisiana	3,698,032,000	1.3%
40	Maine	1,266,422,000	0.5%
14	Maryland	6,502,786,000	2.3%
12	Massachusetts	7,228,123,000	2.6%
10	Michigan	8,818,000,000	3.2%
18	Minnesota	5,323,887,000	1.9%
33	Mississippi	2,078,940,000	0.7%
19	Missouri	4,651,765,000	1.7%
47	Montana	730,250,000	0.3%
36	Nebraska	1,642,220,000	0.6%
35	Nevada	1,946,652,000	0.7%
39	New Hampshire	1,385,181,000	0.5%
5	New Jersey	11,819,295,000	4.2%
37	New Mexico	1,631,212,000	0.6%
2	New York	31,134,786,000	11.2%
13	North Carolina	7,187,140,000	2.6%
50	North Dakota	533,141,000	0.2%
8	Ohio	9,510,645,000	3.4%
30	Oklahoma	2,511,599,000	0.9%
28	Oregon	2,887,048,000	1.0%
6	Pennsylvania	11,471,379,000	4.1%
42	Rhode Island	1,104,914,000	0.4%
25	South Carolina	3,519,871,000	1.3%
49	South Dakota	562,140,000	0.2%
21	Tennessee	4,278,800,000	1.5%
3	Texas	21,577,003,000	7.7%
34	Utah	2,018,339,000	0.7%
46	Vermont	737,268,000	0.3%
11	Virginia	7,710,795,000	2.8%
16	Washington	5,398,728,000	1.9%
38	West Virginia	1,619,360,000	0.6%
15	Wisconsin	5,496,317,000	2.0%
48	Wyoming	681,098,000	0.2%

RANK ORDER

RANK	STATE	EXPENDITURES	% of USA
1	California	$31,712,415,000	11.4%
2	New York	31,134,786,000	11.2%
3	Texas	21,577,003,000	7.7%
4	Illinois	12,192,382,000	4.4%
5	New Jersey	11,819,295,000	4.2%
6	Pennsylvania	11,471,379,000	4.1%
7	Florida	11,456,224,000	4.1%
8	Ohio	9,510,645,000	3.4%
9	Georgia	9,170,995,000	3.3%
10	Michigan	8,818,000,000	3.2%
11	Virginia	7,710,795,000	2.8%
12	Massachusetts	7,228,123,000	2.6%
13	North Carolina	7,187,140,000	2.6%
14	Maryland	6,502,786,000	2.3%
15	Wisconsin	5,496,317,000	2.0%
16	Washington	5,398,728,000	1.9%
17	Indiana	5,370,069,000	1.9%
18	Minnesota	5,323,887,000	1.9%
19	Missouri	4,651,765,000	1.7%
20	Connecticut	4,564,037,000	1.6%
21	Tennessee	4,278,800,000	1.5%
22	Arizona	3,911,631,000	1.4%
23	Louisiana	3,698,032,000	1.3%
24	Colorado	3,641,182,000	1.3%
25	South Carolina	3,519,871,000	1.3%
26	Alabama	3,475,572,000	1.2%
27	Kentucky	3,287,988,000	1.2%
28	Oregon	2,887,048,000	1.0%
29	Iowa	2,710,187,000	1.0%
30	Oklahoma	2,511,599,000	0.9%
31	Kansas	2,397,039,000	0.9%
32	Arkansas	2,105,291,000	0.8%
33	Mississippi	2,078,940,000	0.7%
34	Utah	2,018,339,000	0.7%
35	Nevada	1,946,652,000	0.7%
36	Nebraska	1,642,220,000	0.6%
37	New Mexico	1,631,212,000	0.6%
38	West Virginia	1,619,360,000	0.6%
39	New Hampshire	1,385,181,000	0.5%
40	Maine	1,266,422,000	0.5%
41	Hawaii	1,211,363,000	0.4%
42	Rhode Island	1,104,914,000	0.4%
43	Idaho	1,071,714,000	0.4%
44	Alaska	997,996,000	0.4%
45	Delaware	816,172,000	0.3%
46	Vermont	737,268,000	0.3%
47	Montana	730,250,000	0.3%
48	Wyoming	681,098,000	0.2%
49	South Dakota	562,140,000	0.2%
50	North Dakota	533,141,000	0.2%
	District of Columbia	310,557,000	0.1%

Source: CQ Press using data from U.S. Bureau of the Census, Governments Division
"Public Education Finances: 2009" (http://www.census.gov/govs/school/)
*Current spending for instruction in regular, special, and vocational programs. Excludes support services. Consists of gross compensation before deductions for withheld taxes, retirement contributions, or other purposes. Also includes benefits such as contributions on behalf of employees for retirement coverage, Social Security, group health and life insurance, tuition reimbursement, workers' compensation, and unemployment compensation.

Per Capita Public Elementary and Secondary School Current Expenditures for Salaries, Wages, and Benefits for Instruction in 2009
National Per Capita = $909*

ALPHA ORDER				RANK ORDER		
RANK	STATE	PER CAPITA		RANK	STATE	PER CAPITA
39	Alabama	$738		1	New York	$1,593
2	Alaska	1,429		2	Alaska	1,429
50	Arizona	593		3	New Jersey	1,357
41	Arkansas	729		4	Connecticut	1,297
25	California	858		5	Wyoming	1,251
42	Colorado	725		6	Vermont	1,186
4	Connecticut	1,297		7	Maryland	1,141
18	Delaware	922		8	Massachusetts	1,096
49	Florida	618		9	Rhode Island	1,049
17	Georgia	933		10	New Hampshire	1,046
16	Hawaii	935		11	Minnesota	1,011
45	Idaho	693		12	Virginia	978
15	Illinois	944		13	Wisconsin	972
27	Indiana	836		14	Maine	961
21	Iowa	901		15	Illinois	944
26	Kansas	850		16	Hawaii	935
36	Kentucky	762		17	Georgia	933
30	Louisiana	823		18	Delaware	922
14	Maine	961		19	Nebraska	914
7	Maryland	1,141		20	Pennsylvania	910
8	Massachusetts	1,096		21	Iowa	901
23	Michigan	884		22	West Virginia	890
11	Minnesota	1,011		23	Michigan	884
44	Mississippi	704		24	Texas	871
33	Missouri	777		25	California	858
38	Montana	749		26	Kansas	850
19	Nebraska	914		27	Indiana	836
40	Nevada	737		28	North Dakota	824
10	New Hampshire	1,046		28	Ohio	824
3	New Jersey	1,357		30	Louisiana	823
31	New Mexico	812		31	New Mexico	812
1	New York	1,593		32	Washington	810
35	North Carolina	766		33	Missouri	777
28	North Dakota	824		34	South Carolina	772
28	Ohio	824		35	North Carolina	766
47	Oklahoma	681		36	Kentucky	762
37	Oregon	755		37	Oregon	755
20	Pennsylvania	910		38	Montana	749
9	Rhode Island	1,049		39	Alabama	738
34	South Carolina	772		40	Nevada	737
46	South Dakota	692		41	Arkansas	729
48	Tennessee	680		42	Colorado	725
24	Texas	871		42	Utah	725
42	Utah	725		44	Mississippi	704
6	Vermont	1,186		45	Idaho	693
12	Virginia	978		46	South Dakota	692
32	Washington	810		47	Oklahoma	681
22	West Virginia	890		48	Tennessee	680
13	Wisconsin	972		49	Florida	618
5	Wyoming	1,251		50	Arizona	593
					District of Columbia	518

Source: CQ Press using data from U.S. Bureau of the Census, Governments Division
   "Public Education Finances: 2009" (http://www.census.gov/govs/school/)
*Current spending for instruction in regular, special, and vocational programs. Excludes support services. Consists of gross compensation before deductions for withheld taxes, retirement contributions, or other purposes. Also includes benefits such as contributions on behalf of employees for retirement coverage, Social Security, group health and life insurance, tuition reimbursement, workers' compensation, and unemployment compensation.

Per Pupil Public Elementary and Secondary School Current Expenditures for Salaries, Wages, and Benefits for Instruction in 2009
National Per Pupil = $5,785*

ALPHA ORDER			RANK ORDER		
RANK	STATE	PER PUPIL	RANK	STATE	PER PUPIL
38	Alabama	$4,661	1	New York	$11,545
9	Alaska	7,663	2	New Jersey	8,697
48	Arizona	3,984	3	Vermont	8,368
43	Arkansas	4,438	4	Connecticut	8,345
31	California	5,143	5	Wyoming	7,831
41	Colorado	4,482	6	Rhode Island	7,807
4	Connecticut	8,345	7	Massachusetts	7,752
11	Delaware	6,988	8	Maryland	7,707
45	Florida	4,367	9	Alaska	7,663
24	Georgia	5,560	10	New Hampshire	6,998
14	Hawaii	6,749	11	Delaware	6,988
47	Idaho	4,000	12	Maine	6,782
18	Illinois	5,759	13	Pennsylvania	6,765
27	Indiana	5,222	14	Hawaii	6,749
25	Iowa	5,559	15	Minnesota	6,629
33	Kansas	5,098	16	Wisconsin	6,339
37	Kentucky	4,908	17	Virginia	6,243
23	Louisiana	5,580	18	Illinois	5,759
12	Maine	6,782	19	West Virginia	5,744
8	Maryland	7,707	20	Michigan	5,669
7	Massachusetts	7,752	21	North Dakota	5,633
20	Michigan	5,669	22	Nebraska	5,621
15	Minnesota	6,629	23	Louisiana	5,580
46	Mississippi	4,232	24	Georgia	5,560
29	Missouri	5,177	25	Iowa	5,559
30	Montana	5,157	26	Ohio	5,500
22	Nebraska	5,621	27	Indiana	5,222
40	Nevada	4,517	28	Washington	5,210
10	New Hampshire	6,998	29	Missouri	5,177
2	New Jersey	8,697	30	Montana	5,157
34	New Mexico	4,962	31	California	5,143
1	New York	11,545	32	Oregon	5,137
35	North Carolina	4,950	33	Kansas	5,098
21	North Dakota	5,633	34	New Mexico	4,962
26	Ohio	5,500	35	North Carolina	4,950
49	Oklahoma	3,897	36	South Carolina	4,928
32	Oregon	5,137	37	Kentucky	4,908
13	Pennsylvania	6,765	38	Alabama	4,661
6	Rhode Island	7,807	39	Texas	4,643
36	South Carolina	4,928	40	Nevada	4,517
42	South Dakota	4,439	41	Colorado	4,482
44	Tennessee	4,407	42	South Dakota	4,439
39	Texas	4,643	43	Arkansas	4,438
50	Utah	3,791	44	Tennessee	4,407
3	Vermont	8,368	45	Florida	4,367
17	Virginia	6,243	46	Mississippi	4,232
28	Washington	5,210	47	Idaho	4,000
19	West Virginia	5,744	48	Arizona	3,984
16	Wisconsin	6,339	49	Oklahoma	3,897
5	Wyoming	7,831	50	Utah	3,791
				District of Columbia	7,005

Source: CQ Press using data from U.S. Bureau of the Census, Governments Division
"Public Education Finances: 2009" (http://www.census.gov/govs/school/)

*Based on student membership. Current spending for instruction in regular, special, and vocational programs. Excludes support services. Consists of gross compensation before deductions for withheld taxes, retirement contributions, or other purposes. Includes benefits such as contributions on behalf of employees for retirement coverage, Social Security, group health and life insurance, tuition reimbursement, workers' compensation, and unemployment compensation.

Percent of Public Elementary and Secondary School Current Expenditures Used for Salaries, Wages, and Benefits for Instruction in 2009
National Percent = 53.9%*

ALPHA ORDER

RANK	STATE	PERCENT
38	Alabama	51.7
47	Alaska	49.1
44	Arizona	50.6
49	Arkansas	47.4
36	California	51.9
43	Colorado	50.9
14	Connecticut	55.7
12	Delaware	56.1
48	Florida	48.8
4	Georgia	57.2
22	Hawaii	53.8
11	Idaho	56.3
32	Illinois	52.5
16	Indiana	55.3
7	Iowa	57.0
41	Kansas	51.2
15	Kentucky	55.4
30	Louisiana	52.8
27	Maine	53.0
4	Maryland	57.2
38	Massachusetts	51.7
27	Michigan	53.0
6	Minnesota	57.1
35	Mississippi	52.2
24	Missouri	53.3
42	Montana	51.0
13	Nebraska	55.9
24	Nevada	53.3
9	New Hampshire	56.7
45	New Jersey	50.4
32	New Mexico	52.5
1	New York	61.4
3	North Carolina	57.3
18	North Dakota	55.0
46	Ohio	50.0
50	Oklahoma	47.3
40	Oregon	51.3
26	Pennsylvania	53.1
29	Rhode Island	52.9
34	South Carolina	52.4
36	South Dakota	51.9
17	Tennessee	55.2
21	Texas	54.0
2	Utah	57.9
30	Vermont	52.8
8	Virginia	56.8
20	Washington	54.2
19	West Virginia	54.9
10	Wisconsin	56.6
23	Wyoming	53.4

RANK ORDER

RANK	STATE	PERCENT
1	New York	61.4
2	Utah	57.9
3	North Carolina	57.3
4	Georgia	57.2
4	Maryland	57.2
6	Minnesota	57.1
7	Iowa	57.0
8	Virginia	56.8
9	New Hampshire	56.7
10	Wisconsin	56.6
11	Idaho	56.3
12	Delaware	56.1
13	Nebraska	55.9
14	Connecticut	55.7
15	Kentucky	55.4
16	Indiana	55.3
17	Tennessee	55.2
18	North Dakota	55.0
19	West Virginia	54.9
20	Washington	54.2
21	Texas	54.0
22	Hawaii	53.8
23	Wyoming	53.4
24	Missouri	53.3
24	Nevada	53.3
26	Pennsylvania	53.1
27	Maine	53.0
27	Michigan	53.0
29	Rhode Island	52.9
30	Louisiana	52.8
30	Vermont	52.8
32	Illinois	52.5
32	New Mexico	52.5
34	South Carolina	52.4
35	Mississippi	52.2
36	California	51.9
36	South Dakota	51.9
38	Alabama	51.7
38	Massachusetts	51.7
40	Oregon	51.3
41	Kansas	51.2
42	Montana	51.0
43	Colorado	50.9
44	Arizona	50.6
45	New Jersey	50.4
46	Ohio	50.0
47	Alaska	49.1
48	Florida	48.8
49	Arkansas	47.4
50	Oklahoma	47.3

	District of Columbia	42.0

Source: CQ Press using data from U.S. Bureau of the Census, Governments Division
"Public Education Finances: 2009" (http://www.census.gov/govs/school/)
*Current spending for instruction in regular, special, and vocational programs. Excludes support services. Consists of gross compensation before deductions for withheld taxes, retirement contributions, or other purposes. Also includes benefits such as contributions on behalf of employees for retirement coverage, Social Security, group health and life insurance, tuition reimbursement, workers' compensation, and unemployment compensation.

Public Elementary and Secondary School Current Expenditures for Salaries, Wages, and Benefits for Instruction Per FTE Teacher in 2009
National Per Teacher = $87,130*

ALPHA ORDER				RANK ORDER		
RANK	STATE	PER TEACHER		RANK	STATE	PER TEACHER
35	Alabama	$72,685		1	New York	$142,859
2	Alaska	125,938		2	Alaska	125,938
36	Arizona	71,522		3	Maryland	110,347
50	Arkansas	56,652		4	Virginia	107,975
6	California	105,746		5	Hawaii	107,255
32	Colorado	74,783		6	California	105,746
15	Connecticut	94,200		7	New Jersey	103,035
11	Delaware	98,799		8	Massachusetts	102,679
47	Florida	61,474		9	Minnesota	100,298
28	Georgia	77,173		10	Washington	99,193
5	Hawaii	107,255		11	Delaware	98,799
38	Idaho	70,760		12	Rhode Island	97,564
18	Illinois	89,871		13	Wyoming	97,333
22	Indiana	85,709		14	Oregon	96,034
30	Iowa	75,370		15	Connecticut	94,200
42	Kansas	66,823		16	Michigan	93,064
29	Kentucky	75,676		17	Wisconsin	92,534
31	Louisiana	74,897		18	Illinois	89,871
27	Maine	79,599		19	Nevada	88,519
3	Maryland	110,347		20	Pennsylvania	88,473
8	Massachusetts	102,679		21	New Hampshire	88,456
16	Michigan	93,064		22	Indiana	85,709
9	Minnesota	100,298		23	Utah	85,363
46	Mississippi	62,326		24	Ohio	84,282
41	Missouri	68,760		25	Vermont	84,214
40	Montana	69,778		26	West Virginia	80,133
33	Nebraska	74,459		27	Maine	79,599
19	Nevada	88,519		28	Georgia	77,173
21	New Hampshire	88,456		29	Kentucky	75,676
7	New Jersey	103,035		30	Iowa	75,370
37	New Mexico	71,474		31	Louisiana	74,897
1	New York	142,859		32	Colorado	74,783
39	North Carolina	70,701		33	Nebraska	74,459
45	North Dakota	65,186		34	South Carolina	74,021
24	Ohio	84,282		35	Alabama	72,685
49	Oklahoma	59,583		36	Arizona	71,522
14	Oregon	96,034		37	New Mexico	71,474
20	Pennsylvania	88,473		38	Idaho	70,760
12	Rhode Island	97,564		39	North Carolina	70,701
34	South Carolina	74,021		40	Montana	69,778
48	South Dakota	60,824		41	Missouri	68,760
43	Tennessee	65,906		42	Kansas	66,823
44	Texas	65,803		43	Tennessee	65,906
23	Utah	85,363		44	Texas	65,803
25	Vermont	84,214		45	North Dakota	65,186
4	Virginia	107,975		46	Mississippi	62,326
10	Washington	99,193		47	Florida	61,474
26	West Virginia	80,133		48	South Dakota	60,824
17	Wisconsin	92,534		49	Oklahoma	59,583
13	Wyoming	97,333		50	Arkansas	56,652
					District of Columbia	58,364

Source: CQ Press using data from U.S. Bureau of the Census, Governments Division
"Public Education Finances: 2009" (http://www.census.gov/govs/school/) and
"Common Core of Data (CCD) Database" (http://nces.ed.gov/ccd/)
*Current spending for instruction in regular, special, and vocational programs divided by district full-time equivalent teacher counts for 2008-2009 school year. Excludes support services. Consists of gross compensation before deductions for withheld taxes, retirement contributions, or other purposes. Also includes employee benefits.

Public Elementary and Secondary School Current Expenditures for Salaries and Wages for Instruction in 2009
National Total = $209,007,145,000*

RANK	STATE	EXPENDITURES	% of USA
27	Alabama	$2,479,840,000	1.2%
44	Alaska	603,938,000	0.3%
22	Arizona	3,047,829,000	1.5%
32	Arkansas	1,668,196,000	0.8%
1	California	24,304,934,000	11.6%
23	Colorado	2,957,851,000	1.4%
21	Connecticut	3,290,580,000	1.6%
46	Delaware	565,689,000	0.3%
6	Florida	8,805,125,000	4.2%
9	Georgia	7,129,481,000	3.4%
41	Hawaii	868,444,000	0.4%
42	Idaho	808,824,000	0.4%
4	Illinois	9,183,424,000	4.4%
17	Indiana	3,729,754,000	1.8%
28	Iowa	2,085,545,000	1.0%
31	Kansas	1,901,202,000	0.9%
26	Kentucky	2,498,430,000	1.2%
24	Louisiana	2,772,414,000	1.3%
40	Maine	896,809,000	0.4%
13	Maryland	4,715,495,000	2.3%
14	Massachusetts	4,680,805,000	2.2%
10	Michigan	6,027,815,000	2.9%
16	Minnesota	3,749,532,000	1.8%
33	Mississippi	1,592,833,000	0.8%
19	Missouri	3,668,343,000	1.8%
45	Montana	568,330,000	0.3%
37	Nebraska	1,238,895,000	0.6%
35	Nevada	1,423,181,000	0.7%
39	New Hampshire	1,001,600,000	0.5%
5	New Jersey	8,839,737,000	4.2%
36	New Mexico	1,244,507,000	0.6%
2	New York	21,764,757,000	10.4%
11	North Carolina	5,773,635,000	2.8%
50	North Dakota	412,387,000	0.2%
8	Ohio	7,138,973,000	3.4%
30	Oklahoma	1,926,770,000	0.9%
29	Oregon	1,948,926,000	0.9%
7	Pennsylvania	8,537,511,000	4.1%
43	Rhode Island	782,563,000	0.4%
25	South Carolina	2,736,712,000	1.3%
49	South Dakota	443,088,000	0.2%
20	Tennessee	3,321,803,000	1.6%
3	Texas	18,535,835,000	8.9%
34	Utah	1,428,096,000	0.7%
47	Vermont	545,339,000	0.3%
12	Virginia	5,737,099,000	2.7%
15	Washington	4,056,734,000	1.9%
38	West Virginia	1,084,586,000	0.5%
18	Wisconsin	3,698,415,000	1.8%
48	Wyoming	504,326,000	0.2%

RANK	STATE	EXPENDITURES	% of USA
1	California	$24,304,934,000	11.6%
2	New York	21,764,757,000	10.4%
3	Texas	18,535,835,000	8.9%
4	Illinois	9,183,424,000	4.4%
5	New Jersey	8,839,737,000	4.2%
6	Florida	8,805,125,000	4.2%
7	Pennsylvania	8,537,511,000	4.1%
8	Ohio	7,138,973,000	3.4%
9	Georgia	7,129,481,000	3.4%
10	Michigan	6,027,815,000	2.9%
11	North Carolina	5,773,635,000	2.8%
12	Virginia	5,737,099,000	2.7%
13	Maryland	4,715,495,000	2.3%
14	Massachusetts	4,680,805,000	2.2%
15	Washington	4,056,734,000	1.9%
16	Minnesota	3,749,532,000	1.8%
17	Indiana	3,729,754,000	1.8%
18	Wisconsin	3,698,415,000	1.8%
19	Missouri	3,668,343,000	1.8%
20	Tennessee	3,321,803,000	1.6%
21	Connecticut	3,290,580,000	1.6%
22	Arizona	3,047,829,000	1.5%
23	Colorado	2,957,851,000	1.4%
24	Louisiana	2,772,414,000	1.3%
25	South Carolina	2,736,712,000	1.3%
26	Kentucky	2,498,430,000	1.2%
27	Alabama	2,479,840,000	1.2%
28	Iowa	2,085,545,000	1.0%
29	Oregon	1,948,926,000	0.9%
30	Oklahoma	1,926,770,000	0.9%
31	Kansas	1,901,202,000	0.9%
32	Arkansas	1,668,196,000	0.8%
33	Mississippi	1,592,833,000	0.8%
34	Utah	1,428,096,000	0.7%
35	Nevada	1,423,181,000	0.7%
36	New Mexico	1,244,507,000	0.6%
37	Nebraska	1,238,895,000	0.6%
38	West Virginia	1,084,586,000	0.5%
39	New Hampshire	1,001,600,000	0.5%
40	Maine	896,809,000	0.4%
41	Hawaii	868,444,000	0.4%
42	Idaho	808,824,000	0.4%
43	Rhode Island	782,563,000	0.4%
44	Alaska	603,938,000	0.3%
45	Montana	568,330,000	0.3%
46	Delaware	565,689,000	0.3%
47	Vermont	545,339,000	0.3%
48	Wyoming	504,326,000	0.2%
49	South Dakota	443,088,000	0.2%
50	North Dakota	412,387,000	0.2%
	District of Columbia	280,208,000	0.1%

Source: U.S. Bureau of the Census, Governments Division
"Public Education Finances: 2009" (http://www.census.gov/govs/school/)
*Includes payments from all funds for salaries for instruction. Excludes capital outlay, debt service, and interfund transfers. Instruction covers regular, special, and vocational programs offered in both the academic year and summer school. Excluded are support services (e.g., instructional staff support and administration) and other support activities as well as adult education and community services.

Percent of Public Elementary and Secondary School Current Expenditures Used for Salaries and Wages for Instruction in 2009
National Percent = 40.4%*

ALPHA ORDER

RANK	STATE	PERCENT	RANK	STATE	PERCENT
44	Alabama	36.9	1	Texas	46.4
50	Alaska	29.7	2	North Carolina	46.0
31	Arizona	39.4	3	Georgia	44.5
40	Arkansas	37.5	4	Iowa	43.9
25	California	39.8	5	New York	42.9
14	Colorado	41.4	5	Tennessee	42.9
21	Connecticut	40.2	7	North Dakota	42.6
34	Delaware	38.9	8	Idaho	42.5
40	Florida	37.5	9	Nebraska	42.2
3	Georgia	44.5	9	Virginia	42.2
35	Hawaii	38.6	11	Kentucky	42.1
8	Idaho	42.5	12	Missouri	42.0
27	Illinois	39.6	13	Maryland	41.5
36	Indiana	38.4	14	Colorado	41.4
4	Iowa	43.9	15	New Hampshire	41.0
20	Kansas	40.6	16	South Dakota	40.9
11	Kentucky	42.1	16	Utah	40.9
27	Louisiana	39.6	18	South Carolina	40.7
40	Maine	37.5	18	Washington	40.7
13	Maryland	41.5	20	Kansas	40.6
49	Massachusetts	33.5	21	Connecticut	40.2
47	Michigan	36.2	21	Minnesota	40.2
21	Minnesota	40.2	23	New Mexico	40.1
24	Mississippi	40.0	24	Mississippi	40.0
12	Missouri	42.0	25	California	39.8
26	Montana	39.7	26	Montana	39.7
9	Nebraska	42.2	27	Illinois	39.6
32	Nevada	39.0	27	Louisiana	39.6
15	New Hampshire	41.0	27	Wyoming	39.6
38	New Jersey	37.7	30	Pennsylvania	39.5
23	New Mexico	40.1	31	Arizona	39.4
5	New York	42.9	32	Nevada	39.0
2	North Carolina	46.0	32	Vermont	39.0
7	North Dakota	42.6	34	Delaware	38.9
39	Ohio	37.6	35	Hawaii	38.6
46	Oklahoma	36.3	36	Indiana	38.4
48	Oregon	34.6	37	Wisconsin	38.1
30	Pennsylvania	39.5	38	New Jersey	37.7
40	Rhode Island	37.5	39	Ohio	37.6
18	South Carolina	40.7	40	Arkansas	37.5
16	South Dakota	40.9	40	Florida	37.5
5	Tennessee	42.9	40	Maine	37.5
1	Texas	46.4	40	Rhode Island	37.5
16	Utah	40.9	44	Alabama	36.9
32	Vermont	39.0	45	West Virginia	36.8
9	Virginia	42.2	46	Oklahoma	36.3
18	Washington	40.7	47	Michigan	36.2
45	West Virginia	36.8	48	Oregon	34.6
37	Wisconsin	38.1	49	Massachusetts	33.5
27	Wyoming	39.6	50	Alaska	29.7

District of Columbia 37.9

Source: CQ Press using data from U.S. Bureau of the Census, Governments Division
   "Public Education Finances: 2009" (http://www.census.gov/govs/school/)
*Includes payments from all funds for salaries for instruction. Excludes capital outlay, debt service, and interfund transfers. Instruction covers regular, special, and vocational programs offered in both the academic year and summer school. Excluded are support services (e.g., instructional staff support and administration) and other support activities as well as adult education and community services.

Public Elementary and Secondary School Current Expenditures for Employee Benefits for Instruction in 2009
National Total = $70,058,805,000*

ALPHA ORDER

RANK	STATE	EXPENDITURES	% of USA
20	Alabama	$995,732,000	1.4%
38	Alaska	394,058,000	0.6%
25	Arizona	863,802,000	1.2%
36	Arkansas	437,095,000	0.6%
2	California	7,407,481,000	10.6%
28	Colorado	683,331,000	1.0%
19	Connecticut	1,273,457,000	1.8%
45	Delaware	250,483,000	0.4%
8	Florida	2,651,099,000	3.8%
11	Georgia	2,041,514,000	2.9%
42	Hawaii	342,919,000	0.5%
44	Idaho	262,890,000	0.4%
4	Illinois	3,008,958,000	4.3%
15	Indiana	1,640,315,000	2.3%
29	Iowa	624,642,000	0.9%
34	Kansas	495,837,000	0.7%
26	Kentucky	789,558,000	1.1%
24	Louisiana	925,618,000	1.3%
41	Maine	369,613,000	0.5%
14	Maryland	1,787,291,000	2.6%
9	Massachusetts	2,547,318,000	3.6%
7	Michigan	2,790,185,000	4.0%
16	Minnesota	1,574,355,000	2.2%
35	Mississippi	486,107,000	0.7%
21	Missouri	983,422,000	1.4%
48	Montana	161,920,000	0.2%
37	Nebraska	403,325,000	0.6%
33	Nevada	523,471,000	0.7%
40	New Hampshire	383,581,000	0.5%
5	New Jersey	2,979,558,000	4.3%
39	New Mexico	386,705,000	0.6%
1	New York	9,370,029,000	13.4%
17	North Carolina	1,413,505,000	2.0%
49	North Dakota	120,754,000	0.2%
10	Ohio	2,371,672,000	3.4%
31	Oklahoma	584,829,000	0.8%
23	Oregon	938,122,000	1.3%
6	Pennsylvania	2,933,868,000	4.2%
43	Rhode Island	322,351,000	0.5%
27	South Carolina	783,159,000	1.1%
50	South Dakota	119,052,000	0.2%
22	Tennessee	956,997,000	1.4%
3	Texas	3,041,168,000	4.3%
30	Utah	590,243,000	0.8%
46	Vermont	191,929,000	0.3%
12	Virginia	1,973,696,000	2.8%
18	Washington	1,341,994,000	1.9%
32	West Virginia	534,774,000	0.8%
13	Wisconsin	1,797,902,000	2.6%
47	Wyoming	176,772,000	0.3%

RANK ORDER

RANK	STATE	EXPENDITURES	% of USA
1	New York	$9,370,029,000	13.4%
2	California	7,407,481,000	10.6%
3	Texas	3,041,168,000	4.3%
4	Illinois	3,008,958,000	4.3%
5	New Jersey	2,979,558,000	4.3%
6	Pennsylvania	2,933,868,000	4.2%
7	Michigan	2,790,185,000	4.0%
8	Florida	2,651,099,000	3.8%
9	Massachusetts	2,547,318,000	3.6%
10	Ohio	2,371,672,000	3.4%
11	Georgia	2,041,514,000	2.9%
12	Virginia	1,973,696,000	2.8%
13	Wisconsin	1,797,902,000	2.6%
14	Maryland	1,787,291,000	2.6%
15	Indiana	1,640,315,000	2.3%
16	Minnesota	1,574,355,000	2.2%
17	North Carolina	1,413,505,000	2.0%
18	Washington	1,341,994,000	1.9%
19	Connecticut	1,273,457,000	1.8%
20	Alabama	995,732,000	1.4%
21	Missouri	983,422,000	1.4%
22	Tennessee	956,997,000	1.4%
23	Oregon	938,122,000	1.3%
24	Louisiana	925,618,000	1.3%
25	Arizona	863,802,000	1.2%
26	Kentucky	789,558,000	1.1%
27	South Carolina	783,159,000	1.1%
28	Colorado	683,331,000	1.0%
29	Iowa	624,642,000	0.9%
30	Utah	590,243,000	0.8%
31	Oklahoma	584,829,000	0.8%
32	West Virginia	534,774,000	0.8%
33	Nevada	523,471,000	0.7%
34	Kansas	495,837,000	0.7%
35	Mississippi	486,107,000	0.7%
36	Arkansas	437,095,000	0.6%
37	Nebraska	403,325,000	0.6%
38	Alaska	394,058,000	0.6%
39	New Mexico	386,705,000	0.6%
40	New Hampshire	383,581,000	0.5%
41	Maine	369,613,000	0.5%
42	Hawaii	342,919,000	0.5%
43	Rhode Island	322,351,000	0.5%
44	Idaho	262,890,000	0.4%
45	Delaware	250,483,000	0.4%
46	Vermont	191,929,000	0.3%
47	Wyoming	176,772,000	0.3%
48	Montana	161,920,000	0.2%
49	North Dakota	120,754,000	0.2%
50	South Dakota	119,052,000	0.2%
	District of Columbia	30,349,000	0.0%

Source: U.S. Bureau of the Census, Governments Division
"Public Education Finances: 2009" (http://www.census.gov/govs/school/)
*Includes payments from all funds for employee benefits for instruction. Excludes capital outlay, debt service, and interfund transfers. Instruction covers regular, special, and vocational programs offered in both the academic school year and summer school. It excludes support services (e.g., instructional staff support and administration) and other support activities as well as adult education and community services.

Percent of Public Elementary and Secondary School Current Expenditures Used for Employee Benefits for Instruction in 2009
National Percent = 13.5%*

ALPHA ORDER

RANK	STATE	PERCENT
18	Alabama	14.8
1	Alaska	19.4
44	Arizona	11.2
48	Arkansas	9.8
38	California	12.1
49	Colorado	9.6
14	Connecticut	15.5
6	Delaware	17.2
40	Florida	11.3
31	Georgia	12.7
17	Hawaii	15.2
22	Idaho	13.8
30	Illinois	13.0
7	Indiana	16.9
29	Iowa	13.1
47	Kansas	10.6
27	Kentucky	13.3
28	Louisiana	13.2
14	Maine	15.5
12	Maryland	15.7
4	Massachusetts	18.2
10	Michigan	16.8
7	Minnesota	16.9
37	Mississippi	12.2
40	Missouri	11.3
40	Montana	11.3
23	Nebraska	13.7
20	Nevada	14.3
12	New Hampshire	15.7
31	New Jersey	12.7
35	New Mexico	12.4
2	New York	18.5
40	North Carolina	11.3
33	North Dakota	12.5
33	Ohio	12.5
45	Oklahoma	11.0
11	Oregon	16.7
25	Pennsylvania	13.6
16	Rhode Island	15.4
39	South Carolina	11.7
45	South Dakota	11.0
36	Tennessee	12.3
50	Texas	7.6
7	Utah	16.9
23	Vermont	13.7
19	Virginia	14.5
26	Washington	13.5
5	West Virginia	18.1
2	Wisconsin	18.5
21	Wyoming	13.9

RANK ORDER

RANK	STATE	PERCENT
1	Alaska	19.4
2	New York	18.5
2	Wisconsin	18.5
4	Massachusetts	18.2
5	West Virginia	18.1
6	Delaware	17.2
7	Indiana	16.9
7	Minnesota	16.9
7	Utah	16.9
10	Michigan	16.8
11	Oregon	16.7
12	Maryland	15.7
12	New Hampshire	15.7
14	Connecticut	15.5
14	Maine	15.5
16	Rhode Island	15.4
17	Hawaii	15.2
18	Alabama	14.8
19	Virginia	14.5
20	Nevada	14.3
21	Wyoming	13.9
22	Idaho	13.8
23	Nebraska	13.7
23	Vermont	13.7
25	Pennsylvania	13.6
26	Washington	13.5
27	Kentucky	13.3
28	Louisiana	13.2
29	Iowa	13.1
30	Illinois	13.0
31	Georgia	12.7
31	New Jersey	12.7
33	North Dakota	12.5
33	Ohio	12.5
35	New Mexico	12.4
36	Tennessee	12.3
37	Mississippi	12.2
38	California	12.1
39	South Carolina	11.7
40	Florida	11.3
40	Missouri	11.3
40	Montana	11.3
40	North Carolina	11.3
44	Arizona	11.2
45	Oklahoma	11.0
45	South Dakota	11.0
47	Kansas	10.6
48	Arkansas	9.8
49	Colorado	9.6
50	Texas	7.6

District of Columbia   4.1

Source: CQ Press using data from U.S. Bureau of the Census, Governments Division
"Public Education Finances: 2009" (http://www.census.gov/govs/school/)
*Includes payments from all funds for employee benefits for instruction. Excludes capital outlay, debt service, and interfund transfers. Instruction covers regular, special, and vocational programs offered in both the academic school year and summer school. It excludes support services (e.g., instructional staff support and administration) and other support activities as well as adult education and community services.

Public Elementary and Secondary Current Expenditures for Support Services in 2009
National Total = $178,693,645,000*

ALPHA ORDER

RANK	STATE	EXPENDITURES	% of USA
26	Alabama	$2,331,552,000	1.3%
40	Alaska	832,783,000	0.5%
19	Arizona	2,983,729,000	1.7%
32	Arkansas	1,492,691,000	0.8%
1	California	21,693,675,000	12.1%
22	Colorado	2,708,535,000	1.5%
20	Connecticut	2,805,173,000	1.6%
46	Delaware	496,383,000	0.3%
6	Florida	8,067,350,000	4.5%
10	Georgia	5,135,180,000	2.9%
43	Hawaii	718,309,000	0.4%
44	Idaho	646,213,000	0.4%
4	Illinois	8,764,971,000	4.9%
15	Indiana	3,681,825,000	2.1%
30	Iowa	1,615,189,000	0.9%
31	Kansas	1,578,417,000	0.9%
28	Kentucky	2,050,683,000	1.1%
23	Louisiana	2,542,723,000	1.4%
39	Maine	857,706,000	0.5%
13	Maryland	3,984,072,000	2.2%
12	Massachusetts	4,626,112,000	2.6%
9	Michigan	6,354,021,000	3.6%
21	Minnesota	2,712,430,000	1.5%
33	Mississippi	1,392,119,000	0.8%
18	Missouri	3,023,041,000	1.7%
45	Montana	509,899,000	0.3%
38	Nebraska	905,681,000	0.5%
34	Nevada	1,364,083,000	0.8%
41	New Hampshire	822,081,000	0.5%
5	New Jersey	8,687,138,000	4.9%
35	New Mexico	1,167,618,000	0.7%
2	New York	14,079,990,000	7.9%
14	North Carolina	3,848,021,000	2.2%
50	North Dakota	310,316,000	0.2%
8	Ohio	7,347,959,000	4.1%
29	Oklahoma	1,895,590,000	1.1%
27	Oregon	2,121,378,000	1.2%
7	Pennsylvania	7,637,090,000	4.3%
42	Rhode Island	773,039,000	0.4%
25	South Carolina	2,463,391,000	1.4%
49	South Dakota	379,946,000	0.2%
24	Tennessee	2,480,290,000	1.4%
3	Texas	13,799,383,000	7.7%
36	Utah	1,008,636,000	0.6%
47	Vermont	489,015,000	0.3%
11	Virginia	4,813,706,000	2.7%
16	Washington	3,464,921,000	1.9%
37	West Virginia	994,305,000	0.6%
17	Wisconsin	3,382,519,000	1.9%
48	Wyoming	482,641,000	0.3%

RANK ORDER

RANK	STATE	EXPENDITURES	% of USA
1	California	$21,693,675,000	12.1%
2	New York	14,079,990,000	7.9%
3	Texas	13,799,383,000	7.7%
4	Illinois	8,764,971,000	4.9%
5	New Jersey	8,687,138,000	4.9%
6	Florida	8,067,350,000	4.5%
7	Pennsylvania	7,637,090,000	4.3%
8	Ohio	7,347,959,000	4.1%
9	Michigan	6,354,021,000	3.6%
10	Georgia	5,135,180,000	2.9%
11	Virginia	4,813,706,000	2.7%
12	Massachusetts	4,626,112,000	2.6%
13	Maryland	3,984,072,000	2.2%
14	North Carolina	3,848,021,000	2.2%
15	Indiana	3,681,825,000	2.1%
16	Washington	3,464,921,000	1.9%
17	Wisconsin	3,382,519,000	1.9%
18	Missouri	3,023,041,000	1.7%
19	Arizona	2,983,729,000	1.7%
20	Connecticut	2,805,173,000	1.6%
21	Minnesota	2,712,430,000	1.5%
22	Colorado	2,708,535,000	1.5%
23	Louisiana	2,542,723,000	1.4%
24	Tennessee	2,480,290,000	1.4%
25	South Carolina	2,463,391,000	1.4%
26	Alabama	2,331,552,000	1.3%
27	Oregon	2,121,378,000	1.2%
28	Kentucky	2,050,683,000	1.1%
29	Oklahoma	1,895,590,000	1.1%
30	Iowa	1,615,189,000	0.9%
31	Kansas	1,578,417,000	0.9%
32	Arkansas	1,492,691,000	0.8%
33	Mississippi	1,392,119,000	0.8%
34	Nevada	1,364,083,000	0.8%
35	New Mexico	1,167,618,000	0.7%
36	Utah	1,008,636,000	0.6%
37	West Virginia	994,305,000	0.6%
38	Nebraska	905,681,000	0.5%
39	Maine	857,706,000	0.5%
40	Alaska	832,783,000	0.5%
41	New Hampshire	822,081,000	0.5%
42	Rhode Island	773,039,000	0.4%
43	Hawaii	718,309,000	0.4%
44	Idaho	646,213,000	0.4%
45	Montana	509,899,000	0.3%
46	Delaware	496,383,000	0.3%
47	Vermont	489,015,000	0.3%
48	Wyoming	482,641,000	0.3%
49	South Dakota	379,946,000	0.2%
50	North Dakota	310,316,000	0.2%
	District of Columbia	370,127,000	0.2%

Source: U.S. Bureau of the Census, Governments Division
"Public Education Finances: 2009" (http://www.census.gov/govs/school/)
*Includes payments from all funds for support services. This includes salaries, employee benefits, supplies, materials, and contractual services. Excludes capital outlay, debt service, and interfund transfers. Support services cover regular, special, and vocational programs offered in both the academic school year and summer school. It excludes instruction services as well as adult education and community services.

Per Capita Elementary and Secondary School Current Expenditures for Support Services in 2009
National Per Capita = $582*

ALPHA ORDER				RANK ORDER		
RANK	STATE	PER CAPITA		RANK	STATE	PER CAPITA
40	Alabama	$495		1	Alaska	$1,192
1	Alaska	1,192		2	New Jersey	998
45	Arizona	452		3	Wyoming	887
34	Arkansas	517		4	Connecticut	797
18	California	587		5	Vermont	787
29	Colorado	539		6	Rhode Island	734
4	Connecticut	797		7	New York	721
22	Delaware	561		8	Massachusetts	702
46	Florida	435		9	Maryland	699
32	Georgia	522		10	Illinois	679
25	Hawaii	555		11	Maine	651
47	Idaho	418		12	Michigan	637
10	Illinois	679		12	Ohio	637
20	Indiana	573		14	New Hampshire	621
30	Iowa	537		15	Virginia	611
23	Kansas	560		16	Pennsylvania	606
42	Kentucky	475		17	Wisconsin	598
21	Louisiana	566		18	California	587
11	Maine	651		19	New Mexico	581
9	Maryland	699		20	Indiana	573
8	Massachusetts	702		21	Louisiana	566
12	Michigan	637		22	Delaware	561
36	Minnesota	515		23	Kansas	560
43	Mississippi	472		24	Texas	557
38	Missouri	505		25	Hawaii	555
31	Montana	523		25	Oregon	555
39	Nebraska	504		27	West Virginia	546
35	Nevada	516		28	South Carolina	540
14	New Hampshire	621		29	Colorado	539
2	New Jersey	998		30	Iowa	537
19	New Mexico	581		31	Montana	523
7	New York	721		32	Georgia	522
48	North Carolina	410		33	Washington	520
41	North Dakota	480		34	Arkansas	517
12	Ohio	637		35	Nevada	516
37	Oklahoma	514		36	Minnesota	515
25	Oregon	555		37	Oklahoma	514
16	Pennsylvania	606		38	Missouri	505
6	Rhode Island	734		39	Nebraska	504
28	South Carolina	540		40	Alabama	495
44	South Dakota	468		41	North Dakota	480
49	Tennessee	394		42	Kentucky	475
24	Texas	557		43	Mississippi	472
50	Utah	362		44	South Dakota	468
5	Vermont	787		45	Arizona	452
15	Virginia	611		46	Florida	435
33	Washington	520		47	Idaho	418
27	West Virginia	546		48	North Carolina	410
17	Wisconsin	598		49	Tennessee	394
3	Wyoming	887		50	Utah	362
					District of Columbia	617

Source: CQ Press using data from U.S. Bureau of the Census, Governments Division
    "Public Education Finances: 2009" (http://www.census.gov/govs/school/)
*Includes payments from all funds for support services. This includes salaries, employee benefits, supplies, materials, and contractual services. Excludes capital outlay, debt service, and interfund transfers. Support services cover regular, special, and vocational programs offered in both the academic school year and summer school. It excludes instruction services as well as adult education and community services.

Per Pupil Public Elementary and Secondary School Current Expenditures for Support Services in 2009
National Per Pupil = $3,704*

ALPHA ORDER

RANK	STATE	PER PUPIL
37	Alabama	$3,127
1	Alaska	6,394
42	Arizona	3,039
36	Arkansas	3,146
26	California	3,518
32	Colorado	3,334
7	Connecticut	5,129
12	Delaware	4,250
40	Florida	3,076
38	Georgia	3,113
17	Hawaii	4,002
49	Idaho	2,412
15	Illinois	4,140
23	Indiana	3,580
33	Iowa	3,313
30	Kansas	3,357
41	Kentucky	3,061
20	Louisiana	3,836
10	Maine	4,593
9	Maryland	4,722
8	Massachusetts	4,961
16	Michigan	4,085
28	Minnesota	3,377
46	Mississippi	2,834
29	Missouri	3,364
22	Montana	3,601
39	Nebraska	3,100
35	Nevada	3,165
14	New Hampshire	4,153
2	New Jersey	6,392
24	New Mexico	3,552
6	New York	5,221
47	North Carolina	2,650
34	North Dakota	3,278
12	Ohio	4,250
45	Oklahoma	2,941
21	Oregon	3,775
11	Pennsylvania	4,504
5	Rhode Island	5,462
27	South Carolina	3,449
43	South Dakota	3,001
48	Tennessee	2,555
44	Texas	2,969
50	Utah	1,894
3	Vermont	5,551
19	Virginia	3,898
31	Washington	3,344
25	West Virginia	3,527
18	Wisconsin	3,901
4	Wyoming	5,549

RANK ORDER

RANK	STATE	PER PUPIL
1	Alaska	$6,394
2	New Jersey	6,392
3	Vermont	5,551
4	Wyoming	5,549
5	Rhode Island	5,462
6	New York	5,221
7	Connecticut	5,129
8	Massachusetts	4,961
9	Maryland	4,722
10	Maine	4,593
11	Pennsylvania	4,504
12	Delaware	4,250
12	Ohio	4,250
14	New Hampshire	4,153
15	Illinois	4,140
16	Michigan	4,085
17	Hawaii	4,002
18	Wisconsin	3,901
19	Virginia	3,898
20	Louisiana	3,836
21	Oregon	3,775
22	Montana	3,601
23	Indiana	3,580
24	New Mexico	3,552
25	West Virginia	3,527
26	California	3,518
27	South Carolina	3,449
28	Minnesota	3,377
29	Missouri	3,364
30	Kansas	3,357
31	Washington	3,344
32	Colorado	3,334
33	Iowa	3,313
34	North Dakota	3,278
35	Nevada	3,165
36	Arkansas	3,146
37	Alabama	3,127
38	Georgia	3,113
39	Nebraska	3,100
40	Florida	3,076
41	Kentucky	3,061
42	Arizona	3,039
43	South Dakota	3,001
44	Texas	2,969
45	Oklahoma	2,941
46	Mississippi	2,834
47	North Carolina	2,650
48	Tennessee	2,555
49	Idaho	2,412
50	Utah	1,894
	District of Columbia	8,349

Source: U.S. Bureau of the Census, Governments Division
"Public Education Finances: 2009" (http://www.census.gov/govs/school/)
*Based on student membership. Includes payments from all funds for support services. This includes salaries, employee benefits, supplies, materials, and contractual services. Excludes capital outlay, debt service, and interfund transfers. Support services cover regular, special, and vocational programs offered in both the academic school year and summer school. It excludes instruction services as well as adult education and community services.

Percent of Public Elementary and Secondary School Current Expenditures Used for Support Services in 2009
National Percent = 34.5%*

ALPHA ORDER

RANK	STATE	PERCENT
28	Alabama	34.6
1	Alaska	41.0
2	Arizona	38.6
39	Arkansas	33.6
19	California	35.5
5	Colorado	37.9
32	Connecticut	34.3
34	Delaware	34.1
32	Florida	34.3
42	Georgia	32.0
45	Hawaii	31.9
36	Idaho	33.9
8	Illinois	37.8
5	Indiana	37.9
35	Iowa	34.0
37	Kansas	33.7
28	Kentucky	34.6
15	Louisiana	36.3
16	Maine	35.9
23	Maryland	35.0
41	Massachusetts	33.1
4	Michigan	38.2
48	Minnesota	29.1
25	Mississippi	34.9
28	Missouri	34.6
18	Montana	35.6
46	Nebraska	30.8
11	Nevada	37.4
39	New Hampshire	33.6
12	New Jersey	37.1
10	New Mexico	37.6
50	New York	27.8
47	North Carolina	30.7
42	North Dakota	32.0
2	Ohio	38.6
17	Oklahoma	35.7
9	Oregon	37.7
20	Pennsylvania	35.4
13	Rhode Island	37.0
14	South Carolina	36.7
22	South Dakota	35.1
42	Tennessee	32.0
31	Texas	34.5
49	Utah	28.9
23	Vermont	35.0
20	Virginia	35.4
26	Washington	34.8
37	West Virginia	33.7
26	Wisconsin	34.8
5	Wyoming	37.9

RANK ORDER

RANK	STATE	PERCENT
1	Alaska	41.0
2	Arizona	38.6
2	Ohio	38.6
4	Michigan	38.2
5	Colorado	37.9
5	Indiana	37.9
5	Wyoming	37.9
8	Illinois	37.8
9	Oregon	37.7
10	New Mexico	37.6
11	Nevada	37.4
12	New Jersey	37.1
13	Rhode Island	37.0
14	South Carolina	36.7
15	Louisiana	36.3
16	Maine	35.9
17	Oklahoma	35.7
18	Montana	35.6
19	California	35.5
20	Pennsylvania	35.4
20	Virginia	35.4
22	South Dakota	35.1
23	Maryland	35.0
23	Vermont	35.0
25	Mississippi	34.9
26	Washington	34.8
26	Wisconsin	34.8
28	Alabama	34.6
28	Kentucky	34.6
28	Missouri	34.6
31	Texas	34.5
32	Connecticut	34.3
32	Florida	34.3
34	Delaware	34.1
35	Iowa	34.0
36	Idaho	33.9
37	Kansas	33.7
37	West Virginia	33.7
39	Arkansas	33.6
39	New Hampshire	33.6
41	Massachusetts	33.1
42	Georgia	32.0
42	North Dakota	32.0
42	Tennessee	32.0
45	Hawaii	31.9
46	Nebraska	30.8
47	North Carolina	30.7
48	Minnesota	29.1
49	Utah	28.9
50	New York	27.8

District of Columbia	50.1

Source: CQ Press using data from U.S. Bureau of the Census, Governments Division
"Public Education Finances: 2009" (http://www.census.gov/govs/school/)

*Includes payments from all funds for support services. This includes salaries, employee benefits, supplies, materials, and contractual services. Excludes capital outlay, debt service, and interfund transfers. Support services cover regular, special, and vocational programs offered in both the academic school year and summer school. It excludes instruction services as well as adult education and community services.

Public Elementary and Secondary School Current Expenditures for Salaries and Wages for Support Services in 2009
National Total = $90,999,666,000*

ALPHA ORDER

RANK	STATE	EXPENDITURES	% of USA
26	Alabama	$1,148,375,000	1.3%
44	Alaska	319,126,000	0.4%
18	Arizona	1,512,183,000	1.7%
32	Arkansas	800,788,000	0.9%
1	California	11,582,876,000	12.7%
19	Colorado	1,490,262,000	1.6%
23	Connecticut	1,268,687,000	1.4%
48	Delaware	217,220,000	0.2%
4	Florida	4,430,629,000	4.9%
10	Georgia	2,979,825,000	3.3%
42	Hawaii	340,860,000	0.4%
43	Idaho	333,647,000	0.4%
6	Illinois	4,156,074,000	4.6%
16	Indiana	1,646,724,000	1.8%
29	Iowa	899,280,000	1.0%
31	Kansas	882,120,000	1.0%
27	Kentucky	1,143,534,000	1.3%
24	Louisiana	1,226,864,000	1.3%
39	Maine	394,886,000	0.4%
13	Maryland	2,183,709,000	2.4%
14	Massachusetts	2,056,905,000	2.3%
9	Michigan	3,099,185,000	3.4%
25	Minnesota	1,184,210,000	1.3%
34	Mississippi	697,568,000	0.8%
17	Missouri	1,577,709,000	1.7%
46	Montana	243,104,000	0.3%
38	Nebraska	455,439,000	0.5%
33	Nevada	749,967,000	0.8%
41	New Hampshire	346,042,000	0.4%
5	New Jersey	4,326,856,000	4.8%
35	New Mexico	595,714,000	0.7%
3	New York	6,443,512,000	7.1%
12	North Carolina	2,274,166,000	2.5%
50	North Dakota	155,332,000	0.2%
7	Ohio	3,721,901,000	4.1%
30	Oklahoma	886,310,000	1.0%
28	Oregon	995,622,000	1.1%
8	Pennsylvania	3,418,848,000	3.8%
40	Rhode Island	375,878,000	0.4%
21	South Carolina	1,302,220,000	1.4%
49	South Dakota	181,775,000	0.2%
22	Tennessee	1,279,999,000	1.4%
2	Texas	7,910,456,000	8.7%
36	Utah	561,857,000	0.6%
47	Vermont	231,006,000	0.3%
11	Virginia	2,700,707,000	3.0%
15	Washington	1,965,640,000	2.2%
37	West Virginia	481,430,000	0.5%
20	Wisconsin	1,376,627,000	1.5%
45	Wyoming	262,436,000	0.3%

RANK ORDER

RANK	STATE	EXPENDITURES	% of USA
1	California	$11,582,876,000	12.7%
2	Texas	7,910,456,000	8.7%
3	New York	6,443,512,000	7.1%
4	Florida	4,430,629,000	4.9%
5	New Jersey	4,326,856,000	4.8%
6	Illinois	4,156,074,000	4.6%
7	Ohio	3,721,901,000	4.1%
8	Pennsylvania	3,418,848,000	3.8%
9	Michigan	3,099,185,000	3.4%
10	Georgia	2,979,825,000	3.3%
11	Virginia	2,700,707,000	3.0%
12	North Carolina	2,274,166,000	2.5%
13	Maryland	2,183,709,000	2.4%
14	Massachusetts	2,056,905,000	2.3%
15	Washington	1,965,640,000	2.2%
16	Indiana	1,646,724,000	1.8%
17	Missouri	1,577,709,000	1.7%
18	Arizona	1,512,183,000	1.7%
19	Colorado	1,490,262,000	1.6%
20	Wisconsin	1,376,627,000	1.5%
21	South Carolina	1,302,220,000	1.4%
22	Tennessee	1,279,999,000	1.4%
23	Connecticut	1,268,687,000	1.4%
24	Louisiana	1,226,864,000	1.3%
25	Minnesota	1,184,210,000	1.3%
26	Alabama	1,148,375,000	1.3%
27	Kentucky	1,143,534,000	1.3%
28	Oregon	995,622,000	1.1%
29	Iowa	899,280,000	1.0%
30	Oklahoma	886,310,000	1.0%
31	Kansas	882,120,000	1.0%
32	Arkansas	800,788,000	0.9%
33	Nevada	749,967,000	0.8%
34	Mississippi	697,568,000	0.8%
35	New Mexico	595,714,000	0.7%
36	Utah	561,857,000	0.6%
37	West Virginia	481,430,000	0.5%
38	Nebraska	455,439,000	0.5%
39	Maine	394,886,000	0.4%
40	Rhode Island	375,878,000	0.4%
41	New Hampshire	346,042,000	0.4%
42	Hawaii	340,860,000	0.4%
43	Idaho	333,647,000	0.4%
44	Alaska	319,126,000	0.4%
45	Wyoming	262,436,000	0.3%
46	Montana	243,104,000	0.3%
47	Vermont	231,006,000	0.3%
48	Delaware	217,220,000	0.2%
49	South Dakota	181,775,000	0.2%
50	North Dakota	155,332,000	0.2%
	District of Columbia	183,576,000	0.2%

Source: U.S. Bureau of the Census, Governments Division
"Public Education Finances: 2009" (http://www.census.gov/govs/school/)
*Includes payments from all funds for support services used for salaries and wages. Excludes capital outlay, debt service, and interfund transfers. Support services cover regular, special, and vocational programs offered in both the academic year and summer school. It excludes instruction services as well as adult education and community services.

Percent of Public Elementary and Secondary School Current Expenditures Used for Salaries and Wages for Support Services in 2009
National Percent = 17.6%*

ALPHA ORDER

RANK	STATE	PERCENT
29	Alabama	17.1
41	Alaska	15.7
8	Arizona	19.5
22	Arkansas	18.0
13	California	19.0
1	Colorado	20.9
42	Connecticut	15.5
45	Delaware	14.9
14	Florida	18.9
17	Georgia	18.6
44	Hawaii	15.1
26	Idaho	17.5
24	Illinois	17.9
30	Indiana	17.0
14	Iowa	18.9
16	Kansas	18.8
10	Kentucky	19.3
26	Louisiana	17.5
34	Maine	16.5
11	Maryland	19.2
46	Massachusetts	14.7
17	Michigan	18.6
49	Minnesota	12.7
26	Mississippi	17.5
20	Missouri	18.1
30	Montana	17.0
42	Nebraska	15.5
3	Nevada	20.5
47	New Hampshire	14.2
19	New Jersey	18.5
11	New Mexico	19.2
49	New York	12.7
20	North Carolina	18.1
39	North Dakota	16.0
7	Ohio	19.6
33	Oklahoma	16.7
25	Oregon	17.7
40	Pennsylvania	15.8
22	Rhode Island	18.0
9	South Carolina	19.4
32	South Dakota	16.8
34	Tennessee	16.5
5	Texas	19.8
38	Utah	16.1
34	Vermont	16.5
4	Virginia	19.9
6	Washington	19.7
37	West Virginia	16.3
47	Wisconsin	14.2
2	Wyoming	20.6

RANK ORDER

RANK	STATE	PERCENT
1	Colorado	20.9
2	Wyoming	20.6
3	Nevada	20.5
4	Virginia	19.9
5	Texas	19.8
6	Washington	19.7
7	Ohio	19.6
8	Arizona	19.5
9	South Carolina	19.4
10	Kentucky	19.3
11	Maryland	19.2
11	New Mexico	19.2
13	California	19.0
14	Florida	18.9
14	Iowa	18.9
16	Kansas	18.8
17	Georgia	18.6
17	Michigan	18.6
19	New Jersey	18.5
20	Missouri	18.1
20	North Carolina	18.1
22	Arkansas	18.0
22	Rhode Island	18.0
24	Illinois	17.9
25	Oregon	17.7
26	Idaho	17.5
26	Louisiana	17.5
26	Mississippi	17.5
29	Alabama	17.1
30	Indiana	17.0
30	Montana	17.0
32	South Dakota	16.8
33	Oklahoma	16.7
34	Maine	16.5
34	Tennessee	16.5
34	Vermont	16.5
37	West Virginia	16.3
38	Utah	16.1
39	North Dakota	16.0
40	Pennsylvania	15.8
41	Alaska	15.7
42	Connecticut	15.5
42	Nebraska	15.5
44	Hawaii	15.1
45	Delaware	14.9
46	Massachusetts	14.7
47	New Hampshire	14.2
47	Wisconsin	14.2
49	Minnesota	12.7
49	New York	12.7
	District of Columbia	24.8

Source: CQ Press using data from U.S. Bureau of the Census, Governments Division
    "Public Education Finances: 2009" (http://www.census.gov/govs/school/)
*Includes payments from all funds for support services used for salaries and wages. Excludes capital outlay, debt service, and interfund transfers. Support services cover regular, special, and vocational programs offered in both the academic year and summer school. It excludes instruction services as well as adult education and community services.

Public Elementary and Secondary School Current Expenditures for Employee Benefits for Support Services in 2009
National Total = $31,901,000,000*

ALPHA ORDER

RANK	STATE	EXPENDITURES	% of USA
20	Alabama	$497,017,000	1.6%
36	Alaska	210,902,000	0.7%
22	Arizona	448,120,000	1.4%
37	Arkansas	207,812,000	0.7%
1	California	4,197,815,000	13.2%
28	Colorado	356,364,000	1.1%
18	Connecticut	525,533,000	1.6%
46	Delaware	95,462,000	0.3%
7	Florida	1,453,560,000	4.6%
16	Georgia	662,133,000	2.1%
42	Hawaii	134,908,000	0.4%
44	Idaho	115,618,000	0.4%
4	Illinois	1,540,067,000	4.8%
11	Indiana	943,164,000	3.0%
30	Iowa	280,196,000	0.9%
34	Kansas	227,714,000	0.7%
25	Kentucky	405,704,000	1.3%
24	Louisiana	438,600,000	1.4%
40	Maine	156,465,000	0.5%
14	Maryland	795,133,000	2.5%
12	Massachusetts	853,293,000	2.7%
5	Michigan	1,510,036,000	4.7%
21	Minnesota	475,358,000	1.5%
35	Mississippi	225,220,000	0.7%
23	Missouri	441,473,000	1.4%
48	Montana	73,933,000	0.2%
41	Nebraska	136,489,000	0.4%
29	Nevada	286,998,000	0.9%
43	New Hampshire	132,649,000	0.4%
3	New Jersey	1,636,096,000	5.1%
38	New Mexico	190,514,000	0.6%
2	New York	2,540,371,000	8.0%
17	North Carolina	571,462,000	1.8%
50	North Dakota	45,304,000	0.1%
6	Ohio	1,460,225,000	4.6%
31	Oklahoma	255,277,000	0.8%
19	Oregon	511,324,000	1.6%
9	Pennsylvania	1,246,535,000	3.9%
39	Rhode Island	183,354,000	0.6%
26	South Carolina	399,893,000	1.3%
49	South Dakota	51,856,000	0.2%
27	Tennessee	381,074,000	1.2%
8	Texas	1,405,271,000	4.4%
33	Utah	231,039,000	0.7%
47	Vermont	82,578,000	0.3%
10	Virginia	963,805,000	3.0%
15	Washington	694,543,000	2.2%
32	West Virginia	253,420,000	0.8%
13	Wisconsin	845,798,000	2.7%
45	Wyoming	97,586,000	0.3%

RANK ORDER

RANK	STATE	EXPENDITURES	% of USA
1	California	$4,197,815,000	13.2%
2	New York	2,540,371,000	8.0%
3	New Jersey	1,636,096,000	5.1%
4	Illinois	1,540,067,000	4.8%
5	Michigan	1,510,036,000	4.7%
6	Ohio	1,460,225,000	4.6%
7	Florida	1,453,560,000	4.6%
8	Texas	1,405,271,000	4.4%
9	Pennsylvania	1,246,535,000	3.9%
10	Virginia	963,805,000	3.0%
11	Indiana	943,164,000	3.0%
12	Massachusetts	853,293,000	2.7%
13	Wisconsin	845,798,000	2.7%
14	Maryland	795,133,000	2.5%
15	Washington	694,543,000	2.2%
16	Georgia	662,133,000	2.1%
17	North Carolina	571,462,000	1.8%
18	Connecticut	525,533,000	1.6%
19	Oregon	511,324,000	1.6%
20	Alabama	497,017,000	1.6%
21	Minnesota	475,358,000	1.5%
22	Arizona	448,120,000	1.4%
23	Missouri	441,473,000	1.4%
24	Louisiana	438,600,000	1.4%
25	Kentucky	405,704,000	1.3%
26	South Carolina	399,893,000	1.3%
27	Tennessee	381,074,000	1.2%
28	Colorado	356,364,000	1.1%
29	Nevada	286,998,000	0.9%
30	Iowa	280,196,000	0.9%
31	Oklahoma	255,277,000	0.8%
32	West Virginia	253,420,000	0.8%
33	Utah	231,039,000	0.7%
34	Kansas	227,714,000	0.7%
35	Mississippi	225,220,000	0.7%
36	Alaska	210,902,000	0.7%
37	Arkansas	207,812,000	0.7%
38	New Mexico	190,514,000	0.6%
39	Rhode Island	183,354,000	0.6%
40	Maine	156,465,000	0.5%
41	Nebraska	136,489,000	0.4%
42	Hawaii	134,908,000	0.4%
43	New Hampshire	132,649,000	0.4%
44	Idaho	115,618,000	0.4%
45	Wyoming	97,586,000	0.3%
46	Delaware	95,462,000	0.3%
47	Vermont	82,578,000	0.3%
48	Montana	73,933,000	0.2%
49	South Dakota	51,856,000	0.2%
50	North Dakota	45,304,000	0.1%
	District of Columbia	25,939,000	0.1%

Source: U.S. Bureau of the Census, Governments Division
"Public Education Finances: 2009" (http://www.census.gov/govs/school/)
*Includes payments from all funds for support services used for employee benefits. Excludes capital outlay, debt service, and interfund transfers. Support services cover regular, special, and vocational programs offered in both the academic year and summer school. It excludes instruction services as well as adult education and community services.

Percent of Public Elementary and Secondary School Current Expenditures Used for Employee Benefits for Support Services in 2009
National Percent = 6.2%*

ALPHA ORDER

RANK	STATE	PERCENT
11	Alabama	7.4
1	Alaska	10.4
32	Arizona	5.8
45	Arkansas	4.7
16	California	6.9
39	Colorado	5.0
22	Connecticut	6.4
18	Delaware	6.6
24	Florida	6.2
49	Georgia	4.1
28	Hawaii	6.0
25	Idaho	6.1
18	Illinois	6.6
2	Indiana	9.7
30	Iowa	5.9
41	Kansas	4.9
17	Kentucky	6.8
23	Louisiana	6.3
21	Maine	6.5
13	Maryland	7.0
25	Massachusetts	6.1
3	Michigan	9.1
37	Minnesota	5.1
34	Mississippi	5.7
37	Missouri	5.1
36	Montana	5.2
47	Nebraska	4.6
8	Nevada	7.9
35	New Hampshire	5.4
13	New Jersey	7.0
25	New Mexico	6.1
39	New York	5.0
47	North Carolina	4.6
45	North Dakota	4.7
9	Ohio	7.7
43	Oklahoma	4.8
3	Oregon	9.1
32	Pennsylvania	5.8
5	Rhode Island	8.8
28	South Carolina	6.0
43	South Dakota	4.8
41	Tennessee	4.9
50	Texas	3.5
18	Utah	6.6
30	Vermont	5.9
12	Virginia	7.1
13	Washington	7.0
7	West Virginia	8.6
6	Wisconsin	8.7
9	Wyoming	7.7

RANK ORDER

RANK	STATE	PERCENT
1	Alaska	10.4
2	Indiana	9.7
3	Michigan	9.1
3	Oregon	9.1
5	Rhode Island	8.8
6	Wisconsin	8.7
7	West Virginia	8.6
8	Nevada	7.9
9	Ohio	7.7
9	Wyoming	7.7
11	Alabama	7.4
12	Virginia	7.1
13	Maryland	7.0
13	New Jersey	7.0
13	Washington	7.0
16	California	6.9
17	Kentucky	6.8
18	Delaware	6.6
18	Illinois	6.6
18	Utah	6.6
21	Maine	6.5
22	Connecticut	6.4
23	Louisiana	6.3
24	Florida	6.2
25	Idaho	6.1
25	Massachusetts	6.1
25	New Mexico	6.1
28	Hawaii	6.0
28	South Carolina	6.0
30	Iowa	5.9
30	Vermont	5.9
32	Arizona	5.8
32	Pennsylvania	5.8
34	Mississippi	5.7
35	New Hampshire	5.4
36	Montana	5.2
37	Minnesota	5.1
37	Missouri	5.1
39	Colorado	5.0
39	New York	5.0
41	Kansas	4.9
41	Tennessee	4.9
43	Oklahoma	4.8
43	South Dakota	4.8
45	Arkansas	4.7
45	North Dakota	4.7
47	Nebraska	4.6
47	North Carolina	4.6
49	Georgia	4.1
50	Texas	3.5

District of Columbia 3.5

Source: CQ Press using data from U.S. Bureau of the Census, Governments Division
"Public Education Finances: 2009" (http://www.census.gov/govs/school/)
*Includes payments from all funds for support services used for employee benefits. Excludes capital outlay, debt service, and interfund transfers. Support services cover regular, special, and vocational programs offered in both the academic year and summer school. It excludes instruction services as well as adult education and community services.

Public Elementary and Secondary School Current Expenditures for Pupil Support Services in 2009
National Total = $27,574,807,000*

ALPHA ORDER

RANK	STATE	EXPENDITURES	% of USA
23	Alabama	$373,885,000	1.4%
39	Alaska	164,629,000	0.6%
15	Arizona	542,272,000	2.0%
35	Arkansas	206,128,000	0.7%
1	California	2,992,661,000	10.9%
25	Colorado	330,672,000	1.2%
18	Connecticut	507,084,000	1.8%
48	Delaware	72,398,000	0.3%
9	Florida	1,070,743,000	3.9%
11	Georgia	768,126,000	2.8%
34	Hawaii	211,127,000	0.8%
43	Idaho	108,152,000	0.4%
5	Illinois	1,465,478,000	5.3%
19	Indiana	444,810,000	1.6%
29	Iowa	269,678,000	1.0%
33	Kansas	220,589,000	0.8%
30	Kentucky	262,459,000	1.0%
27	Louisiana	321,363,000	1.2%
40	Maine	145,972,000	0.5%
16	Maryland	531,227,000	1.9%
10	Massachusetts	963,279,000	3.5%
6	Michigan	1,277,487,000	4.6%
32	Minnesota	240,177,000	0.9%
36	Mississippi	185,928,000	0.7%
21	Missouri	408,361,000	1.5%
46	Montana	79,866,000	0.3%
41	Nebraska	126,927,000	0.5%
38	Nevada	173,298,000	0.6%
37	New Hampshire	173,945,000	0.6%
2	New Jersey	2,150,375,000	7.8%
28	New Mexico	307,708,000	1.1%
4	New York	1,477,360,000	5.4%
14	North Carolina	621,983,000	2.3%
50	North Dakota	38,034,000	0.1%
7	Ohio	1,135,884,000	4.1%
24	Oklahoma	350,275,000	1.3%
22	Oregon	397,978,000	1.4%
8	Pennsylvania	1,103,373,000	4.0%
31	Rhode Island	253,892,000	0.9%
17	South Carolina	517,305,000	1.9%
49	South Dakota	58,701,000	0.2%
26	Tennessee	330,166,000	1.2%
3	Texas	1,963,251,000	7.1%
42	Utah	119,776,000	0.4%
45	Vermont	102,870,000	0.4%
13	Virginia	655,443,000	2.4%
12	Washington	660,137,000	2.4%
44	West Virginia	106,102,000	0.4%
20	Wisconsin	428,865,000	1.6%
47	Wyoming	73,057,000	0.3%

RANK ORDER

RANK	STATE	EXPENDITURES	% of USA
1	California	$2,992,661,000	10.9%
2	New Jersey	2,150,375,000	7.8%
3	Texas	1,963,251,000	7.1%
4	New York	1,477,360,000	5.4%
5	Illinois	1,465,478,000	5.3%
6	Michigan	1,277,487,000	4.6%
7	Ohio	1,135,884,000	4.1%
8	Pennsylvania	1,103,373,000	4.0%
9	Florida	1,070,743,000	3.9%
10	Massachusetts	963,279,000	3.5%
11	Georgia	768,126,000	2.8%
12	Washington	660,137,000	2.4%
13	Virginia	655,443,000	2.4%
14	North Carolina	621,983,000	2.3%
15	Arizona	542,272,000	2.0%
16	Maryland	531,227,000	1.9%
17	South Carolina	517,305,000	1.9%
18	Connecticut	507,084,000	1.8%
19	Indiana	444,810,000	1.6%
20	Wisconsin	428,865,000	1.6%
21	Missouri	408,361,000	1.5%
22	Oregon	397,978,000	1.4%
23	Alabama	373,885,000	1.4%
24	Oklahoma	350,275,000	1.3%
25	Colorado	330,672,000	1.2%
26	Tennessee	330,166,000	1.2%
27	Louisiana	321,363,000	1.2%
28	New Mexico	307,708,000	1.1%
29	Iowa	269,678,000	1.0%
30	Kentucky	262,459,000	1.0%
31	Rhode Island	253,892,000	0.9%
32	Minnesota	240,177,000	0.9%
33	Kansas	220,589,000	0.8%
34	Hawaii	211,127,000	0.8%
35	Arkansas	206,128,000	0.7%
36	Mississippi	185,928,000	0.7%
37	New Hampshire	173,945,000	0.6%
38	Nevada	173,298,000	0.6%
39	Alaska	164,629,000	0.6%
40	Maine	145,972,000	0.5%
41	Nebraska	126,927,000	0.5%
42	Utah	119,776,000	0.4%
43	Idaho	108,152,000	0.4%
44	West Virginia	106,102,000	0.4%
45	Vermont	102,870,000	0.4%
46	Montana	79,866,000	0.3%
47	Wyoming	73,057,000	0.3%
48	Delaware	72,398,000	0.3%
49	South Dakota	58,701,000	0.2%
50	North Dakota	38,034,000	0.1%
	District of Columbia	83,551,000	0.3%

Source: U.S. Bureau of the Census, Governments Division
"Public Education Finances: 2009" (http://www.census.gov/govs/school/)
*Pupil support services include social work, counseling, record maintenance, nursing, psychological, and speech services. Includes salaries, benefits, services, and supplies. Census expanded its usual "current expenditures" concept for education finance reports to include all current public elementary and secondary education outlays regardless of the specific unit of government that actually makes the expenditure.

Percent of Public Elementary and Secondary School Current Expenditures Used for Pupil Support Services in 2009
National Percent = 5.3%*

ALPHA ORDER

RANK	STATE	PERCENT
22	Alabama	5.6
5	Alaska	8.1
11	Arizona	7.0
37	Arkansas	4.6
28	California	4.9
37	Colorado	4.6
16	Connecticut	6.2
26	Delaware	5.0
37	Florida	4.6
30	Georgia	4.8
3	Hawaii	9.4
19	Idaho	5.7
15	Illinois	6.3
37	Indiana	4.6
19	Iowa	5.7
32	Kansas	4.7
42	Kentucky	4.4
37	Louisiana	4.6
17	Maine	6.1
32	Maryland	4.7
12	Massachusetts	6.9
6	Michigan	7.7
50	Minnesota	2.6
32	Mississippi	4.7
32	Missouri	4.7
22	Montana	5.6
44	Nebraska	4.3
32	Nevada	4.7
9	New Hampshire	7.1
4	New Jersey	9.2
2	New Mexico	9.9
49	New York	2.9
26	North Carolina	5.0
46	North Dakota	3.9
18	Ohio	6.0
13	Oklahoma	6.6
9	Oregon	7.1
25	Pennsylvania	5.1
1	Rhode Island	12.2
6	South Carolina	7.7
24	South Dakota	5.4
44	Tennessee	4.3
28	Texas	4.9
48	Utah	3.4
8	Vermont	7.4
30	Virginia	4.8
13	Washington	6.6
47	West Virginia	3.6
42	Wisconsin	4.4
19	Wyoming	5.7

RANK ORDER

RANK	STATE	PERCENT
1	Rhode Island	12.2
2	New Mexico	9.9
3	Hawaii	9.4
4	New Jersey	9.2
5	Alaska	8.1
6	Michigan	7.7
6	South Carolina	7.7
8	Vermont	7.4
9	New Hampshire	7.1
9	Oregon	7.1
11	Arizona	7.0
12	Massachusetts	6.9
13	Oklahoma	6.6
13	Washington	6.6
15	Illinois	6.3
16	Connecticut	6.2
17	Maine	6.1
18	Ohio	6.0
19	Idaho	5.7
19	Iowa	5.7
19	Wyoming	5.7
22	Alabama	5.6
22	Montana	5.6
24	South Dakota	5.4
25	Pennsylvania	5.1
26	Delaware	5.0
26	North Carolina	5.0
28	California	4.9
28	Texas	4.9
30	Georgia	4.8
30	Virginia	4.8
32	Kansas	4.7
32	Maryland	4.7
32	Mississippi	4.7
32	Missouri	4.7
32	Nevada	4.7
37	Arkansas	4.6
37	Colorado	4.6
37	Florida	4.6
37	Indiana	4.6
37	Louisiana	4.6
42	Kentucky	4.4
42	Wisconsin	4.4
44	Nebraska	4.3
44	Tennessee	4.3
46	North Dakota	3.9
47	West Virginia	3.6
48	Utah	3.4
49	New York	2.9
50	Minnesota	2.6

District of Columbia   11.3

Source: CQ Press using data from U.S. Bureau of the Census, Governments Division
"Public Education Finances: 2009" (http://www.census.gov/govs/school/)

*Pupil support services include social work, counseling, record maintenance, nursing, psychological, and speech services. Includes salaries, benefits, services, and supplies. Census expanded its usual "current expenditures" concept for education finance reports to include all current public elementary and secondary education outlays regardless of the specific unit of government that actually makes the expenditure.

Public Elementary and Secondary School Current Expenditures for Instructional Staff Support Services in 2009
National Total = $24,696,411,000*

ALPHA ORDER

RANK	STATE	EXPENDITURES	% of USA
26	Alabama	$311,990,000	1.3%
36	Alaska	114,604,000	0.5%
28	Arizona	244,871,000	1.0%
24	Arkansas	330,309,000	1.3%
1	California	3,753,972,000	15.2%
21	Colorado	392,190,000	1.6%
27	Connecticut	258,006,000	1.0%
50	Delaware	16,373,000	0.1%
3	Florida	1,489,251,000	6.0%
9	Georgia	811,828,000	3.3%
44	Hawaii	73,175,000	0.3%
42	Idaho	80,191,000	0.3%
6	Illinois	1,062,952,000	4.3%
23	Indiana	354,949,000	1.4%
30	Iowa	214,087,000	0.9%
31	Kansas	208,828,000	0.8%
25	Kentucky	312,353,000	1.3%
22	Louisiana	380,132,000	1.5%
38	Maine	106,632,000	0.4%
13	Maryland	593,667,000	2.4%
10	Massachusetts	800,065,000	3.2%
11	Michigan	792,089,000	3.2%
19	Minnesota	413,282,000	1.7%
34	Mississippi	181,412,000	0.7%
20	Missouri	399,191,000	1.6%
47	Montana	55,322,000	0.2%
39	Nebraska	98,242,000	0.4%
33	Nevada	190,062,000	0.8%
43	New Hampshire	78,606,000	0.3%
12	New Jersey	772,837,000	3.1%
40	New Mexico	90,265,000	0.4%
4	New York	1,358,844,000	5.5%
16	North Carolina	446,437,000	1.8%
49	North Dakota	28,722,000	0.1%
5	Ohio	1,233,890,000	5.0%
32	Oklahoma	200,243,000	0.8%
29	Oregon	239,091,000	1.0%
8	Pennsylvania	839,483,000	3.4%
45	Rhode Island	65,639,000	0.3%
18	South Carolina	435,618,000	1.8%
48	South Dakota	44,645,000	0.2%
17	Tennessee	442,245,000	1.8%
2	Texas	2,104,130,000	8.5%
35	Utah	150,976,000	0.6%
46	Vermont	55,340,000	0.2%
7	Virginia	906,448,000	3.7%
15	Washington	450,212,000	1.8%
37	West Virginia	108,232,000	0.4%
14	Wisconsin	462,865,000	1.9%
41	Wyoming	83,661,000	0.3%

RANK ORDER

RANK	STATE	EXPENDITURES	% of USA
1	California	$3,753,972,000	15.2%
2	Texas	2,104,130,000	8.5%
3	Florida	1,489,251,000	6.0%
4	New York	1,358,844,000	5.5%
5	Ohio	1,233,890,000	5.0%
6	Illinois	1,062,952,000	4.3%
7	Virginia	906,448,000	3.7%
8	Pennsylvania	839,483,000	3.4%
9	Georgia	811,828,000	3.3%
10	Massachusetts	800,065,000	3.2%
11	Michigan	792,089,000	3.2%
12	New Jersey	772,837,000	3.1%
13	Maryland	593,667,000	2.4%
14	Wisconsin	462,865,000	1.9%
15	Washington	450,212,000	1.8%
16	North Carolina	446,437,000	1.8%
17	Tennessee	442,245,000	1.8%
18	South Carolina	435,618,000	1.8%
19	Minnesota	413,282,000	1.7%
20	Missouri	399,191,000	1.6%
21	Colorado	392,190,000	1.6%
22	Louisiana	380,132,000	1.5%
23	Indiana	354,949,000	1.4%
24	Arkansas	330,309,000	1.3%
25	Kentucky	312,353,000	1.3%
26	Alabama	311,990,000	1.3%
27	Connecticut	258,006,000	1.0%
28	Arizona	244,871,000	1.0%
29	Oregon	239,091,000	1.0%
30	Iowa	214,087,000	0.9%
31	Kansas	208,828,000	0.8%
32	Oklahoma	200,243,000	0.8%
33	Nevada	190,062,000	0.8%
34	Mississippi	181,412,000	0.7%
35	Utah	150,976,000	0.6%
36	Alaska	114,604,000	0.5%
37	West Virginia	108,232,000	0.4%
38	Maine	106,632,000	0.4%
39	Nebraska	98,242,000	0.4%
40	New Mexico	90,265,000	0.4%
41	Wyoming	83,661,000	0.3%
42	Idaho	80,191,000	0.3%
43	New Hampshire	78,606,000	0.3%
44	Hawaii	73,175,000	0.3%
45	Rhode Island	65,639,000	0.3%
46	Vermont	55,340,000	0.2%
47	Montana	55,322,000	0.2%
48	South Dakota	44,645,000	0.2%
49	North Dakota	28,722,000	0.1%
50	Delaware	16,373,000	0.1%
	District of Columbia	57,957,000	0.2%

Source: U.S. Bureau of the Census, Governments Division
"Public Education Finances: 2009" (http://www.census.gov/govs/school/)
*Staff support services include curriculum development, instructional staff training, and media, library, audiovisual, television, and computer-assisted services. Includes salaries, benefits, services, and supplies. Census expanded its usual "current expenditures" concept for education finance reports to include all current public elementary and secondary education outlays regardless of the specific unit of government that actually makes the expenditure.

Percent of Public Elementary and Secondary School Current Expenditures Used for Instructional Staff Support Services in 2009
National Percent = 4.8%*

ALPHA ORDER

RANK	STATE	PERCENT
20	Alabama	4.6
10	Alaska	5.6
43	Arizona	3.2
1	Arkansas	7.4
7	California	6.1
11	Colorado	5.5
43	Connecticut	3.2
50	Delaware	1.1
6	Florida	6.3
17	Georgia	5.1
40	Hawaii	3.3
30	Idaho	4.2
20	Illinois	4.6
37	Indiana	3.7
24	Iowa	4.5
24	Kansas	4.5
13	Kentucky	5.3
12	Louisiana	5.4
24	Maine	4.5
15	Maryland	5.2
8	Massachusetts	5.7
18	Michigan	4.8
28	Minnesota	4.4
20	Mississippi	4.6
20	Missouri	4.6
34	Montana	3.9
40	Nebraska	3.3
15	Nevada	5.2
43	New Hampshire	3.2
40	New Jersey	3.3
48	New Mexico	2.9
49	New York	2.7
39	North Carolina	3.6
47	North Dakota	3.0
4	Ohio	6.5
36	Oklahoma	3.8
30	Oregon	4.2
34	Pennsylvania	3.9
46	Rhode Island	3.1
4	South Carolina	6.5
32	South Dakota	4.1
8	Tennessee	5.7
13	Texas	5.3
29	Utah	4.3
33	Vermont	4.0
2	Virginia	6.7
24	Washington	4.5
37	West Virginia	3.7
18	Wisconsin	4.8
3	Wyoming	6.6

RANK ORDER

RANK	STATE	PERCENT
1	Arkansas	7.4
2	Virginia	6.7
3	Wyoming	6.6
4	Ohio	6.5
4	South Carolina	6.5
6	Florida	6.3
7	California	6.1
8	Massachusetts	5.7
8	Tennessee	5.7
10	Alaska	5.6
11	Colorado	5.5
12	Louisiana	5.4
13	Kentucky	5.3
13	Texas	5.3
15	Maryland	5.2
15	Nevada	5.2
17	Georgia	5.1
18	Michigan	4.8
18	Wisconsin	4.8
20	Alabama	4.6
20	Illinois	4.6
20	Mississippi	4.6
20	Missouri	4.6
24	Iowa	4.5
24	Kansas	4.5
24	Maine	4.5
24	Washington	4.5
28	Minnesota	4.4
29	Utah	4.3
30	Idaho	4.2
30	Oregon	4.2
32	South Dakota	4.1
33	Vermont	4.0
34	Montana	3.9
34	Pennsylvania	3.9
36	Oklahoma	3.8
37	Indiana	3.7
37	West Virginia	3.7
39	North Carolina	3.6
40	Hawaii	3.3
40	Nebraska	3.3
40	New Jersey	3.3
43	Arizona	3.2
43	Connecticut	3.2
43	New Hampshire	3.2
46	Rhode Island	3.1
47	North Dakota	3.0
48	New Mexico	2.9
49	New York	2.7
50	Delaware	1.1

District of Columbia — 7.8

Source: CQ Press using data from U.S. Bureau of the Census, Governments Division
   "Public Education Finances: 2009" (http://www.census.gov/govs/school/)
*Staff support services include curriculum development, instructional staff training, and media, library, audiovisual, television, and computer-assisted services. Includes salaries, benefits, services, and supplies. Census expanded its usual "current expenditures" concept for education finance reports to include all current public elementary and secondary education outlays regardless of the specific unit of government that actually makes the expenditure.

Public Elementary and Secondary School Current Expenditures for General Administration in 2009
National Total = $9,647,865,000*

ALPHA ORDER

RANK	STATE	EXPENDITURES	% of USA
18	Alabama	$172,998,000	1.8%
47	Alaska	31,139,000	0.3%
30	Arizona	101,852,000	1.1%
32	Arkansas	93,645,000	1.0%
5	California	563,797,000	5.8%
27	Colorado	114,320,000	1.2%
16	Connecticut	183,626,000	1.9%
49	Delaware	15,975,000	0.2%
14	Florida	207,579,000	2.2%
12	Georgia	235,318,000	2.4%
50	Hawaii	11,688,000	0.1%
42	Idaho	40,542,000	0.4%
1	Illinois	958,299,000	9.9%
15	Indiana	192,240,000	2.0%
24	Iowa	124,574,000	1.3%
25	Kansas	124,161,000	1.3%
22	Kentucky	139,339,000	1.4%
17	Louisiana	174,629,000	1.8%
29	Maine	105,778,000	1.1%
31	Maryland	97,091,000	1.0%
19	Massachusetts	170,458,000	1.8%
10	Michigan	260,020,000	2.7%
8	Minnesota	348,499,000	3.6%
26	Mississippi	116,839,000	1.2%
9	Missouri	264,926,000	2.7%
43	Montana	40,218,000	0.4%
33	Nebraska	91,104,000	0.9%
39	Nevada	58,863,000	0.6%
34	New Hampshire	83,925,000	0.9%
7	New Jersey	494,990,000	5.1%
37	New Mexico	64,399,000	0.7%
2	New York	814,642,000	8.4%
23	North Carolina	136,885,000	1.4%
41	North Dakota	41,489,000	0.4%
6	Ohio	496,650,000	5.1%
20	Oklahoma	153,523,000	1.6%
36	Oregon	75,707,000	0.8%
3	Pennsylvania	618,349,000	6.4%
40	Rhode Island	50,349,000	0.5%
35	South Carolina	77,522,000	0.8%
45	South Dakota	36,348,000	0.4%
21	Tennessee	151,445,000	1.6%
4	Texas	567,066,000	5.9%
44	Utah	39,788,000	0.4%
46	Vermont	32,899,000	0.3%
13	Virginia	214,383,000	2.2%
28	Washington	110,754,000	1.1%
38	West Virginia	63,009,000	0.7%
11	Wisconsin	246,748,000	2.6%
48	Wyoming	24,525,000	0.3%

RANK ORDER

RANK	STATE	EXPENDITURES	% of USA
1	Illinois	$958,299,000	9.9%
2	New York	814,642,000	8.4%
3	Pennsylvania	618,349,000	6.4%
4	Texas	567,066,000	5.9%
5	California	563,797,000	5.8%
6	Ohio	496,650,000	5.1%
7	New Jersey	494,990,000	5.1%
8	Minnesota	348,499,000	3.6%
9	Missouri	264,926,000	2.7%
10	Michigan	260,020,000	2.7%
11	Wisconsin	246,748,000	2.6%
12	Georgia	235,318,000	2.4%
13	Virginia	214,383,000	2.2%
14	Florida	207,579,000	2.2%
15	Indiana	192,240,000	2.0%
16	Connecticut	183,626,000	1.9%
17	Louisiana	174,629,000	1.8%
18	Alabama	172,998,000	1.8%
19	Massachusetts	170,458,000	1.8%
20	Oklahoma	153,523,000	1.6%
21	Tennessee	151,445,000	1.6%
22	Kentucky	139,339,000	1.4%
23	North Carolina	136,885,000	1.4%
24	Iowa	124,574,000	1.3%
25	Kansas	124,161,000	1.3%
26	Mississippi	116,839,000	1.2%
27	Colorado	114,320,000	1.2%
28	Washington	110,754,000	1.1%
29	Maine	105,778,000	1.1%
30	Arizona	101,852,000	1.1%
31	Maryland	97,091,000	1.0%
32	Arkansas	93,645,000	1.0%
33	Nebraska	91,104,000	0.9%
34	New Hampshire	83,925,000	0.9%
35	South Carolina	77,522,000	0.8%
36	Oregon	75,707,000	0.8%
37	New Mexico	64,399,000	0.7%
38	West Virginia	63,009,000	0.7%
39	Nevada	58,863,000	0.6%
40	Rhode Island	50,349,000	0.5%
41	North Dakota	41,489,000	0.4%
42	Idaho	40,542,000	0.4%
43	Montana	40,218,000	0.4%
44	Utah	39,788,000	0.4%
45	South Dakota	36,348,000	0.4%
46	Vermont	32,899,000	0.3%
47	Alaska	31,139,000	0.3%
48	Wyoming	24,525,000	0.3%
49	Delaware	15,975,000	0.2%
50	Hawaii	11,688,000	0.1%
	District of Columbia	12,953,000	0.1%

Source: U.S. Bureau of the Census, Governments Division
"Public Education Finances: 2009" (http://www.census.gov/govs/school/)
*General administration includes expenditures for board of education and office of the superintendent services. Includes salaries, benefits, services, and supplies. Census expanded its usual "current expenditures" concept for education finance reports to include all current public elementary and secondary education outlays regardless of the specific unit of government that actually makes the expenditure.

Per Pupil Public Elementary and Secondary School
Current Expenditures for General Administration in 2009
National Per Pupil = $200*

ALPHA ORDER

RANK ORDER

RANK	STATE	PER PUPIL		RANK	STATE	PER PUPIL
25	Alabama	$232		1	Maine	$566
22	Alaska	239		2	Illinois	453
45	Arizona	104		3	North Dakota	438
28	Arkansas	197		4	Minnesota	434
47	California	91		5	New Hampshire	424
37	Colorado	141		6	Vermont	373
10	Connecticut	336		7	Pennsylvania	365
38	Delaware	137		8	New Jersey	364
48	Florida	79		9	Rhode Island	356
36	Georgia	143		10	Connecticut	336
50	Hawaii	65		11	Nebraska	312
35	Idaho	151		12	New York	302
2	Illinois	453		13	Missouri	295
30	Indiana	187		14	Ohio	287
21	Iowa	256		14	South Dakota	287
19	Kansas	264		16	Wisconsin	285
27	Kentucky	208		17	Montana	284
20	Louisiana	263		18	Wyoming	282
1	Maine	566		19	Kansas	264
42	Maryland	115		20	Louisiana	263
31	Massachusetts	183		21	Iowa	256
33	Michigan	167		22	Alaska	239
4	Minnesota	434		23	Mississippi	238
23	Mississippi	238		23	Oklahoma	238
13	Missouri	295		25	Alabama	232
17	Montana	284		26	West Virginia	224
11	Nebraska	312		27	Kentucky	208
38	Nevada	137		28	Arkansas	197
5	New Hampshire	424		29	New Mexico	196
8	New Jersey	364		30	Indiana	187
29	New Mexico	196		31	Massachusetts	183
12	New York	302		32	Virginia	174
46	North Carolina	94		33	Michigan	167
3	North Dakota	438		34	Tennessee	156
14	Ohio	287		35	Idaho	151
23	Oklahoma	238		36	Georgia	143
40	Oregon	135		37	Colorado	141
7	Pennsylvania	365		38	Delaware	137
9	Rhode Island	356		38	Nevada	137
43	South Carolina	109		40	Oregon	135
14	South Dakota	287		41	Texas	122
34	Tennessee	156		42	Maryland	115
41	Texas	122		43	South Carolina	109
49	Utah	75		44	Washington	107
6	Vermont	373		45	Arizona	104
32	Virginia	174		46	North Carolina	94
44	Washington	107		47	California	91
26	West Virginia	224		48	Florida	79
16	Wisconsin	285		49	Utah	75
18	Wyoming	282		50	Hawaii	65

District of Columbia   292

Source: U.S. Bureau of the Census, Governments Division
"Public Education Finances: 2009" (http://www.census.gov/govs/school/)
*Based on student membership. General administration includes expenditures for board of education and office of the superintendent services. For this per pupil calculation, Census has excluded current spending for adult education, community services, and other nonelementary-secondary programs.

Public Elementary and Secondary School Current Expenditures for General Administration per $1,000 Personal Income in 2009
National Ratio = $0.78*

ALPHA ORDER

RANK	STATE	RATIO
20	Alabama	$1.09
23	Alaska	1.02
42	Arizona	0.45
24	Arkansas	1.00
47	California	0.35
39	Colorado	0.53
27	Connecticut	0.92
42	Delaware	0.45
49	Florida	0.28
33	Georgia	0.69
50	Hawaii	0.21
31	Idaho	0.80
2	Illinois	1.73
30	Indiana	0.86
20	Iowa	1.09
17	Kansas	1.11
24	Kentucky	1.00
22	Louisiana	1.03
1	Maine	2.19
47	Maryland	0.35
41	Massachusetts	0.51
32	Michigan	0.74
4	Minnesota	1.54
7	Mississippi	1.29
10	Missouri	1.21
12	Montana	1.18
8	Nebraska	1.27
37	Nevada	0.56
5	New Hampshire	1.46
17	New Jersey	1.11
26	New Mexico	0.97
29	New York	0.87
45	North Carolina	0.42
3	North Dakota	1.56
11	Ohio	1.19
16	Oklahoma	1.14
38	Oregon	0.54
9	Pennsylvania	1.22
14	Rhode Island	1.15
40	South Carolina	0.52
14	South Dakota	1.15
33	Tennessee	0.69
36	Texas	0.59
42	Utah	0.45
6	Vermont	1.35
35	Virginia	0.61
46	Washington	0.39
19	West Virginia	1.10
13	Wisconsin	1.16
28	Wyoming	0.91

RANK ORDER

RANK	STATE	RATIO
1	Maine	$2.19
2	Illinois	1.73
3	North Dakota	1.56
4	Minnesota	1.54
5	New Hampshire	1.46
6	Vermont	1.35
7	Mississippi	1.29
8	Nebraska	1.27
9	Pennsylvania	1.22
10	Missouri	1.21
11	Ohio	1.19
12	Montana	1.18
13	Wisconsin	1.16
14	Rhode Island	1.15
14	South Dakota	1.15
16	Oklahoma	1.14
17	Kansas	1.11
17	New Jersey	1.11
19	West Virginia	1.10
20	Alabama	1.09
20	Iowa	1.09
22	Louisiana	1.03
23	Alaska	1.02
24	Arkansas	1.00
24	Kentucky	1.00
26	New Mexico	0.97
27	Connecticut	0.92
28	Wyoming	0.91
29	New York	0.87
30	Indiana	0.86
31	Idaho	0.80
32	Michigan	0.74
33	Georgia	0.69
33	Tennessee	0.69
35	Virginia	0.61
36	Texas	0.59
37	Nevada	0.56
38	Oregon	0.54
39	Colorado	0.53
40	South Carolina	0.52
41	Massachusetts	0.51
42	Arizona	0.45
42	Delaware	0.45
42	Utah	0.45
45	North Carolina	0.42
46	Washington	0.39
47	California	0.35
47	Maryland	0.35
49	Florida	0.28
50	Hawaii	0.21
	District of Columbia	0.32

Source: U.S. Bureau of the Census, Governments Division
   "Public Education Finances: 2009" (http://www.census.gov/govs/school/)
*General administration includes expenditures for board of education and office of the superintendent services. Includes salaries, benefits, services, and supplies.

Percent of Public Elementary and Secondary School Current Expenditures Used for General Administration in 2009
National Percent = 1.9%*

ALPHA ORDER

RANK	STATE	PERCENT
13	Alabama	2.6
36	Alaska	1.5
39	Arizona	1.3
23	Arkansas	2.1
47	California	0.9
31	Colorado	1.6
22	Connecticut	2.2
43	Delaware	1.1
47	Florida	0.9
36	Georgia	1.5
50	Hawaii	0.5
23	Idaho	2.1
3	Illinois	4.1
28	Indiana	2.0
13	Iowa	2.6
13	Kansas	2.6
21	Kentucky	2.3
17	Louisiana	2.5
1	Maine	4.4
47	Maryland	0.9
41	Massachusetts	1.2
31	Michigan	1.6
4	Minnesota	3.7
9	Mississippi	2.9
8	Missouri	3.0
12	Montana	2.8
7	Nebraska	3.1
31	Nevada	1.6
5	New Hampshire	3.4
23	New Jersey	2.1
23	New Mexico	2.1
31	New York	1.6
43	North Carolina	1.1
2	North Dakota	4.3
13	Ohio	2.6
9	Oklahoma	2.9
39	Oregon	1.3
9	Pennsylvania	2.9
19	Rhode Island	2.4
41	South Carolina	1.2
5	South Dakota	3.4
28	Tennessee	2.0
38	Texas	1.4
43	Utah	1.1
19	Vermont	2.4
31	Virginia	1.6
43	Washington	1.1
23	West Virginia	2.1
17	Wisconsin	2.5
30	Wyoming	1.9

RANK ORDER

RANK	STATE	PERCENT
1	Maine	4.4
2	North Dakota	4.3
3	Illinois	4.1
4	Minnesota	3.7
5	New Hampshire	3.4
5	South Dakota	3.4
7	Nebraska	3.1
8	Missouri	3.0
9	Mississippi	2.9
9	Oklahoma	2.9
9	Pennsylvania	2.9
12	Montana	2.8
13	Alabama	2.6
13	Iowa	2.6
13	Kansas	2.6
13	Ohio	2.6
17	Louisiana	2.5
17	Wisconsin	2.5
19	Rhode Island	2.4
19	Vermont	2.4
21	Kentucky	2.3
22	Connecticut	2.2
23	Arkansas	2.1
23	Idaho	2.1
23	New Jersey	2.1
23	New Mexico	2.1
23	West Virginia	2.1
28	Indiana	2.0
28	Tennessee	2.0
30	Wyoming	1.9
31	Colorado	1.6
31	Michigan	1.6
31	Nevada	1.6
31	New York	1.6
31	Virginia	1.6
36	Alaska	1.5
36	Georgia	1.5
38	Texas	1.4
39	Arizona	1.3
39	Oregon	1.3
41	Massachusetts	1.2
41	South Carolina	1.2
43	Delaware	1.1
43	North Carolina	1.1
43	Utah	1.1
43	Washington	1.1
47	California	0.9
47	Florida	0.9
47	Maryland	0.9
50	Hawaii	0.5

District of Columbia	1.8

Source: U.S. Bureau of the Census, Governments Division
   "Public Education Finances: 2009" (http://www.census.gov/govs/school/)
*General administration includes expenditures for board of education and office of the superintendent services. Includes salaries, benefits, services, and supplies. Census expanded its usual "current expenditures" concept for education finance reports to include all current public elementary and secondary education outlays regardless of the specific unit of government that actually makes the expenditure.

Public Elementary and Secondary School Current Expenditures for School Administration in 2009
National Total = $27,914,800,000*

ALPHA ORDER					RANK ORDER			
RANK	STATE	EXPENDITURES	% of USA		RANK	STATE	EXPENDITURES	% of USA
22	Alabama	$416,154,000	1.5%		1	California	$3,966,831,000	14.2%
42	Alaska	122,462,000	0.4%		2	Texas	2,202,798,000	7.9%
25	Arizona	377,272,000	1.4%		3	New York	1,975,174,000	7.1%
34	Arkansas	218,073,000	0.8%		4	Florida	1,311,982,000	4.7%
1	California	3,966,831,000	14.2%		5	Illinois	1,157,531,000	4.1%
19	Colorado	482,658,000	1.7%		6	New Jersey	1,086,420,000	3.9%
20	Connecticut	464,977,000	1.7%		7	Ohio	996,970,000	3.6%
46	Delaware	85,469,000	0.3%		8	Georgia	939,217,000	3.4%
4	Florida	1,311,982,000	4.7%		9	Michigan	912,993,000	3.3%
8	Georgia	939,217,000	3.4%		10	Pennsylvania	879,581,000	3.2%
39	Hawaii	137,433,000	0.5%		11	Maryland	804,519,000	2.9%
43	Idaho	108,137,000	0.4%		12	Virginia	799,234,000	2.9%
5	Illinois	1,157,531,000	4.1%		13	North Carolina	756,100,000	2.7%
16	Indiana	543,699,000	1.9%		14	Washington	579,765,000	2.1%
31	Iowa	274,483,000	1.0%		15	Massachusetts	574,497,000	2.1%
30	Kansas	274,686,000	1.0%		16	Indiana	543,699,000	1.9%
28	Kentucky	329,357,000	1.2%		17	Missouri	488,656,000	1.8%
24	Louisiana	379,843,000	1.4%		18	Wisconsin	484,501,000	1.7%
41	Maine	125,946,000	0.5%		19	Colorado	482,658,000	1.7%
11	Maryland	804,519,000	2.9%		20	Connecticut	464,977,000	1.7%
15	Massachusetts	574,497,000	2.1%		21	Tennessee	440,561,000	1.6%
9	Michigan	912,993,000	3.3%		22	Alabama	416,154,000	1.5%
26	Minnesota	355,617,000	1.3%		23	South Carolina	392,094,000	1.4%
33	Mississippi	228,488,000	0.8%		24	Louisiana	379,843,000	1.4%
17	Missouri	488,656,000	1.8%		25	Arizona	377,272,000	1.4%
47	Montana	77,546,000	0.3%		26	Minnesota	355,617,000	1.3%
38	Nebraska	152,725,000	0.5%		27	Oregon	351,415,000	1.3%
32	Nevada	259,942,000	0.9%		28	Kentucky	329,357,000	1.2%
40	New Hampshire	134,347,000	0.5%		29	Oklahoma	277,417,000	1.0%
6	New Jersey	1,086,420,000	3.9%		30	Kansas	274,686,000	1.0%
36	New Mexico	191,954,000	0.7%		31	Iowa	274,483,000	1.0%
3	New York	1,975,174,000	7.1%		32	Nevada	259,942,000	0.9%
13	North Carolina	756,100,000	2.7%		33	Mississippi	228,488,000	0.8%
50	North Dakota	46,843,000	0.2%		34	Arkansas	218,073,000	0.8%
7	Ohio	996,970,000	3.6%		35	Utah	201,662,000	0.7%
29	Oklahoma	277,417,000	1.0%		36	New Mexico	191,954,000	0.7%
27	Oregon	351,415,000	1.3%		37	West Virginia	155,775,000	0.6%
10	Pennsylvania	879,581,000	3.2%		38	Nebraska	152,725,000	0.5%
44	Rhode Island	98,731,000	0.4%		39	Hawaii	137,433,000	0.5%
23	South Carolina	392,094,000	1.4%		40	New Hampshire	134,347,000	0.5%
49	South Dakota	51,763,000	0.2%		41	Maine	125,946,000	0.5%
21	Tennessee	440,561,000	1.6%		42	Alaska	122,462,000	0.4%
2	Texas	2,202,798,000	7.9%		43	Idaho	108,137,000	0.4%
35	Utah	201,662,000	0.7%		44	Rhode Island	98,731,000	0.4%
45	Vermont	95,150,000	0.3%		45	Vermont	95,150,000	0.3%
12	Virginia	799,234,000	2.9%		46	Delaware	85,469,000	0.3%
14	Washington	579,765,000	2.1%		47	Montana	77,546,000	0.3%
37	West Virginia	155,775,000	0.6%		48	Wyoming	68,672,000	0.2%
18	Wisconsin	484,501,000	1.7%		49	South Dakota	51,763,000	0.2%
48	Wyoming	68,672,000	0.2%		50	North Dakota	46,843,000	0.2%
						District of Columbia	76,680,000	0.3%

Source: U.S. Bureau of the Census, Governments Division
"Public Education Finances: 2009" (http://www.census.gov/govs/school/)
*School administration includes expenditures for the office of principal services. Includes salaries, benefits, services, and supplies. Census expanded its usual "current expenditures" concept for education finance reports to include all current public elementary and secondary education outlays regardless of the specific unit of government that actually makes the expenditure.

Per Pupil Public Elementary and Secondary School Current Expenditures for School Administration in 2009
National Per Pupil = $579*

ALPHA ORDER

RANK	STATE	PER PUPIL
28	Alabama	$558
3	Alaska	940
49	Arizona	384
43	Arkansas	460
14	California	643
18	Colorado	594
4	Connecticut	850
8	Delaware	732
38	Florida	500
24	Georgia	569
7	Hawaii	766
48	Idaho	404
32	Illinois	547
34	Indiana	529
25	Iowa	563
20	Kansas	584
40	Kentucky	492
23	Louisiana	573
12	Maine	674
2	Maryland	953
16	Massachusetts	616
19	Michigan	587
45	Minnesota	443
42	Mississippi	465
33	Missouri	544
31	Montana	548
35	Nebraska	523
17	Nevada	603
11	New Hampshire	679
5	New Jersey	799
20	New Mexico	584
8	New York	732
36	North Carolina	521
39	North Dakota	495
22	Ohio	577
46	Oklahoma	430
15	Oregon	625
37	Pennsylvania	519
10	Rhode Island	698
30	South Carolina	549
47	South Dakota	409
44	Tennessee	454
41	Texas	474
50	Utah	379
1	Vermont	1,080
13	Virginia	647
26	Washington	560
29	West Virginia	553
27	Wisconsin	559
6	Wyoming	790

RANK ORDER

RANK	STATE	PER PUPIL
1	Vermont	$1,080
2	Maryland	953
3	Alaska	940
4	Connecticut	850
5	New Jersey	799
6	Wyoming	790
7	Hawaii	766
8	Delaware	732
8	New York	732
10	Rhode Island	698
11	New Hampshire	679
12	Maine	674
13	Virginia	647
14	California	643
15	Oregon	625
16	Massachusetts	616
17	Nevada	603
18	Colorado	594
19	Michigan	587
20	Kansas	584
20	New Mexico	584
22	Ohio	577
23	Louisiana	573
24	Georgia	569
25	Iowa	563
26	Washington	560
27	Wisconsin	559
28	Alabama	558
29	West Virginia	553
30	South Carolina	549
31	Montana	548
32	Illinois	547
33	Missouri	544
34	Indiana	529
35	Nebraska	523
36	North Carolina	521
37	Pennsylvania	519
38	Florida	500
39	North Dakota	495
40	Kentucky	492
41	Texas	474
42	Mississippi	465
43	Arkansas	460
44	Tennessee	454
45	Minnesota	443
46	Oklahoma	430
47	South Dakota	409
48	Idaho	404
49	Arizona	384
50	Utah	379

District of Columbia — 1,730

Source: U.S. Bureau of the Census, Governments Division
    "Public Education Finances: 2009" (http://www.census.gov/govs/school/)
*Based on student membership. School administration includes expenditures for the office of principal services. For this per pupil calculation, Census has excluded current spending for adult education, community services, and other nonelementary-secondary programs.

Public Elementary and Secondary School Current Expenditures for School Administration per $1,000 Personal Income in 2009
National Ratio = $2.25*

ALPHA ORDER

RANK	STATE	RATIO
8	Alabama	$2.62
1	Alaska	4.01
48	Arizona	1.68
24	Arkansas	2.33
16	California	2.46
33	Colorado	2.25
26	Connecticut	2.32
21	Delaware	2.39
44	Florida	1.78
5	Georgia	2.75
13	Hawaii	2.52
37	Idaho	2.15
40	Illinois	2.09
18	Indiana	2.44
20	Iowa	2.40
17	Kansas	2.45
23	Kentucky	2.37
35	Louisiana	2.24
9	Maine	2.61
3	Maryland	2.94
47	Massachusetts	1.72
10	Michigan	2.58
50	Minnesota	1.57
12	Mississippi	2.53
36	Missouri	2.23
30	Montana	2.27
38	Nebraska	2.14
15	Nevada	2.48
24	New Hampshire	2.33
19	New Jersey	2.43
4	New Mexico	2.88
39	New York	2.11
27	North Carolina	2.30
45	North Dakota	1.76
21	Ohio	2.39
41	Oklahoma	2.06
13	Oregon	2.52
46	Pennsylvania	1.73
33	Rhode Island	2.25
7	South Carolina	2.64
49	South Dakota	1.64
43	Tennessee	2.01
29	Texas	2.28
30	Utah	2.27
2	Vermont	3.90
28	Virginia	2.29
42	Washington	2.02
6	West Virginia	2.72
30	Wisconsin	2.27
11	Wyoming	2.55

RANK ORDER

RANK	STATE	RATIO
1	Alaska	$4.01
2	Vermont	3.90
3	Maryland	2.94
4	New Mexico	2.88
5	Georgia	2.75
6	West Virginia	2.72
7	South Carolina	2.64
8	Alabama	2.62
9	Maine	2.61
10	Michigan	2.58
11	Wyoming	2.55
12	Mississippi	2.53
13	Hawaii	2.52
13	Oregon	2.52
15	Nevada	2.48
16	California	2.46
17	Kansas	2.45
18	Indiana	2.44
19	New Jersey	2.43
20	Iowa	2.40
21	Delaware	2.39
21	Ohio	2.39
23	Kentucky	2.37
24	Arkansas	2.33
24	New Hampshire	2.33
26	Connecticut	2.32
27	North Carolina	2.30
28	Virginia	2.29
29	Texas	2.28
30	Montana	2.27
30	Utah	2.27
30	Wisconsin	2.27
33	Colorado	2.25
33	Rhode Island	2.25
35	Louisiana	2.24
36	Missouri	2.23
37	Idaho	2.15
38	Nebraska	2.14
39	New York	2.11
40	Illinois	2.09
41	Oklahoma	2.06
42	Washington	2.02
43	Tennessee	2.01
44	Florida	1.78
45	North Dakota	1.76
46	Pennsylvania	1.73
47	Massachusetts	1.72
48	Arizona	1.68
49	South Dakota	1.64
50	Minnesota	1.57
	District of Columbia	1.90

Source: U.S. Bureau of the Census, Governments Division
      "Public Education Finances: 2009" (http://www.census.gov/govs/school/)
*School administration includes expenditures for the office of principal services. Includes salaries, benefits, services, and supplies.

Percent of Public Elementary and Secondary School Current Expenditures Used for School Administration in 2009
National Percent = 5.4%*

RANK	STATE	PERCENT
6	Alabama	6.2
10	Alaska	6.0
41	Arizona	4.9
41	Arkansas	4.9
5	California	6.5
3	Colorado	6.8
20	Connecticut	5.7
12	Delaware	5.9
24	Florida	5.6
12	Georgia	5.9
9	Hawaii	6.1
20	Idaho	5.7
39	Illinois	5.0
24	Indiana	5.6
16	Iowa	5.8
12	Kansas	5.9
24	Kentucky	5.6
31	Louisiana	5.4
34	Maine	5.3
1	Maryland	7.1
47	Massachusetts	4.1
28	Michigan	5.5
50	Minnesota	3.8
20	Mississippi	5.7
24	Missouri	5.6
31	Montana	5.4
36	Nebraska	5.2
1	Nevada	7.1
28	New Hampshire	5.5
46	New Jersey	4.6
6	New Mexico	6.2
49	New York	3.9
10	North Carolina	6.0
43	North Dakota	4.8
36	Ohio	5.2
36	Oklahoma	5.2
6	Oregon	6.2
47	Pennsylvania	4.1
45	Rhode Island	4.7
16	South Carolina	5.8
43	South Dakota	4.8
20	Tennessee	5.7
28	Texas	5.5
16	Utah	5.8
3	Vermont	6.8
12	Virginia	5.9
16	Washington	5.8
34	West Virginia	5.3
39	Wisconsin	5.0
31	Wyoming	5.4

RANK	STATE	PERCENT
1	Maryland	7.1
1	Nevada	7.1
3	Colorado	6.8
3	Vermont	6.8
5	California	6.5
6	Alabama	6.2
6	New Mexico	6.2
6	Oregon	6.2
9	Hawaii	6.1
10	Alaska	6.0
10	North Carolina	6.0
12	Delaware	5.9
12	Georgia	5.9
12	Kansas	5.9
12	Virginia	5.9
16	Iowa	5.8
16	South Carolina	5.8
16	Utah	5.8
16	Washington	5.8
20	Connecticut	5.7
20	Idaho	5.7
20	Mississippi	5.7
20	Tennessee	5.7
24	Florida	5.6
24	Indiana	5.6
24	Kentucky	5.6
24	Missouri	5.6
28	Michigan	5.5
28	New Hampshire	5.5
28	Texas	5.5
31	Louisiana	5.4
31	Montana	5.4
31	Wyoming	5.4
34	Maine	5.3
34	West Virginia	5.3
36	Nebraska	5.2
36	Ohio	5.2
36	Oklahoma	5.2
39	Illinois	5.0
39	Wisconsin	5.0
41	Arizona	4.9
41	Arkansas	4.9
43	North Dakota	4.8
43	South Dakota	4.8
45	Rhode Island	4.7
46	New Jersey	4.6
47	Massachusetts	4.1
47	Pennsylvania	4.1
49	New York	3.9
50	Minnesota	3.8

District of Columbia   10.4

Source: CQ Press using data from U.S. Bureau of the Census, Governments Division
   "Public Education Finances: 2009" (http://www.census.gov/govs/school/)
*School administration includes expenditures for the office of principal services. Includes salaries, benefits, services, and supplies. Census expanded its usual "current expenditures" concept for education finance reports to include all current public elementary and secondary education outlays regardless of the specific unit of government that actually makes the expenditure.

Public Elementary and Secondary School Current Expenditures for Pupil Transportation in 2009
National Total = $22,048,971,000*

ALPHA ORDER

RANK	STATE	EXPENDITURES	% of USA
24	Alabama	$314,694,000	1.4%
45	Alaska	60,158,000	0.3%
22	Arizona	353,305,000	1.6%
35	Arkansas	151,034,000	0.7%
2	California	1,532,426,000	7.0%
28	Colorado	212,841,000	1.0%
17	Connecticut	412,162,000	1.9%
42	Delaware	89,849,000	0.4%
7	Florida	932,856,000	4.2%
11	Georgia	663,852,000	3.0%
47	Hawaii	47,397,000	0.2%
41	Idaho	92,327,000	0.4%
5	Illinois	1,122,676,000	5.1%
13	Indiana	559,459,000	2.5%
32	Iowa	168,254,000	0.8%
30	Kansas	180,105,000	0.8%
23	Kentucky	335,705,000	1.5%
20	Louisiana	384,493,000	1.7%
38	Maine	107,573,000	0.5%
12	Maryland	570,853,000	2.6%
14	Massachusetts	556,196,000	2.5%
9	Michigan	734,507,000	3.3%
16	Minnesota	463,915,000	2.1%
31	Mississippi	179,704,000	0.8%
18	Missouri	404,469,000	1.8%
44	Montana	67,305,000	0.3%
43	Nebraska	84,154,000	0.4%
34	Nevada	163,268,000	0.7%
39	New Hampshire	105,721,000	0.5%
4	New Jersey	1,257,000,000	5.7%
37	New Mexico	110,205,000	0.5%
1	New York	2,929,091,000	13.3%
15	North Carolina	515,692,000	2.3%
49	North Dakota	40,265,000	0.2%
8	Ohio	852,198,000	3.9%
33	Oklahoma	167,589,000	0.8%
26	Oregon	241,630,000	1.1%
3	Pennsylvania	1,264,691,000	5.7%
40	Rhode Island	93,513,000	0.4%
27	South Carolina	216,096,000	1.0%
50	South Dakota	37,075,000	0.2%
25	Tennessee	280,350,000	1.3%
6	Texas	1,096,490,000	5.0%
36	Utah	115,544,000	0.5%
48	Vermont	46,837,000	0.2%
10	Virginia	691,336,000	3.1%
19	Washington	390,894,000	1.8%
29	West Virginia	210,604,000	1.0%
21	Wisconsin	382,046,000	1.7%
46	Wyoming	58,482,000	0.3%

RANK ORDER

RANK	STATE	EXPENDITURES	% of USA
1	New York	$2,929,091,000	13.3%
2	California	1,532,426,000	7.0%
3	Pennsylvania	1,264,691,000	5.7%
4	New Jersey	1,257,000,000	5.7%
5	Illinois	1,122,676,000	5.1%
6	Texas	1,096,490,000	5.0%
7	Florida	932,856,000	4.2%
8	Ohio	852,198,000	3.9%
9	Michigan	734,507,000	3.3%
10	Virginia	691,336,000	3.1%
11	Georgia	663,852,000	3.0%
12	Maryland	570,853,000	2.6%
13	Indiana	559,459,000	2.5%
14	Massachusetts	556,196,000	2.5%
15	North Carolina	515,692,000	2.3%
16	Minnesota	463,915,000	2.1%
17	Connecticut	412,162,000	1.9%
18	Missouri	404,469,000	1.8%
19	Washington	390,894,000	1.8%
20	Louisiana	384,493,000	1.7%
21	Wisconsin	382,046,000	1.7%
22	Arizona	353,305,000	1.6%
23	Kentucky	335,705,000	1.5%
24	Alabama	314,694,000	1.4%
25	Tennessee	280,350,000	1.3%
26	Oregon	241,630,000	1.1%
27	South Carolina	216,096,000	1.0%
28	Colorado	212,841,000	1.0%
29	West Virginia	210,604,000	1.0%
30	Kansas	180,105,000	0.8%
31	Mississippi	179,704,000	0.8%
32	Iowa	168,254,000	0.8%
33	Oklahoma	167,589,000	0.8%
34	Nevada	163,268,000	0.7%
35	Arkansas	151,034,000	0.7%
36	Utah	115,544,000	0.5%
37	New Mexico	110,205,000	0.5%
38	Maine	107,573,000	0.5%
39	New Hampshire	105,721,000	0.5%
40	Rhode Island	93,513,000	0.4%
41	Idaho	92,327,000	0.4%
42	Delaware	89,849,000	0.4%
43	Nebraska	84,154,000	0.4%
44	Montana	67,305,000	0.3%
45	Alaska	60,158,000	0.3%
46	Wyoming	58,482,000	0.3%
47	Hawaii	47,397,000	0.2%
48	Vermont	46,837,000	0.2%
49	North Dakota	40,265,000	0.2%
50	South Dakota	37,075,000	0.2%
	District of Columbia	85,000	0.0%

Source: U.S. Bureau of the Census, Governments Division
"Public Education Finances: 2009" (http://www.census.gov/govs/school/)
*Includes transportation of public school students including vehicle operation, monitoring riders, and vehicle servicing and maintenance. Includes salaries, benefits, services, and supplies. Census expanded its usual "current expenditures" concept for education finance reports to include all current public elementary and secondary education outlays regardless of the specific unit of government that actually makes the expenditure.

Percent of Public Elementary and Secondary School Current Expenditures Used for Pupil Transportation in 2009
National Percent = 4.3%*

RANK	STATE	PERCENT
15	Alabama	4.7
45	Alaska	3.0
17	Arizona	4.6
39	Arkansas	3.4
49	California	2.5
45	Colorado	3.0
10	Connecticut	5.0
2	Delaware	6.2
31	Florida	4.0
29	Georgia	4.1
50	Hawaii	2.1
13	Idaho	4.8
13	Illinois	4.8
4	Indiana	5.8
37	Iowa	3.5
35	Kansas	3.8
6	Kentucky	5.7
7	Louisiana	5.5
20	Maine	4.5
10	Maryland	5.0
31	Massachusetts	4.0
25	Michigan	4.4
10	Minnesota	5.0
20	Mississippi	4.5
17	Missouri	4.6
15	Montana	4.7
47	Nebraska	2.9
20	Nevada	4.5
26	New Hampshire	4.3
8	New Jersey	5.4
37	New Mexico	3.5
4	New York	5.8
29	North Carolina	4.1
28	North Dakota	4.2
20	Ohio	4.5
43	Oklahoma	3.2
26	Oregon	4.3
3	Pennsylvania	5.9
20	Rhode Island	4.5
43	South Carolina	3.2
39	South Dakota	3.4
36	Tennessee	3.6
48	Texas	2.7
42	Utah	3.3
39	Vermont	3.4
9	Virginia	5.1
33	Washington	3.9
1	West Virginia	7.1
33	Wisconsin	3.9
17	Wyoming	4.6

RANK	STATE	PERCENT
1	West Virginia	7.1
2	Delaware	6.2
3	Pennsylvania	5.9
4	Indiana	5.8
4	New York	5.8
6	Kentucky	5.7
7	Louisiana	5.5
8	New Jersey	5.4
9	Virginia	5.1
10	Connecticut	5.0
10	Maryland	5.0
10	Minnesota	5.0
13	Idaho	4.8
13	Illinois	4.8
15	Alabama	4.7
15	Montana	4.7
17	Arizona	4.6
17	Missouri	4.6
17	Wyoming	4.6
20	Maine	4.5
20	Mississippi	4.5
20	Nevada	4.5
20	Ohio	4.5
20	Rhode Island	4.5
25	Michigan	4.4
26	New Hampshire	4.3
26	Oregon	4.3
28	North Dakota	4.2
29	Georgia	4.1
29	North Carolina	4.1
31	Florida	4.0
31	Massachusetts	4.0
33	Washington	3.9
33	Wisconsin	3.9
35	Kansas	3.8
36	Tennessee	3.6
37	Iowa	3.5
37	New Mexico	3.5
39	Arkansas	3.4
39	South Dakota	3.4
39	Vermont	3.4
42	Utah	3.3
43	Oklahoma	3.2
43	South Carolina	3.2
45	Alaska	3.0
45	Colorado	3.0
47	Nebraska	2.9
48	Texas	2.7
49	California	2.5
50	Hawaii	2.1
	District of Columbia	0.0

Source: CQ Press using data from U.S. Bureau of the Census, Governments Division
"Public Education Finances: 2009" (http://www.census.gov/govs/school/)
*Includes transportation of public school students including vehicle operation, monitoring riders, and vehicle servicing and maintenance. Includes salaries, benefits, services, and supplies. Census expanded its usual "current expenditures" concept for education finance reports to include all current public elementary and secondary education outlays regardless of the specific unit of government that actually makes the expenditure.

Public Elementary and Secondary School Current Expenditures for Operation and Maintenance of Facilities in 2009
National Total = $49,438,271,000*

ALPHA ORDER

ALPHA ORDER

RANK	STATE	EXPENDITURES	% of USA
26	Alabama	$610,804,000	1.2%
39	Alaska	264,068,000	0.5%
16	Arizona	935,993,000	1.9%
33	Arkansas	394,953,000	0.8%
1	California	5,930,549,000	12.0%
22	Colorado	699,187,000	1.4%
20	Connecticut	800,307,000	1.6%
46	Delaware	146,468,000	0.3%
4	Florida	2,461,851,000	5.0%
12	Georgia	1,188,791,000	2.4%
44	Hawaii	163,588,000	0.3%
42	Idaho	179,727,000	0.4%
7	Illinois	2,175,914,000	4.4%
13	Indiana	1,143,057,000	2.3%
31	Iowa	424,485,000	0.9%
30	Kansas	455,581,000	0.9%
28	Kentucky	538,384,000	1.1%
21	Louisiana	700,231,000	1.4%
40	Maine	246,272,000	0.5%
14	Maryland	1,077,933,000	2.2%
11	Massachusetts	1,258,099,000	2.5%
9	Michigan	1,641,993,000	3.3%
24	Minnesota	658,705,000	1.3%
32	Mississippi	412,107,000	0.8%
19	Missouri	843,693,000	1.7%
45	Montana	155,028,000	0.3%
38	Nebraska	273,655,000	0.6%
34	Nevada	388,345,000	0.8%
41	New Hampshire	220,204,000	0.4%
5	New Jersey	2,383,351,000	4.8%
35	New Mexico	314,969,000	0.6%
3	New York	4,094,933,000	8.3%
15	North Carolina	1,014,619,000	2.1%
50	North Dakota	90,198,000	0.2%
8	Ohio	1,754,204,000	3.5%
27	Oklahoma	593,434,000	1.2%
29	Oregon	460,990,000	0.9%
6	Pennsylvania	2,196,363,000	4.4%
43	Rhode Island	172,943,000	0.3%
25	South Carolina	617,109,000	1.2%
49	South Dakota	113,928,000	0.2%
23	Tennessee	694,776,000	1.4%
2	Texas	4,498,329,000	9.1%
36	Utah	305,576,000	0.6%
48	Vermont	120,265,000	0.2%
10	Virginia	1,324,730,000	2.7%
18	Washington	883,225,000	1.8%
37	West Virginia	304,174,000	0.6%
17	Wisconsin	891,946,000	1.8%
47	Wyoming	125,061,000	0.3%

RANK ORDER

RANK	STATE	EXPENDITURES	% of USA
1	California	$5,930,549,000	12.0%
2	Texas	4,498,329,000	9.1%
3	New York	4,094,933,000	8.3%
4	Florida	2,461,851,000	5.0%
5	New Jersey	2,383,351,000	4.8%
6	Pennsylvania	2,196,363,000	4.4%
7	Illinois	2,175,914,000	4.4%
8	Ohio	1,754,204,000	3.5%
9	Michigan	1,641,993,000	3.3%
10	Virginia	1,324,730,000	2.7%
11	Massachusetts	1,258,099,000	2.5%
12	Georgia	1,188,791,000	2.4%
13	Indiana	1,143,057,000	2.3%
14	Maryland	1,077,933,000	2.2%
15	North Carolina	1,014,619,000	2.1%
16	Arizona	935,993,000	1.9%
17	Wisconsin	891,946,000	1.8%
18	Washington	883,225,000	1.8%
19	Missouri	843,693,000	1.7%
20	Connecticut	800,307,000	1.6%
21	Louisiana	700,231,000	1.4%
22	Colorado	699,187,000	1.4%
23	Tennessee	694,776,000	1.4%
24	Minnesota	658,705,000	1.3%
25	South Carolina	617,109,000	1.2%
26	Alabama	610,804,000	1.2%
27	Oklahoma	593,434,000	1.2%
28	Kentucky	538,384,000	1.1%
29	Oregon	460,990,000	0.9%
30	Kansas	455,581,000	0.9%
31	Iowa	424,485,000	0.9%
32	Mississippi	412,107,000	0.8%
33	Arkansas	394,953,000	0.8%
34	Nevada	388,345,000	0.8%
35	New Mexico	314,969,000	0.6%
36	Utah	305,576,000	0.6%
37	West Virginia	304,174,000	0.6%
38	Nebraska	273,655,000	0.6%
39	Alaska	264,068,000	0.5%
40	Maine	246,272,000	0.5%
41	New Hampshire	220,204,000	0.4%
42	Idaho	179,727,000	0.4%
43	Rhode Island	172,943,000	0.3%
44	Hawaii	163,588,000	0.3%
45	Montana	155,028,000	0.3%
46	Delaware	146,468,000	0.3%
47	Wyoming	125,061,000	0.3%
48	Vermont	120,265,000	0.2%
49	South Dakota	113,928,000	0.2%
50	North Dakota	90,198,000	0.2%
	District of Columbia	93,176,000	0.2%

Source: U.S. Bureau of the Census, Governments Division
   "Public Education Finances: 2009" (http://www.census.gov/govs/school/)
*Includes building services, care and upkeep of grounds and equipment, nonstudent transportation, vehicle maintenance, and security services. Includes salaries, benefits, services, and supplies. Census expanded its usual "current expenditures" concept for education finance reports to include all current public elementary and secondary education outlays regardless of the specific unit of government that actually makes the expenditure.

Percent of Public Elementary and Secondary School Current Expenditures Used for Operations and Maintenance of Facilities in 2009
National Percent = 9.5%*

ALPHA ORDER

RANK ORDER

RANK	STATE	PERCENT	RANK	STATE	PERCENT
34	Alabama	9.1	1	Alaska	13.0
1	Alaska	13.0	2	Arizona	12.1
2	Arizona	12.1	3	Indiana	11.8
39	Arkansas	8.9	4	Texas	11.3
23	California	9.7	5	Oklahoma	11.2
19	Colorado	9.8	6	Montana	10.8
19	Connecticut	9.8	7	Nevada	10.6
15	Delaware	10.1	8	Florida	10.5
8	Florida	10.5	8	South Dakota	10.5
48	Georgia	7.4	10	Maine	10.3
49	Hawaii	7.3	10	Mississippi	10.3
27	Idaho	9.4	10	West Virginia	10.3
27	Illinois	9.4	13	New Jersey	10.2
3	Indiana	11.8	13	Pennsylvania	10.2
39	Iowa	8.9	15	Delaware	10.1
23	Kansas	9.7	15	New Mexico	10.1
34	Kentucky	9.1	17	Louisiana	10.0
17	Louisiana	10.0	18	Michigan	9.9
10	Maine	10.3	19	Colorado	9.8
26	Maryland	9.5	19	Connecticut	9.8
36	Massachusetts	9.0	19	Virginia	9.8
18	Michigan	9.9	19	Wyoming	9.8
50	Minnesota	7.1	23	California	9.7
10	Mississippi	10.3	23	Kansas	9.7
23	Missouri	9.7	23	Missouri	9.7
6	Montana	10.8	26	Maryland	9.5
29	Nebraska	9.3	27	Idaho	9.4
7	Nevada	10.6	27	Illinois	9.4
36	New Hampshire	9.0	29	Nebraska	9.3
13	New Jersey	10.2	29	North Dakota	9.3
15	New Mexico	10.1	31	Ohio	9.2
46	New York	8.1	31	South Carolina	9.2
46	North Carolina	8.1	31	Wisconsin	9.2
29	North Dakota	9.3	34	Alabama	9.1
31	Ohio	9.2	34	Kentucky	9.1
5	Oklahoma	11.2	36	Massachusetts	9.0
45	Oregon	8.2	36	New Hampshire	9.0
13	Pennsylvania	10.2	36	Tennessee	9.0
44	Rhode Island	8.3	39	Arkansas	8.9
31	South Carolina	9.2	39	Iowa	8.9
8	South Dakota	10.5	39	Washington	8.9
36	Tennessee	9.0	42	Utah	8.8
4	Texas	11.3	43	Vermont	8.6
42	Utah	8.8	44	Rhode Island	8.3
43	Vermont	8.6	45	Oregon	8.2
19	Virginia	9.8	46	New York	8.1
39	Washington	8.9	46	North Carolina	8.1
10	West Virginia	10.3	48	Georgia	7.4
31	Wisconsin	9.2	49	Hawaii	7.3
19	Wyoming	9.8	50	Minnesota	7.1

District of Columbia 12.6

Source: CQ Press using data from U.S. Bureau of the Census, Governments Division
    "Public Education Finances: 2009" (http://www.census.gov/govs/school/)
*Includes building services, care and upkeep of grounds and equipment, nonstudent transportation, vehicle maintenance, and security services. Includes salaries, benefits, services, and supplies. Census expanded its usual "current expenditures" concept for education finance reports to include all current public elementary and secondary education outlays regardless of the specific unit of government that actually makes the expenditure.

State and Local Government Expenditures for Elementary and Secondary Education in 2008
National Total = $565,631,236,000*

ALPHA ORDER

RANK	STATE	EXPENDITURES	% of USA
25	Alabama	$7,736,839,000	1.4%
42	Alaska	2,236,207,000	0.4%
20	Arizona	9,183,710,000	1.6%
33	Arkansas	4,456,722,000	0.8%
1	California	70,687,156,000	12.5%
21	Colorado	8,444,895,000	1.5%
23	Connecticut	8,178,903,000	1.4%
45	Delaware	1,718,975,000	0.3%
4	Florida	30,484,206,000	5.4%
9	Georgia	18,615,660,000	3.3%
41	Hawaii	2,248,990,000	0.4%
44	Idaho	1,927,885,000	0.3%
7	Illinois	22,985,805,000	4.1%
18	Indiana	9,684,117,000	1.7%
30	Iowa	5,191,110,000	0.9%
31	Kansas	4,758,174,000	0.8%
27	Kentucky	6,330,937,000	1.1%
26	Louisiana	7,510,264,000	1.3%
40	Maine	2,277,615,000	0.4%
14	Maryland	11,675,002,000	2.1%
13	Massachusetts	12,489,925,000	2.2%
10	Michigan	17,985,160,000	3.2%
17	Minnesota	9,714,168,000	1.7%
34	Mississippi	4,292,984,000	0.8%
19	Missouri	9,536,565,000	1.7%
46	Montana	1,535,395,000	0.3%
37	Nebraska	3,208,957,000	0.6%
32	Nevada	4,633,015,000	0.8%
39	New Hampshire	2,493,623,000	0.4%
5	New Jersey	24,039,648,000	4.3%
36	New Mexico	3,557,284,000	0.6%
2	New York	51,185,161,000	9.0%
12	North Carolina	13,468,428,000	2.4%
50	North Dakota	1,021,318,000	0.2%
8	Ohio	21,135,711,000	3.7%
29	Oklahoma	5,583,723,000	1.0%
28	Oregon	6,112,891,000	1.1%
6	Pennsylvania	23,697,574,000	4.2%
43	Rhode Island	2,165,460,000	0.4%
24	South Carolina	7,920,103,000	1.4%
49	South Dakota	1,129,781,000	0.2%
22	Tennessee	8,355,853,000	1.5%
3	Texas	45,440,154,000	8.0%
35	Utah	4,236,242,000	0.7%
48	Vermont	1,383,151,000	0.2%
11	Virginia	15,228,627,000	2.7%
15	Washington	11,237,122,000	2.0%
38	West Virginia	2,813,769,000	0.5%
16	Wisconsin	10,091,255,000	1.8%
47	Wyoming	1,507,073,000	0.3%

RANK ORDER

RANK	STATE	EXPENDITURES	% of USA
1	California	$70,687,156,000	12.5%
2	New York	51,185,161,000	9.0%
3	Texas	45,440,154,000	8.0%
4	Florida	30,484,206,000	5.4%
5	New Jersey	24,039,648,000	4.3%
6	Pennsylvania	23,697,574,000	4.2%
7	Illinois	22,985,805,000	4.1%
8	Ohio	21,135,711,000	3.7%
9	Georgia	18,615,660,000	3.3%
10	Michigan	17,985,160,000	3.2%
11	Virginia	15,228,627,000	2.7%
12	North Carolina	13,468,428,000	2.4%
13	Massachusetts	12,489,925,000	2.2%
14	Maryland	11,675,002,000	2.1%
15	Washington	11,237,122,000	2.0%
16	Wisconsin	10,091,255,000	1.8%
17	Minnesota	9,714,168,000	1.7%
18	Indiana	9,684,117,000	1.7%
19	Missouri	9,536,565,000	1.7%
20	Arizona	9,183,710,000	1.6%
21	Colorado	8,444,895,000	1.5%
22	Tennessee	8,355,853,000	1.5%
23	Connecticut	8,178,903,000	1.4%
24	South Carolina	7,920,103,000	1.4%
25	Alabama	7,736,839,000	1.4%
26	Louisiana	7,510,264,000	1.3%
27	Kentucky	6,330,937,000	1.1%
28	Oregon	6,112,891,000	1.1%
29	Oklahoma	5,583,723,000	1.0%
30	Iowa	5,191,110,000	0.9%
31	Kansas	4,758,174,000	0.8%
32	Nevada	4,633,015,000	0.8%
33	Arkansas	4,456,722,000	0.8%
34	Mississippi	4,292,984,000	0.8%
35	Utah	4,236,242,000	0.7%
36	New Mexico	3,557,284,000	0.6%
37	Nebraska	3,208,957,000	0.6%
38	West Virginia	2,813,769,000	0.5%
39	New Hampshire	2,493,623,000	0.4%
40	Maine	2,277,615,000	0.4%
41	Hawaii	2,248,990,000	0.4%
42	Alaska	2,236,207,000	0.4%
43	Rhode Island	2,165,460,000	0.4%
44	Idaho	1,927,885,000	0.3%
45	Delaware	1,718,975,000	0.3%
46	Montana	1,535,395,000	0.3%
47	Wyoming	1,507,073,000	0.3%
48	Vermont	1,383,151,000	0.2%
49	South Dakota	1,129,781,000	0.2%
50	North Dakota	1,021,318,000	0.2%
	District of Columbia	2,097,944,000	0.4%

Source: U.S. Bureau of the Census, Governments Division
"State and Local Government Finances 2007-2008" (http://www.census.gov/govs/estimate/)
*Direct general expenditures. Includes capital outlays.

Per Capita State and Local Government Expenditures for Elementary and Secondary Education in 2008
National Per Capita = $1,858*

ALPHA ORDER

RANK	STATE	PER CAPITA
34	Alabama	$1,654
1	Alaska	3,250
47	Arizona	1,413
39	Arkansas	1,554
11	California	1,932
29	Colorado	1,711
5	Connecticut	2,335
9	Delaware	1,962
33	Florida	1,655
12	Georgia	1,920
26	Hawaii	1,747
50	Idaho	1,262
22	Illinois	1,790
43	Indiana	1,516
27	Iowa	1,734
31	Kansas	1,701
44	Kentucky	1,476
32	Louisiana	1,687
28	Maine	1,726
7	Maryland	2,063
13	Massachusetts	1,909
20	Michigan	1,798
17	Minnesota	1,857
45	Mississippi	1,460
36	Missouri	1,601
38	Montana	1,586
19	Nebraska	1,801
24	Nevada	1,771
14	New Hampshire	1,886
3	New Jersey	2,775
22	New Mexico	1,790
4	New York	2,629
46	North Carolina	1,456
37	North Dakota	1,592
18	Ohio	1,833
42	Oklahoma	1,532
35	Oregon	1,616
14	Pennsylvania	1,886
8	Rhode Island	2,055
25	South Carolina	1,759
48	South Dakota	1,404
49	Tennessee	1,339
16	Texas	1,870
40	Utah	1,553
6	Vermont	2,227
10	Virginia	1,954
29	Washington	1,711
41	West Virginia	1,550
21	Wisconsin	1,793
2	Wyoming	2,828

RANK ORDER

RANK	STATE	PER CAPITA
1	Alaska	$3,250
2	Wyoming	2,828
3	New Jersey	2,775
4	New York	2,629
5	Connecticut	2,335
6	Vermont	2,227
7	Maryland	2,063
8	Rhode Island	2,055
9	Delaware	1,962
10	Virginia	1,954
11	California	1,932
12	Georgia	1,920
13	Massachusetts	1,909
14	New Hampshire	1,886
14	Pennsylvania	1,886
16	Texas	1,870
17	Minnesota	1,857
18	Ohio	1,833
19	Nebraska	1,801
20	Michigan	1,798
21	Wisconsin	1,793
22	Illinois	1,790
22	New Mexico	1,790
24	Nevada	1,771
25	South Carolina	1,759
26	Hawaii	1,747
27	Iowa	1,734
28	Maine	1,726
29	Colorado	1,711
29	Washington	1,711
31	Kansas	1,701
32	Louisiana	1,687
33	Florida	1,655
34	Alabama	1,654
35	Oregon	1,616
36	Missouri	1,601
37	North Dakota	1,592
38	Montana	1,586
39	Arkansas	1,554
40	Utah	1,553
41	West Virginia	1,550
42	Oklahoma	1,532
43	Indiana	1,516
44	Kentucky	1,476
45	Mississippi	1,460
46	North Carolina	1,456
47	Arizona	1,413
48	South Dakota	1,404
49	Tennessee	1,339
50	Idaho	1,262

| | District of Columbia | 3,555 |

Source: CQ Press using data from U.S. Bureau of the Census, Governments Division
   "State and Local Government Finances 2007-2008" (http://www.census.gov/govs/estimate/)
*Direct general expenditures. Includes capital outlays.

State and Local Government Expenditures for Elementary and Secondary Education as a Percent of All Education Expenditures in 2008
National Percent = 68.5%*

RANK	STATE	PERCENT
47	Alabama	59.4
4	Alaska	74.3
25	Arizona	65.4
29	Arkansas	63.8
17	California	68.1
22	Colorado	67.0
7	Connecticut	73.5
44	Delaware	59.7
5	Florida	73.8
9	Georgia	72.6
23	Hawaii	66.3
40	Idaho	60.8
13	Illinois	70.2
35	Indiana	62.8
44	Iowa	59.7
32	Kansas	63.4
46	Kentucky	59.5
30	Louisiana	63.6
12	Maine	71.4
18	Maryland	67.9
10	Massachusetts	72.2
31	Michigan	63.5
24	Minnesota	65.6
43	Mississippi	60.0
15	Missouri	68.4
39	Montana	60.9
34	Nebraska	63.0
3	Nevada	74.4
8	New Hampshire	72.9
2	New Jersey	78.8
41	New Mexico	60.2
1	New York	79.1
48	North Carolina	59.1
50	North Dakota	55.4
15	Ohio	68.4
38	Oklahoma	61.1
33	Oregon	63.2
11	Pennsylvania	71.6
6	Rhode Island	73.7
27	South Carolina	64.6
28	South Dakota	64.4
19	Tennessee	67.5
14	Texas	68.9
49	Utah	56.7
36	Vermont	62.5
21	Virginia	67.1
37	Washington	62.3
42	West Virginia	60.1
26	Wisconsin	64.7
20	Wyoming	67.3

RANK	STATE	PERCENT
1	New York	79.1
2	New Jersey	78.8
3	Nevada	74.4
4	Alaska	74.3
5	Florida	73.8
6	Rhode Island	73.7
7	Connecticut	73.5
8	New Hampshire	72.9
9	Georgia	72.6
10	Massachusetts	72.2
11	Pennsylvania	71.6
12	Maine	71.4
13	Illinois	70.2
14	Texas	68.9
15	Missouri	68.4
15	Ohio	68.4
17	California	68.1
18	Maryland	67.9
19	Tennessee	67.5
20	Wyoming	67.3
21	Virginia	67.1
22	Colorado	67.0
23	Hawaii	66.3
24	Minnesota	65.6
25	Arizona	65.4
26	Wisconsin	64.7
27	South Carolina	64.6
28	South Dakota	64.4
29	Arkansas	63.8
30	Louisiana	63.6
31	Michigan	63.5
32	Kansas	63.4
33	Oregon	63.2
34	Nebraska	63.0
35	Indiana	62.8
36	Vermont	62.5
37	Washington	62.3
38	Oklahoma	61.1
39	Montana	60.9
40	Idaho	60.8
41	New Mexico	60.2
42	West Virginia	60.1
43	Mississippi	60.0
44	Delaware	59.7
44	Iowa	59.7
46	Kentucky	59.5
47	Alabama	59.4
48	North Carolina	59.1
49	Utah	56.7
50	North Dakota	55.4
	District of Columbia	94.2

Source: CQ Press using data from U.S. Bureau of the Census, Governments Division
   "State and Local Government Finances 2007-2008" (http://www.census.gov/govs/estimate/)
*Direct general expenditures. Includes capital outlays.

Expenditures for Elementary and Secondary Education
as a Percent of All State and Local Government Expenditures in 2008
National Percent = 23.6%*

ALPHA ORDER

RANK	STATE	PERCENT
19	Alabama	23.7
47	Alaska	19.4
40	Arizona	21.2
11	Arkansas	24.9
42	California	21.1
19	Colorado	23.7
5	Connecticut	26.9
38	Delaware	21.3
32	Florida	22.0
2	Georgia	28.5
48	Hawaii	19.2
46	Idaho	19.9
17	Illinois	23.9
34	Indiana	21.8
27	Iowa	22.5
24	Kansas	22.8
37	Kentucky	21.5
50	Louisiana	18.2
29	Maine	22.1
7	Maryland	25.5
29	Massachusetts	22.1
11	Michigan	24.9
32	Minnesota	22.0
49	Mississippi	19.1
14	Missouri	24.3
40	Montana	21.2
22	Nebraska	23.4
8	Nevada	25.4
3	New Hampshire	27.9
1	New Jersey	30.5
44	New Mexico	20.6
16	New York	24.1
38	North Carolina	21.3
45	North Dakota	20.0
13	Ohio	24.5
23	Oklahoma	23.3
35	Oregon	21.7
10	Pennsylvania	25.0
15	Rhode Island	24.2
21	South Carolina	23.5
36	South Dakota	21.6
29	Tennessee	22.1
3	Texas	27.9
26	Utah	22.6
8	Vermont	25.4
6	Virginia	26.7
43	Washington	21.0
25	West Virginia	22.7
18	Wisconsin	23.8
28	Wyoming	22.2

RANK ORDER

RANK	STATE	PERCENT
1	New Jersey	30.5
2	Georgia	28.5
3	New Hampshire	27.9
3	Texas	27.9
5	Connecticut	26.9
6	Virginia	26.7
7	Maryland	25.5
8	Nevada	25.4
8	Vermont	25.4
10	Pennsylvania	25.0
11	Arkansas	24.9
11	Michigan	24.9
13	Ohio	24.5
14	Missouri	24.3
15	Rhode Island	24.2
16	New York	24.1
17	Illinois	23.9
18	Wisconsin	23.8
19	Alabama	23.7
19	Colorado	23.7
21	South Carolina	23.5
22	Nebraska	23.4
23	Oklahoma	23.3
24	Kansas	22.8
25	West Virginia	22.7
26	Utah	22.6
27	Iowa	22.5
28	Wyoming	22.2
29	Maine	22.1
29	Massachusetts	22.1
29	Tennessee	22.1
32	Florida	22.0
32	Minnesota	22.0
34	Indiana	21.8
35	Oregon	21.7
36	South Dakota	21.6
37	Kentucky	21.5
38	Delaware	21.3
38	North Carolina	21.3
40	Arizona	21.2
40	Montana	21.2
42	California	21.1
43	Washington	21.0
44	New Mexico	20.6
45	North Dakota	20.0
46	Idaho	19.9
47	Alaska	19.4
48	Hawaii	19.2
49	Mississippi	19.1
50	Louisiana	18.2

District of Columbia	19.6

Source: CQ Press using data from U.S. Bureau of the Census, Governments Division
    "State and Local Government Finances 2007-2008" (http://www.census.gov/govs/estimate/)
*Direct general expenditures. Includes capital outlays.

State Expenditures for Preschool in 2010

National Total = $5,442,597,771*

ALPHA ORDER

RANK	STATE	EXPENDITURES	% of USA
30	Alabama	$17,585,880	0.3%
38	Alaska	1,700,000	0.0%
40	Arizona	494,687	0.0%
12	Arkansas	111,000,000	2.0%
1	California	796,320,978	14.6%
25	Colorado	45,246,206	0.8%
16	Connecticut	83,301,663	1.5%
36	Delaware	5,727,800	0.1%
4	Florida	391,819,943	7.2%
6	Georgia	341,470,922	6.3%
41	Hawaii	0	0.0%
41	Idaho	0	0.0%
7	Illinois	295,267,954	5.4%
41	Indiana	0	0.0%
24	Iowa	48,634,416	0.9%
27	Kansas	23,564,928	0.4%
19	Kentucky	69,187,530	1.3%
14	Louisiana	95,757,442	1.8%
35	Maine	6,443,614	0.1%
13	Maryland	107,619,200	2.0%
23	Massachusetts	52,462,817	1.0%
15	Michigan	87,128,000	1.6%
32	Minnesota	13,682,074	0.3%
41	Mississippi	0	0.0%
33	Missouri	13,215,441	0.2%
41	Montana	0	0.0%
34	Nebraska	11,922,004	0.2%
37	Nevada	3,338,875	0.1%
41	New Hampshire	0	0.0%
3	New Jersey	576,996,173	10.6%
31	New Mexico	16,542,407	0.3%
5	New York	378,107,213	6.9%
10	North Carolina	163,451,644	3.0%
41	North Dakota	0	0.0%
28	Ohio	22,243,792	0.4%
9	Oklahoma	167,245,396	3.1%
21	Oregon	54,897,578	1.0%
8	Pennsylvania	189,808,021	3.5%
39	Rhode Island	700,000	0.0%
26	South Carolina	35,513,846	0.7%
41	South Dakota	0	0.0%
17	Tennessee	81,657,785	1.5%
2	Texas	791,378,304	14.5%
41	Utah	0	0.0%
29	Vermont	17,790,714	0.3%
20	Virginia	63,078,873	1.2%
22	Washington	54,716,348	1.0%
18	West Virginia	76,617,241	1.4%
11	Wisconsin	128,960,062	2.4%
41	Wyoming	0	0.0%

RANK ORDER

RANK	STATE	EXPENDITURES	% of USA
1	California	$796,320,978	14.6%
2	Texas	791,378,304	14.5%
3	New Jersey	576,996,173	10.6%
4	Florida	391,819,943	7.2%
5	New York	378,107,213	6.9%
6	Georgia	341,470,922	6.3%
7	Illinois	295,267,954	5.4%
8	Pennsylvania	189,808,021	3.5%
9	Oklahoma	167,245,396	3.1%
10	North Carolina	163,451,644	3.0%
11	Wisconsin	128,960,062	2.4%
12	Arkansas	111,000,000	2.0%
13	Maryland	107,619,200	2.0%
14	Louisiana	95,757,442	1.8%
15	Michigan	87,128,000	1.6%
16	Connecticut	83,301,663	1.5%
17	Tennessee	81,657,785	1.5%
18	West Virginia	76,617,241	1.4%
19	Kentucky	69,187,530	1.3%
20	Virginia	63,078,873	1.2%
21	Oregon	54,897,578	1.0%
22	Washington	54,716,348	1.0%
23	Massachusetts	52,462,817	1.0%
24	Iowa	48,634,416	0.9%
25	Colorado	45,246,206	0.8%
26	South Carolina	35,513,846	0.7%
27	Kansas	23,564,928	0.4%
28	Ohio	22,243,792	0.4%
29	Vermont	17,790,714	0.3%
30	Alabama	17,585,880	0.3%
31	New Mexico	16,542,407	0.3%
32	Minnesota	13,682,074	0.3%
33	Missouri	13,215,441	0.2%
34	Nebraska	11,922,004	0.2%
35	Maine	6,443,614	0.1%
36	Delaware	5,727,800	0.1%
37	Nevada	3,338,875	0.1%
38	Alaska	1,700,000	0.0%
39	Rhode Island	700,000	0.0%
40	Arizona	494,687	0.0%
41	Hawaii	0	0.0%
41	Idaho	0	0.0%
41	Indiana	0	0.0%
41	Mississippi	0	0.0%
41	Montana	0	0.0%
41	New Hampshire	0	0.0%
41	North Dakota	0	0.0%
41	South Dakota	0	0.0%
41	Utah	0	0.0%
41	Wyoming	0	0.0%
	District of Columbia**	NA	NA

Source: Rutgers, The State University of New Jersey, National Institute for Early Education Research
     "The State of Preschool: 2010 State Preschool Yearbook" (http://nieer.org/yearbook/)
*School year 2009-2010. State spending figures do not include all money received from federal and local sources. They are not estimates of total costs. The state figures do include some flow-through money from federal sources. States with no expenditures have no state funded pre-school program.
**Not available.

Per Pupil State Expenditures for Preschool in 2010

National Per Pupil = $4,212*

<table>
<tr><td colspan="3">ALPHA ORDER</td><td colspan="3">RANK ORDER</td></tr>
<tr><td>RANK</td><td>STATE</td><td>PER CHILD</td><td>RANK</td><td>STATE</td><td>PER CHILD</td></tr>
<tr><td>15</td><td>Alabama</td><td>$4,544</td><td>1</td><td>New Jersey</td><td>$11,578</td></tr>
<tr><td>3</td><td>Alaska</td><td>8,500</td><td>2</td><td>Connecticut</td><td>9,297</td></tr>
<tr><td>40</td><td>Arizona</td><td>115</td><td>3</td><td>Alaska</td><td>8,500</td></tr>
<tr><td>11</td><td>Arkansas</td><td>5,414</td><td>4</td><td>Oregon</td><td>8,435</td></tr>
<tr><td>12</td><td>California</td><td>5,410</td><td>5</td><td>Minnesota</td><td>7,301</td></tr>
<tr><td>36</td><td>Colorado</td><td>2,321</td><td>6</td><td>Washington</td><td>6,817</td></tr>
<tr><td>2</td><td>Connecticut</td><td>9,297</td><td>7</td><td>Delaware</td><td>6,795</td></tr>
<tr><td>7</td><td>Delaware</td><td>6,795</td><td>8</td><td>Pennsylvania</td><td>5,924</td></tr>
<tr><td>34</td><td>Florida</td><td>2,514</td><td>9</td><td>Rhode Island</td><td>5,556</td></tr>
<tr><td>20</td><td>Georgia</td><td>4,206</td><td>10</td><td>West Virginia</td><td>5,521</td></tr>
<tr><td>41</td><td>Hawaii</td><td>0</td><td>11</td><td>Arkansas</td><td>5,414</td></tr>
<tr><td>41</td><td>Idaho</td><td>0</td><td>12</td><td>California</td><td>5,410</td></tr>
<tr><td>28</td><td>Illinois</td><td>3,371</td><td>13</td><td>North Carolina</td><td>5,239</td></tr>
<tr><td>41</td><td>Indiana</td><td>0</td><td>14</td><td>Louisiana</td><td>4,706</td></tr>
<tr><td>31</td><td>Iowa</td><td>3,092</td><td>15</td><td>Alabama</td><td>4,544</td></tr>
<tr><td>35</td><td>Kansas</td><td>2,490</td><td>16</td><td>Oklahoma</td><td>4,477</td></tr>
<tr><td>30</td><td>Kentucky</td><td>3,103</td><td>17</td><td>Tennessee</td><td>4,445</td></tr>
<tr><td>14</td><td>Louisiana</td><td>4,706</td><td>18</td><td>Michigan</td><td>4,405</td></tr>
<tr><td>37</td><td>Maine</td><td>1,787</td><td>19</td><td>Virginia</td><td>4,221</td></tr>
<tr><td>21</td><td>Maryland</td><td>4,116</td><td>20</td><td>Georgia</td><td>4,206</td></tr>
<tr><td>24</td><td>Massachusetts</td><td>3,895</td><td>21</td><td>Maryland</td><td>4,116</td></tr>
<tr><td>18</td><td>Michigan</td><td>4,405</td><td>22</td><td>Vermont</td><td>3,980</td></tr>
<tr><td>5</td><td>Minnesota</td><td>7,301</td><td>23</td><td>Ohio</td><td>3,902</td></tr>
<tr><td>41</td><td>Mississippi</td><td>0</td><td>24</td><td>Massachusetts</td><td>3,895</td></tr>
<tr><td>32</td><td>Missouri</td><td>3,051</td><td>25</td><td>Texas</td><td>3,686</td></tr>
<tr><td>41</td><td>Montana</td><td>0</td><td>26</td><td>New York</td><td>3,503</td></tr>
<tr><td>39</td><td>Nebraska</td><td>1,163</td><td>27</td><td>New Mexico</td><td>3,412</td></tr>
<tr><td>33</td><td>Nevada</td><td>2,710</td><td>28</td><td>Illinois</td><td>3,371</td></tr>
<tr><td>41</td><td>New Hampshire</td><td>0</td><td>29</td><td>Wisconsin</td><td>3,282</td></tr>
<tr><td>1</td><td>New Jersey</td><td>11,578</td><td>30</td><td>Kentucky</td><td>3,103</td></tr>
<tr><td>27</td><td>New Mexico</td><td>3,412</td><td>31</td><td>Iowa</td><td>3,092</td></tr>
<tr><td>26</td><td>New York</td><td>3,503</td><td>32</td><td>Missouri</td><td>3,051</td></tr>
<tr><td>13</td><td>North Carolina</td><td>5,239</td><td>33</td><td>Nevada</td><td>2,710</td></tr>
<tr><td>41</td><td>North Dakota</td><td>0</td><td>34</td><td>Florida</td><td>2,514</td></tr>
<tr><td>23</td><td>Ohio</td><td>3,902</td><td>35</td><td>Kansas</td><td>2,490</td></tr>
<tr><td>16</td><td>Oklahoma</td><td>4,477</td><td>36</td><td>Colorado</td><td>2,321</td></tr>
<tr><td>4</td><td>Oregon</td><td>8,435</td><td>37</td><td>Maine</td><td>1,787</td></tr>
<tr><td>8</td><td>Pennsylvania</td><td>5,924</td><td>38</td><td>South Carolina</td><td>1,446</td></tr>
<tr><td>9</td><td>Rhode Island</td><td>5,556</td><td>39</td><td>Nebraska</td><td>1,163</td></tr>
<tr><td>38</td><td>South Carolina</td><td>1,446</td><td>40</td><td>Arizona</td><td>115</td></tr>
<tr><td>41</td><td>South Dakota</td><td>0</td><td>41</td><td>Hawaii</td><td>0</td></tr>
<tr><td>17</td><td>Tennessee</td><td>4,445</td><td>41</td><td>Idaho</td><td>0</td></tr>
<tr><td>25</td><td>Texas</td><td>3,686</td><td>41</td><td>Indiana</td><td>0</td></tr>
<tr><td>41</td><td>Utah</td><td>0</td><td>41</td><td>Mississippi</td><td>0</td></tr>
<tr><td>22</td><td>Vermont</td><td>3,980</td><td>41</td><td>Montana</td><td>0</td></tr>
<tr><td>19</td><td>Virginia</td><td>4,221</td><td>41</td><td>New Hampshire</td><td>0</td></tr>
<tr><td>6</td><td>Washington</td><td>6,817</td><td>41</td><td>North Dakota</td><td>0</td></tr>
<tr><td>10</td><td>West Virginia</td><td>5,521</td><td>41</td><td>South Dakota</td><td>0</td></tr>
<tr><td>29</td><td>Wisconsin</td><td>3,282</td><td>41</td><td>Utah</td><td>0</td></tr>
<tr><td>41</td><td>Wyoming</td><td>0</td><td>41</td><td>Wyoming</td><td>0</td></tr>
<tr><td></td><td></td><td></td><td></td><td>District of Columbia**</td><td>NA</td></tr>
</table>

Source: Rutgers, The State University of New Jersey, National Institute for Early Education Research
   "The State of Preschool: 2010 State Preschool Yearbook" (http://nieer.org/yearbook/)
*School year 2009-2010. State spending figures do not include all money received from federal and local sources. They are not estimates of total costs. The state figures do include some flow-through money from federal sources. States with no expenditures have no state funded pre-school program.
**Not available.

Federal Allocations for Head Start Program in 2009

National Total = $6,871,942,000*

ALPHA ORDER

ALPHA ORDER

RANK ORDER

RANK	STATE	ALLOCATIONS	% of USA
18	Alabama	$110,249,206	1.6%
49	Alaska	12,896,034	0.2%
19	Arizona	107,014,507	1.6%
29	Arkansas	66,717,253	1.0%
1	California	859,903,697	12.5%
28	Colorado	70,658,907	1.0%
32	Connecticut	53,660,157	0.8%
48	Delaware	13,685,159	0.2%
5	Florida	272,067,200	4.0%
9	Georgia	174,228,123	2.5%
40	Hawaii	23,662,982	0.3%
41	Idaho	23,588,259	0.3%
4	Illinois	279,954,144	4.1%
22	Indiana	99,465,458	1.4%
33	Iowa	53,299,350	0.8%
34	Kansas	52,655,405	0.8%
17	Kentucky	111,506,347	1.6%
11	Louisiana	150,854,764	2.2%
38	Maine	28,548,027	0.4%
26	Maryland	80,682,993	1.2%
16	Massachusetts	112,027,847	1.6%
7	Michigan	242,511,360	3.5%
27	Minnesota	74,447,456	1.1%
10	Mississippi	167,178,073	2.4%
15	Missouri	123,030,722	1.8%
43	Montana	21,660,206	0.3%
37	Nebraska	37,282,488	0.5%
39	Nevada	25,104,010	0.4%
47	New Hampshire	13,840,339	0.2%
13	New Jersey	133,392,411	1.9%
31	New Mexico	54,074,855	0.8%
3	New York	447,896,246	6.5%
12	North Carolina	146,070,201	2.1%
45	North Dakota	17,757,780	0.3%
6	Ohio	255,276,707	3.7%
25	Oklahoma	83,800,755	1.2%
30	Oregon	61,487,791	0.9%
8	Pennsylvania	235,917,078	3.4%
42	Rhode Island	22,762,399	0.3%
24	South Carolina	85,302,467	1.2%
44	South Dakota	19,464,308	0.3%
14	Tennessee	123,390,836	1.8%
2	Texas	494,959,267	7.2%
36	Utah	39,046,126	0.6%
46	Vermont	14,019,568	0.2%
21	Virginia	102,461,544	1.5%
20	Washington	103,768,790	1.5%
35	West Virginia	52,362,072	0.8%
23	Wisconsin	93,962,521	1.4%
50	Wyoming	12,791,225	0.2%

RANK	STATE	ALLOCATIONS	% of USA
1	California	$859,903,697	12.5%
2	Texas	494,959,267	7.2%
3	New York	447,896,246	6.5%
4	Illinois	279,954,144	4.1%
5	Florida	272,067,200	4.0%
6	Ohio	255,276,707	3.7%
7	Michigan	242,511,360	3.5%
8	Pennsylvania	235,917,078	3.4%
9	Georgia	174,228,123	2.5%
10	Mississippi	167,178,073	2.4%
11	Louisiana	150,854,764	2.2%
12	North Carolina	146,070,201	2.1%
13	New Jersey	133,392,411	1.9%
14	Tennessee	123,390,836	1.8%
15	Missouri	123,030,722	1.8%
16	Massachusetts	112,027,847	1.6%
17	Kentucky	111,506,347	1.6%
18	Alabama	110,249,206	1.6%
19	Arizona	107,014,507	1.6%
20	Washington	103,768,790	1.5%
21	Virginia	102,461,544	1.5%
22	Indiana	99,465,458	1.4%
23	Wisconsin	93,962,521	1.4%
24	South Carolina	85,302,467	1.2%
25	Oklahoma	83,800,755	1.2%
26	Maryland	80,682,993	1.2%
27	Minnesota	74,447,456	1.1%
28	Colorado	70,658,907	1.0%
29	Arkansas	66,717,253	1.0%
30	Oregon	61,487,791	0.9%
31	New Mexico	54,074,855	0.8%
32	Connecticut	53,660,157	0.8%
33	Iowa	53,299,350	0.8%
34	Kansas	52,655,405	0.8%
35	West Virginia	52,362,072	0.8%
36	Utah	39,046,126	0.6%
37	Nebraska	37,282,488	0.5%
38	Maine	28,548,027	0.4%
39	Nevada	25,104,010	0.4%
40	Hawaii	23,662,982	0.3%
41	Idaho	23,588,259	0.3%
42	Rhode Island	22,762,399	0.3%
43	Montana	21,660,206	0.3%
44	South Dakota	19,464,308	0.3%
45	North Dakota	17,757,780	0.3%
46	Vermont	14,019,568	0.2%
47	New Hampshire	13,840,339	0.2%
48	Delaware	13,685,159	0.2%
49	Alaska	12,896,034	0.2%
50	Wyoming	12,791,225	0.2%
	District of Columbia	25,959,996	0.4%

Source: U.S. Department of Health and Human Services, Administration for Children and Families
   "Head Start Fact Sheet" (http://www.acf.hhs.gov/programs/ohs/about/fy2010.html)
*For fiscal year 2009. National total includes $510,028,911 to Migrant and Native American programs and $273,607,674 to U.S. territories. Does not include $238,341,000 in "support activities" expenditures.

Per Child Federal Allocations for Head Start Program in 2009

National Per Child = $7,600*

ALPHA ORDER			RANK ORDER		
RANK	STATE	PER CHILD	RANK	STATE	PER CHILD
43	Alabama	$6,798	1	New York	$9,329
11	Alaska	8,147	2	Vermont	9,309
10	Arizona	8,266	3	Washington	9,201
47	Arkansas	6,341	4	Nevada	9,115
7	California	8,784	5	New Jersey	8,984
29	Colorado	7,195	6	Massachusetts	8,818
13	Connecticut	7,894	7	California	8,784
45	Delaware	6,647	8	New Hampshire	8,481
17	Florida	7,688	9	Idaho	8,371
24	Georgia	7,459	10	Arizona	8,266
15	Hawaii	7,761	11	Alaska	8,147
9	Idaho	8,371	12	Rhode Island	7,959
32	Illinois	7,099	13	Connecticut	7,894
35	Indiana	7,032	14	Maryland	7,812
39	Iowa	6,943	15	Hawaii	7,761
46	Kansas	6,439	16	North Carolina	7,727
37	Kentucky	6,986	17	Florida	7,688
33	Louisiana	7,073	18	Maine	7,617
18	Maine	7,617	19	Virginia	7,580
14	Maryland	7,812	20	North Dakota	7,563
6	Massachusetts	8,818	21	Tennessee	7,552
31	Michigan	7,101	22	Montana	7,464
26	Minnesota	7,341	23	New Mexico	7,460
48	Mississippi	6,304	24	Georgia	7,459
34	Missouri	7,054	25	Nebraska	7,370
22	Montana	7,464	26	Minnesota	7,341
25	Nebraska	7,370	27	Texas	7,323
4	Nevada	9,115	28	Utah	7,231
8	New Hampshire	8,481	29	Colorado	7,195
5	New Jersey	8,984	30	Wyoming	7,154
23	New Mexico	7,460	31	Michigan	7,101
1	New York	9,329	32	Illinois	7,099
16	North Carolina	7,727	33	Louisiana	7,073
20	North Dakota	7,563	34	Missouri	7,054
40	Ohio	6,886	35	Indiana	7,032
49	Oklahoma	6,219	36	South Carolina	6,995
50	Oregon	5,546	37	Kentucky	6,986
44	Pennsylvania	6,692	38	Wisconsin	6,976
12	Rhode Island	7,959	39	Iowa	6,943
36	South Carolina	6,995	40	Ohio	6,886
41	South Dakota	6,885	41	South Dakota	6,885
21	Tennessee	7,552	42	West Virginia	6,881
27	Texas	7,323	43	Alabama	6,798
28	Utah	7,231	44	Pennsylvania	6,692
2	Vermont	9,309	45	Delaware	6,647
19	Virginia	7,580	46	Kansas	6,439
3	Washington	9,201	47	Arkansas	6,341
42	West Virginia	6,881	48	Mississippi	6,304
38	Wisconsin	6,976	49	Oklahoma	6,219
30	Wyoming	7,154	50	Oregon	5,546
				District of Columbia	7,629

Source: CQ Press using data from U.S. Department of Health and Human Services, Administration for Children and Families "Head Start Fact Sheet" (http://www.acf.hhs.gov/programs/ohs/about/fy2010.html)

*For fiscal year 2009. National rate includes enrollees and expenditures in Migrant and Native American programs and in U.S. territories. Does not include "support activities" expenditures.

III. Graduates and Achievement

Estimated Public High School Graduates in 2011

National Total = 3,175,998 Graduates*

ALPHA ORDER

RANK	STATE	GRADUATES	% of USA
24	Alabama	41,945	1.3%
47	Alaska	7,826	0.2%
13	Arizona	86,966	2.7%
33	Arkansas	30,130	0.9%
1	California	394,959	12.4%
22	Colorado	47,314	1.5%
26	Connecticut	41,291	1.3%
48	Delaware	7,567	0.2%
4	Florida	148,147	4.7%
9	Georgia	101,905	3.2%
42	Hawaii	11,909	0.4%
39	Idaho	17,501	0.6%
6	Illinois	132,104	4.2%
18	Indiana	64,009	2.0%
30	Iowa	34,556	1.1%
31	Kansas	30,868	1.0%
23	Kentucky	42,235	1.3%
28	Louisiana	37,111	1.2%
41	Maine	15,324	0.5%
21	Maryland	61,008	1.9%
19	Massachusetts	63,717	2.0%
8	Michigan	116,158	3.7%
15	Minnesota	67,106	2.1%
35	Mississippi	24,059	0.8%
20	Missouri	63,189	2.0%
43	Montana	10,063	0.3%
36	Nebraska	20,281	0.6%
34	Nevada	24,704	0.8%
40	New Hampshire	15,817	0.5%
10	New Jersey	98,437	3.1%
37	New Mexico	19,352	0.6%
3	New York	181,223	5.7%
11	North Carolina	90,725	2.9%
49	North Dakota	6,621	0.2%
7	Ohio	126,557	4.0%
27	Oklahoma	38,167	1.2%
29	Oregon	36,754	1.2%
5	Pennsylvania	136,623	4.3%
44	Rhode Island	9,715	0.3%
25	South Carolina	41,391	1.3%
46	South Dakota	8,182	0.3%
16	Tennessee	64,939	2.0%
2	Texas	270,882	8.5%
32	Utah	30,737	1.0%
45	Vermont	8,371	0.3%
12	Virginia	90,480	2.8%
17	Washington	64,247	2.0%
38	West Virginia	18,158	0.6%
14	Wisconsin	67,727	2.1%
50	Wyoming	5,521	0.2%

RANK ORDER

RANK	STATE	GRADUATES	% of USA
1	California	394,959	12.4%
2	Texas	270,882	8.5%
3	New York	181,223	5.7%
4	Florida	148,147	4.7%
5	Pennsylvania	136,623	4.3%
6	Illinois	132,104	4.2%
7	Ohio	126,557	4.0%
8	Michigan	116,158	3.7%
9	Georgia	101,905	3.2%
10	New Jersey	98,437	3.1%
11	North Carolina	90,725	2.9%
12	Virginia	90,480	2.8%
13	Arizona	86,966	2.7%
14	Wisconsin	67,727	2.1%
15	Minnesota	67,106	2.1%
16	Tennessee	64,939	2.0%
17	Washington	64,247	2.0%
18	Indiana	64,009	2.0%
19	Massachusetts	63,717	2.0%
20	Missouri	63,189	2.0%
21	Maryland	61,008	1.9%
22	Colorado	47,314	1.5%
23	Kentucky	42,235	1.3%
24	Alabama	41,945	1.3%
25	South Carolina	41,391	1.3%
26	Connecticut	41,291	1.3%
27	Oklahoma	38,167	1.2%
28	Louisiana	37,111	1.2%
29	Oregon	36,754	1.2%
30	Iowa	34,556	1.1%
31	Kansas	30,868	1.0%
32	Utah	30,737	1.0%
33	Arkansas	30,130	0.9%
34	Nevada	24,704	0.8%
35	Mississippi	24,059	0.8%
36	Nebraska	20,281	0.6%
37	New Mexico	19,352	0.6%
38	West Virginia	18,158	0.6%
39	Idaho	17,501	0.6%
40	New Hampshire	15,817	0.5%
41	Maine	15,324	0.5%
42	Hawaii	11,909	0.4%
43	Montana	10,063	0.3%
44	Rhode Island	9,715	0.3%
45	Vermont	8,371	0.3%
46	South Dakota	8,182	0.3%
47	Alaska	7,826	0.2%
48	Delaware	7,567	0.2%
49	North Dakota	6,621	0.2%
50	Wyoming	5,521	0.2%
	District of Columbia	1,420	0.0%

Source: National Education Association, Washington, D.C.
   "Rankings and Estimates" (Copyright © 2011, NEA, used with permission, http://www.nea.org/home/44479.htm)
*Estimates for school year 2010-2011.

Public High School Graduates in 2010

National Total = 3,117,890 Graduates*

ALPHA ORDER

RANK	STATE	GRADUATES	% of USA
24	Alabama	41,003	1.3%
47	Alaska	7,712	0.2%
13	Arizona	82,206	2.6%
33	Arkansas	29,834	1.0%
1	California	383,566	12.3%
22	Colorado	46,811	1.5%
25	Connecticut	40,277	1.3%
48	Delaware	7,538	0.2%
4	Florida	145,793	4.7%
9	Georgia	101,138	3.2%
42	Hawaii	11,451	0.4%
39	Idaho	17,212	0.6%
6	Illinois	131,443	4.2%
18	Indiana	63,071	2.0%
30	Iowa	34,462	1.1%
31	Kansas	30,738	1.0%
23	Kentucky	42,235	1.4%
28	Louisiana	36,408	1.2%
41	Maine	15,039	0.5%
21	Maryland	59,774	1.9%
17	Massachusetts	64,670	2.1%
8	Michigan	114,217	3.7%
15	Minnesota	66,215	2.1%
34	Mississippi	24,027	0.8%
20	Missouri	62,342	2.0%
43	Montana	10,029	0.3%
36	Nebraska	19,970	0.6%
35	Nevada	23,582	0.8%
40	New Hampshire	15,468	0.5%
10	New Jersey	96,589	3.1%
37	New Mexico	18,545	0.6%
3	New York	176,532	5.7%
11	North Carolina	88,698	2.8%
49	North Dakota	6,933	0.2%
7	Ohio	124,264	4.0%
26	Oklahoma	37,782	1.2%
29	Oregon	35,815	1.1%
5	Pennsylvania	134,697	4.3%
44	Rhode Island	9,576	0.3%
27	South Carolina	36,989	1.2%
46	South Dakota	8,170	0.3%
19	Tennessee	62,529	2.0%
2	Texas	270,882	8.7%
32	Utah	29,933	1.0%
45	Vermont	8,201	0.3%
12	Virginia	87,101	2.8%
16	Washington	64,761	2.1%
38	West Virginia	17,836	0.6%
14	Wisconsin	66,603	2.1%
50	Wyoming	5,480	0.2%

RANK ORDER

RANK	STATE	GRADUATES	% of USA
1	California	383,566	12.3%
2	Texas	270,882	8.7%
3	New York	176,532	5.7%
4	Florida	145,793	4.7%
5	Pennsylvania	134,697	4.3%
6	Illinois	131,443	4.2%
7	Ohio	124,264	4.0%
8	Michigan	114,217	3.7%
9	Georgia	101,138	3.2%
10	New Jersey	96,589	3.1%
11	North Carolina	88,698	2.8%
12	Virginia	87,101	2.8%
13	Arizona	82,206	2.6%
14	Wisconsin	66,603	2.1%
15	Minnesota	66,215	2.1%
16	Washington	64,761	2.1%
17	Massachusetts	64,670	2.1%
18	Indiana	63,071	2.0%
19	Tennessee	62,529	2.0%
20	Missouri	62,342	2.0%
21	Maryland	59,774	1.9%
22	Colorado	46,811	1.5%
23	Kentucky	42,235	1.4%
24	Alabama	41,003	1.3%
25	Connecticut	40,277	1.3%
26	Oklahoma	37,782	1.2%
27	South Carolina	36,989	1.2%
28	Louisiana	36,408	1.2%
29	Oregon	35,815	1.1%
30	Iowa	34,462	1.1%
31	Kansas	30,738	1.0%
32	Utah	29,933	1.0%
33	Arkansas	29,834	1.0%
34	Mississippi	24,027	0.8%
35	Nevada	23,582	0.8%
36	Nebraska	19,970	0.6%
37	New Mexico	18,545	0.6%
38	West Virginia	17,836	0.6%
39	Idaho	17,212	0.6%
40	New Hampshire	15,468	0.5%
41	Maine	15,039	0.5%
42	Hawaii	11,451	0.4%
43	Montana	10,029	0.3%
44	Rhode Island	9,576	0.3%
45	Vermont	8,201	0.3%
46	South Dakota	8,170	0.3%
47	Alaska	7,712	0.2%
48	Delaware	7,538	0.2%
49	North Dakota	6,933	0.2%
50	Wyoming	5,480	0.2%
	District of Columbia	1,745	0.1%

Source: National Education Association, Washington, D.C.
   "Rankings and Estimates" (Copyright © 2011, NEA, used with permission, http://www.nea.org/home/44479.htm)
*Revised figures for school year 2009-2010.

Percent of Population Graduated from High School in 2009

National Percent = 85.3%*

RANK	STATE	PERCENT
46	Alabama	82.1
3	Alaska	91.4
37	Arizona	84.2
44	Arkansas	82.4
48	California	80.6
17	Colorado	89.3
20	Connecticut	88.6
26	Delaware	87.4
33	Florida	85.3
38	Georgia	83.9
8	Hawaii	90.4
21	Idaho	88.4
31	Illinois	86.4
29	Indiana	86.6
7	Iowa	90.5
15	Kansas	89.7
47	Kentucky	81.7
45	Louisiana	82.2
10	Maine	90.2
22	Maryland	88.2
19	Massachusetts	89.0
23	Michigan	87.9
2	Minnesota	91.5
49	Mississippi	80.4
28	Missouri	86.8
6	Montana	90.8
13	Nebraska	89.8
38	Nevada	83.9
4	New Hampshire	91.3
26	New Jersey	87.4
42	New Mexico	82.8
34	New York	84.7
36	North Carolina	84.3
11	North Dakota	90.1
25	Ohio	87.6
32	Oklahoma	85.6
18	Oregon	89.1
23	Pennsylvania	87.9
34	Rhode Island	84.7
40	South Carolina	83.6
12	South Dakota	89.9
41	Tennessee	83.1
50	Texas	79.9
8	Utah	90.4
5	Vermont	91.0
29	Virginia	86.6
15	Washington	89.7
42	West Virginia	82.8
13	Wisconsin	89.8
1	Wyoming	91.8

RANK	STATE	PERCENT
1	Wyoming	91.8
2	Minnesota	91.5
3	Alaska	91.4
4	New Hampshire	91.3
5	Vermont	91.0
6	Montana	90.8
7	Iowa	90.5
8	Hawaii	90.4
8	Utah	90.4
10	Maine	90.2
11	North Dakota	90.1
12	South Dakota	89.9
13	Nebraska	89.8
13	Wisconsin	89.8
15	Kansas	89.7
15	Washington	89.7
17	Colorado	89.3
18	Oregon	89.1
19	Massachusetts	89.0
20	Connecticut	88.6
21	Idaho	88.4
22	Maryland	88.2
23	Michigan	87.9
23	Pennsylvania	87.9
25	Ohio	87.6
26	Delaware	87.4
26	New Jersey	87.4
28	Missouri	86.8
29	Indiana	86.6
29	Virginia	86.6
31	Illinois	86.4
32	Oklahoma	85.6
33	Florida	85.3
34	New York	84.7
34	Rhode Island	84.7
36	North Carolina	84.3
37	Arizona	84.2
38	Georgia	83.9
38	Nevada	83.9
40	South Carolina	83.6
41	Tennessee	83.1
42	New Mexico	82.8
42	West Virginia	82.8
44	Arkansas	82.4
45	Louisiana	82.2
46	Alabama	82.1
47	Kentucky	81.7
48	California	80.6
49	Mississippi	80.4
50	Texas	79.9

	District of Columbia	87.1

Source: U.S. Bureau of the Census, American Community Survey
"Percent of People 25 Years and Over Who Have Completed High School" (http://www.census.gov/acs/www/index.html)
*Persons age 25 and older. Includes equivalency status.

Public High School Graduates in 2009

National Total = 3,039,015 Graduates*

<table>
<tr><td colspan="4">ALPHA ORDER</td><td colspan="4">RANK ORDER</td></tr>
<tr><td>RANK</td><td>STATE</td><td>GRADUATES</td><td>% of USA</td><td>RANK</td><td>STATE</td><td>GRADUATES</td><td>% of USA</td></tr>
<tr><td>23</td><td>Alabama</td><td>42,082</td><td>1.4%</td><td>1</td><td>California</td><td>372,310</td><td>12.3%</td></tr>
<tr><td>46</td><td>Alaska</td><td>8,008</td><td>0.3%</td><td>2</td><td>Texas</td><td>264,275</td><td>8.7%</td></tr>
<tr><td>18</td><td>Arizona</td><td>62,374</td><td>2.1%</td><td>3</td><td>New York</td><td>180,917</td><td>6.0%</td></tr>
<tr><td>33</td><td>Arkansas</td><td>28,057</td><td>0.9%</td><td>4</td><td>Florida</td><td>153,461</td><td>5.0%</td></tr>
<tr><td>1</td><td>California</td><td>372,310</td><td>12.3%</td><td>5</td><td>Illinois</td><td>131,670</td><td>4.3%</td></tr>
<tr><td>22</td><td>Colorado</td><td>47,459</td><td>1.6%</td><td>6</td><td>Pennsylvania</td><td>130,658</td><td>4.3%</td></tr>
<tr><td>29</td><td>Connecticut</td><td>34,968</td><td>1.2%</td><td>7</td><td>Ohio</td><td>122,203</td><td>4.0%</td></tr>
<tr><td>47</td><td>Delaware</td><td>7,839</td><td>0.3%</td><td>8</td><td>Michigan</td><td>112,742</td><td>3.7%</td></tr>
<tr><td>4</td><td>Florida</td><td>153,461</td><td>5.0%</td><td>9</td><td>New Jersey</td><td>95,085</td><td>3.1%</td></tr>
<tr><td>10</td><td>Georgia</td><td>88,003</td><td>2.9%</td><td>10</td><td>Georgia</td><td>88,003</td><td>2.9%</td></tr>
<tr><td>42</td><td>Hawaii</td><td>11,508</td><td>0.4%</td><td>11</td><td>North Carolina</td><td>86,712</td><td>2.9%</td></tr>
<tr><td>39</td><td>Idaho</td><td>16,807</td><td>0.6%</td><td>12</td><td>Virginia</td><td>79,651</td><td>2.6%</td></tr>
<tr><td>5</td><td>Illinois</td><td>131,670</td><td>4.3%</td><td>13</td><td>Wisconsin</td><td>65,410</td><td>2.2%</td></tr>
<tr><td>15</td><td>Indiana</td><td>63,663</td><td>2.1%</td><td>14</td><td>Massachusetts</td><td>65,258</td><td>2.1%</td></tr>
<tr><td>30</td><td>Iowa</td><td>33,926</td><td>1.1%</td><td>15</td><td>Indiana</td><td>63,663</td><td>2.1%</td></tr>
<tr><td>32</td><td>Kansas</td><td>30,368</td><td>1.0%</td><td>16</td><td>Missouri</td><td>62,969</td><td>2.1%</td></tr>
<tr><td>24</td><td>Kentucky</td><td>41,851</td><td>1.4%</td><td>17</td><td>Washington</td><td>62,764</td><td>2.1%</td></tr>
<tr><td>27</td><td>Louisiana</td><td>35,622</td><td>1.2%</td><td>18</td><td>Arizona</td><td>62,374</td><td>2.1%</td></tr>
<tr><td>41</td><td>Maine</td><td>14,093</td><td>0.5%</td><td>19</td><td>Tennessee</td><td>60,368</td><td>2.0%</td></tr>
<tr><td>21</td><td>Maryland</td><td>58,304</td><td>1.9%</td><td>20</td><td>Minnesota</td><td>59,729</td><td>2.0%</td></tr>
<tr><td>14</td><td>Massachusetts</td><td>65,258</td><td>2.1%</td><td>21</td><td>Maryland</td><td>58,304</td><td>1.9%</td></tr>
<tr><td>8</td><td>Michigan</td><td>112,742</td><td>3.7%</td><td>22</td><td>Colorado</td><td>47,459</td><td>1.6%</td></tr>
<tr><td>20</td><td>Minnesota</td><td>59,729</td><td>2.0%</td><td>23</td><td>Alabama</td><td>42,082</td><td>1.4%</td></tr>
<tr><td>34</td><td>Mississippi</td><td>24,505</td><td>0.8%</td><td>24</td><td>Kentucky</td><td>41,851</td><td>1.4%</td></tr>
<tr><td>16</td><td>Missouri</td><td>62,969</td><td>2.1%</td><td>25</td><td>South Carolina</td><td>39,114</td><td>1.3%</td></tr>
<tr><td>43</td><td>Montana</td><td>10,077</td><td>0.3%</td><td>26</td><td>Oklahoma</td><td>37,219</td><td>1.2%</td></tr>
<tr><td>36</td><td>Nebraska</td><td>19,501</td><td>0.6%</td><td>27</td><td>Louisiana</td><td>35,622</td><td>1.2%</td></tr>
<tr><td>35</td><td>Nevada</td><td>19,904</td><td>0.7%</td><td>28</td><td>Oregon</td><td>35,138</td><td>1.2%</td></tr>
<tr><td>40</td><td>New Hampshire</td><td>14,757</td><td>0.5%</td><td>29</td><td>Connecticut</td><td>34,968</td><td>1.2%</td></tr>
<tr><td>9</td><td>New Jersey</td><td>95,085</td><td>3.1%</td><td>30</td><td>Iowa</td><td>33,926</td><td>1.1%</td></tr>
<tr><td>37</td><td>New Mexico</td><td>17,931</td><td>0.6%</td><td>31</td><td>Utah</td><td>30,463</td><td>1.0%</td></tr>
<tr><td>3</td><td>New York</td><td>180,917</td><td>6.0%</td><td>32</td><td>Kansas</td><td>30,368</td><td>1.0%</td></tr>
<tr><td>11</td><td>North Carolina</td><td>86,712</td><td>2.9%</td><td>33</td><td>Arkansas</td><td>28,057</td><td>0.9%</td></tr>
<tr><td>48</td><td>North Dakota</td><td>7,232</td><td>0.2%</td><td>34</td><td>Mississippi</td><td>24,505</td><td>0.8%</td></tr>
<tr><td>7</td><td>Ohio</td><td>122,203</td><td>4.0%</td><td>35</td><td>Nevada</td><td>19,904</td><td>0.7%</td></tr>
<tr><td>26</td><td>Oklahoma</td><td>37,219</td><td>1.2%</td><td>36</td><td>Nebraska</td><td>19,501</td><td>0.6%</td></tr>
<tr><td>28</td><td>Oregon</td><td>35,138</td><td>1.2%</td><td>37</td><td>New Mexico</td><td>17,931</td><td>0.6%</td></tr>
<tr><td>6</td><td>Pennsylvania</td><td>130,658</td><td>4.3%</td><td>38</td><td>West Virginia</td><td>17,690</td><td>0.6%</td></tr>
<tr><td>44</td><td>Rhode Island</td><td>10,028</td><td>0.3%</td><td>39</td><td>Idaho</td><td>16,807</td><td>0.6%</td></tr>
<tr><td>25</td><td>South Carolina</td><td>39,114</td><td>1.3%</td><td>40</td><td>New Hampshire</td><td>14,757</td><td>0.5%</td></tr>
<tr><td>45</td><td>South Dakota</td><td>8,123</td><td>0.3%</td><td>41</td><td>Maine</td><td>14,093</td><td>0.5%</td></tr>
<tr><td>19</td><td>Tennessee</td><td>60,368</td><td>2.0%</td><td>42</td><td>Hawaii</td><td>11,508</td><td>0.4%</td></tr>
<tr><td>2</td><td>Texas</td><td>264,275</td><td>8.7%</td><td>43</td><td>Montana</td><td>10,077</td><td>0.3%</td></tr>
<tr><td>31</td><td>Utah</td><td>30,463</td><td>1.0%</td><td>44</td><td>Rhode Island</td><td>10,028</td><td>0.3%</td></tr>
<tr><td>49</td><td>Vermont</td><td>7,209</td><td>0.2%</td><td>45</td><td>South Dakota</td><td>8,123</td><td>0.3%</td></tr>
<tr><td>12</td><td>Virginia</td><td>79,651</td><td>2.6%</td><td>46</td><td>Alaska</td><td>8,008</td><td>0.3%</td></tr>
<tr><td>17</td><td>Washington</td><td>62,764</td><td>2.1%</td><td>47</td><td>Delaware</td><td>7,839</td><td>0.3%</td></tr>
<tr><td>38</td><td>West Virginia</td><td>17,690</td><td>0.6%</td><td>48</td><td>North Dakota</td><td>7,232</td><td>0.2%</td></tr>
<tr><td>13</td><td>Wisconsin</td><td>65,410</td><td>2.2%</td><td>49</td><td>Vermont</td><td>7,209</td><td>0.2%</td></tr>
<tr><td>50</td><td>Wyoming</td><td>5,493</td><td>0.2%</td><td>50</td><td>Wyoming</td><td>5,493</td><td>0.2%</td></tr>
<tr><td></td><td></td><td></td><td></td><td></td><td>District of Columbia</td><td>3,517</td><td>0.1%</td></tr>
</table>

Source: U.S. Department of Education, National Center for Education Statistics
   "Common Core of Data (CCD) Database" (http://nces.ed.gov/ccd/)
*Diploma recipients for school year 2008-2009. Excludes persons receiving high school equivalency certificates.

Percent Change in Public High School Graduates: 2005 to 2009

National Percent Change = 8.7% Increase*

	ALPHA ORDER				RANK ORDER	
RANK	STATE	PERCENT CHANGE		RANK	STATE	PERCENT CHANGE
12	Alabama	12.4		1	Nevada	26.5
6	Alaska	15.9		2	Tennessee	25.9
28	Arizona	4.8		3	Georgia	24.2
27	Arkansas	5.4		4	New York	18.1
28	California	4.8		5	South Carolina	17.0
23	Colorado	6.6		6	Alaska	15.9
45	Connecticut	(1.5)		7	North Carolina	15.6
11	Delaware	13.1		8	Florida	15.1
8	Florida	15.1		9	Indiana	14.8
3	Georgia	24.2		10	Virginia	14.4
26	Hawaii	6.4		11	Delaware	13.1
23	Idaho	6.6		12	Alabama	12.4
25	Illinois	6.5		13	Michigan	11.0
9	Indiana	14.8		14	Texas	10.2
40	Iowa	1.1		15	New Jersey	9.9
43	Kansas	0.0		16	Massachusetts	9.4
17	Kentucky	9.0		17	Kentucky	9.0
44	Louisiana	(1.1)		18	Missouri	8.9
19	Maine	7.8		19	Maine	7.8
21	Maryland	7.6		19	Oregon	7.8
16	Massachusetts	9.4		21	Maryland	7.6
13	Michigan	11.0		22	New Hampshire	7.1
38	Minnesota	2.3		23	Colorado	6.6
32	Mississippi	4.2		23	Idaho	6.6
18	Missouri	8.9		25	Illinois	6.5
48	Montana	(2.5)		26	Hawaii	6.4
46	Nebraska	(2.2)		27	Arkansas	5.4
1	Nevada	26.5		28	Arizona	4.8
22	New Hampshire	7.1		28	California	4.8
15	New Jersey	9.9		30	Ohio	4.7
34	New Mexico	3.3		30	Pennsylvania	4.7
4	New York	18.1		32	Mississippi	4.2
7	North Carolina	15.6		33	Wisconsin	3.4
49	North Dakota	(4.3)		34	New Mexico	3.3
30	Ohio	4.7		35	West Virginia	3.2
36	Oklahoma	2.7		36	Oklahoma	2.7
19	Oregon	7.8		36	Washington	2.7
30	Pennsylvania	4.7		38	Minnesota	2.3
39	Rhode Island	1.5		39	Rhode Island	1.5
5	South Carolina	17.0		40	Iowa	1.1
50	South Dakota	(5.4)		41	Vermont	0.8
2	Tennessee	25.9		42	Utah	0.7
14	Texas	10.2		43	Kansas	0.0
42	Utah	0.7		44	Louisiana	(1.1)
41	Vermont	0.8		45	Connecticut	(1.5)
10	Virginia	14.4		46	Nebraska	(2.2)
36	Washington	2.7		46	Wyoming	(2.2)
35	West Virginia	3.2		48	Montana	(2.5)
33	Wisconsin	3.4		49	North Dakota	(4.3)
46	Wyoming	(2.2)		50	South Dakota	(5.4)

District of Columbia 26.5

Source: CQ Press using data from U.S. Department of Education, National Center for Education Statistics
    "Common Core of Data (CCD) Database" (http://nces.ed.gov/ccd/)
*Based on diploma recipients for school years 2008-2009 and 2004-2005. Excludes persons receiving high school equivalency certificates.

Reported Public High School Equivalency Recipients in 2009

National Total = 147,000 Recipients*

ALPHA ORDER					RANK ORDER			
RANK	STATE		RECIPIENTS	% of USA	RANK	STATE	RECIPIENTS	% of USA
18	Alabama		3,316	2.3%	1	Florida	14,182	9.6%
43	Alaska		599	0.4%	2	Texas	9,549	6.5%
12	Arizona		3,863	2.6%	3	California	8,634	5.9%
19	Arkansas		3,169	2.2%	4	New York	8,109	5.5%
3	California		8,634	5.9%	5	Georgia	5,766	3.9%
15	Colorado		3,568	2.4%	6	Virginia	5,570	3.8%
41	Connecticut		710	0.5%	7	Illinois	4,917	3.3%
50	Delaware		197	0.1%	8	Washington	4,177	2.8%
1	Florida		14,182	9.6%	9	Pennsylvania	4,077	2.8%
5	Georgia		5,766	3.9%	10	North Carolina	4,049	2.8%
40	Hawaii		797	0.5%	11	Missouri	3,909	2.7%
34	Idaho		1,496	1.0%	12	Arizona	3,863	2.6%
7	Illinois		4,917	3.3%	13	Oregon	3,689	2.5%
14	Indiana		3,652	2.5%	14	Indiana	3,652	2.5%
36	Iowa		1,250	0.9%	15	Colorado	3,568	2.4%
35	Kansas		1,266	0.9%	16	Louisiana	3,559	2.4%
25	Kentucky		2,739	1.9%	17	Mississippi	3,359	2.3%
16	Louisiana		3,559	2.4%	18	Alabama	3,316	2.3%
39	Maine		818	0.6%	19	Arkansas	3,169	2.2%
31	Maryland		1,791	1.2%	20	Ohio	2,956	2.0%
24	Massachusetts		2,744	1.9%	21	Michigan	2,889	2.0%
21	Michigan		2,889	2.0%	22	Tennessee	2,847	1.9%
37	Minnesota		1,123	0.8%	23	New Jersey	2,750	1.9%
17	Mississippi		3,359	2.3%	24	Massachusetts	2,744	1.9%
11	Missouri		3,909	2.7%	25	Kentucky	2,739	1.9%
38	Montana		1,036	0.7%	26	South Carolina	2,231	1.5%
42	Nebraska		684	0.5%	27	Utah	2,230	1.5%
33	Nevada		1,566	1.1%	28	New Mexico	2,197	1.5%
45	New Hampshire		548	0.4%	28	Wisconsin	2,197	1.5%
23	New Jersey		2,750	1.9%	30	Oklahoma	2,062	1.4%
28	New Mexico		2,197	1.5%	31	Maryland	1,791	1.2%
4	New York		8,109	5.5%	32	West Virginia	1,690	1.1%
10	North Carolina		4,049	2.8%	33	Nevada	1,566	1.1%
48	North Dakota		394	0.3%	34	Idaho	1,496	1.0%
20	Ohio		2,956	2.0%	35	Kansas	1,266	0.9%
30	Oklahoma		2,062	1.4%	36	Iowa	1,250	0.9%
13	Oregon		3,689	2.5%	37	Minnesota	1,123	0.8%
9	Pennsylvania		4,077	2.8%	38	Montana	1,036	0.7%
46	Rhode Island		477	0.3%	39	Maine	818	0.6%
26	South Carolina		2,231	1.5%	40	Hawaii	797	0.5%
47	South Dakota		460	0.3%	41	Connecticut	710	0.5%
22	Tennessee		2,847	1.9%	42	Nebraska	684	0.5%
2	Texas		9,549	6.5%	43	Alaska	599	0.4%
27	Utah		2,230	1.5%	44	Wyoming	591	0.4%
49	Vermont		387	0.3%	45	New Hampshire	548	0.4%
6	Virginia		5,570	3.8%	46	Rhode Island	477	0.3%
8	Washington		4,177	2.8%	47	South Dakota	460	0.3%
32	West Virginia		1,690	1.1%	48	North Dakota	394	0.3%
28	Wisconsin		2,197	1.5%	49	Vermont	387	0.3%
44	Wyoming		591	0.4%	50	Delaware	197	0.1%
						District of Columbia	164	0.1%

Source: U.S. Department of Education, National Center for Education Statistics
    "Common Core of Data (CCD) Database" (http://nces.ed.gov/ccd/)
*For school year 2008-2009.

Other Public High School Completers in 2009

National Total = 51,954 Students*

ALPHA ORDER

RANK ORDER

RANK	STATE	STUDENTS	% of USA	RANK	STATE	STUDENTS	% of USA
9	Alabama	2,168	4.2%	1	Virginia	8,294	16.0%
23	Alaska	271	0.5%	2	Florida	7,073	13.6%
33	Arizona	0	0.0%	3	New York	5,937	11.4%
NA	Arkansas**	NA	NA	4	Georgia	5,787	11.1%
NA	California**	NA	NA	5	Louisiana	5,172	10.0%
6	Colorado	2,918	5.6%	6	Colorado	2,918	5.6%
21	Connecticut	368	0.7%	7	Tennessee	2,331	4.5%
26	Delaware	154	0.3%	8	Mississippi	2,213	4.3%
2	Florida	7,073	13.6%	9	Alabama	2,168	4.2%
4	Georgia	5,787	11.1%	10	North Carolina	1,497	2.9%
24	Hawaii	256	0.5%	11	Oregon	1,369	2.6%
31	Idaho	88	0.2%	12	Massachusetts	864	1.7%
22	Illinois	319	0.6%	13	Wisconsin	856	1.6%
NA	Indiana**	NA	NA	14	Maryland	698	1.3%
30	Iowa	107	0.2%	15	Utah	602	1.2%
29	Kansas	121	0.2%	16	New Mexico	454	0.9%
20	Kentucky	384	0.7%	17	Michigan	416	0.8%
5	Louisiana	5,172	10.0%	18	New Hampshire	413	0.8%
27	Maine	144	0.3%	19	Washington	397	0.8%
14	Maryland	698	1.3%	20	Kentucky	384	0.7%
12	Massachusetts	864	1.7%	21	Connecticut	368	0.7%
17	Michigan	416	0.8%	22	Illinois	319	0.6%
NA	Minnesota**	NA	NA	23	Alaska	271	0.5%
8	Mississippi	2,213	4.3%	24	Hawaii	256	0.5%
NA	Missouri**	NA	NA	25	Nebraska	157	0.3%
NA	Montana**	NA	NA	26	Delaware	154	0.3%
25	Nebraska	157	0.3%	27	Maine	144	0.3%
NA	Nevada**	NA	NA	28	Wyoming	123	0.2%
18	New Hampshire	413	0.8%	29	Kansas	121	0.2%
NA	New Jersey**	NA	NA	30	Iowa	107	0.2%
16	New Mexico	454	0.9%	31	Idaho	88	0.2%
3	New York	5,937	11.4%	32	Rhode Island	3	0.0%
10	North Carolina	1,497	2.9%	33	Arizona	0	0.0%
NA	North Dakota**	NA	NA	NA	Arkansas**	NA	NA
NA	Ohio**	NA	NA	NA	California**	NA	NA
NA	Oklahoma**	NA	NA	NA	Indiana**	NA	NA
11	Oregon	1,369	2.6%	NA	Minnesota**	NA	NA
NA	Pennsylvania**	NA	NA	NA	Missouri**	NA	NA
32	Rhode Island	3	0.0%	NA	Montana**	NA	NA
NA	South Carolina**	NA	NA	NA	Nevada**	NA	NA
NA	South Dakota**	NA	NA	NA	New Jersey**	NA	NA
7	Tennessee	2,331	4.5%	NA	North Dakota**	NA	NA
NA	Texas**	NA	NA	NA	Ohio**	NA	NA
15	Utah	602	1.2%	NA	Oklahoma**	NA	NA
NA	Vermont**	NA	NA	NA	Pennsylvania**	NA	NA
1	Virginia	8,294	16.0%	NA	South Carolina**	NA	NA
19	Washington	397	0.8%	NA	South Dakota**	NA	NA
NA	West Virginia**	NA	NA	NA	Texas**	NA	NA
13	Wisconsin	856	1.6%	NA	Vermont**	NA	NA
28	Wyoming	123	0.2%	NA	West Virginia**	NA	NA
					District of Columbia**	NA	NA

Source: U.S. Department of Education, National Center for Education Statistics
    "Common Core of Data (CCD) Database" (http://nces.ed.gov/ccd/)
*For school year 2008-2009. Includes students receiving a certificate of attendance or other certificate of completion in lieu of a diploma.
**Either no students in this category or data not available.

Averaged Freshman Graduation Rate for Public High Schools in 2009

National Average = 75.5%*

ALPHA ORDER

RANK	STATE	PERCENT
43	Alabama	69.9
40	Alaska	72.6
41	Arizona	72.5
36	Arkansas	74.0
42	California	71.0
22	Colorado	77.6
28	Connecticut	75.4
37	Delaware	73.7
44	Florida	68.9
45	Georgia	67.8
30	Hawaii	75.3
13	Idaho	80.6
21	Illinois	77.7
33	Indiana	75.2
5	Iowa	85.7
15	Kansas	80.2
22	Kentucky	77.6
46	Louisiana	67.3
17	Maine	79.9
16	Maryland	80.1
8	Massachusetts	83.3
30	Michigan	75.3
3	Minnesota	87.4
49	Mississippi	62.0
9	Missouri	83.1
11	Montana	82.0
10	Nebraska	82.9
50	Nevada	56.3
7	New Hampshire	84.3
6	New Jersey	85.3
48	New Mexico	64.8
39	New York	73.5
35	North Carolina	75.1
3	North Dakota	87.4
18	Ohio	79.6
25	Oklahoma	77.3
27	Oregon	76.5
14	Pennsylvania	80.5
30	Rhode Island	75.3
47	South Carolina	66.0
12	South Dakota	81.7
24	Tennessee	77.4
28	Texas	75.4
19	Utah	79.4
2	Vermont	89.6
20	Virginia	78.4
37	Washington	73.7
26	West Virginia	77.0
1	Wisconsin	90.7
33	Wyoming	75.2

RANK ORDER

RANK	STATE	PERCENT
1	Wisconsin	90.7
2	Vermont	89.6
3	Minnesota	87.4
3	North Dakota	87.4
5	Iowa	85.7
6	New Jersey	85.3
7	New Hampshire	84.3
8	Massachusetts	83.3
9	Missouri	83.1
10	Nebraska	82.9
11	Montana	82.0
12	South Dakota	81.7
13	Idaho	80.6
14	Pennsylvania	80.5
15	Kansas	80.2
16	Maryland	80.1
17	Maine	79.9
18	Ohio	79.6
19	Utah	79.4
20	Virginia	78.4
21	Illinois	77.7
22	Colorado	77.6
22	Kentucky	77.6
24	Tennessee	77.4
25	Oklahoma	77.3
26	West Virginia	77.0
27	Oregon	76.5
28	Connecticut	75.4
28	Texas	75.4
30	Hawaii	75.3
30	Michigan	75.3
30	Rhode Island	75.3
33	Indiana	75.2
33	Wyoming	75.2
35	North Carolina	75.1
36	Arkansas	74.0
37	Delaware	73.7
37	Washington	73.7
39	New York	73.5
40	Alaska	72.6
41	Arizona	72.5
42	California	71.0
43	Alabama	69.9
44	Florida	68.9
45	Georgia	67.8
46	Louisiana	67.3
47	South Carolina	66.0
48	New Mexico	64.8
49	Mississippi	62.0
50	Nevada	56.3

| District of Columbia | | 62.4 |

Source: U.S. Department of Education, National Center for Education Statistics
    "Public School Graduates and Dropouts from the Common Core of Data: School Year 2008-09" (NCES 2011312)
        (http://nces.ed.gov/pubsearch/pubsinfo.asp?pubid=2011312)

*This rate is calculated by comparing the incoming freshman class enrollment of school year 2005-2006 with the number of graduates with regular diplomas four years later (2008-2009). The incoming class enrollment figure is an average of the 8th grade from five years earlier, the 9th grade four years earlier, and the 10th grade from three years earlier.

Percent Change in Averaged Freshman Graduation Rate for Public High Schools: 2005 to 2009
National Percent Change = 1.1% Increase*

ALPHA ORDER

RANK	STATE	PERCENT CHANGE
7	Alabama	6.1
1	Alaska	13.3
50	Arizona	(14.4)
43	Arkansas	(2.2)
46	California	(4.8)
24	Colorado	1.2
49	Connecticut	(6.8)
27	Delaware	0.8
6	Florida	6.7
4	Georgia	9.9
30	Hawaii	0.3
33	Idaho	(0.5)
41	Illinois	(2.1)
17	Indiana	2.7
37	Iowa	(1.0)
22	Kansas	1.3
18	Kentucky	2.2
9	Louisiana	5.3
20	Maine	1.7
25	Maryland	1.0
8	Massachusetts	5.8
14	Michigan	3.2
20	Minnesota	1.7
41	Mississippi	(2.1)
15	Missouri	3.1
28	Montana	0.6
47	Nebraska	(5.6)
26	Nevada	0.9
10	New Hampshire	5.2
31	New Jersey	0.2
36	New Mexico	(0.9)
3	New York	12.6
13	North Carolina	3.4
22	North Dakota	1.3
34	Ohio	(0.7)
29	Oklahoma	0.5
15	Oregon	3.1
44	Pennsylvania	(2.4)
45	Rhode Island	(4.0)
5	South Carolina	9.8
34	South Dakota	(0.7)
2	Tennessee	13.0
19	Texas	1.9
48	Utah	(5.9)
12	Vermont	3.6
38	Virginia	(1.5)
39	Washington	(1.7)
32	West Virginia	(0.4)
11	Wisconsin	4.6
40	Wyoming	(2.0)

RANK ORDER

RANK	STATE	PERCENT CHANGE
1	Alaska	13.3
2	Tennessee	13.0
3	New York	12.6
4	Georgia	9.9
5	South Carolina	9.8
6	Florida	6.7
7	Alabama	6.1
8	Massachusetts	5.8
9	Louisiana	5.3
10	New Hampshire	5.2
11	Wisconsin	4.6
12	Vermont	3.6
13	North Carolina	3.4
14	Michigan	3.2
15	Missouri	3.1
15	Oregon	3.1
17	Indiana	2.7
18	Kentucky	2.2
19	Texas	1.9
20	Maine	1.7
20	Minnesota	1.7
22	Kansas	1.3
22	North Dakota	1.3
24	Colorado	1.2
25	Maryland	1.0
26	Nevada	0.9
27	Delaware	0.8
28	Montana	0.6
29	Oklahoma	0.5
30	Hawaii	0.3
31	New Jersey	0.2
32	West Virginia	(0.4)
33	Idaho	(0.5)
34	Ohio	(0.7)
34	South Dakota	(0.7)
36	New Mexico	(0.9)
37	Iowa	(1.0)
38	Virginia	(1.5)
39	Washington	(1.7)
40	Wyoming	(2.0)
41	Illinois	(2.1)
41	Mississippi	(2.1)
43	Arkansas	(2.2)
44	Pennsylvania	(2.4)
45	Rhode Island	(4.0)
46	California	(4.8)
47	Nebraska	(5.6)
48	Utah	(5.9)
49	Connecticut	(6.8)
50	Arizona	(14.4)

District of Columbia (9.3)

Source: CQ Press using data from U.S. Department of Education, National Center for Education Statistics
"Public School Graduates and Dropouts from the Common Core of Data: School Year 2008-09" (NCES 2011312)
(http://nces.ed.gov/pubsearch/pubsinfo.asp?pubid=2011312)

*This rate is calculated by comparing an averaged incoming freshman class enrollment with the number of graduates with regular diplomas four years later. The incoming class enrollment figure is an average of the 8th grade from five years earlier, the 9th grade four years earlier, and the 10th grade from three years earlier.

Estimated Averaged Freshman Public High School Graduation Rate for White Students in 2009
Reporting States Rate = 82.0% Graduated*

ALPHA ORDER

RANK	STATE	PERCENT
41	Alabama	74.5
40	Alaska	75.2
37	Arizona	75.8
38	Arkansas	75.5
26	California	80.8
17	Colorado	84.3
22	Connecticut	81.8
29	Delaware	79.0
46	Florida	71.1
43	Georgia	73.0
47	Hawaii	70.5
24	Idaho	81.6
9	Illinois	85.7
34	Indiana	77.1
7	Iowa	87.4
19	Kansas	83.7
31	Kentucky	77.8
42	Louisiana	73.2
NA	Maine**	NA
11	Maryland	85.6
8	Massachusetts	86.1
25	Michigan	80.9
2	Minnesota	91.4
48	Mississippi	65.3
9	Missouri	85.7
15	Montana	84.5
6	Nebraska	88.0
NA	Nevada**	NA
18	New Hampshire	84.2
4	New Jersey	89.1
44	New Mexico	72.4
12	New York	85.1
28	North Carolina	79.3
3	North Dakota	91.1
14	Ohio	84.9
29	Oklahoma	79.0
33	Oregon	77.4
16	Pennsylvania	84.4
31	Rhode Island	77.8
45	South Carolina	71.6
12	South Dakota	85.1
27	Tennessee	79.4
20	Texas	82.7
23	Utah	81.7
4	Vermont	89.1
21	Virginia	82.3
39	Washington	75.3
36	West Virginia	77.0
1	Wisconsin	95.0
34	Wyoming	77.1

RANK ORDER

RANK	STATE	PERCENT
1	Wisconsin	95.0
2	Minnesota	91.4
3	North Dakota	91.1
4	New Jersey	89.1
4	Vermont	89.1
6	Nebraska	88.0
7	Iowa	87.4
8	Massachusetts	86.1
9	Illinois	85.7
9	Missouri	85.7
11	Maryland	85.6
12	New York	85.1
12	South Dakota	85.1
14	Ohio	84.9
15	Montana	84.5
16	Pennsylvania	84.4
17	Colorado	84.3
18	New Hampshire	84.2
19	Kansas	83.7
20	Texas	82.7
21	Virginia	82.3
22	Connecticut	81.8
23	Utah	81.7
24	Idaho	81.6
25	Michigan	80.9
26	California	80.8
27	Tennessee	79.4
28	North Carolina	79.3
29	Delaware	79.0
29	Oklahoma	79.0
31	Kentucky	77.8
31	Rhode Island	77.8
33	Oregon	77.4
34	Indiana	77.1
34	Wyoming	77.1
36	West Virginia	77.0
37	Arizona	75.8
38	Arkansas	75.5
39	Washington	75.3
40	Alaska	75.2
41	Alabama	74.5
42	Louisiana	73.2
43	Georgia	73.0
44	New Mexico	72.4
45	South Carolina	71.6
46	Florida	71.1
47	Hawaii	70.5
48	Mississippi	65.3
NA	Maine**	NA
NA	Nevada**	NA

District of Columbia   77.5

Source: U.S. Department of Education, National Center for Education Statistics
   "Public School Graduates and Dropouts: School Year 2008-2009" (http://nces.ed.gov/pubsearch/pubsinfo.asp?pubid=2011312)
*Based on reporting states' totals and excludes students for whom race/ethnicity was not reported. Excludes white Hispanics.
Calculated by comparing estimated number of public high school graduates in 2009 with average membership of the 8th grade in
2004-2005, the 9th grade in 2005-2006, and the 10th grade in 2006-2007. Data exclude ungraded pupils and have not been
adjusted for interstate migration or switching to or from private schools. **Not available.

Estimated Averaged Freshman Public High School Graduation Rate for Black Students in 2009
Reporting States Rate = 63.5% Graduated*

ALPHA ORDER

RANK	STATE	PERCENT
33	Alabama	62.2
48	Alaska	56.3
6	Arizona	78.7
22	Arkansas	68.0
44	California	57.7
19	Colorado	69.8
32	Connecticut	63.5
26	Delaware	66.8
38	Florida	59.8
34	Georgia	61.2
8	Hawaii	75.3
3	Idaho	91.9
36	Illinois	60.8
47	Indiana	56.4
12	Iowa	71.5
27	Kansas	66.6
17	Kentucky	70.2
39	Louisiana	59.6
NA	Maine**	NA
11	Maryland	71.8
9	Massachusetts	73.9
42	Michigan	58.5
20	Minnesota	69.1
41	Mississippi	58.6
14	Missouri	71.3
9	Montana	73.9
46	Nebraska	56.7
NA	Nevada**	NA
1	New Hampshire	100.0
7	New Jersey	75.9
24	New Mexico	67.4
43	New York	58.1
29	North Carolina	65.0
1	North Dakota	100.0
45	Ohio	56.8
21	Oklahoma	68.7
35	Oregon	61.1
31	Pennsylvania	64.0
15	Rhode Island	70.5
40	South Carolina	58.9
4	South Dakota	85.5
13	Tennessee	71.4
22	Texas	68.0
16	Utah	70.3
5	Vermont	84.6
25	Virginia	67.2
37	Washington	60.7
17	West Virginia	70.2
28	Wisconsin	65.3
29	Wyoming	65.0

RANK ORDER

RANK	STATE	PERCENT
1	New Hampshire	100.0
1	North Dakota	100.0
3	Idaho	91.9
4	South Dakota	85.5
5	Vermont	84.6
6	Arizona	78.7
7	New Jersey	75.9
8	Hawaii	75.3
9	Massachusetts	73.9
9	Montana	73.9
11	Maryland	71.8
12	Iowa	71.5
13	Tennessee	71.4
14	Missouri	71.3
15	Rhode Island	70.5
16	Utah	70.3
17	Kentucky	70.2
17	West Virginia	70.2
19	Colorado	69.8
20	Minnesota	69.1
21	Oklahoma	68.7
22	Arkansas	68.0
22	Texas	68.0
24	New Mexico	67.4
25	Virginia	67.2
26	Delaware	66.8
27	Kansas	66.6
28	Wisconsin	65.3
29	North Carolina	65.0
29	Wyoming	65.0
31	Pennsylvania	64.0
32	Connecticut	63.5
33	Alabama	62.2
34	Georgia	61.2
35	Oregon	61.1
36	Illinois	60.8
37	Washington	60.7
38	Florida	59.8
39	Louisiana	59.6
40	South Carolina	58.9
41	Mississippi	58.6
42	Michigan	58.5
43	New York	58.1
44	California	57.7
45	Ohio	56.8
46	Nebraska	56.7
47	Indiana	56.4
48	Alaska	56.3
NA	Maine**	NA
NA	Nevada**	NA

District of Columbia	62.8

Source: U.S. Department of Education, National Center for Education Statistics
"Public School Graduates and Dropouts: School Year 2008-2009" (http://nces.ed.gov/pubsearch/pubsinfo.asp?pubid=2011312)
*Based on reporting states' totals and excludes students for whom race/ethnicity was not reported. Excludes black Hispanics.
Calculated by comparing estimated number of public high school graduates in 2009 with average membership of the 8th grade in 2004-2005, the 9th grade in 2005-2006, and the 10th grade in 2006-2007. Data exclude ungraded pupils and have not been adjusted for interstate migration or switching to or from private schools. **Not available.

Estimated Averaged Freshman Public High School Graduation Rate for Hispanic Students in 2009
Reporting States Rate = 65.9% Graduated*

ALPHA ORDER

RANK	STATE	PERCENT
38	Alabama	63.0
1	Alaska	89.4
21	Arizona	69.2
10	Arkansas	75.7
39	California	61.6
43	Colorado	60.8
47	Connecticut	55.5
40	Delaware	61.3
27	Florida	66.9
46	Georgia	56.6
17	Hawaii	71.0
14	Idaho	72.7
22	Illinois	68.8
29	Indiana	66.8
23	Iowa	68.7
36	Kansas	63.5
5	Kentucky	80.2
13	Louisiana	73.6
NA	Maine**	NA
7	Maryland	76.8
24	Massachusetts	67.7
41	Michigan	61.2
35	Minnesota	63.9
24	Mississippi	67.7
4	Missouri	80.3
8	Montana	76.6
27	Nebraska	66.9
NA	Nevada**	NA
48	New Hampshire	41.6
9	New Jersey	76.1
44	New Mexico	60.7
45	New York	57.4
30	North Carolina	66.5
15	North Dakota	72.4
32	Ohio	66.0
12	Oklahoma	73.7
18	Oregon	70.7
33	Pennsylvania	65.3
26	Rhode Island	67.2
34	South Carolina	64.0
30	South Dakota	66.5
11	Tennessee	74.3
19	Texas	69.6
41	Utah	61.2
3	Vermont	81.3
16	Virginia	71.8
37	Washington	63.1
2	West Virginia	88.1
6	Wisconsin	77.3
19	Wyoming	69.6

RANK ORDER

RANK	STATE	PERCENT
1	Alaska	89.4
2	West Virginia	88.1
3	Vermont	81.3
4	Missouri	80.3
5	Kentucky	80.2
6	Wisconsin	77.3
7	Maryland	76.8
8	Montana	76.6
9	New Jersey	76.1
10	Arkansas	75.7
11	Tennessee	74.3
12	Oklahoma	73.7
13	Louisiana	73.6
14	Idaho	72.7
15	North Dakota	72.4
16	Virginia	71.8
17	Hawaii	71.0
18	Oregon	70.7
19	Texas	69.6
19	Wyoming	69.6
21	Arizona	69.2
22	Illinois	68.8
23	Iowa	68.7
24	Massachusetts	67.7
24	Mississippi	67.7
26	Rhode Island	67.2
27	Florida	66.9
27	Nebraska	66.9
29	Indiana	66.8
30	North Carolina	66.5
30	South Dakota	66.5
32	Ohio	66.0
33	Pennsylvania	65.3
34	South Carolina	64.0
35	Minnesota	63.9
36	Kansas	63.5
37	Washington	63.1
38	Alabama	63.0
39	California	61.6
40	Delaware	61.3
41	Michigan	61.2
41	Utah	61.2
43	Colorado	60.8
44	New Mexico	60.7
45	New York	57.4
46	Georgia	56.6
47	Connecticut	55.5
48	New Hampshire	41.6
NA	Maine**	NA
NA	Nevada**	NA

District of Columbia   50.1

Source: U.S. Department of Education, National Center for Education Statistics
   "Public School Graduates and Dropouts: School Year 2008-2009" (http://nces.ed.gov/pubsearch/pubsinfo.asp?pubid=2011312)
*Based on reporting states' totals and excludes students for whom race/ethnicity was not reported.   Calculated by comparing estimated number of public high school graduates in 2009 with average membership of the 8th grade in 2004-2005, the 9th grade in 2005-2006, and the 10th grade in 2006-2007. Data exclude ungraded pupils and have not been adjusted for interstate migration or switching to or from private schools. **Not available.

Estimated Averaged Freshman Public High School Graduation Rate for Asian Students in 2009
Reporting States Rate = 91.8% Graduated*

ALPHA ORDER

RANK	STATE	PERCENT
38	Alabama	90.2
45	Alaska	79.9
14	Arizona	98.9
22	Arkansas	94.4
33	California	91.9
20	Colorado	96.3
40	Connecticut	88.5
34	Delaware	91.8
25	Florida	94.0
24	Georgia	94.1
47	Hawaii	76.7
19	Idaho	96.7
30	Illinois	92.9
1	Indiana	100.0
17	Iowa	98.1
42	Kansas	87.9
12	Kentucky	99.0
23	Louisiana	94.2
NA	Maine**	NA
15	Maryland	98.8
27	Massachusetts	93.3
21	Michigan	94.5
36	Minnesota	90.4
45	Mississippi	79.9
1	Missouri	100.0
32	Montana	92.0
31	Nebraska	92.4
NA	Nevada**	NA
1	New Hampshire	100.0
11	New Jersey	99.1
27	New Mexico	93.3
41	New York	88.4
27	North Carolina	93.3
26	North Dakota	93.8
16	Ohio	98.7
1	Oklahoma	100.0
39	Oregon	89.8
10	Pennsylvania	99.3
48	Rhode Island	75.7
37	South Carolina	90.3
12	South Dakota	99.0
18	Tennessee	97.8
1	Texas	100.0
35	Utah	91.3
1	Vermont	100.0
9	Virginia	99.4
43	Washington	87.6
1	West Virginia	100.0
8	Wisconsin	99.5
44	Wyoming	87.3

RANK ORDER

RANK	STATE	PERCENT
1	Indiana	100.0
1	Missouri	100.0
1	New Hampshire	100.0
1	Oklahoma	100.0
1	Texas	100.0
1	Vermont	100.0
1	West Virginia	100.0
8	Wisconsin	99.5
9	Virginia	99.4
10	Pennsylvania	99.3
11	New Jersey	99.1
12	Kentucky	99.0
12	South Dakota	99.0
14	Arizona	98.9
15	Maryland	98.8
16	Ohio	98.7
17	Iowa	98.1
18	Tennessee	97.8
19	Idaho	96.7
20	Colorado	96.3
21	Michigan	94.5
22	Arkansas	94.4
23	Louisiana	94.2
24	Georgia	94.1
25	Florida	94.0
26	North Dakota	93.8
27	Massachusetts	93.3
27	New Mexico	93.3
27	North Carolina	93.3
30	Illinois	92.9
31	Nebraska	92.4
32	Montana	92.0
33	California	91.9
34	Delaware	91.8
35	Utah	91.3
36	Minnesota	90.4
37	South Carolina	90.3
38	Alabama	90.2
39	Oregon	89.8
40	Connecticut	88.5
41	New York	88.4
42	Kansas	87.9
43	Washington	87.6
44	Wyoming	87.3
45	Alaska	79.9
45	Mississippi	79.9
47	Hawaii	76.7
48	Rhode Island	75.7
NA	Maine**	NA
NA	Nevada**	NA

District of Columbia 84.6

Source: U.S. Department of Education, National Center for Education Statistics
"Public School Graduates and Dropouts: School Year 2008-2009" (http://nces.ed.gov/pubsearch/pubsinfo.asp?pubid=2011312)
*Based on reporting states' totals and excludes students for whom race/ethnicity was not reported. Includes Pacific Islanders. Calculated by comparing estimated number of public high school graduates in 2009 with average membership of the 8th grade in 2004-2005, the 9th grade in 2005-2006, and the 10th grade in 2006-2007. Data exclude ungraded pupils and have not been adjusted for interstate migration or switching to or from private schools. **Not available.

Estimated Averaged Freshman Public High School Graduation Rate for American Indian Students in 2009
Reporting States Rate = 64.8% Graduated*

ALPHA ORDER

RANK	STATE	PERCENT
1	Alabama	84.7
44	Alaska	51.8
42	Arizona	53.8
9	Arkansas	79.2
26	California	65.8
34	Colorado	61.4
35	Connecticut	61.1
7	Delaware	81.6
24	Florida	68.4
12	Georgia	76.1
11	Hawaii	77.0
33	Idaho	61.5
19	Illinois	70.6
23	Indiana	68.6
28	Iowa	63.6
22	Kansas	69.0
48	Kentucky	7.2
21	Louisiana	70.0
NA	Maine**	NA
18	Maryland	71.5
13	Massachusetts	76.0
27	Michigan	64.7
39	Minnesota	56.7
46	Mississippi	49.3
3	Missouri	83.4
29	Montana	63.1
40	Nebraska	56.3
NA	Nevada**	NA
10	New Hampshire	77.6
20	New Jersey	70.5
37	New Mexico	59.9
36	New York	60.6
25	North Carolina	67.2
43	North Dakota	52.4
2	Ohio	83.9
15	Oklahoma	75.5
32	Oregon	62.3
17	Pennsylvania	72.5
14	Rhode Island	75.9
30	South Carolina	62.9
41	South Dakota	54.4
4	Tennessee	83.2
6	Texas	81.9
30	Utah	62.9
5	Vermont	83.0
8	Virginia	79.7
45	Washington	51.3
38	West Virginia	57.1
16	Wisconsin	74.1
47	Wyoming	45.0

RANK ORDER

RANK	STATE	PERCENT
1	Alabama	84.7
2	Ohio	83.9
3	Missouri	83.4
4	Tennessee	83.2
5	Vermont	83.0
6	Texas	81.9
7	Delaware	81.6
8	Virginia	79.7
9	Arkansas	79.2
10	New Hampshire	77.6
11	Hawaii	77.0
12	Georgia	76.1
13	Massachusetts	76.0
14	Rhode Island	75.9
15	Oklahoma	75.5
16	Wisconsin	74.1
17	Pennsylvania	72.5
18	Maryland	71.5
19	Illinois	70.6
20	New Jersey	70.5
21	Louisiana	70.0
22	Kansas	69.0
23	Indiana	68.6
24	Florida	68.4
25	North Carolina	67.2
26	California	65.8
27	Michigan	64.7
28	Iowa	63.6
29	Montana	63.1
30	South Carolina	62.9
30	Utah	62.9
32	Oregon	62.3
33	Idaho	61.5
34	Colorado	61.4
35	Connecticut	61.1
36	New York	60.6
37	New Mexico	59.9
38	West Virginia	57.1
39	Minnesota	56.7
40	Nebraska	56.3
41	South Dakota	54.4
42	Arizona	53.8
43	North Dakota	52.4
44	Alaska	51.8
45	Washington	51.3
46	Mississippi	49.3
47	Wyoming	45.0
48	Kentucky	7.2
NA	Maine**	NA
NA	Nevada**	NA

District of Columbia	100.0

Source: U.S. Department of Education, National Center for Education Statistics
   "Public School Graduates and Dropouts: School Year 2008-2009" (http://nces.ed.gov/pubsearch/pubsinfo.asp?pubid=2011312)
*Based on reporting states' totals and excludes students for whom race/ethnicity was not reported. Includes Alaska Natives.
Calculated by comparing estimated number of public high school graduates in 2009 with average membership of the 8th grade in 2004-2005, the 9th grade in 2005-2006, and the 10th grade in 2006-2007. Data exclude ungraded pupils and have not been adjusted for interstate migration or switching to or from private schools. **Not available.

Private High School Graduates in 2009

National Total = 308,813 Graduates*

ALPHA ORDER

RANK	STATE	GRADUATES	% of USA
20	Alabama	5,277	1.7%
48	Alaska	189	0.1%
29	Arizona	2,755	0.9%
40	Arkansas	1,330	0.4%
1	California	35,256	11.4%
28	Colorado	2,838	0.9%
16	Connecticut	6,233	2.0%
36	Delaware	1,847	0.6%
4	Florida	18,255	5.9%
12	Georgia	8,322	2.7%
30	Hawaii	2,659	0.9%
45	Idaho	543	0.2%
5	Illinois	15,107	4.9%
21	Indiana	5,232	1.7%
33	Iowa	2,249	0.7%
34	Kansas	2,166	0.7%
24	Kentucky	3,937	1.3%
13	Louisiana	8,136	2.6%
32	Maine	2,362	0.8%
10	Maryland	9,228	3.0%
9	Massachusetts	10,630	3.4%
11	Michigan	8,519	2.8%
23	Minnesota	4,241	1.4%
25	Mississippi	3,358	1.1%
14	Missouri	7,043	2.3%
47	Montana	372	0.1%
35	Nebraska	2,004	0.6%
43	Nevada	824	0.3%
31	New Hampshire	2,463	0.8%
6	New Jersey	14,348	4.6%
39	New Mexico	1,387	0.4%
2	New York	31,245	10.1%
18	North Carolina	5,727	1.9%
NA	North Dakota**	NA	NA
7	Ohio	13,303	4.3%
38	Oklahoma	1,531	0.5%
26	Oregon	3,139	1.0%
3	Pennsylvania	18,663	6.0%
37	Rhode Island	1,818	0.6%
27	South Carolina	3,073	1.0%
46	South Dakota	518	0.2%
17	Tennessee	6,219	2.0%
8	Texas	12,903	4.2%
41	Utah	1,270	0.4%
42	Vermont	1,167	0.4%
15	Virginia	6,511	2.1%
22	Washington	4,448	1.4%
44	West Virginia	739	0.2%
19	Wisconsin	5,607	1.8%
NA	Wyoming**	NA	NA

RANK ORDER

RANK	STATE	GRADUATES	% of USA
1	California	35,256	11.4%
2	New York	31,245	10.1%
3	Pennsylvania	18,663	6.0%
4	Florida	18,255	5.9%
5	Illinois	15,107	4.9%
6	New Jersey	14,348	4.6%
7	Ohio	13,303	4.3%
8	Texas	12,903	4.2%
9	Massachusetts	10,630	3.4%
10	Maryland	9,228	3.0%
11	Michigan	8,519	2.8%
12	Georgia	8,322	2.7%
13	Louisiana	8,136	2.6%
14	Missouri	7,043	2.3%
15	Virginia	6,511	2.1%
16	Connecticut	6,233	2.0%
17	Tennessee	6,219	2.0%
18	North Carolina	5,727	1.9%
19	Wisconsin	5,607	1.8%
20	Alabama	5,277	1.7%
21	Indiana	5,232	1.7%
22	Washington	4,448	1.4%
23	Minnesota	4,241	1.4%
24	Kentucky	3,937	1.3%
25	Mississippi	3,358	1.1%
26	Oregon	3,139	1.0%
27	South Carolina	3,073	1.0%
28	Colorado	2,838	0.9%
29	Arizona	2,755	0.9%
30	Hawaii	2,659	0.9%
31	New Hampshire	2,463	0.8%
32	Maine	2,362	0.8%
33	Iowa	2,249	0.7%
34	Kansas	2,166	0.7%
35	Nebraska	2,004	0.6%
36	Delaware	1,847	0.6%
37	Rhode Island	1,818	0.6%
38	Oklahoma	1,531	0.5%
39	New Mexico	1,387	0.4%
40	Arkansas	1,330	0.4%
41	Utah	1,270	0.4%
42	Vermont	1,167	0.4%
43	Nevada	824	0.3%
44	West Virginia	739	0.2%
45	Idaho	543	0.2%
46	South Dakota	518	0.2%
47	Montana	372	0.1%
48	Alaska	189	0.1%
NA	North Dakota**	NA	NA
NA	Wyoming**	NA	NA
	District of Columbia	1,339	0.4%

Source: U.S. Department of Education, National Center for Education Statistics
  "Characteristics of Private Schools in the United States" (http://nces.ed.gov/pubs2011/2011339.pdf)
*For school year 2008-2009.
**Not available.

Public High School Dropouts in 2009

National Total = 607,789 Dropouts*

ALPHA ORDER

RANK	STATE	DROPOUTS	% of USA
36	Alabama	3,292	0.5%
37	Alaska	2,904	0.5%
5	Arizona	26,173	4.3%
27	Arkansas	5,641	0.9%
1	California	101,188	16.6%
12	Colorado	14,571	2.4%
29	Connecticut	5,392	0.9%
44	Delaware	1,987	0.3%
9	Florida	20,609	3.4%
10	Georgia	19,942	3.3%
39	Hawaii	2,598	0.4%
45	Idaho	1,338	0.2%
2	Illinois	73,480	12.1%
28	Indiana	5,429	0.9%
33	Iowa	4,782	0.8%
38	Kansas	2,895	0.5%
26	Kentucky	5,673	0.9%
14	Louisiana	12,282	2.0%
41	Maine	2,264	0.4%
19	Maryland	7,929	1.3%
18	Massachusetts	8,585	1.4%
8	Michigan	20,714	3.4%
30	Minnesota	5,177	0.9%
25	Mississippi	5,835	1.0%
15	Missouri	12,221	2.0%
40	Montana	2,272	0.4%
42	Nebraska	2,178	0.4%
23	Nevada	6,341	1.0%
46	New Hampshire	1,126	0.2%
21	New Jersey	6,926	1.1%
32	New Mexico	4,804	0.8%
4	New York	36,790	6.1%
7	North Carolina	22,966	3.8%
48	North Dakota	757	0.1%
6	Ohio	24,109	4.0%
34	Oklahoma	4,462	0.7%
24	Oregon	6,132	1.0%
13	Pennsylvania	13,519	2.2%
43	Rhode Island	2,086	0.3%
20	South Carolina	7,074	1.2%
49	South Dakota	683	0.1%
17	Tennessee	9,086	1.5%
3	Texas	41,393	6.8%
31	Utah	5,050	0.8%
47	Vermont	784	0.1%
16	Virginia	9,452	1.6%
11	Washington	15,509	2.6%
35	West Virginia	3,444	0.6%
22	Wisconsin	6,412	1.1%
50	Wyoming	287	0.0%

RANK ORDER

RANK	STATE	DROPOUTS	% of USA
1	California	101,188	16.6%
2	Illinois	73,480	12.1%
3	Texas	41,393	6.8%
4	New York	36,790	6.1%
5	Arizona	26,173	4.3%
6	Ohio	24,109	4.0%
7	North Carolina	22,966	3.8%
8	Michigan	20,714	3.4%
9	Florida	20,609	3.4%
10	Georgia	19,942	3.3%
11	Washington	15,509	2.6%
12	Colorado	14,571	2.4%
13	Pennsylvania	13,519	2.2%
14	Louisiana	12,282	2.0%
15	Missouri	12,221	2.0%
16	Virginia	9,452	1.6%
17	Tennessee	9,086	1.5%
18	Massachusetts	8,585	1.4%
19	Maryland	7,929	1.3%
20	South Carolina	7,074	1.2%
21	New Jersey	6,926	1.1%
22	Wisconsin	6,412	1.1%
23	Nevada	6,341	1.0%
24	Oregon	6,132	1.0%
25	Mississippi	5,835	1.0%
26	Kentucky	5,673	0.9%
27	Arkansas	5,641	0.9%
28	Indiana	5,429	0.9%
29	Connecticut	5,392	0.9%
30	Minnesota	5,177	0.9%
31	Utah	5,050	0.8%
32	New Mexico	4,804	0.8%
33	Iowa	4,782	0.8%
34	Oklahoma	4,462	0.7%
35	West Virginia	3,444	0.6%
36	Alabama	3,292	0.5%
37	Alaska	2,904	0.5%
38	Kansas	2,895	0.5%
39	Hawaii	2,598	0.4%
40	Montana	2,272	0.4%
41	Maine	2,264	0.4%
42	Nebraska	2,178	0.4%
43	Rhode Island	2,086	0.3%
44	Delaware	1,987	0.3%
45	Idaho	1,338	0.2%
46	New Hampshire	1,126	0.2%
47	Vermont	784	0.1%
48	North Dakota	757	0.1%
49	South Dakota	683	0.1%
50	Wyoming	287	0.0%
	District of Columbia	1,246	0.2%

Source: U.S. Department of Education, National Center for Education Statistics
"Public School Graduates and Dropouts: School Year 2008-2009" (http://nces.ed.gov/pubsearch/pubsinfo.asp?pubid=2011312)
*"Event" dropout figures showing the number of 9th-12th grade dropouts.

Public High School Dropout Rate in 2009

National Rate = 4.1%*

ALPHA ORDER

RANK	STATE	RATE
49	Alabama	1.5
3	Alaska	7.0
2	Arizona	8.3
20	Arkansas	4.1
9	California	5.0
5	Colorado	6.1
29	Connecticut	3.1
7	Delaware	5.1
34	Florida	2.6
16	Georgia	4.2
11	Hawaii	4.9
47	Idaho	1.6
1	Illinois	11.5
45	Indiana	1.7
29	Iowa	3.1
42	Kansas	2.1
32	Kentucky	2.9
4	Louisiana	6.8
23	Maine	3.6
31	Maryland	3.0
32	Massachusetts	2.9
22	Michigan	3.8
43	Minnesota	1.9
16	Mississippi	4.2
15	Missouri	4.3
9	Montana	5.0
39	Nebraska	2.4
7	Nevada	5.1
45	New Hampshire	1.7
47	New Jersey	1.6
11	New Mexico	4.9
16	New York	4.2
6	North Carolina	5.3
36	North Dakota	2.5
16	Ohio	4.2
36	Oklahoma	2.5
24	Oregon	3.4
40	Pennsylvania	2.3
14	Rhode Island	4.4
24	South Carolina	3.4
44	South Dakota	1.8
27	Tennessee	3.2
27	Texas	3.2
26	Utah	3.3
34	Vermont	2.6
36	Virginia	2.5
13	Washington	4.7
20	West Virginia	4.1
40	Wisconsin	2.3
50	Wyoming	1.1

RANK ORDER

RANK	STATE	RATE
1	Illinois	11.5
2	Arizona	8.3
3	Alaska	7.0
4	Louisiana	6.8
5	Colorado	6.1
6	North Carolina	5.3
7	Delaware	5.1
7	Nevada	5.1
9	California	5.0
9	Montana	5.0
11	Hawaii	4.9
11	New Mexico	4.9
13	Washington	4.7
14	Rhode Island	4.4
15	Missouri	4.3
16	Georgia	4.2
16	Mississippi	4.2
16	New York	4.2
16	Ohio	4.2
20	Arkansas	4.1
20	West Virginia	4.1
22	Michigan	3.8
23	Maine	3.6
24	Oregon	3.4
24	South Carolina	3.4
26	Utah	3.3
27	Tennessee	3.2
27	Texas	3.2
29	Connecticut	3.1
29	Iowa	3.1
31	Maryland	3.0
32	Kentucky	2.9
32	Massachusetts	2.9
34	Florida	2.6
34	Vermont	2.6
36	North Dakota	2.5
36	Oklahoma	2.5
36	Virginia	2.5
39	Nebraska	2.4
40	Pennsylvania	2.3
40	Wisconsin	2.3
42	Kansas	2.1
43	Minnesota	1.9
44	South Dakota	1.8
45	Indiana	1.7
45	New Hampshire	1.7
47	Idaho	1.6
47	New Jersey	1.6
49	Alabama	1.5
50	Wyoming	1.1

District of Columbia   7.0

Source: U.S. Department of Education, National Center for Education Statistics
"Public School Graduates and Dropouts: School Year 2008-2009" (http://nces.ed.gov/pubsearch/pubsinfo.asp?pubid=2011312)
*"Event" dropout rates showing the number of 9th-12th grade dropouts divided by the number of students enrolled at the beginning of the school year in those grades.

Male Public High School Dropout Rate in 2009

National Rate = 3.6%*

ALPHA ORDER

RANK	STATE	RATE
42	Alabama	1.8
4	Alaska	7.6
3	Arizona	7.9
16	Arkansas	4.7
NA	California**	NA
5	Colorado	6.7
22	Connecticut	3.9
6	Delaware	6.2
29	Florida	3.0
12	Georgia	5.1
9	Hawaii	5.4
42	Idaho	1.8
1	Illinois	11.5
39	Indiana	2.0
26	Iowa	3.6
37	Kansas	2.4
30	Kentucky	2.9
2	Louisiana	8.2
21	Maine	4.0
NA	Maryland**	NA
27	Massachusetts	3.4
19	Michigan	4.4
38	Minnesota	2.1
14	Mississippi	5.0
16	Missouri	4.7
8	Montana	5.6
32	Nebraska	2.8
NA	Nevada**	NA
39	New Hampshire	2.0
42	New Jersey	1.8
9	New Mexico	5.4
15	New York	4.9
6	North Carolina	6.2
35	North Dakota	2.6
20	Ohio	4.3
33	Oklahoma	2.7
24	Oregon	3.7
35	Pennsylvania	2.6
11	Rhode Island	5.2
23	South Carolina	3.8
41	South Dakota	1.9
24	Tennessee	3.7
27	Texas	3.4
NA	Utah**	NA
NA	Vermont**	NA
30	Virginia	2.9
12	Washington	5.1
18	West Virginia	4.5
33	Wisconsin	2.7
45	Wyoming	1.1

RANK ORDER

RANK	STATE	RATE
1	Illinois	11.5
2	Louisiana	8.2
3	Arizona	7.9
4	Alaska	7.6
5	Colorado	6.7
6	Delaware	6.2
6	North Carolina	6.2
8	Montana	5.6
9	Hawaii	5.4
9	New Mexico	5.4
11	Rhode Island	5.2
12	Georgia	5.1
12	Washington	5.1
14	Mississippi	5.0
15	New York	4.9
16	Arkansas	4.7
16	Missouri	4.7
18	West Virginia	4.5
19	Michigan	4.4
20	Ohio	4.3
21	Maine	4.0
22	Connecticut	3.9
23	South Carolina	3.8
24	Oregon	3.7
24	Tennessee	3.7
26	Iowa	3.6
27	Massachusetts	3.4
27	Texas	3.4
29	Florida	3.0
30	Kentucky	2.9
30	Virginia	2.9
32	Nebraska	2.8
33	Oklahoma	2.7
33	Wisconsin	2.7
35	North Dakota	2.6
35	Pennsylvania	2.6
37	Kansas	2.4
38	Minnesota	2.1
39	Indiana	2.0
39	New Hampshire	2.0
41	South Dakota	1.9
42	Alabama	1.8
42	Idaho	1.8
42	New Jersey	1.8
45	Wyoming	1.1
NA	California**	NA
NA	Maryland**	NA
NA	Nevada**	NA
NA	Utah**	NA
NA	Vermont**	NA
	District of Columbia	7.6

Source: U.S. Department of Education, National Center for Education Statistics
"Public School Graduates and Dropouts: School Year 2008-2009" (http://nces.ed.gov/pubsearch/pubsinfo.asp?pubid=2011312)
*"Event" dropout rates showing the number of 9th-12th grade dropouts divided by the number of students enrolled at the beginning of the school year in those grades. National rate is for reporting states.
**Not available.

Female Public High School Dropout Rate in 2009

National Rate = 2.7%*

<table>
<tr><td colspan="3">ALPHA ORDER</td><td colspan="3">RANK ORDER</td></tr>
<tr><td>RANK</td><td>STATE</td><td>RATE</td><td>RANK</td><td>STATE</td><td>RATE</td></tr>
<tr><td>44</td><td>Alabama</td><td>1.2</td><td>1</td><td>Illinois</td><td>8.6</td></tr>
<tr><td>2</td><td>Alaska</td><td>6.4</td><td>2</td><td>Alaska</td><td>6.4</td></tr>
<tr><td>2</td><td>Arizona</td><td>6.4</td><td>2</td><td>Arizona</td><td>6.4</td></tr>
<tr><td>17</td><td>Arkansas</td><td>3.5</td><td>4</td><td>Colorado</td><td>5.6</td></tr>
<tr><td>NA</td><td>California**</td><td>NA</td><td>5</td><td>Louisiana</td><td>5.5</td></tr>
<tr><td>4</td><td>Colorado</td><td>5.6</td><td>6</td><td>Montana</td><td>4.5</td></tr>
<tr><td>32</td><td>Connecticut</td><td>2.2</td><td>7</td><td>New Mexico</td><td>4.4</td></tr>
<tr><td>11</td><td>Delaware</td><td>4.0</td><td>8</td><td>North Carolina</td><td>4.3</td></tr>
<tr><td>29</td><td>Florida</td><td>2.3</td><td>9</td><td>Hawaii</td><td>4.2</td></tr>
<tr><td>18</td><td>Georgia</td><td>3.4</td><td>10</td><td>Washington</td><td>4.1</td></tr>
<tr><td>9</td><td>Hawaii</td><td>4.2</td><td>11</td><td>Delaware</td><td>4.0</td></tr>
<tr><td>40</td><td>Idaho</td><td>1.5</td><td>12</td><td>Ohio</td><td>3.8</td></tr>
<tr><td>1</td><td>Illinois</td><td>8.6</td><td>13</td><td>Missouri</td><td>3.7</td></tr>
<tr><td>41</td><td>Indiana</td><td>1.4</td><td>13</td><td>Rhode Island</td><td>3.7</td></tr>
<tr><td>25</td><td>Iowa</td><td>2.7</td><td>13</td><td>West Virginia</td><td>3.7</td></tr>
<tr><td>37</td><td>Kansas</td><td>1.7</td><td>16</td><td>New York</td><td>3.6</td></tr>
<tr><td>29</td><td>Kentucky</td><td>2.3</td><td>17</td><td>Arkansas</td><td>3.5</td></tr>
<tr><td>5</td><td>Louisiana</td><td>5.5</td><td>18</td><td>Georgia</td><td>3.4</td></tr>
<tr><td>20</td><td>Maine</td><td>3.2</td><td>18</td><td>Mississippi</td><td>3.4</td></tr>
<tr><td>NA</td><td>Maryland**</td><td>NA</td><td>20</td><td>Maine</td><td>3.2</td></tr>
<tr><td>27</td><td>Massachusetts</td><td>2.5</td><td>20</td><td>Michigan</td><td>3.2</td></tr>
<tr><td>20</td><td>Michigan</td><td>3.2</td><td>20</td><td>Oregon</td><td>3.2</td></tr>
<tr><td>38</td><td>Minnesota</td><td>1.6</td><td>23</td><td>Texas</td><td>3.0</td></tr>
<tr><td>18</td><td>Mississippi</td><td>3.4</td><td>24</td><td>South Carolina</td><td>2.9</td></tr>
<tr><td>13</td><td>Missouri</td><td>3.7</td><td>25</td><td>Iowa</td><td>2.7</td></tr>
<tr><td>6</td><td>Montana</td><td>4.5</td><td>26</td><td>Tennessee</td><td>2.6</td></tr>
<tr><td>34</td><td>Nebraska</td><td>2.0</td><td>27</td><td>Massachusetts</td><td>2.5</td></tr>
<tr><td>NA</td><td>Nevada**</td><td>NA</td><td>28</td><td>North Dakota</td><td>2.4</td></tr>
<tr><td>41</td><td>New Hampshire</td><td>1.4</td><td>29</td><td>Florida</td><td>2.3</td></tr>
<tr><td>41</td><td>New Jersey</td><td>1.4</td><td>29</td><td>Kentucky</td><td>2.3</td></tr>
<tr><td>7</td><td>New Mexico</td><td>4.4</td><td>29</td><td>Oklahoma</td><td>2.3</td></tr>
<tr><td>16</td><td>New York</td><td>3.6</td><td>32</td><td>Connecticut</td><td>2.2</td></tr>
<tr><td>8</td><td>North Carolina</td><td>4.3</td><td>33</td><td>Virginia</td><td>2.1</td></tr>
<tr><td>28</td><td>North Dakota</td><td>2.4</td><td>34</td><td>Nebraska</td><td>2.0</td></tr>
<tr><td>12</td><td>Ohio</td><td>3.8</td><td>34</td><td>Pennsylvania</td><td>2.0</td></tr>
<tr><td>29</td><td>Oklahoma</td><td>2.3</td><td>36</td><td>Wisconsin</td><td>1.8</td></tr>
<tr><td>20</td><td>Oregon</td><td>3.2</td><td>37</td><td>Kansas</td><td>1.7</td></tr>
<tr><td>34</td><td>Pennsylvania</td><td>2.0</td><td>38</td><td>Minnesota</td><td>1.6</td></tr>
<tr><td>13</td><td>Rhode Island</td><td>3.7</td><td>38</td><td>South Dakota</td><td>1.6</td></tr>
<tr><td>24</td><td>South Carolina</td><td>2.9</td><td>40</td><td>Idaho</td><td>1.5</td></tr>
<tr><td>38</td><td>South Dakota</td><td>1.6</td><td>41</td><td>Indiana</td><td>1.4</td></tr>
<tr><td>26</td><td>Tennessee</td><td>2.6</td><td>41</td><td>New Hampshire</td><td>1.4</td></tr>
<tr><td>23</td><td>Texas</td><td>3.0</td><td>41</td><td>New Jersey</td><td>1.4</td></tr>
<tr><td>NA</td><td>Utah**</td><td>NA</td><td>44</td><td>Alabama</td><td>1.2</td></tr>
<tr><td>NA</td><td>Vermont**</td><td>NA</td><td>45</td><td>Wyoming</td><td>0.8</td></tr>
<tr><td>33</td><td>Virginia</td><td>2.1</td><td>NA</td><td>California**</td><td>NA</td></tr>
<tr><td>10</td><td>Washington</td><td>4.1</td><td>NA</td><td>Maryland**</td><td>NA</td></tr>
<tr><td>13</td><td>West Virginia</td><td>3.7</td><td>NA</td><td>Nevada**</td><td>NA</td></tr>
<tr><td>36</td><td>Wisconsin</td><td>1.8</td><td>NA</td><td>Utah**</td><td>NA</td></tr>
<tr><td>45</td><td>Wyoming</td><td>0.8</td><td>NA</td><td>Vermont**</td><td>NA</td></tr>
<tr><td></td><td></td><td></td><td></td><td>District of Columbia</td><td>5.9</td></tr>
</table>

Source: U.S. Department of Education, National Center for Education Statistics
    "Public School Graduates and Dropouts: School Year 2008-2009" (http://nces.ed.gov/pubsearch/pubsinfo.asp?pubid=2011312)
*"Event" dropout rates showing the number of 9th-12th grade dropouts divided by the number of students enrolled at the beginning
of the school year in those grades. National rate is for reporting states.
**Not available.

White Public High School Dropout Rate in 2009

National Rate = 2.7%*

ALPHA ORDER

RANK	STATE	RATE
41	Alabama	1.4
49	Alaska	0.2
2	Arizona	6.1
13	Arkansas	3.5
17	California	3.2
11	Colorado	3.7
41	Connecticut	1.4
6	Delaware	4.1
31	Florida	1.8
16	Georgia	3.4
3	Hawaii	5.3
41	Idaho	1.4
1	Illinois	8.0
39	Indiana	1.5
23	Iowa	2.7
31	Kansas	1.8
24	Kentucky	2.6
4	Louisiana	4.7
13	Maine	3.5
27	Maryland	2.3
31	Massachusetts	1.8
24	Michigan	2.6
45	Minnesota	1.2
17	Mississippi	3.2
20	Missouri	3.1
6	Montana	4.1
34	Nebraska	1.7
11	Nevada	3.7
34	New Hampshire	1.7
47	New Jersey	0.9
10	New Mexico	3.8
29	New York	2.0
5	North Carolina	4.6
34	North Dakota	1.7
22	Ohio	2.8
27	Oklahoma	2.3
21	Oregon	2.9
38	Pennsylvania	1.6
13	Rhode Island	3.5
17	South Carolina	3.2
45	South Dakota	1.2
29	Tennessee	2.0
39	Texas	1.5
24	Utah	2.6
NA	Vermont**	NA
34	Virginia	1.7
9	Washington	4.0
6	West Virginia	4.1
44	Wisconsin	1.3
48	Wyoming	0.7

RANK ORDER

RANK	STATE	RATE
1	Illinois	8.0
2	Arizona	6.1
3	Hawaii	5.3
4	Louisiana	4.7
5	North Carolina	4.6
6	Delaware	4.1
6	Montana	4.1
6	West Virginia	4.1
9	Washington	4.0
10	New Mexico	3.8
11	Colorado	3.7
11	Nevada	3.7
13	Arkansas	3.5
13	Maine	3.5
13	Rhode Island	3.5
16	Georgia	3.4
17	California	3.2
17	Mississippi	3.2
17	South Carolina	3.2
20	Missouri	3.1
21	Oregon	2.9
22	Ohio	2.8
23	Iowa	2.7
24	Kentucky	2.6
24	Michigan	2.6
24	Utah	2.6
27	Maryland	2.3
27	Oklahoma	2.3
29	New York	2.0
29	Tennessee	2.0
31	Florida	1.8
31	Kansas	1.8
31	Massachusetts	1.8
34	Nebraska	1.7
34	New Hampshire	1.7
34	North Dakota	1.7
34	Virginia	1.7
38	Pennsylvania	1.6
39	Indiana	1.5
39	Texas	1.5
41	Alabama	1.4
41	Connecticut	1.4
41	Idaho	1.4
44	Wisconsin	1.3
45	Minnesota	1.2
45	South Dakota	1.2
47	New Jersey	0.9
48	Wyoming	0.7
49	Alaska	0.2
NA	Vermont**	NA
	District of Columbia	4.8

Source: U.S. Department of Education, National Center for Education Statistics
"Public School Graduates and Dropouts: School Year 2008-2009" (http://nces.ed.gov/pubsearch/pubsinfo.asp?pubid=2011312)
*"Event" dropout rates showing the number of 9th-12th grade dropouts divided by the number of students enrolled at the beginning of the school year in those grades. National rate is for reporting states. Does not include white Hispanics.
**Not available.

Black Public High School Dropout Rate in 2009

National Rate = 6.6%*

ALPHA ORDER				RANK ORDER		
RANK	STATE	RATE		RANK	STATE	RATE
46	Alabama	1.7		1	Illinois	20.0
49	Alaska	0.5		2	Arizona	10.1
2	Arizona	10.1		3	Ohio	9.9
23	Arkansas	5.7		4	Colorado	9.6
7	California	9.2		4	Missouri	9.6
4	Colorado	9.6		6	Louisiana	9.4
16	Connecticut	6.8		7	California	9.2
14	Delaware	6.9		8	Wisconsin	8.0
37	Florida	4.3		9	Iowa	7.9
26	Georgia	5.3		9	Michigan	7.9
33	Hawaii	4.6		11	New York	7.6
47	Idaho	1.3		12	Montana	7.5
1	Illinois	20.0		13	Washington	7.2
43	Indiana	2.7		14	Delaware	6.9
9	Iowa	7.9		14	Nevada	6.9
42	Kansas	3.1		16	Connecticut	6.8
31	Kentucky	4.8		17	Tennessee	6.4
6	Louisiana	9.4		18	Rhode Island	6.3
35	Maine	4.5		19	Oregon	6.1
38	Maryland	3.9		20	Nebraska	6.0
24	Massachusetts	5.6		20	New Hampshire	6.0
9	Michigan	7.9		20	North Carolina	6.0
32	Minnesota	4.7		23	Arkansas	5.7
28	Mississippi	5.2		24	Massachusetts	5.6
4	Missouri	9.6		25	North Dakota	5.5
12	Montana	7.5		26	Georgia	5.3
20	Nebraska	6.0		26	Utah	5.3
14	Nevada	6.9		28	Mississippi	5.2
20	New Hampshire	6.0		28	New Mexico	5.2
41	New Jersey	3.4		30	Texas	5.0
28	New Mexico	5.2		31	Kentucky	4.8
11	New York	7.6		32	Minnesota	4.7
20	North Carolina	6.0		33	Hawaii	4.6
25	North Dakota	5.5		33	Pennsylvania	4.6
3	Ohio	9.9		35	Maine	4.5
43	Oklahoma	2.7		36	West Virginia	4.4
19	Oregon	6.1		37	Florida	4.3
33	Pennsylvania	4.6		38	Maryland	3.9
18	Rhode Island	6.3		38	Virginia	3.9
40	South Carolina	3.6		40	South Carolina	3.6
48	South Dakota	0.8		41	New Jersey	3.4
17	Tennessee	6.4		42	Kansas	3.1
30	Texas	5.0		43	Indiana	2.7
26	Utah	5.3		43	Oklahoma	2.7
NA	Vermont**	NA		43	Wyoming	2.7
38	Virginia	3.9		46	Alabama	1.7
13	Washington	7.2		47	Idaho	1.3
36	West Virginia	4.4		48	South Dakota	0.8
8	Wisconsin	8.0		49	Alaska	0.5
43	Wyoming	2.7		NA	Vermont**	NA
					District of Columbia	6.9

Source: U.S. Department of Education, National Center for Education Statistics
   "Public School Graduates and Dropouts: School Year 2008-2009" (http://nces.ed.gov/pubsearch/pubsinfo.asp?pubid=2011312)
*"Event" dropout rates showing the number of 9th-12th grade dropouts divided by the number of students enrolled at the beginning of the school year in those grades. National rate is for reporting states. Does not include black Hispanics.
**Not available.

Hispanic Public High School Dropout Rate in 2009

National Rate = 6.0%*

ALPHA ORDER

RANK	STATE	RATE
48	Alabama	1.6
49	Alaska	0.2
3	Arizona	10.2
29	Arkansas	4.7
16	California	6.2
2	Colorado	11.4
8	Connecticut	7.4
14	Delaware	6.6
42	Florida	3.0
29	Georgia	4.7
27	Hawaii	4.8
41	Idaho	3.1
1	Illinois	13.4
46	Indiana	2.3
19	Iowa	5.3
42	Kansas	3.0
35	Kentucky	4.0
4	Louisiana	8.5
32	Maine	4.4
34	Maryland	4.1
7	Massachusetts	7.5
18	Michigan	5.6
23	Minnesota	5.0
40	Mississippi	3.2
26	Missouri	4.9
5	Montana	8.3
29	Nebraska	4.7
14	Nevada	6.6
47	New Hampshire	2.1
44	New Jersey	2.9
23	New Mexico	5.0
11	New York	7.1
9	North Carolina	7.3
20	North Dakota	5.2
6	Ohio	7.8
38	Oklahoma	3.7
22	Oregon	5.1
17	Pennsylvania	5.9
10	Rhode Island	7.2
36	South Carolina	3.9
39	South Dakota	3.5
36	Tennessee	3.9
33	Texas	4.2
12	Utah	6.7
NA	Vermont**	NA
23	Virginia	5.0
12	Washington	6.7
27	West Virginia	4.8
20	Wisconsin	5.2
45	Wyoming	2.7

RANK ORDER

RANK	STATE	RATE
1	Illinois	13.4
2	Colorado	11.4
3	Arizona	10.2
4	Louisiana	8.5
5	Montana	8.3
6	Ohio	7.8
7	Massachusetts	7.5
8	Connecticut	7.4
9	North Carolina	7.3
10	Rhode Island	7.2
11	New York	7.1
12	Utah	6.7
12	Washington	6.7
14	Delaware	6.6
14	Nevada	6.6
16	California	6.2
17	Pennsylvania	5.9
18	Michigan	5.6
19	Iowa	5.3
20	North Dakota	5.2
20	Wisconsin	5.2
22	Oregon	5.1
23	Minnesota	5.0
23	New Mexico	5.0
23	Virginia	5.0
26	Missouri	4.9
27	Hawaii	4.8
27	West Virginia	4.8
29	Arkansas	4.7
29	Georgia	4.7
29	Nebraska	4.7
32	Maine	4.4
33	Texas	4.2
34	Maryland	4.1
35	Kentucky	4.0
36	South Carolina	3.9
36	Tennessee	3.9
38	Oklahoma	3.7
39	South Dakota	3.5
40	Mississippi	3.2
41	Idaho	3.1
42	Florida	3.0
42	Kansas	3.0
44	New Jersey	2.9
45	Wyoming	2.7
46	Indiana	2.3
47	New Hampshire	2.1
48	Alabama	1.6
49	Alaska	0.2
NA	Vermont**	NA
	District of Columbia	8.3

Source: U.S. Department of Education, National Center for Education Statistics
  "Public School Graduates and Dropouts: School Year 2008-2009" (http://nces.ed.gov/pubsearch/pubsinfo.asp?pubid=2011312)
*"Event" dropout rates showing the number of 9th-12th grade dropouts divided by the number of students enrolled at the beginning of the school year in those grades. National rate is for reporting states. Hispanics can be of any race.
**Not available.

Asian Public High School Dropout Rate in 2009

National Rate = 2.4%*

ALPHA ORDER

RANK	STATE	RATE
45	Alabama	0.7
49	Alaska	0.0
2	Arizona	5.0
4	Arkansas	3.8
15	California	2.4
7	Colorado	3.4
42	Connecticut	0.9
18	Delaware	2.3
42	Florida	0.9
27	Georgia	1.8
3	Hawaii	4.6
22	Idaho	2.0
1	Illinois	8.2
39	Indiana	1.0
15	Iowa	2.4
35	Kansas	1.3
19	Kentucky	2.2
9	Louisiana	3.1
12	Maine	2.8
37	Maryland	1.1
27	Massachusetts	1.8
32	Michigan	1.6
24	Minnesota	1.9
24	Mississippi	1.9
19	Missouri	2.2
6	Montana	3.5
29	Nebraska	1.7
7	Nevada	3.4
45	New Hampshire	0.7
47	New Jersey	0.3
9	New Mexico	3.1
14	New York	2.5
21	North Carolina	2.1
39	North Dakota	1.0
29	Ohio	1.7
24	Oklahoma	1.9
15	Oregon	2.4
33	Pennsylvania	1.5
5	Rhode Island	3.7
34	South Carolina	1.4
44	South Dakota	0.8
29	Tennessee	1.7
39	Texas	1.0
12	Utah	2.8
NA	Vermont**	NA
37	Virginia	1.1
9	Washington	3.1
36	West Virginia	1.2
22	Wisconsin	2.0
47	Wyoming	0.3

RANK ORDER

RANK	STATE	RATE
1	Illinois	8.2
2	Arizona	5.0
3	Hawaii	4.6
4	Arkansas	3.8
5	Rhode Island	3.7
6	Montana	3.5
7	Colorado	3.4
7	Nevada	3.4
9	Louisiana	3.1
9	New Mexico	3.1
9	Washington	3.1
12	Maine	2.8
12	Utah	2.8
14	New York	2.5
15	California	2.4
15	Iowa	2.4
15	Oregon	2.4
18	Delaware	2.3
19	Kentucky	2.2
19	Missouri	2.2
21	North Carolina	2.1
22	Idaho	2.0
22	Wisconsin	2.0
24	Minnesota	1.9
24	Mississippi	1.9
24	Oklahoma	1.9
27	Georgia	1.8
27	Massachusetts	1.8
29	Nebraska	1.7
29	Ohio	1.7
29	Tennessee	1.7
32	Michigan	1.6
33	Pennsylvania	1.5
34	South Carolina	1.4
35	Kansas	1.3
36	West Virginia	1.2
37	Maryland	1.1
37	Virginia	1.1
39	Indiana	1.0
39	North Dakota	1.0
39	Texas	1.0
42	Connecticut	0.9
42	Florida	0.9
44	South Dakota	0.8
45	Alabama	0.7
45	New Hampshire	0.7
47	New Jersey	0.3
47	Wyoming	0.3
49	Alaska	0.0
NA	Vermont**	NA

District of Columbia	5.3

Source: U.S. Department of Education, National Center for Education Statistics
   "Public School Graduates and Dropouts: School Year 2008-2009" (http://nces.ed.gov/pubsearch/pubsinfo.asp?pubid=2011312)
*"Event" dropout rates showing the number of 9th-12th grade dropouts divided by the number of students enrolled at the beginning
of the school year in those grades. National rate is for reporting states. Includes Pacific Islanders.
**Not available.

American Indian Public High School Dropout Rate in 2009

National Rate = 6.3%*

<table>
<tr><td colspan="3">ALPHA ORDER</td><td colspan="3">RANK ORDER</td></tr>
<tr><td>RANK</td><td>STATE</td><td>RATE</td><td>RANK</td><td>STATE</td><td>RATE</td></tr>
<tr><td>48</td><td>Alabama</td><td>1.2</td><td>1</td><td>Illinois</td><td>15.3</td></tr>
<tr><td>48</td><td>Alaska</td><td>1.2</td><td>2</td><td>Arizona</td><td>12.9</td></tr>
<tr><td>2</td><td>Arizona</td><td>12.9</td><td>3</td><td>Colorado</td><td>12.3</td></tr>
<tr><td>30</td><td>Arkansas</td><td>4.5</td><td>3</td><td>Montana</td><td>12.3</td></tr>
<tr><td>14</td><td>California</td><td>6.8</td><td>5</td><td>Washington</td><td>9.4</td></tr>
<tr><td>3</td><td>Colorado</td><td>12.3</td><td>6</td><td>Maine</td><td>8.9</td></tr>
<tr><td>45</td><td>Connecticut</td><td>2.4</td><td>7</td><td>North Dakota</td><td>8.7</td></tr>
<tr><td>25</td><td>Delaware</td><td>5.4</td><td>8</td><td>Minnesota</td><td>8.5</td></tr>
<tr><td>41</td><td>Florida</td><td>2.9</td><td>9</td><td>West Virginia</td><td>8.4</td></tr>
<tr><td>46</td><td>Georgia</td><td>2.3</td><td>10</td><td>North Carolina</td><td>7.7</td></tr>
<tr><td>16</td><td>Hawaii</td><td>6.6</td><td>11</td><td>Ohio</td><td>7.6</td></tr>
<tr><td>42</td><td>Idaho</td><td>2.7</td><td>12</td><td>Utah</td><td>7.4</td></tr>
<tr><td>1</td><td>Illinois</td><td>15.3</td><td>13</td><td>New Mexico</td><td>7.1</td></tr>
<tr><td>38</td><td>Indiana</td><td>3.0</td><td>14</td><td>California</td><td>6.8</td></tr>
<tr><td>22</td><td>Iowa</td><td>6.0</td><td>15</td><td>New York</td><td>6.7</td></tr>
<tr><td>38</td><td>Kansas</td><td>3.0</td><td>16</td><td>Hawaii</td><td>6.6</td></tr>
<tr><td>38</td><td>Kentucky</td><td>3.0</td><td>16</td><td>Louisiana</td><td>6.6</td></tr>
<tr><td>16</td><td>Louisiana</td><td>6.6</td><td>18</td><td>Michigan</td><td>6.4</td></tr>
<tr><td>6</td><td>Maine</td><td>8.9</td><td>18</td><td>Oregon</td><td>6.4</td></tr>
<tr><td>27</td><td>Maryland</td><td>5.3</td><td>20</td><td>South Carolina</td><td>6.3</td></tr>
<tr><td>32</td><td>Massachusetts</td><td>4.3</td><td>21</td><td>South Dakota</td><td>6.2</td></tr>
<tr><td>18</td><td>Michigan</td><td>6.4</td><td>22</td><td>Iowa</td><td>6.0</td></tr>
<tr><td>8</td><td>Minnesota</td><td>8.5</td><td>23</td><td>Nevada</td><td>5.8</td></tr>
<tr><td>33</td><td>Mississippi</td><td>3.9</td><td>24</td><td>Nebraska</td><td>5.5</td></tr>
<tr><td>28</td><td>Missouri</td><td>5.0</td><td>25</td><td>Delaware</td><td>5.4</td></tr>
<tr><td>3</td><td>Montana</td><td>12.3</td><td>25</td><td>Rhode Island</td><td>5.4</td></tr>
<tr><td>24</td><td>Nebraska</td><td>5.5</td><td>27</td><td>Maryland</td><td>5.3</td></tr>
<tr><td>23</td><td>Nevada</td><td>5.8</td><td>28</td><td>Missouri</td><td>5.0</td></tr>
<tr><td>37</td><td>New Hampshire</td><td>3.1</td><td>29</td><td>Wisconsin</td><td>4.9</td></tr>
<tr><td>34</td><td>New Jersey</td><td>3.5</td><td>30</td><td>Arkansas</td><td>4.5</td></tr>
<tr><td>13</td><td>New Mexico</td><td>7.1</td><td>30</td><td>Wyoming</td><td>4.5</td></tr>
<tr><td>15</td><td>New York</td><td>6.7</td><td>32</td><td>Massachusetts</td><td>4.3</td></tr>
<tr><td>10</td><td>North Carolina</td><td>7.7</td><td>33</td><td>Mississippi</td><td>3.9</td></tr>
<tr><td>7</td><td>North Dakota</td><td>8.7</td><td>34</td><td>New Jersey</td><td>3.5</td></tr>
<tr><td>11</td><td>Ohio</td><td>7.6</td><td>35</td><td>Pennsylvania</td><td>3.4</td></tr>
<tr><td>44</td><td>Oklahoma</td><td>2.6</td><td>36</td><td>Virginia</td><td>3.2</td></tr>
<tr><td>18</td><td>Oregon</td><td>6.4</td><td>37</td><td>New Hampshire</td><td>3.1</td></tr>
<tr><td>35</td><td>Pennsylvania</td><td>3.4</td><td>38</td><td>Indiana</td><td>3.0</td></tr>
<tr><td>25</td><td>Rhode Island</td><td>5.4</td><td>38</td><td>Kansas</td><td>3.0</td></tr>
<tr><td>20</td><td>South Carolina</td><td>6.3</td><td>38</td><td>Kentucky</td><td>3.0</td></tr>
<tr><td>21</td><td>South Dakota</td><td>6.2</td><td>41</td><td>Florida</td><td>2.9</td></tr>
<tr><td>42</td><td>Tennessee</td><td>2.7</td><td>42</td><td>Idaho</td><td>2.7</td></tr>
<tr><td>47</td><td>Texas</td><td>2.2</td><td>42</td><td>Tennessee</td><td>2.7</td></tr>
<tr><td>12</td><td>Utah</td><td>7.4</td><td>44</td><td>Oklahoma</td><td>2.6</td></tr>
<tr><td>NA</td><td>Vermont**</td><td>NA</td><td>45</td><td>Connecticut</td><td>2.4</td></tr>
<tr><td>36</td><td>Virginia</td><td>3.2</td><td>46</td><td>Georgia</td><td>2.3</td></tr>
<tr><td>5</td><td>Washington</td><td>9.4</td><td>47</td><td>Texas</td><td>2.2</td></tr>
<tr><td>9</td><td>West Virginia</td><td>8.4</td><td>48</td><td>Alabama</td><td>1.2</td></tr>
<tr><td>29</td><td>Wisconsin</td><td>4.9</td><td>48</td><td>Alaska</td><td>1.2</td></tr>
<tr><td>30</td><td>Wyoming</td><td>4.5</td><td>NA</td><td>Vermont**</td><td>NA</td></tr>
<tr><td></td><td></td><td></td><td></td><td>District of Columbia</td><td>0.0</td></tr>
</table>

Source: U.S. Department of Education, National Center for Education Statistics
   "Public School Graduates and Dropouts: School Year 2008-2009" (http://nces.ed.gov/pubsearch/pubsinfo.asp?pubid=2011312)
*"Event" dropout rates showing the number of 9th-12th grade dropouts divided by the number of students enrolled at the beginning of the school year in those grades. National rate is for reporting states. Includes Alaska Natives.
**Not available.

ACT Average Composite Score in 2011

National Average = 21.1*

ALPHA ORDER

RANK	STATE	AVERAGE SCORE
39	Alabama	20.3
31	Alaska	21.2
46	Arizona	19.7
44	Arkansas	19.9
17	California	22.1
34	Colorado	20.7
2	Connecticut	23.9
11	Delaware	22.4
47	Florida	19.6
37	Georgia	20.6
30	Hawaii	21.3
26	Idaho	21.7
32	Illinois	20.9
12	Indiana	22.3
12	Iowa	22.3
21	Kansas	22.0
47	Kentucky	19.6
41	Louisiana	20.2
5	Maine	23.3
17	Maryland	22.1
1	Massachusetts	24.2
43	Michigan	20.0
8	Minnesota	22.9
50	Mississippi	18.7
27	Missouri	21.6
17	Montana	22.1
17	Nebraska	22.1
29	Nevada	21.4
3	New Hampshire	23.7
6	New Jersey	23.2
45	New Mexico	19.8
4	New York	23.4
22	North Carolina	21.9
34	North Dakota	20.7
23	Ohio	21.8
34	Oklahoma	20.7
28	Oregon	21.5
12	Pennsylvania	22.3
7	Rhode Island	23.0
42	South Carolina	20.1
23	South Dakota	21.8
49	Tennessee	19.5
33	Texas	20.8
23	Utah	21.8
10	Vermont	22.7
12	Virginia	22.3
9	Washington	22.8
37	West Virginia	20.6
16	Wisconsin	22.2
39	Wyoming	20.3

RANK ORDER

RANK	STATE	AVERAGE SCORE
1	Massachusetts	24.2
2	Connecticut	23.9
3	New Hampshire	23.7
4	New York	23.4
5	Maine	23.3
6	New Jersey	23.2
7	Rhode Island	23.0
8	Minnesota	22.9
9	Washington	22.8
10	Vermont	22.7
11	Delaware	22.4
12	Indiana	22.3
12	Iowa	22.3
12	Pennsylvania	22.3
12	Virginia	22.3
16	Wisconsin	22.2
17	California	22.1
17	Maryland	22.1
17	Montana	22.1
17	Nebraska	22.1
21	Kansas	22.0
22	North Carolina	21.9
23	Ohio	21.8
23	South Dakota	21.8
23	Utah	21.8
26	Idaho	21.7
27	Missouri	21.6
28	Oregon	21.5
29	Nevada	21.4
30	Hawaii	21.3
31	Alaska	21.2
32	Illinois	20.9
33	Texas	20.8
34	Colorado	20.7
34	North Dakota	20.7
34	Oklahoma	20.7
37	Georgia	20.6
37	West Virginia	20.6
39	Alabama	20.3
39	Wyoming	20.3
41	Louisiana	20.2
42	South Carolina	20.1
43	Michigan	20.0
44	Arkansas	19.9
45	New Mexico	19.8
46	Arizona	19.7
47	Florida	19.6
47	Kentucky	19.6
49	Tennessee	19.5
50	Mississippi	18.7

| | District of Columbia | 20.0 |

Source: The American College Testing Program (Copyright © 2011)
 "Average ACT Scores by State" (http://www.act.org/news/data.html)
*The ACT score range is 1 to 36. Approximately 1.6 million 2011 U.S. high school students took the test. Caution should be used in using ACT scores to compare states. The percentage of high school students taking the test varies greatly from one state to another. For example, all 11th grade students in Colorado, Illinois, Kentucky, Louisiana, Michigan, Mississippi, Tennessee, and Wyoming are required to take the test but, in Maine, only 9 percent of 11th grade students took the test.

ACT Average Mathematics Score in 2011

National Average = 21.1*

ALPHA ORDER

RANK	STATE	AVERAGE SCORE
45	Alabama	19.6
28	Alaska	21.4
37	Arizona	20.3
43	Arkansas	19.7
10	California	22.7
36	Colorado	20.4
2	Connecticut	23.9
13	Delaware	22.4
40	Florida	19.9
35	Georgia	20.7
21	Hawaii	21.8
30	Idaho	21.3
33	Illinois	20.9
13	Indiana	22.4
19	Iowa	21.9
21	Kansas	21.8
48	Kentucky	19.1
43	Louisiana	19.7
6	Maine	23.2
16	Maryland	22.2
1	Massachusetts	24.6
40	Michigan	19.9
7	Minnesota	23.0
50	Mississippi	18.2
32	Missouri	21.0
19	Montana	21.9
24	Nebraska	21.7
28	Nevada	21.4
4	New Hampshire	23.7
4	New Jersey	23.7
46	New Mexico	19.5
3	New York	23.8
13	North Carolina	22.4
34	North Dakota	20.8
26	Ohio	21.5
40	Oklahoma	19.9
25	Oregon	21.6
11	Pennsylvania	22.6
9	Rhode Island	22.8
37	South Carolina	20.3
21	South Dakota	21.8
49	Tennessee	19.0
26	Texas	21.5
31	Utah	21.2
11	Vermont	22.6
16	Virginia	22.2
8	Washington	22.9
46	West Virginia	19.5
18	Wisconsin	22.1
39	Wyoming	20.0

RANK ORDER

RANK	STATE	AVERAGE SCORE
1	Massachusetts	24.6
2	Connecticut	23.9
3	New York	23.8
4	New Hampshire	23.7
4	New Jersey	23.7
6	Maine	23.2
7	Minnesota	23.0
8	Washington	22.9
9	Rhode Island	22.8
10	California	22.7
11	Pennsylvania	22.6
11	Vermont	22.6
13	Delaware	22.4
13	Indiana	22.4
13	North Carolina	22.4
16	Maryland	22.2
16	Virginia	22.2
18	Wisconsin	22.1
19	Iowa	21.9
19	Montana	21.9
21	Hawaii	21.8
21	Kansas	21.8
21	South Dakota	21.8
24	Nebraska	21.7
25	Oregon	21.6
26	Ohio	21.5
26	Texas	21.5
28	Alaska	21.4
28	Nevada	21.4
30	Idaho	21.3
31	Utah	21.2
32	Missouri	21.0
33	Illinois	20.9
34	North Dakota	20.8
35	Georgia	20.7
36	Colorado	20.4
37	Arizona	20.3
37	South Carolina	20.3
39	Wyoming	20.0
40	Florida	19.9
40	Michigan	19.9
40	Oklahoma	19.9
43	Arkansas	19.7
43	Louisiana	19.7
45	Alabama	19.6
46	New Mexico	19.5
46	West Virginia	19.5
48	Kentucky	19.1
49	Tennessee	19.0
50	Mississippi	18.2
	District of Columbia	20.2

Source: The American College Testing Program (Copyright © 2011)
   "Average ACT Scores by State" (http://www.act.org/news/data.html)
*The ACT score range is 1 to 36. Approximately 1.6 million 2011 U.S. high school students took the test. Caution should be used in using ACT scores to compare states. The percentage of high school students taking the test varies greatly from one state to another. For example, all 11th grade students in Colorado, Illinois, Kentucky, Louisiana, Michigan, Mississippi, Tennessee, and Wyoming are required to take the test but, in Maine, only 9 percent of 11th grade students took the test.

ACT Average Reading Score in 2011

National Average = 21.3*

ALPHA ORDER

RANK	STATE	AVERAGE SCORE
39	Alabama	20.7
30	Alaska	21.7
48	Arizona	19.9
43	Arkansas	20.2
25	California	22.0
34	Colorado	20.9
2	Connecticut	24.1
11	Delaware	22.7
43	Florida	20.2
35	Georgia	20.8
31	Hawaii	21.3
20	Idaho	22.2
35	Illinois	20.8
14	Indiana	22.6
14	Iowa	22.6
17	Kansas	22.3
47	Kentucky	20.0
41	Louisiana	20.3
4	Maine	23.8
20	Maryland	22.2
1	Massachusetts	24.4
46	Michigan	20.1
10	Minnesota	22.9
50	Mississippi	18.8
27	Missouri	21.9
11	Montana	22.7
17	Nebraska	22.3
28	Nevada	21.8
2	New Hampshire	24.1
7	New Jersey	23.3
43	New Mexico	20.2
5	New York	23.5
20	North Carolina	22.2
35	North Dakota	20.8
24	Ohio	22.1
31	Oklahoma	21.3
28	Oregon	21.8
14	Pennsylvania	22.6
5	Rhode Island	23.5
41	South Carolina	20.3
25	South Dakota	22.0
49	Tennessee	19.7
39	Texas	20.7
17	Utah	22.3
9	Vermont	23.0
11	Virginia	22.7
8	Washington	23.1
33	West Virginia	21.2
20	Wisconsin	22.2
35	Wyoming	20.8

RANK ORDER

RANK	STATE	AVERAGE SCORE
1	Massachusetts	24.4
2	Connecticut	24.1
2	New Hampshire	24.1
4	Maine	23.8
5	New York	23.5
5	Rhode Island	23.5
7	New Jersey	23.3
8	Washington	23.1
9	Vermont	23.0
10	Minnesota	22.9
11	Delaware	22.7
11	Montana	22.7
11	Virginia	22.7
14	Indiana	22.6
14	Iowa	22.6
14	Pennsylvania	22.6
17	Kansas	22.3
17	Nebraska	22.3
17	Utah	22.3
20	Idaho	22.2
20	Maryland	22.2
20	North Carolina	22.2
20	Wisconsin	22.2
24	Ohio	22.1
25	California	22.0
25	South Dakota	22.0
27	Missouri	21.9
28	Nevada	21.8
28	Oregon	21.8
30	Alaska	21.7
31	Hawaii	21.3
31	Oklahoma	21.3
33	West Virginia	21.2
34	Colorado	20.9
35	Georgia	20.8
35	Illinois	20.8
35	North Dakota	20.8
35	Wyoming	20.8
39	Alabama	20.7
39	Texas	20.7
41	Louisiana	20.3
41	South Carolina	20.3
43	Arkansas	20.2
43	Florida	20.2
43	New Mexico	20.2
46	Michigan	20.1
47	Kentucky	20.0
48	Arizona	19.9
49	Tennessee	19.7
50	Mississippi	18.8
	District of Columbia	20.4

Source: The American College Testing Program (Copyright © 2011)
    "Average ACT Scores by State" (http://www.act.org/news/data.html)
*The ACT score range is 1 to 36. Approximately 1.6 million 2011 U.S. high school students took the test. Caution should be used in using ACT scores to compare states. The percentage of high school students taking the test varies greatly from one state to another. For example, all 11th grade students in Colorado, Illinois, Kentucky, Louisiana, Michigan, Mississippi, Tennessee, and Wyoming are required to take the test but, in Maine, only 9 percent of 11th grade students took the test.

Average Mathematics SAT Score in 2010

National Average Score = 516*

ALPHA ORDER				RANK ORDER		
RANK	STATE	AVERAGE SCORE		RANK	STATE	AVERAGE SCORE
18	Alabama	550		1	Iowa	613
32	Alaska	515		2	Minnesota	607
27	Arizona	525		3	Michigan	605
16	Arkansas	566		4	Wisconsin	604
31	California	516		5	South Dakota	603
12	Colorado	572		6	Illinois	600
33	Connecticut	514		7	Kansas	595
46	Delaware	495		7	Missouri	595
45	Florida	498		9	North Dakota	594
49	Georgia	490		10	Nebraska	593
39	Hawaii	505		11	Kentucky	575
23	Idaho	541		12	Colorado	572
6	Illinois	600		13	Tennessee	571
39	Indiana	505		14	Oklahoma	568
1	Iowa	613		15	Wyoming	567
7	Kansas	595		16	Arkansas	566
11	Kentucky	575		17	Utah	559
18	Louisiana	550		18	Alabama	550
50	Maine	467		18	Louisiana	550
38	Maryland	506		20	New Mexico	549
26	Massachusetts	526		21	Mississippi	548
3	Michigan	605		21	Ohio	548
2	Minnesota	607		23	Idaho	541
21	Mississippi	548		24	Montana	538
7	Missouri	595		25	Washington	532
24	Montana	538		26	Massachusetts	526
10	Nebraska	593		27	Arizona	525
42	Nevada	501		28	New Hampshire	524
28	New Hampshire	524		28	Oregon	524
33	New Jersey	514		30	Vermont	521
20	New Mexico	549		31	California	516
44	New York	499		32	Alaska	515
36	North Carolina	511		33	Connecticut	514
9	North Dakota	594		33	New Jersey	514
21	Ohio	548		35	Virginia	512
14	Oklahoma	568		36	North Carolina	511
28	Oregon	524		37	West Virginia	507
42	Pennsylvania	501		38	Maryland	506
46	Rhode Island	495		39	Hawaii	505
46	South Carolina	495		39	Indiana	505
5	South Dakota	603		39	Texas	505
13	Tennessee	571		42	Nevada	501
39	Texas	505		42	Pennsylvania	501
17	Utah	559		44	New York	499
30	Vermont	521		45	Florida	498
35	Virginia	512		46	Delaware	495
25	Washington	532		46	Rhode Island	495
37	West Virginia	507		46	South Carolina	495
4	Wisconsin	604		49	Georgia	490
15	Wyoming	567		50	Maine	467
					District of Columbia	464

Source: The College Board, New York, NY
"College-Bound Seniors 2010" (http://professionals.collegeboard.com/data-reports-research/sat/cb-seniors-2010)
*The SAT score range is 200 to 800. The College Board strongly cautions against comparing states based on SAT scores alone. The percentage of high school students taking the test varies greatly from one state to another. For example, 3 percent of graduating seniors in Iowa took the test compared to 92 percent of such students in Maine. The SAT was formerly known as the Scholastic Aptitude Test.

Average Critical Reading SAT Score in 2010

National Average Score = 501*

ALPHA ORDER

RANK	STATE	AVERAGE SCORE
19	Alabama	556
30	Alaska	518
28	Arizona	519
17	Arkansas	566
35	California	501
15	Colorado	568
34	Connecticut	509
43	Delaware	493
38	Florida	496
45	Georgia	488
49	Hawaii	483
22	Idaho	543
7	Illinois	585
41	Indiana	494
1	Iowa	603
6	Kansas	590
12	Kentucky	575
20	Louisiana	555
50	Maine	468
35	Maryland	501
32	Massachusetts	512
7	Michigan	585
3	Minnesota	594
17	Mississippi	566
4	Missouri	593
23	Montana	538
7	Nebraska	585
38	Nevada	496
27	New Hampshire	520
40	New Jersey	495
21	New Mexico	553
46	New York	484
37	North Carolina	497
10	North Dakota	580
23	Ohio	538
14	Oklahoma	569
26	Oregon	523
44	Pennsylvania	492
41	Rhode Island	494
46	South Carolina	484
5	South Dakota	592
11	Tennessee	576
46	Texas	484
15	Utah	568
28	Vermont	519
32	Virginia	512
25	Washington	524
31	West Virginia	515
2	Wisconsin	595
13	Wyoming	570

RANK ORDER

RANK	STATE	AVERAGE SCORE
1	Iowa	603
2	Wisconsin	595
3	Minnesota	594
4	Missouri	593
5	South Dakota	592
6	Kansas	590
7	Illinois	585
7	Michigan	585
7	Nebraska	585
10	North Dakota	580
11	Tennessee	576
12	Kentucky	575
13	Wyoming	570
14	Oklahoma	569
15	Colorado	568
15	Utah	568
17	Arkansas	566
17	Mississippi	566
19	Alabama	556
20	Louisiana	555
21	New Mexico	553
22	Idaho	543
23	Montana	538
23	Ohio	538
25	Washington	524
26	Oregon	523
27	New Hampshire	520
28	Arizona	519
28	Vermont	519
30	Alaska	518
31	West Virginia	515
32	Massachusetts	512
32	Virginia	512
34	Connecticut	509
35	California	501
35	Maryland	501
37	North Carolina	497
38	Florida	496
38	Nevada	496
40	New Jersey	495
41	Indiana	494
41	Rhode Island	494
43	Delaware	493
44	Pennsylvania	492
45	Georgia	488
46	New York	484
46	South Carolina	484
46	Texas	484
49	Hawaii	483
50	Maine	468
	District of Columbia	474

Source: The College Board, New York, NY
"College-Bound Seniors 2010" (http://professionals.collegeboard.com/data-reports-research/sat/cb-seniors-2010)
*The SAT score range is 200 to 800. The College Board strongly cautions against comparing states based on SAT scores alone. The percentage of high school students taking the test varies greatly from one state to another. For example, 3 percent of graduating seniors in Iowa took the test compared to 92 percent of such students in Maine. The SAT was formerly known as the Scholastic Aptitude Test.

Average Writing SAT Score in 2010

National Average Score = 492*

RANK	STATE	AVERAGE SCORE
20	Alabama	544
37	Alaska	491
30	Arizona	500
14	Arkansas	552
30	California	500
13	Colorado	555
25	Connecticut	513
39	Delaware	481
41	Florida	479
45	Georgia	475
48	Hawaii	470
23	Idaho	517
5	Illinois	577
43	Indiana	477
1	Iowa	582
9	Kansas	567
11	Kentucky	563
16	Louisiana	547
50	Maine	454
36	Maryland	495
27	Massachusetts	509
6	Michigan	576
2	Minnesota	580
14	Mississippi	552
2	Missouri	580
23	Montana	517
8	Nebraska	568
46	Nevada	473
26	New Hampshire	510
34	New Jersey	497
21	New Mexico	534
42	New York	478
43	North Carolina	477
12	North Dakota	559
22	Ohio	522
16	Oklahoma	547
33	Oregon	499
40	Pennsylvania	480
38	Rhode Island	488
49	South Carolina	468
7	South Dakota	571
10	Tennessee	565
46	Texas	473
16	Utah	547
29	Vermont	506
34	Virginia	497
28	Washington	508
30	West Virginia	500
4	Wisconsin	579
19	Wyoming	546

RANK	STATE	AVERAGE SCORE
1	Iowa	582
2	Minnesota	580
2	Missouri	580
4	Wisconsin	579
5	Illinois	577
6	Michigan	576
7	South Dakota	571
8	Nebraska	568
9	Kansas	567
10	Tennessee	565
11	Kentucky	563
12	North Dakota	559
13	Colorado	555
14	Arkansas	552
14	Mississippi	552
16	Louisiana	547
16	Oklahoma	547
16	Utah	547
19	Wyoming	546
20	Alabama	544
21	New Mexico	534
22	Ohio	522
23	Idaho	517
23	Montana	517
25	Connecticut	513
26	New Hampshire	510
27	Massachusetts	509
28	Washington	508
29	Vermont	506
30	Arizona	500
30	California	500
30	West Virginia	500
33	Oregon	499
34	New Jersey	497
34	Virginia	497
36	Maryland	495
37	Alaska	491
38	Rhode Island	488
39	Delaware	481
40	Pennsylvania	480
41	Florida	479
42	New York	478
43	Indiana	477
43	North Carolina	477
45	Georgia	475
46	Nevada	473
46	Texas	473
48	Hawaii	470
49	South Carolina	468
50	Maine	454
	District of Columbia	466

Source: The College Board, New York, NY
    "College-Bound Seniors 2010" (http://professionals.collegeboard.com/data-reports-research/sat/cb-seniors-2010)
*The SAT score range is 200 to 800. The College Board strongly cautions against comparing states based on SAT scores alone.
The percentage of high school students taking the test varies greatly from one state to another. For example, 3 percent of
graduating seniors in Iowa took the test compared to 92 percent of such students in Maine. The SAT was formerly known as the
Scholastic Aptitude Test.

Average Reading Score for Public School Fourth Graders in 2009

National Average Score = 220*

ALPHA ORDER

RANK	STATE	AVERAGE SCORE
39	Alabama	216
43	Alaska	211
47	Arizona	210
39	Arkansas	216
47	California	210
7	Colorado	226
2	Connecticut	229
7	Delaware	226
7	Florida	226
34	Georgia	218
43	Hawaii	211
26	Idaho	221
30	Illinois	219
20	Indiana	223
26	Iowa	221
15	Kansas	224
7	Kentucky	226
50	Louisiana	207
15	Maine	224
7	Maryland	226
1	Massachusetts	234
34	Michigan	218
20	Minnesota	223
43	Mississippi	211
15	Missouri	224
13	Montana	225
20	Nebraska	223
43	Nevada	211
2	New Hampshire	229
2	New Jersey	229
49	New Mexico	208
15	New York	224
30	North Carolina	219
7	North Dakota	226
13	Ohio	225
37	Oklahoma	217
34	Oregon	218
15	Pennsylvania	224
20	Rhode Island	223
39	South Carolina	216
25	South Dakota	222
37	Tennessee	217
30	Texas	219
30	Utah	219
2	Vermont	229
6	Virginia	227
26	Washington	221
42	West Virginia	215
29	Wisconsin	220
20	Wyoming	223

RANK ORDER

RANK	STATE	AVERAGE SCORE
1	Massachusetts	234
2	Connecticut	229
2	New Hampshire	229
2	New Jersey	229
2	Vermont	229
6	Virginia	227
7	Colorado	226
7	Delaware	226
7	Florida	226
7	Kentucky	226
7	Maryland	226
7	North Dakota	226
13	Montana	225
13	Ohio	225
15	Kansas	224
15	Maine	224
15	Missouri	224
15	New York	224
15	Pennsylvania	224
20	Indiana	223
20	Minnesota	223
20	Nebraska	223
20	Rhode Island	223
20	Wyoming	223
25	South Dakota	222
26	Idaho	221
26	Iowa	221
26	Washington	221
29	Wisconsin	220
30	Illinois	219
30	North Carolina	219
30	Texas	219
30	Utah	219
34	Georgia	218
34	Michigan	218
34	Oregon	218
37	Oklahoma	217
37	Tennessee	217
39	Alabama	216
39	Arkansas	216
39	South Carolina	216
42	West Virginia	215
43	Alaska	211
43	Hawaii	211
43	Mississippi	211
43	Nevada	211
47	Arizona	210
47	California	210
49	New Mexico	208
50	Louisiana	207

	District of Columbia	202

Source: U.S. Department of Education, National Center for Education Statistics
      "The Nation's Report Card: Reading 2009" (http://nces.ed.gov/nationsreportcard/)
*These scores are from the National Assessment of Educational Progress (NAEP). Scale ranges from 0 to 500.

Average Reading Score for Public School Fourth Grade Males in 2009

National Average = 216*

ALPHA ORDER

ALPHA ORDER

RANK ORDER

RANK	STATE	AVERAGE SCORE		RANK	STATE	AVERAGE SCORE
40	Alabama	212		1	Massachusetts	231
45	Alaska	207		2	New Jersey	227
45	Arizona	207		3	New Hampshire	226
41	Arkansas	211		3	Vermont	226
45	California	207		5	Connecticut	225
11	Colorado	222		6	Delaware	223
5	Connecticut	225		6	Florida	223
6	Delaware	223		6	Maryland	223
6	Florida	223		6	North Dakota	223
34	Georgia	214		6	Virginia	223
48	Hawaii	205		11	Colorado	222
26	Idaho	217		11	Kansas	222
32	Illinois	215		11	Kentucky	222
24	Indiana	218		11	Montana	222
26	Iowa	217		11	Ohio	222
11	Kansas	222		16	New York	221
11	Kentucky	222		16	Pennsylvania	221
49	Louisiana	203		18	Maine	220
18	Maine	220		18	Minnesota	220
6	Maryland	223		18	Nebraska	220
1	Massachusetts	231		18	South Dakota	220
34	Michigan	214		22	Missouri	219
18	Minnesota	220		22	Wyoming	219
43	Mississippi	208		24	Indiana	218
22	Missouri	219		24	Rhode Island	218
11	Montana	222		26	Idaho	217
18	Nebraska	220		26	Iowa	217
43	Nevada	208		26	Utah	217
3	New Hampshire	226		26	Washington	217
2	New Jersey	227		26	Wisconsin	217
49	New Mexico	203		31	Texas	216
16	New York	221		32	Illinois	215
32	North Carolina	215		32	North Carolina	215
6	North Dakota	223		34	Georgia	214
11	Ohio	222		34	Michigan	214
34	Oklahoma	214		34	Oklahoma	214
34	Oregon	214		34	Oregon	214
16	Pennsylvania	221		34	Tennessee	214
24	Rhode Island	218		39	South Carolina	213
39	South Carolina	213		40	Alabama	212
18	South Dakota	220		41	Arkansas	211
34	Tennessee	214		41	West Virginia	211
31	Texas	216		43	Mississippi	208
26	Utah	217		43	Nevada	208
3	Vermont	226		45	Alaska	207
6	Virginia	223		45	Arizona	207
26	Washington	217		45	California	207
41	West Virginia	211		48	Hawaii	205
26	Wisconsin	217		49	Louisiana	203
22	Wyoming	219		49	New Mexico	203
					District of Columbia	198

Source: U.S. Department of Education, National Center for Education Statistics
   "The Nation's Report Card: Reading 2009" (http://nces.ed.gov/nationsreportcard/)
*These scores are from the National Assessment of Educational Progress (NAEP). Scale ranges from 0 to 500.

Average Reading Score for Public School Fourth Grade Females in 2009

National Average Score = 223*

ALPHA ORDER			RANK ORDER		
RANK	STATE	AVERAGE SCORE	RANK	STATE	AVERAGE SCORE
37	Alabama	221	1	Massachusetts	236
44	Alaska	216	2	Connecticut	234
46	Arizona	213	3	New Hampshire	233
33	Arkansas	222	4	New Jersey	232
46	California	213	5	Vermont	231
7	Colorado	229	6	Virginia	230
2	Connecticut	234	7	Colorado	229
13	Delaware	228	7	Florida	229
7	Florida	229	7	Kentucky	229
37	Georgia	221	7	Maryland	229
43	Hawaii	217	7	Missouri	229
21	Idaho	226	7	North Dakota	229
29	Illinois	224	13	Delaware	228
18	Indiana	227	13	Maine	228
21	Iowa	226	13	Montana	228
21	Kansas	226	13	New York	228
7	Kentucky	229	13	Rhode Island	228
50	Louisiana	212	18	Indiana	227
13	Maine	228	18	Minnesota	227
7	Maryland	229	18	Ohio	227
1	Massachusetts	236	21	Idaho	226
33	Michigan	222	21	Iowa	226
18	Minnesota	227	21	Kansas	226
46	Mississippi	213	21	Pennsylvania	226
7	Missouri	229	21	Washington	226
13	Montana	228	21	Wyoming	226
27	Nebraska	225	27	Nebraska	225
45	Nevada	214	27	South Dakota	225
3	New Hampshire	233	29	Illinois	224
4	New Jersey	232	29	North Carolina	224
46	New Mexico	213	29	Wisconsin	224
13	New York	228	32	Oregon	223
29	North Carolina	224	33	Arkansas	222
7	North Dakota	229	33	Michigan	222
18	Ohio	227	33	Texas	222
39	Oklahoma	220	33	Utah	222
32	Oregon	223	37	Alabama	221
21	Pennsylvania	226	37	Georgia	221
13	Rhode Island	228	39	Oklahoma	220
41	South Carolina	219	39	Tennessee	220
27	South Dakota	225	41	South Carolina	219
39	Tennessee	220	42	West Virginia	218
33	Texas	222	43	Hawaii	217
33	Utah	222	44	Alaska	216
5	Vermont	231	45	Nevada	214
6	Virginia	230	46	Arizona	213
21	Washington	226	46	California	213
42	West Virginia	218	46	Mississippi	213
29	Wisconsin	224	46	New Mexico	213
21	Wyoming	226	50	Louisiana	212
				District of Columbia	206

Source: U.S. Department of Education, National Center for Education Statistics
    "The Nation's Report Card: Reading 2009" (http://nces.ed.gov/nationsreportcard/)
*These scores are from the National Assessment of Educational Progress (NAEP). Scale ranges from 0 to 500.

Average Reading Score for Public School Fourth Graders
Eligible for Free or Reduced Price Lunch Program in 2009
National Average Score = 206*

ALPHA ORDER

ALPHA ORDER

RANK	STATE	AVERAGE SCORE
36	Alabama	204
50	Alaska	194
48	Arizona	197
25	Arkansas	207
49	California	196
29	Colorado	206
25	Connecticut	207
6	Delaware	214
1	Florida	217
25	Georgia	207
47	Hawaii	198
13	Idaho	211
42	Illinois	202
15	Indiana	210
22	Iowa	208
9	Kansas	213
3	Kentucky	215
44	Louisiana	201
11	Maine	212
15	Maryland	210
3	Massachusetts	215
36	Michigan	204
40	Minnesota	203
40	Mississippi	203
15	Missouri	210
6	Montana	214
15	Nebraska	210
45	Nevada	200
9	New Hampshire	213
13	New Jersey	211
46	New Mexico	199
6	New York	214
32	North Carolina	205
2	North Dakota	216
22	Ohio	208
25	Oklahoma	207
36	Oregon	204
29	Pennsylvania	206
32	Rhode Island	205
36	South Carolina	204
20	South Dakota	209
32	Tennessee	205
20	Texas	209
32	Utah	205
3	Vermont	215
15	Virginia	210
22	Washington	208
29	West Virginia	206
42	Wisconsin	202
11	Wyoming	212

RANK ORDER

RANK	STATE	AVERAGE SCORE
1	Florida	217
2	North Dakota	216
3	Kentucky	215
3	Massachusetts	215
3	Vermont	215
6	Delaware	214
6	Montana	214
6	New York	214
9	Kansas	213
9	New Hampshire	213
11	Maine	212
11	Wyoming	212
13	Idaho	211
13	New Jersey	211
15	Indiana	210
15	Maryland	210
15	Missouri	210
15	Nebraska	210
15	Virginia	210
20	South Dakota	209
20	Texas	209
22	Iowa	208
22	Ohio	208
22	Washington	208
25	Arkansas	207
25	Connecticut	207
25	Georgia	207
25	Oklahoma	207
29	Colorado	206
29	Pennsylvania	206
29	West Virginia	206
32	North Carolina	205
32	Rhode Island	205
32	Tennessee	205
32	Utah	205
36	Alabama	204
36	Michigan	204
36	Oregon	204
36	South Carolina	204
40	Minnesota	203
40	Mississippi	203
42	Illinois	202
42	Wisconsin	202
44	Louisiana	201
45	Nevada	200
46	New Mexico	199
47	Hawaii	198
48	Arizona	197
49	California	196
50	Alaska	194
	District of Columbia	193

Source: U.S. Department of Education, National Center for Education Statistics
    "The Nation's Report Card: Reading 2009" (http://nces.ed.gov/nationsreportcard/)
*These scores are from the National Assessment of Educational Progress (NAEP). Scale ranges from 0 to 500.

Percent of Public School Fourth Graders
Proficient or Better in Reading in 2009
National Percent = 32%*

ALPHA ORDER

RANK	STATE	PERCENT
37	Alabama	28
42	Alaska	27
45	Arizona	25
35	Arkansas	29
46	California	24
5	Colorado	40
2	Connecticut	42
17	Delaware	35
11	Florida	36
35	Georgia	29
43	Hawaii	26
29	Idaho	32
29	Illinois	32
23	Indiana	34
23	Iowa	34
17	Kansas	35
11	Kentucky	36
50	Louisiana	18
17	Maine	35
8	Maryland	37
1	Massachusetts	47
34	Michigan	30
8	Minnesota	37
48	Mississippi	22
11	Missouri	36
17	Montana	35
17	Nebraska	35
46	Nevada	24
3	New Hampshire	41
5	New Jersey	40
49	New Mexico	20
11	New York	36
29	North Carolina	32
17	North Dakota	35
11	Ohio	36
37	Oklahoma	28
32	Oregon	31
8	Pennsylvania	37
11	Rhode Island	36
37	South Carolina	28
25	South Dakota	33
37	Tennessee	28
37	Texas	28
32	Utah	31
3	Vermont	41
7	Virginia	38
25	Washington	33
43	West Virginia	26
25	Wisconsin	33
25	Wyoming	33

RANK ORDER

RANK	STATE	PERCENT
1	Massachusetts	47
2	Connecticut	42
3	New Hampshire	41
3	Vermont	41
5	Colorado	40
5	New Jersey	40
7	Virginia	38
8	Maryland	37
8	Minnesota	37
8	Pennsylvania	37
11	Florida	36
11	Kentucky	36
11	Missouri	36
11	New York	36
11	Ohio	36
11	Rhode Island	36
17	Delaware	35
17	Kansas	35
17	Maine	35
17	Montana	35
17	Nebraska	35
17	North Dakota	35
23	Indiana	34
23	Iowa	34
25	South Dakota	33
25	Washington	33
25	Wisconsin	33
25	Wyoming	33
29	Idaho	32
29	Illinois	32
29	North Carolina	32
32	Oregon	31
32	Utah	31
34	Michigan	30
35	Arkansas	29
35	Georgia	29
37	Alabama	28
37	Oklahoma	28
37	South Carolina	28
37	Tennessee	28
37	Texas	28
42	Alaska	27
43	Hawaii	26
43	West Virginia	26
45	Arizona	25
46	California	24
46	Nevada	24
48	Mississippi	22
49	New Mexico	20
50	Louisiana	18
	District of Columbia	17

Source: U.S. Department of Education, National Center for Education Statistics
    "The Nation's Report Card: Reading 2009" (http://nces.ed.gov/nationsreportcard/)
*There are four achievement levels: Below Basic, Basic, Proficient, and Advanced. Proficient represents solid academic
mastery for 4th graders. Students reaching this level have demonstrated competency over challenging subject matter, including
subject matter knowledge, application of such knowledge to real-world situations, and analytical skills appropriate to the subject
matter.

Percent of Public School Fourth Grade Males
Proficient or Better in Reading in 2009
National Percent = 28%*

ALPHA ORDER

RANK	STATE	PERCENT
39	Alabama	25
42	Alaska	24
44	Arizona	22
39	Arkansas	25
44	California	22
6	Colorado	36
2	Connecticut	38
12	Delaware	33
12	Florida	33
34	Georgia	26
44	Hawaii	22
31	Idaho	28
25	Illinois	29
25	Indiana	29
25	Iowa	29
9	Kansas	34
15	Kentucky	32
50	Louisiana	15
19	Maine	31
9	Maryland	34
1	Massachusetts	45
34	Michigan	26
9	Minnesota	34
48	Mississippi	20
19	Missouri	31
15	Montana	32
12	Nebraska	33
44	Nevada	22
4	New Hampshire	37
4	New Jersey	37
49	New Mexico	17
15	New York	32
25	North Carolina	29
23	North Dakota	30
15	Ohio	32
34	Oklahoma	26
31	Oregon	28
7	Pennsylvania	35
19	Rhode Island	31
34	South Carolina	26
19	South Dakota	31
34	Tennessee	26
39	Texas	25
31	Utah	28
2	Vermont	38
7	Virginia	35
25	Washington	29
43	West Virginia	23
25	Wisconsin	29
23	Wyoming	30

RANK ORDER

RANK	STATE	PERCENT
1	Massachusetts	45
2	Connecticut	38
2	Vermont	38
4	New Hampshire	37
4	New Jersey	37
6	Colorado	36
7	Pennsylvania	35
7	Virginia	35
9	Kansas	34
9	Maryland	34
9	Minnesota	34
12	Delaware	33
12	Florida	33
12	Nebraska	33
15	Kentucky	32
15	Montana	32
15	New York	32
15	Ohio	32
19	Maine	31
19	Missouri	31
19	Rhode Island	31
19	South Dakota	31
23	North Dakota	30
23	Wyoming	30
25	Illinois	29
25	Indiana	29
25	Iowa	29
25	North Carolina	29
25	Washington	29
25	Wisconsin	29
31	Idaho	28
31	Oregon	28
31	Utah	28
34	Georgia	26
34	Michigan	26
34	Oklahoma	26
34	South Carolina	26
34	Tennessee	26
39	Alabama	25
39	Arkansas	25
39	Texas	25
42	Alaska	24
43	West Virginia	23
44	Arizona	22
44	California	22
44	Hawaii	22
44	Nevada	22
48	Mississippi	20
49	New Mexico	17
50	Louisiana	15
	District of Columbia	16

Source: U.S. Department of Education, National Center for Education Statistics
"The Nation's Report Card: Reading 2009" (http://nces.ed.gov/nationsreportcard/)
*There are four achievement levels: Below Basic, Basic, Proficient, and Advanced. Proficient represents solid academic mastery for 4th graders. Students reaching this level have demonstrated competency over challenging subject matter, including subject matter knowledge, application of such knowledge to real-world situations, and analytical skills appropriate to the subject matter.

Percent of Public School Fourth Grade Females
Proficient or Better in Reading in 2009
National Percent = 35%*

ALPHA ORDER

RANK	STATE	PERCENT
37	Alabama	32
38	Alaska	31
45	Arizona	27
35	Arkansas	33
46	California	26
5	Colorado	44
2	Connecticut	47
19	Delaware	38
16	Florida	39
35	Georgia	33
39	Hawaii	30
23	Idaho	37
28	Illinois	36
19	Indiana	38
16	Iowa	39
23	Kansas	37
10	Kentucky	40
50	Louisiana	22
10	Maine	40
10	Maryland	40
1	Massachusetts	50
32	Michigan	34
8	Minnesota	41
48	Mississippi	24
8	Missouri	41
23	Montana	37
23	Nebraska	37
46	Nevada	26
3	New Hampshire	46
5	New Jersey	44
49	New Mexico	23
10	New York	40
28	North Carolina	36
16	North Dakota	39
10	Ohio	40
42	Oklahoma	29
32	Oregon	34
19	Pennsylvania	38
10	Rhode Island	40
42	South Carolina	29
31	South Dakota	35
39	Tennessee	30
39	Texas	30
32	Utah	34
4	Vermont	45
7	Virginia	42
19	Washington	38
42	West Virginia	29
23	Wisconsin	37
28	Wyoming	36

RANK ORDER

RANK	STATE	PERCENT
1	Massachusetts	50
2	Connecticut	47
3	New Hampshire	46
4	Vermont	45
5	Colorado	44
5	New Jersey	44
7	Virginia	42
8	Minnesota	41
8	Missouri	41
10	Kentucky	40
10	Maine	40
10	Maryland	40
10	New York	40
10	Ohio	40
10	Rhode Island	40
16	Florida	39
16	Iowa	39
16	North Dakota	39
19	Delaware	38
19	Indiana	38
19	Pennsylvania	38
19	Washington	38
23	Idaho	37
23	Kansas	37
23	Montana	37
23	Nebraska	37
23	Wisconsin	37
28	Illinois	36
28	North Carolina	36
28	Wyoming	36
31	South Dakota	35
32	Michigan	34
32	Oregon	34
32	Utah	34
35	Arkansas	33
35	Georgia	33
37	Alabama	32
38	Alaska	31
39	Hawaii	30
39	Tennessee	30
39	Texas	30
42	Oklahoma	29
42	South Carolina	29
42	West Virginia	29
45	Arizona	27
46	California	26
46	Nevada	26
48	Mississippi	24
49	New Mexico	23
50	Louisiana	22
	District of Columbia	18

Source: U.S. Department of Education, National Center for Education Statistics
     "The Nation's Report Card: Reading 2009" (http://nces.ed.gov/nationsreportcard/)
*There are four achievement levels: Below Basic, Basic, Proficient, and Advanced. Proficient represents solid academic mastery for 4th graders. Students reaching this level have demonstrated competency over challenging subject matter, including subject matter knowledge, application of such knowledge to real-world situations, and analytical skills appropriate to the subject matter.

Percent of Public School Fourth Graders Eligible for Free or Reduced Price Lunch Program Proficient or Better in Reading in 2009
National Percent = 17%*

ALPHA ORDER

RANK	STATE	PERCENT
38	Alabama	16
44	Alaska	14
46	Arizona	13
17	Arkansas	20
50	California	10
20	Colorado	19
23	Connecticut	18
10	Delaware	21
2	Florida	25
23	Georgia	18
39	Hawaii	15
10	Idaho	21
39	Illinois	15
17	Indiana	20
10	Iowa	21
7	Kansas	22
3	Kentucky	24
46	Louisiana	13
10	Maine	21
23	Maryland	18
5	Massachusetts	23
39	Michigan	15
29	Minnesota	17
44	Mississippi	14
10	Missouri	21
10	Montana	21
7	Nebraska	22
46	Nevada	13
5	New Hampshire	23
29	New Jersey	17
49	New Mexico	12
3	New York	24
29	North Carolina	17
7	North Dakota	22
29	Ohio	17
23	Oklahoma	18
29	Oregon	17
20	Pennsylvania	19
29	Rhode Island	17
39	South Carolina	15
17	South Dakota	20
29	Tennessee	17
29	Texas	17
20	Utah	19
1	Vermont	26
23	Virginia	18
23	Washington	18
29	West Virginia	17
39	Wisconsin	15
10	Wyoming	21

RANK ORDER

RANK	STATE	PERCENT
1	Vermont	26
2	Florida	25
3	Kentucky	24
3	New York	24
5	Massachusetts	23
5	New Hampshire	23
7	Kansas	22
7	Nebraska	22
7	North Dakota	22
10	Delaware	21
10	Idaho	21
10	Iowa	21
10	Maine	21
10	Missouri	21
10	Montana	21
10	Wyoming	21
17	Arkansas	20
17	Indiana	20
17	South Dakota	20
20	Colorado	19
20	Pennsylvania	19
20	Utah	19
23	Connecticut	18
23	Georgia	18
23	Maryland	18
23	Oklahoma	18
23	Virginia	18
23	Washington	18
29	Minnesota	17
29	New Jersey	17
29	North Carolina	17
29	Ohio	17
29	Oregon	17
29	Rhode Island	17
29	Tennessee	17
29	Texas	17
29	West Virginia	17
38	Alabama	16
39	Hawaii	15
39	Illinois	15
39	Michigan	15
39	South Carolina	15
39	Wisconsin	15
44	Alaska	14
44	Mississippi	14
46	Arizona	13
46	Louisiana	13
46	Nevada	13
49	New Mexico	12
50	California	10
	District of Columbia	9

Source: U.S. Department of Education, National Center for Education Statistics
  "The Nation's Report Card: Reading 2009" (http://nces.ed.gov/nationsreportcard/)
*There are four achievement levels: Below Basic, Basic, Proficient, and Advanced. Proficient represents solid academic mastery for 4th graders. Students reaching this level have demonstrated competency over challenging subject matter, including subject matter knowledge, application of such knowledge to real-world situations, and analytical skills appropriate to the subject matter.

Percent of White Public School Fourth Graders
Proficient or Better in Reading in 2009
National Percent = 41%*

<table>
<tr><td colspan="3">ALPHA ORDER</td><td colspan="3">RANK ORDER</td></tr>
<tr><td>RANK</td><td>STATE</td><td>PERCENT</td><td>RANK</td><td>STATE</td><td>PERCENT</td></tr>
<tr><td>35</td><td>Alabama</td><td>36</td><td>1</td><td>Massachusetts</td><td>56</td></tr>
<tr><td>27</td><td>Alaska</td><td>38</td><td>2</td><td>Connecticut</td><td>52</td></tr>
<tr><td>31</td><td>Arizona</td><td>37</td><td>3</td><td>Colorado</td><td>51</td></tr>
<tr><td>41</td><td>Arkansas</td><td>35</td><td>3</td><td>New Jersey</td><td>51</td></tr>
<tr><td>25</td><td>California</td><td>39</td><td>5</td><td>Maryland</td><td>50</td></tr>
<tr><td>3</td><td>Colorado</td><td>51</td><td>6</td><td>Delaware</td><td>47</td></tr>
<tr><td>2</td><td>Connecticut</td><td>52</td><td>6</td><td>Virginia</td><td>47</td></tr>
<tr><td>6</td><td>Delaware</td><td>47</td><td>8</td><td>Florida</td><td>45</td></tr>
<tr><td>8</td><td>Florida</td><td>45</td><td>8</td><td>New York</td><td>45</td></tr>
<tr><td>20</td><td>Georgia</td><td>40</td><td>10</td><td>Illinois</td><td>44</td></tr>
<tr><td>15</td><td>Hawaii</td><td>42</td><td>10</td><td>North Carolina</td><td>44</td></tr>
<tr><td>35</td><td>Idaho</td><td>36</td><td>10</td><td>Rhode Island</td><td>44</td></tr>
<tr><td>10</td><td>Illinois</td><td>44</td><td>13</td><td>Minnesota</td><td>43</td></tr>
<tr><td>27</td><td>Indiana</td><td>38</td><td>13</td><td>Texas</td><td>43</td></tr>
<tr><td>35</td><td>Iowa</td><td>36</td><td>15</td><td>Hawaii</td><td>42</td></tr>
<tr><td>20</td><td>Kansas</td><td>40</td><td>15</td><td>New Hampshire</td><td>42</td></tr>
<tr><td>25</td><td>Kentucky</td><td>39</td><td>15</td><td>Ohio</td><td>42</td></tr>
<tr><td>49</td><td>Louisiana</td><td>28</td><td>15</td><td>Pennsylvania</td><td>42</td></tr>
<tr><td>35</td><td>Maine</td><td>36</td><td>15</td><td>Vermont</td><td>42</td></tr>
<tr><td>5</td><td>Maryland</td><td>50</td><td>20</td><td>Georgia</td><td>40</td></tr>
<tr><td>1</td><td>Massachusetts</td><td>56</td><td>20</td><td>Kansas</td><td>40</td></tr>
<tr><td>35</td><td>Michigan</td><td>36</td><td>20</td><td>Missouri</td><td>40</td></tr>
<tr><td>13</td><td>Minnesota</td><td>43</td><td>20</td><td>Nebraska</td><td>40</td></tr>
<tr><td>41</td><td>Mississippi</td><td>35</td><td>20</td><td>Washington</td><td>40</td></tr>
<tr><td>20</td><td>Missouri</td><td>40</td><td>25</td><td>California</td><td>39</td></tr>
<tr><td>31</td><td>Montana</td><td>37</td><td>25</td><td>Kentucky</td><td>39</td></tr>
<tr><td>20</td><td>Nebraska</td><td>40</td><td>27</td><td>Alaska</td><td>38</td></tr>
<tr><td>45</td><td>Nevada</td><td>34</td><td>27</td><td>Indiana</td><td>38</td></tr>
<tr><td>15</td><td>New Hampshire</td><td>42</td><td>27</td><td>South Carolina</td><td>38</td></tr>
<tr><td>3</td><td>New Jersey</td><td>51</td><td>27</td><td>Wisconsin</td><td>38</td></tr>
<tr><td>41</td><td>New Mexico</td><td>35</td><td>31</td><td>Arizona</td><td>37</td></tr>
<tr><td>8</td><td>New York</td><td>45</td><td>31</td><td>Montana</td><td>37</td></tr>
<tr><td>10</td><td>North Carolina</td><td>44</td><td>31</td><td>North Dakota</td><td>37</td></tr>
<tr><td>31</td><td>North Dakota</td><td>37</td><td>31</td><td>South Dakota</td><td>37</td></tr>
<tr><td>15</td><td>Ohio</td><td>42</td><td>35</td><td>Alabama</td><td>36</td></tr>
<tr><td>48</td><td>Oklahoma</td><td>33</td><td>35</td><td>Idaho</td><td>36</td></tr>
<tr><td>41</td><td>Oregon</td><td>35</td><td>35</td><td>Iowa</td><td>36</td></tr>
<tr><td>15</td><td>Pennsylvania</td><td>42</td><td>35</td><td>Maine</td><td>36</td></tr>
<tr><td>10</td><td>Rhode Island</td><td>44</td><td>35</td><td>Michigan</td><td>36</td></tr>
<tr><td>27</td><td>South Carolina</td><td>38</td><td>35</td><td>Utah</td><td>36</td></tr>
<tr><td>31</td><td>South Dakota</td><td>37</td><td>41</td><td>Arkansas</td><td>35</td></tr>
<tr><td>45</td><td>Tennessee</td><td>34</td><td>41</td><td>Mississippi</td><td>35</td></tr>
<tr><td>13</td><td>Texas</td><td>43</td><td>41</td><td>New Mexico</td><td>35</td></tr>
<tr><td>35</td><td>Utah</td><td>36</td><td>41</td><td>Oregon</td><td>35</td></tr>
<tr><td>15</td><td>Vermont</td><td>42</td><td>45</td><td>Nevada</td><td>34</td></tr>
<tr><td>6</td><td>Virginia</td><td>47</td><td>45</td><td>Tennessee</td><td>34</td></tr>
<tr><td>20</td><td>Washington</td><td>40</td><td>45</td><td>Wyoming</td><td>34</td></tr>
<tr><td>50</td><td>West Virginia</td><td>26</td><td>48</td><td>Oklahoma</td><td>33</td></tr>
<tr><td>27</td><td>Wisconsin</td><td>38</td><td>49</td><td>Louisiana</td><td>28</td></tr>
<tr><td>45</td><td>Wyoming</td><td>34</td><td>50</td><td>West Virginia</td><td>26</td></tr>
<tr><td colspan="3"></td><td colspan="2">District of Columbia</td><td>75</td></tr>
</table>

Source: U.S. Department of Education, National Center for Education Statistics
"The Nation's Report Card: Reading 2009" (http://nces.ed.gov/nationsreportcard/)
*There are four achievement levels: Below Basic, Basic, Proficient, and Advanced. Proficient represents solid academic mastery for 4th graders. Students reaching this level have demonstrated competency over challenging subject matter, including subject matter knowledge, application of such knowledge to real-world situations, and analytical skills appropriate to the subject matter.

Percent of Black Public School Fourth Graders
Proficient or Better in Reading in 2009
National Percent = 15%*

ALPHA ORDER

RANK	STATE	PERCENT
32	Alabama	13
32	Alaska	13
8	Arizona	20
27	Arkansas	14
27	California	14
3	Colorado	27
5	Connecticut	22
11	Delaware	19
14	Florida	18
24	Georgia	15
14	Hawaii	18
NA	Idaho**	NA
39	Illinois	11
24	Indiana	15
5	Iowa	22
8	Kansas	20
32	Kentucky	13
43	Louisiana	9
14	Maine	18
11	Maryland	19
4	Massachusetts	23
43	Michigan	9
37	Minnesota	12
42	Mississippi	10
22	Missouri	16
NA	Montana**	NA
11	Nebraska	19
27	Nevada	14
2	New Hampshire	28
14	New Jersey	18
32	New Mexico	13
14	New York	18
27	North Carolina	14
NA	North Dakota**	NA
32	Ohio	13
39	Oklahoma	11
20	Oregon	17
24	Pennsylvania	15
20	Rhode Island	17
39	South Carolina	11
NA	South Dakota**	NA
37	Tennessee	12
8	Texas	20
27	Utah	14
1	Vermont	29
14	Virginia	18
7	Washington	21
22	West Virginia	16
43	Wisconsin	9
NA	Wyoming**	NA

RANK ORDER

RANK	STATE	PERCENT
1	Vermont	29
2	New Hampshire	28
3	Colorado	27
4	Massachusetts	23
5	Connecticut	22
5	Iowa	22
7	Washington	21
8	Arizona	20
8	Kansas	20
8	Texas	20
11	Delaware	19
11	Maryland	19
11	Nebraska	19
14	Florida	18
14	Hawaii	18
14	Maine	18
14	New Jersey	18
14	New York	18
14	Virginia	18
20	Oregon	17
20	Rhode Island	17
22	Missouri	16
22	West Virginia	16
24	Georgia	15
24	Indiana	15
24	Pennsylvania	15
27	Arkansas	14
27	California	14
27	Nevada	14
27	North Carolina	14
27	Utah	14
32	Alabama	13
32	Alaska	13
32	Kentucky	13
32	New Mexico	13
32	Ohio	13
37	Minnesota	12
37	Tennessee	12
39	Illinois	11
39	Oklahoma	11
39	South Carolina	11
42	Mississippi	10
43	Louisiana	9
43	Michigan	9
43	Wisconsin	9
NA	Idaho**	NA
NA	Montana**	NA
NA	North Dakota**	NA
NA	South Dakota**	NA
NA	Wyoming**	NA
	District of Columbia	11

Source: U.S. Department of Education, National Center for Education Statistics
   "The Nation's Report Card: Reading 2009" (http://nces.ed.gov/nationsreportcard/)
*There are four achievement levels: Below Basic, Basic, Proficient, and Advanced. Proficient represents solid academic
mastery for 4th graders. Students reaching this level have demonstrated competency over challenging subject matter, including
subject matter knowledge, application of such knowledge to real-world situations, and analytical skills appropriate to the subject
matter. **Sample size insufficient.

Percent of Hispanic Public School Fourth Graders
Proficient or Better in Reading in 2009
National Percent = 16%*

RANK	STATE	PERCENT
22	Alabama	18
6	Alaska	27
36	Arizona	14
29	Arkansas	16
45	California	11
22	Colorado	18
34	Connecticut	15
11	Delaware	24
1	Florida	31
15	Georgia	20
6	Hawaii	27
36	Idaho	14
29	Illinois	16
34	Indiana	15
15	Iowa	20
15	Kansas	20
12	Kentucky	22
29	Louisiana	16
NA	Maine**	NA
2	Maryland	30
15	Massachusetts	20
25	Michigan	17
42	Minnesota	13
20	Mississippi	19
8	Missouri	26
8	Montana	26
15	Nebraska	20
42	Nevada	13
2	New Hampshire	30
20	New Jersey	19
36	New Mexico	14
12	New York	22
25	North Carolina	17
NA	North Dakota**	NA
2	Ohio	30
25	Oklahoma	17
42	Oregon	13
36	Pennsylvania	14
36	Rhode Island	14
25	South Carolina	17
5	South Dakota	29
29	Tennessee	16
22	Texas	18
46	Utah	10
NA	Vermont**	NA
8	Virginia	26
36	Washington	14
NA	West Virginia**	NA
29	Wisconsin	16
12	Wyoming	22

RANK	STATE	PERCENT
1	Florida	31
2	Maryland	30
2	New Hampshire	30
2	Ohio	30
5	South Dakota	29
6	Alaska	27
6	Hawaii	27
8	Missouri	26
8	Montana	26
8	Virginia	26
11	Delaware	24
12	Kentucky	22
12	New York	22
12	Wyoming	22
15	Georgia	20
15	Iowa	20
15	Kansas	20
15	Massachusetts	20
15	Nebraska	20
20	Mississippi	19
20	New Jersey	19
22	Alabama	18
22	Colorado	18
22	Texas	18
25	Michigan	17
25	North Carolina	17
25	Oklahoma	17
25	South Carolina	17
29	Arkansas	16
29	Illinois	16
29	Louisiana	16
29	Tennessee	16
29	Wisconsin	16
34	Connecticut	15
34	Indiana	15
36	Arizona	14
36	Idaho	14
36	New Mexico	14
36	Pennsylvania	14
36	Rhode Island	14
36	Washington	14
42	Minnesota	13
42	Nevada	13
42	Oregon	13
45	California	11
46	Utah	10
NA	Maine**	NA
NA	North Dakota**	NA
NA	Vermont**	NA
NA	West Virginia**	NA
	District of Columbia	17

Source: U.S. Department of Education, National Center for Education Statistics
   "The Nation's Report Card: Reading 2009" (http://nces.ed.gov/nationsreportcard/)
*There are four achievement levels: Below Basic, Basic, Proficient, and Advanced. Proficient represents solid academic mastery for 4th graders. Students reaching this level have demonstrated competency over challenging subject matter, including subject matter knowledge, application of such knowledge to real-world situations, and analytical skills appropriate to the subject matter. **Sample size insufficient.

Percent of Asian Public School Fourth Graders
Proficient or Better in Reading in 2009
National Percent = 48%*

ALPHA ORDER

RANK	STATE	PERCENT
NA	Alabama**	NA
33	Alaska	19
22	Arizona	41
NA	Arkansas**	NA
17	California	48
11	Colorado	53
10	Connecticut	55
5	Delaware	57
7	Florida	56
11	Georgia	53
32	Hawaii	22
29	Idaho	33
1	Illinois	63
NA	Indiana**	NA
18	Iowa	46
16	Kansas	50
7	Kentucky	56
NA	Louisiana**	NA
NA	Maine**	NA
4	Maryland	59
7	Massachusetts	56
21	Michigan	42
28	Minnesota	34
NA	Mississippi**	NA
NA	Missouri**	NA
NA	Montana**	NA
23	Nebraska	40
25	Nevada	38
19	New Hampshire	45
2	New Jersey	62
24	New Mexico	39
13	New York	52
13	North Carolina	52
NA	North Dakota**	NA
NA	Ohio**	NA
NA	Oklahoma**	NA
20	Oregon	43
3	Pennsylvania	61
30	Rhode Island	30
NA	South Carolina**	NA
NA	South Dakota**	NA
NA	Tennessee**	NA
13	Texas	52
30	Utah	30
NA	Vermont**	NA
5	Virginia	57
27	Washington	35
NA	West Virginia**	NA
26	Wisconsin	36
NA	Wyoming**	NA

RANK ORDER

RANK	STATE	PERCENT
1	Illinois	63
2	New Jersey	62
3	Pennsylvania	61
4	Maryland	59
5	Delaware	57
5	Virginia	57
7	Florida	56
7	Kentucky	56
7	Massachusetts	56
10	Connecticut	55
11	Colorado	53
11	Georgia	53
13	New York	52
13	North Carolina	52
13	Texas	52
16	Kansas	50
17	California	48
18	Iowa	46
19	New Hampshire	45
20	Oregon	43
21	Michigan	42
22	Arizona	41
23	Nebraska	40
24	New Mexico	39
25	Nevada	38
26	Wisconsin	36
27	Washington	35
28	Minnesota	34
29	Idaho	33
30	Rhode Island	30
30	Utah	30
32	Hawaii	22
33	Alaska	19
NA	Alabama**	NA
NA	Arkansas**	NA
NA	Indiana**	NA
NA	Louisiana**	NA
NA	Maine**	NA
NA	Mississippi**	NA
NA	Missouri**	NA
NA	Montana**	NA
NA	North Dakota**	NA
NA	Ohio**	NA
NA	Oklahoma**	NA
NA	South Carolina**	NA
NA	South Dakota**	NA
NA	Tennessee**	NA
NA	Vermont**	NA
NA	West Virginia**	NA
NA	Wyoming**	NA
	District of Columbia**	NA

Source: U.S. Department of Education, National Center for Education Statistics
"The Nation's Report Card: Reading 2009" (http://nces.ed.gov/nationsreportcard/)
*There are four achievement levels: Below Basic, Basic, Proficient, and Advanced. Proficient represents solid academic
mastery for 4th graders. Students reaching this level have demonstrated competency over challenging subject matter, including
subject matter knowledge, application of such knowledge to real-world situations, and analytical skills appropriate to the subject
matter. **Sample size insufficient.

Percent of Disabled Public School Fourth Graders Proficient or Better in Reading in 2009
National Percent = 12%*

RANK	STATE	PERCENT
41	Alabama	8
45	Alaska	6
18	Arizona	13
41	Arkansas	8
36	California	9
11	Colorado	15
18	Connecticut	13
11	Delaware	15
5	Florida	17
15	Georgia	14
50	Hawaii	3
47	Idaho	5
11	Illinois	15
4	Indiana	19
47	Iowa	5
31	Kansas	10
8	Kentucky	16
43	Louisiana	7
23	Maine	12
1	Maryland	21
1	Massachusetts	21
31	Michigan	10
8	Minnesota	16
43	Mississippi	7
31	Missouri	10
29	Montana	11
8	Nebraska	16
31	Nevada	10
15	New Hampshire	14
1	New Jersey	21
47	New Mexico	5
23	New York	12
23	North Carolina	12
5	North Dakota	17
36	Ohio	9
36	Oklahoma	9
18	Oregon	13
15	Pennsylvania	14
36	Rhode Island	9
23	South Carolina	12
5	South Dakota	17
23	Tennessee	12
45	Texas	6
18	Utah	13
29	Vermont	11
11	Virginia	15
23	Washington	12
18	West Virginia	13
36	Wisconsin	9
31	Wyoming	10

RANK	STATE	PERCENT
1	Maryland	21
1	Massachusetts	21
1	New Jersey	21
4	Indiana	19
5	Florida	17
5	North Dakota	17
5	South Dakota	17
8	Kentucky	16
8	Minnesota	16
8	Nebraska	16
11	Colorado	15
11	Delaware	15
11	Illinois	15
11	Virginia	15
15	Georgia	14
15	New Hampshire	14
15	Pennsylvania	14
18	Arizona	13
18	Connecticut	13
18	Oregon	13
18	Utah	13
18	West Virginia	13
23	Maine	12
23	New York	12
23	North Carolina	12
23	South Carolina	12
23	Tennessee	12
23	Washington	12
29	Montana	11
29	Vermont	11
31	Kansas	10
31	Michigan	10
31	Missouri	10
31	Nevada	10
31	Wyoming	10
36	California	9
36	Ohio	9
36	Oklahoma	9
36	Rhode Island	9
36	Wisconsin	9
41	Alabama	8
41	Arkansas	8
43	Louisiana	7
43	Mississippi	7
45	Alaska	6
45	Texas	6
47	Idaho	5
47	Iowa	5
47	New Mexico	5
50	Hawaii	3
	District of Columbia	6

Source: U.S. Department of Education, National Center for Education Statistics
   "The Nation's Report Card: Reading 2009" (http://nces.ed.gov/nationsreportcard/)
*There are four achievement levels: Below Basic, Basic, Proficient, and Advanced. Proficient represents solid academic mastery for 4th graders. Students reaching this level have demonstrated competency over challenging subject matter, including subject matter knowledge, application of such knowledge to real-world situations, and analytical skills appropriate to the subject matter. Based only on disabled students who were assessed.

Percent of English Language Learner Public School Fourth Graders Proficient or Better in Reading in 2009
National Percent = 6%*

ALPHA ORDER			RANK ORDER		
RANK	STATE	PERCENT	RANK	STATE	PERCENT
NA	Alabama**	NA	1	South Carolina	20
29	Alaska	4	2	Kansas	17
39	Arizona	2	2	Maryland	17
10	Arkansas	9	4	New Hampshire	15
29	California	4	5	Florida	13
29	Colorado	4	6	Massachusetts	12
20	Connecticut	6	6	Virginia	12
10	Delaware	9	8	North Carolina	11
5	Florida	13	9	Louisiana	10
20	Georgia	6	10	Arkansas	9
25	Hawaii	5	10	Delaware	9
35	Idaho	3	10	Iowa	9
18	Illinois	7	10	Michigan	9
20	Indiana	6	10	Oklahoma	9
10	Iowa	9	15	Ohio	8
2	Kansas	17	15	Texas	8
NA	Kentucky**	NA	15	Wisconsin	8
9	Louisiana	10	18	Illinois	7
NA	Maine**	NA	18	Minnesota	7
2	Maryland	17	20	Connecticut	6
6	Massachusetts	12	20	Georgia	6
10	Michigan	9	20	Indiana	6
18	Minnesota	7	20	New York	6
NA	Mississippi**	NA	20	Rhode Island	6
NA	Missouri**	NA	25	Hawaii	5
25	Montana	5	25	Montana	5
29	Nebraska	4	25	Nevada	5
25	Nevada	5	25	Utah	5
4	New Hampshire	15	29	Alaska	4
NA	New Jersey**	NA	29	California	4
35	New Mexico	3	29	Colorado	4
20	New York	6	29	Nebraska	4
8	North Carolina	11	29	Pennsylvania	4
NA	North Dakota**	NA	29	Tennessee	4
15	Ohio	8	35	Idaho	3
10	Oklahoma	9	35	New Mexico	3
35	Oregon	3	35	Oregon	3
29	Pennsylvania	4	35	Washington	3
20	Rhode Island	6	39	Arizona	2
1	South Carolina	20	NA	Alabama**	NA
NA	South Dakota**	NA	NA	Kentucky**	NA
29	Tennessee	4	NA	Maine**	NA
15	Texas	8	NA	Mississippi**	NA
25	Utah	5	NA	Missouri**	NA
NA	Vermont**	NA	NA	New Jersey**	NA
6	Virginia	12	NA	North Dakota**	NA
35	Washington	3	NA	South Dakota**	NA
NA	West Virginia**	NA	NA	Vermont**	NA
15	Wisconsin	8	NA	West Virginia**	NA
NA	Wyoming**	NA	NA	Wyoming**	NA
				District of Columbia	6

Source: U.S. Department of Education, National Center for Education Statistics
"The Nation's Report Card: Reading 2009" (http://nces.ed.gov/nationsreportcard/)
*There are four achievement levels: Below Basic, Basic, Proficient, and Advanced. Proficient represents solid academic mastery for 4th graders. Students reaching this level have demonstrated competency over challenging subject matter, including subject matter knowledge, application of such knowledge to real-world situations, and analytical skills appropriate to the subject matter. **Sample size insufficient.

Average Reading Score for Public School Eighth Graders in 2009

National Average Score = 262*

RANK	STATE	AVERAGE SCORE
43	Alabama	255
38	Alaska	259
40	Arizona	258
40	Arkansas	258
48	California	253
20	Colorado	266
3	Connecticut	272
25	Delaware	265
30	Florida	264
34	Georgia	260
43	Hawaii	255
25	Idaho	265
25	Illinois	265
20	Indiana	266
25	Iowa	265
14	Kansas	267
14	Kentucky	267
48	Louisiana	253
12	Maine	268
14	Maryland	267
1	Massachusetts	274
32	Michigan	262
7	Minnesota	270
50	Mississippi	251
14	Missouri	267
7	Montana	270
14	Nebraska	267
46	Nevada	254
5	New Hampshire	271
2	New Jersey	273
46	New Mexico	254
30	New York	264
34	North Carolina	260
10	North Dakota	269
10	Ohio	269
38	Oklahoma	259
25	Oregon	265
5	Pennsylvania	271
34	Rhode Island	260
42	South Carolina	257
7	South Dakota	270
33	Tennessee	261
34	Texas	260
20	Utah	266
3	Vermont	272
20	Virginia	266
14	Washington	267
43	West Virginia	255
20	Wisconsin	266
12	Wyoming	268

RANK ORDER

RANK	STATE	AVERAGE SCORE
1	Massachusetts	274
2	New Jersey	273
3	Connecticut	272
3	Vermont	272
5	New Hampshire	271
5	Pennsylvania	271
7	Minnesota	270
7	Montana	270
7	South Dakota	270
10	North Dakota	269
10	Ohio	269
12	Maine	268
12	Wyoming	268
14	Kansas	267
14	Kentucky	267
14	Maryland	267
14	Missouri	267
14	Nebraska	267
14	Washington	267
20	Colorado	266
20	Indiana	266
20	Utah	266
20	Virginia	266
20	Wisconsin	266
25	Delaware	265
25	Idaho	265
25	Illinois	265
25	Iowa	265
25	Oregon	265
30	Florida	264
30	New York	264
32	Michigan	262
33	Tennessee	261
34	Georgia	260
34	North Carolina	260
34	Rhode Island	260
34	Texas	260
38	Alaska	259
38	Oklahoma	259
40	Arizona	258
40	Arkansas	258
42	South Carolina	257
43	Alabama	255
43	Hawaii	255
43	West Virginia	255
46	Nevada	254
46	New Mexico	254
48	California	253
48	Louisiana	253
50	Mississippi	251

	District of Columbia	242

Source: U.S. Department of Education, National Center for Education Statistics
"The Nation's Report Card: Reading 2009" (http://nces.ed.gov/nationsreportcard/)
*These scores are from the National Assessment of Educational Progress (NAEP). Scale ranges from 0 to 500.

Average Reading Score for Public School Eighth Grade Males in 2009

National Average Score = 258*

<table>
<tr><td colspan="3">ALPHA ORDER</td><td colspan="3">RANK ORDER</td></tr>
<tr><td>RANK</td><td>STATE</td><td>AVERAGE SCORE</td><td>RANK</td><td>STATE</td><td>AVERAGE SCORE</td></tr>
<tr><td>44</td><td>Alabama</td><td>249</td><td>1</td><td>Massachusetts</td><td>269</td></tr>
<tr><td>38</td><td>Alaska</td><td>254</td><td>1</td><td>New Jersey</td><td>269</td></tr>
<tr><td>38</td><td>Arizona</td><td>254</td><td>3</td><td>Connecticut</td><td>267</td></tr>
<tr><td>38</td><td>Arkansas</td><td>254</td><td>3</td><td>Pennsylvania</td><td>267</td></tr>
<tr><td>45</td><td>California</td><td>248</td><td>3</td><td>Vermont</td><td>267</td></tr>
<tr><td>17</td><td>Colorado</td><td>262</td><td>6</td><td>South Dakota</td><td>266</td></tr>
<tr><td>3</td><td>Connecticut</td><td>267</td><td>7</td><td>Kansas</td><td>265</td></tr>
<tr><td>23</td><td>Delaware</td><td>260</td><td>7</td><td>Minnesota</td><td>265</td></tr>
<tr><td>29</td><td>Florida</td><td>259</td><td>7</td><td>Montana</td><td>265</td></tr>
<tr><td>35</td><td>Georgia</td><td>255</td><td>7</td><td>North Dakota</td><td>265</td></tr>
<tr><td>45</td><td>Hawaii</td><td>248</td><td>7</td><td>Ohio</td><td>265</td></tr>
<tr><td>29</td><td>Idaho</td><td>259</td><td>7</td><td>Wyoming</td><td>265</td></tr>
<tr><td>23</td><td>Illinois</td><td>260</td><td>13</td><td>New Hampshire</td><td>264</td></tr>
<tr><td>14</td><td>Indiana</td><td>263</td><td>14</td><td>Indiana</td><td>263</td></tr>
<tr><td>21</td><td>Iowa</td><td>261</td><td>14</td><td>Kentucky</td><td>263</td></tr>
<tr><td>7</td><td>Kansas</td><td>265</td><td>14</td><td>Nebraska</td><td>263</td></tr>
<tr><td>14</td><td>Kentucky</td><td>263</td><td>17</td><td>Colorado</td><td>262</td></tr>
<tr><td>45</td><td>Louisiana</td><td>248</td><td>17</td><td>Maine</td><td>262</td></tr>
<tr><td>17</td><td>Maine</td><td>262</td><td>17</td><td>Maryland</td><td>262</td></tr>
<tr><td>17</td><td>Maryland</td><td>262</td><td>17</td><td>Missouri</td><td>262</td></tr>
<tr><td>1</td><td>Massachusetts</td><td>269</td><td>21</td><td>Iowa</td><td>261</td></tr>
<tr><td>32</td><td>Michigan</td><td>257</td><td>21</td><td>Washington</td><td>261</td></tr>
<tr><td>7</td><td>Minnesota</td><td>265</td><td>23</td><td>Delaware</td><td>260</td></tr>
<tr><td>45</td><td>Mississippi</td><td>248</td><td>23</td><td>Illinois</td><td>260</td></tr>
<tr><td>17</td><td>Missouri</td><td>262</td><td>23</td><td>Oregon</td><td>260</td></tr>
<tr><td>7</td><td>Montana</td><td>265</td><td>23</td><td>Utah</td><td>260</td></tr>
<tr><td>14</td><td>Nebraska</td><td>263</td><td>23</td><td>Virginia</td><td>260</td></tr>
<tr><td>45</td><td>Nevada</td><td>248</td><td>23</td><td>Wisconsin</td><td>260</td></tr>
<tr><td>13</td><td>New Hampshire</td><td>264</td><td>29</td><td>Florida</td><td>259</td></tr>
<tr><td>1</td><td>New Jersey</td><td>269</td><td>29</td><td>Idaho</td><td>259</td></tr>
<tr><td>42</td><td>New Mexico</td><td>251</td><td>29</td><td>New York</td><td>259</td></tr>
<tr><td>29</td><td>New York</td><td>259</td><td>32</td><td>Michigan</td><td>257</td></tr>
<tr><td>41</td><td>North Carolina</td><td>253</td><td>32</td><td>Tennessee</td><td>257</td></tr>
<tr><td>7</td><td>North Dakota</td><td>265</td><td>34</td><td>Texas</td><td>256</td></tr>
<tr><td>7</td><td>Ohio</td><td>265</td><td>35</td><td>Georgia</td><td>255</td></tr>
<tr><td>35</td><td>Oklahoma</td><td>255</td><td>35</td><td>Oklahoma</td><td>255</td></tr>
<tr><td>23</td><td>Oregon</td><td>260</td><td>35</td><td>Rhode Island</td><td>255</td></tr>
<tr><td>3</td><td>Pennsylvania</td><td>267</td><td>38</td><td>Alaska</td><td>254</td></tr>
<tr><td>35</td><td>Rhode Island</td><td>255</td><td>38</td><td>Arizona</td><td>254</td></tr>
<tr><td>42</td><td>South Carolina</td><td>251</td><td>38</td><td>Arkansas</td><td>254</td></tr>
<tr><td>6</td><td>South Dakota</td><td>266</td><td>41</td><td>North Carolina</td><td>253</td></tr>
<tr><td>32</td><td>Tennessee</td><td>257</td><td>42</td><td>New Mexico</td><td>251</td></tr>
<tr><td>34</td><td>Texas</td><td>256</td><td>42</td><td>South Carolina</td><td>251</td></tr>
<tr><td>23</td><td>Utah</td><td>260</td><td>44</td><td>Alabama</td><td>249</td></tr>
<tr><td>3</td><td>Vermont</td><td>267</td><td>45</td><td>California</td><td>248</td></tr>
<tr><td>23</td><td>Virginia</td><td>260</td><td>45</td><td>Hawaii</td><td>248</td></tr>
<tr><td>21</td><td>Washington</td><td>261</td><td>45</td><td>Louisiana</td><td>248</td></tr>
<tr><td>45</td><td>West Virginia</td><td>248</td><td>45</td><td>Mississippi</td><td>248</td></tr>
<tr><td>23</td><td>Wisconsin</td><td>260</td><td>45</td><td>Nevada</td><td>248</td></tr>
<tr><td>7</td><td>Wyoming</td><td>265</td><td>45</td><td>West Virginia</td><td>248</td></tr>
<tr><td></td><td></td><td></td><td></td><td>District of Columbia</td><td>236</td></tr>
</table>

Source: U.S. Department of Education, National Center for Education Statistics
    "The Nation's Report Card: Reading 2009" (http://nces.ed.gov/nationsreportcard/)
*These scores are from the National Assessment of Educational Progress (NAEP). Scale ranges from 0 to 500.

Average Reading Score for Public School Eighth Grade Females in 2009

National Average Score = 267*

ALPHA ORDER				RANK ORDER		
RANK	STATE	AVERAGE SCORE		RANK	STATE	AVERAGE SCORE
44	Alabama	261		1	Massachusetts	279
35	Alaska	265		2	Vermont	278
44	Arizona	261		3	Connecticut	277
41	Arkansas	262		3	New Hampshire	277
48	California	257		3	New Jersey	277
23	Colorado	270		6	Montana	276
3	Connecticut	277		7	Minnesota	275
23	Delaware	270		7	South Dakota	275
27	Florida	269		9	North Dakota	274
34	Georgia	266		9	Pennsylvania	274
41	Hawaii	262		11	Maine	273
17	Idaho	271		11	Washington	273
27	Illinois	269		13	Maryland	272
27	Indiana	269		13	Missouri	272
27	Iowa	269		13	Nebraska	272
27	Kansas	269		13	Ohio	272
17	Kentucky	271		17	Idaho	271
47	Louisiana	258		17	Kentucky	271
11	Maine	273		17	Utah	271
13	Maryland	272		17	Virginia	271
1	Massachusetts	279		17	Wisconsin	271
32	Michigan	267		17	Wyoming	271
7	Minnesota	275		23	Colorado	270
50	Mississippi	255		23	Delaware	270
13	Missouri	272		23	New York	270
6	Montana	276		23	Oregon	270
13	Nebraska	272		27	Florida	269
46	Nevada	260		27	Illinois	269
3	New Hampshire	277		27	Indiana	269
3	New Jersey	277		27	Iowa	269
48	New Mexico	257		27	Kansas	269
23	New York	270		32	Michigan	267
32	North Carolina	267		32	North Carolina	267
9	North Dakota	274		34	Georgia	266
13	Ohio	272		35	Alaska	265
38	Oklahoma	264		35	Rhode Island	265
23	Oregon	270		35	Tennessee	265
9	Pennsylvania	274		38	Oklahoma	264
35	Rhode Island	265		38	South Carolina	264
38	South Carolina	264		38	Texas	264
7	South Dakota	275		41	Arkansas	262
35	Tennessee	265		41	Hawaii	262
38	Texas	264		41	West Virginia	262
17	Utah	271		44	Alabama	261
2	Vermont	278		44	Arizona	261
17	Virginia	271		46	Nevada	260
11	Washington	273		47	Louisiana	258
41	West Virginia	262		48	California	257
17	Wisconsin	271		48	New Mexico	257
17	Wyoming	271		50	Mississippi	255
					District of Columbia	248

Source: U.S. Department of Education, National Center for Education Statistics
"The Nation's Report Card: Reading 2009" (http://nces.ed.gov/nationsreportcard/)
*These scores are from the National Assessment of Educational Progress (NAEP). Scale ranges from 0 to 500.

Average Reading Score for Public School Eighth Graders Eligible for Free or Reduced Price Lunch Program in 2009
National Average Score = 249*

ALPHA ORDER

RANK	STATE	AVERAGE SCORE
47	Alabama	243
37	Alaska	247
46	Arizona	244
36	Arkansas	248
50	California	241
25	Colorado	251
28	Connecticut	250
16	Delaware	253
9	Florida	255
32	Georgia	249
39	Hawaii	246
12	Idaho	254
32	Illinois	249
12	Indiana	254
16	Iowa	253
9	Kansas	255
6	Kentucky	257
39	Louisiana	246
4	Maine	259
28	Maryland	250
12	Massachusetts	254
37	Michigan	247
22	Minnesota	252
47	Mississippi	243
16	Missouri	253
1	Montana	261
16	Nebraska	253
47	Nevada	243
6	New Hampshire	257
16	New Jersey	253
39	New Mexico	246
22	New York	252
44	North Carolina	245
2	North Dakota	260
9	Ohio	255
28	Oklahoma	250
22	Oregon	252
16	Pennsylvania	253
44	Rhode Island	245
39	South Carolina	246
5	South Dakota	258
28	Tennessee	250
32	Texas	249
25	Utah	251
2	Vermont	260
25	Virginia	251
12	Washington	254
39	West Virginia	246
32	Wisconsin	249
6	Wyoming	257

RANK ORDER

RANK	STATE	AVERAGE SCORE
1	Montana	261
2	North Dakota	260
2	Vermont	260
4	Maine	259
5	South Dakota	258
6	Kentucky	257
6	New Hampshire	257
6	Wyoming	257
9	Florida	255
9	Kansas	255
9	Ohio	255
12	Idaho	254
12	Indiana	254
12	Massachusetts	254
12	Washington	254
16	Delaware	253
16	Iowa	253
16	Missouri	253
16	Nebraska	253
16	New Jersey	253
16	Pennsylvania	253
22	Minnesota	252
22	New York	252
22	Oregon	252
25	Colorado	251
25	Utah	251
25	Virginia	251
28	Connecticut	250
28	Maryland	250
28	Oklahoma	250
28	Tennessee	250
32	Georgia	249
32	Illinois	249
32	Texas	249
32	Wisconsin	249
36	Arkansas	248
37	Alaska	247
37	Michigan	247
39	Hawaii	246
39	Louisiana	246
39	New Mexico	246
39	South Carolina	246
39	West Virginia	246
44	North Carolina	245
44	Rhode Island	245
46	Arizona	244
47	Alabama	243
47	Mississippi	243
47	Nevada	243
50	California	241
	District of Columbia	237

Source: U.S. Department of Education, National Center for Education Statistics
   "The Nation's Report Card: Reading 2009" (http://nces.ed.gov/nationsreportcard/)
*These scores are from the National Assessment of Educational Progress (NAEP). Scale ranges from 0 to 500.

Percent of Public School Eighth Graders
Proficient or Better in Reading in 2009
National Percent = 30%*

RANK	STATE	PERCENT
42	Alabama	24
36	Alaska	27
36	Arizona	27
36	Arkansas	27
44	California	22
26	Colorado	32
1	Connecticut	43
31	Delaware	31
26	Florida	32
36	Georgia	27
44	Hawaii	22
19	Idaho	33
19	Illinois	33
26	Indiana	32
26	Iowa	32
19	Kansas	33
19	Kentucky	33
49	Louisiana	20
13	Maine	35
11	Maryland	36
1	Massachusetts	43
31	Michigan	31
7	Minnesota	38
50	Mississippi	19
15	Missouri	34
7	Montana	38
13	Nebraska	35
44	Nevada	22
6	New Hampshire	39
3	New Jersey	42
44	New Mexico	22
19	New York	33
33	North Carolina	29
15	North Dakota	34
9	Ohio	37
41	Oklahoma	26
19	Oregon	33
5	Pennsylvania	40
34	Rhode Island	28
42	South Carolina	24
9	South Dakota	37
34	Tennessee	28
36	Texas	27
19	Utah	33
4	Vermont	41
26	Virginia	32
11	Washington	36
44	West Virginia	22
15	Wisconsin	34
15	Wyoming	34

RANK	STATE	PERCENT
1	Connecticut	43
1	Massachusetts	43
3	New Jersey	42
4	Vermont	41
5	Pennsylvania	40
6	New Hampshire	39
7	Minnesota	38
7	Montana	38
9	Ohio	37
9	South Dakota	37
11	Maryland	36
11	Washington	36
13	Maine	35
13	Nebraska	35
15	Missouri	34
15	North Dakota	34
15	Wisconsin	34
15	Wyoming	34
19	Idaho	33
19	Illinois	33
19	Kansas	33
19	Kentucky	33
19	New York	33
19	Oregon	33
19	Utah	33
26	Colorado	32
26	Florida	32
26	Indiana	32
26	Iowa	32
26	Virginia	32
31	Delaware	31
31	Michigan	31
33	North Carolina	29
34	Rhode Island	28
34	Tennessee	28
36	Alaska	27
36	Arizona	27
36	Arkansas	27
36	Georgia	27
36	Texas	27
41	Oklahoma	26
42	Alabama	24
42	South Carolina	24
44	California	22
44	Hawaii	22
44	Nevada	22
44	New Mexico	22
44	West Virginia	22
49	Louisiana	20
50	Mississippi	19

	District of Columbia	14

Source: U.S. Department of Education, National Center for Education Statistics
"The Nation's Report Card: Reading 2009" (http://nces.ed.gov/nationsreportcard/)
*There are four achievement levels: Below Basic, Basic, Proficient, and Advanced. Proficient represents solid academic mastery for 8th graders. Students reaching this level have demonstrated competency over challenging subject matter, including subject matter knowledge, application of such knowledge to real-world situations, and analytical skills appropriate to the subject matter.

Percent of Public School Eighth Grade Males
Proficient or Better in Reading in 2009
National Percent = 26%*

ALPHA ORDER			RANK ORDER		
RANK	STATE	PERCENT	RANK	STATE	PERCENT
43	Alabama	19	1	Connecticut	37
40	Alaska	21	1	Massachusetts	37
33	Arizona	24	3	New Jersey	36
35	Arkansas	23	4	Pennsylvania	35
43	California	19	5	Vermont	34
17	Colorado	28	6	Minnesota	32
1	Connecticut	37	6	New Hampshire	32
30	Delaware	25	6	Ohio	32
24	Florida	27	9	Kansas	31
38	Georgia	22	9	Maryland	31
48	Hawaii	16	11	Montana	30
28	Idaho	26	11	South Dakota	30
17	Illinois	28	11	Washington	30
15	Indiana	29	11	Wyoming	30
28	Iowa	26	15	Indiana	29
9	Kansas	31	15	Kentucky	29
15	Kentucky	29	17	Colorado	28
48	Louisiana	16	17	Illinois	28
17	Maine	28	17	Maine	28
9	Maryland	31	17	Missouri	28
1	Massachusetts	37	17	Nebraska	28
30	Michigan	25	17	New York	28
6	Minnesota	32	17	Oregon	28
46	Mississippi	17	24	Florida	27
17	Missouri	28	24	North Dakota	27
11	Montana	30	24	Utah	27
17	Nebraska	28	24	Wisconsin	27
48	Nevada	16	28	Idaho	26
6	New Hampshire	32	28	Iowa	26
3	New Jersey	36	30	Delaware	25
42	New Mexico	20	30	Michigan	25
17	New York	28	30	Virginia	25
38	North Carolina	22	33	Arizona	24
24	North Dakota	27	33	Tennessee	24
6	Ohio	32	35	Arkansas	23
40	Oklahoma	21	35	Rhode Island	23
17	Oregon	28	35	Texas	23
4	Pennsylvania	35	38	Georgia	22
35	Rhode Island	23	38	North Carolina	22
43	South Carolina	19	40	Alaska	21
11	South Dakota	30	40	Oklahoma	21
33	Tennessee	24	42	New Mexico	20
35	Texas	23	43	Alabama	19
24	Utah	27	43	California	19
5	Vermont	34	43	South Carolina	19
30	Virginia	25	46	Mississippi	17
11	Washington	30	46	West Virginia	17
46	West Virginia	17	48	Hawaii	16
24	Wisconsin	27	48	Louisiana	16
11	Wyoming	30	48	Nevada	16
				District of Columbia	11

Source: U.S. Department of Education, National Center for Education Statistics
     "The Nation's Report Card: Reading 2009" (http://nces.ed.gov/nationsreportcard/)
*There are four achievement levels: Below Basic, Basic, Proficient, and Advanced. Proficient represents solid academic
mastery for 8th graders. Students reaching this level have demonstrated competency over challenging subject matter, including
subject matter knowledge, application of such knowledge to real-world situations, and analytical skills appropriate to the subject
matter.

Percent of Public School Eighth Grade Females
Proficient or Better in Reading in 2009
National Percent = 35%*

ALPHA ORDER

RANK	STATE	PERCENT
43	Alabama	28
34	Alaska	33
40	Arizona	30
40	Arkansas	30
47	California	26
26	Colorado	37
2	Connecticut	48
26	Delaware	37
26	Florida	37
35	Georgia	32
43	Hawaii	28
18	Idaho	40
26	Illinois	37
33	Indiana	35
24	Iowa	38
30	Kansas	36
24	Kentucky	38
48	Louisiana	24
11	Maine	41
11	Maryland	41
1	Massachusetts	49
30	Michigan	36
6	Minnesota	45
50	Mississippi	21
11	Missouri	41
6	Montana	45
11	Nebraska	41
43	Nevada	28
4	New Hampshire	47
4	New Jersey	47
49	New Mexico	23
19	New York	39
30	North Carolina	36
11	North Dakota	41
11	Ohio	41
38	Oklahoma	31
19	Oregon	39
6	Pennsylvania	45
35	Rhode Island	32
40	South Carolina	30
9	South Dakota	44
35	Tennessee	32
38	Texas	31
19	Utah	39
2	Vermont	48
19	Virginia	39
10	Washington	42
43	West Virginia	28
11	Wisconsin	41
19	Wyoming	39

RANK ORDER

RANK	STATE	PERCENT
1	Massachusetts	49
2	Connecticut	48
2	Vermont	48
4	New Hampshire	47
4	New Jersey	47
6	Minnesota	45
6	Montana	45
6	Pennsylvania	45
9	South Dakota	44
10	Washington	42
11	Maine	41
11	Maryland	41
11	Missouri	41
11	Nebraska	41
11	North Dakota	41
11	Ohio	41
11	Wisconsin	41
18	Idaho	40
19	New York	39
19	Oregon	39
19	Utah	39
19	Virginia	39
19	Wyoming	39
24	Iowa	38
24	Kentucky	38
26	Colorado	37
26	Delaware	37
26	Florida	37
26	Illinois	37
30	Kansas	36
30	Michigan	36
30	North Carolina	36
33	Indiana	35
34	Alaska	33
35	Georgia	32
35	Rhode Island	32
35	Tennessee	32
38	Oklahoma	31
38	Texas	31
40	Arizona	30
40	Arkansas	30
40	South Carolina	30
43	Alabama	28
43	Hawaii	28
43	Nevada	28
43	West Virginia	28
47	California	26
48	Louisiana	24
49	New Mexico	23
50	Mississippi	21

| | District of Columbia | 16 |

Source: U.S. Department of Education, National Center for Education Statistics
    "The Nation's Report Card: Reading 2009" (http://nces.ed.gov/nationsreportcard/)
*There are four achievement levels: Below Basic, Basic, Proficient, and Advanced. Proficient represents solid academic mastery for 8th graders. Students reaching this level have demonstrated competency over challenging subject matter, including subject matter knowledge, application of such knowledge to real-world situations, and analytical skills appropriate to the subject matter.

Percent of Public School Eighth Graders Eligible for Free or Reduced Lunch Program Proficient or Better in Reading in 2009
National Percent = 16%*

ALPHA ORDER				RANK ORDER		
RANK	STATE	PERCENT		RANK	STATE	PERCENT
48	Alabama	12		1	Montana	26
33	Alaska	15		2	North Dakota	25
39	Arizona	14		3	New Hampshire	24
27	Arkansas	17		3	Vermont	24
50	California	11		5	Maine	23
29	Colorado	16		6	South Dakota	22
20	Connecticut	18		7	Florida	21
27	Delaware	17		7	Idaho	21
7	Florida	21		7	Iowa	21
39	Georgia	14		7	Kentucky	21
39	Hawaii	14		7	Ohio	21
7	Idaho	21		7	Washington	21
29	Illinois	16		13	Massachusetts	20
20	Indiana	18		14	Kansas	19
7	Iowa	21		14	Nebraska	19
14	Kansas	19		14	New York	19
7	Kentucky	21		14	Oregon	19
45	Louisiana	13		14	Pennsylvania	19
5	Maine	23		14	Wyoming	19
29	Maryland	16		20	Connecticut	18
13	Massachusetts	20		20	Indiana	18
33	Michigan	15		20	Minnesota	18
20	Minnesota	18		20	Missouri	18
48	Mississippi	12		20	New Jersey	18
20	Missouri	18		20	Utah	18
1	Montana	26		20	Wisconsin	18
14	Nebraska	19		27	Arkansas	17
45	Nevada	13		27	Delaware	17
3	New Hampshire	24		29	Colorado	16
20	New Jersey	18		29	Illinois	16
39	New Mexico	14		29	Maryland	16
14	New York	19		29	Oklahoma	16
39	North Carolina	14		33	Alaska	15
2	North Dakota	25		33	Michigan	15
7	Ohio	21		33	Tennessee	15
29	Oklahoma	16		33	Texas	15
14	Oregon	19		33	Virginia	15
14	Pennsylvania	19		33	West Virginia	15
39	Rhode Island	14		39	Arizona	14
45	South Carolina	13		39	Georgia	14
6	South Dakota	22		39	Hawaii	14
33	Tennessee	15		39	New Mexico	14
33	Texas	15		39	North Carolina	14
20	Utah	18		39	Rhode Island	14
3	Vermont	24		45	Louisiana	13
33	Virginia	15		45	Nevada	13
7	Washington	21		45	South Carolina	13
33	West Virginia	15		48	Alabama	12
20	Wisconsin	18		48	Mississippi	12
14	Wyoming	19		50	California	11
					District of Columbia	9

Source: U.S. Department of Education, National Center for Education Statistics
   "The Nation's Report Card: Reading 2009" (http://nces.ed.gov/nationsreportcard/)
*There are four achievement levels: Below Basic, Basic, Proficient, and Advanced. Proficient represents solid academic mastery for 8th graders. Students reaching this level have demonstrated competency over challenging subject matter, including subject matter knowledge, application of such knowledge to real-world situations, and analytical skills appropriate to the subject matter.

Percent of White Public School Eighth Graders
Proficient or Better in Reading in 2009
National Percent = 39%*

ALPHA ORDER

RANK	STATE	PERCENT
45	Alabama	31
31	Alaska	36
20	Arizona	39
44	Arkansas	33
27	California	37
11	Colorado	41
1	Connecticut	51
11	Delaware	41
15	Florida	40
35	Georgia	35
35	Hawaii	35
27	Idaho	37
8	Illinois	42
31	Indiana	36
40	Iowa	34
20	Kansas	39
35	Kentucky	35
49	Louisiana	28
35	Maine	35
4	Maryland	48
3	Massachusetts	49
31	Michigan	36
6	Minnesota	44
45	Mississippi	31
25	Missouri	38
15	Montana	40
20	Nebraska	39
45	Nevada	31
15	New Hampshire	40
1	New Jersey	51
25	New Mexico	38
6	New York	44
20	North Carolina	39
35	North Dakota	35
8	Ohio	42
48	Oklahoma	29
27	Oregon	37
5	Pennsylvania	46
40	Rhode Island	34
40	South Carolina	34
15	South Dakota	40
40	Tennessee	34
8	Texas	42
27	Utah	37
11	Vermont	41
15	Virginia	40
11	Washington	41
50	West Virginia	22
20	Wisconsin	39
31	Wyoming	36

RANK ORDER

RANK	STATE	PERCENT
1	Connecticut	51
1	New Jersey	51
3	Massachusetts	49
4	Maryland	48
5	Pennsylvania	46
6	Minnesota	44
6	New York	44
8	Illinois	42
8	Ohio	42
8	Texas	42
11	Colorado	41
11	Delaware	41
11	Vermont	41
11	Washington	41
15	Florida	40
15	Montana	40
15	New Hampshire	40
15	South Dakota	40
15	Virginia	40
20	Arizona	39
20	Kansas	39
20	Nebraska	39
20	North Carolina	39
20	Wisconsin	39
25	Missouri	38
25	New Mexico	38
27	California	37
27	Idaho	37
27	Oregon	37
27	Utah	37
31	Alaska	36
31	Indiana	36
31	Michigan	36
31	Wyoming	36
35	Georgia	35
35	Hawaii	35
35	Kentucky	35
35	Maine	35
35	North Dakota	35
40	Iowa	34
40	Rhode Island	34
40	South Carolina	34
40	Tennessee	34
44	Arkansas	33
45	Alabama	31
45	Mississippi	31
45	Nevada	31
48	Oklahoma	29
49	Louisiana	28
50	West Virginia	22
	District of Columbia**	NA

Source: U.S. Department of Education, National Center for Education Statistics
"The Nation's Report Card: Reading 2009" (http://nces.ed.gov/nationsreportcard/)
*There are four achievement levels: Below Basic, Basic, Proficient, and Advanced. Proficient represents solid academic mastery for 8th graders. Students reaching this level have demonstrated competency over challenging subject matter, including subject matter knowledge, application of such knowledge to real-world situations, and analytical skills appropriate to the subject matter. **Sample size insufficient.

Percent of Black Public School Eighth Graders
Proficient or Better in Reading in 2009
National Percent = 13%*

<table>
<tr><th colspan="3">ALPHA ORDER</th><th colspan="3">RANK ORDER</th></tr>
<tr><th>RANK</th><th>STATE</th><th>PERCENT</th><th>RANK</th><th>STATE</th><th>PERCENT</th></tr>
<tr><td>36</td><td>Alabama</td><td>9</td><td>1</td><td>Maine</td><td>22</td></tr>
<tr><td>24</td><td>Alaska</td><td>12</td><td>2</td><td>Arizona</td><td>21</td></tr>
<tr><td>2</td><td>Arizona</td><td>21</td><td>3</td><td>Hawaii</td><td>20</td></tr>
<tr><td>40</td><td>Arkansas</td><td>8</td><td>4</td><td>West Virginia</td><td>18</td></tr>
<tr><td>28</td><td>California</td><td>11</td><td>5</td><td>Massachusetts</td><td>17</td></tr>
<tr><td>12</td><td>Colorado</td><td>15</td><td>5</td><td>New Jersey</td><td>17</td></tr>
<tr><td>28</td><td>Connecticut</td><td>11</td><td>7</td><td>Delaware</td><td>16</td></tr>
<tr><td>7</td><td>Delaware</td><td>16</td><td>7</td><td>Maryland</td><td>16</td></tr>
<tr><td>12</td><td>Florida</td><td>15</td><td>7</td><td>New Mexico</td><td>16</td></tr>
<tr><td>12</td><td>Georgia</td><td>15</td><td>7</td><td>Oklahoma</td><td>16</td></tr>
<tr><td>3</td><td>Hawaii</td><td>20</td><td>7</td><td>Pennsylvania</td><td>16</td></tr>
<tr><td>NA</td><td>Idaho**</td><td>NA</td><td>12</td><td>Colorado</td><td>15</td></tr>
<tr><td>31</td><td>Illinois</td><td>10</td><td>12</td><td>Florida</td><td>15</td></tr>
<tr><td>12</td><td>Indiana</td><td>15</td><td>12</td><td>Georgia</td><td>15</td></tr>
<tr><td>24</td><td>Iowa</td><td>12</td><td>12</td><td>Indiana</td><td>15</td></tr>
<tr><td>17</td><td>Kansas</td><td>14</td><td>12</td><td>Kentucky</td><td>15</td></tr>
<tr><td>12</td><td>Kentucky</td><td>15</td><td>17</td><td>Kansas</td><td>14</td></tr>
<tr><td>31</td><td>Louisiana</td><td>10</td><td>17</td><td>Missouri</td><td>14</td></tr>
<tr><td>1</td><td>Maine</td><td>22</td><td>17</td><td>Virginia</td><td>14</td></tr>
<tr><td>7</td><td>Maryland</td><td>16</td><td>20</td><td>New York</td><td>13</td></tr>
<tr><td>5</td><td>Massachusetts</td><td>17</td><td>20</td><td>Ohio</td><td>13</td></tr>
<tr><td>36</td><td>Michigan</td><td>9</td><td>20</td><td>Texas</td><td>13</td></tr>
<tr><td>31</td><td>Minnesota</td><td>10</td><td>20</td><td>Washington</td><td>13</td></tr>
<tr><td>40</td><td>Mississippi</td><td>8</td><td>24</td><td>Alaska</td><td>12</td></tr>
<tr><td>17</td><td>Missouri</td><td>14</td><td>24</td><td>Iowa</td><td>12</td></tr>
<tr><td>NA</td><td>Montana**</td><td>NA</td><td>24</td><td>Nebraska</td><td>12</td></tr>
<tr><td>24</td><td>Nebraska</td><td>12</td><td>24</td><td>North Carolina</td><td>12</td></tr>
<tr><td>31</td><td>Nevada</td><td>10</td><td>28</td><td>California</td><td>11</td></tr>
<tr><td>NA</td><td>New Hampshire**</td><td>NA</td><td>28</td><td>Connecticut</td><td>11</td></tr>
<tr><td>5</td><td>New Jersey</td><td>17</td><td>28</td><td>Tennessee</td><td>11</td></tr>
<tr><td>7</td><td>New Mexico</td><td>16</td><td>31</td><td>Illinois</td><td>10</td></tr>
<tr><td>20</td><td>New York</td><td>13</td><td>31</td><td>Louisiana</td><td>10</td></tr>
<tr><td>24</td><td>North Carolina</td><td>12</td><td>31</td><td>Minnesota</td><td>10</td></tr>
<tr><td>NA</td><td>North Dakota**</td><td>NA</td><td>31</td><td>Nevada</td><td>10</td></tr>
<tr><td>20</td><td>Ohio</td><td>13</td><td>31</td><td>South Carolina</td><td>10</td></tr>
<tr><td>7</td><td>Oklahoma</td><td>16</td><td>36</td><td>Alabama</td><td>9</td></tr>
<tr><td>NA</td><td>Oregon**</td><td>NA</td><td>36</td><td>Michigan</td><td>9</td></tr>
<tr><td>7</td><td>Pennsylvania</td><td>16</td><td>36</td><td>Rhode Island</td><td>9</td></tr>
<tr><td>36</td><td>Rhode Island</td><td>9</td><td>36</td><td>Wisconsin</td><td>9</td></tr>
<tr><td>31</td><td>South Carolina</td><td>10</td><td>40</td><td>Arkansas</td><td>8</td></tr>
<tr><td>NA</td><td>South Dakota**</td><td>NA</td><td>40</td><td>Mississippi</td><td>8</td></tr>
<tr><td>28</td><td>Tennessee</td><td>11</td><td>NA</td><td>Idaho**</td><td>NA</td></tr>
<tr><td>20</td><td>Texas</td><td>13</td><td>NA</td><td>Montana**</td><td>NA</td></tr>
<tr><td>NA</td><td>Utah**</td><td>NA</td><td>NA</td><td>New Hampshire**</td><td>NA</td></tr>
<tr><td>NA</td><td>Vermont**</td><td>NA</td><td>NA</td><td>North Dakota**</td><td>NA</td></tr>
<tr><td>17</td><td>Virginia</td><td>14</td><td>NA</td><td>Oregon**</td><td>NA</td></tr>
<tr><td>20</td><td>Washington</td><td>13</td><td>NA</td><td>South Dakota**</td><td>NA</td></tr>
<tr><td>4</td><td>West Virginia</td><td>18</td><td>NA</td><td>Utah**</td><td>NA</td></tr>
<tr><td>36</td><td>Wisconsin</td><td>9</td><td>NA</td><td>Vermont**</td><td>NA</td></tr>
<tr><td>NA</td><td>Wyoming**</td><td>NA</td><td>NA</td><td>Wyoming**</td><td>NA</td></tr>
<tr><td></td><td></td><td></td><td></td><td>District of Columbia</td><td>10</td></tr>
</table>

Source: U.S. Department of Education, National Center for Education Statistics
    "The Nation's Report Card: Reading 2009" (http://nces.ed.gov/nationsreportcard/)
*There are four achievement levels: Below Basic, Basic, Proficient, and Advanced. Proficient represents solid academic
mastery for 8th graders. Students reaching this level have demonstrated competency over challenging subject matter, including
subject matter knowledge, application of such knowledge to real-world situations, and analytical skills appropriate to the subject
matter. **Sample size insufficient.

Percent of Hispanic Public School Eighth Graders
Proficient or Better in Reading in 2009
National Percent = 16%*

ALPHA ORDER			RANK ORDER		
RANK	STATE	PERCENT	RANK	STATE	PERCENT
10	Alabama	23	1	Kentucky	30
6	Alaska	25	1	South Carolina	30
31	Arizona	15	3	Florida	27
17	Arkansas	19	3	New Hampshire	27
37	California	13	5	Michigan	26
26	Colorado	16	6	Alaska	25
17	Connecticut	19	6	Maryland	25
13	Delaware	21	6	Missouri	25
3	Florida	27	9	Hawaii	24
15	Georgia	20	10	Alabama	23
9	Hawaii	24	10	Wyoming	23
41	Idaho	11	12	Virginia	22
21	Illinois	18	13	Delaware	21
31	Indiana	15	13	Tennessee	21
21	Iowa	18	15	Georgia	20
26	Kansas	16	15	New Jersey	20
1	Kentucky	30	17	Arkansas	19
NA	Louisiana**	NA	17	Connecticut	19
NA	Maine**	NA	17	Nebraska	19
6	Maryland	25	17	North Carolina	19
23	Massachusetts	17	21	Illinois	18
5	Michigan	26	21	Iowa	18
26	Minnesota	16	23	Massachusetts	17
NA	Mississippi**	NA	23	Texas	17
6	Missouri	25	23	Washington	17
NA	Montana**	NA	26	Colorado	16
17	Nebraska	19	26	Kansas	16
37	Nevada	13	26	Minnesota	16
3	New Hampshire	27	26	New York	16
15	New Jersey	20	26	Ohio	16
34	New Mexico	14	31	Arizona	15
26	New York	16	31	Indiana	15
17	North Carolina	19	31	Wisconsin	15
NA	North Dakota**	NA	34	New Mexico	14
26	Ohio	16	34	Oklahoma	14
34	Oklahoma	14	34	Oregon	14
34	Oregon	14	37	California	13
40	Pennsylvania	12	37	Nevada	13
41	Rhode Island	11	37	Utah	13
1	South Carolina	30	40	Pennsylvania	12
NA	South Dakota**	NA	41	Idaho	11
13	Tennessee	21	41	Rhode Island	11
23	Texas	17	NA	Louisiana**	NA
37	Utah	13	NA	Maine**	NA
NA	Vermont**	NA	NA	Mississippi**	NA
12	Virginia	22	NA	Montana**	NA
23	Washington	17	NA	North Dakota**	NA
NA	West Virginia**	NA	NA	South Dakota**	NA
31	Wisconsin	15	NA	Vermont**	NA
10	Wyoming	23	NA	West Virginia**	NA
				District of Columbia	21

Source: U.S. Department of Education, National Center for Education Statistics
   "The Nation's Report Card: Reading 2009" (http://nces.ed.gov/nationsreportcard/)
*There are four achievement levels: Below Basic, Basic, Proficient, and Advanced. Proficient represents solid academic mastery for 8th graders. Students reaching this level have demonstrated competency over challenging subject matter, including subject matter knowledge, application of such knowledge to real-world situations, and analytical skills appropriate to the subject matter. **Sample size insufficient.

Percent of Asian Public School Eighth Graders
Proficient or Better in Reading in 2009
National Percent = 44%*

ALPHA ORDER				RANK ORDER		
RANK	STATE	PERCENT		RANK	STATE	PERCENT
NA	Alabama**	NA		1	Connecticut	64
25	Alaska	21		1	Florida	64
8	Arizona	56		1	New Jersey	64
NA	Arkansas**	NA		4	Georgia	61
19	California	35		5	Illinois	60
15	Colorado	43		5	Maryland	60
1	Connecticut	64		5	Pennsylvania	60
17	Delaware	38		8	Arizona	56
1	Florida	64		9	Texas	53
4	Georgia	61		10	Massachusetts	50
26	Hawaii	19		11	New York	49
NA	Idaho**	NA		12	Oregon	48
5	Illinois	60		12	Virginia	48
NA	Indiana**	NA		14	North Carolina	46
NA	Iowa**	NA		15	Colorado	43
18	Kansas	36		16	Washington	42
NA	Kentucky**	NA		17	Delaware	38
NA	Louisiana**	NA		18	Kansas	36
NA	Maine**	NA		19	California	35
5	Maryland	60		19	Rhode Island	35
10	Massachusetts	50		21	Wisconsin	34
NA	Michigan**	NA		22	Utah	33
23	Minnesota	30		23	Minnesota	30
NA	Mississippi**	NA		24	Nevada	28
NA	Missouri**	NA		25	Alaska	21
NA	Montana**	NA		26	Hawaii	19
NA	Nebraska**	NA		NA	Alabama**	NA
24	Nevada	28		NA	Arkansas**	NA
NA	New Hampshire**	NA		NA	Idaho**	NA
1	New Jersey	64		NA	Indiana**	NA
NA	New Mexico**	NA		NA	Iowa**	NA
11	New York	49		NA	Kentucky**	NA
14	North Carolina	46		NA	Louisiana**	NA
NA	North Dakota**	NA		NA	Maine**	NA
NA	Ohio**	NA		NA	Michigan**	NA
NA	Oklahoma**	NA		NA	Mississippi**	NA
12	Oregon	48		NA	Missouri**	NA
5	Pennsylvania	60		NA	Montana**	NA
19	Rhode Island	35		NA	Nebraska**	NA
NA	South Carolina**	NA		NA	New Hampshire**	NA
NA	South Dakota**	NA		NA	New Mexico**	NA
NA	Tennessee**	NA		NA	North Dakota**	NA
9	Texas	53		NA	Ohio**	NA
22	Utah	33		NA	Oklahoma**	NA
NA	Vermont**	NA		NA	South Carolina**	NA
12	Virginia	48		NA	South Dakota**	NA
16	Washington	42		NA	Tennessee**	NA
NA	West Virginia**	NA		NA	Vermont**	NA
21	Wisconsin	34		NA	West Virginia**	NA
NA	Wyoming**	NA		NA	Wyoming**	NA
					District of Columbia**	NA

Source: U.S. Department of Education, National Center for Education Statistics
   "The Nation's Report Card: Reading 2009" (http://nces.ed.gov/nationsreportcard/)
*There are four achievement levels: Below Basic, Basic, Proficient, and Advanced. Proficient represents solid academic mastery for 8th graders. Students reaching this level have demonstrated competency over challenging subject matter, including subject matter knowledge, application of such knowledge to real-world situations, and analytical skills appropriate to the subject matter. **Sample size insufficient.

Percent of Disabled Public School Eighth Graders
Proficient or Better in Reading in 2009
National Percent = 8%*

ALPHA ORDER			RANK ORDER		
RANK	STATE	PERCENT	RANK	STATE	PERCENT
48	Alabama	2	1	New Jersey	19
32	Alaska	5	2	Maryland	18
26	Arizona	6	2	Massachusetts	18
32	Arkansas	5	4	Vermont	14
48	California	2	5	Connecticut	13
21	Colorado	7	5	Ohio	13
5	Connecticut	13	7	Kentucky	12
13	Delaware	9	7	New Hampshire	12
9	Florida	11	9	Florida	11
42	Georgia	4	10	Illinois	10
46	Hawaii	3	10	Maine	10
32	Idaho	5	10	Pennsylvania	10
10	Illinois	10	13	Delaware	9
13	Indiana	9	13	Indiana	9
32	Iowa	5	13	Minnesota	9
26	Kansas	6	13	New York	9
7	Kentucky	12	13	Oregon	9
32	Louisiana	5	13	Washington	9
10	Maine	10	19	Missouri	8
2	Maryland	18	19	Virginia	8
2	Massachusetts	18	21	Colorado	7
32	Michigan	5	21	Montana	7
13	Minnesota	9	21	North Dakota	7
48	Mississippi	2	21	Rhode Island	7
19	Missouri	8	21	South Carolina	7
21	Montana	7	26	Arizona	6
26	Nebraska	6	26	Kansas	6
42	Nevada	4	26	Nebraska	6
7	New Hampshire	12	26	Oklahoma	6
1	New Jersey	19	26	Wisconsin	6
32	New Mexico	5	26	Wyoming	6
13	New York	9	32	Alaska	5
32	North Carolina	5	32	Arkansas	5
21	North Dakota	7	32	Idaho	5
5	Ohio	13	32	Iowa	5
26	Oklahoma	6	32	Louisiana	5
13	Oregon	9	32	Michigan	5
10	Pennsylvania	10	32	New Mexico	5
21	Rhode Island	7	32	North Carolina	5
21	South Carolina	7	32	Tennessee	5
42	South Dakota	4	32	West Virginia	5
32	Tennessee	5	42	Georgia	4
42	Texas	4	42	Nevada	4
46	Utah	3	42	South Dakota	4
4	Vermont	14	42	Texas	4
19	Virginia	8	46	Hawaii	3
13	Washington	9	46	Utah	3
32	West Virginia	5	48	Alabama	2
26	Wisconsin	6	48	California	2
26	Wyoming	6	48	Mississippi	2
				District of Columbia	2

Source: U.S. Department of Education, National Center for Education Statistics
   "The Nation's Report Card: Reading 2009" (http://nces.ed.gov/nationsreportcard/)
*There are four achievement levels: Below Basic, Basic, Proficient, and Advanced. Proficient represents solid academic mastery for 8th graders. Students reaching this level have demonstrated competency over challenging subject matter, including subject matter knowledge, application of such knowledge to real-world situations, and analytical skills appropriate to the subject matter. Based only on disabled students who were assessed.

Percent of English Language Learner Public School Eighth Graders Proficient or Better in Reading in 2009
National Percent = 3%*

ALPHA ORDER

RANK	STATE	PERCENT
NA	Alabama**	NA
18	Alaska	2
22	Arizona	1
4	Arkansas	7
18	California	2
11	Colorado	3
NA	Connecticut**	NA
NA	Delaware**	NA
4	Florida	7
NA	Georgia**	NA
11	Hawaii	3
11	Idaho	3
10	Illinois	4
NA	Indiana**	NA
NA	Iowa**	NA
7	Kansas	5
NA	Kentucky**	NA
NA	Louisiana**	NA
NA	Maine**	NA
NA	Maryland**	NA
11	Massachusetts	3
3	Michigan	8
11	Minnesota	3
NA	Mississippi**	NA
NA	Missouri**	NA
NA	Montana**	NA
NA	Nebraska**	NA
22	Nevada	1
NA	New Hampshire**	NA
NA	New Jersey**	NA
22	New Mexico	1
18	New York	2
7	North Carolina	5
NA	North Dakota**	NA
NA	Ohio**	NA
11	Oklahoma	3
22	Oregon	1
7	Pennsylvania	5
22	Rhode Island	1
1	South Carolina	18
NA	South Dakota**	NA
NA	Tennessee**	NA
22	Texas	1
11	Utah	3
NA	Vermont**	NA
2	Virginia	9
18	Washington	2
NA	West Virginia**	NA
4	Wisconsin	7
NA	Wyoming**	NA

RANK ORDER

RANK	STATE	PERCENT
1	South Carolina	18
2	Virginia	9
3	Michigan	8
4	Arkansas	7
4	Florida	7
4	Wisconsin	7
7	Kansas	5
7	North Carolina	5
7	Pennsylvania	5
10	Illinois	4
11	Colorado	3
11	Hawaii	3
11	Idaho	3
11	Massachusetts	3
11	Minnesota	3
11	Oklahoma	3
11	Utah	3
18	Alaska	2
18	California	2
18	New York	2
18	Washington	2
22	Arizona	1
22	Nevada	1
22	New Mexico	1
22	Oregon	1
22	Rhode Island	1
22	Texas	1
NA	Alabama**	NA
NA	Connecticut**	NA
NA	Delaware**	NA
NA	Georgia**	NA
NA	Indiana**	NA
NA	Iowa**	NA
NA	Kentucky**	NA
NA	Louisiana**	NA
NA	Maine**	NA
NA	Maryland**	NA
NA	Mississippi**	NA
NA	Missouri**	NA
NA	Montana**	NA
NA	Nebraska**	NA
NA	New Hampshire**	NA
NA	New Jersey**	NA
NA	North Dakota**	NA
NA	Ohio**	NA
NA	South Dakota**	NA
NA	Tennessee**	NA
NA	Vermont**	NA
NA	West Virginia**	NA
NA	Wyoming**	NA
	District of Columbia**	NA

Source: U.S. Department of Education, National Center for Education Statistics
   "The Nation's Report Card: Reading 2009" (http://nces.ed.gov/nationsreportcard/)
*There are four achievement levels: Below Basic, Basic, Proficient, and Advanced. Proficient represents solid academic mastery for 8th graders. Students reaching this level have demonstrated competency over challenging subject matter, including subject matter knowledge, application of such knowledge to real-world situations, and analytical skills appropriate to the subject matter. **Sample size insufficient.

Average Public School Fourth Grade Mathematics Score in 2009

National Average Score = 239*

ALPHA ORDER				RANK ORDER		
RANK	STATE	AVERAGE SCORE		RANK	STATE	AVERAGE SCORE
49	Alabama	228		1	Massachusetts	252
36	Alaska	237		2	New Hampshire	251
46	Arizona	230		3	Minnesota	249
33	Arkansas	238		4	Vermont	248
44	California	232		5	New Jersey	247
16	Colorado	243		6	Connecticut	245
6	Connecticut	245		6	Kansas	245
29	Delaware	239		6	North Dakota	245
20	Florida	242		9	Maine	244
38	Georgia	236		9	Maryland	244
38	Hawaii	236		9	Montana	244
24	Idaho	241		9	North Carolina	244
33	Illinois	238		9	Ohio	244
16	Indiana	243		9	Pennsylvania	244
16	Iowa	243		9	Wisconsin	244
6	Kansas	245		16	Colorado	243
29	Kentucky	239		16	Indiana	243
48	Louisiana	229		16	Iowa	243
9	Maine	244		16	Virginia	243
9	Maryland	244		20	Florida	242
1	Massachusetts	252		20	South Dakota	242
38	Michigan	236		20	Washington	242
3	Minnesota	249		20	Wyoming	242
50	Mississippi	227		24	Idaho	241
24	Missouri	241		24	Missouri	241
9	Montana	244		24	New York	241
29	Nebraska	239		27	Texas	240
42	Nevada	235		27	Utah	240
2	New Hampshire	251		29	Delaware	239
5	New Jersey	247		29	Kentucky	239
46	New Mexico	230		29	Nebraska	239
24	New York	241		29	Rhode Island	239
9	North Carolina	244		33	Arkansas	238
6	North Dakota	245		33	Illinois	238
9	Ohio	244		33	Oregon	238
36	Oklahoma	237		36	Alaska	237
33	Oregon	238		36	Oklahoma	237
9	Pennsylvania	244		38	Georgia	236
29	Rhode Island	239		38	Hawaii	236
38	South Carolina	236		38	Michigan	236
20	South Dakota	242		38	South Carolina	236
44	Tennessee	232		42	Nevada	235
27	Texas	240		43	West Virginia	233
27	Utah	240		44	California	232
4	Vermont	248		44	Tennessee	232
16	Virginia	243		46	Arizona	230
20	Washington	242		46	New Mexico	230
43	West Virginia	233		48	Louisiana	229
9	Wisconsin	244		49	Alabama	228
20	Wyoming	242		50	Mississippi	227

District of Columbia 219

Source: U.S. Department of Education, National Center for Education Statistics
    "The Nation's Report Card: Mathematics 2009" (http://nces.ed.gov/nationsreportcard/)
*These scores are from the National Assessment of Educational Progress (NAEP). Scale ranges from 0 to 500.

Average Mathematics Score for Public School Fourth Grade Males in 2009

National Average Score = 240*

RANK	STATE	AVERAGE SCORE
49	Alabama	228
36	Alaska	238
47	Arizona	230
34	Arkansas	239
44	California	233
15	Colorado	244
9	Connecticut	246
26	Delaware	241
18	Florida	243
39	Georgia	237
42	Hawaii	235
23	Idaho	242
30	Illinois	240
18	Indiana	243
18	Iowa	243
9	Kansas	246
30	Kentucky	240
47	Louisiana	230
6	Maine	247
15	Maryland	244
1	Massachusetts	253
36	Michigan	238
3	Minnesota	251
50	Mississippi	227
26	Missouri	241
6	Montana	247
34	Nebraska	239
40	Nevada	236
2	New Hampshire	252
5	New Jersey	248
46	New Mexico	231
23	New York	242
15	North Carolina	244
6	North Dakota	247
11	Ohio	245
36	Oklahoma	238
30	Oregon	240
11	Pennsylvania	245
30	Rhode Island	240
40	South Carolina	236
18	South Dakota	243
45	Tennessee	232
26	Texas	241
26	Utah	241
4	Vermont	249
11	Virginia	245
23	Washington	242
43	West Virginia	234
11	Wisconsin	245
18	Wyoming	243

RANK	STATE	AVERAGE SCORE
1	Massachusetts	253
2	New Hampshire	252
3	Minnesota	251
4	Vermont	249
5	New Jersey	248
6	Maine	247
6	Montana	247
6	North Dakota	247
9	Connecticut	246
9	Kansas	246
11	Ohio	245
11	Pennsylvania	245
11	Virginia	245
11	Wisconsin	245
15	Colorado	244
15	Maryland	244
15	North Carolina	244
18	Florida	243
18	Indiana	243
18	Iowa	243
18	South Dakota	243
18	Wyoming	243
23	Idaho	242
23	New York	242
23	Washington	242
26	Delaware	241
26	Missouri	241
26	Texas	241
26	Utah	241
30	Illinois	240
30	Kentucky	240
30	Oregon	240
30	Rhode Island	240
34	Arkansas	239
34	Nebraska	239
36	Alaska	238
36	Michigan	238
36	Oklahoma	238
39	Georgia	237
40	Nevada	236
40	South Carolina	236
42	Hawaii	235
43	West Virginia	234
44	California	233
45	Tennessee	232
46	New Mexico	231
47	Arizona	230
47	Louisiana	230
49	Alabama	228
50	Mississippi	227
	District of Columbia	218

Source: U.S. Department of Education, National Center for Education Statistics
   "The Nation's Report Card: Mathematics 2009" (http://nces.ed.gov/nationsreportcard/)
*These scores are from the National Assessment of Educational Progress (NAEP). Scale ranges from 0 to 500.

Average Mathematics Score for Public School Fourth Grade Females in 2009

National Average Score = 238*

ALPHA ORDER

RANK	STATE	AVERAGE SCORE
49	Alabama	228
34	Alaska	236
46	Arizona	230
34	Arkansas	236
44	California	231
11	Colorado	242
9	Connecticut	243
30	Delaware	238
20	Florida	241
34	Georgia	236
34	Hawaii	236
24	Idaho	240
32	Illinois	237
11	Indiana	242
11	Iowa	242
6	Kansas	244
30	Kentucky	238
47	Louisiana	229
11	Maine	242
9	Maryland	243
1	Massachusetts	251
40	Michigan	235
3	Minnesota	248
49	Mississippi	228
24	Missouri	240
11	Montana	242
27	Nebraska	239
42	Nevada	234
2	New Hampshire	250
5	New Jersey	245
47	New Mexico	229
27	New York	239
6	North Carolina	244
6	North Dakota	244
11	Ohio	242
34	Oklahoma	236
34	Oregon	236
11	Pennsylvania	242
32	Rhode Island	237
40	South Carolina	235
20	South Dakota	241
44	Tennessee	231
24	Texas	240
27	Utah	239
4	Vermont	247
20	Virginia	241
11	Washington	242
43	West Virginia	232
11	Wisconsin	242
20	Wyoming	241

RANK ORDER

RANK	STATE	AVERAGE SCORE
1	Massachusetts	251
2	New Hampshire	250
3	Minnesota	248
4	Vermont	247
5	New Jersey	245
6	Kansas	244
6	North Carolina	244
6	North Dakota	244
9	Connecticut	243
9	Maryland	243
11	Colorado	242
11	Indiana	242
11	Iowa	242
11	Maine	242
11	Montana	242
11	Ohio	242
11	Pennsylvania	242
11	Washington	242
11	Wisconsin	242
20	Florida	241
20	South Dakota	241
20	Virginia	241
20	Wyoming	241
24	Idaho	240
24	Missouri	240
24	Texas	240
27	Nebraska	239
27	New York	239
27	Utah	239
30	Delaware	238
30	Kentucky	238
32	Illinois	237
32	Rhode Island	237
34	Alaska	236
34	Arkansas	236
34	Georgia	236
34	Hawaii	236
34	Oklahoma	236
34	Oregon	236
40	Michigan	235
40	South Carolina	235
42	Nevada	234
43	West Virginia	232
44	California	231
44	Tennessee	231
46	Arizona	230
47	Louisiana	229
47	New Mexico	229
49	Alabama	228
49	Mississippi	228

| | District of Columbia | 221 |

Source: U.S. Department of Education, National Center for Education Statistics
   "The Nation's Report Card: Mathematics 2009" (http://nces.ed.gov/nationsreportcard/)
*These scores are from the National Assessment of Educational Progress (NAEP). Scale ranges from 0 to 500.

Average Mathematics Score for Public School Fourth Graders
Eligible for Free or Reduced Price Lunch Program in 2009
National Average Score = 228*

<table>
<tr><td colspan="3">ALPHA ORDER</td><td colspan="3">RANK ORDER</td></tr>
<tr><td>RANK</td><td>STATE</td><td>AVERAGE SCORE</td><td>RANK</td><td>STATE</td><td>AVERAGE SCORE</td></tr>
<tr><td>50</td><td>Alabama</td><td>217</td><td>1</td><td>Massachusetts</td><td>237</td></tr>
<tr><td>35</td><td>Alaska</td><td>226</td><td>1</td><td>New Hampshire</td><td>237</td></tr>
<tr><td>49</td><td>Arizona</td><td>219</td><td>3</td><td>Kansas</td><td>236</td></tr>
<tr><td>22</td><td>Arkansas</td><td>229</td><td>3</td><td>North Dakota</td><td>236</td></tr>
<tr><td>48</td><td>California</td><td>220</td><td>5</td><td>Florida</td><td>235</td></tr>
<tr><td>29</td><td>Colorado</td><td>228</td><td>5</td><td>Maine</td><td>235</td></tr>
<tr><td>38</td><td>Connecticut</td><td>225</td><td>5</td><td>Montana</td><td>235</td></tr>
<tr><td>22</td><td>Delaware</td><td>229</td><td>5</td><td>Vermont</td><td>235</td></tr>
<tr><td>5</td><td>Florida</td><td>235</td><td>9</td><td>Idaho</td><td>234</td></tr>
<tr><td>38</td><td>Georgia</td><td>225</td><td>9</td><td>Minnesota</td><td>234</td></tr>
<tr><td>40</td><td>Hawaii</td><td>224</td><td>9</td><td>Wyoming</td><td>234</td></tr>
<tr><td>9</td><td>Idaho</td><td>234</td><td>12</td><td>New York</td><td>233</td></tr>
<tr><td>40</td><td>Illinois</td><td>224</td><td>12</td><td>Texas</td><td>233</td></tr>
<tr><td>14</td><td>Indiana</td><td>232</td><td>14</td><td>Indiana</td><td>232</td></tr>
<tr><td>14</td><td>Iowa</td><td>232</td><td>14</td><td>Iowa</td><td>232</td></tr>
<tr><td>3</td><td>Kansas</td><td>236</td><td>14</td><td>North Carolina</td><td>232</td></tr>
<tr><td>22</td><td>Kentucky</td><td>229</td><td>14</td><td>South Dakota</td><td>232</td></tr>
<tr><td>43</td><td>Louisiana</td><td>223</td><td>18</td><td>Oklahoma</td><td>231</td></tr>
<tr><td>5</td><td>Maine</td><td>235</td><td>18</td><td>Washington</td><td>231</td></tr>
<tr><td>22</td><td>Maryland</td><td>229</td><td>20</td><td>Ohio</td><td>230</td></tr>
<tr><td>1</td><td>Massachusetts</td><td>237</td><td>20</td><td>Virginia</td><td>230</td></tr>
<tr><td>45</td><td>Michigan</td><td>222</td><td>22</td><td>Arkansas</td><td>229</td></tr>
<tr><td>9</td><td>Minnesota</td><td>234</td><td>22</td><td>Delaware</td><td>229</td></tr>
<tr><td>47</td><td>Mississippi</td><td>221</td><td>22</td><td>Kentucky</td><td>229</td></tr>
<tr><td>22</td><td>Missouri</td><td>229</td><td>22</td><td>Maryland</td><td>229</td></tr>
<tr><td>5</td><td>Montana</td><td>235</td><td>22</td><td>Missouri</td><td>229</td></tr>
<tr><td>31</td><td>Nebraska</td><td>227</td><td>22</td><td>New Jersey</td><td>229</td></tr>
<tr><td>35</td><td>Nevada</td><td>226</td><td>22</td><td>Wisconsin</td><td>229</td></tr>
<tr><td>1</td><td>New Hampshire</td><td>237</td><td>29</td><td>Colorado</td><td>228</td></tr>
<tr><td>22</td><td>New Jersey</td><td>229</td><td>29</td><td>Pennsylvania</td><td>228</td></tr>
<tr><td>43</td><td>New Mexico</td><td>223</td><td>31</td><td>Nebraska</td><td>227</td></tr>
<tr><td>12</td><td>New York</td><td>233</td><td>31</td><td>Oregon</td><td>227</td></tr>
<tr><td>14</td><td>North Carolina</td><td>232</td><td>31</td><td>Utah</td><td>227</td></tr>
<tr><td>3</td><td>North Dakota</td><td>236</td><td>31</td><td>West Virginia</td><td>227</td></tr>
<tr><td>20</td><td>Ohio</td><td>230</td><td>35</td><td>Alaska</td><td>226</td></tr>
<tr><td>18</td><td>Oklahoma</td><td>231</td><td>35</td><td>Nevada</td><td>226</td></tr>
<tr><td>31</td><td>Oregon</td><td>227</td><td>35</td><td>South Carolina</td><td>226</td></tr>
<tr><td>29</td><td>Pennsylvania</td><td>228</td><td>38</td><td>Connecticut</td><td>225</td></tr>
<tr><td>40</td><td>Rhode Island</td><td>224</td><td>38</td><td>Georgia</td><td>225</td></tr>
<tr><td>35</td><td>South Carolina</td><td>226</td><td>40</td><td>Hawaii</td><td>224</td></tr>
<tr><td>14</td><td>South Dakota</td><td>232</td><td>40</td><td>Illinois</td><td>224</td></tr>
<tr><td>45</td><td>Tennessee</td><td>222</td><td>40</td><td>Rhode Island</td><td>224</td></tr>
<tr><td>12</td><td>Texas</td><td>233</td><td>43</td><td>Louisiana</td><td>223</td></tr>
<tr><td>31</td><td>Utah</td><td>227</td><td>43</td><td>New Mexico</td><td>223</td></tr>
<tr><td>5</td><td>Vermont</td><td>235</td><td>45</td><td>Michigan</td><td>222</td></tr>
<tr><td>20</td><td>Virginia</td><td>230</td><td>45</td><td>Tennessee</td><td>222</td></tr>
<tr><td>18</td><td>Washington</td><td>231</td><td>47</td><td>Mississippi</td><td>221</td></tr>
<tr><td>31</td><td>West Virginia</td><td>227</td><td>48</td><td>California</td><td>220</td></tr>
<tr><td>22</td><td>Wisconsin</td><td>229</td><td>49</td><td>Arizona</td><td>219</td></tr>
<tr><td>9</td><td>Wyoming</td><td>234</td><td>50</td><td>Alabama</td><td>217</td></tr>
<tr><td></td><td></td><td></td><td></td><td>District of Columbia</td><td>211</td></tr>
</table>

Source: U.S. Department of Education, National Center for Education Statistics
   "The Nation's Report Card: Mathematics 2009" (http://nces.ed.gov/nationsreportcard/)
*These scores are from the National Assessment of Educational Progress (NAEP). Scale ranges from 0 to 500.

Percent of Public School Fourth Graders Proficient or Better in Mathematics in 2009
National Percent = 38%*

ALPHA ORDER

RANK	STATE	PERCENT
48	Alabama	24
29	Alaska	38
44	Arizona	28
36	Arkansas	36
43	California	30
9	Colorado	45
6	Connecticut	46
36	Delaware	36
25	Florida	40
39	Georgia	34
33	Hawaii	37
21	Idaho	41
29	Illinois	38
19	Indiana	42
21	Iowa	41
6	Kansas	46
33	Kentucky	37
49	Louisiana	23
9	Maine	45
15	Maryland	44
1	Massachusetts	57
38	Michigan	35
3	Minnesota	54
50	Mississippi	22
21	Missouri	41
9	Montana	45
29	Nebraska	38
42	Nevada	32
2	New Hampshire	56
5	New Jersey	49
47	New Mexico	26
25	New York	40
16	North Carolina	43
9	North Dakota	45
9	Ohio	45
41	Oklahoma	33
33	Oregon	37
6	Pennsylvania	46
28	Rhode Island	39
39	South Carolina	34
19	South Dakota	42
44	Tennessee	28
29	Texas	38
21	Utah	41
4	Vermont	51
16	Virginia	43
16	Washington	43
44	West Virginia	28
9	Wisconsin	45
25	Wyoming	40

RANK ORDER

RANK	STATE	PERCENT
1	Massachusetts	57
2	New Hampshire	56
3	Minnesota	54
4	Vermont	51
5	New Jersey	49
6	Connecticut	46
6	Kansas	46
6	Pennsylvania	46
9	Colorado	45
9	Maine	45
9	Montana	45
9	North Dakota	45
9	Ohio	45
9	Wisconsin	45
15	Maryland	44
16	North Carolina	43
16	Virginia	43
16	Washington	43
19	Indiana	42
19	South Dakota	42
21	Idaho	41
21	Iowa	41
21	Missouri	41
21	Utah	41
25	Florida	40
25	New York	40
25	Wyoming	40
28	Rhode Island	39
29	Alaska	38
29	Illinois	38
29	Nebraska	38
29	Texas	38
33	Hawaii	37
33	Kentucky	37
33	Oregon	37
36	Arkansas	36
36	Delaware	36
38	Michigan	35
39	Georgia	34
39	South Carolina	34
41	Oklahoma	33
42	Nevada	32
43	California	30
44	Arizona	28
44	Tennessee	28
44	West Virginia	28
47	New Mexico	26
48	Alabama	24
49	Louisiana	23
50	Mississippi	22
	District of Columbia	17

Source: U.S. Department of Education, National Center for Education Statistics
   "The Nation's Report Card: Mathematics 2009" (http://nces.ed.gov/nationsreportcard/)
*There are four achievement levels: Below Basic, Basic, Proficient, and Advanced. Proficient represents solid academic mastery for 4th graders. Students reaching this level have demonstrated competency over challenging subject matter, including subject matter knowledge, application of such knowledge to real-world situations, and analytical skills appropriate to the subject matter.

Percent of Public School Fourth Grade Males
Proficient or Better in Mathematics in 2009
National Percent = 40%*

ALPHA ORDER

RANK	STATE	PERCENT
48	Alabama	25
30	Alaska	40
44	Arizona	30
33	Arkansas	39
43	California	32
14	Colorado	46
6	Connecticut	49
30	Delaware	40
25	Florida	42
40	Georgia	35
37	Hawaii	37
25	Idaho	42
29	Illinois	41
25	Indiana	42
20	Iowa	43
8	Kansas	48
33	Kentucky	39
49	Louisiana	24
8	Maine	48
17	Maryland	44
1	Massachusetts	59
37	Michigan	37
3	Minnesota	56
50	Mississippi	23
20	Missouri	43
6	Montana	49
33	Nebraska	39
42	Nevada	34
2	New Hampshire	58
5	New Jersey	51
47	New Mexico	27
20	New York	43
17	North Carolina	44
12	North Dakota	47
8	Ohio	48
40	Oklahoma	35
30	Oregon	40
8	Pennsylvania	48
20	Rhode Island	43
39	South Carolina	36
17	South Dakota	44
46	Tennessee	29
33	Texas	39
25	Utah	42
4	Vermont	53
14	Virginia	46
16	Washington	45
44	West Virginia	30
12	Wisconsin	47
20	Wyoming	43

RANK ORDER

RANK	STATE	PERCENT
1	Massachusetts	59
2	New Hampshire	58
3	Minnesota	56
4	Vermont	53
5	New Jersey	51
6	Connecticut	49
6	Montana	49
8	Kansas	48
8	Maine	48
8	Ohio	48
8	Pennsylvania	48
12	North Dakota	47
12	Wisconsin	47
14	Colorado	46
14	Virginia	46
16	Washington	45
17	Maryland	44
17	North Carolina	44
17	South Dakota	44
20	Iowa	43
20	Missouri	43
20	New York	43
20	Rhode Island	43
20	Wyoming	43
25	Florida	42
25	Idaho	42
25	Indiana	42
25	Utah	42
29	Illinois	41
30	Alaska	40
30	Delaware	40
30	Oregon	40
33	Arkansas	39
33	Kentucky	39
33	Nebraska	39
33	Texas	39
37	Hawaii	37
37	Michigan	37
39	South Carolina	36
40	Georgia	35
40	Oklahoma	35
42	Nevada	34
43	California	32
44	Arizona	30
44	West Virginia	30
46	Tennessee	29
47	New Mexico	27
48	Alabama	25
49	Louisiana	24
50	Mississippi	23
	District of Columbia	17

Source: U.S. Department of Education, National Center for Education Statistics
"The Nation's Report Card: Mathematics 2009" (http://nces.ed.gov/nationsreportcard/)
*There are four achievement levels: Below Basic, Basic, Proficient, and Advanced. Proficient represents solid academic mastery for 4th graders. Students reaching this level have demonstrated competency over challenging subject matter, including subject matter knowledge, application of such knowledge to real-world situations, and analytical skills appropriate to the subject matter.

Percent of Public School Fourth Grade Females
Proficient or Better in Mathematics in 2009
National Percent = 37%*

ALPHA ORDER

RANK	STATE	PERCENT
48	Alabama	24
31	Alaska	36
45	Arizona	26
34	Arkansas	34
43	California	29
6	Colorado	44
6	Connecticut	44
37	Delaware	33
21	Florida	39
39	Georgia	32
27	Hawaii	37
21	Idaho	39
33	Illinois	35
17	Indiana	41
19	Iowa	40
6	Kansas	44
34	Kentucky	34
49	Louisiana	21
13	Maine	42
9	Maryland	43
1	Massachusetts	55
37	Michigan	33
3	Minnesota	51
49	Mississippi	21
21	Missouri	39
17	Montana	41
27	Nebraska	37
41	Nevada	30
2	New Hampshire	54
5	New Jersey	46
47	New Mexico	25
27	New York	37
13	North Carolina	42
13	North Dakota	42
9	Ohio	43
41	Oklahoma	30
34	Oregon	34
9	Pennsylvania	43
31	Rhode Island	36
39	South Carolina	32
21	South Dakota	39
44	Tennessee	28
27	Texas	37
19	Utah	40
4	Vermont	49
21	Virginia	39
13	Washington	42
45	West Virginia	26
9	Wisconsin	43
26	Wyoming	38

RANK ORDER

RANK	STATE	PERCENT
1	Massachusetts	55
2	New Hampshire	54
3	Minnesota	51
4	Vermont	49
5	New Jersey	46
6	Colorado	44
6	Connecticut	44
6	Kansas	44
9	Maryland	43
9	Ohio	43
9	Pennsylvania	43
9	Wisconsin	43
13	Maine	42
13	North Carolina	42
13	North Dakota	42
13	Washington	42
17	Indiana	41
17	Montana	41
19	Iowa	40
19	Utah	40
21	Florida	39
21	Idaho	39
21	Missouri	39
21	South Dakota	39
21	Virginia	39
26	Wyoming	38
27	Hawaii	37
27	Nebraska	37
27	New York	37
27	Texas	37
31	Alaska	36
31	Rhode Island	36
33	Illinois	35
34	Arkansas	34
34	Kentucky	34
34	Oregon	34
37	Delaware	33
37	Michigan	33
39	Georgia	32
39	South Carolina	32
41	Nevada	30
41	Oklahoma	30
43	California	29
44	Tennessee	28
45	Arizona	26
45	West Virginia	26
47	New Mexico	25
48	Alabama	24
49	Louisiana	21
49	Mississippi	21

	District of Columbia	17

Source: U.S. Department of Education, National Center for Education Statistics
  "The Nation's Report Card: Mathematics 2009" (http://nces.ed.gov/nationsreportcard/)
*There are four achievement levels: Below Basic, Basic, Proficient, and Advanced. Proficient represents solid academic mastery for 4th graders. Students reaching this level have demonstrated competency over challenging subject matter, including subject matter knowledge, application of such knowledge to real-world situations, and analytical skills appropriate to the subject matter.

Percent of Public School Fourth Graders Eligible for Free or Reduced Price Lunch Program Proficient or Better in Mathematics in 2009
National Percent = 22%*

ALPHA ORDER

RANK	STATE	PERCENT
50	Alabama	13
19	Alaska	24
46	Arizona	15
25	Arkansas	23
46	California	15
19	Colorado	24
40	Connecticut	18
33	Delaware	21
9	Florida	29
39	Georgia	19
25	Hawaii	23
8	Idaho	30
40	Illinois	18
15	Indiana	26
17	Iowa	25
2	Kansas	32
33	Kentucky	21
48	Louisiana	14
4	Maine	31
35	Maryland	20
4	Massachusetts	31
43	Michigan	17
4	Minnesota	31
48	Mississippi	14
19	Missouri	24
4	Montana	31
25	Nebraska	23
35	Nevada	20
1	New Hampshire	35
31	New Jersey	22
43	New Mexico	17
12	New York	28
17	North Carolina	25
9	North Dakota	29
19	Ohio	24
25	Oklahoma	23
31	Oregon	22
25	Pennsylvania	23
40	Rhode Island	18
35	South Carolina	20
13	South Dakota	27
45	Tennessee	16
15	Texas	26
19	Utah	24
2	Vermont	32
25	Virginia	23
13	Washington	27
35	West Virginia	20
19	Wisconsin	24
9	Wyoming	29

RANK ORDER

RANK	STATE	PERCENT
1	New Hampshire	35
2	Kansas	32
2	Vermont	32
4	Maine	31
4	Massachusetts	31
4	Minnesota	31
4	Montana	31
8	Idaho	30
9	Florida	29
9	North Dakota	29
9	Wyoming	29
12	New York	28
13	South Dakota	27
13	Washington	27
15	Indiana	26
15	Texas	26
17	Iowa	25
17	North Carolina	25
19	Alaska	24
19	Colorado	24
19	Missouri	24
19	Ohio	24
19	Utah	24
19	Wisconsin	24
25	Arkansas	23
25	Hawaii	23
25	Nebraska	23
25	Oklahoma	23
25	Pennsylvania	23
25	Virginia	23
31	New Jersey	22
31	Oregon	22
33	Delaware	21
33	Kentucky	21
35	Maryland	20
35	Nevada	20
35	South Carolina	20
35	West Virginia	20
39	Georgia	19
40	Connecticut	18
40	Illinois	18
40	Rhode Island	18
43	Michigan	17
43	New Mexico	17
45	Tennessee	16
46	Arizona	15
46	California	15
48	Louisiana	14
48	Mississippi	14
50	Alabama	13
	District of Columbia	8

Source: U.S. Department of Education, National Center for Education Statistics
   "The Nation's Report Card: Mathematics 2009" (http://nces.ed.gov/nationsreportcard/)
*There are four achievement levels: Below Basic, Basic, Proficient, and Advanced. Proficient represents solid academic mastery for 4th graders. Students reaching this level have demonstrated competency over challenging subject matter, including subject matter knowledge, application of such knowledge to real-world situations, and analytical skills appropriate to the subject matter.

Percent of White Public School Fourth Graders Proficient or Better in Mathematics in 2009
National Percent = 50%*

ALPHA ORDER

RANK	STATE	PERCENT
49	Alabama	34
16	Alaska	52
39	Arizona	44
32	Arkansas	46
18	California	51
8	Colorado	57
7	Connecticut	58
22	Delaware	50
13	Florida	53
27	Georgia	48
18	Hawaii	51
39	Idaho	44
16	Illinois	52
27	Indiana	48
37	Iowa	45
10	Kansas	55
45	Kentucky	39
46	Louisiana	37
32	Maine	46
5	Maryland	60
1	Massachusetts	67
42	Michigan	43
3	Minnesota	61
46	Mississippi	37
32	Missouri	46
25	Montana	49
37	Nebraska	45
32	Nevada	46
8	New Hampshire	57
2	New Jersey	63
30	New Mexico	47
22	New York	50
6	North Carolina	59
25	North Dakota	49
11	Ohio	54
44	Oklahoma	40
42	Oregon	43
13	Pennsylvania	53
22	Rhode Island	50
32	South Carolina	46
30	South Dakota	47
48	Tennessee	36
3	Texas	61
27	Utah	48
18	Vermont	51
11	Virginia	54
18	Washington	51
50	West Virginia	28
13	Wisconsin	53
39	Wyoming	44

RANK ORDER

RANK	STATE	PERCENT
1	Massachusetts	67
2	New Jersey	63
3	Minnesota	61
3	Texas	61
5	Maryland	60
6	North Carolina	59
7	Connecticut	58
8	Colorado	57
8	New Hampshire	57
10	Kansas	55
11	Ohio	54
11	Virginia	54
13	Florida	53
13	Pennsylvania	53
13	Wisconsin	53
16	Alaska	52
16	Illinois	52
18	California	51
18	Hawaii	51
18	Vermont	51
18	Washington	51
22	Delaware	50
22	New York	50
22	Rhode Island	50
25	Montana	49
25	North Dakota	49
27	Georgia	48
27	Indiana	48
27	Utah	48
30	New Mexico	47
30	South Dakota	47
32	Arkansas	46
32	Maine	46
32	Missouri	46
32	Nevada	46
32	South Carolina	46
37	Iowa	45
37	Nebraska	45
39	Arizona	44
39	Idaho	44
39	Wyoming	44
42	Michigan	43
42	Oregon	43
44	Oklahoma	40
45	Kentucky	39
46	Louisiana	37
46	Mississippi	37
48	Tennessee	36
49	Alabama	34
50	West Virginia	28
	District of Columbia	81

Source: U.S. Department of Education, National Center for Education Statistics
   "The Nation's Report Card: Mathematics 2009" (http://nces.ed.gov/nationsreportcard/)
*There are four achievement levels: Below Basic, Basic, Proficient, and Advanced. Proficient represents solid academic mastery for 4th graders. Students reaching this level have demonstrated competency over challenging subject matter, including subject matter knowledge, application of such knowledge to real-world situations, and analytical skills appropriate to the subject matter.

Percent of Black Public School Fourth Graders Proficient or Better in Mathematics in 2009
National Percent = 15%*

ALPHA ORDER

ALPHA ORDER

RANK	STATE	PERCENT
43	Alabama	7
18	Alaska	17
11	Arizona	19
35	Arkansas	12
33	California	13
6	Colorado	23
28	Connecticut	14
18	Delaware	17
9	Florida	20
25	Georgia	15
1	Hawaii	33
NA	Idaho**	NA
37	Illinois	11
33	Indiana	13
18	Iowa	17
15	Kansas	18
28	Kentucky	14
41	Louisiana	8
3	Maine	28
8	Maryland	21
2	Massachusetts	30
40	Michigan	9
4	Minnesota	25
41	Mississippi	8
18	Missouri	17
NA	Montana**	NA
39	Nebraska	10
35	Nevada	12
NA	New Hampshire**	NA
11	New Jersey	19
11	New Mexico	19
11	New York	19
15	North Carolina	18
NA	North Dakota**	NA
28	Ohio	14
28	Oklahoma	14
15	Oregon	18
18	Pennsylvania	17
25	Rhode Island	15
28	South Carolina	14
18	South Dakota	17
43	Tennessee	7
6	Texas	23
25	Utah	15
NA	Vermont**	NA
24	Virginia	16
5	Washington	24
9	West Virginia	20
37	Wisconsin	11
NA	Wyoming**	NA

RANK ORDER

RANK	STATE	PERCENT
1	Hawaii	33
2	Massachusetts	30
3	Maine	28
4	Minnesota	25
5	Washington	24
6	Colorado	23
6	Texas	23
8	Maryland	21
9	Florida	20
9	West Virginia	20
11	Arizona	19
11	New Jersey	19
11	New Mexico	19
11	New York	19
15	Kansas	18
15	North Carolina	18
15	Oregon	18
18	Alaska	17
18	Delaware	17
18	Iowa	17
18	Missouri	17
18	Pennsylvania	17
18	South Dakota	17
24	Virginia	16
25	Georgia	15
25	Rhode Island	15
25	Utah	15
28	Connecticut	14
28	Kentucky	14
28	Ohio	14
28	Oklahoma	14
28	South Carolina	14
33	California	13
33	Indiana	13
35	Arkansas	12
35	Nevada	12
37	Illinois	11
37	Wisconsin	11
39	Nebraska	10
40	Michigan	9
41	Louisiana	8
41	Mississippi	8
43	Alabama	7
43	Tennessee	7
NA	Idaho**	NA
NA	Montana**	NA
NA	New Hampshire**	NA
NA	North Dakota**	NA
NA	Vermont**	NA
NA	Wyoming**	NA

District of Columbia   9

Source: U.S. Department of Education, National Center for Education Statistics
"The Nation's Report Card: Mathematics 2009" (http://nces.ed.gov/nationsreportcard/)
*There are four achievement levels: Below Basic, Basic, Proficient, and Advanced. Proficient represents solid academic mastery for 4th graders. Students reaching this level have demonstrated competency over challenging subject matter, including subject matter knowledge, application of such knowledge to real-world situations, and analytical skills appropriate to the subject matter. **Sample size insufficient.

Percent of Hispanic Public School Fourth Graders Proficient or Better in Mathematics in 2009
National Percent = 21%*

ALPHA ORDER

RANK	STATE	PERCENT
45	Alabama	11
10	Alaska	27
42	Arizona	15
13	Arkansas	26
43	California	14
20	Colorado	24
35	Connecticut	18
25	Delaware	22
3	Florida	33
13	Georgia	26
7	Hawaii	28
35	Idaho	18
29	Illinois	20
22	Indiana	23
38	Iowa	17
20	Kansas	24
25	Kentucky	22
22	Louisiana	23
NA	Maine**	NA
4	Maryland	32
16	Massachusetts	25
29	Michigan	20
6	Minnesota	29
NA	Mississippi**	NA
2	Missouri	37
1	Montana	41
39	Nebraska	16
33	Nevada	19
5	New Hampshire	31
16	New Jersey	25
35	New Mexico	18
16	New York	25
10	North Carolina	27
NA	North Dakota**	NA
16	Ohio	25
29	Oklahoma	20
39	Oregon	16
22	Pennsylvania	23
43	Rhode Island	14
7	South Carolina	28
10	South Dakota	27
33	Tennessee	19
13	Texas	26
39	Utah	16
NA	Vermont**	NA
7	Virginia	28
29	Washington	20
NA	West Virginia**	NA
25	Wisconsin	22
25	Wyoming	22

RANK ORDER

RANK	STATE	PERCENT
1	Montana	41
2	Missouri	37
3	Florida	33
4	Maryland	32
5	New Hampshire	31
6	Minnesota	29
7	Hawaii	28
7	South Carolina	28
7	Virginia	28
10	Alaska	27
10	North Carolina	27
10	South Dakota	27
13	Arkansas	26
13	Georgia	26
13	Texas	26
16	Massachusetts	25
16	New Jersey	25
16	New York	25
16	Ohio	25
20	Colorado	24
20	Kansas	24
22	Indiana	23
22	Louisiana	23
22	Pennsylvania	23
25	Delaware	22
25	Kentucky	22
25	Wisconsin	22
25	Wyoming	22
29	Illinois	20
29	Michigan	20
29	Oklahoma	20
29	Washington	20
33	Nevada	19
33	Tennessee	19
35	Connecticut	18
35	Idaho	18
35	New Mexico	18
38	Iowa	17
39	Nebraska	16
39	Oregon	16
39	Utah	16
42	Arizona	15
43	California	14
43	Rhode Island	14
45	Alabama	11
NA	Maine**	NA
NA	Mississippi**	NA
NA	North Dakota**	NA
NA	Vermont**	NA
NA	West Virginia**	NA

District of Columbia	24

Source: U.S. Department of Education, National Center for Education Statistics
  "The Nation's Report Card: Mathematics 2009" (http://nces.ed.gov/nationsreportcard/)
*There are four achievement levels: Below Basic, Basic, Proficient, and Advanced. Proficient represents solid academic mastery for 4th graders. Students reaching this level have demonstrated competency over challenging subject matter, including subject matter knowledge, application of such knowledge to real-world situations, and analytical skills appropriate to the subject matter. **Sample size insufficient.

Percent of Asian Public School Fourth Graders Proficient or Better in Mathematics in 2009
National Percent = 61%*

ALPHA ORDER

RANK	STATE	PERCENT
NA	Alabama**	NA
31	Alaska	35
25	Arizona	45
NA	Arkansas**	NA
18	California	61
23	Colorado	51
12	Connecticut	65
10	Delaware	66
1	Florida	73
19	Georgia	60
31	Hawaii	35
NA	Idaho**	NA
1	Illinois	73
NA	Indiana**	NA
10	Iowa	66
13	Kansas	64
6	Kentucky	69
NA	Louisiana**	NA
NA	Maine**	NA
7	Maryland	67
5	Massachusetts	70
21	Michigan	55
27	Minnesota	44
NA	Mississippi**	NA
15	Missouri	62
NA	Montana**	NA
21	Nebraska	55
25	Nevada	45
7	New Hampshire	67
3	New Jersey	72
NA	New Mexico**	NA
7	New York	67
15	North Carolina	62
NA	North Dakota**	NA
NA	Ohio**	NA
NA	Oklahoma**	NA
24	Oregon	48
15	Pennsylvania	62
28	Rhode Island	40
NA	South Carolina**	NA
NA	South Dakota**	NA
NA	Tennessee**	NA
4	Texas	71
29	Utah	39
NA	Vermont**	NA
13	Virginia	64
20	Washington	56
NA	West Virginia**	NA
29	Wisconsin	39
NA	Wyoming**	NA

RANK ORDER

RANK	STATE	PERCENT
1	Florida	73
1	Illinois	73
3	New Jersey	72
4	Texas	71
5	Massachusetts	70
6	Kentucky	69
7	Maryland	67
7	New Hampshire	67
7	New York	67
10	Delaware	66
10	Iowa	66
12	Connecticut	65
13	Kansas	64
13	Virginia	64
15	Missouri	62
15	North Carolina	62
15	Pennsylvania	62
18	California	61
19	Georgia	60
20	Washington	56
21	Michigan	55
21	Nebraska	55
23	Colorado	51
24	Oregon	48
25	Arizona	45
25	Nevada	45
27	Minnesota	44
28	Rhode Island	40
29	Utah	39
29	Wisconsin	39
31	Alaska	35
31	Hawaii	35
NA	Alabama**	NA
NA	Arkansas**	NA
NA	Idaho**	NA
NA	Indiana**	NA
NA	Louisiana**	NA
NA	Maine**	NA
NA	Mississippi**	NA
NA	Montana**	NA
NA	New Mexico**	NA
NA	North Dakota**	NA
NA	Ohio**	NA
NA	Oklahoma**	NA
NA	South Carolina**	NA
NA	South Dakota**	NA
NA	Tennessee**	NA
NA	Vermont**	NA
NA	West Virginia**	NA
NA	Wyoming**	NA
	District of Columbia**	NA

Source: U.S. Department of Education, National Center for Education Statistics
   "The Nation's Report Card: Mathematics 2009" (http://nces.ed.gov/nationsreportcard/)
*There are four achievement levels: Below Basic, Basic, Proficient, and Advanced. Proficient represents solid academic mastery for 4th graders. Students reaching this level have demonstrated competency over challenging subject matter, including subject matter knowledge, application of such knowledge to real-world situations, and analytical skills appropriate to the subject matter. **Sample size insufficient.

Percent of Disabled Public School Fourth Graders Proficient or Better in Mathematics in 2009
National Percent = 19%*

ALPHA ORDER				RANK ORDER		
RANK	STATE	PERCENT		RANK	STATE	PERCENT
50	Alabama	5		1	Massachusetts	32
29	Alaska	16		1	Minnesota	32
36	Arizona	15		3	Maryland	27
38	Arkansas	14		3	New Hampshire	27
29	California	16		3	New Jersey	27
36	Colorado	15		6	Florida	26
18	Connecticut	19		6	Missouri	26
29	Delaware	16		8	Indiana	24
6	Florida	26		9	Illinois	23
40	Georgia	13		9	Kansas	23
49	Hawaii	9		9	North Carolina	23
29	Idaho	16		12	South Dakota	22
9	Illinois	23		12	Vermont	22
8	Indiana	24		14	Kentucky	21
44	Iowa	12		14	North Dakota	21
9	Kansas	23		14	Virginia	21
14	Kentucky	21		17	Wyoming	20
46	Louisiana	10		18	Connecticut	19
18	Maine	19		18	Maine	19
3	Maryland	27		18	Michigan	19
1	Massachusetts	32		18	Pennsylvania	19
18	Michigan	19		22	Nebraska	18
1	Minnesota	32		22	Ohio	18
46	Mississippi	10		22	Texas	18
6	Missouri	26		22	Utah	18
29	Montana	16		22	Wisconsin	18
22	Nebraska	18		27	Oregon	17
29	Nevada	16		27	Washington	17
3	New Hampshire	27		29	Alaska	16
3	New Jersey	27		29	California	16
46	New Mexico	10		29	Delaware	16
40	New York	13		29	Idaho	16
9	North Carolina	23		29	Montana	16
14	North Dakota	21		29	Nevada	16
22	Ohio	18		29	Oklahoma	16
29	Oklahoma	16		36	Arizona	15
27	Oregon	17		36	Colorado	15
18	Pennsylvania	19		38	Arkansas	14
40	Rhode Island	13		38	West Virginia	14
40	South Carolina	13		40	Georgia	13
12	South Dakota	22		40	New York	13
45	Tennessee	11		40	Rhode Island	13
22	Texas	18		40	South Carolina	13
22	Utah	18		44	Iowa	12
12	Vermont	22		45	Tennessee	11
14	Virginia	21		46	Louisiana	10
27	Washington	17		46	Mississippi	10
38	West Virginia	14		46	New Mexico	10
22	Wisconsin	18		49	Hawaii	9
17	Wyoming	20		50	Alabama	5
					District of Columbia	4

Source: U.S. Department of Education, National Center for Education Statistics
   "The Nation's Report Card: Mathematics 2009" (http://nces.ed.gov/nationsreportcard/)
*There are four achievement levels: Below Basic, Basic, Proficient, and Advanced. Proficient represents solid academic mastery for 4th graders. Students reaching this level have demonstrated competency over challenging subject matter, including subject matter knowledge, application of such knowledge to real-world situations, and analytical skills appropriate to the subject matter. Based only on disabled students who were assessed.

Percent of English Language Learner Public School Fourth Graders Proficient or Better in Mathematics in 2009
National Percent = 12%*

ALPHA ORDER

RANK	STATE	PERCENT
NA	Alabama**	NA
40	Alaska	4
41	Arizona	2
5	Arkansas	21
35	California	6
30	Colorado	9
30	Connecticut	9
25	Delaware	11
8	Florida	19
17	Georgia	14
21	Hawaii	12
34	Idaho	7
25	Illinois	11
8	Indiana	19
17	Iowa	14
5	Kansas	21
2	Kentucky	28
13	Louisiana	15
NA	Maine**	NA
12	Maryland	17
13	Massachusetts	15
21	Michigan	12
13	Minnesota	15
NA	Mississippi**	NA
NA	Missouri**	NA
27	Montana	10
35	Nebraska	6
21	Nevada	12
2	New Hampshire	28
27	New Jersey	10
39	New Mexico	5
19	New York	13
11	North Carolina	18
NA	North Dakota**	NA
1	Ohio	36
30	Oklahoma	9
35	Oregon	6
21	Pennsylvania	12
27	Rhode Island	10
2	South Carolina	28
NA	South Dakota**	NA
19	Tennessee	13
7	Texas	20
35	Utah	6
NA	Vermont**	NA
8	Virginia	19
33	Washington	8
NA	West Virginia**	NA
13	Wisconsin	15
NA	Wyoming**	NA

RANK ORDER

RANK	STATE	PERCENT
1	Ohio	36
2	Kentucky	28
2	New Hampshire	28
2	South Carolina	28
5	Arkansas	21
5	Kansas	21
7	Texas	20
8	Florida	19
8	Indiana	19
8	Virginia	19
11	North Carolina	18
12	Maryland	17
13	Louisiana	15
13	Massachusetts	15
13	Minnesota	15
13	Wisconsin	15
17	Georgia	14
17	Iowa	14
19	New York	13
19	Tennessee	13
21	Hawaii	12
21	Michigan	12
21	Nevada	12
21	Pennsylvania	12
25	Delaware	11
25	Illinois	11
27	Montana	10
27	New Jersey	10
27	Rhode Island	10
30	Colorado	9
30	Connecticut	9
30	Oklahoma	9
33	Washington	8
34	Idaho	7
35	California	6
35	Nebraska	6
35	Oregon	6
35	Utah	6
39	New Mexico	5
40	Alaska	4
41	Arizona	2
NA	Alabama**	NA
NA	Maine**	NA
NA	Mississippi**	NA
NA	Missouri**	NA
NA	North Dakota**	NA
NA	South Dakota**	NA
NA	Vermont**	NA
NA	West Virginia**	NA
NA	Wyoming**	NA

District of Columbia — 14

Source: U.S. Department of Education, National Center for Education Statistics
    "The Nation's Report Card: Mathematics 2009" (http://nces.ed.gov/nationsreportcard/)
*There are four achievement levels: Below Basic, Basic, Proficient, and Advanced. Proficient represents solid academic mastery for 4th graders. Students reaching this level have demonstrated competency over challenging subject matter, including subject matter knowledge, application of such knowledge to real-world situations, and analytical skills appropriate to the subject matter. **Sample size insufficient.

Average Public School Eighth Grade Mathematics Score in 2009

National Average Score = 282*

ALPHA ORDER

RANK	STATE	AVERAGE SCORE
49	Alabama	269
30	Alaska	283
39	Arizona	277
40	Arkansas	276
46	California	270
15	Colorado	287
9	Connecticut	289
25	Delaware	284
34	Florida	279
36	Georgia	278
43	Hawaii	274
15	Idaho	287
32	Illinois	282
15	Indiana	287
25	Iowa	284
9	Kansas	289
34	Kentucky	279
45	Louisiana	272
19	Maine	286
12	Maryland	288
1	Massachusetts	299
36	Michigan	278
2	Minnesota	294
50	Mississippi	265
19	Missouri	286
6	Montana	292
25	Nebraska	284
43	Nevada	274
6	New Hampshire	292
3	New Jersey	293
46	New Mexico	270
30	New York	283
25	North Carolina	284
3	North Dakota	293
19	Ohio	286
40	Oklahoma	276
24	Oregon	285
12	Pennsylvania	288
36	Rhode Island	278
33	South Carolina	280
8	South Dakota	291
42	Tennessee	275
15	Texas	287
25	Utah	284
3	Vermont	293
19	Virginia	286
9	Washington	289
46	West Virginia	270
12	Wisconsin	288
19	Wyoming	286

RANK ORDER

RANK	STATE	AVERAGE SCORE
1	Massachusetts	299
2	Minnesota	294
3	New Jersey	293
3	North Dakota	293
3	Vermont	293
6	Montana	292
6	New Hampshire	292
8	South Dakota	291
9	Connecticut	289
9	Kansas	289
9	Washington	289
12	Maryland	288
12	Pennsylvania	288
12	Wisconsin	288
15	Colorado	287
15	Idaho	287
15	Indiana	287
15	Texas	287
19	Maine	286
19	Missouri	286
19	Ohio	286
19	Virginia	286
19	Wyoming	286
24	Oregon	285
25	Delaware	284
25	Iowa	284
25	Nebraska	284
25	North Carolina	284
25	Utah	284
30	Alaska	283
30	New York	283
32	Illinois	282
33	South Carolina	280
34	Florida	279
34	Kentucky	279
36	Georgia	278
36	Michigan	278
36	Rhode Island	278
39	Arizona	277
40	Arkansas	276
40	Oklahoma	276
42	Tennessee	275
43	Hawaii	274
43	Nevada	274
45	Louisiana	272
46	California	270
46	New Mexico	270
46	West Virginia	270
49	Alabama	269
50	Mississippi	265
	District of Columbia	254

Source: U.S. Department of Education, National Center for Education Statistics
    "The Nation's Report Card: Mathematics 2009" (http://nces.ed.gov/nationsreportcard/)
*These scores are from the National Assessment of Educational Progress (NAEP). Scale ranges from 0 to 500.

Average Mathematics Score for Public School Eighth Grade Males in 2009

National Average Score = 283*

ALPHA ORDER			RANK ORDER		
RANK	STATE	AVERAGE SCORE	RANK	STATE	AVERAGE SCORE
49	Alabama	268	1	Massachusetts	300
31	Alaska	283	2	Minnesota	296
37	Arizona	279	3	New Jersey	295
41	Arkansas	275	4	North Dakota	294
44	California	272	4	Vermont	294
13	Colorado	289	6	New Hampshire	293
15	Connecticut	288	7	Montana	292
28	Delaware	284	7	South Dakota	292
33	Florida	281	9	Kansas	290
40	Georgia	277	9	Maryland	290
46	Hawaii	271	9	Pennsylvania	290
15	Idaho	288	9	Washington	290
28	Illinois	284	13	Colorado	289
15	Indiana	288	13	Wisconsin	289
26	Iowa	285	15	Connecticut	288
9	Kansas	290	15	Idaho	288
33	Kentucky	281	15	Indiana	288
44	Louisiana	272	15	Maine	288
15	Maine	288	15	Wyoming	288
9	Maryland	290	20	Missouri	287
1	Massachusetts	300	20	Ohio	287
36	Michigan	280	20	Oregon	287
2	Minnesota	296	20	Texas	287
50	Mississippi	265	20	Virginia	287
20	Missouri	287	25	Nebraska	286
7	Montana	292	26	Iowa	285
25	Nebraska	286	26	Utah	285
41	Nevada	275	28	Delaware	284
6	New Hampshire	293	28	Illinois	284
3	New Jersey	295	28	North Carolina	284
46	New Mexico	271	31	Alaska	283
31	New York	283	31	New York	283
28	North Carolina	284	33	Florida	281
4	North Dakota	294	33	Kentucky	281
20	Ohio	287	33	South Carolina	281
38	Oklahoma	278	36	Michigan	280
20	Oregon	287	37	Arizona	279
9	Pennsylvania	290	38	Oklahoma	278
38	Rhode Island	278	38	Rhode Island	278
33	South Carolina	281	40	Georgia	277
7	South Dakota	292	41	Arkansas	275
41	Tennessee	275	41	Nevada	275
20	Texas	287	41	Tennessee	275
26	Utah	285	44	California	272
4	Vermont	294	44	Louisiana	272
20	Virginia	287	46	Hawaii	271
9	Washington	290	46	New Mexico	271
46	West Virginia	271	46	West Virginia	271
13	Wisconsin	289	49	Alabama	268
15	Wyoming	288	50	Mississippi	265
				District of Columbia	252

Source: U.S. Department of Education, National Center for Education Statistics
   "The Nation's Report Card: Mathematics 2009" (http://nces.ed.gov/nationsreportcard/)
*These scores are from the National Assessment of Educational Progress (NAEP). Scale ranges from 0 to 500.

Average Mathematics Score for Public School Eighth Grade Females in 2009

National Average Score = 281*

RANK	STATE	AVERAGE SCORE
47	Alabama	269
26	Alaska	283
40	Arizona	276
38	Arkansas	277
49	California	268
15	Colorado	286
8	Connecticut	289
26	Delaware	283
34	Florida	278
34	Georgia	278
40	Hawaii	276
15	Idaho	286
32	Illinois	280
18	Indiana	285
21	Iowa	284
11	Kansas	287
34	Kentucky	278
44	Louisiana	273
21	Maine	284
11	Maryland	287
1	Massachusetts	298
38	Michigan	277
2	Minnesota	293
50	Mississippi	265
18	Missouri	285
5	Montana	291
26	Nebraska	283
44	Nevada	273
3	New Hampshire	292
7	New Jersey	290
47	New Mexico	269
31	New York	282
21	North Carolina	284
5	North Dakota	291
21	Ohio	284
43	Oklahoma	274
26	Oregon	283
11	Pennsylvania	287
34	Rhode Island	278
32	South Carolina	280
8	South Dakota	289
42	Tennessee	275
15	Texas	286
26	Utah	283
3	Vermont	292
18	Virginia	285
10	Washington	288
46	West Virginia	270
11	Wisconsin	287
21	Wyoming	284

RANK	STATE	AVERAGE SCORE
1	Massachusetts	298
2	Minnesota	293
3	New Hampshire	292
3	Vermont	292
5	Montana	291
5	North Dakota	291
7	New Jersey	290
8	Connecticut	289
8	South Dakota	289
10	Washington	288
11	Kansas	287
11	Maryland	287
11	Pennsylvania	287
11	Wisconsin	287
15	Colorado	286
15	Idaho	286
15	Texas	286
18	Indiana	285
18	Missouri	285
18	Virginia	285
21	Iowa	284
21	Maine	284
21	North Carolina	284
21	Ohio	284
21	Wyoming	284
26	Alaska	283
26	Delaware	283
26	Nebraska	283
26	Oregon	283
26	Utah	283
31	New York	282
32	Illinois	280
32	South Carolina	280
34	Florida	278
34	Georgia	278
34	Kentucky	278
34	Rhode Island	278
38	Arkansas	277
38	Michigan	277
40	Arizona	276
40	Hawaii	276
42	Tennessee	275
43	Oklahoma	274
44	Louisiana	273
44	Nevada	273
46	West Virginia	270
47	Alabama	269
47	New Mexico	269
49	California	268
50	Mississippi	265
	District of Columbia	255

Source: U.S. Department of Education, National Center for Education Statistics
   "The Nation's Report Card: Mathematics 2009" (http://nces.ed.gov/nationsreportcard/)
*These scores are from the National Assessment of Educational Progress (NAEP). Scale ranges from 0 to 500.

Average Mathematics Score for Public School Eighth Graders
Eligible for Free or Reduced Price Lunch Program in 2009
National Average Score = 266*

ALPHA ORDER

RANK	STATE	AVERAGE SCORE
50	Alabama	255
20	Alaska	269
41	Arizona	262
36	Arkansas	264
48	California	258
31	Colorado	267
38	Connecticut	263
15	Delaware	271
20	Florida	269
35	Georgia	265
43	Hawaii	261
5	Idaho	276
36	Illinois	264
11	Indiana	273
20	Iowa	269
5	Kansas	276
25	Kentucky	268
38	Louisiana	263
13	Maine	272
31	Maryland	267
2	Massachusetts	278
47	Michigan	260
11	Minnesota	273
49	Mississippi	256
13	Missouri	272
3	Montana	277
31	Nebraska	267
38	Nevada	263
5	New Hampshire	276
17	New Jersey	270
43	New Mexico	261
17	New York	270
25	North Carolina	268
1	North Dakota	280
20	Ohio	269
34	Oklahoma	266
17	Oregon	270
25	Pennsylvania	268
43	Rhode Island	261
25	South Carolina	268
5	South Dakota	276
43	Tennessee	261
5	Texas	276
25	Utah	268
3	Vermont	277
25	Virginia	268
15	Washington	271
41	West Virginia	262
20	Wisconsin	269
10	Wyoming	274

RANK ORDER

RANK	STATE	AVERAGE SCORE
1	North Dakota	280
2	Massachusetts	278
3	Montana	277
3	Vermont	277
5	Idaho	276
5	Kansas	276
5	New Hampshire	276
5	South Dakota	276
5	Texas	276
10	Wyoming	274
11	Indiana	273
11	Minnesota	273
13	Maine	272
13	Missouri	272
15	Delaware	271
15	Washington	271
17	New Jersey	270
17	New York	270
17	Oregon	270
20	Alaska	269
20	Florida	269
20	Iowa	269
20	Ohio	269
20	Wisconsin	269
25	Kentucky	268
25	North Carolina	268
25	Pennsylvania	268
25	South Carolina	268
25	Utah	268
25	Virginia	268
31	Colorado	267
31	Maryland	267
31	Nebraska	267
34	Oklahoma	266
35	Georgia	265
36	Arkansas	264
36	Illinois	264
38	Connecticut	263
38	Louisiana	263
38	Nevada	263
41	Arizona	262
41	West Virginia	262
43	Hawaii	261
43	New Mexico	261
43	Rhode Island	261
43	Tennessee	261
47	Michigan	260
48	California	258
49	Mississippi	256
50	Alabama	255
	District of Columbia	247

Source: U.S. Department of Education, National Center for Education Statistics
    "The Nation's Report Card: Mathematics 2009" (http://nces.ed.gov/nationsreportcard/)
*These scores are from the National Assessment of Educational Progress (NAEP). Scale ranges from 0 to 500.

Percent of Public School Eighth Graders Proficient or Better in Mathematics in 2009
National Percent = 33%*

ALPHA ORDER

RANK	STATE	PERCENT
46	Alabama	20
30	Alaska	33
35	Arizona	29
38	Arkansas	27
45	California	23
9	Colorado	40
9	Connecticut	40
32	Delaware	32
35	Florida	29
38	Georgia	27
41	Hawaii	25
16	Idaho	38
30	Illinois	33
18	Indiana	36
28	Iowa	34
13	Kansas	39
38	Kentucky	27
46	Louisiana	20
23	Maine	35
9	Maryland	40
1	Massachusetts	52
33	Michigan	31
2	Minnesota	47
50	Mississippi	15
23	Missouri	35
3	Montana	44
23	Nebraska	35
41	Nevada	25
5	New Hampshire	43
3	New Jersey	44
46	New Mexico	20
28	New York	34
18	North Carolina	36
5	North Dakota	43
18	Ohio	36
44	Oklahoma	24
17	Oregon	37
9	Pennsylvania	40
37	Rhode Island	28
34	South Carolina	30
8	South Dakota	42
41	Tennessee	25
18	Texas	36
23	Utah	35
5	Vermont	43
18	Virginia	36
13	Washington	39
49	West Virginia	19
13	Wisconsin	39
23	Wyoming	35

RANK ORDER

RANK	STATE	PERCENT
1	Massachusetts	52
2	Minnesota	47
3	Montana	44
3	New Jersey	44
5	New Hampshire	43
5	North Dakota	43
5	Vermont	43
8	South Dakota	42
9	Colorado	40
9	Connecticut	40
9	Maryland	40
9	Pennsylvania	40
13	Kansas	39
13	Washington	39
13	Wisconsin	39
16	Idaho	38
17	Oregon	37
18	Indiana	36
18	North Carolina	36
18	Ohio	36
18	Texas	36
18	Virginia	36
23	Maine	35
23	Missouri	35
23	Nebraska	35
23	Utah	35
23	Wyoming	35
28	Iowa	34
28	New York	34
30	Alaska	33
30	Illinois	33
32	Delaware	32
33	Michigan	31
34	South Carolina	30
35	Arizona	29
35	Florida	29
37	Rhode Island	28
38	Arkansas	27
38	Georgia	27
38	Kentucky	27
41	Hawaii	25
41	Nevada	25
41	Tennessee	25
44	Oklahoma	24
45	California	23
46	Alabama	20
46	Louisiana	20
46	New Mexico	20
49	West Virginia	19
50	Mississippi	15
	District of Columbia	11

Source: U.S. Department of Education, National Center for Education Statistics
    "The Nation's Report Card: Mathematics 2009" (http://nces.ed.gov/nationsreportcard/)
*There are four achievement levels: Below Basic, Basic, Proficient, and Advanced. Proficient represents solid academic mastery for 8th graders. Students reaching this level have demonstrated competency over challenging subject matter, including subject matter knowledge, application of such knowledge to real-world situations, and analytical skills appropriate to the subject matter.

Percent of Public School Eighth Grade Males
Proficient or Better in Mathematics in 2009
National Percent = 34%*

ALPHA ORDER

RANK	STATE	PERCENT
46	Alabama	21
31	Alaska	34
34	Arizona	31
39	Arkansas	27
41	California	26
12	Colorado	41
16	Connecticut	39
32	Delaware	32
34	Florida	31
39	Georgia	27
45	Hawaii	24
16	Idaho	39
29	Illinois	35
16	Indiana	39
29	Iowa	35
9	Kansas	43
37	Kentucky	30
46	Louisiana	21
19	Maine	38
10	Maryland	42
1	Massachusetts	53
32	Michigan	32
2	Minnesota	49
50	Mississippi	15
24	Missouri	37
4	Montana	45
24	Nebraska	37
41	Nevada	26
4	New Hampshire	45
3	New Jersey	47
46	New Mexico	21
28	New York	36
24	North Carolina	37
4	North Dakota	45
19	Ohio	38
41	Oklahoma	26
15	Oregon	40
10	Pennsylvania	42
38	Rhode Island	29
34	South Carolina	31
8	South Dakota	44
41	Tennessee	26
19	Texas	38
24	Utah	37
4	Vermont	45
19	Virginia	38
12	Washington	41
46	West Virginia	21
12	Wisconsin	41
19	Wyoming	38

RANK ORDER

RANK	STATE	PERCENT
1	Massachusetts	53
2	Minnesota	49
3	New Jersey	47
4	Montana	45
4	New Hampshire	45
4	North Dakota	45
4	Vermont	45
8	South Dakota	44
9	Kansas	43
10	Maryland	42
10	Pennsylvania	42
12	Colorado	41
12	Washington	41
12	Wisconsin	41
15	Oregon	40
16	Connecticut	39
16	Idaho	39
16	Indiana	39
19	Maine	38
19	Ohio	38
19	Texas	38
19	Virginia	38
19	Wyoming	38
24	Missouri	37
24	Nebraska	37
24	North Carolina	37
24	Utah	37
28	New York	36
29	Illinois	35
29	Iowa	35
31	Alaska	34
32	Delaware	32
32	Michigan	32
34	Arizona	31
34	Florida	31
34	South Carolina	31
37	Kentucky	30
38	Rhode Island	29
39	Arkansas	27
39	Georgia	27
41	California	26
41	Nevada	26
41	Oklahoma	26
41	Tennessee	26
45	Hawaii	24
46	Alabama	21
46	Louisiana	21
46	New Mexico	21
46	West Virginia	21
50	Mississippi	15
	District of Columbia	12

Source: U.S. Department of Education, National Center for Education Statistics
   "The Nation's Report Card: Mathematics 2009" (http://nces.ed.gov/nationsreportcard/)
*There are four achievement levels: Below Basic, Basic, Proficient, and Advanced.   Proficient represents solid academic mastery for 8th graders. Students reaching this level have demonstrated competency over challenging subject matter, including subject matter knowledge, application of such knowledge to real-world situations, and analytical skills appropriate to the subject matter.

Percent of Public School Eighth Grade Females
Proficient or Better in Mathematics in 2009
National Percent = 31%*

ALPHA ORDER

RANK	STATE	PERCENT
46	Alabama	20
22	Alaska	33
35	Arizona	27
35	Arkansas	27
44	California	21
10	Colorado	38
8	Connecticut	41
30	Delaware	31
35	Florida	27
35	Georgia	27
35	Hawaii	27
14	Idaho	37
30	Illinois	31
18	Indiana	34
22	Iowa	33
16	Kansas	36
41	Kentucky	25
46	Louisiana	20
27	Maine	32
10	Maryland	38
1	Massachusetts	50
33	Michigan	29
2	Minnesota	45
50	Mississippi	15
18	Missouri	34
3	Montana	42
27	Nebraska	32
43	Nevada	24
3	New Hampshire	42
3	New Jersey	42
48	New Mexico	19
27	New York	32
18	North Carolina	34
3	North Dakota	42
18	Ohio	34
44	Oklahoma	21
22	Oregon	33
14	Pennsylvania	37
40	Rhode Island	26
33	South Carolina	29
9	South Dakota	39
41	Tennessee	25
17	Texas	35
22	Utah	33
3	Vermont	42
22	Virginia	33
10	Washington	38
49	West Virginia	18
10	Wisconsin	38
30	Wyoming	31

RANK ORDER

RANK	STATE	PERCENT
1	Massachusetts	50
2	Minnesota	45
3	Montana	42
3	New Hampshire	42
3	New Jersey	42
3	North Dakota	42
3	Vermont	42
8	Connecticut	41
9	South Dakota	39
10	Colorado	38
10	Maryland	38
10	Washington	38
10	Wisconsin	38
14	Idaho	37
14	Pennsylvania	37
16	Kansas	36
17	Texas	35
18	Indiana	34
18	Missouri	34
18	North Carolina	34
18	Ohio	34
22	Alaska	33
22	Iowa	33
22	Oregon	33
22	Utah	33
22	Virginia	33
27	Maine	32
27	Nebraska	32
27	New York	32
30	Delaware	31
30	Illinois	31
30	Wyoming	31
33	Michigan	29
33	South Carolina	29
35	Arizona	27
35	Arkansas	27
35	Florida	27
35	Georgia	27
35	Hawaii	27
40	Rhode Island	26
41	Kentucky	25
41	Tennessee	25
43	Nevada	24
44	California	21
44	Oklahoma	21
46	Alabama	20
46	Louisiana	20
48	New Mexico	19
49	West Virginia	18
50	Mississippi	15
	District of Columbia	11

Source: U.S. Department of Education, National Center for Education Statistics
   "The Nation's Report Card: Mathematics 2009" (http://nces.ed.gov/nationsreportcard/)
*There are four achievement levels: Below Basic, Basic, Proficient, and Advanced. Proficient represents solid academic mastery for 8th graders. Students reaching this level have demonstrated competency over challenging subject matter, including subject matter knowledge, application of such knowledge to real-world situations, and analytical skills appropriate to the subject matter.

Percent of Public School Eighth Graders Eligible for Free or Reduced Price Lunch Program Proficient or Better in Mathematics in 2009
National Percent = 17%*

ALPHA ORDER				RANK ORDER		
RANK	STATE	PERCENT		RANK	STATE	PERCENT
49	Alabama	10		1	Massachusetts	29
19	Alaska	19		2	Montana	27
36	Arizona	14		2	North Dakota	27
32	Arkansas	15		4	Idaho	25
44	California	12		5	Kansas	24
19	Colorado	19		5	New Hampshire	24
40	Connecticut	13		5	South Dakota	24
27	Delaware	17		5	Vermont	24
23	Florida	18		9	Texas	23
40	Georgia	13		10	New York	22
32	Hawaii	15		11	Indiana	21
4	Idaho	25		11	Minnesota	21
36	Illinois	14		11	Oregon	21
11	Indiana	21		14	New Jersey	20
27	Iowa	17		14	Utah	20
5	Kansas	24		14	Washington	20
32	Kentucky	15		14	Wisconsin	20
46	Louisiana	11		14	Wyoming	20
19	Maine	19		19	Alaska	19
27	Maryland	17		19	Colorado	19
1	Massachusetts	29		19	Maine	19
40	Michigan	13		19	Missouri	19
11	Minnesota	21		23	Florida	18
50	Mississippi	8		23	North Carolina	18
19	Missouri	19		23	Ohio	18
2	Montana	27		23	Pennsylvania	18
27	Nebraska	17		27	Delaware	17
36	Nevada	14		27	Iowa	17
5	New Hampshire	24		27	Maryland	17
14	New Jersey	20		27	Nebraska	17
46	New Mexico	11		31	South Carolina	16
10	New York	22		32	Arkansas	15
23	North Carolina	18		32	Hawaii	15
2	North Dakota	27		32	Kentucky	15
23	Ohio	18		32	Virginia	15
36	Oklahoma	14		36	Arizona	14
11	Oregon	21		36	Illinois	14
23	Pennsylvania	18		36	Nevada	14
44	Rhode Island	12		36	Oklahoma	14
31	South Carolina	16		40	Connecticut	13
5	South Dakota	24		40	Georgia	13
40	Tennessee	13		40	Michigan	13
9	Texas	23		40	Tennessee	13
14	Utah	20		44	California	12
5	Vermont	24		44	Rhode Island	12
32	Virginia	15		46	Louisiana	11
14	Washington	20		46	New Mexico	11
46	West Virginia	11		46	West Virginia	11
14	Wisconsin	20		49	Alabama	10
14	Wyoming	20		50	Mississippi	8
					District of Columbia	7

Source: U.S. Department of Education, National Center for Education Statistics
"The Nation's Report Card: Mathematics 2009" (http://nces.ed.gov/nationsreportcard/)
*There are four achievement levels: Below Basic, Basic, Proficient, and Advanced. Proficient represents solid academic mastery for 8th graders. Students reaching this level have demonstrated competency over challenging subject matter, including subject matter knowledge, application of such knowledge to real-world situations, and analytical skills appropriate to the subject matter.

Percent of White Public School Eighth Graders Proficient or Better in Mathematics in 2009
National Percent = 43%*

ALPHA ORDER

RANK	STATE	PERCENT
45	Alabama	29
16	Alaska	44
25	Arizona	42
42	Arkansas	34
31	California	39
6	Colorado	51
7	Connecticut	49
22	Delaware	43
31	Florida	39
31	Georgia	39
43	Hawaii	31
22	Idaho	43
16	Illinois	44
26	Indiana	41
37	Iowa	37
13	Kansas	45
45	Kentucky	29
45	Louisiana	29
39	Maine	36
2	Maryland	56
1	Massachusetts	59
37	Michigan	37
5	Minnesota	53
49	Mississippi	25
31	Missouri	39
9	Montana	47
26	Nebraska	41
39	Nevada	36
16	New Hampshire	44
3	New Jersey	54
31	New Mexico	39
16	New York	44
7	North Carolina	49
10	North Dakota	46
26	Ohio	41
45	Oklahoma	29
26	Oregon	41
13	Pennsylvania	45
41	Rhode Island	35
22	South Carolina	43
10	South Dakota	46
44	Tennessee	30
3	Texas	54
30	Utah	40
16	Vermont	44
16	Virginia	44
10	Washington	46
50	West Virginia	20
13	Wisconsin	45
36	Wyoming	38

RANK ORDER

RANK	STATE	PERCENT
1	Massachusetts	59
2	Maryland	56
3	New Jersey	54
3	Texas	54
5	Minnesota	53
6	Colorado	51
7	Connecticut	49
7	North Carolina	49
9	Montana	47
10	North Dakota	46
10	South Dakota	46
10	Washington	46
13	Kansas	45
13	Pennsylvania	45
13	Wisconsin	45
16	Alaska	44
16	Illinois	44
16	New Hampshire	44
16	New York	44
16	Vermont	44
16	Virginia	44
22	Delaware	43
22	Idaho	43
22	South Carolina	43
25	Arizona	42
26	Indiana	41
26	Nebraska	41
26	Ohio	41
26	Oregon	41
30	Utah	40
31	California	39
31	Florida	39
31	Georgia	39
31	Missouri	39
31	New Mexico	39
36	Wyoming	38
37	Iowa	37
37	Michigan	37
39	Maine	36
39	Nevada	36
41	Rhode Island	35
42	Arkansas	34
43	Hawaii	31
44	Tennessee	30
45	Alabama	29
45	Kentucky	29
45	Louisiana	29
45	Oklahoma	29
49	Mississippi	25
50	West Virginia	20

District of Columbia**	NA

Source: U.S. Department of Education, National Center for Education Statistics
    "The Nation's Report Card: Mathematics 2009" (http://nces.ed.gov/nationsreportcard/)
*There are four achievement levels: Below Basic, Basic, Proficient, and Advanced. Proficient represents solid academic mastery for 8th graders. Students reaching this level have demonstrated competency over challenging subject matter, including subject matter knowledge, application of such knowledge to real-world situations, and analytical skills appropriate to the subject matter. **Sample size insufficient.

Percent of Black Public School Eighth Graders Proficient or Better in Mathematics in 2009
National Percent = 12%*

ALPHA ORDER

RANK	STATE	PERCENT
40	Alabama	6
4	Alaska	17
1	Arizona	23
36	Arkansas	8
28	California	10
7	Colorado	16
28	Connecticut	10
14	Delaware	13
14	Florida	13
23	Georgia	11
3	Hawaii	21
NA	Idaho**	NA
34	Illinois	9
11	Indiana	14
34	Iowa	9
9	Kansas	15
36	Kentucky	8
39	Louisiana	7
11	Maine	14
9	Maryland	15
1	Massachusetts	23
41	Michigan	5
14	Minnesota	13
41	Mississippi	5
23	Missouri	11
NA	Montana**	NA
28	Nebraska	10
28	Nevada	10
NA	New Hampshire**	NA
4	New Jersey	17
14	New Mexico	13
14	New York	13
20	North Carolina	12
NA	North Dakota**	NA
23	Ohio	11
28	Oklahoma	10
20	Oregon	12
14	Pennsylvania	13
36	Rhode Island	8
20	South Carolina	12
NA	South Dakota**	NA
28	Tennessee	10
4	Texas	17
NA	Utah**	NA
NA	Vermont**	NA
11	Virginia	14
7	Washington	16
23	West Virginia	11
23	Wisconsin	11
NA	Wyoming**	NA

RANK ORDER

RANK	STATE	PERCENT
1	Arizona	23
1	Massachusetts	23
3	Hawaii	21
4	Alaska	17
4	New Jersey	17
4	Texas	17
7	Colorado	16
7	Washington	16
9	Kansas	15
9	Maryland	15
11	Indiana	14
11	Maine	14
11	Virginia	14
14	Delaware	13
14	Florida	13
14	Minnesota	13
14	New Mexico	13
14	New York	13
14	Pennsylvania	13
20	North Carolina	12
20	Oregon	12
20	South Carolina	12
23	Georgia	11
23	Missouri	11
23	Ohio	11
23	West Virginia	11
23	Wisconsin	11
28	California	10
28	Connecticut	10
28	Nebraska	10
28	Nevada	10
28	Oklahoma	10
28	Tennessee	10
34	Illinois	9
34	Iowa	9
36	Arkansas	8
36	Kentucky	8
36	Rhode Island	8
39	Louisiana	7
40	Alabama	6
41	Michigan	5
41	Mississippi	5
NA	Idaho**	NA
NA	Montana**	NA
NA	New Hampshire**	NA
NA	North Dakota**	NA
NA	South Dakota**	NA
NA	Utah**	NA
NA	Vermont**	NA
NA	Wyoming**	NA

	District of Columbia	8

Source: U.S. Department of Education, National Center for Education Statistics
   "The Nation's Report Card: Mathematics 2009" (http://nces.ed.gov/nationsreportcard/)
*There are four achievement levels: Below Basic, Basic, Proficient, and Advanced. Proficient represents solid academic mastery for 8th graders. Students reaching this level have demonstrated competency over challenging subject matter, including subject matter knowledge, application of such knowledge to real-world situations, and analytical skills appropriate to the subject matter. **Sample size insufficient.

Percent of Hispanic Public School Eighth Graders Proficient or Better in Mathematics in 2009
National Percent = 17%*

ALPHA ORDER

RANK	STATE	PERCENT
42	Alabama	10
7	Alaska	23
25	Arizona	16
28	Arkansas	15
40	California	11
20	Colorado	18
34	Connecticut	14
9	Delaware	22
9	Florida	22
20	Georgia	18
3	Hawaii	26
28	Idaho	15
23	Illinois	17
18	Indiana	19
28	Iowa	15
9	Kansas	22
9	Kentucky	22
NA	Louisiana**	NA
NA	Maine**	NA
3	Maryland	26
15	Massachusetts	21
23	Michigan	17
15	Minnesota	21
NA	Mississippi**	NA
1	Missouri	37
2	Montana	27
42	Nebraska	10
35	Nevada	13
9	New Hampshire	22
9	New Jersey	22
38	New Mexico	12
28	New York	15
6	North Carolina	24
NA	North Dakota**	NA
25	Ohio	16
38	Oklahoma	12
28	Oregon	15
20	Pennsylvania	18
44	Rhode Island	8
25	South Carolina	16
35	South Dakota	13
18	Tennessee	19
5	Texas	25
40	Utah	11
NA	Vermont**	NA
7	Virginia	23
35	Washington	13
NA	West Virginia**	NA
17	Wisconsin	20
28	Wyoming	15

RANK ORDER

RANK	STATE	PERCENT
1	Missouri	37
2	Montana	27
3	Hawaii	26
3	Maryland	26
5	Texas	25
6	North Carolina	24
7	Alaska	23
7	Virginia	23
9	Delaware	22
9	Florida	22
9	Kansas	22
9	Kentucky	22
9	New Hampshire	22
9	New Jersey	22
15	Massachusetts	21
15	Minnesota	21
17	Wisconsin	20
18	Indiana	19
18	Tennessee	19
20	Colorado	18
20	Georgia	18
20	Pennsylvania	18
23	Illinois	17
23	Michigan	17
25	Arizona	16
25	Ohio	16
25	South Carolina	16
28	Arkansas	15
28	Idaho	15
28	Iowa	15
28	New York	15
28	Oregon	15
28	Wyoming	15
34	Connecticut	14
35	Nevada	13
35	South Dakota	13
35	Washington	13
38	New Mexico	12
38	Oklahoma	12
40	California	11
40	Utah	11
42	Alabama	10
42	Nebraska	10
44	Rhode Island	8
NA	Louisiana**	NA
NA	Maine**	NA
NA	Mississippi**	NA
NA	North Dakota**	NA
NA	Vermont**	NA
NA	West Virginia**	NA

District of Columbia	18

Source: U.S. Department of Education, National Center for Education Statistics
   "The Nation's Report Card: Mathematics 2009" (http://nces.ed.gov/nationsreportcard/)
*There are four achievement levels: Below Basic, Basic, Proficient, and Advanced. Proficient represents solid academic mastery for 8th graders. Students reaching this level have demonstrated competency over challenging subject matter, including subject matter knowledge, application of such knowledge to real-world situations, and analytical skills appropriate to the subject matter. **Sample size insufficient.

Percent of Asian Public School Eighth Graders Proficient or Better in Mathematics in 2009
National Percent = 53%*

ALPHA ORDER

RANK	STATE	PERCENT
NA	Alabama**	NA
26	Alaska	31
17	Arizona	52
NA	Arkansas**	NA
20	California	46
13	Colorado	55
9	Connecticut	61
3	Delaware	69
13	Florida	55
19	Georgia	49
28	Hawaii	25
NA	Idaho**	NA
10	Illinois	60
NA	Indiana**	NA
NA	Iowa**	NA
NA	Kansas**	NA
NA	Kentucky**	NA
NA	Louisiana**	NA
NA	Maine**	NA
2	Maryland	76
5	Massachusetts	66
12	Michigan	59
24	Minnesota	35
NA	Mississippi**	NA
NA	Missouri**	NA
NA	Montana**	NA
NA	Nebraska**	NA
25	Nevada	33
8	New Hampshire	62
1	New Jersey	77
NA	New Mexico**	NA
7	New York	63
6	North Carolina	65
NA	North Dakota**	NA
NA	Ohio**	NA
23	Oklahoma	38
18	Oregon	50
10	Pennsylvania	60
21	Rhode Island	40
NA	South Carolina**	NA
NA	South Dakota**	NA
NA	Tennessee**	NA
4	Texas	67
27	Utah	27
NA	Vermont**	NA
13	Virginia	55
16	Washington	53
NA	West Virginia**	NA
21	Wisconsin	40
NA	Wyoming**	NA

RANK ORDER

RANK	STATE	PERCENT
1	New Jersey	77
2	Maryland	76
3	Delaware	69
4	Texas	67
5	Massachusetts	66
6	North Carolina	65
7	New York	63
8	New Hampshire	62
9	Connecticut	61
10	Illinois	60
10	Pennsylvania	60
12	Michigan	59
13	Colorado	55
13	Florida	55
13	Virginia	55
16	Washington	53
17	Arizona	52
18	Oregon	50
19	Georgia	49
20	California	46
21	Rhode Island	40
21	Wisconsin	40
23	Oklahoma	38
24	Minnesota	35
25	Nevada	33
26	Alaska	31
27	Utah	27
28	Hawaii	25
NA	Alabama**	NA
NA	Arkansas**	NA
NA	Idaho**	NA
NA	Indiana**	NA
NA	Iowa**	NA
NA	Kansas**	NA
NA	Kentucky**	NA
NA	Louisiana**	NA
NA	Maine**	NA
NA	Mississippi**	NA
NA	Missouri**	NA
NA	Montana**	NA
NA	Nebraska**	NA
NA	New Mexico**	NA
NA	North Dakota**	NA
NA	Ohio**	NA
NA	South Carolina**	NA
NA	South Dakota**	NA
NA	Tennessee**	NA
NA	Vermont**	NA
NA	West Virginia**	NA
NA	Wyoming**	NA
	District of Columbia**	NA

Source: U.S. Department of Education, National Center for Education Statistics
"The Nation's Report Card: Mathematics 2009" (http://nces.ed.gov/nationsreportcard/)
*There are four achievement levels: Below Basic, Basic, Proficient, and Advanced. Proficient represents solid academic mastery for 8th graders. Students reaching this level have demonstrated competency over challenging subject matter, including subject matter knowledge, application of such knowledge to real-world situations, and analytical skills appropriate to the subject matter. **Sample size insufficient.

Percent of Disabled Public School Eighth Graders Proficient or Better in Mathematics in 2009
National Percent = 9%*

ALPHA ORDER

RANK	STATE	PERCENT
49	Alabama	1
31	Alaska	6
40	Arizona	5
44	Arkansas	4
45	California	3
10	Colorado	11
6	Connecticut	13
20	Delaware	9
24	Florida	8
31	Georgia	6
45	Hawaii	3
24	Idaho	8
24	Illinois	8
9	Indiana	12
40	Iowa	5
20	Kansas	9
29	Kentucky	7
31	Louisiana	6
14	Maine	10
2	Maryland	18
1	Massachusetts	21
45	Michigan	3
3	Minnesota	16
49	Mississippi	1
20	Missouri	9
31	Montana	6
14	Nebraska	10
20	Nevada	9
4	New Hampshire	14
6	New Jersey	13
31	New Mexico	6
14	New York	10
10	North Carolina	11
6	North Dakota	13
10	Ohio	11
40	Oklahoma	5
31	Oregon	6
14	Pennsylvania	10
40	Rhode Island	5
29	South Carolina	7
24	South Dakota	8
31	Tennessee	6
4	Texas	14
31	Utah	6
10	Vermont	11
14	Virginia	10
31	Washington	6
48	West Virginia	2
14	Wisconsin	10
24	Wyoming	8

RANK ORDER

RANK	STATE	PERCENT
1	Massachusetts	21
2	Maryland	18
3	Minnesota	16
4	New Hampshire	14
4	Texas	14
6	Connecticut	13
6	New Jersey	13
6	North Dakota	13
9	Indiana	12
10	Colorado	11
10	North Carolina	11
10	Ohio	11
10	Vermont	11
14	Maine	10
14	Nebraska	10
14	New York	10
14	Pennsylvania	10
14	Virginia	10
14	Wisconsin	10
20	Delaware	9
20	Kansas	9
20	Missouri	9
20	Nevada	9
24	Florida	8
24	Idaho	8
24	Illinois	8
24	South Dakota	8
24	Wyoming	8
29	Kentucky	7
29	South Carolina	7
31	Alaska	6
31	Georgia	6
31	Louisiana	6
31	Montana	6
31	New Mexico	6
31	Oregon	6
31	Tennessee	6
31	Utah	6
31	Washington	6
40	Arizona	5
40	Iowa	5
40	Oklahoma	5
40	Rhode Island	5
44	Arkansas	4
45	California	3
45	Hawaii	3
45	Michigan	3
48	West Virginia	2
49	Alabama	1
49	Mississippi	1
	District of Columbia	1

Source: U.S. Department of Education, National Center for Education Statistics
   "The Nation's Report Card: Mathematics 2009" (http://nces.ed.gov/nationsreportcard/)
*There are four achievement levels: Below Basic, Basic, Proficient, and Advanced. Proficient represents solid academic mastery for 8th graders. Students reaching this level have demonstrated competency over challenging subject matter, including subject matter knowledge, application of such knowledge to real-world situations, and analytical skills appropriate to the subject matter. Based only on disabled students who were assessed.

Percent of English Language Learner Public School Eighth Graders Proficient or Better in Mathematics in 2009
National Percent = 5%*

ALPHA ORDER

RANK	STATE	PERCENT
NA	Alabama**	NA
27	Alaska	2
27	Arizona	2
12	Arkansas	8
22	California	3
19	Colorado	4
17	Connecticut	6
NA	Delaware**	NA
19	Florida	4
NA	Georgia**	NA
27	Hawaii	2
32	Idaho	1
16	Illinois	7
1	Indiana	19
NA	Iowa**	NA
8	Kansas	10
NA	Kentucky**	NA
NA	Louisiana**	NA
NA	Maine**	NA
12	Maryland	8
12	Massachusetts	8
8	Michigan	10
10	Minnesota	9
NA	Mississippi**	NA
NA	Missouri**	NA
32	Montana	1
22	Nebraska	3
27	Nevada	2
NA	New Hampshire**	NA
4	New Jersey	11
22	New Mexico	3
19	New York	4
4	North Carolina	11
NA	North Dakota**	NA
4	Ohio	11
32	Oklahoma	1
22	Oregon	3
4	Pennsylvania	11
12	Rhode Island	8
2	South Carolina	17
NA	South Dakota**	NA
NA	Tennessee**	NA
17	Texas	6
27	Utah	2
NA	Vermont**	NA
3	Virginia	13
22	Washington	3
NA	West Virginia**	NA
10	Wisconsin	9
NA	Wyoming**	NA

RANK ORDER

RANK	STATE	PERCENT
1	Indiana	19
2	South Carolina	17
3	Virginia	13
4	New Jersey	11
4	North Carolina	11
4	Ohio	11
4	Pennsylvania	11
8	Kansas	10
8	Michigan	10
10	Minnesota	9
10	Wisconsin	9
12	Arkansas	8
12	Maryland	8
12	Massachusetts	8
12	Rhode Island	8
16	Illinois	7
17	Connecticut	6
17	Texas	6
19	Colorado	4
19	Florida	4
19	New York	4
22	California	3
22	Nebraska	3
22	New Mexico	3
22	Oregon	3
22	Washington	3
27	Alaska	2
27	Arizona	2
27	Hawaii	2
27	Nevada	2
27	Utah	2
32	Idaho	1
32	Montana	1
32	Oklahoma	1
NA	Alabama**	NA
NA	Delaware**	NA
NA	Georgia**	NA
NA	Iowa**	NA
NA	Kentucky**	NA
NA	Louisiana**	NA
NA	Maine**	NA
NA	Mississippi**	NA
NA	Missouri**	NA
NA	New Hampshire**	NA
NA	North Dakota**	NA
NA	South Dakota**	NA
NA	Tennessee**	NA
NA	Vermont**	NA
NA	West Virginia**	NA
NA	Wyoming**	NA
	District of Columbia**	NA

Source: U.S. Department of Education, National Center for Education Statistics
"The Nation's Report Card: Mathematics 2009" (http://nces.ed.gov/nationsreportcard/)
*There are four achievement levels: Below Basic, Basic, Proficient, and Advanced. Proficient represents solid academic mastery for 8th graders. Students reaching this level have demonstrated competency over challenging subject matter, including subject matter knowledge, application of such knowledge to real-world situations, and analytical skills appropriate to the subject matter. **Sample size insufficient.

Average Science Score for Public School Fourth Graders in 2009

National Average Score = 149*

ALPHA ORDER

RANK	STATE	AVERAGE SCORE
38	Alabama	143
NA	Alaska**	NA
43	Arizona	138
36	Arkansas	146
44	California	136
16	Colorado	155
13	Connecticut	156
46	Delaware	23
22	Florida	151
37	Georgia	144
42	Hawaii	140
18	Idaho	154
29	Illinois	148
21	Indiana	153
9	Iowa	157
NA	Kansas**	NA
4	Kentucky	161
40	Louisiana	141
5	Maine	160
25	Maryland	150
5	Massachusetts	160
25	Michigan	150
8	Minnesota	158
45	Mississippi	133
13	Missouri	156
5	Montana	160
NA	Nebraska**	NA
40	Nevada	141
1	New Hampshire	163
16	New Jersey	155
39	New Mexico	142
29	New York	148
29	North Carolina	148
2	North Dakota	162
9	Ohio	157
29	Oklahoma	148
22	Oregon	151
18	Pennsylvania	154
25	Rhode Island	150
28	South Carolina	149
9	South Dakota	157
29	Tennessee	148
29	Texas	148
18	Utah	154
NA	Vermont**	NA
2	Virginia	162
22	Washington	151
29	West Virginia	148
9	Wisconsin	157
13	Wyoming	156

RANK ORDER

RANK	STATE	AVERAGE SCORE
1	New Hampshire	163
2	North Dakota	162
2	Virginia	162
4	Kentucky	161
5	Maine	160
5	Massachusetts	160
5	Montana	160
8	Minnesota	158
9	Iowa	157
9	Ohio	157
9	South Dakota	157
9	Wisconsin	157
13	Connecticut	156
13	Missouri	156
13	Wyoming	156
16	Colorado	155
16	New Jersey	155
18	Idaho	154
18	Pennsylvania	154
18	Utah	154
21	Indiana	153
22	Florida	151
22	Oregon	151
22	Washington	151
25	Maryland	150
25	Michigan	150
25	Rhode Island	150
28	South Carolina	149
29	Illinois	148
29	New York	148
29	North Carolina	148
29	Oklahoma	148
29	Tennessee	148
29	Texas	148
29	West Virginia	148
36	Arkansas	146
37	Georgia	144
38	Alabama	143
39	New Mexico	142
40	Louisiana	141
40	Nevada	141
42	Hawaii	140
43	Arizona	138
44	California	136
45	Mississippi	133
46	Delaware	23
NA	Alaska**	NA
NA	Kansas**	NA
NA	Nebraska**	NA
NA	Vermont**	NA
	District of Columbia**	NA

Source: U.S. Department of Education, National Center for Education Statistics
"The Nation's Report Card: Science 2009" (http://nces.ed.gov/nationsreportcard/)
*These scores are from the National Assessment of Educational Progress (NAEP). Scale ranges from 0 to 300.
**Not available.

Average Science Score for Public School Fourth Grade Males in 2009

National Average Score = 149*

ALPHA ORDER				RANK ORDER		
RANK	STATE	AVERAGE SCORE		RANK	STATE	AVERAGE SCORE
39	Alabama	144		1	North Dakota	164
NA	Alaska**	NA		2	New Hampshire	163
43	Arizona	137		3	Massachusetts	162
37	Arkansas	146		4	Kentucky	161
45	California	136		4	Maine	161
14	Colorado	156		4	Virginia	161
14	Connecticut	156		7	Montana	160
21	Delaware	153		8	Minnesota	159
23	Florida	151		8	Ohio	159
38	Georgia	145		10	Iowa	158
43	Hawaii	137		10	South Dakota	158
20	Idaho	154		12	Wisconsin	157
33	Illinois	148		12	Wyoming	157
21	Indiana	153		14	Colorado	156
10	Iowa	158		14	Connecticut	156
NA	Kansas**	NA		14	New Jersey	156
4	Kentucky	161		14	Pennsylvania	156
42	Louisiana	141		18	Missouri	155
4	Maine	161		18	Utah	155
23	Maryland	151		20	Idaho	154
3	Massachusetts	162		21	Delaware	153
23	Michigan	151		21	Indiana	153
8	Minnesota	159		23	Florida	151
46	Mississippi	134		23	Maryland	151
18	Missouri	155		23	Michigan	151
7	Montana	160		23	Oregon	151
NA	Nebraska**	NA		23	Rhode Island	151
40	Nevada	142		23	Washington	151
2	New Hampshire	163		29	South Carolina	150
14	New Jersey	156		30	North Carolina	149
40	New Mexico	142		30	Tennessee	149
33	New York	148		30	West Virginia	149
30	North Carolina	149		33	Illinois	148
1	North Dakota	164		33	New York	148
8	Ohio	159		33	Oklahoma	148
33	Oklahoma	148		33	Texas	148
23	Oregon	151		37	Arkansas	146
14	Pennsylvania	156		38	Georgia	145
23	Rhode Island	151		39	Alabama	144
29	South Carolina	150		40	Nevada	142
10	South Dakota	158		40	New Mexico	142
30	Tennessee	149		42	Louisiana	141
33	Texas	148		43	Arizona	137
18	Utah	155		43	Hawaii	137
NA	Vermont**	NA		45	California	136
4	Virginia	161		46	Mississippi	134
23	Washington	151		NA	Alaska**	NA
30	West Virginia	149		NA	Kansas**	NA
12	Wisconsin	157		NA	Nebraska**	NA
12	Wyoming	157		NA	Vermont**	NA
					District of Columbia**	NA

Source: U.S. Department of Education, National Center for Education Statistics
    "The Nation's Report Card: Science 2009" (http://nces.ed.gov/nationsreportcard/)
*These scores are from the National Assessment of Educational Progress (NAEP). Scale ranges from 0 to 300.
**Not available.

Average Science Score for Public School Fourth Grade Females in 2009

National Average Score = 148*

RANK	STATE	AVERAGE SCORE
40	Alabama	142
NA	Alaska**	NA
44	Arizona	138
36	Arkansas	146
45	California	137
17	Colorado	153
13	Connecticut	155
20	Delaware	152
25	Florida	150
38	Georgia	143
38	Hawaii	143
17	Idaho	153
32	Illinois	147
20	Indiana	152
10	Iowa	157
NA	Kansas**	NA
3	Kentucky	160
41	Louisiana	141
7	Maine	158
26	Maryland	149
6	Massachusetts	159
26	Michigan	149
7	Minnesota	158
46	Mississippi	132
7	Missouri	158
3	Montana	160
NA	Nebraska**	NA
43	Nevada	139
1	New Hampshire	163
15	New Jersey	154
41	New Mexico	141
32	New York	147
36	North Carolina	146
3	North Dakota	160
13	Ohio	155
30	Oklahoma	148
22	Oregon	151
22	Pennsylvania	151
26	Rhode Island	149
26	South Carolina	149
11	South Dakota	156
30	Tennessee	148
32	Texas	147
17	Utah	153
NA	Vermont**	NA
2	Virginia	162
22	Washington	151
32	West Virginia	147
11	Wisconsin	156
15	Wyoming	154

RANK	STATE	AVERAGE SCORE
1	New Hampshire	163
2	Virginia	162
3	Kentucky	160
3	Montana	160
3	North Dakota	160
6	Massachusetts	159
7	Maine	158
7	Minnesota	158
7	Missouri	158
10	Iowa	157
11	South Dakota	156
11	Wisconsin	156
13	Connecticut	155
13	Ohio	155
15	New Jersey	154
15	Wyoming	154
17	Colorado	153
17	Idaho	153
17	Utah	153
20	Delaware	152
20	Indiana	152
22	Oregon	151
22	Pennsylvania	151
22	Washington	151
25	Florida	150
26	Maryland	149
26	Michigan	149
26	Rhode Island	149
26	South Carolina	149
30	Oklahoma	148
30	Tennessee	148
32	Illinois	147
32	New York	147
32	Texas	147
32	West Virginia	147
36	Arkansas	146
36	North Carolina	146
38	Georgia	143
38	Hawaii	143
40	Alabama	142
41	Louisiana	141
41	New Mexico	141
43	Nevada	139
44	Arizona	138
45	California	137
46	Mississippi	132
NA	Alaska**	NA
NA	Kansas**	NA
NA	Nebraska**	NA
NA	Vermont**	NA
	District of Columbia**	NA

Source: U.S. Department of Education, National Center for Education Statistics
   "The Nation's Report Card: Science 2009" (http://nces.ed.gov/nationsreportcard/)
*These scores are from the National Assessment of Educational Progress (NAEP). Scale ranges from 0 to 300.
**Not available.

Average Science Score for Public School Fourth Graders Eligible for Free or Reduced Price Lunch Program in 2009
National Average Score = 134*

ALPHA ORDER

RANK ORDER

RANK	STATE	AVERAGE SCORE	RANK	STATE	AVERAGE SCORE
41	Alabama	129	1	Maine	151
NA	Alaska**	NA	2	Kentucky	150
44	Arizona	125	3	Montana	149
26	Arkansas	135	3	New Hampshire	149
46	California	122	3	North Dakota	149
24	Colorado	136	6	Idaho	145
39	Connecticut	130	6	Virginia	145
21	Delaware	138	6	Wyoming	145
12	Florida	141	9	Missouri	143
35	Georgia	132	9	South Dakota	143
43	Hawaii	126	11	Iowa	142
6	Idaho	145	12	Florida	141
41	Illinois	129	12	Indiana	141
12	Indiana	141	12	West Virginia	141
11	Iowa	142	12	Wisconsin	141
NA	Kansas**	NA	16	Massachusetts	140
2	Kentucky	150	16	Minnesota	140
35	Louisiana	132	18	Ohio	139
1	Maine	151	18	Oklahoma	139
38	Maryland	131	18	Utah	139
16	Massachusetts	140	21	Delaware	138
30	Michigan	134	21	Oregon	138
16	Minnesota	140	23	South Carolina	137
44	Mississippi	125	24	Colorado	136
9	Missouri	143	24	Tennessee	136
3	Montana	149	26	Arkansas	135
NA	Nebraska**	NA	26	New York	135
39	Nevada	130	26	Texas	135
3	New Hampshire	149	26	Washington	135
30	New Jersey	134	30	Michigan	134
32	New Mexico	133	30	New Jersey	134
26	New York	135	32	New Mexico	133
32	North Carolina	133	32	North Carolina	133
3	North Dakota	149	32	Pennsylvania	133
18	Ohio	139	35	Georgia	132
18	Oklahoma	139	35	Louisiana	132
21	Oregon	138	35	Rhode Island	132
32	Pennsylvania	133	38	Maryland	131
35	Rhode Island	132	39	Connecticut	130
23	South Carolina	137	39	Nevada	130
9	South Dakota	143	41	Alabama	129
24	Tennessee	136	41	Illinois	129
26	Texas	135	43	Hawaii	126
18	Utah	139	44	Arizona	125
NA	Vermont**	NA	44	Mississippi	125
6	Virginia	145	46	California	122
26	Washington	135	NA	Alaska**	NA
12	West Virginia	141	NA	Kansas**	NA
12	Wisconsin	141	NA	Nebraska**	NA
6	Wyoming	145	NA	Vermont**	NA
				District of Columbia**	NA

Source: U.S. Department of Education, National Center for Education Statistics
"The Nation's Report Card: Science 2009" (http://nces.ed.gov/nationsreportcard/)
*These scores are from the National Assessment of Educational Progress (NAEP). Scale ranges from 0 to 300.
**Not available.

Percent of Public School Fourth Graders
Proficient or Better in Science in 2009
National Percent = 32%*

ALPHA ORDER

RANK	STATE	PERCENT
38	Alabama	27
NA	Alaska**	NA
45	Arizona	21
35	Arkansas	28
44	California	22
15	Colorado	38
9	Connecticut	40
25	Delaware	33
30	Florida	31
38	Georgia	27
40	Hawaii	24
20	Idaho	35
30	Illinois	31
21	Indiana	34
9	Iowa	40
NA	Kansas**	NA
3	Kentucky	44
40	Louisiana	24
8	Maine	41
29	Maryland	32
3	Massachusetts	44
21	Michigan	34
6	Minnesota	42
46	Mississippi	17
14	Missouri	39
6	Montana	42
NA	Nebraska**	NA
43	Nevada	23
1	New Hampshire	47
15	New Jersey	38
40	New Mexico	24
32	New York	30
33	North Carolina	29
2	North Dakota	45
9	Ohio	40
35	Oklahoma	28
25	Oregon	33
15	Pennsylvania	38
21	Rhode Island	34
25	South Carolina	33
9	South Dakota	40
25	Tennessee	33
33	Texas	29
18	Utah	37
NA	Vermont**	NA
3	Virginia	44
21	Washington	34
35	West Virginia	28
9	Wisconsin	40
18	Wyoming	37

RANK ORDER

RANK	STATE	PERCENT
1	New Hampshire	47
2	North Dakota	45
3	Kentucky	44
3	Massachusetts	44
3	Virginia	44
6	Minnesota	42
6	Montana	42
8	Maine	41
9	Connecticut	40
9	Iowa	40
9	Ohio	40
9	South Dakota	40
9	Wisconsin	40
14	Missouri	39
15	Colorado	38
15	New Jersey	38
15	Pennsylvania	38
18	Utah	37
18	Wyoming	37
20	Idaho	35
21	Indiana	34
21	Michigan	34
21	Rhode Island	34
21	Washington	34
25	Delaware	33
25	Oregon	33
25	South Carolina	33
25	Tennessee	33
29	Maryland	32
30	Florida	31
30	Illinois	31
32	New York	30
33	North Carolina	29
33	Texas	29
35	Arkansas	28
35	Oklahoma	28
35	West Virginia	28
38	Alabama	27
38	Georgia	27
40	Hawaii	24
40	Louisiana	24
40	New Mexico	24
43	Nevada	23
44	California	22
45	Arizona	21
46	Mississippi	17
NA	Alaska**	NA
NA	Kansas**	NA
NA	Nebraska**	NA
NA	Vermont**	NA
	District of Columbia**	NA

Source: U.S. Department of Education, National Center for Education Statistics
    "The Nation's Report Card: Science 2009" (http://nces.ed.gov/nationsreportcard/)
*There are four achievement levels: Below Basic, Basic, Proficient, and Advanced. Proficient represents solid academic
mastery for 4th graders. Students reaching this level have demonstrated competency over challenging subject matter, including
subject matter knowledge, application of such knowledge to real-world situations, and analytical skills appropriate to the subject
matter. **Not available.

Percent of Public School Fourth Grade Males
Proficient or Better in Science in 2009
National Percent = 34%*

ALPHA ORDER

RANK	STATE	PERCENT
37	Alabama	29
NA	Alaska**	NA
44	Arizona	23
34	Arkansas	30
45	California	22
16	Colorado	40
10	Connecticut	42
24	Delaware	35
29	Florida	33
37	Georgia	29
43	Hawaii	24
20	Idaho	37
25	Illinois	34
22	Indiana	36
10	Iowa	42
NA	Kansas**	NA
4	Kentucky	46
40	Louisiana	26
8	Maine	44
29	Maryland	33
2	Massachusetts	47
20	Michigan	37
5	Minnesota	45
46	Mississippi	18
16	Missouri	40
9	Montana	43
NA	Nebraska**	NA
40	Nevada	26
2	New Hampshire	47
13	New Jersey	41
42	New Mexico	25
33	New York	31
29	North Carolina	33
1	North Dakota	49
5	Ohio	45
37	Oklahoma	29
25	Oregon	34
13	Pennsylvania	41
22	Rhode Island	36
25	South Carolina	34
10	South Dakota	42
29	Tennessee	33
34	Texas	30
18	Utah	39
NA	Vermont**	NA
5	Virginia	45
25	Washington	34
34	West Virginia	30
13	Wisconsin	41
19	Wyoming	38

RANK ORDER

RANK	STATE	PERCENT
1	North Dakota	49
2	Massachusetts	47
2	New Hampshire	47
4	Kentucky	46
5	Minnesota	45
5	Ohio	45
5	Virginia	45
8	Maine	44
9	Montana	43
10	Connecticut	42
10	Iowa	42
10	South Dakota	42
13	New Jersey	41
13	Pennsylvania	41
13	Wisconsin	41
16	Colorado	40
16	Missouri	40
18	Utah	39
19	Wyoming	38
20	Idaho	37
20	Michigan	37
22	Indiana	36
22	Rhode Island	36
24	Delaware	35
25	Illinois	34
25	Oregon	34
25	South Carolina	34
25	Washington	34
29	Florida	33
29	Maryland	33
29	North Carolina	33
29	Tennessee	33
33	New York	31
34	Arkansas	30
34	Texas	30
34	West Virginia	30
37	Alabama	29
37	Georgia	29
37	Oklahoma	29
40	Louisiana	26
40	Nevada	26
42	New Mexico	25
43	Hawaii	24
44	Arizona	23
45	California	22
46	Mississippi	18
NA	Alaska**	NA
NA	Kansas**	NA
NA	Nebraska**	NA
NA	Vermont**	NA
	District of Columbia**	NA

Source: U.S. Department of Education, National Center for Education Statistics
"The Nation's Report Card: Science 2009" (http://nces.ed.gov/nationsreportcard/)
*There are four achievement levels: Below Basic, Basic, Proficient, and Advanced. Proficient represents solid academic mastery for 4th graders. Students reaching this level have demonstrated competency over challenging subject matter, including subject matter knowledge, application of such knowledge to real-world situations, and analytical skills appropriate to the subject matter. **Not available.

Percent of Public School Fourth Grade Females
Proficient or Better in Science in 2009
National Percent = 31%*

ALPHA ORDER

ALPHA ORDER

RANK	STATE	PERCENT
38	Alabama	25
NA	Alaska**	NA
44	Arizona	21
35	Arkansas	27
43	California	22
15	Colorado	37
12	Connecticut	38
26	Delaware	32
30	Florida	31
38	Georgia	25
38	Hawaii	25
21	Idaho	34
31	Illinois	30
21	Indiana	34
8	Iowa	40
NA	Kansas**	NA
3	Kentucky	43
41	Louisiana	24
11	Maine	39
26	Maryland	32
3	Massachusetts	43
26	Michigan	32
7	Minnesota	41
46	Mississippi	16
8	Missouri	40
5	Montana	42
NA	Nebraska**	NA
44	Nevada	21
1	New Hampshire	48
15	New Jersey	37
42	New Mexico	23
32	New York	29
35	North Carolina	27
5	North Dakota	42
12	Ohio	38
33	Oklahoma	28
21	Oregon	34
17	Pennsylvania	36
26	Rhode Island	32
24	South Carolina	33
12	South Dakota	38
24	Tennessee	33
33	Texas	28
17	Utah	36
NA	Vermont**	NA
2	Virginia	47
20	Washington	35
37	West Virginia	26
8	Wisconsin	40
17	Wyoming	36

RANK ORDER

RANK	STATE	PERCENT
1	New Hampshire	48
2	Virginia	47
3	Kentucky	43
3	Massachusetts	43
5	Montana	42
5	North Dakota	42
7	Minnesota	41
8	Iowa	40
8	Missouri	40
8	Wisconsin	40
11	Maine	39
12	Connecticut	38
12	Ohio	38
12	South Dakota	38
15	Colorado	37
15	New Jersey	37
17	Pennsylvania	36
17	Utah	36
17	Wyoming	36
20	Washington	35
21	Idaho	34
21	Indiana	34
21	Oregon	34
24	South Carolina	33
24	Tennessee	33
26	Delaware	32
26	Maryland	32
26	Michigan	32
26	Rhode Island	32
30	Florida	31
31	Illinois	30
32	New York	29
33	Oklahoma	28
33	Texas	28
35	Arkansas	27
35	North Carolina	27
37	West Virginia	26
38	Alabama	25
38	Georgia	25
38	Hawaii	25
41	Louisiana	24
42	New Mexico	23
43	California	22
44	Arizona	21
44	Nevada	21
46	Mississippi	16
NA	Alaska**	NA
NA	Kansas**	NA
NA	Nebraska**	NA
NA	Vermont**	NA
	District of Columbia**	NA

Source: U.S. Department of Education, National Center for Education Statistics
"The Nation's Report Card: Science 2009" (http://nces.ed.gov/nationsreportcard/)
*There are four achievement levels: Below Basic, Basic, Proficient, and Advanced. Proficient represents solid academic mastery for 4th graders. Students reaching this level have demonstrated competency over challenging subject matter, including subject matter knowledge, application of such knowledge to real-world situations, and analytical skills appropriate to the subject matter. **Not available.

Percent of Public School Fourth Graders Eligible for
Free or Reduced Price Lunch Program Proficient or Better in Science in 2009
National Percent = 16%*

ALPHA ORDER

RANK	STATE	PERCENT
37	Alabama	13
NA	Alaska**	NA
44	Arizona	11
19	Arkansas	19
45	California	10
29	Colorado	16
42	Connecticut	12
29	Delaware	16
16	Florida	20
37	Georgia	13
37	Hawaii	13
6	Idaho	24
35	Illinois	14
13	Indiana	21
13	Iowa	21
NA	Kansas**	NA
1	Kentucky	30
31	Louisiana	15
3	Maine	29
42	Maryland	12
19	Massachusetts	19
24	Michigan	18
13	Minnesota	21
45	Mississippi	10
6	Missouri	24
4	Montana	28
NA	Nebraska**	NA
31	Nevada	15
4	New Hampshire	28
37	New Jersey	13
31	New Mexico	15
26	New York	17
37	North Carolina	13
1	North Dakota	30
16	Ohio	20
24	Oklahoma	18
19	Oregon	19
26	Pennsylvania	17
35	Rhode Island	14
19	South Carolina	19
9	South Dakota	23
16	Tennessee	20
31	Texas	15
12	Utah	22
NA	Vermont**	NA
9	Virginia	23
26	Washington	17
19	West Virginia	19
9	Wisconsin	23
6	Wyoming	24

RANK ORDER

RANK	STATE	PERCENT
1	Kentucky	30
1	North Dakota	30
3	Maine	29
4	Montana	28
4	New Hampshire	28
6	Idaho	24
6	Missouri	24
6	Wyoming	24
9	South Dakota	23
9	Virginia	23
9	Wisconsin	23
12	Utah	22
13	Indiana	21
13	Iowa	21
13	Minnesota	21
16	Florida	20
16	Ohio	20
16	Tennessee	20
19	Arkansas	19
19	Massachusetts	19
19	Oregon	19
19	South Carolina	19
19	West Virginia	19
24	Michigan	18
24	Oklahoma	18
26	New York	17
26	Pennsylvania	17
26	Washington	17
29	Colorado	16
29	Delaware	16
31	Louisiana	15
31	Nevada	15
31	New Mexico	15
31	Texas	15
35	Illinois	14
35	Rhode Island	14
37	Alabama	13
37	Georgia	13
37	Hawaii	13
37	New Jersey	13
37	North Carolina	13
42	Connecticut	12
42	Maryland	12
44	Arizona	11
45	California	10
45	Mississippi	10
NA	Alaska**	NA
NA	Kansas**	NA
NA	Nebraska**	NA
NA	Vermont**	NA
	District of Columbia**	NA

Source: U.S. Department of Education, National Center for Education Statistics
    "The Nation's Report Card: Science 2009" (http://nces.ed.gov/nationsreportcard/)
*There are four achievement levels: Below Basic, Basic, Proficient, and Advanced. Proficient represents solid academic
mastery for 4th graders. Students reaching this level have demonstrated competency over challenging subject matter, including
subject matter knowledge, application of such knowledge to real-world situations, and analytical skills appropriate to the subject
matter. **Not available.

Average Science Score for Public School Eighth Graders in 2009

National Average Score = 149*

ALPHA ORDER

RANK	STATE	AVERAGE SCORE
42	Alabama	139
NA	Alaska**	NA
40	Arizona	141
36	Arkansas	144
45	California	137
13	Colorado	156
18	Connecticut	155
27	Delaware	148
32	Florida	146
31	Georgia	147
42	Hawaii	139
7	Idaho	158
27	Illinois	148
24	Indiana	152
13	Iowa	156
NA	Kansas**	NA
13	Kentucky	156
42	Louisiana	139
7	Maine	158
27	Maryland	148
4	Massachusetts	160
23	Michigan	153
6	Minnesota	159
46	Mississippi	132
13	Missouri	156
1	Montana	162
NA	Nebraska**	NA
40	Nevada	141
4	New Hampshire	160
18	New Jersey	155
38	New Mexico	143
26	New York	149
36	North Carolina	144
1	North Dakota	162
7	Ohio	158
32	Oklahoma	146
21	Oregon	154
21	Pennsylvania	154
32	Rhode Island	146
38	South Carolina	143
3	South Dakota	161
27	Tennessee	148
25	Texas	150
7	Utah	158
NA	Vermont**	NA
13	Virginia	156
18	Washington	155
35	West Virginia	145
12	Wisconsin	157
7	Wyoming	158

RANK ORDER

RANK	STATE	AVERAGE SCORE
1	Montana	162
1	North Dakota	162
3	South Dakota	161
4	Massachusetts	160
4	New Hampshire	160
6	Minnesota	159
7	Idaho	158
7	Maine	158
7	Ohio	158
7	Utah	158
7	Wyoming	158
12	Wisconsin	157
13	Colorado	156
13	Iowa	156
13	Kentucky	156
13	Missouri	156
13	Virginia	156
18	Connecticut	155
18	New Jersey	155
18	Washington	155
21	Oregon	154
21	Pennsylvania	154
23	Michigan	153
24	Indiana	152
25	Texas	150
26	New York	149
27	Delaware	148
27	Illinois	148
27	Maryland	148
27	Tennessee	148
31	Georgia	147
32	Florida	146
32	Oklahoma	146
32	Rhode Island	146
35	West Virginia	145
36	Arkansas	144
36	North Carolina	144
38	New Mexico	143
38	South Carolina	143
40	Arizona	141
40	Nevada	141
42	Alabama	139
42	Hawaii	139
42	Louisiana	139
45	California	137
46	Mississippi	132
NA	Alaska**	NA
NA	Kansas**	NA
NA	Nebraska**	NA
NA	Vermont**	NA
	District of Columbia**	NA

Source: U.S. Department of Education, National Center for Education Statistics
"The Nation's Report Card: Science 2009" (http://nces.ed.gov/nationsreportcard/)
*These scores are from the National Assessment of Educational Progress (NAEP). Scale ranges from 0 to 300.
**Not available.

Average Science Score for Public School Eighth Grade Males in 2009

National Average Score = 151*

ALPHA ORDER				RANK ORDER		
RANK	STATE	AVERAGE SCORE		RANK	STATE	AVERAGE SCORE
41	Alabama	142		1	North Dakota	166
NA	Alaska**	NA		2	Montana	165
40	Arizona	143		3	New Hampshire	164
37	Arkansas	145		3	South Dakota	164
45	California	138		5	Massachusetts	162
14	Colorado	158		5	Wyoming	162
17	Connecticut	157		7	Minnesota	161
26	Delaware	151		7	Ohio	161
34	Florida	148		9	Idaho	160
27	Georgia	150		9	Maine	160
44	Hawaii	140		9	Wisconsin	160
9	Idaho	160		12	Kentucky	159
27	Illinois	150		12	Utah	159
23	Indiana	155		14	Colorado	158
14	Iowa	158		14	Iowa	158
NA	Kansas**	NA		14	Missouri	158
12	Kentucky	159		17	Connecticut	157
43	Louisiana	141		17	Pennsylvania	157
9	Maine	160		17	Virginia	157
27	Maryland	150		20	New Jersey	156
5	Massachusetts	162		20	Oregon	156
23	Michigan	155		20	Washington	156
7	Minnesota	161		23	Indiana	155
46	Mississippi	134		23	Michigan	155
14	Missouri	158		25	Texas	152
2	Montana	165		26	Delaware	151
NA	Nebraska**	NA		27	Georgia	150
41	Nevada	142		27	Illinois	150
3	New Hampshire	164		27	Maryland	150
20	New Jersey	156		27	New York	150
36	New Mexico	147		31	Oklahoma	149
27	New York	150		31	Rhode Island	149
37	North Carolina	145		31	Tennessee	149
1	North Dakota	166		34	Florida	148
7	Ohio	161		34	West Virginia	148
31	Oklahoma	149		36	New Mexico	147
20	Oregon	156		37	Arkansas	145
17	Pennsylvania	157		37	North Carolina	145
31	Rhode Island	149		39	South Carolina	144
39	South Carolina	144		40	Arizona	143
3	South Dakota	164		41	Alabama	142
31	Tennessee	149		41	Nevada	142
25	Texas	152		43	Louisiana	141
12	Utah	159		44	Hawaii	140
NA	Vermont**	NA		45	California	138
17	Virginia	157		46	Mississippi	134
20	Washington	156		NA	Alaska**	NA
34	West Virginia	148		NA	Kansas**	NA
9	Wisconsin	160		NA	Nebraska**	NA
5	Wyoming	162		NA	Vermont**	NA
					District of Columbia**	NA

Source: U.S. Department of Education, National Center for Education Statistics
    "The Nation's Report Card: Science 2009" (http://nces.ed.gov/nationsreportcard/)
*These scores are from the National Assessment of Educational Progress (NAEP). Scale ranges from 0 to 300.
**Not available.

Average Science Score for Public School Eighth Grade Females in 2009

National Average Score = 147*

ALPHA ORDER

RANK	STATE	AVERAGE SCORE
43	Alabama	136
NA	Alaska**	NA
40	Arizona	139
35	Arkansas	142
44	California	135
17	Colorado	153
17	Connecticut	153
27	Delaware	146
30	Florida	144
30	Georgia	144
42	Hawaii	137
9	Idaho	155
27	Illinois	146
24	Indiana	150
12	Iowa	154
NA	Kansas**	NA
12	Kentucky	154
41	Louisiana	138
7	Maine	156
46	Maryland	41
3	Massachusetts	158
21	Michigan	152
4	Minnesota	157
45	Mississippi	130
12	Missouri	154
1	Montana	159
NA	Nebraska**	NA
38	Nevada	140
4	New Hampshire	157
17	New Jersey	153
38	New Mexico	140
26	New York	147
33	North Carolina	143
1	North Dakota	159
12	Ohio	154
30	Oklahoma	144
21	Oregon	152
23	Pennsylvania	151
33	Rhode Island	143
35	South Carolina	142
4	South Dakota	157
27	Tennessee	146
25	Texas	148
7	Utah	156
NA	Vermont**	NA
9	Virginia	155
17	Washington	153
35	West Virginia	142
9	Wisconsin	155
12	Wyoming	154

RANK ORDER

RANK	STATE	AVERAGE SCORE
1	Montana	159
1	North Dakota	159
3	Massachusetts	158
4	Minnesota	157
4	New Hampshire	157
4	South Dakota	157
7	Maine	156
7	Utah	156
9	Idaho	155
9	Virginia	155
9	Wisconsin	155
12	Iowa	154
12	Kentucky	154
12	Missouri	154
12	Ohio	154
12	Wyoming	154
17	Colorado	153
17	Connecticut	153
17	New Jersey	153
17	Washington	153
21	Michigan	152
21	Oregon	152
23	Pennsylvania	151
24	Indiana	150
25	Texas	148
26	New York	147
27	Delaware	146
27	Illinois	146
27	Tennessee	146
30	Florida	144
30	Georgia	144
30	Oklahoma	144
33	North Carolina	143
33	Rhode Island	143
35	Arkansas	142
35	South Carolina	142
35	West Virginia	142
38	Nevada	140
38	New Mexico	140
40	Arizona	139
41	Louisiana	138
42	Hawaii	137
43	Alabama	136
44	California	135
45	Mississippi	130
46	Maryland	41
NA	Alaska**	NA
NA	Kansas**	NA
NA	Nebraska**	NA
NA	Vermont**	NA
	District of Columbia**	NA

Source: U.S. Department of Education, National Center for Education Statistics
"The Nation's Report Card: Science 2009" (http://nces.ed.gov/nationsreportcard/)
*These scores are from the National Assessment of Educational Progress (NAEP). Scale ranges from 0 to 300.
**Not available.

Average Science Score for Public School Eighth Graders
Eligible for Free or Reduced Price Lunch Program in 2009
National Average Score = 133*

ALPHA ORDER

RANK	STATE	AVERAGE SCORE
44	Alabama	125
NA	Alaska**	NA
40	Arizona	127
32	Arkansas	131
45	California	122
15	Colorado	140
34	Connecticut	130
25	Delaware	135
25	Florida	135
28	Georgia	133
40	Hawaii	127
7	Idaho	146
40	Illinois	127
23	Indiana	136
9	Iowa	142
NA	Kansas**	NA
5	Kentucky	147
35	Louisiana	129
3	Maine	148
35	Maryland	129
21	Massachusetts	137
20	Michigan	138
15	Minnesota	140
45	Mississippi	122
9	Missouri	142
1	Montana	151
NA	Nebraska**	NA
35	Nevada	129
8	New Hampshire	144
31	New Jersey	132
27	New Mexico	134
32	New York	131
35	North Carolina	129
1	North Dakota	151
9	Ohio	142
21	Oklahoma	137
13	Oregon	141
28	Pennsylvania	133
40	Rhode Island	127
35	South Carolina	129
3	South Dakota	148
28	Tennessee	133
15	Texas	140
9	Utah	142
NA	Vermont**	NA
13	Virginia	141
18	Washington	139
23	West Virginia	136
18	Wisconsin	139
5	Wyoming	147

RANK ORDER

RANK	STATE	AVERAGE SCORE
1	Montana	151
1	North Dakota	151
3	Maine	148
3	South Dakota	148
5	Kentucky	147
5	Wyoming	147
7	Idaho	146
8	New Hampshire	144
9	Iowa	142
9	Missouri	142
9	Ohio	142
9	Utah	142
13	Oregon	141
13	Virginia	141
15	Colorado	140
15	Minnesota	140
15	Texas	140
18	Washington	139
18	Wisconsin	139
20	Michigan	138
21	Massachusetts	137
21	Oklahoma	137
23	Indiana	136
23	West Virginia	136
25	Delaware	135
25	Florida	135
27	New Mexico	134
28	Georgia	133
28	Pennsylvania	133
28	Tennessee	133
31	New Jersey	132
32	Arkansas	131
32	New York	131
34	Connecticut	130
35	Louisiana	129
35	Maryland	129
35	Nevada	129
35	North Carolina	129
35	South Carolina	129
40	Arizona	127
40	Hawaii	127
40	Illinois	127
40	Rhode Island	127
44	Alabama	125
45	California	122
45	Mississippi	122
NA	Alaska**	NA
NA	Kansas**	NA
NA	Nebraska**	NA
NA	Vermont**	NA
	District of Columbia**	NA

Source: U.S. Department of Education, National Center for Education Statistics
    "The Nation's Report Card: Science 2009" (http://nces.ed.gov/nationsreportcard/)
*These scores are from the National Assessment of Educational Progress (NAEP). Scale ranges from 0 to 300.
**Not available.

Percent of Public School Eighth Graders
Proficient or Better in Science in 2009
National Percent = 28%*

ALPHA ORDER

RANK	STATE	PERCENT
42	Alabama	19
NA	Alaska**	NA
38	Arizona	21
32	Arkansas	24
42	California	19
12	Colorado	34
17	Connecticut	33
32	Delaware	24
35	Florida	23
30	Georgia	26
45	Hawaii	17
9	Idaho	35
27	Illinois	27
24	Indiana	31
12	Iowa	34
NA	Kansas**	NA
21	Kentucky	32
42	Louisiana	19
12	Maine	34
27	Maryland	27
3	Massachusetts	38
21	Michigan	32
3	Minnesota	38
46	Mississippi	15
12	Missouri	34
1	Montana	41
NA	Nebraska**	NA
40	Nevada	20
6	New Hampshire	37
21	New Jersey	32
40	New Mexico	20
25	New York	29
35	North Carolina	23
1	North Dakota	41
9	Ohio	35
32	Oklahoma	24
17	Oregon	33
17	Pennsylvania	33
31	Rhode Island	25
37	South Carolina	22
3	South Dakota	38
27	Tennessee	27
26	Texas	28
6	Utah	37
NA	Vermont**	NA
12	Virginia	34
17	Washington	33
38	West Virginia	21
8	Wisconsin	36
9	Wyoming	35

RANK ORDER

RANK	STATE	PERCENT
1	Montana	41
1	North Dakota	41
3	Massachusetts	38
3	Minnesota	38
3	South Dakota	38
6	New Hampshire	37
6	Utah	37
8	Wisconsin	36
9	Idaho	35
9	Ohio	35
9	Wyoming	35
12	Colorado	34
12	Iowa	34
12	Maine	34
12	Missouri	34
12	Virginia	34
17	Connecticut	33
17	Oregon	33
17	Pennsylvania	33
17	Washington	33
21	Kentucky	32
21	Michigan	32
21	New Jersey	32
24	Indiana	31
25	New York	29
26	Texas	28
27	Illinois	27
27	Maryland	27
27	Tennessee	27
30	Georgia	26
31	Rhode Island	25
32	Arkansas	24
32	Delaware	24
32	Oklahoma	24
35	Florida	23
35	North Carolina	23
37	South Carolina	22
38	Arizona	21
38	West Virginia	21
40	Nevada	20
40	New Mexico	20
42	Alabama	19
42	California	19
42	Louisiana	19
45	Hawaii	17
46	Mississippi	15
NA	Alaska**	NA
NA	Kansas**	NA
NA	Nebraska**	NA
NA	Vermont**	NA
	District of Columbia**	NA

Source: U.S. Department of Education, National Center for Education Statistics
"The Nation's Report Card: Science 2009" (http://nces.ed.gov/nationsreportcard/)
*There are four achievement levels: Below Basic, Basic, Proficient, and Advanced. Proficient represents solid academic mastery for 8th graders. Students reaching this level have demonstrated competency over challenging subject matter, including subject matter knowledge, application of such knowledge to real-world situations, and analytical skills appropriate to the subject matter. **Not available.

Percent of Public School Eighth Grade Males
Proficient or Better in Science in 2009
National Percent = 32%*

ALPHA ORDER

RANK	STATE	PERCENT
38	Alabama	24
NA	Alaska**	NA
35	Arizona	26
32	Arkansas	28
41	California	22
12	Colorado	39
15	Connecticut	38
31	Delaware	29
32	Florida	28
29	Georgia	30
44	Hawaii	19
9	Idaho	42
26	Illinois	32
24	Indiana	35
15	Iowa	38
NA	Kansas**	NA
21	Kentucky	37
41	Louisiana	22
15	Maine	38
46	Maryland	2
4	Massachusetts	44
15	Michigan	38
6	Minnesota	43
45	Mississippi	17
15	Missouri	38
1	Montana	47
NA	Nebraska**	NA
43	Nevada	21
4	New Hampshire	44
21	New Jersey	37
38	New Mexico	24
25	New York	34
37	North Carolina	25
1	North Dakota	47
11	Ohio	41
32	Oklahoma	28
21	Oregon	37
12	Pennsylvania	39
29	Rhode Island	30
38	South Carolina	24
3	South Dakota	45
26	Tennessee	32
26	Texas	32
6	Utah	43
NA	Vermont**	NA
12	Virginia	39
15	Washington	38
35	West Virginia	26
6	Wisconsin	43
9	Wyoming	42

RANK ORDER

RANK	STATE	PERCENT
1	Montana	47
1	North Dakota	47
3	South Dakota	45
4	Massachusetts	44
4	New Hampshire	44
6	Minnesota	43
6	Utah	43
6	Wisconsin	43
9	Idaho	42
9	Wyoming	42
11	Ohio	41
12	Colorado	39
12	Pennsylvania	39
12	Virginia	39
15	Connecticut	38
15	Iowa	38
15	Maine	38
15	Michigan	38
15	Missouri	38
15	Washington	38
21	Kentucky	37
21	New Jersey	37
21	Oregon	37
24	Indiana	35
25	New York	34
26	Illinois	32
26	Tennessee	32
26	Texas	32
29	Georgia	30
29	Rhode Island	30
31	Delaware	29
32	Arkansas	28
32	Florida	28
32	Oklahoma	28
35	Arizona	26
35	West Virginia	26
37	North Carolina	25
38	Alabama	24
38	New Mexico	24
38	South Carolina	24
41	California	22
41	Louisiana	22
43	Nevada	21
44	Hawaii	19
45	Mississippi	17
46	Maryland	2
NA	Alaska**	NA
NA	Kansas**	NA
NA	Nebraska**	NA
NA	Vermont**	NA

District of Columbia**   NA

Source: U.S. Department of Education, National Center for Education Statistics
    "The Nation's Report Card: Science 2009" (http://nces.ed.gov/nationsreportcard/)
*There are four achievement levels: Below Basic, Basic, Proficient, and Advanced. Proficient represents solid academic mastery for 8th graders. Students reaching this level have demonstrated competency over challenging subject matter, including subject matter knowledge, application of such knowledge to real-world situations, and analytical skills appropriate to the subject matter. **Not available.

Percent of Public School Eighth Grade Females
Proficient or Better in Science in 2009
National Percent = 26%*

RANK	STATE	PERCENT
44	Alabama	15
NA	Alaska**	NA
39	Arizona	18
37	Arkansas	20
43	California	17
13	Colorado	32
13	Connecticut	32
35	Delaware	21
35	Florida	21
29	Georgia	24
44	Hawaii	15
7	Idaho	33
27	Illinois	25
24	Indiana	28
17	Iowa	31
NA	Kansas**	NA
21	Kentucky	30
39	Louisiana	18
7	Maine	33
27	Maryland	25
1	Massachusetts	38
17	Michigan	31
4	Minnesota	36
46	Mississippi	13
7	Missouri	33
1	Montana	38
NA	Nebraska**	NA
38	Nevada	19
7	New Hampshire	33
17	New Jersey	31
39	New Mexico	18
25	New York	27
31	North Carolina	22
3	North Dakota	37
13	Ohio	32
31	Oklahoma	22
13	Oregon	32
17	Pennsylvania	31
31	Rhode Island	22
31	South Carolina	22
6	South Dakota	35
29	Tennessee	24
26	Texas	26
4	Utah	36
NA	Vermont**	NA
7	Virginia	33
21	Washington	30
39	West Virginia	18
7	Wisconsin	33
21	Wyoming	30

RANK	STATE	PERCENT
1	Massachusetts	38
1	Montana	38
3	North Dakota	37
4	Minnesota	36
4	Utah	36
6	South Dakota	35
7	Idaho	33
7	Maine	33
7	Missouri	33
7	New Hampshire	33
7	Virginia	33
7	Wisconsin	33
13	Colorado	32
13	Connecticut	32
13	Ohio	32
13	Oregon	32
17	Iowa	31
17	Michigan	31
17	New Jersey	31
17	Pennsylvania	31
21	Kentucky	30
21	Washington	30
21	Wyoming	30
24	Indiana	28
25	New York	27
26	Texas	26
27	Illinois	25
27	Maryland	25
29	Georgia	24
29	Tennessee	24
31	North Carolina	22
31	Oklahoma	22
31	Rhode Island	22
31	South Carolina	22
35	Delaware	21
35	Florida	21
37	Arkansas	20
38	Nevada	19
39	Arizona	18
39	Louisiana	18
39	New Mexico	18
39	West Virginia	18
43	California	17
44	Alabama	15
44	Hawaii	15
46	Mississippi	13
NA	Alaska**	NA
NA	Kansas**	NA
NA	Nebraska**	NA
NA	Vermont**	NA
	District of Columbia**	NA

Source: U.S. Department of Education, National Center for Education Statistics
   "The Nation's Report Card: Science 2009" (http://nces.ed.gov/nationsreportcard/)
*There are four achievement levels: Below Basic, Basic, Proficient, and Advanced. Proficient represents solid academic mastery for 8th graders. Students reaching this level have demonstrated competency over challenging subject matter, including subject matter knowledge, application of such knowledge to real-world situations, and analytical skills appropriate to the subject matter. **Not available.

Percent of Public School Eighth Graders Eligible for
Free or Reduced Price Lunch Program Proficient or Better in Science in 2009
National Percent = 14%*

<table>
<tr><td colspan="3">ALPHA ORDER</td><td colspan="3">RANK ORDER</td></tr>
<tr><td>RANK</td><td>STATE</td><td>PERCENT</td><td>RANK</td><td>STATE</td><td>PERCENT</td></tr>
<tr><td>39</td><td>Alabama</td><td>9</td><td>1</td><td>Montana</td><td>28</td></tr>
<tr><td>NA</td><td>Alaska**</td><td>NA</td><td>1</td><td>North Dakota</td><td>28</td></tr>
<tr><td>37</td><td>Arizona</td><td>10</td><td>3</td><td>South Dakota</td><td>25</td></tr>
<tr><td>23</td><td>Arkansas</td><td>14</td><td>4</td><td>Utah</td><td>24</td></tr>
<tr><td>45</td><td>California</td><td>8</td><td>5</td><td>Idaho</td><td>23</td></tr>
<tr><td>16</td><td>Colorado</td><td>18</td><td>5</td><td>Kentucky</td><td>23</td></tr>
<tr><td>31</td><td>Connecticut</td><td>12</td><td>5</td><td>Wyoming</td><td>23</td></tr>
<tr><td>31</td><td>Delaware</td><td>12</td><td>8</td><td>Maine</td><td>22</td></tr>
<tr><td>27</td><td>Florida</td><td>13</td><td>9</td><td>New Hampshire</td><td>21</td></tr>
<tr><td>27</td><td>Georgia</td><td>13</td><td>10</td><td>Iowa</td><td>20</td></tr>
<tr><td>39</td><td>Hawaii</td><td>9</td><td>10</td><td>Michigan</td><td>20</td></tr>
<tr><td>5</td><td>Idaho</td><td>23</td><td>10</td><td>Ohio</td><td>20</td></tr>
<tr><td>39</td><td>Illinois</td><td>9</td><td>10</td><td>Oregon</td><td>20</td></tr>
<tr><td>19</td><td>Indiana</td><td>17</td><td>14</td><td>Minnesota</td><td>19</td></tr>
<tr><td>10</td><td>Iowa</td><td>20</td><td>14</td><td>Missouri</td><td>19</td></tr>
<tr><td>NA</td><td>Kansas**</td><td>NA</td><td>16</td><td>Colorado</td><td>18</td></tr>
<tr><td>5</td><td>Kentucky</td><td>23</td><td>16</td><td>Washington</td><td>18</td></tr>
<tr><td>34</td><td>Louisiana</td><td>11</td><td>16</td><td>Wisconsin</td><td>18</td></tr>
<tr><td>8</td><td>Maine</td><td>22</td><td>19</td><td>Indiana</td><td>17</td></tr>
<tr><td>39</td><td>Maryland</td><td>9</td><td>19</td><td>Oklahoma</td><td>17</td></tr>
<tr><td>34</td><td>Massachusetts</td><td>11</td><td>19</td><td>Texas</td><td>17</td></tr>
<tr><td>10</td><td>Michigan</td><td>20</td><td>19</td><td>Virginia</td><td>17</td></tr>
<tr><td>14</td><td>Minnesota</td><td>19</td><td>23</td><td>Arkansas</td><td>14</td></tr>
<tr><td>46</td><td>Mississippi</td><td>7</td><td>23</td><td>Pennsylvania</td><td>14</td></tr>
<tr><td>14</td><td>Missouri</td><td>19</td><td>23</td><td>Tennessee</td><td>14</td></tr>
<tr><td>1</td><td>Montana</td><td>28</td><td>23</td><td>West Virginia</td><td>14</td></tr>
<tr><td>NA</td><td>Nebraska**</td><td>NA</td><td>27</td><td>Florida</td><td>13</td></tr>
<tr><td>39</td><td>Nevada</td><td>9</td><td>27</td><td>Georgia</td><td>13</td></tr>
<tr><td>9</td><td>New Hampshire</td><td>21</td><td>27</td><td>New Mexico</td><td>13</td></tr>
<tr><td>31</td><td>New Jersey</td><td>12</td><td>27</td><td>New York</td><td>13</td></tr>
<tr><td>27</td><td>New Mexico</td><td>13</td><td>31</td><td>Connecticut</td><td>12</td></tr>
<tr><td>27</td><td>New York</td><td>13</td><td>31</td><td>Delaware</td><td>12</td></tr>
<tr><td>37</td><td>North Carolina</td><td>10</td><td>31</td><td>New Jersey</td><td>12</td></tr>
<tr><td>1</td><td>North Dakota</td><td>28</td><td>34</td><td>Louisiana</td><td>11</td></tr>
<tr><td>10</td><td>Ohio</td><td>20</td><td>34</td><td>Massachusetts</td><td>11</td></tr>
<tr><td>19</td><td>Oklahoma</td><td>17</td><td>34</td><td>South Carolina</td><td>11</td></tr>
<tr><td>10</td><td>Oregon</td><td>20</td><td>37</td><td>Arizona</td><td>10</td></tr>
<tr><td>23</td><td>Pennsylvania</td><td>14</td><td>37</td><td>North Carolina</td><td>10</td></tr>
<tr><td>39</td><td>Rhode Island</td><td>9</td><td>39</td><td>Alabama</td><td>9</td></tr>
<tr><td>34</td><td>South Carolina</td><td>11</td><td>39</td><td>Hawaii</td><td>9</td></tr>
<tr><td>3</td><td>South Dakota</td><td>25</td><td>39</td><td>Illinois</td><td>9</td></tr>
<tr><td>23</td><td>Tennessee</td><td>14</td><td>39</td><td>Maryland</td><td>9</td></tr>
<tr><td>19</td><td>Texas</td><td>17</td><td>39</td><td>Nevada</td><td>9</td></tr>
<tr><td>4</td><td>Utah</td><td>24</td><td>39</td><td>Rhode Island</td><td>9</td></tr>
<tr><td>NA</td><td>Vermont**</td><td>NA</td><td>45</td><td>California</td><td>8</td></tr>
<tr><td>19</td><td>Virginia</td><td>17</td><td>46</td><td>Mississippi</td><td>7</td></tr>
<tr><td>16</td><td>Washington</td><td>18</td><td>NA</td><td>Alaska**</td><td>NA</td></tr>
<tr><td>23</td><td>West Virginia</td><td>14</td><td>NA</td><td>Kansas**</td><td>NA</td></tr>
<tr><td>16</td><td>Wisconsin</td><td>18</td><td>NA</td><td>Nebraska**</td><td>NA</td></tr>
<tr><td>5</td><td>Wyoming</td><td>23</td><td>NA</td><td>Vermont**</td><td>NA</td></tr>
<tr><td></td><td></td><td></td><td></td><td>District of Columbia**</td><td>NA</td></tr>
</table>

Source: U.S. Department of Education, National Center for Education Statistics
  "The Nation's Report Card: Science 2009" (http://nces.ed.gov/nationsreportcard/)
*There are four achievement levels: Below Basic, Basic, Proficient, and Advanced. Proficient represents solid academic
mastery for 8th graders. Students reaching this level have demonstrated competency over challenging subject matter, including
subject matter knowledge, application of such knowledge to real-world situations, and analytical skills appropriate to the subject
matter. **Not available.

Average Writing Score for Public School Eighth Graders in 2007

National Average Score = 154*

ALPHA ORDER

ALPHA ORDER | RANK ORDER

RANK	STATE	AVERAGE SCORE	RANK	STATE	AVERAGE SCORE
36	Alabama	148	1	New Jersey	175
NA	Alaska**	NA	2	Connecticut	172
36	Arizona	148	3	Massachusetts	167
32	Arkansas	151	4	Vermont	162
36	California	148	5	Colorado	161
5	Colorado	161	5	Maine	161
2	Connecticut	172	7	Illinois	160
10	Delaware	158	7	New Hampshire	160
10	Florida	158	9	Pennsylvania	159
27	Georgia	153	10	Delaware	158
42	Hawaii	144	10	Florida	158
23	Idaho	154	10	Washington	158
7	Illinois	160	10	Wisconsin	158
21	Indiana	155	10	Wyoming	158
21	Iowa	155	15	Montana	157
17	Kansas	156	15	Virginia	157
32	Kentucky	151	17	Kansas	156
40	Louisiana	147	17	Minnesota	156
5	Maine	161	17	Ohio	156
NA	Maryland**	NA	17	Tennessee	156
3	Massachusetts	167	21	Indiana	155
32	Michigan	151	21	Iowa	155
17	Minnesota	156	23	Idaho	154
45	Mississippi	142	23	New York	154
27	Missouri	153	23	North Dakota	154
15	Montana	157	23	Rhode Island	154
NA	Nebraska**	NA	27	Georgia	153
43	Nevada	143	27	Missouri	153
7	New Hampshire	160	27	North Carolina	153
1	New Jersey	175	27	Oklahoma	153
43	New Mexico	143	31	Utah	152
23	New York	154	32	Arkansas	151
27	North Carolina	153	32	Kentucky	151
23	North Dakota	154	32	Michigan	151
17	Ohio	156	32	Texas	151
27	Oklahoma	153	36	Alabama	148
NA	Oregon**	NA	36	Arizona	148
9	Pennsylvania	159	36	California	148
23	Rhode Island	154	36	South Carolina	148
36	South Carolina	148	40	Louisiana	147
NA	South Dakota**	NA	41	West Virginia	146
17	Tennessee	156	42	Hawaii	144
32	Texas	151	43	Nevada	143
31	Utah	152	43	New Mexico	143
4	Vermont	162	45	Mississippi	142
15	Virginia	157	NA	Alaska**	NA
10	Washington	158	NA	Maryland**	NA
41	West Virginia	146	NA	Nebraska**	NA
10	Wisconsin	158	NA	Oregon**	NA
10	Wyoming	158	NA	South Dakota**	NA
				District of Columbia**	NA

Source: U.S. Department of Education, National Center for Education Statistics
"The Nation's Report Card: Writing 2007" (http://nces.ed.gov/nationsreportcard/)
*These scores are from the National Assessment of Educational Progress (NAEP). Scale ranges from 0 to 300.
**Not available.

Average Writing Score for Public School Eighth Grade Males in 2007

National Average Score = 144*

ALPHA ORDER

RANK	STATE	AVERAGE SCORE
38	Alabama	138
NA	Alaska**	NA
35	Arizona	139
35	Arkansas	139
35	California	139
4	Colorado	152
2	Connecticut	163
5	Delaware	151
11	Florida	147
23	Georgia	143
41	Hawaii	134
23	Idaho	143
7	Illinois	150
20	Indiana	144
23	Iowa	143
20	Kansas	144
29	Kentucky	142
38	Louisiana	138
8	Maine	149
NA	Maryland**	NA
3	Massachusetts	157
33	Michigan	140
20	Minnesota	144
44	Mississippi	132
23	Missouri	143
18	Montana	145
NA	Nebraska**	NA
45	Nevada	131
8	New Hampshire	149
1	New Jersey	168
42	New Mexico	133
18	New York	145
29	North Carolina	142
29	North Dakota	142
11	Ohio	147
23	Oklahoma	143
NA	Oregon**	NA
5	Pennsylvania	151
23	Rhode Island	143
40	South Carolina	137
NA	South Dakota**	NA
13	Tennessee	146
29	Texas	142
33	Utah	140
8	Vermont	149
13	Virginia	146
13	Washington	146
42	West Virginia	133
13	Wisconsin	146
13	Wyoming	146

RANK ORDER

RANK	STATE	AVERAGE SCORE
1	New Jersey	168
2	Connecticut	163
3	Massachusetts	157
4	Colorado	152
5	Delaware	151
5	Pennsylvania	151
7	Illinois	150
8	Maine	149
8	New Hampshire	149
8	Vermont	149
11	Florida	147
11	Ohio	147
13	Tennessee	146
13	Virginia	146
13	Washington	146
13	Wisconsin	146
13	Wyoming	146
18	Montana	145
18	New York	145
20	Indiana	144
20	Kansas	144
20	Minnesota	144
23	Georgia	143
23	Idaho	143
23	Iowa	143
23	Missouri	143
23	Oklahoma	143
23	Rhode Island	143
29	Kentucky	142
29	North Carolina	142
29	North Dakota	142
29	Texas	142
33	Michigan	140
33	Utah	140
35	Arizona	139
35	Arkansas	139
35	California	139
38	Alabama	138
38	Louisiana	138
40	South Carolina	137
41	Hawaii	134
42	New Mexico	133
42	West Virginia	133
44	Mississippi	132
45	Nevada	131
NA	Alaska**	NA
NA	Maryland**	NA
NA	Nebraska**	NA
NA	Oregon**	NA
NA	South Dakota**	NA
	District of Columbia**	NA

Source: U.S. Department of Education, National Center for Education Statistics
  "The Nation's Report Card: Writing 2007" (http://nces.ed.gov/nationsreportcard/)
*These scores are from the National Assessment of Educational Progress (NAEP). Scale ranges from 0 to 300.
**Not available.

Average Writing Score for Public School Eighth Grade Females in 2007

National Average Score = 164*

ALPHA ORDER

RANK	STATE	AVERAGE SCORE
38	Alabama	157
NA	Alaska**	NA
38	Arizona	157
27	Arkansas	164
38	California	157
11	Colorado	169
2	Connecticut	181
21	Delaware	166
11	Florida	169
27	Georgia	164
43	Hawaii	155
18	Idaho	167
8	Illinois	170
24	Indiana	165
18	Iowa	167
14	Kansas	168
34	Kentucky	161
41	Louisiana	156
5	Maine	174
NA	Maryland**	NA
3	Massachusetts	178
32	Michigan	162
14	Minnesota	168
44	Mississippi	152
30	Missouri	163
11	Montana	169
NA	Nebraska**	NA
41	Nevada	156
6	New Hampshire	173
1	New Jersey	183
44	New Mexico	152
30	New York	163
27	North Carolina	164
21	North Dakota	166
21	Ohio	166
32	Oklahoma	162
NA	Oregon**	NA
14	Pennsylvania	168
24	Rhode Island	165
36	South Carolina	159
NA	South Dakota**	NA
18	Tennessee	167
35	Texas	160
24	Utah	165
4	Vermont	176
14	Virginia	168
8	Washington	170
36	West Virginia	159
8	Wisconsin	170
7	Wyoming	171

RANK ORDER

RANK	STATE	AVERAGE SCORE
1	New Jersey	183
2	Connecticut	181
3	Massachusetts	178
4	Vermont	176
5	Maine	174
6	New Hampshire	173
7	Wyoming	171
8	Illinois	170
8	Washington	170
8	Wisconsin	170
11	Colorado	169
11	Florida	169
11	Montana	169
14	Kansas	168
14	Minnesota	168
14	Pennsylvania	168
14	Virginia	168
18	Idaho	167
18	Iowa	167
18	Tennessee	167
21	Delaware	166
21	North Dakota	166
21	Ohio	166
24	Indiana	165
24	Rhode Island	165
24	Utah	165
27	Arkansas	164
27	Georgia	164
27	North Carolina	164
30	Missouri	163
30	New York	163
32	Michigan	162
32	Oklahoma	162
34	Kentucky	161
35	Texas	160
36	South Carolina	159
36	West Virginia	159
38	Alabama	157
38	Arizona	157
38	California	157
41	Louisiana	156
41	Nevada	156
43	Hawaii	155
44	Mississippi	152
44	New Mexico	152
NA	Alaska**	NA
NA	Maryland**	NA
NA	Nebraska**	NA
NA	Oregon**	NA
NA	South Dakota**	NA
	District of Columbia**	NA

Source: U.S. Department of Education, National Center for Education Statistics
    "The Nation's Report Card: Writing 2007" (http://nces.ed.gov/nationsreportcard/)
*These scores are from the National Assessment of Educational Progress (NAEP). Scale ranges from 0 to 300.
**Not available.

Average Writing Score for Public School Eighth Graders Eligible for Free or Reduced Lunch Program in 2007
National Average Score = 141*

<table>
<tr><td colspan="3">ALPHA ORDER</td><td colspan="3">RANK ORDER</td></tr>
<tr><td>RANK</td><td>STATE</td><td>AVERAGE SCORE</td><td>RANK</td><td>STATE</td><td>AVERAGE SCORE</td></tr>
<tr><td>43</td><td>Alabama</td><td>135</td><td>1</td><td>New Jersey</td><td>155</td></tr>
<tr><td>NA</td><td>Alaska**</td><td>NA</td><td>2</td><td>Maine</td><td>150</td></tr>
<tr><td>39</td><td>Arizona</td><td>136</td><td>3</td><td>Connecticut</td><td>149</td></tr>
<tr><td>23</td><td>Arkansas</td><td>141</td><td>4</td><td>Delaware</td><td>146</td></tr>
<tr><td>39</td><td>California</td><td>136</td><td>4</td><td>Florida</td><td>146</td></tr>
<tr><td>16</td><td>Colorado</td><td>143</td><td>4</td><td>Massachusetts</td><td>146</td></tr>
<tr><td>3</td><td>Connecticut</td><td>149</td><td>4</td><td>Oklahoma</td><td>146</td></tr>
<tr><td>4</td><td>Delaware</td><td>146</td><td>4</td><td>Tennessee</td><td>146</td></tr>
<tr><td>4</td><td>Florida</td><td>146</td><td>9</td><td>New York</td><td>145</td></tr>
<tr><td>23</td><td>Georgia</td><td>141</td><td>9</td><td>North Dakota</td><td>145</td></tr>
<tr><td>44</td><td>Hawaii</td><td>132</td><td>9</td><td>Wyoming</td><td>145</td></tr>
<tr><td>12</td><td>Idaho</td><td>144</td><td>12</td><td>Idaho</td><td>144</td></tr>
<tr><td>19</td><td>Illinois</td><td>142</td><td>12</td><td>Pennsylvania</td><td>144</td></tr>
<tr><td>19</td><td>Indiana</td><td>142</td><td>12</td><td>Vermont</td><td>144</td></tr>
<tr><td>29</td><td>Iowa</td><td>140</td><td>12</td><td>Washington</td><td>144</td></tr>
<tr><td>19</td><td>Kansas</td><td>142</td><td>16</td><td>Colorado</td><td>143</td></tr>
<tr><td>23</td><td>Kentucky</td><td>141</td><td>16</td><td>Montana</td><td>143</td></tr>
<tr><td>29</td><td>Louisiana</td><td>140</td><td>16</td><td>New Hampshire</td><td>143</td></tr>
<tr><td>2</td><td>Maine</td><td>150</td><td>19</td><td>Illinois</td><td>142</td></tr>
<tr><td>NA</td><td>Maryland**</td><td>NA</td><td>19</td><td>Indiana</td><td>142</td></tr>
<tr><td>4</td><td>Massachusetts</td><td>146</td><td>19</td><td>Kansas</td><td>142</td></tr>
<tr><td>36</td><td>Michigan</td><td>137</td><td>19</td><td>Wisconsin</td><td>142</td></tr>
<tr><td>29</td><td>Minnesota</td><td>140</td><td>23</td><td>Arkansas</td><td>141</td></tr>
<tr><td>39</td><td>Mississippi</td><td>136</td><td>23</td><td>Georgia</td><td>141</td></tr>
<tr><td>23</td><td>Missouri</td><td>141</td><td>23</td><td>Kentucky</td><td>141</td></tr>
<tr><td>16</td><td>Montana</td><td>143</td><td>23</td><td>Missouri</td><td>141</td></tr>
<tr><td>NA</td><td>Nebraska**</td><td>NA</td><td>23</td><td>North Carolina</td><td>141</td></tr>
<tr><td>44</td><td>Nevada</td><td>132</td><td>23</td><td>Virginia</td><td>141</td></tr>
<tr><td>16</td><td>New Hampshire</td><td>143</td><td>29</td><td>Iowa</td><td>140</td></tr>
<tr><td>1</td><td>New Jersey</td><td>155</td><td>29</td><td>Louisiana</td><td>140</td></tr>
<tr><td>36</td><td>New Mexico</td><td>137</td><td>29</td><td>Minnesota</td><td>140</td></tr>
<tr><td>9</td><td>New York</td><td>145</td><td>29</td><td>Ohio</td><td>140</td></tr>
<tr><td>23</td><td>North Carolina</td><td>141</td><td>29</td><td>Texas</td><td>140</td></tr>
<tr><td>9</td><td>North Dakota</td><td>145</td><td>34</td><td>South Carolina</td><td>139</td></tr>
<tr><td>29</td><td>Ohio</td><td>140</td><td>34</td><td>Utah</td><td>139</td></tr>
<tr><td>4</td><td>Oklahoma</td><td>146</td><td>36</td><td>Michigan</td><td>137</td></tr>
<tr><td>NA</td><td>Oregon**</td><td>NA</td><td>36</td><td>New Mexico</td><td>137</td></tr>
<tr><td>12</td><td>Pennsylvania</td><td>144</td><td>36</td><td>West Virginia</td><td>137</td></tr>
<tr><td>39</td><td>Rhode Island</td><td>136</td><td>39</td><td>Arizona</td><td>136</td></tr>
<tr><td>34</td><td>South Carolina</td><td>139</td><td>39</td><td>California</td><td>136</td></tr>
<tr><td>NA</td><td>South Dakota**</td><td>NA</td><td>39</td><td>Mississippi</td><td>136</td></tr>
<tr><td>4</td><td>Tennessee</td><td>146</td><td>39</td><td>Rhode Island</td><td>136</td></tr>
<tr><td>29</td><td>Texas</td><td>140</td><td>43</td><td>Alabama</td><td>135</td></tr>
<tr><td>34</td><td>Utah</td><td>139</td><td>44</td><td>Hawaii</td><td>132</td></tr>
<tr><td>12</td><td>Vermont</td><td>144</td><td>44</td><td>Nevada</td><td>132</td></tr>
<tr><td>23</td><td>Virginia</td><td>141</td><td>NA</td><td>Alaska**</td><td>NA</td></tr>
<tr><td>12</td><td>Washington</td><td>144</td><td>NA</td><td>Maryland**</td><td>NA</td></tr>
<tr><td>36</td><td>West Virginia</td><td>137</td><td>NA</td><td>Nebraska**</td><td>NA</td></tr>
<tr><td>19</td><td>Wisconsin</td><td>142</td><td>NA</td><td>Oregon**</td><td>NA</td></tr>
<tr><td>9</td><td>Wyoming</td><td>145</td><td>NA</td><td>South Dakota**</td><td>NA</td></tr>
<tr><td></td><td></td><td></td><td></td><td>District of Columbia**</td><td>NA</td></tr>
</table>

Source: U.S. Department of Education, National Center for Education Statistics
   "The Nation's Report Card: Writing 2007" (http://nces.ed.gov/nationsreportcard/)
*These scores are from the National Assessment of Educational Progress (NAEP). Scale ranges from 0 to 300.
**Not available.

Percent of Public School Eighth Graders
Proficient or Better in Writing in 2007
National Percent = 31%*

RANK	STATE	PERCENT
37	Alabama	24
NA	Alaska**	NA
38	Arizona	23
29	Arkansas	27
36	California	25
6	Colorado	38
2	Connecticut	53
13	Delaware	34
9	Florida	36
26	Georgia	29
42	Hawaii	20
26	Idaho	29
8	Illinois	37
24	Indiana	30
17	Iowa	32
15	Kansas	33
32	Kentucky	26
43	Louisiana	17
6	Maine	38
NA	Maryland**	NA
3	Massachusetts	46
29	Michigan	27
17	Minnesota	32
45	Mississippi	15
32	Missouri	26
15	Montana	33
NA	Nebraska**	NA
41	Nevada	21
5	New Hampshire	39
1	New Jersey	56
43	New Mexico	17
21	New York	31
26	North Carolina	29
29	North Dakota	27
17	Ohio	32
32	Oklahoma	26
NA	Oregon**	NA
9	Pennsylvania	36
17	Rhode Island	32
38	South Carolina	23
NA	South Dakota**	NA
24	Tennessee	30
32	Texas	26
21	Utah	31
4	Vermont	40
21	Virginia	31
12	Washington	35
40	West Virginia	22
9	Wisconsin	36
13	Wyoming	34

RANK	STATE	PERCENT
1	New Jersey	56
2	Connecticut	53
3	Massachusetts	46
4	Vermont	40
5	New Hampshire	39
6	Colorado	38
6	Maine	38
8	Illinois	37
9	Florida	36
9	Pennsylvania	36
9	Wisconsin	36
12	Washington	35
13	Delaware	34
13	Wyoming	34
15	Kansas	33
15	Montana	33
17	Iowa	32
17	Minnesota	32
17	Ohio	32
17	Rhode Island	32
21	New York	31
21	Utah	31
21	Virginia	31
24	Indiana	30
24	Tennessee	30
26	Georgia	29
26	Idaho	29
26	North Carolina	29
29	Arkansas	27
29	Michigan	27
29	North Dakota	27
32	Kentucky	26
32	Missouri	26
32	Oklahoma	26
32	Texas	26
36	California	25
37	Alabama	24
38	Arizona	23
38	South Carolina	23
40	West Virginia	22
41	Nevada	21
42	Hawaii	20
43	Louisiana	17
43	New Mexico	17
45	Mississippi	15
NA	Alaska**	NA
NA	Maryland**	NA
NA	Nebraska**	NA
NA	Oregon**	NA
NA	South Dakota**	NA
	District of Columbia**	NA

Source: U.S. Department of Education, National Center for Education Statistics
   "The Nation's Report Card: Writing 2007" (http://nces.ed.gov/nationsreportcard/)
*There are four achievement levels: Below Basic, Basic, Proficient, and Advanced. Proficient represents solid academic mastery for 8th graders. Students reaching this level have demonstrated competency over challenging subject matter, including subject matter knowledge, application of such knowledge to real-world situations, and analytical skills appropriate to the subject matter. **Not available.

Percent of Public School Eighth Grade Males
Proficient or Better in Writing in 2007
National Percent = 20%*

ALPHA ORDER

RANK	STATE	PERCENT
33	Alabama	15
NA	Alaska**	NA
37	Arizona	13
35	Arkansas	14
27	California	17
4	Colorado	28
2	Connecticut	42
9	Delaware	24
9	Florida	24
27	Georgia	17
39	Hawaii	12
22	Idaho	18
5	Illinois	27
27	Indiana	17
27	Iowa	17
15	Kansas	21
31	Kentucky	16
43	Louisiana	9
9	Maine	24
NA	Maryland**	NA
3	Massachusetts	32
35	Michigan	14
22	Minnesota	18
45	Mississippi	6
33	Missouri	15
19	Montana	19
NA	Nebraska**	NA
41	Nevada	11
7	New Hampshire	26
1	New Jersey	47
43	New Mexico	9
13	New York	22
22	North Carolina	18
37	North Dakota	13
15	Ohio	21
31	Oklahoma	16
NA	Oregon**	NA
7	Pennsylvania	26
17	Rhode Island	20
39	South Carolina	12
NA	South Dakota**	NA
19	Tennessee	19
22	Texas	18
22	Utah	18
5	Vermont	27
19	Virginia	19
12	Washington	23
41	West Virginia	11
13	Wisconsin	22
17	Wyoming	20

RANK ORDER

RANK	STATE	PERCENT
1	New Jersey	47
2	Connecticut	42
3	Massachusetts	32
4	Colorado	28
5	Illinois	27
5	Vermont	27
7	New Hampshire	26
7	Pennsylvania	26
9	Delaware	24
9	Florida	24
9	Maine	24
12	Washington	23
13	New York	22
13	Wisconsin	22
15	Kansas	21
15	Ohio	21
17	Rhode Island	20
17	Wyoming	20
19	Montana	19
19	Tennessee	19
19	Virginia	19
22	Idaho	18
22	Minnesota	18
22	North Carolina	18
22	Texas	18
22	Utah	18
27	California	17
27	Georgia	17
27	Indiana	17
27	Iowa	17
31	Kentucky	16
31	Oklahoma	16
33	Alabama	15
33	Missouri	15
35	Arkansas	14
35	Michigan	14
37	Arizona	13
37	North Dakota	13
39	Hawaii	12
39	South Carolina	12
41	Nevada	11
41	West Virginia	11
43	Louisiana	9
43	New Mexico	9
45	Mississippi	6
NA	Alaska**	NA
NA	Maryland**	NA
NA	Nebraska**	NA
NA	Oregon**	NA
NA	South Dakota**	NA
	District of Columbia**	NA

Source: U.S. Department of Education, National Center for Education Statistics
   "The Nation's Report Card: Writing 2007" (http://nces.ed.gov/nationsreportcard/)
*There are four achievement levels: Below Basic, Basic, Proficient, and Advanced. Proficient represents solid academic mastery for 8th graders. Students reaching this level have demonstrated competency over challenging subject matter, including subject matter knowledge, application of such knowledge to real-world situations, and analytical skills appropriate to the subject matter. **Not available.

Percent of Public School Eighth Grade Females
Proficient or Better in Writing in 2007
National Percent = 41%*

ALPHA ORDER

RANK	STATE	PERCENT
36	Alabama	33
NA	Alaska**	NA
39	Arizona	32
28	Arkansas	40
36	California	33
9	Colorado	49
2	Connecticut	63
21	Delaware	43
10	Florida	48
28	Georgia	40
42	Hawaii	29
23	Idaho	42
10	Illinois	48
23	Indiana	42
13	Iowa	47
16	Kansas	46
34	Kentucky	36
43	Louisiana	26
5	Maine	53
NA	Maryland**	NA
3	Massachusetts	60
31	Michigan	39
16	Minnesota	46
45	Mississippi	23
32	Missouri	38
13	Montana	47
NA	Nebraska**	NA
41	Nevada	31
5	New Hampshire	53
1	New Jersey	65
44	New Mexico	25
26	New York	41
28	North Carolina	40
26	North Dakota	41
21	Ohio	43
33	Oklahoma	37
NA	Oregon**	NA
13	Pennsylvania	47
18	Rhode Island	45
39	South Carolina	32
NA	South Dakota**	NA
23	Tennessee	42
34	Texas	36
19	Utah	44
4	Vermont	56
19	Virginia	44
10	Washington	48
36	West Virginia	33
7	Wisconsin	50
7	Wyoming	50

RANK ORDER

RANK	STATE	PERCENT
1	New Jersey	65
2	Connecticut	63
3	Massachusetts	60
4	Vermont	56
5	Maine	53
5	New Hampshire	53
7	Wisconsin	50
7	Wyoming	50
9	Colorado	49
10	Florida	48
10	Illinois	48
10	Washington	48
13	Iowa	47
13	Montana	47
13	Pennsylvania	47
16	Kansas	46
16	Minnesota	46
18	Rhode Island	45
19	Utah	44
19	Virginia	44
21	Delaware	43
21	Ohio	43
23	Idaho	42
23	Indiana	42
23	Tennessee	42
26	New York	41
26	North Dakota	41
28	Arkansas	40
28	Georgia	40
28	North Carolina	40
31	Michigan	39
32	Missouri	38
33	Oklahoma	37
34	Kentucky	36
34	Texas	36
36	Alabama	33
36	California	33
36	West Virginia	33
39	Arizona	32
39	South Carolina	32
41	Nevada	31
42	Hawaii	29
43	Louisiana	26
44	New Mexico	25
45	Mississippi	23
NA	Alaska**	NA
NA	Maryland**	NA
NA	Nebraska**	NA
NA	Oregon**	NA
NA	South Dakota**	NA

District of Columbia**   NA

Source: U.S. Department of Education, National Center for Education Statistics
"The Nation's Report Card: Writing 2007" (http://nces.ed.gov/nationsreportcard/)
*There are four achievement levels: Below Basic, Basic, Proficient, and Advanced. Proficient represents solid academic mastery for 8th graders. Students reaching this level have demonstrated competency over challenging subject matter, including subject matter knowledge, application of such knowledge to real-world situations, and analytical skills appropriate to the subject matter. **Not available.

Percent of Public School Eighth Graders Eligible for
Free or Reduced Price Lunch Proficient or Better in Writing in 2007
National Percent = 17%*

ALPHA ORDER

RANK	STATE	PERCENT
39	Alabama	12
NA	Alaska**	NA
43	Arizona	10
23	Arkansas	17
35	California	13
17	Colorado	18
2	Connecticut	28
17	Delaware	18
4	Florida	23
26	Georgia	16
42	Hawaii	11
17	Idaho	18
23	Illinois	17
23	Indiana	17
17	Iowa	18
17	Kansas	18
26	Kentucky	16
43	Louisiana	10
3	Maine	26
NA	Maryland**	NA
7	Massachusetts	21
33	Michigan	14
26	Minnesota	16
45	Mississippi	9
35	Missouri	13
9	Montana	20
NA	Nebraska**	NA
39	Nevada	12
9	New Hampshire	20
1	New Jersey	33
39	New Mexico	12
6	New York	22
26	North Carolina	16
13	North Dakota	19
30	Ohio	15
13	Oklahoma	19
NA	Oregon**	NA
13	Pennsylvania	19
30	Rhode Island	15
35	South Carolina	13
NA	South Dakota**	NA
13	Tennessee	19
30	Texas	15
17	Utah	18
4	Vermont	23
35	Virginia	13
9	Washington	20
33	West Virginia	14
9	Wisconsin	20
7	Wyoming	21

RANK ORDER

RANK	STATE	PERCENT
1	New Jersey	33
2	Connecticut	28
3	Maine	26
4	Florida	23
4	Vermont	23
6	New York	22
7	Massachusetts	21
7	Wyoming	21
9	Montana	20
9	New Hampshire	20
9	Washington	20
9	Wisconsin	20
13	North Dakota	19
13	Oklahoma	19
13	Pennsylvania	19
13	Tennessee	19
17	Colorado	18
17	Delaware	18
17	Idaho	18
17	Iowa	18
17	Kansas	18
17	Utah	18
23	Arkansas	17
23	Illinois	17
23	Indiana	17
26	Georgia	16
26	Kentucky	16
26	Minnesota	16
26	North Carolina	16
30	Ohio	15
30	Rhode Island	15
30	Texas	15
33	Michigan	14
33	West Virginia	14
35	California	13
35	Missouri	13
35	South Carolina	13
35	Virginia	13
39	Alabama	12
39	Nevada	12
39	New Mexico	12
42	Hawaii	11
43	Arizona	10
43	Louisiana	10
45	Mississippi	9
NA	Alaska**	NA
NA	Maryland**	NA
NA	Nebraska**	NA
NA	Oregon**	NA
NA	South Dakota**	NA
	District of Columbia**	NA

Source: U.S. Department of Education, National Center for Education Statistics
    "The Nation's Report Card: Writing 2007" (http://nces.ed.gov/nationsreportcard/)
*There are four achievement levels: Below Basic, Basic, Proficient, and Advanced. Proficient represents solid academic
mastery for 8th graders. Students reaching this level have demonstrated competency over challenging subject matter, including
subject matter knowledge, application of such knowledge to real-world situations, and analytical skills appropriate to the subject
matter. **Not available.

Percent of White Public School Eighth Graders
Proficient or Better in Writing in 2007
National Percent = 39%*

ALPHA ORDER

RANK	STATE	PERCENT
29	Alabama	33
NA	Alaska**	NA
27	Arizona	34
32	Arkansas	32
17	California	38
4	Colorado	49
2	Connecticut	63
6	Delaware	45
6	Florida	45
14	Georgia	39
42	Hawaii	26
32	Idaho	32
5	Illinois	48
29	Indiana	33
29	Iowa	33
21	Kansas	37
40	Kentucky	27
43	Louisiana	24
17	Maine	38
NA	Maryland**	NA
3	Massachusetts	52
34	Michigan	30
25	Minnesota	35
44	Mississippi	23
34	Missouri	30
25	Montana	35
NA	Nebraska**	NA
38	Nevada	28
10	New Hampshire	40
1	New Jersey	66
40	New Mexico	27
17	New York	38
17	North Carolina	38
38	North Dakota	28
22	Ohio	36
34	Oklahoma	30
NA	Oregon**	NA
8	Pennsylvania	42
14	Rhode Island	39
34	South Carolina	30
NA	South Dakota**	NA
22	Tennessee	36
9	Texas	41
27	Utah	34
10	Vermont	40
14	Virginia	39
10	Washington	40
45	West Virginia	22
10	Wisconsin	40
22	Wyoming	36

RANK ORDER

RANK	STATE	PERCENT
1	New Jersey	66
2	Connecticut	63
3	Massachusetts	52
4	Colorado	49
5	Illinois	48
6	Delaware	45
6	Florida	45
8	Pennsylvania	42
9	Texas	41
10	New Hampshire	40
10	Vermont	40
10	Washington	40
10	Wisconsin	40
14	Georgia	39
14	Rhode Island	39
14	Virginia	39
17	California	38
17	Maine	38
17	New York	38
17	North Carolina	38
21	Kansas	37
22	Ohio	36
22	Tennessee	36
22	Wyoming	36
25	Minnesota	35
25	Montana	35
27	Arizona	34
27	Utah	34
29	Alabama	33
29	Indiana	33
29	Iowa	33
32	Arkansas	32
32	Idaho	32
34	Michigan	30
34	Missouri	30
34	Oklahoma	30
34	South Carolina	30
38	Nevada	28
38	North Dakota	28
40	Kentucky	27
40	New Mexico	27
42	Hawaii	26
43	Louisiana	24
44	Mississippi	23
45	West Virginia	22
NA	Alaska**	NA
NA	Maryland**	NA
NA	Nebraska**	NA
NA	Oregon**	NA
NA	South Dakota**	NA
	District of Columbia**	NA

Source: U.S. Department of Education, National Center for Education Statistics
    "The Nation's Report Card: Writing 2007" (http://nces.ed.gov/nationsreportcard/)
*There are four achievement levels: Below Basic, Basic, Proficient, and Advanced. Proficient represents solid academic
mastery for 8th graders. Students reaching this level have demonstrated competency over challenging subject matter, including
subject matter knowledge, application of such knowledge to real-world situations, and analytical skills appropriate to the subject
matter. **Not available.

Percent of Black Public School Eighth Graders
Proficient or Better in Writing in 2007
National Percent = 15%*

ALPHA ORDER				RANK ORDER		
RANK	STATE	PERCENT		RANK	STATE	PERCENT
34	Alabama	9		1	Connecticut	27
NA	Alaska**	NA		1	New Jersey	27
13	Arizona	16		3	Washington	24
17	Arkansas	14		4	Florida	22
20	California	13		5	Colorado	21
5	Colorado	21		6	Kansas	20
1	Connecticut	27		7	Massachusetts	19
8	Delaware	18		8	Delaware	18
4	Florida	22		8	Illinois	18
11	Georgia	17		8	Tennessee	18
14	Hawaii	15		11	Georgia	17
NA	Idaho**	NA		11	Texas	17
8	Illinois	18		13	Arizona	16
26	Indiana	12		14	Hawaii	15
20	Iowa	13		14	New York	15
6	Kansas	20		14	West Virginia	15
17	Kentucky	14		17	Arkansas	14
34	Louisiana	9		17	Kentucky	14
NA	Maine**	NA		17	Virginia	14
NA	Maryland**	NA		20	California	13
7	Massachusetts	19		20	Iowa	13
32	Michigan	10		20	Minnesota	13
20	Minnesota	13		20	Nevada	13
36	Mississippi	8		20	Ohio	13
26	Missouri	12		20	Pennsylvania	13
NA	Montana**	NA		26	Indiana	12
NA	Nebraska**	NA		26	Missouri	12
20	Nevada	13		26	North Carolina	12
NA	New Hampshire**	NA		26	Oklahoma	12
1	New Jersey	27		26	Rhode Island	12
NA	New Mexico**	NA		26	South Carolina	12
14	New York	15		32	Michigan	10
26	North Carolina	12		32	Wisconsin	10
NA	North Dakota**	NA		34	Alabama	9
20	Ohio	13		34	Louisiana	9
26	Oklahoma	12		36	Mississippi	8
NA	Oregon**	NA		NA	Alaska**	NA
20	Pennsylvania	13		NA	Idaho**	NA
26	Rhode Island	12		NA	Maine**	NA
26	South Carolina	12		NA	Maryland**	NA
NA	South Dakota**	NA		NA	Montana**	NA
8	Tennessee	18		NA	Nebraska**	NA
11	Texas	17		NA	New Hampshire**	NA
NA	Utah**	NA		NA	New Mexico**	NA
NA	Vermont**	NA		NA	North Dakota**	NA
17	Virginia	14		NA	Oregon**	NA
3	Washington	24		NA	South Dakota**	NA
14	West Virginia	15		NA	Utah**	NA
32	Wisconsin	10		NA	Vermont**	NA
NA	Wyoming**	NA		NA	Wyoming**	NA
					District of Columbia**	NA

Source: U.S. Department of Education, National Center for Education Statistics
   "The Nation's Report Card: Writing 2007" (http://nces.ed.gov/nationsreportcard/)
*There are four achievement levels: Below Basic, Basic, Proficient, and Advanced. Proficient represents solid academic
mastery for 8th graders. Students reaching this level have demonstrated competency over challenging subject matter, including
subject matter knowledge, application of such knowledge to real-world situations, and analytical skills appropriate to the subject
matter. **Not available.

Percent of Hispanic Public School Eighth Graders
Proficient or Better in Writing in 2007
National Percent = 17%*

ALPHA ORDER

RANK	STATE	PERCENT
NA	Alabama**	NA
NA	Alaska**	NA
35	Arizona	10
16	Arkansas	17
30	California	13
21	Colorado	16
3	Connecticut	27
16	Delaware	17
2	Florida	28
10	Georgia	19
21	Hawaii	16
30	Idaho	13
16	Illinois	17
11	Indiana	18
27	Iowa	14
27	Kansas	14
NA	Kentucky**	NA
NA	Louisiana**	NA
NA	Maine**	NA
NA	Maryland**	NA
21	Massachusetts	16
16	Michigan	17
16	Minnesota	17
NA	Mississippi**	NA
21	Missouri	16
NA	Montana**	NA
NA	Nebraska**	NA
32	Nevada	12
7	New Hampshire	21
1	New Jersey	41
32	New Mexico	12
8	New York	20
21	North Carolina	16
NA	North Dakota**	NA
6	Ohio	22
27	Oklahoma	14
NA	Oregon**	NA
8	Pennsylvania	20
34	Rhode Island	11
11	South Carolina	18
NA	South Dakota**	NA
11	Tennessee	18
21	Texas	16
35	Utah	10
NA	Vermont**	NA
11	Virginia	18
11	Washington	18
NA	West Virginia**	NA
4	Wisconsin	26
5	Wyoming	23

RANK ORDER

RANK	STATE	PERCENT
1	New Jersey	41
2	Florida	28
3	Connecticut	27
4	Wisconsin	26
5	Wyoming	23
6	Ohio	22
7	New Hampshire	21
8	New York	20
8	Pennsylvania	20
10	Georgia	19
11	Indiana	18
11	South Carolina	18
11	Tennessee	18
11	Virginia	18
11	Washington	18
16	Arkansas	17
16	Delaware	17
16	Illinois	17
16	Michigan	17
16	Minnesota	17
21	Colorado	16
21	Hawaii	16
21	Massachusetts	16
21	Missouri	16
21	North Carolina	16
21	Texas	16
27	Iowa	14
27	Kansas	14
27	Oklahoma	14
30	California	13
30	Idaho	13
32	Nevada	12
32	New Mexico	12
34	Rhode Island	11
35	Arizona	10
35	Utah	10
NA	Alabama**	NA
NA	Alaska**	NA
NA	Kentucky**	NA
NA	Louisiana**	NA
NA	Maine**	NA
NA	Maryland**	NA
NA	Mississippi**	NA
NA	Montana**	NA
NA	Nebraska**	NA
NA	North Dakota**	NA
NA	Oregon**	NA
NA	South Dakota**	NA
NA	Vermont**	NA
NA	West Virginia**	NA
	District of Columbia**	NA

Source: U.S. Department of Education, National Center for Education Statistics
   "The Nation's Report Card: Writing 2007" (http://nces.ed.gov/nationsreportcard/)
*There are four achievement levels: Below Basic, Basic, Proficient, and Advanced. Proficient represents solid academic mastery for 8th graders. Students reaching this level have demonstrated competency over challenging subject matter, including subject matter knowledge, application of such knowledge to real-world situations, and analytical skills appropriate to the subject matter. **Not available.

Percent of Asian Public School Eighth Graders
Proficient or Better in Writing in 2007
National Percent = 45%*

ALPHA ORDER

RANK	STATE	PERCENT
NA	Alabama**	NA
NA	Alaska**	NA
12	Arizona	45
NA	Arkansas**	NA
14	California	44
5	Colorado	52
5	Connecticut	52
3	Delaware	56
9	Florida	50
NA	Georgia**	NA
22	Hawaii	19
NA	Idaho**	NA
2	Illinois	60
NA	Indiana**	NA
11	Iowa	49
NA	Kansas**	NA
NA	Kentucky**	NA
NA	Louisiana**	NA
NA	Maine**	NA
NA	Maryland**	NA
4	Massachusetts	55
NA	Michigan**	NA
20	Minnesota	27
NA	Mississippi**	NA
NA	Missouri**	NA
NA	Montana**	NA
NA	Nebraska**	NA
21	Nevada	26
NA	New Hampshire**	NA
1	New Jersey	73
NA	New Mexico**	NA
5	New York	52
12	North Carolina	45
NA	North Dakota**	NA
NA	Ohio**	NA
NA	Oklahoma**	NA
NA	Oregon**	NA
9	Pennsylvania	50
15	Rhode Island	43
NA	South Carolina**	NA
NA	South Dakota**	NA
NA	Tennessee**	NA
17	Texas	41
19	Utah	36
NA	Vermont**	NA
8	Virginia	51
18	Washington	37
NA	West Virginia**	NA
16	Wisconsin	42
NA	Wyoming**	NA

RANK ORDER

RANK	STATE	PERCENT
1	New Jersey	73
2	Illinois	60
3	Delaware	56
4	Massachusetts	55
5	Colorado	52
5	Connecticut	52
5	New York	52
8	Virginia	51
9	Florida	50
9	Pennsylvania	50
11	Iowa	49
12	Arizona	45
12	North Carolina	45
14	California	44
15	Rhode Island	43
16	Wisconsin	42
17	Texas	41
18	Washington	37
19	Utah	36
20	Minnesota	27
21	Nevada	26
22	Hawaii	19
NA	Alabama**	NA
NA	Alaska**	NA
NA	Arkansas**	NA
NA	Georgia**	NA
NA	Idaho**	NA
NA	Indiana**	NA
NA	Kansas**	NA
NA	Kentucky**	NA
NA	Louisiana**	NA
NA	Maine**	NA
NA	Maryland**	NA
NA	Michigan**	NA
NA	Mississippi**	NA
NA	Missouri**	NA
NA	Montana**	NA
NA	Nebraska**	NA
NA	New Hampshire**	NA
NA	New Mexico**	NA
NA	North Dakota**	NA
NA	Ohio**	NA
NA	Oklahoma**	NA
NA	Oregon**	NA
NA	South Carolina**	NA
NA	South Dakota**	NA
NA	Tennessee**	NA
NA	Vermont**	NA
NA	West Virginia**	NA
NA	Wyoming**	NA
	District of Columbia**	NA

Source: U.S. Department of Education, National Center for Education Statistics
    "The Nation's Report Card: Writing 2007" (http://nces.ed.gov/nationsreportcard/)
*There are four achievement levels: Below Basic, Basic, Proficient, and Advanced. Proficient represents solid academic
mastery for 8th graders. Students reaching this level have demonstrated competency over challenging subject matter, including
subject matter knowledge, application of such knowledge to real-world situations, and analytical skills appropriate to the subject
matter. **Not available.

Percent of Disabled Public School Eighth Graders
Proficient or Better in Writing in 2007
National Percent = 6%*

ALPHA ORDER

RANK	STATE	PERCENT
37	Alabama	2
NA	Alaska**	NA
27	Arizona	4
27	Arkansas	4
15	California	6
7	Colorado	8
1	Connecticut	18
10	Delaware	7
6	Florida	9
20	Georgia	5
37	Hawaii	2
15	Idaho	6
15	Illinois	6
20	Indiana	5
37	Iowa	2
7	Kansas	8
32	Kentucky	3
37	Louisiana	2
10	Maine	7
NA	Maryland**	NA
3	Massachusetts	14
32	Michigan	3
27	Minnesota	4
45	Mississippi	1
32	Missouri	3
20	Montana	5
NA	Nebraska**	NA
10	Nevada	7
4	New Hampshire	11
1	New Jersey	18
37	New Mexico	2
32	New York	3
15	North Carolina	6
20	North Dakota	5
27	Ohio	4
37	Oklahoma	2
NA	Oregon**	NA
7	Pennsylvania	8
15	Rhode Island	6
37	South Carolina	2
NA	South Dakota**	NA
4	Tennessee	11
20	Texas	5
32	Utah	3
10	Vermont	7
20	Virginia	5
20	Washington	5
37	West Virginia	2
27	Wisconsin	4
10	Wyoming	7

RANK ORDER

RANK	STATE	PERCENT
1	Connecticut	18
1	New Jersey	18
3	Massachusetts	14
4	New Hampshire	11
4	Tennessee	11
6	Florida	9
7	Colorado	8
7	Kansas	8
7	Pennsylvania	8
10	Delaware	7
10	Maine	7
10	Nevada	7
10	Vermont	7
10	Wyoming	7
15	California	6
15	Idaho	6
15	Illinois	6
15	North Carolina	6
15	Rhode Island	6
20	Georgia	5
20	Indiana	5
20	Montana	5
20	North Dakota	5
20	Texas	5
20	Virginia	5
20	Washington	5
27	Arizona	4
27	Arkansas	4
27	Minnesota	4
27	Ohio	4
27	Wisconsin	4
32	Kentucky	3
32	Michigan	3
32	Missouri	3
32	New York	3
32	Utah	3
37	Alabama	2
37	Hawaii	2
37	Iowa	2
37	Louisiana	2
37	New Mexico	2
37	Oklahoma	2
37	South Carolina	2
37	West Virginia	2
45	Mississippi	1
NA	Alaska**	NA
NA	Maryland**	NA
NA	Nebraska**	NA
NA	Oregon**	NA
NA	South Dakota**	NA
	District of Columbia**	NA

Source: U.S. Department of Education, National Center for Education Statistics
    "The Nation's Report Card: Writing 2007" (http://nces.ed.gov/nationsreportcard/)
*There are four achievement levels: Below Basic, Basic, Proficient, and Advanced. Proficient represents solid academic mastery for 8th graders. Students reaching this level have demonstrated competency over challenging subject matter, including subject matter knowledge, application of such knowledge to real-world situations, and analytical skills appropriate to the subject matter. Based only on disabled students who were assessed. **Not available.

Percent of English Language Learner Public School Eighth Graders Proficient or Better in Writing in 2007
National Percent = 5%*

RANK	STATE	PERCENT
NA	Alabama**	NA
NA	Alaska**	NA
22	Arizona	2
6	Arkansas	11
13	California	5
18	Colorado	4
18	Connecticut	4
NA	Delaware**	NA
9	Florida	9
NA	Georgia**	NA
13	Hawaii	5
6	Idaho	11
13	Illinois	5
3	Indiana	14
NA	Iowa**	NA
10	Kansas	7
NA	Kentucky**	NA
NA	Louisiana**	NA
NA	Maine**	NA
NA	Maryland**	NA
13	Massachusetts	5
NA	Michigan**	NA
4	Minnesota	13
NA	Mississippi**	NA
NA	Missouri**	NA
10	Montana	7
NA	Nebraska**	NA
20	Nevada	3
NA	New Hampshire**	NA
NA	New Jersey**	NA
20	New Mexico	3
22	New York	2
10	North Carolina	7
NA	North Dakota**	NA
NA	Ohio**	NA
2	Oklahoma	15
NA	Oregon**	NA
NA	Pennsylvania**	NA
NA	Rhode Island**	NA
NA	South Carolina**	NA
NA	South Dakota**	NA
NA	Tennessee**	NA
24	Texas	1
4	Utah	13
NA	Vermont**	NA
6	Virginia	11
13	Washington	5
NA	West Virginia**	NA
1	Wisconsin	17
NA	Wyoming**	NA

RANK	STATE	PERCENT
1	Wisconsin	17
2	Oklahoma	15
3	Indiana	14
4	Minnesota	13
4	Utah	13
6	Arkansas	11
6	Idaho	11
6	Virginia	11
9	Florida	9
10	Kansas	7
10	Montana	7
10	North Carolina	7
13	California	5
13	Hawaii	5
13	Illinois	5
13	Massachusetts	5
13	Washington	5
18	Colorado	4
18	Connecticut	4
20	Nevada	3
20	New Mexico	3
22	Arizona	2
22	New York	2
24	Texas	1
NA	Alabama**	NA
NA	Alaska**	NA
NA	Delaware**	NA
NA	Georgia**	NA
NA	Iowa**	NA
NA	Kentucky**	NA
NA	Louisiana**	NA
NA	Maine**	NA
NA	Maryland**	NA
NA	Michigan**	NA
NA	Mississippi**	NA
NA	Missouri**	NA
NA	Nebraska**	NA
NA	New Hampshire**	NA
NA	New Jersey**	NA
NA	North Dakota**	NA
NA	Ohio**	NA
NA	Oregon**	NA
NA	Pennsylvania**	NA
NA	Rhode Island**	NA
NA	South Carolina**	NA
NA	South Dakota**	NA
NA	Tennessee**	NA
NA	Vermont**	NA
NA	West Virginia**	NA
NA	Wyoming**	NA
	District of Columbia**	NA

Source: U.S. Department of Education, National Center for Education Statistics
   "The Nation's Report Card: Writing 2007" (http://nces.ed.gov/nationsreportcard/)
*There are four achievement levels: Below Basic, Basic, Proficient, and Advanced. Proficient represents solid academic mastery for 8th graders. Students reaching this level have demonstrated competency over challenging subject matter, including subject matter knowledge, application of such knowledge to real-world situations, and analytical skills appropriate to the subject matter. **Not available.

IV. Safety and Discipline

Percent of Public School Teachers Who Reported
Being Threatened or Injured by a Student in 2008
National Percent = 8.1% of Teachers*

ALPHA ORDER

RANK	STATE	PERCENT
35	Alabama	6.8
23	Alaska	7.8
36	Arizona	6.6
44	Arkansas	5.7
18	California	8.6
34	Colorado	6.9
31	Connecticut	7.2
3	Delaware	11.7
4	Florida	11.4
43	Georgia	5.8
26	Hawaii	7.6
42	Idaho	5.9
20	Illinois	8.2
8	Indiana	10.2
36	Iowa	6.6
44	Kansas	5.7
9	Kentucky	9.9
7	Louisiana	10.4
12	Maine	9.5
2	Maryland	12.7
10	Massachusetts	9.7
41	Michigan	6.0
30	Minnesota	7.3
5	Mississippi	10.7
15	Missouri	8.7
39	Montana	6.4
31	Nebraska	7.2
13	Nevada	9.3
38	New Hampshire	6.5
48	New Jersey	4.7
1	New Mexico	12.8
6	New York	10.5
11	North Carolina	9.6
50	North Dakota	3.2
15	Ohio	8.7
29	Oklahoma	7.4
40	Oregon	6.3
49	Pennsylvania	4.6
15	Rhode Island	8.7
19	South Carolina	8.5
24	South Dakota	7.7
24	Tennessee	7.7
26	Texas	7.6
44	Utah	5.7
26	Vermont	7.6
20	Virginia	8.2
33	Washington	7.0
22	West Virginia	8.0
14	Wisconsin	9.0
47	Wyoming	5.4

RANK ORDER

RANK	STATE	PERCENT
1	New Mexico	12.8
2	Maryland	12.7
3	Delaware	11.7
4	Florida	11.4
5	Mississippi	10.7
6	New York	10.5
7	Louisiana	10.4
8	Indiana	10.2
9	Kentucky	9.9
10	Massachusetts	9.7
11	North Carolina	9.6
12	Maine	9.5
13	Nevada	9.3
14	Wisconsin	9.0
15	Missouri	8.7
15	Ohio	8.7
15	Rhode Island	8.7
18	California	8.6
19	South Carolina	8.5
20	Illinois	8.2
20	Virginia	8.2
22	West Virginia	8.0
23	Alaska	7.8
24	South Dakota	7.7
24	Tennessee	7.7
26	Hawaii	7.6
26	Texas	7.6
26	Vermont	7.6
29	Oklahoma	7.4
30	Minnesota	7.3
31	Connecticut	7.2
31	Nebraska	7.2
33	Washington	7.0
34	Colorado	6.9
35	Alabama	6.8
36	Arizona	6.6
36	Iowa	6.6
38	New Hampshire	6.5
39	Montana	6.4
40	Oregon	6.3
41	Michigan	6.0
42	Idaho	5.9
43	Georgia	5.8
44	Arkansas	5.7
44	Kansas	5.7
44	Utah	5.7
47	Wyoming	5.4
48	New Jersey	4.7
49	Pennsylvania	4.6
50	North Dakota	3.2
	District of Columbia	16.9

Source: U.S. Department of Justice, Bureau of Justice Statistics and
U.S. Department of Education, National Center for Education Statistics
"Indicators of School Crime and Safety: 2009" (http://nces.ed.gov/pubsearch/pubsinfo.asp?pubid=2010012)
*For school year 2007-2008.

Percent of Public School Teachers Who Reported Being Physically Attacked by a Student in 2008
National Percent = 4.3% of Teachers*

RANK	STATE	PERCENT
39	Alabama	3.2
2	Alaska	6.7
12	Arizona	5.0
28	Arkansas	3.9
35	California	3.6
14	Colorado	4.7
37	Connecticut	3.3
9	Delaware	5.4
24	Florida	4.0
24	Georgia	4.0
21	Hawaii	4.1
43	Idaho	2.9
28	Illinois	3.9
14	Indiana	4.7
40	Iowa	3.1
12	Kansas	5.0
8	Kentucky	5.8
24	Louisiana	4.0
11	Maine	5.2
1	Maryland	8.4
21	Massachusetts	4.1
36	Michigan	3.5
3	Minnesota	6.6
43	Mississippi	2.9
10	Missouri	5.3
24	Montana	4.0
18	Nebraska	4.2
37	Nevada	3.3
46	New Hampshire	2.2
48	New Jersey	1.8
17	New Mexico	4.3
5	New York	6.4
7	North Carolina	5.9
49	North Dakota	1.7
46	Ohio	2.2
40	Oklahoma	3.1
28	Oregon	3.9
33	Pennsylvania	3.8
NA	Rhode Island**	NA
43	South Carolina	2.9
16	South Dakota	4.5
28	Tennessee	3.9
18	Texas	4.2
33	Utah	3.8
18	Vermont	4.2
6	Virginia	6.0
21	Washington	4.1
28	West Virginia	3.9
3	Wisconsin	6.6
42	Wyoming	3.0

RANK	STATE	PERCENT
1	Maryland	8.4
2	Alaska	6.7
3	Minnesota	6.6
3	Wisconsin	6.6
5	New York	6.4
6	Virginia	6.0
7	North Carolina	5.9
8	Kentucky	5.8
9	Delaware	5.4
10	Missouri	5.3
11	Maine	5.2
12	Arizona	5.0
12	Kansas	5.0
14	Colorado	4.7
14	Indiana	4.7
16	South Dakota	4.5
17	New Mexico	4.3
18	Nebraska	4.2
18	Texas	4.2
18	Vermont	4.2
21	Hawaii	4.1
21	Massachusetts	4.1
21	Washington	4.1
24	Florida	4.0
24	Georgia	4.0
24	Louisiana	4.0
24	Montana	4.0
28	Arkansas	3.9
28	Illinois	3.9
28	Oregon	3.9
28	Tennessee	3.9
28	West Virginia	3.9
33	Pennsylvania	3.8
33	Utah	3.8
35	California	3.6
36	Michigan	3.5
37	Connecticut	3.3
37	Nevada	3.3
39	Alabama	3.2
40	Iowa	3.1
40	Oklahoma	3.1
42	Wyoming	3.0
43	Idaho	2.9
43	Mississippi	2.9
43	South Carolina	2.9
46	New Hampshire	2.2
46	Ohio	2.2
48	New Jersey	1.8
49	North Dakota	1.7
NA	Rhode Island**	NA

	District of Columbia	7.1

Source: U.S. Department of Justice, Bureau of Justice Statistics and
  U.S. Department of Education, National Center for Education Statistics
   "Indicators of School Crime and Safety: 2009" (http://nces.ed.gov/pubsearch/pubsinfo.asp?pubid=2010012)
*For school year 2007-2008.
**Not available.

Percent of High School Students Who Felt Too Unsafe to Go to School at Some Point in 2009
National Percent = 5.0%*

ALPHA ORDER

RANK	STATE	PERCENT
2	Alabama	9.6
20	Alaska	6.0
7	Arizona	7.4
1	Arkansas	10.4
NA	California**	NA
29	Colorado	5.1
31	Connecticut	4.9
17	Delaware	6.3
13	Florida	6.9
13	Georgia	6.9
4	Hawaii	7.9
37	Idaho	4.0
7	Illinois	7.4
34	Indiana	4.1
NA	Iowa**	NA
40	Kansas	3.5
25	Kentucky	5.4
3	Louisiana	9.1
24	Maine	5.5
12	Maryland	7.1
37	Massachusetts	4.0
7	Michigan	7.4
NA	Minnesota**	NA
34	Mississippi	4.1
21	Missouri	5.7
27	Montana	5.2
NA	Nebraska**	NA
6	Nevada	7.5
33	New Hampshire	4.5
27	New Jersey	5.2
11	New Mexico	7.2
17	New York	6.3
22	North Carolina	5.6
NA	North Dakota**	NA
NA	Ohio**	NA
34	Oklahoma	4.1
NA	Oregon**	NA
25	Pennsylvania	5.4
7	Rhode Island	7.4
15	South Carolina	6.5
41	South Dakota	2.9
22	Tennessee	5.6
29	Texas	5.1
15	Utah	6.5
31	Vermont	4.9
NA	Virginia**	NA
NA	Washington**	NA
5	West Virginia	7.8
39	Wisconsin	3.7
19	Wyoming	6.1

RANK ORDER

RANK	STATE	PERCENT
1	Arkansas	10.4
2	Alabama	9.6
3	Louisiana	9.1
4	Hawaii	7.9
5	West Virginia	7.8
6	Nevada	7.5
7	Arizona	7.4
7	Illinois	7.4
7	Michigan	7.4
7	Rhode Island	7.4
11	New Mexico	7.2
12	Maryland	7.1
13	Florida	6.9
13	Georgia	6.9
15	South Carolina	6.5
15	Utah	6.5
17	Delaware	6.3
17	New York	6.3
19	Wyoming	6.1
20	Alaska	6.0
21	Missouri	5.7
22	North Carolina	5.6
22	Tennessee	5.6
24	Maine	5.5
25	Kentucky	5.4
25	Pennsylvania	5.4
27	Montana	5.2
27	New Jersey	5.2
29	Colorado	5.1
29	Texas	5.1
31	Connecticut	4.9
31	Vermont	4.9
33	New Hampshire	4.5
34	Indiana	4.1
34	Mississippi	4.1
34	Oklahoma	4.1
37	Idaho	4.0
37	Massachusetts	4.0
39	Wisconsin	3.7
40	Kansas	3.5
41	South Dakota	2.9
NA	California**	NA
NA	Iowa**	NA
NA	Minnesota**	NA
NA	Nebraska**	NA
NA	North Dakota**	NA
NA	Ohio**	NA
NA	Oregon**	NA
NA	Virginia**	NA
NA	Washington**	NA
	District of Columbia**	NA

Source: U.S. Department of Health and Human Services, Centers for Disease Control and Prevention
"Youth Risk Behavior Surveillance--U.S., 2009" (http://www.cdc.gov/HealthyYouth/yrbs/)
*On at least one of the 30 days preceding the survey. National percent includes nonreporting states.
**Not available.

Percent of High School Students Who Were Bullied on School Property in 2009

National Percent = 19.9%*

ALPHA ORDER

RANK	STATE	PERCENT
19	Alabama	19.3
14	Alaska	20.7
NA	Arizona**	NA
NA	Arkansas**	NA
NA	California**	NA
21	Colorado	18.8
NA	Connecticut**	NA
31	Delaware	15.9
34	Florida	13.4
NA	Georgia**	NA
NA	Hawaii**	NA
9	Idaho	22.3
16	Illinois	19.6
5	Indiana	22.8
NA	Iowa**	NA
24	Kansas	18.5
13	Kentucky	20.8
31	Louisiana	15.9
8	Maine	22.4
12	Maryland	20.9
18	Massachusetts	19.4
2	Michigan	24.0
NA	Minnesota**	NA
30	Mississippi	16.0
5	Missouri	22.8
4	Montana	23.1
NA	Nebraska**	NA
NA	Nevada**	NA
10	New Hampshire	22.1
14	New Jersey	20.7
17	New Mexico	19.5
25	New York	18.2
28	North Carolina	16.6
11	North Dakota	21.1
NA	Ohio**	NA
26	Oklahoma	17.5
NA	Oregon**	NA
20	Pennsylvania	19.2
29	Rhode Island	16.3
33	South Carolina	15.1
NA	South Dakota**	NA
27	Tennessee	17.3
23	Texas	18.7
21	Utah	18.8
NA	Vermont**	NA
NA	Virginia**	NA
NA	Washington**	NA
3	West Virginia	23.5
7	Wisconsin	22.5
1	Wyoming	24.4

RANK ORDER

RANK	STATE	PERCENT
1	Wyoming	24.4
2	Michigan	24.0
3	West Virginia	23.5
4	Montana	23.1
5	Indiana	22.8
5	Missouri	22.8
7	Wisconsin	22.5
8	Maine	22.4
9	Idaho	22.3
10	New Hampshire	22.1
11	North Dakota	21.1
12	Maryland	20.9
13	Kentucky	20.8
14	Alaska	20.7
14	New Jersey	20.7
16	Illinois	19.6
17	New Mexico	19.5
18	Massachusetts	19.4
19	Alabama	19.3
20	Pennsylvania	19.2
21	Colorado	18.8
21	Utah	18.8
23	Texas	18.7
24	Kansas	18.5
25	New York	18.2
26	Oklahoma	17.5
27	Tennessee	17.3
28	North Carolina	16.6
29	Rhode Island	16.3
30	Mississippi	16.0
31	Delaware	15.9
31	Louisiana	15.9
33	South Carolina	15.1
34	Florida	13.4
NA	Arizona**	NA
NA	Arkansas**	NA
NA	California**	NA
NA	Connecticut**	NA
NA	Georgia**	NA
NA	Hawaii**	NA
NA	Iowa**	NA
NA	Minnesota**	NA
NA	Nebraska**	NA
NA	Nevada**	NA
NA	Ohio**	NA
NA	Oregon**	NA
NA	South Dakota**	NA
NA	Vermont**	NA
NA	Virginia**	NA
NA	Washington**	NA
	District of Columbia**	NA

Source: U.S. Department of Health and Human Services, Centers for Disease Control and Prevention
   "Youth Risk Behavior Surveillance--U.S., 2009" (http://www.cdc.gov/HealthyYouth/yrbs/)
*One or more times during the 12 months preceding the survey. National percent includes nonreporting states.
**Not available.

Percent of High School Students Who Carried a
Weapon on School Property in 2009
National Percent = 5.6%*

ALPHA ORDER

RANK	STATE	PERCENT
5	Alabama	8.7
9	Alaska	7.8
11	Arizona	6.5
6	Arkansas	8.4
NA	California**	NA
20	Colorado	5.5
38	Connecticut	3.9
24	Delaware	5.1
29	Florida	4.7
16	Georgia	6.0
29	Hawaii	4.7
10	Idaho	6.7
27	Illinois	4.8
18	Indiana	5.7
NA	Iowa**	NA
24	Kansas	5.1
11	Kentucky	6.5
17	Louisiana	5.8
NA	Maine**	NA
32	Maryland	4.6
36	Massachusetts	4.4
21	Michigan	5.4
NA	Minnesota**	NA
35	Mississippi	4.5
23	Missouri	5.3
8	Montana	7.9
NA	Nebraska**	NA
15	Nevada	6.2
4	New Hampshire	8.8
41	New Jersey	3.1
7	New Mexico	8.1
27	New York	4.8
29	North Carolina	4.7
21	North Dakota	5.4
NA	Ohio**	NA
19	Oklahoma	5.6
NA	Oregon**	NA
40	Pennsylvania	3.3
37	Rhode Island	4.0
32	South Carolina	4.6
2	South Dakota	9.2
24	Tennessee	5.1
14	Texas	6.4
32	Utah	4.6
3	Vermont	9.0
NA	Virginia**	NA
NA	Washington**	NA
11	West Virginia	6.5
39	Wisconsin	3.4
1	Wyoming	11.5

RANK ORDER

RANK	STATE	PERCENT
1	Wyoming	11.5
2	South Dakota	9.2
3	Vermont	9.0
4	New Hampshire	8.8
5	Alabama	8.7
6	Arkansas	8.4
7	New Mexico	8.1
8	Montana	7.9
9	Alaska	7.8
10	Idaho	6.7
11	Arizona	6.5
11	Kentucky	6.5
11	West Virginia	6.5
14	Texas	6.4
15	Nevada	6.2
16	Georgia	6.0
17	Louisiana	5.8
18	Indiana	5.7
19	Oklahoma	5.6
20	Colorado	5.5
21	Michigan	5.4
21	North Dakota	5.4
23	Missouri	5.3
24	Delaware	5.1
24	Kansas	5.1
24	Tennessee	5.1
27	Illinois	4.8
27	New York	4.8
29	Florida	4.7
29	Hawaii	4.7
29	North Carolina	4.7
32	Maryland	4.6
32	South Carolina	4.6
32	Utah	4.6
35	Mississippi	4.5
36	Massachusetts	4.4
37	Rhode Island	4.0
38	Connecticut	3.9
39	Wisconsin	3.4
40	Pennsylvania	3.3
41	New Jersey	3.1
NA	California**	NA
NA	Iowa**	NA
NA	Maine**	NA
NA	Minnesota**	NA
NA	Nebraska**	NA
NA	Ohio**	NA
NA	Oregon**	NA
NA	Virginia**	NA
NA	Washington**	NA
	District of Columbia**	NA

Source: U.S. Department of Health and Human Services, Centers for Disease Control and Prevention
   "Youth Risk Behavior Surveillance--U.S., 2009" (http://www.cdc.gov/HealthyYouth/yrbs/)
*Weapons include guns, knives, clubs, or other instrument. National percent includes nonreporting states.
**Not available.

Percent of High School Students Who Were Threatened or Injured with a Weapon on School Property in 2009
National Percent = 7.7%*

ALPHA ORDER

RANK	STATE	PERCENT
3	Alabama	10.4
25	Alaska	7.3
7	Arizona	9.3
1	Arkansas	11.9
NA	California**	NA
14	Colorado	8.0
27	Connecticut	7.0
18	Delaware	7.8
12	Florida	8.2
12	Georgia	8.2
20	Hawaii	7.7
16	Idaho	7.9
10	Illinois	8.8
34	Indiana	6.5
NA	Iowa**	NA
36	Kansas	6.2
16	Kentucky	7.9
4	Louisiana	9.5
20	Maine	7.7
9	Maryland	9.1
27	Massachusetts	7.0
5	Michigan	9.4
NA	Minnesota**	NA
14	Mississippi	8.0
18	Missouri	7.8
24	Montana	7.4
NA	Nebraska**	NA
2	Nevada	10.7
NA	New Hampshire**	NA
33	New Jersey	6.6
NA	New Mexico**	NA
23	New York	7.5
30	North Carolina	6.8
NA	North Dakota**	NA
NA	Ohio**	NA
38	Oklahoma	5.8
NA	Oregon**	NA
39	Pennsylvania	5.6
34	Rhode Island	6.5
10	South Carolina	8.8
30	South Dakota	6.8
27	Tennessee	7.0
26	Texas	7.2
20	Utah	7.7
37	Vermont	6.0
NA	Virginia**	NA
NA	Washington**	NA
8	West Virginia	9.2
32	Wisconsin	6.7
5	Wyoming	9.4

RANK ORDER

RANK	STATE	PERCENT
1	Arkansas	11.9
2	Nevada	10.7
3	Alabama	10.4
4	Louisiana	9.5
5	Michigan	9.4
5	Wyoming	9.4
7	Arizona	9.3
8	West Virginia	9.2
9	Maryland	9.1
10	Illinois	8.8
10	South Carolina	8.8
12	Florida	8.2
12	Georgia	8.2
14	Colorado	8.0
14	Mississippi	8.0
16	Idaho	7.9
16	Kentucky	7.9
18	Delaware	7.8
18	Missouri	7.8
20	Hawaii	7.7
20	Maine	7.7
20	Utah	7.7
23	New York	7.5
24	Montana	7.4
25	Alaska	7.3
26	Texas	7.2
27	Connecticut	7.0
27	Massachusetts	7.0
27	Tennessee	7.0
30	North Carolina	6.8
30	South Dakota	6.8
32	Wisconsin	6.7
33	New Jersey	6.6
34	Indiana	6.5
34	Rhode Island	6.5
36	Kansas	6.2
37	Vermont	6.0
38	Oklahoma	5.8
39	Pennsylvania	5.6
NA	California**	NA
NA	Iowa**	NA
NA	Minnesota**	NA
NA	Nebraska**	NA
NA	New Hampshire**	NA
NA	New Mexico**	NA
NA	North Dakota**	NA
NA	Ohio**	NA
NA	Oregon**	NA
NA	Virginia**	NA
NA	Washington**	NA
	District of Columbia**	NA

Source: U.S. Department of Health and Human Services, Centers for Disease Control and Prevention
   "Youth Risk Behavior Surveillance--U.S., 2009" (http://www.cdc.gov/HealthyYouth/yrbs/)
*One or more times during the 12 months preceding the survey. National percent includes nonreporting states.
**Not available.

Percent of High School Students Who Engaged in a
Physical Fight on School Property in 2009
National Percent = 11.1%*

ALPHA ORDER

RANK	STATE	PERCENT
5	Alabama	13.1
27	Alaska	9.8
10	Arizona	12.0
2	Arkansas	14.8
NA	California**	NA
20	Colorado	10.7
28	Connecticut	9.6
39	Delaware	8.6
22	Florida	10.5
11	Georgia	11.7
23	Hawaii	10.2
23	Idaho	10.2
12	Illinois	11.5
30	Indiana	9.5
NA	Iowa**	NA
36	Kansas	9.0
30	Kentucky	9.5
3	Louisiana	13.7
33	Maine	9.1
17	Maryland	11.2
38	Massachusetts	8.7
14	Michigan	11.3
NA	Minnesota**	NA
7	Mississippi	12.6
36	Missouri	9.0
19	Montana	10.8
NA	Nebraska**	NA
25	Nevada	10.0
33	New Hampshire	9.1
NA	New Jersey**	NA
1	New Mexico	15.0
13	New York	11.4
32	North Carolina	9.4
41	North Dakota	7.4
NA	Ohio**	NA
6	Oklahoma	12.8
NA	Oregon**	NA
26	Pennsylvania	9.9
33	Rhode Island	9.1
9	South Carolina	12.1
40	South Dakota	8.3
14	Tennessee	11.3
4	Texas	13.2
21	Utah	10.6
18	Vermont	11.0
NA	Virginia**	NA
NA	Washington**	NA
14	West Virginia	11.3
28	Wisconsin	9.6
7	Wyoming	12.6

RANK ORDER

RANK	STATE	PERCENT
1	New Mexico	15.0
2	Arkansas	14.8
3	Louisiana	13.7
4	Texas	13.2
5	Alabama	13.1
6	Oklahoma	12.8
7	Mississippi	12.6
7	Wyoming	12.6
9	South Carolina	12.1
10	Arizona	12.0
11	Georgia	11.7
12	Illinois	11.5
13	New York	11.4
14	Michigan	11.3
14	Tennessee	11.3
14	West Virginia	11.3
17	Maryland	11.2
18	Vermont	11.0
19	Montana	10.8
20	Colorado	10.7
21	Utah	10.6
22	Florida	10.5
23	Hawaii	10.2
23	Idaho	10.2
25	Nevada	10.0
26	Pennsylvania	9.9
27	Alaska	9.8
28	Connecticut	9.6
28	Wisconsin	9.6
30	Indiana	9.5
30	Kentucky	9.5
32	North Carolina	9.4
33	Maine	9.1
33	New Hampshire	9.1
33	Rhode Island	9.1
36	Kansas	9.0
36	Missouri	9.0
38	Massachusetts	8.7
39	Delaware	8.6
40	South Dakota	8.3
41	North Dakota	7.4
NA	California**	NA
NA	Iowa**	NA
NA	Minnesota**	NA
NA	Nebraska**	NA
NA	New Jersey**	NA
NA	Ohio**	NA
NA	Oregon**	NA
NA	Virginia**	NA
NA	Washington**	NA
	District of Columbia**	NA

Source: U.S. Department of Health and Human Services, Centers for Disease Control and Prevention
  "Youth Risk Behavior Surveillance--U.S., 2009" (http://www.cdc.gov/HealthyYouth/yrbs/)
*One or more times during the 12 months preceding the survey. National percent includes nonreporting states.
**Not available.

Percent of High School Students Who Smoked Cigarettes in 2009

National Percent = 19.5%*

ALPHA ORDER

RANK ORDER

RANK	STATE	PERCENT	RANK	STATE	PERCENT
11	Alabama	20.8	1	Kentucky	26.1
36	Alaska	15.7	2	New Mexico	24.0
15	Arizona	19.7	3	Indiana	23.5
14	Arkansas	20.3	4	South Dakota	23.2
NA	California**	NA	5	Oklahoma	22.6
25	Colorado	17.7	6	North Dakota	22.4
24	Connecticut	17.8	7	Wyoming	22.1
17	Delaware	19.0	8	West Virginia	21.8
34	Florida	16.1	9	Texas	21.2
31	Georgia	16.9	10	Tennessee	20.9
37	Hawaii	15.2	11	Alabama	20.8
39	Idaho	14.5	11	New Hampshire	20.8
22	Illinois	18.1	13	South Carolina	20.5
3	Indiana	23.5	14	Arkansas	20.3
NA	Iowa**	NA	15	Arizona	19.7
31	Kansas	16.9	16	Mississippi	19.6
1	Kentucky	26.1	17	Delaware	19.0
27	Louisiana	17.6	18	Missouri	18.9
22	Maine	18.1	19	Michigan	18.8
41	Maryland	11.9	20	Montana	18.7
35	Massachusetts	16.0	21	Pennsylvania	18.4
19	Michigan	18.8	22	Illinois	18.1
NA	Minnesota**	NA	22	Maine	18.1
16	Mississippi	19.6	24	Connecticut	17.8
18	Missouri	18.9	25	Colorado	17.7
20	Montana	18.7	25	North Carolina	17.7
NA	Nebraska**	NA	27	Louisiana	17.6
29	Nevada	17.0	27	Vermont	17.6
11	New Hampshire	20.8	29	Nevada	17.0
29	New Jersey	17.0	29	New Jersey	17.0
2	New Mexico	24.0	31	Georgia	16.9
38	New York	14.8	31	Kansas	16.9
25	North Carolina	17.7	31	Wisconsin	16.9
6	North Dakota	22.4	34	Florida	16.1
NA	Ohio**	NA	35	Massachusetts	16.0
5	Oklahoma	22.6	36	Alaska	15.7
NA	Oregon**	NA	37	Hawaii	15.2
21	Pennsylvania	18.4	38	New York	14.8
40	Rhode Island	13.3	39	Idaho	14.5
13	South Carolina	20.5	40	Rhode Island	13.3
4	South Dakota	23.2	41	Maryland	11.9
10	Tennessee	20.9	42	Utah	8.5
9	Texas	21.2	NA	California**	NA
42	Utah	8.5	NA	Iowa**	NA
27	Vermont	17.6	NA	Minnesota**	NA
NA	Virginia**	NA	NA	Nebraska**	NA
NA	Washington**	NA	NA	Ohio**	NA
8	West Virginia	21.8	NA	Oregon**	NA
31	Wisconsin	16.9	NA	Virginia**	NA
7	Wyoming	22.1	NA	Washington**	NA
				District of Columbia**	NA

Source: U.S. Department of Health and Human Services, Centers for Disease Control and Prevention
  "Youth Risk Behavior Surveillance--U.S., 2009" (http://www.cdc.gov/HealthyYouth/yrbs/)

*Smoked cigarettes on one or more of the 30 days preceding the survey. National percent includes nonreporting states.
**Not available.

Percent of High School Students Who Smoked Cigarettes on School Property in 2009
National Percent = 5.1%*

ALPHA ORDER

RANK	STATE	PERCENT
11	Alabama	6.0
27	Alaska	4.5
23	Arizona	4.7
19	Arkansas	5.3
NA	California**	NA
3	Colorado	8.3
NA	Connecticut**	NA
6	Delaware	6.9
19	Florida	5.3
23	Georgia	4.7
NA	Hawaii**	NA
32	Idaho	3.4
14	Illinois	5.8
5	Indiana	7.5
NA	Iowa**	NA
28	Kansas	4.3
1	Kentucky	9.4
32	Louisiana	3.4
NA	Maine**	NA
31	Maryland	3.7
7	Massachusetts	6.7
13	Michigan	5.9
NA	Minnesota**	NA
29	Mississippi	4.2
26	Missouri	4.6
17	Montana	5.4
NA	Nebraska**	NA
15	Nevada	5.6
NA	New Hampshire**	NA
NA	New Jersey**	NA
2	New Mexico	8.7
8	New York	6.5
NA	North Carolina**	NA
NA	North Dakota**	NA
NA	Ohio**	NA
21	Oklahoma	5.2
NA	Oregon**	NA
29	Pennsylvania	4.2
17	Rhode Island	5.4
9	South Carolina	6.2
9	South Dakota	6.2
11	Tennessee	6.0
23	Texas	4.7
34	Utah	2.4
NA	Vermont**	NA
NA	Virginia**	NA
NA	Washington**	NA
16	West Virginia	5.5
22	Wisconsin	4.8
4	Wyoming	8.2

RANK ORDER

RANK	STATE	PERCENT
1	Kentucky	9.4
2	New Mexico	8.7
3	Colorado	8.3
4	Wyoming	8.2
5	Indiana	7.5
6	Delaware	6.9
7	Massachusetts	6.7
8	New York	6.5
9	South Carolina	6.2
9	South Dakota	6.2
11	Alabama	6.0
11	Tennessee	6.0
13	Michigan	5.9
14	Illinois	5.8
15	Nevada	5.6
16	West Virginia	5.5
17	Montana	5.4
17	Rhode Island	5.4
19	Arkansas	5.3
19	Florida	5.3
21	Oklahoma	5.2
22	Wisconsin	4.8
23	Arizona	4.7
23	Georgia	4.7
23	Texas	4.7
26	Missouri	4.6
27	Alaska	4.5
28	Kansas	4.3
29	Mississippi	4.2
29	Pennsylvania	4.2
31	Maryland	3.7
32	Idaho	3.4
32	Louisiana	3.4
34	Utah	2.4
NA	California**	NA
NA	Connecticut**	NA
NA	Hawaii**	NA
NA	Iowa**	NA
NA	Maine**	NA
NA	Minnesota**	NA
NA	Nebraska**	NA
NA	New Hampshire**	NA
NA	New Jersey**	NA
NA	North Carolina**	NA
NA	North Dakota**	NA
NA	Ohio**	NA
NA	Oregon**	NA
NA	Vermont**	NA
NA	Virginia**	NA
NA	Washington**	NA
	District of Columbia**	NA

Source: U.S. Department of Health and Human Services, Centers for Disease Control and Prevention
    "Youth Risk Behavior Surveillance--U.S., 2009" (http://www.cdc.gov/HealthyYouth/yrbs/)
*Smoked cigarettes on one or more of the 30 days preceding the survey on school property. National percent includes nonreporting states.
**Not available.

Percent of High School Students Who Used Smokeless Tobacco on School Property in 2009
National Percent = 5.5%*

ALPHA ORDER

RANK	STATE	PERCENT
8	Alabama	7.4
9	Alaska	6.7
24	Arizona	3.3
6	Arkansas	7.8
NA	California**	NA
11	Colorado	5.9
NA	Connecticut**	NA
20	Delaware	4.2
NA	Florida**	NA
17	Georgia	5.0
NA	Hawaii**	NA
13	Idaho	5.5
19	Illinois	4.7
17	Indiana	5.0
NA	Iowa**	NA
21	Kansas	4.0
2	Kentucky	9.3
12	Louisiana	5.6
NA	Maine**	NA
27	Maryland	2.8
NA	Massachusetts**	NA
NA	Michigan**	NA
NA	Minnesota**	NA
15	Mississippi	5.3
13	Missouri	5.5
4	Montana	8.8
NA	Nebraska**	NA
25	Nevada	3.2
NA	New Hampshire**	NA
NA	New Jersey**	NA
NA	New Mexico**	NA
NA	New York**	NA
NA	North Carolina**	NA
NA	North Dakota**	NA
NA	Ohio**	NA
16	Oklahoma	5.1
NA	Oregon**	NA
21	Pennsylvania	4.0
NA	Rhode Island**	NA
9	South Carolina	6.7
5	South Dakota	8.0
7	Tennessee	7.5
23	Texas	3.8
26	Utah	3.0
NA	Vermont**	NA
NA	Virginia**	NA
NA	Washington**	NA
2	West Virginia	9.3
NA	Wisconsin**	NA
1	Wyoming	10.3

RANK ORDER

RANK	STATE	PERCENT
1	Wyoming	10.3
2	Kentucky	9.3
2	West Virginia	9.3
4	Montana	8.8
5	South Dakota	8.0
6	Arkansas	7.8
7	Tennessee	7.5
8	Alabama	7.4
9	Alaska	6.7
9	South Carolina	6.7
11	Colorado	5.9
12	Louisiana	5.6
13	Idaho	5.5
13	Missouri	5.5
15	Mississippi	5.3
16	Oklahoma	5.1
17	Georgia	5.0
17	Indiana	5.0
19	Illinois	4.7
20	Delaware	4.2
21	Kansas	4.0
21	Pennsylvania	4.0
23	Texas	3.8
24	Arizona	3.3
25	Nevada	3.2
26	Utah	3.0
27	Maryland	2.8
NA	California**	NA
NA	Connecticut**	NA
NA	Florida**	NA
NA	Hawaii**	NA
NA	Iowa**	NA
NA	Maine**	NA
NA	Massachusetts**	NA
NA	Michigan**	NA
NA	Minnesota**	NA
NA	Nebraska**	NA
NA	New Hampshire**	NA
NA	New Jersey**	NA
NA	New Mexico**	NA
NA	New York**	NA
NA	North Carolina**	NA
NA	North Dakota**	NA
NA	Ohio**	NA
NA	Oregon**	NA
NA	Rhode Island**	NA
NA	Vermont**	NA
NA	Virginia**	NA
NA	Washington**	NA
NA	Wisconsin**	NA
	District of Columbia**	NA

Source: U.S. Department of Health and Human Services, Centers for Disease Control and Prevention
   "Youth Risk Behavior Surveillance--U.S., 2009" (http://www.cdc.gov/HealthyYouth/yrbs/)
*Used chewing tobacco, snuff, or dip on one or more of the 30 days preceding the survey on school property. National percent includes nonreporting states.
**Not available.

Percent of High School Students Who Drank Alcohol in 2009

National Percent = 41.8%*

ALPHA ORDER				RANK ORDER		
RANK	STATE	PERCENT		RANK	STATE	PERCENT
20	Alabama	39.5		1	Louisiana	47.5
40	Alaska	33.2		2	New Jersey	45.2
4	Arizona	44.5		3	Texas	44.8
19	Arkansas	39.7		4	Arizona	44.5
NA	California**	NA		5	Delaware	43.7
13	Colorado	40.8		6	Massachusetts	43.6
7	Connecticut	43.5		7	Connecticut	43.5
5	Delaware	43.7		8	North Dakota	43.3
14	Florida	40.5		9	Montana	42.8
36	Georgia	34.3		10	Wyoming	41.7
30	Hawaii	37.8		11	New York	41.4
37	Idaho	34.2		12	Wisconsin	41.3
18	Illinois	39.8		13	Colorado	40.8
28	Indiana	38.5		14	Florida	40.5
NA	Iowa**	NA		14	New Mexico	40.5
26	Kansas	38.7		16	West Virginia	40.4
30	Kentucky	37.8		17	South Dakota	40.1
1	Louisiana	47.5		18	Illinois	39.8
41	Maine	32.2		19	Arkansas	39.7
32	Maryland	37.0		20	Alabama	39.5
6	Massachusetts	43.6		21	Missouri	39.3
32	Michigan	37.0		21	New Hampshire	39.3
NA	Minnesota**	NA		23	Mississippi	39.2
23	Mississippi	39.2		24	Oklahoma	39.0
21	Missouri	39.3		24	Vermont	39.0
9	Montana	42.8		26	Kansas	38.7
NA	Nebraska**	NA		27	Nevada	38.6
27	Nevada	38.6		28	Indiana	38.5
21	New Hampshire	39.3		29	Pennsylvania	38.4
2	New Jersey	45.2		30	Hawaii	37.8
14	New Mexico	40.5		30	Kentucky	37.8
11	New York	41.4		32	Maryland	37.0
35	North Carolina	35.0		32	Michigan	37.0
8	North Dakota	43.3		34	South Carolina	35.2
NA	Ohio**	NA		35	North Carolina	35.0
24	Oklahoma	39.0		36	Georgia	34.3
NA	Oregon**	NA		37	Idaho	34.2
29	Pennsylvania	38.4		38	Rhode Island	34.0
38	Rhode Island	34.0		39	Tennessee	33.5
34	South Carolina	35.2		40	Alaska	33.2
17	South Dakota	40.1		41	Maine	32.2
39	Tennessee	33.5		42	Utah	18.2
3	Texas	44.8		NA	California**	NA
42	Utah	18.2		NA	Iowa**	NA
24	Vermont	39.0		NA	Minnesota**	NA
NA	Virginia**	NA		NA	Nebraska**	NA
NA	Washington**	NA		NA	Ohio**	NA
16	West Virginia	40.4		NA	Oregon**	NA
12	Wisconsin	41.3		NA	Virginia**	NA
10	Wyoming	41.7		NA	Washington**	NA
				District of Columbia**		NA

Source: U.S. Department of Health and Human Services, Centers for Disease Control and Prevention
    "Youth Risk Behavior Surveillance--U.S., 2009" (http://www.cdc.gov/HealthyYouth/yrbs/)
*Drank alcohol on one or more of the 30 days preceding the survey. National percent includes nonreporting states.
**Not available.

Percent of High School Students Who Drank Alcohol on School Property in 2009

National Percent = 4.5%*

ALPHA ORDER

RANK ORDER

RANK	STATE	PERCENT		RANK	STATE	PERCENT
8	Alabama	5.4		1	New Mexico	8.0
34	Alaska	3.0		2	Hawaii	7.9
5	Arizona	5.9		3	Wyoming	6.4
4	Arkansas	6.1		4	Arkansas	6.1
NA	California**	NA		5	Arizona	5.9
22	Colorado	4.1		6	West Virginia	5.7
11	Connecticut	5.0		7	Louisiana	5.6
11	Delaware	5.0		8	Alabama	5.4
13	Florida	4.9		9	Kentucky	5.2
20	Georgia	4.2		10	Montana	5.1
2	Hawaii	7.9		11	Connecticut	5.0
29	Idaho	3.5		11	Delaware	5.0
16	Illinois	4.4		13	Florida	4.9
29	Indiana	3.5		14	Maryland	4.8
NA	Iowa**	NA		15	Texas	4.7
32	Kansas	3.2		16	Illinois	4.4
9	Kentucky	5.2		16	Nevada	4.4
7	Louisiana	5.6		18	Mississippi	4.3
24	Maine	4.0		18	New Hampshire	4.3
14	Maryland	4.8		20	Georgia	4.2
26	Massachusetts	3.8		20	North Dakota	4.2
27	Michigan	3.7		22	Colorado	4.1
NA	Minnesota**	NA		22	North Carolina	4.1
18	Mississippi	4.3		24	Maine	4.0
34	Missouri	3.0		25	Oklahoma	3.9
10	Montana	5.1		26	Massachusetts	3.8
NA	Nebraska**	NA		27	Michigan	3.7
16	Nevada	4.4		28	South Carolina	3.6
18	New Hampshire	4.3		29	Idaho	3.5
NA	New Jersey**	NA		29	Indiana	3.5
1	New Mexico	8.0		31	Vermont	3.3
NA	New York**	NA		32	Kansas	3.2
22	North Carolina	4.1		32	Rhode Island	3.2
20	North Dakota	4.2		34	Alaska	3.0
NA	Ohio**	NA		34	Missouri	3.0
25	Oklahoma	3.9		34	Tennessee	3.0
NA	Oregon**	NA		37	Pennsylvania	2.8
37	Pennsylvania	2.8		38	Utah	2.7
32	Rhode Island	3.2		NA	California**	NA
28	South Carolina	3.6		NA	Iowa**	NA
NA	South Dakota**	NA		NA	Minnesota**	NA
34	Tennessee	3.0		NA	Nebraska**	NA
15	Texas	4.7		NA	New Jersey**	NA
38	Utah	2.7		NA	New York**	NA
31	Vermont	3.3		NA	Ohio**	NA
NA	Virginia**	NA		NA	Oregon**	NA
NA	Washington**	NA		NA	South Dakota**	NA
6	West Virginia	5.7		NA	Virginia**	NA
NA	Wisconsin**	NA		NA	Washington**	NA
3	Wyoming	6.4		NA	Wisconsin**	NA
					District of Columbia**	NA

Source: U.S. Department of Health and Human Services, Centers for Disease Control and Prevention
   "Youth Risk Behavior Surveillance--U.S., 2009" (http://www.cdc.gov/HealthyYouth/yrbs/)
*Drank alcohol on one or more of the 30 days preceding the survey on school property. National percent includes nonreporting states.
**Not available.

Percent of High School Students Who Used Marijuana in 2009

National Percent = 20.8%*

ALPHA ORDER

RANK	STATE	PERCENT
37	Alabama	16.2
10	Alaska	22.7
8	Arizona	23.7
31	Arkansas	17.8
NA	California**	NA
6	Colorado	24.8
13	Connecticut	21.8
4	Delaware	25.8
14	Florida	21.4
30	Georgia	18.3
11	Hawaii	22.1
41	Idaho	13.7
15	Illinois	21.0
16	Indiana	20.9
NA	Iowa**	NA
40	Kansas	14.7
38	Kentucky	16.1
36	Louisiana	16.3
20	Maine	20.5
12	Maryland	21.9
2	Massachusetts	27.1
18	Michigan	20.7
NA	Minnesota**	NA
32	Mississippi	17.7
19	Missouri	20.6
9	Montana	23.1
NA	Nebraska**	NA
25	Nevada	20.0
5	New Hampshire	25.6
22	New Jersey	20.3
1	New Mexico	28.0
16	New York	20.9
26	North Carolina	19.8
34	North Dakota	16.9
NA	Ohio**	NA
33	Oklahoma	17.2
NA	Oregon**	NA
28	Pennsylvania	19.3
3	Rhode Island	26.3
21	South Carolina	20.4
39	South Dakota	15.2
24	Tennessee	20.1
27	Texas	19.5
42	Utah	10.0
7	Vermont	24.6
NA	Virginia**	NA
NA	Washington**	NA
22	West Virginia	20.3
29	Wisconsin	18.9
34	Wyoming	16.9

RANK ORDER

RANK	STATE	PERCENT
1	New Mexico	28.0
2	Massachusetts	27.1
3	Rhode Island	26.3
4	Delaware	25.8
5	New Hampshire	25.6
6	Colorado	24.8
7	Vermont	24.6
8	Arizona	23.7
9	Montana	23.1
10	Alaska	22.7
11	Hawaii	22.1
12	Maryland	21.9
13	Connecticut	21.8
14	Florida	21.4
15	Illinois	21.0
16	Indiana	20.9
16	New York	20.9
18	Michigan	20.7
19	Missouri	20.6
20	Maine	20.5
21	South Carolina	20.4
22	New Jersey	20.3
22	West Virginia	20.3
24	Tennessee	20.1
25	Nevada	20.0
26	North Carolina	19.8
27	Texas	19.5
28	Pennsylvania	19.3
29	Wisconsin	18.9
30	Georgia	18.3
31	Arkansas	17.8
32	Mississippi	17.7
33	Oklahoma	17.2
34	North Dakota	16.9
34	Wyoming	16.9
36	Louisiana	16.3
37	Alabama	16.2
38	Kentucky	16.1
39	South Dakota	15.2
40	Kansas	14.7
41	Idaho	13.7
42	Utah	10.0
NA	California**	NA
NA	Iowa**	NA
NA	Minnesota**	NA
NA	Nebraska**	NA
NA	Ohio**	NA
NA	Oregon**	NA
NA	Virginia**	NA
NA	Washington**	NA
	District of Columbia**	NA

Source: U.S. Department of Health and Human Services, Centers for Disease Control and Prevention
"Youth Risk Behavior Surveillance--U.S., 2009" (http://www.cdc.gov/HealthyYouth/yrbs/)
*Used marijuana one or more times in the 30 days preceding the survey. National percent includes nonreporting states.
**Not available.

Percent of High School Students Who Used
Marijuana on School Property in 2009
National Percent = 4.6%*

ALPHA ORDER

RANK	STATE	PERCENT
19	Alabama	4.6
8	Alaska	5.9
4	Arizona	6.4
21	Arkansas	4.5
NA	California**	NA
7	Colorado	6.1
6	Connecticut	6.2
11	Delaware	5.6
13	Florida	5.2
30	Georgia	3.4
2	Hawaii	8.3
33	Idaho	3.0
15	Illinois	5.0
22	Indiana	4.4
NA	Iowa**	NA
36	Kansas	2.7
32	Kentucky	3.1
28	Louisiana	3.6
NA	Maine**	NA
15	Maryland	5.0
8	Massachusetts	5.9
18	Michigan	4.8
NA	Minnesota**	NA
37	Mississippi	2.5
30	Missouri	3.4
10	Montana	5.8
NA	Nebraska**	NA
17	Nevada	4.9
3	New Hampshire	6.8
NA	New Jersey**	NA
1	New Mexico	9.7
NA	New York**	NA
23	North Carolina	4.0
25	North Dakota	3.8
NA	Ohio**	NA
34	Oklahoma	2.9
NA	Oregon**	NA
29	Pennsylvania	3.5
14	Rhode Island	5.1
27	South Carolina	3.7
34	South Dakota	2.9
25	Tennessee	3.8
19	Texas	4.6
37	Utah	2.5
5	Vermont	6.3
NA	Virginia**	NA
NA	Washington**	NA
24	West Virginia	3.9
NA	Wisconsin**	NA
12	Wyoming	5.3

RANK ORDER

RANK	STATE	PERCENT
1	New Mexico	9.7
2	Hawaii	8.3
3	New Hampshire	6.8
4	Arizona	6.4
5	Vermont	6.3
6	Connecticut	6.2
7	Colorado	6.1
8	Alaska	5.9
8	Massachusetts	5.9
10	Montana	5.8
11	Delaware	5.6
12	Wyoming	5.3
13	Florida	5.2
14	Rhode Island	5.1
15	Illinois	5.0
15	Maryland	5.0
17	Nevada	4.9
18	Michigan	4.8
19	Alabama	4.6
19	Texas	4.6
21	Arkansas	4.5
22	Indiana	4.4
23	North Carolina	4.0
24	West Virginia	3.9
25	North Dakota	3.8
25	Tennessee	3.8
27	South Carolina	3.7
28	Louisiana	3.6
29	Pennsylvania	3.5
30	Georgia	3.4
30	Missouri	3.4
32	Kentucky	3.1
33	Idaho	3.0
34	Oklahoma	2.9
34	South Dakota	2.9
36	Kansas	2.7
37	Mississippi	2.5
37	Utah	2.5
NA	California**	NA
NA	Iowa**	NA
NA	Maine**	NA
NA	Minnesota**	NA
NA	Nebraska**	NA
NA	New Jersey**	NA
NA	New York**	NA
NA	Ohio**	NA
NA	Oregon**	NA
NA	Virginia**	NA
NA	Washington**	NA
NA	Wisconsin**	NA
	District of Columbia**	NA

Source: U.S. Department of Health and Human Services, Centers for Disease Control and Prevention
   "Youth Risk Behavior Surveillance--U.S., 2009" (http://www.cdc.gov/HealthyYouth/yrbs/)
*Used marijuana one or more times in the 30 days preceding the survey on school property. National percent includes nonreporting states.
**Not available.

Percent of High School Students Who Were Offered, Sold, or Given an Illegal Drug on School Property in 2009
National Percent = 22.7%*

ALPHA ORDER

RANK	STATE	PERCENT
13	Alabama	27.6
21	Alaska	24.8
3	Arizona	34.6
6	Arkansas	31.4
NA	California**	NA
25	Colorado	22.7
11	Connecticut	28.9
31	Delaware	20.9
28	Florida	21.8
4	Georgia	32.9
1	Hawaii	36.1
25	Idaho	22.7
15	Illinois	27.5
19	Indiana	25.5
NA	Iowa**	NA
42	Kansas	15.1
18	Kentucky	25.6
24	Louisiana	22.8
29	Maine	21.2
10	Maryland	29.3
16	Massachusetts	26.1
9	Michigan	29.5
NA	Minnesota**	NA
37	Mississippi	18.0
39	Missouri	17.3
32	Montana	20.7
NA	Nebraska**	NA
2	Nevada	35.6
27	New Hampshire	22.1
5	New Jersey	32.2
7	New Mexico	30.9
22	New York	24.0
8	North Carolina	30.2
35	North Dakota	19.5
NA	Ohio**	NA
40	Oklahoma	16.8
NA	Oregon**	NA
41	Pennsylvania	16.1
20	Rhode Island	25.2
13	South Carolina	27.6
38	South Dakota	17.7
36	Tennessee	18.8
17	Texas	25.9
34	Utah	19.7
30	Vermont	21.1
NA	Virginia**	NA
NA	Washington**	NA
12	West Virginia	28.0
33	Wisconsin	20.5
23	Wyoming	23.7

RANK ORDER

RANK	STATE	PERCENT
1	Hawaii	36.1
2	Nevada	35.6
3	Arizona	34.6
4	Georgia	32.9
5	New Jersey	32.2
6	Arkansas	31.4
7	New Mexico	30.9
8	North Carolina	30.2
9	Michigan	29.5
10	Maryland	29.3
11	Connecticut	28.9
12	West Virginia	28.0
13	Alabama	27.6
13	South Carolina	27.6
15	Illinois	27.5
16	Massachusetts	26.1
17	Texas	25.9
18	Kentucky	25.6
19	Indiana	25.5
20	Rhode Island	25.2
21	Alaska	24.8
22	New York	24.0
23	Wyoming	23.7
24	Louisiana	22.8
25	Colorado	22.7
25	Idaho	22.7
27	New Hampshire	22.1
28	Florida	21.8
29	Maine	21.2
30	Vermont	21.1
31	Delaware	20.9
32	Montana	20.7
33	Wisconsin	20.5
34	Utah	19.7
35	North Dakota	19.5
36	Tennessee	18.8
37	Mississippi	18.0
38	South Dakota	17.7
39	Missouri	17.3
40	Oklahoma	16.8
41	Pennsylvania	16.1
42	Kansas	15.1
NA	California**	NA
NA	Iowa**	NA
NA	Minnesota**	NA
NA	Nebraska**	NA
NA	Ohio**	NA
NA	Oregon**	NA
NA	Virginia**	NA
NA	Washington**	NA
	District of Columbia**	NA

Source: U.S. Department of Health and Human Services, Centers for Disease Control and Prevention
"Youth Risk Behavior Surveillance--U.S., 2009" (http://www.cdc.gov/HealthyYouth/yrbs/)
*One or more times during the 12 months preceding the survey. National percent includes nonreporting states.
**Not available.

Percent of High School Students Who Have Ever Had Sexual Intercourse as of 2009
National Percent = 46.0%*

ALPHA ORDER

RANK	STATE	PERCENT
3	Alabama	56.6
31	Alaska	43.5
16	Arizona	48.6
5	Arkansas	53.6
NA	California**	NA
35	Colorado	40.0
34	Connecticut	40.5
2	Delaware	57.5
11	Florida	50.6
NA	Georgia**	NA
29	Hawaii	44.3
36	Idaho	39.0
19	Illinois	48.1
13	Indiana	49.2
NA	Iowa**	NA
22	Kansas	46.6
17	Kentucky	48.3
NA	Louisiana**	NA
26	Maine	46.0
NA	Maryland**	NA
23	Massachusetts	46.4
27	Michigan	45.6
NA	Minnesota**	NA
1	Mississippi	61.0
15	Missouri	48.7
20	Montana	47.6
NA	Nebraska**	NA
14	Nevada	49.0
24	New Hampshire	46.3
24	New Jersey	46.3
NA	New Mexico**	NA
32	New York	42.0
9	North Carolina	51.1
28	North Dakota	44.6
NA	Ohio**	NA
9	Oklahoma	51.1
NA	Oregon**	NA
17	Pennsylvania	48.3
30	Rhode Island	44.2
6	South Carolina	53.4
21	South Dakota	47.0
6	Tennessee	53.4
8	Texas	51.6
NA	Utah**	NA
NA	Vermont**	NA
NA	Virginia**	NA
NA	Washington**	NA
4	West Virginia	54.1
33	Wisconsin	40.9
11	Wyoming	50.6

RANK ORDER

RANK	STATE	PERCENT
1	Mississippi	61.0
2	Delaware	57.5
3	Alabama	56.6
4	West Virginia	54.1
5	Arkansas	53.6
6	South Carolina	53.4
6	Tennessee	53.4
8	Texas	51.6
9	North Carolina	51.1
9	Oklahoma	51.1
11	Florida	50.6
11	Wyoming	50.6
13	Indiana	49.2
14	Nevada	49.0
15	Missouri	48.7
16	Arizona	48.6
17	Kentucky	48.3
17	Pennsylvania	48.3
19	Illinois	48.1
20	Montana	47.6
21	South Dakota	47.0
22	Kansas	46.6
23	Massachusetts	46.4
24	New Hampshire	46.3
24	New Jersey	46.3
26	Maine	46.0
27	Michigan	45.6
28	North Dakota	44.6
29	Hawaii	44.3
30	Rhode Island	44.2
31	Alaska	43.5
32	New York	42.0
33	Wisconsin	40.9
34	Connecticut	40.5
35	Colorado	40.0
36	Idaho	39.0
NA	California**	NA
NA	Georgia**	NA
NA	Iowa**	NA
NA	Louisiana**	NA
NA	Maryland**	NA
NA	Minnesota**	NA
NA	Nebraska**	NA
NA	New Mexico**	NA
NA	Ohio**	NA
NA	Oregon**	NA
NA	Utah**	NA
NA	Vermont**	NA
NA	Virginia**	NA
NA	Washington**	NA
	District of Columbia**	NA

Source: U.S. Department of Health and Human Services, Centers for Disease Control and Prevention
   "Youth Risk Behavior Surveillance--U.S., 2009" (http://www.cdc.gov/HealthyYouth/yrbs/)
*Have had sexual intercourse at least once during their life. National percent includes nonreporting states.
**Not available.

Percent of High School Students Who Were Sexually Active in 2009

National Percent = 34.2%*

ALPHA ORDER

RANK ORDER

RANK	STATE	PERCENT	RANK	STATE	PERCENT
3	Alabama	41.5	1	Mississippi	44.9
33	Alaska	30.4	2	Delaware	42.9
21	Arizona	34.5	3	Alabama	41.5
6	Arkansas	38.9	4	West Virginia	40.3
NA	California**	NA	5	Oklahoma	39.8
36	Colorado	27.4	6	Arkansas	38.9
34	Connecticut	29.6	7	Tennessee	38.8
2	Delaware	42.9	8	South Carolina	38.6
11	Florida	37.0	9	Wyoming	37.8
NA	Georgia**	NA	10	Texas	37.7
32	Hawaii	30.5	11	Florida	37.0
NA	Idaho**	NA	12	Pennsylvania	36.9
17	Illinois	36.2	13	Indiana	36.7
13	Indiana	36.7	14	North Carolina	36.6
NA	Iowa**	NA	15	New Hampshire	36.3
22	Kansas	34.2	15	South Dakota	36.3
24	Kentucky	33.6	17	Illinois	36.2
NA	Louisiana**	NA	18	Missouri	35.5
19	Maine	35.3	19	Maine	35.3
NA	Maryland**	NA	20	Massachusetts	34.6
20	Massachusetts	34.6	21	Arizona	34.5
23	Michigan	34.1	22	Kansas	34.2
NA	Minnesota**	NA	23	Michigan	34.1
1	Mississippi	44.9	24	Kentucky	33.6
18	Missouri	35.5	24	New Jersey	33.6
30	Montana	32.2	26	North Dakota	33.3
NA	Nebraska**	NA	27	Nevada	32.7
27	Nevada	32.7	28	New Mexico	32.6
15	New Hampshire	36.3	29	Rhode Island	32.3
24	New Jersey	33.6	30	Montana	32.2
28	New Mexico	32.6	31	New York	31.5
31	New York	31.5	32	Hawaii	30.5
14	North Carolina	36.6	33	Alaska	30.4
26	North Dakota	33.3	34	Connecticut	29.6
NA	Ohio**	NA	35	Wisconsin	29.3
5	Oklahoma	39.8	36	Colorado	27.4
NA	Oregon**	NA	NA	California**	NA
12	Pennsylvania	36.9	NA	Georgia**	NA
29	Rhode Island	32.3	NA	Idaho**	NA
8	South Carolina	38.6	NA	Iowa**	NA
15	South Dakota	36.3	NA	Louisiana**	NA
7	Tennessee	38.8	NA	Maryland**	NA
10	Texas	37.7	NA	Minnesota**	NA
NA	Utah**	NA	NA	Nebraska**	NA
NA	Vermont**	NA	NA	Ohio**	NA
NA	Virginia**	NA	NA	Oregon**	NA
NA	Washington**	NA	NA	Utah**	NA
4	West Virginia	40.3	NA	Vermont**	NA
35	Wisconsin	29.3	NA	Virginia**	NA
9	Wyoming	37.8	NA	Washington**	NA
				District of Columbia**	NA

Source: U.S. Department of Health and Human Services, Centers for Disease Control and Prevention
"Youth Risk Behavior Surveillance--U.S., 2009" (http://www.cdc.gov/HealthyYouth/yrbs/)
*Sexual intercourse during the 3 months preceding the survey. National percent includes nonreporting states.
**Not available.

Percent of Sexually Active High School Students Who Used Condoms in 2009

National Percent = 61.1%*

ALPHA ORDER

RANK	STATE	PERCENT
27	Alabama	58.5
11	Alaska	62.2
23	Arizona	59.7
26	Arkansas	58.7
NA	California**	NA
8	Colorado	63.2
25	Connecticut	59.4
12	Delaware	62.0
5	Florida	65.1
NA	Georgia**	NA
35	Hawaii	47.7
NA	Idaho**	NA
8	Illinois	63.2
28	Indiana	58.0
NA	Iowa**	NA
19	Kansas	60.1
21	Kentucky	59.9
NA	Louisiana**	NA
18	Maine	60.5
NA	Maryland**	NA
30	Massachusetts	57.5
15	Michigan	61.4
NA	Minnesota**	NA
3	Mississippi	65.7
22	Missouri	59.8
2	Montana	67.5
NA	Nebraska**	NA
10	Nevada	62.9
32	New Hampshire	56.8
4	New Jersey	65.5
30	New Mexico	57.5
1	New York	67.6
17	North Carolina	60.7
NA	North Dakota**	NA
NA	Ohio**	NA
33	Oklahoma	56.7
NA	Oregon**	NA
6	Pennsylvania	64.8
16	Rhode Island	61.2
20	South Carolina	60.0
14	South Dakota	61.6
24	Tennessee	59.5
29	Texas	57.7
NA	Utah**	NA
NA	Vermont**	NA
NA	Virginia**	NA
NA	Washington**	NA
34	West Virginia	54.4
7	Wisconsin	63.7
13	Wyoming	61.7

RANK ORDER

RANK	STATE	PERCENT
1	New York	67.6
2	Montana	67.5
3	Mississippi	65.7
4	New Jersey	65.5
5	Florida	65.1
6	Pennsylvania	64.8
7	Wisconsin	63.7
8	Colorado	63.2
8	Illinois	63.2
10	Nevada	62.9
11	Alaska	62.2
12	Delaware	62.0
13	Wyoming	61.7
14	South Dakota	61.6
15	Michigan	61.4
16	Rhode Island	61.2
17	North Carolina	60.7
18	Maine	60.5
19	Kansas	60.1
20	South Carolina	60.0
21	Kentucky	59.9
22	Missouri	59.8
23	Arizona	59.7
24	Tennessee	59.5
25	Connecticut	59.4
26	Arkansas	58.7
27	Alabama	58.5
28	Indiana	58.0
29	Texas	57.7
30	Massachusetts	57.5
30	New Mexico	57.5
32	New Hampshire	56.8
33	Oklahoma	56.7
34	West Virginia	54.4
35	Hawaii	47.7
NA	California**	NA
NA	Georgia**	NA
NA	Idaho**	NA
NA	Iowa**	NA
NA	Louisiana**	NA
NA	Maryland**	NA
NA	Minnesota**	NA
NA	Nebraska**	NA
NA	North Dakota**	NA
NA	Ohio**	NA
NA	Oregon**	NA
NA	Utah**	NA
NA	Vermont**	NA
NA	Virginia**	NA
NA	Washington**	NA
	District of Columbia**	NA

Source: U.S. Department of Health and Human Services, Centers for Disease Control and Prevention
 "Youth Risk Behavior Surveillance--U.S., 2009" (http://www.cdc.gov/HealthyYouth/yrbs/)
*Reported that they or their partner used a condom during last sexual intercourse. National percent includes nonreporting states.
**Not available.

Teenage Birth Rate in 2008

National Rate = 41.5 Live Births per 1,000 Women 15 to 19 Years Old*

ALPHA ORDER

RANK	STATE	RATE
12	Alabama	53.0
17	Alaska	46.8
6	Arizona	56.2
4	Arkansas	61.8
29	California	38.4
22	Colorado	42.5
47	Connecticut	22.9
27	Delaware	40.4
21	Florida	42.8
13	Georgia	51.8
23	Hawaii	42.1
24	Idaho	41.2
30	Illinois	38.1
20	Indiana	43.7
35	Iowa	33.9
18	Kansas	45.6
7	Kentucky	55.6
9	Louisiana	54.1
44	Maine	26.1
38	Maryland	32.8
49	Massachusetts	20.1
37	Michigan	33.2
43	Minnesota	27.2
1	Mississippi	65.7
19	Missouri	45.5
26	Montana	40.7
32	Nebraska	36.5
10	Nevada	53.5
50	New Hampshire	19.8
46	New Jersey	24.5
2	New Mexico	64.1
45	New York	25.2
14	North Carolina	49.4
41	North Dakota	28.6
25	Ohio	41.0
5	Oklahoma	61.6
31	Oregon	37.2
39	Pennsylvania	31.5
42	Rhode Island	28.5
11	South Carolina	53.1
28	South Dakota	40.0
7	Tennessee	55.6
3	Texas	63.4
33	Utah	35.1
48	Vermont	21.3
36	Virginia	33.5
34	Washington	34.6
16	West Virginia	48.8
40	Wisconsin	31.3
15	Wyoming	49.2

RANK ORDER

RANK	STATE	RATE
1	Mississippi	65.7
2	New Mexico	64.1
3	Texas	63.4
4	Arkansas	61.8
5	Oklahoma	61.6
6	Arizona	56.2
7	Kentucky	55.6
7	Tennessee	55.6
9	Louisiana	54.1
10	Nevada	53.5
11	South Carolina	53.1
12	Alabama	53.0
13	Georgia	51.8
14	North Carolina	49.4
15	Wyoming	49.2
16	West Virginia	48.8
17	Alaska	46.8
18	Kansas	45.6
19	Missouri	45.5
20	Indiana	43.7
21	Florida	42.8
22	Colorado	42.5
23	Hawaii	42.1
24	Idaho	41.2
25	Ohio	41.0
26	Montana	40.7
27	Delaware	40.4
28	South Dakota	40.0
29	California	38.4
30	Illinois	38.1
31	Oregon	37.2
32	Nebraska	36.5
33	Utah	35.1
34	Washington	34.6
35	Iowa	33.9
36	Virginia	33.5
37	Michigan	33.2
38	Maryland	32.8
39	Pennsylvania	31.5
40	Wisconsin	31.3
41	North Dakota	28.6
42	Rhode Island	28.5
43	Minnesota	27.2
44	Maine	26.1
45	New York	25.2
46	New Jersey	24.5
47	Connecticut	22.9
48	Vermont	21.3
49	Massachusetts	20.1
50	New Hampshire	19.8
	District of Columbia	50.9

Source: U.S. Department of Health and Human Services, National Center for Health Statistics
   "National Vital Statistics Reports" (Vol. 59, No. 1, December 2010, http://www.cdc.gov/nchs/births.htm)
*Final data by state of residence.

Percent of Children Living in Poverty in 2009

National Percent = 20.0%*

RANK	STATE	PERCENT
5	Alabama	24.7
45	Alaska	12.8
11	Arizona	23.4
2	Arkansas	27.2
22	California	19.9
29	Colorado	17.4
48	Connecticut	12.1
34	Delaware	16.5
18	Florida	21.3
14	Georgia	22.3
40	Hawaii	13.8
26	Idaho	18.1
24	Illinois	18.9
20	Indiana	20.0
36	Iowa	15.7
27	Kansas	17.6
3	Kentucky	25.6
8	Louisiana	24.2
30	Maine	17.1
49	Maryland	11.6
43	Massachusetts	13.1
12	Michigan	22.5
38	Minnesota	14.1
1	Mississippi	31.0
19	Missouri	20.7
17	Montana	21.4
37	Nebraska	15.2
27	Nevada	17.6
50	New Hampshire	10.8
41	New Jersey	13.5
4	New Mexico	25.3
20	New York	20.0
12	North Carolina	22.5
44	North Dakota	13.0
16	Ohio	21.9
15	Oklahoma	22.2
23	Oregon	19.2
30	Pennsylvania	17.1
32	Rhode Island	16.9
6	South Carolina	24.4
25	South Dakota	18.5
9	Tennessee	23.9
6	Texas	24.4
47	Utah	12.2
42	Vermont	13.3
39	Virginia	13.9
35	Washington	16.2
10	West Virginia	23.6
33	Wisconsin	16.7
46	Wyoming	12.6

RANK	STATE	PERCENT
1	Mississippi	31.0
2	Arkansas	27.2
3	Kentucky	25.6
4	New Mexico	25.3
5	Alabama	24.7
6	South Carolina	24.4
6	Texas	24.4
8	Louisiana	24.2
9	Tennessee	23.9
10	West Virginia	23.6
11	Arizona	23.4
12	Michigan	22.5
12	North Carolina	22.5
14	Georgia	22.3
15	Oklahoma	22.2
16	Ohio	21.9
17	Montana	21.4
18	Florida	21.3
19	Missouri	20.7
20	Indiana	20.0
20	New York	20.0
22	California	19.9
23	Oregon	19.2
24	Illinois	18.9
25	South Dakota	18.5
26	Idaho	18.1
27	Kansas	17.6
27	Nevada	17.6
29	Colorado	17.4
30	Maine	17.1
30	Pennsylvania	17.1
32	Rhode Island	16.9
33	Wisconsin	16.7
34	Delaware	16.5
35	Washington	16.2
36	Iowa	15.7
37	Nebraska	15.2
38	Minnesota	14.1
39	Virginia	13.9
40	Hawaii	13.8
41	New Jersey	13.5
42	Vermont	13.3
43	Massachusetts	13.1
44	North Dakota	13.0
45	Alaska	12.8
46	Wyoming	12.6
47	Utah	12.2
48	Connecticut	12.1
49	Maryland	11.6
50	New Hampshire	10.8
	District of Columbia	29.4

Source: U.S. Bureau of the Census
   "2009 American Community Survey" (http://www.census.gov/acs/www/)
*Children 17 and under living in families with incomes below the poverty level.

Rate of Child Abuse and Neglect in 2009

National Rate = 10.1 Abused Children per 1,000 Population Under 18*

ALPHA ORDER

RANK	STATE	RATE
34	Alabama	7.3
2	Alaska	21.6
48	Arizona	2.3
9	Arkansas	14.9
30	California	8.5
25	Colorado	9.7
16	Connecticut	12.1
23	Delaware	10.0
16	Florida	12.1
27	Georgia	9.3
35	Hawaii	7.1
42	Idaho	3.9
26	Illinois	9.4
7	Indiana	15.2
4	Iowa	18.2
49	Kansas	1.9
5	Kentucky	17.2
29	Louisiana	8.6
8	Maine	15.0
15	Maryland	12.4
1	Massachusetts	27.2
11	Michigan	13.8
42	Minnesota	3.9
22	Mississippi	10.3
44	Missouri	3.8
33	Montana	7.4
16	Nebraska	12.1
36	Nevada	6.9
46	New Hampshire	3.4
40	New Jersey	4.5
21	New Mexico	10.5
3	New York	20.4
20	North Carolina	10.8
28	North Dakota	8.7
14	Ohio	12.6
31	Oklahoma	8.3
12	Oregon	13.5
50	Pennsylvania	1.5
12	Rhode Island	13.5
19	South Carolina	11.8
32	South Dakota	7.6
37	Tennessee	6.2
23	Texas	10.0
6	Utah	15.8
38	Vermont	6.0
47	Virginia	3.3
41	Washington	4.2
10	West Virginia	14.2
44	Wisconsin	3.8
39	Wyoming	5.5

RANK ORDER

RANK	STATE	RATE
1	Massachusetts	27.2
2	Alaska	21.6
3	New York	20.4
4	Iowa	18.2
5	Kentucky	17.2
6	Utah	15.8
7	Indiana	15.2
8	Maine	15.0
9	Arkansas	14.9
10	West Virginia	14.2
11	Michigan	13.8
12	Oregon	13.5
12	Rhode Island	13.5
14	Ohio	12.6
15	Maryland	12.4
16	Connecticut	12.1
16	Florida	12.1
16	Nebraska	12.1
19	South Carolina	11.8
20	North Carolina	10.8
21	New Mexico	10.5
22	Mississippi	10.3
23	Delaware	10.0
23	Texas	10.0
25	Colorado	9.7
26	Illinois	9.4
27	Georgia	9.3
28	North Dakota	8.7
29	Louisiana	8.6
30	California	8.5
31	Oklahoma	8.3
32	South Dakota	7.6
33	Montana	7.4
34	Alabama	7.3
35	Hawaii	7.1
36	Nevada	6.9
37	Tennessee	6.2
38	Vermont	6.0
39	Wyoming	5.5
40	New Jersey	4.5
41	Washington	4.2
42	Idaho	3.9
42	Minnesota	3.9
44	Missouri	3.8
44	Wisconsin	3.8
46	New Hampshire	3.4
47	Virginia	3.3
48	Arizona	2.3
49	Kansas	1.9
50	Pennsylvania	1.5
	District of Columbia	29.9

Source: U.S. Department of Health and Human Services, Children's Bureau
   "Child Maltreatment 2009" (http://www.acf.hhs.gov/programs/cb/pubs/cm09/index.htm)
*State-substantiated or indicated incidents.

Reported Juvenile Arrest Rate in 2009

National Rate = 5,920.6 Reported Arrests per 100,000 Juvenile Population*

ALPHA ORDER				RANK ORDER		
RANK	STATE	RATE		RANK	STATE	RATE
46	Alabama	2,800.9		1	Wisconsin	15,012.5
38	Alaska	4,858.3		2	Wyoming	10,925.2
16	Arizona	7,181.0		3	Hawaii	10,490.5
41	Arkansas	4,443.7		4	North Dakota	10,291.9
35	California	4,981.8		5	Nevada	8,721.0
8	Colorado	8,210.4		6	Nebraska	8,569.2
36	Connecticut	4,958.1		7	South Dakota	8,516.0
13	Delaware	7,369.0		8	Colorado	8,210.4
26	Florida	5,952.9		9	Minnesota	7,912.1
28	Georgia	5,617.2		10	Idaho	7,860.0
3	Hawaii	10,490.5		11	Utah	7,776.6
10	Idaho	7,860.0		12	Montana	7,594.0
NA	Illinois**	NA		13	Delaware	7,369.0
19	Indiana	6,874.8		14	Pennsylvania	7,281.8
23	Iowa	6,335.9		15	Missouri	7,250.8
37	Kansas	4,894.1		16	Arizona	7,181.0
45	Kentucky	3,328.3		17	Louisiana	7,043.4
17	Louisiana	7,043.4		18	Maryland	6,948.5
29	Maine	5,400.5		19	Indiana	6,874.8
18	Maryland	6,948.5		20	Tennessee	6,842.2
47	Massachusetts	2,649.3		21	Oregon	6,690.6
44	Michigan	3,398.1		22	Mississippi	6,357.3
9	Minnesota	7,912.1		23	Iowa	6,335.9
22	Mississippi	6,357.3		24	New Hampshire	6,145.9
15	Missouri	7,250.8		25	Texas	6,095.2
12	Montana	7,594.0		26	Florida	5,952.9
6	Nebraska	8,569.2		27	New Mexico	5,898.3
5	Nevada	8,721.0		28	Georgia	5,617.2
24	New Hampshire	6,145.9		29	Maine	5,400.5
31	New Jersey	5,358.5		30	Oklahoma	5,374.0
27	New Mexico	5,898.3		31	New Jersey	5,358.5
43	New York	3,811.2		32	Washington	5,138.2
33	North Carolina	5,107.9		33	North Carolina	5,107.9
4	North Dakota	10,291.9		34	Rhode Island	5,090.8
40	Ohio	4,616.1		35	California	4,981.8
30	Oklahoma	5,374.0		36	Connecticut	4,958.1
21	Oregon	6,690.6		37	Kansas	4,894.1
14	Pennsylvania	7,281.8		38	Alaska	4,858.3
34	Rhode Island	5,090.8		39	South Carolina	4,665.1
39	South Carolina	4,665.1		40	Ohio	4,616.1
7	South Dakota	8,516.0		41	Arkansas	4,443.7
20	Tennessee	6,842.2		42	Virginia	4,427.9
25	Texas	6,095.2		43	New York	3,811.2
11	Utah	7,776.6		44	Michigan	3,398.1
48	Vermont	2,606.5		45	Kentucky	3,328.3
42	Virginia	4,427.9		46	Alabama	2,800.9
32	Washington	5,138.2		47	Massachusetts	2,649.3
49	West Virginia	2,526.3		48	Vermont	2,606.5
1	Wisconsin	15,012.5		49	West Virginia	2,526.3
2	Wyoming	10,925.2		NA	Illinois**	NA
					District of Columbia**	NA

Source: CQ Press using reported data from the Federal Bureau of Investigation
   "Crime in the United States 2009" (Uniform Crime Reports, September 13, 2010, http://www.fbi.gov/ucr/ucr.htm)
*By law enforcement agencies submitting complete reports to the F.B.I. for 12 months in 2009. Arrests of youths 17 years and younger divided into population of 10 to 17 year olds.
**Not available.

Inmates under Age 18 Held in State Prisons in 2009

National Total = 2,778 Prisoners*

ALPHA ORDER					RANK ORDER			
RANK	STATE	PRISONERS	% of USA		RANK	STATE	PRISONERS	% of USA
8	Alabama	118	4.2%		1	Florida	393	14.1%
33	Alaska	7	0.3%		2	Connecticut	332	12.0%
5	Arizona	157	5.7%		3	North Carolina	215	7.7%
26	Arkansas	17	0.6%		4	New York	190	6.8%
44	California	0	0.0%		5	Arizona	157	5.7%
14	Colorado	79	2.8%		6	Texas	156	5.6%
2	Connecticut	332	12.0%		7	Michigan	132	4.8%
20	Delaware	28	1.0%		8	Alabama	118	4.2%
1	Florida	393	14.1%		8	Nevada	118	4.2%
11	Georgia	99	3.6%		10	Illinois	106	3.8%
38	Hawaii	2	0.1%		11	Georgia	99	3.6%
44	Idaho	0	0.0%		12	South Carolina	89	3.2%
10	Illinois	106	3.8%		13	Ohio	86	3.1%
17	Indiana	54	1.9%		14	Colorado	79	2.8%
29	Iowa	13	0.5%		15	Pennsylvania	61	2.2%
35	Kansas	5	0.2%		16	Maryland	58	2.1%
44	Kentucky	0	0.0%		17	Indiana	54	1.9%
28	Louisiana	15	0.5%		18	Wisconsin	37	1.3%
44	Maine	0	0.0%		19	Missouri	31	1.1%
16	Maryland	58	2.1%		20	Delaware	28	1.0%
32	Massachusetts	8	0.3%		20	Mississippi	28	1.0%
7	Michigan	132	4.8%		22	Tennessee	22	0.8%
29	Minnesota	13	0.5%		23	Nebraska	21	0.8%
20	Mississippi	28	1.0%		23	New Jersey	21	0.8%
19	Missouri	31	1.1%		25	Oklahoma	19	0.7%
40	Montana	1	0.0%		26	Arkansas	17	0.6%
23	Nebraska	21	0.8%		27	Virginia	16	0.6%
8	Nevada	118	4.2%		28	Louisiana	15	0.5%
44	New Hampshire	0	0.0%		29	Iowa	13	0.5%
23	New Jersey	21	0.8%		29	Minnesota	13	0.5%
37	New Mexico	3	0.1%		29	Oregon	13	0.5%
4	New York	190	6.8%		32	Massachusetts	8	0.3%
3	North Carolina	215	7.7%		33	Alaska	7	0.3%
44	North Dakota	0	0.0%		34	Utah	6	0.2%
13	Ohio	86	3.1%		35	Kansas	5	0.2%
25	Oklahoma	19	0.7%		36	Vermont	4	0.1%
29	Oregon	13	0.5%		37	New Mexico	3	0.1%
15	Pennsylvania	61	2.2%		38	Hawaii	2	0.1%
40	Rhode Island	1	0.0%		38	Washington	2	0.1%
12	South Carolina	89	3.2%		40	Montana	1	0.0%
40	South Dakota	1	0.0%		40	Rhode Island	1	0.0%
22	Tennessee	22	0.8%		40	South Dakota	1	0.0%
6	Texas	156	5.6%		40	Wyoming	1	0.0%
34	Utah	6	0.2%		44	California	0	0.0%
36	Vermont	4	0.1%		44	Idaho	0	0.0%
27	Virginia	16	0.6%		44	Kentucky	0	0.0%
38	Washington	2	0.1%		44	Maine	0	0.0%
44	West Virginia	0	0.0%		44	New Hampshire	0	0.0%
18	Wisconsin	37	1.3%		44	North Dakota	0	0.0%
40	Wyoming	1	0.0%		44	West Virginia	0	0.0%
						District of Columbia**	NA	NA

Source: U.S. Department of Justice, Bureau of Justice Statistics
   "Prison and Jail Inmates at Midyear 2009" (June 2010, NCJ 230113, http://bjs.ojp.usdoj.gov/)
*As of June 30, 2009.
**Not available. Responsibility for sentenced felons in D.C. was transferred to the Federal Bureau of Prisons.

Juveniles in Residential Placement in 2007

National Total = 86,814 Juveniles*

ALPHA ORDER

RANK	STATE	JUVENILES	% of USA
14	Alabama	1,650	1.9%
42	Alaska	321	0.4%
16	Arizona	1,485	1.7%
33	Arkansas	810	0.9%
1	California	14,034	16.2%
12	Colorado	1,752	2.0%
39	Connecticut	426	0.5%
41	Delaware	369	0.4%
3	Florida	5,733	6.6%
8	Georgia	2,736	3.2%
49	Hawaii	129	0.1%
36	Idaho	528	0.6%
10	Illinois	2,565	3.0%
9	Indiana	2,727	3.1%
29	Iowa	954	1.1%
24	Kansas	1,146	1.3%
25	Kentucky	1,116	1.3%
18	Louisiana	1,350	1.6%
47	Maine	204	0.2%
30	Maryland	930	1.1%
28	Massachusetts	969	1.1%
7	Michigan	2,748	3.2%
19	Minnesota	1,317	1.5%
38	Mississippi	450	0.5%
22	Missouri	1,227	1.4%
46	Montana	210	0.2%
34	Nebraska	708	0.8%
27	Nevada	996	1.1%
48	New Hampshire	156	0.2%
13	New Jersey	1,677	1.9%
40	New Mexico	378	0.4%
6	New York	3,612	4.2%
26	North Carolina	1,035	1.2%
45	North Dakota	213	0.2%
5	Ohio	4,332	5.0%
32	Oklahoma	864	1.0%
20	Oregon	1,299	1.5%
4	Pennsylvania	4,554	5.2%
43	Rhode Island	312	0.4%
23	South Carolina	1,200	1.4%
37	South Dakota	456	0.5%
21	Tennessee	1,263	1.5%
2	Texas	7,035	8.1%
31	Utah	867	1.0%
50	Vermont	45	0.1%
11	Virginia	2,124	2.4%
15	Washington	1,527	1.8%
35	West Virginia	570	0.7%
17	Wisconsin	1,422	1.6%
44	Wyoming	249	0.3%

RANK ORDER

RANK	STATE	JUVENILES	% of USA
1	California	14,034	16.2%
2	Texas	7,035	8.1%
3	Florida	5,733	6.6%
4	Pennsylvania	4,554	5.2%
5	Ohio	4,332	5.0%
6	New York	3,612	4.2%
7	Michigan	2,748	3.2%
8	Georgia	2,736	3.2%
9	Indiana	2,727	3.1%
10	Illinois	2,565	3.0%
11	Virginia	2,124	2.4%
12	Colorado	1,752	2.0%
13	New Jersey	1,677	1.9%
14	Alabama	1,650	1.9%
15	Washington	1,527	1.8%
16	Arizona	1,485	1.7%
17	Wisconsin	1,422	1.6%
18	Louisiana	1,350	1.6%
19	Minnesota	1,317	1.5%
20	Oregon	1,299	1.5%
21	Tennessee	1,263	1.5%
22	Missouri	1,227	1.4%
23	South Carolina	1,200	1.4%
24	Kansas	1,146	1.3%
25	Kentucky	1,116	1.3%
26	North Carolina	1,035	1.2%
27	Nevada	996	1.1%
28	Massachusetts	969	1.1%
29	Iowa	954	1.1%
30	Maryland	930	1.1%
31	Utah	867	1.0%
32	Oklahoma	864	1.0%
33	Arkansas	810	0.9%
34	Nebraska	708	0.8%
35	West Virginia	570	0.7%
36	Idaho	528	0.6%
37	South Dakota	456	0.5%
38	Mississippi	450	0.5%
39	Connecticut	426	0.5%
40	New Mexico	378	0.4%
41	Delaware	369	0.4%
42	Alaska	321	0.4%
43	Rhode Island	312	0.4%
44	Wyoming	249	0.3%
45	North Dakota	213	0.2%
46	Montana	210	0.2%
47	Maine	204	0.2%
48	New Hampshire	156	0.2%
49	Hawaii	129	0.1%
50	Vermont	45	0.1%
	District of Columbia	288	0.3%

Source: U.S. Department of Justice, Office of Juvenile Justice and Delinquency Prevention
"Juveniles in Residential Placement, 1997-2008" (OJJDP Fact Sheet, February 2010)
(http://www.ncjrs.gov/pdffiles1/ojjdp/229379.pdf)
*Juveniles include youths age 10 through each state's upper age of original juvenile court jurisdiction. This age is 16 or 17 for most states. Residential placement refers to those juveniles assigned a bed in a public or private facility. National total includes 1,748 juveniles not shown by state.

Rate of Juveniles in Residential Placement in 2007

National Rate = 279 Juveniles in Custody Per 100,000 Juvenile Population*

ALPHA ORDER				RANK ORDER		
RANK	STATE	RATE		RANK	STATE	RATE
14	Alabama	325		1	South Dakota	513
4	Alaska	383		2	Wyoming	443
36	Arizona	208		3	Delaware	401
28	Arkansas	261		4	Alaska	383
13	California	329		5	Indiana	382
11	Colorado	339		6	Kansas	370
45	Connecticut	148		7	Nebraska	359
3	Delaware	401		8	Nevada	348
18	Florida	315		9	Pennsylvania	344
23	Georgia	286		10	Ohio	341
49	Hawaii	101		11	Colorado	339
19	Idaho	298		12	Oregon	330
37	Illinois	204		13	California	329
5	Indiana	382		14	Alabama	325
20	Iowa	294		15	North Dakota	322
6	Kansas	370		16	Louisiana	321
30	Kentucky	247		17	West Virginia	320
16	Louisiana	321		18	Florida	315
43	Maine	150		19	Idaho	298
44	Maryland	149		20	Iowa	294
42	Massachusetts	167		21	South Carolina	292
25	Michigan	274		22	Texas	287
32	Minnesota	230		23	Georgia	286
47	Mississippi	131		24	Rhode Island	282
34	Missouri	218		25	Michigan	274
37	Montana	204		26	Wisconsin	269
7	Nebraska	359		27	Utah	262
8	Nevada	348		28	Arkansas	261
48	New Hampshire	125		28	Virginia	261
40	New Jersey	176		30	Kentucky	247
41	New Mexico	170		31	New York	239
31	New York	239		32	Minnesota	230
46	North Carolina	144		33	Oklahoma	219
15	North Dakota	322		34	Missouri	218
10	Ohio	341		34	Washington	218
33	Oklahoma	219		36	Arizona	208
12	Oregon	330		37	Illinois	204
9	Pennsylvania	344		37	Montana	204
24	Rhode Island	282		39	Tennessee	191
21	South Carolina	292		40	New Jersey	176
1	South Dakota	513		41	New Mexico	170
39	Tennessee	191		42	Massachusetts	167
22	Texas	287		43	Maine	150
27	Utah	262		44	Maryland	149
50	Vermont	69		45	Connecticut	148
28	Virginia	261		46	North Carolina	144
34	Washington	218		47	Mississippi	131
17	West Virginia	320		48	New Hampshire	125
26	Wisconsin	269		49	Hawaii	101
2	Wyoming	443		50	Vermont	69
					District of Columbia	588

Source: U.S. Department of Justice, Office of Juvenile Justice and Delinquency Prevention
   "Juveniles in Residential Placement, 1997-2008" (OJJDP Fact Sheet, February 2010)
      (http://www.ncjrs.gov/pdffiles1/ojjdp/229379.pdf)
*Juveniles include youths age 10 through each state's upper age of original juvenile court jurisdiction. This age is 16 or 17 for
most states. Residential placement refers to those juveniles assigned a bed in a public or private facility.

Percent of High School Students Who Were Obese or Overweight in 2009

National Percent = 27.8%*

ALPHA ORDER				RANK ORDER		
RANK	STATE	PERCENT		RANK	STATE	PERCENT
6	Alabama	31.0		1	Mississippi	34.8
25	Alaska	26.2		2	Kentucky	33.2
18	Arizona	27.7		3	Louisiana	32.7
8	Arkansas	30.1		4	Tennessee	31.9
NA	California**	NA		5	South Carolina	31.7
41	Colorado	18.2		6	Alabama	31.0
32	Connecticut	24.9		7	Oklahoma	30.5
9	Delaware	29.5		8	Arkansas	30.1
31	Florida	25.0		9	Delaware	29.5
22	Georgia	27.2		10	Texas	29.2
14	Hawaii	28.5		11	Missouri	28.8
40	Idaho	20.8		12	Indiana	28.7
21	Illinois	27.4		13	West Virginia	28.6
12	Indiana	28.7		14	Hawaii	28.5
NA	Iowa**	NA		15	New Mexico	28.1
29	Kansas	25.5		16	North Carolina	28.0
2	Kentucky	33.2		17	Maryland	27.8
3	Louisiana	32.7		18	Arizona	27.7
20	Maine	27.6		18	Pennsylvania	27.7
17	Maryland	27.8		20	Maine	27.6
30	Massachusetts	25.2		21	Illinois	27.4
26	Michigan	26.1		22	Georgia	27.2
NA	Minnesota**	NA		23	Rhode Island	27.1
1	Mississippi	34.8		24	New York	26.6
11	Missouri	28.8		25	Alaska	26.2
38	Montana	22.3		26	Michigan	26.1
NA	Nebraska**	NA		27	Vermont	25.8
35	Nevada	24.4		28	New Hampshire	25.7
28	New Hampshire	25.7		29	Kansas	25.5
33	New Jersey	24.5		30	Massachusetts	25.2
15	New Mexico	28.1		31	Florida	25.0
24	New York	26.6		32	Connecticut	24.9
16	North Carolina	28.0		33	New Jersey	24.5
33	North Dakota	24.5		33	North Dakota	24.5
NA	Ohio**	NA		35	Nevada	24.4
7	Oklahoma	30.5		36	Wisconsin	23.3
NA	Oregon**	NA		37	Wyoming	22.4
18	Pennsylvania	27.7		38	Montana	22.3
23	Rhode Island	27.1		39	South Dakota	22.2
5	South Carolina	31.7		40	Idaho	20.8
39	South Dakota	22.2		41	Colorado	18.2
4	Tennessee	31.9		42	Utah	16.9
10	Texas	29.2		NA	California**	NA
42	Utah	16.9		NA	Iowa**	NA
27	Vermont	25.8		NA	Minnesota**	NA
NA	Virginia**	NA		NA	Nebraska**	NA
NA	Washington**	NA		NA	Ohio**	NA
13	West Virginia	28.6		NA	Oregon**	NA
36	Wisconsin	23.3		NA	Virginia**	NA
37	Wyoming	22.4		NA	Washington**	NA
				District of Columbia**		NA

Source: CQ Press using data from U.S. Department of Health and Human Services, Centers for Disease Control and Prevention
"Youth Risk Behavior Surveillance--U.S., 2009" (http://www.cdc.gov/HealthyYouth/yrbs/)
*Overweight includes students who were equal to or greater than 85th percentile for body mass index, by age and sex, based on reference data. Obese includes students at the 95th percentile or higher. National figure includes 12.0 percent obese and 15.8 percent overweight. National figure includes nonreporting states.
**Not available.

Percent of High School Students Who Attempted Suicide in 2009

National Percent = 6.3%*

<table>
<tr><td colspan="3">ALPHA ORDER</td><td colspan="3">RANK ORDER</td></tr>
<tr><th>RANK</th><th>STATE</th><th>PERCENT</th><th>RANK</th><th>STATE</th><th>PERCENT</th></tr>
<tr><td>5</td><td>Alabama</td><td>10.7</td><td>1</td><td>Hawaii</td><td>12.8</td></tr>
<tr><td>18</td><td>Alaska</td><td>8.5</td><td>2</td><td>Arkansas</td><td>12.0</td></tr>
<tr><td>11</td><td>Arizona</td><td>9.5</td><td>3</td><td>Louisiana</td><td>10.9</td></tr>
<tr><td>2</td><td>Arkansas</td><td>12.0</td><td>4</td><td>South Carolina</td><td>10.8</td></tr>
<tr><td>NA</td><td>California**</td><td>NA</td><td>5</td><td>Alabama</td><td>10.7</td></tr>
<tr><td>24</td><td>Colorado</td><td>7.6</td><td>5</td><td>West Virginia</td><td>10.7</td></tr>
<tr><td>25</td><td>Connecticut</td><td>7.4</td><td>7</td><td>Maryland</td><td>10.4</td></tr>
<tr><td>20</td><td>Delaware</td><td>8.2</td><td>8</td><td>Nevada</td><td>10.2</td></tr>
<tr><td>34</td><td>Florida</td><td>6.5</td><td>9</td><td>North Carolina</td><td>9.9</td></tr>
<tr><td>19</td><td>Georgia</td><td>8.3</td><td>10</td><td>New Mexico</td><td>9.7</td></tr>
<tr><td>1</td><td>Hawaii</td><td>12.8</td><td>11</td><td>Arizona</td><td>9.5</td></tr>
<tr><td>31</td><td>Idaho</td><td>6.9</td><td>12</td><td>Wyoming</td><td>9.4</td></tr>
<tr><td>16</td><td>Illinois</td><td>8.9</td><td>13</td><td>Indiana</td><td>9.3</td></tr>
<tr><td>13</td><td>Indiana</td><td>9.3</td><td>13</td><td>Michigan</td><td>9.3</td></tr>
<tr><td>NA</td><td>Iowa**</td><td>NA</td><td>13</td><td>Mississippi</td><td>9.3</td></tr>
<tr><td>36</td><td>Kansas</td><td>6.1</td><td>16</td><td>Illinois</td><td>8.9</td></tr>
<tr><td>17</td><td>Kentucky</td><td>8.8</td><td>17</td><td>Kentucky</td><td>8.8</td></tr>
<tr><td>3</td><td>Louisiana</td><td>10.9</td><td>18</td><td>Alaska</td><td>8.5</td></tr>
<tr><td>21</td><td>Maine</td><td>7.9</td><td>19</td><td>Georgia</td><td>8.3</td></tr>
<tr><td>7</td><td>Maryland</td><td>10.4</td><td>20</td><td>Delaware</td><td>8.2</td></tr>
<tr><td>32</td><td>Massachusetts</td><td>6.8</td><td>21</td><td>Maine</td><td>7.9</td></tr>
<tr><td>13</td><td>Michigan</td><td>9.3</td><td>22</td><td>Montana</td><td>7.7</td></tr>
<tr><td>NA</td><td>Minnesota**</td><td>NA</td><td>22</td><td>Rhode Island</td><td>7.7</td></tr>
<tr><td>13</td><td>Mississippi</td><td>9.3</td><td>24</td><td>Colorado</td><td>7.6</td></tr>
<tr><td>35</td><td>Missouri</td><td>6.4</td><td>25</td><td>Connecticut</td><td>7.4</td></tr>
<tr><td>22</td><td>Montana</td><td>7.7</td><td>25</td><td>New York</td><td>7.4</td></tr>
<tr><td>NA</td><td>Nebraska**</td><td>NA</td><td>25</td><td>Texas</td><td>7.4</td></tr>
<tr><td>8</td><td>Nevada</td><td>10.2</td><td>28</td><td>Utah</td><td>7.2</td></tr>
<tr><td>40</td><td>New Hampshire</td><td>4.7</td><td>29</td><td>Tennessee</td><td>7.1</td></tr>
<tr><td>NA</td><td>New Jersey**</td><td>NA</td><td>30</td><td>Oklahoma</td><td>7.0</td></tr>
<tr><td>10</td><td>New Mexico</td><td>9.7</td><td>31</td><td>Idaho</td><td>6.9</td></tr>
<tr><td>25</td><td>New York</td><td>7.4</td><td>32</td><td>Massachusetts</td><td>6.8</td></tr>
<tr><td>9</td><td>North Carolina</td><td>9.9</td><td>33</td><td>South Dakota</td><td>6.7</td></tr>
<tr><td>38</td><td>North Dakota</td><td>5.7</td><td>34</td><td>Florida</td><td>6.5</td></tr>
<tr><td>NA</td><td>Ohio**</td><td>NA</td><td>35</td><td>Missouri</td><td>6.4</td></tr>
<tr><td>30</td><td>Oklahoma</td><td>7.0</td><td>36</td><td>Kansas</td><td>6.1</td></tr>
<tr><td>NA</td><td>Oregon**</td><td>NA</td><td>37</td><td>Wisconsin</td><td>5.8</td></tr>
<tr><td>38</td><td>Pennsylvania</td><td>5.7</td><td>38</td><td>North Dakota</td><td>5.7</td></tr>
<tr><td>22</td><td>Rhode Island</td><td>7.7</td><td>38</td><td>Pennsylvania</td><td>5.7</td></tr>
<tr><td>4</td><td>South Carolina</td><td>10.8</td><td>40</td><td>New Hampshire</td><td>4.7</td></tr>
<tr><td>33</td><td>South Dakota</td><td>6.7</td><td>41</td><td>Vermont</td><td>4.3</td></tr>
<tr><td>29</td><td>Tennessee</td><td>7.1</td><td>NA</td><td>California**</td><td>NA</td></tr>
<tr><td>25</td><td>Texas</td><td>7.4</td><td>NA</td><td>Iowa**</td><td>NA</td></tr>
<tr><td>28</td><td>Utah</td><td>7.2</td><td>NA</td><td>Minnesota**</td><td>NA</td></tr>
<tr><td>41</td><td>Vermont</td><td>4.3</td><td>NA</td><td>Nebraska**</td><td>NA</td></tr>
<tr><td>NA</td><td>Virginia**</td><td>NA</td><td>NA</td><td>New Jersey**</td><td>NA</td></tr>
<tr><td>NA</td><td>Washington**</td><td>NA</td><td>NA</td><td>Ohio**</td><td>NA</td></tr>
<tr><td>5</td><td>West Virginia</td><td>10.7</td><td>NA</td><td>Oregon**</td><td>NA</td></tr>
<tr><td>37</td><td>Wisconsin</td><td>5.8</td><td>NA</td><td>Virginia**</td><td>NA</td></tr>
<tr><td>12</td><td>Wyoming</td><td>9.4</td><td>NA</td><td>Washington**</td><td>NA</td></tr>
<tr><td></td><td></td><td></td><td>NA</td><td>District of Columbia**</td><td>NA</td></tr>
</table>

Source: U.S. Department of Health and Human Services, Centers for Disease Control and Prevention
   "Youth Risk Behavior Surveillance--U.S., 2009" (http://www.cdc.gov/HealthyYouth/yrbs/)
*Percent who actually attempted suicide one or more times during the preceding 12 months. The national percent of students who attempted suicide and required treatment by a doctor or a nurse was 1.9 percent. National percent includes nonreporting states.
**Not available.

Percent of High School Students Who Played on One or More Sports Teams in 2009
National Percent = 58.3%*

ALPHA ORDER

RANK	STATE	PERCENT
26	Alabama	50.8
5	Alaska	61.9
24	Arizona	51.9
22	Arkansas	52.2
NA	California**	NA
2	Colorado	63.9
NA	Connecticut**	NA
20	Delaware	53.2
29	Florida	50.0
18	Georgia	54.3
NA	Hawaii**	NA
6	Idaho	61.2
13	Illinois	58.7
17	Indiana	54.5
NA	Iowa**	NA
8	Kansas	60.1
30	Kentucky	48.2
27	Louisiana	50.6
NA	Maine**	NA
15	Maryland	57.5
11	Massachusetts	58.9
NA	Michigan**	NA
NA	Minnesota**	NA
19	Mississippi	53.8
9	Missouri	59.6
14	Montana	57.7
NA	Nebraska**	NA
NA	Nevada**	NA
NA	New Hampshire**	NA
4	New Jersey	62.2
NA	New Mexico**	NA
9	New York	59.6
NA	North Carolina**	NA
NA	North Dakota**	NA
NA	Ohio**	NA
21	Oklahoma	52.4
NA	Oregon**	NA
16	Pennsylvania	57.4
NA	Rhode Island**	NA
25	South Carolina	51.3
1	South Dakota	64.4
28	Tennessee	50.1
12	Texas	58.8
3	Utah	63.6
NA	Vermont**	NA
NA	Virginia**	NA
NA	Washington**	NA
22	West Virginia	52.2
NA	Wisconsin**	NA
7	Wyoming	60.3

RANK ORDER

RANK	STATE	PERCENT
1	South Dakota	64.4
2	Colorado	63.9
3	Utah	63.6
4	New Jersey	62.2
5	Alaska	61.9
6	Idaho	61.2
7	Wyoming	60.3
8	Kansas	60.1
9	Missouri	59.6
9	New York	59.6
11	Massachusetts	58.9
12	Texas	58.8
13	Illinois	58.7
14	Montana	57.7
15	Maryland	57.5
16	Pennsylvania	57.4
17	Indiana	54.5
18	Georgia	54.3
19	Mississippi	53.8
20	Delaware	53.2
21	Oklahoma	52.4
22	Arkansas	52.2
22	West Virginia	52.2
24	Arizona	51.9
25	South Carolina	51.3
26	Alabama	50.8
27	Louisiana	50.6
28	Tennessee	50.1
29	Florida	50.0
30	Kentucky	48.2
NA	California**	NA
NA	Connecticut**	NA
NA	Hawaii**	NA
NA	Iowa**	NA
NA	Maine**	NA
NA	Michigan**	NA
NA	Minnesota**	NA
NA	Nebraska**	NA
NA	Nevada**	NA
NA	New Hampshire**	NA
NA	New Mexico**	NA
NA	North Carolina**	NA
NA	North Dakota**	NA
NA	Ohio**	NA
NA	Oregon**	NA
NA	Rhode Island**	NA
NA	Vermont**	NA
NA	Virginia**	NA
NA	Washington**	NA
NA	Wisconsin**	NA
	District of Columbia**	NA

Source: U.S. Department of Health and Human Services, Centers for Disease Control and Prevention
"Youth Risk Behavior Surveillance--U.S., 2009" (http://www.cdc.gov/HealthyYouth/yrbs/)
*Teams run either by their school or community group during the 12 months before the survey. National percent includes nonreporting states.
**Not available.

Percent of High School Students Not Participating in
60 or More Minutes of Physical Activity in the Past Week in 2009
National Percent = 23.1%*

ALPHA ORDER

RANK	STATE	PERCENT
2	Alabama	22.4
21	Alaska	16.2
23	Arizona	15.6
6	Arkansas	19.5
NA	California**	NA
40	Colorado	11.3
30	Connecticut	14.0
5	Delaware	19.7
8	Florida	19.4
15	Georgia	17.6
11	Hawaii	18.3
41	Idaho	10.8
19	Illinois	16.5
6	Indiana	19.5
NA	Iowa**	NA
27	Kansas	14.4
17	Kentucky	17.0
9	Louisiana	18.5
13	Maine	18.0
9	Maryland	18.5
1	Massachusetts	23.3
28	Michigan	14.2
NA	Minnesota**	NA
4	Mississippi	21.2
26	Missouri	14.7
34	Montana	13.4
NA	Nebraska**	NA
28	Nevada	14.2
36	New Hampshire	13.2
11	New Jersey	18.3
24	New Mexico	15.5
17	New York	17.0
25	North Carolina	15.4
32	North Dakota	13.7
NA	Ohio**	NA
20	Oklahoma	16.3
NA	Oregon**	NA
38	Pennsylvania	13.1
35	Rhode Island	13.3
3	South Carolina	21.3
30	South Dakota	14.0
14	Tennessee	17.7
22	Texas	16.0
42	Utah	10.5
36	Vermont	13.2
NA	Virginia**	NA
NA	Washington**	NA
16	West Virginia	17.3
39	Wisconsin	12.9
33	Wyoming	13.6

RANK ORDER

RANK	STATE	PERCENT
1	Massachusetts	23.3
2	Alabama	22.4
3	South Carolina	21.3
4	Mississippi	21.2
5	Delaware	19.7
6	Arkansas	19.5
6	Indiana	19.5
8	Florida	19.4
9	Louisiana	18.5
9	Maryland	18.5
11	Hawaii	18.3
11	New Jersey	18.3
13	Maine	18.0
14	Tennessee	17.7
15	Georgia	17.6
16	West Virginia	17.3
17	Kentucky	17.0
17	New York	17.0
19	Illinois	16.5
20	Oklahoma	16.3
21	Alaska	16.2
22	Texas	16.0
23	Arizona	15.6
24	New Mexico	15.5
25	North Carolina	15.4
26	Missouri	14.7
27	Kansas	14.4
28	Michigan	14.2
28	Nevada	14.2
30	Connecticut	14.0
30	South Dakota	14.0
32	North Dakota	13.7
33	Wyoming	13.6
34	Montana	13.4
35	Rhode Island	13.3
36	New Hampshire	13.2
36	Vermont	13.2
38	Pennsylvania	13.1
39	Wisconsin	12.9
40	Colorado	11.3
41	Idaho	10.8
42	Utah	10.5
NA	California**	NA
NA	Iowa**	NA
NA	Minnesota**	NA
NA	Nebraska**	NA
NA	Ohio**	NA
NA	Oregon**	NA
NA	Virginia**	NA
NA	Washington**	NA
	District of Columbia**	NA

Source: U.S. Department of Health and Human Services, Centers for Disease Control and Prevention
"Youth Risk Behavior Surveillance--U.S., 2009" (http://www.cdc.gov/HealthyYouth/yrbs/)
*Did not participate in 60 or more minutes of any kind of physical activity that increased their heart rate and made them breathe hard some of the time on at least 1 day during the 7 days before the survey. National percent includes nonreporting states.
**Not available.

Percent of High School Students Who Watched
Three or More Hours of Television Daily in 2009
National Percent = 32.8%*

ALPHA ORDER

RANK	STATE	PERCENT
7	Alabama	37.8
34	Alaska	24.8
15	Arizona	33.3
10	Arkansas	36.4
NA	California**	NA
33	Colorado	25.1
23	Connecticut	30.2
8	Delaware	37.7
6	Florida	38.2
4	Georgia	39.2
24	Hawaii	30.1
40	Idaho	21.9
13	Illinois	35.7
27	Indiana	29.0
NA	Iowa**	NA
30	Kansas	28.3
29	Kentucky	28.8
2	Louisiana	40.3
32	Maine	25.4
5	Maryland	39.1
22	Massachusetts	30.4
25	Michigan	29.6
NA	Minnesota**	NA
1	Mississippi	44.9
19	Missouri	32.4
35	Montana	23.7
NA	Nebraska**	NA
14	Nevada	35.1
37	New Hampshire	23.0
17	New Jersey	32.6
17	New Mexico	32.6
16	New York	32.7
12	North Carolina	36.2
31	North Dakota	25.6
NA	Ohio**	NA
27	Oklahoma	29.0
NA	Oregon**	NA
21	Pennsylvania	30.8
26	Rhode Island	29.1
3	South Carolina	39.7
38	South Dakota	22.6
8	Tennessee	37.7
11	Texas	36.3
41	Utah	16.3
NA	Vermont**	NA
NA	Virginia**	NA
NA	Washington**	NA
20	West Virginia	31.5
36	Wisconsin	23.1
39	Wyoming	22.0

RANK ORDER

RANK	STATE	PERCENT
1	Mississippi	44.9
2	Louisiana	40.3
3	South Carolina	39.7
4	Georgia	39.2
5	Maryland	39.1
6	Florida	38.2
7	Alabama	37.8
8	Delaware	37.7
8	Tennessee	37.7
10	Arkansas	36.4
11	Texas	36.3
12	North Carolina	36.2
13	Illinois	35.7
14	Nevada	35.1
15	Arizona	33.3
16	New York	32.7
17	New Jersey	32.6
17	New Mexico	32.6
19	Missouri	32.4
20	West Virginia	31.5
21	Pennsylvania	30.8
22	Massachusetts	30.4
23	Connecticut	30.2
24	Hawaii	30.1
25	Michigan	29.6
26	Rhode Island	29.1
27	Indiana	29.0
27	Oklahoma	29.0
29	Kentucky	28.8
30	Kansas	28.3
31	North Dakota	25.6
32	Maine	25.4
33	Colorado	25.1
34	Alaska	24.8
35	Montana	23.7
36	Wisconsin	23.1
37	New Hampshire	23.0
38	South Dakota	22.6
39	Wyoming	22.0
40	Idaho	21.9
41	Utah	16.3
NA	California**	NA
NA	Iowa**	NA
NA	Minnesota**	NA
NA	Nebraska**	NA
NA	Ohio**	NA
NA	Oregon**	NA
NA	Vermont**	NA
NA	Virginia**	NA
NA	Washington**	NA

District of Columbia**   NA

Source: U.S. Department of Health and Human Services, Centers for Disease Control and Prevention
"Youth Risk Behavior Surveillance--U.S., 2009" (http://www.cdc.gov/HealthyYouth/yrbs/)
*National figure includes nonreporting states.
**Not available.

Percent of High School Students Who Used Computers
Three or More Hours Daily in 2009
National Percent = 24.9%*

ALPHA ORDER

RANK	STATE	PERCENT
16	Alabama	24.1
20	Alaska	23.6
30	Arizona	22.1
31	Arkansas	21.0
NA	California**	NA
36	Colorado	18.4
6	Connecticut	27.9
8	Delaware	27.4
1	Florida	31.0
24	Georgia	22.9
8	Hawaii	27.4
39	Idaho	17.2
14	Illinois	24.5
19	Indiana	23.7
NA	Iowa**	NA
33	Kansas	19.8
23	Kentucky	23.0
15	Louisiana	24.4
24	Maine	22.9
4	Maryland	28.9
2	Massachusetts	29.9
22	Michigan	23.3
NA	Minnesota**	NA
29	Mississippi	22.3
24	Missouri	22.9
38	Montana	17.9
NA	Nebraska**	NA
11	Nevada	26.2
18	New Hampshire	23.9
4	New Jersey	28.9
31	New Mexico	21.0
3	New York	29.2
21	North Carolina	23.5
36	North Dakota	18.4
NA	Ohio**	NA
28	Oklahoma	22.5
NA	Oregon**	NA
10	Pennsylvania	26.7
7	Rhode Island	27.8
27	South Carolina	22.7
33	South Dakota	19.8
12	Tennessee	26.0
13	Texas	25.1
41	Utah	12.1
NA	Vermont**	NA
NA	Virginia**	NA
NA	Washington**	NA
16	West Virginia	24.1
35	Wisconsin	19.2
40	Wyoming	16.3

RANK ORDER

RANK	STATE	PERCENT
1	Florida	31.0
2	Massachusetts	29.9
3	New York	29.2
4	Maryland	28.9
4	New Jersey	28.9
6	Connecticut	27.9
7	Rhode Island	27.8
8	Delaware	27.4
8	Hawaii	27.4
10	Pennsylvania	26.7
11	Nevada	26.2
12	Tennessee	26.0
13	Texas	25.1
14	Illinois	24.5
15	Louisiana	24.4
16	Alabama	24.1
16	West Virginia	24.1
18	New Hampshire	23.9
19	Indiana	23.7
20	Alaska	23.6
21	North Carolina	23.5
22	Michigan	23.3
23	Kentucky	23.0
24	Georgia	22.9
24	Maine	22.9
24	Missouri	22.9
27	South Carolina	22.7
28	Oklahoma	22.5
29	Mississippi	22.3
30	Arizona	22.1
31	Arkansas	21.0
31	New Mexico	21.0
33	Kansas	19.8
33	South Dakota	19.8
35	Wisconsin	19.2
36	Colorado	18.4
36	North Dakota	18.4
38	Montana	17.9
39	Idaho	17.2
40	Wyoming	16.3
41	Utah	12.1
NA	California**	NA
NA	Iowa**	NA
NA	Minnesota**	NA
NA	Nebraska**	NA
NA	Ohio**	NA
NA	Oregon**	NA
NA	Vermont**	NA
NA	Virginia**	NA
NA	Washington**	NA
	District of Columbia**	NA

Source: U.S. Department of Health and Human Services, Centers for Disease Control and Prevention
    "Youth Risk Behavior Surveillance--U.S., 2009" (http://www.cdc.gov/HealthyYouth/yrbs/)
*National figure includes nonreporting states.
**Not available.

V. Special Education

Total Federal Government Special Education Grants to States in 2011

National Total = $11,855,551,380*

ALPHA ORDER

RANK	STATE	GRANTS	% of USA
23	Alabama	$185,730,470	1.6%
45	Alaska	37,357,786	0.3%
22	Arizona	188,988,875	1.6%
32	Arkansas	116,434,710	1.0%
1	California	1,253,536,457	10.6%
26	Colorado	157,984,691	1.3%
28	Connecticut	136,610,444	1.2%
46	Delaware	34,898,477	0.3%
4	Florida	644,678,039	5.4%
11	Georgia	332,633,436	2.8%
43	Hawaii	40,538,800	0.3%
39	Idaho	56,970,363	0.5%
5	Illinois	519,288,861	4.4%
14	Indiana	264,427,945	2.2%
30	Iowa	124,934,931	1.1%
34	Kansas	110,170,953	0.9%
25	Kentucky	166,766,124	1.4%
21	Louisiana	193,956,036	1.6%
40	Maine	56,708,500	0.5%
19	Maryland	205,006,905	1.7%
12	Massachusetts	291,097,989	2.5%
8	Michigan	409,312,404	3.5%
20	Minnesota	195,442,067	1.6%
31	Mississippi	123,262,979	1.0%
16	Missouri	231,048,719	1.9%
44	Montana	38,029,041	0.3%
37	Nebraska	76,231,539	0.6%
38	Nevada	71,300,218	0.6%
41	New Hampshire	48,571,011	0.4%
9	New Jersey	369,467,122	3.1%
35	New Mexico	93,469,070	0.8%
3	New York	785,595,902	6.6%
10	North Carolina	334,830,490	2.8%
49	North Dakota	28,128,085	0.2%
6	Ohio	446,076,511	3.8%
27	Oklahoma	150,168,322	1.3%
29	Oregon	131,607,016	1.1%
7	Pennsylvania	437,047,979	3.7%
42	Rhode Island	44,988,886	0.4%
24	South Carolina	182,548,196	1.5%
47	South Dakota	34,003,707	0.3%
15	Tennessee	241,506,810	2.0%
2	Texas	995,975,291	8.4%
33	Utah	112,160,052	0.9%
50	Vermont	27,199,708	0.2%
13	Virginia	288,387,761	2.4%
17	Washington	227,375,518	1.9%
36	West Virginia	78,701,760	0.7%
18	Wisconsin	215,646,347	1.8%
48	Wyoming	28,686,740	0.2%

RANK ORDER

RANK	STATE	GRANTS	% of USA
1	California	$1,253,536,457	10.6%
2	Texas	995,975,291	8.4%
3	New York	785,595,902	6.6%
4	Florida	644,678,039	5.4%
5	Illinois	519,288,861	4.4%
6	Ohio	446,076,511	3.8%
7	Pennsylvania	437,047,979	3.7%
8	Michigan	409,312,404	3.5%
9	New Jersey	369,467,122	3.1%
10	North Carolina	334,830,490	2.8%
11	Georgia	332,633,436	2.8%
12	Massachusetts	291,097,989	2.5%
13	Virginia	288,387,761	2.4%
14	Indiana	264,427,945	2.2%
15	Tennessee	241,506,810	2.0%
16	Missouri	231,048,719	1.9%
17	Washington	227,375,518	1.9%
18	Wisconsin	215,646,347	1.8%
19	Maryland	205,006,905	1.7%
20	Minnesota	195,442,067	1.6%
21	Louisiana	193,956,036	1.6%
22	Arizona	188,988,875	1.6%
23	Alabama	185,730,470	1.6%
24	South Carolina	182,548,196	1.5%
25	Kentucky	166,766,124	1.4%
26	Colorado	157,984,691	1.3%
27	Oklahoma	150,168,322	1.3%
28	Connecticut	136,610,444	1.2%
29	Oregon	131,607,016	1.1%
30	Iowa	124,934,931	1.1%
31	Mississippi	123,262,979	1.0%
32	Arkansas	116,434,710	1.0%
33	Utah	112,160,052	0.9%
34	Kansas	110,170,953	0.9%
35	New Mexico	93,469,070	0.8%
36	West Virginia	78,701,760	0.7%
37	Nebraska	76,231,539	0.6%
38	Nevada	71,300,218	0.6%
39	Idaho	56,970,363	0.5%
40	Maine	56,708,500	0.5%
41	New Hampshire	48,571,011	0.4%
42	Rhode Island	44,988,886	0.4%
43	Hawaii	40,538,800	0.3%
44	Montana	38,029,041	0.3%
45	Alaska	37,357,786	0.3%
46	Delaware	34,898,477	0.3%
47	South Dakota	34,003,707	0.3%
48	Wyoming	28,686,740	0.2%
49	North Dakota	28,128,085	0.2%
50	Vermont	27,199,708	0.2%
	District of Columbia	17,166,502	0.1%

Source: CQ Press using data from U.S. Department of Education, Budget Office
   "Fiscal Year 2010-2012 State Tables" (http://www2.ed.gov/about/overview/budget/statetables/index.html)
*Estimates for fiscal year 2011 appropriation. Includes grants for special education of children with disabilities from birth through age 21. Total includes $272,894,835 in grants to U.S. territories and Indian tribe set-aside.

Per Capita Total Federal Government
Special Education Grants to States in 2011
National Per Capita = $37.48*

RANK	STATE	PER CAPITA
25	Alabama	$39.27
1	Alaska	52.70
49	Arizona	28.31
21	Arkansas	40.01
45	California	33.64
48	Colorado	31.01
29	Connecticut	38.73
26	Delaware	39.15
42	Florida	34.52
46	Georgia	33.57
47	Hawaii	31.18
37	Idaho	36.52
20	Illinois	40.12
17	Indiana	41.03
15	Iowa	41.33
28	Kansas	38.78
31	Kentucky	38.43
9	Louisiana	42.82
6	Maine	43.19
39	Maryland	35.73
4	Massachusetts	43.90
16	Michigan	41.21
35	Minnesota	36.94
13	Mississippi	41.64
31	Missouri	38.43
27	Montana	38.80
12	Nebraska	42.09
50	Nevada	26.86
36	New Hampshire	36.70
11	New Jersey	42.31
3	New Mexico	45.96
19	New York	40.13
40	North Carolina	35.40
8	North Dakota	43.02
30	Ohio	38.68
18	Oklahoma	40.32
43	Oregon	34.13
41	Pennsylvania	34.60
10	Rhode Island	42.57
22	South Carolina	39.71
14	South Dakota	41.46
33	Tennessee	38.10
24	Texas	39.50
23	Utah	39.62
5	Vermont	43.70
38	Virginia	36.27
44	Washington	33.70
7	West Virginia	43.11
34	Wisconsin	38.04
2	Wyoming	52.38

RANK	STATE	PER CAPITA
1	Alaska	$52.70
2	Wyoming	52.38
3	New Mexico	45.96
4	Massachusetts	43.90
5	Vermont	43.70
6	Maine	43.19
7	West Virginia	43.11
8	North Dakota	43.02
9	Louisiana	42.82
10	Rhode Island	42.57
11	New Jersey	42.31
12	Nebraska	42.09
13	Mississippi	41.64
14	South Dakota	41.46
15	Iowa	41.33
16	Michigan	41.21
17	Indiana	41.03
18	Oklahoma	40.32
19	New York	40.13
20	Illinois	40.12
21	Arkansas	40.01
22	South Carolina	39.71
23	Utah	39.62
24	Texas	39.50
25	Alabama	39.27
26	Delaware	39.15
27	Montana	38.80
28	Kansas	38.78
29	Connecticut	38.73
30	Ohio	38.68
31	Kentucky	38.43
31	Missouri	38.43
33	Tennessee	38.10
34	Wisconsin	38.04
35	Minnesota	36.94
36	New Hampshire	36.70
37	Idaho	36.52
38	Virginia	36.27
39	Maryland	35.73
40	North Carolina	35.40
41	Pennsylvania	34.60
42	Florida	34.52
43	Oregon	34.13
44	Washington	33.70
45	California	33.64
46	Georgia	33.57
47	Hawaii	31.18
48	Colorado	31.01
49	Arizona	28.31
50	Nevada	26.86
	District of Columbia	28.11

Source: CQ Press using data from U.S. Department of Education, Budget Office
"Fiscal Year 2010-2012 State Tables" (http://www2.ed.gov/about/overview/budget/statetables/index.html)
*Estimates for fiscal year 2010 appropriation. Includes grants for special education of children with disabilities from birth through age 21. Does not include grants or population in U.S. territories and Indian tribe set-aside. Per capita calculated using 2010 population estimates.

Percent Change in Federal Government
Special Education Grants to States: 2007 to 2011
National Percent Change = 6.1% Increase*

ALPHA ORDER

RANK	STATE	PERCENT CHANGE
22	Alabama	5.5
13	Alaska	7.3
1	Arizona	9.1
50	Arkansas	5.3
38	California	5.4
11	Colorado	7.5
38	Connecticut	5.4
6	Delaware	9.0
20	Florida	5.9
1	Georgia	9.1
22	Hawaii	5.5
13	Idaho	7.3
22	Illinois	5.5
19	Indiana	6.3
22	Iowa	5.5
38	Kansas	5.4
38	Kentucky	5.4
38	Louisiana	5.4
38	Maine	5.4
22	Maryland	5.5
22	Massachusetts	5.5
22	Michigan	5.5
38	Minnesota	5.4
17	Mississippi	6.4
22	Missouri	5.5
17	Montana	6.4
22	Nebraska	5.5
1	Nevada	9.1
22	New Hampshire	5.5
22	New Jersey	5.5
22	New Mexico	5.5
38	New York	5.4
9	North Carolina	8.2
1	North Dakota	9.1
22	Ohio	5.5
22	Oklahoma	5.5
22	Oregon	5.5
22	Pennsylvania	5.5
38	Rhode Island	5.4
16	South Carolina	6.5
6	South Dakota	9.0
15	Tennessee	7.1
11	Texas	7.5
9	Utah	8.2
1	Vermont	9.1
21	Virginia	5.6
38	Washington	5.4
38	West Virginia	5.4
38	Wisconsin	5.4
6	Wyoming	9.0

RANK ORDER

RANK	STATE	PERCENT CHANGE
1	Arizona	9.1
1	Georgia	9.1
1	Nevada	9.1
1	North Dakota	9.1
1	Vermont	9.1
6	Delaware	9.0
6	South Dakota	9.0
6	Wyoming	9.0
9	North Carolina	8.2
9	Utah	8.2
11	Colorado	7.5
11	Texas	7.5
13	Alaska	7.3
13	Idaho	7.3
15	Tennessee	7.1
16	South Carolina	6.5
17	Mississippi	6.4
17	Montana	6.4
19	Indiana	6.3
20	Florida	5.9
21	Virginia	5.6
22	Alabama	5.5
22	Hawaii	5.5
22	Illinois	5.5
22	Iowa	5.5
22	Maryland	5.5
22	Massachusetts	5.5
22	Michigan	5.5
22	Missouri	5.5
22	Nebraska	5.5
22	New Hampshire	5.5
22	New Jersey	5.5
22	New Mexico	5.5
22	Ohio	5.5
22	Oklahoma	5.5
22	Oregon	5.5
22	Pennsylvania	5.5
38	California	5.4
38	Connecticut	5.4
38	Kansas	5.4
38	Kentucky	5.4
38	Louisiana	5.4
38	Maine	5.4
38	Minnesota	5.4
38	New York	5.4
38	Rhode Island	5.4
38	Washington	5.4
38	West Virginia	5.4
38	Wisconsin	5.4
50	Arkansas	5.3

District of Columbia 9.3

Source: CQ Press using data from U.S. Department of Education, Budget Office
"Fiscal Year 2010-2012 State Tables" (http://www2.ed.gov/about/overview/budget/statetables/index.html)
*Based on estimates for fiscal year 2011 appropriation. Includes grants for special education of children with disabilities from birth through age 21. Does not include grants to U.S. territories and Indian tribe set-aside.

Percent Change in Per Capita Federal Government
Special Education Grants to States: 2007 to 2011
National Percent Change = 2.8% Increase*

ALPHA ORDER

RANK	STATE	PERCENT CHANGE
26	Alabama	2.6
38	Alaska	1.4
44	Arizona	0.8
36	Arkansas	1.8
21	California	3.2
45	Colorado	0.3
9	Connecticut	4.8
13	Delaware	4.4
26	Florida	2.6
23	Georgia	3.1
14	Hawaii	4.3
43	Idaho	0.9
12	Illinois	4.5
15	Indiana	4.2
16	Iowa	4.1
26	Kansas	2.6
34	Kentucky	2.2
49	Louisiana	(0.2)
4	Maine	6.1
21	Maryland	3.2
33	Massachusetts	2.4
2	Michigan	7.2
24	Minnesota	3.0
11	Mississippi	4.6
30	Missouri	2.5
30	Montana	2.5
24	Nebraska	3.0
26	Nevada	2.6
9	New Hampshire	4.8
6	New Jersey	5.4
40	New Mexico	1.3
17	New York	3.9
40	North Carolina	1.3
4	North Dakota	6.1
7	Ohio	5.0
38	Oklahoma	1.4
42	Oregon	1.2
17	Pennsylvania	3.9
3	Rhode Island	6.5
46	South Carolina	0.2
17	South Dakota	3.9
35	Tennessee	2.0
46	Texas	0.2
50	Utah	(2.5)
1	Vermont	9.3
37	Virginia	1.5
48	Washington	(0.1)
7	West Virginia	5.0
20	Wisconsin	3.3
30	Wyoming	2.5

RANK ORDER

RANK	STATE	PERCENT CHANGE
1	Vermont	9.3
2	Michigan	7.2
3	Rhode Island	6.5
4	Maine	6.1
4	North Dakota	6.1
6	New Jersey	5.4
7	Ohio	5.0
7	West Virginia	5.0
9	Connecticut	4.8
9	New Hampshire	4.8
11	Mississippi	4.6
12	Illinois	4.5
13	Delaware	4.4
14	Hawaii	4.3
15	Indiana	4.2
16	Iowa	4.1
17	New York	3.9
17	Pennsylvania	3.9
17	South Dakota	3.9
20	Wisconsin	3.3
21	California	3.2
21	Maryland	3.2
23	Georgia	3.1
24	Minnesota	3.0
24	Nebraska	3.0
26	Alabama	2.6
26	Florida	2.6
26	Kansas	2.6
26	Nevada	2.6
30	Missouri	2.5
30	Montana	2.5
30	Wyoming	2.5
33	Massachusetts	2.4
34	Kentucky	2.2
35	Tennessee	2.0
36	Arkansas	1.8
37	Virginia	1.5
38	Alaska	1.4
38	Oklahoma	1.4
40	New Mexico	1.3
40	North Carolina	1.3
42	Oregon	1.2
43	Idaho	0.9
44	Arizona	0.8
45	Colorado	0.3
46	South Carolina	0.2
46	Texas	0.2
48	Washington	(0.1)
49	Louisiana	(0.2)
50	Utah	(2.5)

| | District of Columbia | 4.1 |

Source: CQ Press using data from U.S. Department of Education, Budget Office
"Fiscal Year 2010-2012 State Tables" (http://www2.ed.gov/about/overview/budget/statetables/index.html)
*Based on estimates for fiscal year 2011 appropriation. Includes grants for special education of children with disabilities from birth through age 21. Does not include grants or population in U.S. territories and Indian tribe set-aside. Per capita for 2011 calculated using 2010 population estimates.

Federal Government Preschool Special Education Grants to States in 2011

National Total = $373,350,802*

ALPHA ORDER

RANK	STATE	GRANTS	% of USA
24	Alabama	$5,495,480	1.5%
44	Alaska	1,239,512	0.3%
26	Arizona	5,246,435	1.4%
25	Arkansas	5,269,918	1.4%
1	California	37,746,603	10.1%
27	Colorado	4,861,610	1.3%
28	Connecticut	4,818,610	1.3%
45	Delaware	1,233,036	0.3%
4	Florida	18,135,111	4.9%
13	Georgia	9,616,887	2.6%
48	Hawaii	975,921	0.3%
40	Idaho	2,148,215	0.6%
5	Illinois	17,337,847	4.6%
16	Indiana	8,741,965	2.3%
31	Iowa	3,921,348	1.1%
29	Kansas	4,257,655	1.1%
11	Kentucky	10,033,703	2.7%
22	Louisiana	6,360,712	1.7%
37	Maine	2,469,146	0.7%
21	Maryland	6,553,868	1.8%
12	Massachusetts	9,718,123	2.6%
7	Michigan	12,332,211	3.3%
18	Minnesota	7,297,787	2.0%
30	Mississippi	4,152,914	1.1%
23	Missouri	5,887,301	1.6%
46	Montana	1,160,520	0.3%
38	Nebraska	2,216,070	0.6%
39	Nevada	2,200,299	0.6%
42	New Hampshire	1,530,429	0.4%
9	New Jersey	11,177,681	3.0%
36	New Mexico	3,131,729	0.8%
2	New York	33,156,784	8.9%
10	North Carolina	11,113,496	3.0%
50	North Dakota	792,151	0.2%
8	Ohio	12,295,481	3.3%
33	Oklahoma	3,571,920	1.0%
32	Oregon	3,786,322	1.0%
6	Pennsylvania	13,723,720	3.7%
41	Rhode Island	1,642,085	0.4%
19	South Carolina	7,014,967	1.9%
43	South Dakota	1,439,498	0.4%
20	Tennessee	6,762,357	1.8%
3	Texas	22,380,344	6.0%
34	Utah	3,497,488	0.9%
49	Vermont	842,648	0.2%
15	Virginia	8,967,283	2.4%
17	Washington	8,025,225	2.1%
35	West Virginia	3,422,571	0.9%
14	Wisconsin	9,305,597	2.5%
47	Wyoming	1,035,572	0.3%

RANK ORDER

RANK	STATE	GRANTS	% of USA
1	California	$37,746,603	10.1%
2	New York	33,156,784	8.9%
3	Texas	22,380,344	6.0%
4	Florida	18,135,111	4.9%
5	Illinois	17,337,847	4.6%
6	Pennsylvania	13,723,720	3.7%
7	Michigan	12,332,211	3.3%
8	Ohio	12,295,481	3.3%
9	New Jersey	11,177,681	3.0%
10	North Carolina	11,113,496	3.0%
11	Kentucky	10,033,703	2.7%
12	Massachusetts	9,718,123	2.6%
13	Georgia	9,616,887	2.6%
14	Wisconsin	9,305,597	2.5%
15	Virginia	8,967,283	2.4%
16	Indiana	8,741,965	2.3%
17	Washington	8,025,225	2.1%
18	Minnesota	7,297,787	2.0%
19	South Carolina	7,014,967	1.9%
20	Tennessee	6,762,357	1.8%
21	Maryland	6,553,868	1.8%
22	Louisiana	6,360,712	1.7%
23	Missouri	5,887,301	1.6%
24	Alabama	5,495,480	1.5%
25	Arkansas	5,269,918	1.4%
26	Arizona	5,246,435	1.4%
27	Colorado	4,861,610	1.3%
28	Connecticut	4,818,610	1.3%
29	Kansas	4,257,655	1.1%
30	Mississippi	4,152,914	1.1%
31	Iowa	3,921,348	1.1%
32	Oregon	3,786,322	1.0%
33	Oklahoma	3,571,920	1.0%
34	Utah	3,497,488	0.9%
35	West Virginia	3,422,571	0.9%
36	New Mexico	3,131,729	0.8%
37	Maine	2,469,146	0.7%
38	Nebraska	2,216,070	0.6%
39	Nevada	2,200,299	0.6%
40	Idaho	2,148,215	0.6%
41	Rhode Island	1,642,085	0.4%
42	New Hampshire	1,530,429	0.4%
43	South Dakota	1,439,498	0.4%
44	Alaska	1,239,512	0.3%
45	Delaware	1,233,036	0.3%
46	Montana	1,160,520	0.3%
47	Wyoming	1,035,572	0.3%
48	Hawaii	975,921	0.3%
49	Vermont	842,648	0.2%
50	North Dakota	792,151	0.2%
	District of Columbia	239,418	0.1%

Source: U.S. Department of Education, Budget Office
   "Fiscal Year 2010-2012 State Tables" (http://www2.ed.gov/about/overview/budget/statetables/index.html)
*Estimates for fiscal year 2011 appropriation. Grants for special education of children with disabilities ages 3 through 5. Includes $3,067,229 in grants to Puerto Rico.

Per Capita Federal Government Preschool
Special Education Grants to States in 2011
National Per Capita = $1.20*

ALPHA ORDER

RANK	STATE	PER CAPITA
33	Alabama	$1.16
7	Alaska	1.75
49	Arizona	0.79
5	Arkansas	1.81
40	California	1.01
46	Colorado	0.95
20	Connecticut	1.37
17	Delaware	1.38
43	Florida	0.97
43	Georgia	0.97
50	Hawaii	0.75
17	Idaho	1.38
23	Illinois	1.34
21	Indiana	1.36
24	Iowa	1.30
13	Kansas	1.50
1	Kentucky	2.31
15	Louisiana	1.40
3	Maine	1.88
35	Maryland	1.14
14	Massachusetts	1.47
26	Michigan	1.24
17	Minnesota	1.38
15	Mississippi	1.40
41	Missouri	0.98
31	Montana	1.18
28	Nebraska	1.22
48	Nevada	0.83
33	New Hampshire	1.16
25	New Jersey	1.28
11	New Mexico	1.54
8	New York	1.69
32	North Carolina	1.17
29	North Dakota	1.21
38	Ohio	1.07
45	Oklahoma	0.96
41	Oregon	0.98
37	Pennsylvania	1.09
10	Rhode Island	1.55
12	South Carolina	1.53
6	South Dakota	1.76
38	Tennessee	1.07
47	Texas	0.89
26	Utah	1.24
22	Vermont	1.35
36	Virginia	1.13
30	Washington	1.19
4	West Virginia	1.87
9	Wisconsin	1.64
2	Wyoming	1.89

RANK ORDER

RANK	STATE	PER CAPITA
1	Kentucky	$2.31
2	Wyoming	1.89
3	Maine	1.88
4	West Virginia	1.87
5	Arkansas	1.81
6	South Dakota	1.76
7	Alaska	1.75
8	New York	1.69
9	Wisconsin	1.64
10	Rhode Island	1.55
11	New Mexico	1.54
12	South Carolina	1.53
13	Kansas	1.50
14	Massachusetts	1.47
15	Louisiana	1.40
15	Mississippi	1.40
17	Delaware	1.38
17	Idaho	1.38
17	Minnesota	1.38
20	Connecticut	1.37
21	Indiana	1.36
22	Vermont	1.35
23	Illinois	1.34
24	Iowa	1.30
25	New Jersey	1.28
26	Michigan	1.24
26	Utah	1.24
28	Nebraska	1.22
29	North Dakota	1.21
30	Washington	1.19
31	Montana	1.18
32	North Carolina	1.17
33	Alabama	1.16
33	New Hampshire	1.16
35	Maryland	1.14
36	Virginia	1.13
37	Pennsylvania	1.09
38	Ohio	1.07
38	Tennessee	1.07
40	California	1.01
41	Missouri	0.98
41	Oregon	0.98
43	Florida	0.97
43	Georgia	0.97
45	Oklahoma	0.96
46	Colorado	0.95
47	Texas	0.89
48	Nevada	0.83
49	Arizona	0.79
50	Hawaii	0.75
	District of Columbia	0.39

Source: CQ Press using data from U.S. Department of Education, Budget Office
   "Fiscal Year 2010-2012 State Tables" (http://www2.ed.gov/about/overview/budget/statetables/index.html)
*Estimates for fiscal year 2011 appropriation. Grants for special education of children with disabilities ages 3 through 5. Does not include grants or population in Puerto Rico. Per capita calculated using 2010 population estimates.

Federal Government Special Education Grants to States
for Youths Age 6 to 21 in 2011
National Total = $11,482,200,578*

ALPHA ORDER

RANK	STATE	GRANTS	% of USA
23	Alabama	$180,234,990	1.6%
45	Alaska	36,118,274	0.3%
22	Arizona	183,742,440	1.6%
32	Arkansas	111,164,792	1.0%
1	California	1,215,789,854	10.6%
26	Colorado	153,123,081	1.3%
28	Connecticut	131,791,834	1.1%
46	Delaware	33,665,441	0.3%
4	Florida	626,542,928	5.5%
11	Georgia	323,016,549	2.8%
43	Hawaii	39,562,879	0.3%
39	Idaho	54,822,148	0.5%
5	Illinois	501,951,014	4.4%
14	Indiana	255,685,980	2.2%
30	Iowa	121,013,583	1.1%
34	Kansas	105,913,298	0.9%
25	Kentucky	156,732,421	1.4%
21	Louisiana	187,595,324	1.6%
40	Maine	54,239,354	0.5%
19	Maryland	198,453,037	1.7%
12	Massachusetts	281,379,866	2.5%
8	Michigan	396,980,193	3.5%
20	Minnesota	188,144,280	1.6%
31	Mississippi	119,110,065	1.0%
16	Missouri	225,161,418	2.0%
44	Montana	36,868,521	0.3%
37	Nebraska	74,015,469	0.6%
38	Nevada	69,099,919	0.6%
41	New Hampshire	47,040,582	0.4%
9	New Jersey	358,289,441	3.1%
35	New Mexico	90,337,341	0.8%
3	New York	752,439,118	6.6%
10	North Carolina	323,716,994	2.8%
49	North Dakota	27,335,934	0.2%
6	Ohio	433,781,030	3.8%
27	Oklahoma	146,596,402	1.3%
29	Oregon	127,820,694	1.1%
7	Pennsylvania	423,324,259	3.7%
42	Rhode Island	43,346,801	0.4%
24	South Carolina	175,533,229	1.5%
47	South Dakota	32,564,209	0.3%
15	Tennessee	234,744,453	2.0%
2	Texas	973,594,947	8.5%
33	Utah	108,662,564	0.9%
50	Vermont	26,357,060	0.2%
13	Virginia	279,420,478	2.4%
17	Washington	219,350,293	1.9%
36	West Virginia	75,279,189	0.7%
18	Wisconsin	206,340,750	1.8%
48	Wyoming	27,651,168	0.2%

RANK ORDER

RANK	STATE	GRANTS	% of USA
1	California	$1,215,789,854	10.6%
2	Texas	973,594,947	8.5%
3	New York	752,439,118	6.6%
4	Florida	626,542,928	5.5%
5	Illinois	501,951,014	4.4%
6	Ohio	433,781,030	3.8%
7	Pennsylvania	423,324,259	3.7%
8	Michigan	396,980,193	3.5%
9	New Jersey	358,289,441	3.1%
10	North Carolina	323,716,994	2.8%
11	Georgia	323,016,549	2.8%
12	Massachusetts	281,379,866	2.5%
13	Virginia	279,420,478	2.4%
14	Indiana	255,685,980	2.2%
15	Tennessee	234,744,453	2.0%
16	Missouri	225,161,418	2.0%
17	Washington	219,350,293	1.9%
18	Wisconsin	206,340,750	1.8%
19	Maryland	198,453,037	1.7%
20	Minnesota	188,144,280	1.6%
21	Louisiana	187,595,324	1.6%
22	Arizona	183,742,440	1.6%
23	Alabama	180,234,990	1.6%
24	South Carolina	175,533,229	1.5%
25	Kentucky	156,732,421	1.4%
26	Colorado	153,123,081	1.3%
27	Oklahoma	146,596,402	1.3%
28	Connecticut	131,791,834	1.1%
29	Oregon	127,820,694	1.1%
30	Iowa	121,013,583	1.1%
31	Mississippi	119,110,065	1.0%
32	Arkansas	111,164,792	1.0%
33	Utah	108,662,564	0.9%
34	Kansas	105,913,298	0.9%
35	New Mexico	90,337,341	0.8%
36	West Virginia	75,279,189	0.7%
37	Nebraska	74,015,469	0.6%
38	Nevada	69,099,919	0.6%
39	Idaho	54,822,148	0.5%
40	Maine	54,239,354	0.5%
41	New Hampshire	47,040,582	0.4%
42	Rhode Island	43,346,801	0.4%
43	Hawaii	39,562,879	0.3%
44	Montana	36,868,521	0.3%
45	Alaska	36,118,274	0.3%
46	Delaware	33,665,441	0.3%
47	South Dakota	32,564,209	0.3%
48	Wyoming	27,651,168	0.2%
49	North Dakota	27,335,934	0.2%
50	Vermont	26,357,060	0.2%
	District of Columbia	16,927,084	0.1%

Source: U.S. Department of Education, Budget Office
   "Fiscal Year 2010-2012 State Tables" (http://www2.ed.gov/about/overview/budget/statetables/index.html)
*Estimates for fiscal year 2011 appropriation. Grants for special education of children with disabilities ages 6 through 21 years.
Includes $269,827,606 in grants to U.S. territories and Indian tribe set-aside.

Per Capita Federal Government Special Education Grants to States for Youths Age 6 to 21 in 2011
National Per Capita = $36.28*

ALPHA ORDER

RANK	STATE	PER CAPITA
25	Alabama	$38.11
1	Alaska	50.95
49	Arizona	27.52
23	Arkansas	38.20
44	California	32.62
48	Colorado	30.05
30	Connecticut	37.37
26	Delaware	37.76
41	Florida	33.54
45	Georgia	32.60
47	Hawaii	30.43
37	Idaho	35.15
19	Illinois	38.78
17	Indiana	39.67
14	Iowa	40.03
31	Kansas	37.28
34	Kentucky	36.12
7	Louisiana	41.42
8	Maine	41.31
39	Maryland	34.59
4	Massachusetts	42.43
15	Michigan	39.97
35	Minnesota	35.56
13	Mississippi	40.23
29	Missouri	37.45
27	Montana	37.62
12	Nebraska	40.87
50	Nevada	26.03
36	New Hampshire	35.54
10	New Jersey	41.03
3	New Mexico	44.42
21	New York	38.43
40	North Carolina	34.22
6	North Dakota	41.81
27	Ohio	37.62
18	Oklahoma	39.36
43	Oregon	33.15
42	Pennsylvania	33.51
11	Rhode Island	41.01
24	South Carolina	38.18
16	South Dakota	39.71
32	Tennessee	37.04
20	Texas	38.61
22	Utah	38.39
5	Vermont	42.35
38	Virginia	35.14
46	Washington	32.51
9	West Virginia	41.24
33	Wisconsin	36.40
2	Wyoming	50.49

RANK ORDER

RANK	STATE	PER CAPITA
1	Alaska	$50.95
2	Wyoming	50.49
3	New Mexico	44.42
4	Massachusetts	42.43
5	Vermont	42.35
6	North Dakota	41.81
7	Louisiana	41.42
8	Maine	41.31
9	West Virginia	41.24
10	New Jersey	41.03
11	Rhode Island	41.01
12	Nebraska	40.87
13	Mississippi	40.23
14	Iowa	40.03
15	Michigan	39.97
16	South Dakota	39.71
17	Indiana	39.67
18	Oklahoma	39.36
19	Illinois	38.78
20	Texas	38.61
21	New York	38.43
22	Utah	38.39
23	Arkansas	38.20
24	South Carolina	38.18
25	Alabama	38.11
26	Delaware	37.76
27	Montana	37.62
27	Ohio	37.62
29	Missouri	37.45
30	Connecticut	37.37
31	Kansas	37.28
32	Tennessee	37.04
33	Wisconsin	36.40
34	Kentucky	36.12
35	Minnesota	35.56
36	New Hampshire	35.54
37	Idaho	35.15
38	Virginia	35.14
39	Maryland	34.59
40	North Carolina	34.22
41	Florida	33.54
42	Pennsylvania	33.51
43	Oregon	33.15
44	California	32.62
45	Georgia	32.60
46	Washington	32.51
47	Hawaii	30.43
48	Colorado	30.05
49	Arizona	27.52
50	Nevada	26.03
	District of Columbia	27.72

Source: CQ Press using data from U.S. Department of Education, Budget Office
   "Fiscal Year 2010-2012 State Tables" (http://www2.ed.gov/about/overview/budget/statetables/index.html)
*Estimates for fiscal year 2011 appropriation. Grants for special education of children with disabilities ages 6 through 21. Does not include grants or population in U.S. territories and Indian tribe set-aside. Per capita calculated using 2010 population estimates.

Infants and Toddlers Receiving Early Intervention Services under Individuals with Disabilities Education Act (IDEA) in 2010
National Total = 343,203 Children Aged Birth through Two Years*

ALPHA ORDER   RANK ORDER

RANK	STATE	CHILDREN	% of USA	RANK	STATE	CHILDREN	% of USA
31	Alabama	3,098	0.9%	1	California	38,338	11.2%
49	Alaska	675	0.2%	2	New York	32,876	9.6%
17	Arizona	5,372	1.6%	3	Texas	28,574	8.3%
34	Arkansas	2,720	0.8%	4	Illinois	18,266	5.3%
1	California	38,338	11.2%	5	Pennsylvania	17,160	5.0%
18	Colorado	5,156	1.5%	6	Massachusetts	15,132	4.4%
22	Connecticut	4,743	1.4%	7	Florida	14,477	4.2%
47	Delaware	840	0.2%	8	Ohio	14,336	4.2%
7	Florida	14,477	4.2%	9	Michigan	10,663	3.1%
16	Georgia	5,632	1.6%	10	New Jersey	10,505	3.1%
37	Hawaii	2,080	0.6%	11	Indiana	10,064	2.9%
38	Idaho	1,916	0.6%	12	North Carolina	9,971	2.9%
4	Illinois	18,266	5.3%	13	Maryland	7,178	2.1%
11	Indiana	10,064	2.9%	14	Virginia	6,288	1.8%
28	Iowa	3,772	1.1%	15	Wisconsin	6,000	1.7%
29	Kansas	3,563	1.0%	16	Georgia	5,632	1.6%
19	Kentucky	5,077	1.5%	17	Arizona	5,372	1.6%
25	Louisiana	4,548	1.3%	18	Colorado	5,156	1.5%
45	Maine	999	0.3%	19	Kentucky	5,077	1.5%
13	Maryland	7,178	2.1%	20	Washington	5,006	1.5%
6	Massachusetts	15,132	4.4%	21	Minnesota	4,749	1.4%
9	Michigan	10,663	3.1%	22	Connecticut	4,743	1.4%
21	Minnesota	4,749	1.4%	23	New Mexico	4,669	1.4%
36	Mississippi	2,263	0.7%	24	South Carolina	4,600	1.3%
27	Missouri	4,200	1.2%	25	Louisiana	4,548	1.3%
50	Montana	649	0.2%	26	Tennessee	4,257	1.2%
42	Nebraska	1,534	0.4%	27	Missouri	4,200	1.2%
39	Nevada	1,892	0.6%	28	Iowa	3,772	1.1%
41	New Hampshire	1,744	0.5%	29	Kansas	3,563	1.0%
10	New Jersey	10,505	3.1%	30	Utah	3,284	1.0%
23	New Mexico	4,669	1.4%	31	Alabama	3,098	0.9%
2	New York	32,876	9.6%	32	Oklahoma	3,080	0.9%
12	North Carolina	9,971	2.9%	33	Oregon	2,762	0.8%
46	North Dakota	909	0.3%	34	Arkansas	2,720	0.8%
8	Ohio	14,336	4.2%	35	West Virginia	2,472	0.7%
32	Oklahoma	3,080	0.9%	36	Mississippi	2,263	0.7%
33	Oregon	2,762	0.8%	37	Hawaii	2,080	0.6%
5	Pennsylvania	17,160	5.0%	38	Idaho	1,916	0.6%
40	Rhode Island	1,871	0.5%	39	Nevada	1,892	0.6%
24	South Carolina	4,600	1.3%	40	Rhode Island	1,871	0.5%
44	South Dakota	1,029	0.3%	41	New Hampshire	1,744	0.5%
26	Tennessee	4,257	1.2%	42	Nebraska	1,534	0.4%
3	Texas	28,574	8.3%	43	Wyoming	1,107	0.3%
30	Utah	3,284	1.0%	44	South Dakota	1,029	0.3%
48	Vermont	776	0.2%	45	Maine	999	0.3%
14	Virginia	6,288	1.8%	46	North Dakota	909	0.3%
20	Washington	5,006	1.5%	47	Delaware	840	0.2%
35	West Virginia	2,472	0.7%	48	Vermont	776	0.2%
15	Wisconsin	6,000	1.7%	49	Alaska	675	0.2%
43	Wyoming	1,107	0.3%	50	Montana	649	0.2%
					District of Columbia	331	0.1%

Source: U.S. Department of Education, Office of Special Education Programs
    "Data Tables for OSEP State Reported Data" (https://www.ideadata.org/arc_toc11.asp)
*2009-2010 school year. IDEA authorizes funding to states and other organizations to support research, demonstrations, technical assistance, and other programs to ensure that the rights of infants, toddlers, children, and youth with disabilities and their parents are protected. National total does not include recipients served in U.S. territories and Bureau of Indian Education programs.

Percent of Infants and Toddlers Receiving Early Intervention Services under Individuals with Disabilities Education Act (IDEA) in 2010
National Percent = 2.7% of Children Aged Birth through 2 Years*

ALPHA ORDER

RANK ORDER

RANK	STATE	PERCENT	RANK	STATE	PERCENT
48	Alabama	1.6	1	Massachusetts	6.5
36	Alaska	2.0	2	New Mexico	5.1
43	Arizona	1.7	2	Rhode Island	5.1
33	Arkansas	2.2	4	Wyoming	4.5
29	California	2.3	5	New York	4.4
26	Colorado	2.4	6	New Hampshire	4.0
9	Connecticut	3.8	7	Vermont	3.9
29	Delaware	2.3	7	West Virginia	3.9
35	Florida	2.1	9	Connecticut	3.8
50	Georgia	1.2	9	Hawaii	3.8
9	Hawaii	3.8	9	Pennsylvania	3.8
24	Idaho	2.5	12	Indiana	3.7
13	Illinois	3.4	13	Illinois	3.4
12	Indiana	3.7	13	North Dakota	3.4
16	Iowa	3.1	15	Ohio	3.2
21	Kansas	2.8	16	Iowa	3.1
19	Kentucky	2.9	16	Maryland	3.1
29	Louisiana	2.3	16	New Jersey	3.1
26	Maine	2.4	19	Kentucky	2.9
16	Maryland	3.1	19	Michigan	2.9
1	Massachusetts	6.5	21	Kansas	2.8
19	Michigan	2.9	21	South Dakota	2.8
33	Minnesota	2.2	23	Wisconsin	2.7
43	Mississippi	1.7	24	Idaho	2.5
43	Missouri	1.7	24	North Carolina	2.5
43	Montana	1.7	26	Colorado	2.4
39	Nebraska	1.9	26	Maine	2.4
49	Nevada	1.5	26	South Carolina	2.4
6	New Hampshire	4.0	29	California	2.3
16	New Jersey	3.1	29	Delaware	2.3
2	New Mexico	5.1	29	Louisiana	2.3
5	New York	4.4	29	Texas	2.3
24	North Carolina	2.5	33	Arkansas	2.2
13	North Dakota	3.4	33	Minnesota	2.2
15	Ohio	3.2	35	Florida	2.1
39	Oklahoma	1.9	36	Alaska	2.0
41	Oregon	1.8	36	Utah	2.0
9	Pennsylvania	3.8	36	Virginia	2.0
2	Rhode Island	5.1	39	Nebraska	1.9
26	South Carolina	2.4	39	Oklahoma	1.9
21	South Dakota	2.8	41	Oregon	1.8
43	Tennessee	1.7	41	Washington	1.8
29	Texas	2.3	43	Arizona	1.7
36	Utah	2.0	43	Mississippi	1.7
7	Vermont	3.9	43	Missouri	1.7
36	Virginia	2.0	43	Montana	1.7
41	Washington	1.8	43	Tennessee	1.7
7	West Virginia	3.9	48	Alabama	1.6
23	Wisconsin	2.7	49	Nevada	1.5
4	Wyoming	4.5	50	Georgia	1.2
				District of Columbia	1.4

Source: U.S. Department of Education, Office of Special Education Programs
"Data Tables for OSEP State Reported Data" (https://www.ideadata.org/arc_toc11.asp)
*2009-2010 school year. IDEA authorizes funding to states and other organizations to support research, demonstrations, technical assistance, and other programs to ensure that the rights of infants, toddlers, children, and youth with disabilities and their parents are protected. National percent does not include recipients or population in U.S. territories.

Children Age 3 to 21 Served under the
Individuals with Disabilities Education Act (IDEA) in 2010
National Total = 6,480,540 Children*

ALPHA ORDER

RANK	STATE	CHILDREN	% of USA
27	Alabama	82,997	1.3%
46	Alaska	17,893	0.3%
17	Arizona	125,866	1.9%
33	Arkansas	65,039	1.0%
1	California	673,428	10.4%
26	Colorado	83,765	1.3%
29	Connecticut	68,738	1.1%
44	Delaware	19,348	0.3%
4	Florida	376,576	5.8%
11	Georgia	177,070	2.7%
43	Hawaii	19,957	0.3%
41	Idaho	27,787	0.4%
5	Illinois	313,583	4.8%
12	Indiana	172,095	2.7%
31	Iowa	66,636	1.0%
32	Kansas	66,219	1.0%
21	Kentucky	106,045	1.6%
25	Louisiana	85,119	1.3%
39	Maine	32,766	0.5%
22	Maryland	103,018	1.6%
13	Massachusetts	167,297	2.6%
9	Michigan	227,973	3.5%
19	Minnesota	121,359	1.9%
34	Mississippi	63,988	1.0%
15	Missouri	129,886	2.0%
47	Montana	17,213	0.3%
38	Nebraska	43,470	0.7%
35	Nevada	48,115	0.7%
40	New Hampshire	30,210	0.5%
8	New Jersey	229,066	3.5%
37	New Mexico	45,782	0.7%
2	New York	461,470	7.1%
10	North Carolina	184,893	2.9%
50	North Dakota	13,262	0.2%
7	Ohio	263,396	4.1%
24	Oklahoma	95,186	1.5%
28	Oregon	80,062	1.2%
6	Pennsylvania	294,595	4.5%
42	Rhode Island	26,332	0.4%
23	South Carolina	101,039	1.6%
45	South Dakota	17,907	0.3%
20	Tennessee	119,016	1.8%
3	Texas	444,198	6.9%
30	Utah	67,781	1.0%
49	Vermont	14,163	0.2%
14	Virginia	164,771	2.5%
16	Washington	126,024	1.9%
36	West Virginia	46,169	0.7%
18	Wisconsin	125,503	1.9%
48	Wyoming	15,098	0.2%

RANK ORDER

RANK	STATE	CHILDREN	% of USA
1	California	673,428	10.4%
2	New York	461,470	7.1%
3	Texas	444,198	6.9%
4	Florida	376,576	5.8%
5	Illinois	313,583	4.8%
6	Pennsylvania	294,595	4.5%
7	Ohio	263,396	4.1%
8	New Jersey	229,066	3.5%
9	Michigan	227,973	3.5%
10	North Carolina	184,893	2.9%
11	Georgia	177,070	2.7%
12	Indiana	172,095	2.7%
13	Massachusetts	167,297	2.6%
14	Virginia	164,771	2.5%
15	Missouri	129,886	2.0%
16	Washington	126,024	1.9%
17	Arizona	125,866	1.9%
18	Wisconsin	125,503	1.9%
19	Minnesota	121,359	1.9%
20	Tennessee	119,016	1.8%
21	Kentucky	106,045	1.6%
22	Maryland	103,018	1.6%
23	South Carolina	101,039	1.6%
24	Oklahoma	95,186	1.5%
25	Louisiana	85,119	1.3%
26	Colorado	83,765	1.3%
27	Alabama	82,997	1.3%
28	Oregon	80,062	1.2%
29	Connecticut	68,738	1.1%
30	Utah	67,781	1.0%
31	Iowa	66,636	1.0%
32	Kansas	66,219	1.0%
33	Arkansas	65,039	1.0%
34	Mississippi	63,988	1.0%
35	Nevada	48,115	0.7%
36	West Virginia	46,169	0.7%
37	New Mexico	45,782	0.7%
38	Nebraska	43,470	0.7%
39	Maine	32,766	0.5%
40	New Hampshire	30,210	0.5%
41	Idaho	27,787	0.4%
42	Rhode Island	26,332	0.4%
43	Hawaii	19,957	0.3%
44	Delaware	19,348	0.3%
45	South Dakota	17,907	0.3%
46	Alaska	17,893	0.3%
47	Montana	17,213	0.3%
48	Wyoming	15,098	0.2%
49	Vermont	14,163	0.2%
50	North Dakota	13,262	0.2%
	District of Columbia	11,371	0.2%

Source: U.S. Department of Education, Office of Special Education Programs
    "Data Tables for OSEP State Reported Data" (https://www.ideadata.org/arc_toc11.asp)
*2009-2010 school year. IDEA authorizes funding to states and other organizations to support research, demonstrations, technical assistance, and other programs to ensure that the rights of infants, toddlers, children, and youth with disabilities and their parents are protected. National total does not include children served in U.S. territories and Bureau of Indian Education programs.

Percent of All Children Age 3 to 21 Served under the Individuals with Disabilities Education Act (IDEA) in 2010
National Percent = 8.2%*

RANK	STATE	PERCENT
44	Alabama	6.9
13	Alaska	9.3
39	Arizona	7.2
23	Arkansas	8.7
45	California	6.8
48	Colorado	6.5
34	Connecticut	7.7
20	Delaware	8.8
20	Florida	8.8
46	Georgia	6.6
46	Hawaii	6.6
49	Idaho	6.4
15	Illinois	9.2
6	Indiana	10.1
28	Iowa	8.5
20	Kansas	8.8
8	Kentucky	9.9
39	Louisiana	7.2
2	Maine	10.9
39	Maryland	7.2
5	Massachusetts	10.4
19	Michigan	8.9
17	Minnesota	9.0
32	Mississippi	7.9
28	Missouri	8.5
39	Montana	7.2
17	Nebraska	9.0
43	Nevada	7.1
13	New Hampshire	9.3
4	New Jersey	10.7
26	New Mexico	8.6
10	New York	9.6
36	North Carolina	7.6
32	North Dakota	7.9
16	Ohio	9.1
9	Oklahoma	9.8
26	Oregon	8.6
10	Pennsylvania	9.6
6	Rhode Island	10.1
23	South Carolina	8.7
30	South Dakota	8.4
36	Tennessee	7.6
50	Texas	6.3
34	Utah	7.7
12	Vermont	9.5
31	Virginia	8.3
36	Washington	7.6
1	West Virginia	11.0
23	Wisconsin	8.7
3	Wyoming	10.8

RANK	STATE	PERCENT
1	West Virginia	11.0
2	Maine	10.9
3	Wyoming	10.8
4	New Jersey	10.7
5	Massachusetts	10.4
6	Indiana	10.1
6	Rhode Island	10.1
8	Kentucky	9.9
9	Oklahoma	9.8
10	New York	9.6
10	Pennsylvania	9.6
12	Vermont	9.5
13	Alaska	9.3
13	New Hampshire	9.3
15	Illinois	9.2
16	Ohio	9.1
17	Minnesota	9.0
17	Nebraska	9.0
19	Michigan	8.9
20	Delaware	8.8
20	Florida	8.8
20	Kansas	8.8
23	Arkansas	8.7
23	South Carolina	8.7
23	Wisconsin	8.7
26	New Mexico	8.6
26	Oregon	8.6
28	Iowa	8.5
28	Missouri	8.5
30	South Dakota	8.4
31	Virginia	8.3
32	Mississippi	7.9
32	North Dakota	7.9
34	Connecticut	7.7
34	Utah	7.7
36	North Carolina	7.6
36	Tennessee	7.6
36	Washington	7.6
39	Arizona	7.2
39	Louisiana	7.2
39	Maryland	7.2
39	Montana	7.2
43	Nevada	7.1
44	Alabama	6.9
45	California	6.8
46	Georgia	6.6
46	Hawaii	6.6
48	Colorado	6.5
49	Idaho	6.4
50	Texas	6.3
	District of Columbia	8.6

Source: CQ Press using data from U.S. Department of Education, Office of Special Education Programs
"Data Tables for OSEP State Reported Data" (https://www.ideadata.org/arc_toc11.asp)
*2009-2010 school year. IDEA authorizes funding to states and other organizations to support research, demonstrations, technical assistance, and other programs to ensure that the rights of infants, toddlers, children, and youth with disabilities and their parents are protected. National percent does not include children served in U.S. territories and Bureau of Indian Education programs.

Percent of All Children Age 3 to 5 Served under the Individuals with Disabilities Education Act (IDEA) in 2010
National Percent = 5.7%*

ALPHA ORDER

RANK	STATE	PERCENT
48	Alabama	3.9
24	Alaska	6.4
44	Arizona	4.7
3	Arkansas	10.7
47	California	4.5
36	Colorado	5.2
25	Connecticut	6.2
13	Delaware	7.3
39	Florida	5.1
49	Georgia	3.7
42	Hawaii	4.8
31	Idaho	5.4
17	Illinois	6.9
15	Indiana	7.0
34	Iowa	5.3
8	Kansas	8.7
2	Kentucky	11.1
31	Louisiana	5.4
7	Maine	8.9
29	Maryland	5.6
15	Massachusetts	7.0
23	Michigan	6.5
18	Minnesota	6.8
11	Mississippi	7.5
21	Missouri	6.6
42	Montana	4.8
44	Nebraska	4.7
28	Nevada	5.7
21	New Hampshire	6.6
40	New Jersey	4.9
12	New Mexico	7.4
4	New York	9.0
46	North Carolina	4.6
18	North Dakota	6.8
34	Ohio	5.3
40	Oklahoma	4.9
25	Oregon	6.2
18	Pennsylvania	6.8
9	Rhode Island	8.0
27	South Carolina	6.0
10	South Dakota	7.8
36	Tennessee	5.2
50	Texas	3.3
30	Utah	5.5
4	Vermont	9.0
31	Virginia	5.4
36	Washington	5.2
4	West Virginia	9.0
13	Wisconsin	7.3
1	Wyoming	14.4

RANK ORDER

RANK	STATE	PERCENT
1	Wyoming	14.4
2	Kentucky	11.1
3	Arkansas	10.7
4	New York	9.0
4	Vermont	9.0
4	West Virginia	9.0
7	Maine	8.9
8	Kansas	8.7
9	Rhode Island	8.0
10	South Dakota	7.8
11	Mississippi	7.5
12	New Mexico	7.4
13	Delaware	7.3
13	Wisconsin	7.3
15	Indiana	7.0
15	Massachusetts	7.0
17	Illinois	6.9
18	Minnesota	6.8
18	North Dakota	6.8
18	Pennsylvania	6.8
21	Missouri	6.6
21	New Hampshire	6.6
23	Michigan	6.5
24	Alaska	6.4
25	Connecticut	6.2
25	Oregon	6.2
27	South Carolina	6.0
28	Nevada	5.7
29	Maryland	5.6
30	Utah	5.5
31	Idaho	5.4
31	Louisiana	5.4
31	Virginia	5.4
34	Iowa	5.3
34	Ohio	5.3
36	Colorado	5.2
36	Tennessee	5.2
36	Washington	5.2
39	Florida	5.1
40	New Jersey	4.9
40	Oklahoma	4.9
42	Hawaii	4.8
42	Montana	4.8
44	Arizona	4.7
44	Nebraska	4.7
46	North Carolina	4.6
47	California	4.5
48	Alabama	3.9
49	Georgia	3.7
50	Texas	3.3
	District of Columbia	3.3

Source: CQ Press using data from U.S. Department of Education, Office of Special Education Programs
    "Data Tables for OSEP State Reported Data" (https://www.ideadata.org/arc_toc11.asp)
*2009-2010 school year. IDEA authorizes funding to states and other organizations to support research, demonstrations, technical assistance, and other programs to ensure that the rights of infants, toddlers, children, and youth with disabilities and their parents are protected. National percent does not include children served in U.S. territories and Bureau of Indian Education programs.

Percent of All Children Age 6 to 17 Served under the Individuals with Disabilities Education Act (IDEA) in 2010
National Percent = 11.0%*

RANK	STATE	PERCENT
43	Alabama	9.4
14	Alaska	12.5
40	Arizona	9.5
32	Arkansas	10.6
45	California	9.1
48	Colorado	8.6
35	Connecticut	10.3
26	Delaware	11.5
20	Florida	11.9
46	Georgia	9.0
44	Hawaii	9.2
50	Idaho	8.4
16	Illinois	12.3
7	Indiana	13.6
17	Iowa	12.1
26	Kansas	11.5
15	Kentucky	12.4
40	Louisiana	9.5
1	Maine	14.7
40	Maryland	9.5
1	Massachusetts	14.7
20	Michigan	11.9
19	Minnesota	12.0
38	Mississippi	10.1
29	Missouri	11.2
37	Montana	10.2
11	Nebraska	13.0
46	Nevada	9.0
12	New Hampshire	12.8
1	New Jersey	14.7
31	New Mexico	11.1
13	New York	12.6
32	North Carolina	10.6
22	North Dakota	11.8
17	Ohio	12.1
6	Oklahoma	13.9
25	Oregon	11.6
10	Pennsylvania	13.1
5	Rhode Island	14.2
22	South Carolina	11.8
29	South Dakota	11.2
38	Tennessee	10.1
48	Texas	8.6
34	Utah	10.4
8	Vermont	13.3
28	Virginia	11.4
35	Washington	10.3
1	West Virginia	14.7
22	Wisconsin	11.8
9	Wyoming	13.2

RANK	STATE	PERCENT
1	Maine	14.7
1	Massachusetts	14.7
1	New Jersey	14.7
1	West Virginia	14.7
5	Rhode Island	14.2
6	Oklahoma	13.9
7	Indiana	13.6
8	Vermont	13.3
9	Wyoming	13.2
10	Pennsylvania	13.1
11	Nebraska	13.0
12	New Hampshire	12.8
13	New York	12.6
14	Alaska	12.5
15	Kentucky	12.4
16	Illinois	12.3
17	Iowa	12.1
17	Ohio	12.1
19	Minnesota	12.0
20	Florida	11.9
20	Michigan	11.9
22	North Dakota	11.8
22	South Carolina	11.8
22	Wisconsin	11.8
25	Oregon	11.6
26	Delaware	11.5
26	Kansas	11.5
28	Virginia	11.4
29	Missouri	11.2
29	South Dakota	11.2
31	New Mexico	11.1
32	Arkansas	10.6
32	North Carolina	10.6
34	Utah	10.4
35	Connecticut	10.3
35	Washington	10.3
37	Montana	10.2
38	Mississippi	10.1
38	Tennessee	10.1
40	Arizona	9.5
40	Louisiana	9.5
40	Maryland	9.5
43	Alabama	9.4
44	Hawaii	9.2
45	California	9.1
46	Georgia	9.0
46	Nevada	9.0
48	Colorado	8.6
48	Texas	8.6
50	Idaho	8.4

	District of Columbia	13.6

Source: CQ Press using data from U.S. Department of Education, Office of Special Education Programs "Data Tables for OSEP State Reported Data" (https://www.ideadata.org/arc_toc11.asp)
*2009-2010 school year. IDEA authorizes funding to states and other organizations to support research, demonstrations, technical assistance, and other programs to ensure that the rights of infants, toddlers, children, and youth with disabilities and their parents are protected. National percent does not include children served in U.S. territories and Bureau of Indian Education programs.

Percent of All Young Adults Age 18 to 21 Served under the Individuals with Disabilities Education Act (IDEA) in 2010
National Percent = 2.0%*

ALPHA ORDER

RANK	STATE	PERCENT
20	Alabama	2.0
8	Alaska	2.3
43	Arizona	1.6
28	Arkansas	1.8
28	California	1.8
37	Colorado	1.7
28	Connecticut	1.8
8	Delaware	2.3
4	Florida	2.5
44	Georgia	1.5
50	Hawaii	1.0
47	Idaho	1.4
8	Illinois	2.3
2	Indiana	2.7
28	Iowa	1.8
37	Kansas	1.7
37	Kentucky	1.7
37	Louisiana	1.7
13	Maine	2.2
28	Maryland	1.8
18	Massachusetts	2.1
13	Michigan	2.2
3	Minnesota	2.6
26	Mississippi	1.9
13	Missouri	2.2
49	Montana	1.2
37	Nebraska	1.7
44	Nevada	1.5
20	New Hampshire	2.0
8	New Jersey	2.3
13	New Mexico	2.2
18	New York	2.1
28	North Carolina	1.8
47	North Dakota	1.4
1	Ohio	3.0
20	Oklahoma	2.0
20	Oregon	2.0
6	Pennsylvania	2.4
8	Rhode Island	2.3
6	South Carolina	2.4
37	South Dakota	1.7
20	Tennessee	2.0
28	Texas	1.8
44	Utah	1.5
26	Vermont	1.9
13	Virginia	2.2
28	Washington	1.8
4	West Virginia	2.5
28	Wisconsin	1.8
20	Wyoming	2.0

RANK ORDER

RANK	STATE	PERCENT
1	Ohio	3.0
2	Indiana	2.7
3	Minnesota	2.6
4	Florida	2.5
4	West Virginia	2.5
6	Pennsylvania	2.4
6	South Carolina	2.4
8	Alaska	2.3
8	Delaware	2.3
8	Illinois	2.3
8	New Jersey	2.3
8	Rhode Island	2.3
13	Maine	2.2
13	Michigan	2.2
13	Missouri	2.2
13	New Mexico	2.2
13	Virginia	2.2
18	Massachusetts	2.1
18	New York	2.1
20	Alabama	2.0
20	New Hampshire	2.0
20	Oklahoma	2.0
20	Oregon	2.0
20	Tennessee	2.0
20	Wyoming	2.0
26	Mississippi	1.9
26	Vermont	1.9
28	Arkansas	1.8
28	California	1.8
28	Connecticut	1.8
28	Iowa	1.8
28	Maryland	1.8
28	North Carolina	1.8
28	Texas	1.8
28	Washington	1.8
28	Wisconsin	1.8
37	Colorado	1.7
37	Kansas	1.7
37	Kentucky	1.7
37	Louisiana	1.7
37	Nebraska	1.7
37	South Dakota	1.7
43	Arizona	1.6
44	Georgia	1.5
44	Nevada	1.5
44	Utah	1.5
47	Idaho	1.4
47	North Dakota	1.4
49	Montana	1.2
50	Hawaii	1.0

	District of Columbia	2.8

Source: CQ Press using data from U.S. Department of Education, Office of Special Education Programs
"Data Tables for OSEP State Reported Data" (https://www.ideadata.org/arc_toc11.asp)
*2009-2010 school year. IDEA authorizes funding to states and other organizations to support research, demonstrations, technical assistance, and other programs to ensure that the rights of infants, toddlers, children, and youth with disabilities and their parents are protected. National percent does not include children served in U.S. territories and Bureau of Indian Education programs.

Percent of Children Age 6 to 21 Served under the Individuals with Disabilities Education Act (IDEA) for Specific Learning Disabilities in 2010
National Percent = 3.6%*

ALPHA ORDER

RANK ORDER

RANK	STATE	PERCENT	RANK	STATE	PERCENT
NA	Alabama**	NA	1	Iowa	5.5
NA	Alaska**	NA	2	Pennsylvania	5.1
18	Arizona	3.8	3	Oklahoma	5.0
30	Arkansas	3.1	4	Delaware	4.9
23	California	3.4	5	New Jersey	4.8
33	Colorado	2.8	6	Florida	4.4
33	Connecticut	2.8	6	Illinois	4.4
4	Delaware	4.9	6	South Carolina	4.4
6	Florida	4.4	9	Rhode Island	4.3
37	Georgia	2.3	10	New Hampshire	4.2
NA	Hawaii**	NA	11	Massachusetts	4.1
37	Idaho	2.3	11	Nevada	4.1
6	Illinois	4.4	11	Ohio	4.1
14	Indiana	4.0	14	Indiana	4.0
1	Iowa	5.5	14	New Mexico	4.0
19	Kansas	3.7	14	New York	4.0
NA	Kentucky**	NA	14	Utah	4.0
NA	Louisiana**	NA	18	Arizona	3.8
19	Maine	3.7	19	Kansas	3.7
35	Maryland	2.7	19	Maine	3.7
11	Massachusetts	4.1	19	Michigan	3.7
19	Michigan	3.7	22	Montana	3.5
35	Minnesota	2.7	23	California	3.4
NA	Mississippi**	NA	23	Nebraska	3.4
32	Missouri	2.9	23	South Dakota	3.4
22	Montana	3.5	23	Virginia	3.4
23	Nebraska	3.4	27	Tennessee	3.3
11	Nevada	4.1	28	Texas	3.2
10	New Hampshire	4.2	28	Washington	3.2
5	New Jersey	4.8	30	Arkansas	3.1
14	New Mexico	4.0	30	North Carolina	3.1
14	New York	4.0	32	Missouri	2.9
30	North Carolina	3.1	33	Colorado	2.8
NA	North Dakota**	NA	33	Connecticut	2.8
11	Ohio	4.1	35	Maryland	2.7
3	Oklahoma	5.0	35	Minnesota	2.7
NA	Oregon**	NA	37	Georgia	2.3
2	Pennsylvania	5.1	37	Idaho	2.3
9	Rhode Island	4.3	NA	Alabama**	NA
6	South Carolina	4.4	NA	Alaska**	NA
23	South Dakota	3.4	NA	Hawaii**	NA
27	Tennessee	3.3	NA	Kentucky**	NA
28	Texas	3.2	NA	Louisiana**	NA
14	Utah	4.0	NA	Mississippi**	NA
NA	Vermont**	NA	NA	North Dakota**	NA
23	Virginia	3.4	NA	Oregon**	NA
28	Washington	3.2	NA	Vermont**	NA
NA	West Virginia**	NA	NA	West Virginia**	NA
NA	Wisconsin**	NA	NA	Wisconsin**	NA
NA	Wyoming**	NA	NA	Wyoming**	NA

District of Columbia   4.2

Source: CQ Press using data from U.S. Department of Education, Office of Special Education Programs
"Data Tables for OSEP State Reported Data" (https://www.ideadata.org/arc_toc11.asp)
*2009-2010 school year. IDEA authorizes funding to states and other organizations to support research, demonstrations, technical assistance, and other programs to ensure that the rights of infants, toddlers, children, and youth with disabilities and their parents are protected. National percent does not include children served in U.S. territories and Bureau of Indian Education programs.
**Not available.

Percent of Children Age 6 to 21 Served under the Individuals with Disabilities Education Act (IDEA) for Speech Impairments in 2010
National Percent = 1.6%*

RANK	STATE	PERCENT		RANK	STATE	PERCENT
36	Alabama	1.3		1	West Virginia	3.2
26	Alaska	1.6		2	Wyoming	2.7
31	Arizona	1.4		3	Indiana	2.4
12	Arkansas	2.0		3	Mississippi	2.4
28	California	1.5		3	Missouri	2.4
36	Colorado	1.3		3	Nebraska	2.4
28	Connecticut	1.5		3	New Jersey	2.4
49	Delaware	0.7		8	Florida	2.2
8	Florida	2.2		8	Kentucky	2.2
45	Georgia	1.1		10	New York	2.1
50	Hawaii	0.2		10	Oregon	2.1
31	Idaho	1.4		12	Arkansas	2.0
19	Illinois	1.8		12	Maine	2.0
3	Indiana	2.4		12	New Mexico	2.0
48	Iowa	0.8		12	Tennessee	2.0
31	Kansas	1.4		16	Louisiana	1.9
8	Kentucky	2.2		16	Michigan	1.9
16	Louisiana	1.9		16	South Dakota	1.9
12	Maine	2.0		19	Illinois	1.8
36	Maryland	1.3		19	Massachusetts	1.8
19	Massachusetts	1.8		19	North Dakota	1.8
16	Michigan	1.9		19	Wisconsin	1.8
31	Minnesota	1.4		23	Montana	1.7
3	Mississippi	2.4		23	South Carolina	1.7
3	Missouri	2.4		23	Utah	1.7
23	Montana	1.7		26	Alaska	1.6
3	Nebraska	2.4		26	Rhode Island	1.6
45	Nevada	1.1		28	California	1.5
31	New Hampshire	1.4		28	Connecticut	1.5
3	New Jersey	2.4		28	Pennsylvania	1.5
12	New Mexico	2.0		31	Arizona	1.4
10	New York	2.1		31	Idaho	1.4
40	North Carolina	1.2		31	Kansas	1.4
19	North Dakota	1.8		31	Minnesota	1.4
40	Ohio	1.2		31	New Hampshire	1.4
40	Oklahoma	1.2		36	Alabama	1.3
10	Oregon	2.1		36	Colorado	1.3
28	Pennsylvania	1.5		36	Maryland	1.3
26	Rhode Island	1.6		36	Virginia	1.3
23	South Carolina	1.7		40	North Carolina	1.2
16	South Dakota	1.9		40	Ohio	1.2
12	Tennessee	2.0		40	Oklahoma	1.2
45	Texas	1.1		40	Vermont	1.2
23	Utah	1.7		40	Washington	1.2
40	Vermont	1.2		45	Georgia	1.1
36	Virginia	1.3		45	Nevada	1.1
40	Washington	1.2		45	Texas	1.1
1	West Virginia	3.2		48	Iowa	0.8
19	Wisconsin	1.8		49	Delaware	0.7
2	Wyoming	2.7		50	Hawaii	0.2
					District of Columbia	0.7

ALPHA ORDER

RANK ORDER

Source: CQ Press using data from U.S. Department of Education, Office of Special Education Programs
"Data Tables for OSEP State Reported Data" (https://www.ideadata.org/arc_toc11.asp)
*2009-2010 school year. IDEA authorizes funding to states and other organizations to support research, demonstrations, technical assistance, and other programs to ensure that the rights of infants, toddlers, children, and youth with disabilities and their parents are protected. National percent does not include children served in U.S. territories and Bureau of Indian Education programs.

Percent of Children Age 6 to 21 Served under the Individuals with Disabilities Education Act (IDEA) for Mental Retardation in 2010
National Percent = 0.7%*

ALPHA ORDER

RANK	STATE	PERCENT
49	Alabama	0.0
37	Alaska	0.4
29	Arizona	0.5
7	Arkansas	1.0
29	California	0.5
42	Colorado	0.3
42	Connecticut	0.3
7	Delaware	1.0
12	Florida	0.8
12	Georgia	0.8
29	Hawaii	0.5
29	Idaho	0.5
12	Illinois	0.8
4	Indiana	1.3
3	Iowa	1.6
24	Kansas	0.6
2	Kentucky	1.8
12	Louisiana	0.8
42	Maine	0.3
37	Maryland	0.4
12	Massachusetts	0.8
7	Michigan	1.0
12	Minnesota	0.8
24	Mississippi	0.6
12	Missouri	0.8
29	Montana	0.5
6	Nebraska	1.1
42	Nevada	0.3
49	New Hampshire	0.0
42	New Jersey	0.3
37	New Mexico	0.4
42	New York	0.3
7	North Carolina	1.0
24	North Dakota	0.6
5	Ohio	1.2
22	Oklahoma	0.7
29	Oregon	0.5
12	Pennsylvania	0.8
37	Rhode Island	0.4
11	South Carolina	0.9
12	South Dakota	0.8
24	Tennessee	0.6
29	Texas	0.5
37	Utah	0.4
22	Vermont	0.7
24	Virginia	0.6
42	Washington	0.3
1	West Virginia	2.1
12	Wisconsin	0.8
29	Wyoming	0.5

RANK ORDER

RANK	STATE	PERCENT
1	West Virginia	2.1
2	Kentucky	1.8
3	Iowa	1.6
4	Indiana	1.3
5	Ohio	1.2
6	Nebraska	1.1
7	Arkansas	1.0
7	Delaware	1.0
7	Michigan	1.0
7	North Carolina	1.0
11	South Carolina	0.9
12	Florida	0.8
12	Georgia	0.8
12	Illinois	0.8
12	Louisiana	0.8
12	Massachusetts	0.8
12	Minnesota	0.8
12	Missouri	0.8
12	Pennsylvania	0.8
12	South Dakota	0.8
12	Wisconsin	0.8
22	Oklahoma	0.7
22	Vermont	0.7
24	Kansas	0.6
24	Mississippi	0.6
24	North Dakota	0.6
24	Tennessee	0.6
24	Virginia	0.6
29	Arizona	0.5
29	California	0.5
29	Hawaii	0.5
29	Idaho	0.5
29	Montana	0.5
29	Oregon	0.5
29	Texas	0.5
29	Wyoming	0.5
37	Alaska	0.4
37	Maryland	0.4
37	New Mexico	0.4
37	Rhode Island	0.4
37	Utah	0.4
42	Colorado	0.3
42	Connecticut	0.3
42	Maine	0.3
42	Nevada	0.3
42	New Jersey	0.3
42	New York	0.3
42	Washington	0.3
49	Alabama	0.0
49	New Hampshire	0.0
	District of Columbia	0.0

Source: CQ Press using data from U.S. Department of Education, Office of Special Education Programs
"Data Tables for OSEP State Reported Data" (https://www.ideadata.org/arc_toc11.asp)
*2009-2010 school year. IDEA authorizes funding to states and other organizations to support research, demonstrations, technical assistance, and other programs to ensure that the rights of infants, toddlers, children, and youth with disabilities and their parents are protected. National percent does not include children served in U.S. territories and Bureau of Indian Education programs.
**Not available.

Percent of Children Age 6 to 21 Served under the Individuals with Disabilities Education Act (IDEA) for Emotional Disturbance in 2010

National Percent = 0.6%*

<table>
<tr><td colspan="3">ALPHA ORDER</td><td colspan="3">RANK ORDER</td></tr>
<tr><td>RANK</td><td>STATE</td><td>PERCENT</td><td>RANK</td><td>STATE</td><td>PERCENT</td></tr>
<tr><td>40</td><td>Alabama</td><td>0.0</td><td>1</td><td>Minnesota</td><td>1.4</td></tr>
<tr><td>34</td><td>Alaska</td><td>0.4</td><td>2</td><td>Rhode Island</td><td>1.1</td></tr>
<tr><td>20</td><td>Arizona</td><td>0.6</td><td>2</td><td>Wisconsin</td><td>1.1</td></tr>
<tr><td>40</td><td>Arkansas</td><td>0.0</td><td>4</td><td>Indiana</td><td>1.0</td></tr>
<tr><td>36</td><td>California</td><td>0.3</td><td>4</td><td>Maine</td><td>1.0</td></tr>
<tr><td>13</td><td>Colorado</td><td>0.7</td><td>4</td><td>Massachusetts</td><td>1.0</td></tr>
<tr><td>13</td><td>Connecticut</td><td>0.7</td><td>7</td><td>Iowa</td><td>0.9</td></tr>
<tr><td>34</td><td>Delaware</td><td>0.4</td><td>7</td><td>Pennsylvania</td><td>0.9</td></tr>
<tr><td>13</td><td>Florida</td><td>0.7</td><td>9</td><td>Georgia</td><td>0.8</td></tr>
<tr><td>9</td><td>Georgia</td><td>0.8</td><td>9</td><td>Illinois</td><td>0.8</td></tr>
<tr><td>20</td><td>Hawaii</td><td>0.6</td><td>9</td><td>New Hampshire</td><td>0.8</td></tr>
<tr><td>40</td><td>Idaho</td><td>0.0</td><td>9</td><td>New York</td><td>0.8</td></tr>
<tr><td>9</td><td>Illinois</td><td>0.8</td><td>13</td><td>Colorado</td><td>0.7</td></tr>
<tr><td>4</td><td>Indiana</td><td>1.0</td><td>13</td><td>Connecticut</td><td>0.7</td></tr>
<tr><td>7</td><td>Iowa</td><td>0.9</td><td>13</td><td>Florida</td><td>0.7</td></tr>
<tr><td>27</td><td>Kansas</td><td>0.5</td><td>13</td><td>Maryland</td><td>0.7</td></tr>
<tr><td>20</td><td>Kentucky</td><td>0.6</td><td>13</td><td>Michigan</td><td>0.7</td></tr>
<tr><td>40</td><td>Louisiana</td><td>0.0</td><td>13</td><td>Ohio</td><td>0.7</td></tr>
<tr><td>4</td><td>Maine</td><td>1.0</td><td>13</td><td>Wyoming</td><td>0.7</td></tr>
<tr><td>13</td><td>Maryland</td><td>0.7</td><td>20</td><td>Arizona</td><td>0.6</td></tr>
<tr><td>4</td><td>Massachusetts</td><td>1.0</td><td>20</td><td>Hawaii</td><td>0.6</td></tr>
<tr><td>13</td><td>Michigan</td><td>0.7</td><td>20</td><td>Kentucky</td><td>0.6</td></tr>
<tr><td>1</td><td>Minnesota</td><td>1.4</td><td>20</td><td>Oklahoma</td><td>0.6</td></tr>
<tr><td>40</td><td>Mississippi</td><td>0.0</td><td>20</td><td>Oregon</td><td>0.6</td></tr>
<tr><td>27</td><td>Missouri</td><td>0.5</td><td>20</td><td>South Dakota</td><td>0.6</td></tr>
<tr><td>40</td><td>Montana</td><td>0.0</td><td>20</td><td>Virginia</td><td>0.6</td></tr>
<tr><td>27</td><td>Nebraska</td><td>0.5</td><td>27</td><td>Kansas</td><td>0.5</td></tr>
<tr><td>40</td><td>Nevada</td><td>0.0</td><td>27</td><td>Missouri</td><td>0.5</td></tr>
<tr><td>9</td><td>New Hampshire</td><td>0.8</td><td>27</td><td>Nebraska</td><td>0.5</td></tr>
<tr><td>27</td><td>New Jersey</td><td>0.5</td><td>27</td><td>New Jersey</td><td>0.5</td></tr>
<tr><td>27</td><td>New Mexico</td><td>0.5</td><td>27</td><td>New Mexico</td><td>0.5</td></tr>
<tr><td>9</td><td>New York</td><td>0.8</td><td>27</td><td>Texas</td><td>0.5</td></tr>
<tr><td>40</td><td>North Carolina</td><td>0.0</td><td>27</td><td>West Virginia</td><td>0.5</td></tr>
<tr><td>40</td><td>North Dakota</td><td>0.0</td><td>34</td><td>Alaska</td><td>0.4</td></tr>
<tr><td>13</td><td>Ohio</td><td>0.7</td><td>34</td><td>Delaware</td><td>0.4</td></tr>
<tr><td>20</td><td>Oklahoma</td><td>0.6</td><td>36</td><td>California</td><td>0.3</td></tr>
<tr><td>20</td><td>Oregon</td><td>0.6</td><td>36</td><td>Tennessee</td><td>0.3</td></tr>
<tr><td>7</td><td>Pennsylvania</td><td>0.9</td><td>36</td><td>Utah</td><td>0.3</td></tr>
<tr><td>2</td><td>Rhode Island</td><td>1.1</td><td>36</td><td>Washington</td><td>0.3</td></tr>
<tr><td>40</td><td>South Carolina</td><td>0.0</td><td>40</td><td>Alabama</td><td>0.0</td></tr>
<tr><td>20</td><td>South Dakota</td><td>0.6</td><td>40</td><td>Arkansas</td><td>0.0</td></tr>
<tr><td>36</td><td>Tennessee</td><td>0.3</td><td>40</td><td>Idaho</td><td>0.0</td></tr>
<tr><td>27</td><td>Texas</td><td>0.5</td><td>40</td><td>Louisiana</td><td>0.0</td></tr>
<tr><td>36</td><td>Utah</td><td>0.3</td><td>40</td><td>Mississippi</td><td>0.0</td></tr>
<tr><td>40</td><td>Vermont</td><td>0.0</td><td>40</td><td>Montana</td><td>0.0</td></tr>
<tr><td>20</td><td>Virginia</td><td>0.6</td><td>40</td><td>Nevada</td><td>0.0</td></tr>
<tr><td>36</td><td>Washington</td><td>0.3</td><td>40</td><td>North Carolina</td><td>0.0</td></tr>
<tr><td>27</td><td>West Virginia</td><td>0.5</td><td>40</td><td>North Dakota</td><td>0.0</td></tr>
<tr><td>2</td><td>Wisconsin</td><td>1.1</td><td>40</td><td>South Carolina</td><td>0.0</td></tr>
<tr><td>13</td><td>Wyoming</td><td>0.7</td><td>40</td><td>Vermont</td><td>0.0</td></tr>
<tr><td></td><td></td><td></td><td></td><td>District of Columbia</td><td>1.4</td></tr>
</table>

Source: CQ Press using data from U.S. Department of Education, Office of Special Education Programs
"Data Tables for OSEP State Reported Data" (https://www.ideadata.org/arc_toc11.asp)
*2009-2010 school year. IDEA authorizes funding to states and other organizations to support research, demonstrations, technical assistance, and other programs to ensure that the rights of infants, toddlers, children, and youth with disabilities and their parents are protected. National percent does not include children served in U.S. territories and Bureau of Indian Education programs.

Percent of Children Age 6 to 21 Served under the Individuals with Disabilities Education Act (IDEA) for Autism in 2010
National Percent = 0.5%*

RANK	STATE	PERCENT
38	Alabama	0.3
25	Alaska	0.4
25	Arizona	0.4
25	Arkansas	0.4
6	California	0.6
38	Colorado	0.3
4	Connecticut	0.7
25	Delaware	0.4
25	Florida	0.4
25	Georgia	0.4
25	Hawaii	0.4
14	Idaho	0.5
14	Illinois	0.5
4	Indiana	0.7
50	Iowa	0.1
38	Kansas	0.3
38	Kentucky	0.3
38	Louisiana	0.3
3	Maine	0.8
6	Maryland	0.6
6	Massachusetts	0.6
6	Michigan	0.6
1	Minnesota	1.1
38	Mississippi	0.3
14	Missouri	0.5
49	Montana	0.2
25	Nebraska	0.4
14	Nevada	0.5
14	New Hampshire	0.5
6	New Jersey	0.6
38	New Mexico	0.3
14	New York	0.5
14	North Carolina	0.5
25	North Dakota	0.4
14	Ohio	0.5
38	Oklahoma	0.3
2	Oregon	0.9
6	Pennsylvania	0.6
6	Rhode Island	0.6
38	South Carolina	0.3
38	South Dakota	0.3
25	Tennessee	0.4
25	Texas	0.4
25	Utah	0.4
14	Vermont	0.5
14	Virginia	0.5
14	Washington	0.5
38	West Virginia	0.3
6	Wisconsin	0.6
25	Wyoming	0.4

RANK	STATE	PERCENT
1	Minnesota	1.1
2	Oregon	0.9
3	Maine	0.8
4	Connecticut	0.7
4	Indiana	0.7
6	California	0.6
6	Maryland	0.6
6	Massachusetts	0.6
6	Michigan	0.6
6	New Jersey	0.6
6	Pennsylvania	0.6
6	Rhode Island	0.6
6	Wisconsin	0.6
14	Idaho	0.5
14	Illinois	0.5
14	Missouri	0.5
14	Nevada	0.5
14	New Hampshire	0.5
14	New York	0.5
14	North Carolina	0.5
14	Ohio	0.5
14	Vermont	0.5
14	Virginia	0.5
14	Washington	0.5
25	Alaska	0.4
25	Arizona	0.4
25	Arkansas	0.4
25	Delaware	0.4
25	Florida	0.4
25	Georgia	0.4
25	Hawaii	0.4
25	Nebraska	0.4
25	North Dakota	0.4
25	Tennessee	0.4
25	Texas	0.4
25	Utah	0.4
25	Wyoming	0.4
38	Alabama	0.3
38	Colorado	0.3
38	Kansas	0.3
38	Kentucky	0.3
38	Louisiana	0.3
38	Mississippi	0.3
38	New Mexico	0.3
38	Oklahoma	0.3
38	South Carolina	0.3
38	South Dakota	0.3
38	West Virginia	0.3
49	Montana	0.2
50	Iowa	0.1

	District of Columbia	0.3

Source: CQ Press using data from U.S. Department of Education, Office of Special Education Programs
"Data Tables for OSEP State Reported Data" (https://www.ideadata.org/arc_toc11.asp)
*2009-2010 school year. IDEA authorizes funding to states and other organizations to support research, demonstrations, technical assistance, and other programs to ensure that the rights of infants, toddlers, children, and youth with disabilities and their parents are protected. National percent does not include children served in U.S. territories and Bureau of Indian Education programs.

Percent of Children Age 6 to 21 Served under IDEA
Who Spend More than 80% of Their Time in a Regular Classroom in 2010
National Percent = 59.4%*

ALPHA ORDER

RANK	STATE	PERCENT
1	Alabama	82.3
34	Alaska	56.9
32	Arizona	58.1
43	Arkansas	53.1
44	California	51.4
9	Colorado	70.0
7	Connecticut	70.4
31	Delaware	58.2
14	Florida	66.2
23	Georgia	61.7
50	Hawaii	16.6
19	Idaho	62.8
46	Illinois	50.5
15	Indiana	64.9
23	Iowa	61.7
19	Kansas	62.8
6	Kentucky	70.8
26	Louisiana	60.9
38	Maine	55.7
16	Maryland	64.8
35	Massachusetts	56.7
27	Michigan	60.0
25	Minnesota	61.4
13	Mississippi	66.4
30	Missouri	58.4
44	Montana	51.4
4	Nebraska	72.1
17	Nevada	63.8
48	New Hampshire	48.7
49	New Jersey	44.8
40	New Mexico	54.9
39	New York	55.2
18	North Carolina	63.1
2	North Dakota	76.4
37	Ohio	55.8
22	Oklahoma	61.9
8	Oregon	70.1
33	Pennsylvania	57.5
3	Rhode Island	73.1
36	South Carolina	56.2
11	South Dakota	67.4
21	Tennessee	62.3
12	Texas	67.1
42	Utah	53.6
5	Vermont	71.7
28	Virginia	59.7
47	Washington	50.1
10	West Virginia	68.1
41	Wisconsin	54.6
29	Wyoming	58.8

RANK ORDER

RANK	STATE	PERCENT
1	Alabama	82.3
2	North Dakota	76.4
3	Rhode Island	73.1
4	Nebraska	72.1
5	Vermont	71.7
6	Kentucky	70.8
7	Connecticut	70.4
8	Oregon	70.1
9	Colorado	70.0
10	West Virginia	68.1
11	South Dakota	67.4
12	Texas	67.1
13	Mississippi	66.4
14	Florida	66.2
15	Indiana	64.9
16	Maryland	64.8
17	Nevada	63.8
18	North Carolina	63.1
19	Idaho	62.8
19	Kansas	62.8
21	Tennessee	62.3
22	Oklahoma	61.9
23	Georgia	61.7
23	Iowa	61.7
25	Minnesota	61.4
26	Louisiana	60.9
27	Michigan	60.0
28	Virginia	59.7
29	Wyoming	58.8
30	Missouri	58.4
31	Delaware	58.2
32	Arizona	58.1
33	Pennsylvania	57.5
34	Alaska	56.9
35	Massachusetts	56.7
36	South Carolina	56.2
37	Ohio	55.8
38	Maine	55.7
39	New York	55.2
40	New Mexico	54.9
41	Wisconsin	54.6
42	Utah	53.6
43	Arkansas	53.1
44	California	51.4
44	Montana	51.4
46	Illinois	50.5
47	Washington	50.1
48	New Hampshire	48.7
49	New Jersey	44.8
50	Hawaii	16.6

| | District of Columbia | 35.5 |

Source: U.S. Department of Education, Office of Special Education Programs
   "Data Tables for OSEP State Reported Data" (https://www.ideadata.org/arc_toc11.asp)
*2009-2010 school year. IDEA authorizes funding to states and other organizations to support research, demonstrations, technical assistance, and other programs to ensure that the rights of infants, toddlers, children, and youth with disabilities and their parents are protected. National percent does not include children served in U.S. territories and Bureau of Indian Education programs.

Percent of Children Age 6 to 21 Served under IDEA
Who Are Served in a Separate School in 2010
National Percent = 3.0%*

ALPHA ORDER			RANK ORDER		
RANK	STATE	PERCENT	RANK	STATE	PERCENT
31	Alabama	1.2	1	New Jersey	7.0
29	Alaska	1.4	2	Maryland	6.9
19	Arizona	2.4	3	Massachusetts	5.8
33	Arkansas	1.1	4	Connecticut	5.6
11	California	3.9	5	Illinois	5.3
22	Colorado	2.1	5	New York	5.3
4	Connecticut	5.6	7	Delaware	5.1
7	Delaware	5.1	8	Vermont	4.9
17	Florida	2.6	9	Michigan	4.6
25	Georgia	1.6	10	Rhode Island	4.2
37	Hawaii	0.9	11	California	3.9
33	Idaho	1.1	11	Minnesota	3.9
5	Illinois	5.3	13	Pennsylvania	3.8
33	Indiana	1.1	14	Ohio	3.4
25	Iowa	1.6	15	Missouri	3.1
23	Kansas	1.9	16	Utah	2.7
41	Kentucky	0.7	17	Florida	2.6
48	Louisiana	0.4	17	Maine	2.6
17	Maine	2.6	19	Arizona	2.4
2	Maryland	6.9	20	Nebraska	2.3
3	Massachusetts	5.8	20	Virginia	2.3
9	Michigan	4.6	22	Colorado	2.1
11	Minnesota	3.9	23	Kansas	1.9
39	Mississippi	0.8	24	New Hampshire	1.8
15	Missouri	3.1	25	Georgia	1.6
36	Montana	1.0	25	Iowa	1.6
20	Nebraska	2.3	27	Nevada	1.5
27	Nevada	1.5	27	South Dakota	1.5
24	New Hampshire	1.8	29	Alaska	1.4
1	New Jersey	7.0	30	North Carolina	1.3
44	New Mexico	0.6	31	Alabama	1.2
5	New York	5.3	31	Oregon	1.2
30	North Carolina	1.3	33	Arkansas	1.1
45	North Dakota	0.5	33	Idaho	1.1
14	Ohio	3.4	33	Indiana	1.1
48	Oklahoma	0.4	36	Montana	1.0
31	Oregon	1.2	37	Hawaii	0.9
13	Pennsylvania	3.8	37	Tennessee	0.9
10	Rhode Island	4.2	39	Mississippi	0.8
41	South Carolina	0.7	39	Wisconsin	0.8
27	South Dakota	1.5	41	Kentucky	0.7
37	Tennessee	0.9	41	South Carolina	0.7
45	Texas	0.5	41	Washington	0.7
16	Utah	2.7	44	New Mexico	0.6
8	Vermont	4.9	45	North Dakota	0.5
20	Virginia	2.3	45	Texas	0.5
41	Washington	0.7	45	Wyoming	0.5
50	West Virginia	0.0	48	Louisiana	0.4
39	Wisconsin	0.8	48	Oklahoma	0.4
45	Wyoming	0.5	50	West Virginia	0.0
				District of Columbia	27.5

Source: U.S. Department of Education, Office of Special Education Programs
   "Data Tables for OSEP State Reported Data" (https://www.ideadata.org/arc_toc11.asp)
*2009-2010 school year. IDEA authorizes funding to states and other organizations to support research, demonstrations, technical assistance, and other programs to ensure that the rights of infants, toddlers, children, and youth with disabilities and their parents are protected. National percent does not include children served in U.S. territories and Bureau of Indian Education programs.

Special Education Students Who Graduated with a Diploma in 2009

National Total = 245,131 Students*

ALPHA ORDER					RANK ORDER			
RANK	STATE	STUDENTS	% of USA		RANK	STATE	STUDENTS	% of USA
34	Alabama	1,678	0.7%		1	Pennsylvania	18,731	7.6%
48	Alaska	512	0.2%		2	Texas	16,251	6.6%
19	Arizona	4,910	2.0%		3	New York	15,937	6.5%
26	Arkansas	3,364	1.4%		4	California	14,630	6.0%
4	California	14,630	6.0%		5	Illinois	14,263	5.8%
28	Colorado	3,050	1.2%		6	New Jersey	14,234	5.8%
23	Connecticut	3,556	1.5%		7	Florida	11,588	4.7%
47	Delaware	569	0.2%		8	Michigan	10,359	4.2%
7	Florida	11,588	4.7%		9	Massachusetts	7,775	3.2%
20	Georgia	4,579	1.9%		10	Ohio	7,674	3.1%
40	Hawaii	1,199	0.5%		11	Missouri	7,100	2.9%
44	Idaho	684	0.3%		12	North Carolina	6,484	2.6%
5	Illinois	14,263	5.8%		13	Wisconsin	6,075	2.5%
15	Indiana	5,898	2.4%		14	Virginia	6,007	2.5%
24	Iowa	3,479	1.4%		15	Indiana	5,898	2.4%
27	Kansas	3,113	1.3%		16	Tennessee	5,758	2.3%
25	Kentucky	3,365	1.4%		17	Minnesota	5,757	2.3%
38	Louisiana	1,461	0.6%		18	Oklahoma	5,134	2.1%
36	Maine	1,557	0.6%		19	Arizona	4,910	2.0%
22	Maryland	4,112	1.7%		20	Georgia	4,579	1.9%
9	Massachusetts	7,775	3.2%		21	Washington	4,511	1.8%
8	Michigan	10,359	4.2%		22	Maryland	4,112	1.7%
17	Minnesota	5,757	2.3%		23	Connecticut	3,556	1.5%
42	Mississippi	807	0.3%		24	Iowa	3,479	1.4%
11	Missouri	7,100	2.9%		25	Kentucky	3,365	1.4%
41	Montana	852	0.3%		26	Arkansas	3,364	1.4%
35	Nebraska	1,591	0.6%		27	Kansas	3,113	1.3%
43	Nevada	703	0.3%		28	Colorado	3,050	1.2%
33	New Hampshire	1,825	0.7%		29	Utah	2,476	1.0%
6	New Jersey	14,234	5.8%		30	South Carolina	2,308	0.9%
37	New Mexico	1,486	0.6%		31	Oregon	2,224	0.9%
3	New York	15,937	6.5%		32	West Virginia	2,122	0.9%
12	North Carolina	6,484	2.6%		33	New Hampshire	1,825	0.7%
46	North Dakota	576	0.2%		34	Alabama	1,678	0.7%
10	Ohio	7,674	3.1%		35	Nebraska	1,591	0.6%
18	Oklahoma	5,134	2.1%		36	Maine	1,557	0.6%
31	Oregon	2,224	0.9%		37	New Mexico	1,486	0.6%
1	Pennsylvania	18,731	7.6%		38	Louisiana	1,461	0.6%
39	Rhode Island	1,205	0.5%		39	Rhode Island	1,205	0.5%
30	South Carolina	2,308	0.9%		40	Hawaii	1,199	0.5%
45	South Dakota	577	0.2%		41	Montana	852	0.3%
16	Tennessee	5,758	2.3%		42	Mississippi	807	0.3%
2	Texas	16,251	6.6%		43	Nevada	703	0.3%
29	Utah	2,476	1.0%		44	Idaho	684	0.3%
NA	Vermont**	NA	NA		45	South Dakota	577	0.2%
14	Virginia	6,007	2.5%		46	North Dakota	576	0.2%
21	Washington	4,511	1.8%		47	Delaware	569	0.2%
32	West Virginia	2,122	0.9%		48	Alaska	512	0.2%
13	Wisconsin	6,075	2.5%		49	Wyoming	408	0.2%
49	Wyoming	408	0.2%		NA	Vermont**	NA	NA
						District of Columbia	617	0.3%

Source: U.S. Department of Education, Office of Special Education Programs
   "Data Tables for OSEP State Reported Data" (https://www.ideadata.org/arc_toc11.asp)
*2008-2009 school year. National total does not include graduates served in U.S. territories and Bureau of Indian Education programs.
**Not available.

Special Education Students Who Dropped Out of School in 2009

National Total = 90,028 Students*

ALPHA ORDER

RANK	STATE	STUDENTS	% of USA
35	Alabama	636	0.7%
43	Alaska	309	0.3%
24	Arizona	1,321	1.5%
34	Arkansas	669	0.7%
3	California	6,833	7.6%
19	Colorado	1,674	1.9%
28	Connecticut	879	1.0%
40	Delaware	322	0.4%
4	Florida	5,588	6.2%
9	Georgia	3,154	3.5%
49	Hawaii	41	0.0%
41	Idaho	321	0.4%
7	Illinois	3,486	3.9%
11	Indiana	2,700	3.0%
22	Iowa	1,493	1.7%
27	Kansas	988	1.1%
29	Kentucky	873	1.0%
14	Louisiana	2,336	2.6%
37	Maine	497	0.6%
21	Maryland	1,637	1.8%
13	Massachusetts	2,381	2.6%
5	Michigan	4,912	5.5%
33	Minnesota	695	0.8%
38	Mississippi	445	0.5%
15	Missouri	2,299	2.6%
45	Montana	285	0.3%
44	Nebraska	306	0.3%
30	Nevada	870	1.0%
36	New Hampshire	530	0.6%
8	New Jersey	3,270	3.6%
41	New Mexico	321	0.4%
1	New York	7,788	8.7%
6	North Carolina	3,559	4.0%
47	North Dakota	231	0.3%
16	Ohio	1,839	2.0%
23	Oklahoma	1,480	1.6%
25	Oregon	1,211	1.3%
12	Pennsylvania	2,388	2.7%
39	Rhode Island	378	0.4%
10	South Carolina	3,002	3.3%
48	South Dakota	138	0.2%
26	Tennessee	1,073	1.2%
2	Texas	7,066	7.8%
32	Utah	789	0.9%
NA	Vermont**	NA	NA
17	Virginia	1,803	2.0%
18	Washington	1,796	2.0%
31	West Virginia	822	0.9%
20	Wisconsin	1,656	1.8%
46	Wyoming	265	0.3%

RANK ORDER

RANK	STATE	STUDENTS	% of USA
1	New York	7,788	8.7%
2	Texas	7,066	7.8%
3	California	6,833	7.6%
4	Florida	5,588	6.2%
5	Michigan	4,912	5.5%
6	North Carolina	3,559	4.0%
7	Illinois	3,486	3.9%
8	New Jersey	3,270	3.6%
9	Georgia	3,154	3.5%
10	South Carolina	3,002	3.3%
11	Indiana	2,700	3.0%
12	Pennsylvania	2,388	2.7%
13	Massachusetts	2,381	2.6%
14	Louisiana	2,336	2.6%
15	Missouri	2,299	2.6%
16	Ohio	1,839	2.0%
17	Virginia	1,803	2.0%
18	Washington	1,796	2.0%
19	Colorado	1,674	1.9%
20	Wisconsin	1,656	1.8%
21	Maryland	1,637	1.8%
22	Iowa	1,493	1.7%
23	Oklahoma	1,480	1.6%
24	Arizona	1,321	1.5%
25	Oregon	1,211	1.3%
26	Tennessee	1,073	1.2%
27	Kansas	988	1.1%
28	Connecticut	879	1.0%
29	Kentucky	873	1.0%
30	Nevada	870	1.0%
31	West Virginia	822	0.9%
32	Utah	789	0.9%
33	Minnesota	695	0.8%
34	Arkansas	669	0.7%
35	Alabama	636	0.7%
36	New Hampshire	530	0.6%
37	Maine	497	0.6%
38	Mississippi	445	0.5%
39	Rhode Island	378	0.4%
40	Delaware	322	0.4%
41	Idaho	321	0.4%
41	New Mexico	321	0.4%
43	Alaska	309	0.3%
44	Nebraska	306	0.3%
45	Montana	285	0.3%
46	Wyoming	265	0.3%
47	North Dakota	231	0.3%
48	South Dakota	138	0.2%
49	Hawaii	41	0.0%
NA	Vermont**	NA	NA
	District of Columbia	673	0.7%

Source: U.S. Department of Education, Office of Special Education Programs
"Data Tables for OSEP State Reported Data" (https://www.ideadata.org/arc_toc11.asp)
*2008-2009 school year. "Dropped out" is defined as the total who were enrolled at some point in the reporting year, were not enrolled at the end of the reporting year, and who did not graduate, receive a certificate, die, or reach maximum age. Drop outs includes runaways, GED recipients, expulsions, status unknown, and other exiters.
**Not available.

Public Elementary and Secondary School Students with Individualized Educational Plans (IEPs) in 2009
National Total = 6,450,858 Students*

<table>
<tr><td colspan="4">ALPHA ORDER</td><td colspan="4">RANK ORDER</td></tr>
<tr><td>RANK</td><td>STATE</td><td>STUDENTS</td><td>% of USA</td><td>RANK</td><td>STATE</td><td>STUDENTS</td><td>% of USA</td></tr>
<tr><td>27</td><td>Alabama</td><td>82,988</td><td>1.3%</td><td>1</td><td>California</td><td>663,004</td><td>10.3%</td></tr>
<tr><td>46</td><td>Alaska</td><td>17,893</td><td>0.3%</td><td>2</td><td>New York</td><td>460,336</td><td>7.1%</td></tr>
<tr><td>17</td><td>Arizona</td><td>125,839</td><td>2.0%</td><td>3</td><td>Texas</td><td>444,198</td><td>6.9%</td></tr>
<tr><td>33</td><td>Arkansas</td><td>65,039</td><td>1.0%</td><td>4</td><td>Florida</td><td>374,669</td><td>5.8%</td></tr>
<tr><td>1</td><td>California</td><td>663,004</td><td>10.3%</td><td>5</td><td>Illinois</td><td>312,534</td><td>4.8%</td></tr>
<tr><td>26</td><td>Colorado</td><td>83,765</td><td>1.3%</td><td>6</td><td>Pennsylvania</td><td>294,592</td><td>4.6%</td></tr>
<tr><td>29</td><td>Connecticut</td><td>68,687</td><td>1.1%</td><td>7</td><td>Ohio</td><td>263,394</td><td>4.1%</td></tr>
<tr><td>44</td><td>Delaware</td><td>19,348</td><td>0.3%</td><td>8</td><td>New Jersey</td><td>228,989</td><td>3.5%</td></tr>
<tr><td>4</td><td>Florida</td><td>374,669</td><td>5.8%</td><td>9</td><td>Michigan</td><td>227,640</td><td>3.5%</td></tr>
<tr><td>11</td><td>Georgia</td><td>177,070</td><td>2.7%</td><td>10</td><td>North Carolina</td><td>184,583</td><td>2.9%</td></tr>
<tr><td>43</td><td>Hawaii</td><td>19,957</td><td>0.3%</td><td>11</td><td>Georgia</td><td>177,070</td><td>2.7%</td></tr>
<tr><td>41</td><td>Idaho</td><td>27,787</td><td>0.4%</td><td>12</td><td>Indiana</td><td>172,095</td><td>2.7%</td></tr>
<tr><td>5</td><td>Illinois</td><td>312,534</td><td>4.8%</td><td>13</td><td>Massachusetts</td><td>167,297</td><td>2.6%</td></tr>
<tr><td>12</td><td>Indiana</td><td>172,095</td><td>2.7%</td><td>14</td><td>Virginia</td><td>164,717</td><td>2.6%</td></tr>
<tr><td>31</td><td>Iowa</td><td>66,630</td><td>1.0%</td><td>15</td><td>Missouri</td><td>129,879</td><td>2.0%</td></tr>
<tr><td>32</td><td>Kansas</td><td>66,219</td><td>1.0%</td><td>16</td><td>Washington</td><td>126,021</td><td>2.0%</td></tr>
<tr><td>21</td><td>Kentucky</td><td>106,045</td><td>1.6%</td><td>17</td><td>Arizona</td><td>125,839</td><td>2.0%</td></tr>
<tr><td>25</td><td>Louisiana</td><td>85,119</td><td>1.3%</td><td>18</td><td>Wisconsin</td><td>125,503</td><td>1.9%</td></tr>
<tr><td>40</td><td>Maine</td><td>29,925</td><td>0.5%</td><td>19</td><td>Minnesota</td><td>121,359</td><td>1.9%</td></tr>
<tr><td>22</td><td>Maryland</td><td>102,327</td><td>1.6%</td><td>20</td><td>Tennessee</td><td>118,587</td><td>1.8%</td></tr>
<tr><td>13</td><td>Massachusetts</td><td>167,297</td><td>2.6%</td><td>21</td><td>Kentucky</td><td>106,045</td><td>1.6%</td></tr>
<tr><td>9</td><td>Michigan</td><td>227,640</td><td>3.5%</td><td>22</td><td>Maryland</td><td>102,327</td><td>1.6%</td></tr>
<tr><td>19</td><td>Minnesota</td><td>121,359</td><td>1.9%</td><td>23</td><td>South Carolina</td><td>101,020</td><td>1.6%</td></tr>
<tr><td>34</td><td>Mississippi</td><td>63,721</td><td>1.0%</td><td>24</td><td>Oklahoma</td><td>95,186</td><td>1.5%</td></tr>
<tr><td>15</td><td>Missouri</td><td>129,879</td><td>2.0%</td><td>25</td><td>Louisiana</td><td>85,119</td><td>1.3%</td></tr>
<tr><td>47</td><td>Montana</td><td>17,210</td><td>0.3%</td><td>26</td><td>Colorado</td><td>83,765</td><td>1.3%</td></tr>
<tr><td>38</td><td>Nebraska</td><td>43,470</td><td>0.7%</td><td>27</td><td>Alabama</td><td>82,988</td><td>1.3%</td></tr>
<tr><td>35</td><td>Nevada</td><td>48,115</td><td>0.7%</td><td>28</td><td>Oregon</td><td>79,301</td><td>1.2%</td></tr>
<tr><td>39</td><td>New Hampshire</td><td>30,155</td><td>0.5%</td><td>29</td><td>Connecticut</td><td>68,687</td><td>1.1%</td></tr>
<tr><td>8</td><td>New Jersey</td><td>228,989</td><td>3.5%</td><td>30</td><td>Utah</td><td>67,787</td><td>1.1%</td></tr>
<tr><td>37</td><td>New Mexico</td><td>45,776</td><td>0.7%</td><td>31</td><td>Iowa</td><td>66,630</td><td>1.0%</td></tr>
<tr><td>2</td><td>New York</td><td>460,336</td><td>7.1%</td><td>32</td><td>Kansas</td><td>66,219</td><td>1.0%</td></tr>
<tr><td>10</td><td>North Carolina</td><td>184,583</td><td>2.9%</td><td>33</td><td>Arkansas</td><td>65,039</td><td>1.0%</td></tr>
<tr><td>48</td><td>North Dakota</td><td>13,218</td><td>0.2%</td><td>34</td><td>Mississippi</td><td>63,721</td><td>1.0%</td></tr>
<tr><td>7</td><td>Ohio</td><td>263,394</td><td>4.1%</td><td>35</td><td>Nevada</td><td>48,115</td><td>0.7%</td></tr>
<tr><td>24</td><td>Oklahoma</td><td>95,186</td><td>1.5%</td><td>36</td><td>West Virginia</td><td>46,086</td><td>0.7%</td></tr>
<tr><td>28</td><td>Oregon</td><td>79,301</td><td>1.2%</td><td>37</td><td>New Mexico</td><td>45,776</td><td>0.7%</td></tr>
<tr><td>6</td><td>Pennsylvania</td><td>294,592</td><td>4.6%</td><td>38</td><td>Nebraska</td><td>43,470</td><td>0.7%</td></tr>
<tr><td>42</td><td>Rhode Island</td><td>26,332</td><td>0.4%</td><td>39</td><td>New Hampshire</td><td>30,155</td><td>0.5%</td></tr>
<tr><td>23</td><td>South Carolina</td><td>101,020</td><td>1.6%</td><td>40</td><td>Maine</td><td>29,925</td><td>0.5%</td></tr>
<tr><td>45</td><td>South Dakota</td><td>17,904</td><td>0.3%</td><td>41</td><td>Idaho</td><td>27,787</td><td>0.4%</td></tr>
<tr><td>20</td><td>Tennessee</td><td>118,587</td><td>1.8%</td><td>42</td><td>Rhode Island</td><td>26,332</td><td>0.4%</td></tr>
<tr><td>3</td><td>Texas</td><td>444,198</td><td>6.9%</td><td>43</td><td>Hawaii</td><td>19,957</td><td>0.3%</td></tr>
<tr><td>30</td><td>Utah</td><td>67,787</td><td>1.1%</td><td>44</td><td>Delaware</td><td>19,348</td><td>0.3%</td></tr>
<tr><td>50</td><td>Vermont</td><td>7,791</td><td>0.1%</td><td>45</td><td>South Dakota</td><td>17,904</td><td>0.3%</td></tr>
<tr><td>14</td><td>Virginia</td><td>164,717</td><td>2.6%</td><td>46</td><td>Alaska</td><td>17,893</td><td>0.3%</td></tr>
<tr><td>16</td><td>Washington</td><td>126,021</td><td>2.0%</td><td>47</td><td>Montana</td><td>17,210</td><td>0.3%</td></tr>
<tr><td>36</td><td>West Virginia</td><td>46,086</td><td>0.7%</td><td>48</td><td>North Dakota</td><td>13,218</td><td>0.2%</td></tr>
<tr><td>18</td><td>Wisconsin</td><td>125,503</td><td>1.9%</td><td>49</td><td>Wyoming</td><td>12,405</td><td>0.2%</td></tr>
<tr><td>49</td><td>Wyoming</td><td>12,405</td><td>0.2%</td><td>50</td><td>Vermont</td><td>7,791</td><td>0.1%</td></tr>
<tr><td></td><td></td><td></td><td></td><td></td><td>District of Columbia</td><td>11,346</td><td>0.2%</td></tr>
</table>

Source: U.S. Department of Education, National Center for Education Statistics
"Common Core of Data (CCD) Database" (http://nces.ed.gov/ccd/)
*These plans are for students participating in various special education services. For school year 2008-2009.

Percent of Public Elementary and Secondary School Students with Individualized Education Plans (IEPs) in 2009
National Percent = 13.1%*

ALPHA ORDER

RANK	STATE	PERCENT
43	Alabama	11.1
28	Alaska	13.6
40	Arizona	11.7
30	Arkansas	13.5
45	California	10.7
47	Colorado	10.1
35	Connecticut	12.2
10	Delaware	15.3
19	Florida	14.2
46	Georgia	10.6
43	Hawaii	11.1
47	Idaho	10.1
12	Illinois	14.9
5	Indiana	16.4
28	Iowa	13.6
24	Kansas	14.0
9	Kentucky	15.6
34	Louisiana	12.3
8	Maine	15.8
38	Maryland	12.1
2	Massachusetts	17.5
26	Michigan	13.9
15	Minnesota	14.5
32	Mississippi	12.9
19	Missouri	14.2
38	Montana	12.1
14	Nebraska	14.7
42	Nevada	11.2
10	New Hampshire	15.3
5	New Jersey	16.4
27	New Mexico	13.7
3	New York	16.6
33	North Carolina	12.4
19	North Dakota	14.2
12	Ohio	14.9
15	Oklahoma	14.5
22	Oregon	14.1
3	Pennsylvania	16.6
1	Rhode Island	18.1
24	South Carolina	14.0
15	South Dakota	14.5
35	Tennessee	12.2
49	Texas	9.2
41	Utah	11.6
50	Vermont	8.4
31	Virginia	13.2
35	Washington	12.2
7	West Virginia	16.3
18	Wisconsin	14.4
22	Wyoming	14.1

RANK ORDER

RANK	STATE	PERCENT
1	Rhode Island	18.1
2	Massachusetts	17.5
3	New York	16.6
3	Pennsylvania	16.6
5	Indiana	16.4
5	New Jersey	16.4
7	West Virginia	16.3
8	Maine	15.8
9	Kentucky	15.6
10	Delaware	15.3
10	New Hampshire	15.3
12	Illinois	14.9
12	Ohio	14.9
14	Nebraska	14.7
15	Minnesota	14.5
15	Oklahoma	14.5
15	South Dakota	14.5
18	Wisconsin	14.4
19	Florida	14.2
19	Missouri	14.2
19	North Dakota	14.2
22	Oregon	14.1
22	Wyoming	14.1
24	Kansas	14.0
24	South Carolina	14.0
26	Michigan	13.9
27	New Mexico	13.7
28	Alaska	13.6
28	Iowa	13.6
30	Arkansas	13.5
31	Virginia	13.2
32	Mississippi	12.9
33	North Carolina	12.4
34	Louisiana	12.3
35	Connecticut	12.2
35	Tennessee	12.2
35	Washington	12.2
38	Maryland	12.1
38	Montana	12.1
40	Arizona	11.7
41	Utah	11.6
42	Nevada	11.2
43	Alabama	11.1
43	Hawaii	11.1
45	California	10.7
46	Georgia	10.6
47	Colorado	10.1
47	Idaho	10.1
49	Texas	9.2
50	Vermont	8.4

| | District of Columbia | 16.3 |

Source: CQ Press using data from U.S. Department of Education, National Center for Education Statistics
"Common Core of Data (CCD) Database" (http://nces.ed.gov/ccd/)
*These plans are for students participating in various special education services. For school year 2008-2009.

Public Elementary and Secondary School Students Receiving English Language Learner (ELL) Services in 2009
National Total = 4,723,926 Students*

ALPHA ORDER

RANK	STATE	STUDENTS	% of USA
33	Alabama	19,497	0.4%
37	Alaska	14,670	0.3%
10	Arizona	83,625	1.8%
29	Arkansas	29,752	0.6%
1	California	1,779,102	37.7%
7	Colorado	95,141	2.0%
28	Connecticut	30,090	0.6%
40	Delaware	7,685	0.2%
3	Florida	230,540	4.9%
8	Georgia	86,755	1.8%
35	Hawaii	18,097	0.4%
36	Idaho	15,965	0.3%
5	Illinois	179,857	3.8%
19	Indiana	49,271	1.0%
31	Iowa	20,867	0.4%
25	Kansas	38,011	0.8%
38	Kentucky	14,244	0.3%
39	Louisiana	13,012	0.3%
43	Maine	4,478	0.1%
23	Maryland	43,179	0.9%
17	Massachusetts	51,667	1.1%
15	Michigan	58,740	1.2%
14	Minnesota	61,396	1.3%
42	Mississippi	6,061	0.1%
32	Missouri	20,473	0.4%
46	Montana	3,807	0.1%
34	Nebraska	19,339	0.4%
11	Nevada	67,874	1.4%
45	New Hampshire	3,821	0.1%
16	New Jersey	55,656	1.2%
18	New Mexico	51,493	1.1%
4	New York	200,805	4.3%
6	North Carolina	106,335	2.3%
47	North Dakota	3,031	0.1%
26	Ohio	37,478	0.8%
24	Oklahoma	39,285	0.8%
13	Oregon	61,865	1.3%
21	Pennsylvania	46,352	1.0%
41	Rhode Island	6,775	0.1%
27	South Carolina	34,685	0.7%
44	South Dakota	4,005	0.1%
30	Tennessee	27,550	0.6%
2	Texas	726,062	15.4%
20	Utah	47,390	1.0%
50	Vermont	1,525	0.0%
9	Virginia	86,751	1.8%
12	Washington	65,101	1.4%
49	West Virginia	1,609	0.0%
22	Wisconsin	45,168	1.0%
48	Wyoming	2,099	0.0%

RANK ORDER

RANK	STATE	STUDENTS	% of USA
1	California	1,779,102	37.7%
2	Texas	726,062	15.4%
3	Florida	230,540	4.9%
4	New York	200,805	4.3%
5	Illinois	179,857	3.8%
6	North Carolina	106,335	2.3%
7	Colorado	95,141	2.0%
8	Georgia	86,755	1.8%
9	Virginia	86,751	1.8%
10	Arizona	83,625	1.8%
11	Nevada	67,874	1.4%
12	Washington	65,101	1.4%
13	Oregon	61,865	1.3%
14	Minnesota	61,396	1.3%
15	Michigan	58,740	1.2%
16	New Jersey	55,656	1.2%
17	Massachusetts	51,667	1.1%
18	New Mexico	51,493	1.1%
19	Indiana	49,271	1.0%
20	Utah	47,390	1.0%
21	Pennsylvania	46,352	1.0%
22	Wisconsin	45,168	1.0%
23	Maryland	43,179	0.9%
24	Oklahoma	39,285	0.8%
25	Kansas	38,011	0.8%
26	Ohio	37,478	0.8%
27	South Carolina	34,685	0.7%
28	Connecticut	30,090	0.6%
29	Arkansas	29,752	0.6%
30	Tennessee	27,550	0.6%
31	Iowa	20,867	0.4%
32	Missouri	20,473	0.4%
33	Alabama	19,497	0.4%
34	Nebraska	19,339	0.4%
35	Hawaii	18,097	0.4%
36	Idaho	15,965	0.3%
37	Alaska	14,670	0.3%
38	Kentucky	14,244	0.3%
39	Louisiana	13,012	0.3%
40	Delaware	7,685	0.2%
41	Rhode Island	6,775	0.1%
42	Mississippi	6,061	0.1%
43	Maine	4,478	0.1%
44	South Dakota	4,005	0.1%
45	New Hampshire	3,821	0.1%
46	Montana	3,807	0.1%
47	North Dakota	3,031	0.1%
48	Wyoming	2,099	0.0%
49	West Virginia	1,609	0.0%
50	Vermont	1,525	0.0%
	District of Columbia	5,890	0.1%

Source: U.S. Department of Education, National Center for Education Statistics
 "Common Core of Data (CCD) Database" (http://nces.ed.gov/ccd/)
*For school year 2008-2009. Increasingly, English language learner (ELL) or English learner (EL) is used in place of Limited English proficient (LEP) as the term to identify those students who have insufficient English to succeed in English-only classrooms.

Percent of Public Elementary and Secondary School Students Receiving English Language Learner (ELL) Services in 2009
Reporting States Percent = 9.6%*

RANK	STATE	PERCENT
39	Alabama	2.6
6	Alaska	11.1
13	Arizona	7.8
20	Arkansas	6.2
1	California	28.7
5	Colorado	11.4
25	Connecticut	5.3
21	Delaware	6.1
9	Florida	8.8
26	Georgia	5.2
8	Hawaii	10.0
23	Idaho	5.8
10	Illinois	8.5
30	Indiana	4.7
32	Iowa	4.2
12	Kansas	8.0
44	Kentucky	2.1
46	Louisiana	1.9
41	Maine	2.4
28	Maryland	5.1
24	Massachusetts	5.4
34	Michigan	3.6
14	Minnesota	7.3
49	Mississippi	1.2
43	Missouri	2.2
38	Montana	2.7
18	Nebraska	6.5
2	Nevada	15.8
46	New Hampshire	1.9
33	New Jersey	4.0
3	New Mexico	15.4
14	New York	7.3
16	North Carolina	7.2
35	North Dakota	3.3
44	Ohio	2.1
22	Oklahoma	6.0
7	Oregon	11.0
39	Pennsylvania	2.6
30	Rhode Island	4.7
29	South Carolina	4.8
36	South Dakota	3.2
37	Tennessee	2.8
4	Texas	15.0
11	Utah	8.1
48	Vermont	1.7
17	Virginia	7.0
19	Washington	6.3
50	West Virginia	0.6
26	Wisconsin	5.2
41	Wyoming	2.4

RANK	STATE	PERCENT
1	California	28.7
2	Nevada	15.8
3	New Mexico	15.4
4	Texas	15.0
5	Colorado	11.4
6	Alaska	11.1
7	Oregon	11.0
8	Hawaii	10.0
9	Florida	8.8
10	Illinois	8.5
11	Utah	8.1
12	Kansas	8.0
13	Arizona	7.8
14	Minnesota	7.3
14	New York	7.3
16	North Carolina	7.2
17	Virginia	7.0
18	Nebraska	6.5
19	Washington	6.3
20	Arkansas	6.2
21	Delaware	6.1
22	Oklahoma	6.0
23	Idaho	5.8
24	Massachusetts	5.4
25	Connecticut	5.3
26	Georgia	5.2
26	Wisconsin	5.2
28	Maryland	5.1
29	South Carolina	4.8
30	Indiana	4.7
30	Rhode Island	4.7
32	Iowa	4.2
33	New Jersey	4.0
34	Michigan	3.6
35	North Dakota	3.3
36	South Dakota	3.2
37	Tennessee	2.8
38	Montana	2.7
39	Alabama	2.6
39	Pennsylvania	2.6
41	Maine	2.4
41	Wyoming	2.4
43	Missouri	2.2
44	Kentucky	2.1
44	Ohio	2.1
46	Louisiana	1.9
46	New Hampshire	1.9
48	Vermont	1.7
49	Mississippi	1.2
50	West Virginia	0.6

	District of Columbia	8.5

Source: CQ Press using data from U.S. Department of Education, National Center for Education Statistics "Common Core of Data (CCD) Database" (http://nces.ed.gov/ccd/)

*For school year 2008-2009. Increasingly, English language learner (ELL) or English learner (EL) is used in place of Limited English proficient (LEP) as the term to identify those students who have insufficient English to succeed in English-only classrooms.

Special Education Teachers in 2009

National Total = 397,469 Teachers*

ALPHA ORDER				RANK ORDER			
RANK	STATE	TEACHERS	% of USA	RANK	STATE	TEACHERS	% of USA
26	Alabama	5,338	1.3%	1	New York	47,047	11.8%
45	Alaska	1,103	0.3%	2	California	22,821	5.7%
21	Arizona	7,002	1.8%	3	Texas	22,686	5.7%
30	Arkansas	4,442	1.1%	4	Pennsylvania	21,932	5.5%
2	California	22,821	5.7%	5	Illinois	21,918	5.5%
27	Colorado	5,190	1.3%	6	Ohio	19,906	5.0%
25	Connecticut	5,754	1.4%	7	Georgia	17,586	4.4%
41	Delaware	1,746	0.4%	8	Florida	16,663	4.2%
8	Florida	16,663	4.2%	9	Virginia	14,677	3.7%
7	Georgia	17,586	4.4%	10	Michigan	14,172	3.6%
39	Hawaii	2,175	0.5%	11	North Carolina	11,784	3.0%
43	Idaho	1,105	0.3%	12	Massachusetts	9,728	2.4%
5	Illinois	21,918	5.5%	13	Maryland	9,418	2.4%
18	Indiana	7,254	1.8%	14	Missouri	8,770	2.2%
23	Iowa	6,337	1.6%	15	Wisconsin	8,508	2.1%
29	Kansas	4,627	1.2%	16	Minnesota	8,422	2.1%
19	Kentucky	7,033	1.8%	17	Tennessee	7,782	2.0%
20	Louisiana	7,025	1.8%	18	Indiana	7,254	1.8%
35	Maine	2,858	0.7%	19	Kentucky	7,033	1.8%
13	Maryland	9,418	2.4%	20	Louisiana	7,025	1.8%
12	Massachusetts	9,728	2.4%	21	Arizona	7,002	1.8%
10	Michigan	14,172	3.6%	22	South Carolina	6,462	1.6%
16	Minnesota	8,422	2.1%	23	Iowa	6,337	1.6%
44	Mississippi	1,104	0.3%	24	Washington	5,849	1.5%
14	Missouri	8,770	2.2%	25	Connecticut	5,754	1.4%
46	Montana	918	0.2%	26	Alabama	5,338	1.3%
37	Nebraska	2,506	0.6%	27	Colorado	5,190	1.3%
32	Nevada	3,149	0.8%	28	Oklahoma	4,775	1.2%
36	New Hampshire	2,721	0.7%	29	Kansas	4,627	1.2%
NA	New Jersey**	NA	NA	30	Arkansas	4,442	1.1%
38	New Mexico	2,267	0.6%	31	Oregon	3,282	0.8%
1	New York	47,047	11.8%	32	Nevada	3,149	0.8%
11	North Carolina	11,784	3.0%	33	West Virginia	3,059	0.8%
47	North Dakota	837	0.2%	34	Utah	3,021	0.8%
6	Ohio	19,906	5.0%	35	Maine	2,858	0.7%
28	Oklahoma	4,775	1.2%	36	New Hampshire	2,721	0.7%
31	Oregon	3,282	0.8%	37	Nebraska	2,506	0.6%
4	Pennsylvania	21,932	5.5%	38	New Mexico	2,267	0.6%
40	Rhode Island	1,767	0.4%	39	Hawaii	2,175	0.5%
22	South Carolina	6,462	1.6%	40	Rhode Island	1,767	0.4%
48	South Dakota	792	0.2%	41	Delaware	1,746	0.4%
17	Tennessee	7,782	2.0%	42	Vermont	1,257	0.3%
3	Texas	22,686	5.7%	43	Idaho	1,105	0.3%
34	Utah	3,021	0.8%	44	Mississippi	1,104	0.3%
42	Vermont	1,257	0.3%	45	Alaska	1,103	0.3%
9	Virginia	14,677	3.7%	46	Montana	918	0.2%
24	Washington	5,849	1.5%	47	North Dakota	837	0.2%
33	West Virginia	3,059	0.8%	48	South Dakota	792	0.2%
15	Wisconsin	8,508	2.1%	49	Wyoming	704	0.2%
49	Wyoming	704	0.2%	NA	New Jersey**	NA	NA
					District of Columbia	191	0.0%

Source: CQ Press using data from U.S. Department of Education, Office of Special Education Programs
"Data Tables for OSEP State Reported Data" (https://www.ideadata.org/arc_toc11.asp)
*Figures are full-time equivalent (FTE). Includes teachers, whether meeting the standards of highly qualified or not, of disabled children ages 3 to 21 for school year 2008-2009. National total does not include 6,134 teachers in U.S. territories and Bureau of Indian Education programs.
**Not available.

Preschool Special Education Teachers in 2009

National Total = 33,009 Teachers*

ALPHA ORDER				RANK ORDER			
RANK	STATE	TEACHERS	% of USA	RANK	STATE	TEACHERS	% of USA
33	Alabama	235	0.7%	1	New York	4,779	14.5%
44	Alaska	93	0.3%	2	Texas	2,510	7.6%
15	Arizona	722	2.2%	3	California	2,217	6.7%
19	Arkansas	609	1.8%	4	Ohio	1,660	5.0%
3	California	2,217	6.7%	5	Florida	1,551	4.7%
30	Colorado	357	1.1%	6	Illinois	1,464	4.4%
26	Connecticut	478	1.4%	7	Massachusetts	1,242	3.8%
46	Delaware	80	0.2%	8	Pennsylvania	1,236	3.7%
5	Florida	1,551	4.7%	9	North Carolina	1,005	3.0%
11	Georgia	811	2.5%	10	Minnesota	822	2.5%
32	Hawaii	285	0.9%	11	Georgia	811	2.5%
37	Idaho	140	0.4%	12	Missouri	794	2.4%
6	Illinois	1,464	4.4%	13	Michigan	787	2.4%
27	Indiana	417	1.3%	14	Virginia	776	2.4%
23	Iowa	563	1.7%	15	Arizona	722	2.2%
25	Kansas	480	1.5%	16	Wisconsin	719	2.2%
28	Kentucky	410	1.2%	17	Louisiana	686	2.1%
17	Louisiana	686	2.1%	18	Maryland	647	2.0%
35	Maine	212	0.6%	19	Arkansas	609	1.8%
18	Maryland	647	2.0%	20	Washington	580	1.8%
7	Massachusetts	1,242	3.8%	21	South Carolina	577	1.7%
13	Michigan	787	2.4%	22	Oklahoma	576	1.7%
10	Minnesota	822	2.5%	23	Iowa	563	1.7%
43	Mississippi	100	0.3%	24	Tennessee	502	1.5%
12	Missouri	794	2.4%	25	Kansas	480	1.5%
47	Montana	45	0.1%	26	Connecticut	478	1.4%
36	Nebraska	190	0.6%	27	Indiana	417	1.3%
29	Nevada	406	1.2%	28	Kentucky	410	1.2%
48	New Hampshire	26	0.1%	29	Nevada	406	1.2%
NA	New Jersey**	NA	NA	30	Colorado	357	1.1%
49	New Mexico	20	0.1%	31	West Virginia	302	0.9%
1	New York	4,779	14.5%	32	Hawaii	285	0.9%
9	North Carolina	1,005	3.0%	33	Alabama	235	0.7%
45	North Dakota	86	0.3%	34	Utah	226	0.7%
4	Ohio	1,660	5.0%	35	Maine	212	0.6%
22	Oklahoma	576	1.7%	36	Nebraska	190	0.6%
40	Oregon	117	0.4%	37	Idaho	140	0.4%
8	Pennsylvania	1,236	3.7%	38	Vermont	125	0.4%
41	Rhode Island	115	0.3%	39	South Dakota	119	0.4%
21	South Carolina	577	1.7%	40	Oregon	117	0.4%
39	South Dakota	119	0.4%	41	Rhode Island	115	0.3%
24	Tennessee	502	1.5%	42	Wyoming	105	0.3%
2	Texas	2,510	7.6%	43	Mississippi	100	0.3%
34	Utah	226	0.7%	44	Alaska	93	0.3%
38	Vermont	125	0.4%	45	North Dakota	86	0.3%
14	Virginia	776	2.4%	46	Delaware	80	0.2%
20	Washington	580	1.8%	47	Montana	45	0.1%
31	West Virginia	302	0.9%	48	New Hampshire	26	0.1%
16	Wisconsin	719	2.2%	49	New Mexico	20	0.1%
42	Wyoming	105	0.3%	NA	New Jersey**	NA	NA
					District of Columbia	7	0.0%

Source: U.S. Department of Education, Office of Special Education Programs
"Data Tables for OSEP State Reported Data" (https://www.ideadata.org/arc_toc11.asp)
*Figures are full-time equivalent (FTE). Includes teachers, whether meeting the standards of highly qualified or not, of disabled children ages 3 to 5 for school year 2008-2009. National total does not include teachers in U.S. territories and Bureau of Indian Education programs.
**Not available.

Highly Qualified Preschool Special Education Teachers in 2009

National Total = 29,529 Teachers*

ALPHA ORDER

RANK	STATE	TEACHERS	% of USA
31	Alabama	226	0.8%
44	Alaska	71	0.2%
16	Arizona	574	1.9%
22	Arkansas	503	1.7%
3	California	1,999	6.8%
28	Colorado	279	0.9%
24	Connecticut	478	1.6%
47	Delaware	23	0.1%
49	Florida	15	0.1%
9	Georgia	800	2.7%
30	Hawaii	254	0.9%
36	Idaho	124	0.4%
5	Illinois	1,461	4.9%
26	Indiana	405	1.4%
20	Iowa	563	1.9%
23	Kansas	480	1.6%
27	Kentucky	397	1.3%
15	Louisiana	578	2.0%
34	Maine	212	0.7%
18	Maryland	565	1.9%
7	Massachusetts	1,187	4.0%
11	Michigan	780	2.6%
12	Minnesota	773	2.6%
41	Mississippi	93	0.3%
10	Missouri	781	2.6%
45	Montana	45	0.2%
35	Nebraska	173	0.6%
29	Nevada	273	0.9%
46	New Hampshire	26	0.1%
NA	New Jersey**	NA	NA
48	New Mexico	20	0.1%
1	New York	4,436	15.0%
8	North Carolina	966	3.3%
43	North Dakota	79	0.3%
4	Ohio	1,596	5.4%
19	Oklahoma	564	1.9%
38	Oregon	114	0.4%
6	Pennsylvania	1,202	4.1%
39	Rhode Island	110	0.4%
20	South Carolina	563	1.9%
37	South Dakota	115	0.4%
25	Tennessee	459	1.6%
2	Texas	2,494	8.4%
33	Utah	213	0.7%
40	Vermont	109	0.4%
13	Virginia	772	2.6%
17	Washington	567	1.9%
32	West Virginia	224	0.8%
14	Wisconsin	702	2.4%
42	Wyoming	80	0.3%

RANK ORDER

RANK	STATE	TEACHERS	% of USA
1	New York	4,436	15.0%
2	Texas	2,494	8.4%
3	California	1,999	6.8%
4	Ohio	1,596	5.4%
5	Illinois	1,461	4.9%
6	Pennsylvania	1,202	4.1%
7	Massachusetts	1,187	4.0%
8	North Carolina	966	3.3%
9	Georgia	800	2.7%
10	Missouri	781	2.6%
11	Michigan	780	2.6%
12	Minnesota	773	2.6%
13	Virginia	772	2.6%
14	Wisconsin	702	2.4%
15	Louisiana	578	2.0%
16	Arizona	574	1.9%
17	Washington	567	1.9%
18	Maryland	565	1.9%
19	Oklahoma	564	1.9%
20	Iowa	563	1.9%
20	South Carolina	563	1.9%
22	Arkansas	503	1.7%
23	Kansas	480	1.6%
24	Connecticut	478	1.6%
25	Tennessee	459	1.6%
26	Indiana	405	1.4%
27	Kentucky	397	1.3%
28	Colorado	279	0.9%
29	Nevada	273	0.9%
30	Hawaii	254	0.9%
31	Alabama	226	0.8%
32	West Virginia	224	0.8%
33	Utah	213	0.7%
34	Maine	212	0.7%
35	Nebraska	173	0.6%
36	Idaho	124	0.4%
37	South Dakota	115	0.4%
38	Oregon	114	0.4%
39	Rhode Island	110	0.4%
40	Vermont	109	0.4%
41	Mississippi	93	0.3%
42	Wyoming	80	0.3%
43	North Dakota	79	0.3%
44	Alaska	71	0.2%
45	Montana	45	0.2%
46	New Hampshire	26	0.1%
47	Delaware	23	0.1%
48	New Mexico	20	0.1%
49	Florida	15	0.1%
NA	New Jersey**	NA	NA
	District of Columbia	7	0.0%

Source: U.S. Department of Education, Office of Special Education Programs
   "Data Tables for OSEP State Reported Data" (https://www.ideadata.org/arc_toc11.asp)
*Figures are full-time equivalent (FTE). Includes highly qualified teachers of disabled children ages 3 to 5 for school year
2008-2009. National total does not include teachers in U.S. territories and Bureau of Indian Education programs.
**Not available.

Percent of Preschool Special Education Teachers Highly Qualified in 2009

National Percent = 89.5%*

ALPHA ORDER

RANK ORDER

RANK	STATE	PERCENT		RANK	STATE	PERCENT
23	Alabama	96.2		1	Connecticut	100.0
44	Alaska	76.3		1	Iowa	100.0
42	Arizona	79.5		1	Kansas	100.0
41	Arkansas	82.6		1	Maine	100.0
35	California	90.2		1	Montana	100.0
43	Colorado	78.2		1	New Hampshire	100.0
1	Connecticut	100.0		1	New Mexico	100.0
48	Delaware	28.8		8	Illinois	99.8
49	Florida	1.0		9	Virginia	99.5
12	Georgia	98.6		10	Texas	99.4
36	Hawaii	89.1		11	Michigan	99.1
37	Idaho	88.6		12	Georgia	98.6
8	Illinois	99.8		13	Missouri	98.4
20	Indiana	97.1		14	Oklahoma	97.9
1	Iowa	100.0		15	Washington	97.8
1	Kansas	100.0		16	South Carolina	97.6
21	Kentucky	96.8		16	Wisconsin	97.6
40	Louisiana	84.3		18	Oregon	97.4
1	Maine	100.0		19	Pennsylvania	97.2
38	Maryland	87.3		20	Indiana	97.1
27	Massachusetts	95.6		21	Kentucky	96.8
11	Michigan	99.1		22	South Dakota	96.6
29	Minnesota	94.0		23	Alabama	96.2
30	Mississippi	93.0		24	North Carolina	96.1
13	Missouri	98.4		24	Ohio	96.1
1	Montana	100.0		26	Rhode Island	95.7
34	Nebraska	91.1		27	Massachusetts	95.6
47	Nevada	67.2		28	Utah	94.2
1	New Hampshire	100.0		29	Minnesota	94.0
NA	New Jersey**	NA		30	Mississippi	93.0
1	New Mexico	100.0		31	New York	92.8
31	New York	92.8		32	North Dakota	91.9
24	North Carolina	96.1		33	Tennessee	91.4
32	North Dakota	91.9		34	Nebraska	91.1
24	Ohio	96.1		35	California	90.2
14	Oklahoma	97.9		36	Hawaii	89.1
18	Oregon	97.4		37	Idaho	88.6
19	Pennsylvania	97.2		38	Maryland	87.3
26	Rhode Island	95.7		39	Vermont	87.2
16	South Carolina	97.6		40	Louisiana	84.3
22	South Dakota	96.6		41	Arkansas	82.6
33	Tennessee	91.4		42	Arizona	79.5
10	Texas	99.4		43	Colorado	78.2
28	Utah	94.2		44	Alaska	76.3
39	Vermont	87.2		45	Wyoming	76.2
9	Virginia	99.5		46	West Virginia	74.2
15	Washington	97.8		47	Nevada	67.2
46	West Virginia	74.2		48	Delaware	28.8
16	Wisconsin	97.6		49	Florida	1.0
45	Wyoming	76.2		NA	New Jersey**	NA
					District of Columbia	100.0

Source: CQ Press using data from U.S. Department of Education, Office of Special Education Programs
  "Data Tables for OSEP State Reported Data" (https://www.ideadata.org/arc_toc11.asp)
*Figures are based on full-time equivalent (FTE). Includes teachers of disabled children ages 3 to 5 for school year 2008-2009.
National percent does not include teachers in U.S. territories and Bureau of Indian Education programs.
**Not available.

Elementary and Secondary Special Education Teachers in 2009

National Total = 364,460 Teachers*

ALPHA ORDER				RANK ORDER			
RANK	STATE	TEACHERS	% of USA	RANK	STATE	TEACHERS	% of USA
26	Alabama	5,103	1.4%	1	New York	42,268	11.6%
43	Alaska	1,010	0.3%	2	Pennsylvania	20,696	5.7%
21	Arizona	6,280	1.7%	3	California	20,604	5.7%
30	Arkansas	3,833	1.1%	4	Illinois	20,454	5.6%
3	California	20,604	5.7%	5	Texas	20,176	5.5%
27	Colorado	4,833	1.3%	6	Ohio	18,246	5.0%
24	Connecticut	5,276	1.4%	7	Georgia	16,775	4.6%
40	Delaware	1,666	0.5%	8	Florida	15,112	4.1%
8	Florida	15,112	4.1%	9	Virginia	13,901	3.8%
7	Georgia	16,775	4.6%	10	Michigan	13,385	3.7%
39	Hawaii	1,890	0.5%	11	North Carolina	10,779	3.0%
45	Idaho	965	0.3%	12	Maryland	8,771	2.4%
4	Illinois	20,454	5.6%	13	Massachusetts	8,486	2.3%
18	Indiana	6,837	1.9%	14	Missouri	7,976	2.2%
23	Iowa	5,774	1.6%	15	Wisconsin	7,789	2.1%
29	Kansas	4,147	1.1%	16	Minnesota	7,600	2.1%
19	Kentucky	6,623	1.8%	17	Tennessee	7,280	2.0%
20	Louisiana	6,339	1.7%	18	Indiana	6,837	1.9%
36	Maine	2,646	0.7%	19	Kentucky	6,623	1.8%
12	Maryland	8,771	2.4%	20	Louisiana	6,339	1.7%
13	Massachusetts	8,486	2.3%	21	Arizona	6,280	1.7%
10	Michigan	13,385	3.7%	22	South Carolina	5,885	1.6%
16	Minnesota	7,600	2.1%	23	Iowa	5,774	1.6%
44	Mississippi	1,004	0.3%	24	Connecticut	5,276	1.4%
14	Missouri	7,976	2.2%	25	Washington	5,269	1.4%
46	Montana	873	0.2%	26	Alabama	5,103	1.4%
37	Nebraska	2,316	0.6%	27	Colorado	4,833	1.3%
34	Nevada	2,743	0.8%	28	Oklahoma	4,199	1.2%
35	New Hampshire	2,695	0.7%	29	Kansas	4,147	1.1%
NA	New Jersey**	NA	NA	30	Arkansas	3,833	1.1%
38	New Mexico	2,247	0.6%	31	Oregon	3,165	0.9%
1	New York	42,268	11.6%	32	Utah	2,795	0.8%
11	North Carolina	10,779	3.0%	33	West Virginia	2,757	0.8%
47	North Dakota	751	0.2%	34	Nevada	2,743	0.8%
6	Ohio	18,246	5.0%	35	New Hampshire	2,695	0.7%
28	Oklahoma	4,199	1.2%	36	Maine	2,646	0.7%
31	Oregon	3,165	0.9%	37	Nebraska	2,316	0.6%
2	Pennsylvania	20,696	5.7%	38	New Mexico	2,247	0.6%
41	Rhode Island	1,652	0.5%	39	Hawaii	1,890	0.5%
22	South Carolina	5,885	1.6%	40	Delaware	1,666	0.5%
48	South Dakota	673	0.2%	41	Rhode Island	1,652	0.5%
17	Tennessee	7,280	2.0%	42	Vermont	1,132	0.3%
5	Texas	20,176	5.5%	43	Alaska	1,010	0.3%
32	Utah	2,795	0.8%	44	Mississippi	1,004	0.3%
42	Vermont	1,132	0.3%	45	Idaho	965	0.3%
9	Virginia	13,901	3.8%	46	Montana	873	0.2%
25	Washington	5,269	1.4%	47	North Dakota	751	0.2%
33	West Virginia	2,757	0.8%	48	South Dakota	673	0.2%
15	Wisconsin	7,789	2.1%	49	Wyoming	599	0.2%
49	Wyoming	599	0.2%	NA	New Jersey**	NA	NA
					District of Columbia	184	0.1%

Source: U.S. Department of Education, Office of Special Education Programs
    "Data Tables for OSEP State Reported Data" (https://www.ideadata.org/arc_toc11.asp)
*Figures are full-time equivalent (FTE). Includes teachers, whether meeting the standards of highly qualified or not, of disabled children ages 6 to 21 for school year 200-2008. National total does not include teachers in U.S. territories and Bureau of Indian Education programs.
**Not available.

Highly Qualified Elementary and Secondary Special Education Teachers in 2009

National Total = 332,863 Teachers*

ALPHA ORDER				RANK ORDER			
RANK	STATE	TEACHERS	% of USA	RANK	STATE	TEACHERS	% of USA
26	Alabama	4,821	1.4%	1	New York	37,746	11.3%
44	Alaska	843	0.3%	2	Illinois	20,408	6.1%
22	Arizona	5,454	1.6%	3	Pennsylvania	19,995	6.0%
29	Arkansas	3,542	1.1%	4	Texas	19,816	6.0%
5	California	19,163	5.8%	5	California	19,163	5.8%
28	Colorado	4,113	1.2%	6	Ohio	17,170	5.2%
23	Connecticut	5,242	1.6%	7	Georgia	15,274	4.6%
44	Delaware	843	0.3%	8	Michigan	12,730	3.8%
11	Florida	9,544	2.9%	9	Virginia	12,044	3.6%
7	Georgia	15,274	4.6%	10	North Carolina	10,475	3.1%
40	Hawaii	1,400	0.4%	11	Florida	9,544	2.9%
42	Idaho	911	0.3%	12	Massachusetts	8,004	2.4%
2	Illinois	20,408	6.1%	13	Missouri	7,709	2.3%
18	Indiana	6,569	2.0%	14	Wisconsin	7,555	2.3%
20	Iowa	5,774	1.7%	15	Minnesota	7,222	2.2%
31	Kansas	2,885	0.9%	16	Maryland	6,820	2.0%
19	Kentucky	6,431	1.9%	17	Tennessee	6,644	2.0%
25	Louisiana	4,957	1.5%	18	Indiana	6,569	2.0%
33	Maine	2,485	0.7%	19	Kentucky	6,431	1.9%
16	Maryland	6,820	2.0%	20	Iowa	5,774	1.7%
12	Massachusetts	8,004	2.4%	21	South Carolina	5,590	1.7%
8	Michigan	12,730	3.8%	22	Arizona	5,454	1.6%
15	Minnesota	7,222	2.2%	23	Connecticut	5,242	1.6%
47	Mississippi	717	0.2%	24	Washington	5,106	1.5%
13	Missouri	7,709	2.3%	25	Louisiana	4,957	1.5%
43	Montana	863	0.3%	26	Alabama	4,821	1.4%
37	Nebraska	2,199	0.7%	27	Oklahoma	4,115	1.2%
36	Nevada	2,365	0.7%	28	Colorado	4,113	1.2%
32	New Hampshire	2,695	0.8%	29	Arkansas	3,542	1.1%
NA	New Jersey**	NA	NA	30	Oregon	2,969	0.9%
38	New Mexico	2,069	0.6%	31	Kansas	2,885	0.9%
1	New York	37,746	11.3%	32	New Hampshire	2,695	0.8%
10	North Carolina	10,475	3.1%	33	Maine	2,485	0.7%
46	North Dakota	738	0.2%	34	West Virginia	2,449	0.7%
6	Ohio	17,170	5.2%	35	Utah	2,366	0.7%
27	Oklahoma	4,115	1.2%	36	Nevada	2,365	0.7%
30	Oregon	2,969	0.9%	37	Nebraska	2,199	0.7%
3	Pennsylvania	19,995	6.0%	38	New Mexico	2,069	0.6%
39	Rhode Island	1,617	0.5%	39	Rhode Island	1,617	0.5%
21	South Carolina	5,590	1.7%	40	Hawaii	1,400	0.4%
48	South Dakota	655	0.2%	41	Vermont	1,038	0.3%
17	Tennessee	6,644	2.0%	42	Idaho	911	0.3%
4	Texas	19,816	6.0%	43	Montana	863	0.3%
35	Utah	2,366	0.7%	44	Alaska	843	0.3%
41	Vermont	1,038	0.3%	44	Delaware	843	0.3%
9	Virginia	12,044	3.6%	46	North Dakota	738	0.2%
24	Washington	5,106	1.5%	47	Mississippi	717	0.2%
34	West Virginia	2,449	0.7%	48	South Dakota	655	0.2%
14	Wisconsin	7,555	2.3%	49	Wyoming	571	0.2%
49	Wyoming	571	0.2%	NA	New Jersey**	NA	NA
					District of Columbia	152	0.0%

Source: U.S. Department of Education, Office of Special Education Programs
   "Data Tables for OSEP State Reported Data" (https://www.ideadata.org/arc_toc11.asp)
*Figures are full-time equivalent (FTE). Includes highly qualified teachers of disabled children ages 6 to 21 for school year 2008-2009. National total does not include 5,050 teachers in U.S. territories and Bureau of Indian Education programs.
**Not available.

Percent of Elementary and Secondary Special Education Teachers Highly Qualified in 2009
National Percent = 91.3%*

ALPHA ORDER

RANK	STATE	PERCENT
23	Alabama	94.5
42	Alaska	83.5
37	Arizona	86.8
30	Arkansas	92.4
29	California	93.0
40	Colorado	85.1
4	Connecticut	99.4
49	Delaware	50.6
48	Florida	63.2
34	Georgia	91.1
45	Hawaii	74.1
24	Idaho	94.4
3	Illinois	99.8
17	Indiana	96.1
1	Iowa	100.0
47	Kansas	69.6
12	Kentucky	97.1
43	Louisiana	78.2
27	Maine	93.9
44	Maryland	77.8
25	Massachusetts	94.3
19	Michigan	95.1
20	Minnesota	95.0
46	Mississippi	71.4
15	Missouri	96.7
5	Montana	98.9
22	Nebraska	94.9
39	Nevada	86.2
1	New Hampshire	100.0
NA	New Jersey**	NA
31	New Mexico	92.1
35	New York	89.3
11	North Carolina	97.2
6	North Dakota	98.3
26	Ohio	94.1
8	Oklahoma	98.0
28	Oregon	93.8
16	Pennsylvania	96.6
9	Rhode Island	97.9
20	South Carolina	95.0
10	South Dakota	97.3
33	Tennessee	91.3
7	Texas	98.2
41	Utah	84.7
32	Vermont	91.7
38	Virginia	86.6
14	Washington	96.9
36	West Virginia	88.8
13	Wisconsin	97.0
18	Wyoming	95.3

RANK ORDER

RANK	STATE	PERCENT
1	Iowa	100.0
1	New Hampshire	100.0
3	Illinois	99.8
4	Connecticut	99.4
5	Montana	98.9
6	North Dakota	98.3
7	Texas	98.2
8	Oklahoma	98.0
9	Rhode Island	97.9
10	South Dakota	97.3
11	North Carolina	97.2
12	Kentucky	97.1
13	Wisconsin	97.0
14	Washington	96.9
15	Missouri	96.7
16	Pennsylvania	96.6
17	Indiana	96.1
18	Wyoming	95.3
19	Michigan	95.1
20	Minnesota	95.0
20	South Carolina	95.0
22	Nebraska	94.9
23	Alabama	94.5
24	Idaho	94.4
25	Massachusetts	94.3
26	Ohio	94.1
27	Maine	93.9
28	Oregon	93.8
29	California	93.0
30	Arkansas	92.4
31	New Mexico	92.1
32	Vermont	91.7
33	Tennessee	91.3
34	Georgia	91.1
35	New York	89.3
36	West Virginia	88.8
37	Arizona	86.8
38	Virginia	86.6
39	Nevada	86.2
40	Colorado	85.1
41	Utah	84.7
42	Alaska	83.5
43	Louisiana	78.2
44	Maryland	77.8
45	Hawaii	74.1
46	Mississippi	71.4
47	Kansas	69.6
48	Florida	63.2
49	Delaware	50.6
NA	New Jersey**	NA

	District of Columbia	82.6

Source: CQ Press using data from U.S. Department of Education, Office of Special Education Programs
"Data Tables for OSEP State Reported Data" (https://www.ideadata.org/arc_toc11.asp)
*Figures are based on full-time equivalent (FTE). Includes highly qualified teachers of disabled children ages 6 to 21 for school year 2008-2009. National percent does not include teachers in U.S. territories and Bureau of Indian Education programs.
**Not available.

Special Education Pupil-Teacher Ratio in 2009

National Ratio = 16.3 Students Per Fully Certified Teacher*

ALPHA ORDER

RANK	STATE	RATIO
24	Alabama	15.5
18	Alaska	16.2
15	Arizona	18.0
32	Arkansas	14.6
2	California	29.5
19	Colorado	16.1
39	Connecticut	11.9
43	Delaware	11.1
6	Florida	22.6
47	Georgia	10.1
49	Hawaii	9.2
3	Idaho	25.1
34	Illinois	14.3
5	Indiana	23.7
46	Iowa	10.5
34	Kansas	14.3
27	Kentucky	15.1
38	Louisiana	12.1
40	Maine	11.5
45	Maryland	10.9
17	Massachusetts	17.2
19	Michigan	16.1
33	Minnesota	14.4
1	Mississippi	58.0
30	Missouri	14.8
14	Montana	18.8
16	Nebraska	17.3
25	Nevada	15.3
43	New Hampshire	11.1
NA	New Jersey**	NA
11	New Mexico	20.2
48	New York	9.8
22	North Carolina	15.7
21	North Dakota	15.8
37	Ohio	13.2
12	Oklahoma	19.9
4	Oregon	24.4
36	Pennsylvania	13.4
29	Rhode Island	14.9
23	South Carolina	15.6
6	South Dakota	22.6
25	Tennessee	15.3
13	Texas	19.6
8	Utah	22.4
41	Vermont	11.3
42	Virginia	11.2
9	Washington	21.5
27	West Virginia	15.1
30	Wisconsin	14.8
10	Wyoming	21.4

RANK ORDER

RANK	STATE	RATIO
1	Mississippi	58.0
2	California	29.5
3	Idaho	25.1
4	Oregon	24.4
5	Indiana	23.7
6	Florida	22.6
6	South Dakota	22.6
8	Utah	22.4
9	Washington	21.5
10	Wyoming	21.4
11	New Mexico	20.2
12	Oklahoma	19.9
13	Texas	19.6
14	Montana	18.8
15	Arizona	18.0
16	Nebraska	17.3
17	Massachusetts	17.2
18	Alaska	16.2
19	Colorado	16.1
19	Michigan	16.1
21	North Dakota	15.8
22	North Carolina	15.7
23	South Carolina	15.6
24	Alabama	15.5
25	Nevada	15.3
25	Tennessee	15.3
27	Kentucky	15.1
27	West Virginia	15.1
29	Rhode Island	14.9
30	Missouri	14.8
30	Wisconsin	14.8
32	Arkansas	14.6
33	Minnesota	14.4
34	Illinois	14.3
34	Kansas	14.3
36	Pennsylvania	13.4
37	Ohio	13.2
38	Louisiana	12.1
39	Connecticut	11.9
40	Maine	11.5
41	Vermont	11.3
42	Virginia	11.2
43	Delaware	11.1
43	New Hampshire	11.1
45	Maryland	10.9
46	Iowa	10.5
47	Georgia	10.1
48	New York	9.8
49	Hawaii	9.2
NA	New Jersey**	NA
	District of Columbia	59.5

Source: CQ Press using data from U.S. Department of Education, Office of Special Education Programs
   "Data Tables for OSEP State Reported Data" (https://www.ideadata.org/arc_toc11.asp)
*Figures for teachers are full-time equivalent (FTE). Includes highly qualified teachers of disabled children ages 3 to 21 for school year 2008-2009. National rate does not include teachers or students in U.S. territories and Bureau of Indian Education programs.
**Not available.

Special Education Paraprofessionals in 2009

National Total = 430,279 Paraprofessionals*

ALPHA ORDER

RANK	STATE	PARAS	% of USA
30	Alabama	4,714	1.1%
46	Alaska	1,338	0.3%
14	Arizona	8,996	2.1%
36	Arkansas	3,187	0.7%
1	California	50,053	11.6%
26	Colorado	6,416	1.5%
16	Connecticut	8,951	2.1%
49	Delaware	1,059	0.2%
8	Florida	14,553	3.4%
9	Georgia	12,796	3.0%
38	Hawaii	2,723	0.6%
39	Idaho	2,665	0.6%
3	Illinois	31,177	7.2%
17	Indiana	8,807	2.0%
19	Iowa	8,019	1.9%
11	Kansas	11,455	2.7%
28	Kentucky	5,815	1.4%
21	Louisiana	6,976	1.6%
31	Maine	4,120	1.0%
18	Maryland	8,586	2.0%
7	Massachusetts	14,729	3.4%
12	Michigan	11,254	2.6%
13	Minnesota	11,111	2.6%
45	Mississippi	1,360	0.3%
25	Missouri	6,669	1.5%
47	Montana	1,230	0.3%
34	Nebraska	3,321	0.8%
40	Nevada	2,496	0.6%
22	New Hampshire	6,931	1.6%
6	New Jersey	17,686	4.1%
37	New Mexico	3,054	0.7%
2	New York	35,664	8.3%
15	North Carolina	8,972	2.1%
50	North Dakota	994	0.2%
48	Ohio	1,072	0.2%
33	Oklahoma	3,468	0.8%
27	Oregon	5,949	1.4%
4	Pennsylvania	20,210	4.7%
41	Rhode Island	1,967	0.5%
29	South Carolina	4,990	1.2%
43	South Dakota	1,568	0.4%
20	Tennessee	7,975	1.9%
5	Texas	18,312	4.3%
32	Utah	4,051	0.9%
35	Vermont	3,300	0.8%
10	Virginia	12,390	2.9%
23	Washington	6,825	1.6%
42	West Virginia	1,844	0.4%
24	Wisconsin	6,811	1.6%
44	Wyoming	1,377	0.3%

RANK ORDER

RANK	STATE	PARAS	% of USA
1	California	50,053	11.6%
2	New York	35,664	8.3%
3	Illinois	31,177	7.2%
4	Pennsylvania	20,210	4.7%
5	Texas	18,312	4.3%
6	New Jersey	17,686	4.1%
7	Massachusetts	14,729	3.4%
8	Florida	14,553	3.4%
9	Georgia	12,796	3.0%
10	Virginia	12,390	2.9%
11	Kansas	11,455	2.7%
12	Michigan	11,254	2.6%
13	Minnesota	11,111	2.6%
14	Arizona	8,996	2.1%
15	North Carolina	8,972	2.1%
16	Connecticut	8,951	2.1%
17	Indiana	8,807	2.0%
18	Maryland	8,586	2.0%
19	Iowa	8,019	1.9%
20	Tennessee	7,975	1.9%
21	Louisiana	6,976	1.6%
22	New Hampshire	6,931	1.6%
23	Washington	6,825	1.6%
24	Wisconsin	6,811	1.6%
25	Missouri	6,669	1.5%
26	Colorado	6,416	1.5%
27	Oregon	5,949	1.4%
28	Kentucky	5,815	1.4%
29	South Carolina	4,990	1.2%
30	Alabama	4,714	1.1%
31	Maine	4,120	1.0%
32	Utah	4,051	0.9%
33	Oklahoma	3,468	0.8%
34	Nebraska	3,321	0.8%
35	Vermont	3,300	0.8%
36	Arkansas	3,187	0.7%
37	New Mexico	3,054	0.7%
38	Hawaii	2,723	0.6%
39	Idaho	2,665	0.6%
40	Nevada	2,496	0.6%
41	Rhode Island	1,967	0.5%
42	West Virginia	1,844	0.4%
43	South Dakota	1,568	0.4%
44	Wyoming	1,377	0.3%
45	Mississippi	1,360	0.3%
46	Alaska	1,338	0.3%
47	Montana	1,230	0.3%
48	Ohio	1,072	0.2%
49	Delaware	1,059	0.2%
50	North Dakota	994	0.2%
	District of Columbia	294	0.1%

Source: CQ Press using data from U.S. Department of Education, Office of Special Education Programs
"Data Tables for OSEP State Reported Data" (https://www.ideadata.org/arc_toc11.asp)
*Figures are full-time equivalent (FTE). Includes paraprofessional, whether meeting the standards of highly qualified or not, working with disabled children ages 3 to 21 for school year 2008-2009. National total does not include paraprofessionals in U.S. territories and Bureau of Indian Education programs.

Highly Qualified Special Education Paraprofessionals in 2009

National Total = 402,286 Paraprofessionals*

RANK	STATE	PARAS	% of USA
29	Alabama	4,470	1.1%
44	Alaska	1,297	0.3%
20	Arizona	7,185	1.8%
36	Arkansas	2,721	0.7%
1	California	47,902	11.9%
26	Colorado	6,416	1.6%
13	Connecticut	8,951	2.2%
47	Delaware	1,025	0.3%
19	Florida	7,226	1.8%
8	Georgia	12,796	3.2%
38	Hawaii	2,529	0.6%
37	Idaho	2,665	0.7%
3	Illinois	31,177	7.7%
14	Indiana	8,807	2.2%
17	Iowa	8,019	2.0%
10	Kansas	11,455	2.8%
27	Kentucky	5,806	1.4%
25	Louisiana	6,627	1.6%
31	Maine	3,981	1.0%
15	Maryland	8,586	2.1%
7	Massachusetts	13,931	3.5%
11	Michigan	11,246	2.8%
12	Minnesota	11,111	2.8%
43	Mississippi	1,360	0.3%
24	Missouri	6,669	1.7%
45	Montana	1,230	0.3%
32	Nebraska	3,321	0.8%
39	Nevada	2,496	0.6%
21	New Hampshire	6,931	1.7%
6	New Jersey	17,686	4.4%
35	New Mexico	3,010	0.7%
2	New York	31,893	7.9%
16	North Carolina	8,080	2.0%
49	North Dakota	603	0.1%
46	Ohio	1,072	0.3%
34	Oklahoma	3,037	0.8%
30	Oregon	4,415	1.1%
4	Pennsylvania	18,205	4.5%
40	Rhode Island	1,967	0.5%
28	South Carolina	4,828	1.2%
42	South Dakota	1,567	0.4%
18	Tennessee	7,654	1.9%
5	Texas	18,147	4.5%
50	Utah	84	0.0%
33	Vermont	3,228	0.8%
9	Virginia	12,390	3.1%
22	Washington	6,825	1.7%
41	West Virginia	1,768	0.4%
23	Wisconsin	6,780	1.7%
48	Wyoming	864	0.2%

RANK	STATE	PARAS	% of USA
1	California	47,902	11.9%
2	New York	31,893	7.9%
3	Illinois	31,177	7.7%
4	Pennsylvania	18,205	4.5%
5	Texas	18,147	4.5%
6	New Jersey	17,686	4.4%
7	Massachusetts	13,931	3.5%
8	Georgia	12,796	3.2%
9	Virginia	12,390	3.1%
10	Kansas	11,455	2.8%
11	Michigan	11,246	2.8%
12	Minnesota	11,111	2.8%
13	Connecticut	8,951	2.2%
14	Indiana	8,807	2.2%
15	Maryland	8,586	2.1%
16	North Carolina	8,080	2.0%
17	Iowa	8,019	2.0%
18	Tennessee	7,654	1.9%
19	Florida	7,226	1.8%
20	Arizona	7,185	1.8%
21	New Hampshire	6,931	1.7%
22	Washington	6,825	1.7%
23	Wisconsin	6,780	1.7%
24	Missouri	6,669	1.7%
25	Louisiana	6,627	1.6%
26	Colorado	6,416	1.6%
27	Kentucky	5,806	1.4%
28	South Carolina	4,828	1.2%
29	Alabama	4,470	1.1%
30	Oregon	4,415	1.1%
31	Maine	3,981	1.0%
32	Nebraska	3,321	0.8%
33	Vermont	3,228	0.8%
34	Oklahoma	3,037	0.8%
35	New Mexico	3,010	0.7%
36	Arkansas	2,721	0.7%
37	Idaho	2,665	0.7%
38	Hawaii	2,529	0.6%
39	Nevada	2,496	0.6%
40	Rhode Island	1,967	0.5%
41	West Virginia	1,768	0.4%
42	South Dakota	1,567	0.4%
43	Mississippi	1,360	0.3%
44	Alaska	1,297	0.3%
45	Montana	1,230	0.3%
46	Ohio	1,072	0.3%
47	Delaware	1,025	0.3%
48	Wyoming	864	0.2%
49	North Dakota	603	0.1%
50	Utah	84	0.0%
	District of Columbia	246	0.1%

Source: CQ Press using data from U.S. Department of Education, Office of Special Education Programs
    "Data Tables for OSEP State Reported Data" (https://www.ideadata.org/arc_toc11.asp)
*Figures are full-time equivalent (FTE). Includes highly qualified paraprofessionals working with disabled children ages 3 to 21 for school year 2008-2009. National total does not include paraprofessionals in U.S. territories and Bureau of Indian Education programs.

Percent of Special Education Paraprofessionals Highly Qualified in 2009

National Percent = 93.5%*

ALPHA ORDER

RANK	STATE	PERCENT
37	Alabama	94.8
29	Alaska	96.9
45	Arizona	79.9
44	Arkansas	85.4
35	California	95.7
1	Colorado	100.0
1	Connecticut	100.0
30	Delaware	96.8
49	Florida	49.7
1	Georgia	100.0
39	Hawaii	92.9
1	Idaho	100.0
1	Illinois	100.0
1	Indiana	100.0
1	Iowa	100.0
1	Kansas	100.0
24	Kentucky	99.8
36	Louisiana	95.0
32	Maine	96.6
1	Maryland	100.0
38	Massachusetts	94.6
22	Michigan	99.9
1	Minnesota	100.0
1	Mississippi	100.0
1	Missouri	100.0
1	Montana	100.0
1	Nebraska	100.0
1	Nevada	100.0
1	New Hampshire	100.0
1	New Jersey	100.0
27	New Mexico	98.6
42	New York	89.4
40	North Carolina	90.1
48	North Dakota	60.7
1	Ohio	100.0
43	Oklahoma	87.6
46	Oregon	74.2
40	Pennsylvania	90.1
1	Rhode Island	100.0
30	South Carolina	96.8
22	South Dakota	99.9
33	Tennessee	96.0
26	Texas	99.1
50	Utah	2.1
28	Vermont	97.8
1	Virginia	100.0
1	Washington	100.0
34	West Virginia	95.9
25	Wisconsin	99.5
47	Wyoming	62.7

RANK ORDER

RANK	STATE	PERCENT
1	Colorado	100.0
1	Connecticut	100.0
1	Georgia	100.0
1	Idaho	100.0
1	Illinois	100.0
1	Indiana	100.0
1	Iowa	100.0
1	Kansas	100.0
1	Maryland	100.0
1	Minnesota	100.0
1	Mississippi	100.0
1	Missouri	100.0
1	Montana	100.0
1	Nebraska	100.0
1	Nevada	100.0
1	New Hampshire	100.0
1	New Jersey	100.0
1	Ohio	100.0
1	Rhode Island	100.0
1	Virginia	100.0
1	Washington	100.0
22	Michigan	99.9
22	South Dakota	99.9
24	Kentucky	99.8
25	Wisconsin	99.5
26	Texas	99.1
27	New Mexico	98.6
28	Vermont	97.8
29	Alaska	96.9
30	Delaware	96.8
30	South Carolina	96.8
32	Maine	96.6
33	Tennessee	96.0
34	West Virginia	95.9
35	California	95.7
36	Louisiana	95.0
37	Alabama	94.8
38	Massachusetts	94.6
39	Hawaii	92.9
40	North Carolina	90.1
40	Pennsylvania	90.1
42	New York	89.4
43	Oklahoma	87.6
44	Arkansas	85.4
45	Arizona	79.9
46	Oregon	74.2
47	Wyoming	62.7
48	North Dakota	60.7
49	Florida	49.7
50	Utah	2.1

District of Columbia — 83.7

Source: CQ Press using data from U.S. Department of Education, Office of Special Education Programs
"Data Tables for OSEP State Reported Data" (https://www.ideadata.org/arc_toc11.asp)
*Figures are full-time equivalent (FTE). Includes paraprofessional working with disabled children ages 3 to 21 for school year 2008-2009. National percent does not include paraprofessionals in U.S. territories and Bureau of Indian Education programs.

Special Education Staff in 2009

National Total = 1,015,687 Staff*

ALPHA ORDER

RANK	STATE	STAFF	% of USA
28	Alabama	12,673	1.2%
46	Alaska	2,791	0.3%
15	Arizona	20,540	2.0%
33	Arkansas	8,360	0.8%
2	California	87,721	8.6%
26	Colorado	14,581	1.4%
17	Connecticut	18,809	1.9%
44	Delaware	3,245	0.3%
6	Florida	39,215	3.9%
7	Georgia	34,122	3.4%
40	Hawaii	5,677	0.6%
43	Idaho	4,339	0.4%
3	Illinois	64,965	6.4%
18	Indiana	18,506	1.8%
24	Iowa	15,796	1.6%
19	Kansas	18,265	1.8%
25	Kentucky	15,151	1.5%
21	Louisiana	16,988	1.7%
34	Maine	8,269	0.8%
14	Maryland	22,032	2.2%
10	Massachusetts	28,352	2.8%
9	Michigan	30,152	3.0%
13	Minnesota	24,179	2.4%
42	Mississippi	4,864	0.5%
22	Missouri	16,438	1.6%
48	Montana	2,576	0.3%
35	Nebraska	7,759	0.8%
37	Nevada	6,859	0.7%
29	New Hampshire	10,754	1.1%
NA	New Jersey**	NA	NA
36	New Mexico	6,884	0.7%
1	New York	112,526	11.1%
11	North Carolina	26,488	2.6%
49	North Dakota	2,252	0.2%
12	Ohio	25,059	2.5%
31	Oklahoma	9,812	1.0%
30	Oregon	10,672	1.1%
4	Pennsylvania	52,033	5.1%
39	Rhode Island	5,756	0.6%
27	South Carolina	12,808	1.3%
45	South Dakota	2,832	0.3%
20	Tennessee	18,107	1.8%
5	Texas	47,513	4.7%
32	Utah	8,426	0.8%
41	Vermont	5,035	0.5%
8	Virginia	31,330	3.1%
23	Washington	16,134	1.6%
38	West Virginia	5,826	0.6%
16	Wisconsin	19,325	1.9%
47	Wyoming	2,640	0.3%

RANK ORDER

RANK	STATE	STAFF	% of USA
1	New York	112,526	11.1%
2	California	87,721	8.6%
3	Illinois	64,965	6.4%
4	Pennsylvania	52,033	5.1%
5	Texas	47,513	4.7%
6	Florida	39,215	3.9%
7	Georgia	34,122	3.4%
8	Virginia	31,330	3.1%
9	Michigan	30,152	3.0%
10	Massachusetts	28,352	2.8%
11	North Carolina	26,488	2.6%
12	Ohio	25,059	2.5%
13	Minnesota	24,179	2.4%
14	Maryland	22,032	2.2%
15	Arizona	20,540	2.0%
16	Wisconsin	19,325	1.9%
17	Connecticut	18,809	1.9%
18	Indiana	18,506	1.8%
19	Kansas	18,265	1.8%
20	Tennessee	18,107	1.8%
21	Louisiana	16,988	1.7%
22	Missouri	16,438	1.6%
23	Washington	16,134	1.6%
24	Iowa	15,796	1.6%
25	Kentucky	15,151	1.5%
26	Colorado	14,581	1.4%
27	South Carolina	12,808	1.3%
28	Alabama	12,673	1.2%
29	New Hampshire	10,754	1.1%
30	Oregon	10,672	1.1%
31	Oklahoma	9,812	1.0%
32	Utah	8,426	0.8%
33	Arkansas	8,360	0.8%
34	Maine	8,269	0.8%
35	Nebraska	7,759	0.8%
36	New Mexico	6,884	0.7%
37	Nevada	6,859	0.7%
38	West Virginia	5,826	0.6%
39	Rhode Island	5,756	0.6%
40	Hawaii	5,677	0.6%
41	Vermont	5,035	0.5%
42	Mississippi	4,864	0.5%
43	Idaho	4,339	0.4%
44	Delaware	3,245	0.3%
45	South Dakota	2,832	0.3%
46	Alaska	2,791	0.3%
47	Wyoming	2,640	0.3%
48	Montana	2,576	0.3%
49	North Dakota	2,252	0.2%
NA	New Jersey**	NA	NA

District of Columbia 817 0.1%

Source: CQ Press using data from U.S. Department of Education, Office of Special Education Programs
"Data Tables for OSEP State Reported Data" (https://www.ideadata.org/arc_toc11.asp)
*Full-time equivalent (FTE) employed all staff for disabled children ages 3 to 21 in 2008-2009. National total does not include staff in U.S. territories and Bureau of Indian Education programs. Includes teachers; social workers; occupational, recreation, and physical therapists; aides; phys ed teachers; administrators; psychologists; diagnostic staff; audiologists; work study coord.; vocational ed; counselors; rehab counselors; interpreters; speech pathologists; and other staff. **Not available.

Special Education Pupil-Staff Ratio in 2009

National Ratio = 6.4 Students Per Staff Person*

<table>
<tr><td colspan="3">ALPHA ORDER</td><td colspan="3">RANK ORDER</td></tr>
<tr><th>RANK</th><th>STATE</th><th>RATIO</th><th>RANK</th><th>STATE</th><th>RATIO</th></tr>
<tr><td>22</td><td>Alabama</td><td>6.5</td><td>1</td><td>Mississippi</td><td>13.2</td></tr>
<tr><td>24</td><td>Alaska</td><td>6.4</td><td>2</td><td>Ohio</td><td>10.5</td></tr>
<tr><td>27</td><td>Arizona</td><td>6.1</td><td>3</td><td>Oklahoma</td><td>9.7</td></tr>
<tr><td>11</td><td>Arkansas</td><td>7.8</td><td>4</td><td>Florida</td><td>9.6</td></tr>
<tr><td>13</td><td>California</td><td>7.7</td><td>5</td><td>Indiana</td><td>9.3</td></tr>
<tr><td>31</td><td>Colorado</td><td>5.7</td><td>5</td><td>Texas</td><td>9.3</td></tr>
<tr><td>45</td><td>Connecticut</td><td>3.7</td><td>7</td><td>Utah</td><td>8.0</td></tr>
<tr><td>28</td><td>Delaware</td><td>6.0</td><td>8</td><td>Missouri</td><td>7.9</td></tr>
<tr><td>4</td><td>Florida</td><td>9.6</td><td>8</td><td>South Carolina</td><td>7.9</td></tr>
<tr><td>36</td><td>Georgia</td><td>5.2</td><td>8</td><td>West Virginia</td><td>7.9</td></tr>
<tr><td>47</td><td>Hawaii</td><td>3.5</td><td>11</td><td>Arkansas</td><td>7.8</td></tr>
<tr><td>24</td><td>Idaho</td><td>6.4</td><td>11</td><td>Washington</td><td>7.8</td></tr>
<tr><td>39</td><td>Illinois</td><td>4.8</td><td>13</td><td>California</td><td>7.7</td></tr>
<tr><td>5</td><td>Indiana</td><td>9.3</td><td>14</td><td>Michigan</td><td>7.6</td></tr>
<tr><td>42</td><td>Iowa</td><td>4.2</td><td>15</td><td>Oregon</td><td>7.5</td></tr>
<tr><td>46</td><td>Kansas</td><td>3.6</td><td>16</td><td>Kentucky</td><td>7.0</td></tr>
<tr><td>16</td><td>Kentucky</td><td>7.0</td><td>16</td><td>Nevada</td><td>7.0</td></tr>
<tr><td>37</td><td>Louisiana</td><td>5.0</td><td>16</td><td>North Carolina</td><td>7.0</td></tr>
<tr><td>44</td><td>Maine</td><td>4.0</td><td>19</td><td>Montana</td><td>6.7</td></tr>
<tr><td>40</td><td>Maryland</td><td>4.7</td><td>19</td><td>New Mexico</td><td>6.7</td></tr>
<tr><td>29</td><td>Massachusetts</td><td>5.9</td><td>21</td><td>Tennessee</td><td>6.6</td></tr>
<tr><td>14</td><td>Michigan</td><td>7.6</td><td>22</td><td>Alabama</td><td>6.5</td></tr>
<tr><td>37</td><td>Minnesota</td><td>5.0</td><td>22</td><td>Wisconsin</td><td>6.5</td></tr>
<tr><td>1</td><td>Mississippi</td><td>13.2</td><td>24</td><td>Alaska</td><td>6.4</td></tr>
<tr><td>8</td><td>Missouri</td><td>7.9</td><td>24</td><td>Idaho</td><td>6.4</td></tr>
<tr><td>19</td><td>Montana</td><td>6.7</td><td>26</td><td>South Dakota</td><td>6.3</td></tr>
<tr><td>34</td><td>Nebraska</td><td>5.6</td><td>27</td><td>Arizona</td><td>6.1</td></tr>
<tr><td>16</td><td>Nevada</td><td>7.0</td><td>28</td><td>Delaware</td><td>6.0</td></tr>
<tr><td>48</td><td>New Hampshire</td><td>2.8</td><td>29</td><td>Massachusetts</td><td>5.9</td></tr>
<tr><td>NA</td><td>New Jersey**</td><td>NA</td><td>29</td><td>North Dakota</td><td>5.9</td></tr>
<tr><td>19</td><td>New Mexico</td><td>6.7</td><td>31</td><td>Colorado</td><td>5.7</td></tr>
<tr><td>43</td><td>New York</td><td>4.1</td><td>31</td><td>Pennsylvania</td><td>5.7</td></tr>
<tr><td>16</td><td>North Carolina</td><td>7.0</td><td>31</td><td>Wyoming</td><td>5.7</td></tr>
<tr><td>29</td><td>North Dakota</td><td>5.9</td><td>34</td><td>Nebraska</td><td>5.6</td></tr>
<tr><td>2</td><td>Ohio</td><td>10.5</td><td>35</td><td>Virginia</td><td>5.3</td></tr>
<tr><td>3</td><td>Oklahoma</td><td>9.7</td><td>36</td><td>Georgia</td><td>5.2</td></tr>
<tr><td>15</td><td>Oregon</td><td>7.5</td><td>37</td><td>Louisiana</td><td>5.0</td></tr>
<tr><td>31</td><td>Pennsylvania</td><td>5.7</td><td>37</td><td>Minnesota</td><td>5.0</td></tr>
<tr><td>41</td><td>Rhode Island</td><td>4.6</td><td>39</td><td>Illinois</td><td>4.8</td></tr>
<tr><td>8</td><td>South Carolina</td><td>7.9</td><td>40</td><td>Maryland</td><td>4.7</td></tr>
<tr><td>26</td><td>South Dakota</td><td>6.3</td><td>41</td><td>Rhode Island</td><td>4.6</td></tr>
<tr><td>21</td><td>Tennessee</td><td>6.6</td><td>42</td><td>Iowa</td><td>4.2</td></tr>
<tr><td>5</td><td>Texas</td><td>9.3</td><td>43</td><td>New York</td><td>4.1</td></tr>
<tr><td>7</td><td>Utah</td><td>8.0</td><td>44</td><td>Maine</td><td>4.0</td></tr>
<tr><td>48</td><td>Vermont</td><td>2.8</td><td>45</td><td>Connecticut</td><td>3.7</td></tr>
<tr><td>35</td><td>Virginia</td><td>5.3</td><td>46</td><td>Kansas</td><td>3.6</td></tr>
<tr><td>11</td><td>Washington</td><td>7.8</td><td>47</td><td>Hawaii</td><td>3.5</td></tr>
<tr><td>8</td><td>West Virginia</td><td>7.9</td><td>48</td><td>New Hampshire</td><td>2.8</td></tr>
<tr><td>22</td><td>Wisconsin</td><td>6.5</td><td>48</td><td>Vermont</td><td>2.8</td></tr>
<tr><td>31</td><td>Wyoming</td><td>5.7</td><td>NA</td><td>New Jersey**</td><td>NA</td></tr>
<tr><td></td><td></td><td></td><td></td><td>District of Columbia</td><td>13.9</td></tr>
</table>

Source: CQ Press using data from U.S. Department of Education, Office of Special Education Programs
    "Data Tables for OSEP State Reported Data" (https://www.ideadata.org/arc_toc10.asp)
*Full-time equivalent (FTE) employed all staff for disabled children ages 3 to 21 in 2008-2009. National rate does not include
staff or students in U.S. territories and Bureau of Indian Education programs. Includes teachers; social workers; occupational,
recreation, and physical therapists; aides; phys ed teachers; administrators; psychologists; diagnostic staff; audiologists; work
study coord.; vocational ed; counselors; rehab counselors; interpreters; speech pathologists; and other staff. **Not available.

Average Annual Salary of Preschool, Kindergarten, and Elementary Special Education Teachers in 2010
National Average = $55,220*

ALPHA ORDER

RANK	STATE	SALARY
28	Alabama	$48,610
1	Alaska	72,770
47	Arizona	41,450
38	Arkansas	45,340
5	California	64,320
22	Colorado	52,010
2	Connecticut	70,020
32	Delaware	48,090
18	Florida	52,940
21	Georgia	52,070
27	Hawaii	49,770
46	Idaho	42,960
11	Illinois	57,150
31	Indiana	48,190
42	Iowa	44,860
34	Kansas	47,300
30	Kentucky	48,450
33	Louisiana	47,830
44	Maine	44,420
7	Maryland	63,950
10	Massachusetts	58,510
9	Michigan	58,640
16	Minnesota	53,630
43	Mississippi	44,650
41	Missouri	45,020
50	Montana	37,870
29	Nebraska	48,520
24	Nevada	50,780
26	New Hampshire	50,370
8	New Jersey	63,390
14	New Mexico	55,550
3	New York	66,850
40	North Carolina	45,110
45	North Dakota	44,070
20	Ohio	52,090
39	Oklahoma	45,130
19	Oregon	52,650
15	Pennsylvania	55,410
4	Rhode Island	64,370
35	South Carolina	46,890
49	South Dakota	38,710
37	Tennessee	46,240
25	Texas	50,390
36	Utah	46,430
17	Vermont	53,330
6	Virginia	64,230
13	Washington	56,430
48	West Virginia	41,100
23	Wisconsin	51,130
12	Wyoming	56,650

RANK ORDER

RANK	STATE	SALARY
1	Alaska	$72,770
2	Connecticut	70,020
3	New York	66,850
4	Rhode Island	64,370
5	California	64,320
6	Virginia	64,230
7	Maryland	63,950
8	New Jersey	63,390
9	Michigan	58,640
10	Massachusetts	58,510
11	Illinois	57,150
12	Wyoming	56,650
13	Washington	56,430
14	New Mexico	55,550
15	Pennsylvania	55,410
16	Minnesota	53,630
17	Vermont	53,330
18	Florida	52,940
19	Oregon	52,650
20	Ohio	52,090
21	Georgia	52,070
22	Colorado	52,010
23	Wisconsin	51,130
24	Nevada	50,780
25	Texas	50,390
26	New Hampshire	50,370
27	Hawaii	49,770
28	Alabama	48,610
29	Nebraska	48,520
30	Kentucky	48,450
31	Indiana	48,190
32	Delaware	48,090
33	Louisiana	47,830
34	Kansas	47,300
35	South Carolina	46,890
36	Utah	46,430
37	Tennessee	46,240
38	Arkansas	45,340
39	Oklahoma	45,130
40	North Carolina	45,110
41	Missouri	45,020
42	Iowa	44,860
43	Mississippi	44,650
44	Maine	44,420
45	North Dakota	44,070
46	Idaho	42,960
47	Arizona	41,450
48	West Virginia	41,100
49	South Dakota	38,710
50	Montana	37,870
	District of Columbia	49,430

Source: U.S. Department of Labor, Bureau of Labor Statistics
"National Occupational Employment and Wage Estimates" (http://www.bls.gov/oes/)
*As of May 2010.

Average Annual Salary of Middle School Special Education Teachers in 2010

National Average = $56,500*

RANK	STATE	SALARY
33	Alabama	$48,820
2	Alaska	67,370
45	Arizona	42,940
40	Arkansas	46,350
6	California	65,110
23	Colorado	52,290
3	Connecticut	67,250
16	Delaware	55,670
20	Florida	52,960
25	Georgia	50,740
NA	Hawaii**	NA
37	Idaho	46,970
11	Illinois	59,740
31	Indiana	49,880
42	Iowa	43,980
36	Kansas	47,200
34	Kentucky	48,790
35	Louisiana	48,270
39	Maine	46,490
5	Maryland	65,890
10	Massachusetts	60,760
13	Michigan	58,690
17	Minnesota	54,580
44	Mississippi	43,200
32	Missouri	49,330
48	Montana	39,300
18	Nebraska	53,920
21	Nevada	52,810
27	New Hampshire	50,420
9	New Jersey	61,380
15	New Mexico	57,190
1	New York	70,680
41	North Carolina	44,070
NA	North Dakota**	NA
24	Ohio	50,960
43	Oklahoma	43,290
28	Oregon	50,400
8	Pennsylvania	62,040
4	Rhode Island	66,140
30	South Carolina	50,080
47	South Dakota	39,520
38	Tennessee	46,780
26	Texas	50,530
29	Utah	50,350
19	Vermont	53,640
7	Virginia	63,350
14	Washington	57,260
46	West Virginia	39,870
22	Wisconsin	52,750
12	Wyoming	58,780

RANK	STATE	SALARY
1	New York	$70,680
2	Alaska	67,370
3	Connecticut	67,250
4	Rhode Island	66,140
5	Maryland	65,890
6	California	65,110
7	Virginia	63,350
8	Pennsylvania	62,040
9	New Jersey	61,380
10	Massachusetts	60,760
11	Illinois	59,740
12	Wyoming	58,780
13	Michigan	58,690
14	Washington	57,260
15	New Mexico	57,190
16	Delaware	55,670
17	Minnesota	54,580
18	Nebraska	53,920
19	Vermont	53,640
20	Florida	52,960
21	Nevada	52,810
22	Wisconsin	52,750
23	Colorado	52,290
24	Ohio	50,960
25	Georgia	50,740
26	Texas	50,530
27	New Hampshire	50,420
28	Oregon	50,400
29	Utah	50,350
30	South Carolina	50,080
31	Indiana	49,880
32	Missouri	49,330
33	Alabama	48,820
34	Kentucky	48,790
35	Louisiana	48,270
36	Kansas	47,200
37	Idaho	46,970
38	Tennessee	46,780
39	Maine	46,490
40	Arkansas	46,350
41	North Carolina	44,070
42	Iowa	43,980
43	Oklahoma	43,290
44	Mississippi	43,200
45	Arizona	42,940
46	West Virginia	39,870
47	South Dakota	39,520
48	Montana	39,300
NA	Hawaii**	NA
NA	North Dakota**	NA
	District of Columbia	44,280

Source: U.S. Department of Labor, Bureau of Labor Statistics
    "National Occupational Employment and Wage Estimates" (http://www.bls.gov/oes/)
*As of May 2010.
**Not available.

Average Annual Salary of Secondary School Special Education Teachers in 2010
National Average = $58,080*

ALPHA ORDER

RANK	STATE	SALARY
33	Alabama	$49,100
4	Alaska	69,500
36	Arizona	47,850
37	Arkansas	46,440
3	California	69,800
21	Colorado	53,890
2	Connecticut	70,630
9	Delaware	61,230
24	Florida	52,490
22	Georgia	53,880
NA	Hawaii**	NA
43	Idaho	44,740
11	Illinois	59,620
29	Indiana	50,710
46	Iowa	43,630
31	Kansas	49,700
32	Kentucky	49,610
34	Louisiana	49,000
38	Maine	46,250
8	Maryland	62,680
10	Massachusetts	60,500
17	Michigan	56,820
20	Minnesota	54,460
45	Mississippi	44,100
30	Missouri	50,290
48	Montana	40,110
28	Nebraska	51,190
26	Nevada	51,990
23	New Hampshire	52,870
6	New Jersey	66,980
24	New Mexico	52,490
1	New York	73,510
40	North Carolina	45,470
44	North Dakota	44,430
14	Ohio	56,950
42	Oklahoma	45,050
19	Oregon	54,680
12	Pennsylvania	58,360
7	Rhode Island	63,850
35	South Carolina	48,090
49	South Dakota	39,500
41	Tennessee	45,380
27	Texas	51,690
39	Utah	45,670
16	Vermont	56,850
5	Virginia	67,250
13	Washington	57,270
47	West Virginia	42,940
18	Wisconsin	54,700
15	Wyoming	56,920

RANK ORDER

RANK	STATE	SALARY
1	New York	$73,510
2	Connecticut	70,630
3	California	69,800
4	Alaska	69,500
5	Virginia	67,250
6	New Jersey	66,980
7	Rhode Island	63,850
8	Maryland	62,680
9	Delaware	61,230
10	Massachusetts	60,500
11	Illinois	59,620
12	Pennsylvania	58,360
13	Washington	57,270
14	Ohio	56,950
15	Wyoming	56,920
16	Vermont	56,850
17	Michigan	56,820
18	Wisconsin	54,700
19	Oregon	54,680
20	Minnesota	54,460
21	Colorado	53,890
22	Georgia	53,880
23	New Hampshire	52,870
24	Florida	52,490
24	New Mexico	52,490
26	Nevada	51,990
27	Texas	51,690
28	Nebraska	51,190
29	Indiana	50,710
30	Missouri	50,290
31	Kansas	49,700
32	Kentucky	49,610
33	Alabama	49,100
34	Louisiana	49,000
35	South Carolina	48,090
36	Arizona	47,850
37	Arkansas	46,440
38	Maine	46,250
39	Utah	45,670
40	North Carolina	45,470
41	Tennessee	45,380
42	Oklahoma	45,050
43	Idaho	44,740
44	North Dakota	44,430
45	Mississippi	44,100
46	Iowa	43,630
47	West Virginia	42,940
48	Montana	40,110
49	South Dakota	39,500
NA	Hawaii**	NA
	District of Columbia	49,490

Source: U.S. Department of Labor, Bureau of Labor Statistics
"National Occupational Employment and Wage Estimates" (http://www.bls.gov/oes/)
*As of May 2010.
**Not available.

VI. Staff

Estimated Public Elementary and Secondary School Teachers in 2011

National Total = 3,238,795 Teachers*

ALPHA ORDER

RANK	STATE	TEACHERS	% of USA
25	Alabama	47,478	1.5%
46	Alaska	9,102	0.3%
19	Arizona	58,305	1.8%
29	Arkansas	36,759	1.1%
2	California	295,496	9.1%
23	Colorado	49,877	1.5%
26	Connecticut	43,405	1.3%
48	Delaware	8,740	0.3%
4	Florida	163,160	5.0%
7	Georgia	122,193	3.8%
42	Hawaii	10,851	0.3%
40	Idaho	15,670	0.5%
5	Illinois	145,267	4.5%
16	Indiana	63,157	2.0%
31	Iowa	35,913	1.1%
32	Kansas	35,074	1.1%
28	Kentucky	41,700	1.3%
24	Louisiana	48,209	1.5%
39	Maine	17,248	0.5%
17	Maryland	61,308	1.9%
13	Massachusetts	70,217	2.2%
11	Michigan	96,663	3.0%
21	Minnesota	52,281	1.6%
30	Mississippi	35,978	1.1%
14	Missouri	68,544	2.1%
43	Montana	10,570	0.3%
36	Nebraska	22,223	0.7%
35	Nevada	25,049	0.8%
41	New Hampshire	15,622	0.5%
8	New Jersey	115,368	3.6%
37	New Mexico	21,882	0.7%
3	New York	223,862	6.9%
12	North Carolina	95,377	2.9%
49	North Dakota	7,706	0.2%
10	Ohio	107,275	3.3%
27	Oklahoma	43,344	1.3%
33	Oregon	31,135	1.0%
6	Pennsylvania	127,479	3.9%
44	Rhode Island	10,050	0.3%
22	South Carolina	51,551	1.6%
45	South Dakota	9,212	0.3%
15	Tennessee	66,213	2.0%
1	Texas	333,103	10.3%
34	Utah	26,328	0.8%
47	Vermont	8,901	0.3%
9	Virginia	107,879	3.3%
20	Washington	54,517	1.7%
38	West Virginia	19,805	0.6%
18	Wisconsin	58,722	1.8%
50	Wyoming	7,191	0.2%

RANK ORDER

RANK	STATE	TEACHERS	% of USA
1	Texas	333,103	10.3%
2	California	295,496	9.1%
3	New York	223,862	6.9%
4	Florida	163,160	5.0%
5	Illinois	145,267	4.5%
6	Pennsylvania	127,479	3.9%
7	Georgia	122,193	3.8%
8	New Jersey	115,368	3.6%
9	Virginia	107,879	3.3%
10	Ohio	107,275	3.3%
11	Michigan	96,663	3.0%
12	North Carolina	95,377	2.9%
13	Massachusetts	70,217	2.2%
14	Missouri	68,544	2.1%
15	Tennessee	66,213	2.0%
16	Indiana	63,157	2.0%
17	Maryland	61,308	1.9%
18	Wisconsin	58,722	1.8%
19	Arizona	58,305	1.8%
20	Washington	54,517	1.7%
21	Minnesota	52,281	1.6%
22	South Carolina	51,551	1.6%
23	Colorado	49,877	1.5%
24	Louisiana	48,209	1.5%
25	Alabama	47,478	1.5%
26	Connecticut	43,405	1.3%
27	Oklahoma	43,344	1.3%
28	Kentucky	41,700	1.3%
29	Arkansas	36,759	1.1%
30	Mississippi	35,978	1.1%
31	Iowa	35,913	1.1%
32	Kansas	35,074	1.1%
33	Oregon	31,135	1.0%
34	Utah	26,328	0.8%
35	Nevada	25,049	0.8%
36	Nebraska	22,223	0.7%
37	New Mexico	21,882	0.7%
38	West Virginia	19,805	0.6%
39	Maine	17,248	0.5%
40	Idaho	15,670	0.5%
41	New Hampshire	15,622	0.5%
42	Hawaii	10,851	0.3%
43	Montana	10,570	0.3%
44	Rhode Island	10,050	0.3%
45	South Dakota	9,212	0.3%
46	Alaska	9,102	0.3%
47	Vermont	8,901	0.3%
48	Delaware	8,740	0.3%
49	North Dakota	7,706	0.2%
50	Wyoming	7,191	0.2%
	District of Columbia	5,835	0.2%

Source: National Education Association, Washington, D.C.
    "Rankings and Estimates" (Copyright © 2011, NEA, used with permission, http://www.nea.org/home/44479.htm)
*Estimates for school year 2010-2011.

Public Elementary and Secondary School Teachers in 2010

National Total = 3,209,637 Teachers*

ALPHA ORDER

RANK	STATE	TEACHERS	% of USA
24	Alabama	47,492	1.5%
49	Alaska	8,083	0.3%
21	Arizona	51,947	1.6%
29	Arkansas	37,240	1.2%
2	California	313,795	9.8%
23	Colorado	49,060	1.5%
27	Connecticut	43,593	1.4%
47	Delaware	8,640	0.3%
4	Florida	183,827	5.7%
7	Georgia	115,918	3.6%
42	Hawaii	11,404	0.4%
41	Idaho	15,201	0.5%
5	Illinois	138,483	4.3%
16	Indiana	62,258	1.9%
30	Iowa	35,842	1.1%
31	Kansas	34,700	1.1%
26	Kentucky	44,371	1.4%
22	Louisiana	49,646	1.5%
39	Maine	16,275	0.5%
18	Maryland	58,235	1.8%
13	Massachusetts	69,909	2.2%
11	Michigan	92,691	2.9%
20	Minnesota	52,839	1.6%
32	Mississippi	33,103	1.0%
14	Missouri	67,796	2.1%
44	Montana	10,521	0.3%
36	Nebraska	22,256	0.7%
37	Nevada	22,104	0.7%
40	New Hampshire	15,491	0.5%
8	New Jersey	115,248	3.6%
35	New Mexico	22,724	0.7%
3	New York	214,804	6.7%
10	North Carolina	105,046	3.3%
48	North Dakota	8,366	0.3%
9	Ohio	111,378	3.5%
28	Oklahoma	42,678	1.3%
33	Oregon	28,751	0.9%
6	Pennsylvania	130,984	4.1%
43	Rhode Island	11,365	0.4%
25	South Carolina	46,980	1.5%
45	South Dakota	9,326	0.3%
15	Tennessee	65,361	2.0%
1	Texas	333,164	10.4%
34	Utah	25,474	0.8%
46	Vermont	8,734	0.3%
12	Virginia	70,827	2.2%
19	Washington	53,448	1.7%
38	West Virginia	20,299	0.6%
17	Wisconsin	58,426	1.8%
50	Wyoming	7,166	0.2%

RANK ORDER

RANK	STATE	TEACHERS	% of USA
1	Texas	333,164	10.4%
2	California	313,795	9.8%
3	New York	214,804	6.7%
4	Florida	183,827	5.7%
5	Illinois	138,483	4.3%
6	Pennsylvania	130,984	4.1%
7	Georgia	115,918	3.6%
8	New Jersey	115,248	3.6%
9	Ohio	111,378	3.5%
10	North Carolina	105,046	3.3%
11	Michigan	92,691	2.9%
12	Virginia	70,827	2.2%
13	Massachusetts	69,909	2.2%
14	Missouri	67,796	2.1%
15	Tennessee	65,361	2.0%
16	Indiana	62,258	1.9%
17	Wisconsin	58,426	1.8%
18	Maryland	58,235	1.8%
19	Washington	53,448	1.7%
20	Minnesota	52,839	1.6%
21	Arizona	51,947	1.6%
22	Louisiana	49,646	1.5%
23	Colorado	49,060	1.5%
24	Alabama	47,492	1.5%
25	South Carolina	46,980	1.5%
26	Kentucky	44,371	1.4%
27	Connecticut	43,593	1.4%
28	Oklahoma	42,678	1.3%
29	Arkansas	37,240	1.2%
30	Iowa	35,842	1.1%
31	Kansas	34,700	1.1%
32	Mississippi	33,103	1.0%
33	Oregon	28,751	0.9%
34	Utah	25,474	0.8%
35	New Mexico	22,724	0.7%
36	Nebraska	22,256	0.7%
37	Nevada	22,104	0.7%
38	West Virginia	20,299	0.6%
39	Maine	16,275	0.5%
40	New Hampshire	15,491	0.5%
41	Idaho	15,201	0.5%
42	Hawaii	11,404	0.4%
43	Rhode Island	11,365	0.4%
44	Montana	10,521	0.3%
45	South Dakota	9,326	0.3%
46	Vermont	8,734	0.3%
47	Delaware	8,640	0.3%
48	North Dakota	8,366	0.3%
49	Alaska	8,083	0.3%
50	Wyoming	7,166	0.2%
	District of Columbia	6,370	0.2%

Source: U.S. Department of Education, National Center for Education Statistics
   "Common Core of Data (CCD) Database" (http://nces.ed.gov/ccd/)
*School year 2009-2010. Counts are full-time equivalent figures.

Percent Change in Number of Public Elementary and Secondary School Teachers: 2000 to 2010
National Percent Change = 10.3% Increase*

ALPHA ORDER				RANK ORDER		
RANK	STATE	PERCENT CHANGE		RANK	STATE	PERCENT CHANGE
43	Alabama	(2.3)		1	Florida	41.0
34	Alaska	3.1		2	North Carolina	28.2
9	Arizona	18.4		3	Georgia	27.9
8	Arkansas	18.7		4	Nevada	27.2
18	California	9.2		5	Texas	24.3
6	Colorado	20.3		6	Colorado	20.3
18	Connecticut	9.2		7	New Jersey	20.2
10	Delaware	18.1		8	Arkansas	18.7
1	Florida	41.0		9	Arizona	18.4
3	Georgia	27.9		10	Delaware	18.1
30	Hawaii	5.0		11	Utah	16.7
15	Idaho	11.4		12	New Mexico	14.8
16	Illinois	11.0		13	Pennsylvania	14.4
27	Indiana	5.8		14	Maryland	14.2
23	Iowa	7.1		15	Idaho	11.4
29	Kansas	5.3		16	Illinois	11.0
27	Kentucky	5.8		17	New Hampshire	10.4
42	Louisiana	(0.8)		18	California	9.2
40	Maine	(0.5)		18	Connecticut	9.2
14	Maryland	14.2		20	Mississippi	7.8
49	Massachusetts	(9.9)		21	Tennessee	7.7
44	Michigan	(3.5)		22	Nebraska	7.2
48	Minnesota	(5.7)		23	Iowa	7.1
20	Mississippi	7.8		24	New York	6.3
25	Missouri	6.1		25	Missouri	6.1
39	Montana	1.6		25	Washington	6.1
22	Nebraska	7.2		27	Indiana	5.8
4	Nevada	27.2		27	Kentucky	5.8
17	New Hampshire	10.4		29	Kansas	5.3
7	New Jersey	20.2		30	Hawaii	5.0
12	New Mexico	14.8		31	Oregon	3.4
24	New York	6.3		32	South Carolina	3.3
2	North Carolina	28.2		32	Wyoming	3.3
38	North Dakota	2.7		34	Alaska	3.1
47	Ohio	(4.1)		34	Vermont	3.1
37	Oklahoma	2.8		36	Rhode Island	2.9
31	Oregon	3.4		37	Oklahoma	2.8
13	Pennsylvania	14.4		38	North Dakota	2.7
36	Rhode Island	2.9		39	Montana	1.6
32	South Carolina	3.3		40	Maine	(0.5)
41	South Dakota	(0.6)		41	South Dakota	(0.6)
21	Tennessee	7.7		42	Louisiana	(0.8)
5	Texas	24.3		43	Alabama	(2.3)
11	Utah	16.7		44	Michigan	(3.5)
34	Vermont	3.1		45	West Virginia	(3.7)
50	Virginia	(16.7)		46	Wisconsin	(3.9)
25	Washington	6.1		47	Ohio	(4.1)
45	West Virginia	(3.7)		48	Minnesota	(5.7)
46	Wisconsin	(3.9)		49	Massachusetts	(9.9)
32	Wyoming	3.3		50	Virginia	(16.7)
					District of Columbia	32.4

Source: CQ Press using data from U.S. Department of Education, National Center for Education Statistics
  "Common Core of Data (CCD) Database" (http://nces.ed.gov/ccd/)
*School year 1999-2000 to 2009-2010. Counts are full-time equivalent figures.

Public School Pre-Kindergarten Teachers in 2010

National Total = 56,663 Teachers*

ALPHA ORDER					RANK ORDER			

RANK	STATE	TEACHERS	% of USA		RANK	STATE	TEACHERS	% of USA
28	Alabama	537	0.9%		1	Texas	8,862	15.6%
45	Alaska	118	0.2%		2	California	3,970	7.0%
34	Arizona	327	0.6%		3	New York	2,827	5.0%
27	Arkansas	562	1.0%		4	Georgia	2,744	4.8%
2	California	3,970	7.0%		5	New Jersey	2,718	4.8%
19	Colorado	1,081	1.9%		6	Illinois	2,697	4.8%
35	Connecticut	326	0.6%		7	Florida	2,054	3.6%
49	Delaware	89	0.2%		8	Ohio	1,956	3.5%
7	Florida	2,054	3.6%		9	Virginia	1,923	3.4%
4	Georgia	2,744	4.8%		10	Missouri	1,828	3.2%
36	Hawaii	290	0.5%		11	Wisconsin	1,791	3.2%
42	Idaho	145	0.3%		12	North Carolina	1,637	2.9%
6	Illinois	2,697	4.8%		13	Minnesota	1,567	2.8%
26	Indiana	612	1.1%		14	Oklahoma	1,455	2.6%
17	Iowa	1,195	2.1%		15	Massachusetts	1,252	2.2%
25	Kansas	724	1.3%		16	Louisiana	1,233	2.2%
23	Kentucky	936	1.7%		17	Iowa	1,195	2.1%
16	Louisiana	1,233	2.2%		18	Tennessee	1,124	2.0%
44	Maine	124	0.2%		19	Colorado	1,081	1.9%
22	Maryland	943	1.7%		20	Pennsylvania	1,011	1.8%
15	Massachusetts	1,252	2.2%		21	Michigan	1,006	1.8%
21	Michigan	1,006	1.8%		22	Maryland	943	1.7%
13	Minnesota	1,567	2.8%		23	Kentucky	936	1.7%
33	Mississippi	359	0.6%		24	South Carolina	903	1.6%
10	Missouri	1,828	3.2%		25	Kansas	724	1.3%
39	Montana	236	0.4%		26	Indiana	612	1.1%
29	Nebraska	521	0.9%		27	Arkansas	562	1.0%
46	Nevada	108	0.2%		28	Alabama	537	0.9%
40	New Hampshire	175	0.3%		29	Nebraska	521	0.9%
5	New Jersey	2,718	4.8%		30	New Mexico	419	0.7%
30	New Mexico	419	0.7%		31	West Virginia	407	0.7%
3	New York	2,827	5.0%		32	Washington	383	0.7%
12	North Carolina	1,637	2.9%		33	Mississippi	359	0.6%
43	North Dakota	136	0.2%		34	Arizona	327	0.6%
8	Ohio	1,956	3.5%		35	Connecticut	326	0.6%
14	Oklahoma	1,455	2.6%		36	Hawaii	290	0.5%
38	Oregon	242	0.4%		37	Utah	258	0.5%
20	Pennsylvania	1,011	1.8%		38	Oregon	242	0.4%
46	Rhode Island	108	0.2%		39	Montana	236	0.4%
24	South Carolina	903	1.6%		40	New Hampshire	175	0.3%
41	South Dakota	156	0.3%		41	South Dakota	156	0.3%
18	Tennessee	1,124	2.0%		42	Idaho	145	0.3%
1	Texas	8,862	15.6%		43	North Dakota	136	0.2%
37	Utah	258	0.5%		44	Maine	124	0.2%
48	Vermont	90	0.2%		45	Alaska	118	0.2%
9	Virginia	1,923	3.4%		46	Nevada	108	0.2%
32	Washington	383	0.7%		46	Rhode Island	108	0.2%
31	West Virginia	407	0.7%		48	Vermont	90	0.2%
11	Wisconsin	1,791	3.2%		49	Delaware	89	0.2%
50	Wyoming	23	0.0%		50	Wyoming	23	0.0%
						District of Columbia	477	0.8%

Source: U.S. Department of Education, National Center for Education Statistics
    "Common Core of Data (CCD) Database" (http://nces.ed.gov/ccd/)
*School year 2009-2010. Counts are full-time equivalent figures.

Percent of Public School Teachers Who Teach Pre-Kindergarten in 2010

National Percent = 1.8% of Teachers*

ALPHA ORDER

RANK	STATE	PERCENT
32	Alabama	1.1
28	Alaska	1.5
48	Arizona	0.6
28	Arkansas	1.5
30	California	1.3
13	Colorado	2.2
46	Connecticut	0.7
37	Delaware	1.0
32	Florida	1.1
10	Georgia	2.4
8	Hawaii	2.5
37	Idaho	1.0
18	Illinois	1.9
37	Indiana	1.0
2	Iowa	3.3
15	Kansas	2.1
15	Kentucky	2.1
8	Louisiana	2.5
43	Maine	0.8
25	Maryland	1.6
20	Massachusetts	1.8
32	Michigan	1.1
4	Minnesota	3.0
32	Mississippi	1.1
5	Missouri	2.7
13	Montana	2.2
12	Nebraska	2.3
49	Nevada	0.5
32	New Hampshire	1.1
10	New Jersey	2.4
20	New Mexico	1.8
30	New York	1.3
25	North Carolina	1.6
25	North Dakota	1.6
20	Ohio	1.8
1	Oklahoma	3.4
43	Oregon	0.8
43	Pennsylvania	0.8
37	Rhode Island	1.0
18	South Carolina	1.9
23	South Dakota	1.7
23	Tennessee	1.7
5	Texas	2.7
37	Utah	1.0
37	Vermont	1.0
5	Virginia	2.7
46	Washington	0.7
17	West Virginia	2.0
3	Wisconsin	3.1
50	Wyoming	0.3

RANK ORDER

RANK	STATE	PERCENT
1	Oklahoma	3.4
2	Iowa	3.3
3	Wisconsin	3.1
4	Minnesota	3.0
5	Missouri	2.7
5	Texas	2.7
5	Virginia	2.7
8	Hawaii	2.5
8	Louisiana	2.5
10	Georgia	2.4
10	New Jersey	2.4
12	Nebraska	2.3
13	Colorado	2.2
13	Montana	2.2
15	Kansas	2.1
15	Kentucky	2.1
17	West Virginia	2.0
18	Illinois	1.9
18	South Carolina	1.9
20	Massachusetts	1.8
20	New Mexico	1.8
20	Ohio	1.8
23	South Dakota	1.7
23	Tennessee	1.7
25	Maryland	1.6
25	North Carolina	1.6
25	North Dakota	1.6
28	Alaska	1.5
28	Arkansas	1.5
30	California	1.3
30	New York	1.3
32	Alabama	1.1
32	Florida	1.1
32	Michigan	1.1
32	Mississippi	1.1
32	New Hampshire	1.1
37	Delaware	1.0
37	Idaho	1.0
37	Indiana	1.0
37	Rhode Island	1.0
37	Utah	1.0
37	Vermont	1.0
43	Maine	0.8
43	Oregon	0.8
43	Pennsylvania	0.8
46	Connecticut	0.7
46	Washington	0.7
48	Arizona	0.6
49	Nevada	0.5
50	Wyoming	0.3

District of Columbia 7.5

Source: CQ Press using data from U.S. Department of Education, National Center for Education Statistics
    "Common Core of Data (CCD) Database" (http://nces.ed.gov/ccd/)
*School year 2009-2010. Counts are full-time equivalent figures.

Public School Kindergarten Teachers in 2010

National Total = 179,612 Teachers*

ALPHA ORDER

RANK	STATE	TEACHERS	% of USA
10	Alabama	4,768	2.7%
46	Alaska	425	0.2%
22	Arizona	3,031	1.7%
18	Arkansas	3,425	1.9%
1	California	21,498	12.0%
16	Colorado	3,466	1.9%
31	Connecticut	1,721	1.0%
50	Delaware	373	0.2%
4	Florida	9,761	5.4%
5	Georgia	7,396	4.1%
42	Hawaii	591	0.3%
41	Idaho	627	0.3%
9	Illinois	4,887	2.7%
15	Indiana	3,953	2.2%
25	Iowa	2,645	1.5%
32	Kansas	1,690	0.9%
36	Kentucky	1,230	0.7%
27	Louisiana	2,347	1.3%
39	Maine	837	0.5%
21	Maryland	3,108	1.7%
17	Massachusetts	3,437	1.9%
11	Michigan	4,247	2.4%
24	Minnesota	2,770	1.5%
29	Mississippi	1,914	1.1%
14	Missouri	3,965	2.2%
40	Montana	688	0.4%
34	Nebraska	1,265	0.7%
38	Nevada	913	0.5%
43	New Hampshire	500	0.3%
19	New Jersey	3,371	1.9%
33	New Mexico	1,281	0.7%
3	New York	13,139	7.3%
6	North Carolina	6,702	3.7%
44	North Dakota	490	0.3%
7	Ohio	6,061	3.4%
26	Oklahoma	2,408	1.3%
30	Oregon	1,859	1.0%
8	Pennsylvania	5,250	2.9%
47	Rhode Island	407	0.2%
28	South Carolina	2,309	1.3%
45	South Dakota	487	0.3%
13	Tennessee	4,033	2.2%
2	Texas	20,591	11.5%
35	Utah	1,244	0.7%
49	Vermont	388	0.2%
12	Virginia	4,202	2.3%
23	Washington	2,794	1.6%
37	West Virginia	1,076	0.6%
20	Wisconsin	3,324	1.9%
48	Wyoming	406	0.2%

RANK ORDER

RANK	STATE	TEACHERS	% of USA
1	California	21,498	12.0%
2	Texas	20,591	11.5%
3	New York	13,139	7.3%
4	Florida	9,761	5.4%
5	Georgia	7,396	4.1%
6	North Carolina	6,702	3.7%
7	Ohio	6,061	3.4%
8	Pennsylvania	5,250	2.9%
9	Illinois	4,887	2.7%
10	Alabama	4,768	2.7%
11	Michigan	4,247	2.4%
12	Virginia	4,202	2.3%
13	Tennessee	4,033	2.2%
14	Missouri	3,965	2.2%
15	Indiana	3,953	2.2%
16	Colorado	3,466	1.9%
17	Massachusetts	3,437	1.9%
18	Arkansas	3,425	1.9%
19	New Jersey	3,371	1.9%
20	Wisconsin	3,324	1.9%
21	Maryland	3,108	1.7%
22	Arizona	3,031	1.7%
23	Washington	2,794	1.6%
24	Minnesota	2,770	1.5%
25	Iowa	2,645	1.5%
26	Oklahoma	2,408	1.3%
27	Louisiana	2,347	1.3%
28	South Carolina	2,309	1.3%
29	Mississippi	1,914	1.1%
30	Oregon	1,859	1.0%
31	Connecticut	1,721	1.0%
32	Kansas	1,690	0.9%
33	New Mexico	1,281	0.7%
34	Nebraska	1,265	0.7%
35	Utah	1,244	0.7%
36	Kentucky	1,230	0.7%
37	West Virginia	1,076	0.6%
38	Nevada	913	0.5%
39	Maine	837	0.5%
40	Montana	688	0.4%
41	Idaho	627	0.3%
42	Hawaii	591	0.3%
43	New Hampshire	500	0.3%
44	North Dakota	490	0.3%
45	South Dakota	487	0.3%
46	Alaska	425	0.2%
47	Rhode Island	407	0.2%
48	Wyoming	406	0.2%
49	Vermont	388	0.2%
50	Delaware	373	0.2%
	District of Columbia	314	0.2%

Source: U.S. Department of Education, National Center for Education Statistics
    "Common Core of Data (CCD) Database" (http://nces.ed.gov/ccd/)
*School year 2009-2010. Counts are full-time equivalent figures.

Percent of Public School Teachers Who Teach Kindergarten in 2010

National Percent = 5.6% of Teachers*

ALPHA ORDER

RANK	STATE	PERCENT
1	Alabama	10.0
25	Alaska	5.3
16	Arizona	5.8
2	Arkansas	9.2
5	California	6.9
4	Colorado	7.1
45	Connecticut	3.9
41	Delaware	4.3
25	Florida	5.3
8	Georgia	6.4
29	Hawaii	5.2
42	Idaho	4.1
47	Illinois	3.5
10	Indiana	6.3
3	Iowa	7.4
34	Kansas	4.9
50	Kentucky	2.8
38	Louisiana	4.7
33	Maine	5.1
25	Maryland	5.3
34	Massachusetts	4.9
39	Michigan	4.6
29	Minnesota	5.2
16	Mississippi	5.8
16	Missouri	5.8
6	Montana	6.5
19	Nebraska	5.7
42	Nevada	4.1
48	New Hampshire	3.2
49	New Jersey	2.9
22	New Mexico	5.6
13	New York	6.1
8	North Carolina	6.4
14	North Dakota	5.9
24	Ohio	5.4
22	Oklahoma	5.6
6	Oregon	6.5
44	Pennsylvania	4.0
46	Rhode Island	3.6
34	South Carolina	4.9
29	South Dakota	5.2
11	Tennessee	6.2
11	Texas	6.2
34	Utah	4.9
40	Vermont	4.4
14	Virginia	5.9
29	Washington	5.2
25	West Virginia	5.3
19	Wisconsin	5.7
19	Wyoming	5.7

RANK ORDER

RANK	STATE	PERCENT
1	Alabama	10.0
2	Arkansas	9.2
3	Iowa	7.4
4	Colorado	7.1
5	California	6.9
6	Montana	6.5
6	Oregon	6.5
8	Georgia	6.4
8	North Carolina	6.4
10	Indiana	6.3
11	Tennessee	6.2
11	Texas	6.2
13	New York	6.1
14	North Dakota	5.9
14	Virginia	5.9
16	Arizona	5.8
16	Mississippi	5.8
16	Missouri	5.8
19	Nebraska	5.7
19	Wisconsin	5.7
19	Wyoming	5.7
22	New Mexico	5.6
22	Oklahoma	5.6
24	Ohio	5.4
25	Alaska	5.3
25	Florida	5.3
25	Maryland	5.3
25	West Virginia	5.3
29	Hawaii	5.2
29	Minnesota	5.2
29	South Dakota	5.2
29	Washington	5.2
33	Maine	5.1
34	Kansas	4.9
34	Massachusetts	4.9
34	South Carolina	4.9
34	Utah	4.9
38	Louisiana	4.7
39	Michigan	4.6
40	Vermont	4.4
41	Delaware	4.3
42	Idaho	4.1
42	Nevada	4.1
44	Pennsylvania	4.0
45	Connecticut	3.9
46	Rhode Island	3.6
47	Illinois	3.5
48	New Hampshire	3.2
49	New Jersey	2.9
50	Kentucky	2.8
	District of Columbia	4.9

Source: CQ Press using data from U.S. Department of Education, National Center for Education Statistics
"Common Core of Data (CCD) Database" (http://nces.ed.gov/ccd/)
*School year 2009-2010. Counts are full-time equivalent figures.

Public School Elementary Teachers in 2010

National Total = 1,540,873 Teachers*

ALPHA ORDER

RANK	STATE	TEACHERS	% of USA
26	Alabama	21,770	1.4%
48	Alaska	3,721	0.2%
13	Arizona	33,650	2.2%
31	Arkansas	15,718	1.0%
1	California	199,176	12.9%
23	Colorado	23,525	1.5%
21	Connecticut	26,256	1.7%
47	Delaware	3,801	0.2%
5	Florida	62,341	4.0%
6	Georgia	60,372	3.9%
43	Hawaii	5,332	0.3%
41	Idaho	7,252	0.5%
4	Illinois	85,829	5.6%
19	Indiana	29,120	1.9%
30	Iowa	15,953	1.0%
32	Kansas	14,604	0.9%
27	Kentucky	19,821	1.3%
15	Louisiana	30,712	2.0%
36	Maine	10,161	0.7%
16	Maryland	30,237	2.0%
11	Massachusetts	41,546	2.7%
14	Michigan	31,684	2.1%
25	Minnesota	23,123	1.5%
33	Mississippi	13,482	0.9%
18	Missouri	29,138	1.9%
42	Montana	6,209	0.4%
34	Nebraska	11,988	0.8%
37	Nevada	10,159	0.7%
38	New Hampshire	9,856	0.6%
7	New Jersey	56,002	3.6%
39	New Mexico	8,277	0.5%
3	New York	87,718	5.7%
9	North Carolina	47,262	3.1%
46	North Dakota	4,617	0.3%
10	Ohio	46,381	3.0%
28	Oklahoma	19,028	1.2%
29	Oregon	18,047	1.2%
8	Pennsylvania	55,661	3.6%
45	Rhode Island	4,928	0.3%
17	South Carolina	29,710	1.9%
44	South Dakota	5,233	0.3%
12	Tennessee	39,426	2.6%
2	Texas	137,180	8.9%
35	Utah	11,325	0.7%
50	Vermont	2,873	0.2%
20	Virginia	29,053	1.9%
22	Washington	24,129	1.6%
40	West Virginia	7,991	0.5%
24	Wisconsin	23,204	1.5%
49	Wyoming	3,306	0.2%

RANK ORDER

RANK	STATE	TEACHERS	% of USA
1	California	199,176	12.9%
2	Texas	137,180	8.9%
3	New York	87,718	5.7%
4	Illinois	85,829	5.6%
5	Florida	62,341	4.0%
6	Georgia	60,372	3.9%
7	New Jersey	56,002	3.6%
8	Pennsylvania	55,661	3.6%
9	North Carolina	47,262	3.1%
10	Ohio	46,381	3.0%
11	Massachusetts	41,546	2.7%
12	Tennessee	39,426	2.6%
13	Arizona	33,650	2.2%
14	Michigan	31,684	2.1%
15	Louisiana	30,712	2.0%
16	Maryland	30,237	2.0%
17	South Carolina	29,710	1.9%
18	Missouri	29,138	1.9%
19	Indiana	29,120	1.9%
20	Virginia	29,053	1.9%
21	Connecticut	26,256	1.7%
22	Washington	24,129	1.6%
23	Colorado	23,525	1.5%
24	Wisconsin	23,204	1.5%
25	Minnesota	23,123	1.5%
26	Alabama	21,770	1.4%
27	Kentucky	19,821	1.3%
28	Oklahoma	19,028	1.2%
29	Oregon	18,047	1.2%
30	Iowa	15,953	1.0%
31	Arkansas	15,718	1.0%
32	Kansas	14,604	0.9%
33	Mississippi	13,482	0.9%
34	Nebraska	11,988	0.8%
35	Utah	11,325	0.7%
36	Maine	10,161	0.7%
37	Nevada	10,159	0.7%
38	New Hampshire	9,856	0.6%
39	New Mexico	8,277	0.5%
40	West Virginia	7,991	0.5%
41	Idaho	7,252	0.5%
42	Montana	6,209	0.4%
43	Hawaii	5,332	0.3%
44	South Dakota	5,233	0.3%
45	Rhode Island	4,928	0.3%
46	North Dakota	4,617	0.3%
47	Delaware	3,801	0.2%
48	Alaska	3,721	0.2%
49	Wyoming	3,306	0.2%
50	Vermont	2,873	0.2%
	District of Columbia	2,991	0.2%

Source: U.S. Department of Education, National Center for Education Statistics
    "Common Core of Data (CCD) Database" (http://nces.ed.gov/ccd/)
*School year 2009-2010. Counts are full-time equivalent figures.

Percent of Public School Teachers Who Teach Elementary Grades in 2010

National Percent = 48.0% of Teachers*

<table>
<tr><th colspan="3">ALPHA ORDER</th><th colspan="3">RANK ORDER</th></tr>
<tr><th>RANK</th><th>STATE</th><th>PERCENT</th><th>RANK</th><th>STATE</th><th>PERCENT</th></tr>
<tr><td>26</td><td>Alabama</td><td>45.8</td><td>1</td><td>Arizona</td><td>64.8</td></tr>
<tr><td>24</td><td>Alaska</td><td>46.0</td><td>2</td><td>New Hampshire</td><td>63.6</td></tr>
<tr><td>1</td><td>Arizona</td><td>64.8</td><td>3</td><td>California</td><td>63.5</td></tr>
<tr><td>38</td><td>Arkansas</td><td>42.2</td><td>4</td><td>South Carolina</td><td>63.2</td></tr>
<tr><td>3</td><td>California</td><td>63.5</td><td>5</td><td>Oregon</td><td>62.8</td></tr>
<tr><td>19</td><td>Colorado</td><td>48.0</td><td>6</td><td>Maine</td><td>62.4</td></tr>
<tr><td>10</td><td>Connecticut</td><td>60.2</td><td>7</td><td>Illinois</td><td>62.0</td></tr>
<tr><td>33</td><td>Delaware</td><td>44.0</td><td>8</td><td>Louisiana</td><td>61.9</td></tr>
<tr><td>49</td><td>Florida</td><td>33.9</td><td>9</td><td>Tennessee</td><td>60.3</td></tr>
<tr><td>16</td><td>Georgia</td><td>52.1</td><td>10</td><td>Connecticut</td><td>60.2</td></tr>
<tr><td>21</td><td>Hawaii</td><td>46.8</td><td>11</td><td>Massachusetts</td><td>59.4</td></tr>
<tr><td>20</td><td>Idaho</td><td>47.7</td><td>12</td><td>Montana</td><td>59.0</td></tr>
<tr><td>7</td><td>Illinois</td><td>62.0</td><td>13</td><td>South Dakota</td><td>56.1</td></tr>
<tr><td>21</td><td>Indiana</td><td>46.8</td><td>14</td><td>North Dakota</td><td>55.2</td></tr>
<tr><td>31</td><td>Iowa</td><td>44.5</td><td>15</td><td>Nebraska</td><td>53.9</td></tr>
<tr><td>39</td><td>Kansas</td><td>42.1</td><td>16</td><td>Georgia</td><td>52.1</td></tr>
<tr><td>29</td><td>Kentucky</td><td>44.7</td><td>17</td><td>Maryland</td><td>51.9</td></tr>
<tr><td>8</td><td>Louisiana</td><td>61.9</td><td>18</td><td>New Jersey</td><td>48.6</td></tr>
<tr><td>6</td><td>Maine</td><td>62.4</td><td>19</td><td>Colorado</td><td>48.0</td></tr>
<tr><td>17</td><td>Maryland</td><td>51.9</td><td>20</td><td>Idaho</td><td>47.7</td></tr>
<tr><td>11</td><td>Massachusetts</td><td>59.4</td><td>21</td><td>Hawaii</td><td>46.8</td></tr>
<tr><td>48</td><td>Michigan</td><td>34.2</td><td>21</td><td>Indiana</td><td>46.8</td></tr>
<tr><td>34</td><td>Minnesota</td><td>43.8</td><td>23</td><td>Wyoming</td><td>46.1</td></tr>
<tr><td>44</td><td>Mississippi</td><td>40.7</td><td>24</td><td>Alaska</td><td>46.0</td></tr>
<tr><td>36</td><td>Missouri</td><td>43.0</td><td>24</td><td>Nevada</td><td>46.0</td></tr>
<tr><td>12</td><td>Montana</td><td>59.0</td><td>26</td><td>Alabama</td><td>45.8</td></tr>
<tr><td>15</td><td>Nebraska</td><td>53.9</td><td>27</td><td>Washington</td><td>45.1</td></tr>
<tr><td>24</td><td>Nevada</td><td>46.0</td><td>28</td><td>North Carolina</td><td>45.0</td></tr>
<tr><td>2</td><td>New Hampshire</td><td>63.6</td><td>29</td><td>Kentucky</td><td>44.7</td></tr>
<tr><td>18</td><td>New Jersey</td><td>48.6</td><td>30</td><td>Oklahoma</td><td>44.6</td></tr>
<tr><td>47</td><td>New Mexico</td><td>36.4</td><td>31</td><td>Iowa</td><td>44.5</td></tr>
<tr><td>43</td><td>New York</td><td>40.8</td><td>31</td><td>Utah</td><td>44.5</td></tr>
<tr><td>28</td><td>North Carolina</td><td>45.0</td><td>33</td><td>Delaware</td><td>44.0</td></tr>
<tr><td>14</td><td>North Dakota</td><td>55.2</td><td>34</td><td>Minnesota</td><td>43.8</td></tr>
<tr><td>40</td><td>Ohio</td><td>41.6</td><td>35</td><td>Rhode Island</td><td>43.4</td></tr>
<tr><td>30</td><td>Oklahoma</td><td>44.6</td><td>36</td><td>Missouri</td><td>43.0</td></tr>
<tr><td>5</td><td>Oregon</td><td>62.8</td><td>37</td><td>Pennsylvania</td><td>42.5</td></tr>
<tr><td>37</td><td>Pennsylvania</td><td>42.5</td><td>38</td><td>Arkansas</td><td>42.2</td></tr>
<tr><td>35</td><td>Rhode Island</td><td>43.4</td><td>39</td><td>Kansas</td><td>42.1</td></tr>
<tr><td>4</td><td>South Carolina</td><td>63.2</td><td>40</td><td>Ohio</td><td>41.6</td></tr>
<tr><td>13</td><td>South Dakota</td><td>56.1</td><td>41</td><td>Texas</td><td>41.2</td></tr>
<tr><td>9</td><td>Tennessee</td><td>60.3</td><td>42</td><td>Virginia</td><td>41.0</td></tr>
<tr><td>41</td><td>Texas</td><td>41.2</td><td>43</td><td>New York</td><td>40.8</td></tr>
<tr><td>31</td><td>Utah</td><td>44.5</td><td>44</td><td>Mississippi</td><td>40.7</td></tr>
<tr><td>50</td><td>Vermont</td><td>32.9</td><td>45</td><td>Wisconsin</td><td>39.7</td></tr>
<tr><td>42</td><td>Virginia</td><td>41.0</td><td>46</td><td>West Virginia</td><td>39.4</td></tr>
<tr><td>27</td><td>Washington</td><td>45.1</td><td>47</td><td>New Mexico</td><td>36.4</td></tr>
<tr><td>46</td><td>West Virginia</td><td>39.4</td><td>48</td><td>Michigan</td><td>34.2</td></tr>
<tr><td>45</td><td>Wisconsin</td><td>39.7</td><td>49</td><td>Florida</td><td>33.9</td></tr>
<tr><td>23</td><td>Wyoming</td><td>46.1</td><td>50</td><td>Vermont</td><td>32.9</td></tr>
<tr><td></td><td></td><td></td><td></td><td>District of Columbia</td><td>47.0</td></tr>
</table>

Source: CQ Press using data from U.S. Department of Education, National Center for Education Statistics
"Common Core of Data (CCD) Database" (http://nces.ed.gov/ccd/)
*School year 2009-2010. Counts are full-time equivalent figures.

Public Secondary School Teachers in 2010

National Total = 1,227,484 Teachers*

ALPHA ORDER

RANK	STATE	TEACHERS	% of USA
21	Alabama	20,417	1.7%
45	Alaska	3,819	0.3%
27	Arizona	14,939	1.2%
28	Arkansas	14,577	1.2%
2	California	89,151	7.3%
20	Colorado	20,989	1.7%
29	Connecticut	14,236	1.2%
44	Delaware	4,378	0.4%
4	Florida	65,821	5.4%
8	Georgia	45,344	3.7%
42	Hawaii	5,151	0.4%
39	Idaho	7,177	0.6%
9	Illinois	45,062	3.7%
15	Indiana	28,171	2.3%
25	Iowa	16,049	1.3%
24	Kansas	16,816	1.4%
33	Kentucky	10,329	0.8%
26	Louisiana	15,355	1.3%
41	Maine	5,154	0.4%
16	Maryland	23,948	2.0%
18	Massachusetts	23,674	1.9%
11	Michigan	36,706	3.0%
17	Minnesota	23,884	1.9%
31	Mississippi	13,270	1.1%
13	Missouri	32,865	2.7%
48	Montana	3,388	0.3%
37	Nebraska	8,482	0.7%
38	Nevada	7,982	0.7%
43	New Hampshire	4,960	0.4%
10	New Jersey	40,615	3.3%
35	New Mexico	8,657	0.7%
3	New York	72,408	5.9%
7	North Carolina	47,923	3.9%
49	North Dakota	3,123	0.3%
6	Ohio	53,016	4.3%
22	Oklahoma	19,788	1.6%
36	Oregon	8,604	0.7%
5	Pennsylvania	59,973	4.9%
40	Rhode Island	5,922	0.5%
30	South Carolina	14,058	1.1%
50	South Dakota	2,566	0.2%
23	Tennessee	18,946	1.5%
1	Texas	131,239	10.7%
34	Utah	9,979	0.8%
46	Vermont	3,563	0.3%
12	Virginia	35,649	2.9%
19	Washington	22,852	1.9%
32	West Virginia	10,825	0.9%
14	Wisconsin	29,962	2.4%
47	Wyoming	3,431	0.3%

RANK ORDER

RANK	STATE	TEACHERS	% of USA
1	Texas	131,239	10.7%
2	California	89,151	7.3%
3	New York	72,408	5.9%
4	Florida	65,821	5.4%
5	Pennsylvania	59,973	4.9%
6	Ohio	53,016	4.3%
7	North Carolina	47,923	3.9%
8	Georgia	45,344	3.7%
9	Illinois	45,062	3.7%
10	New Jersey	40,615	3.3%
11	Michigan	36,706	3.0%
12	Virginia	35,649	2.9%
13	Missouri	32,865	2.7%
14	Wisconsin	29,962	2.4%
15	Indiana	28,171	2.3%
16	Maryland	23,948	2.0%
17	Minnesota	23,884	1.9%
18	Massachusetts	23,674	1.9%
19	Washington	22,852	1.9%
20	Colorado	20,989	1.7%
21	Alabama	20,417	1.7%
22	Oklahoma	19,788	1.6%
23	Tennessee	18,946	1.5%
24	Kansas	16,816	1.4%
25	Iowa	16,049	1.3%
26	Louisiana	15,355	1.3%
27	Arizona	14,939	1.2%
28	Arkansas	14,577	1.2%
29	Connecticut	14,236	1.2%
30	South Carolina	14,058	1.1%
31	Mississippi	13,270	1.1%
32	West Virginia	10,825	0.9%
33	Kentucky	10,329	0.8%
34	Utah	9,979	0.8%
35	New Mexico	8,657	0.7%
36	Oregon	8,604	0.7%
37	Nebraska	8,482	0.7%
38	Nevada	7,982	0.7%
39	Idaho	7,177	0.6%
40	Rhode Island	5,922	0.5%
41	Maine	5,154	0.4%
42	Hawaii	5,151	0.4%
43	New Hampshire	4,960	0.4%
44	Delaware	4,378	0.4%
45	Alaska	3,819	0.3%
46	Vermont	3,563	0.3%
47	Wyoming	3,431	0.3%
48	Montana	3,388	0.3%
49	North Dakota	3,123	0.3%
50	South Dakota	2,566	0.2%
	District of Columbia	2,291	0.2%

Source: U.S. Department of Education, National Center for Education Statistics
"Common Core of Data (CCD) Database" (http://nces.ed.gov/ccd/)
*School year 2009-2010. Counts are full-time equivalent figures.

Percent of Public School Teachers Who Teach Secondary Grades in 2010

National Percent = 38.2% of Teachers*

ALPHA ORDER

RANK ORDER

RANK	STATE	PERCENT	RANK	STATE	PERCENT
19	Alabama	43.0	1	West Virginia	53.3
10	Alaska	47.2	2	Rhode Island	52.1
47	Arizona	28.8	3	Wisconsin	51.3
28	Arkansas	39.1	4	Delaware	50.7
48	California	28.4	5	Virginia	50.3
20	Colorado	42.8	6	Kansas	48.5
38	Connecticut	32.7	6	Missouri	48.5
4	Delaware	50.7	8	Wyoming	47.9
34	Florida	35.8	9	Ohio	47.6
28	Georgia	39.1	10	Alaska	47.2
15	Hawaii	45.2	10	Idaho	47.2
10	Idaho	47.2	12	Oklahoma	46.4
39	Illinois	32.5	13	Pennsylvania	45.8
15	Indiana	45.2	14	North Carolina	45.6
18	Iowa	44.8	15	Hawaii	45.2
6	Kansas	48.5	15	Indiana	45.2
50	Kentucky	23.3	15	Minnesota	45.2
43	Louisiana	30.9	18	Iowa	44.8
42	Maine	31.7	19	Alabama	43.0
22	Maryland	41.1	20	Colorado	42.8
36	Massachusetts	33.9	20	Washington	42.8
25	Michigan	39.6	22	Maryland	41.1
15	Minnesota	45.2	23	Vermont	40.8
24	Mississippi	40.1	24	Mississippi	40.1
6	Missouri	48.5	25	Michigan	39.6
40	Montana	32.2	26	Texas	39.4
30	Nebraska	38.1	27	Utah	39.2
33	Nevada	36.1	28	Arkansas	39.1
41	New Hampshire	32.0	28	Georgia	39.1
35	New Jersey	35.2	30	Nebraska	38.1
30	New Mexico	38.1	30	New Mexico	38.1
37	New York	33.7	32	North Dakota	37.3
14	North Carolina	45.6	33	Nevada	36.1
32	North Dakota	37.3	34	Florida	35.8
9	Ohio	47.6	35	New Jersey	35.2
12	Oklahoma	46.4	36	Massachusetts	33.9
44	Oregon	29.9	37	New York	33.7
13	Pennsylvania	45.8	38	Connecticut	32.7
2	Rhode Island	52.1	39	Illinois	32.5
44	South Carolina	29.9	40	Montana	32.2
49	South Dakota	27.5	41	New Hampshire	32.0
46	Tennessee	29.0	42	Maine	31.7
26	Texas	39.4	43	Louisiana	30.9
27	Utah	39.2	44	Oregon	29.9
23	Vermont	40.8	44	South Carolina	29.9
5	Virginia	50.3	46	Tennessee	29.0
20	Washington	42.8	47	Arizona	28.8
1	West Virginia	53.3	48	California	28.4
3	Wisconsin	51.3	49	South Dakota	27.5
8	Wyoming	47.9	50	Kentucky	23.3

District of Columbia   36.0

Source: CQ Press using data from U.S. Department of Education, National Center for Education Statistics
      "Common Core of Data (CCD) Database" (http://nces.ed.gov/ccd/)
*School year 2009-2010. Counts are full-time equivalent figures.

Public Elementary and Secondary School Teachers of Ungraded Classes in 2010
National Total = 205,004 Teachers*

ALPHA ORDER

RANK	STATE	TEACHERS	% of USA
27	Alabama	0	0.0%
27	Alaska	0	0.0%
27	Arizona	0	0.0%
12	Arkansas	2,958	1.4%
27	California	0	0.0%
27	Colorado	0	0.0%
19	Connecticut	1,054	0.5%
27	Delaware	0	0.0%
1	Florida	43,851	21.4%
24	Georgia	61	0.0%
25	Hawaii	40	0.0%
27	Idaho	0	0.0%
26	Illinois	8	0.0%
22	Indiana	402	0.2%
27	Iowa	0	0.0%
21	Kansas	867	0.4%
6	Kentucky	12,056	5.9%
27	Louisiana	0	0.0%
27	Maine	0	0.0%
27	Maryland	0	0.0%
27	Massachusetts	0	0.0%
4	Michigan	19,047	9.3%
18	Minnesota	1,496	0.7%
9	Mississippi	4,078	2.0%
27	Missouri	0	0.0%
27	Montana	0	0.0%
27	Nebraska	0	0.0%
13	Nevada	2,942	1.4%
27	New Hampshire	0	0.0%
5	New Jersey	12,542	6.1%
8	New Mexico	4,090	2.0%
2	New York	38,712	18.9%
17	North Carolina	1,522	0.7%
27	North Dakota	0	0.0%
10	Ohio	3,963	1.9%
27	Oklahoma	0	0.0%
27	Oregon	0	0.0%
7	Pennsylvania	9,089	4.4%
27	Rhode Island	0	0.0%
27	South Carolina	0	0.0%
20	South Dakota	884	0.4%
15	Tennessee	1,832	0.9%
3	Texas	35,292	17.2%
14	Utah	2,667	1.3%
16	Vermont	1,819	0.9%
27	Virginia	0	0.0%
11	Washington	3,290	1.6%
27	West Virginia	0	0.0%
23	Wisconsin	145	0.1%
27	Wyoming	0	0.0%

RANK ORDER

RANK	STATE	TEACHERS	% of USA
1	Florida	43,851	21.4%
2	New York	38,712	18.9%
3	Texas	35,292	17.2%
4	Michigan	19,047	9.3%
5	New Jersey	12,542	6.1%
6	Kentucky	12,056	5.9%
7	Pennsylvania	9,089	4.4%
8	New Mexico	4,090	2.0%
9	Mississippi	4,078	2.0%
10	Ohio	3,963	1.9%
11	Washington	3,290	1.6%
12	Arkansas	2,958	1.4%
13	Nevada	2,942	1.4%
14	Utah	2,667	1.3%
15	Tennessee	1,832	0.9%
16	Vermont	1,819	0.9%
17	North Carolina	1,522	0.7%
18	Minnesota	1,496	0.7%
19	Connecticut	1,054	0.5%
20	South Dakota	884	0.4%
21	Kansas	867	0.4%
22	Indiana	402	0.2%
23	Wisconsin	145	0.1%
24	Georgia	61	0.0%
25	Hawaii	40	0.0%
26	Illinois	8	0.0%
27	Alabama	0	0.0%
27	Alaska	0	0.0%
27	Arizona	0	0.0%
27	California	0	0.0%
27	Colorado	0	0.0%
27	Delaware	0	0.0%
27	Idaho	0	0.0%
27	Iowa	0	0.0%
27	Louisiana	0	0.0%
27	Maine	0	0.0%
27	Maryland	0	0.0%
27	Massachusetts	0	0.0%
27	Missouri	0	0.0%
27	Montana	0	0.0%
27	Nebraska	0	0.0%
27	New Hampshire	0	0.0%
27	North Dakota	0	0.0%
27	Oklahoma	0	0.0%
27	Oregon	0	0.0%
27	Rhode Island	0	0.0%
27	South Carolina	0	0.0%
27	Virginia	0	0.0%
27	West Virginia	0	0.0%
27	Wyoming	0	0.0%
	District of Columbia	297	0.1%

Source: U.S. Department of Education, National Center for Education Statistics
    "Common Core of Data (CCD) Database" (http://nces.ed.gov/ccd/)
*School year 2009-2010. Counts are full-time equivalent figures. These are teachers who instruct classes or programs to which students are assigned without standard grade designation.

Percent of Public Elementary and Secondary Teachers Who Teach Ungraded Classes in 2010
National Percent = 6.4% of Teachers*

ALPHA ORDER

ALPHA ORDER

RANK	STATE	PERCENT
26	Alabama	0.0
26	Alaska	0.0
26	Arizona	0.0
13	Arkansas	7.9
26	California	0.0
26	Colorado	0.0
20	Connecticut	2.4
26	Delaware	0.0
2	Florida	23.9
25	Georgia	0.1
23	Hawaii	0.4
26	Idaho	0.0
26	Illinois	0.0
22	Indiana	0.6
26	Iowa	0.0
19	Kansas	2.5
1	Kentucky	27.2
26	Louisiana	0.0
26	Maine	0.0
26	Maryland	0.0
26	Massachusetts	0.0
4	Michigan	20.5
17	Minnesota	2.8
8	Mississippi	12.3
26	Missouri	0.0
26	Montana	0.0
26	Nebraska	0.0
7	Nevada	13.3
26	New Hampshire	0.0
9	New Jersey	10.9
5	New Mexico	18.0
5	New York	18.0
21	North Carolina	1.4
26	North Dakota	0.0
16	Ohio	3.6
26	Oklahoma	0.0
26	Oregon	0.0
14	Pennsylvania	6.9
26	Rhode Island	0.0
26	South Carolina	0.0
12	South Dakota	9.5
17	Tennessee	2.8
10	Texas	10.6
11	Utah	10.5
3	Vermont	20.8
26	Virginia	0.0
15	Washington	6.2
26	West Virginia	0.0
24	Wisconsin	0.2
26	Wyoming	0.0

RANK ORDER

RANK	STATE	PERCENT
1	Kentucky	27.2
2	Florida	23.9
3	Vermont	20.8
4	Michigan	20.5
5	New Mexico	18.0
5	New York	18.0
7	Nevada	13.3
8	Mississippi	12.3
9	New Jersey	10.9
10	Texas	10.6
11	Utah	10.5
12	South Dakota	9.5
13	Arkansas	7.9
14	Pennsylvania	6.9
15	Washington	6.2
16	Ohio	3.6
17	Minnesota	2.8
17	Tennessee	2.8
19	Kansas	2.5
20	Connecticut	2.4
21	North Carolina	1.4
22	Indiana	0.6
23	Hawaii	0.4
24	Wisconsin	0.2
25	Georgia	0.1
26	Alabama	0.0
26	Alaska	0.0
26	Arizona	0.0
26	California	0.0
26	Colorado	0.0
26	Delaware	0.0
26	Idaho	0.0
26	Illinois	0.0
26	Iowa	0.0
26	Louisiana	0.0
26	Maine	0.0
26	Maryland	0.0
26	Massachusetts	0.0
26	Missouri	0.0
26	Montana	0.0
26	Nebraska	0.0
26	New Hampshire	0.0
26	North Dakota	0.0
26	Oklahoma	0.0
26	Oregon	0.0
26	Rhode Island	0.0
26	South Carolina	0.0
26	Virginia	0.0
26	West Virginia	0.0
26	Wyoming	0.0

	District of Columbia	4.7

Source: CQ Press using data from U.S. Department of Education, National Center for Education Statistics
    "Common Core of Data (CCD) Database" (http://nces.ed.gov/ccd/)
*School year 2009-2010. Counts are full-time equivalent figures. These are teachers who instruct classes or programs to which students are assigned without standard grade designation.

Estimated Percent of Public Elementary and Secondary Teachers Who Are Men in 2011
National Percent = 23.9%*

<table>
<tr><td colspan="3"><u>ALPHA ORDER</u></td><td colspan="3"><u>RANK ORDER</u></td></tr>
<tr><th>RANK</th><th>STATE</th><th>PERCENT</th><th>RANK</th><th>STATE</th><th>PERCENT</th></tr>
<tr><td>37</td><td>Alabama</td><td>22.0</td><td>1</td><td>Kansas</td><td>33.1</td></tr>
<tr><td>2</td><td>Alaska</td><td>31.5</td><td>2</td><td>Alaska</td><td>31.5</td></tr>
<tr><td>29</td><td>Arizona</td><td>23.6</td><td>3</td><td>Oregon</td><td>30.8</td></tr>
<tr><td>50</td><td>Arkansas</td><td>14.8</td><td>4</td><td>Indiana</td><td>30.5</td></tr>
<tr><td>10</td><td>California</td><td>28.0</td><td>5</td><td>Vermont</td><td>30.2</td></tr>
<tr><td>19</td><td>Colorado</td><td>25.1</td><td>6</td><td>Wyoming</td><td>29.7</td></tr>
<tr><td>15</td><td>Connecticut</td><td>25.8</td><td>7</td><td>Minnesota</td><td>29.5</td></tr>
<tr><td>28</td><td>Delaware</td><td>23.8</td><td>8</td><td>Pennsylvania</td><td>28.8</td></tr>
<tr><td>43</td><td>Florida</td><td>21.0</td><td>8</td><td>Washington</td><td>28.8</td></tr>
<tr><td>45</td><td>Georgia</td><td>19.8</td><td>10</td><td>California</td><td>28.0</td></tr>
<tr><td>16</td><td>Hawaii</td><td>25.5</td><td>11</td><td>Idaho</td><td>27.1</td></tr>
<tr><td>11</td><td>Idaho</td><td>27.1</td><td>12</td><td>Maine</td><td>27.0</td></tr>
<tr><td>34</td><td>Illinois</td><td>22.7</td><td>13</td><td>Montana</td><td>26.9</td></tr>
<tr><td>4</td><td>Indiana</td><td>30.5</td><td>14</td><td>Wisconsin</td><td>26.7</td></tr>
<tr><td>21</td><td>Iowa</td><td>24.8</td><td>15</td><td>Connecticut</td><td>25.8</td></tr>
<tr><td>1</td><td>Kansas</td><td>33.1</td><td>16</td><td>Hawaii</td><td>25.5</td></tr>
<tr><td>41</td><td>Kentucky</td><td>21.4</td><td>16</td><td>New Mexico</td><td>25.5</td></tr>
<tr><td>47</td><td>Louisiana</td><td>18.4</td><td>18</td><td>North Dakota</td><td>25.4</td></tr>
<tr><td>12</td><td>Maine</td><td>27.0</td><td>19</td><td>Colorado</td><td>25.1</td></tr>
<tr><td>36</td><td>Maryland</td><td>22.4</td><td>19</td><td>Ohio</td><td>25.1</td></tr>
<tr><td>26</td><td>Massachusetts</td><td>24.1</td><td>21</td><td>Iowa</td><td>24.8</td></tr>
<tr><td>25</td><td>Michigan</td><td>24.3</td><td>21</td><td>Nebraska</td><td>24.8</td></tr>
<tr><td>7</td><td>Minnesota</td><td>29.5</td><td>23</td><td>Nevada</td><td>24.7</td></tr>
<tr><td>48</td><td>Mississippi</td><td>17.9</td><td>24</td><td>New York</td><td>24.5</td></tr>
<tr><td>40</td><td>Missouri</td><td>21.5</td><td>25</td><td>Michigan</td><td>24.3</td></tr>
<tr><td>13</td><td>Montana</td><td>26.9</td><td>26</td><td>Massachusetts</td><td>24.1</td></tr>
<tr><td>21</td><td>Nebraska</td><td>24.8</td><td>26</td><td>New Jersey</td><td>24.1</td></tr>
<tr><td>23</td><td>Nevada</td><td>24.7</td><td>28</td><td>Delaware</td><td>23.8</td></tr>
<tr><td>34</td><td>New Hampshire</td><td>22.7</td><td>29</td><td>Arizona</td><td>23.6</td></tr>
<tr><td>26</td><td>New Jersey</td><td>24.1</td><td>29</td><td>Utah</td><td>23.6</td></tr>
<tr><td>16</td><td>New Mexico</td><td>25.5</td><td>31</td><td>West Virginia</td><td>23.4</td></tr>
<tr><td>24</td><td>New York</td><td>24.5</td><td>32</td><td>South Dakota</td><td>23.3</td></tr>
<tr><td>44</td><td>North Carolina</td><td>20.1</td><td>33</td><td>Texas</td><td>23.0</td></tr>
<tr><td>18</td><td>North Dakota</td><td>25.4</td><td>34</td><td>Illinois</td><td>22.7</td></tr>
<tr><td>19</td><td>Ohio</td><td>25.1</td><td>34</td><td>New Hampshire</td><td>22.7</td></tr>
<tr><td>39</td><td>Oklahoma</td><td>21.9</td><td>36</td><td>Maryland</td><td>22.4</td></tr>
<tr><td>3</td><td>Oregon</td><td>30.8</td><td>37</td><td>Alabama</td><td>22.0</td></tr>
<tr><td>8</td><td>Pennsylvania</td><td>28.8</td><td>37</td><td>Rhode Island</td><td>22.0</td></tr>
<tr><td>37</td><td>Rhode Island</td><td>22.0</td><td>39</td><td>Oklahoma</td><td>21.9</td></tr>
<tr><td>46</td><td>South Carolina</td><td>18.6</td><td>40</td><td>Missouri</td><td>21.5</td></tr>
<tr><td>32</td><td>South Dakota</td><td>23.3</td><td>41</td><td>Kentucky</td><td>21.4</td></tr>
<tr><td>42</td><td>Tennessee</td><td>21.3</td><td>42</td><td>Tennessee</td><td>21.3</td></tr>
<tr><td>33</td><td>Texas</td><td>23.0</td><td>43</td><td>Florida</td><td>21.0</td></tr>
<tr><td>29</td><td>Utah</td><td>23.6</td><td>44</td><td>North Carolina</td><td>20.1</td></tr>
<tr><td>5</td><td>Vermont</td><td>30.2</td><td>45</td><td>Georgia</td><td>19.8</td></tr>
<tr><td>49</td><td>Virginia</td><td>17.8</td><td>46</td><td>South Carolina</td><td>18.6</td></tr>
<tr><td>8</td><td>Washington</td><td>28.8</td><td>47</td><td>Louisiana</td><td>18.4</td></tr>
<tr><td>31</td><td>West Virginia</td><td>23.4</td><td>48</td><td>Mississippi</td><td>17.9</td></tr>
<tr><td>14</td><td>Wisconsin</td><td>26.7</td><td>49</td><td>Virginia</td><td>17.8</td></tr>
<tr><td>6</td><td>Wyoming</td><td>29.7</td><td>50</td><td>Arkansas</td><td>14.8</td></tr>
<tr><td></td><td></td><td></td><td></td><td>District of Columbia</td><td>23.0</td></tr>
</table>

Source: CQ Press using data from National Education Association, Washington, D.C.
   "Rankings and Estimates" (Copyright © 2011, NEA, used with permission, http://www.nea.org/home/44479.htm)
*Estimates for school year 2010-2011.

National Board Certified Teachers as of 2010

National Total = 91,022 Teachers*

Source: National Board for Professional Teaching Standards
"NBCTs by State" (http://www.nbpts.org/resources/nbct_directory/nbcts_by_state)

ALPHA ORDER

RANK	STATE	TEACHERS	% of USA
13	Alabama	2,009	2.2%
45	Alaska	121	0.1%
20	Arizona	767	0.8%
15	Arkansas	1,689	1.9%
5	California	4,910	5.4%
26	Colorado	548	0.6%
43	Connecticut	136	0.1%
30	Delaware	440	0.5%
2	Florida	13,530	14.9%
10	Georgia	2,600	2.9%
37	Hawaii	284	0.3%
32	Idaho	369	0.4%
6	Illinois	4,692	5.2%
42	Indiana	151	0.2%
22	Iowa	663	0.7%
35	Kansas	342	0.4%
12	Kentucky	2,157	2.4%
16	Louisiana	1,682	1.8%
41	Maine	202	0.2%
14	Maryland	1,973	2.2%
27	Massachusetts	519	0.6%
34	Michigan	348	0.4%
33	Minnesota	352	0.4%
8	Mississippi	3,224	3.5%
21	Missouri	671	0.7%
46	Montana	92	0.1%
47	Nebraska	86	0.1%
28	Nevada	487	0.5%
50	New Hampshire	19	0.0%
39	New Jersey	211	0.2%
25	New Mexico	580	0.6%
17	New York	1,136	1.2%
1	North Carolina	17,952	19.7%
49	North Dakota	32	0.0%
7	Ohio	3,267	3.6%
9	Oklahoma	2,820	3.1%
38	Oregon	244	0.3%
19	Pennsylvania	770	0.8%
31	Rhode Island	417	0.5%
3	South Carolina	7,783	8.6%
48	South Dakota	74	0.1%
29	Tennessee	486	0.5%
23	Texas	630	0.7%
40	Utah	204	0.2%
44	Vermont	124	0.1%
11	Virginia	2,180	2.4%
4	Washington	5,229	5.7%
24	West Virginia	583	0.6%
18	Wisconsin	784	0.9%
36	Wyoming	314	0.3%

RANK ORDER

RANK	STATE	TEACHERS	% of USA
1	North Carolina	17,952	19.7%
2	Florida	13,530	14.9%
3	South Carolina	7,783	8.6%
4	Washington	5,229	5.7%
5	California	4,910	5.4%
6	Illinois	4,692	5.2%
7	Ohio	3,267	3.6%
8	Mississippi	3,224	3.5%
9	Oklahoma	2,820	3.1%
10	Georgia	2,600	2.9%
11	Virginia	2,180	2.4%
12	Kentucky	2,157	2.4%
13	Alabama	2,009	2.2%
14	Maryland	1,973	2.2%
15	Arkansas	1,689	1.9%
16	Louisiana	1,682	1.8%
17	New York	1,136	1.2%
18	Wisconsin	784	0.9%
19	Pennsylvania	770	0.8%
20	Arizona	767	0.8%
21	Missouri	671	0.7%
22	Iowa	663	0.7%
23	Texas	630	0.7%
24	West Virginia	583	0.6%
25	New Mexico	580	0.6%
26	Colorado	548	0.6%
27	Massachusetts	519	0.6%
28	Nevada	487	0.5%
29	Tennessee	486	0.5%
30	Delaware	440	0.5%
31	Rhode Island	417	0.5%
32	Idaho	369	0.4%
33	Minnesota	352	0.4%
34	Michigan	348	0.4%
35	Kansas	342	0.4%
36	Wyoming	314	0.3%
37	Hawaii	284	0.3%
38	Oregon	244	0.3%
39	New Jersey	211	0.2%
40	Utah	204	0.2%
41	Maine	202	0.2%
42	Indiana	151	0.2%
43	Connecticut	136	0.1%
44	Vermont	124	0.1%
45	Alaska	121	0.1%
46	Montana	92	0.1%
47	Nebraska	86	0.1%
48	South Dakota	74	0.1%
49	North Dakota	32	0.0%
50	New Hampshire	19	0.0%
	District of Columbia	66	0.1%

*To be certified, teachers must demonstrate their knowledge and skills through a series of performance-based assessments that include student work samples, videotapes, and rigorous analyses of their classroom teaching and student learning. National total includes 73 teachers not shown by state.

Estimated Average Salary of Public School Teachers in 2011

National Average = $56,069*

ALPHA ORDER

RANK	STATE	SALARY
32	Alabama	$48,282
8	Alaska	61,093
35	Arizona	47,553
34	Arkansas	47,700
3	California	69,434
28	Colorado	49,938
5	Connecticut	65,571
12	Delaware	57,934
46	Florida	46,702
17	Georgia	53,906
16	Hawaii	55,063
37	Idaho	47,416
7	Illinois	63,005
25	Indiana	50,407
24	Iowa	50,634
41	Kansas	47,080
27	Kentucky	50,038
29	Louisiana	49,634
39	Maine	47,182
6	Maryland	65,113
2	Massachusetts	71,017
11	Michigan	58,595
19	Minnesota	53,215
45	Mississippi	46,818
48	Missouri	46,411
40	Montana	47,132
36	Nebraska	47,521
20	Nevada	53,023
21	New Hampshire	52,792
4	New Jersey	66,985
43	New Mexico	46,950
1	New York	72,708
44	North Carolina	46,850
49	North Dakota	44,266
13	Ohio	57,291
31	Oklahoma	49,039
15	Oregon	56,387
10	Pennsylvania	60,536
9	Rhode Island	60,923
30	South Carolina	49,434
50	South Dakota	35,201
42	Tennessee	47,043
33	Texas	48,261
47	Utah	46,571
26	Vermont	50,141
23	Virginia	51,559
18	Washington	53,796
38	West Virginia	47,253
22	Wisconsin	52,031
14	Wyoming	56,978

RANK ORDER

RANK	STATE	SALARY
1	New York	$72,708
2	Massachusetts	71,017
3	California	69,434
4	New Jersey	66,985
5	Connecticut	65,571
6	Maryland	65,113
7	Illinois	63,005
8	Alaska	61,093
9	Rhode Island	60,923
10	Pennsylvania	60,536
11	Michigan	58,595
12	Delaware	57,934
13	Ohio	57,291
14	Wyoming	56,978
15	Oregon	56,387
16	Hawaii	55,063
17	Georgia	53,906
18	Washington	53,796
19	Minnesota	53,215
20	Nevada	53,023
21	New Hampshire	52,792
22	Wisconsin	52,031
23	Virginia	51,559
24	Iowa	50,634
25	Indiana	50,407
26	Vermont	50,141
27	Kentucky	50,038
28	Colorado	49,938
29	Louisiana	49,634
30	South Carolina	49,434
31	Oklahoma	49,039
32	Alabama	48,282
33	Texas	48,261
34	Arkansas	47,700
35	Arizona	47,553
36	Nebraska	47,521
37	Idaho	47,416
38	West Virginia	47,253
39	Maine	47,182
40	Montana	47,132
41	Kansas	47,080
42	Tennessee	47,043
43	New Mexico	46,950
44	North Carolina	46,850
45	Mississippi	46,818
46	Florida	46,702
47	Utah	46,571
48	Missouri	46,411
49	North Dakota	44,266
50	South Dakota	35,201
	District of Columbia	66,601

Source: National Education Association, Washington, D.C.
    "Rankings and Estimates" (Copyright © 2011, NEA, used with permission, http://www.nea.org/home/44479.htm)
*Estimates for school year 2010-2011 for classroom teachers.

Average Teacher Salary as a Percent of
Average Annual Pay of All Workers in 2009
National Percent = 120.1% of Average Annual Pay*

ALPHA ORDER

RANK	STATE	PERCENT
31	Alabama	119.8
20	Alaska	125.3
47	Arizona	108.9
15	Arkansas	129.5
11	California	131.1
49	Colorado	104.2
46	Connecticut	110.4
34	Delaware	119.1
40	Florida	114.3
24	Georgia	123.5
8	Hawaii	133.1
5	Idaho	134.0
18	Illinois	127.6
14	Indiana	130.1
9	Iowa	132.2
28	Kansas	121.7
17	Kentucky	128.2
30	Louisiana	120.2
23	Maine	124.0
19	Maryland	125.4
29	Massachusetts	121.6
10	Michigan	132.1
39	Minnesota	115.7
7	Mississippi	133.2
43	Missouri	111.9
6	Montana	133.6
22	Nebraska	124.4
36	Nevada	118.8
42	New Hampshire	113.0
38	New Jersey	116.2
33	New Mexico	119.4
27	New York	121.9
32	North Carolina	119.6
37	North Dakota	117.6
3	Ohio	135.2
25	Oklahoma	122.9
4	Oregon	134.1
13	Pennsylvania	130.4
1	Rhode Island	136.0
16	South Carolina	129.1
45	South Dakota	110.8
41	Tennessee	114.1
48	Texas	104.4
35	Utah	118.9
21	Vermont	125.0
50	Virginia	102.0
44	Washington	111.2
25	West Virginia	122.9
12	Wisconsin	130.8
2	Wyoming	135.7

RANK ORDER

RANK	STATE	PERCENT
1	Rhode Island	136.0
2	Wyoming	135.7
3	Ohio	135.2
4	Oregon	134.1
5	Idaho	134.0
6	Montana	133.6
7	Mississippi	133.2
8	Hawaii	133.1
9	Iowa	132.2
10	Michigan	132.1
11	California	131.1
12	Wisconsin	130.8
13	Pennsylvania	130.4
14	Indiana	130.1
15	Arkansas	129.5
16	South Carolina	129.1
17	Kentucky	128.2
18	Illinois	127.6
19	Maryland	125.4
20	Alaska	125.3
21	Vermont	125.0
22	Nebraska	124.4
23	Maine	124.0
24	Georgia	123.5
25	Oklahoma	122.9
25	West Virginia	122.9
27	New York	121.9
28	Kansas	121.7
29	Massachusetts	121.6
30	Louisiana	120.2
31	Alabama	119.8
32	North Carolina	119.6
33	New Mexico	119.4
34	Delaware	119.1
35	Utah	118.9
36	Nevada	118.8
37	North Dakota	117.6
38	New Jersey	116.2
39	Minnesota	115.7
40	Florida	114.3
41	Tennessee	114.1
42	New Hampshire	113.0
43	Missouri	111.9
44	Washington	111.2
45	South Dakota	110.8
46	Connecticut	110.4
47	Arizona	108.9
48	Texas	104.4
49	Colorado	104.2
50	Virginia	102.0

District of Columbia 82.0

Source: CQ Press using data from National Education Association, Washington, D.C.
"Rankings and Estimates" (Copyright © 2011, NEA, used with permission, http://www.nea.org/home/44479.htm) and
"Quarterly Census of Employment and Wages" (http://www.bls.gov/cew/home.htm)
*Average of public elementary and secondary teacher salary for school years 2008-2009 and estimated 2009-2010 compared to
each state's 2009 average annual pay for all workers covered by federal unemployment.

Average Annual Salary of Preschool Teachers in 2010

National Average = $29,200*

ALPHA ORDER

RANK	STATE	SALARY
28	Alabama	$26,920
10	Alaska	31,120
30	Arizona	26,510
33	Arkansas	26,390
7	California	31,230
6	Colorado	31,480
13	Connecticut	30,080
40	Delaware	24,700
36	Florida	25,480
20	Georgia	28,790
5	Hawaii	31,770
49	Idaho	21,750
18	Illinois	29,010
39	Indiana	25,000
22	Iowa	27,930
8	Kansas	31,200
21	Kentucky	28,160
38	Louisiana	25,290
NA	Maine**	NA
14	Maryland	29,700
3	Massachusetts	33,450
9	Michigan	31,160
4	Minnesota	32,310
48	Mississippi	22,750
42	Missouri	24,650
40	Montana	24,700
32	Nebraska	26,460
37	Nevada	25,380
29	New Hampshire	26,580
2	New Jersey	35,680
15	New Mexico	29,370
1	New York	38,200
47	North Carolina	22,800
23	North Dakota	27,810
45	Ohio	23,570
25	Oklahoma	27,310
44	Oregon	24,360
34	Pennsylvania	26,180
12	Rhode Island	30,290
27	South Carolina	27,040
25	South Dakota	27,310
35	Tennessee	25,870
17	Texas	29,060
46	Utah	23,450
11	Vermont	30,620
16	Virginia	29,350
19	Washington	28,840
24	West Virginia	27,430
43	Wisconsin	24,590
31	Wyoming	26,480

RANK ORDER

RANK	STATE	SALARY
1	New York	$38,200
2	New Jersey	35,680
3	Massachusetts	33,450
4	Minnesota	32,310
5	Hawaii	31,770
6	Colorado	31,480
7	California	31,230
8	Kansas	31,200
9	Michigan	31,160
10	Alaska	31,120
11	Vermont	30,620
12	Rhode Island	30,290
13	Connecticut	30,080
14	Maryland	29,700
15	New Mexico	29,370
16	Virginia	29,350
17	Texas	29,060
18	Illinois	29,010
19	Washington	28,840
20	Georgia	28,790
21	Kentucky	28,160
22	Iowa	27,930
23	North Dakota	27,810
24	West Virginia	27,430
25	Oklahoma	27,310
25	South Dakota	27,310
27	South Carolina	27,040
28	Alabama	26,920
29	New Hampshire	26,580
30	Arizona	26,510
31	Wyoming	26,480
32	Nebraska	26,460
33	Arkansas	26,390
34	Pennsylvania	26,180
35	Tennessee	25,870
36	Florida	25,480
37	Nevada	25,380
38	Louisiana	25,290
39	Indiana	25,000
40	Delaware	24,700
40	Montana	24,700
42	Missouri	24,650
43	Wisconsin	24,590
44	Oregon	24,360
45	Ohio	23,570
46	Utah	23,450
47	North Carolina	22,800
48	Mississippi	22,750
49	Idaho	21,750
NA	Maine**	NA
	District of Columbia	32,890

Source: U.S. Department of Labor, Bureau of Labor Statistics
"National Occupational Employment and Wage Estimates" (http://www.bls.gov/oes/)
*As of May 2010. Does not include special education pre-school teachers.
**Not available.

Average Annual Salary of Kindergarten Teachers in 2010

National Average = $51,550*

ALPHA ORDER

RANK	STATE	SALARY
23	Alabama	$47,720
3	Alaska	65,930
41	Arizona	40,700
37	Arkansas	43,220
6	California	58,970
24	Colorado	47,660
4	Connecticut	62,190
11	Delaware	52,520
20	Florida	49,220
15	Georgia	50,280
45	Hawaii	40,230
49	Idaho	37,440
30	Illinois	46,380
26	Indiana	47,070
38	Iowa	43,100
32	Kansas	45,330
17	Kentucky	49,720
28	Louisiana	46,690
33	Maine	45,210
31	Maryland	45,750
7	Massachusetts	56,090
12	Michigan	52,370
14	Minnesota	51,190
43	Mississippi	40,590
36	Missouri	43,590
48	Montana	38,220
29	Nebraska	46,420
42	Nevada	40,660
39	New Hampshire	42,230
5	New Jersey	58,990
13	New Mexico	51,920
1	New York	70,180
40	North Carolina	41,760
47	North Dakota	39,290
19	Ohio	49,320
44	Oklahoma	40,260
27	Oregon	47,060
10	Pennsylvania	53,880
2	Rhode Island	67,460
16	South Carolina	49,990
50	South Dakota	37,250
35	Tennessee	44,760
21	Texas	48,430
46	Utah	40,120
22	Vermont	48,200
8	Virginia	55,370
18	Washington	49,370
34	West Virginia	45,070
25	Wisconsin	47,410
9	Wyoming	54,140

RANK ORDER

RANK	STATE	SALARY
1	New York	$70,180
2	Rhode Island	67,460
3	Alaska	65,930
4	Connecticut	62,190
5	New Jersey	58,990
6	California	58,970
7	Massachusetts	56,090
8	Virginia	55,370
9	Wyoming	54,140
10	Pennsylvania	53,880
11	Delaware	52,520
12	Michigan	52,370
13	New Mexico	51,920
14	Minnesota	51,190
15	Georgia	50,280
16	South Carolina	49,990
17	Kentucky	49,720
18	Washington	49,370
19	Ohio	49,320
20	Florida	49,220
21	Texas	48,430
22	Vermont	48,200
23	Alabama	47,720
24	Colorado	47,660
25	Wisconsin	47,410
26	Indiana	47,070
27	Oregon	47,060
28	Louisiana	46,690
29	Nebraska	46,420
30	Illinois	46,380
31	Maryland	45,750
32	Kansas	45,330
33	Maine	45,210
34	West Virginia	45,070
35	Tennessee	44,760
36	Missouri	43,590
37	Arkansas	43,220
38	Iowa	43,100
39	New Hampshire	42,230
40	North Carolina	41,760
41	Arizona	40,700
42	Nevada	40,660
43	Mississippi	40,590
44	Oklahoma	40,260
45	Hawaii	40,230
46	Utah	40,120
47	North Dakota	39,290
48	Montana	38,220
49	Idaho	37,440
50	South Dakota	37,250
	District of Columbia	42,420

Source: U.S. Department of Labor, Bureau of Labor Statistics
   "National Occupational Employment and Wage Estimates" (http://www.bls.gov/oes/)
*As of May 2010. Does not include special education kindergarten teachers.

Average Annual Salary of Elementary School Teachers in 2010

National Average = $54,330*

RANK	ALPHA ORDER STATE	SALARY		RANK	RANK ORDER STATE	SALARY
33	Alabama	$47,840		1	Alaska	$69,130
1	Alaska	69,130		2	New York	67,940
47	Arizona	42,110		3	Connecticut	66,500
42	Arkansas	43,380		4	Rhode Island	65,020
5	California	63,010		5	California	63,010
29	Colorado	49,150		6	New Jersey	62,990
3	Connecticut	66,500		7	Massachusetts	62,570
14	Delaware	54,700		8	Virginia	60,390
27	Florida	49,820		9	Maryland	59,840
18	Georgia	53,190		10	Illinois	59,460
30	Hawaii	49,030		11	Washington	57,760
26	Idaho	49,990		12	Michigan	56,870
10	Illinois	59,460		13	Wyoming	56,330
31	Indiana	48,550		14	Delaware	54,700
40	Iowa	44,040		15	Ohio	54,180
45	Kansas	42,910		16	Minnesota	54,040
32	Kentucky	48,300		17	Pennsylvania	53,960
35	Louisiana	46,530		18	Georgia	53,190
38	Maine	45,420		19	Vermont	52,750
9	Maryland	59,840		20	Wisconsin	52,110
7	Massachusetts	62,570		21	Oregon	51,820
12	Michigan	56,870		22	New Mexico	51,660
16	Minnesota	54,040		23	Texas	51,090
49	Mississippi	41,720		24	New Hampshire	50,450
39	Missouri	44,070		25	Nebraska	50,150
48	Montana	41,900		26	Idaho	49,990
25	Nebraska	50,150		27	Florida	49,820
28	Nevada	49,450		28	Nevada	49,450
24	New Hampshire	50,450		29	Colorado	49,150
6	New Jersey	62,990		30	Hawaii	49,030
22	New Mexico	51,660		31	Indiana	48,550
2	New York	67,940		32	Kentucky	48,300
43	North Carolina	43,200		33	Alabama	47,840
44	North Dakota	43,110		34	South Carolina	47,090
15	Ohio	54,180		35	Louisiana	46,530
46	Oklahoma	42,450		36	Utah	46,270
21	Oregon	51,820		37	Tennessee	45,790
17	Pennsylvania	53,960		38	Maine	45,420
4	Rhode Island	65,020		39	Missouri	44,070
34	South Carolina	47,090		40	Iowa	44,040
50	South Dakota	39,350		41	West Virginia	43,700
37	Tennessee	45,790		42	Arkansas	43,380
23	Texas	51,090		43	North Carolina	43,200
36	Utah	46,270		44	North Dakota	43,110
19	Vermont	52,750		45	Kansas	42,910
8	Virginia	60,390		46	Oklahoma	42,450
11	Washington	57,760		47	Arizona	42,110
41	West Virginia	43,700		48	Montana	41,900
20	Wisconsin	52,110		49	Mississippi	41,720
13	Wyoming	56,330		50	South Dakota	39,350
					District of Columbia	63,370

Source: U.S. Department of Labor, Bureau of Labor Statistics
   "National Occupational Employment and Wage Estimates" (http://www.bls.gov/oes/)
*As of May 2010. Does not include special education elementary school teachers.

Average Annual Salary of Middle School Teachers in 2010

National Average = $54,880*

ALPHA ORDER

RANK	STATE	SALARY
33	Alabama	$47,630
3	Alaska	66,890
44	Arizona	42,040
40	Arkansas	45,210
7	California	62,970
26	Colorado	49,410
2	Connecticut	68,420
16	Delaware	54,230
24	Florida	50,770
17	Georgia	53,620
49	Hawaii	34,620
28	Idaho	49,050
9	Illinois	61,360
31	Indiana	47,660
38	Iowa	45,730
41	Kansas	44,420
27	Kentucky	49,060
36	Louisiana	46,710
35	Maine	46,720
4	Maryland	65,440
8	Massachusetts	61,670
14	Michigan	58,020
34	Minnesota	47,550
47	Mississippi	40,700
37	Missouri	46,690
42	Montana	42,730
21	Nebraska	51,290
25	Nevada	49,450
29	New Hampshire	48,910
5	New Jersey	63,930
18	New Mexico	52,930
1	New York	70,670
43	North Carolina	42,670
NA	North Dakota**	NA
19	Ohio	52,680
46	Oklahoma	41,310
23	Oregon	51,170
11	Pennsylvania	58,740
6	Rhode Island	63,590
31	South Carolina	47,660
48	South Dakota	40,300
39	Tennessee	45,310
22	Texas	51,230
30	Utah	48,880
15	Vermont	54,250
10	Virginia	59,670
12	Washington	58,490
45	West Virginia	42,030
20	Wisconsin	52,240
13	Wyoming	58,290

RANK ORDER

RANK	STATE	SALARY
1	New York	$70,670
2	Connecticut	68,420
3	Alaska	66,890
4	Maryland	65,440
5	New Jersey	63,930
6	Rhode Island	63,590
7	California	62,970
8	Massachusetts	61,670
9	Illinois	61,360
10	Virginia	59,670
11	Pennsylvania	58,740
12	Washington	58,490
13	Wyoming	58,290
14	Michigan	58,020
15	Vermont	54,250
16	Delaware	54,230
17	Georgia	53,620
18	New Mexico	52,930
19	Ohio	52,680
20	Wisconsin	52,240
21	Nebraska	51,290
22	Texas	51,230
23	Oregon	51,170
24	Florida	50,770
25	Nevada	49,450
26	Colorado	49,410
27	Kentucky	49,060
28	Idaho	49,050
29	New Hampshire	48,910
30	Utah	48,880
31	Indiana	47,660
31	South Carolina	47,660
33	Alabama	47,630
34	Minnesota	47,550
35	Maine	46,720
36	Louisiana	46,710
37	Missouri	46,690
38	Iowa	45,730
39	Tennessee	45,310
40	Arkansas	45,210
41	Kansas	44,420
42	Montana	42,730
43	North Carolina	42,670
44	Arizona	42,040
45	West Virginia	42,030
46	Oklahoma	41,310
47	Mississippi	40,700
48	South Dakota	40,300
49	Hawaii	34,620
NA	North Dakota**	NA
	District of Columbia	56,850

Source: U.S. Department of Labor, Bureau of Labor Statistics
   "National Occupational Employment and Wage Estimates" (http://www.bls.gov/oes/)
*As of May 2010. Does not include special and career/technical education middle school teachers.
**Not available.

Average Annual Salary of Secondary School Teachers in 2010

National Average = $55,990*

ALPHA ORDER

RANK	STATE	SALARY
32	Alabama	$48,390
2	Alaska	67,790
42	Arizona	43,880
38	Arkansas	45,770
6	California	64,860
25	Colorado	50,920
5	Connecticut	66,600
15	Delaware	55,480
20	Florida	52,640
19	Georgia	52,830
31	Hawaii	48,700
23	Idaho	51,190
3	Illinois	67,110
37	Indiana	46,630
41	Iowa	44,080
43	Kansas	43,620
27	Kentucky	50,040
33	Louisiana	48,090
35	Maine	47,340
8	Maryland	63,000
9	Massachusetts	62,850
16	Michigan	55,210
26	Minnesota	50,460
47	Mississippi	41,490
45	Missouri	43,280
49	Montana	40,290
34	Nebraska	48,080
29	Nevada	49,690
27	New Hampshire	50,040
4	New Jersey	67,010
17	New Mexico	54,700
1	New York	70,400
40	North Carolina	44,730
48	North Dakota	41,240
14	Ohio	55,870
46	Oklahoma	43,060
21	Oregon	52,180
13	Pennsylvania	56,740
7	Rhode Island	64,550
30	South Carolina	48,930
50	South Dakota	39,310
36	Tennessee	46,660
18	Texas	53,160
39	Utah	45,560
22	Vermont	51,470
10	Virginia	60,450
11	Washington	59,470
44	West Virginia	43,410
24	Wisconsin	51,040
12	Wyoming	57,750

RANK ORDER

RANK	STATE	SALARY
1	New York	$70,400
2	Alaska	67,790
3	Illinois	67,110
4	New Jersey	67,010
5	Connecticut	66,600
6	California	64,860
7	Rhode Island	64,550
8	Maryland	63,000
9	Massachusetts	62,850
10	Virginia	60,450
11	Washington	59,470
12	Wyoming	57,750
13	Pennsylvania	56,740
14	Ohio	55,870
15	Delaware	55,480
16	Michigan	55,210
17	New Mexico	54,700
18	Texas	53,160
19	Georgia	52,830
20	Florida	52,640
21	Oregon	52,180
22	Vermont	51,470
23	Idaho	51,190
24	Wisconsin	51,040
25	Colorado	50,920
26	Minnesota	50,460
27	Kentucky	50,040
27	New Hampshire	50,040
29	Nevada	49,690
30	South Carolina	48,930
31	Hawaii	48,700
32	Alabama	48,390
33	Louisiana	48,090
34	Nebraska	48,080
35	Maine	47,340
36	Tennessee	46,660
37	Indiana	46,630
38	Arkansas	45,770
39	Utah	45,560
40	North Carolina	44,730
41	Iowa	44,080
42	Arizona	43,880
43	Kansas	43,620
44	West Virginia	43,410
45	Missouri	43,280
46	Oklahoma	43,060
47	Mississippi	41,490
48	North Dakota	41,240
49	Montana	40,290
50	South Dakota	39,310
	District of Columbia	56,270

Source: U.S. Department of Labor, Bureau of Labor Statistics
    "National Occupational Employment and Wage Estimates" (http://www.bls.gov/oes/)
*As of May 2010. Does not include special and career/technical education secondary school teachers.

Average Annual Salary of Elementary and Secondary School Administrators in 2010
National Average = $89,990*

ALPHA ORDER

ALPHA ORDER

RANK	STATE	SALARY		RANK	STATE	SALARY
35	Alabama	$76,950		1	New York	$118,490
8	Alaska	100,940		2	New Jersey	115,960
37	Arizona	76,540		3	Connecticut	112,030
39	Arkansas	74,600		4	California	105,250
4	California	105,250		5	Maryland	102,620
30	Colorado	80,920		6	Delaware	102,310
3	Connecticut	112,030		7	Illinois	101,970
6	Delaware	102,310		8	Alaska	100,940
16	Florida	88,670		9	Washington	97,690
22	Georgia	85,690		10	Massachusetts	94,330
14	Hawaii	89,480		11	Rhode Island	93,520
36	Idaho	76,570		12	Pennsylvania	93,190
7	Illinois	101,970		13	Minnesota	93,110
31	Indiana	80,460		14	Hawaii	89,480
24	Iowa	84,120		15	Wisconsin	88,970
34	Kansas	77,400		16	Florida	88,670
32	Kentucky	80,190		17	Oregon	88,600
42	Louisiana	71,770		18	Virginia	88,250
41	Maine	72,620		19	Wyoming	87,640
5	Maryland	102,620		20	Michigan	87,180
10	Massachusetts	94,330		21	Nevada	86,790
20	Michigan	87,180		22	Georgia	85,690
13	Minnesota	93,110		23	Ohio	85,330
45	Mississippi	69,920		24	Iowa	84,120
29	Missouri	81,520		25	Utah	83,830
48	Montana	67,140		26	Vermont	83,680
27	Nebraska	82,540		27	Nebraska	82,540
21	Nevada	86,790		28	South Carolina	81,630
40	New Hampshire	74,470		29	Missouri	81,520
2	New Jersey	115,960		30	Colorado	80,920
33	New Mexico	79,890		31	Indiana	80,460
1	New York	118,490		32	Kentucky	80,190
46	North Carolina	68,590		33	New Mexico	79,890
43	North Dakota	71,500		34	Kansas	77,400
23	Ohio	85,330		35	Alabama	76,950
49	Oklahoma	65,910		36	Idaho	76,570
17	Oregon	88,600		37	Arizona	76,540
12	Pennsylvania	93,190		38	Texas	76,330
11	Rhode Island	93,520		39	Arkansas	74,600
28	South Carolina	81,630		40	New Hampshire	74,470
47	South Dakota	68,120		41	Maine	72,620
44	Tennessee	70,730		42	Louisiana	71,770
38	Texas	76,330		43	North Dakota	71,500
25	Utah	83,830		44	Tennessee	70,730
26	Vermont	83,680		45	Mississippi	69,920
18	Virginia	88,250		46	North Carolina	68,590
9	Washington	97,690		47	South Dakota	68,120
50	West Virginia	63,180		48	Montana	67,140
15	Wisconsin	88,970		49	Oklahoma	65,910
19	Wyoming	87,640		50	West Virginia	63,180
					District of Columbia	84,380

Source: U.S. Department of Labor, Bureau of Labor Statistics
   "National Occupational Employment and Wage Estimates" (http://www.bls.gov/oes/)
*As of May 2010.

Staff Employed by Public Elementary and Secondary School Systems in 2010

National Total = 6,355,351 Staff*

ALPHA ORDER

RANK	STATE	STAFF	% of USA
25	Alabama	94,058	1.5%
47	Alaska	17,743	0.3%
24	Arizona	100,320	1.6%
28	Arkansas	74,311	1.2%
2	California	594,796	9.4%
22	Colorado	103,354	1.6%
26	Connecticut	92,877	1.5%
48	Delaware	16,977	0.3%
4	Florida	335,446	5.3%
7	Georgia	234,694	3.7%
42	Hawaii	21,653	0.3%
41	Idaho	27,701	0.4%
8	Illinois	221,771	3.5%
13	Indiana	142,724	2.2%
29	Iowa	72,546	1.1%
31	Kansas	67,531	1.1%
17	Kentucky	118,431	1.9%
23	Louisiana	102,874	1.6%
38	Maine	37,081	0.6%
18	Maryland	115,288	1.8%
16	Massachusetts	123,167	1.9%
10	Michigan	204,625	3.2%
19	Minnesota	109,066	1.7%
30	Mississippi	70,782	1.1%
14	Missouri	132,047	2.1%
43	Montana	19,429	0.3%
36	Nebraska	45,835	0.7%
39	Nevada	33,747	0.5%
40	New Hampshire	32,911	0.5%
9	New Jersey	213,783	3.4%
35	New Mexico	47,565	0.7%
3	New York	421,929	6.6%
12	North Carolina	200,461	3.2%
50	North Dakota	15,983	0.3%
6	Ohio	244,232	3.8%
27	Oklahoma	85,036	1.3%
33	Oregon	62,969	1.0%
5	Pennsylvania	253,869	4.0%
45	Rhode Island	18,638	0.3%
32	South Carolina	67,358	1.1%
46	South Dakota	18,631	0.3%
15	Tennessee	127,743	2.0%
1	Texas	662,369	10.4%
34	Utah	51,660	0.8%
44	Vermont	19,337	0.3%
11	Virginia	202,907	3.2%
21	Washington	103,938	1.6%
37	West Virginia	39,205	0.6%
20	Wisconsin	105,229	1.7%
49	Wyoming	16,468	0.3%

RANK ORDER

RANK	STATE	STAFF	% of USA
1	Texas	662,369	10.4%
2	California	594,796	9.4%
3	New York	421,929	6.6%
4	Florida	335,446	5.3%
5	Pennsylvania	253,869	4.0%
6	Ohio	244,232	3.8%
7	Georgia	234,694	3.7%
8	Illinois	221,771	3.5%
9	New Jersey	213,783	3.4%
10	Michigan	204,625	3.2%
11	Virginia	202,907	3.2%
12	North Carolina	200,461	3.2%
13	Indiana	142,724	2.2%
14	Missouri	132,047	2.1%
15	Tennessee	127,743	2.0%
16	Massachusetts	123,167	1.9%
17	Kentucky	118,431	1.9%
18	Maryland	115,288	1.8%
19	Minnesota	109,066	1.7%
20	Wisconsin	105,229	1.7%
21	Washington	103,938	1.6%
22	Colorado	103,354	1.6%
23	Louisiana	102,874	1.6%
24	Arizona	100,320	1.6%
25	Alabama	94,058	1.5%
26	Connecticut	92,877	1.5%
27	Oklahoma	85,036	1.3%
28	Arkansas	74,311	1.2%
29	Iowa	72,546	1.1%
30	Mississippi	70,782	1.1%
31	Kansas	67,531	1.1%
32	South Carolina	67,358	1.1%
33	Oregon	62,969	1.0%
34	Utah	51,660	0.8%
35	New Mexico	47,565	0.7%
36	Nebraska	45,835	0.7%
37	West Virginia	39,205	0.6%
38	Maine	37,081	0.6%
39	Nevada	33,747	0.5%
40	New Hampshire	32,911	0.5%
41	Idaho	27,701	0.4%
42	Hawaii	21,653	0.3%
43	Montana	19,429	0.3%
44	Vermont	19,337	0.3%
45	Rhode Island	18,638	0.3%
46	South Dakota	18,631	0.3%
47	Alaska	17,743	0.3%
48	Delaware	16,977	0.3%
49	Wyoming	16,468	0.3%
50	North Dakota	15,983	0.3%
	District of Columbia	12,256	0.2%

Source: U.S. Department of Education, National Center for Education Statistics
"Public Elementary and Secondary School Student Enrollment and Staff" (http://nces.ed.gov/pubs2011/2011347.pdf)
*School year 2009-2010. Counts are full-time equivalent figures. Staff includes teachers, administrators, support staff, aides, counselors, and coordinators.

Percent of Public Elementary and Secondary School Staff Who Are School District Administrators in 2010
National Percent = 1.0%*

ALPHA ORDER

RANK	STATE	PERCENT
23	Alabama	1.0
1	Alaska	3.8
47	Arizona	0.4
28	Arkansas	0.9
37	California	0.7
19	Colorado	1.1
8	Connecticut	1.9
7	Delaware	2.1
44	Florida	0.6
23	Georgia	1.0
28	Hawaii	0.9
45	Idaho	0.5
17	Illinois	1.2
33	Indiana	0.8
17	Iowa	1.2
37	Kansas	0.7
23	Kentucky	1.0
47	Louisiana	0.4
11	Maine	1.8
3	Maryland	2.9
11	Massachusetts	1.8
14	Michigan	1.6
8	Minnesota	1.9
15	Mississippi	1.4
19	Missouri	1.1
28	Montana	0.9
16	Nebraska	1.3
49	Nevada	0.1
6	New Hampshire	2.2
37	New Jersey	0.7
11	New Mexico	1.8
37	New York	0.7
33	North Carolina	0.8
4	North Dakota	2.8
28	Ohio	0.9
37	Oklahoma	0.7
37	Oregon	0.7
19	Pennsylvania	1.1
45	Rhode Island	0.5
23	South Carolina	1.0
1	South Dakota	3.8
49	Tennessee	0.1
23	Texas	1.0
33	Utah	0.8
37	Vermont	0.7
33	Virginia	0.8
19	Washington	1.1
8	West Virginia	1.9
28	Wisconsin	0.9
5	Wyoming	2.3

RANK ORDER

RANK	STATE	PERCENT
1	Alaska	3.8
1	South Dakota	3.8
3	Maryland	2.9
4	North Dakota	2.8
5	Wyoming	2.3
6	New Hampshire	2.2
7	Delaware	2.1
8	Connecticut	1.9
8	Minnesota	1.9
8	West Virginia	1.9
11	Maine	1.8
11	Massachusetts	1.8
11	New Mexico	1.8
14	Michigan	1.6
15	Mississippi	1.4
16	Nebraska	1.3
17	Illinois	1.2
17	Iowa	1.2
19	Colorado	1.1
19	Missouri	1.1
19	Pennsylvania	1.1
19	Washington	1.1
23	Alabama	1.0
23	Georgia	1.0
23	Kentucky	1.0
23	South Carolina	1.0
23	Texas	1.0
28	Arkansas	0.9
28	Hawaii	0.9
28	Montana	0.9
28	Ohio	0.9
28	Wisconsin	0.9
33	Indiana	0.8
33	North Carolina	0.8
33	Utah	0.8
33	Virginia	0.8
37	California	0.7
37	Kansas	0.7
37	New Jersey	0.7
37	New York	0.7
37	Oklahoma	0.7
37	Oregon	0.7
37	Vermont	0.7
44	Florida	0.6
45	Idaho	0.5
45	Rhode Island	0.5
47	Arizona	0.4
47	Louisiana	0.4
49	Nevada	0.1
49	Tennessee	0.1
	District of Columbia	1.4

Source: CQ Press using data from U.S. Department of Education, National Center for Education Statistics "Public Elementary and Secondary School Student Enrollment and Staff" (http://nces.ed.gov/pubs2011/2011347.pdf)
*School year 2009-2010. Percents are based on full-time equivalent figures. Includes superintendents, assistant superintendents, and other school district administrators.

Percent of Public Elementary and Secondary School Staff Who Are School Administrators in 2010
National Percent = 2.7%*

ALPHA ORDER

RANK	STATE	PERCENT
10	Alabama	2.9
1	Alaska	4.9
27	Arizona	2.5
31	Arkansas	2.4
12	California	2.8
18	Colorado	2.7
31	Connecticut	2.4
31	Delaware	2.4
38	Florida	2.3
12	Georgia	2.8
31	Hawaii	2.4
22	Idaho	2.6
4	Illinois	3.4
44	Indiana	2.2
27	Iowa	2.5
18	Kansas	2.7
8	Kentucky	3.1
12	Louisiana	2.8
5	Maine	3.3
5	Maryland	3.3
3	Massachusetts	3.5
31	Michigan	2.4
49	Minnesota	1.9
12	Mississippi	2.8
38	Missouri	2.3
12	Montana	2.8
44	Nebraska	2.2
9	Nevada	3.0
50	New Hampshire	1.6
38	New Jersey	2.3
12	New Mexico	2.8
44	New York	2.2
22	North Carolina	2.6
18	North Dakota	2.7
48	Ohio	2.1
22	Oklahoma	2.6
27	Oregon	2.5
38	Pennsylvania	2.3
31	Rhode Island	2.4
2	South Carolina	3.8
38	South Dakota	2.3
22	Tennessee	2.6
5	Texas	3.3
27	Utah	2.5
22	Vermont	2.6
38	Virginia	2.3
18	Washington	2.7
10	West Virginia	2.9
31	Wisconsin	2.4
44	Wyoming	2.2

RANK ORDER

RANK	STATE	PERCENT
1	Alaska	4.9
2	South Carolina	3.8
3	Massachusetts	3.5
4	Illinois	3.4
5	Maine	3.3
5	Maryland	3.3
5	Texas	3.3
8	Kentucky	3.1
9	Nevada	3.0
10	Alabama	2.9
10	West Virginia	2.9
12	California	2.8
12	Georgia	2.8
12	Louisiana	2.8
12	Mississippi	2.8
12	Montana	2.8
12	New Mexico	2.8
18	Colorado	2.7
18	Kansas	2.7
18	North Dakota	2.7
18	Washington	2.7
22	Idaho	2.6
22	North Carolina	2.6
22	Oklahoma	2.6
22	Tennessee	2.6
22	Vermont	2.6
27	Arizona	2.5
27	Iowa	2.5
27	Oregon	2.5
27	Utah	2.5
31	Arkansas	2.4
31	Connecticut	2.4
31	Delaware	2.4
31	Hawaii	2.4
31	Michigan	2.4
31	Rhode Island	2.4
31	Wisconsin	2.4
38	Florida	2.3
38	Missouri	2.3
38	New Jersey	2.3
38	Pennsylvania	2.3
38	South Dakota	2.3
38	Virginia	2.3
44	Indiana	2.2
44	Nebraska	2.2
44	New York	2.2
44	Wyoming	2.2
48	Ohio	2.1
49	Minnesota	1.9
50	New Hampshire	1.6

	District of Columbia	4.1

Source: CQ Press using data from U.S. Department of Education, National Center for Education Statistics
    "Public Elementary and Secondary School Student Enrollment and Staff" (http://nces.ed.gov/pubs2011/2011347.pdf)
*School year 2009-2010. Percents are based on full-time equivalent figures. Composed mostly of principals and assistant principals. Does not include school district administrators.

Percent of Public Elementary and Secondary School Staff
Who Are Administrative Support Staff in 2010
National Percent = 6.9%*

ALPHA ORDER

RANK	STATE	PERCENT
38	Alabama	5.3
2	Alaska	11.1
36	Arizona	5.5
12	Arkansas	7.5
5	California	9.5
6	Colorado	9.0
39	Connecticut	5.2
43	Delaware	4.4
6	Florida	9.0
41	Georgia	5.0
11	Hawaii	7.6
36	Idaho	5.5
49	Illinois	1.9
31	Indiana	5.8
34	Iowa	5.6
39	Kansas	5.2
4	Kentucky	10.2
24	Louisiana	6.2
10	Maine	7.7
15	Maryland	7.1
13	Massachusetts	7.4
19	Michigan	6.7
31	Minnesota	5.8
22	Mississippi	6.5
19	Missouri	6.7
48	Montana	2.8
34	Nebraska	5.6
17	Nevada	6.9
45	New Hampshire	4.1
19	New Jersey	6.7
8	New Mexico	8.2
14	New York	7.2
24	North Carolina	6.2
47	North Dakota	2.9
3	Ohio	10.6
9	Oklahoma	7.8
1	Oregon	11.3
17	Pennsylvania	6.9
24	Rhode Island	6.2
49	South Carolina	1.9
42	South Dakota	4.6
44	Tennessee	4.2
16	Texas	7.0
31	Utah	5.8
28	Vermont	6.1
29	Virginia	6.0
30	Washington	5.9
45	West Virginia	4.1
24	Wisconsin	6.2
22	Wyoming	6.5

RANK ORDER

RANK	STATE	PERCENT
1	Oregon	11.3
2	Alaska	11.1
3	Ohio	10.6
4	Kentucky	10.2
5	California	9.5
6	Colorado	9.0
6	Florida	9.0
8	New Mexico	8.2
9	Oklahoma	7.8
10	Maine	7.7
11	Hawaii	7.6
12	Arkansas	7.5
13	Massachusetts	7.4
14	New York	7.2
15	Maryland	7.1
16	Texas	7.0
17	Nevada	6.9
17	Pennsylvania	6.9
19	Michigan	6.7
19	Missouri	6.7
19	New Jersey	6.7
22	Mississippi	6.5
22	Wyoming	6.5
24	Louisiana	6.2
24	North Carolina	6.2
24	Rhode Island	6.2
24	Wisconsin	6.2
28	Vermont	6.1
29	Virginia	6.0
30	Washington	5.9
31	Indiana	5.8
31	Minnesota	5.8
31	Utah	5.8
34	Iowa	5.6
34	Nebraska	5.6
36	Arizona	5.5
36	Idaho	5.5
38	Alabama	5.3
39	Connecticut	5.2
39	Kansas	5.2
41	Georgia	5.0
42	South Dakota	4.6
43	Delaware	4.4
44	Tennessee	4.2
45	New Hampshire	4.1
45	West Virginia	4.1
47	North Dakota	2.9
48	Montana	2.8
49	Illinois	1.9
49	South Carolina	1.9

District of Columbia	9.2

Source: CQ Press using data from U.S. Department of Education, National Center for Education Statistics
"Public Elementary and Secondary School Student Enrollment and Staff" (http://nces.ed.gov/pubs2011/2011347.pdf)
*School year 2009-2010. Percents are based on full-time equivalent figures. Includes secretarial and other clerical staff and persons whose activities are concerned with support of the teaching and administrative duties of the office of the principal or department chairpersons or central office administrators.

Percent of Public Elementary and Secondary School Staff
Who Are Teachers in 2010
National Percent = 50.5%*

ALPHA ORDER

RANK	STATE	PERCENT
24	Alabama	50.5
42	Alaska	45.6
15	Arizona	51.8
28	Arkansas	50.1
11	California	52.8
37	Colorado	47.5
39	Connecticut	46.9
22	Delaware	50.9
8	Florida	54.8
30	Georgia	49.4
12	Hawaii	52.7
7	Idaho	54.9
3	Illinois	62.4
47	Indiana	43.6
30	Iowa	49.4
18	Kansas	51.4
49	Kentucky	37.5
35	Louisiana	48.3
46	Maine	43.9
24	Maryland	50.5
5	Massachusetts	56.8
44	Michigan	45.3
34	Minnesota	48.4
40	Mississippi	46.8
20	Missouri	51.3
9	Montana	54.2
33	Nebraska	48.6
2	Nevada	65.5
38	New Hampshire	47.1
10	New Jersey	53.9
36	New Mexico	47.8
22	New York	50.9
13	North Carolina	52.4
14	North Dakota	52.3
42	Ohio	45.6
27	Oklahoma	50.2
41	Oregon	45.7
17	Pennsylvania	51.6
4	Rhode Island	61.0
1	South Carolina	69.7
28	South Dakota	50.1
21	Tennessee	51.2
26	Texas	50.3
32	Utah	49.3
45	Vermont	45.2
50	Virginia	34.9
18	Washington	51.4
15	West Virginia	51.8
6	Wisconsin	55.5
48	Wyoming	43.5

RANK ORDER

RANK	STATE	PERCENT
1	South Carolina	69.7
2	Nevada	65.5
3	Illinois	62.4
4	Rhode Island	61.0
5	Massachusetts	56.8
6	Wisconsin	55.5
7	Idaho	54.9
8	Florida	54.8
9	Montana	54.2
10	New Jersey	53.9
11	California	52.8
12	Hawaii	52.7
13	North Carolina	52.4
14	North Dakota	52.3
15	Arizona	51.8
15	West Virginia	51.8
17	Pennsylvania	51.6
18	Kansas	51.4
18	Washington	51.4
20	Missouri	51.3
21	Tennessee	51.2
22	Delaware	50.9
22	New York	50.9
24	Alabama	50.5
24	Maryland	50.5
26	Texas	50.3
27	Oklahoma	50.2
28	Arkansas	50.1
28	South Dakota	50.1
30	Georgia	49.4
30	Iowa	49.4
32	Utah	49.3
33	Nebraska	48.6
34	Minnesota	48.4
35	Louisiana	48.3
36	New Mexico	47.8
37	Colorado	47.5
38	New Hampshire	47.1
39	Connecticut	46.9
40	Mississippi	46.8
41	Oregon	45.7
42	Alaska	45.6
42	Ohio	45.6
44	Michigan	45.3
45	Vermont	45.2
46	Maine	43.9
47	Indiana	43.6
48	Wyoming	43.5
49	Kentucky	37.5
50	Virginia	34.9

| | District of Columbia | 52.0 |

Source: CQ Press using data from U.S. Department of Education, National Center for Education Statistics
"Public Elementary and Secondary School Student Enrollment and Staff" (http://nces.ed.gov/pubs2011/2011347.pdf)
*School year 2009-2010. Counts are full-time equivalent figures.

Percent of Public Elementary and Secondary School Staff
Who Are Guidance Counselors in 2010
National Percent = 1.7%*

ALPHA ORDER

RANK	STATE	PERCENT
13	Alabama	2.0
30	Alaska	1.7
45	Arizona	1.3
18	Arkansas	1.9
45	California	1.3
10	Colorado	2.1
48	Connecticut	1.2
36	Delaware	1.6
30	Florida	1.7
36	Georgia	1.6
1	Hawaii	3.0
8	Idaho	2.2
43	Illinois	1.4
43	Indiana	1.4
30	Iowa	1.7
36	Kansas	1.6
45	Kentucky	1.3
18	Louisiana	1.9
30	Maine	1.7
10	Maryland	2.1
24	Massachusetts	1.8
48	Michigan	1.2
50	Minnesota	1.0
36	Mississippi	1.6
13	Missouri	2.0
6	Montana	2.4
24	Nebraska	1.8
4	Nevada	2.6
4	New Hampshire	2.6
13	New Jersey	2.0
24	New Mexico	1.8
36	New York	1.6
18	North Carolina	1.9
24	North Dakota	1.8
42	Ohio	1.5
13	Oklahoma	2.0
30	Oregon	1.7
18	Pennsylvania	1.9
10	Rhode Island	2.1
3	South Carolina	2.8
24	South Dakota	1.8
8	Tennessee	2.2
30	Texas	1.7
36	Utah	1.6
7	Vermont	2.3
18	Virginia	1.9
13	Washington	2.0
18	West Virginia	1.9
24	Wisconsin	1.8
2	Wyoming	2.9

RANK ORDER

RANK	STATE	PERCENT
1	Hawaii	3.0
2	Wyoming	2.9
3	South Carolina	2.8
4	Nevada	2.6
4	New Hampshire	2.6
6	Montana	2.4
7	Vermont	2.3
8	Idaho	2.2
8	Tennessee	2.2
10	Colorado	2.1
10	Maryland	2.1
10	Rhode Island	2.1
13	Alabama	2.0
13	Missouri	2.0
13	New Jersey	2.0
13	Oklahoma	2.0
13	Washington	2.0
18	Arkansas	1.9
18	Louisiana	1.9
18	North Carolina	1.9
18	Pennsylvania	1.9
18	Virginia	1.9
18	West Virginia	1.9
24	Massachusetts	1.8
24	Nebraska	1.8
24	New Mexico	1.8
24	North Dakota	1.8
24	South Dakota	1.8
24	Wisconsin	1.8
30	Alaska	1.7
30	Florida	1.7
30	Iowa	1.7
30	Maine	1.7
30	Oregon	1.7
30	Texas	1.7
36	Delaware	1.6
36	Georgia	1.6
36	Kansas	1.6
36	Mississippi	1.6
36	New York	1.6
36	Utah	1.6
42	Ohio	1.5
43	Illinois	1.4
43	Indiana	1.4
45	Arizona	1.3
45	California	1.3
45	Kentucky	1.3
48	Connecticut	1.2
48	Michigan	1.2
50	Minnesota	1.0

District of Columbia   2.8

Source: CQ Press using data from U.S. Department of Education, National Center for Education Statistics
    "Public Elementary and Secondary School Student Enrollment and Staff" (http://nces.ed.gov/pubs2011/2011347.pdf)
*School year 2009-2010. Counts are full-time equivalent figures.

Percent of Public Elementary and Secondary School Staff
Who Are Librarians in 2010
National Percent = 0.8%*

ALPHA ORDER

RANK	STATE	PERCENT	RANK	STATE	PERCENT
4	Alabama	1.5	1	Montana	1.9
21	Alaska	1.0	2	South Carolina	1.7
41	Arizona	0.6	3	Rhode Island	1.6
6	Arkansas	1.4	4	Alabama	1.5
50	California	0.2	4	Tennessee	1.5
30	Colorado	0.8	6	Arkansas	1.4
27	Connecticut	0.9	6	Mississippi	1.4
30	Delaware	0.8	8	Oklahoma	1.3
30	Florida	0.8	9	Kansas	1.2
21	Georgia	1.0	9	Louisiana	1.2
21	Hawaii	1.0	9	Missouri	1.2
45	Idaho	0.5	9	Nebraska	1.2
30	Illinois	0.8	9	North Carolina	1.2
41	Indiana	0.6	9	North Dakota	1.2
30	Iowa	0.8	15	Maryland	1.1
9	Kansas	1.2	15	Nevada	1.1
21	Kentucky	1.0	15	Vermont	1.1
9	Louisiana	1.2	15	Washington	1.1
41	Maine	0.6	15	Wisconsin	1.1
15	Maryland	1.1	15	Wyoming	1.1
37	Massachusetts	0.7	21	Alaska	1.0
45	Michigan	0.5	21	Georgia	1.0
37	Minnesota	0.7	21	Hawaii	1.0
6	Mississippi	1.4	21	Kentucky	1.0
9	Missouri	1.2	21	New Hampshire	1.0
1	Montana	1.9	21	Virginia	1.0
9	Nebraska	1.2	27	Connecticut	0.9
15	Nevada	1.1	27	Pennsylvania	0.9
21	New Hampshire	1.0	27	West Virginia	0.9
30	New Jersey	0.8	30	Colorado	0.8
41	New Mexico	0.6	30	Delaware	0.8
37	New York	0.7	30	Florida	0.8
9	North Carolina	1.2	30	Illinois	0.8
9	North Dakota	1.2	30	Iowa	0.8
45	Ohio	0.5	30	New Jersey	0.8
8	Oklahoma	1.3	30	Texas	0.8
45	Oregon	0.5	37	Massachusetts	0.7
27	Pennsylvania	0.9	37	Minnesota	0.7
3	Rhode Island	1.6	37	New York	0.7
2	South Carolina	1.7	37	South Dakota	0.7
37	South Dakota	0.7	41	Arizona	0.6
4	Tennessee	1.5	41	Indiana	0.6
30	Texas	0.8	41	Maine	0.6
45	Utah	0.5	41	New Mexico	0.6
15	Vermont	1.1	45	Idaho	0.5
21	Virginia	1.0	45	Michigan	0.5
15	Washington	1.1	45	Ohio	0.5
27	West Virginia	0.9	45	Oregon	0.5
15	Wisconsin	1.1	45	Utah	0.5
15	Wyoming	1.1	50	California	0.2

RANK ORDER

District of Columbia 1.0

Source: CQ Press using data from U.S. Department of Education, National Center for Education Statistics
"Public Elementary and Secondary School Student Enrollment and Staff" (http://nces.ed.gov/pubs2011/2011347.pdf)
*School year 2009-2010. Counts are full-time equivalent figures.

Percent of Public Elementary and Secondary School Staff
Who Are Instructional Aides in 2010
National Percent = 11.6%*

ALPHA ORDER

RANK ORDER

RANK	STATE	PERCENT	RANK	STATE	PERCENT
50	Alabama	7.1	1	Vermont	23.0
18	Alaska	13.7	2	New Hampshire	21.9
11	Arizona	14.7	3	Massachusetts	18.9
37	Arkansas	10.8	4	Indiana	16.8
38	California	10.2	5	Oregon	16.4
11	Colorado	14.7	6	Maine	16.3
8	Connecticut	15.5	7	Utah	15.8
29	Delaware	11.9	8	Connecticut	15.5
48	Florida	8.4	9	Iowa	15.0
32	Georgia	11.5	10	Minnesota	14.9
34	Hawaii	11.2	11	Arizona	14.7
35	Idaho	11.0	11	Colorado	14.7
17	Illinois	13.9	13	Wyoming	14.2
4	Indiana	16.8	14	Kentucky	14.1
9	Iowa	15.0	14	Nebraska	14.1
16	Kansas	14.0	16	Kansas	14.0
14	Kentucky	14.1	17	Illinois	13.9
32	Louisiana	11.5	18	Alaska	13.7
6	Maine	16.3	19	North Dakota	13.4
43	Maryland	9.9	20	North Carolina	13.3
3	Massachusetts	18.9	21	New Jersey	12.9
36	Michigan	10.9	21	New Mexico	12.9
10	Minnesota	14.9	21	South Carolina	12.9
25	Mississippi	12.6	21	South Dakota	12.9
40	Missouri	10.0	25	Mississippi	12.6
28	Montana	12.1	25	Tennessee	12.6
14	Nebraska	14.1	27	Nevada	12.5
27	Nevada	12.5	28	Montana	12.1
2	New Hampshire	21.9	29	Delaware	11.9
21	New Jersey	12.9	30	Pennsylvania	11.8
21	New Mexico	12.9	30	Rhode Island	11.8
46	New York	9.3	32	Georgia	11.5
20	North Carolina	13.3	32	Louisiana	11.5
19	North Dakota	13.4	34	Hawaii	11.2
49	Ohio	8.0	35	Idaho	11.0
38	Oklahoma	10.2	36	Michigan	10.9
5	Oregon	16.4	37	Arkansas	10.8
30	Pennsylvania	11.8	38	California	10.2
30	Rhode Island	11.8	38	Oklahoma	10.2
21	South Carolina	12.9	40	Missouri	10.0
21	South Dakota	12.9	40	Washington	10.0
25	Tennessee	12.6	40	Wisconsin	10.0
44	Texas	9.8	43	Maryland	9.9
7	Utah	15.8	44	Texas	9.8
1	Vermont	23.0	44	Virginia	9.8
44	Virginia	9.8	46	New York	9.3
40	Washington	10.0	47	West Virginia	9.2
47	West Virginia	9.2	48	Florida	8.4
40	Wisconsin	10.0	49	Ohio	8.0
13	Wyoming	14.2	50	Alabama	7.1
				District of Columbia	12.6

Source: CQ Press using data from U.S. Department of Education, National Center for Education Statistics
   "Public Elementary and Secondary School Student Enrollment and Staff" (http://nces.ed.gov/pubs2011/2011347.pdf)
*School year 2009-2010. Percents are based on full-time equivalent figures. Aides directly assist teachers in providing
instruction to students.

Percent of Public Elementary and Secondary School Staff Who Are Instructional Coordinators and Supervisors in 2010
National Percent = 1.2%*

ALPHA ORDER

ALPHA ORDER

RANK	STATE	PERCENT
21	Alabama	1.1
21	Alaska	1.1
50	Arizona	0.1
21	Arkansas	1.1
19	California	1.2
7	Colorado	2.4
3	Connecticut	3.8
9	Delaware	2.0
48	Florida	0.2
24	Georgia	1.0
5	Hawaii	2.8
26	Idaho	0.9
48	Illinois	0.2
15	Indiana	1.5
39	Iowa	0.6
15	Kansas	1.5
30	Kentucky	0.8
9	Louisiana	2.0
26	Maine	0.9
15	Maryland	1.5
46	Massachusetts	0.4
12	Michigan	1.7
11	Minnesota	1.8
24	Mississippi	1.0
30	Missouri	0.8
30	Montana	0.8
8	Nebraska	2.1
2	Nevada	4.1
30	New Hampshire	0.8
13	New Jersey	1.6
13	New Mexico	1.6
41	New York	0.5
39	North Carolina	0.6
26	North Dakota	0.9
34	Ohio	0.7
41	Oklahoma	0.5
34	Oregon	0.7
34	Pennsylvania	0.7
46	Rhode Island	0.4
34	South Carolina	0.7
41	South Dakota	0.5
34	Tennessee	0.7
41	Texas	0.5
4	Utah	3.2
19	Vermont	1.2
1	Virginia	6.6
41	Washington	0.5
26	West Virginia	0.9
18	Wisconsin	1.3
6	Wyoming	2.7

RANK ORDER

RANK	STATE	PERCENT
1	Virginia	6.6
2	Nevada	4.1
3	Connecticut	3.8
4	Utah	3.2
5	Hawaii	2.8
6	Wyoming	2.7
7	Colorado	2.4
8	Nebraska	2.1
9	Delaware	2.0
9	Louisiana	2.0
11	Minnesota	1.8
12	Michigan	1.7
13	New Jersey	1.6
13	New Mexico	1.6
15	Indiana	1.5
15	Kansas	1.5
15	Maryland	1.5
18	Wisconsin	1.3
19	California	1.2
19	Vermont	1.2
21	Alabama	1.1
21	Alaska	1.1
21	Arkansas	1.1
24	Georgia	1.0
24	Mississippi	1.0
26	Idaho	0.9
26	Maine	0.9
26	North Dakota	0.9
26	West Virginia	0.9
30	Kentucky	0.8
30	Missouri	0.8
30	Montana	0.8
30	New Hampshire	0.8
34	Ohio	0.7
34	Oregon	0.7
34	Pennsylvania	0.7
34	South Carolina	0.7
34	Tennessee	0.7
39	Iowa	0.6
39	North Carolina	0.6
41	New York	0.5
41	Oklahoma	0.5
41	South Dakota	0.5
41	Texas	0.5
41	Washington	0.5
46	Massachusetts	0.4
46	Rhode Island	0.4
48	Florida	0.2
48	Illinois	0.2
50	Arizona	0.1

	District of Columbia	3.0

Source: CQ Press using data from U.S. Department of Education, National Center for Education Statistics
"Public Elementary and Secondary School Student Enrollment and Staff" (http://nces.ed.gov/pubs2011/2011347.pdf)
*School year 2009-2010. Percents are based on full-time equivalent figures. Coordinators oversee functions such as curriculum development and in-service training.

Percent of Public Elementary and Secondary School Staff
Who Are Student and Other Support Staff in 2010
National Percent = 23.6%*

ALPHA ORDER

RANK	STATE	PERCENT
5	Alabama	28.7
45	Alaska	17.2
25	Arizona	23.0
18	Arkansas	23.9
35	California	21.3
40	Colorado	19.7
28	Connecticut	22.2
20	Delaware	23.8
30	Florida	22.0
7	Georgia	26.7
43	Hawaii	18.4
32	Idaho	21.8
46	Illinois	14.8
6	Indiana	27.2
24	Iowa	23.1
33	Kansas	21.7
2	Kentucky	31.1
11	Louisiana	25.8
18	Maine	23.9
34	Maryland	21.6
48	Massachusetts	8.9
4	Michigan	29.8
21	Minnesota	23.5
10	Mississippi	25.9
15	Missouri	24.7
28	Montana	22.2
23	Nebraska	23.2
50	Nevada	4.2
42	New Hampshire	18.8
41	New Jersey	19.0
27	New Mexico	22.5
7	New York	26.7
36	North Carolina	21.0
30	North Dakota	22.0
3	Ohio	30.1
17	Oklahoma	24.5
38	Oregon	20.6
25	Pennsylvania	23.0
47	Rhode Island	14.0
49	South Carolina	5.4
21	South Dakota	23.5
14	Tennessee	24.9
12	Texas	25.6
39	Utah	20.4
44	Vermont	17.8
1	Virginia	36.7
13	Washington	25.3
9	West Virginia	26.5
37	Wisconsin	20.9
15	Wyoming	24.7

RANK ORDER

RANK	STATE	PERCENT
1	Virginia	36.7
2	Kentucky	31.1
3	Ohio	30.1
4	Michigan	29.8
5	Alabama	28.7
6	Indiana	27.2
7	Georgia	26.7
7	New York	26.7
9	West Virginia	26.5
10	Mississippi	25.9
11	Louisiana	25.8
12	Texas	25.6
13	Washington	25.3
14	Tennessee	24.9
15	Missouri	24.7
15	Wyoming	24.7
17	Oklahoma	24.5
18	Arkansas	23.9
18	Maine	23.9
20	Delaware	23.8
21	Minnesota	23.5
21	South Dakota	23.5
23	Nebraska	23.2
24	Iowa	23.1
25	Arizona	23.0
25	Pennsylvania	23.0
27	New Mexico	22.5
28	Connecticut	22.2
28	Montana	22.2
30	Florida	22.0
30	North Dakota	22.0
32	Idaho	21.8
33	Kansas	21.7
34	Maryland	21.6
35	California	21.3
36	North Carolina	21.0
37	Wisconsin	20.9
38	Oregon	20.6
39	Utah	20.4
40	Colorado	19.7
41	New Jersey	19.0
42	New Hampshire	18.8
43	Hawaii	18.4
44	Vermont	17.8
45	Alaska	17.2
46	Illinois	14.8
47	Rhode Island	14.0
48	Massachusetts	8.9
49	South Carolina	5.4
50	Nevada	4.2

District of Columbia		13.9

Source: CQ Press using data from U.S. Department of Education, National Center for Education Statistics
"Public Elementary and Secondary School Student Enrollment and Staff" (http://nces.ed.gov/pubs2011/2011347.pdf)
*School year 2009-2010. Percents are based on full-time equivalent figures. Includes library support staff, student support services staff, and all other support staff.

Private Elementary and Secondary School Teachers in 2010

National Total = 437,414 Teachers*

ALPHA ORDER

RANK	STATE	TEACHERS	% of USA
18	Alabama	8,775	2.0%
49	Alaska	529	0.1%
29	Arizona	3,896	0.9%
36	Arkansas	2,392	0.5%
1	California	45,741	10.5%
26	Colorado	4,793	1.1%
21	Connecticut	7,431	1.7%
38	Delaware	2,064	0.5%
3	Florida	26,591	6.1%
10	Georgia	13,246	3.0%
32	Hawaii	3,044	0.7%
43	Idaho	1,364	0.3%
6	Illinois	20,289	4.6%
20	Indiana	8,420	1.9%
31	Iowa	3,218	0.7%
30	Kansas	3,367	0.8%
24	Kentucky	5,282	1.2%
14	Louisiana	10,061	2.3%
40	Maine	1,885	0.4%
11	Maryland	13,230	3.0%
9	Massachusetts	14,917	3.4%
13	Michigan	10,888	2.5%
23	Minnesota	6,424	1.5%
27	Mississippi	4,507	1.0%
17	Missouri	9,028	2.1%
46	Montana	880	0.2%
34	Nebraska	2,658	0.6%
42	Nevada	1,601	0.4%
35	New Hampshire	2,611	0.6%
7	New Jersey	19,018	4.3%
39	New Mexico	2,041	0.5%
2	New York	41,959	9.6%
15	North Carolina	9,962	2.3%
48	North Dakota	585	0.1%
8	Ohio	16,787	3.8%
33	Oklahoma	2,936	0.7%
28	Oregon	4,372	1.0%
5	Pennsylvania	23,699	5.4%
37	Rhode Island	2,296	0.5%
25	South Carolina	5,058	1.2%
47	South Dakota	849	0.2%
19	Tennessee	8,579	2.0%
4	Texas	25,659	5.9%
41	Utah	1,849	0.4%
44	Vermont	1,317	0.3%
12	Virginia	11,357	2.6%
22	Washington	6,957	1.6%
45	West Virginia	1,279	0.3%
16	Wisconsin	9,580	2.2%
50	Wyoming	270	0.1%

RANK ORDER

RANK	STATE	TEACHERS	% of USA
1	California	45,741	10.5%
2	New York	41,959	9.6%
3	Florida	26,591	6.1%
4	Texas	25,659	5.9%
5	Pennsylvania	23,699	5.4%
6	Illinois	20,289	4.6%
7	New Jersey	19,018	4.3%
8	Ohio	16,787	3.8%
9	Massachusetts	14,917	3.4%
10	Georgia	13,246	3.0%
11	Maryland	13,230	3.0%
12	Virginia	11,357	2.6%
13	Michigan	10,888	2.5%
14	Louisiana	10,061	2.3%
15	North Carolina	9,962	2.3%
16	Wisconsin	9,580	2.2%
17	Missouri	9,028	2.1%
18	Alabama	8,775	2.0%
19	Tennessee	8,579	2.0%
20	Indiana	8,420	1.9%
21	Connecticut	7,431	1.7%
22	Washington	6,957	1.6%
23	Minnesota	6,424	1.5%
24	Kentucky	5,282	1.2%
25	South Carolina	5,058	1.2%
26	Colorado	4,793	1.1%
27	Mississippi	4,507	1.0%
28	Oregon	4,372	1.0%
29	Arizona	3,896	0.9%
30	Kansas	3,367	0.8%
31	Iowa	3,218	0.7%
32	Hawaii	3,044	0.7%
33	Oklahoma	2,936	0.7%
34	Nebraska	2,658	0.6%
35	New Hampshire	2,611	0.6%
36	Arkansas	2,392	0.5%
37	Rhode Island	2,296	0.5%
38	Delaware	2,064	0.5%
39	New Mexico	2,041	0.5%
40	Maine	1,885	0.4%
41	Utah	1,849	0.4%
42	Nevada	1,601	0.4%
43	Idaho	1,364	0.3%
44	Vermont	1,317	0.3%
45	West Virginia	1,279	0.3%
46	Montana	880	0.2%
47	South Dakota	849	0.2%
48	North Dakota	585	0.1%
49	Alaska	529	0.1%
50	Wyoming	270	0.1%
	District of Columbia	1,873	0.4%

Source: U.S. Department of Education, National Center for Education Statistics
   "Characteristics of Private Schools in the United States" (http://nces.ed.gov/pubs2011/2011339.pdf)
*For school year 2009-2010. Figures are full-time equivalent (FTE) teachers.

VII. Students

Estimated Percent of School-Age Population in Public Schools in 2010

National Percent = 92.7%*

ALPHA ORDER

RANK	STATE	PERCENT
29	Alabama	92.0
1	Alaska	102.0
43	Arizona	88.8
10	Arkansas	95.1
19	California	93.7
8	Colorado	96.4
15	Connecticut	94.4
49	Delaware	86.1
34	Florida	91.1
36	Georgia	91.0
40	Hawaii	89.5
17	Idaho	93.9
28	Illinois	92.1
32	Indiana	91.5
7	Iowa	96.6
12	Kansas	95.0
21	Kentucky	93.6
50	Louisiana	85.9
15	Maine	94.4
46	Maryland	87.3
33	Massachusetts	91.4
10	Michigan	95.1
22	Minnesota	93.3
37	Mississippi	90.3
41	Missouri	89.3
38	Montana	90.1
25	Nebraska	93.2
39	Nevada	89.8
29	New Hampshire	92.0
19	New Jersey	93.7
22	New Mexico	93.3
48	New York	86.4
29	North Carolina	92.0
14	North Dakota	94.5
41	Ohio	89.3
2	Oklahoma	101.2
22	Oregon	93.3
45	Pennsylvania	88.1
47	Rhode Island	87.1
17	South Carolina	93.9
44	South Dakota	88.4
34	Tennessee	91.1
4	Texas	100.6
6	Utah	97.9
5	Vermont	98.5
13	Virginia	94.8
26	Washington	92.5
3	West Virginia	100.8
27	Wisconsin	92.2
9	Wyoming	96.2

RANK ORDER

RANK	STATE	PERCENT
1	Alaska	102.0
2	Oklahoma	101.2
3	West Virginia	100.8
4	Texas	100.6
5	Vermont	98.5
6	Utah	97.9
7	Iowa	96.6
8	Colorado	96.4
9	Wyoming	96.2
10	Arkansas	95.1
10	Michigan	95.1
12	Kansas	95.0
13	Virginia	94.8
14	North Dakota	94.5
15	Connecticut	94.4
15	Maine	94.4
17	Idaho	93.9
17	South Carolina	93.9
19	California	93.7
19	New Jersey	93.7
21	Kentucky	93.6
22	Minnesota	93.3
22	New Mexico	93.3
22	Oregon	93.3
25	Nebraska	93.2
26	Washington	92.5
27	Wisconsin	92.2
28	Illinois	92.1
29	Alabama	92.0
29	New Hampshire	92.0
29	North Carolina	92.0
32	Indiana	91.5
33	Massachusetts	91.4
34	Florida	91.1
34	Tennessee	91.1
36	Georgia	91.0
37	Mississippi	90.3
38	Montana	90.1
39	Nevada	89.8
40	Hawaii	89.5
41	Missouri	89.3
41	Ohio	89.3
43	Arizona	88.8
44	South Dakota	88.4
45	Pennsylvania	88.1
46	Maryland	87.3
47	Rhode Island	87.1
48	New York	86.4
49	Delaware	86.1
50	Louisiana	85.9

District of Columbia — 90.3

Source: CQ Press using data from U.S. Department of Education, National Center for Education Statistics
"Public Elementary and Secondary School Student Enrollment and Staff" (http://nces.ed.gov/pubs2011/2011347.pdf)
*Estimate based on 2009 Census population estimates for 5- to 17-year-olds compared to estimated 2009-2010 school year public school student membership. Student membership figures include counts for pre-kindergarten programs. Figures higher than 100 percent reflect using different sources for population and for student membership.

Estimated Enrollment in Public Elementary and Secondary Schools in 2011

National Total = 49,162,463 Students*

ALPHA ORDER

RANK	STATE	STUDENTS	% of USA
23	Alabama	740,975	1.5%
45	Alaska	132,000	0.3%
13	Arizona	1,071,484	2.2%
34	Arkansas	459,419	0.9%
1	California	6,219,649	12.7%
20	Colorado	843,958	1.7%
29	Connecticut	566,030	1.2%
46	Delaware	128,530	0.3%
4	Florida	2,621,085	5.3%
8	Georgia	1,689,648	3.4%
42	Hawaii	179,122	0.4%
38	Idaho	285,236	0.6%
5	Illinois	2,106,925	4.3%
14	Indiana	1,051,696	2.1%
32	Iowa	491,431	1.0%
33	Kansas	481,000	1.0%
26	Kentucky	658,328	1.3%
25	Louisiana	702,133	1.4%
41	Maine	187,401	0.4%
21	Maryland	840,628	1.7%
17	Massachusetts	953,223	1.9%
9	Michigan	1,662,067	3.4%
22	Minnesota	810,123	1.6%
31	Mississippi	496,504	1.0%
18	Missouri	903,887	1.8%
43	Montana	140,533	0.3%
37	Nebraska	297,563	0.6%
35	Nevada	456,844	0.9%
40	New Hampshire	193,264	0.4%
11	New Jersey	1,366,067	2.8%
36	New Mexico	326,940	0.7%
3	New York	2,642,524	5.4%
10	North Carolina	1,405,706	2.9%
48	North Dakota	92,074	0.2%
6	Ohio	1,914,222	3.9%
27	Oklahoma	656,655	1.3%
30	Oregon	564,620	1.1%
7	Pennsylvania	1,763,946	3.6%
44	Rhode Island	138,803	0.3%
24	South Carolina	716,524	1.5%
47	South Dakota	123,900	0.3%
16	Tennessee	971,537	2.0%
2	Texas	4,824,778	9.8%
28	Utah	587,198	1.2%
50	Vermont	85,635	0.2%
12	Virginia	1,252,529	2.5%
15	Washington	1,038,156	2.1%
39	West Virginia	283,469	0.6%
19	Wisconsin	871,929	1.8%
49	Wyoming	88,355	0.2%

RANK ORDER

RANK	STATE	STUDENTS	% of USA
1	California	6,219,649	12.7%
2	Texas	4,824,778	9.8%
3	New York	2,642,524	5.4%
4	Florida	2,621,085	5.3%
5	Illinois	2,106,925	4.3%
6	Ohio	1,914,222	3.9%
7	Pennsylvania	1,763,946	3.6%
8	Georgia	1,689,648	3.4%
9	Michigan	1,662,067	3.4%
10	North Carolina	1,405,706	2.9%
11	New Jersey	1,366,067	2.8%
12	Virginia	1,252,529	2.5%
13	Arizona	1,071,484	2.2%
14	Indiana	1,051,696	2.1%
15	Washington	1,038,156	2.1%
16	Tennessee	971,537	2.0%
17	Massachusetts	953,223	1.9%
18	Missouri	903,887	1.8%
19	Wisconsin	871,929	1.8%
20	Colorado	843,958	1.7%
21	Maryland	840,628	1.7%
22	Minnesota	810,123	1.6%
23	Alabama	740,975	1.5%
24	South Carolina	716,524	1.5%
25	Louisiana	702,133	1.4%
26	Kentucky	658,328	1.3%
27	Oklahoma	656,655	1.3%
28	Utah	587,198	1.2%
29	Connecticut	566,030	1.2%
30	Oregon	564,620	1.1%
31	Mississippi	496,504	1.0%
32	Iowa	491,431	1.0%
33	Kansas	481,000	1.0%
34	Arkansas	459,419	0.9%
35	Nevada	456,844	0.9%
36	New Mexico	326,940	0.7%
37	Nebraska	297,563	0.6%
38	Idaho	285,236	0.6%
39	West Virginia	283,469	0.6%
40	New Hampshire	193,264	0.4%
41	Maine	187,401	0.4%
42	Hawaii	179,122	0.4%
43	Montana	140,533	0.3%
44	Rhode Island	138,803	0.3%
45	Alaska	132,000	0.3%
46	Delaware	128,530	0.3%
47	South Dakota	123,900	0.3%
48	North Dakota	92,074	0.2%
49	Wyoming	88,355	0.2%
50	Vermont	85,635	0.2%
	District of Columbia	76,210	0.2%

Source: National Education Association, Washington, D.C.
 "Rankings and Estimates" (Copyright © 2011, NEA, used with permission, http://www.nea.org/home/44479.htm)
*Estimates for school year 2010-2011.

Enrollment in Public Elementary and Secondary Schools in 2010

National Total = 49,373,307 Students*

ALPHA ORDER					RANK ORDER			
RANK	**STATE**	**STUDENTS**	**% of USA**		**RANK**	**STATE**	**STUDENTS**	**% of USA**
23	Alabama	748,889	1.5%		1	California	6,263,449	12.7%
45	Alaska	131,661	0.3%		2	Texas	4,850,210	9.8%
13	Arizona	1,077,831	2.2%		3	New York	2,766,052	5.6%
33	Arkansas	480,559	1.0%		4	Florida	2,634,522	5.3%
1	California	6,263,449	12.7%		5	Illinois	2,104,175	4.3%
22	Colorado	832,368	1.7%		6	Pennsylvania	1,786,103	3.6%
30	Connecticut	563,985	1.1%		7	Ohio	1,764,297	3.6%
46	Delaware	126,801	0.3%		8	Georgia	1,667,685	3.4%
4	Florida	2,634,522	5.3%		9	Michigan	1,649,082	3.3%
8	Georgia	1,667,685	3.4%		10	North Carolina	1,483,397	3.0%
42	Hawaii	180,196	0.4%		11	New Jersey	1,396,029	2.8%
39	Idaho	276,299	0.6%		12	Virginia	1,245,340	2.5%
5	Illinois	2,104,175	4.3%		13	Arizona	1,077,831	2.2%
14	Indiana	1,046,661	2.1%		14	Indiana	1,046,661	2.1%
32	Iowa	491,842	1.0%		15	Washington	1,035,347	2.1%
34	Kansas	474,489	1.0%		16	Tennessee	972,549	2.0%
26	Kentucky	680,089	1.4%		17	Massachusetts	957,053	1.9%
25	Louisiana	690,915	1.4%		18	Missouri	917,982	1.9%
41	Maine	189,225	0.4%		19	Wisconsin	872,436	1.8%
20	Maryland	848,412	1.7%		20	Maryland	848,412	1.7%
17	Massachusetts	957,053	1.9%		21	Minnesota	837,053	1.7%
9	Michigan	1,649,082	3.3%		22	Colorado	832,368	1.7%
21	Minnesota	837,053	1.7%		23	Alabama	748,889	1.5%
31	Mississippi	492,481	1.0%		24	South Carolina	723,143	1.5%
18	Missouri	917,982	1.9%		25	Louisiana	690,915	1.4%
44	Montana	141,807	0.3%		26	Kentucky	680,089	1.4%
37	Nebraska	295,368	0.6%		27	Oklahoma	654,802	1.3%
35	Nevada	428,947	0.9%		28	Oregon	582,839	1.2%
40	New Hampshire	197,140	0.4%		29	Utah	582,793	1.2%
11	New Jersey	1,396,029	2.8%		30	Connecticut	563,985	1.1%
36	New Mexico	334,419	0.7%		31	Mississippi	492,481	1.0%
3	New York	2,766,052	5.6%		32	Iowa	491,842	1.0%
10	North Carolina	1,483,397	3.0%		33	Arkansas	480,559	1.0%
48	North Dakota	95,073	0.2%		34	Kansas	474,489	1.0%
7	Ohio	1,764,297	3.6%		35	Nevada	428,947	0.9%
27	Oklahoma	654,802	1.3%		36	New Mexico	334,419	0.7%
28	Oregon	582,839	1.2%		37	Nebraska	295,368	0.6%
6	Pennsylvania	1,786,103	3.6%		38	West Virginia	282,662	0.6%
43	Rhode Island	145,118	0.3%		39	Idaho	276,299	0.6%
24	South Carolina	723,143	1.5%		40	New Hampshire	197,140	0.4%
47	South Dakota	123,713	0.3%		41	Maine	189,225	0.4%
16	Tennessee	972,549	2.0%		42	Hawaii	180,196	0.4%
2	Texas	4,850,210	9.8%		43	Rhode Island	145,118	0.3%
29	Utah	582,793	1.2%		44	Montana	141,807	0.3%
49	Vermont	92,431	0.2%		45	Alaska	131,661	0.3%
12	Virginia	1,245,340	2.5%		46	Delaware	126,801	0.3%
15	Washington	1,035,347	2.1%		47	South Dakota	123,713	0.3%
38	West Virginia	282,662	0.6%		48	North Dakota	95,073	0.2%
19	Wisconsin	872,436	1.8%		49	Vermont	92,431	0.2%
50	Wyoming	88,155	0.2%		50	Wyoming	88,155	0.2%
						District of Columbia	69,433	0.1%

Source: U.S. Department of Education, National Center for Education Statistics
"Public Elementary and Secondary School Student Enrollment and Staff" (http://nces.ed.gov/pubs2011/2011347.pdf)
*School year 2009-2010.

Percent Change in Enrollment in Public
Elementary and Secondary Schools: 2000 to 2010
National Percent Change = 5.4% Increase*

ALPHA ORDER				RANK ORDER		
RANK	STATE	PERCENT CHANGE		RANK	STATE	PERCENT CHANGE
26	Alabama	1.1		1	Nevada	31.7
35	Alaska	(2.0)		2	Arizona	26.4
2	Arizona	26.4		3	Texas	21.5
15	Arkansas	6.5		4	Utah	21.4
21	California	3.7		5	Colorado	17.5
5	Colorado	17.5		6	Georgia	17.2
25	Connecticut	1.8		7	North Carolina	16.3
9	Delaware	12.4		8	Idaho	12.7
10	Florida	10.6		9	Delaware	12.4
6	Georgia	17.2		10	Florida	10.6
37	Hawaii	(3.0)		11	Virginia	9.8
8	Idaho	12.7		12	South Carolina	8.5
20	Illinois	3.8		13	New Jersey	8.3
17	Indiana	5.9		14	Oregon	6.9
31	Iowa	(1.1)		15	Arkansas	6.5
27	Kansas	0.5		16	Tennessee	6.2
18	Kentucky	4.9		17	Indiana	5.9
46	Louisiana	(8.7)		18	Kentucky	4.9
47	Maine	(9.6)		19	Oklahoma	4.4
29	Maryland	0.2		20	Illinois	3.8
32	Massachusetts	(1.5)		21	California	3.7
42	Michigan	(4.4)		22	Washington	3.2
35	Minnesota	(2.0)		23	New Mexico	3.1
33	Mississippi	(1.6)		24	Nebraska	2.5
28	Missouri	0.4		25	Connecticut	1.8
48	Montana	(10.0)		26	Alabama	1.1
24	Nebraska	2.5		27	Kansas	0.5
1	Nevada	31.7		28	Missouri	0.4
43	New Hampshire	(4.7)		29	Maryland	0.2
13	New Jersey	8.3		30	Wisconsin	(0.6)
23	New Mexico	3.1		31	Iowa	(1.1)
40	New York	(4.2)		32	Massachusetts	(1.5)
7	North Carolina	16.3		33	Mississippi	(1.6)
50	North Dakota	(15.7)		34	Pennsylvania	(1.7)
39	Ohio	(3.9)		35	Alaska	(2.0)
19	Oklahoma	4.4		35	Minnesota	(2.0)
14	Oregon	6.9		37	Hawaii	(3.0)
34	Pennsylvania	(1.7)		38	West Virginia	(3.1)
45	Rhode Island	(7.2)		39	Ohio	(3.9)
12	South Carolina	8.5		40	New York	(4.2)
44	South Dakota	(5.6)		41	Wyoming	(4.3)
16	Tennessee	6.2		42	Michigan	(4.4)
3	Texas	21.5		43	New Hampshire	(4.7)
4	Utah	21.4		44	South Dakota	(5.6)
49	Vermont	(11.6)		45	Rhode Island	(7.2)
11	Virginia	9.8		46	Louisiana	(8.7)
22	Washington	3.2		47	Maine	(9.6)
38	West Virginia	(3.1)		48	Montana	(10.0)
30	Wisconsin	(0.6)		49	Vermont	(11.6)
41	Wyoming	(4.3)		50	North Dakota	(15.7)
					District of Columbia	(10.1)

Source: CQ Press using data from U.S. Department of Education, National Center for Education Statistics
   "Public Elementary and Secondary School Student Enrollment and Staff" (http://nces.ed.gov/pubs2011/2011347.pdf)
*Calculated comparing data for school years 2009-2010 and 1999-2000.

Male Public Elementary and Secondary School Students in 2010

National Total = 25,058,982 Male Students*

RANK	STATE	MALES	% of USA
23	Alabama	382,516	1.5%
45	Alaska	67,979	0.3%
13	Arizona	555,226	2.2%
33	Arkansas	245,808	1.0%
1	California	3,180,868	12.7%
22	Colorado	426,619	1.7%
28	Connecticut	290,680	1.2%
46	Delaware	65,027	0.3%
4	Florida	1,309,388	5.2%
8	Georgia	852,689	3.4%
42	Hawaii	93,815	0.4%
39	Idaho	142,737	0.6%
5	Illinois	1,049,490	4.2%
15	Indiana	513,545	2.0%
31	Iowa	253,311	1.0%
34	Kansas	244,049	1.0%
26	Kentucky	342,656	1.4%
25	Louisiana	353,721	1.4%
41	Maine	97,890	0.4%
20	Maryland	435,071	1.7%
17	Massachusetts	491,377	2.0%
9	Michigan	840,629	3.4%
21	Minnesota	431,517	1.7%
32	Mississippi	251,344	1.0%
18	Missouri	473,044	1.9%
44	Montana	73,298	0.3%
37	Nebraska	152,466	0.6%
35	Nevada	221,106	0.9%
40	New Hampshire	101,935	0.4%
11	New Jersey	720,999	2.9%
36	New Mexico	171,240	0.7%
3	New York	1,398,897	5.6%
10	North Carolina	756,336	3.0%
48	North Dakota	49,108	0.2%
7	Ohio	870,039	3.5%
27	Oklahoma	337,500	1.3%
29	Oregon	278,140	1.1%
6	Pennsylvania	907,388	3.6%
43	Rhode Island	75,238	0.3%
24	South Carolina	368,862	1.5%
47	South Dakota	63,884	0.3%
16	Tennessee	500,107	2.0%
2	Texas	2,491,255	9.9%
30	Utah	267,807	1.1%
49	Vermont	47,868	0.2%
12	Virginia	622,168	2.5%
14	Washington	516,493	2.1%
38	West Virginia	145,960	0.6%
19	Wisconsin	449,894	1.8%
50	Wyoming	45,609	0.2%

RANK	STATE	MALES	% of USA
1	California	3,180,868	12.7%
2	Texas	2,491,255	9.9%
3	New York	1,398,897	5.6%
4	Florida	1,309,388	5.2%
5	Illinois	1,049,490	4.2%
6	Pennsylvania	907,388	3.6%
7	Ohio	870,039	3.5%
8	Georgia	852,689	3.4%
9	Michigan	840,629	3.4%
10	North Carolina	756,336	3.0%
11	New Jersey	720,999	2.9%
12	Virginia	622,168	2.5%
13	Arizona	555,226	2.2%
14	Washington	516,493	2.1%
15	Indiana	513,545	2.0%
16	Tennessee	500,107	2.0%
17	Massachusetts	491,377	2.0%
18	Missouri	473,044	1.9%
19	Wisconsin	449,894	1.8%
20	Maryland	435,071	1.7%
21	Minnesota	431,517	1.7%
22	Colorado	426,619	1.7%
23	Alabama	382,516	1.5%
24	South Carolina	368,862	1.5%
25	Louisiana	353,721	1.4%
26	Kentucky	342,656	1.4%
27	Oklahoma	337,500	1.3%
28	Connecticut	290,680	1.2%
29	Oregon	278,140	1.1%
30	Utah	267,807	1.1%
31	Iowa	253,311	1.0%
32	Mississippi	251,344	1.0%
33	Arkansas	245,808	1.0%
34	Kansas	244,049	1.0%
35	Nevada	221,106	0.9%
36	New Mexico	171,240	0.7%
37	Nebraska	152,466	0.6%
38	West Virginia	145,960	0.6%
39	Idaho	142,737	0.6%
40	New Hampshire	101,935	0.4%
41	Maine	97,890	0.4%
42	Hawaii	93,815	0.4%
43	Rhode Island	75,238	0.3%
44	Montana	73,298	0.3%
45	Alaska	67,979	0.3%
46	Delaware	65,027	0.3%
47	South Dakota	63,884	0.3%
48	North Dakota	49,108	0.2%
49	Vermont	47,868	0.2%
50	Wyoming	45,609	0.2%
	District of Columbia	34,389	0.1%

Source: U.S. Department of Education, National Center for Education Statistics
"Common Core of Data (CCD) Database" (http://nces.ed.gov/ccd/)
*For school year 2009-2010.

Percent of Public Elementary and Secondary School Students Who Are Male in 2010
National Percent = 51.4% Male*

ALPHA ORDER

RANK	STATE	PERCENT
38	Alabama	51.3
11	Alaska	51.6
21	Arizona	51.5
44	Arkansas	51.2
28	California	51.4
38	Colorado	51.3
21	Connecticut	51.5
38	Delaware	51.3
21	Florida	51.5
47	Georgia	51.1
1	Hawaii	52.1
5	Idaho	51.7
28	Illinois	51.4
28	Indiana	51.4
21	Iowa	51.5
28	Kansas	51.4
11	Kentucky	51.6
44	Louisiana	51.2
5	Maine	51.7
38	Maryland	51.3
38	Massachusetts	51.3
2	Michigan	51.8
11	Minnesota	51.6
48	Mississippi	51.0
21	Missouri	51.5
5	Montana	51.7
11	Nebraska	51.6
21	Nevada	51.5
5	New Hampshire	51.7
11	New Jersey	51.6
44	New Mexico	51.2
50	New York	50.8
48	North Carolina	51.0
5	North Dakota	51.7
28	Ohio	51.4
21	Oklahoma	51.5
28	Oregon	51.4
28	Pennsylvania	51.4
2	Rhode Island	51.8
38	South Carolina	51.3
11	South Dakota	51.6
28	Tennessee	51.4
28	Texas	51.4
11	Utah	51.6
2	Vermont	51.8
28	Virginia	51.4
11	Washington	51.6
11	West Virginia	51.6
11	Wisconsin	51.6
5	Wyoming	51.7

RANK ORDER

RANK	STATE	PERCENT
1	Hawaii	52.1
2	Michigan	51.8
2	Rhode Island	51.8
2	Vermont	51.8
5	Idaho	51.7
5	Maine	51.7
5	Montana	51.7
5	New Hampshire	51.7
5	North Dakota	51.7
5	Wyoming	51.7
11	Alaska	51.6
11	Kentucky	51.6
11	Minnesota	51.6
11	Nebraska	51.6
11	New Jersey	51.6
11	South Dakota	51.6
11	Utah	51.6
11	Washington	51.6
11	West Virginia	51.6
11	Wisconsin	51.6
21	Arizona	51.5
21	Connecticut	51.5
21	Florida	51.5
21	Iowa	51.5
21	Missouri	51.5
21	Nevada	51.5
21	Oklahoma	51.5
28	California	51.4
28	Illinois	51.4
28	Indiana	51.4
28	Kansas	51.4
28	Ohio	51.4
28	Oregon	51.4
28	Pennsylvania	51.4
28	Tennessee	51.4
28	Texas	51.4
28	Virginia	51.4
38	Alabama	51.3
38	Colorado	51.3
38	Delaware	51.3
38	Maryland	51.3
38	Massachusetts	51.3
38	South Carolina	51.3
44	Arkansas	51.2
44	Louisiana	51.2
44	New Mexico	51.2
47	Georgia	51.1
48	Mississippi	51.0
48	North Carolina	51.0
50	New York	50.8

District of Columbia 49.5

Source: CQ Press using data from U.S. Department of Education, National Center for Education Statistics "Common Core of Data (CCD) Database" (http://nces.ed.gov/ccd/)
*For school year 2009-2010. Based on enrollment where gender is known.

Female Public Elementary and Secondary School Students in 2010

National Total = 23,712,836 Female Students*

ALPHA ORDER

RANK	STATE	FEMALES	% of USA
23	Alabama	363,257	1.5%
45	Alaska	63,682	0.3%
13	Arizona	522,605	2.2%
33	Arkansas	234,751	1.0%
1	California	3,010,798	12.7%
21	Colorado	405,749	1.7%
28	Connecticut	273,305	1.2%
46	Delaware	61,774	0.3%
4	Florida	1,235,527	5.2%
8	Georgia	814,996	3.4%
42	Hawaii	86,381	0.4%
39	Idaho	133,562	0.6%
5	Illinois	993,114	4.2%
14	Indiana	486,388	2.1%
32	Iowa	238,531	1.0%
34	Kansas	230,440	1.0%
26	Kentucky	320,997	1.4%
25	Louisiana	337,194	1.4%
41	Maine	91,330	0.4%
20	Maryland	413,341	1.7%
17	Massachusetts	465,676	2.0%
9	Michigan	783,291	3.3%
22	Minnesota	405,536	1.7%
31	Mississippi	241,137	1.0%
18	Missouri	444,938	1.9%
44	Montana	68,509	0.3%
37	Nebraska	142,902	0.6%
35	Nevada	207,841	0.9%
40	New Hampshire	95,205	0.4%
11	New Jersey	675,030	2.8%
36	New Mexico	163,179	0.7%
3	New York	1,354,682	5.7%
10	North Carolina	725,797	3.1%
48	North Dakota	45,965	0.2%
7	Ohio	821,783	3.5%
27	Oklahoma	317,302	1.3%
29	Oregon	263,000	1.1%
6	Pennsylvania	856,784	3.6%
43	Rhode Island	69,880	0.3%
24	South Carolina	350,027	1.5%
47	South Dakota	59,829	0.3%
16	Tennessee	472,442	2.0%
2	Texas	2,358,955	9.9%
30	Utah	251,652	1.1%
49	Vermont	44,563	0.2%
12	Virginia	587,154	2.5%
15	Washington	485,248	2.0%
38	West Virginia	136,702	0.6%
19	Wisconsin	422,542	1.8%
50	Wyoming	42,546	0.2%

RANK ORDER

RANK	STATE	FEMALES	% of USA
1	California	3,010,798	12.7%
2	Texas	2,358,955	9.9%
3	New York	1,354,682	5.7%
4	Florida	1,235,527	5.2%
5	Illinois	993,114	4.2%
6	Pennsylvania	856,784	3.6%
7	Ohio	821,783	3.5%
8	Georgia	814,996	3.4%
9	Michigan	783,291	3.3%
10	North Carolina	725,797	3.1%
11	New Jersey	675,030	2.8%
12	Virginia	587,154	2.5%
13	Arizona	522,605	2.2%
14	Indiana	486,388	2.1%
15	Washington	485,248	2.0%
16	Tennessee	472,442	2.0%
17	Massachusetts	465,676	2.0%
18	Missouri	444,938	1.9%
19	Wisconsin	422,542	1.8%
20	Maryland	413,341	1.7%
21	Colorado	405,749	1.7%
22	Minnesota	405,536	1.7%
23	Alabama	363,257	1.5%
24	South Carolina	350,027	1.5%
25	Louisiana	337,194	1.4%
26	Kentucky	320,997	1.4%
27	Oklahoma	317,302	1.3%
28	Connecticut	273,305	1.2%
29	Oregon	263,000	1.1%
30	Utah	251,652	1.1%
31	Mississippi	241,137	1.0%
32	Iowa	238,531	1.0%
33	Arkansas	234,751	1.0%
34	Kansas	230,440	1.0%
35	Nevada	207,841	0.9%
36	New Mexico	163,179	0.7%
37	Nebraska	142,902	0.6%
38	West Virginia	136,702	0.6%
39	Idaho	133,562	0.6%
40	New Hampshire	95,205	0.4%
41	Maine	91,330	0.4%
42	Hawaii	86,381	0.4%
43	Rhode Island	69,880	0.3%
44	Montana	68,509	0.3%
45	Alaska	63,682	0.3%
46	Delaware	61,774	0.3%
47	South Dakota	59,829	0.3%
48	North Dakota	45,965	0.2%
49	Vermont	44,563	0.2%
50	Wyoming	42,546	0.2%
	District of Columbia	35,017	0.1%

Source: U.S. Department of Education, National Center for Education Statistics
   "Common Core of Data (CCD) Database" (http://nces.ed.gov/ccd/)
*For school year 2009-2010.

Percent of Public Elementary and Secondary School Students Who Are Female in 2010
National Percent = 48.6% Female*

ALPHA ORDER

RANK	STATE	PERCENT
8	Alabama	48.7
31	Alaska	48.4
24	Arizona	48.5
5	Arkansas	48.8
14	California	48.6
8	Colorado	48.7
24	Connecticut	48.5
8	Delaware	48.7
24	Florida	48.5
4	Georgia	48.9
50	Hawaii	47.9
41	Idaho	48.3
14	Illinois	48.6
14	Indiana	48.6
24	Iowa	48.5
14	Kansas	48.6
31	Kentucky	48.4
5	Louisiana	48.8
41	Maine	48.3
8	Maryland	48.7
8	Massachusetts	48.7
47	Michigan	48.2
31	Minnesota	48.4
2	Mississippi	49.0
24	Missouri	48.5
41	Montana	48.3
31	Nebraska	48.4
24	Nevada	48.5
41	New Hampshire	48.3
31	New Jersey	48.4
5	New Mexico	48.8
1	New York	49.2
2	North Carolina	49.0
41	North Dakota	48.3
14	Ohio	48.6
24	Oklahoma	48.5
14	Oregon	48.6
14	Pennsylvania	48.6
47	Rhode Island	48.2
8	South Carolina	48.7
31	South Dakota	48.4
14	Tennessee	48.6
14	Texas	48.6
31	Utah	48.4
47	Vermont	48.2
14	Virginia	48.6
31	Washington	48.4
31	West Virginia	48.4
31	Wisconsin	48.4
41	Wyoming	48.3

RANK ORDER

RANK	STATE	PERCENT
1	New York	49.2
2	Mississippi	49.0
2	North Carolina	49.0
4	Georgia	48.9
5	Arkansas	48.8
5	Louisiana	48.8
5	New Mexico	48.8
8	Alabama	48.7
8	Colorado	48.7
8	Delaware	48.7
8	Maryland	48.7
8	Massachusetts	48.7
8	South Carolina	48.7
14	California	48.6
14	Illinois	48.6
14	Indiana	48.6
14	Kansas	48.6
14	Ohio	48.6
14	Oregon	48.6
14	Pennsylvania	48.6
14	Tennessee	48.6
14	Texas	48.6
14	Virginia	48.6
24	Arizona	48.5
24	Connecticut	48.5
24	Florida	48.5
24	Iowa	48.5
24	Missouri	48.5
24	Nevada	48.5
24	Oklahoma	48.5
31	Alaska	48.4
31	Kentucky	48.4
31	Minnesota	48.4
31	Nebraska	48.4
31	New Jersey	48.4
31	South Dakota	48.4
31	Utah	48.4
31	Washington	48.4
31	West Virginia	48.4
31	Wisconsin	48.4
41	Idaho	48.3
41	Maine	48.3
41	Montana	48.3
41	New Hampshire	48.3
41	North Dakota	48.3
41	Wyoming	48.3
47	Michigan	48.2
47	Rhode Island	48.2
47	Vermont	48.2
50	Hawaii	47.9

District of Columbia — 50.5

Source: CQ Press using data from U.S. Department of Education, National Center for Education Statistics
"Common Core of Data (CCD) Database" (http://nces.ed.gov/ccd/)
*For school year 2009-2010. Based on enrollment where gender is known.

Pupil-Teacher Ratio in Public Elementary and Secondary Schools in 2010

National Ratio = 15.4 Pupils Per Teacher*

ALPHA ORDER

RANK	STATE	RATIO
13	Alabama	15.8
12	Alaska	16.3
2	Arizona	20.7
41	Arkansas	12.9
4	California	20.0
10	Colorado	17.0
41	Connecticut	12.9
24	Delaware	14.7
29	Florida	14.3
28	Georgia	14.4
13	Hawaii	15.8
7	Idaho	18.2
20	Illinois	15.2
11	Indiana	16.8
33	Iowa	13.7
33	Kansas	13.7
18	Kentucky	15.3
31	Louisiana	13.9
48	Maine	11.6
26	Maryland	14.6
33	Massachusetts	13.7
8	Michigan	17.8
13	Minnesota	15.8
21	Mississippi	14.9
37	Missouri	13.5
37	Montana	13.5
39	Nebraska	13.3
5	Nevada	19.4
45	New Hampshire	12.7
47	New Jersey	12.1
24	New Mexico	14.7
41	New York	12.9
30	North Carolina	14.1
49	North Dakota	11.4
13	Ohio	15.8
18	Oklahoma	15.3
3	Oregon	20.3
36	Pennsylvania	13.6
44	Rhode Island	12.8
17	South Carolina	15.4
39	South Dakota	13.3
21	Tennessee	14.9
26	Texas	14.6
1	Utah	22.9
50	Vermont	10.6
9	Virginia	17.6
5	Washington	19.4
31	West Virginia	13.9
21	Wisconsin	14.9
46	Wyoming	12.3

RANK ORDER

RANK	STATE	RATIO
1	Utah	22.9
2	Arizona	20.7
3	Oregon	20.3
4	California	20.0
5	Nevada	19.4
5	Washington	19.4
7	Idaho	18.2
8	Michigan	17.8
9	Virginia	17.6
10	Colorado	17.0
11	Indiana	16.8
12	Alaska	16.3
13	Alabama	15.8
13	Hawaii	15.8
13	Minnesota	15.8
13	Ohio	15.8
17	South Carolina	15.4
18	Kentucky	15.3
18	Oklahoma	15.3
20	Illinois	15.2
21	Mississippi	14.9
21	Tennessee	14.9
21	Wisconsin	14.9
24	Delaware	14.7
24	New Mexico	14.7
26	Maryland	14.6
26	Texas	14.6
28	Georgia	14.4
29	Florida	14.3
30	North Carolina	14.1
31	Louisiana	13.9
31	West Virginia	13.9
33	Iowa	13.7
33	Kansas	13.7
33	Massachusetts	13.7
36	Pennsylvania	13.6
37	Missouri	13.5
37	Montana	13.5
39	Nebraska	13.3
39	South Dakota	13.3
41	Arkansas	12.9
41	Connecticut	12.9
41	New York	12.9
44	Rhode Island	12.8
45	New Hampshire	12.7
46	Wyoming	12.3
47	New Jersey	12.1
48	Maine	11.6
49	North Dakota	11.4
50	Vermont	10.6

| | District of Columbia | 10.9 |

Source: U.S. Department of Education, National Center for Education Statistics
   "Public Elementary and Secondary School Student Enrollment and Staff" (http://nces.ed.gov/pubs2011/2011347.pdf)
*For school year 2009-2010. Based on full-time equivalency counts of teachers.

Public Kindergarten Pupil-Teacher Ratio in 2010

National Ratio = 20.5 Students Per Teacher*

ALPHA ORDER

RANK	STATE	RATIO
49	Alabama	12.0
17	Alaska	23.1
8	Arizona	27.8
50	Arkansas	11.1
21	California	21.9
36	Colorado	18.5
15	Connecticut	23.2
11	Delaware	25.6
29	Florida	20.1
40	Georgia	17.8
9	Hawaii	27.5
4	Idaho	34.5
5	Illinois	30.3
32	Indiana	19.8
47	Iowa	14.7
24	Kansas	21.6
1	Kentucky	41.7
18	Louisiana	22.9
42	Maine	16.4
32	Maryland	19.8
30	Massachusetts	19.9
6	Michigan	29.7
19	Minnesota	22.8
27	Mississippi	20.5
41	Missouri	17.4
43	Montana	16.2
35	Nebraska	18.6
3	Nevada	35.1
14	New Hampshire	23.9
7	New Jersey	28.3
27	New Mexico	20.5
48	New York	14.5
45	North Carolina	15.7
46	North Dakota	15.2
24	Ohio	21.6
26	Oklahoma	21.2
22	Oregon	21.8
13	Pennsylvania	24.6
12	Rhode Island	25.2
15	South Carolina	23.2
23	South Dakota	21.7
34	Tennessee	19.0
39	Texas	17.9
2	Utah	39.0
43	Vermont	16.2
20	Virginia	22.0
10	Washington	26.7
30	West Virginia	19.9
37	Wisconsin	18.4
38	Wyoming	18.2

RANK ORDER

RANK	STATE	RATIO
1	Kentucky	41.7
2	Utah	39.0
3	Nevada	35.1
4	Idaho	34.5
5	Illinois	30.3
6	Michigan	29.7
7	New Jersey	28.3
8	Arizona	27.8
9	Hawaii	27.5
10	Washington	26.7
11	Delaware	25.6
12	Rhode Island	25.2
13	Pennsylvania	24.6
14	New Hampshire	23.9
15	Connecticut	23.2
15	South Carolina	23.2
17	Alaska	23.1
18	Louisiana	22.9
19	Minnesota	22.8
20	Virginia	22.0
21	California	21.9
22	Oregon	21.8
23	South Dakota	21.7
24	Kansas	21.6
24	Ohio	21.6
26	Oklahoma	21.2
27	Mississippi	20.5
27	New Mexico	20.5
29	Florida	20.1
30	Massachusetts	19.9
30	West Virginia	19.9
32	Indiana	19.8
32	Maryland	19.8
34	Tennessee	19.0
35	Nebraska	18.6
36	Colorado	18.5
37	Wisconsin	18.4
38	Wyoming	18.2
39	Texas	17.9
40	Georgia	17.8
41	Missouri	17.4
42	Maine	16.4
43	Montana	16.2
43	Vermont	16.2
45	North Carolina	15.7
46	North Dakota	15.2
47	Iowa	14.7
48	New York	14.5
49	Alabama	12.0
50	Arkansas	11.1

District of Columbia   16.5

Source: U.S. Department of Education, National Center for Education Statistics
  "Public Elementary and Secondary School Student Enrollment and Staff" (http://nces.ed.gov/pubs2011/2011347.pdf)
*For school year 2009-2010. Ratios are based on full-time equivalent counts.

Public Elementary School Pupil-Teacher Ratio in 2010

National Ratio = 19.1 Students Per Teacher*

<table>
<tr><td colspan="3">ALPHA ORDER</td><td colspan="3">RANK ORDER</td></tr>
<tr><td>RANK</td><td>STATE</td><td>RATIO</td><td>RANK</td><td>STATE</td><td>RATIO</td></tr>
<tr><td>12</td><td>Alabama</td><td>21.3</td><td>1</td><td>Utah</td><td>32.1</td></tr>
<tr><td>14</td><td>Alaska</td><td>21.1</td><td>2</td><td>Michigan</td><td>29.9</td></tr>
<tr><td>23</td><td>Arizona</td><td>19.8</td><td>3</td><td>Nevada</td><td>26.5</td></tr>
<tr><td>30</td><td>Arkansas</td><td>18.6</td><td>4</td><td>Florida</td><td>25.7</td></tr>
<tr><td>28</td><td>California</td><td>18.7</td><td>4</td><td>Washington</td><td>25.7</td></tr>
<tr><td>14</td><td>Colorado</td><td>21.1</td><td>6</td><td>Virginia</td><td>25.5</td></tr>
<tr><td>47</td><td>Connecticut</td><td>12.7</td><td>7</td><td>New Mexico</td><td>24.4</td></tr>
<tr><td>20</td><td>Delaware</td><td>20.4</td><td>8</td><td>Idaho</td><td>23.5</td></tr>
<tr><td>4</td><td>Florida</td><td>25.7</td><td>9</td><td>Ohio</td><td>23.0</td></tr>
<tr><td>35</td><td>Georgia</td><td>16.9</td><td>10</td><td>Mississippi</td><td>22.6</td></tr>
<tr><td>18</td><td>Hawaii</td><td>20.6</td><td>11</td><td>Indiana</td><td>22.0</td></tr>
<tr><td>8</td><td>Idaho</td><td>23.5</td><td>12</td><td>Alabama</td><td>21.3</td></tr>
<tr><td>40</td><td>Illinois</td><td>14.3</td><td>13</td><td>Texas</td><td>21.2</td></tr>
<tr><td>11</td><td>Indiana</td><td>22.0</td><td>14</td><td>Alaska</td><td>21.1</td></tr>
<tr><td>33</td><td>Iowa</td><td>17.6</td><td>14</td><td>Colorado</td><td>21.1</td></tr>
<tr><td>25</td><td>Kansas</td><td>19.4</td><td>14</td><td>Minnesota</td><td>21.1</td></tr>
<tr><td>20</td><td>Kentucky</td><td>20.4</td><td>17</td><td>Wisconsin</td><td>20.9</td></tr>
<tr><td>44</td><td>Louisiana</td><td>13.9</td><td>18</td><td>Hawaii</td><td>20.6</td></tr>
<tr><td>50</td><td>Maine</td><td>10.9</td><td>18</td><td>West Virginia</td><td>20.6</td></tr>
<tr><td>36</td><td>Maryland</td><td>16.3</td><td>20</td><td>Delaware</td><td>20.4</td></tr>
<tr><td>46</td><td>Massachusetts</td><td>13.7</td><td>20</td><td>Kentucky</td><td>20.4</td></tr>
<tr><td>2</td><td>Michigan</td><td>29.9</td><td>22</td><td>Oklahoma</td><td>20.2</td></tr>
<tr><td>14</td><td>Minnesota</td><td>21.1</td><td>23</td><td>Arizona</td><td>19.8</td></tr>
<tr><td>10</td><td>Mississippi</td><td>22.6</td><td>24</td><td>North Carolina</td><td>19.5</td></tr>
<tr><td>28</td><td>Missouri</td><td>18.7</td><td>25</td><td>Kansas</td><td>19.4</td></tr>
<tr><td>45</td><td>Montana</td><td>13.8</td><td>26</td><td>Oregon</td><td>19.0</td></tr>
<tr><td>40</td><td>Nebraska</td><td>14.3</td><td>26</td><td>Pennsylvania</td><td>19.0</td></tr>
<tr><td>3</td><td>Nevada</td><td>26.5</td><td>28</td><td>California</td><td>18.7</td></tr>
<tr><td>49</td><td>New Hampshire</td><td>12.0</td><td>28</td><td>Missouri</td><td>18.7</td></tr>
<tr><td>40</td><td>New Jersey</td><td>14.3</td><td>30</td><td>Arkansas</td><td>18.6</td></tr>
<tr><td>7</td><td>New Mexico</td><td>24.4</td><td>31</td><td>Vermont</td><td>18.0</td></tr>
<tr><td>32</td><td>New York</td><td>17.7</td><td>32</td><td>New York</td><td>17.7</td></tr>
<tr><td>24</td><td>North Carolina</td><td>19.5</td><td>33</td><td>Iowa</td><td>17.6</td></tr>
<tr><td>48</td><td>North Dakota</td><td>12.1</td><td>34</td><td>Rhode Island</td><td>17.4</td></tr>
<tr><td>9</td><td>Ohio</td><td>23.0</td><td>35</td><td>Georgia</td><td>16.9</td></tr>
<tr><td>22</td><td>Oklahoma</td><td>20.2</td><td>36</td><td>Maryland</td><td>16.3</td></tr>
<tr><td>26</td><td>Oregon</td><td>19.0</td><td>36</td><td>Wyoming</td><td>16.3</td></tr>
<tr><td>26</td><td>Pennsylvania</td><td>19.0</td><td>38</td><td>Tennessee</td><td>15.1</td></tr>
<tr><td>34</td><td>Rhode Island</td><td>17.4</td><td>39</td><td>South Carolina</td><td>14.6</td></tr>
<tr><td>39</td><td>South Carolina</td><td>14.6</td><td>40</td><td>Illinois</td><td>14.3</td></tr>
<tr><td>43</td><td>South Dakota</td><td>14.1</td><td>40</td><td>Nebraska</td><td>14.3</td></tr>
<tr><td>38</td><td>Tennessee</td><td>15.1</td><td>40</td><td>New Jersey</td><td>14.3</td></tr>
<tr><td>13</td><td>Texas</td><td>21.2</td><td>43</td><td>South Dakota</td><td>14.1</td></tr>
<tr><td>1</td><td>Utah</td><td>32.1</td><td>44</td><td>Louisiana</td><td>13.9</td></tr>
<tr><td>31</td><td>Vermont</td><td>18.0</td><td>45</td><td>Montana</td><td>13.8</td></tr>
<tr><td>6</td><td>Virginia</td><td>25.5</td><td>46</td><td>Massachusetts</td><td>13.7</td></tr>
<tr><td>4</td><td>Washington</td><td>25.7</td><td>47</td><td>Connecticut</td><td>12.7</td></tr>
<tr><td>18</td><td>West Virginia</td><td>20.6</td><td>48</td><td>North Dakota</td><td>12.1</td></tr>
<tr><td>17</td><td>Wisconsin</td><td>20.9</td><td>49</td><td>New Hampshire</td><td>12.0</td></tr>
<tr><td>36</td><td>Wyoming</td><td>16.3</td><td>50</td><td>Maine</td><td>10.9</td></tr>
<tr><td></td><td></td><td></td><td></td><td>District of Columbia</td><td>12.6</td></tr>
</table>

Source: U.S. Department of Education, National Center for Education Statistics
    "Public Elementary and Secondary School Student Enrollment and Staff" (http://nces.ed.gov/pubs2011/2011347.pdf)
*For school year 2009-2010. Ratios are based on full-time equivalent counts. Includes grades 1-8.

Public Secondary School Pupil-Teacher Ratio in 2010

National Ratio = 12.1 Students Per Teacher*

ALPHA ORDER

RANK	STATE	RATIO
27	Alabama	10.8
28	Alaska	10.7
2	Arizona	21.2
40	Arkansas	9.3
1	California	22.4
21	Colorado	11.5
16	Connecticut	12.2
44	Delaware	8.9
17	Florida	11.9
30	Georgia	10.4
33	Hawaii	10.2
22	Idaho	11.4
12	Illinois	14.2
25	Indiana	11.2
39	Iowa	9.4
46	Kansas	8.3
4	Kentucky	18.9
19	Louisiana	11.8
19	Maine	11.8
26	Maryland	11.1
15	Massachusetts	12.3
10	Michigan	14.4
22	Minnesota	11.4
30	Mississippi	10.4
45	Missouri	8.5
13	Montana	13.0
30	Nebraska	10.4
6	Nevada	15.5
13	New Hampshire	13.0
33	New Jersey	10.2
22	New Mexico	11.4
17	New York	11.9
42	North Carolina	9.0
37	North Dakota	9.8
33	Ohio	10.2
42	Oklahoma	9.0
3	Oregon	20.7
38	Pennsylvania	9.7
48	Rhode Island	7.9
8	South Carolina	15.0
9	South Dakota	14.8
7	Tennessee	15.1
36	Texas	10.1
5	Utah	16.2
46	Vermont	8.3
28	Virginia	10.7
10	Washington	14.4
50	West Virginia	7.6
40	Wisconsin	9.3
49	Wyoming	7.7

RANK ORDER

RANK	STATE	RATIO
1	California	22.4
2	Arizona	21.2
3	Oregon	20.7
4	Kentucky	18.9
5	Utah	16.2
6	Nevada	15.5
7	Tennessee	15.1
8	South Carolina	15.0
9	South Dakota	14.8
10	Michigan	14.4
10	Washington	14.4
12	Illinois	14.2
13	Montana	13.0
13	New Hampshire	13.0
15	Massachusetts	12.3
16	Connecticut	12.2
17	Florida	11.9
17	New York	11.9
19	Louisiana	11.8
19	Maine	11.8
21	Colorado	11.5
22	Idaho	11.4
22	Minnesota	11.4
22	New Mexico	11.4
25	Indiana	11.2
26	Maryland	11.1
27	Alabama	10.8
28	Alaska	10.7
28	Virginia	10.7
30	Georgia	10.4
30	Mississippi	10.4
30	Nebraska	10.4
33	Hawaii	10.2
33	New Jersey	10.2
33	Ohio	10.2
36	Texas	10.1
37	North Dakota	9.8
38	Pennsylvania	9.7
39	Iowa	9.4
40	Arkansas	9.3
40	Wisconsin	9.3
42	North Carolina	9.0
42	Oklahoma	9.0
44	Delaware	8.9
45	Missouri	8.5
46	Kansas	8.3
46	Vermont	8.3
48	Rhode Island	7.9
49	Wyoming	7.7
50	West Virginia	7.6
	District of Columbia	7.7

Source: U.S. Department of Education, National Center for Education Statistics
   "Public Elementary and Secondary School Student Enrollment and Staff" (http://nces.ed.gov/pubs2011/2011347.pdf)
*For school year 2009-2010. Ratios are based on full-time equivalent counts. Includes grades 9-12.

Pupil-Staff Ratio in Public Elementary and Secondary Schools in 2010

National Ratio = 7.8 Students Per Staff*

ALPHA ORDER

RANK	STATE	RATIO
14	Alabama	8.0
22	Alaska	7.4
3	Arizona	10.7
40	Arkansas	6.5
5	California	10.5
12	Colorado	8.1
43	Connecticut	6.1
21	Delaware	7.5
15	Florida	7.9
30	Georgia	7.1
10	Hawaii	8.3
6	Idaho	10.0
8	Illinois	9.5
25	Indiana	7.3
36	Iowa	6.8
31	Kansas	7.0
47	Kentucky	5.7
37	Louisiana	6.7
49	Maine	5.1
22	Maryland	7.4
16	Massachusetts	7.8
12	Michigan	8.1
18	Minnesota	7.7
31	Mississippi	7.0
31	Missouri	7.0
25	Montana	7.3
42	Nebraska	6.4
1	Nevada	12.7
45	New Hampshire	6.0
40	New Jersey	6.5
31	New Mexico	7.0
38	New York	6.6
22	North Carolina	7.4
46	North Dakota	5.9
28	Ohio	7.2
18	Oklahoma	7.7
9	Oregon	9.3
31	Pennsylvania	7.0
16	Rhode Island	7.8
3	South Carolina	10.7
38	South Dakota	6.6
20	Tennessee	7.6
25	Texas	7.3
2	Utah	11.3
50	Vermont	4.8
43	Virginia	6.1
6	Washington	10.0
28	West Virginia	7.2
10	Wisconsin	8.3
48	Wyoming	5.4

RANK ORDER

RANK	STATE	RATIO
1	Nevada	12.7
2	Utah	11.3
3	Arizona	10.7
3	South Carolina	10.7
5	California	10.5
6	Idaho	10.0
6	Washington	10.0
8	Illinois	9.5
9	Oregon	9.3
10	Hawaii	8.3
10	Wisconsin	8.3
12	Colorado	8.1
12	Michigan	8.1
14	Alabama	8.0
15	Florida	7.9
16	Massachusetts	7.8
16	Rhode Island	7.8
18	Minnesota	7.7
18	Oklahoma	7.7
20	Tennessee	7.6
21	Delaware	7.5
22	Alaska	7.4
22	Maryland	7.4
22	North Carolina	7.4
25	Indiana	7.3
25	Montana	7.3
25	Texas	7.3
28	Ohio	7.2
28	West Virginia	7.2
30	Georgia	7.1
31	Kansas	7.0
31	Mississippi	7.0
31	Missouri	7.0
31	New Mexico	7.0
31	Pennsylvania	7.0
36	Iowa	6.8
37	Louisiana	6.7
38	New York	6.6
38	South Dakota	6.6
40	Arkansas	6.5
40	New Jersey	6.5
42	Nebraska	6.4
43	Connecticut	6.1
43	Virginia	6.1
45	New Hampshire	6.0
46	North Dakota	5.9
47	Kentucky	5.7
48	Wyoming	5.4
49	Maine	5.1
50	Vermont	4.8
	District of Columbia	5.7

Source: CQ Press using data from U.S. Department of Education, National Center for Education Statistics
"Public Elementary and Secondary School Student Enrollment and Staff" (http://nces.ed.gov/pubs2011/2011347.pdf)
*For school year 2009-2010. Ratios are based on full-time equivalent counts. Includes grades K-12. Includes administration, instructional, and all support staff.

Pupil-Administrative Staff Ratio in Public Elementary and Secondary Schools in 2010
National Ratio = 211.6 Students Per Staff*

ALPHA ORDER

RANK	STATE	RATIO
22	Alabama	209.1
50	Alaska	85.5
2	Arizona	365.5
31	Arkansas	194.4
5	California	301.2
24	Colorado	206.6
44	Connecticut	141.5
37	Delaware	164.0
8	Florida	269.7
32	Georgia	187.6
12	Hawaii	247.5
4	Idaho	317.6
23	Illinois	208.3
14	Indiana	242.3
33	Iowa	184.7
26	Kansas	204.2
43	Kentucky	142.8
20	Louisiana	212.3
49	Maine	100.7
46	Maryland	117.6
41	Massachusetts	146.0
27	Michigan	201.8
28	Minnesota	201.6
36	Mississippi	164.7
25	Missouri	204.5
29	Montana	198.6
34	Nebraska	181.4
1	Nevada	411.4
38	New Hampshire	160.6
19	New Jersey	217.1
40	New Mexico	151.7
17	New York	219.6
18	North Carolina	217.6
48	North Dakota	108.8
13	Ohio	247.2
15	Oklahoma	231.7
6	Oregon	284.9
21	Pennsylvania	211.0
8	Rhode Island	269.7
16	South Carolina	221.6
47	South Dakota	109.3
7	Tennessee	278.8
35	Texas	170.9
3	Utah	342.4
42	Vermont	144.2
30	Virginia	198.5
10	Washington	263.4
39	West Virginia	152.5
11	Wisconsin	253.6
45	Wyoming	120.8

RANK ORDER

RANK	STATE	RATIO
1	Nevada	411.4
2	Arizona	365.5
3	Utah	342.4
4	Idaho	317.6
5	California	301.2
6	Oregon	284.9
7	Tennessee	278.8
8	Florida	269.7
8	Rhode Island	269.7
10	Washington	263.4
11	Wisconsin	253.6
12	Hawaii	247.5
13	Ohio	247.2
14	Indiana	242.3
15	Oklahoma	231.7
16	South Carolina	221.6
17	New York	219.6
18	North Carolina	217.6
19	New Jersey	217.1
20	Louisiana	212.3
21	Pennsylvania	211.0
22	Alabama	209.1
23	Illinois	208.3
24	Colorado	206.6
25	Missouri	204.5
26	Kansas	204.2
27	Michigan	201.8
28	Minnesota	201.6
29	Montana	198.6
30	Virginia	198.5
31	Arkansas	194.4
32	Georgia	187.6
33	Iowa	184.7
34	Nebraska	181.4
35	Texas	170.9
36	Mississippi	164.7
37	Delaware	164.0
38	New Hampshire	160.6
39	West Virginia	152.5
40	New Mexico	151.7
41	Massachusetts	146.0
42	Vermont	144.2
43	Kentucky	142.8
44	Connecticut	141.5
45	Wyoming	120.8
46	Maryland	117.6
47	South Dakota	109.3
48	North Dakota	108.8
49	Maine	100.7
50	Alaska	85.5
	District of Columbia	101.4

Source: U.S. Department of Education, National Center for Education Statistics
"Public Elementary and Secondary School Student Enrollment and Staff" (http://nces.ed.gov/pubs2011/2011347.pdf)
*For school year 2009-2010. Ratios are based on full-time equivalent counts. Includes grades K-12.

Average Daily Attendance in Public Elementary and Secondary Schools in 2011

National Total = 46,700,381 Students*

ALPHA ORDER

RANK	STATE	STUDENTS	% of USA
23	Alabama	703,472	1.5%
44	Alaska	117,585	0.3%
13	Arizona	1,029,915	2.2%
35	Arkansas	365,075	0.8%
1	California	6,066,540	13.0%
21	Colorado	782,686	1.7%
28	Connecticut	574,120	1.2%
46	Delaware	114,683	0.2%
4	Florida	2,476,962	5.3%
8	Georgia	1,638,203	3.5%
42	Hawaii	163,105	0.3%
38	Idaho	267,099	0.6%
5	Illinois	1,984,594	4.2%
14	Indiana	992,304	2.1%
34	Iowa	434,039	0.9%
32	Kansas	454,449	1.0%
26	Kentucky	622,041	1.3%
25	Louisiana	638,034	1.4%
41	Maine	173,864	0.4%
19	Maryland	833,251	1.8%
16	Massachusetts	899,799	1.9%
9	Michigan	1,527,733	3.3%
22	Minnesota	766,845	1.6%
30	Mississippi	474,902	1.0%
17	Missouri	837,024	1.8%
47	Montana	113,470	0.2%
37	Nebraska	267,156	0.6%
31	Nevada	465,098	1.0%
40	New Hampshire	182,544	0.4%
10	New Jersey	1,431,418	3.1%
36	New Mexico	312,793	0.7%
3	New York	3,085,515	6.6%
11	North Carolina	1,298,190	2.8%
48	North Dakota	85,260	0.2%
7	Ohio	1,643,439	3.5%
27	Oklahoma	612,284	1.3%
29	Oregon	499,563	1.1%
6	Pennsylvania	1,681,858	3.6%
43	Rhode Island	117,999	0.3%
24	South Carolina	673,061	1.4%
45	South Dakota	116,884	0.3%
18	Tennessee	835,882	1.8%
2	Texas	4,485,884	9.6%
33	Utah	443,449	0.9%
50	Vermont	67,559	0.1%
12	Virginia	1,155,324	2.5%
15	Washington	974,870	2.1%
39	West Virginia	255,830	0.5%
20	Wisconsin	798,302	1.7%
49	Wyoming	82,214	0.2%

RANK ORDER

RANK	STATE	STUDENTS	% of USA
1	California	6,066,540	13.0%
2	Texas	4,485,884	9.6%
3	New York	3,085,515	6.6%
4	Florida	2,476,962	5.3%
5	Illinois	1,984,594	4.2%
6	Pennsylvania	1,681,858	3.6%
7	Ohio	1,643,439	3.5%
8	Georgia	1,638,203	3.5%
9	Michigan	1,527,733	3.3%
10	New Jersey	1,431,418	3.1%
11	North Carolina	1,298,190	2.8%
12	Virginia	1,155,324	2.5%
13	Arizona	1,029,915	2.2%
14	Indiana	992,304	2.1%
15	Washington	974,870	2.1%
16	Massachusetts	899,799	1.9%
17	Missouri	837,024	1.8%
18	Tennessee	835,882	1.8%
19	Maryland	833,251	1.8%
20	Wisconsin	798,302	1.7%
21	Colorado	782,686	1.7%
22	Minnesota	766,845	1.6%
23	Alabama	703,472	1.5%
24	South Carolina	673,061	1.4%
25	Louisiana	638,034	1.4%
26	Kentucky	622,041	1.3%
27	Oklahoma	612,284	1.3%
28	Connecticut	574,120	1.2%
29	Oregon	499,563	1.1%
30	Mississippi	474,902	1.0%
31	Nevada	465,098	1.0%
32	Kansas	454,449	1.0%
33	Utah	443,449	0.9%
34	Iowa	434,039	0.9%
35	Arkansas	365,075	0.8%
36	New Mexico	312,793	0.7%
37	Nebraska	267,156	0.6%
38	Idaho	267,099	0.6%
39	West Virginia	255,830	0.5%
40	New Hampshire	182,544	0.4%
41	Maine	173,864	0.4%
42	Hawaii	163,105	0.3%
43	Rhode Island	117,999	0.3%
44	Alaska	117,585	0.3%
45	South Dakota	116,884	0.3%
46	Delaware	114,683	0.2%
47	Montana	113,470	0.2%
48	North Dakota	85,260	0.2%
49	Wyoming	82,214	0.2%
50	Vermont	67,559	0.1%
	District of Columbia	76,210	0.2%

Source: National Education Association, Washington, D.C.
    "Rankings and Estimates" (Copyright © 2011, NEA, used with permission, http://www.nea.org/home/44479.htm)
*Estimates for school year 2010-2011.

Average Daily Attendance as a Percent of Fall Enrollment in Public Elementary and Secondary Schools in 2011
National Percent = 95.0%*

ALPHA ORDER

RANK	STATE	PERCENT
12	Alabama	94.9
41	Alaska	89.1
8	Arizona	96.1
48	Arkansas	79.5
6	California	97.5
29	Colorado	92.7
4	Connecticut	101.4
40	Delaware	89.2
14	Florida	94.5
7	Georgia	97.0
36	Hawaii	91.1
24	Idaho	93.6
21	Illinois	94.2
18	Indiana	94.4
43	Iowa	88.3
14	Kansas	94.5
14	Kentucky	94.5
37	Louisiana	90.9
28	Maine	92.8
5	Maryland	99.1
18	Massachusetts	94.4
34	Michigan	91.9
13	Minnesota	94.7
10	Mississippi	95.6
30	Missouri	92.6
47	Montana	80.7
39	Nebraska	89.8
3	Nevada	101.8
14	New Hampshire	94.5
2	New Jersey	104.8
9	New Mexico	95.7
1	New York	116.8
32	North Carolina	92.4
30	North Dakota	92.6
45	Ohio	85.9
25	Oklahoma	93.2
42	Oregon	88.5
11	Pennsylvania	95.3
46	Rhode Island	85.0
22	South Carolina	93.9
20	South Dakota	94.3
44	Tennessee	86.0
26	Texas	93.0
50	Utah	75.5
49	Vermont	78.9
33	Virginia	92.2
22	Washington	93.9
38	West Virginia	90.2
35	Wisconsin	91.6
26	Wyoming	93.0

RANK ORDER

RANK	STATE	PERCENT
1	New York	116.8
2	New Jersey	104.8
3	Nevada	101.8
4	Connecticut	101.4
5	Maryland	99.1
6	California	97.5
7	Georgia	97.0
8	Arizona	96.1
9	New Mexico	95.7
10	Mississippi	95.6
11	Pennsylvania	95.3
12	Alabama	94.9
13	Minnesota	94.7
14	Florida	94.5
14	Kansas	94.5
14	Kentucky	94.5
14	New Hampshire	94.5
18	Indiana	94.4
18	Massachusetts	94.4
20	South Dakota	94.3
21	Illinois	94.2
22	South Carolina	93.9
22	Washington	93.9
24	Idaho	93.6
25	Oklahoma	93.2
26	Texas	93.0
26	Wyoming	93.0
28	Maine	92.8
29	Colorado	92.7
30	Missouri	92.6
30	North Dakota	92.6
32	North Carolina	92.4
33	Virginia	92.2
34	Michigan	91.9
35	Wisconsin	91.6
36	Hawaii	91.1
37	Louisiana	90.9
38	West Virginia	90.2
39	Nebraska	89.8
40	Delaware	89.2
41	Alaska	89.1
42	Oregon	88.5
43	Iowa	88.3
44	Tennessee	86.0
45	Ohio	85.9
46	Rhode Island	85.0
47	Montana	80.7
48	Arkansas	79.5
49	Vermont	78.9
50	Utah	75.5
	District of Columbia	100.0

Source: National Education Association, Washington, D.C.
"Rankings and Estimates" (Copyright © 2011, NEA, used with permission, http://www.nea.org/home/44479.htm)
*Estimates for school year 2010-2011.

Students in Average Daily Attendance Per Teacher in Public Elementary and Secondary Schools in 2011
National Average = 14.4 Students*

ALPHA ORDER

RANK	STATE	STUDENTS
15	Alabama	14.8
33	Alaska	12.9
4	Arizona	17.7
49	Arkansas	9.9
1	California	20.5
9	Colorado	15.7
26	Connecticut	13.2
30	Delaware	13.1
12	Florida	15.2
25	Georgia	13.4
13	Hawaii	15.0
5	Idaho	17.0
20	Illinois	13.7
9	Indiana	15.7
40	Iowa	12.1
32	Kansas	13.0
14	Kentucky	14.9
26	Louisiana	13.2
48	Maine	10.1
21	Maryland	13.6
35	Massachusetts	12.8
8	Michigan	15.8
16	Minnesota	14.7
26	Mississippi	13.2
39	Missouri	12.2
46	Montana	10.7
41	Nebraska	12.0
2	Nevada	18.6
42	New Hampshire	11.7
38	New Jersey	12.4
17	New Mexico	14.3
19	New York	13.8
21	North Carolina	13.6
45	North Dakota	11.1
11	Ohio	15.3
18	Oklahoma	14.1
7	Oregon	16.0
26	Pennsylvania	13.2
42	Rhode Island	11.7
30	South Carolina	13.1
36	South Dakota	12.7
37	Tennessee	12.6
24	Texas	13.5
6	Utah	16.8
50	Vermont	7.6
46	Virginia	10.7
3	Washington	17.9
33	West Virginia	12.9
21	Wisconsin	13.6
44	Wyoming	11.4

RANK ORDER

RANK	STATE	STUDENTS
1	California	20.5
2	Nevada	18.6
3	Washington	17.9
4	Arizona	17.7
5	Idaho	17.0
6	Utah	16.8
7	Oregon	16.0
8	Michigan	15.8
9	Colorado	15.7
9	Indiana	15.7
11	Ohio	15.3
12	Florida	15.2
13	Hawaii	15.0
14	Kentucky	14.9
15	Alabama	14.8
16	Minnesota	14.7
17	New Mexico	14.3
18	Oklahoma	14.1
19	New York	13.8
20	Illinois	13.7
21	Maryland	13.6
21	North Carolina	13.6
21	Wisconsin	13.6
24	Texas	13.5
25	Georgia	13.4
26	Connecticut	13.2
26	Louisiana	13.2
26	Mississippi	13.2
26	Pennsylvania	13.2
30	Delaware	13.1
30	South Carolina	13.1
32	Kansas	13.0
33	Alaska	12.9
33	West Virginia	12.9
35	Massachusetts	12.8
36	South Dakota	12.7
37	Tennessee	12.6
38	New Jersey	12.4
39	Missouri	12.2
40	Iowa	12.1
41	Nebraska	12.0
42	New Hampshire	11.7
42	Rhode Island	11.7
44	Wyoming	11.4
45	North Dakota	11.1
46	Montana	10.7
46	Virginia	10.7
48	Maine	10.1
49	Arkansas	9.9
50	Vermont	7.6

| | District of Columbia | 13.1 |

Source: CQ Press using data from National Education Association, Washington, D.C.
   "Rankings and Estimates" (Copyright © 2011, NEA, used with permission, http://www.nea.org/home/44479.htm)
*Estimates for school year 2010-2011.

Students Attending Regular Public Elementary and Secondary Schools in 2010

National Total = 48,238,807 Students*

ALPHA ORDER

RANK	STATE	STUDENTS	% of USA
23	Alabama	744,895	1.5%
46	Alaska	117,598	0.2%
13	Arizona	1,060,293	2.2%
32	Arkansas	478,796	1.0%
1	California	5,975,132	12.4%
21	Colorado	814,926	1.7%
30	Connecticut	546,358	1.1%
47	Delaware	114,744	0.2%
4	Florida	2,570,257	5.3%
8	Georgia	1,656,245	3.4%
42	Hawaii	179,981	0.4%
39	Idaho	271,080	0.6%
5	Illinois	2,080,034	4.3%
14	Indiana	1,043,004	2.2%
33	Iowa	478,318	1.0%
34	Kansas	468,926	1.0%
25	Kentucky	669,531	1.4%
27	Louisiana	652,595	1.4%
41	Maine	184,180	0.4%
20	Maryland	827,977	1.7%
17	Massachusetts	913,332	1.9%
9	Michigan	1,549,893	3.2%
22	Minnesota	806,143	1.7%
31	Mississippi	492,279	1.0%
18	Missouri	905,503	1.9%
43	Montana	141,693	0.3%
37	Nebraska	294,792	0.6%
35	Nevada	422,124	0.9%
40	New Hampshire	197,140	0.4%
11	New Jersey	1,353,840	2.8%
36	New Mexico	327,362	0.7%
3	New York	2,729,395	5.7%
10	North Carolina	1,476,561	3.1%
48	North Dakota	93,032	0.2%
6	Ohio	1,754,349	3.6%
26	Oklahoma	653,603	1.4%
29	Oregon	548,032	1.1%
7	Pennsylvania	1,741,393	3.6%
44	Rhode Island	139,781	0.3%
24	South Carolina	721,466	1.5%
45	South Dakota	122,383	0.3%
16	Tennessee	967,003	2.0%
2	Texas	4,770,849	9.9%
28	Utah	569,093	1.2%
50	Vermont	86,118	0.2%
12	Virginia	1,241,919	2.6%
15	Washington	984,052	2.0%
38	West Virginia	281,537	0.6%
19	Wisconsin	866,214	1.8%
49	Wyoming	86,947	0.2%

RANK ORDER

RANK	STATE	STUDENTS	% of USA
1	California	5,975,132	12.4%
2	Texas	4,770,849	9.9%
3	New York	2,729,395	5.7%
4	Florida	2,570,257	5.3%
5	Illinois	2,080,034	4.3%
6	Ohio	1,754,349	3.6%
7	Pennsylvania	1,741,393	3.6%
8	Georgia	1,656,245	3.4%
9	Michigan	1,549,893	3.2%
10	North Carolina	1,476,561	3.1%
11	New Jersey	1,353,840	2.8%
12	Virginia	1,241,919	2.6%
13	Arizona	1,060,293	2.2%
14	Indiana	1,043,004	2.2%
15	Washington	984,052	2.0%
16	Tennessee	967,003	2.0%
17	Massachusetts	913,332	1.9%
18	Missouri	905,503	1.9%
19	Wisconsin	866,214	1.8%
20	Maryland	827,977	1.7%
21	Colorado	814,926	1.7%
22	Minnesota	806,143	1.7%
23	Alabama	744,895	1.5%
24	South Carolina	721,466	1.5%
25	Kentucky	669,531	1.4%
26	Oklahoma	653,603	1.4%
27	Louisiana	652,595	1.4%
28	Utah	569,093	1.2%
29	Oregon	548,032	1.1%
30	Connecticut	546,358	1.1%
31	Mississippi	492,279	1.0%
32	Arkansas	478,796	1.0%
33	Iowa	478,318	1.0%
34	Kansas	468,926	1.0%
35	Nevada	422,124	0.9%
36	New Mexico	327,362	0.7%
37	Nebraska	294,792	0.6%
38	West Virginia	281,537	0.6%
39	Idaho	271,080	0.6%
40	New Hampshire	197,140	0.4%
41	Maine	184,180	0.4%
42	Hawaii	179,981	0.4%
43	Montana	141,693	0.3%
44	Rhode Island	139,781	0.3%
45	South Dakota	122,383	0.3%
46	Alaska	117,598	0.2%
47	Delaware	114,744	0.2%
48	North Dakota	93,032	0.2%
49	Wyoming	86,947	0.2%
50	Vermont	86,118	0.2%
	District of Columbia	66,109	0.1%

Source: U.S. Department of Education, National Center for Education Statistics
"Numbers and Types of Public Elementary and Secondary Schools" (http://nces.ed.gov/pubs2011/2011345.pdf)
*For school year 2009-2010. Does not include special education, vocational education, or alternative education schools.
However, many regular schools include these programs.

Percent of Students Attending Regular
Public Elementary and Secondary Schools in 2010
National Percent = 98.2%*

ALPHA ORDER

RANK	STATE	PERCENT
17	Alabama	99.5
50	Alaska	89.3
31	Arizona	98.5
15	Arkansas	99.6
43	California	96.7
36	Colorado	98.0
42	Connecticut	96.9
49	Delaware	91.9
37	Florida	97.6
20	Georgia	99.3
6	Hawaii	99.9
35	Idaho	98.1
22	Illinois	99.2
13	Indiana	99.7
22	Iowa	99.2
6	Kansas	99.9
24	Kentucky	99.0
48	Louisiana	94.5
1	Maine	100.0
37	Maryland	97.6
46	Massachusetts	95.4
45	Michigan	95.8
44	Minnesota	96.3
1	Mississippi	100.0
28	Missouri	98.7
6	Montana	99.9
10	Nebraska	99.8
32	Nevada	98.4
1	New Hampshire	100.0
37	New Jersey	97.6
32	New Mexico	98.4
28	New York	98.7
6	North Carolina	99.9
1	North Dakota	100.0
17	Ohio	99.5
10	Oklahoma	99.8
24	Oregon	99.0
27	Pennsylvania	98.8
41	Rhode Island	97.3
10	South Carolina	99.8
26	South Dakota	98.9
19	Tennessee	99.4
32	Texas	98.4
37	Utah	97.6
1	Vermont	100.0
13	Virginia	99.7
47	Washington	95.0
15	West Virginia	99.6
20	Wisconsin	99.3
30	Wyoming	98.6

RANK ORDER

RANK	STATE	PERCENT
1	Maine	100.0
1	Mississippi	100.0
1	New Hampshire	100.0
1	North Dakota	100.0
1	Vermont	100.0
6	Hawaii	99.9
6	Kansas	99.9
6	Montana	99.9
6	North Carolina	99.9
10	Nebraska	99.8
10	Oklahoma	99.8
10	South Carolina	99.8
13	Indiana	99.7
13	Virginia	99.7
15	Arkansas	99.6
15	West Virginia	99.6
17	Alabama	99.5
17	Ohio	99.5
19	Tennessee	99.4
20	Georgia	99.3
20	Wisconsin	99.3
22	Illinois	99.2
22	Iowa	99.2
24	Kentucky	99.0
24	Oregon	99.0
26	South Dakota	98.9
27	Pennsylvania	98.8
28	Missouri	98.7
28	New York	98.7
30	Wyoming	98.6
31	Arizona	98.5
32	Nevada	98.4
32	New Mexico	98.4
32	Texas	98.4
35	Idaho	98.1
36	Colorado	98.0
37	Florida	97.6
37	Maryland	97.6
37	New Jersey	97.6
37	Utah	97.6
41	Rhode Island	97.3
42	Connecticut	96.9
43	California	96.7
44	Minnesota	96.3
45	Michigan	95.8
46	Massachusetts	95.4
47	Washington	95.0
48	Louisiana	94.5
49	Delaware	91.9
50	Alaska	89.3

	District of Columbia	95.5

Source: CQ Press using data from U.S. Department of Education, National Center for Education Statistics
"Numbers and Types of Public Elementary and Secondary Schools" (http://nces.ed.gov/pubs2011/2011345.pdf)
*For school year 2009-2010. Does not include special education, vocational education, or alternative education schools.
However, many regular schools include these programs.

Students Attending Public Elementary and Secondary
Title I Eligible Schools in 2010
National Total = 31,859,293 Students*

RANK	STATE	STUDENTS	% of USA
21	Alabama	454,301	1.4%
47	Alaska	69,966	0.2%
15	Arizona	649,074	2.0%
27	Arkansas	324,890	1.0%
1	California	3,748,045	11.8%
32	Colorado	241,229	0.8%
31	Connecticut	253,569	0.8%
45	Delaware	101,223	0.3%
4	Florida	1,876,355	5.9%
10	Georgia	997,571	3.1%
42	Hawaii	114,176	0.4%
35	Idaho	194,563	0.6%
5	Illinois	1,568,443	4.9%
13	Indiana	726,120	2.3%
29	Iowa	299,208	0.9%
24	Kansas	359,687	1.1%
17	Kentucky	564,883	1.8%
19	Louisiana	553,848	1.7%
38	Maine	150,925	0.5%
36	Maryland	178,305	0.6%
20	Massachusetts	503,449	1.6%
7	Michigan	1,281,414	4.0%
28	Minnesota	323,010	1.0%
25	Mississippi	342,900	1.1%
23	Missouri	368,750	1.2%
43	Montana	111,543	0.4%
39	Nebraska	136,040	0.4%
34	Nevada	217,086	0.7%
37	New Hampshire	161,939	0.5%
11	New Jersey	760,848	2.4%
30	New Mexico	290,574	0.9%
3	New York	2,448,874	7.7%
9	North Carolina	1,042,315	3.3%
49	North Dakota	48,220	0.2%
8	Ohio	1,274,888	4.0%
22	Oklahoma	410,996	1.3%
33	Oregon	225,041	0.7%
6	Pennsylvania	1,283,368	4.0%
41	Rhode Island	116,462	0.4%
16	South Carolina	588,616	1.8%
46	South Dakota	91,528	0.3%
12	Tennessee	752,613	2.4%
2	Texas	3,707,223	11.6%
40	Utah	131,444	0.4%
48	Vermont	63,603	0.2%
26	Virginia	330,062	1.0%
14	Washington	657,296	2.1%
44	West Virginia	106,954	0.3%
18	Wisconsin	561,921	1.8%
50	Wyoming	36,341	0.1%

RANK	STATE	STUDENTS	% of USA
1	California	3,748,045	11.8%
2	Texas	3,707,223	11.6%
3	New York	2,448,874	7.7%
4	Florida	1,876,355	5.9%
5	Illinois	1,568,443	4.9%
6	Pennsylvania	1,283,368	4.0%
7	Michigan	1,281,414	4.0%
8	Ohio	1,274,888	4.0%
9	North Carolina	1,042,315	3.3%
10	Georgia	997,571	3.1%
11	New Jersey	760,848	2.4%
12	Tennessee	752,613	2.4%
13	Indiana	726,120	2.3%
14	Washington	657,296	2.1%
15	Arizona	649,074	2.0%
16	South Carolina	588,616	1.8%
17	Kentucky	564,883	1.8%
18	Wisconsin	561,921	1.8%
19	Louisiana	553,848	1.7%
20	Massachusetts	503,449	1.6%
21	Alabama	454,301	1.4%
22	Oklahoma	410,996	1.3%
23	Missouri	368,750	1.2%
24	Kansas	359,687	1.1%
25	Mississippi	342,900	1.1%
26	Virginia	330,062	1.0%
27	Arkansas	324,890	1.0%
28	Minnesota	323,010	1.0%
29	Iowa	299,208	0.9%
30	New Mexico	290,574	0.9%
31	Connecticut	253,569	0.8%
32	Colorado	241,229	0.8%
33	Oregon	225,041	0.7%
34	Nevada	217,086	0.7%
35	Idaho	194,563	0.6%
36	Maryland	178,305	0.6%
37	New Hampshire	161,939	0.5%
38	Maine	150,925	0.5%
39	Nebraska	136,040	0.4%
40	Utah	131,444	0.4%
41	Rhode Island	116,462	0.4%
42	Hawaii	114,176	0.4%
43	Montana	111,543	0.4%
44	West Virginia	106,954	0.3%
45	Delaware	101,223	0.3%
46	South Dakota	91,528	0.3%
47	Alaska	69,966	0.2%
48	Vermont	63,603	0.2%
49	North Dakota	48,220	0.2%
50	Wyoming	36,341	0.1%
	District of Columbia	57,594	0.2%

Source: U.S. Department of Education, National Center for Education Statistics
 "Numbers and Types of Public Elementary and Secondary Schools" (http://nces.ed.gov/pubs2011/2011345.pdf)
*Estimate for school year 2009-2010. Title I schools are eligible for Title I federal funding to assist disadvantaged students.
Includes schools with and without school-wide Title I programs.

Percent of Students Attending Public Elementary and Secondary Title I Eligible Schools in 2010
National Percent = 64.8%*

<table>
<tr><td colspan="3">ALPHA ORDER</td><td colspan="3">RANK ORDER</td></tr>
<tr><td>RANK</td><td>STATE</td><td>PERCENT</td><td>RANK</td><td>STATE</td><td>PERCENT</td></tr>
<tr><td>31</td><td>Alabama</td><td>60.7</td><td>1</td><td>New York</td><td>88.5</td></tr>
<tr><td>36</td><td>Alaska</td><td>53.1</td><td>2</td><td>New Mexico</td><td>87.4</td></tr>
<tr><td>33</td><td>Arizona</td><td>60.3</td><td>3</td><td>Kentucky</td><td>83.5</td></tr>
<tr><td>25</td><td>Arkansas</td><td>67.6</td><td>4</td><td>New Hampshire</td><td>82.1</td></tr>
<tr><td>31</td><td>California</td><td>60.7</td><td>5</td><td>Maine</td><td>81.9</td></tr>
<tr><td>47</td><td>Colorado</td><td>29.0</td><td>6</td><td>South Carolina</td><td>81.4</td></tr>
<tr><td>41</td><td>Connecticut</td><td>45.0</td><td>7</td><td>Delaware</td><td>81.1</td></tr>
<tr><td>7</td><td>Delaware</td><td>81.1</td><td>7</td><td>Rhode Island</td><td>81.1</td></tr>
<tr><td>20</td><td>Florida</td><td>71.2</td><td>9</td><td>Louisiana</td><td>80.2</td></tr>
<tr><td>34</td><td>Georgia</td><td>59.8</td><td>10</td><td>Michigan</td><td>79.2</td></tr>
<tr><td>28</td><td>Hawaii</td><td>63.4</td><td>11</td><td>Montana</td><td>78.7</td></tr>
<tr><td>22</td><td>Idaho</td><td>70.4</td><td>12</td><td>Tennessee</td><td>77.4</td></tr>
<tr><td>15</td><td>Illinois</td><td>74.8</td><td>13</td><td>Kansas</td><td>76.6</td></tr>
<tr><td>24</td><td>Indiana</td><td>69.4</td><td>14</td><td>Texas</td><td>76.4</td></tr>
<tr><td>30</td><td>Iowa</td><td>62.1</td><td>15</td><td>Illinois</td><td>74.8</td></tr>
<tr><td>13</td><td>Kansas</td><td>76.6</td><td>16</td><td>South Dakota</td><td>74.0</td></tr>
<tr><td>3</td><td>Kentucky</td><td>83.5</td><td>17</td><td>Vermont</td><td>73.8</td></tr>
<tr><td>9</td><td>Louisiana</td><td>80.2</td><td>18</td><td>Pennsylvania</td><td>72.8</td></tr>
<tr><td>5</td><td>Maine</td><td>81.9</td><td>19</td><td>Ohio</td><td>72.3</td></tr>
<tr><td>50</td><td>Maryland</td><td>21.0</td><td>20</td><td>Florida</td><td>71.2</td></tr>
<tr><td>37</td><td>Massachusetts</td><td>52.6</td><td>21</td><td>North Carolina</td><td>70.6</td></tr>
<tr><td>10</td><td>Michigan</td><td>79.2</td><td>22</td><td>Idaho</td><td>70.4</td></tr>
<tr><td>45</td><td>Minnesota</td><td>38.6</td><td>23</td><td>Mississippi</td><td>69.6</td></tr>
<tr><td>23</td><td>Mississippi</td><td>69.6</td><td>24</td><td>Indiana</td><td>69.4</td></tr>
<tr><td>44</td><td>Missouri</td><td>40.2</td><td>25</td><td>Arkansas</td><td>67.6</td></tr>
<tr><td>11</td><td>Montana</td><td>78.7</td><td>26</td><td>Wisconsin</td><td>64.4</td></tr>
<tr><td>40</td><td>Nebraska</td><td>46.1</td><td>27</td><td>Washington</td><td>63.5</td></tr>
<tr><td>39</td><td>Nevada</td><td>50.6</td><td>28</td><td>Hawaii</td><td>63.4</td></tr>
<tr><td>4</td><td>New Hampshire</td><td>82.1</td><td>29</td><td>Oklahoma</td><td>62.8</td></tr>
<tr><td>35</td><td>New Jersey</td><td>54.9</td><td>30</td><td>Iowa</td><td>62.1</td></tr>
<tr><td>2</td><td>New Mexico</td><td>87.4</td><td>31</td><td>Alabama</td><td>60.7</td></tr>
<tr><td>1</td><td>New York</td><td>88.5</td><td>31</td><td>California</td><td>60.7</td></tr>
<tr><td>21</td><td>North Carolina</td><td>70.6</td><td>33</td><td>Arizona</td><td>60.3</td></tr>
<tr><td>38</td><td>North Dakota</td><td>51.8</td><td>34</td><td>Georgia</td><td>59.8</td></tr>
<tr><td>19</td><td>Ohio</td><td>72.3</td><td>35</td><td>New Jersey</td><td>54.9</td></tr>
<tr><td>29</td><td>Oklahoma</td><td>62.8</td><td>36</td><td>Alaska</td><td>53.1</td></tr>
<tr><td>43</td><td>Oregon</td><td>40.6</td><td>37</td><td>Massachusetts</td><td>52.6</td></tr>
<tr><td>18</td><td>Pennsylvania</td><td>72.8</td><td>38</td><td>North Dakota</td><td>51.8</td></tr>
<tr><td>7</td><td>Rhode Island</td><td>81.1</td><td>39</td><td>Nevada</td><td>50.6</td></tr>
<tr><td>6</td><td>South Carolina</td><td>81.4</td><td>40</td><td>Nebraska</td><td>46.1</td></tr>
<tr><td>16</td><td>South Dakota</td><td>74.0</td><td>41</td><td>Connecticut</td><td>45.0</td></tr>
<tr><td>12</td><td>Tennessee</td><td>77.4</td><td>42</td><td>Wyoming</td><td>41.2</td></tr>
<tr><td>14</td><td>Texas</td><td>76.4</td><td>43</td><td>Oregon</td><td>40.6</td></tr>
<tr><td>49</td><td>Utah</td><td>22.6</td><td>44</td><td>Missouri</td><td>40.2</td></tr>
<tr><td>17</td><td>Vermont</td><td>73.8</td><td>45</td><td>Minnesota</td><td>38.6</td></tr>
<tr><td>48</td><td>Virginia</td><td>26.5</td><td>46</td><td>West Virginia</td><td>37.8</td></tr>
<tr><td>27</td><td>Washington</td><td>63.5</td><td>47</td><td>Colorado</td><td>29.0</td></tr>
<tr><td>46</td><td>West Virginia</td><td>37.8</td><td>48</td><td>Virginia</td><td>26.5</td></tr>
<tr><td>26</td><td>Wisconsin</td><td>64.4</td><td>49</td><td>Utah</td><td>22.6</td></tr>
<tr><td>42</td><td>Wyoming</td><td>41.2</td><td>50</td><td>Maryland</td><td>21.0</td></tr>
<tr><td></td><td></td><td></td><td></td><td>District of Columbia</td><td>83.2</td></tr>
</table>

Source: CQ Press using data from U.S. Department of Education, National Center for Education Statistics
"Numbers and Types of Public Elementary and Secondary Schools" (http://nces.ed.gov/pubs2011/2011345.pdf)
*Estimate for school year 2009-2010. Title I schools are eligible for Title I federal funding to assist disadvantaged students. Includes schools with and without school-wide Title I programs.

Students Attending Title I School-Wide
Public Elementary and Secondary Schools in 2010
National Total = 22,266,028 Students*

ALPHA ORDER

RANK	STATE	STUDENTS	% of USA
18	Alabama	436,081	2.0%
45	Alaska	54,531	0.2%
15	Arizona	505,441	2.3%
21	Arkansas	273,875	1.2%
2	California	2,834,898	12.7%
29	Colorado	174,339	0.8%
40	Connecticut	89,038	0.4%
41	Delaware	86,610	0.4%
3	Florida	1,676,830	7.5%
7	Georgia	801,719	3.6%
36	Hawaii	101,822	0.5%
32	Idaho	166,437	0.7%
8	Illinois	714,108	3.2%
16	Indiana	489,621	2.2%
30	Iowa	172,991	0.8%
24	Kansas	237,724	1.1%
13	Kentucky	515,574	2.3%
14	Louisiana	513,311	2.3%
37	Maine	98,805	0.4%
34	Maryland	132,559	0.6%
23	Massachusetts	245,079	1.1%
11	Michigan	657,309	3.0%
39	Minnesota	89,976	0.4%
20	Mississippi	330,899	1.5%
31	Missouri	166,518	0.7%
43	Montana	62,854	0.3%
42	Nebraska	72,394	0.3%
26	Nevada	187,839	0.8%
48	New Hampshire	32,360	0.1%
25	New Jersey	223,683	1.0%
22	New Mexico	271,965	1.2%
4	New York	954,436	4.3%
5	North Carolina	915,597	4.1%
50	North Dakota	13,140	0.1%
6	Ohio	830,916	3.7%
19	Oklahoma	338,787	1.5%
33	Oregon	160,033	0.7%
10	Pennsylvania	671,011	3.0%
44	Rhode Island	54,887	0.2%
12	South Carolina	527,887	2.4%
47	South Dakota	42,416	0.2%
9	Tennessee	686,628	3.1%
1	Texas	3,509,130	15.8%
38	Utah	93,341	0.4%
46	Vermont	45,990	0.2%
28	Virginia	178,971	0.8%
17	Washington	457,388	2.1%
35	West Virginia	106,656	0.5%
27	Wisconsin	187,342	0.8%
49	Wyoming	17,907	0.1%

RANK ORDER

RANK	STATE	STUDENTS	% of USA
1	Texas	3,509,130	15.8%
2	California	2,834,898	12.7%
3	Florida	1,676,830	7.5%
4	New York	954,436	4.3%
5	North Carolina	915,597	4.1%
6	Ohio	830,916	3.7%
7	Georgia	801,719	3.6%
8	Illinois	714,108	3.2%
9	Tennessee	686,628	3.1%
10	Pennsylvania	671,011	3.0%
11	Michigan	657,309	3.0%
12	South Carolina	527,887	2.4%
13	Kentucky	515,574	2.3%
14	Louisiana	513,311	2.3%
15	Arizona	505,441	2.3%
16	Indiana	489,621	2.2%
17	Washington	457,388	2.1%
18	Alabama	436,081	2.0%
19	Oklahoma	338,787	1.5%
20	Mississippi	330,899	1.5%
21	Arkansas	273,875	1.2%
22	New Mexico	271,965	1.2%
23	Massachusetts	245,079	1.1%
24	Kansas	237,724	1.1%
25	New Jersey	223,683	1.0%
26	Nevada	187,839	0.8%
27	Wisconsin	187,342	0.8%
28	Virginia	178,971	0.8%
29	Colorado	174,339	0.8%
30	Iowa	172,991	0.8%
31	Missouri	166,518	0.7%
32	Idaho	166,437	0.7%
33	Oregon	160,033	0.7%
34	Maryland	132,559	0.6%
35	West Virginia	106,656	0.5%
36	Hawaii	101,822	0.5%
37	Maine	98,805	0.4%
38	Utah	93,341	0.4%
39	Minnesota	89,976	0.4%
40	Connecticut	89,038	0.4%
41	Delaware	86,610	0.4%
42	Nebraska	72,394	0.3%
43	Montana	62,854	0.3%
44	Rhode Island	54,887	0.2%
45	Alaska	54,531	0.2%
46	Vermont	45,990	0.2%
47	South Dakota	42,416	0.2%
48	New Hampshire	32,360	0.1%
49	Wyoming	17,907	0.1%
50	North Dakota	13,140	0.1%
	District of Columbia	56,375	0.3%

Source: U.S. Department of Education, National Center for Education Statistics
"Numbers and Types of Public Elementary and Secondary Schools" (http://nces.ed.gov/pubs2011/2011345.pdf)
*Estimate for school year 2009-2010. Title I school-wide schools are those in which all of the pupils enrolled are eligible for Title I federal funding, which assists disadvantaged students.

Percent of Students Attending Title I School-Wide
Public Elementary and Secondary Schools in 2010
National Percent = 45.3%*

ALPHA ORDER

ALPHA ORDER

RANK ORDER

RANK	STATE	PERCENT		RANK	STATE	PERCENT
12	Alabama	58.2		1	New Mexico	81.8
27	Alaska	41.4		2	Kentucky	76.2
21	Arizona	47.0		3	Louisiana	74.3
13	Arkansas	57.0		4	South Carolina	73.0
23	California	45.9		5	Texas	72.4
40	Colorado	21.0		6	Tennessee	70.6
46	Connecticut	15.8		7	Delaware	69.4
7	Delaware	69.4		8	Mississippi	67.2
9	Florida	63.6		9	Florida	63.6
19	Georgia	48.1		10	North Carolina	62.0
14	Hawaii	56.5		11	Idaho	60.2
11	Idaho	60.2		12	Alabama	58.2
35	Illinois	34.1		13	Arkansas	57.0
22	Indiana	46.8		14	Hawaii	56.5
32	Iowa	35.9		15	Maine	53.6
18	Kansas	50.7		16	Vermont	53.4
2	Kentucky	76.2		17	Oklahoma	51.7
3	Louisiana	74.3		18	Kansas	50.7
15	Maine	53.6		19	Georgia	48.1
47	Maryland	15.6		20	Ohio	47.1
37	Massachusetts	25.6		21	Arizona	47.0
28	Michigan	40.6		22	Indiana	46.8
50	Minnesota	10.8		23	California	45.9
8	Mississippi	67.2		24	Montana	44.3
42	Missouri	18.2		25	Washington	44.2
24	Montana	44.3		26	Nevada	43.8
38	Nebraska	24.5		27	Alaska	41.4
26	Nevada	43.8		28	Michigan	40.6
43	New Hampshire	16.4		29	Rhode Island	38.2
44	New Jersey	16.1		30	Pennsylvania	38.1
1	New Mexico	81.8		31	West Virginia	37.7
33	New York	34.5		32	Iowa	35.9
10	North Carolina	62.0		33	New York	34.5
49	North Dakota	14.1		34	South Dakota	34.3
20	Ohio	47.1		35	Illinois	34.1
17	Oklahoma	51.7		36	Oregon	28.9
36	Oregon	28.9		37	Massachusetts	25.6
30	Pennsylvania	38.1		38	Nebraska	24.5
29	Rhode Island	38.2		39	Wisconsin	21.5
4	South Carolina	73.0		40	Colorado	21.0
34	South Dakota	34.3		41	Wyoming	20.3
6	Tennessee	70.6		42	Missouri	18.2
5	Texas	72.4		43	New Hampshire	16.4
45	Utah	16.0		44	New Jersey	16.1
16	Vermont	53.4		45	Utah	16.0
48	Virginia	14.4		46	Connecticut	15.8
25	Washington	44.2		47	Maryland	15.6
31	West Virginia	37.7		48	Virginia	14.4
39	Wisconsin	21.5		49	North Dakota	14.1
41	Wyoming	20.3		50	Minnesota	10.8

District of Columbia 81.4

Source: CQ Press using data from U.S. Department of Education, National Center for Education Statistics
"Numbers and Types of Public Elementary and Secondary Schools" (http://nces.ed.gov/pubs2011/2011345.pdf)
*Estimate for school year 2009-2010. Title I school-wide schools are those in which all of the pupils enrolled are eligible for Title I federal funding, which assists disadvantaged students.

Public Elementary and Secondary School Students Eligible for Free or Reduced-Price Meals in 2010
National Total = 22,423,407 Students*

	ALPHA ORDER					RANK ORDER		
RANK	STATE	STUDENTS	% of USA		RANK	STATE	STUDENTS	% of USA
18	Alabama	411,067	1.8%		1	California	3,393,827	15.1%
45	Alaska	47,678	0.2%		2	Texas	2,450,265	10.9%
12	Arizona	501,403	2.2%		3	Florida	1,408,677	6.3%
29	Arkansas	286,477	1.3%		4	Georgia	934,899	4.2%
1	California	3,393,827	15.1%		5	Illinois	901,912	4.0%
26	Colorado	319,404	1.4%		6	Michigan	742,138	3.3%
36	Connecticut	179,586	0.8%		7	North Carolina	720,798	3.2%
43	Delaware	58,375	0.3%		8	Ohio	710,381	3.2%
3	Florida	1,408,677	6.3%		9	Pennsylvania	663,132	3.0%
4	Georgia	934,899	4.2%		10	New York	569,659	2.5%
40	Hawaii	77,947	0.3%		11	Tennessee	516,176	2.3%
39	Idaho	118,932	0.5%		12	Arizona	501,403	2.2%
5	Illinois	901,912	4.0%		13	Indiana	474,326	2.1%
13	Indiana	474,326	2.1%		14	Louisiana	454,338	2.0%
35	Iowa	179,921	0.8%		15	New Jersey	445,174	2.0%
33	Kansas	214,437	1.0%		16	Virginia	444,715	2.0%
22	Kentucky	370,264	1.7%		17	Washington	428,263	1.9%
14	Louisiana	454,338	2.0%		18	Alabama	411,067	1.8%
41	Maine	76,715	0.3%		19	Missouri	401,947	1.8%
24	Maryland	324,904	1.4%		20	South Carolina	394,018	1.8%
27	Massachusetts	315,153	1.4%		21	Oklahoma	384,448	1.7%
6	Michigan	742,138	3.3%		22	Kentucky	370,264	1.7%
28	Minnesota	296,756	1.3%		23	Mississippi	348,050	1.6%
23	Mississippi	348,050	1.6%		24	Maryland	324,904	1.4%
19	Missouri	401,947	1.8%		25	Wisconsin	323,634	1.4%
44	Montana	56,201	0.3%		26	Colorado	319,404	1.4%
38	Nebraska	121,915	0.5%		27	Massachusetts	315,153	1.4%
34	Nevada	181,688	0.8%		28	Minnesota	296,756	1.3%
46	New Hampshire	46,246	0.2%		29	Arkansas	286,477	1.3%
15	New Jersey	445,174	2.0%		30	Oregon	272,196	1.2%
32	New Mexico	218,130	1.0%		31	Utah	244,458	1.1%
10	New York	569,659	2.5%		32	New Mexico	218,130	1.0%
7	North Carolina	720,798	3.2%		33	Kansas	214,437	1.0%
49	North Dakota	30,693	0.1%		34	Nevada	181,688	0.8%
8	Ohio	710,381	3.2%		35	Iowa	179,921	0.8%
21	Oklahoma	384,448	1.7%		36	Connecticut	179,586	0.8%
30	Oregon	272,196	1.2%		37	West Virginia	147,036	0.7%
9	Pennsylvania	663,132	3.0%		38	Nebraska	121,915	0.5%
42	Rhode Island	60,179	0.3%		39	Idaho	118,932	0.5%
20	South Carolina	394,018	1.8%		40	Hawaii	77,947	0.3%
47	South Dakota	45,956	0.2%		41	Maine	76,715	0.3%
11	Tennessee	516,176	2.3%		42	Rhode Island	60,179	0.3%
2	Texas	2,450,265	10.9%		43	Delaware	58,375	0.3%
31	Utah	244,458	1.1%		44	Montana	56,201	0.3%
50	Vermont	29,529	0.1%		45	Alaska	47,678	0.2%
16	Virginia	444,715	2.0%		46	New Hampshire	46,246	0.2%
17	Washington	428,263	1.9%		47	South Dakota	45,956	0.2%
37	West Virginia	147,036	0.7%		48	Wyoming	31,054	0.1%
25	Wisconsin	323,634	1.4%		49	North Dakota	30,693	0.1%
48	Wyoming	31,054	0.1%		50	Vermont	29,529	0.1%
						District of Columbia	48,330	0.2%

Source: U.S. Department of Education, National Center for Education Statistics
"Common Core of Data (CCD) Database" (http://nces.ed.gov/ccd/)
*For school year 2009-2010.

Percent of Public Elementary and Secondary School Students Eligible for Free or Reduced-Price Meals in 2010
National Percent = 45.6%*

ALPHA ORDER

RANK	STATE	PERCENT
7	Alabama	54.9
40	Alaska	36.2
18	Arizona	46.6
4	Arkansas	59.6
7	California	54.9
34	Colorado	38.4
48	Connecticut	31.9
17	Delaware	46.8
11	Florida	53.5
6	Georgia	56.1
23	Hawaii	43.3
24	Idaho	43.0
24	Illinois	43.0
21	Indiana	45.3
37	Iowa	37.3
20	Kansas	45.7
9	Kentucky	54.7
2	Louisiana	65.8
29	Maine	41.6
35	Maryland	38.3
46	Massachusetts	32.9
19	Michigan	45.9
42	Minnesota	35.5
1	Mississippi	70.7
22	Missouri	43.8
33	Montana	39.6
31	Nebraska	41.3
26	Nevada	42.4
49	New Hampshire	23.5
47	New Jersey	32.1
3	New Mexico	65.6
50	New York	20.6
16	North Carolina	48.8
45	North Dakota	33.0
32	Ohio	40.3
5	Oklahoma	58.7
15	Oregon	49.1
36	Pennsylvania	37.6
27	Rhode Island	41.9
10	South Carolina	54.5
38	South Dakota	37.1
12	Tennessee	53.1
14	Texas	50.5
27	Utah	41.9
44	Vermont	34.3
41	Virginia	35.7
30	Washington	41.4
13	West Virginia	52.0
38	Wisconsin	37.1
43	Wyoming	35.2

RANK ORDER

RANK	STATE	PERCENT
1	Mississippi	70.7
2	Louisiana	65.8
3	New Mexico	65.6
4	Arkansas	59.6
5	Oklahoma	58.7
6	Georgia	56.1
7	Alabama	54.9
7	California	54.9
9	Kentucky	54.7
10	South Carolina	54.5
11	Florida	53.5
12	Tennessee	53.1
13	West Virginia	52.0
14	Texas	50.5
15	Oregon	49.1
16	North Carolina	48.8
17	Delaware	46.8
18	Arizona	46.6
19	Michigan	45.9
20	Kansas	45.7
21	Indiana	45.3
22	Missouri	43.8
23	Hawaii	43.3
24	Idaho	43.0
24	Illinois	43.0
26	Nevada	42.4
27	Rhode Island	41.9
27	Utah	41.9
29	Maine	41.6
30	Washington	41.4
31	Nebraska	41.3
32	Ohio	40.3
33	Montana	39.6
34	Colorado	38.4
35	Maryland	38.3
36	Pennsylvania	37.6
37	Iowa	37.3
38	South Dakota	37.1
38	Wisconsin	37.1
40	Alaska	36.2
41	Virginia	35.7
42	Minnesota	35.5
43	Wyoming	35.2
44	Vermont	34.3
45	North Dakota	33.0
46	Massachusetts	32.9
47	New Jersey	32.1
48	Connecticut	31.9
49	New Hampshire	23.5
50	New York	20.6

District of Columbia	69.8

Source: CQ Press using data from U.S. Department of Education, National Center for Education Statistics
"Common Core of Data (CCD) Database" (http://nces.ed.gov/ccd/)
*For school year 2009-2010.

Students Attending Public Elementary and Secondary Magnet Schools in 2010

Reporting States Total = 1,516,392 Students*

ALPHA ORDER

RANK	STATE	STUDENTS	% of USA
17	Alabama	14,792	1.0%
23	Alaska	4,288	0.3%
NA	Arizona**	NA	NA
13	Arkansas	23,286	1.5%
NA	California**	NA	NA
21	Colorado	10,090	0.7%
14	Connecticut	21,126	1.4%
24	Delaware	1,920	0.1%
1	Florida	377,367	24.9%
7	Georgia	74,063	4.9%
NA	Hawaii**	NA	NA
26	Idaho	1,224	0.1%
6	Illinois	75,685	5.0%
19	Indiana	12,745	0.8%
NA	Iowa**	NA	NA
18	Kansas	14,108	0.9%
9	Kentucky	38,384	2.5%
8	Louisiana	47,064	3.1%
28	Maine	132	0.0%
5	Maryland	75,877	5.0%
NA	Massachusetts**	NA	NA
2	Michigan	218,989	14.4%
10	Minnesota	36,667	2.4%
22	Mississippi	4,441	0.3%
16	Missouri	16,013	1.1%
NA	Montana**	NA	NA
NA	Nebraska**	NA	NA
11	Nevada	34,727	2.3%
NA	New Hampshire**	NA	NA
NA	New Jersey**	NA	NA
29	New Mexico	18	0.0%
NA	New York**	NA	NA
4	North Carolina	89,562	5.9%
NA	North Dakota**	NA	NA
NA	Ohio**	NA	NA
NA	Oklahoma**	NA	NA
NA	Oregon**	NA	NA
12	Pennsylvania	26,945	1.8%
NA	Rhode Island**	NA	NA
NA	South Carolina**	NA	NA
NA	South Dakota**	NA	NA
15	Tennessee	17,899	1.2%
NA	Texas**	NA	NA
20	Utah	11,004	0.7%
27	Vermont	431	0.0%
3	Virginia	151,625	10.0%
NA	Washington**	NA	NA
NA	West Virginia**	NA	NA
25	Wisconsin	1,581	0.1%
NA	Wyoming**	NA	NA

RANK ORDER

RANK	STATE	STUDENTS	% of USA
1	Florida	377,367	24.9%
2	Michigan	218,989	14.4%
3	Virginia	151,625	10.0%
4	North Carolina	89,562	5.9%
5	Maryland	75,877	5.0%
6	Illinois	75,685	5.0%
7	Georgia	74,063	4.9%
8	Louisiana	47,064	3.1%
9	Kentucky	38,384	2.5%
10	Minnesota	36,667	2.4%
11	Nevada	34,727	2.3%
12	Pennsylvania	26,945	1.8%
13	Arkansas	23,286	1.5%
14	Connecticut	21,126	1.4%
15	Tennessee	17,899	1.2%
16	Missouri	16,013	1.1%
17	Alabama	14,792	1.0%
18	Kansas	14,108	0.9%
19	Indiana	12,745	0.8%
20	Utah	11,004	0.7%
21	Colorado	10,090	0.7%
22	Mississippi	4,441	0.3%
23	Alaska	4,288	0.3%
24	Delaware	1,920	0.1%
25	Wisconsin	1,581	0.1%
26	Idaho	1,224	0.1%
27	Vermont	431	0.0%
28	Maine	132	0.0%
29	New Mexico	18	0.0%
NA	Arizona**	NA	NA
NA	California**	NA	NA
NA	Hawaii**	NA	NA
NA	Iowa**	NA	NA
NA	Massachusetts**	NA	NA
NA	Montana**	NA	NA
NA	Nebraska**	NA	NA
NA	New Hampshire**	NA	NA
NA	New Jersey**	NA	NA
NA	New York**	NA	NA
NA	North Dakota**	NA	NA
NA	Ohio**	NA	NA
NA	Oklahoma**	NA	NA
NA	Oregon**	NA	NA
NA	Rhode Island**	NA	NA
NA	South Carolina**	NA	NA
NA	South Dakota**	NA	NA
NA	Texas**	NA	NA
NA	Washington**	NA	NA
NA	West Virginia**	NA	NA
NA	Wyoming**	NA	NA
	District of Columbia	2,269	0.1%

Source: U.S. Department of Education, National Center for Education Statistics
"Numbers and Types of Public Elementary and Secondary Schools" (http://nces.ed.gov/pubs2011/2011345.pdf)
*For school year 2009-2010.
**Either no magnet schools designated or not available.

Percent of Students Attending Public Elementary and Secondary Magnet Schools in 2010
Reporting States Percent = 3.1%*

<table>
<tr><th colspan="3">ALPHA ORDER</th><th colspan="3">RANK ORDER</th></tr>
<tr><th>RANK</th><th>STATE</th><th>PERCENT</th><th>RANK</th><th>STATE</th><th>PERCENT</th></tr>
<tr><td>16</td><td>Alabama</td><td>2.0</td><td>1</td><td>Florida</td><td>14.3</td></tr>
<tr><td>14</td><td>Alaska</td><td>3.3</td><td>2</td><td>Michigan</td><td>13.5</td></tr>
<tr><td>NA</td><td>Arizona**</td><td>NA</td><td>3</td><td>Virginia</td><td>12.2</td></tr>
<tr><td>9</td><td>Arkansas</td><td>4.8</td><td>4</td><td>Maryland</td><td>8.9</td></tr>
<tr><td>NA</td><td>California**</td><td>NA</td><td>5</td><td>Nevada</td><td>8.1</td></tr>
<tr><td>22</td><td>Colorado</td><td>1.2</td><td>6</td><td>Louisiana</td><td>6.8</td></tr>
<tr><td>12</td><td>Connecticut</td><td>3.7</td><td>7</td><td>North Carolina</td><td>6.1</td></tr>
<tr><td>20</td><td>Delaware</td><td>1.5</td><td>8</td><td>Kentucky</td><td>5.7</td></tr>
<tr><td>1</td><td>Florida</td><td>14.3</td><td>9</td><td>Arkansas</td><td>4.8</td></tr>
<tr><td>10</td><td>Georgia</td><td>4.4</td><td>10</td><td>Georgia</td><td>4.4</td></tr>
<tr><td>NA</td><td>Hawaii**</td><td>NA</td><td>10</td><td>Minnesota</td><td>4.4</td></tr>
<tr><td>26</td><td>Idaho</td><td>0.4</td><td>12</td><td>Connecticut</td><td>3.7</td></tr>
<tr><td>13</td><td>Illinois</td><td>3.6</td><td>13</td><td>Illinois</td><td>3.6</td></tr>
<tr><td>22</td><td>Indiana</td><td>1.2</td><td>14</td><td>Alaska</td><td>3.3</td></tr>
<tr><td>NA</td><td>Iowa**</td><td>NA</td><td>15</td><td>Kansas</td><td>3.0</td></tr>
<tr><td>15</td><td>Kansas</td><td>3.0</td><td>16</td><td>Alabama</td><td>2.0</td></tr>
<tr><td>8</td><td>Kentucky</td><td>5.7</td><td>17</td><td>Utah</td><td>1.9</td></tr>
<tr><td>6</td><td>Louisiana</td><td>6.8</td><td>18</td><td>Tennessee</td><td>1.8</td></tr>
<tr><td>28</td><td>Maine</td><td>0.1</td><td>19</td><td>Missouri</td><td>1.7</td></tr>
<tr><td>4</td><td>Maryland</td><td>8.9</td><td>20</td><td>Delaware</td><td>1.5</td></tr>
<tr><td>NA</td><td>Massachusetts**</td><td>NA</td><td>20</td><td>Pennsylvania</td><td>1.5</td></tr>
<tr><td>2</td><td>Michigan</td><td>13.5</td><td>22</td><td>Colorado</td><td>1.2</td></tr>
<tr><td>10</td><td>Minnesota</td><td>4.4</td><td>22</td><td>Indiana</td><td>1.2</td></tr>
<tr><td>24</td><td>Mississippi</td><td>0.9</td><td>24</td><td>Mississippi</td><td>0.9</td></tr>
<tr><td>19</td><td>Missouri</td><td>1.7</td><td>25</td><td>Vermont</td><td>0.5</td></tr>
<tr><td>NA</td><td>Montana**</td><td>NA</td><td>26</td><td>Idaho</td><td>0.4</td></tr>
<tr><td>NA</td><td>Nebraska**</td><td>NA</td><td>27</td><td>Wisconsin</td><td>0.2</td></tr>
<tr><td>5</td><td>Nevada</td><td>8.1</td><td>28</td><td>Maine</td><td>0.1</td></tr>
<tr><td>NA</td><td>New Hampshire**</td><td>NA</td><td>29</td><td>New Mexico</td><td>0.0</td></tr>
<tr><td>NA</td><td>New Jersey**</td><td>NA</td><td>NA</td><td>Arizona**</td><td>NA</td></tr>
<tr><td>29</td><td>New Mexico</td><td>0.0</td><td>NA</td><td>California**</td><td>NA</td></tr>
<tr><td>NA</td><td>New York**</td><td>NA</td><td>NA</td><td>Hawaii**</td><td>NA</td></tr>
<tr><td>7</td><td>North Carolina</td><td>6.1</td><td>NA</td><td>Iowa**</td><td>NA</td></tr>
<tr><td>NA</td><td>North Dakota**</td><td>NA</td><td>NA</td><td>Massachusetts**</td><td>NA</td></tr>
<tr><td>NA</td><td>Ohio**</td><td>NA</td><td>NA</td><td>Montana**</td><td>NA</td></tr>
<tr><td>NA</td><td>Oklahoma**</td><td>NA</td><td>NA</td><td>Nebraska**</td><td>NA</td></tr>
<tr><td>NA</td><td>Oregon**</td><td>NA</td><td>NA</td><td>New Hampshire**</td><td>NA</td></tr>
<tr><td>20</td><td>Pennsylvania</td><td>1.5</td><td>NA</td><td>New Jersey**</td><td>NA</td></tr>
<tr><td>NA</td><td>Rhode Island**</td><td>NA</td><td>NA</td><td>New York**</td><td>NA</td></tr>
<tr><td>NA</td><td>South Carolina**</td><td>NA</td><td>NA</td><td>North Dakota**</td><td>NA</td></tr>
<tr><td>NA</td><td>South Dakota**</td><td>NA</td><td>NA</td><td>Ohio**</td><td>NA</td></tr>
<tr><td>18</td><td>Tennessee</td><td>1.8</td><td>NA</td><td>Oklahoma**</td><td>NA</td></tr>
<tr><td>NA</td><td>Texas**</td><td>NA</td><td>NA</td><td>Oregon**</td><td>NA</td></tr>
<tr><td>17</td><td>Utah</td><td>1.9</td><td>NA</td><td>Rhode Island**</td><td>NA</td></tr>
<tr><td>25</td><td>Vermont</td><td>0.5</td><td>NA</td><td>South Carolina**</td><td>NA</td></tr>
<tr><td>3</td><td>Virginia</td><td>12.2</td><td>NA</td><td>South Dakota**</td><td>NA</td></tr>
<tr><td>NA</td><td>Washington**</td><td>NA</td><td>NA</td><td>Texas**</td><td>NA</td></tr>
<tr><td>NA</td><td>West Virginia**</td><td>NA</td><td>NA</td><td>Washington**</td><td>NA</td></tr>
<tr><td>27</td><td>Wisconsin</td><td>0.2</td><td>NA</td><td>West Virginia**</td><td>NA</td></tr>
<tr><td>NA</td><td>Wyoming**</td><td>NA</td><td>NA</td><td>Wyoming**</td><td>NA</td></tr>
</table>

District of Columbia   3.3

Source: CQ Press using data from U.S. Department of Education, National Center for Education Statistics
"Numbers and Types of Public Elementary and Secondary Schools" (http://nces.ed.gov/pubs2011/2011345.pdf)
*For school year 2009-2010.
**Either no magnet schools designated or not available.

Students Attending Public Elementary and Secondary Charter Schools in 2010

National Total = 1,611,332 Students*

ALPHA ORDER

RANK	STATE	STUDENTS	% of USA
NA	Alabama**	NA	NA
32	Alaska	5,196	0.3%
4	Arizona	113,974	7.1%
28	Arkansas	8,662	0.5%
1	California	317,363	19.7%
8	Colorado	66,826	4.1%
31	Connecticut	5,215	0.3%
27	Delaware	9,173	0.6%
3	Florida	137,887	8.6%
11	Georgia	37,545	2.3%
29	Hawaii	7,869	0.5%
22	Idaho	14,529	0.9%
13	Illinois	35,836	2.2%
19	Indiana	18,488	1.1%
37	Iowa	593	0.0%
33	Kansas	4,684	0.3%
NA	Kentucky**	NA	NA
16	Louisiana	31,467	2.0%
NA	Maine**	NA	NA
25	Maryland	11,995	0.7%
17	Massachusetts	27,393	1.7%
5	Michigan	110,845	6.9%
14	Minnesota	35,375	2.2%
38	Mississippi	375	0.0%
20	Missouri	18,415	1.1%
NA	Montana**	NA	NA
NA	Nebraska**	NA	NA
26	Nevada	11,614	0.7%
36	New Hampshire	816	0.1%
18	New Jersey	22,981	1.4%
23	New Mexico	13,090	0.8%
9	New York	43,963	2.7%
10	North Carolina	38,973	2.4%
NA	North Dakota**	NA	NA
6	Ohio	90,989	5.6%
30	Oklahoma	6,315	0.4%
21	Oregon	18,334	1.1%
7	Pennsylvania	79,167	4.9%
35	Rhode Island	3,233	0.2%
24	South Carolina	13,035	0.8%
NA	South Dakota**	NA	NA
34	Tennessee	4,343	0.3%
2	Texas	148,392	9.2%
15	Utah	33,968	2.1%
NA	Vermont**	NA	NA
40	Virginia	179	0.0%
NA	Washington**	NA	NA
NA	West Virginia**	NA	NA
12	Wisconsin	36,153	2.2%
39	Wyoming	269	0.0%

RANK ORDER

RANK	STATE	STUDENTS	% of USA
1	California	317,363	19.7%
2	Texas	148,392	9.2%
3	Florida	137,887	8.6%
4	Arizona	113,974	7.1%
5	Michigan	110,845	6.9%
6	Ohio	90,989	5.6%
7	Pennsylvania	79,167	4.9%
8	Colorado	66,826	4.1%
9	New York	43,963	2.7%
10	North Carolina	38,973	2.4%
11	Georgia	37,545	2.3%
12	Wisconsin	36,153	2.2%
13	Illinois	35,836	2.2%
14	Minnesota	35,375	2.2%
15	Utah	33,968	2.1%
16	Louisiana	31,467	2.0%
17	Massachusetts	27,393	1.7%
18	New Jersey	22,981	1.4%
19	Indiana	18,488	1.1%
20	Missouri	18,415	1.1%
21	Oregon	18,334	1.1%
22	Idaho	14,529	0.9%
23	New Mexico	13,090	0.8%
24	South Carolina	13,035	0.8%
25	Maryland	11,995	0.7%
26	Nevada	11,614	0.7%
27	Delaware	9,173	0.6%
28	Arkansas	8,662	0.5%
29	Hawaii	7,869	0.5%
30	Oklahoma	6,315	0.4%
31	Connecticut	5,215	0.3%
32	Alaska	5,196	0.3%
33	Kansas	4,684	0.3%
34	Tennessee	4,343	0.3%
35	Rhode Island	3,233	0.2%
36	New Hampshire	816	0.1%
37	Iowa	593	0.0%
38	Mississippi	375	0.0%
39	Wyoming	269	0.0%
40	Virginia	179	0.0%
NA	Alabama**	NA	NA
NA	Kentucky**	NA	NA
NA	Maine**	NA	NA
NA	Montana**	NA	NA
NA	Nebraska**	NA	NA
NA	North Dakota**	NA	NA
NA	South Dakota**	NA	NA
NA	Vermont**	NA	NA
NA	Washington**	NA	NA
NA	West Virginia**	NA	NA
	District of Columbia	25,813	1.6%

Source: U.S. Department of Education, National Center for Education Statistics
    "Numbers and Types of Public Elementary and Secondary Schools" (http://nces.ed.gov/pubs2011/2011345.pdf)
*For school year 2009-2010. Charter schools provide free public elementary/secondary education under a charter granted by the state legislature or other appropriate authority.
**Not applicable.

Percent of Students Attending Public Elementary and Secondary Charter Schools in 2010
Reporting States Percent = 3.3%*

<table>
<tr><td colspan="3"><u>ALPHA ORDER</u></td><td colspan="3"><u>RANK ORDER</u></td></tr>
<tr><td>RANK</td><td>STATE</td><td>PERCENT</td><td>RANK</td><td>STATE</td><td>PERCENT</td></tr>
<tr><td>NA</td><td>Alabama**</td><td>NA</td><td>1</td><td>Arizona</td><td>10.6</td></tr>
<tr><td>15</td><td>Alaska</td><td>3.9</td><td>2</td><td>Colorado</td><td>8.0</td></tr>
<tr><td>1</td><td>Arizona</td><td>10.6</td><td>3</td><td>Delaware</td><td>7.3</td></tr>
<tr><td>25</td><td>Arkansas</td><td>1.8</td><td>4</td><td>Michigan</td><td>6.9</td></tr>
<tr><td>9</td><td>California</td><td>5.1</td><td>5</td><td>Utah</td><td>5.8</td></tr>
<tr><td>2</td><td>Colorado</td><td>8.0</td><td>6</td><td>Idaho</td><td>5.3</td></tr>
<tr><td>34</td><td>Connecticut</td><td>0.9</td><td>7</td><td>Florida</td><td>5.2</td></tr>
<tr><td>3</td><td>Delaware</td><td>7.3</td><td>7</td><td>Ohio</td><td>5.2</td></tr>
<tr><td>7</td><td>Florida</td><td>5.2</td><td>9</td><td>California</td><td>5.1</td></tr>
<tr><td>22</td><td>Georgia</td><td>2.3</td><td>10</td><td>Louisiana</td><td>4.6</td></tr>
<tr><td>12</td><td>Hawaii</td><td>4.4</td><td>11</td><td>Pennsylvania</td><td>4.5</td></tr>
<tr><td>6</td><td>Idaho</td><td>5.3</td><td>12</td><td>Hawaii</td><td>4.4</td></tr>
<tr><td>28</td><td>Illinois</td><td>1.7</td><td>13</td><td>Minnesota</td><td>4.2</td></tr>
<tr><td>25</td><td>Indiana</td><td>1.8</td><td>14</td><td>Wisconsin</td><td>4.1</td></tr>
<tr><td>38</td><td>Iowa</td><td>0.1</td><td>15</td><td>Alaska</td><td>3.9</td></tr>
<tr><td>32</td><td>Kansas</td><td>1.0</td><td>15</td><td>New Mexico</td><td>3.9</td></tr>
<tr><td>NA</td><td>Kentucky**</td><td>NA</td><td>17</td><td>Oregon</td><td>3.3</td></tr>
<tr><td>10</td><td>Louisiana</td><td>4.6</td><td>18</td><td>Texas</td><td>3.1</td></tr>
<tr><td>NA</td><td>Maine**</td><td>NA</td><td>19</td><td>Massachusetts</td><td>2.9</td></tr>
<tr><td>31</td><td>Maryland</td><td>1.4</td><td>20</td><td>Nevada</td><td>2.7</td></tr>
<tr><td>19</td><td>Massachusetts</td><td>2.9</td><td>21</td><td>North Carolina</td><td>2.6</td></tr>
<tr><td>4</td><td>Michigan</td><td>6.9</td><td>22</td><td>Georgia</td><td>2.3</td></tr>
<tr><td>13</td><td>Minnesota</td><td>4.2</td><td>22</td><td>Rhode Island</td><td>2.3</td></tr>
<tr><td>38</td><td>Mississippi</td><td>0.1</td><td>24</td><td>Missouri</td><td>2.0</td></tr>
<tr><td>24</td><td>Missouri</td><td>2.0</td><td>25</td><td>Arkansas</td><td>1.8</td></tr>
<tr><td>NA</td><td>Montana**</td><td>NA</td><td>25</td><td>Indiana</td><td>1.8</td></tr>
<tr><td>NA</td><td>Nebraska**</td><td>NA</td><td>25</td><td>South Carolina</td><td>1.8</td></tr>
<tr><td>20</td><td>Nevada</td><td>2.7</td><td>28</td><td>Illinois</td><td>1.7</td></tr>
<tr><td>35</td><td>New Hampshire</td><td>0.4</td><td>28</td><td>New Jersey</td><td>1.7</td></tr>
<tr><td>28</td><td>New Jersey</td><td>1.7</td><td>30</td><td>New York</td><td>1.6</td></tr>
<tr><td>15</td><td>New Mexico</td><td>3.9</td><td>31</td><td>Maryland</td><td>1.4</td></tr>
<tr><td>30</td><td>New York</td><td>1.6</td><td>32</td><td>Kansas</td><td>1.0</td></tr>
<tr><td>21</td><td>North Carolina</td><td>2.6</td><td>32</td><td>Oklahoma</td><td>1.0</td></tr>
<tr><td>NA</td><td>North Dakota**</td><td>NA</td><td>34</td><td>Connecticut</td><td>0.9</td></tr>
<tr><td>7</td><td>Ohio</td><td>5.2</td><td>35</td><td>New Hampshire</td><td>0.4</td></tr>
<tr><td>32</td><td>Oklahoma</td><td>1.0</td><td>35</td><td>Tennessee</td><td>0.4</td></tr>
<tr><td>17</td><td>Oregon</td><td>3.3</td><td>37</td><td>Wyoming</td><td>0.3</td></tr>
<tr><td>11</td><td>Pennsylvania</td><td>4.5</td><td>38</td><td>Iowa</td><td>0.1</td></tr>
<tr><td>22</td><td>Rhode Island</td><td>2.3</td><td>38</td><td>Mississippi</td><td>0.1</td></tr>
<tr><td>25</td><td>South Carolina</td><td>1.8</td><td>40</td><td>Virginia</td><td>0.0</td></tr>
<tr><td>NA</td><td>South Dakota**</td><td>NA</td><td>NA</td><td>Alabama**</td><td>NA</td></tr>
<tr><td>35</td><td>Tennessee</td><td>0.4</td><td>NA</td><td>Kentucky**</td><td>NA</td></tr>
<tr><td>18</td><td>Texas</td><td>3.1</td><td>NA</td><td>Maine**</td><td>NA</td></tr>
<tr><td>5</td><td>Utah</td><td>5.8</td><td>NA</td><td>Montana**</td><td>NA</td></tr>
<tr><td>NA</td><td>Vermont**</td><td>NA</td><td>NA</td><td>Nebraska**</td><td>NA</td></tr>
<tr><td>40</td><td>Virginia</td><td>0.0</td><td>NA</td><td>North Dakota**</td><td>NA</td></tr>
<tr><td>NA</td><td>Washington**</td><td>NA</td><td>NA</td><td>South Dakota**</td><td>NA</td></tr>
<tr><td>NA</td><td>West Virginia**</td><td>NA</td><td>NA</td><td>Vermont**</td><td>NA</td></tr>
<tr><td>14</td><td>Wisconsin</td><td>4.1</td><td>NA</td><td>Washington**</td><td>NA</td></tr>
<tr><td>37</td><td>Wyoming</td><td>0.3</td><td>NA</td><td>West Virginia**</td><td>NA</td></tr>
</table>

District of Columbia   37.3

Source: CQ Press using data from U.S. Department of Education, National Center for Education Statistics
    "Numbers and Types of Public Elementary and Secondary Schools" (http://nces.ed.gov/pubs2011/2011345.pdf)
*For school year 2009-2010. Charter schools provide free public elementary/secondary education under a charter granted by the state legislature or other appropriate authority.
**Not applicable.

Students Attending Public Elementary and Secondary
Special Education Schools in 2010
National Total = 193,212 Students*

ALPHA ORDER

RANK	STATE	STUDENTS	% of USA
24	Alabama	998	0.5%
43	Alaska	84	0.0%
19	Arizona	1,419	0.7%
35	Arkansas	222	0.1%
2	California	26,293	13.6%
22	Colorado	1,154	0.6%
15	Connecticut	3,312	1.7%
18	Delaware	1,737	0.9%
4	Florida	17,964	9.3%
7	Georgia	8,154	4.2%
44	Hawaii	79	0.0%
41	Idaho	135	0.1%
8	Illinois	8,088	4.2%
23	Indiana	1,153	0.6%
30	Iowa	547	0.3%
33	Kansas	326	0.2%
29	Kentucky	572	0.3%
21	Louisiana	1,179	0.6%
47	Maine	16	0.0%
13	Maryland	4,338	2.2%
11	Massachusetts	4,759	2.5%
1	Michigan	31,418	16.3%
5	Minnesota	15,100	7.8%
36	Mississippi	202	0.1%
12	Missouri	4,480	2.3%
45	Montana	35	0.0%
28	Nebraska	576	0.3%
26	Nevada	709	0.4%
48	New Hampshire	0	0.0%
6	New Jersey	9,149	4.7%
27	New Mexico	619	0.3%
3	New York	22,844	11.8%
31	North Carolina	458	0.2%
46	North Dakota	23	0.0%
9	Ohio	6,060	3.1%
34	Oklahoma	237	0.1%
39	Oregon	148	0.1%
20	Pennsylvania	1,257	0.7%
40	Rhode Island	147	0.1%
25	South Carolina	825	0.4%
42	South Dakota	98	0.1%
17	Tennessee	1,822	0.9%
16	Texas	2,412	1.2%
10	Utah	5,948	3.1%
48	Vermont	0	0.0%
32	Virginia	391	0.2%
14	Washington	3,863	2.0%
38	West Virginia	160	0.1%
37	Wisconsin	192	0.1%
48	Wyoming	0	0.0%

RANK ORDER

RANK	STATE	STUDENTS	% of USA
1	Michigan	31,418	16.3%
2	California	26,293	13.6%
3	New York	22,844	11.8%
4	Florida	17,964	9.3%
5	Minnesota	15,100	7.8%
6	New Jersey	9,149	4.7%
7	Georgia	8,154	4.2%
8	Illinois	8,088	4.2%
9	Ohio	6,060	3.1%
10	Utah	5,948	3.1%
11	Massachusetts	4,759	2.5%
12	Missouri	4,480	2.3%
13	Maryland	4,338	2.2%
14	Washington	3,863	2.0%
15	Connecticut	3,312	1.7%
16	Texas	2,412	1.2%
17	Tennessee	1,822	0.9%
18	Delaware	1,737	0.9%
19	Arizona	1,419	0.7%
20	Pennsylvania	1,257	0.7%
21	Louisiana	1,179	0.6%
22	Colorado	1,154	0.6%
23	Indiana	1,153	0.6%
24	Alabama	998	0.5%
25	South Carolina	825	0.4%
26	Nevada	709	0.4%
27	New Mexico	619	0.3%
28	Nebraska	576	0.3%
29	Kentucky	572	0.3%
30	Iowa	547	0.3%
31	North Carolina	458	0.2%
32	Virginia	391	0.2%
33	Kansas	326	0.2%
34	Oklahoma	237	0.1%
35	Arkansas	222	0.1%
36	Mississippi	202	0.1%
37	Wisconsin	192	0.1%
38	West Virginia	160	0.1%
39	Oregon	148	0.1%
40	Rhode Island	147	0.1%
41	Idaho	135	0.1%
42	South Dakota	98	0.1%
43	Alaska	84	0.0%
44	Hawaii	79	0.0%
45	Montana	35	0.0%
46	North Dakota	23	0.0%
47	Maine	16	0.0%
48	New Hampshire	0	0.0%
48	Vermont	0	0.0%
48	Wyoming	0	0.0%
	District of Columbia	1,510	0.8%

Source: U.S. Department of Education, National Center for Education Statistics
   "Numbers and Types of Public Elementary and Secondary Schools" (http://nces.ed.gov/pubs2011/2011345.pdf)
*For school year 2009-2010.

Percent of Students Attending Public Elementary and Secondary Special Education Schools in 2010
National Percent = 0.4%*

ALPHA ORDER

RANK	STATE	PERCENT
22	Alabama	0.1
22	Alaska	0.1
22	Arizona	0.1
35	Arkansas	0.0
13	California	0.4
22	Colorado	0.1
8	Connecticut	0.6
3	Delaware	1.4
6	Florida	0.7
9	Georgia	0.5
35	Hawaii	0.0
35	Idaho	0.0
13	Illinois	0.4
22	Indiana	0.1
22	Iowa	0.1
22	Kansas	0.1
22	Kentucky	0.1
17	Louisiana	0.2
35	Maine	0.0
9	Maryland	0.5
9	Massachusetts	0.5
1	Michigan	1.9
2	Minnesota	1.8
35	Mississippi	0.0
9	Missouri	0.5
35	Montana	0.0
17	Nebraska	0.2
17	Nevada	0.2
35	New Hampshire	0.0
6	New Jersey	0.7
17	New Mexico	0.2
5	New York	0.8
35	North Carolina	0.0
35	North Dakota	0.0
16	Ohio	0.3
35	Oklahoma	0.0
35	Oregon	0.0
22	Pennsylvania	0.1
22	Rhode Island	0.1
22	South Carolina	0.1
22	South Dakota	0.1
17	Tennessee	0.2
35	Texas	0.0
4	Utah	1.0
35	Vermont	0.0
35	Virginia	0.0
13	Washington	0.4
22	West Virginia	0.1
35	Wisconsin	0.0
35	Wyoming	0.0

RANK ORDER

RANK	STATE	PERCENT
1	Michigan	1.9
2	Minnesota	1.8
3	Delaware	1.4
4	Utah	1.0
5	New York	0.8
6	Florida	0.7
6	New Jersey	0.7
8	Connecticut	0.6
9	Georgia	0.5
9	Maryland	0.5
9	Massachusetts	0.5
9	Missouri	0.5
13	California	0.4
13	Illinois	0.4
13	Washington	0.4
16	Ohio	0.3
17	Louisiana	0.2
17	Nebraska	0.2
17	Nevada	0.2
17	New Mexico	0.2
17	Tennessee	0.2
22	Alabama	0.1
22	Alaska	0.1
22	Arizona	0.1
22	Colorado	0.1
22	Indiana	0.1
22	Iowa	0.1
22	Kansas	0.1
22	Kentucky	0.1
22	Pennsylvania	0.1
22	Rhode Island	0.1
22	South Carolina	0.1
22	South Dakota	0.1
22	West Virginia	0.1
35	Arkansas	0.0
35	Hawaii	0.0
35	Idaho	0.0
35	Maine	0.0
35	Mississippi	0.0
35	Montana	0.0
35	New Hampshire	0.0
35	North Carolina	0.0
35	North Dakota	0.0
35	Oklahoma	0.0
35	Oregon	0.0
35	Texas	0.0
35	Vermont	0.0
35	Virginia	0.0
35	Wisconsin	0.0
35	Wyoming	0.0

	District of Columbia	2.2

Source: CQ Press using data from U.S. Department of Education, National Center for Education Statistics
   "Numbers and Types of Public Elementary and Secondary Schools" (http://nces.ed.gov/pubs2011/2011345.pdf)
*For school year 2009-2010.

Students Attending Public Elementary and Secondary Vocational Education Schools in 2010
National Total = 129,840 Students*

ALPHA ORDER

RANK	STATE	STUDENTS	% of USA
25	Alabama	41	0.0%
17	Alaska	769	0.6%
9	Arizona	3,495	2.7%
29	Arkansas	0	0.0%
18	California	611	0.5%
16	Colorado	797	0.6%
4	Connecticut	10,469	8.1%
6	Delaware	7,069	5.4%
10	Florida	3,298	2.5%
29	Georgia	0	0.0%
29	Hawaii	0	0.0%
24	Idaho	81	0.1%
22	Illinois	220	0.2%
29	Indiana	0	0.0%
29	Iowa	0	0.0%
29	Kansas	0	0.0%
29	Kentucky	0	0.0%
29	Louisiana	0	0.0%
29	Maine	0	0.0%
5	Maryland	8,122	6.3%
1	Massachusetts	35,423	27.3%
12	Michigan	1,473	1.1%
28	Minnesota	9	0.0%
29	Mississippi	0	0.0%
8	Missouri	4,518	3.5%
29	Montana	0	0.0%
29	Nebraska	0	0.0%
23	Nevada	157	0.1%
29	New Hampshire	0	0.0%
2	New Jersey	21,891	16.9%
20	New Mexico	319	0.2%
7	New York	6,429	5.0%
21	North Carolina	235	0.2%
29	North Dakota	0	0.0%
14	Ohio	965	0.7%
29	Oklahoma	0	0.0%
29	Oregon	0	0.0%
3	Pennsylvania	18,115	14.0%
11	Rhode Island	1,771	1.4%
29	South Carolina	0	0.0%
26	South Dakota	19	0.0%
13	Tennessee	1,379	1.1%
29	Texas	0	0.0%
29	Utah	0	0.0%
29	Vermont	0	0.0%
29	Virginia	0	0.0%
19	Washington	398	0.3%
27	West Virginia	10	0.0%
15	Wisconsin	803	0.6%
29	Wyoming	0	0.0%

RANK ORDER

RANK	STATE	STUDENTS	% of USA
1	Massachusetts	35,423	27.3%
2	New Jersey	21,891	16.9%
3	Pennsylvania	18,115	14.0%
4	Connecticut	10,469	8.1%
5	Maryland	8,122	6.3%
6	Delaware	7,069	5.4%
7	New York	6,429	5.0%
8	Missouri	4,518	3.5%
9	Arizona	3,495	2.7%
10	Florida	3,298	2.5%
11	Rhode Island	1,771	1.4%
12	Michigan	1,473	1.1%
13	Tennessee	1,379	1.1%
14	Ohio	965	0.7%
15	Wisconsin	803	0.6%
16	Colorado	797	0.6%
17	Alaska	769	0.6%
18	California	611	0.5%
19	Washington	398	0.3%
20	New Mexico	319	0.2%
21	North Carolina	235	0.2%
22	Illinois	220	0.2%
23	Nevada	157	0.1%
24	Idaho	81	0.1%
25	Alabama	41	0.0%
26	South Dakota	19	0.0%
27	West Virginia	10	0.0%
28	Minnesota	9	0.0%
29	Arkansas	0	0.0%
29	Georgia	0	0.0%
29	Hawaii	0	0.0%
29	Indiana	0	0.0%
29	Iowa	0	0.0%
29	Kansas	0	0.0%
29	Kentucky	0	0.0%
29	Louisiana	0	0.0%
29	Maine	0	0.0%
29	Mississippi	0	0.0%
29	Montana	0	0.0%
29	Nebraska	0	0.0%
29	New Hampshire	0	0.0%
29	North Dakota	0	0.0%
29	Oklahoma	0	0.0%
29	Oregon	0	0.0%
29	South Carolina	0	0.0%
29	Texas	0	0.0%
29	Utah	0	0.0%
29	Vermont	0	0.0%
29	Virginia	0	0.0%
29	Wyoming	0	0.0%
	District of Columbia	954	0.7%

Source: U.S. Department of Education, National Center for Education Statistics
   "Numbers and Types of Public Elementary and Secondary Schools" (http://nces.ed.gov/pubs2011/2011345.pdf)
*For school year 2009-2010.

Percent of Students Attending Public Elementary and Secondary Vocational Education Schools in 2010
National Percent = 0.3%*

ALPHA ORDER

RANK	STATE	PERCENT
19	Alabama	0.0
8	Alaska	0.6
10	Arizona	0.3
19	Arkansas	0.0
19	California	0.0
12	Colorado	0.1
3	Connecticut	1.9
1	Delaware	5.7
12	Florida	0.1
19	Georgia	0.0
19	Hawaii	0.0
19	Idaho	0.0
19	Illinois	0.0
19	Indiana	0.0
19	Iowa	0.0
19	Kansas	0.0
19	Kentucky	0.0
19	Louisiana	0.0
19	Maine	0.0
6	Maryland	1.0
2	Massachusetts	3.7
12	Michigan	0.1
19	Minnesota	0.0
19	Mississippi	0.0
9	Missouri	0.5
19	Montana	0.0
19	Nebraska	0.0
19	Nevada	0.0
19	New Hampshire	0.0
4	New Jersey	1.6
12	New Mexico	0.1
11	New York	0.2
19	North Carolina	0.0
19	North Dakota	0.0
12	Ohio	0.1
19	Oklahoma	0.0
19	Oregon	0.0
6	Pennsylvania	1.0
5	Rhode Island	1.2
19	South Carolina	0.0
19	South Dakota	0.0
12	Tennessee	0.1
19	Texas	0.0
19	Utah	0.0
19	Vermont	0.0
19	Virginia	0.0
19	Washington	0.0
19	West Virginia	0.0
12	Wisconsin	0.1
19	Wyoming	0.0

RANK ORDER

RANK	STATE	PERCENT
1	Delaware	5.7
2	Massachusetts	3.7
3	Connecticut	1.9
4	New Jersey	1.6
5	Rhode Island	1.2
6	Maryland	1.0
6	Pennsylvania	1.0
8	Alaska	0.6
9	Missouri	0.5
10	Arizona	0.3
11	New York	0.2
12	Colorado	0.1
12	Florida	0.1
12	Michigan	0.1
12	New Mexico	0.1
12	Ohio	0.1
12	Tennessee	0.1
12	Wisconsin	0.1
19	Alabama	0.0
19	Arkansas	0.0
19	California	0.0
19	Georgia	0.0
19	Hawaii	0.0
19	Idaho	0.0
19	Illinois	0.0
19	Indiana	0.0
19	Iowa	0.0
19	Kansas	0.0
19	Kentucky	0.0
19	Louisiana	0.0
19	Maine	0.0
19	Minnesota	0.0
19	Mississippi	0.0
19	Montana	0.0
19	Nebraska	0.0
19	Nevada	0.0
19	New Hampshire	0.0
19	North Carolina	0.0
19	North Dakota	0.0
19	Oklahoma	0.0
19	Oregon	0.0
19	South Carolina	0.0
19	South Dakota	0.0
19	Texas	0.0
19	Utah	0.0
19	Vermont	0.0
19	Virginia	0.0
19	Washington	0.0
19	West Virginia	0.0
19	Wyoming	0.0

District of Columbia	1.4

Source: CQ Press using data from U.S. Department of Education, National Center for Education Statistics
"Numbers and Types of Public Elementary and Secondary Schools" (http://nces.ed.gov/pubs2011/2011345.pdf)
*For school year 2009-2010.

Students Attending Public Elementary and Secondary
Alternative Education Schools in 2010
National Total = 574,381 Students*

RANK	STATE	STUDENTS	% of USA
26	Alabama	2,902	0.5%
9	Alaska	13,210	2.3%
10	Arizona	10,892	1.9%
32	Arkansas	1,541	0.3%
1	California	175,001	30.5%
8	Colorado	15,029	2.6%
21	Connecticut	3,662	0.6%
33	Delaware	1,259	0.2%
4	Florida	43,003	7.5%
23	Georgia	3,286	0.6%
41	Hawaii	136	0.0%
19	Idaho	5,003	0.9%
11	Illinois	8,199	1.4%
27	Indiana	2,504	0.4%
24	Iowa	3,258	0.6%
44	Kansas	41	0.0%
15	Kentucky	6,183	1.1%
5	Louisiana	36,967	6.4%
45	Maine	36	0.0%
12	Maryland	7,975	1.4%
22	Massachusetts	3,539	0.6%
6	Michigan	35,085	6.1%
7	Minnesota	15,684	2.7%
47	Mississippi	0	0.0%
28	Missouri	2,483	0.4%
43	Montana	79	0.0%
47	Nebraska	0	0.0%
16	Nevada	5,957	1.0%
47	New Hampshire	0	0.0%
30	New Jersey	2,216	0.4%
20	New Mexico	4,284	0.7%
14	New York	7,384	1.3%
42	North Carolina	100	0.0%
47	North Dakota	0	0.0%
39	Ohio	941	0.2%
37	Oklahoma	962	0.2%
17	Oregon	5,666	1.0%
36	Pennsylvania	1,095	0.2%
31	Rhode Island	1,975	0.3%
40	South Carolina	851	0.1%
34	South Dakota	1,209	0.2%
29	Tennessee	2,345	0.4%
2	Texas	76,742	13.4%
13	Utah	7,752	1.3%
46	Vermont	19	0.0%
25	Virginia	2,975	0.5%
3	Washington	47,034	8.2%
38	West Virginia	954	0.2%
18	Wisconsin	5,112	0.9%
35	Wyoming	1,205	0.2%

RANK	STATE	STUDENTS	% of USA
1	California	175,001	30.5%
2	Texas	76,742	13.4%
3	Washington	47,034	8.2%
4	Florida	43,003	7.5%
5	Louisiana	36,967	6.4%
6	Michigan	35,085	6.1%
7	Minnesota	15,684	2.7%
8	Colorado	15,029	2.6%
9	Alaska	13,210	2.3%
10	Arizona	10,892	1.9%
11	Illinois	8,199	1.4%
12	Maryland	7,975	1.4%
13	Utah	7,752	1.3%
14	New York	7,384	1.3%
15	Kentucky	6,183	1.1%
16	Nevada	5,957	1.0%
17	Oregon	5,666	1.0%
18	Wisconsin	5,112	0.9%
19	Idaho	5,003	0.9%
20	New Mexico	4,284	0.7%
21	Connecticut	3,662	0.6%
22	Massachusetts	3,539	0.6%
23	Georgia	3,286	0.6%
24	Iowa	3,258	0.6%
25	Virginia	2,975	0.5%
26	Alabama	2,902	0.5%
27	Indiana	2,504	0.4%
28	Missouri	2,483	0.4%
29	Tennessee	2,345	0.4%
30	New Jersey	2,216	0.4%
31	Rhode Island	1,975	0.3%
32	Arkansas	1,541	0.3%
33	Delaware	1,259	0.2%
34	South Dakota	1,209	0.2%
35	Wyoming	1,205	0.2%
36	Pennsylvania	1,095	0.2%
37	Oklahoma	962	0.2%
38	West Virginia	954	0.2%
39	Ohio	941	0.2%
40	South Carolina	851	0.1%
41	Hawaii	136	0.0%
42	North Carolina	100	0.0%
43	Montana	79	0.0%
44	Kansas	41	0.0%
45	Maine	36	0.0%
46	Vermont	19	0.0%
47	Mississippi	0	0.0%
47	Nebraska	0	0.0%
47	New Hampshire	0	0.0%
47	North Dakota	0	0.0%
	District of Columbia	646	0.1%

Source: U.S. Department of Education, National Center for Education Statistics
"Numbers and Types of Public Elementary and Secondary Schools" (http://nces.ed.gov/pubs2011/2011345.pdf)
*For school year 2009-2010.

Percent of Students Attending Public Elementary and Secondary Alternative Education Schools in 2010
National Percent = 1.2%*

ALPHA ORDER

RANK ORDER

RANK	STATE	PERCENT		RANK	STATE	PERCENT
25	Alabama	0.4		1	Alaska	10.0
1	Alaska	10.0		2	Louisiana	5.4
16	Arizona	1.0		3	Washington	4.5
28	Arkansas	0.3		4	California	2.8
4	California	2.8		5	Michigan	2.2
7	Colorado	1.8		6	Minnesota	1.9
23	Connecticut	0.6		7	Colorado	1.8
16	Delaware	1.0		7	Idaho	1.8
9	Florida	1.6		9	Florida	1.6
32	Georgia	0.2		9	Texas	1.6
37	Hawaii	0.1		11	Nevada	1.4
7	Idaho	1.8		11	Rhode Island	1.4
25	Illinois	0.4		11	Wyoming	1.4
32	Indiana	0.2		14	New Mexico	1.3
22	Iowa	0.7		14	Utah	1.3
43	Kansas	0.0		16	Arizona	1.0
20	Kentucky	0.9		16	Delaware	1.0
2	Louisiana	5.4		16	Oregon	1.0
43	Maine	0.0		16	South Dakota	1.0
20	Maryland	0.9		20	Kentucky	0.9
25	Massachusetts	0.4		20	Maryland	0.9
5	Michigan	2.2		22	Iowa	0.7
6	Minnesota	1.9		23	Connecticut	0.6
43	Mississippi	0.0		23	Wisconsin	0.6
28	Missouri	0.3		25	Alabama	0.4
37	Montana	0.1		25	Illinois	0.4
43	Nebraska	0.0		25	Massachusetts	0.4
11	Nevada	1.4		28	Arkansas	0.3
43	New Hampshire	0.0		28	Missouri	0.3
32	New Jersey	0.2		28	New York	0.3
14	New Mexico	1.3		28	West Virginia	0.3
28	New York	0.3		32	Georgia	0.2
43	North Carolina	0.0		32	Indiana	0.2
43	North Dakota	0.0		32	New Jersey	0.2
37	Ohio	0.1		32	Tennessee	0.2
37	Oklahoma	0.1		32	Virginia	0.2
16	Oregon	1.0		37	Hawaii	0.1
37	Pennsylvania	0.1		37	Montana	0.1
11	Rhode Island	1.4		37	Ohio	0.1
37	South Carolina	0.1		37	Oklahoma	0.1
16	South Dakota	1.0		37	Pennsylvania	0.1
32	Tennessee	0.2		37	South Carolina	0.1
9	Texas	1.6		43	Kansas	0.0
14	Utah	1.3		43	Maine	0.0
43	Vermont	0.0		43	Mississippi	0.0
32	Virginia	0.2		43	Nebraska	0.0
3	Washington	4.5		43	New Hampshire	0.0
28	West Virginia	0.3		43	North Carolina	0.0
23	Wisconsin	0.6		43	North Dakota	0.0
11	Wyoming	1.4		43	Vermont	0.0

District of Columbia   0.9

Source: CQ Press using data from U.S. Department of Education, National Center for Education Statistics
    "Numbers and Types of Public Elementary and Secondary Schools" (http://nces.ed.gov/pubs2011/2011345.pdf)
*For school year 2009-2010.

Minority Students Enrolled in Public Elementary and Secondary Schools in 2010
National Total = 22,382,598 Students*

ALPHA ORDER

RANK	STATE	STUDENTS	% of USA
20	Alabama	308,316	1.4%
39	Alaska	61,606	0.3%
9	Arizona	602,825	2.7%
31	Arkansas	166,650	0.7%
1	California	4,518,099	20.2%
18	Colorado	327,634	1.5%
30	Connecticut	204,502	0.9%
40	Delaware	61,386	0.3%
3	Florida	1,377,510	6.2%
6	Georgia	917,856	4.1%
34	Hawaii	144,644	0.6%
41	Idaho	54,149	0.2%
5	Illinois	934,948	4.2%
27	Indiana	221,964	1.0%
37	Iowa	87,344	0.4%
33	Kansas	147,813	0.7%
36	Kentucky	104,039	0.5%
15	Louisiana	355,856	1.6%
49	Maine	12,433	0.1%
13	Maryland	462,630	2.1%
21	Massachusetts	295,761	1.3%
12	Michigan	469,862	2.1%
29	Minnesota	208,990	0.9%
23	Mississippi	265,626	1.2%
26	Missouri	222,824	1.0%
43	Montana	24,023	0.1%
38	Nebraska	77,456	0.3%
24	Nevada	251,470	1.1%
46	New Hampshire	18,039	0.1%
8	New Jersey	655,711	2.9%
25	New Mexico	248,994	1.1%
4	New York	1,355,843	6.1%
7	North Carolina	683,670	3.1%
48	North Dakota	14,712	0.1%
14	Ohio	370,415	1.7%
22	Oklahoma	285,331	1.3%
32	Oregon	162,104	0.7%
11	Pennsylvania	475,426	2.1%
42	Rhode Island	46,403	0.2%
17	South Carolina	332,544	1.5%
44	South Dakota	23,135	0.1%
19	Tennessee	309,708	1.4%
2	Texas	3,234,075	14.4%
35	Utah	108,483	0.5%
50	Vermont	6,008	0.0%
10	Virginia	511,831	2.3%
16	Washington	339,530	1.5%
45	West Virginia	21,542	0.1%
28	Wisconsin	209,737	0.9%
47	Wyoming	16,356	0.1%

RANK ORDER

RANK	STATE	STUDENTS	% of USA
1	California	4,518,099	20.2%
2	Texas	3,234,075	14.4%
3	Florida	1,377,510	6.2%
4	New York	1,355,843	6.1%
5	Illinois	934,948	4.2%
6	Georgia	917,856	4.1%
7	North Carolina	683,670	3.1%
8	New Jersey	655,711	2.9%
9	Arizona	602,825	2.7%
10	Virginia	511,831	2.3%
11	Pennsylvania	475,426	2.1%
12	Michigan	469,862	2.1%
13	Maryland	462,630	2.1%
14	Ohio	370,415	1.7%
15	Louisiana	355,856	1.6%
16	Washington	339,530	1.5%
17	South Carolina	332,544	1.5%
18	Colorado	327,634	1.5%
19	Tennessee	309,708	1.4%
20	Alabama	308,316	1.4%
21	Massachusetts	295,761	1.3%
22	Oklahoma	285,331	1.3%
23	Mississippi	265,626	1.2%
24	Nevada	251,470	1.1%
25	New Mexico	248,994	1.1%
26	Missouri	222,824	1.0%
27	Indiana	221,964	1.0%
28	Wisconsin	209,737	0.9%
29	Minnesota	208,990	0.9%
30	Connecticut	204,502	0.9%
31	Arkansas	166,650	0.7%
32	Oregon	162,104	0.7%
33	Kansas	147,813	0.7%
34	Hawaii	144,644	0.6%
35	Utah	108,483	0.5%
36	Kentucky	104,039	0.5%
37	Iowa	87,344	0.4%
38	Nebraska	77,456	0.3%
39	Alaska	61,606	0.3%
40	Delaware	61,386	0.3%
41	Idaho	54,149	0.2%
42	Rhode Island	46,403	0.2%
43	Montana	24,023	0.1%
44	South Dakota	23,135	0.1%
45	West Virginia	21,542	0.1%
46	New Hampshire	18,039	0.1%
47	Wyoming	16,356	0.1%
48	North Dakota	14,712	0.1%
49	Maine	12,433	0.1%
50	Vermont	6,008	0.0%
	District of Columbia	64,785	0.3%

Source: CQ Press using data from U.S. Department of Education, National Center for Education Statistics
"Public Elementary and Secondary School Student Enrollment and Staff" (http://nces.ed.gov/pubs2011/2011347.pdf)
*For school year 2009-2010. Minority includes all groups except non-Hispanic white.

Percent of Public Elementary and Secondary Students
Who Are Minorities in 2010
National Percent = 45.9%*

ALPHA ORDER

RANK	STATE	PERCENT
21	Alabama	41.3
15	Alaska	46.8
6	Arizona	55.9
24	Arkansas	34.7
3	California	73.0
22	Colorado	39.4
23	Connecticut	36.3
13	Delaware	48.4
9	Florida	54.1
7	Georgia	55.0
1	Hawaii	80.3
40	Idaho	19.6
18	Illinois	45.8
37	Indiana	22.2
43	Iowa	17.8
28	Kansas	31.2
45	Kentucky	15.7
11	Louisiana	51.5
49	Maine	6.6
8	Maryland	54.5
29	Massachusetts	30.9
31	Michigan	28.9
34	Minnesota	25.0
10	Mississippi	53.9
35	Missouri	24.3
44	Montana	16.9
33	Nebraska	26.2
5	Nevada	58.6
47	New Hampshire	9.2
14	New Jersey	47.0
2	New Mexico	74.5
12	New York	49.2
17	North Carolina	46.1
46	North Dakota	15.5
38	Ohio	21.9
19	Oklahoma	43.6
30	Oregon	30.0
32	Pennsylvania	26.9
26	Rhode Island	32.0
16	South Carolina	46.3
41	South Dakota	18.7
27	Tennessee	31.8
4	Texas	66.7
39	Utah	20.9
50	Vermont	6.5
20	Virginia	42.3
25	Washington	33.9
48	West Virginia	7.6
36	Wisconsin	24.0
42	Wyoming	18.6

RANK ORDER

RANK	STATE	PERCENT
1	Hawaii	80.3
2	New Mexico	74.5
3	California	73.0
4	Texas	66.7
5	Nevada	58.6
6	Arizona	55.9
7	Georgia	55.0
8	Maryland	54.5
9	Florida	54.1
10	Mississippi	53.9
11	Louisiana	51.5
12	New York	49.2
13	Delaware	48.4
14	New Jersey	47.0
15	Alaska	46.8
16	South Carolina	46.3
17	North Carolina	46.1
18	Illinois	45.8
19	Oklahoma	43.6
20	Virginia	42.3
21	Alabama	41.3
22	Colorado	39.4
23	Connecticut	36.3
24	Arkansas	34.7
25	Washington	33.9
26	Rhode Island	32.0
27	Tennessee	31.8
28	Kansas	31.2
29	Massachusetts	30.9
30	Oregon	30.0
31	Michigan	28.9
32	Pennsylvania	26.9
33	Nebraska	26.2
34	Minnesota	25.0
35	Missouri	24.3
36	Wisconsin	24.0
37	Indiana	22.2
38	Ohio	21.9
39	Utah	20.9
40	Idaho	19.6
41	South Dakota	18.7
42	Wyoming	18.6
43	Iowa	17.8
44	Montana	16.9
45	Kentucky	15.7
46	North Dakota	15.5
47	New Hampshire	9.2
48	West Virginia	7.6
49	Maine	6.6
50	Vermont	6.5

District of Columbia 93.3

Source: CQ Press using data from U.S. Department of Education, National Center for Education Statistics
   "Public Elementary and Secondary School Student Enrollment and Staff" (http://nces.ed.gov/pubs2011/2011347.pdf)
*For school year 2009-2010. Minority includes all groups except non-Hispanic white.

Percent of Public Elementary and Secondary Students Who Are White in 2010

National Percent = 54.1%*

ALPHA ORDER

RANK	STATE	PERCENT
30	Alabama	58.7
36	Alaska	53.2
45	Arizona	44.1
27	Arkansas	65.3
48	California	27.0
29	Colorado	60.6
28	Connecticut	63.7
38	Delaware	51.6
42	Florida	45.9
44	Georgia	45.0
50	Hawaii	19.7
11	Idaho	80.4
33	Illinois	54.2
14	Indiana	77.8
8	Iowa	82.2
23	Kansas	68.8
6	Kentucky	84.3
40	Louisiana	48.5
2	Maine	93.4
43	Maryland	45.5
22	Massachusetts	69.1
20	Michigan	71.1
17	Minnesota	75.0
41	Mississippi	46.1
16	Missouri	75.7
7	Montana	83.1
18	Nebraska	73.8
46	Nevada	41.4
4	New Hampshire	90.8
37	New Jersey	53.0
49	New Mexico	25.5
39	New York	50.8
34	North Carolina	53.9
5	North Dakota	84.5
13	Ohio	78.1
32	Oklahoma	56.4
21	Oregon	70.0
19	Pennsylvania	73.1
25	Rhode Island	68.0
35	South Carolina	53.7
10	South Dakota	81.3
24	Tennessee	68.2
47	Texas	33.3
12	Utah	79.1
1	Vermont	93.5
31	Virginia	57.7
26	Washington	66.1
3	West Virginia	92.4
15	Wisconsin	76.0
9	Wyoming	81.4

RANK ORDER

RANK	STATE	PERCENT
1	Vermont	93.5
2	Maine	93.4
3	West Virginia	92.4
4	New Hampshire	90.8
5	North Dakota	84.5
6	Kentucky	84.3
7	Montana	83.1
8	Iowa	82.2
9	Wyoming	81.4
10	South Dakota	81.3
11	Idaho	80.4
12	Utah	79.1
13	Ohio	78.1
14	Indiana	77.8
15	Wisconsin	76.0
16	Missouri	75.7
17	Minnesota	75.0
18	Nebraska	73.8
19	Pennsylvania	73.1
20	Michigan	71.1
21	Oregon	70.0
22	Massachusetts	69.1
23	Kansas	68.8
24	Tennessee	68.2
25	Rhode Island	68.0
26	Washington	66.1
27	Arkansas	65.3
28	Connecticut	63.7
29	Colorado	60.6
30	Alabama	58.7
31	Virginia	57.7
32	Oklahoma	56.4
33	Illinois	54.2
34	North Carolina	53.9
35	South Carolina	53.7
36	Alaska	53.2
37	New Jersey	53.0
38	Delaware	51.6
39	New York	50.8
40	Louisiana	48.5
41	Mississippi	46.1
42	Florida	45.9
43	Maryland	45.5
44	Georgia	45.0
45	Arizona	44.1
46	Nevada	41.4
47	Texas	33.3
48	California	27.0
49	New Mexico	25.5
50	Hawaii	19.7

| | District of Columbia | 6.7 |

Source: U.S. Department of Education, National Center for Education Statistics
"Public Elementary and Secondary School Student Enrollment and Staff" (http://nces.ed.gov/pubs2011/2011347.pdf)
*For school year 2009-2010. Excludes white Hispanics.

Percent of Public Elementary and Secondary Students Who Are Black in 2010

National Percent = 16.8%*

RANK	STATE	PERCENT
6	Alabama	35.0
38	Alaska	3.8
33	Arizona	6.0
12	Arkansas	21.9
32	California	6.9
34	Colorado	5.9
21	Connecticut	13.9
7	Delaware	33.3
11	Florida	23.9
5	Georgia	37.4
43	Hawaii	2.3
48	Idaho	1.2
14	Illinois	19.5
22	Indiana	12.8
37	Iowa	5.1
31	Kansas	7.7
24	Kentucky	11.0
2	Louisiana	46.0
39	Maine	2.9
4	Maryland	37.9
29	Massachusetts	8.2
13	Michigan	20.3
27	Minnesota	9.7
1	Mississippi	50.1
16	Missouri	17.8
50	Montana	1.1
30	Nebraska	8.0
23	Nevada	11.4
45	New Hampshire	2.0
17	New Jersey	17.1
44	New Mexico	2.1
15	New York	19.1
8	North Carolina	31.0
42	North Dakota	2.4
18	Ohio	17.0
24	Oklahoma	11.0
39	Oregon	2.9
19	Pennsylvania	15.8
28	Rhode Island	9.2
3	South Carolina	38.4
41	South Dakota	2.6
10	Tennessee	24.3
20	Texas	14.0
47	Utah	1.5
46	Vermont	1.8
9	Virginia	26.2
35	Washington	5.8
36	West Virginia	5.3
26	Wisconsin	10.4
48	Wyoming	1.2

RANK	STATE	PERCENT
1	Mississippi	50.1
2	Louisiana	46.0
3	South Carolina	38.4
4	Maryland	37.9
5	Georgia	37.4
6	Alabama	35.0
7	Delaware	33.3
8	North Carolina	31.0
9	Virginia	26.2
10	Tennessee	24.3
11	Florida	23.9
12	Arkansas	21.9
13	Michigan	20.3
14	Illinois	19.5
15	New York	19.1
16	Missouri	17.8
17	New Jersey	17.1
18	Ohio	17.0
19	Pennsylvania	15.8
20	Texas	14.0
21	Connecticut	13.9
22	Indiana	12.8
23	Nevada	11.4
24	Kentucky	11.0
24	Oklahoma	11.0
26	Wisconsin	10.4
27	Minnesota	9.7
28	Rhode Island	9.2
29	Massachusetts	8.2
30	Nebraska	8.0
31	Kansas	7.7
32	California	6.9
33	Arizona	6.0
34	Colorado	5.9
35	Washington	5.8
36	West Virginia	5.3
37	Iowa	5.1
38	Alaska	3.8
39	Maine	2.9
39	Oregon	2.9
41	South Dakota	2.6
42	North Dakota	2.4
43	Hawaii	2.3
44	New Mexico	2.1
45	New Hampshire	2.0
46	Vermont	1.8
47	Utah	1.5
48	Idaho	1.2
48	Wyoming	1.2
50	Montana	1.1

District of Columbia   80.2

Source: U.S. Department of Education, National Center for Education Statistics
"Public Elementary and Secondary School Student Enrollment and Staff" (http://nces.ed.gov/pubs2011/2011347.pdf)
*For school year 2009-2010. Excludes black Hispanics.

Percent of Public Elementary and Secondary Students
Who Are Hispanic in 2010
National Percent = 22.1%*

ALPHA ORDER

RANK	STATE	PERCENT
38	Alabama	4.3
33	Alaska	5.8
4	Arizona	41.4
27	Arkansas	9.2
2	California	50.4
6	Colorado	28.6
13	Connecticut	17.6
21	Delaware	11.3
7	Florida	27.2
21	Georgia	11.3
37	Hawaii	4.6
16	Idaho	15.0
8	Illinois	21.7
31	Indiana	7.4
29	Iowa	8.1
15	Kansas	15.7
41	Kentucky	3.3
42	Louisiana	3.2
48	Maine	1.2
25	Maryland	10.0
17	Massachusetts	14.8
36	Michigan	4.9
32	Minnesota	6.7
47	Mississippi	2.2
39	Missouri	4.1
44	Montana	2.8
19	Nebraska	14.3
5	Nevada	37.5
40	New Hampshire	3.5
10	New Jersey	20.6
1	New Mexico	59.9
8	New York	21.7
24	North Carolina	11.1
46	North Dakota	2.5
43	Ohio	3.0
23	Oklahoma	11.2
11	Oregon	20.3
30	Pennsylvania	7.9
12	Rhode Island	18.6
33	South Carolina	5.8
44	South Dakota	2.8
35	Tennessee	5.5
3	Texas	48.6
18	Utah	14.6
48	Vermont	1.2
26	Virginia	9.7
14	Washington	16.5
50	West Virginia	1.0
28	Wisconsin	8.4
20	Wyoming	12.1

RANK ORDER

RANK	STATE	PERCENT
1	New Mexico	59.9
2	California	50.4
3	Texas	48.6
4	Arizona	41.4
5	Nevada	37.5
6	Colorado	28.6
7	Florida	27.2
8	Illinois	21.7
8	New York	21.7
10	New Jersey	20.6
11	Oregon	20.3
12	Rhode Island	18.6
13	Connecticut	17.6
14	Washington	16.5
15	Kansas	15.7
16	Idaho	15.0
17	Massachusetts	14.8
18	Utah	14.6
19	Nebraska	14.3
20	Wyoming	12.1
21	Delaware	11.3
21	Georgia	11.3
23	Oklahoma	11.2
24	North Carolina	11.1
25	Maryland	10.0
26	Virginia	9.7
27	Arkansas	9.2
28	Wisconsin	8.4
29	Iowa	8.1
30	Pennsylvania	7.9
31	Indiana	7.4
32	Minnesota	6.7
33	Alaska	5.8
33	South Carolina	5.8
35	Tennessee	5.5
36	Michigan	4.9
37	Hawaii	4.6
38	Alabama	4.3
39	Missouri	4.1
40	New Hampshire	3.5
41	Kentucky	3.3
42	Louisiana	3.2
43	Ohio	3.0
44	Montana	2.8
44	South Dakota	2.8
46	North Dakota	2.5
47	Mississippi	2.2
48	Maine	1.2
48	Vermont	1.2
50	West Virginia	1.0

District of Columbia — 11.5

Source: U.S. Department of Education, National Center for Education Statistics
"Public Elementary and Secondary School Student Enrollment and Staff" (http://nces.ed.gov/pubs2011/2011347.pdf)
*For school year 2009-2010. Hispanic is an ethnic designation, not a race. People of any race can be Hispanic.

Percent of Public Elementary and Secondary Students Who Are Asian in 2010

National Percent = 5.1%*

<table>
<tr><td colspan="3"><u>ALPHA ORDER</u></td><td colspan="3"><u>RANK ORDER</u></td></tr>
<tr><td>RANK</td><td>STATE</td><td>PERCENT</td><td>RANK</td><td>STATE</td><td>PERCENT</td></tr>
<tr><td>43</td><td>Alabama</td><td>1.3</td><td>1</td><td>Hawaii</td><td>72.7</td></tr>
<tr><td>6</td><td>Alaska</td><td>8.0</td><td>2</td><td>California</td><td>11.6</td></tr>
<tr><td>22</td><td>Arizona</td><td>3.1</td><td>3</td><td>Washington</td><td>9.1</td></tr>
<tr><td>33</td><td>Arkansas</td><td>1.8</td><td>4</td><td>New Jersey</td><td>8.6</td></tr>
<tr><td>2</td><td>California</td><td>11.6</td><td>5</td><td>Nevada</td><td>8.2</td></tr>
<tr><td>15</td><td>Colorado</td><td>3.7</td><td>6</td><td>Alaska</td><td>8.0</td></tr>
<tr><td>13</td><td>Connecticut</td><td>4.4</td><td>6</td><td>New York</td><td>8.0</td></tr>
<tr><td>18</td><td>Delaware</td><td>3.5</td><td>8</td><td>Minnesota</td><td>6.3</td></tr>
<tr><td>24</td><td>Florida</td><td>2.7</td><td>9</td><td>Maryland</td><td>6.1</td></tr>
<tr><td>20</td><td>Georgia</td><td>3.3</td><td>9</td><td>Virginia</td><td>6.1</td></tr>
<tr><td>1</td><td>Hawaii</td><td>72.7</td><td>11</td><td>Massachusetts</td><td>5.4</td></tr>
<tr><td>33</td><td>Idaho</td><td>1.8</td><td>12</td><td>Oregon</td><td>4.8</td></tr>
<tr><td>14</td><td>Illinois</td><td>4.3</td><td>13</td><td>Connecticut</td><td>4.4</td></tr>
<tr><td>36</td><td>Indiana</td><td>1.7</td><td>14</td><td>Illinois</td><td>4.3</td></tr>
<tr><td>31</td><td>Iowa</td><td>2.1</td><td>15</td><td>Colorado</td><td>3.7</td></tr>
<tr><td>27</td><td>Kansas</td><td>2.5</td><td>15</td><td>Texas</td><td>3.7</td></tr>
<tr><td>43</td><td>Kentucky</td><td>1.3</td><td>15</td><td>Wisconsin</td><td>3.7</td></tr>
<tr><td>41</td><td>Louisiana</td><td>1.5</td><td>18</td><td>Delaware</td><td>3.5</td></tr>
<tr><td>36</td><td>Maine</td><td>1.7</td><td>19</td><td>Rhode Island</td><td>3.4</td></tr>
<tr><td>9</td><td>Maryland</td><td>6.1</td><td>20</td><td>Georgia</td><td>3.3</td></tr>
<tr><td>11</td><td>Massachusetts</td><td>5.4</td><td>20</td><td>Utah</td><td>3.3</td></tr>
<tr><td>24</td><td>Michigan</td><td>2.7</td><td>22</td><td>Arizona</td><td>3.1</td></tr>
<tr><td>8</td><td>Minnesota</td><td>6.3</td><td>22</td><td>Pennsylvania</td><td>3.1</td></tr>
<tr><td>48</td><td>Mississippi</td><td>0.9</td><td>24</td><td>Florida</td><td>2.7</td></tr>
<tr><td>32</td><td>Missouri</td><td>2.0</td><td>24</td><td>Michigan</td><td>2.7</td></tr>
<tr><td>46</td><td>Montana</td><td>1.2</td><td>26</td><td>North Carolina</td><td>2.6</td></tr>
<tr><td>29</td><td>Nebraska</td><td>2.2</td><td>27</td><td>Kansas</td><td>2.5</td></tr>
<tr><td>5</td><td>Nevada</td><td>8.2</td><td>27</td><td>New Hampshire</td><td>2.5</td></tr>
<tr><td>27</td><td>New Hampshire</td><td>2.5</td><td>29</td><td>Nebraska</td><td>2.2</td></tr>
<tr><td>4</td><td>New Jersey</td><td>8.6</td><td>29</td><td>Oklahoma</td><td>2.2</td></tr>
<tr><td>43</td><td>New Mexico</td><td>1.3</td><td>31</td><td>Iowa</td><td>2.1</td></tr>
<tr><td>6</td><td>New York</td><td>8.0</td><td>32</td><td>Missouri</td><td>2.0</td></tr>
<tr><td>26</td><td>North Carolina</td><td>2.6</td><td>33</td><td>Arkansas</td><td>1.8</td></tr>
<tr><td>46</td><td>North Dakota</td><td>1.2</td><td>33</td><td>Idaho</td><td>1.8</td></tr>
<tr><td>36</td><td>Ohio</td><td>1.7</td><td>33</td><td>Tennessee</td><td>1.8</td></tr>
<tr><td>29</td><td>Oklahoma</td><td>2.2</td><td>36</td><td>Indiana</td><td>1.7</td></tr>
<tr><td>12</td><td>Oregon</td><td>4.8</td><td>36</td><td>Maine</td><td>1.7</td></tr>
<tr><td>22</td><td>Pennsylvania</td><td>3.1</td><td>36</td><td>Ohio</td><td>1.7</td></tr>
<tr><td>19</td><td>Rhode Island</td><td>3.4</td><td>39</td><td>South Carolina</td><td>1.6</td></tr>
<tr><td>39</td><td>South Carolina</td><td>1.6</td><td>39</td><td>Vermont</td><td>1.6</td></tr>
<tr><td>42</td><td>South Dakota</td><td>1.4</td><td>41</td><td>Louisiana</td><td>1.5</td></tr>
<tr><td>33</td><td>Tennessee</td><td>1.8</td><td>42</td><td>South Dakota</td><td>1.4</td></tr>
<tr><td>15</td><td>Texas</td><td>3.7</td><td>43</td><td>Alabama</td><td>1.3</td></tr>
<tr><td>20</td><td>Utah</td><td>3.3</td><td>43</td><td>Kentucky</td><td>1.3</td></tr>
<tr><td>39</td><td>Vermont</td><td>1.6</td><td>43</td><td>New Mexico</td><td>1.3</td></tr>
<tr><td>9</td><td>Virginia</td><td>6.1</td><td>46</td><td>Montana</td><td>1.2</td></tr>
<tr><td>3</td><td>Washington</td><td>9.1</td><td>46</td><td>North Dakota</td><td>1.2</td></tr>
<tr><td>50</td><td>West Virginia</td><td>0.7</td><td>48</td><td>Mississippi</td><td>0.9</td></tr>
<tr><td>15</td><td>Wisconsin</td><td>3.7</td><td>48</td><td>Wyoming</td><td>0.9</td></tr>
<tr><td>48</td><td>Wyoming</td><td>0.9</td><td>50</td><td>West Virginia</td><td>0.7</td></tr>
<tr><td></td><td></td><td></td><td></td><td>District of Columbia</td><td>1.6</td></tr>
</table>

Source: U.S. Department of Education, National Center for Education Statistics
    "Public Elementary and Secondary School Student Enrollment and Staff" (http://nces.ed.gov/pubs2011/2011347.pdf)
*For school year 2009-2010. Includes Pacific Islander.

Percent of Public Elementary and Secondary Students
Who Are American Indian in 2010
National Percent = 1.2%*

<table>
<tr><td colspan="3">ALPHA ORDER</td><td colspan="3">RANK ORDER</td></tr>
<tr><td>RANK</td><td>STATE</td><td>PERCENT</td><td>RANK</td><td>STATE</td><td>PERCENT</td></tr>
<tr><td>22</td><td>Alabama</td><td>0.8</td><td>1</td><td>Alaska</td><td>23.0</td></tr>
<tr><td>1</td><td>Alaska</td><td>23.0</td><td>2</td><td>Oklahoma</td><td>19.3</td></tr>
<tr><td>7</td><td>Arizona</td><td>5.5</td><td>3</td><td>South Dakota</td><td>12.0</td></tr>
<tr><td>24</td><td>Arkansas</td><td>0.7</td><td>4</td><td>Montana</td><td>11.8</td></tr>
<tr><td>24</td><td>California</td><td>0.7</td><td>5</td><td>New Mexico</td><td>10.4</td></tr>
<tr><td>18</td><td>Colorado</td><td>1.2</td><td>6</td><td>North Dakota</td><td>9.4</td></tr>
<tr><td>31</td><td>Connecticut</td><td>0.4</td><td>7</td><td>Arizona</td><td>5.5</td></tr>
<tr><td>31</td><td>Delaware</td><td>0.4</td><td>8</td><td>Wyoming</td><td>3.2</td></tr>
<tr><td>31</td><td>Florida</td><td>0.4</td><td>9</td><td>Washington</td><td>2.5</td></tr>
<tr><td>37</td><td>Georgia</td><td>0.3</td><td>10</td><td>Minnesota</td><td>2.2</td></tr>
<tr><td>27</td><td>Hawaii</td><td>0.6</td><td>11</td><td>Oregon</td><td>2.0</td></tr>
<tr><td>12</td><td>Idaho</td><td>1.7</td><td>12</td><td>Idaho</td><td>1.7</td></tr>
<tr><td>42</td><td>Illinois</td><td>0.2</td><td>12</td><td>Nebraska</td><td>1.7</td></tr>
<tr><td>37</td><td>Indiana</td><td>0.3</td><td>14</td><td>Nevada</td><td>1.5</td></tr>
<tr><td>28</td><td>Iowa</td><td>0.5</td><td>14</td><td>Wisconsin</td><td>1.5</td></tr>
<tr><td>18</td><td>Kansas</td><td>1.2</td><td>16</td><td>North Carolina</td><td>1.4</td></tr>
<tr><td>48</td><td>Kentucky</td><td>0.1</td><td>16</td><td>Utah</td><td>1.4</td></tr>
<tr><td>22</td><td>Louisiana</td><td>0.8</td><td>18</td><td>Colorado</td><td>1.2</td></tr>
<tr><td>24</td><td>Maine</td><td>0.7</td><td>18</td><td>Kansas</td><td>1.2</td></tr>
<tr><td>31</td><td>Maryland</td><td>0.4</td><td>20</td><td>Michigan</td><td>0.9</td></tr>
<tr><td>37</td><td>Massachusetts</td><td>0.3</td><td>20</td><td>Rhode Island</td><td>0.9</td></tr>
<tr><td>20</td><td>Michigan</td><td>0.9</td><td>22</td><td>Alabama</td><td>0.8</td></tr>
<tr><td>10</td><td>Minnesota</td><td>2.2</td><td>22</td><td>Louisiana</td><td>0.8</td></tr>
<tr><td>42</td><td>Mississippi</td><td>0.2</td><td>24</td><td>Arkansas</td><td>0.7</td></tr>
<tr><td>28</td><td>Missouri</td><td>0.5</td><td>24</td><td>California</td><td>0.7</td></tr>
<tr><td>4</td><td>Montana</td><td>11.8</td><td>24</td><td>Maine</td><td>0.7</td></tr>
<tr><td>12</td><td>Nebraska</td><td>1.7</td><td>27</td><td>Hawaii</td><td>0.6</td></tr>
<tr><td>14</td><td>Nevada</td><td>1.5</td><td>28</td><td>Iowa</td><td>0.5</td></tr>
<tr><td>37</td><td>New Hampshire</td><td>0.3</td><td>28</td><td>Missouri</td><td>0.5</td></tr>
<tr><td>42</td><td>New Jersey</td><td>0.2</td><td>28</td><td>New York</td><td>0.5</td></tr>
<tr><td>5</td><td>New Mexico</td><td>10.4</td><td>31</td><td>Connecticut</td><td>0.4</td></tr>
<tr><td>28</td><td>New York</td><td>0.5</td><td>31</td><td>Delaware</td><td>0.4</td></tr>
<tr><td>16</td><td>North Carolina</td><td>1.4</td><td>31</td><td>Florida</td><td>0.4</td></tr>
<tr><td>6</td><td>North Dakota</td><td>9.4</td><td>31</td><td>Maryland</td><td>0.4</td></tr>
<tr><td>48</td><td>Ohio</td><td>0.1</td><td>31</td><td>South Carolina</td><td>0.4</td></tr>
<tr><td>2</td><td>Oklahoma</td><td>19.3</td><td>31</td><td>Texas</td><td>0.4</td></tr>
<tr><td>11</td><td>Oregon</td><td>2.0</td><td>37</td><td>Georgia</td><td>0.3</td></tr>
<tr><td>42</td><td>Pennsylvania</td><td>0.2</td><td>37</td><td>Indiana</td><td>0.3</td></tr>
<tr><td>20</td><td>Rhode Island</td><td>0.9</td><td>37</td><td>Massachusetts</td><td>0.3</td></tr>
<tr><td>31</td><td>South Carolina</td><td>0.4</td><td>37</td><td>New Hampshire</td><td>0.3</td></tr>
<tr><td>3</td><td>South Dakota</td><td>12.0</td><td>37</td><td>Virginia</td><td>0.3</td></tr>
<tr><td>42</td><td>Tennessee</td><td>0.2</td><td>42</td><td>Illinois</td><td>0.2</td></tr>
<tr><td>31</td><td>Texas</td><td>0.4</td><td>42</td><td>Mississippi</td><td>0.2</td></tr>
<tr><td>16</td><td>Utah</td><td>1.4</td><td>42</td><td>New Jersey</td><td>0.2</td></tr>
<tr><td>42</td><td>Vermont</td><td>0.2</td><td>42</td><td>Pennsylvania</td><td>0.2</td></tr>
<tr><td>37</td><td>Virginia</td><td>0.3</td><td>42</td><td>Tennessee</td><td>0.2</td></tr>
<tr><td>9</td><td>Washington</td><td>2.5</td><td>42</td><td>Vermont</td><td>0.2</td></tr>
<tr><td>48</td><td>West Virginia</td><td>0.1</td><td>48</td><td>Kentucky</td><td>0.1</td></tr>
<tr><td>14</td><td>Wisconsin</td><td>1.5</td><td>48</td><td>Ohio</td><td>0.1</td></tr>
<tr><td>8</td><td>Wyoming</td><td>3.2</td><td>48</td><td>West Virginia</td><td>0.1</td></tr>
<tr><td></td><td></td><td></td><td></td><td>District of Columbia</td><td>0.1</td></tr>
</table>

Source: U.S. Department of Education, National Center for Education Statistics
  "Public Elementary and Secondary School Student Enrollment and Staff" (http://nces.ed.gov/pubs2011/2011347.pdf)
*For school year 2009-2010. Includes Alaska Native.

Children Enrolled in State Funded Pre-Kindergarten Programs in 2010

National Total = 1,283,890 Children*

<table>
<tr><td colspan="4">ALPHA ORDER</td><td colspan="4">RANK ORDER</td></tr>
<tr><td>RANK</td><td>STATE</td><td>CHILDREN</td><td>% of USA</td><td>RANK</td><td>STATE</td><td>CHILDREN</td><td>% of USA</td></tr>
<tr><td>34</td><td>Alabama</td><td>3,870</td><td>0.3%</td><td>1</td><td>Texas</td><td>214,172</td><td>16.7%</td></tr>
<tr><td>39</td><td>Alaska</td><td>200</td><td>0.0%</td><td>2</td><td>Florida</td><td>155,877</td><td>12.1%</td></tr>
<tr><td>33</td><td>Arizona</td><td>4,319</td><td>0.3%</td><td>3</td><td>California</td><td>144,427</td><td>11.2%</td></tr>
<tr><td>16</td><td>Arkansas</td><td>20,064</td><td>1.6%</td><td>4</td><td>New York</td><td>107,927</td><td>8.4%</td></tr>
<tr><td>3</td><td>California</td><td>144,427</td><td>11.2%</td><td>5</td><td>Illinois</td><td>87,451</td><td>6.8%</td></tr>
<tr><td>18</td><td>Colorado</td><td>19,197</td><td>1.5%</td><td>6</td><td>Georgia</td><td>81,177</td><td>6.3%</td></tr>
<tr><td>26</td><td>Connecticut</td><td>8,508</td><td>0.7%</td><td>7</td><td>New Jersey</td><td>49,835</td><td>3.9%</td></tr>
<tr><td>38</td><td>Delaware</td><td>843</td><td>0.1%</td><td>8</td><td>Wisconsin</td><td>37,504</td><td>2.9%</td></tr>
<tr><td>2</td><td>Florida</td><td>155,877</td><td>12.1%</td><td>9</td><td>Oklahoma</td><td>37,356</td><td>2.9%</td></tr>
<tr><td>6</td><td>Georgia</td><td>81,177</td><td>6.3%</td><td>10</td><td>Pennsylvania</td><td>31,796</td><td>2.5%</td></tr>
<tr><td>41</td><td>Hawaii</td><td>0</td><td>0.0%</td><td>11</td><td>North Carolina</td><td>31,197</td><td>2.4%</td></tr>
<tr><td>41</td><td>Idaho</td><td>0</td><td>0.0%</td><td>12</td><td>Maryland</td><td>26,147</td><td>2.0%</td></tr>
<tr><td>5</td><td>Illinois</td><td>87,451</td><td>6.8%</td><td>13</td><td>South Carolina</td><td>24,563</td><td>1.9%</td></tr>
<tr><td>41</td><td>Indiana</td><td>0</td><td>0.0%</td><td>14</td><td>Kentucky</td><td>22,299</td><td>1.7%</td></tr>
<tr><td>20</td><td>Iowa</td><td>15,615</td><td>1.2%</td><td>15</td><td>Louisiana</td><td>20,348</td><td>1.6%</td></tr>
<tr><td>25</td><td>Kansas</td><td>9,463</td><td>0.7%</td><td>16</td><td>Arkansas</td><td>20,064</td><td>1.6%</td></tr>
<tr><td>14</td><td>Kentucky</td><td>22,299</td><td>1.7%</td><td>17</td><td>Michigan</td><td>19,781</td><td>1.5%</td></tr>
<tr><td>15</td><td>Louisiana</td><td>20,348</td><td>1.6%</td><td>18</td><td>Colorado</td><td>19,197</td><td>1.5%</td></tr>
<tr><td>35</td><td>Maine</td><td>3,605</td><td>0.3%</td><td>19</td><td>Tennessee</td><td>18,252</td><td>1.4%</td></tr>
<tr><td>12</td><td>Maryland</td><td>26,147</td><td>2.0%</td><td>20</td><td>Iowa</td><td>15,615</td><td>1.2%</td></tr>
<tr><td>22</td><td>Massachusetts</td><td>13,468</td><td>1.0%</td><td>21</td><td>Virginia</td><td>14,944</td><td>1.2%</td></tr>
<tr><td>17</td><td>Michigan</td><td>19,781</td><td>1.5%</td><td>22</td><td>Massachusetts</td><td>13,468</td><td>1.0%</td></tr>
<tr><td>36</td><td>Minnesota</td><td>1,732</td><td>0.1%</td><td>23</td><td>West Virginia</td><td>13,345</td><td>1.0%</td></tr>
<tr><td>41</td><td>Mississippi</td><td>0</td><td>0.0%</td><td>24</td><td>Nebraska</td><td>9,950</td><td>0.8%</td></tr>
<tr><td>32</td><td>Missouri</td><td>4,331</td><td>0.3%</td><td>25</td><td>Kansas</td><td>9,463</td><td>0.7%</td></tr>
<tr><td>41</td><td>Montana</td><td>0</td><td>0.0%</td><td>26</td><td>Connecticut</td><td>8,508</td><td>0.7%</td></tr>
<tr><td>24</td><td>Nebraska</td><td>9,950</td><td>0.8%</td><td>27</td><td>Washington</td><td>8,026</td><td>0.6%</td></tr>
<tr><td>37</td><td>Nevada</td><td>1,210</td><td>0.1%</td><td>28</td><td>Oregon</td><td>6,460</td><td>0.5%</td></tr>
<tr><td>41</td><td>New Hampshire</td><td>0</td><td>0.0%</td><td>29</td><td>Ohio</td><td>5,201</td><td>0.4%</td></tr>
<tr><td>7</td><td>New Jersey</td><td>49,835</td><td>3.9%</td><td>30</td><td>New Mexico</td><td>4,848</td><td>0.4%</td></tr>
<tr><td>30</td><td>New Mexico</td><td>4,848</td><td>0.4%</td><td>31</td><td>Vermont</td><td>4,456</td><td>0.3%</td></tr>
<tr><td>4</td><td>New York</td><td>107,927</td><td>8.4%</td><td>32</td><td>Missouri</td><td>4,331</td><td>0.3%</td></tr>
<tr><td>11</td><td>North Carolina</td><td>31,197</td><td>2.4%</td><td>33</td><td>Arizona</td><td>4,319</td><td>0.3%</td></tr>
<tr><td>41</td><td>North Dakota</td><td>0</td><td>0.0%</td><td>34</td><td>Alabama</td><td>3,870</td><td>0.3%</td></tr>
<tr><td>29</td><td>Ohio</td><td>5,201</td><td>0.4%</td><td>35</td><td>Maine</td><td>3,605</td><td>0.3%</td></tr>
<tr><td>9</td><td>Oklahoma</td><td>37,356</td><td>2.9%</td><td>36</td><td>Minnesota</td><td>1,732</td><td>0.1%</td></tr>
<tr><td>28</td><td>Oregon</td><td>6,460</td><td>0.5%</td><td>37</td><td>Nevada</td><td>1,210</td><td>0.1%</td></tr>
<tr><td>10</td><td>Pennsylvania</td><td>31,796</td><td>2.5%</td><td>38</td><td>Delaware</td><td>843</td><td>0.1%</td></tr>
<tr><td>40</td><td>Rhode Island</td><td>126</td><td>0.0%</td><td>39</td><td>Alaska</td><td>200</td><td>0.0%</td></tr>
<tr><td>13</td><td>South Carolina</td><td>24,563</td><td>1.9%</td><td>40</td><td>Rhode Island</td><td>126</td><td>0.0%</td></tr>
<tr><td>41</td><td>South Dakota</td><td>0</td><td>0.0%</td><td>41</td><td>Hawaii</td><td>0</td><td>0.0%</td></tr>
<tr><td>19</td><td>Tennessee</td><td>18,252</td><td>1.4%</td><td>41</td><td>Idaho</td><td>0</td><td>0.0%</td></tr>
<tr><td>1</td><td>Texas</td><td>214,172</td><td>16.7%</td><td>41</td><td>Indiana</td><td>0</td><td>0.0%</td></tr>
<tr><td>41</td><td>Utah</td><td>0</td><td>0.0%</td><td>41</td><td>Mississippi</td><td>0</td><td>0.0%</td></tr>
<tr><td>31</td><td>Vermont</td><td>4,456</td><td>0.3%</td><td>41</td><td>Montana</td><td>0</td><td>0.0%</td></tr>
<tr><td>21</td><td>Virginia</td><td>14,944</td><td>1.2%</td><td>41</td><td>New Hampshire</td><td>0</td><td>0.0%</td></tr>
<tr><td>27</td><td>Washington</td><td>8,026</td><td>0.6%</td><td>41</td><td>North Dakota</td><td>0</td><td>0.0%</td></tr>
<tr><td>23</td><td>West Virginia</td><td>13,345</td><td>1.0%</td><td>41</td><td>South Dakota</td><td>0</td><td>0.0%</td></tr>
<tr><td>8</td><td>Wisconsin</td><td>37,504</td><td>2.9%</td><td>41</td><td>Utah</td><td>0</td><td>0.0%</td></tr>
<tr><td>41</td><td>Wyoming</td><td>0</td><td>0.0%</td><td>41</td><td>Wyoming</td><td>0</td><td>0.0%</td></tr>
<tr><td></td><td></td><td></td><td></td><td></td><td>District of Columbia**</td><td>NA</td><td>NA</td></tr>
</table>

Source: Rutgers, The State University of New Jersey, National Institute for Early Education Research
   "The State of Preschool: 2010 State Preschool Yearbook" (http://nieer.org/yearbook/)
*Children age 3 and 4 for school year 2009-2010.
**Not available.

Percent of Children Enrolled in State Funded Pre-Kindergarten Programs in 2010
National Percent = 15.3%*

RANK	STATE	PERCENT
33	Alabama	3.1
39	Alaska	1.0
35	Arizona	2.1
8	Arkansas	24.8
18	California	13.4
19	Colorado	13.2
25	Connecticut	10.0
32	Delaware	3.6
3	Florida	33.7
5	Georgia	27.2
41	Hawaii	0.0
41	Idaho	0.0
8	Illinois	24.8
41	Indiana	0.0
14	Iowa	19.4
22	Kansas	11.8
13	Kentucky	19.5
17	Louisiana	17.0
20	Maine	12.6
16	Maryland	17.5
26	Massachusetts	8.8
28	Michigan	8.0
38	Minnesota	1.2
41	Mississippi	0.0
34	Missouri	2.7
41	Montana	0.0
15	Nebraska	19.0
37	Nevada	1.5
41	New Hampshire	0.0
10	New Jersey	22.6
27	New Mexico	8.1
10	New York	22.6
21	North Carolina	11.9
41	North Dakota	0.0
36	Ohio	1.8
1	Oklahoma	35.1
30	Oregon	6.6
24	Pennsylvania	10.7
40	Rhode Island	0.5
12	South Carolina	20.1
41	South Dakota	0.0
23	Tennessee	10.9
7	Texas	25.9
41	Utah	0.0
1	Vermont	35.1
29	Virginia	7.1
31	Washington	4.5
4	West Virginia	31.7
6	Wisconsin	26.1
41	Wyoming	0.0

RANK	STATE	PERCENT
1	Oklahoma	35.1
1	Vermont	35.1
3	Florida	33.7
4	West Virginia	31.7
5	Georgia	27.2
6	Wisconsin	26.1
7	Texas	25.9
8	Arkansas	24.8
8	Illinois	24.8
10	New Jersey	22.6
10	New York	22.6
12	South Carolina	20.1
13	Kentucky	19.5
14	Iowa	19.4
15	Nebraska	19.0
16	Maryland	17.5
17	Louisiana	17.0
18	California	13.4
19	Colorado	13.2
20	Maine	12.6
21	North Carolina	11.9
22	Kansas	11.8
23	Tennessee	10.9
24	Pennsylvania	10.7
25	Connecticut	10.0
26	Massachusetts	8.8
27	New Mexico	8.1
28	Michigan	8.0
29	Virginia	7.1
30	Oregon	6.6
31	Washington	4.5
32	Delaware	3.6
33	Alabama	3.1
34	Missouri	2.7
35	Arizona	2.1
36	Ohio	1.8
37	Nevada	1.5
38	Minnesota	1.2
39	Alaska	1.0
40	Rhode Island	0.5
41	Hawaii	0.0
41	Idaho	0.0
41	Indiana	0.0
41	Mississippi	0.0
41	Montana	0.0
41	New Hampshire	0.0
41	North Dakota	0.0
41	South Dakota	0.0
41	Utah	0.0
41	Wyoming	0.0
	District of Columbia**	NA

Source: Rutgers, The State University of New Jersey, National Institute for Early Education Research
"The State of Preschool: 2010 State Preschool Yearbook" (http://nieer.org/yearbook/)
*Children age 3 and 4 for school year 2009-2010.
**Not available.

Head Start Program Enrollment in 2009

National Total = 904,153 Children*

ALPHA ORDER

RANK	STATE	CHILDREN	% of USA
15	Alabama	16,218	1.8%
49	Alaska	1,583	0.2%
22	Arizona	12,946	1.4%
27	Arkansas	10,521	1.2%
1	California	97,894	10.8%
30	Colorado	9,820	1.1%
35	Connecticut	6,798	0.8%
46	Delaware	2,059	0.2%
6	Florida	35,390	3.9%
10	Georgia	23,359	2.6%
39	Hawaii	3,049	0.3%
43	Idaho	2,818	0.3%
4	Illinois	39,435	4.4%
18	Indiana	14,145	1.6%
32	Iowa	7,677	0.8%
31	Kansas	8,178	0.9%
16	Kentucky	15,961	1.8%
11	Louisiana	21,327	2.4%
38	Maine	3,748	0.4%
28	Maryland	10,328	1.1%
23	Massachusetts	12,704	1.4%
8	Michigan	34,152	3.8%
29	Minnesota	10,142	1.1%
9	Mississippi	26,520	2.9%
13	Missouri	17,441	1.9%
40	Montana	2,902	0.3%
37	Nebraska	5,059	0.6%
44	Nevada	2,754	0.3%
48	New Hampshire	1,632	0.2%
17	New Jersey	14,848	1.6%
34	New Mexico	7,249	0.8%
3	New York	48,013	5.3%
12	North Carolina	18,903	2.1%
45	North Dakota	2,348	0.3%
5	Ohio	37,072	4.1%
20	Oklahoma	13,474	1.5%
26	Oregon	11,086	1.2%
7	Pennsylvania	35,253	3.9%
41	Rhode Island	2,860	0.3%
24	South Carolina	12,195	1.3%
42	South Dakota	2,827	0.3%
14	Tennessee	16,339	1.8%
2	Texas	67,591	7.5%
36	Utah	5,400	0.6%
50	Vermont	1,506	0.2%
19	Virginia	13,518	1.5%
25	Washington	11,278	1.2%
33	West Virginia	7,610	0.8%
21	Wisconsin	13,470	1.5%
47	Wyoming	1,788	0.2%

RANK ORDER

RANK	STATE	CHILDREN	% of USA
1	California	97,894	10.8%
2	Texas	67,591	7.5%
3	New York	48,013	5.3%
4	Illinois	39,435	4.4%
5	Ohio	37,072	4.1%
6	Florida	35,390	3.9%
7	Pennsylvania	35,253	3.9%
8	Michigan	34,152	3.8%
9	Mississippi	26,520	2.9%
10	Georgia	23,359	2.6%
11	Louisiana	21,327	2.4%
12	North Carolina	18,903	2.1%
13	Missouri	17,441	1.9%
14	Tennessee	16,339	1.8%
15	Alabama	16,218	1.8%
16	Kentucky	15,961	1.8%
17	New Jersey	14,848	1.6%
18	Indiana	14,145	1.6%
19	Virginia	13,518	1.5%
20	Oklahoma	13,474	1.5%
21	Wisconsin	13,470	1.5%
22	Arizona	12,946	1.4%
23	Massachusetts	12,704	1.4%
24	South Carolina	12,195	1.3%
25	Washington	11,278	1.2%
26	Oregon	11,086	1.2%
27	Arkansas	10,521	1.2%
28	Maryland	10,328	1.1%
29	Minnesota	10,142	1.1%
30	Colorado	9,820	1.1%
31	Kansas	8,178	0.9%
32	Iowa	7,677	0.8%
33	West Virginia	7,610	0.8%
34	New Mexico	7,249	0.8%
35	Connecticut	6,798	0.8%
36	Utah	5,400	0.6%
37	Nebraska	5,059	0.6%
38	Maine	3,748	0.4%
39	Hawaii	3,049	0.3%
40	Montana	2,902	0.3%
41	Rhode Island	2,860	0.3%
42	South Dakota	2,827	0.3%
43	Idaho	2,818	0.3%
44	Nevada	2,754	0.3%
45	North Dakota	2,348	0.3%
46	Delaware	2,059	0.2%
47	Wyoming	1,788	0.2%
48	New Hampshire	1,632	0.2%
49	Alaska	1,583	0.2%
50	Vermont	1,506	0.2%
	District of Columbia	3,403	0.4%

Source: U.S. Department of Health and Human Services, Administration for Children and Families
"Head Start Fact Sheet" (http://www.acf.hhs.gov/programs/ohs/about/fy2010.html)
*For fiscal year 2009. National total includes 58,939 enrollees in Migrant and Native American programs and 40,623 enrollees in U.S. territories.

Private Elementary and Secondary School Enrollment in 2010

National Total = 4,700,119 Students*

RANK	STATE	STUDENTS	% of USA
21	Alabama	78,351	1.1%
49	Alaska	4,426	0.1%
29	Arizona	44,559	0.6%
35	Arkansas	23,889	0.3%
1	California	539,726	7.3%
26	Colorado	48,545	0.7%
23	Connecticut	64,384	0.9%
36	Delaware	22,758	0.3%
3	Florida	287,689	3.9%
11	Georgia	130,263	1.8%
33	Hawaii	33,536	0.5%
43	Idaho**	14,507	0.2%
6	Illinois	243,405	3.3%
16	Indiana	104,169	1.4%
31	Iowa	39,694	0.5%
30	Kansas	40,252	0.5%
24	Kentucky	61,384	0.8%
10	Louisiana	131,866	1.8%
42	Maine	16,933	0.2%
12	Maryland	126,415	1.7%
13	Massachusetts	119,112	1.6%
9	Michigan	134,125	1.8%
20	Minnesota	78,389	1.1%
27	Mississippi	47,361	0.6%
15	Missouri	105,548	1.4%
47	Montana	7,987	0.1%
32	Nebraska	34,819	0.5%
40	Nevada	20,108	0.3%
38	New Hampshire	20,807	0.3%
8	New Jersey	188,307	2.5%
39	New Mexico	20,548	0.3%
2	New York	430,605	5.8%
18	North Carolina	98,582	1.3%
48	North Dakota	6,732	0.1%
7	Ohio	222,218	3.0%
34	Oklahoma	28,159	0.4%
28	Oregon	47,123	0.6%
4	Pennsylvania	265,399	3.6%
37	Rhode Island	21,871	0.3%
25	South Carolina	49,203	0.7%
46	South Dakota	9,394	0.1%
19	Tennessee	87,754	1.2%
5	Texas	245,568	3.3%
41	Utah	18,038	0.2%
45	Vermont	9,542	0.1%
17	Virginia	103,076	1.4%
22	Washington	77,024	1.0%
44	West Virginia	12,321	0.2%
14	Wisconsin	115,985	1.6%
50	Wyoming	1,998	0.0%

RANK	STATE	STUDENTS	% of USA
1	California	539,726	7.3%
2	New York	430,605	5.8%
3	Florida	287,689	3.9%
4	Pennsylvania	265,399	3.6%
5	Texas	245,568	3.3%
6	Illinois	243,405	3.3%
7	Ohio	222,218	3.0%
8	New Jersey	188,307	2.5%
9	Michigan	134,125	1.8%
10	Louisiana	131,866	1.8%
11	Georgia	130,263	1.8%
12	Maryland	126,415	1.7%
13	Massachusetts	119,112	1.6%
14	Wisconsin	115,985	1.6%
15	Missouri	105,548	1.4%
16	Indiana	104,169	1.4%
17	Virginia	103,076	1.4%
18	North Carolina	98,582	1.3%
19	Tennessee	87,754	1.2%
20	Minnesota	78,389	1.1%
21	Alabama	78,351	1.1%
22	Washington	77,024	1.0%
23	Connecticut	64,384	0.9%
24	Kentucky	61,384	0.8%
25	South Carolina	49,203	0.7%
26	Colorado	48,545	0.7%
27	Mississippi	47,361	0.6%
28	Oregon	47,123	0.6%
29	Arizona	44,559	0.6%
30	Kansas	40,252	0.5%
31	Iowa	39,694	0.5%
32	Nebraska	34,819	0.5%
33	Hawaii	33,536	0.5%
34	Oklahoma	28,159	0.4%
35	Arkansas	23,889	0.3%
36	Delaware	22,758	0.3%
37	Rhode Island	21,871	0.3%
38	New Hampshire	20,807	0.3%
39	New Mexico	20,548	0.3%
40	Nevada	20,108	0.3%
41	Utah	18,038	0.2%
42	Maine	16,933	0.2%
43	Idaho**	14,507	0.2%
44	West Virginia	12,321	0.2%
45	Vermont	9,542	0.1%
46	South Dakota	9,394	0.1%
47	Montana	7,987	0.1%
48	North Dakota	6,732	0.1%
49	Alaska	4,426	0.1%
50	Wyoming	1,998	0.0%
	District of Columbia	15,667	0.2%

Source: U.S. Department of Education, National Center for Education Statistics
"Characteristics of Private Schools in the United States" (http://nces.ed.gov/pubs2011/2011339.pdf)
*For school year 2009-2010.
**Interpret data for these states with caution.

Glossary

Achievement levels: Performance standards that provide a context for interpreting student performance on the National Assessment of Educational Progress (NAEP) student assessments, based on recommendations from panels of educators and members of the public. The levels, which include Basic, Proficient, and Advanced, measure what students should know at each grade assessed.

ACT: American College Testing Program. Founded in 1959, this is a national college entrance-testing program administered by ACT Inc., an independent, not-for-profit organization. Students are assessed in English, math, reading, and science. There is an optional writing test. The ACT score range is 1 to 36.

Adequate Yearly Progress (AYP): A statewide accountability system mandated by the No Child Left Behind Act of 2001 which requires each state to ensure that all schools and districts make progress in reading, math, graduation rates (for high schools) and attendance rates (for junior high/middle schools.)

Administrative support staff: Comprised of (1) school district staff who provide direct support to superintendents, assistant superintendents, and other local agency administrators; and (2) school building support staff who work to support the teaching and administrative duties of the office of the principal or department chairpersons.

Advanced: One of the three NAEP achievement levels, denoting superior performance at each grade assessed.

Advanced Placement (A.P.) courses: A course designed to prepare students for the Advanced Placement subject assessments administered by The College Board.

Alternative education schools: Schools that provide nontraditional education and address the needs of students that typically cannot be met in the regular school setting.

Average daily attendance (ADA): The total number of days of student attendance divided by the total number of days in the regular school year. A student attending every school day would equal one ADA. Generally ADA is lower than enrollment due to transience, dropouts and illness.

Averaged freshman graduation rate: A measurement of the percentage of high school students who graduate on time. The rate uses enrollment data for a freshman class and the number of diplomas awarded four years later. The incoming freshman class is estimated by summing the enrollment in eighth grade in one year, ninth grade for the next year, and tenth grade for the year after and then dividing by three. The averaged freshman graduation rate is considered an interim step in the process to develop a more comprehensive and accurate assessment of how many students graduate from high school.

Basic: One of the three National Assessment of Educational Progress (NAEP) achievement levels, denoting partial mastery of prerequisite knowledge and skills that are fundamental for proficient work at each grade assessed.

Board certified teachers: Teachers who have demonstrated their knowledge and skills through a series of performance-based assessments that include student work samples, videotapes, and rigorous analyses of their classroom teaching and student learning.

Capital outlay: Direct expenditure for construction of buildings, roads, and other improvements undertaken either on a contractual basis by private contractors or through a government's own staff (i.e., force account); for purchases of equipment, land, and existing structures; and for payments on capital leases. Includes amounts for additions, replacements, and major alterations to fixed works and structures. However, expenditure for maintenance and repairs to such works and structures is classified as current spending.

Charter schools: Schools that provide free public elementary/secondary education under a charter granted by the state legislature or other appropriate authority.

Child nutrition programs: Payments by the Department of Agriculture for the National School Lunch, Special Milk, School Breakfast, and Ala Carte programs. Excludes the value of donated commodities.

Class size: Number of students taught by a teacher in a self-contained classroom, or average number of students per class taught by a teacher who provides departmentalized instruction.

Common Core of Data: A group of surveys administered by the National Center for Education Statistics that acquire and maintain public elementary and secondary education data from the 50 states, District of Columbia and outlying areas.

Compensatory program revenue: Revenue for "at risk" or other economically disadvantaged students including migratory children. Also includes monies from state programs directed toward the attainment of basic skills and categorical education excellence and quality education programs that provide more than staff enhancements such as materials, resource centers, and equipment.

Current expenditures: Direct expenditures for salaries, employee benefits, purchased professional and technical services, purchased property and other services, and supplies. It includes gross school system expenditure for instruction, support services, and non-instructional functions. It excludes expenditure for debt service, capital outlay, and reimbursement to other governments (including other school systems.

Dropout rate: The high school dropout rate shown in *Education State Rankings* is an "event" dropout rate. It measures the proportion of students who leave school each year without completing a high school program. This annual measure of recent dropout occurrences provides important information about how effective educators are in keeping students enrolled in school.

Elementary teachers: The full-time equivalent count of the number of teachers in a state who are of general level instruction classified by state and local practice as elementary and composed of any span of grades not above grade 8. Excludes pre-kindergarten and kindergarten teachers.

Employee benefit expenditures: Amounts paid by a school system for fringe benefits. These amounts are not included in salaries and wages paid directly to employees. Includes contributions on behalf of employees for retirement coverage, social security, group health and life insurance, tuition reimbursement, workers's compensation, and unemployment compensation.

English Language Learners (ELL): Students served in appropriate programs of language assistance (English as a Second Language, High Intensity Language Training, bilingual education). Does not include students enrolled in programs to learn a language other than English. Students may be referred to as Limited English proficiency students (LEP).

Federal aid direct: Aid from project grants for programs such as Impact Aid, Indian Education, Bilingual Education, Head Start, Follow Through, Magnet Schools, Dropout Demonstration Assistance, and Gifted and Talented.

Federal aid distributed by state governments: Aid from formula grants distributed through state government agencies. Includes revenue from programs such as child nutrition, Title I, special education, vocational, and other federal aid distributed by state governments.

Formula assistance: Revenue from general non-categorical state assistance programs such as foundation, minimum or basic formula support, apportionment, equalization, flat or block grants, and state public school fund distributions. This category also includes revenue dedicated from major state taxes, such as income and sales taxes.

Free or reduced-price meal eligibility: Number of students in a school who are eligible to receive free or reduced price meals under the National School Lunch Act.

General administration expenditures: Spending for board of education and executive administration (office of the superintendent) services.

Graduates: High school students who received diplomas during the previous school year and subsequent summer school. A diploma recognizes that the recipient has successfully completed a state's prescribed course of studies at the secondary school level.

Graduation rate: The graduation rates shown in *Education State Rankings* compare numbers of public high school graduates with 9th grade enrollment four years prior. These are basic completion ratios that exclude ungraded pupils and are not adjusted for interstate migration or students switching to private schools. They should be viewed as estimates. The U.S. Department of Education now issues averaged freshman graduation rates (see definition above) as an interim step in the process to develop a more comprehensive and accurate assessment of how many students graduate from high school.

Head Start: The federal government's preschool program for disadvantaged children. Its goal is to increase school readiness of young children in low income families.

High schools: Schools with a low grade of 7 to 12, and must extend through grade 12.

Highly Qualified Teachers: Under the No Child Left Behind Act, highly qualified teachers must hold a bachelor's degree, demonstrate competence in his or her academic subject, obtain full state certification or pass the state licensure exam, and hold a license to teach.

IDEA: The Individuals with Disabilities Education Act. Originally passed in 1975 as the Education for All Handicapped Children Act, the IDEA supports states and localities in protecting the rights of, meeting the individual needs of, and improving the educational results for infants, toddlers, children, and youth with disabilities and their families.

IEP: Individualized Education Programs as defined by the Individuals with Disabilities Education Act (IDEA)—Part B. Each public school student who receives special education and related services must have an IEP. Each IEP is designed specifically for that student. It provides a plan for teachers, parents, school administrators, related services personnel, and students (where appropriate) to improve educational results for children with disabilities.

Instruction expenditures: Includes payments from all funds for salaries, employee benefits (paid by school system only if under "current operation" or paid by both school and state if under "current spending"), supplies, materials, and contractual services. It excludes capital outlay, debt service, and inter-fund transfers. Instruction covers regular, special, and vocational programs offered in both the regular school year and summer school. It excludes instructional, student, and other support activities, as well as adult education, community services, and student enterprise activities.

Instructional aides: The full-time equivalent count in a state for the number of staff members assigned to assist a teachers in activities requiring minor decisions regarding students, and in such activities as monitoring, conducting rote exercises, operating equipment and clerking and includes only paid staff.

Instructional coordinators and supervisors: The full-time equivalent count in a state for the number of staff supervising instructional programs at the school or district of sub-district level.

Instructional staff support expenditures: Spending for supervision of instruction service improvements, curriculum development, instructional staff training, and media, library, audiovisual, television, and computer-assisted instruction services.

Kindergarten teachers: The full-time equivalent count of the number of teachers in a state who teach a group or class that is part of a public school program and is taught during the year preceding the first grade.

Librarians: The full-time equivalent count in a state of professional staff members and supervisors who are assigned specific duties and school time for professional library and media service activities.

Magnet schools: Schools that are designed to attract students of different racial/ethnic backgrounds for the purpose of reducing racial isolation, or to provide an academic or social focus on a specific theme (ex. performing arts.)

Membership count: Annual headcount of students enrolled in school on October 1st.

Middle schools: Schools with a low grade of 4 to 7 and a high grade ranging from 4 to 9. (A 4th grade center is a middle school.)

NAEP: National Assessment of Educational Progress. Since 1969, this program, administered by the U.S. Department of Education's National Center for Education Statistics, has assessed students on their knowledge of reading, mathematics, science, writing, U.S. history, civics, geography, and the arts.

No Child Left Behind: The federal government's reauthorization of the Elementary and Secondary Education Act. Passed in 2001, the law aims at bringing reform and greater accountability to public elementary and secondary education in the United States.

Operation and maintenance of facilities expenditures: Spending for building services (heating, electricity, air conditioning, property insurance), care and upkeep of grounds and equipment, non-student transportation vehicle operation and maintenance, and security services.

Other high school completer: Student who has received a certificate of attendance or other certificate of completion in lieu of a diploma.

"Other" schools: Schools that have grade configurations other than those of primary, middle, and high school. Ungraded schools are included.

Paraprofessional: A special education staff member who is not licensed to teach, but performs many duties, both individually with students and organizationally in the classroom.

Parent government contributions: Tax receipts and other amounts appropriated by a parent government and transferred to its dependent school system. Excludes intergovernmental revenue, current charges, and miscellaneous general revenue.

Pre-kindergarten teachers: The full-time equivalent count of the number of teachers in a state who teach a group or class that is part of a public school program and is taught during the year or years preceding kindergarten.

Primary schools: Schools with a low grade of pre-kindergarten through grade 3, and a high grade of up to 8.

Proficient: One of the three NAEP achievement levels, representing solid academic performance for each grade assessed. Students reaching this level have demonstrated competency over challenging subject matter, including subject-matter knowledge, application of such knowledge to real-world situations, and analytical skills appropriate to the subject matter.

Property taxes: Taxes conditioned on ownership of property and measured by its value. Includes general property taxes relating to property as a whole, taxed at a single rate or at classified rates according to the class of property. Property refers to real property (e.g., land and structures), as well as personal property. Personal property can be either tangible (e.g., automobiles and boats) or intangible (e.g., bank accounts and stocks and bonds).

Public schools: Schools that provide education services to students, have an assigned administrator, receive public funds as their primary support, and are operated by an education agency.

Pupil support service expenditures: Spending for attendance record keeping, social work, student accounting, counseling, student appraisal, record maintenance, and placement services. This category also includes medical, dental, nursing, psychological, and speech services.

Pupil transportation service expenditures: Spending for the transportation of public school students including vehicle operation, monitoring riders, and vehicle servicing and maintenance.

Pupil-teacher ratio: The total number of students divided by the number of full-time equivalent teachers in schools.

Race/Ethnicity categories: Student race and ethnicity categories are American Indian/Alaskan Native; Asian/Pacific Islander; Black, not Hispanic; Hispanic and White, not Hispanic. They are mutually exclusive. "Minority" students include all categories but White, not Hispanic.

Regular school districts: Agencies responsible for providing free public education for school-age children residing within their jurisdiction. This category excludes local supervisory unions that provide management services for a group of associated school districts, although it includes the "component" districts that receive these services.

Regular schools: Schools that do not focus primarily on special, vocational, or alternative education, although they may offer these programs in addition to the regular curriculum.

Revenue: All amounts of money received by a school system from external sources net of refunds and other correcting transactions other than from issuance of debt, liquidation of investments, or as agency and private trust transactions. Note that revenue excludes noncash transactions, such as receipt of services, commodities, or other "receipts in-kind."

Salaries and wages: Amounts paid for compensation of school system officers and employees. Consists of gross compensation before deductions for withheld taxes, retirement contributions, or other purposes.

SAT: Formerly known as the Scholastic Aptitude Test, the SAT is a national college entrance exam that assesses student reasoning based on knowledge and skills developed by the student in school coursework. The SAT assesses students in reading and mathematics and, as of March of 2005, includes a writing assessment. Each subject area is scored separately on a scale from

200 to 800. The SAT is administered by The College Board, a not-for-profit membership organization founded in 1900.

School administration expenditures: Spending for the office of principal services.

School administrators: The full-time equivalent count in a state of staff members whose activities are concerned with directing and managing the operation of a particular school.

School district administrators: The full-time equivalent count in a state of local education agency superintendents, deputy and assistant superintendents, and other persons with district-wide responsibilities such as business managers and administrative assistants.

Secondary school teachers: The full-time equivalent count of the number of teachers in a state who are of general level instruction classified by state and local practice as secondary and composed of any span of grades beginning with the next grade following the elementary grades and ending with or below grade 12.

Special education programs: Revenue for the education of physically and mentally disabled students.

Special education schools: Schools that focus primarily on special education, with materials and instructional approaches adapted to meet students' needs.

Support services expenditures: Spending for general administration, instructional staff support, operation and maintenance of plant, pupil support services, pupil transportation services, school administration, other support services and nonspecified support services. Excluded is spending for capital outlay, debt service and interfund transfers.

Support staff: Comprised of library, student support services, and all other support staff. Library support staff oversee library or media services such as preparing, caring for, and making available to members of the instructional staff the equipment, films, filmstrips, transparencies, tapes, TV programs, and similar materials. Student support services staff provide non-instructional services to students.

Talented/gifted program: Programs designed for students with specifically identified talents or exceptional academic achievement.

Title I schools: Schools designated as eligible for programs authorized by Title I of Public Law 107-110, the Elementary and Secondary Education Act of 2002. This federally-funded program provides educational services, such as remedial reading or mathematics, to children who live in areas with high concentrations of low-income families.

Title I school-wide schools: Schools in which all students enrolled are designated as eligible for programs authorized by

Title I of Public Law 107-110, the Elementary and Secondary Education Act of 2002. This federally-funded program provides educational services, such as remedial reading or mathematics, to children who live in areas with high concentrations of low-income families.

Transportation programs: Payments for various state transportation aid programs, such as those that compensate the school system for part of its transportation expense and those that provide reimbursement for transportation salaries or school bus purchase.

Ungraded students: Students who are assigned to programs or classes without standard grade designation. States are requested to report teachers of ungraded classes even if all students are assigned a grade level of record. In many states, ungraded students are special education students.

Vocational education schools: Schools that focus primarily on vocational, technical, or career education and provide education or training in at least one semi-skilled or technical occupation.

Sources

ACT, Inc.
500 ACT Drive, P.O. Box 168
Iowa City, IA 52243-0168
319-337-1000
Internet: www.act.org

Administration for Children and Families
370 L'Enfant Promenade, S.W.
Washington, DC 20447
202-401-9215
Internet: www.acf.hhs.gov

Budget Office
U.S. Department of Education
400 Maryland Avenue, S.W.
Washington, DC 20202
800-USA-LEARN
Internet: www.ed.gov/about/overview/budget/index.html

Bureau of Labor Statistics
2 Massachusetts Avenue, N.E.
Washington, DC 20212
202-691-5200
Internet: www.bls.gov

Bureau of the Census
Governments Division
Elementary and Secondary Education Statistics Branch
GOVS, CENHQ, Room 6K060
Washington, DC 20233
800-622-6193
Internet: www.census.gov

Centers for Disease Control and Prevention
Youth Risk Behavior Surveillance System
1600 Clifton Road
Atlanta, GA 30333
800-232-4636
Internet: www.cdc.gov/HealthyYouth/yrbs/index.htm

College Board
45 Columbus Avenue
New York, NY 10023-6992
212-713-8000
Internet: www.collegeboard.com

Federal Bureau of Investigation
Criminal Justice Information Services Division
1000 Custer Hollow Road
Clarksburg, WV 26306
304-625-4995
Internet: www.fbi.gov

Head Start (Office of)
Early Childhood Learning and Knowledge Center
1250 Maryland Avenue, S.W., 8th Floor
Washington, DC 20024
866-763-6481
Internet: http://eclkc.ohs.acf.hhs.gov/hslc

Juvenile Justice Clearinghouse
National Criminal Justice Reference Service
P.O. Box 6000
Rockville, MD 20849-6000
800-851-3420
Internet: www.ojjdp.gov

National Board for Professional Teaching Standards
1525 Wilson Blvd
Arlington, VA 22209
800-228-3224
Internet: www.nbpts.org

National Center for Education Statistics
U.S. Department of Education
1990 K Street, N.W.
Washington, DC 20006
202-502-7300
Internet: http://nces.ed.gov

National Education Association
1201 16th Street, N.W.
Washington, DC 20036
202-833-4000
Internet: www.nea.org

National Institute for Early Education Research
Rutgers University
120 Albany Street, Suite 500
New Brunswick, NJ 08901
732-932-4350
Internet: www.nieer.org

National Library of Education
U.S. Department of Education
400 Maryland Ave, S.W.
Washington, DC 20202
800-424-1616
Internet: www.ed.gov/NLE (case sensitive)

Office of Juvenile Justice and Delinquency Prevention
810 Seventh Street, N.W.
Washington, DC 20531
202-307-5911
Internet: www.ojjdp.gov

Special Education and Rehabilitative Services
U.S. Department of Education
400 Maryland Ave, S.W.
Washington, DC 20202
800-872-5327 or 202-245-7868
Internet: www.ed.gov/about/offices/list/osers/index.html

Index